x peritissimorum totius orbis Gæographorum operibus desumta.
S0-BGP-889
ASIA
AFRICA
Polus Arcticus
Polus Antarcticus
Circulus Antarcticus
Aequator
OCEANUS ÆTHIOPICUS
OCEANUS INDICUS
SINENSIS OCEANUS
Oceanus Tartaricus
Mare Lantchidol
TERRA AUSTRALIS MAGALLANICA
EUROPA
AFRICA
ASIA
Mediterraneum
Mare major
Petzorke morie
Noua Zemla
Russia
Tartaria
Cathaia
India
Persis
Golfo Bengala
Iapan
Philippinæ
Mindana
Borneo
Iaua
Timor
Noua Guinea
Madagascar
Monomotapa
Anzica
Nubia
Guinea
Libya
Canaria insulæ
La Ascension
S. Elena
Santa Croce
Tristan d'Acunna
Los Romeros
C. Bone spei
C. das Aguilhas
De Iaua minori
Insulam Sumatram M. Paulo Veneto esse Iauam minorem, tum ex loco, rum distantia ac situ, tum ex aliis circumstantiis attento Lectori satis superque constat.
Vastissimas hic esse regiones ex M. Pauli Veneti & Ludo: vici Vartomanni scriptis peregrinationibus liquido constat.
Psittacorum regio sic a Lusitanis appellata ob incredibilem earum aui um ibidem magnitudinem.
Inter S. Laurentii & Los Romeros insulas vehementi admodum sursum fluxus & refluxus maris.
Cetus
Orion
Canis minor
Argo
Hydra
Crater
Pegasus
Aquila
Capricornus
Sagittarius
Serpentarius
Serpens
Scorpius
Libra
Virgo
à Langren fratres sculpserunt.

Reader's Digest

GREAT WORLD ATLAS

THE
READER'S DIGEST
ASSOCIATION
Pleasantville, New York

READER'S DIGEST GREAT WORLD ATLAS

THIRD EDITION

PUBLISHED BY
THE READER'S DIGEST ASSOCIATION, INC.
Pleasantville, New York

Relief maps on pages 24-29 © Babson Institute
Relief maps on pages 15, 22-23 and 30-41 © Aero Service Corp.
Maps on pages 46-136 and 146-147 © John Bartholomew & Son Ltd.

Library of Congress Catalog Card Number: Map 63-10

ACKNOWLEDGMENTS

Special Consulting Editors

CHARLES B. HITCHCOCK

M.A., D.SC. (Hon.), Director Emeritus, American Geographical Society, New York, N.Y.

and

FRANK DEBENHAM

O.B.E., M.A., D.SC. (Hon.), Emeritus Professor of Geography, Cambridge University, Cambridge, England

---

The Reader's Digest expresses its gratitude to the following, who have generously contributed to and advised on the preparation of this Atlas:

J. B. Allen, B.SC., PH.D., F.G.S., Institute of Geological Sciences, London

American Geographical Society, New York, N. Y.

American Waterways Operators, Inc., Washington, D. C.

Peter Bartholomew, John Bartholomew and Son Ltd., Edinburgh

Franklyn M. Branley, ED.D., Chairman and Astronomer, The American Museum— Hayden Planetarium, New York, N. Y.

British Broadcasting Corporation, London

Wm. Collins, Sons & Co. Ltd., London

David J. deLaubenfels, PH.D., Associate Professor of Geography, Syracuse University, Syracuse, N. Y.

F. W. Dunning, B.SC., F.G.S., Institute of Geological Sciences, London

Rhodes W. Fairbridge, B.SC., D.SC., Professor of Geology, Columbia University, New York, N. Y.

Anthony W. Gatrell, London

George H. Hamlin, Jr.

James G. Hawk, formerly of the Babson Institute, Babson Park, Mass.

Institut de la Statistique et des Études Économiques, Paris

Preston E. James, PH.D., Professor of Geography, Syracuse University, Syracuse, N. Y.

Robert Jastrow, PH.D., Adjunct Professor of Geology, Columbia University; Director, Goddard Institute for Space Studies, National Aeronautics and Space Administration, New York, N. Y.

E. A. Jobbins, B.SC., F.G.S., Institute of Geological Sciences, London

H. C. King, PH.D., M.SC., F.R.A.S., F.B.O.A., The London Planetarium, London

H. A. G. Lewis, Directorate of Military Survey (War Office and Air Ministry), London

Library of Congress, Washington, D.C.

Lick Observatory, Mount Hamilton, Calif.

Longmans, Green & Co. Ltd., London

Mount Wilson Observatory, Mount Wilson, Calif.

Thomas D. Nicholson, PH.D., Assistant Director, The American Museum of Natural History, New York, N. Y.

Palomar Observatory, Mount Palomar, Calif.

Nicholas Panagakos, Science Editor, Goddard Institute for Space Studies, National Aeronautics and Space Administration, New York, N. Y.

G. Etzel Pearcy, B.E., M.A., PH.D., The Geographer, Department of State, Washington, D. C.

E. Penkala, F.R.G.S., A.A.A.S., Amsterdam

James S. Pickering, Astronomer Emeritus, American Museum–Hayden Planetarium, New York, N. Y.

The Polar Institute, London

Erwin Raisz, Cambridge, Mass.

C. S. Roetter, LL.B., London

C. A. Ronan, M.SC., F.R.A.S., Royal Society, London

Scientific Liaison Office, Australia, New Zealand, Canada

David Stern, PH.D., Theoretical Division, National Aeronautics and Space Administration, Greenbelt, Md.

United Nations Information Centre, London

United Nations Statistical Office, New York, N. Y.

U.S. Department of Commerce, Bureau of the Census, Washington, D.C.

U.S. Department of Interior, Washington, D.C.

U.S. Naval Photographic Interpretation Center, Washington, D.C.

U.S.S.R. Academy of Science, Moscow

William Warntz, PH.D., Professor of Theoretical Geography, Harvard University, Cambridge, Mass.

Bernard Workman, M.A., London

Yerkes Observatory, Williams Bay, Wisconsin

We also wish to thank all the others—geographers, cartographers, designers, editors and technicians—who gave valuable assistance in the preparation of this Atlas.

Illustrations on page 15: Lunar flight — based on a drawing, courtesy of American Rocket Society, Inc., New York, N. Y. Earth-Mars flight—based on a drawing, courtesy of Jet Propulsion Laboratory, California Institute of Technology, Pasadena, Calif. Earth-Venus flight—based on a drawing, courtesy of American Rocket Society and Jet Propulsion Laboratory. Moon crater—photograph from National Aeronautics and Space Administration. Mars—from tricolor separation negatives made July 4, 1954, by the National Geographic Society-Lowell Observatory Expedition to the Lamont-Hussey Observatory, Bloemfontein, South Africa, by E. C. Slipher; color print prepared by the Air Force Aeronautical Chart and Information Center, St. Louis, Mo. Venus — photo, Mount Wilson and Palomar Observatories. Jupiter—original photograph by E. C. Slipher; color copy by J. B. Edson, Lowell Observatory.

Aero Service Corporation, Philadelphia, Pa., a subsidiary of Nystrom Raised Relief Map Co., produces many three-dimensional relief maps, including those photographed on pages 15, 22-23 and 30-41, as well as special maps for space navigation. It is the largest aerial mapping company in the world.

The three-dimensional relief maps of the North Atlantic and North Pacific Ocean floors, photographed on pages 42-44, were prepared by the United States Naval Photographic Interpretation Center, Washington, D.C. Highway information on pages 46-75 is based on data from General Drafting Co., Convent Station, N. J.

The Fairbridge Geotectonic World Map, pages 138-139, is reproduced by courtesy of Rhodes W. Fairbridge, with special acknowledgment to Professor H. W. Menard and Professor Bruce C. Heezen. The photograph of the relief model on page 140 is also reproduced by courtesy of Professor Fairbridge.

The maps on pages 146-147 are based on the work of Preston E. James and others.

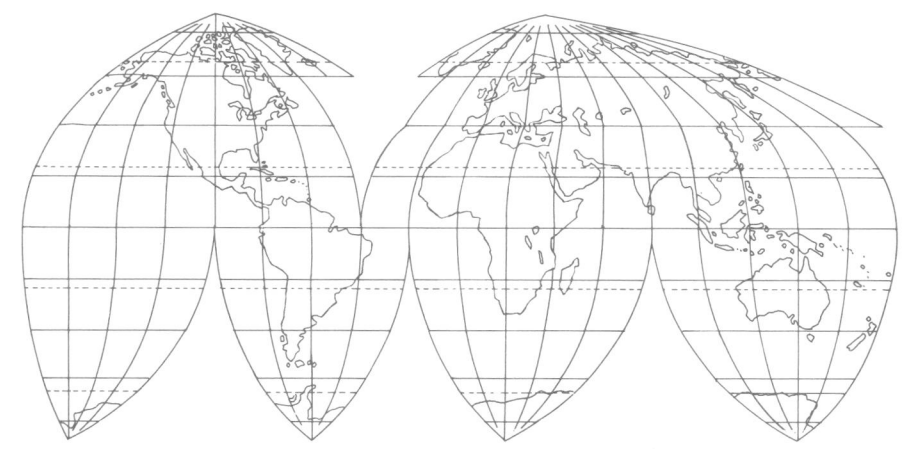

CONTENTS

PART ONE

THE UNIVERSE AND THE EARTH

PART TWO

THE COUNTRIES OF THE WORLD

CONTENTS

CONTENTS

PART THREE

THE WORLD ABOUT US

PART FOUR

INDEXES

From the center of the Earth to the outermost limits of space

Paradise is somewhere in the Far East, Jerusalem is the center of all nations, and the world itself is a flat disk surrounded by vast oceans. So the monks, mapmakers of the Middle Ages, saw the world they lived in.

Today our knowledge of the world has been greatly enriched through scientific discovery, travel and exploration. This Atlas has drawn upon the sum of that knowledge, accumulated through many lifetimes of research.

In *The Universe and the Earth*, Part One of this Atlas, we first view our Earth in space. Incurably inquisitive, man searches continually into every facet of our world and other worlds beyond. He knows that the Sun, around which our planet revolves, is a minor star at the edge of the Milky Way. A galaxy of many millions of stars, the Milky Way is itself only one among a million other galaxies moving in the infinity of space where traditional concepts of distance and time are meaningless.

The universe is a vision that dwarfs the globe on which we live and makes our tiny planet seem insignificant, but here life has been created and has developed. As yet we do not know whether the delicate balance of conditions which has made evolution possible on this planet has ever occurred on any other.

In the opening section of this Atlas, maps made from scientifically designed models show us how our world would appear to an observer hundreds of miles above the surface. Great mountain peaks stand out in sharp contrast to the worn surfaces of older ranges and the plains traversed by mighty rivers. The levels of the ocean floor tell the history of submerged lands and of deeps only recently explored.

Next come *The Countries of the World*. Towns and cities, rivers and railways can all be found easily, for the coloring is subdued and the place names are clear. Together with the relief section, these maps complete a picture of the landscape of our Earth and of the places where we live.

The third Part portrays *The World About Us*. The marvel of its creation cannot be told by any single map or chart. Each feature in this section of the Atlas has been devised to illustrate a most important aspect of the Earth — the evolution of the terrain beneath our feet and man's exploration of it, patterns of climate and vegetation, facts about world population and about the Earth's natural features. Each subject is linked to another, for none of the world's wonders or problems can be seen or understood in isolation.

If this Atlas is new in its manner of presenting geographically the facts about Earth and life and space, it is also new in another way: it provides the background for, and it points the way to, the discoveries and explorations that lie in the future.

The Editors

PART ONE

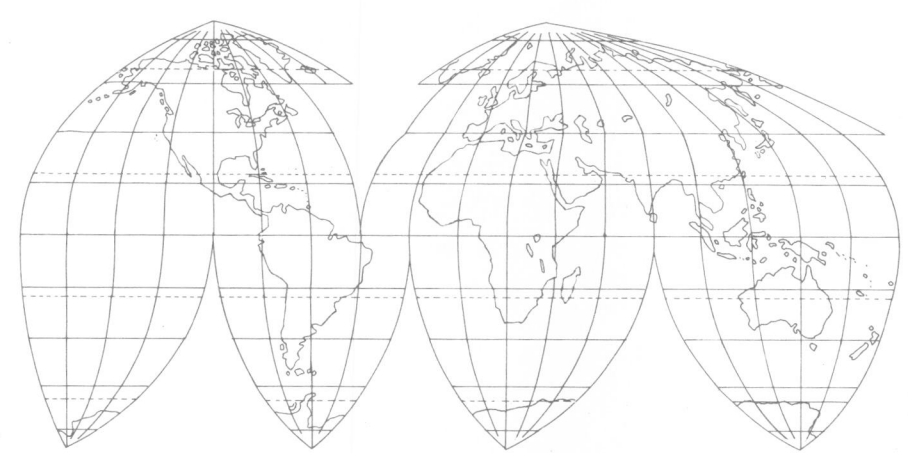

THE UNIVERSE
AND THE EARTH

THE GEOGRAPHY OF SPACE

THE FACE OF THE EARTH: Relief Maps

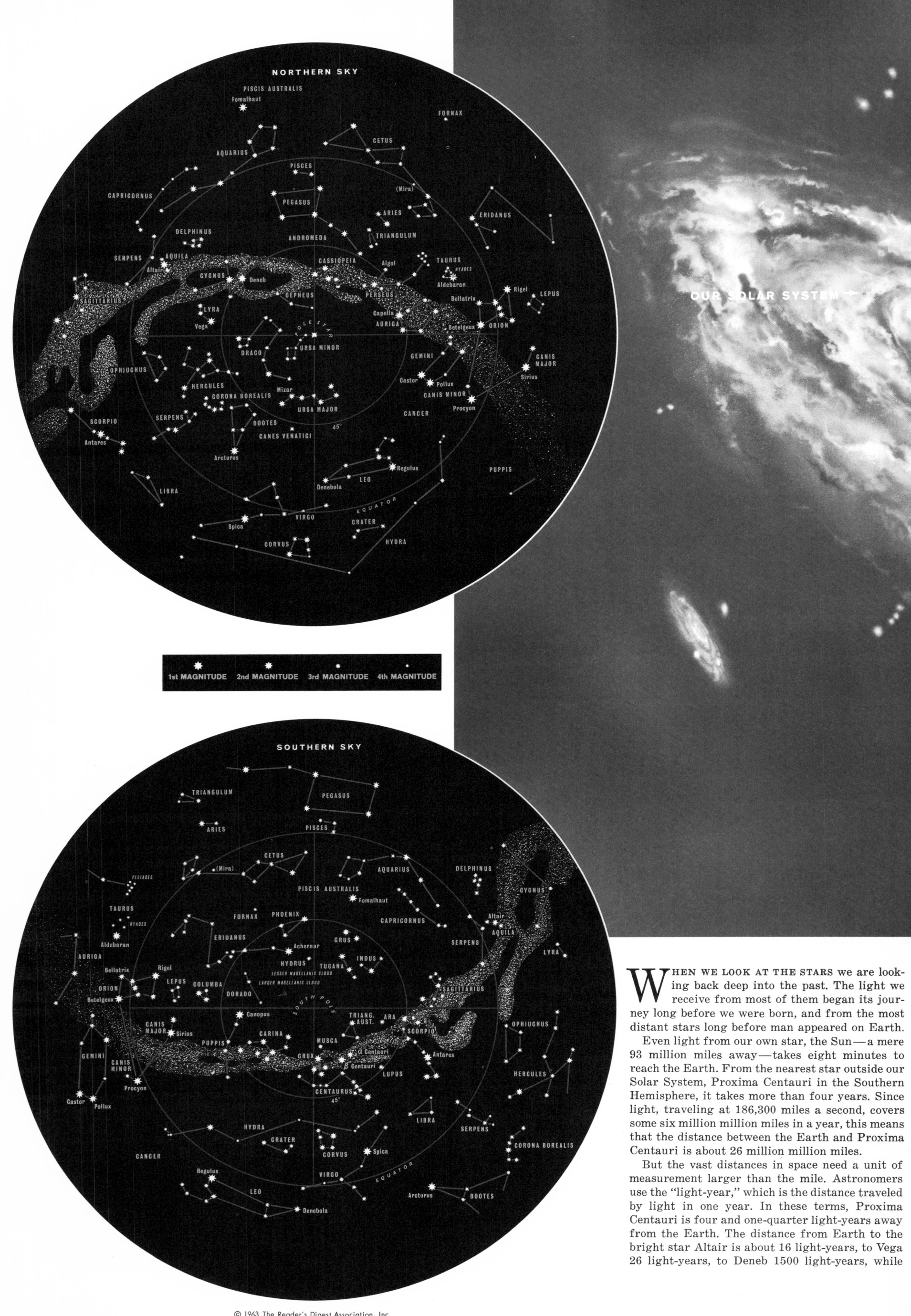

PISCIS AUSTRALIS
Fomalhaut

FORNAX

AQUARIUS

CETUS

PISCES

CAPRICORNUS

PEGASUS

(Mira)

ARIES

ERIDANUS

DELPHINUS

ANDROMEDA

TRIANGULUM

SERPENS

AQUILA

CASSIOPEIA

Algol

TAURUS

HYADES

Altair

CYGNUS

Deneb

PERSEUS

Aldebaran

SAGITTARIUS

CEPHEUS

Capella

Bellatrix

Rigel

LEPUS

LYRA

AURIGA

Betelgeux

ORION

Vega

POLE STAR

OPHIUCHUS

DRACO

URSA MINOR

GEMINI

CANIS
MAJOR

HERCULES

Mizar

Castor

Pollux

Sirius

CORONA BOREALIS

CANIS MINOR

SCORPIO

SERPENS

URSA MAJOR

CANCER

Procyon

Antares

BOOTES

45°

CANES VENATICI

Arcturus

LIBRA

LEO

Regulus

PUPPIS

Denebola

EQUATOR

Spica

VIRGO

CRATER

CORVUS

HYDRA

| 1st MAGNITUDE | 2nd MAGNITUDE | 3rd MAGNITUDE | 4th MAGNITUDE |

TRIANGULUM

PEGASUS

ARIES

PISCES

CETUS

(Mira)

AQUARIUS

DELPHINUS

PLEIADES

PISCIS AUSTRALIS

CYGNUS

TAURUS

Fomalhaut

HYADES

FORNAX

PHOENIX

Altair

Aldebaran

ERIDANUS

CAPRICORNUS

AQUILA

AURIGA

Achernar

GRUS

SERPENS

LYRA

Bellatrix

Rigel

HYDRUS

ORION

LEPUS

COLUMBA

TUCANA

INDUS

Betelgeux

LESSER MAGELLANIC CLOUD

DORADO

LARGER MAGELLANIC CLOUD

SAGITTARIUS

SOUTH POLE

OPHIUCHUS

Canopus

TRIANG.
AUST.

ARA

CANIS
MAJOR

Sirius

CARINA

MUSCA

SCORPIO

GEMINI

PUPPIS

α Centauri

Antares

HERCULES

CANIS
MINOR

CRUX

β Centauri

LUPUS

Procyon

CENTAURUS

Castor

45°

Pollux

LIBRA

SERPENS

HYDRA

CRATER

Spica

CORONA BOREALIS

CANCER

CORVUS

Regulus

VIRGO

EQUATOR

LEO

Arcturus

BOOTES

Denebola

W HEN WE LOOK AT THE STARS we are looking back deep into the past. The light we
receive from most of them began its journey long before we were born, and from the most
distant stars long before man appeared on Earth.

Even light from our own star, the Sun—a mere
93 million miles away—takes eight minutes to
reach the Earth. From the nearest star outside our
Solar System, Proxima Centauri in the Southern
Hemisphere, it takes more than four years. Since
light, traveling at 186,300 miles a second, covers
some six million million miles in a year, this means
that the distance between the Earth and Proxima
Centauri is about 26 million million miles.

But the vast distances in space need a unit of
measurement larger than the mile. Astronomers
use the "light-year," which is the distance traveled
by light in one year. In these terms, Proxima
Centauri is four and one-quarter light-years away
from the Earth. The distance from Earth to the
bright star Altair is about 16 light-years, to Vega
26 light-years, to Deneb 1500 light-years, while

OUTER SPACE: THE BOUNDLESS SKY

some stars of the Milky Way are so distant their light takes thousands of years to reach us.

The stars vary greatly in size. Some, called super-giants, make our Sun seem a dwarf. Others are only a few thousandths of the Sun's size.

Stars also vary considerably in brightness, and so are graded into different "magnitudes." A star of the first magnitude is 100 times brighter than a star of the sixth magnitude.

The brighter stars—such as Rigel and Regulus—are not necessarily the nearest to us. Several very faint stars are in fact nearer to Earth than most of the bright ones.

From earliest times, men have grouped the stars under names of animals and legendary heroes. A few of these constellation figures, as they are called, such as Orion and Corona Borealis (the Northern Crown), do look something like the figures they are supposed to represent, though most call for powerful feats of imagination.

Because the Earth rotates on its axis, the stars —like the Sun by day—*appear* to wheel from east to west across the sky. In the Northern Hemisphere, only Polaris seems to stand still because it is almost directly above the North Pole.

With the unaided eye, we can see from 2000 to 2500 stars on a clear night. Binoculars will show thousands more, and a large telescope can reach out to thousands of millions of stars. Most of these lie in the bright girdle of our own galaxy, the Milky Way.

The Milky Way is a vast rotating system of a hundred billion stars. It is just one galaxy among billions of others in the Universe. The galactic structures in the Universe range from single galaxies to mammoth clusters containing as many as 500 galaxies.

Although the cluster of galaxies to which our Milky Way belongs is comparatively small (it has only 19 members), our galaxy itself ranks among the larger of the known stellar systems. The distance across it is 100,000 light-years.

In the illustration we see the Milky Way Galaxy from the viewpoint of an observer out in space.

In the foreground near the bottom of the picture are two huge masses of stars and nebulae known as the Magellanic Clouds. Our galaxy lies 160,000 light-years from the Large Magellanic Cloud and 190,000 light-years from the Small-Magellanic Cloud. The Andromeda Galaxy (far left), with a diameter greater than 100,000 light-years, appears small because it is two million light-years beyond the Milky Way.

Clusters of hundreds and thousands of stars move as units around the galaxy. Reddish stars are concentrated toward the center of the formation, blue stars in the outer portions. Dark gases and interstellar dust are grouped so close together here and there that starlight from beyond cannot be seen. Our Solar System—the Sun and nine planets—is just a faint dot in one of the spiral arms of the Milky Way, some 27,000 light-years from the center.

As man probes deeper into a Universe that may be boundless, the number of galaxies seems to grow as vast as the space through which they speed.

THE Sun dominates and dwarfs its solar family of the nine major planets and the several thousand smaller ones called "asteroids." Jupiter, the largest dependent planet of the Sun, is no more than a speck by comparison with it, and Jupiter is roughly 1300 times the size of the Earth. The Sun comprises over 99.87 percent of the entire mass in our Solar System. Yet, despite the comparative smallness of the planets and the enormous distances of empty space that separate them from the Sun and from one another, the Sun keeps them under strict control.

Revolving around it in elliptical orbits, these planets are held in their course by the gravitational attraction of the Sun, and are kept from being drawn into it by the speed with which they move through space. The closer they are to the Sun, the faster they move.

Mercury—at an average distance of 36 million miles, the planet nearest the Sun—takes only about 88 days to travel around it, at a speed of 107,280 miles per hour. Venus, 67 million miles from the Sun, takes 224.7 days to complete its solar orbit at a speed of about 78,000 miles per hour. Evidence recorded by radio telescopes indicates that Venus turns so slowly that its day-night period would exceed its year—the direction of its rotation being retrograde (clockwise), opposite to that of the other planets. If this is so, on Venus the sun rises in the west and sets in the east, and the stars would shift very gradually, if they could be seen through the opaque atmosphere.

The Earth, 92,900,000 miles from the Sun, in its yearly orbit travels at a speed of 66,000 miles per hour. Pluto, now thought to be more than twice as large as was once estimated, is the most distant known planet. Pluto, 3664 million miles from the Sun, takes just over 247 years at a speed of 10,440 miles per hour to make one journey around it.

Six of the planets have one or more moons revolving about them, with twelve belonging to Jupiter, ten to Saturn, five to Uranus, two each to Neptune and Mars and one to Earth. Two of Jupiter's moons, Callisto and Ganymede, are very large, exceeding even the planet Mercury in size.

Traveling in a great elliptical belt between Mars and Jupiter are uncounted numbers of asteroids. They range in size from a few yards in diameter to several hundreds of miles. The largest on record is Ceres, 480 miles in diameter. Asteroids have no moisture or air, and therefore no life as we know it can exist on them.

It is doubtful, indeed, if such life can exist on any planet except Earth. Mercury is so close to the Sun that the temperature on its sunlit side is estimated to reach 700° F. Venus, although almost twice as far from the Sun as Mercury, is believed to have a surface temperature of 625° F. uniformly distributed by strong winds. This high temperature may be due to the greenhouse effect of Venus' thick cloud covering, which traps the Sun's heat. Jupiter, Saturn, Uranus, Neptune and Pluto are all too cold to sustain life, and their surfaces are enveloped by layers of the poisonous gases methane and ammonia.

There has been much speculation as to whether a form of life exists on Mars. This planet has an atmosphere with water vapor and carbon dioxide present. The white caps at the Martian poles, probably hoarfrost, vanish in the summer and reappear in the winter. There are also seasonal color changes in what appears to be a kind of vegetation. The belief that the hundreds of miles of Martian "canals" were the work of intelligent beings has now been discounted. However, many authorities agree that some primitive life forms may exist on Mars.

A planet that has long aroused great interest is the giant of the Solar System, Jupiter. Spinning on its axis faster than any other planet, Jupiter has the shortest day of all, approximately 10 hours long. This rapid rotation has caused a bulging of its equator and a flattening of the polar regions. Striking in appearance with its great irregular bands of yellow and brown, Jupiter is best known for its mysterious Great Red Spot, which was discovered in 1665 and about which little is known.

Saturn with its vast rings is one of the most interesting and beautiful planets. The rings, 170,000 miles in diameter, are extremely thin — not more than 10 miles thick — and are composed of millions of small particles, all performing as independent satellites as they speed around the mother planet.

WHERE EARTH

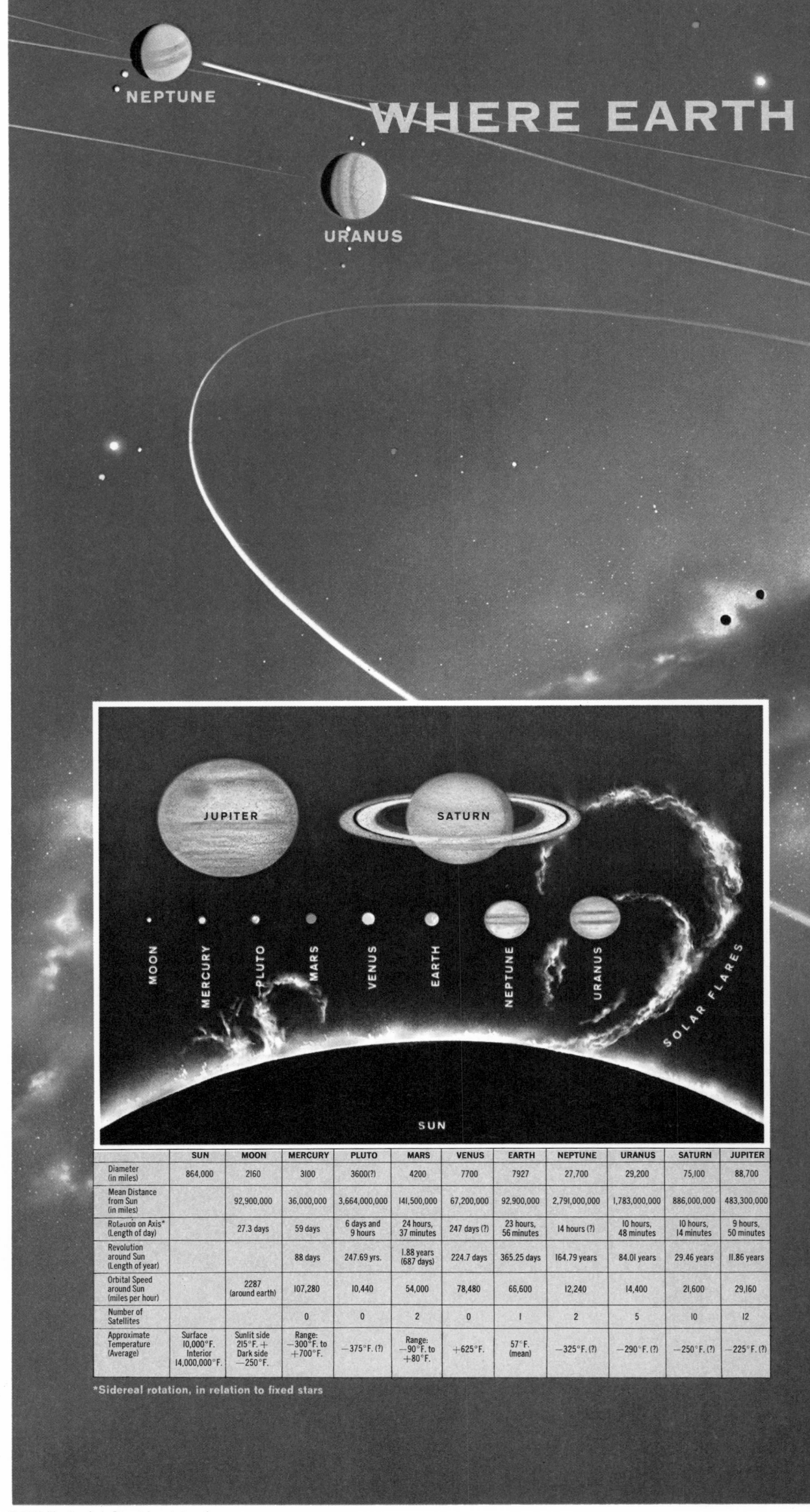

	SUN	MOON	MERCURY	PLUTO	MARS	VENUS	EARTH	NEPTUNE	URANUS	SATURN	JUPITER
Diameter (in miles)	864,000	2160	3100	3600(?)	4200	7700	7927	27,700	29,200	75,100	88,700
Mean Distance from Sun (in miles)		92,900,000	36,000,000	3,664,000,000	141,500,000	67,200,000	92,900,000	2,791,000,000	1,783,000,000	886,000,000	483,300,000
Rotation on Axis* (Length of day)		27.3 days	59 days	6 days and 9 hours	24 hours, 37 minutes	247 days (?)	23 hours, 56 minutes	14 hours (?)	10 hours, 48 minutes	10 hours, 14 minutes	9 hours, 50 minutes
Revolution around Sun (Length of year)			88 days	247.69 yrs.	1.88 years (687 days)	224.7 days	365.25 days	164.79 years	84.01 years	29.46 years	11.86 years
Orbital Speed around Sun (miles per hour)		2287 (around earth)	107,280	10,440	54,000	78,480	66,600	12,240	14,400	21,600	29,160
Number of Satellites			0	0	2	0	1	2	5	10	12
Approximate Temperature (Average)	Surface 10,000°F. Interior 14,000,000°F.	Sunlit side 215°F.+ Dark side −250°F.	Sunlit side −300°F. to +700°F.	−375°F. (?)	Range: −90°F. to +80°F.	+625°F.	57°F. (mean)	−325°F. (?)	−290°F. (?)	−250°F. (?)	−225°F. (?)

*Sidereal rotation, in relation to fixed stars

Another spectacular part of our Solar System is provided by comets. More than a million comets swing around the Sun in flat elliptical orbits. Some take only a few years to make the trip, but most have periods so lengthy that their return cannot be accurately predicted. The head of a comet, sometimes 50,000 miles wide, is composed mainly of dust and gases. When a comet comes near the Sun on its elliptical flight, gaseous matter in the head streams out to form a great glowing tail sometimes millions of miles long. This tail vanishes when the comet speeds away from the Sun. One of the most famous comets is named after the English astronomer Edmund Halley. He observed it in 1682 and accurately predicted its return every 76 years. Halley's Comet was last seen in 1910 and should be visible again in 1986.

Also racing through interplanetary space in regular orbits are billions upon billions of particles called meteorids. Some scientists believe that these bits of stone or metal, whose average size is no larger than a grain of sand, are fragments left

BELONGS: THE SOLAR SYSTEM

PLUTO

MERCURY

VENUS

SUN

MARS

ASTEROID BELT

MOON

EARTH

JUPITER

SATURN

THE SUN AND ITS PLANETS IN THE WINTER OF THE YEAR 2000

from disintegrated comets. When these particles plunge into the Earth's atmosphere they grow white hot and vaporize, becoming "shooting stars." Once in a while a mass of cosmic matter weighing tons plunges through the atmosphere to bury itself in the surface of the Earth. These large meteorites probably originate in the asteroid belt.

The composition of our Earth and its distance from the Sun seem to have provided exactly the right conditions in which an advanced form of life could develop. The life-giving energy of the

Sun, the source of all the heat and light in our Solar System, is generated by nuclear fusion in the Sun's interior. This raises the temperature deep inside the Sun to perhaps as high as 14,000,-000°F. So tremendous is the radiation rate of the Sun's energy that it loses millions of tons in weight every second. This rate of loss has been going on for five billion years, and the likelihood is that another five billion years will pass before the Sun's fuel is finally consumed and our great mother star winks out forever.

The planets of our Solar System not only travel around the Sun in the same direction, they also all lie in practically the same plane. Pluto is the exception. That faraway planet follows a path that is tilted 17 degrees from "the plane of the ecliptic," which is the name of the plane in which our Earth revolves.

13

THE REACH INTO SPACE

OR THOUSANDS OF YEARS man has gazed up at the sky and wondered what lay beyond. Early astronomers studied the pinpoints of light in the heavens and drew star charts. They examined the Moon and the planets, too, as best they could. They learned much, yet the geography of space remained a mystery that would never be really solved until man found a way to travel to the celestial regions and explore and map them himself. But, unlike the birds he observed, man was bound to the ground by a mysterious force he later called "gravity."

When, in 1783, the balloon was invented, it was thought that a means had been found to break free. Within the next century daring "aerostatists" did soar to the upper limits of the breathable atmosphere and scientists succeeded in sending up recording devices to still greater heights. Even so, the balloon proved not to be the answer. The balloon needed the pressure of air to make it rise. It could not function in the vacuum of space.

In 1903 the Wright brothers flew the first engine-driven heavier-than-air machine and another era of sky adventuring began. But the great ocean of space beyond the atmosphere was still unreachable. The airplane, too, was helpless at extreme heights. It could not fly without air flowing across its wings, nor could its internal-combustion engine operate without air.

Finally, after 25 years of experimentation, the modern rocket was developed. Carrying its own oxygen, the rocket needed no air to make its fuel burn. Neither did it need air to buoy it up, or air for its jet stream of exhaust gases to push against. The rocket operated on the principle contained in Sir Isaac Newton's Third Law of Motion: *For every action there is an equal and opposite reaction.* It "kicked" itself forward in the same manner that a gun recoils when it is fired. The rocket functioned even better in the vacuum of space than in the atmosphere of Earth.

It was the rocket, then, that introduced the space age. This amazingly simple device, invented by the Chinese over 700 years before, now stood ready to carry man's recording instruments—and man himself—into the outer deeps of space. On October 4, 1957, such an engine launched an artificial satellite, Sputnik I, into orbit around the Earth—the first man-made object to gain freedom from the remorseless force of gravity.

Since the launching of the first satellite, a great many others have been sent speeding into space. Packed with delicate instruments, these satellites perform a multitude of tasks. They have discovered belts of radiation encircling the Earth, relayed trans-oceanic messages, measured the Earth's shape, located tropical storms and transmitted information from the Moon and the planets.

The first man-carrying satellite was placed in orbital flight around the Earth by the Soviets on April 12, 1961. Numerous other manned flights have followed, some orbiting the Earth many times and covering millions of miles.

To launch a rocket, a great amount of thrust is necessary. Thrust is the propelling force produced by the exhaust stream of a rocket motor and is measured in pounds. The thrust force of a rocket must be much greater than the total rocket weight (including fuel and pay load) before the rocket lifts. Early rocket motors developed a mere 100 pounds of thrust. But by the end of World War II, 56,000 pounds were being delivered by the German V-2 rockets, which bombed London. During the early 1960s there were giant rocket engines rated at over a million pounds. Huge "solid-fuel" boosters are supplementing the liquid-fuel types. Nuclear energy, the ultimate power source, is also being harnessed.

We are, in fact, in a new era of manned space voyages—landings on the Moon, visits to our nearest neighbors, Mars and Venus, and even to the satellites of Jupiter. Our most ancient dreams are at the point of realization, and what the future holds for coming generations is barely imaginable.

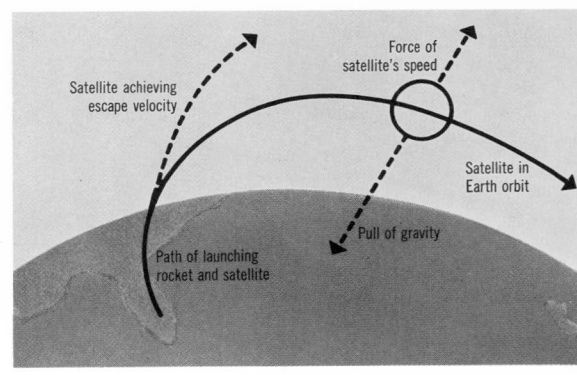

THE LAUNCHING OF A SATELLITE INTO ORBIT

A satellite in orbit maintains a balance between the gravitational attraction of the Earth, which is trying to pull the satellite down from the sky, and its own speed. To be launched into orbit around the Earth, a satellite must be accelerated to 18,000 miles per hour at an altitude of 100 to several thousand miles. This speed produces in the satellite the exact amount of centrifugal force necessary to counteract the pull of gravity. When this balance of forces occurs, the satellite is in orbit, whirling around the Earth once every 90 minutes on an elliptical path.

If the satellite were to slow down, the balance of the two forces would be upset, with the gravitational attraction becoming dominant. The satellite would then be drawn toward the Earth.

If the opposite occurred—if the speed of the satellite should increase—its centrifugal force would become the stronger of the two pulls. This would result in the elliptical orbit of the satellite becoming more and more elongated as the satellite moved farther away from the Earth. At the speed of 25,000 miles per hour the satellite would attain "escape velocity" and travel out into space, never to return.

In orbital flight, with his rocket engines shut off, an astronaut experiences a state of "weightlessness." He and his satellite are falling "freely" around the Earth with nothing to resist their plunge. The feeling of weight will return to the astronaut only when some resisting force begins to operate, such as the firing of rockets or the re-entry into the Earth's atmosphere.

FLIGHT PATH OF AN ORBITING SATELLITE

The flight path of a satellite in orbit around the Earth is plotted on a map of the world as a wavy track—not as a straight line. While the satellite is swinging around the Earth at an angle to the Equator, the Earth itself is rotating on its own axis beneath the satellite. Therefore the satellite is never observed continuously along one circumference of the globe, but appears to swing intermittently north and south as it goes.

Each time the satellite completes a circuit (in 90 minutes for a 200-mile-altitude orbit), the Earth will have turned about 25 degrees under it. Thus, on its second trip the satellite will pass, not over its launching site, but over a point about 25 degrees to the west of this site.

Every subsequent orbit will bring about a similar 25-degree shift westward until, after approximately 16 orbits, the satellite (unless redirected) repeats its first orbital path. The track of each orbit will cross the previous track twice.

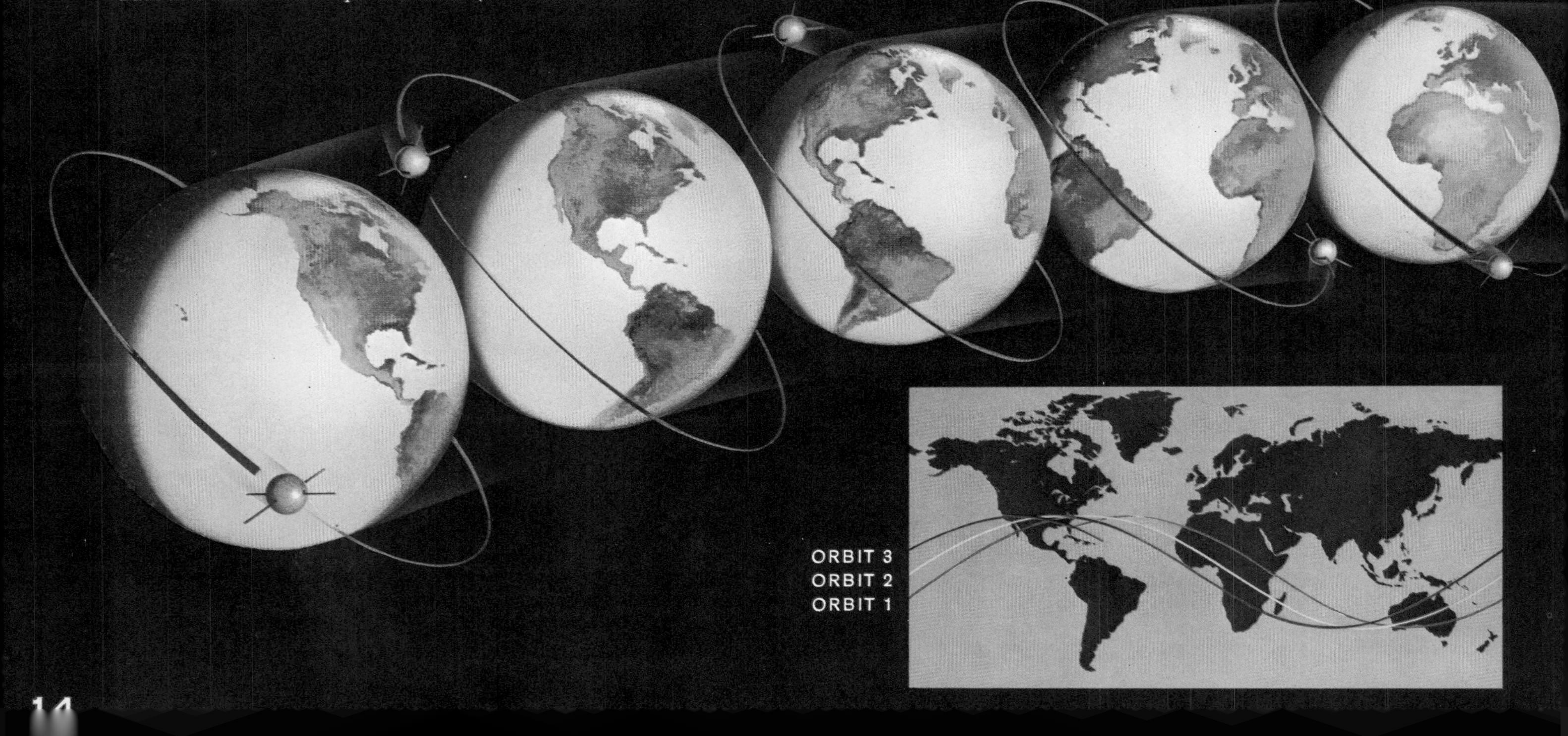

ORBIT 3
ORBIT 2
ORBIT 1

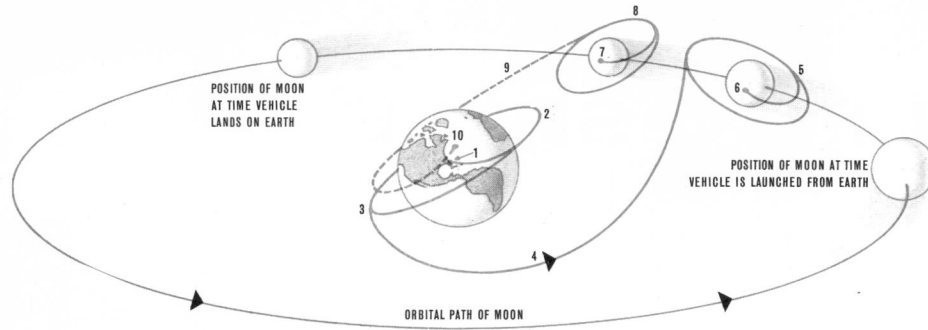

LUNAR FLIGHT

A number of flight patterns for a journey to the Moon have been plotted. The one illustrated here involves the use of a small lunar excursion vehicle, termed a "bug." The parent spacecraft carrying three astronauts and the bug is launched (1) by a three-stage rocket into an orbit (2) around the Earth at an altitude of 100 miles. At the proper moment for a Moon shot the third stage is fired (3) to give the spacecraft escape velocity. The spacecraft is sent on a 70-hour journey (4) to the Moon. Upon arrival in the Moon's vicinity, the craft is maneuvered into a 100-mile-high orbit (5) around the Moon. Two of the crew now enter the bug, de-

tach it from the mother ship and land on the Moon (6). After a period of exploration the lunar astronauts re-enter the bug and take off (7), using its own small rocket engines. Because of the low gravitational pull of the Moon (one sixth of Earth's gravity), relatively little thrust is needed. The bug links up with the mother ship (8), the Moon explorers enter the main ship, and the bug is cut loose and abandoned. The astronauts head back for the Earth in the mother craft (9) and a landing is made (10).

Another favored lunar flight plan involves an Earth-orbiting fuel tanker rather than the bug, but the excursion path is the same.

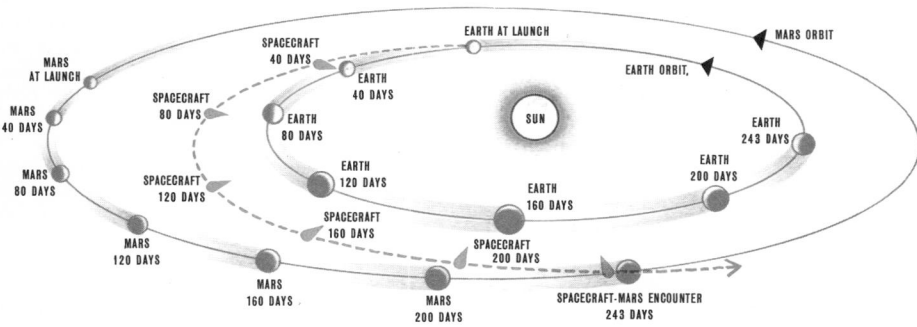

INTERPLANETARY FLIGHT PATHS

When a space vehicle leaves Earth to travel to another planet, it must first attain escape velocity (25,000 miles per hour). The craft then becomes, in effect, an independent satellite of the Sun, traveling in an orbit planned to intersect that of the planet to be visited.

If the objective is Mars or any of the other outer planets, the space vehicle must be launched from Earth in the same direction as the Earth's orbital movement around the Sun (see diagram above). This gives the vehicle an independent velocity greater than that of the Earth (Earth's orbital speed is 66,600 miles per hour). As a result, the spacecraft will travel outward, away from the Sun, with enough speed to counter the gravitational pull of the Sun. The spacecraft's orbit can be timed to intersect the path of an outer planet, such as Mars, at a given point in space. The duration of a flight to Mars would be about 243 days.

If the space vehicle is to rendezvous with an inner planet, such as Venus, the procedure is reversed (see diagram below). To go inward to-

ward the Sun, the vehicle must travel at less than the Earth's orbital speed. It is therefore launched counter to the direction of the Earth's orbital movement. This lowers the craft's speed below that of the Earth, even though the space vehicle will still travel around the Sun in the same direction as the Earth. The spacecraft will now pass inward toward the Sun and can be timed so that it will meet the oncoming Venus in approximately 108 days.

By extremely careful calculations and aiming, such orbits can be designed so that a space vehicle will rendezvous with any one of the planets, using very little more energy than is required to leave the Earth. Such a maneuver is called a "Hohmann transfer" after the engineer who developed the theory in the 1920s.

Venus and Mars probes have been undertaken, using this type of orbit strategy, and plans are being made for sending instrument probes to Jupiter. The first manned landing on that planet will be made probably on one of Jupiter's "moons" rather than on Jupiter itself.

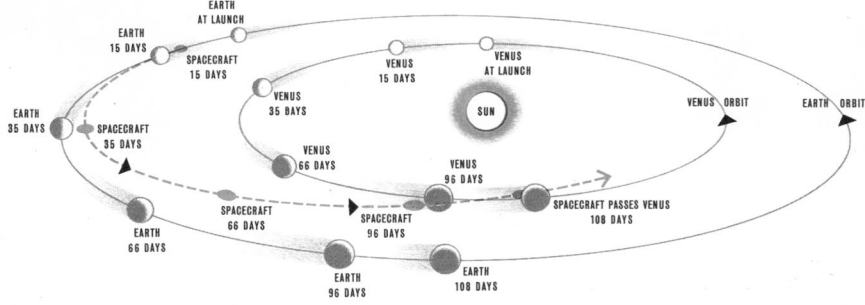

Planet	Minimum Distance from Earth (miles)	Maximum Distance from Earth (miles)	Surface Gravity (compared to 100 Earth pounds)	Escape Velocity (miles per hour)	Approximate Transit Time from Earth
Mercury	49,100,000	136,900,000	38 lbs.	9360	110 days
Venus	25,700,000	160,900,000	88 lbs.	23,040	108 days
Earth			100 lbs.	25,000	
Moon	221,463	252,710	16 lbs.	5400	72 hours
Mars	34,000,000	247,000,000	39 lbs.	14,400	243 days
Jupiter	362,000,000	597,000,000	265 lbs.	133,200	2.7 years
Saturn	773,000,000	1,023,000,000	117 lbs.	79,200	6 years
Uranus	1,594,000,000	1,946,000,000	92 lbs.	46,800	16 years
Neptune	2,654,000,000	2,891,000,000	123 lbs.	50,400	31 years
Pluto	2,605,000,000	4,506,000,000	16 (?)lbs.	5400 (?)	46 years

THE MOON has thousands of craters pitting its surface. Tycho Crater is shown above in a photograph taken by the spacecraft Lunar Orbiter V at a height of 134.9 miles. Tycho is a young crater whose debris, thrown across the face of the Moon, can still be seen.

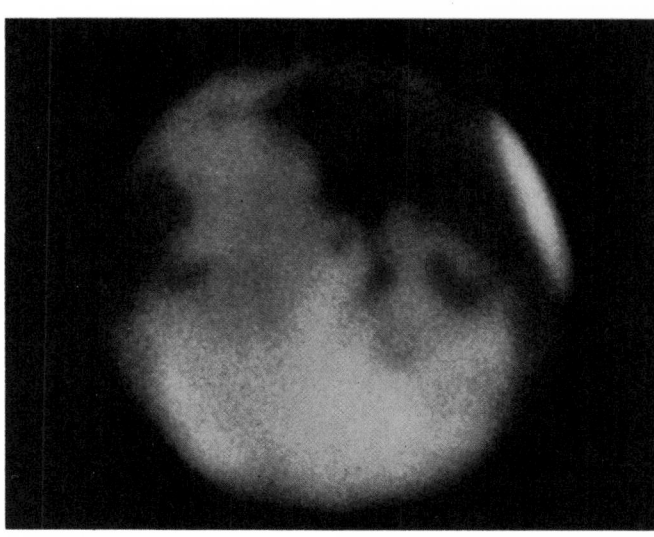

MARS is believed to have no canals, as was once suggested, for none show in close-up photographs. The patches of color in this picture have been suspected to be zones of vegetation, yet there is no evidence to support this contention. The white area is thought to be a thin coating of ice.

VENUS' surface, with a temperature of 625° F., is an inferno darkened by a curtain of clouds. Venus is the brightest of the planets which can be seen from the Earth. When full, it is farthest from us and appears small; when crescent-shaped, it is considerably closer and appears large.

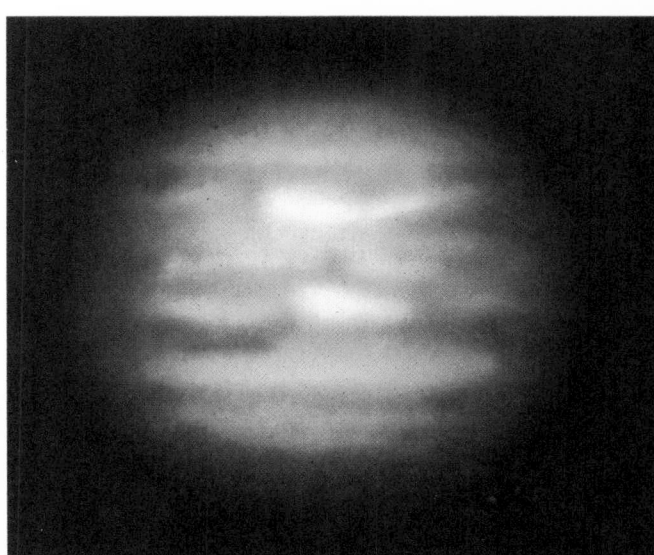

JUPITER is renowned for its Great Red Spot, over 30,000 miles long and 7000 miles wide. The Spot undergoes strange color changes (as in this photograph, where it appears almost white). The dark bands circling Jupiter are believed to be atmospheric, the yellowish areas to be the planet itself.

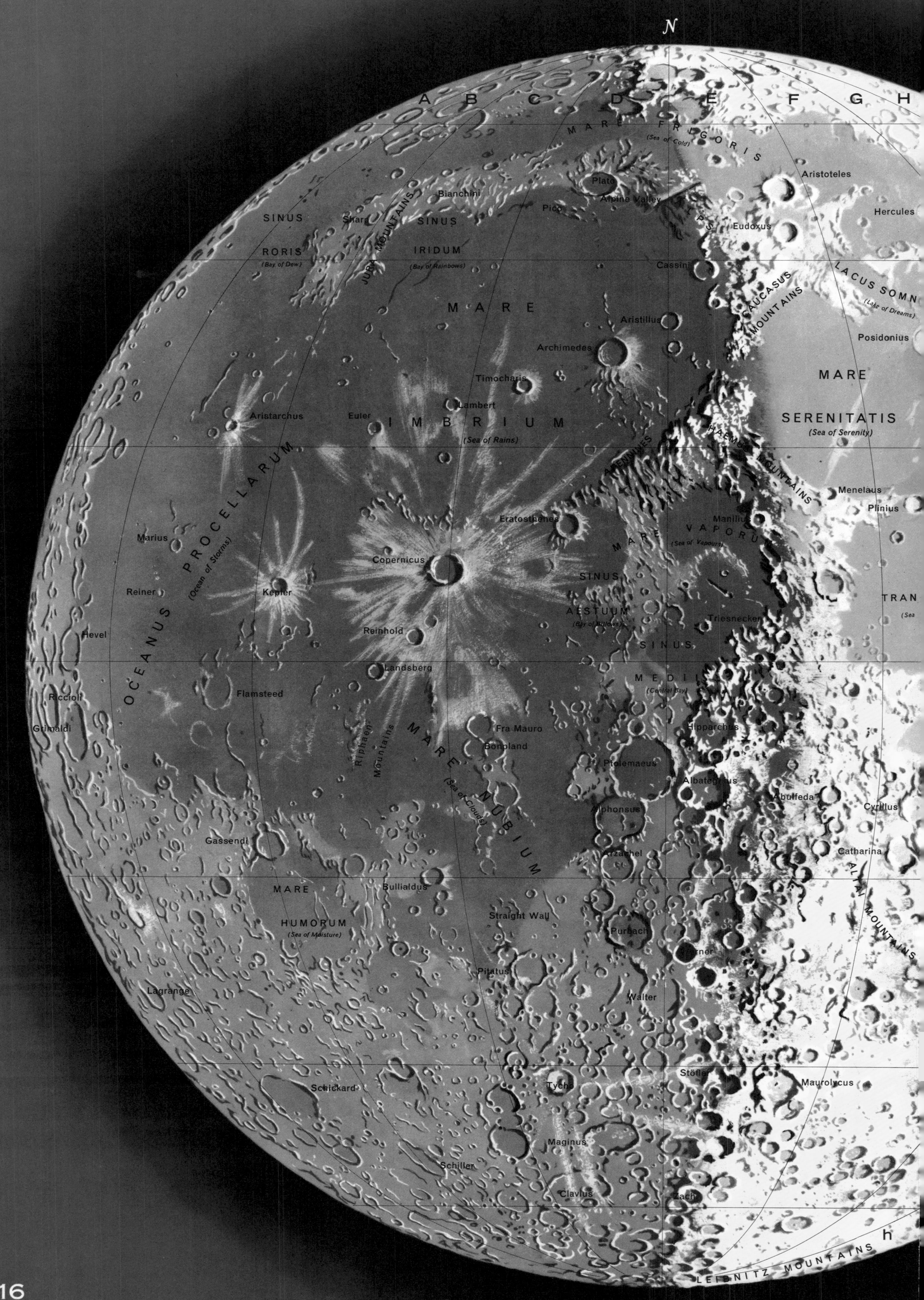

A B C D E F G H

MARE FRIGORIS
(Sea of Cold)

Plato   Aristoteles
Bianchini
Sharp   Pico   Alpine Valley   Hercules
SINUS   Eudoxus
RORIS   SINUS
(Bay of Dew)   IRIDUM   Cassini   CAUCASUS   LACUS SOMN
(Bay of Rainbows)   MOUNTAINS   (Lake of Dreams)

MARE   Aristillus   Posidonius
Archimedes
MARE
Timocharis   SERENITATIS
Lambert   (Sea of Serenity)
Aristarchus   Euler   IMBRIUM
(Sea of Rains)   HAEMUS MOUNTAINS   Menelaus
APENNINES   Plinius
Marius   Eratosthenes   Manilius
Copernicus   MARE VAPORUM
Reiner   (Sea of Vapours)   TRAN
Kepler   SINUS   (Sea
Hevel   Reinhold   AESTUUM   Triesnecker
(Bay of Billows)
Landsberg   SINUS
Riccioli   Flamsteed   MEDII
(Central Bay)
Grimaldi   Fra Mauro   Hipparchus
Ripahean   Bonpland   Ptolemaeus   Albategnius
Mountains   Alphonsus   Abulfeda   Cyrillus
Gassendi   Arzachel
Catharina
MARE   Bullialdus
HUMORUM   Straight Wall   Purbach
(Sea of Moisture)   Werner
Pitatus
Walter
Lagrange
Stöfler   Maurolycus
Schickard   Tycho
Maginus
Schiller
Clavius   Zach

LEIBNITZ MOUNTAINS

OCEANUS PROCELLARUM (Ocean of Storms)

MARE NUBIUM (Sea of Clouds)

ALTAI MOUNTAINS

JURA MOUNTAINS

16

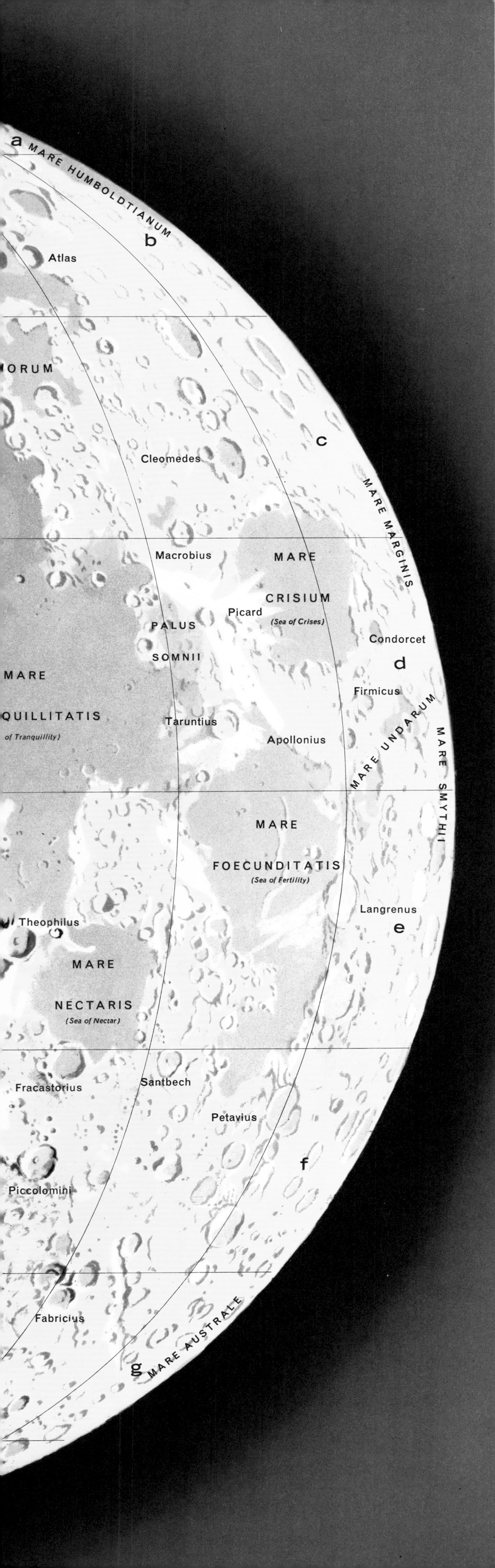

On the large moon map (left), the following labels appear:

a
MARE HUMBOLDTIANUM
b
Atlas
ORUM
Cleomedes
c
MARE MARGINIS
Macrobius
MARE
CRISIUM
Picard
PALUS
(Sea of Crises)
Condorcet
SOMNII
d
MARE
Firmicus
QUILLITATIS
Taruntius
MARE UNDARUM
MARE SMYTHII
(of Tranquillity)
Apollonius
MARE
FOECUNDITATIS
(Sea of Fertility)
Langrenus
e
Theophilus
MARE
NECTARIS
(Sea of Nectar)
Fracastorius
Santbech
Petavius
f
Piccolomini
Fabricius
g
MARE AUSTRALE

THE MOON

EARTH'S NATURAL SATELLITE

THE MOON IS UNIQUE in our Solar System. Many planets have satellites, but these are small in relation to their mother planets. The Moon is the only satellite of a size comparable to its planet, Earth.

The large map shows the near side of the Moon, which always faces the Earth; the far side is therefore never seen from Earth. As the Moon orbits the Earth, its periods of sunlight (its "day") and darkness (its "night") are each a half-month long.

To the naked eye the Moon seems to be made up of bright and darker patches. The bright parts are mountains and craters which catch the light of the Sun; the large darker areas are the low-lying plains. Once thought to be seas, these plains are still called by such names as Mare Imbrium (Sea of Rains) and Oceanus Procellarum (Ocean of Storms), though in fact the Moon is entirely without water.

High, sharp-peaked mountains, similar to the Apennines, rise to 20,000 feet. The highest are the Leibnitz Mountains, near the Moon's south pole, which reach 35,000 feet, higher than Mount Everest.

The most striking features are the many thousands of craters, named after philosophers and men of science. Possibly caused by the impact of meteorites, they range in size from pits a mile or less across, to magnificent walled plains such as Clavius, which is some 150 miles in diameter. Two of the finest, Copernicus and Tycho, are both over 50 miles across and have walls rising to heights above two miles. From these two craters and some others, bright streaks radiate for thousands of miles across mountains and valleys. Their origin is unknown; they may be some whitish material that welled up through cracks in the Moon's crust, or surface deposits thrown out when the craters were formed.

With a diameter about one quarter of the Earth's, the Moon has a surface area less than half that of the Atlantic Ocean. Its gravitational pull is correspondingly smaller, only about one sixth of the Earth's.

The Moon is without atmosphere, its gravity being too weak to hold down gas in any quantity. There is no erosion due to weather, and the Moon's features have therefore undergone little major change since they were formed. There is no sound, which is a vibration transmitted through air. With no atmosphere to protect it from the Sun by day or to imprison the heat by night, the Moon has great extremes of temperature. At the equator, the daytime temperature at the Moon's surface rises to 215°F., higher than that of boiling water, and at night the temperature sinks to −250°F. Under these conditions no life as we know it can exist.

Average distance from Earth......238,900 miles	Mass in terms of Earth 1:81
Diameter .... 2160 miles (Earth's diameter 7918 miles)	Sidereal Period ....27.3 days (approx.) (time taken to make one complete circuit of Earth)
Density ....3.3 times that of water (Earth's density 5.5 times that of water)	Synodic Period ....29.5 days (approx.) (interval between one new Moon and the next)

THE FAR SIDE OF THE MOON

Chart of the reverse side of the Moon, compiled from photographic positions obtained by the U.S. Orbiter vehicles and the Soviet Zond–3. When this chart was made in the autumn of 1967 only a very small portion of the far side of the Moon had not been photographed.

Near the edge of the chart appear some features which can be identified on the map of the visible hemisphere: Mare Marginis and Mare Smythii. Mare Orientalis is of special interest as it can just be seen from the Earth as a foreshortened plain, but the far-side photographs show that it is of very complex structure. It is important to studies of how the Moon's features were molded.

Names for the features on the far side of the Moon are under consideration by the International Astronomical Union.

EARTH'S ATMOSPHERE

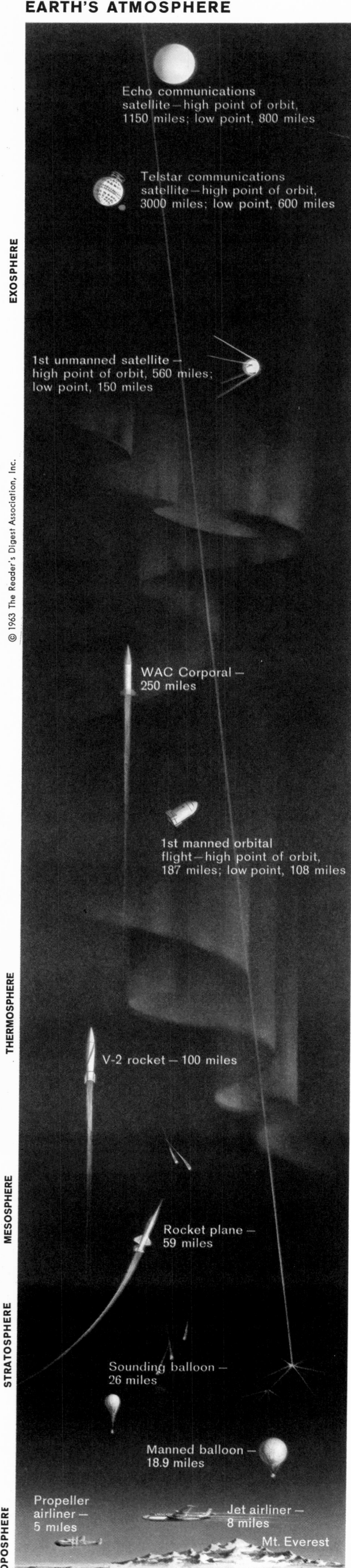

EXOSPHERE

Echo communications satellite—high point of orbit, 1150 miles; low point, 800 miles

Telstar communications satellite—high point of orbit, 3000 miles; low point, 600 miles

1st unmanned satellite—high point of orbit, 560 miles; low point, 150 miles

WAC Corporal—250 miles

THERMOSPHERE

1st manned orbital flight—high point of orbit, 187 miles; low point, 108 miles

V-2 rocket — 100 miles

MESOSPHERE

Rocket plane — 59 miles

STRATOSPHERE

Sounding balloon — 26 miles

Manned balloon — 18.9 miles

TROPOSPHERE

Propeller airliner — 5 miles

Jet airliner — 8 miles

Mt. Everest

Earth's atmosphere, the blanket of gases surrounding the planet, is the factor that, more than any other, enables life to exist. Without its protective insulation, temperatures would swing from unbearable cold at night to unbearable heat during the day and deadly solar radiation would penetrate to the Earth's surface. No one knows how far above the Earth the atmosphere extends, but it is probably at least 1000 miles. The air is not a uniform mass but can be divided into layers, each with its own characteristics.

The air here is so rarefied that its density is only one million-millionth of that at ground level. Air particles move freely, some escaping into the near-vacuum of outer space.

In the ionosphere the air particles are electrically charged (ionized) by the Sun's ultraviolet radiation, and congregate in four main layers: D, E, F_1 and F_2. It is these layers which reflect radio waves back to the ground.

F_2 Layer (150-250 miles) Ionosphere

The glowing auroras (northern and southern lights) are caused by streams of solar electrons and protons impinging upon the atmosphere. The auroras occur at varying heights between 40 and 600 miles.

F_1 Layer (90-150 miles) Ionosphere

It is mainly in the lower ionosphere that meteors burn up as they meet the increased air resistance. F_2 and F_1 layers reflect short radio waves. E layer reflects long radio waves. Also called the Heaviside layer, it is the lowest stable layer. D layer is unstable and unpredictable, and disappears at night.

E Layer (60-90 miles) Ionosphere

D Layer (45-60 miles) Ionosphere

The middle and upper stratosphere, between 15 and 30 miles from the Earth's surface, is a region of increasing temperature, rising from −70° to about 40° F. This is because a layer of ozone absorbs the Sun's ultraviolet rays and is the Earth's defense against the Sun's harmful radiation effects. The absorption of solar ultraviolet radiation causes heating within the stratospheric ozone layer.

Throughout the lower stratosphere, temperature varies little, and is usually about −70° F. At the lower boundary, the tropopause, the direct effects of Earth's weather are not usually felt.

From the ground to the tropopause the temperature drops steadily from about 59° F. at sea level (in temperate zones) to about −70° F. at seven miles (the average height of the troposphere), while the air thins out rapidly with increasing height.

EARTH'S

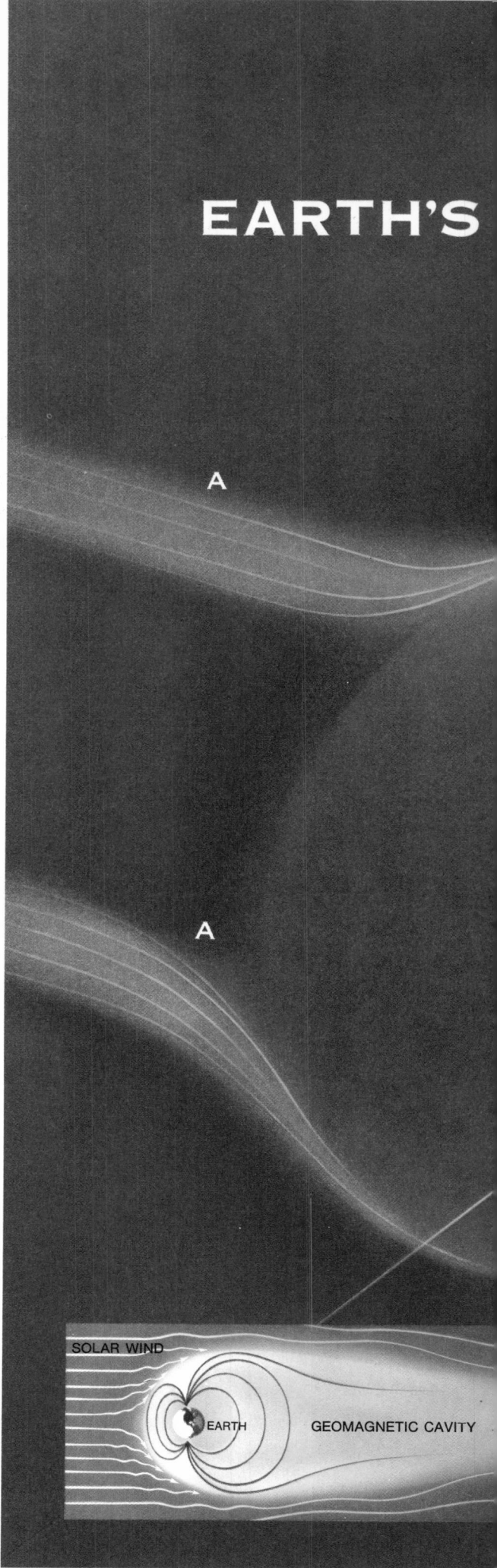

SOLAR WIND

EARTH

GEOMAGNETIC CAVITY

THE EARTH IS A GREAT MAGNET. The holding force of its magnetic field, arching from pole to pole, entraps vast belts of radiation about the Earth. These are called the Van Allen Belts, named after Dr. James A. Van Allen, whose dramatic discovery came in 1958 when he launched recording instruments aboard the first U.S. Explorer satellites. He found that high energy protons and electrons are held within the belts. Such trapped particles may be produced when strong cosmic rays which penetrate the Earth's atmosphere collide with molecules of air.

The Van Allen Belts are broad—their inner limit beginning about 600 miles above the Earth and the outer limits reaching some 35,000 miles into space. Crescent-shaped, their rim dips down toward the North and South Poles, where the Earth's magnetic field is most powerful. The Van Allen Belts pose a serious problem for the space traveler. Manned orbital flights are safe enough at 200 miles or so above the Earth, far under the

ENVIRONS

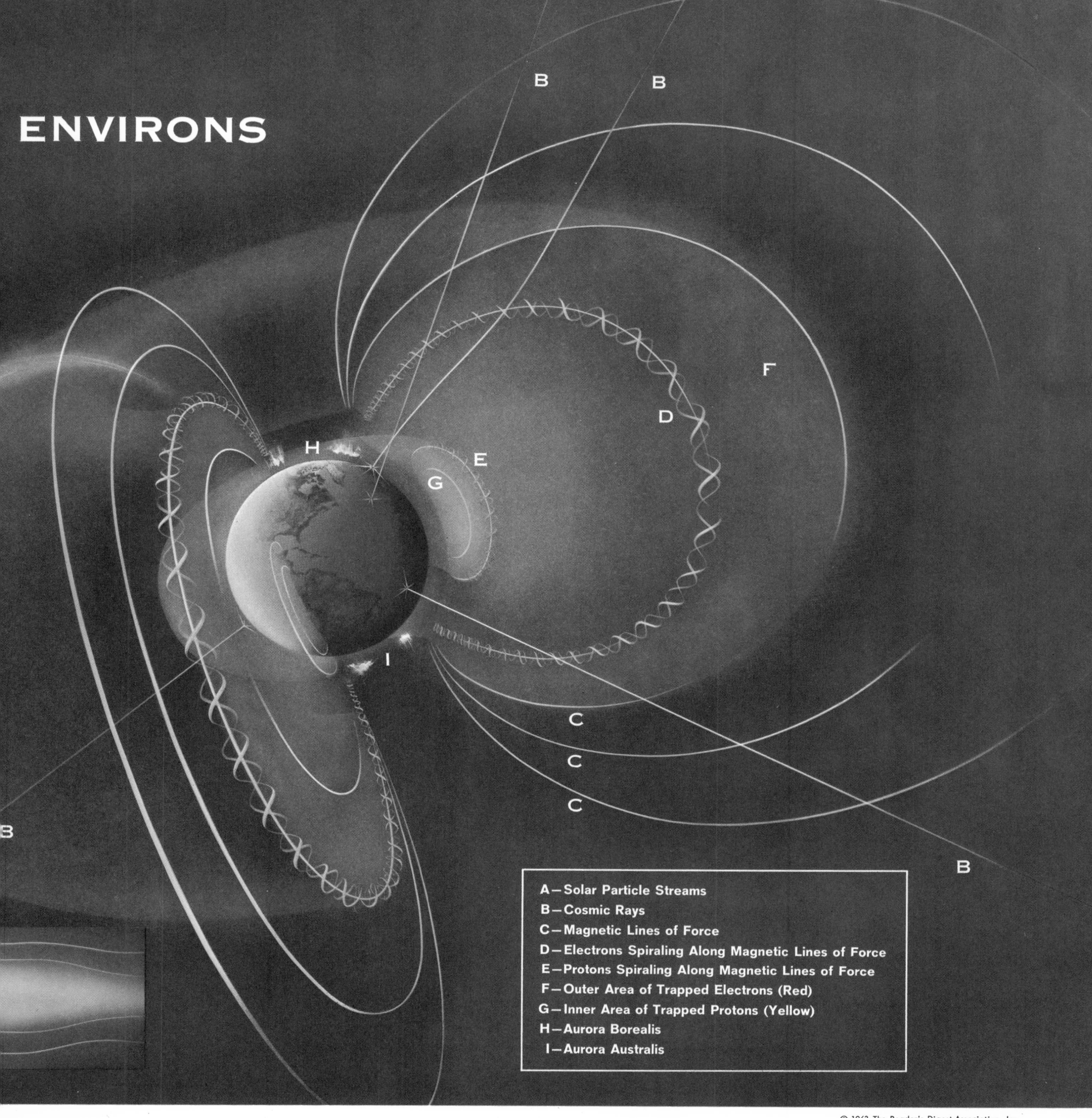

A — Solar Particle Streams
B — Cosmic Rays
C — Magnetic Lines of Force
D — Electrons Spiraling Along Magnetic Lines of Force
E — Protons Spiraling Along Magnetic Lines of Force
F — Outer Area of Trapped Electrons (Red)
G — Inner Area of Trapped Protons (Yellow)
H — Aurora Borealis
I — Aurora Australis

inner rim of the belts. But when a manned spacecraft sets out for the Moon, Venus or Mars, great care must be taken to shield the humans aboard from the lethal effect of radiation until the spacecraft has passed through the belts.

The Earth and its magnetic field are immersed in a never-ending stream of protons and electrons called the solar wind, which flows radially outward from the Sun. As the slow-moving particles approach within 40,000 miles of the planet, they are turned aside by our magnetic field; they divide and flow around the Earth, coming together again on the far side of the Earth, away from the Sun, at a distance of approximately 300,000 miles. The teardrop-shaped hole in the solar wind created by the Earth's magnetic boundary is called the Earth's *geomagnetic cavity* (see inset above). Trailing behind the cavity is a turbulent wake of particles—the *geomagnetic tail*—extending several million miles from the Earth.

The vast ocean of space that surrounds our Earth is ever active. Through it surge still other currents and tides of heat, light—various kinds of radiation. These powerful streams of energy come almost entirely from one source—the Sun. The Sun is more than a ball of raging hot gases; it is a tremendous thermonuclear furnace, slowly fusing hydrogen atoms into helium to produce incredible amounts of energy.

The substance of the Sun is never still. Short-lived eruptions, gigantic and dark, are constantly appearing across its face. About every 11 years (the last time was in 1957) these sunspots—looking like whirlpools—become especially numerous. Some are so large they could swallow up our Earth a hundred times over.

During the solar eruptions, great flares leap from the vicinity of the sunspots and slash out hundreds of thousands of miles across space. The flares spew out clouds of X rays and high energy particles in all directions. Shooting toward the Earth and traveling at tremendous speeds, they impinge on the boundary of the geomagnetic cavity, causing the magnetic field lines within the cavity to quiver and vibrate. The disturbance shakes loose some of the trapped Van Allen particles—fast electrons and protons—which escape from the Van Allen belt through the horns of the crescent near the North and South Poles. There, draining down from the upper atmosphere to the ground, they collide with molecules in the atmosphere to produce one of the grand displays of the Earth—the aurora borealis and aurora australis, or the northern and southern lights. Unusually brilliant displays of these luminous arcs and draperies follow large sunflares.

Much information has been gathered about the sunflare particles, gamma rays, X rays and all the others that make up the electromagnetic spectrum. As man continues to explore space beyond the Earth, more will be learned about the nature of space between the planets, the stars and the galaxies.

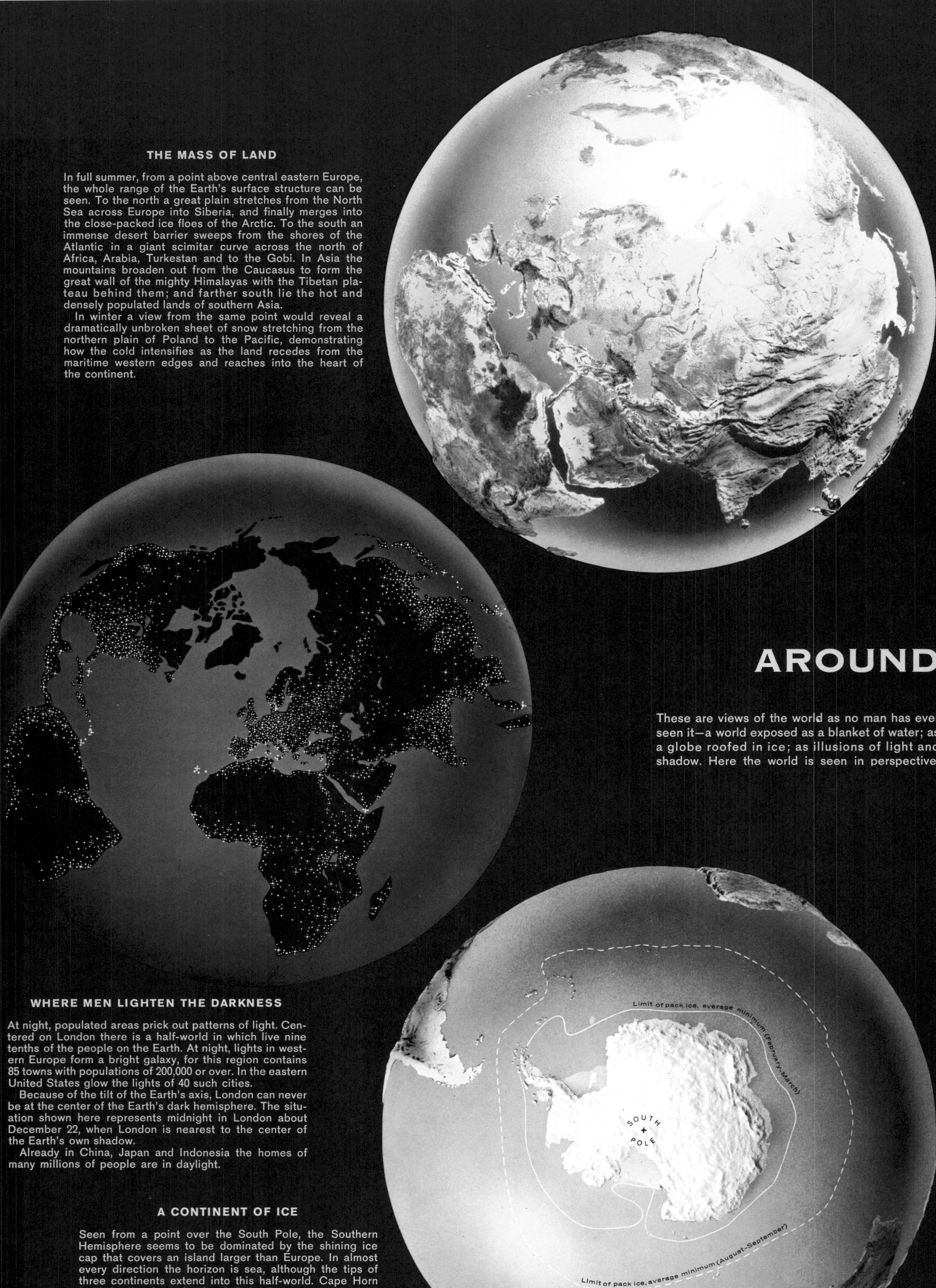

THE MASS OF LAND

In full summer, from a point above central eastern Europe, the whole range of the Earth's surface structure can be seen. To the north a great plain stretches from the North Sea across Europe into Siberia, and finally merges into the close-packed ice floes of the Arctic. To the south an immense desert barrier sweeps from the shores of the Atlantic in a giant scimitar curve across the north of Africa, Arabia, Turkestan and to the Gobi. In Asia the mountains broaden out from the Caucasus to form the great wall of the mighty Himalayas with the Tibetan plateau behind them; and farther south lie the hot and densely populated lands of southern Asia.

In winter a view from the same point would reveal a dramatically unbroken sheet of snow stretching from the northern plain of Poland to the Pacific, demonstrating how the cold intensifies as the land recedes from the maritime western edges and reaches into the heart of the continent.

AROUND

These are views of the world as no man has ever seen it—a world exposed as a blanket of water; as a globe roofed in ice; as illusions of light and shadow. Here the world is seen in perspective,

WHERE MEN LIGHTEN THE DARKNESS

At night, populated areas prick out patterns of light. Centered on London there is a half-world in which live nine tenths of the people on the Earth. At night, lights in western Europe form a bright galaxy, for this region contains 85 towns with populations of 200,000 or over. In the eastern United States glow the lights of 40 such cities.

Because of the tilt of the Earth's axis, London can never be at the center of the Earth's dark hemisphere. The situation shown here represents midnight in London about December 22, when London is nearest to the center of the Earth's own shadow.

Already in China, Japan and Indonesia the homes of many millions of people are in daylight.

A CONTINENT OF ICE

Seen from a point over the South Pole, the Southern Hemisphere seems to be dominated by the shining ice cap that covers an island larger than Europe. In almost every direction the horizon is sea, although the tips of three continents extend into this half-world. Cape Horn is 2350 miles from the South Pole; Buenos Aires is 3800 miles from it; the Cape of Good Hope lies a similar distance away; Christchurch in New Zealand and Hobart in Tasmania, the largest towns near to the Pole, are 3200 miles away.

The ice continent is itself uninhabited, and the stormy southern seas are deserted except for icebergs broken adrift from the polar ice cap.

THE WATER PLANET

Tahiti is at the center of this half-world that is almost all water. To the east and south of Tahiti are thousands of square miles of the Pacific Ocean without a single island or reef. In the western Pacific, groups of tiny islands gleam white in the sunlight; far to the north lies Hawaii, a solitary stepping-stone on the 6200-mile hop from North America to Asia. Solid land masses are far away. To the southwest is Australia—with Sydney 3801 miles from the island of Tahiti. The vast semicircle of the Americas serrates the opposite skyline; Vancouver is 4888 miles from Tahiti, Panama 5180, Cape Horn 4950, Tokyo 5893.

Compare this hemisphere with the one to its left. There, millions of people live in the heart of Asia. Here, in the water hemisphere, live only a few hundred thousand people, thousands of miles from any sizable land.

THE WORLD

night and day, and from four directions. Hold these pages 18 inches from your eyes. Each of the half-worlds will reveal the Earth the same size you would see it if you were 25,000 miles out in space.

DAWN ADVANCES

Part of the world is in shadow: dawn is just reaching the Americas. The first rays of the rising sun break on the hills of Nova Scotia and Brazil, while the glaciers of Greenland are already in full daylight. It is nine in London and breakfast is over, four in the morning in New York, an hour after midnight in San Francisco and noon in Baghdad.

Only at the equinoxes in March and September does every place in the world have an equal number of hours of darkness and light. In June the tilt of the Earth's axis brings full daylight all round the clock to the North Pole. It is then midsummer in the Northern Hemisphere and midwinter in the Southern.

THE ROOF OF THE WORLD

The North Pole, with its waste of broken ice, is the hub of this view. The floating ice of the North Pole merges into the frozen northlands of Russia and Canada. Below comes the belt of coniferous forest which rings the world from the Atlantic Ocean to the Pacific and, jumping the 50-mile gap between Siberia and North America, sweeps on again from the Pacific Ocean to the Atlantic. Below the forest region, great towns describe another circle round the globe—Leningrad 2070 miles from the North Pole, Glasgow 2360, Quebec 3000 and Edmonton 2520. Along this ring the railways, highways and air routes make a web of communications that continues across the oceans by ship and plane. Far on the horizon lies the belt of desert and mountain between temperate and tropical lands.

Map labels (west to east, north to south):

ST. OF JUAN DE FUCA · Seattle · C. Disappointment · MT. RAINIER 14,410 · COAST RANGES · Columbia R. · CASCADE RANGE · SELKIRK MTS. · ROCKY MOUNTAINS · MT. CLEVELAND 10,448 · C · 120° · 100° · N

Portland · MT. HOOD 11,245 · Columbia R. · BLUE MTS. · SAGUAWEAN PK. 10,033 · BITTERROOT RANGE · SALMON RIVER MTS. · ABSAROKA RANGE · BIG HORN MTS. · Yellowstone R. · Billings · Missouri R. · 45°

C. Mendocino · Great Sandy Desert · Snake R. · Boise · Snake River Plain · GANNETT PEAK 13,785 · BLACK HILLS

MT. SHASTA 14,162 · LASSEN PEAK 10,457 · Desert Valley · Great Salt Lake · WASATCH RANGE · South Pass · LARAMIE RANGE

Pt. Arena · COAST RANGES · Sacramento R. · Reno · Donner Pass · SHOSHONE MTS. · Salt Lake City · KINGS PEAK 13,498 · MEDICINE BOW PK. 12,005 · Cheyenne · Platte R. · Republican R.

San Francisco · SIERRA NEVADA · San Joaquin R. · ARC DOME 11,775 · LONGS PEAK 14,255 · Denver · MT. ELBERT 14,420 · PIKES PEAK 14,109 · SAN JUAN MTS. · ROCKY MOUNTAINS

Pt. Sur · DIABLO RANGE · COAST RANGES · WHEELER PEAK 13,058 · Colorado R. · Arkansas R.

Pt. Arguello · MT. WHITNEY 14,495 · Grand Canyon · COLORADO PLATEAU · Painted Desert · Colorado

Mojave Desert · HUMPHREYS PK. 12,655 · Oklahoma City

Los Angeles · SAN GORGONIO MT. 11,485 · SANTA CATALINA I. · Albuquerque · Llano Estacado · Pecos R.

San Diego · Salton Sea · Colorado R. · Phoenix · GALIURO MTS. · SACRAMENTO MTS. · Edwards Plateau

Pta. Banda · CERRO LA ENCANTADA 10,100 · Rio Grande · GUADALUPE PEAK 8751 · 30° · 100°

GULF OF CALIFORNIA · SIERRA MADRE OCCIDENTAL · BOLSON DE MAPIMI · SIERRA MADRE ORIENTAL · EMORY PEAK 7835 · M E X I C O · Rio Grande

PACIFIC OCEAN

Inset map:

HAWAII

160° · 155° · KAUAI I. · OAHU I. · Honolulu · MOLOKAI I. · PACIFIC OCEAN · MAUI I. · 20° · HAWAII I. · 155° · 160°

50 · 0 · 100 Miles

For Alaska see page 30.

THE COUNTRIES of the world, as they might be seen by an astronaut, appear on the relief maps on this and the following pages. Looking down, we see the snow- and ice-covered regions edging the Arctic Ocean; the Antarctic, bleak and formidable in its cold isolation; the lands becoming warmer as we approach the Equator; the shadowy forms of hills rising above the general level of the Earth; the great mountain ranges in all their ruggedness, forming immense natural barriers as they sweep across the continents regardless of man-imposed boundaries; the low-lying plains, some richly fertile, others wide, arid wastes.

In magnificent relief, we see the coastline, sometimes falling abruptly, sometimes sloping gently,

STATES

LAKE SUPERIOR

LAKE MICHIGAN

LAKE HURON

LAKE ERIE

L. ONTARIO

APPALACHIAN MOUNTAINS

ADIRONDACK MTS.

CATSKILL MTS.

BLUE RIDGE

ALLEGHENY

BOSTON MTS.

OUACHITA MTS.

OZARK Plateau

ATLANTIC OCEAN

GULF OF MEXICO

BAHAMA IS.

Relief map copyright: Aero Service Corp., courtesy Nystrom Raised Relief Map Co.

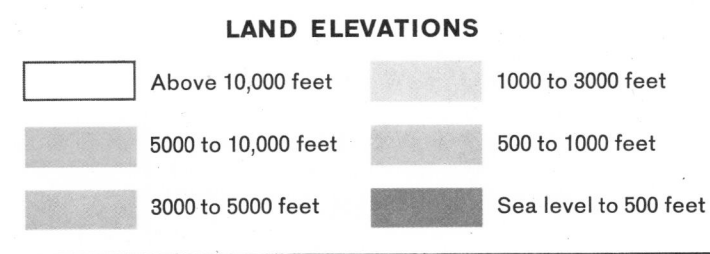

LAND ELEVATIONS

Above 10,000 feet	1000 to 3000 feet
5000 to 10,000 feet	500 to 1000 feet
3000 to 5000 feet	Sea level to 500 feet

down into the sea, which gives a clear pattern of the shapes of continents in their early evolution. We become aware of the vastness of the oceans, the great depths in many of them, and their submerged peaks and mountain ranges.

This map and the reliefs on pages 30-35 and 42-44 are vertically magnified 20 times. On the maps on pages 24-29 and 36-37 the vertical magnification is 30 times; on pages 38-41 it is 25 times.

THE APPALACHIAN RANGE

THE APPALACHIAN RANGE, the oldest chain in the United States, sweeps from Canada 1500 miles southward to central Alabama. It includes the White Mountains of New Hampshire, the Green Mountains of Vermont, the Alleghenies, the Blue Ridge Mountains, the Black Mountains, the Great Smokies and lesser ranges. These form the divide that separates the rivers flowing into the Atlantic Ocean from those entering the Gulf of Mexico.

A number of these rivers have cut deep valleys known as "gaps," among which are the Delaware Water Gap, the Shenandoah Valley and the Cumberland Gap. (There are also wind gaps.) Through the Cumberland Gap, on the borders of Kentucky, Tennessee and Virginia, Daniel Boone blazed one of the principal routes to the west in 1775 — the Wilderness Road.

Other early routes through the mountains were the Forbes Road, between what are now Harrisburg and Pittsburgh, and the National —or Cumberland—Road from Maryland to Illinois, worn by generations of settlers.

The Appalachians have been worn down by the weathering of centuries, and the highest of them—such as Mount Washington in New Hampshire and Mount Mitchell in North Carolina—do not exceed 7000 feet.

An unusual feature of the chain is its longitudinal system of valleys, known as the Great Appalachian Valley, extending north to separate the Appalachians from the Adirondacks and south to divide the Alleghenies from the Blue Ridge.

The Alleghenies have been among the most productive of American mountains, their slopes in the neighborhood of Pittsburgh yielding coal, coke and—once—the iron ore that contributed to the rise of such men as Andrew Carnegie.

Indeed, the Pittsburgh coal seam, discovered by Colonel James Burd in 1759, proved richer in value than any other mineral source ever worked by man. It covers some 5700 square miles in four states. Great labor unions found their origin here among the workers in mining and steel. The first petroleum well was drilled in this region in 1859.

Historically, too, these mountains have been significant. The Appalachians kept the early settlers confined to the Atlantic Coast and delayed the opening of the west. On the other hand, they provided a natural barrier from would-be attackers across the mountains—the Indians and the French—and brought about the denser settlement of the coastal lands.

The combination of protection from enemies and the community spirit fostered among Americans forced to live close together brought the original 13 colonies to a higher degree of development than might otherwise have been the case. The Appalachian barrier therefore played a role in the ultimate success of the American Revolution.

The view to the right shows the upper Appalachians from northern New Hampshire to Pennsylvania. The Great Lakes are seen in the distance. Below, one follows the range from Pennsylvania to Tennessee.

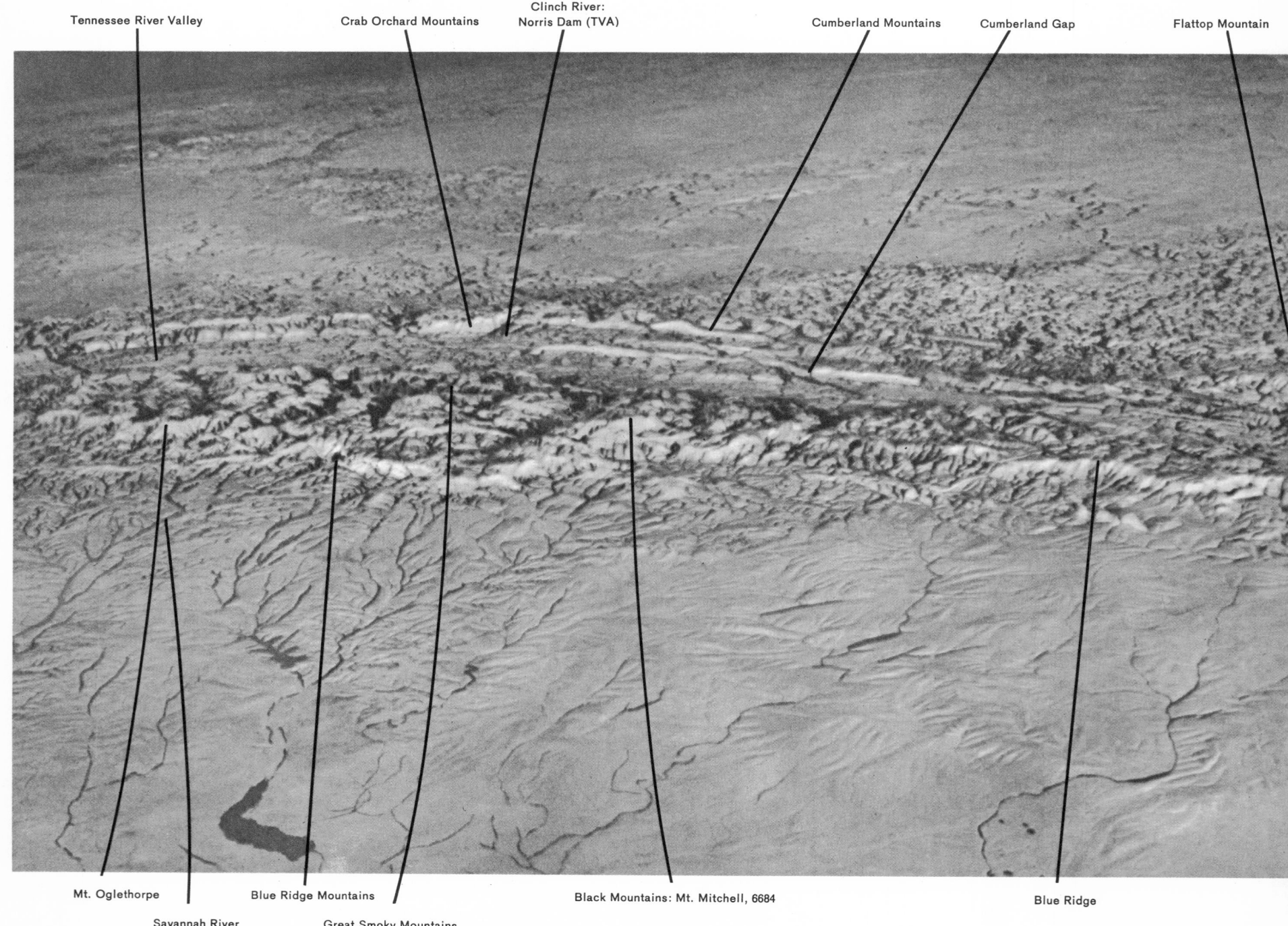

Tennessee River Valley   Crab Orchard Mountains   Clinch River: Norris Dam (TVA)   Cumberland Mountains   Cumberland Gap   Flattop Mountain

Mt. Oglethorpe   Blue Ridge Mountains   Black Mountains: Mt. Mitchell, 6684   Blue Ridge

Savannah River   Great Smoky Mountains

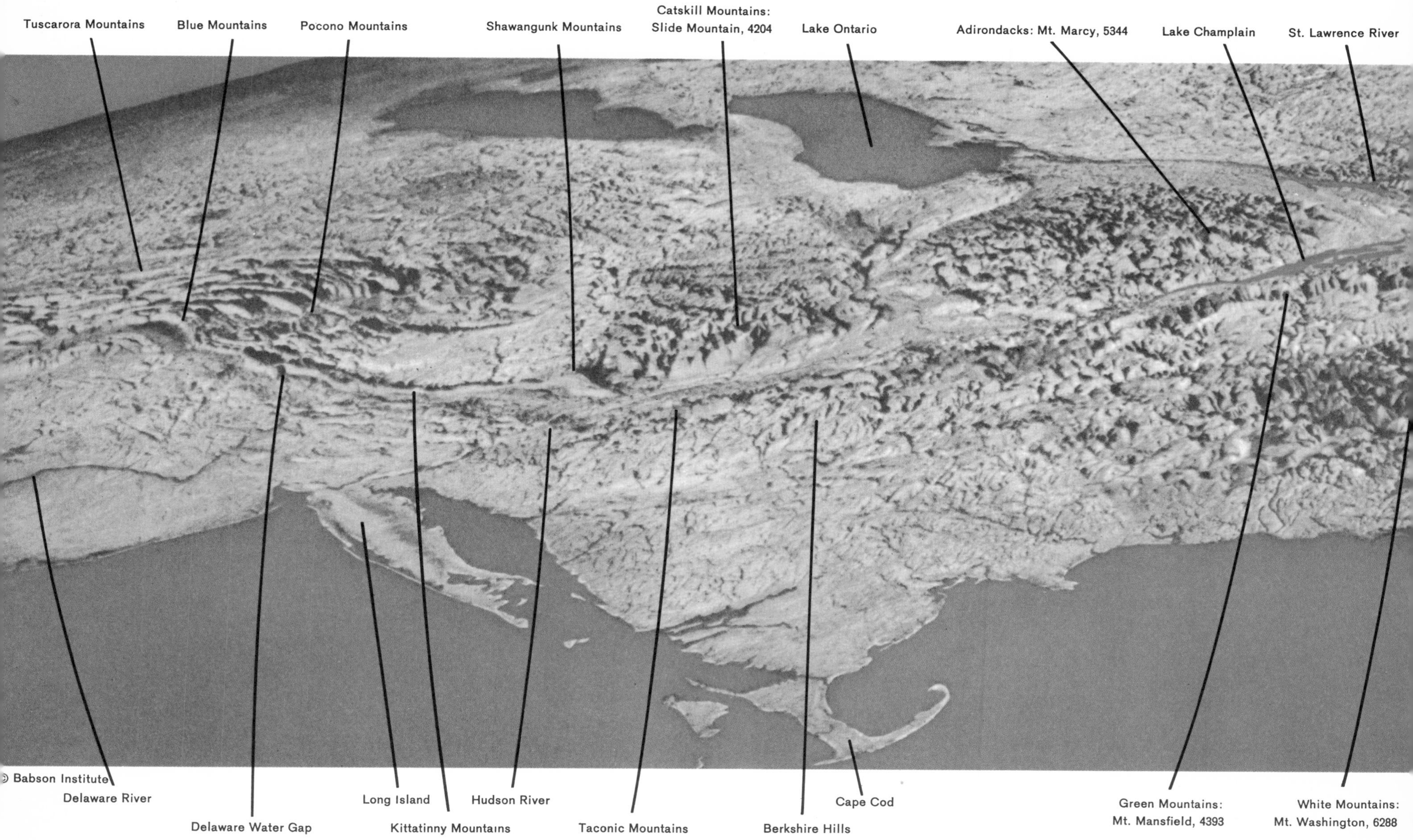
Tuscarora Mountains
Blue Mountains
Pocono Mountains
Shawangunk Mountains
Catskill Mountains:
Slide Mountain, 4204
Lake Ontario
Adirondacks: Mt. Marcy, 5344
Lake Champlain
St. Lawrence River
© Babson Institute
Delaware River
Delaware Water Gap
Long Island
Kittatinny Mountains
Hudson River
Taconic Mountains
Berkshire Hills
Cape Cod
Green Mountains:
Mt. Mansfield, 4393
White Mountains:
Mt. Washington, 6288

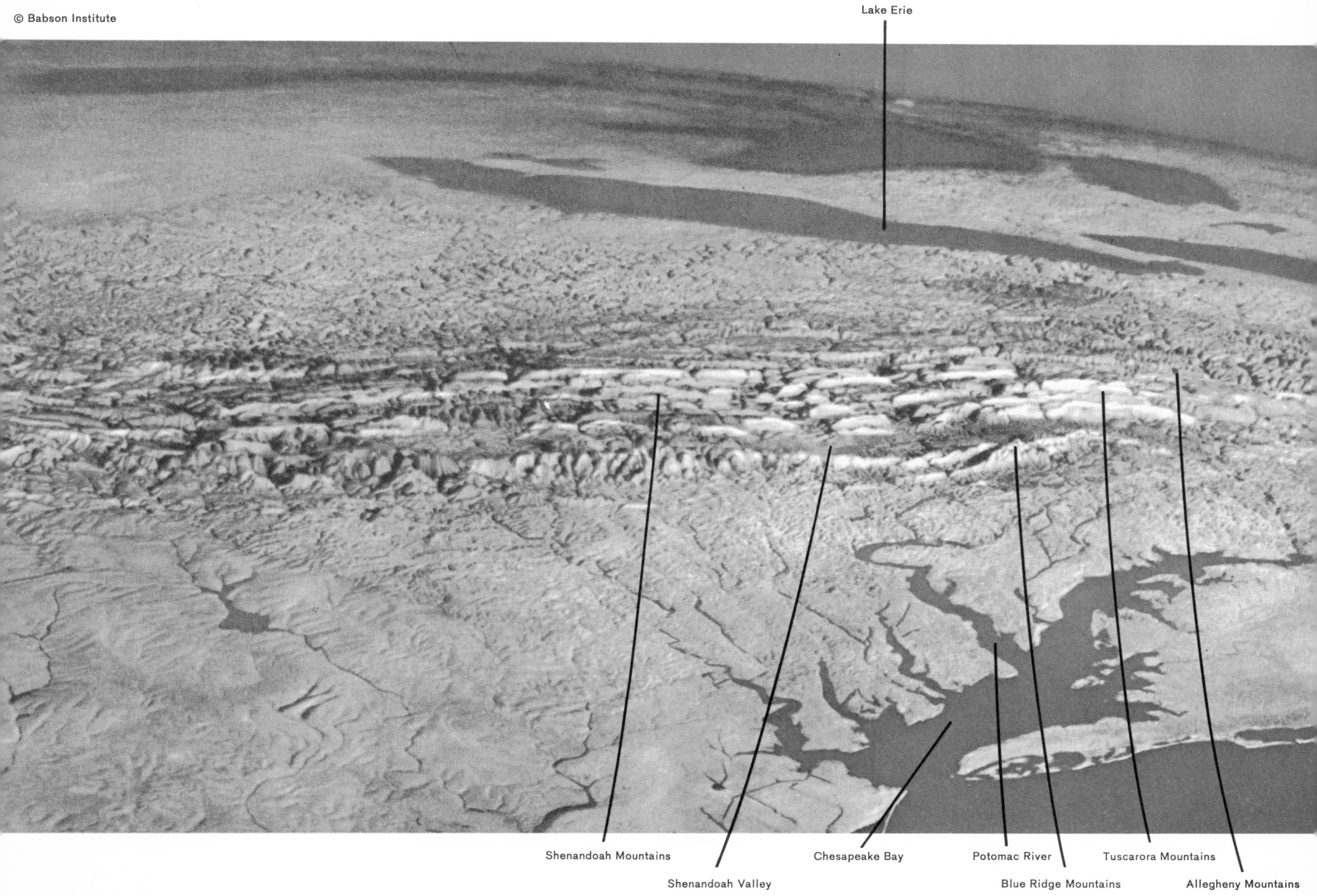
© Babson Institute
Lake Erie
Shenandoah Mountains
Shenandoah Valley
Chesapeake Bay
Potomac River
Blue Ridge Mountains
Tuscarora Mountains
Allegheny Mountains

THE ROCKY MOUNTAINS

THE ROCKY MOUNTAINS, the newest range in the United States, extend some 2800 miles, of which 1290 are below the Canadian border. The latter mark the Continental Divide, which separates the rivers flowing into the Gulf of Mexico from those emptying into the Pacific Ocean.

The highest peaks below Canada are found in Colorado, which has more than 250 mountains of over 13,000 feet and 55 of over 14,000 feet.

Early American pioneers such as Zebulon Pike and the much-traveled John C. Frémont endured hazardous journeys to cross the mountain barriers. South Pass on the Oregon Trail and Raton Pass on the Santa Fe Trail provided passage through the Rockies for later settlers and adventurers traveling westward.

Great rivers, such as the Yukon, the Mackenzie, the Columbia, the Missouri, the Arkansas, the Colorado and the Rio Grande, rise in this range to water the continent.

The views shown here are taken looking westward from eastern Wyoming (top) and eastern Colorado (bottom).

Mt. Shasta, 14,162 — Snake River Plain — Wind River Range: Gannett Peak, 13,785

Great Salt Lake

Bridger Basin

South Pass (Oregon Trail)

Wind River

N. Platte River — Absaroka Range

Painted Desert — San Francisco Peaks, 12,655 — Grand Canyon — Gunnison River Valley

Spanish Peaks, 13,623 — San Luis Valley — Arkansas River — Pikes Peak, 14,109

Raton Pass (Santa Fe Trail) — Sangre de Cristo Range: Blanca Peak, 14,390 — San Juan Mountains: Summit Peak, 13,272

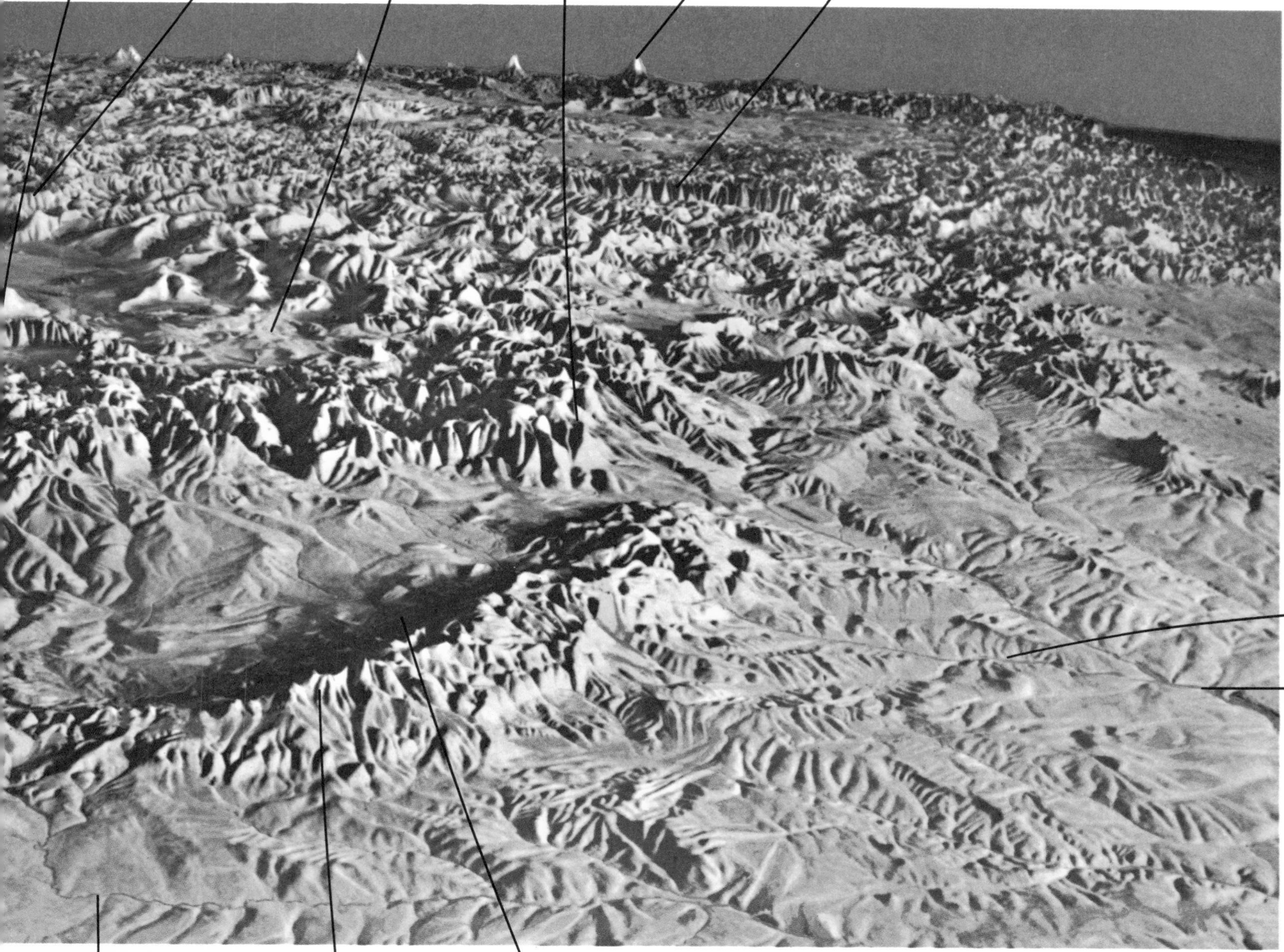

Teton Mountains | Sawtooth Range | Yellowstone National Park | Snowy Range | Mt. Rainier, 14,410 | Bitterroot Range

Bighorn River

Yellowstone River

© Babson Institute

Powder River | Bighorn Range: Cloud Peak, 13,175 | Bighorn Basin

Great Salt Lake Desert | Wasatch Range

Great Salt Lake

North Park

Medicine Bow Mountains

© Babson Institute

South Park | Sawatch Range: Mt. Elbert, 14,420 | Mt. Lincoln, 14,300 | Front Range: Longs Peak, 14,255 | S. Platte River

THE WESTERN COASTAL RANGES

T HE WESTERN COASTAL MOUNTAINS of the United States stretch from Oregon through California, descending into Mexico. Bordering the Pacific are the Coast Ranges. In Washington they include the wild fastnesses of the Olympic Mountains. Farther inland are the Cascade Mountains, of which one, Mount Rainier, rises to a snow-clad peak two and a half miles above sea level.

The Cascade Range continues into Oregon. Through the Blue Mountains of this state, along the valley of the Columbia River, wound the Oregon Trail, blazed by early fur traders. One of these was John Jacob Astor, who founded Astoria at the Columbia River's mouth in 1811. Washington and Oregon and the states east of them are shown to the right.

Below are views of California and the states to the east. The Coast Ranges here are the area of earthquakes, of which the most famous was that at San Francisco in 1906. Inland are the majestic Sierra Nevadas. Mount Whitney (14,495 feet), in this range, is the highest peak below Canada.

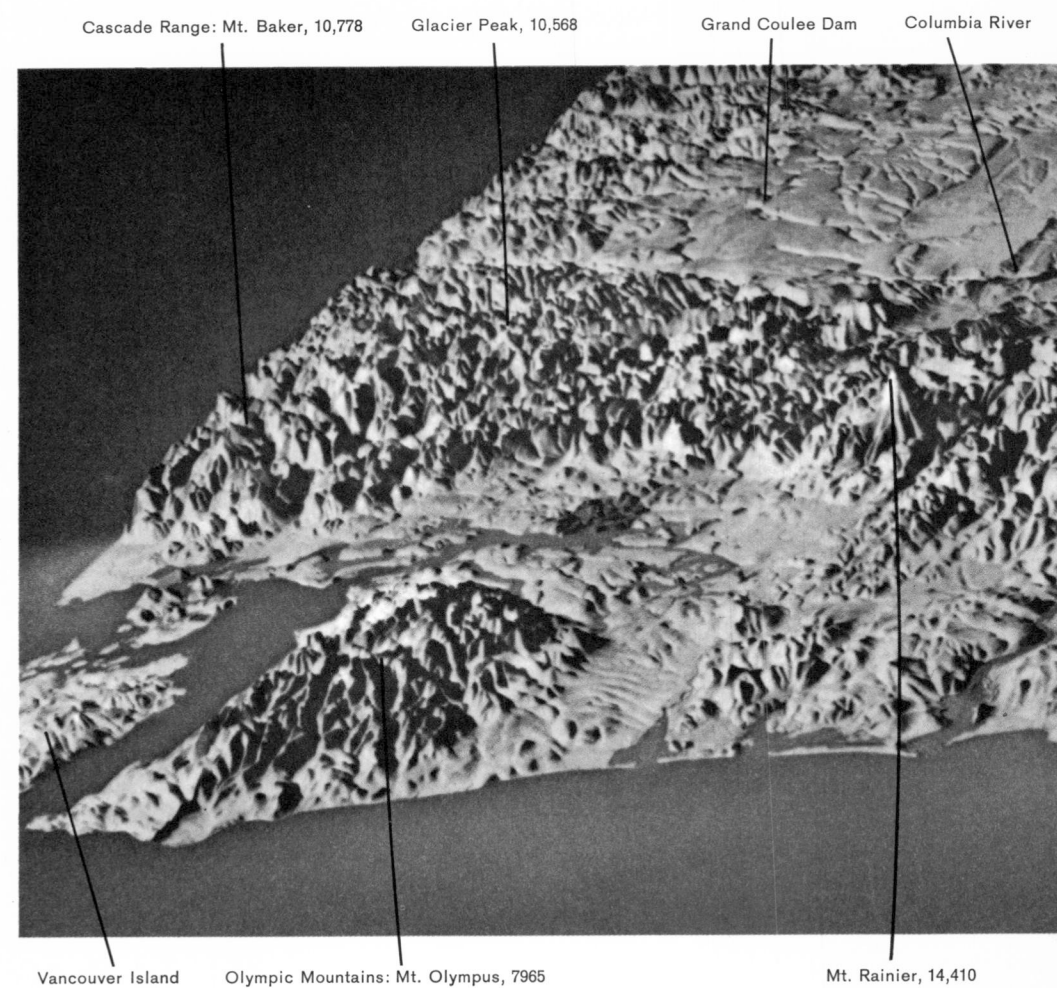

Cascade Range: Mt. Baker, 10,778   Glacier Peak, 10,568   Grand Coulee Dam   Columbia River

Vancouver Island   Olympic Mountains: Mt. Olympus, 7965   Mt. Rainier, 14,410

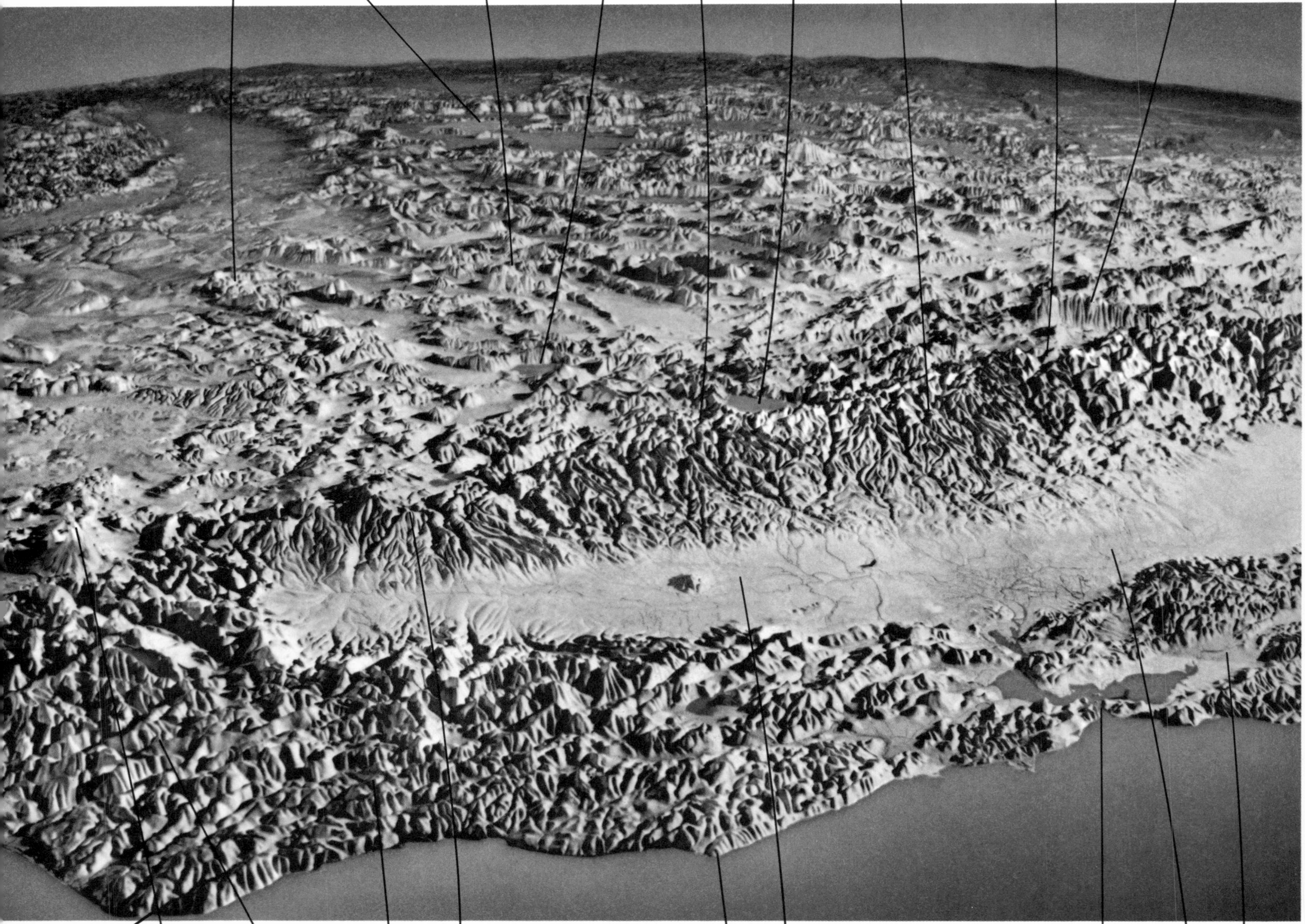

Santa Rosa Range   Great Salt Lake   Shoshone Mountains   Pyramid Lake   Donner Pass   Lake Tahoe   Sierra Nevada Range   Yosemite National Park   White Mountains

Cape Mendocino   Klamath Mountains   Coast Ranges   Point Arena   Golden Gate   Santa Clara Valley

Cascade Range: Mt. Shasta, 14,162   Mt. Lassen, 10,457 (active volcano)   Sacramento Valley   San Joaquin Valley

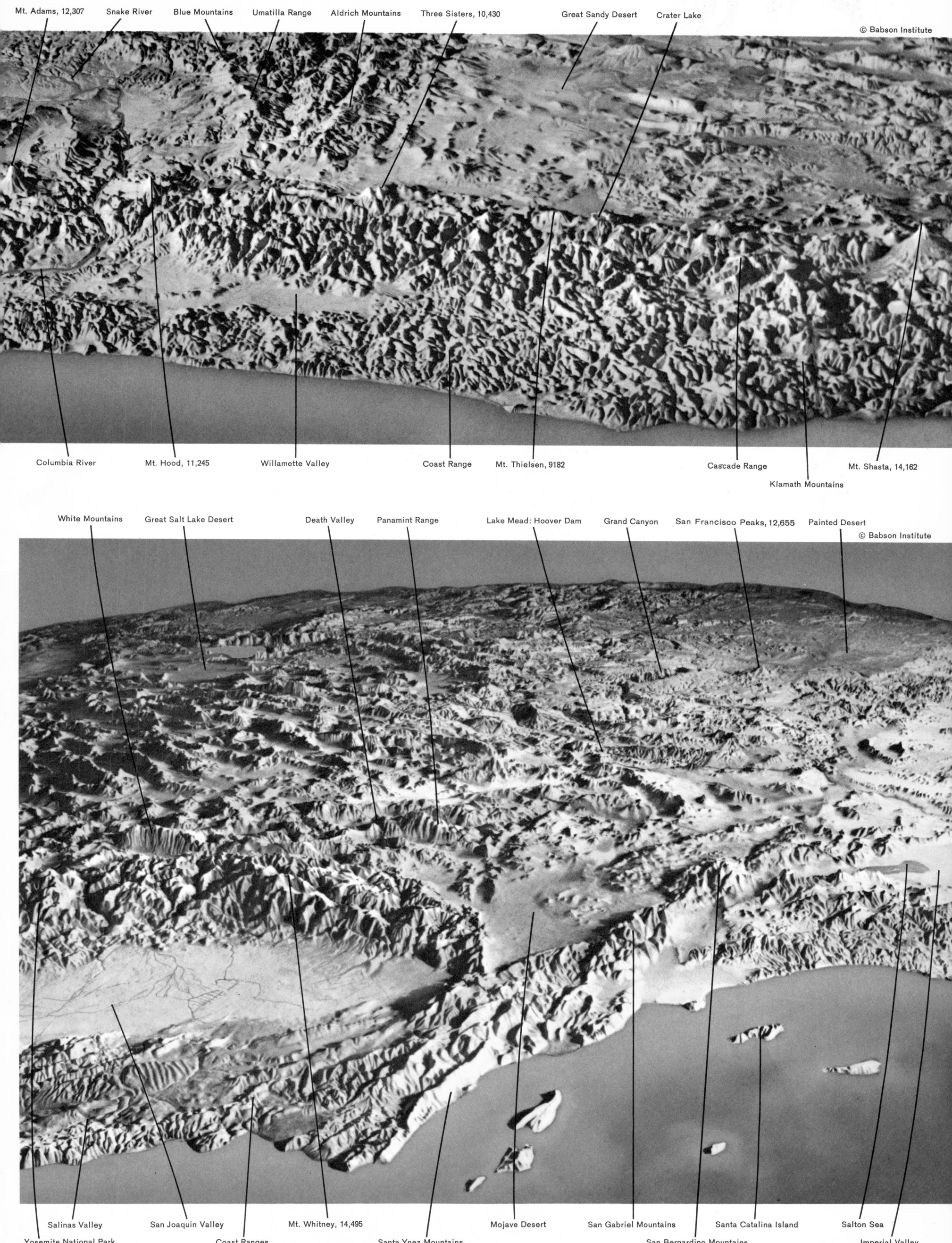

Mt. Adams, 12,307   Snake River   Blue Mountains   Umatilla Range   Aldrich Mountains   Three Sisters, 10,430   Great Sandy Desert   Crater Lake

Columbia River   Mt. Hood, 11,245   Willamette Valley   Coast Range   Mt. Thielsen, 9182   Cascade Range   Mt. Shasta, 14,162

Klamath Mountains

White Mountains   Great Salt Lake Desert   Death Valley   Panamint Range   Lake Mead: Hoover Dam   Grand Canyon   San Francisco Peaks, 12,655   Painted Desert

Salinas Valley   San Joaquin Valley   Mt. Whitney, 14,495   Mojave Desert   San Gabriel Mountains   Santa Catalina Island   Salton Sea

Yosemite National Park   Coast Ranges   Santa Ynez Mountains   San Bernardino Mountains   Imperial Valley

CANADA AND ALASKA

100 0 100 200 300 400 500
Miles

LAND ELEVATIONS

Above 9840 feet

6560 to 9840 feet

3280 to 6560 feet

1640 to 3280 feet

660 to 1640 feet

Sea level to 660 feet

ALEUTIAN ISLANDS

50 0 100 200 MILES

GREENLAND

ICELAND

Reykjavík

DENMARK STRAIT

20°

60°

40°

NORTH

ATLANTIC

OCEAN

80°

ELLESMERE ISLAND

DEVON I.

BAFFIN

BAY

Thule

DISKO I.

DAVIS STRAIT

FOXE

BASIN

MELVILLE PEN.

KEEWATIN

PEN.

SOUTHAMPTON I.

HUDSON STRAIT

UNGAVA BAY

UNGAVA PEN.

L A B R A D O R

NEWFOUNDLAND

Gander

H U D S O N

B A Y

James

Bay

LAURENTIDE MTS.

GULF OF

ST. LAWRENCE

St. Lawrence

NOVA SCOTIA

Halifax

Lake Winnipeg

Winnipeg

E S

Quebec

APPALACHIAN MOUNTAINS

Montreal

Ottawa

LAKE SUPERIOR

Mississippi

LAKE MICHIGAN

LAKE HURON

Toronto

L. ONTARIO

80°

60°

Relief map copyright: Aero Service Corp., courtesy Nystrom Raised Relief Map Co.

CARIBBEAN SEA
LESSER ANTILLES
ARUBA
CURAÇAO
BONAIRE
ST. VINCENT
GRENADA
TOBAGO
TRINIDAD
Port-of-Spain
I. MARGARITA
Caracas
P. Gallinas
G. DE VENEZUELA
PICO CRISTOBAL COLON 18,947
Barranquilla
Maracaibo
L. Maracaibo
CANAL ZONE (U.S.A.)
Panamá
G. DE URABÁ
G. DE PANAMA
I. MALPELO
VENEZUELA
Orinoco
CORD. DOMERIDA
San Cristóbal
C. ORIENTAL
Magdalena
Meta
Bogotá
COLOMBIA
CORD. OCCIDENTAL
CORD. CENTRAL
Cali
NEV. DEL HUILA 18,865
MT. RORAIMA 9094
SIERRA PACARAIMA
GUYANA
Georgetown
Paramaribo
SURINAM (NETH.)
FRENCH GUIANA
Cayenne
C. Orange
SA. DE ACARAI
SA. DE TUMUCUMAQUE
Branco
Negro
Manaus
EQUATOR
80°
60°
40°
0°
20°
Quito
CHIMBORAZO 20,577
ECUADOR
Guayaquil
Putumayo
Solimões
Amazon
Leticia
Marañón
Ucayali
Juruá
Purus
Madeira
Tapajóz
Xingu
Tocantins
Belém
BAÍA DE SÃO MARCOS
Parnaíba
Fortaleza
C. de São Roque
Natal
Recife
Maceió
Salvador
SA. DOS CARAJÁS
Araguaia
SA. DA DESORDEM
SA. NEGRA
SA. DO PENITENTE
SERRA URUÇUÍ
SA. DA IBIAPABA
São Francisco
SERRA GERAL DE GOIÁS
CHAPADA DIAMANTINA
BRAZIL
Pôrto Velho
SERRA DOS PARECIS
SA. DO RONCADOR
Planalto de Mato Grosso
SA. DO VERDINHO
Brasília
SA. DA CANASTRA
PICO DO ITAMBÉ 6155
SERRA DO ESPINHAÇO
SA. DOS AIMORÉS
Belo Horizonte
Corumbá
CERRO YERUPAJÁ 21,758
Lima
PERU
CERRO PUMASILLO 20,492
Cuzco
NEV. COROPUNA 21,690
L. Titicaca
NEV. ILLAMPU 21,270
La Paz
BOLIVIA
Mamoré
CORDILLERA ORIENTAL
CORDILLERA CENTRAL
NEV. SAJAMA 21,390
Sucre
Poopó
Salar de Uyuni
ANDES
Atacama

SOUTH AMERICA

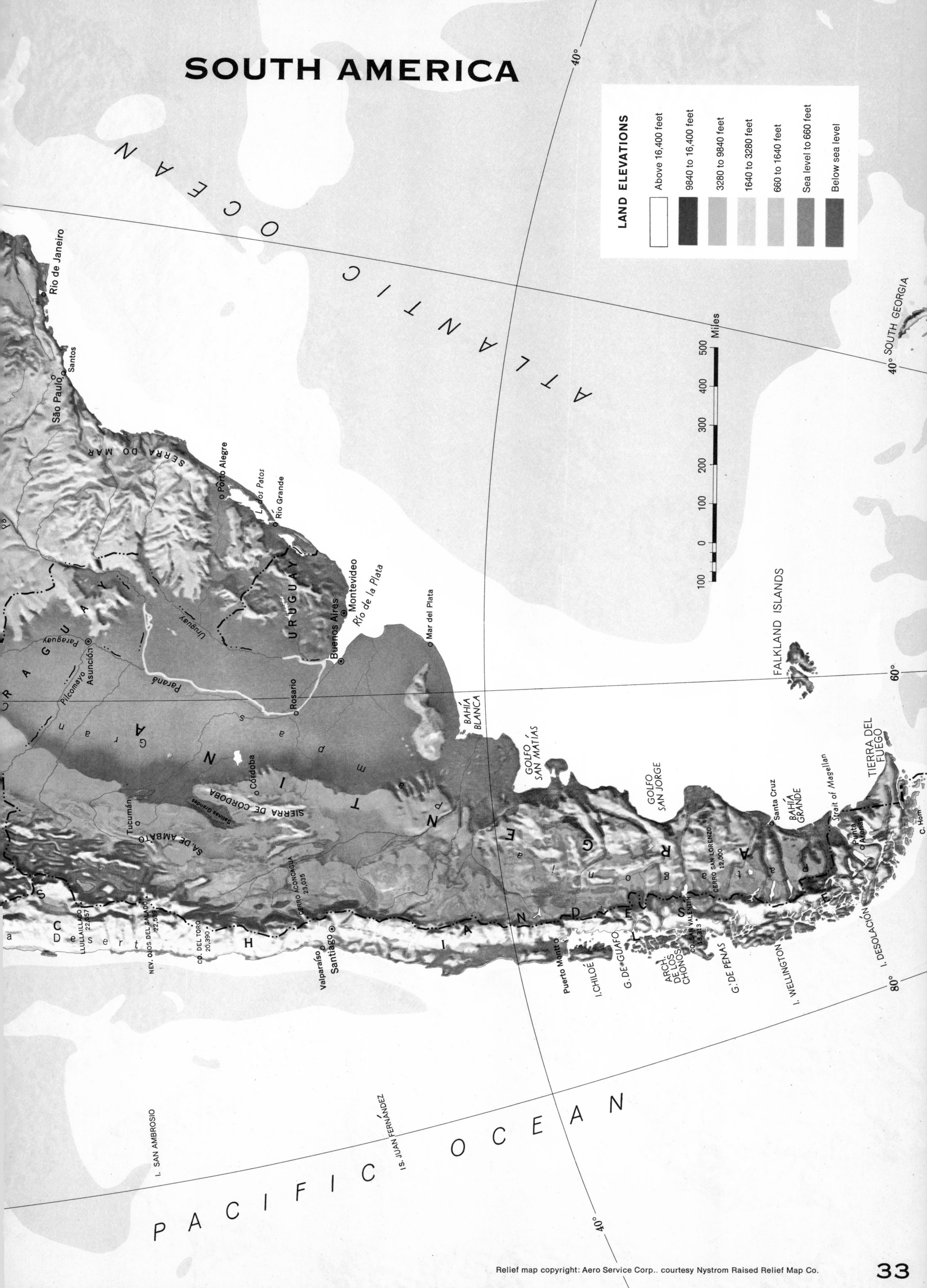

LAND ELEVATIONS

Above 16,400 feet
9840 to 16,400 feet
3280 to 9840 feet
1640 to 3280 feet
660 to 1640 feet
Sea level to 660 feet
Below sea level

ATLANTIC OCEAN

PACIFIC OCEAN

Miles

500
400
300
200
100
0
100

Rio de Janeiro
Santos
São Paulo
SERRA DO MAR
Porto Alegre
L. dos Patos
Rio Grande
URUGUAY
Montevideo
Río de la Plata
Buenos Aires
Mar del Plata
Uruguay
PARAGUAY
Paraguay
Asunción
Pilcomayo
Paraná
Rosario
Gran
Córdoba
SIERRA DE CORDOBA
Salinas Grandes
Tucumán
S. DE AMBATO
CERRO ACONCAGUA 23,035
CO. DEL TORO 20,390
NEV. OJOS DEL SALADO 22,539
LLULLAILLACO 22,057
Valparaíso
Santiago
Desert
Atacama
BAHÍA BLANCA
GOLFO SAN MATÍAS
ARGENTINA
GOLFO SAN JORGE
CERRO SAN LORENZO 12,000
Santa Cruz
BAHÍA GRANDE
Strait of Magellan
TIERRA DEL FUEGO
C. Horn
Punta Arenas
I. DESOLACIÓN
I. WELLINGTON
CO. SAN VALENTIN 13,213
G. DE PENAS
ARCH. DE LOS CHONOS
G. DE GUAFO
I. CHILOÉ
Puerto Montt
FALKLAND ISLANDS
SOUTH GEORGIA

I. SAN AMBROSIO
IS. JUAN FERNÁNDEZ

40°
60°
80°
40°
40°

EUROPE

75 50 25 0   100   200   300
Miles

ICELAND

Reykjavik

NORWEGIAN SEA

0°

60°

20°

ATLANTIC OCEAN

FAERÖE IS.

SHETLAND IS.

ORKNEY IS.

IRELAND

Dublin

Edinburgh

GREAT BRITAIN

NORTH SEA

London

ENGLISH CHANNEL

BAY OF BISCAY

PORTUGAL

Lisbon

Tagus

SPAIN

Madrid

PYRENEES

Barcelona

BALEARIC ISLANDS

40°

0°

MEDITERRANEAN SEA

Algiers

NORWAY

Bergen

Oslo

L. Vänern

SWEDEN

Stockholm

GULF OF BOTHNIA

FINL

GULF

BALTIC SEA

DENMARK

POLAND

Berlin

Warsaw

Oder

NETHERLANDS

BELGIUM

Rhine

Bonn

GERMANY

Frankfurt

LUXEMBOURG

L

Seine

Paris

FRANCE

Massif Central

Prague

CZECHOSLOVAKIA

Danube

Vienna

AUSTRIA

Bern

SWITZERLAND

MONT BLANC 15,771

ALPS

Rhône

Po

Budapest

HUNGARY

YUGOSLAVIA

Belgrade

ADRIATIC SEA

APENNINES

CORSICA

ITALY

Rome

SARDINIA

TYRRHENIAN SEA

MT. VESUVIUS 4190

Tirana

ALBANIA

IONIAN SEA

GREECE

20°

MALTA

SICILY

Tunis

LAND ELEVATIONS

	Above 13,120 feet
	6560 to 13,120 feet
	3280 to 6560 feet
	1640 to 3280 feet
	660 to 1640 feet
	Sea level to 660 feet
	Below sea level

BARENTS SEA

WHITE SEA

Archangel

Lake Onega

Lake Ladoga

Helsinki

OF FINLAND

Leningrad

UNION OF

SOVIET SOCIALIST REPUBLICS

Volga

Volga

Moscow

Dvina

URAL MOUNTAINS

Ural

Volga

Volgograd (Stalingrad)

Pripyat

Marshes

Kiev

Don

CASPIAN SEA

CARPATHIAN MOUNTAINS

Dnepr

Sea of Azov

ROMANIA

Odessa

MT. EL'BRUS 18,482

CAUCASUS MTS.

Bucharest

Danube

BLACK SEA

BULGARIA

Trabzon

Sofia

Istanbul

Tabriz

ELBORZ MTS.

AEGEAN SEA

Ankara

TURKEY

IRAN

Athens

SYRIA

IRAQ

CYPRUS

Euphrates

Baghdad

Tigris

35

MEDITERRANEAN SEA
CORSICA
Rome
Barcelona
Madrid
SPAIN
PORTUGAL
Lisbon
Tagus
MENORCA
MALLORCA
IBIZA
SARDINIA
TYRRHENIAN SEA
Tirana
ALBANIA
CORFU
IONIAN SEA
SICILY
MALTA
C. Bon
Tunis
TUNISIA
G. OF GABÈS
Tripoli
GULF OF SIRTE
Benghazi
GREECE
Athens
AEGEAN SEA
Istanbul
Bosporus
Ankara
TURKEY
RHODES
CRETE
CYPRUS
LEBANON
SYRIA
Damascus
ISRAEL
Tel Aviv
Jerusalem
JORDAN
Syrian Desert
IRAQ
Baghdad
Euphrates
Tigris
ELBURZ MOUNTAINS
Teheran
IRAN
KUWAIT
PERSIAN GULF
SAUDI ARABIA
Riyadh
Mecca
RED SEA
YEMEN
Mocha
Aden
GULF OF ADEN
SOMALILAND
Djibouti
Berbera
ETHIOPIA
Addis Ababa
L. Tana
RAS DASHAN 15,158
ERITREA
L. Rudolf
SOMALI REP.
GULF OF CÁDIZ
Strait of Gibraltar
Tangier
Rabat
Casablanca
Oran
Algiers
ATLAS MOUNTAINS
MOROCCO
Great Western Erg
Great Eastern Erg
ALGERIA
Erg Iguidi
Erg Chech
Djouf
MT. TAHAT 9574
AHAGGAR
Sahara
ADRAR DES IFORAS
AIR OR AZBINE
Teneré
LIBYA
Libyan Desert
UNITED ARAB REPUBLIC (EGYPT)
Alexandria
Port Said
Cairo
Suez
Suez C.
MT. SINAI 7497
Arabian Desert
Nile
Aswan
L. Nasser
Wadi Halfa
Nubian Desert
Port Sudan
SUDAN
Khartoum
Wad Medani
Blue Nile
White Nile
MT. MARRA 10,100
MALI
Timbuktu
Niger
Bani
NIGER
Bodélé
CHAD
L. Chad
UPPER VOLTA
IVORY COAST
Volta Lake
Accra
TOGO
DAHOMEY
Lagos
NIGERIA
CAMEROON
CAMEROONS MT. 13,353
CENTRAL AFRICAN REPUBLIC
40°
20°

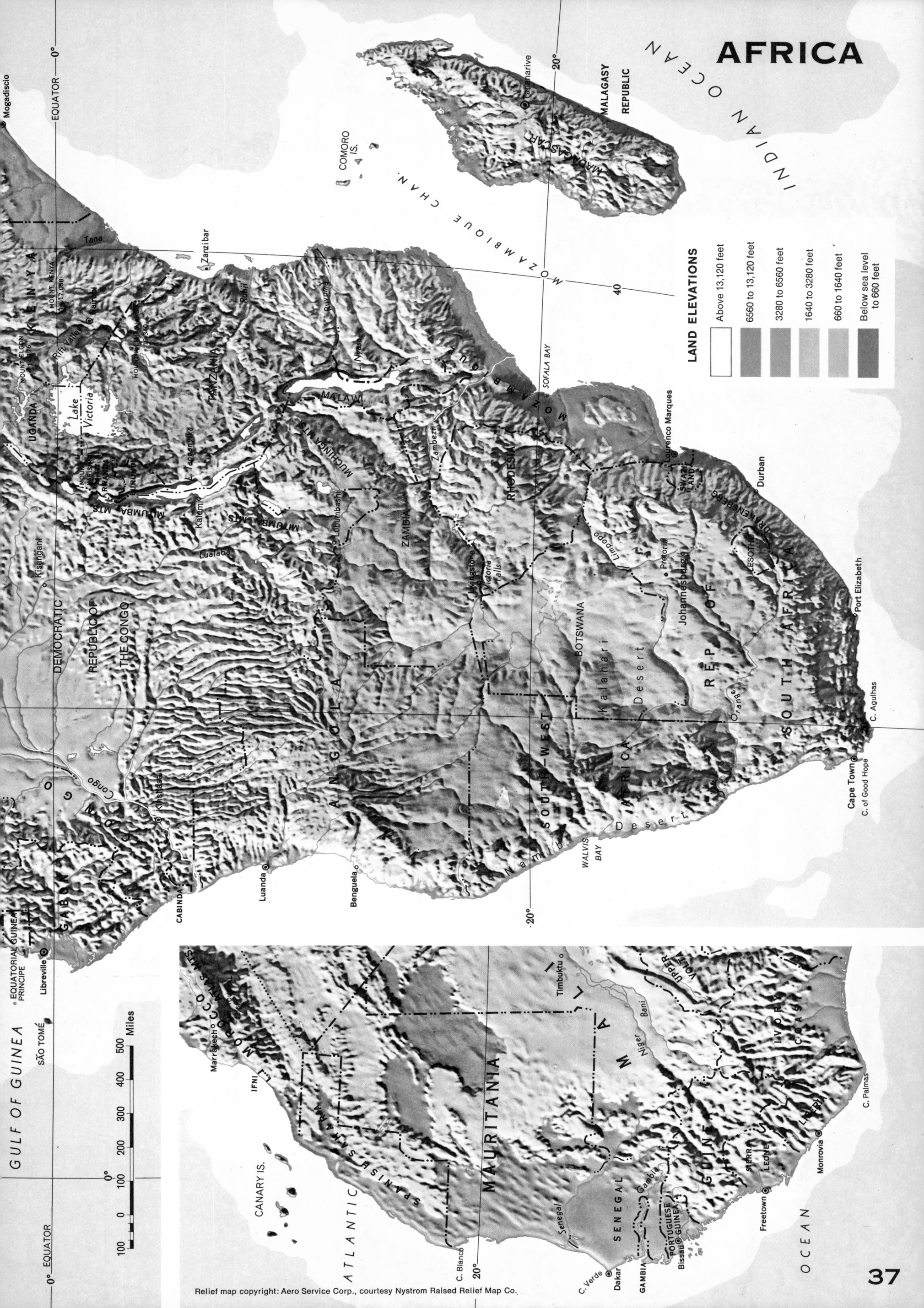

AFERICA

INDIAN OCEAN

MALAGASY REPUBLIC

MADAGASCAR

Tananarive

COMORO IS.

MOZAMBIQUE CHAN.

LAND ELEVATIONS

Above 13,120 feet	6560 to 13,120 feet	3280 to 6560 feet	1640 to 3280 feet	660 to 1640 feet	Below sea level to 660 feet

Zanzibar

Tana

EQUATOR

Mogadiscio

KENYA

MOUNT KENYA 17,058

Nairobi

Rift Valley

MOUNT ELGON

Mount Kilimanjaro 19,565

UGANDA

Lake Victoria

TANZANIA

Rufiji

Ruvuma

Ruvuma

Nyasa

MALAWI

MUCHINGA MTS.

SOFALA BAY

Lourenço Marques

SWAZI LAND

Durban

DRAKENSBERG

MOUNT KIRISIMBI RWANDA BURUNDI

MUMBA MTS.

MITUMBA MTS.

Kalemie

Tanganyika

Lualaba

Lubumbashi

ZAMBIA

Zambezi

RHODESIA

Livingstone

Victoria Falls

Limpopo

Pretoria

Johannesburg

LESOTHO

Kisangani

DEMOCRATIC REPUBLIC OF THE CONGO

ANGOLA

BOTSWANA

Kalahari Desert

Orange

REP. OF SOUTH AFRICA

Port Elizabeth

C. Agulhas

CONGO

Congo

Kinshasa

SOUTH-WEST AFRICA

Namib

Desert

Cape Town

C. of Good Hope

GABON

EQUATORIAL GUINEA

PRINCIPE

Libreville

Luanda

Benguela

CABINDA

WALVIS BAY

20°

SÃO TOMÉ

GULF OF GUINEA

Miles

500
400
300
200
100

0

100

MOROCCO

ATLAS MTS.

Marrakech

IFNI

SPANISH SAHARA

CANARY IS.

ATLANTIC

Timbuktu

MALI

MAURITANIA

Niger

Bani

UPPER VOLTA

IVORY COAST

GUINEA

SIERRA LEONE

Freetown

Monrovia

C. Palmas

C. Blanco

C. Verde

Dakar

SENEGAL

Senegal

GAMBIA

Gambia

PORTUGUESE GUINEA

Bissau

OCEAN

EQUATOR

20°

Relief map copyright: Aero Service Corp., courtesy Nystrom Raised Relief Map Co.

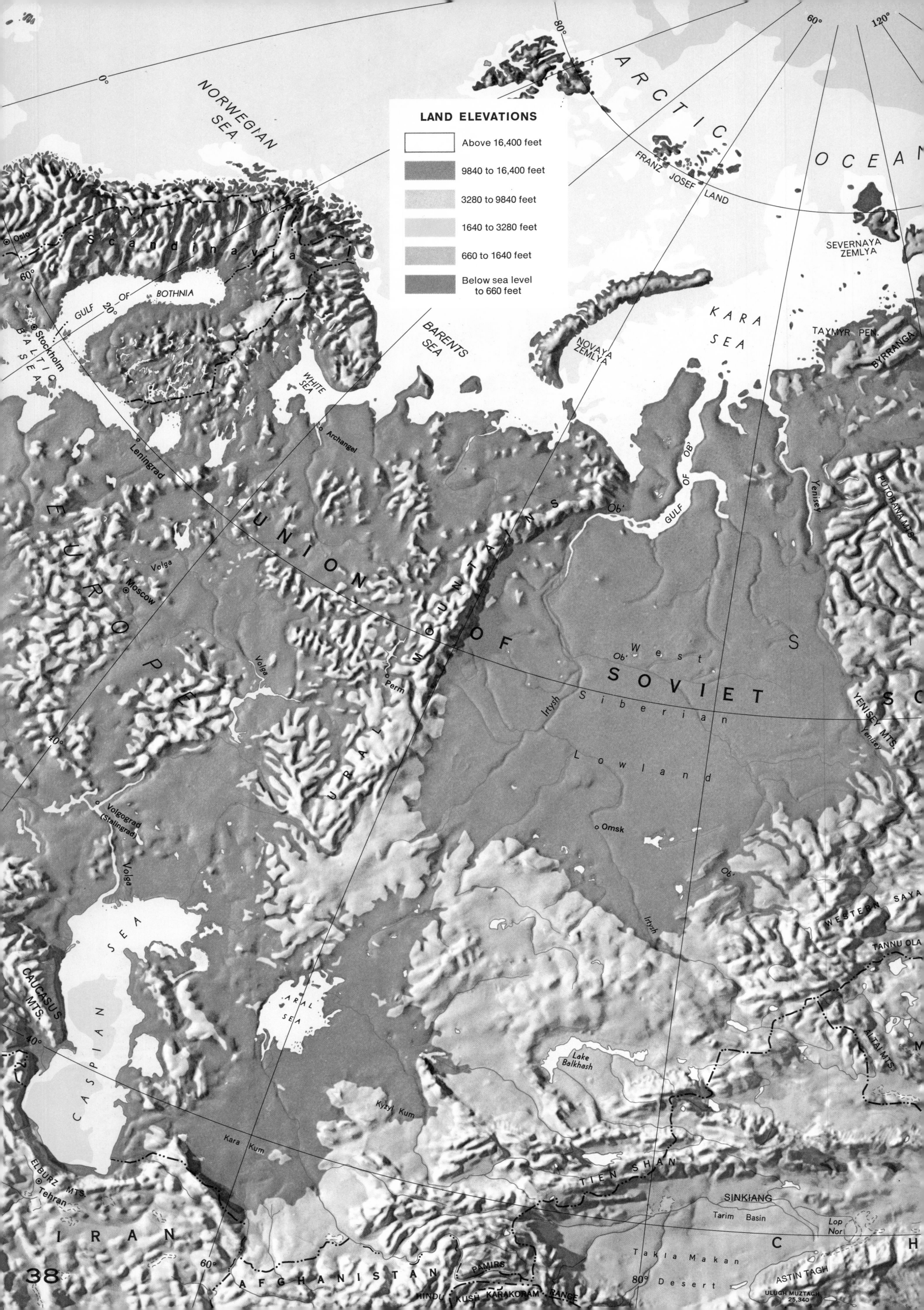

LAND ELEVATIONS

	Above 16,400 feet
	9840 to 16,400 feet
	3280 to 9840 feet
	1640 to 3280 feet
	660 to 1640 feet
	Below sea level to 660 feet

NORWEGIAN SEA

ARCTIC OCEAN

FRANZ JOSEF LAND

SEVERNAYA ZEMLYA

Oslo

60°

GULF OF BOTHNIA

20°

Stockholm

BALTIC SEA

Scandinavia

BARENTS SEA

WHITE SEA

NOVAYA ZEMLYA

KARA SEA

TAYMYR PEN.

BYRRANGA

Leningrad

Archangel

GULF OF OB'

Ob'

Yenisey

PUTORANA Mts.

EUROPE

UNION

Volga

Moscow

Volga

Perm

U R A L   M O U N T A I N S

OF

West

Ob'

S O V I E T

Siberian

S O

YENISEY MTS.

Yenisey

40°

Irtysh

Lowland

Volgograd (Stalingrad)

Volga

Omsk

Ob'

Irtysh

WESTERN SAYA

CASPIAN SEA

TANNU OLA

CAUCASUS MTS.

40°

ARAL SEA

Lake Balkhash

ALTAI MTS.

Kyzyl Kum

Kara Kum

TIEN SHAN

ELBURZ MTS.

Tehran

SINKIANG

Tarim Basin

Lop Nor

IRAN

AFGHANISTAN

60°

80°

PAMIRS

Takla Makan Desert

ASTIN TAGH

CH

HINDU KUSH   KARAKORAM   RANGE

ULUGH MUZTAGH 25,340

38

NORTHERN ASIA

100   0   100   200   300   400   500
Miles

LAPTEV SEA

NEW SIBERIAN IS.

EAST SIBERIAN SEA

WRANGEL I.

ANADYR MTS.

BERING SEA

KORYAK MTS.

KOLYMA MTS.

KOMANDORSKIYE IS.

CHERSKIY MTS.

VERKHOYANSK MTS.

Lena

Central

Siberian

Upland

Yakutsk

SOCIALIST REPUBLICS

DZHUGDZHUR MTS.

Mt. KLYUCHEVSKAYA 15,913

KAMCHATKA PEN.

SEA OF OKHOTSK

SAKHALIN

KURILE IS.

STANOVOY MTS.

Lena

Amur

L. Baykal

YABLONOVY MTS.

EASTERN SAYAN

GREAT KHINGAN MTS.

Amur

Amur

SIKHOTE ALIN MTS.

Vladivostok

MANCHURIA

SEA OF JAPAN

JAPAN

HANGAY MTS.

Ulan Bator

MONGOLIA

Gobi Desert

Mukden

NORTH KOREA

SOUTH KOREA

Seoul

Tokyo

FUJIYAMA 12,388

NAN SHAN

Koko Nor

Yellow

CHINA

Peking

Yellow

YELLOW SEA

Relief map copyright: Aero Service Corp., courtesy Nystrom Raised Relief Map Co.

39

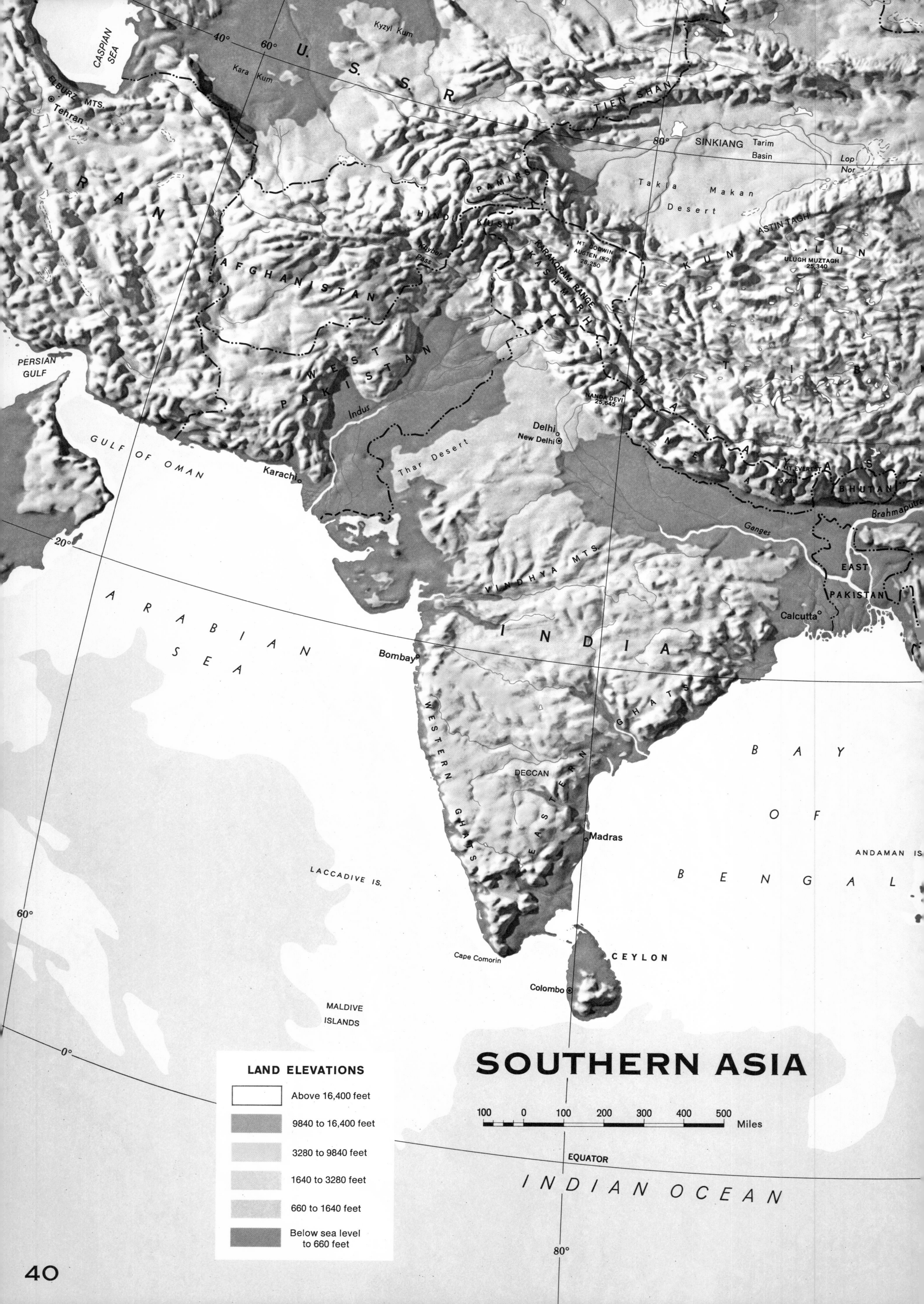

CASPIAN
SEA

U. S. S. R.

Kyzyl Kum

40°   60°

Kara Kum

ELBURZ
MTS.

Tehran

IRAN

PERSIAN
GULF

AFGHANISTAN

TIEN SHAN

80°   SINKIANG   Tarim
Basin

Takla   Makan
Desert

Lop
Nor

PAMIRS

HINDU

KUSH

Khyber
Pass

MT. GODWIN
AUSTEN (K2)
28,250

KARAKORAM RANGE

KASHMIR

ASTIN TAGH

ULUGH MUZTAGH
25,340

KUN   LUN

WEST

PAKISTAN

Indus

GULF OF OMAN

Karachi

NANDA DEVI
25,645

Delhi

New Delhi

T   I   B   E   T

H   I   M   A   L   A   Y   A   S

N   E   P   A   L

MT. EVEREST
9,028

BHUTAN

Brahmaputra

20°

Thar Desert

Ganges

EAST

PAKISTAN

Calcutta

A   R   A   B   I   A   N

S   E   A

Bombay

VINDHYA MTS.

I   N   D   I   A

B   A   Y

O   F

B   E   N   G   A   L

ANDAMAN IS.

WESTERN GHATS

DECCAN

EASTERN GHATS

Madras

LACCADIVE IS.

60°

Cape Comorin

CEYLON

Colombo

MALDIVE
ISLANDS

0°

LAND ELEVATIONS

	Above 16,400 feet
	9840 to 16,400 feet
	3280 to 9840 feet
	1640 to 3280 feet
	660 to 1640 feet
	Below sea level to 660 feet

SOUTHERN ASIA

100   0   100   200   300   400   500
Miles

EQUATOR

I   N   D   I   A   N   O   C   E   A   N

80°

MONGOLIA
Gobi Desert

NAN SHAN

Koko Nor

Yellow

C H I N A

CHIN LING SHAN

Yellow

Yangtze

Peking

40°

120°

NORTH KOREA

Seoul

SOUTH KOREA

SEA OF JAPAN

JAPAN

CHIYAMA 12,461

YELLOW SEA

Shanghai

EAST CHINA SEA

RYUKYU IS.

MINYA KONKA 24,900

Wuhan

Chungking

TIBET

URMA

NAGA HILLS

Irrawaddy

Hanoi

Canton

Hong Kong

TAIWAN

PHILIPPINE SEA

20°

HAINAN

NORTH VIETNAM

PHILIPPINES

Quezon City

Manila

THAILAND

LAOS

Bangkok

CAMBODIA

SOUTH VIETNAM

Saigon

SOUTH CHINA SEA

ANDAMAN SEA

GULF OF SIAM

NICOBAR IS.

CELEBES SEA

MALAYSIA

MALAYSIA

BORNEO

EQUATOR

CELEBES

0°

Singapore

SUMATRA

JAVA SEA

INDONESIA

JAVA

BANDA SEA

Djakarta

100°

120°

Relief map copyright: Aero Service Corp., courtesy Nystrom Raised Relief Map Co.

41

THE GREAT OCEANS

THE OCEANS of our planet are still largely unexplored. Oceanography, the fascinating study of oceans, has developed only in the past fifty years. The resources of a number of sciences, particularly engineering, are required to plumb the three-to-seven-mile deeps of the great ocean beds. Until recently the equipment for such research has not been available. The ocean bottoms, once believed to be almost level, have mountains greater than the highest on land, this new study has revealed, and depths in which Mount Everest would sink more than 5000 feet beneath the surface.

Recently, dramatic experiments have taken place in this field. The Mohole Project attempted experimental drillings to bore through the Earth's crust (see page 138) at sea, where it is only three miles thick, instead of 25 miles as it is on land. The International Indian Ocean Expedition with twenty participating nations began a three-year oceanographic effort in 1962 that disclosed the Ninetyeast Ridge, longest in any ocean. During 1965, thirty men lived and worked for fifteen days at 205 feet in Sealab II of the U.S. Navy, off the coast of California. The world's record for this depth was achieved by M. Scott Carpenter, who stayed down for thirty days. French oceanaut Jacques Cousteau has maintained six men in an undersea Mediterranean station for three weeks at 325 feet.

The continents, which sit on the crust, are surrounded by CONTINENTAL SHELVES, or the shallow edges of the ancient land masses, edges later drowned by the rising sea. Most of these end quite abruptly at the steep CONTINENTAL SLOPES, which are cut by deep-sea canyons, continuing riverbeds of present-day rivers—for example, the Hudson Canyon off the east coast of the United States. The transition from the sharp slopes to the more gradual inclines marks the beginning of the CONTINENTAL RISE, ending in the OCEAN BASINS. In the centers of the ocean basins are often found the flat ABYSSAL PLAINS.

Much of the scenery of the ocean floor is craggy, irregular and complex. The DEEPS (beginning at 18,000 feet below sea level) are the lowest points of oceanic depressions. TRENCHES often occur along mountainous coastal regions or on the convex side of an arc-shaped ridge, whose uppermost points may comprise an island chain. It is in the trenches of the Pacific that the greatest deeps have been found. RIDGES with steep, irregular sides may occur independently of trenches. SEAMOUNTS are isolated sea mountains.

SEASCARPS are long, steep slopes or escarpments. A FRACTURE ZONE is an area of geological cracking, as in the Northeast Pacific, related to the upthrust of mountains on land. Most ISLANDS are volcanic in origin; on the tops of some submerged islands, calcareous animals and plants have built coral ATOLLS and REEFS. Volcanoes under the sea erupt as readily as those on land, often causing whole islands to disappear. In the valleys of the ocean the silt of rivers, the shells and remains of sea creatures, volcanic ash and other debris form a thick layer of SEDIMENT.

The tides and currents of the great oceans are not the least of their marvels. Tides are governed by the gravitational pull of the Moon and, to a lesser extent, of the Sun. Currents are determined by the position of land masses, the ceaseless revolutions of the Earth, and by the winds and the heat of the Sun. The Atlantic and Pacific each have two great current systems; it is the Earth's rotation that causes the currents north of the Equator to flow generally clockwise and those south of it to move in a counterclockwise direction. The Sargasso Sea, part of the West Atlantic, is an area of floating plankton, almost devoid of current. Currents strongly influence the local climate on land and provide swimmers with unexpected contrasts, such as that between the chill waters off the coast of Maine (from the Labrador Current) and the comfortable seas around the more northerly Nova Scotia (tempered by the Gulf Stream).

THE NORTH ATLANTIC

The legend of the lost Atlantis appears to have been fable, but the dark abysses of the Atlantic Ocean (shown at the right) are dramatic in their own right. Here are the bold and jagged mountains of the Mid-Atlantic Ridge—a range outstripping the Rockies in height and as majestic as the Himalayas. A 10,000-mile stretch, it is now thought to be only a part of a 40,000-mile Earth-girdling chain. The trench that has been discovered to run along its uppermost ridge is almost exactly the midpoint between the bordering continents, which are believed to have "drifted" apart or to have been separated by the gradual expansion of the Earth,

leaving the yawning chasms of the oceans between the land masses. (See "The Earth's Structure," p. 138.)

There is only one break in this Ridge, one link between its eastern and western valleys—that of the Romanche Trench on the Equator. The Atlantic has only three other small trenches, two in the West Indies and one in the Antarctic. The Milwaukee Deep near Puerto Rico is its deepest point—30,180 feet. The North Atlantic is characterized by its great basins, ridges, plateaus, deep-sea channels and relatively few seamounts. Only 4150 miles wide at its broadest, the Atlantic has the heaviest shipping of any ocean.

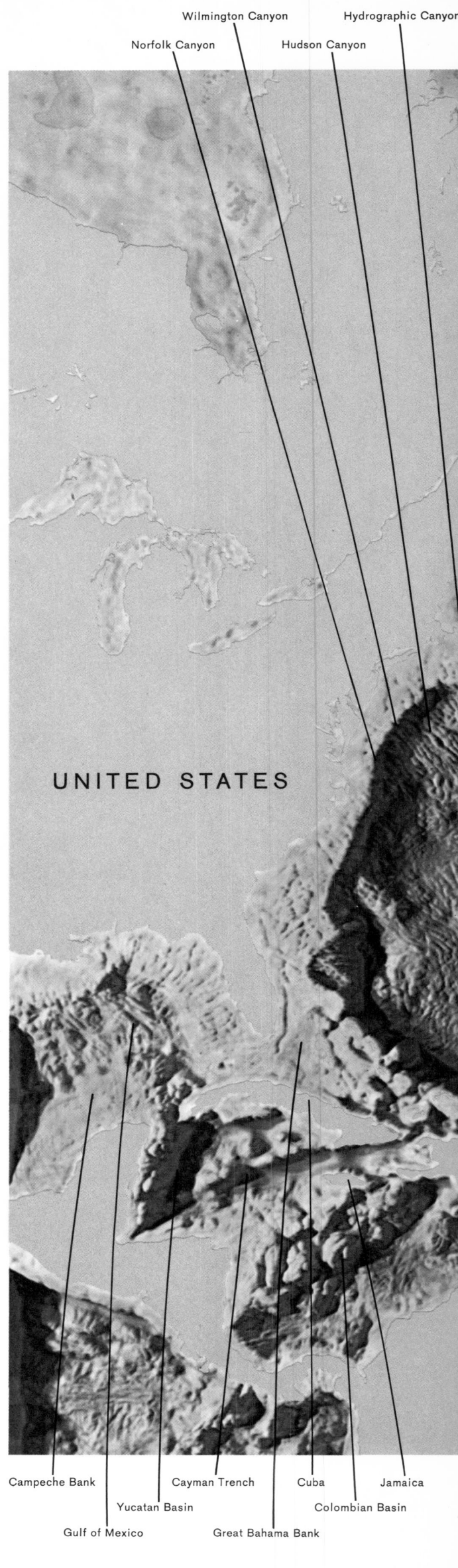

Wilmington Canyon Hydrographic Canyon
Norfolk Canyon Hudson Canyon

UNITED STATES

Campeche Bank Cayman Trench Cuba Jamaica
Yucatan Basin Colombian Basin
Gulf of Mexico Great Bahama Bank

Nova Scotia

Abyssal Plain

Sable Island Bank

Newfoundland

Thoulette Deep

Grand Banks

Flemish Cap

Newfoundland Rise

Milne Seamount

Faraday Hills

Azores Plateau

Rockall Bank

Josephine Seamount

Porcupine Bank

LABRADOR
BASIN

WEST
EUROPEAN
BASIN

IBERIAN
BASIN

EUROPE

NEW ENGLAND
SEAMOUNTS

NORTH AMERICAN

SARGASSO SEA

BASIN

CANARY
BASIN

AFRICA

GUIANA
BASIN

CAPE
VERDE
BASIN

ST. PAUL'S
ROCKS

GUINEA
BASIN

Milwaukee Deep

Venezuelan Basin

Puerto Rico Trench

Bermuda Islands

Barbados Ridge

Muir Seamount

Echo Seamount

Nares Deep

Mid-Atlantic Ridge

Great Meteor Seamount

Cape Verde Islands

Sierra Leone Rise

Cape Verde Plateau

Romanche Trench

Madeira Island

Concepcion Bank

Martha's Vineyard

Azores

Gibraltar

© 1963 The Reader's Digest Association, Inc.

This section of the sea bed between Martha's Vineyard, off Massachusetts, and Gibraltar magnifies vertical distances about 40 times in relation to horizontal distances, to highlight the steepness of slopes. It shows the continental shelves and slopes which fringe the land masses, the deep ocean floors and interrupting seamounts.

43

Mendocino Seascarp

Murray Seascarp

Middle America Trench

Clipperton Fracture Zone

Equator

NORTH AMERICA

Albatross Plateau

EAST PACIFIC BASIN

Clarion Fracture Zone

GULF OF ALASKA

NORTH PACIFIC BASIN

Aleutian Trench

Mid-Pacific Mountains

Aleutian Arc

ALEUTIAN BASIN (BERING SEA)

Midway Island

Emperor Seamounts

Marcus-Wake Seamounts

SEA OF OKHOTSK

Kurile Ridge

Marianas Trench

Kurile Trench

Japan Trench

Philippine Sea

Sea of Japan

Nansei Shoto Trench

E. China Sea

Yellow Sea

ASIA

South China Sea

Nansei Shoto Ridge

Philippine Trench

Mindanao Deep

Kyushu-Palau Ridge

West Caroline Basin

New Guinea Rise

Challenger Deep

East Caroline Basin

Caroline-Solomon Ridge

Caroline Islands

Marianas Islands

Magellan Seamounts

Gilbert Islands

Marshall Islands

Marcus-Necker Rise

Kingman Reef

Hawaiian Ridge

Christmas Island Ridge

CENTRAL PACIFIC BASIN

THE NORTH PACIFIC

T HE PACIFIC OCEAN—11,000 miles wide between Panama and the China Sea—has a border of volcanic activity of which the ridge-trench arcs of islands are part. This border is sometimes called the "Ring of Fire." It also possesses great depths. In 1960 the U.S. bathyscaphe *Trieste* touched bottom at 36,198 feet in the Marianas Trench. The Pacific is characterized by its volcanic activity; its island chains, many of them coral; its trenches with their great deeps; and its many seamounts. Peculiar to the Northeast are the four regular extensions of seascarps and fracture zones. The mid-Pacific islands are the peaks of the globe-encircling mountain range, thought to connect with the Mid-Atlantic Ridge via the Arctic and Indian Oceans.

Cape Mendocino

Mendocino Seascarp

Hawaii

Hawaiian Ridge

Marcus-Necker Rise

Bikini

This section of the sea bed between Bikini, in the Marshall Islands, and Cape Mendocino, California, magnifies vertical distances about 40 times in relation to horizontal distances to highlight the steepness of the slopes. It shows the rough and irregular floor of the Pacific, which contains mountains and deep trenches. The island of Hawaii is not on a line with Bikini and Cape Mendocino, but is included to show the highest land point of the Pacific in comparison with its depths.

PART TWO

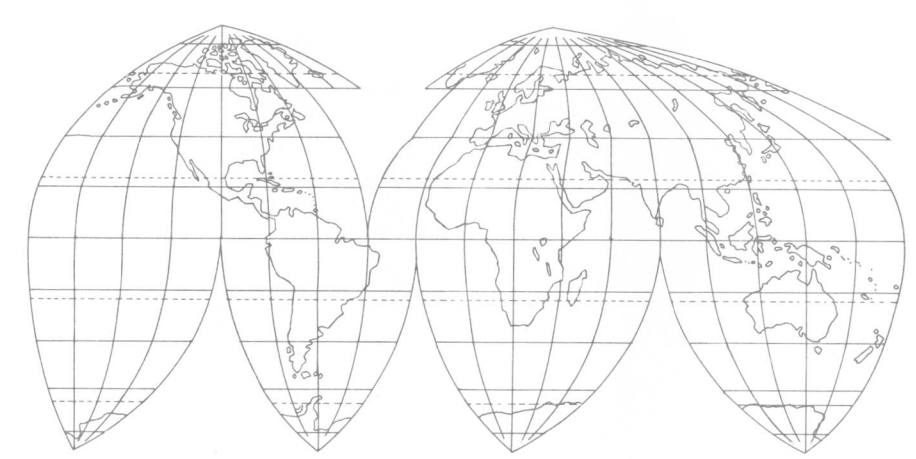

THE COUNTRIES
OF THE WORLD

PACIFIC OCEAN
WASHINGTON
OREGON
CALIFORNIA
NEVADA
IDAHO
MONTANA
WYOMING
UTAH
ARIZONA
COLORADO
NEW MEXICO
NORTH DAKO
SOUTH DAKO
NEBRASK
TEX
MEXICO
BAJA CALIFORNIA
Golfo de California
Vancouver Island
Vancouver
Victoria
Seattle
Tacoma
Spokane
Portland
Salem
Eugene
Boise
Helena
Butte
Billings
Calgary
Lethbridge
Medicine Hat
Regina
Saskatoon
Moose Jaw
Bismarck
Pierre
Casper
Cheyenne
Denver
Colorado Springs
Pueblo
Salt Lake City
Ogden
Provo
Reno
Carson City
San Francisco
Oakland
Sacramento
San Jose
Fresno
Bakersfield
Los Angeles
Long Beach
Pasadena
San Diego
Mexicali
Phoenix
Tucson
Albuquerque
Santa Fe
El Paso
Ciudad Juárez
Amarillo
Lubbock
Chihuahua
Hermosillo
Guaymas
Monterrey
Torreón
Saltillo
Durango
Mazatlán
Culiacán
Tropic of Cancer
Main Highways
Other Main Roads
Main Railroads
Other Railroads
International Boundaries
Swamp and Flood Areas
Spot Heights in Feet 14,109

UNITED STATES OF AMERICA

SEE PAGE 72 FOR STATE OF HAWAII
AND PAGES 76-77 FOR STATE OF ALASKA

SCALE: 1 INCH TO 142 MILES

1:9,000,000

100 80 60 40 20 0   100   200   300 Miles

AREA: 3,615,211 SQUARE MILES
POPULATION: 200,616,000 (March 15, 1968, estimate)

Feet 3281   0   600   1500   3000   6000   9000   12000 Feet
          Below
          Sea Level

© JOHN BARTHOLOMEW & SON LTD.

47

LEGEND AND INDEX TO UNITED STATES MAPS

International Boundaries ▭▭▭▭ Special Highways ━━━ Railroads ━━ ━━ Deserts and Salt Flats
State Boundaries ▭▭▭▭ U.S. Highways ━ ━ ━ U.S. Interstate ㊸ Projected Canals ━━━━ Salt Marshes
State Capitals are underlined ━━━ State Highways and Other Main Roads ━━━ Main Civil Airports ▲ ▲ Glaciers and Ice Caps
Spot Heights in Feet ▲ 20,320 Trails ┄┄┄ Swamp and Flood Areas Lagoons, Reefs and Banks

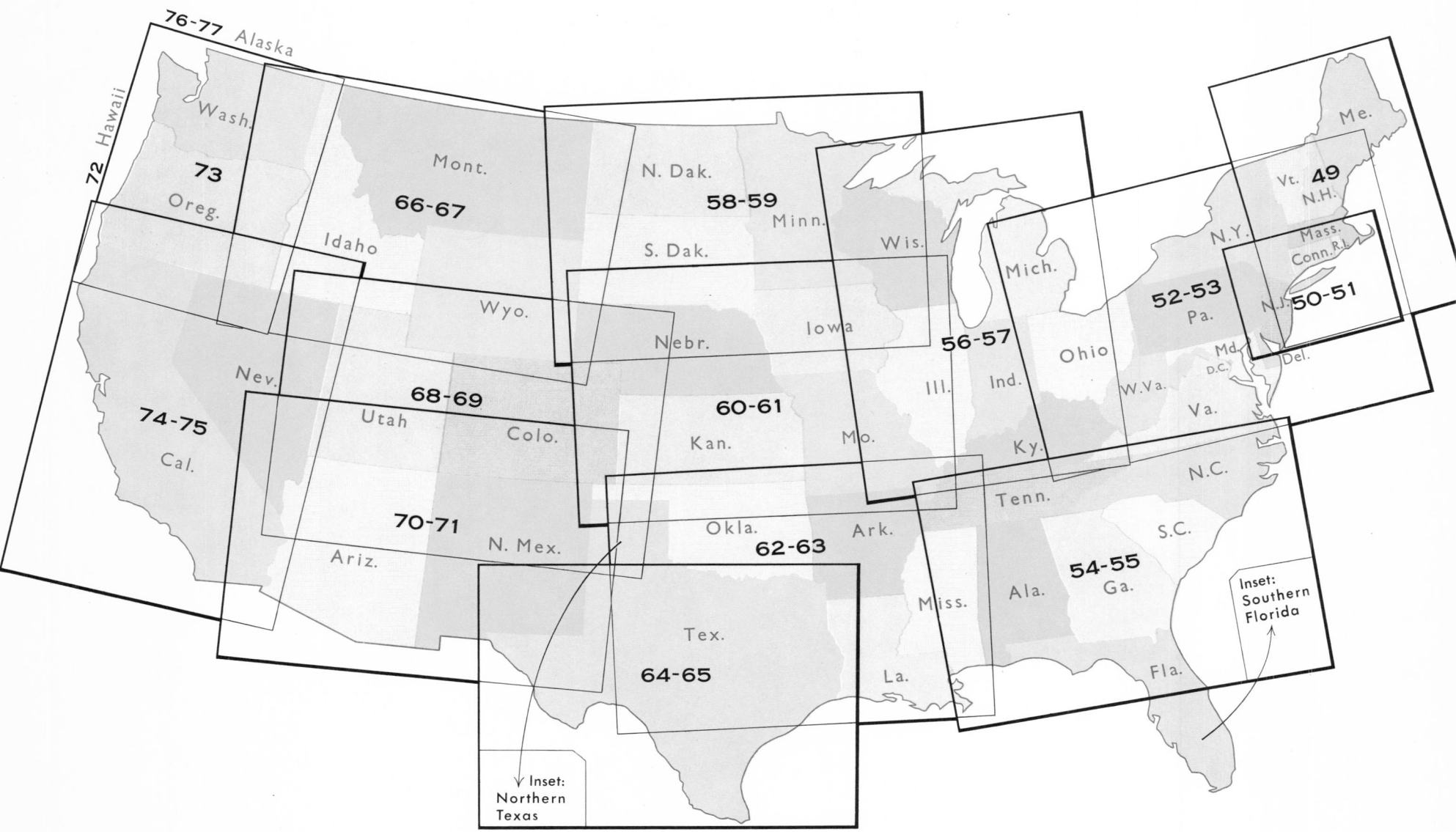

The frames outline the geographical areas mapped on the pages indicated.

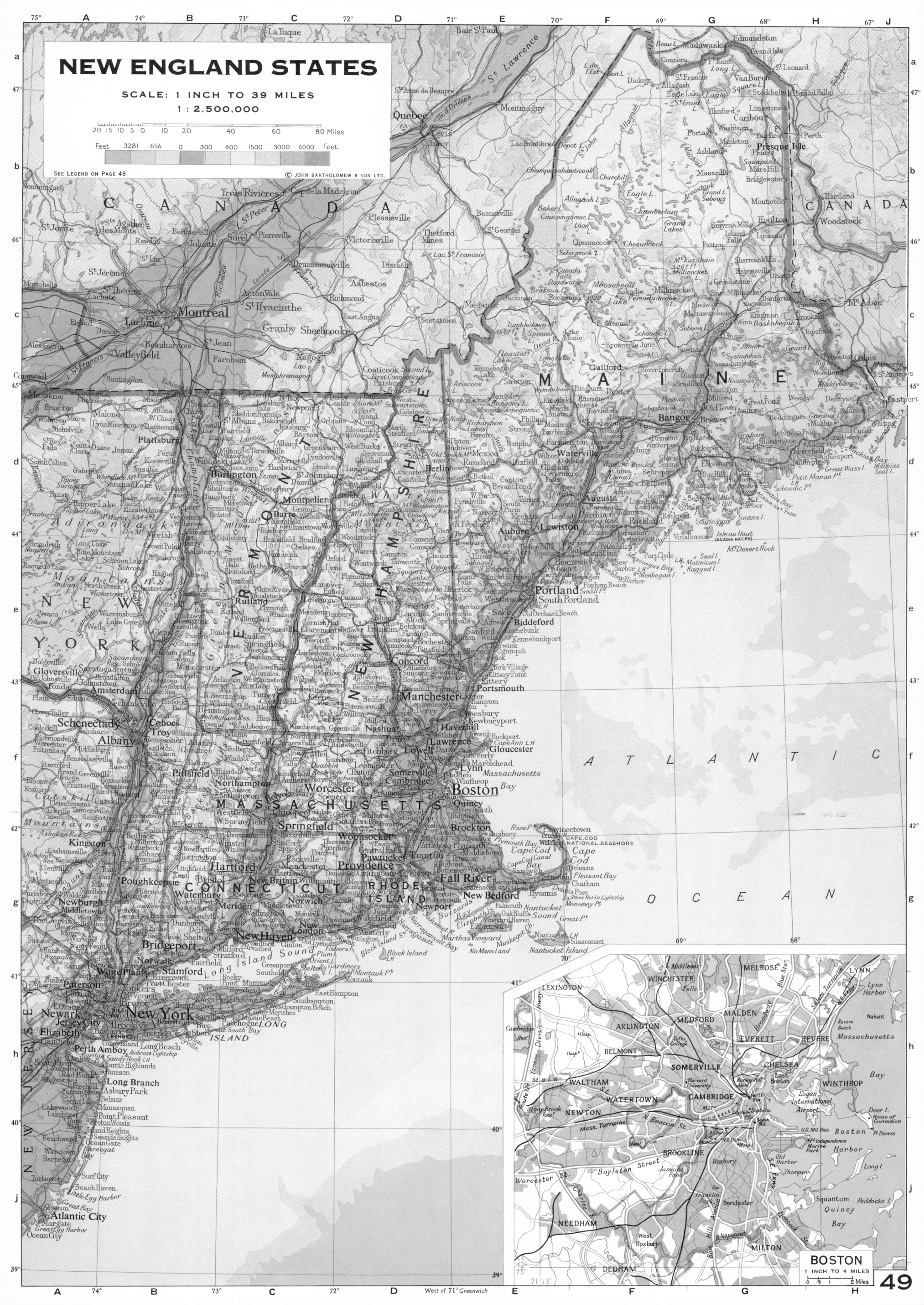

NEW ENGLAND STATES

SCALE: 1 INCH TO 39 MILES

1 : 2,500,000

20 15 10 5 0   10   20   40   60   80 Miles

Feet 3281 656   0   300 600 1500 3000 6000 Feet

See Legend on Page 48

© JOHN BARTHOLOMEW & SON LTD.

BOSTON

1 INCH TO 4 MILES

0   1   2 Miles

49

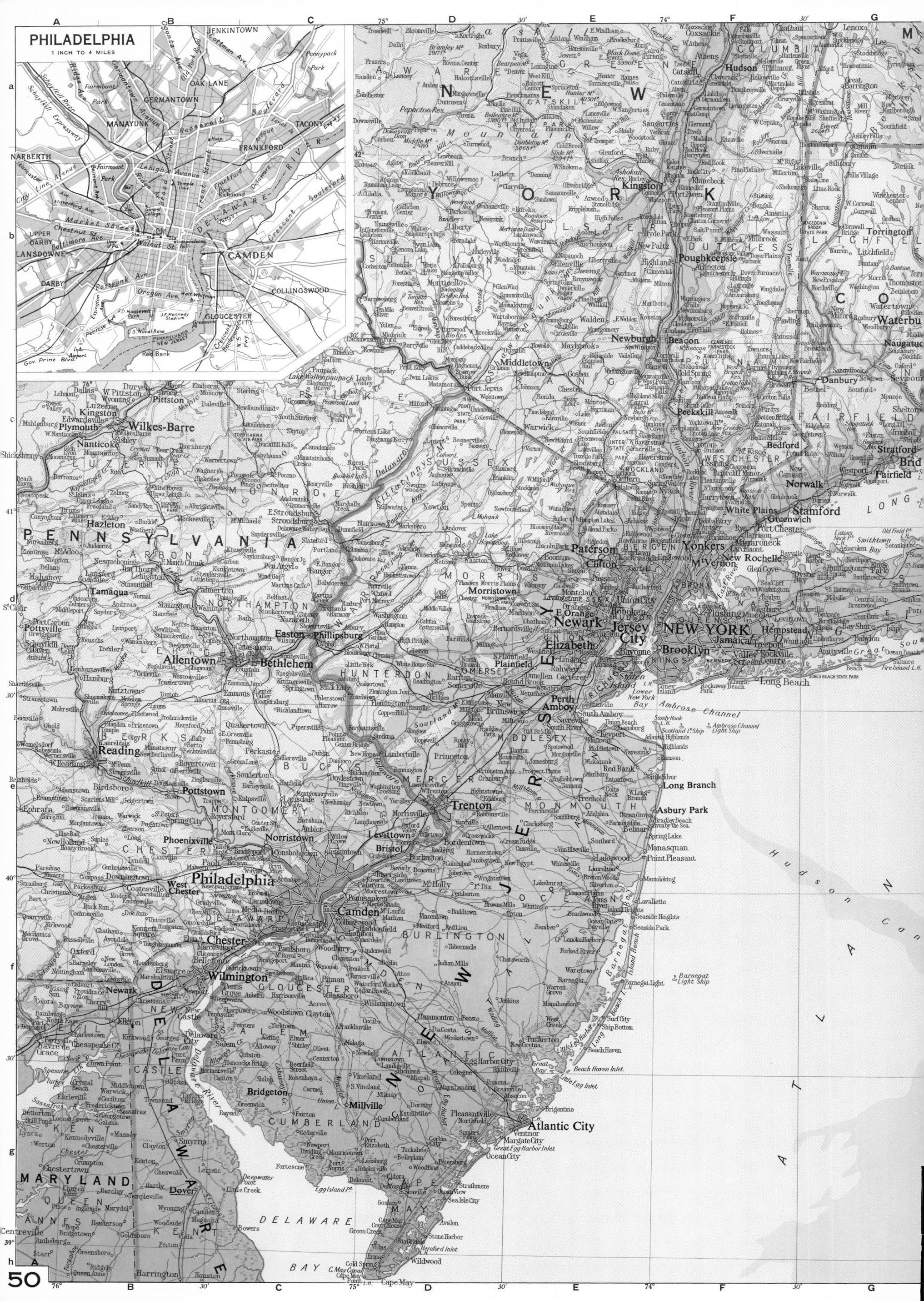

PHILADELPHIA
1 INCH TO 4 MILES
JENKINTOWN
OAK LANE
GERMANTOWN
MANAYUNK
TACONY
FRANKFORD
NARBERTH
UPPER DARBY
LANSDOWNE
DARBY
CAMDEN
COLLINGSWOOD
GLOUCESTER CITY
PENNSYLVANIA
NEW JERSEY
Red Bank
NEW YORK
PENNSYLVANIA
NEW JERSEY
DELAWARE
MARYLAND
ATLANTIC OCEAN
Hudson Canyon
DELAWARE BAY
Catskill Mountains
Kittatinny Mts.
Philadelphia
Camden
Trenton
Wilmington
Chester
Allentown
Bethlehem
Reading
Easton
Phillipsburg
Wilkes-Barre
Hazleton
Pottsville
Norristown
Newark
Elizabeth
Jersey City
Paterson
Clifton
NEW YORK
Brooklyn
Yonkers
White Plains
Stamford
Norwalk
Kingston
Poughkeepsie
Newburgh
Middletown
Atlantic City
Asbury Park
Long Branch
Millville
Bridgeton
Dover
Cape May
Ambrose Channel
Long Beach
75°
74°
76°
42°
41°
40°
39°

MIDDLE ATLANTIC
SEABOARD
SCALE: 1 INCH TO 16 MILES
1 : 1,000,000
10 5 0 5 10 20 30 Miles
Feet 656 164 0 300 600 1500 3000 Feet
SEE LEGEND ON PAGE 48
© JOHN BARTHOLOMEW & SON LTD.
NEW YORK
AND ENVIRONS
1 INCH TO 4 MILES
0 1 2 3 Miles
MASSACHUSETTS
CONNECTICUT
RHODE ISLAND
CAPE COD BAY
BUZZARDS BAY
NANTUCKET SOUND
BLOCK ISLAND SOUND
LONG ISLAND SOUND
OCEAN
Boston
Worcester
Springfield
Hartford
Providence
New Haven
New London
Newport
Fall River
New Bedford
Brockton
Plymouth
Martha's Vineyard
Nantucket Island
Block Island
PATERSON
NEWARK
JERSEY CITY
ELIZABETH
BAYONNE
HOBOKEN
YONKERS
BRONX
QUEENS
BROOKLYN
STATEN ISLAND
MANHATTAN
Upper New York Bay
Lower New York Bay
Jamaica Bay
John F. Kennedy Intern'l Airport (Idlewild)
La Guardia Airport
Newark Airport

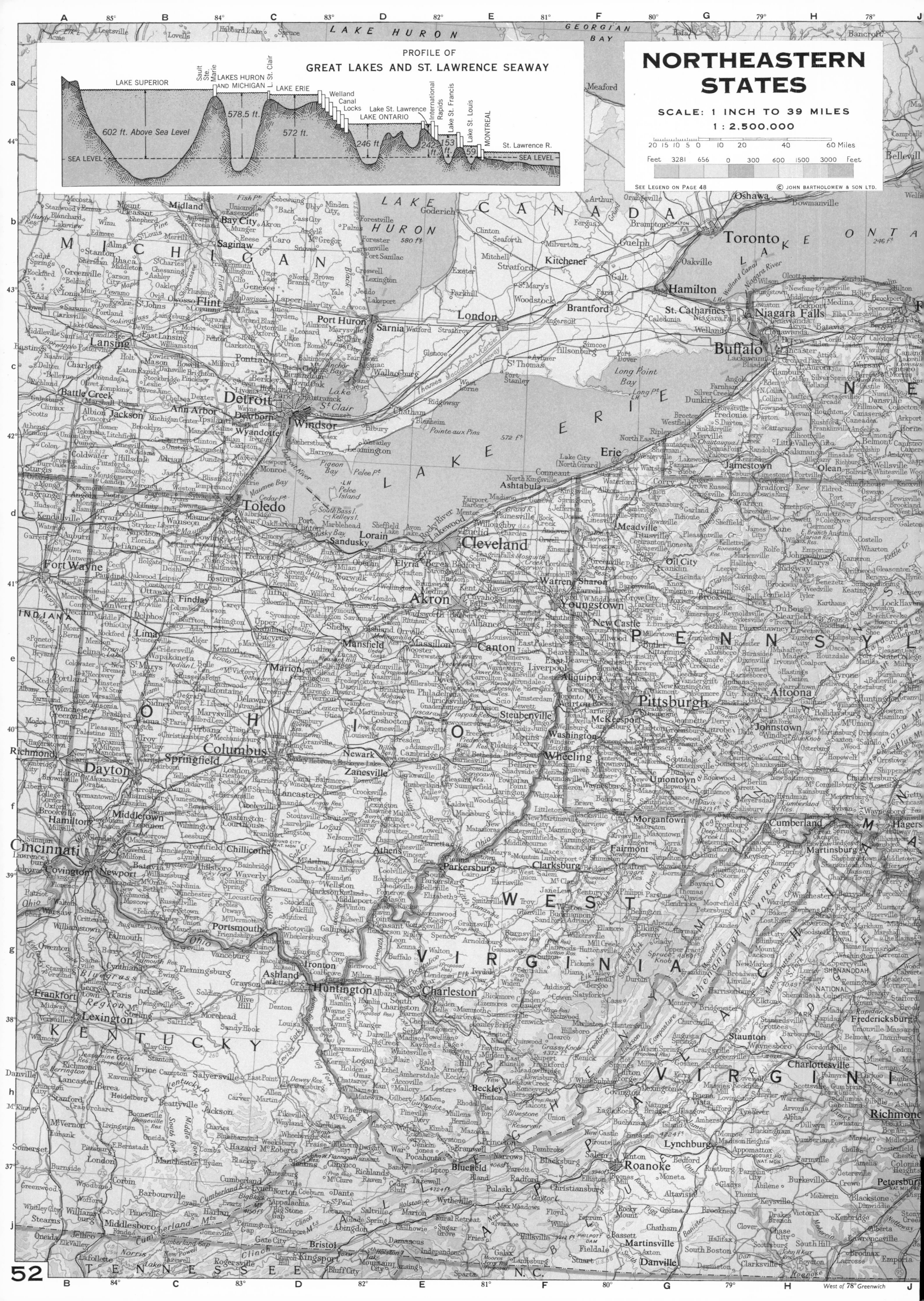

NORTHEASTERN STATES

SCALE: 1 INCH TO 39 MILES

1 : 2,500,000

PROFILE OF
GREAT LAKES AND ST. LAWRENCE SEAWAY

SEE LEGEND ON PAGE 48

© JOHN BARTHOLOMEW & SON LTD.

PITTSBURGH
1 INCH TO 4 MILES
BALTIMORE
1 INCH TO 4 MILES
WASHINGTON
1 INCH TO 4 MILES
NEW YORK
MASSACHUSETTS
CONNECTICUT
RHODE ISLAND
NEW JERSEY
DELAWARE
MARYLAND
VERMONT
PENNSYLVANIA
DIST. OF COLUMBIA
VIRGINIA
ARLINGTON
ATLANTIC
OCEAN
Adirondack Mountains
Catskill Mountains
Long Island Sound
LONG ISLAND
Cape Cod
Nantucket Island
Block Island
New York
Philadelphia
Boston
Baltimore
WASHINGTON D.C.
Albany
Syracuse
Binghamton
Scranton
Trenton
Camden
Wilmington
Atlantic City
Hartford
Providence
Springfield
Worcester
New Haven
Bridgeport
Newark
Norfolk
Newport News
Portsmouth
Annapolis
Harrisburg
Lancaster
Reading
Allentown
Bethlehem
Wilkes Barre
Schenectady
Utica
Rome
Watertown
Ogdensburg
Plattsburg
Burlington
Kingston
Poughkeepsie
Newburgh
Paterson
Elizabeth
Perth Amboy
Long Branch
Dover
Salisbury
Williamsburg
Fall River
New Bedford
Brockton
Pawtucket
Woonsocket
Waterbury
Meriden
New Britain
Norwich
New London
Stamford
Norwalk
White Plains
Elmira
Ithaca
Oswego
Saratoga Springs
Amsterdam
Troy
Cohoes
Gloversville
Pittsfield
Northampton
Cambridge
Somerville
Quincy
Chesapeake Bay
Delaware Bay

SOUTHEASTERN STATES

SCALE: 1 INCH TO 39 MILES

1 : 2,500,000

Feet 3281 656 0 300 600 1500 3000 6000 Feet

SEE LEGEND ON PAGE 48

© JOHN BARTHOLOMEW & SON LTD.

MIAMI

1 INCH TO 8 MILES

PUERTO RICO AND VIRGIN ISLANDS

ON THE SAME SCALE

54

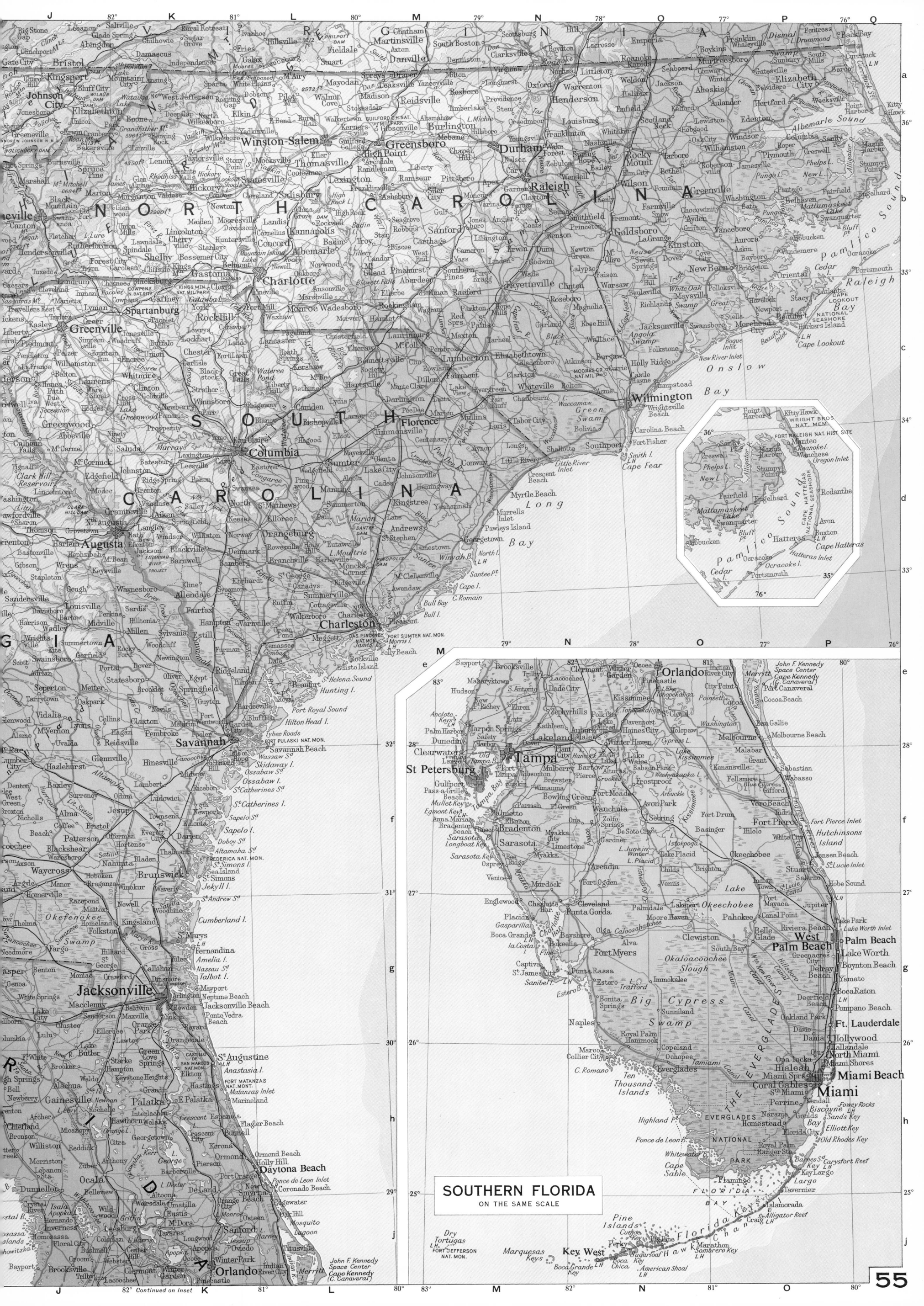

SOUTHERN FLORIDA
ON THE SAME SCALE
NORTH CAROLINA
SOUTH CAROLINA
GEORGIA
FLORIDA
Winston-Salem
Greensboro
Durham
Raleigh
Charlotte
Greenville
Spartanburg
Columbia
Florence
Wilmington
Augusta
Charleston
Savannah
Jacksonville
Daytona Beach
Orlando
Tampa
St Petersburg
West Palm Beach
Ft. Lauderdale
Miami Beach
Miami
Key West
Onslow Bay
Long Bay
Raleigh Bay
Pamlico Sound
Albemarle Sound
Cape Fear
Cape Lookout
Cape Hatteras
Lake Okeechobee
Big Cypress Swamp
THE EVERGLADES
EVERGLADES NATIONAL PARK
Florida Bay
Florida Keys
Ten Thousand Islands
Dry Tortugas
Okefenokee Swamp
Continued on Inset

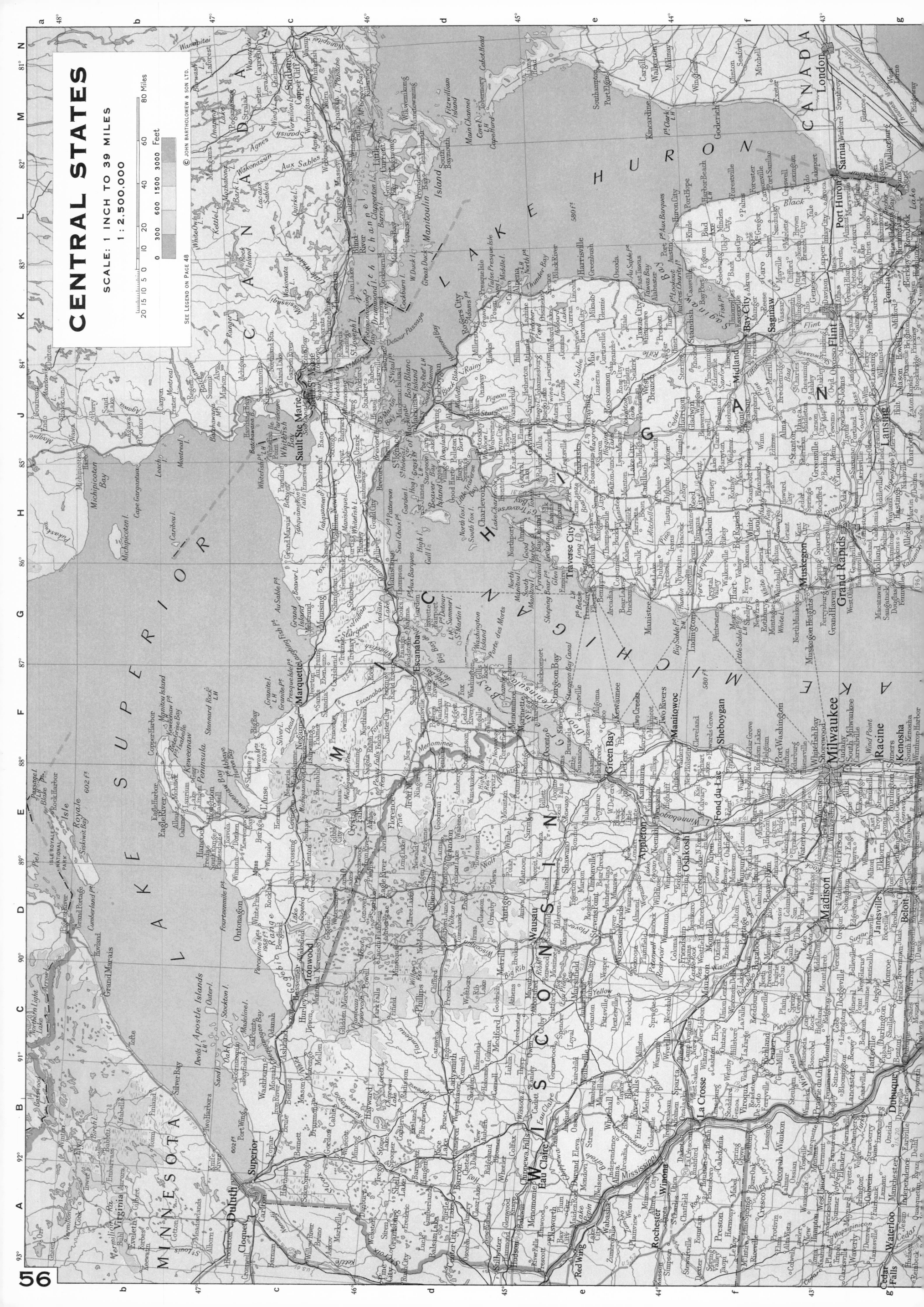
CENTRAL STATES
SCALE: 1 INCH TO 39 MILES
1 : 2,500,000
20 15 10 5 0 10 20 40 60 80 Miles
0 300 600 1500 3000 Feet
SEE LEGEND ON PAGE 48
© JOHN BARTHOLOMEW & SON LTD.
LAKE SUPERIOR
LAKE MICHIGAN
LAKE HURON
MINNESOTA
WISCONSIN
MICHIGAN
CANADA
Duluth
Superior
Marquette
Sault Ste Marie
Green Bay
Milwaukee
Madison
Racine
Kenosha
Grand Rapids
Lansing
Flint
Saginaw
Bay City
Port Huron
Sarnia
London
Dubuque
La Crosse
Rochester
Winona
Eau Claire
Wausau
Oshkosh
Appleton
Sheboygan
Manitowoc
Muskegon
Traverse City
Escanaba
Manitoulin Island
Isle Royale

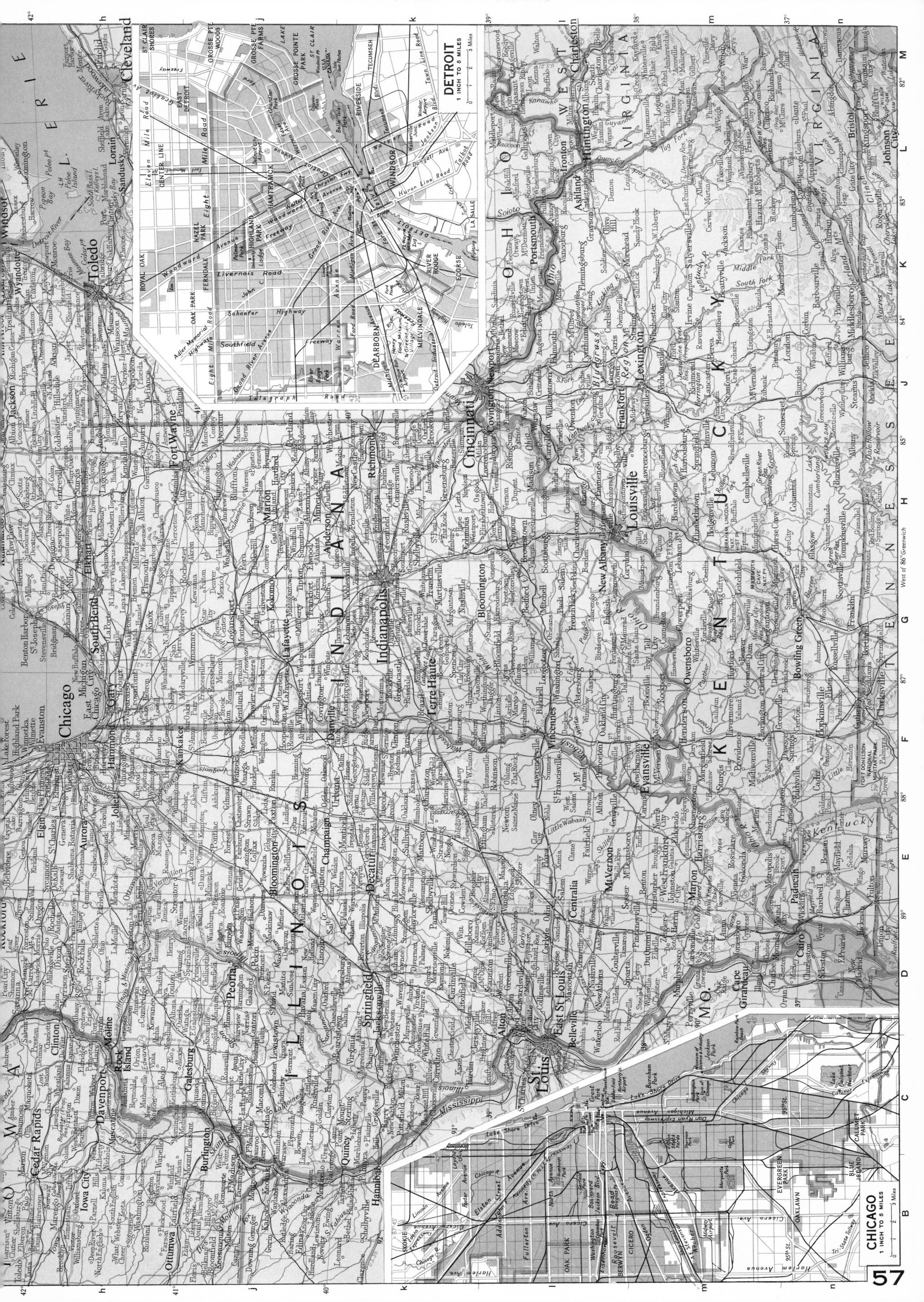

DETROIT
1 INCH TO 5 MILES
CHICAGO
1 INCH TO 5 MILES
ILLINOIS
INDIANA
OHIO
KENTUCKY
WEST VIRGINIA
VIRGINIA
TENNESSEE
MO.
IOWA
L. ERIE
Chicago
Indianapolis
Cincinnati
Louisville
Toledo
Cleveland
Fort Wayne
South Bend
Springfield
Peoria
Terre Haute
Evansville
Lexington
Frankfort
St. Louis
East St Louis
Davenport
Cedar Rapids
Rock Island
Moline
Joliet
Aurora
Elgin
Gary
Hammond
Kankakee
Danville
Champaign
Urbana
Bloomington
Decatur
Lafayette
Kokomo
Muncie
Anderson
Marion
Richmond
Paducah
Owensboro
Henderson
Bowling Green
Covington
Newport
Huntington
Charleston
Portsmouth
Ashland
Lorain
Sandusky
Galesburg
Quincy
Hannibal
Burlington
Keokuk
Iowa City
Ottumwa
Cairo
Cape Girardeau
Jacksonville
Belleville
Alton
Centralia
Vincennes
Mt Vernon
New Albany
Elkhart
Clinton
West of 86° Greenwich

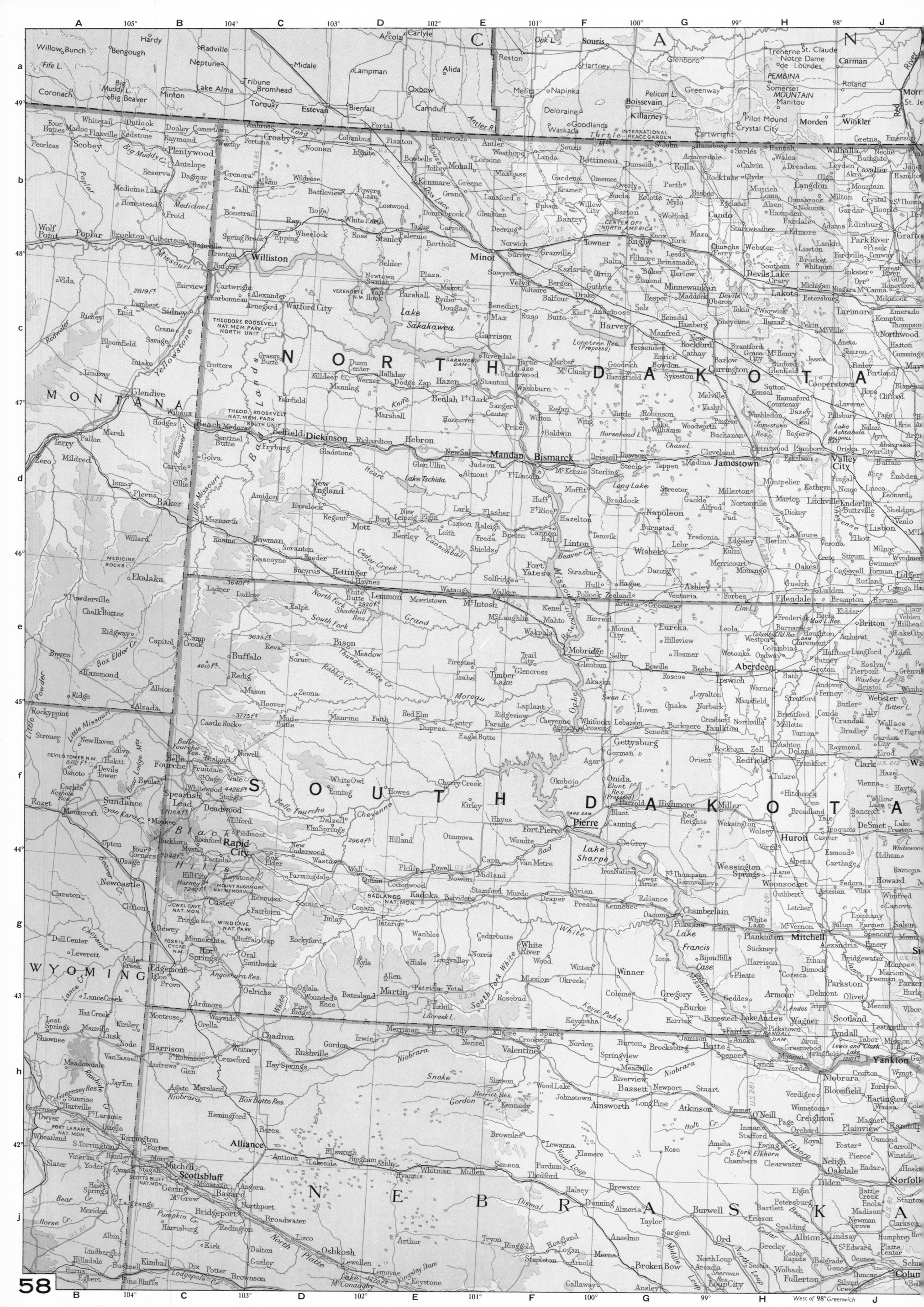
NORTH DAKOTA
SOUTH DAKOTA
MONTANA
WYOMING
NEBRASKA
CANADA
Williston
Minot
Bismarck
Mandan
Dickinson
Jamestown
Valley City
Devils Lake
Aberdeen
Pierre
Rapid City
Huron
Mitchell
Yankton
Scottsbluff
Alliance
Lake Sakakawea
Lake Sharpe
Lake Oahe
Missouri
Black Hills
West of 98° Greenwich

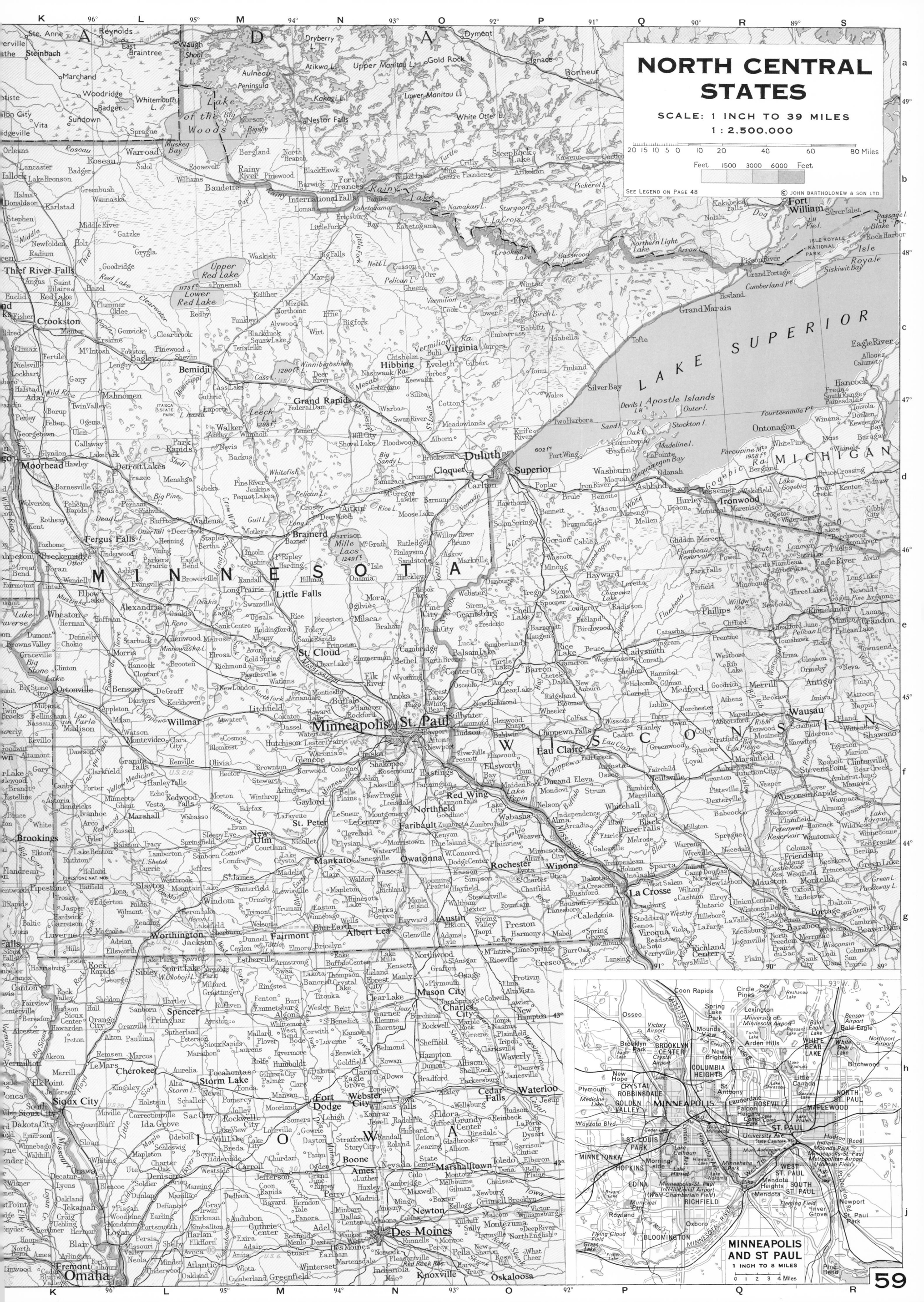
NORTH CENTRAL STATES
SCALE: 1 INCH TO 39 MILES
1 : 2,500,000
20 15 10 5 0 10 20 40 60 80 Miles
Feet 1500 3000 6000 Feet
See Legend on Page 48
© JOHN BARTHOLOMEW & SON LTD.
LAKE SUPERIOR
MINNESOTA
WISCONSIN
MICHIGAN
IOWA
Minneapolis
St. Paul
Duluth
Des Moines
Omaha
MINNEAPOLIS AND ST PAUL
1 INCH TO 8 MILES
0 1 2 3 4 Miles

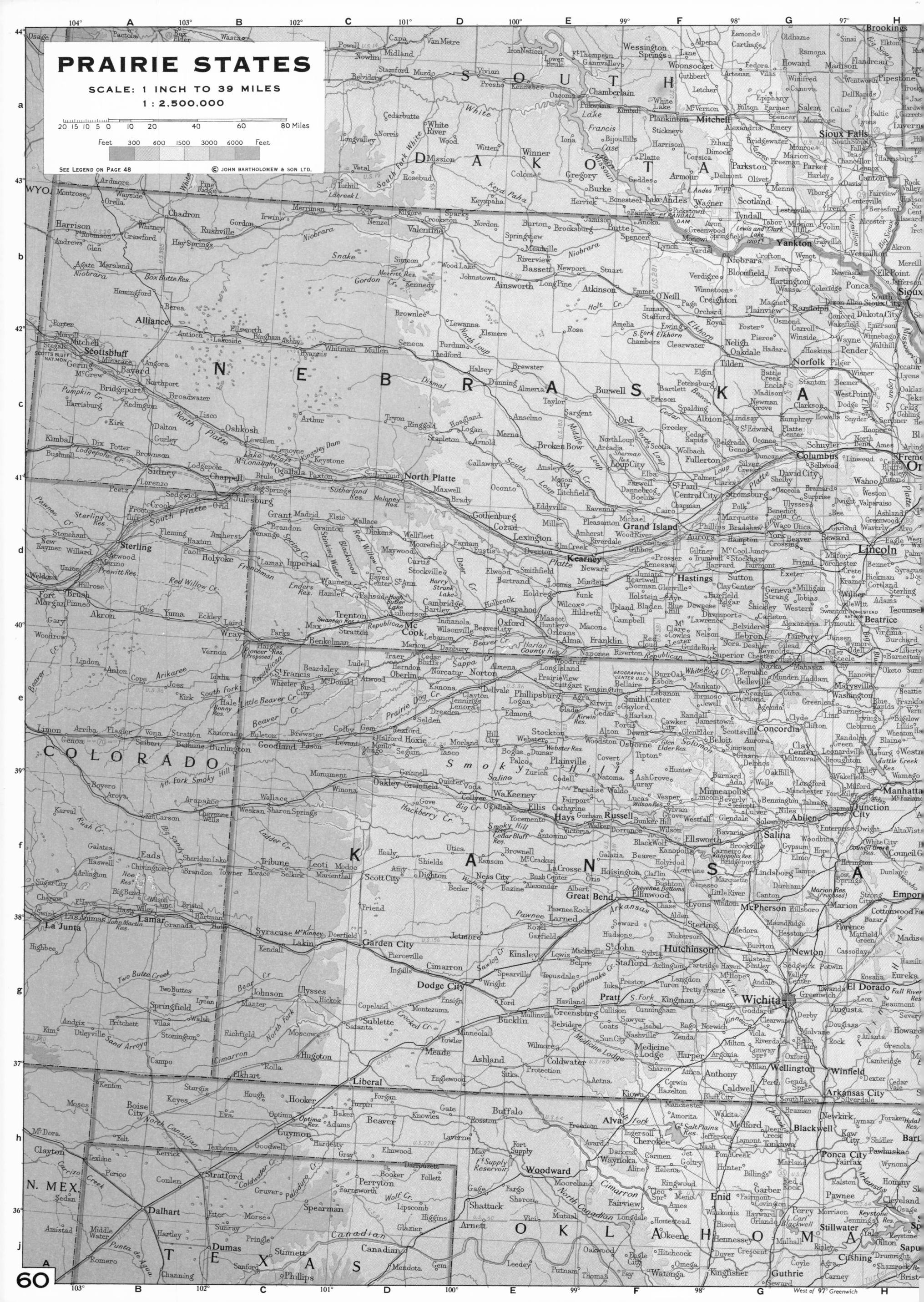
PRAIRIE STATES
SCALE: 1 INCH TO 39 MILES
1 : 2,500,000
20 15 10 5 0 10 20 40 60 80 Miles
Feet 300 600 1500 3000 6000 Feet
See Legend on Page 48
© JOHN BARTHOLOMEW & SON LTD.
SOUTH DAKOTA
NEBRASKA
COLORADO
KANSAS
OKLAHOMA
TEXAS
N. MEX.
WYO.
104° A 103° B 102° C 101° D 100° E 99° F 98° G 97° H
44° a 43° b 42° c 41° d 40° e 39° f 38° g 37° h 36° j
103° B 102° C 101° D 100° E 99° F 98° G West of 97° Greenwich H

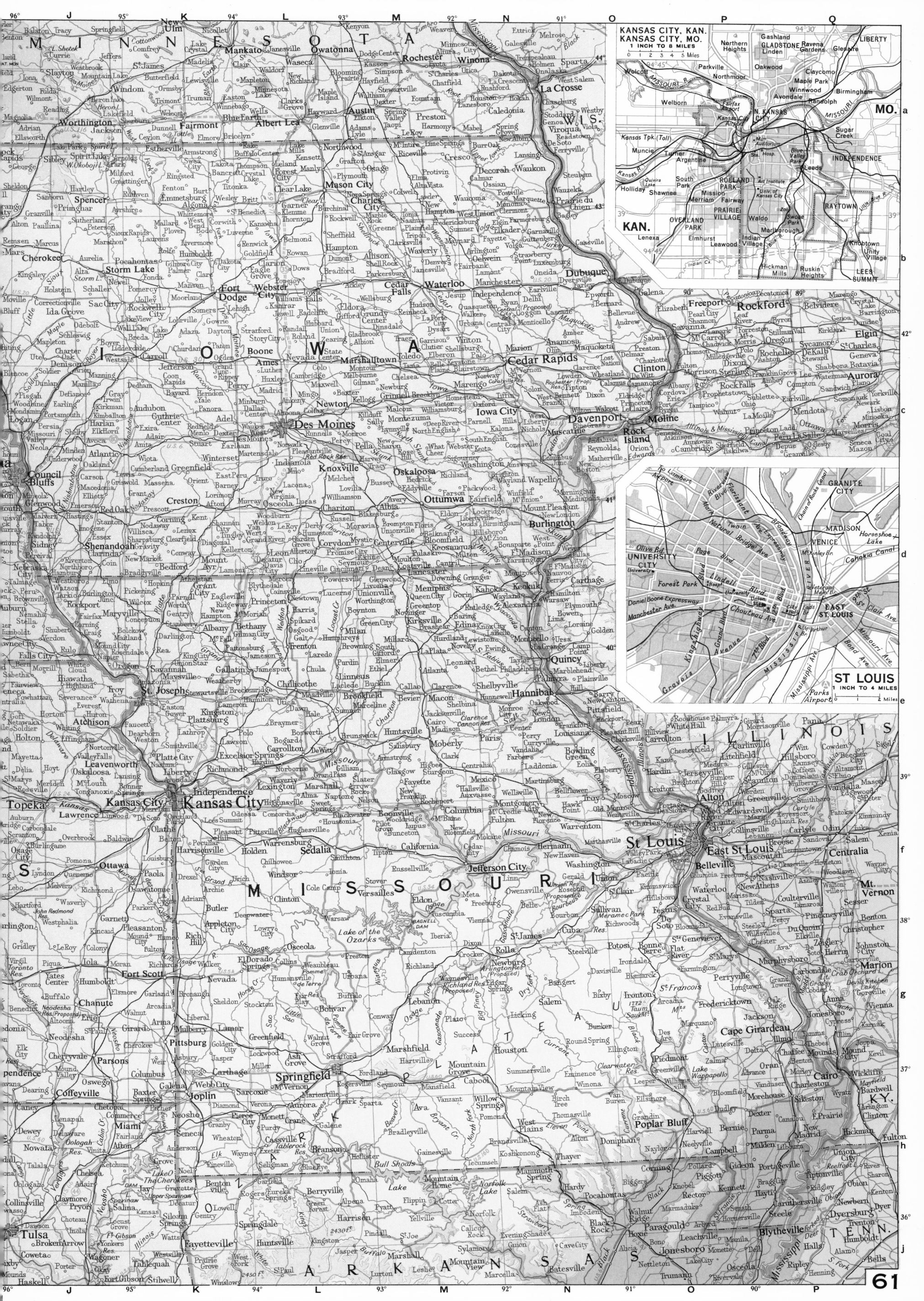

MINNESOTA
WIS.
IOWA
ILLINOIS
MISSOURI
KAN.
MO.
KY.
TENN.
ARKANSAS
OZARK PLATEAU
KANSAS CITY, KAN.
KANSAS CITY, MO.
1 INCH TO 8 MILES
ST LOUIS
1 INCH TO 4 MILES

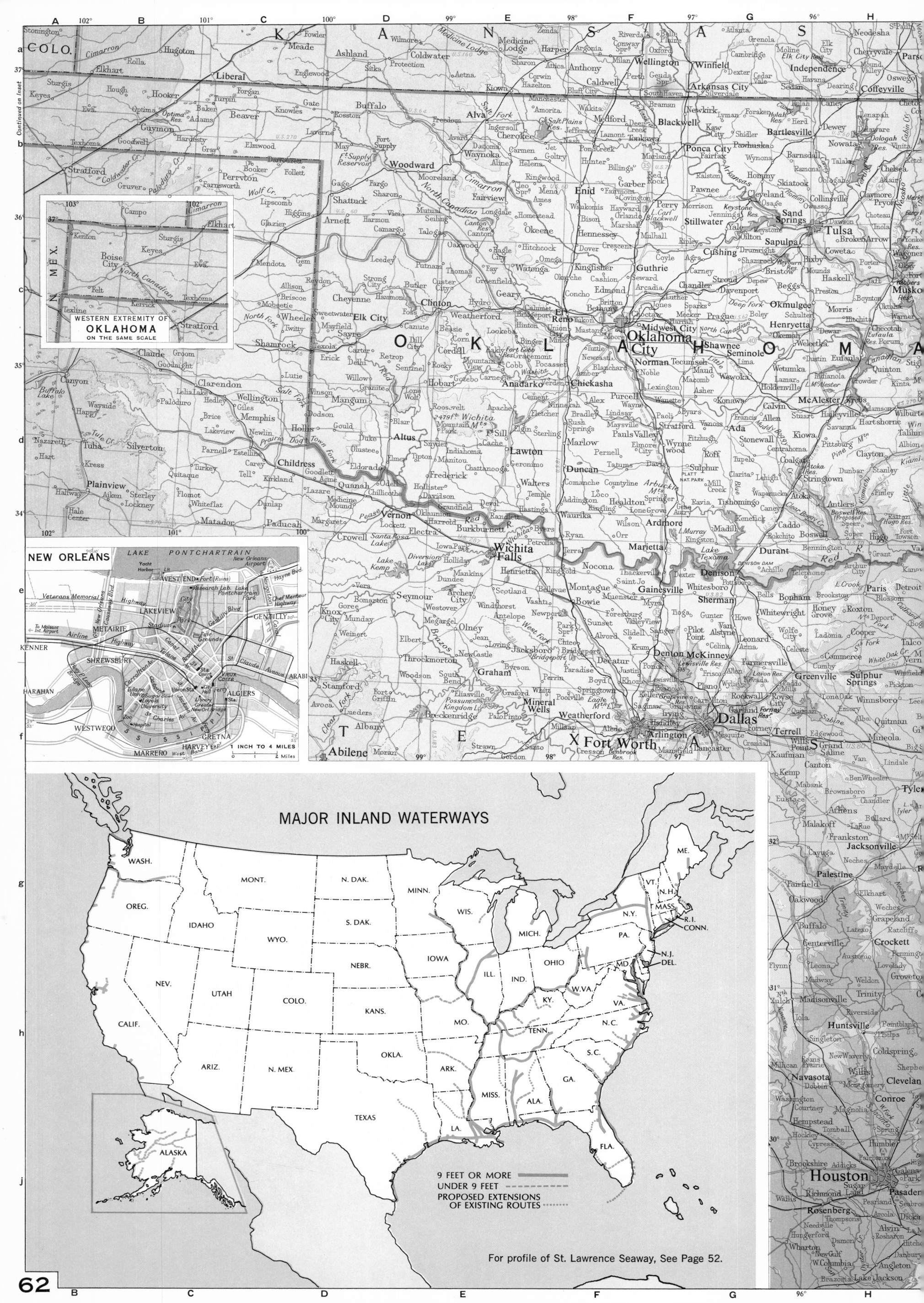
KANSAS
OKLAHOMA
TEXAS
COLO.
Continued on Inset
WESTERN EXTREMITY OF
OKLAHOMA
ON THE SAME SCALE
N. MEX.
NEW ORLEANS
LAKE PONTCHARTRAIN
1 INCH TO 4 MILES
MISSISSIPPI
MAJOR INLAND WATERWAYS
9 FEET OR MORE
UNDER 9 FEET
PROPOSED EXTENSIONS
OF EXISTING ROUTES
For profile of St. Lawrence Seaway, See Page 52.
Oklahoma City
Tulsa
Dallas
Fort Worth
Wichita Falls
Houston

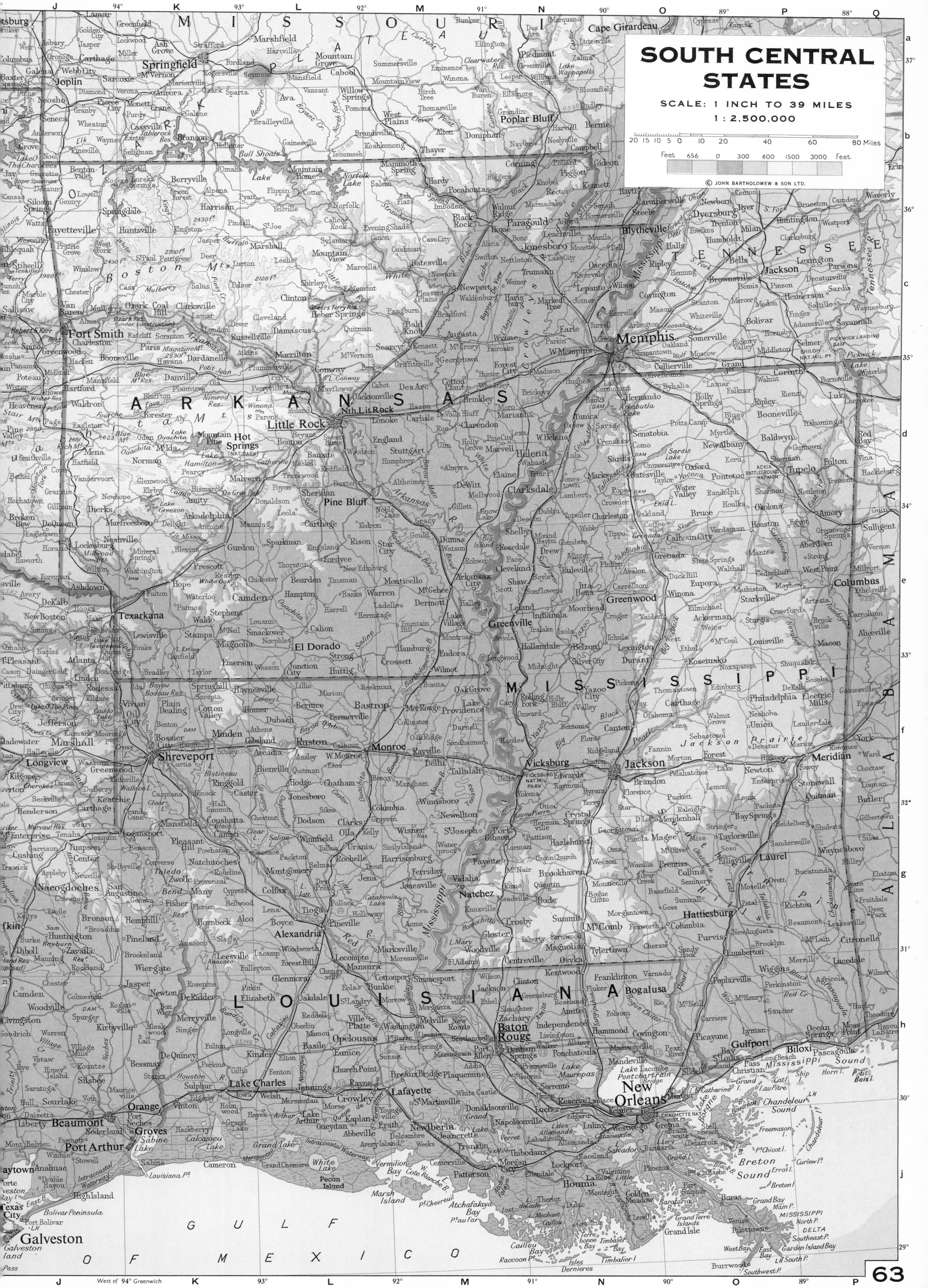
SOUTH CENTRAL STATES
SCALE: 1 INCH TO 39 MILES
1 : 2,500,000
20 15 10 5 0 10 20 40 60 80 Miles
Feet 656 0 300 600 1500 3000 Feet
© JOHN BARTHOLOMEW & SON LTD.
MISSOURI
ARKANSAS
LOUISIANA
MISSISSIPPI
TENNESSEE
ALABAMA
GULF OF MEXICO
Springfield
Joplin
Poplar Bluff
Cape Girardeau
Fort Smith
Little Rock
Pine Bluff
Hot Springs
Texarkana
El Dorado
Memphis
Jackson
Greenwood
Greenville
Vicksburg
Meridian
Hattiesburg
Gulfport
Biloxi
Shreveport
Monroe
Alexandria
Baton Rouge
New Orleans
Lafayette
Lake Charles
Beaumont
Port Arthur
Galveston
Natchez
Columbus
Tupelo
West of 94° Greenwich

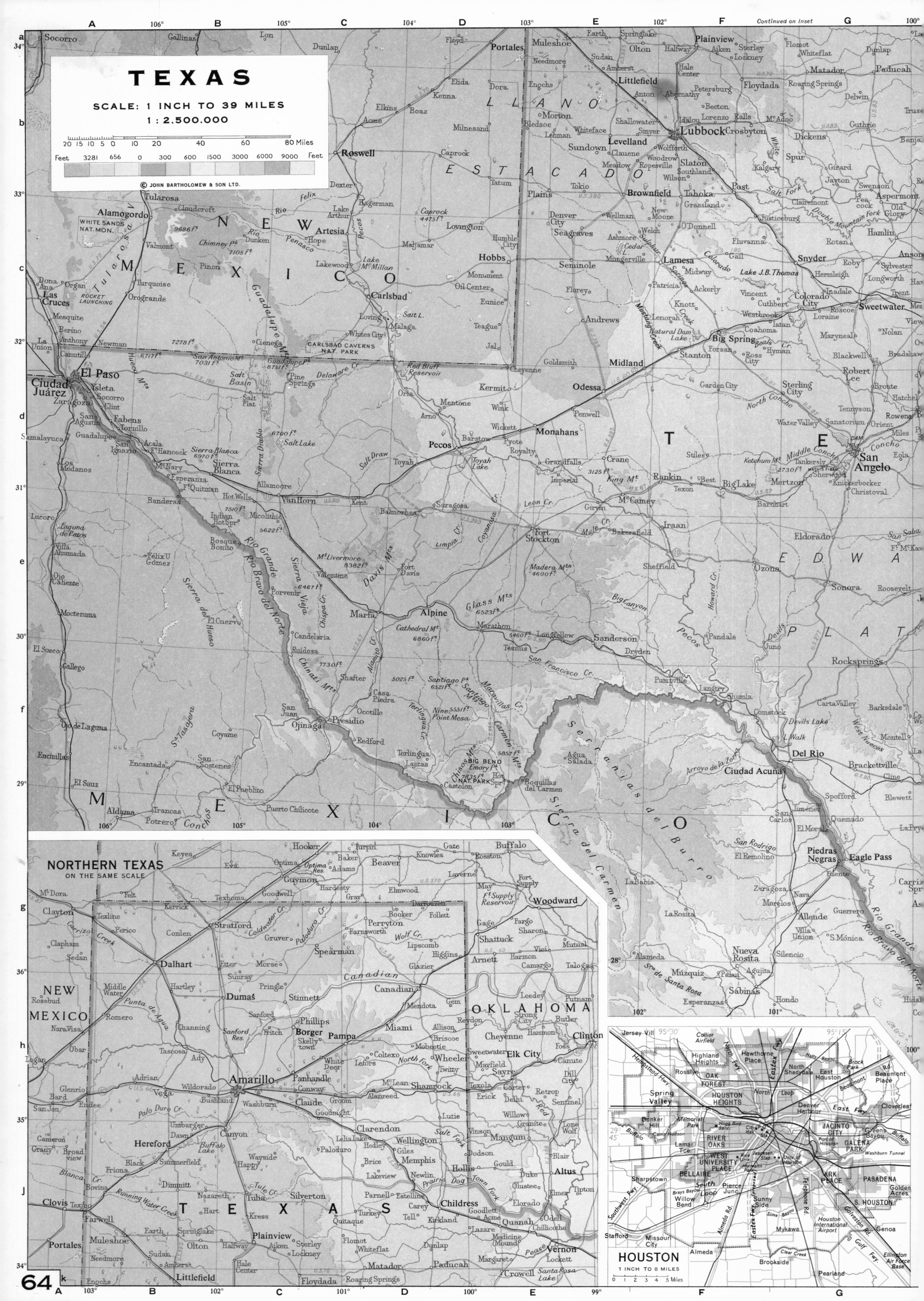

TEXAS

SCALE: 1 INCH TO 39 MILES
1 : 2.500.000

20 15 10 5 0 10 20 40 60 80 Miles

Feet 3281 656 0 300 1500 3000 6000 9000 Feet

© JOHN BARTHOLOMEW & SON LTD.

NEW MEXICO

LLANO

ESTACADO

T E X A S

E D W A R D S

P L A T

M E X I C O

NORTHERN TEXAS
ON THE SAME SCALE

NEW MEXICO

OKLAHOMA

TEXAS

HOUSTON
1 INCH TO 8 MILES
0 1 2 3 4 5 Miles

64

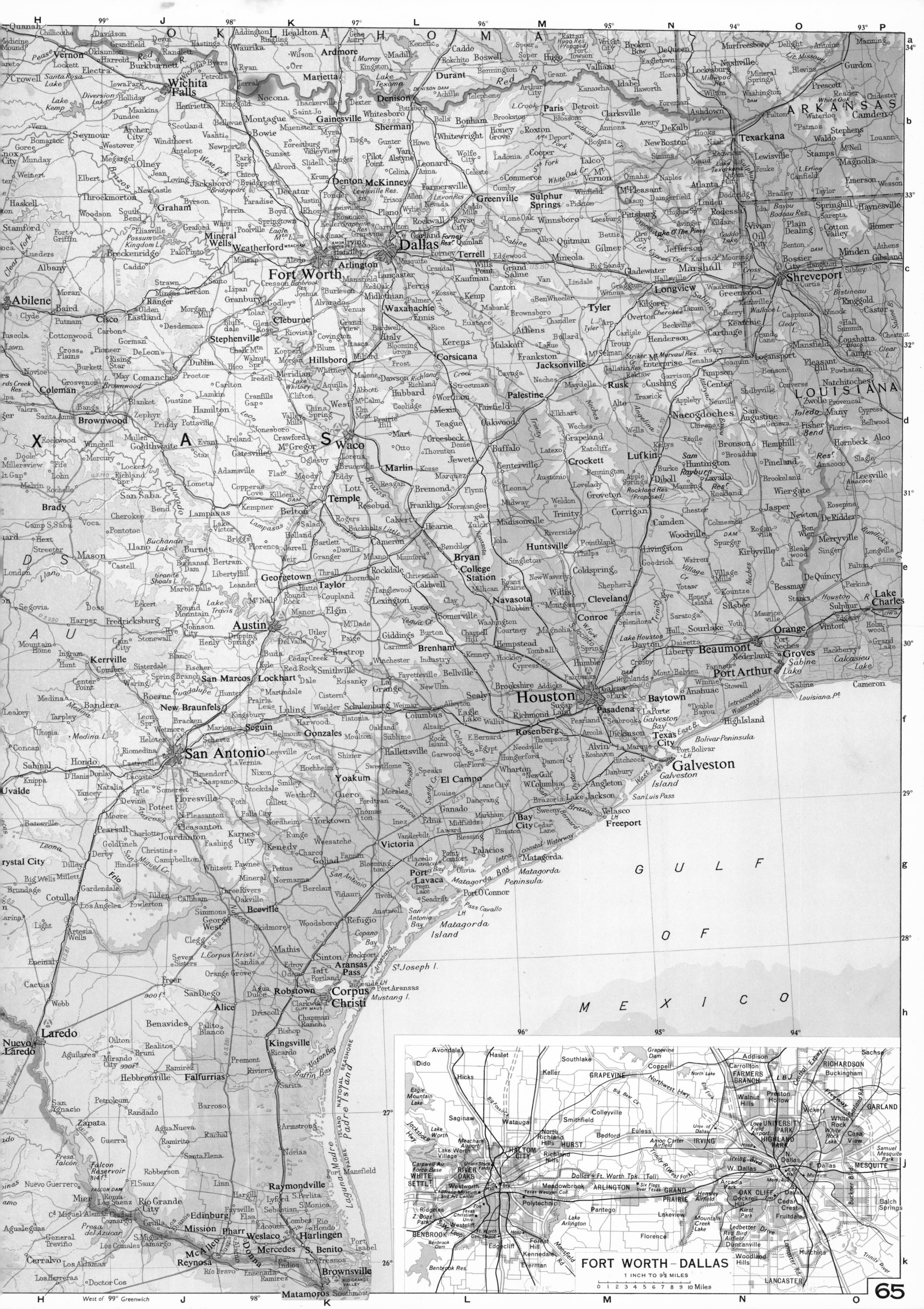

FORT WORTH – DALLAS

1 INCH TO 9½ MILES

0 1 2 3 4 5 6 7 8 9 10 Miles

65

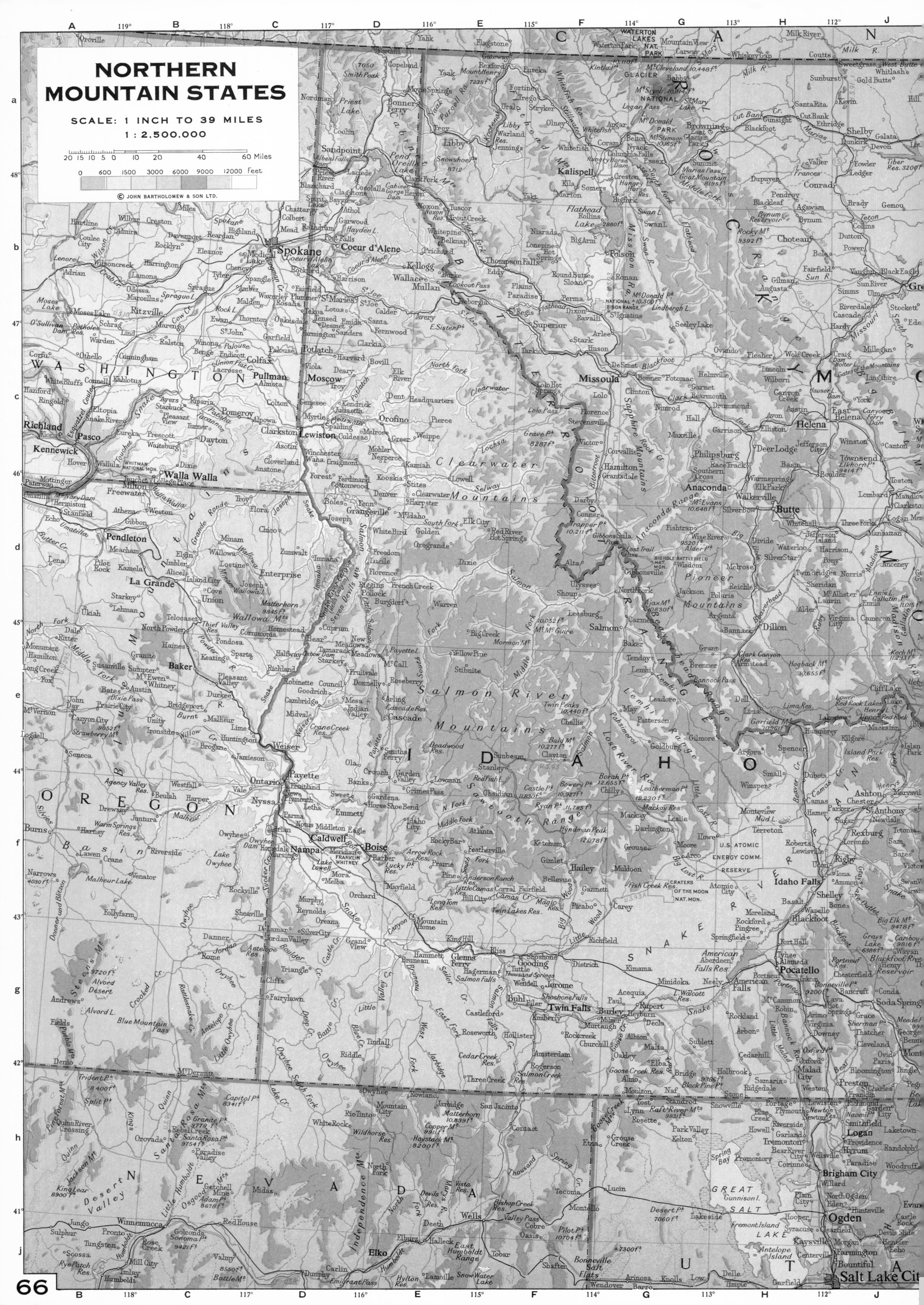

NORTHERN MOUNTAIN STATES

SCALE: 1 INCH TO 39 MILES
1 : 2,500,000

20 15 10 5 0   10   20   40   60 Miles

600 1500 3000 6000 9000 12000 Feet

© JOHN BARTHOLOMEW & SON LTD.

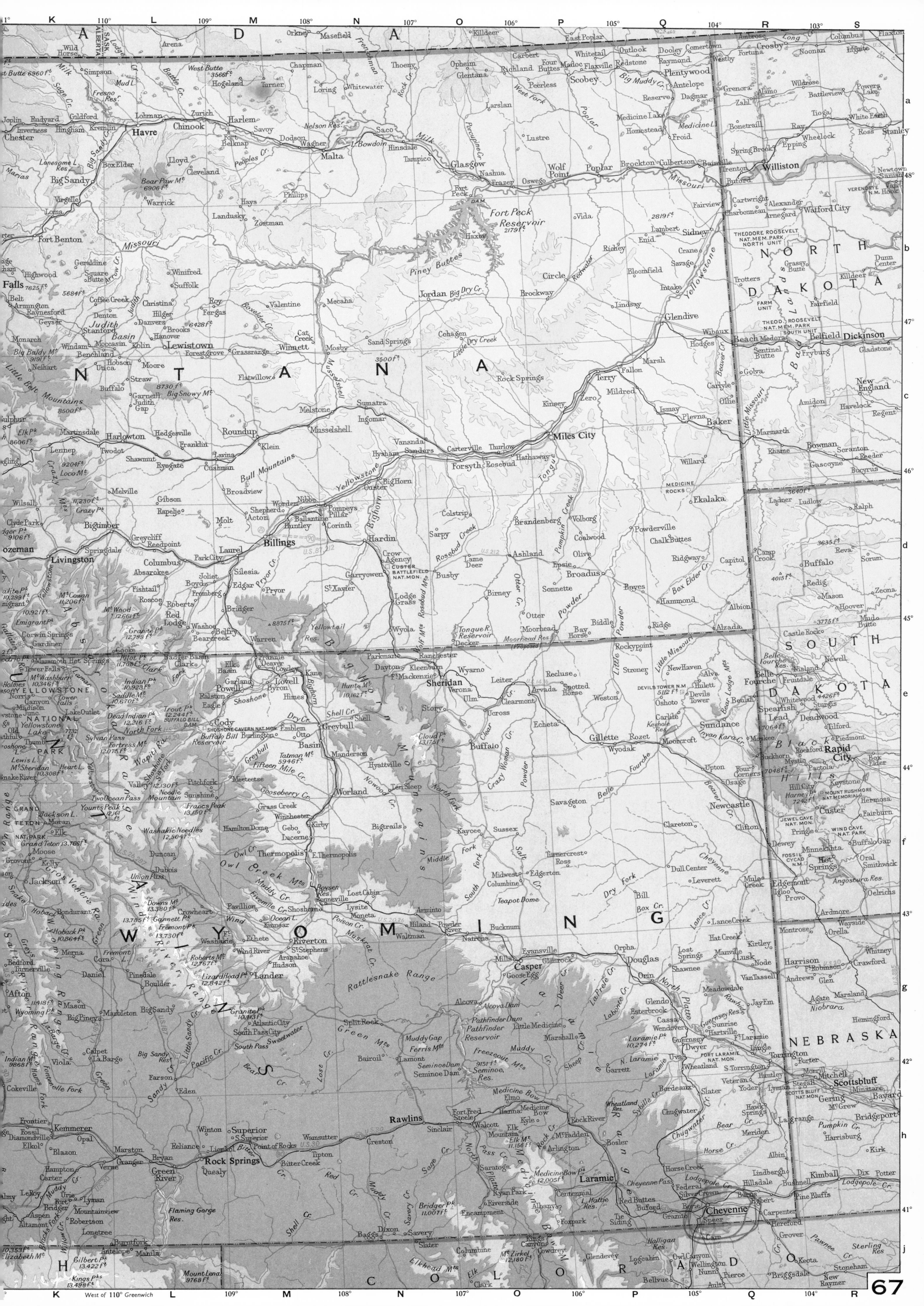

K L M N O P Q R S
110° 109° 108° 107° 106° 105° 104° 103°
CANADA
SASK. ALBERTA
NORTH DAKOTA
SOUTH DAKOTA
NEBRASKA
WYOMING
COLORADO
MONTANA
Havre
Chinook
Harlem
Malta
Glasgow
Wolf Point
Poplar
Plentywood
Scobey
Williston
Sidney
Glendive
Circle
Jordan
Lewistown
Roundup
Miles City
Forsyth
Terry
Baker
Billings
Laurel
Hardin
Livingston
Bigtimber
Big Sandy
Fort Benton
Fort Peck Reservoir
Missouri
Yellowstone
Musselshell
Bighorn
Powder
Tongue
Little Missouri
Dickinson
Beach
Belfield
Bowman
Buffalo
Rapid City
Belle Fourche
Spearfish
Lead
Deadwood
Sturgis
Custer
Hot Springs
Edgemont
Black Hills
Sheridan
Buffalo
Gillette
Sundance
Newcastle
Cody
Powell
Lovell
Greybull
Basin
Worland
Thermopolis
Riverton
Lander
Casper
Douglas
Glenrock
Wheatland
Torrington
Scottsbluff
Gering
Rawlins
Laramie
Cheyenne
Rock Springs
Green River
Kemmerer
Jackson
YELLOWSTONE NATIONAL PARK
GRAND TETON NAT. PARK
Yellowstone Lake
Big Horn Mountains
Absaroka Range
Wind River Range
Laramie Range
Medicine Bow Mts.
Rattlesnake Range
Owl Creek Mts.
Green Mts.
North Platte
Pathfinder Reservoir
Seminoe Res.
DEVILS TOWER N.M.
CUSTER BATTLEFIELD NAT. MON.
THEODORE ROOSEVELT NAT. MEM. PARK
MOUNT RUSHMORE NAT. MEMORIAL
WIND CAVE NAT. PARK
JEWEL CAVE NAT. MON.
SCOTTS BLUFF NAT. MON.
FORT LARAMIE NAT. MON.
SHOSHONE CAVERN NAT. MON.
48° 47° 46° 45° 44° 43° 42° 41°
a b c d e f g h j
West of 110° Greenwich

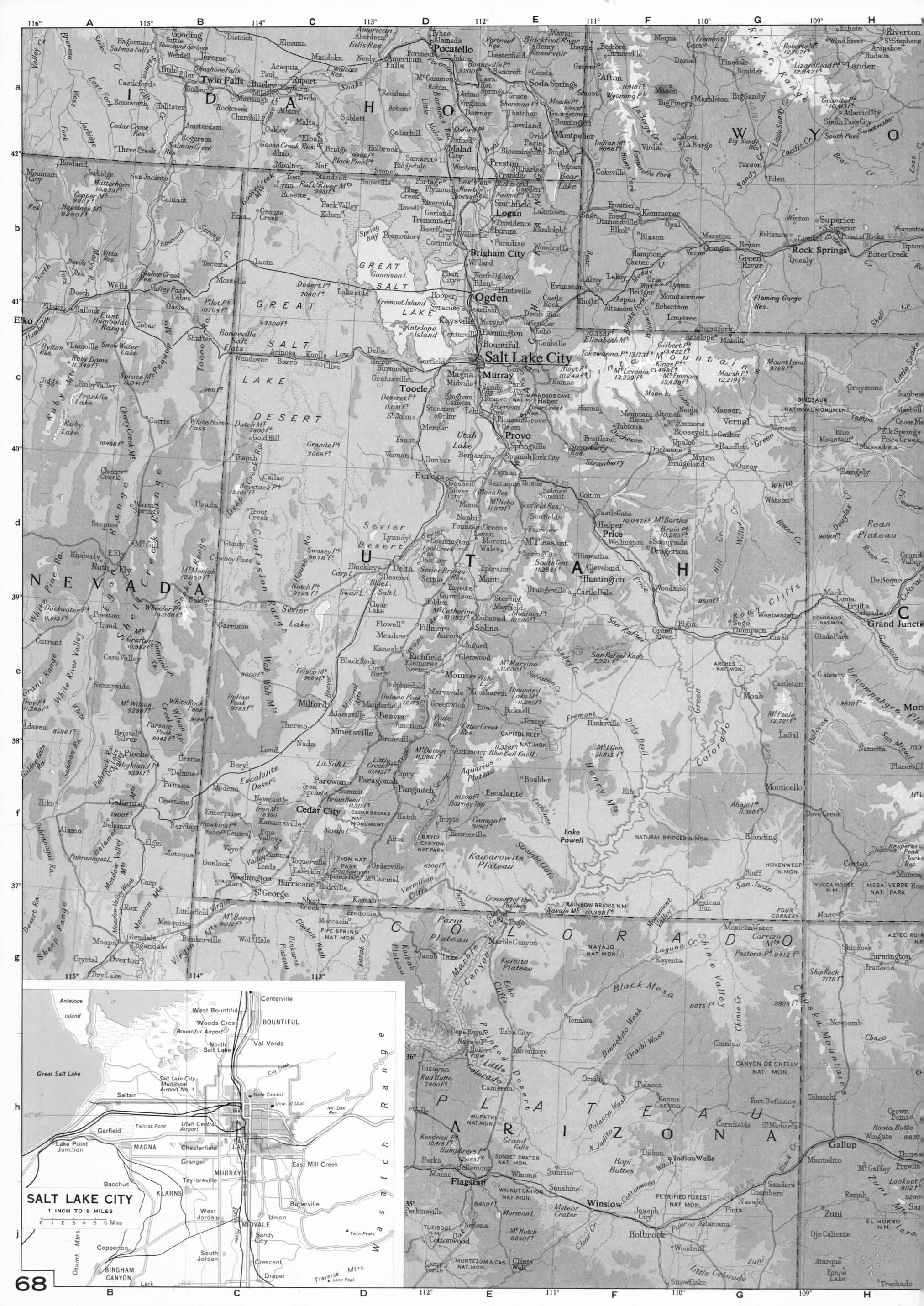

IDAHO
WYOMING
NEVADA
UTAH
COLORADO
ARIZONA
PLATEAU
GREAT SALT LAKE
GREAT SALT LAKE DESERT
Sevier Desert
Sevier Lake
Utah Lake
Bear Lake
Salt Lake City
Ogden
Provo
Logan
Brigham City
Pocatello
Twin Falls
Rock Springs
Kemmerer
Evanston
Elko
Ely
Price
Vernal
Moab
Cedar City
St. George
Kanab
Flagstaff
Winslow
Holbrook
Gallup
Farmington
Grand Junction
Tooele
Murray
Kaysville
Bountiful
Uinta Mountains
Wasatch Range
Lake Powell
Grand Canyon
Painted Desert
Black Mesa
Kaiparowits Plateau
Roan Cliffs
Vermilion Cliffs
Echo Cliffs
Henry Mts.
San Rafael Knob
BRYCE CANYON NAT. PARK
ZION NAT. PARK
CEDAR BREAKS NAT. MONUMENT
CAPITOL REEF NAT. MON.
ARCHES NAT. MON.
NATURAL BRIDGES N. MON.
RAINBOW BRIDGE N.M.
DINOSAUR NATIONAL MONUMENT
MESA VERDE NAT. PARK
CANYON DE CHELLY NAT. MON.
NAVAJO NAT. MON.
WUPATKI NAT. MON.
SUNSET CRATER NAT. MON.
WALNUT CANYON NAT. MON.
PETRIFIED FOREST NAT. MON.
MONTEZUMA CAS. NAT. MON.
TUZIGOOT N. MON.
PIPE SPRING NAT. MON.
HOVENWEEP N. MON.
YUCCA HOUSE N.M.
AZTEC RUINS
EL MORRO N.M.
TIMPANOGOS CAVE NAT. MON.
FOUR CORNERS
SALT LAKE CITY
1 INCH TO 8 MILES
Miles
Great Salt Lake
Antelope Island
Centerville
West Bountiful
Woods Cross
BOUNTIFUL
Bountiful Airport
North Salt Lake
Val Verda
Salt Lake City Municipal Airport No. 1
State Capitol
Univ. of Utah
Mt. Dell Res.
Saltair
Garfield
Tailings Pond
Utah Central Airport
Lake Point Junction
MAGNA
Chesterfield
S. SALT LAKE
Granger
East Mill Creek
MURRAY
Taylorsville
Bacchus
KEARNS
Butlerville
West Jordan
Union
MIDVALE
Sandy City
Twin Peaks
Copperton
South Jordan
Oquirrh Mtns.
Jordan River
Wasatch Range
BINGHAM CANYON
Crescent
Draper
Traverse Mtns.
Lone Peak
Lark

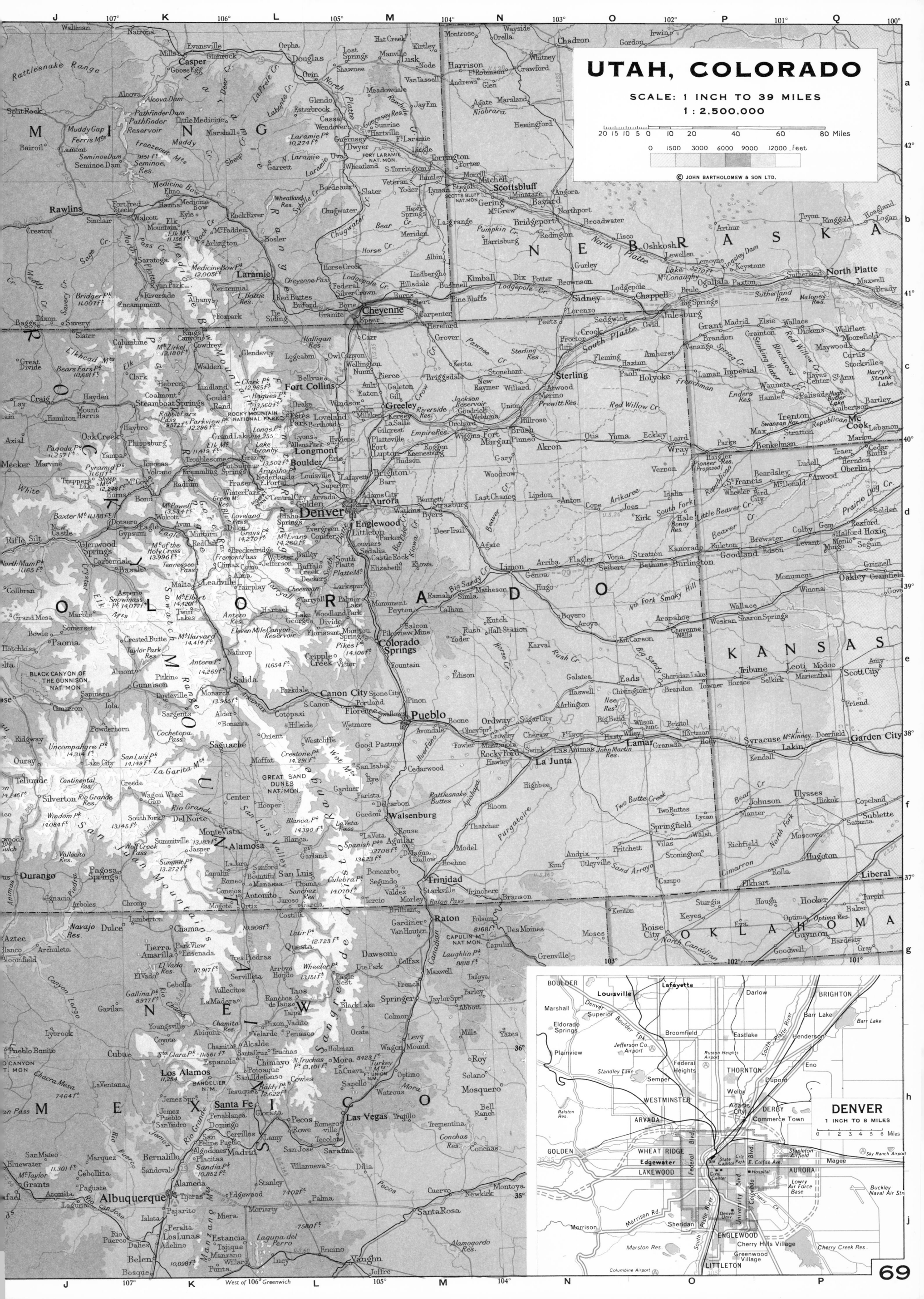

UTAH, COLORADO

SCALE: 1 INCH TO 39 MILES
1:2,500,000

20 15 10 5 0   10   20   40   60   80 Miles

0   1500   3000 6000 9000 12000 Feet

© JOHN BARTHOLOMEW & SON LTD.

DENVER
1 INCH TO 8 MILES
0 1 2 3 4 5 6 Miles

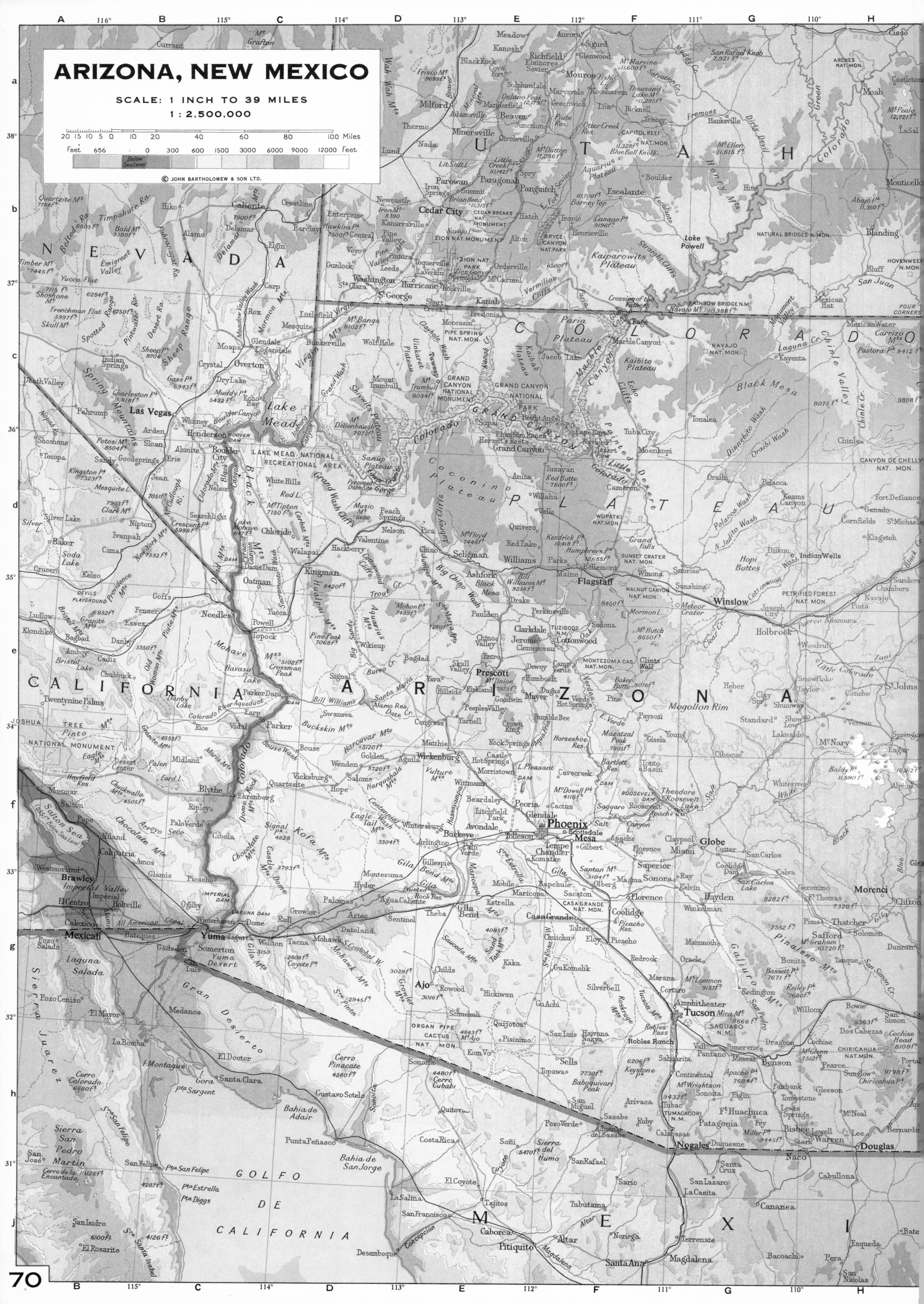

ARIZONA, NEW MEXICO

SCALE: 1 INCH TO 39 MILES

1 : 2,500,000

© JOHN BARTHOLOMEW & SON LTD.

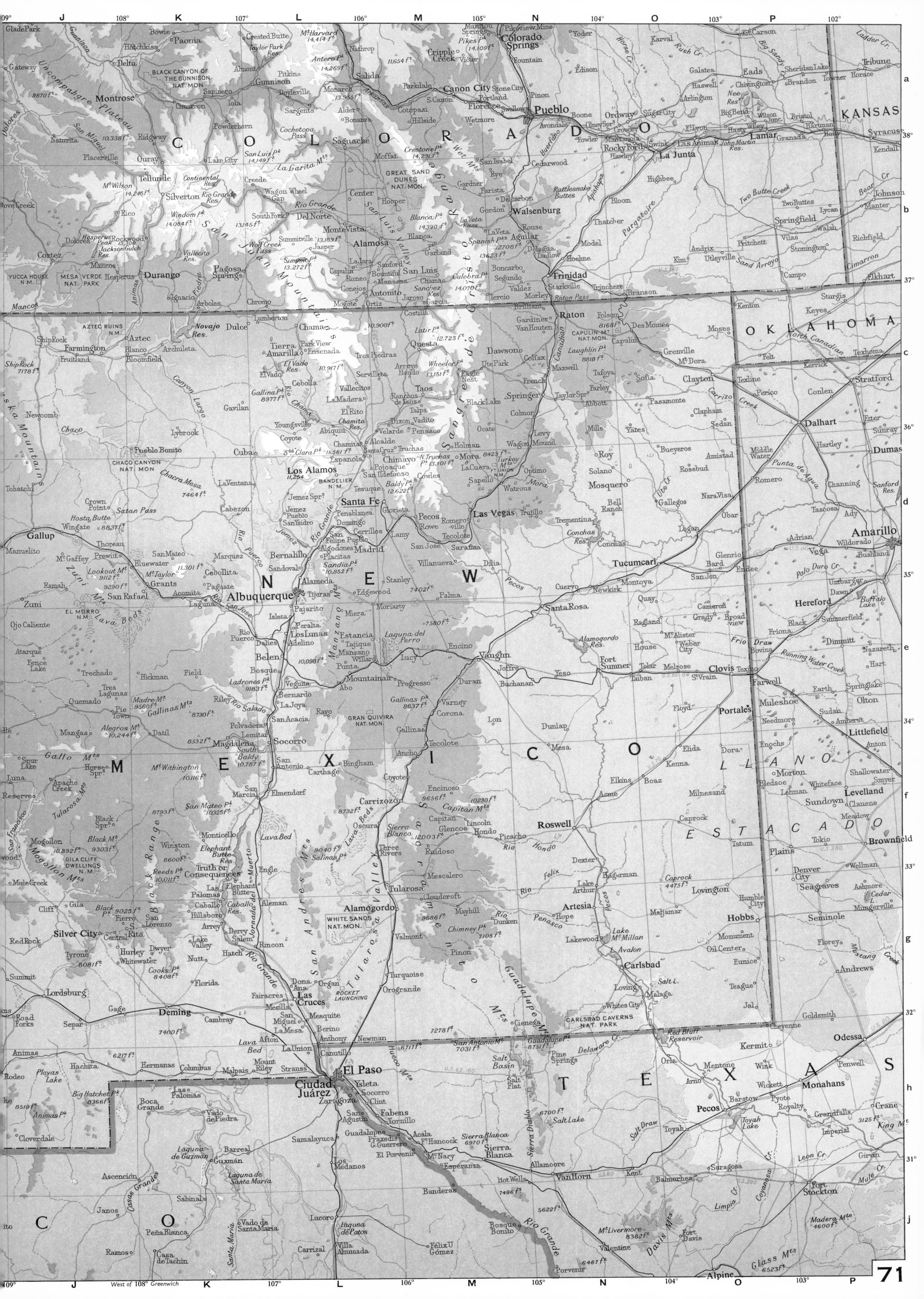
COLORADO
NEW MEXICO
TEXAS
KANSAS
OKLAHOMA
MEXICO
LLANO ESTACADO
Colorado Springs
Pueblo
Canon City
Trinidad
Walsenburg
La Junta
Lamar
Alamosa
Durango
Montrose
Gunnison
Raton
Santa Fe
Las Vegas
Los Alamos
Albuquerque
Gallup
Farmington
Taos
Socorro
Tucumcari
Clovis
Roswell
Artesia
Carlsbad
Alamogordo
Las Cruces
Deming
Lordsburg
Silver City
El Paso
Ciudad Juárez
Amarillo
Dalhart
Hereford
Lubbock
Odessa
Pecos
Monahans
Fort Stockton
Alpine
Hobbs
Portales
West of 108° Greenwich
109° 108° 107° 106° 105° 104° 103° 102°
38° 37° 36° 35° 34° 33° 32° 31°
J K L M N O P
a b c d e f g h j

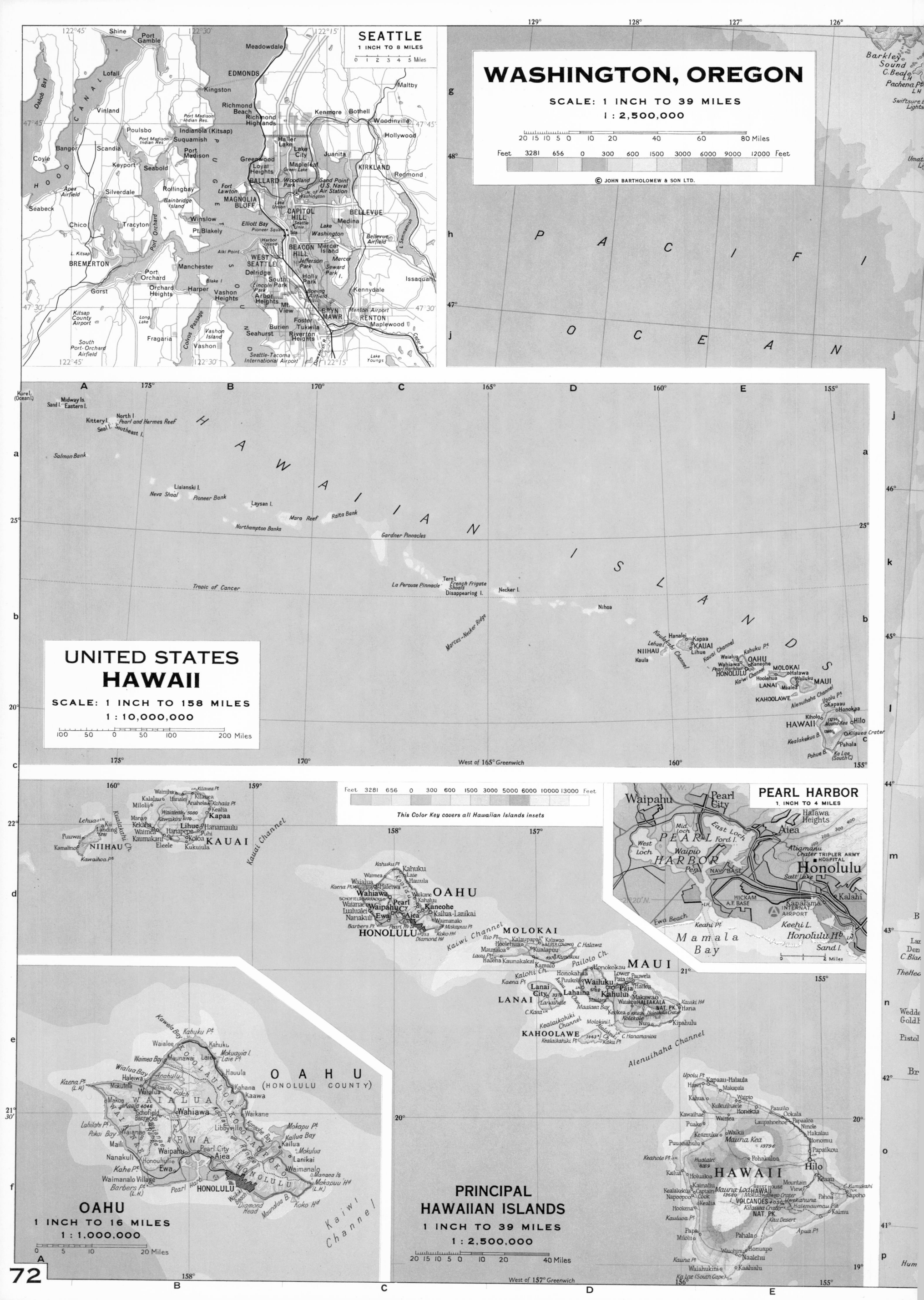

SEATTLE
1 INCH TO 8 MILES
0 1 2 3 4 5 Miles

WASHINGTON, OREGON
SCALE: 1 INCH TO 39 MILES
1 : 2,500,000
20 15 10 5 0   10   20   40   60   80 Miles
Feet 3281 656 0 300 600 1500 3000 6000 9000 12000 Feet
© JOHN BARTHOLOMEW & SON LTD.

UNITED STATES
HAWAII
SCALE: 1 INCH TO 158 MILES
1 : 10,000,000
100 50 0 50 100   200 Miles

Feet 3281 656 0 300 600 1500 3000 5000 6000 10000 13000 Feet
This Color Key covers all Hawaiian Islands insets

PEARL HARBOR
1 INCH TO 4 MILES

OAHU
1 INCH TO 16 MILES
1 : 1,000,000
0 5 10   20 Miles

PRINCIPAL
HAWAIIAN ISLANDS
1 INCH TO 39 MILES
1 : 2,500,000
20 15 10 5 0   10   20   40 Miles

72

C A N A D A
W A S H I N G T O N
O R E G O N
C A L I F O R N I A
N E V A D A
I D A H O
VANCOUVER ISLAND
STRAIT OF JUAN DE FUCA
Victoria
Bellingham
Anacortes
Port Angeles
Everett
Seattle
Bremerton
Tacoma
Olympia
Aberdeen
Hoquiam
Centralia
Chehalis
Longview
Kelso
Astoria
Vancouver
Portland
Oregon City
Salem
Albany
Corvallis
Eugene
Springfield
Roseburg
Coos Bay
Grants Pass
Medford
Ashland
Klamath Falls
Altamont
Bend
The Dalles
Pendleton
La Grande
Baker
Walla Walla
Pasco
Kennewick
Richland
Yakima
Ellensburg
Wenatchee
Spokane
Pullman
Moscow
Lewiston
Coeur d'Alene
Sandpoint
Ontario
Nampa
Eureka
Arcata
Yreka
Dunsmuir
Alturas
Lakeview
Burns
Columbia
Snake
Willamette
OLYMPIC NATIONAL PARK
MOUNT RAINIER NATIONAL PARK
CRATER LAKE NAT. PARK
LAVA BEDS NAT. MON.
Mt Olympus 7965 ft
Mt Rainier 14,410 ft
Mt St Helens 9677
Mt Adams 12,307 ft
Mt Hood 11,245 ft
Mt Jefferson 10,495 ft
Mt Shasta 14,162 ft
Mt Baker
Cascade Range
Blue Mountains
Wallowa Mts
Harney Basin
High Desert
Low Desert
Steens Mt 9720 ft
Alvord Desert
Black Rock Desert
Columbia Basin
Grand Coulee Dam
West of 120° Greenwich
125° 124° 123° 122° 121° 120° 119° 118° 117°
49° 48° 47° 46° 45° 44° 43° 42° 41°
F G H J K L M N O

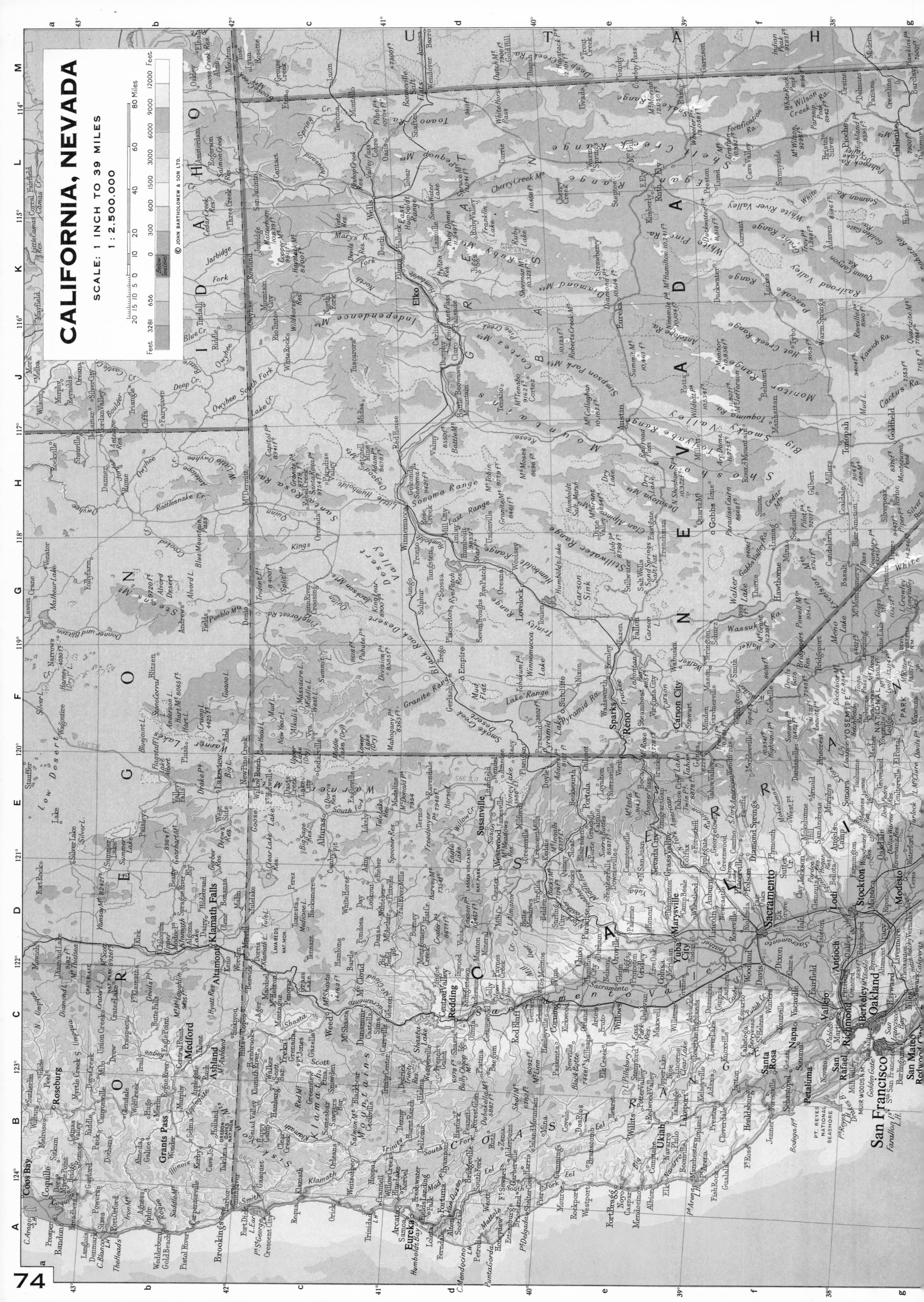

CALIFORNIA, NEVADA

SCALE: 1 INCH TO 39 MILES

1 : 2.500.000

© JOHN BARTHOLOMEW & SON LTD.

74

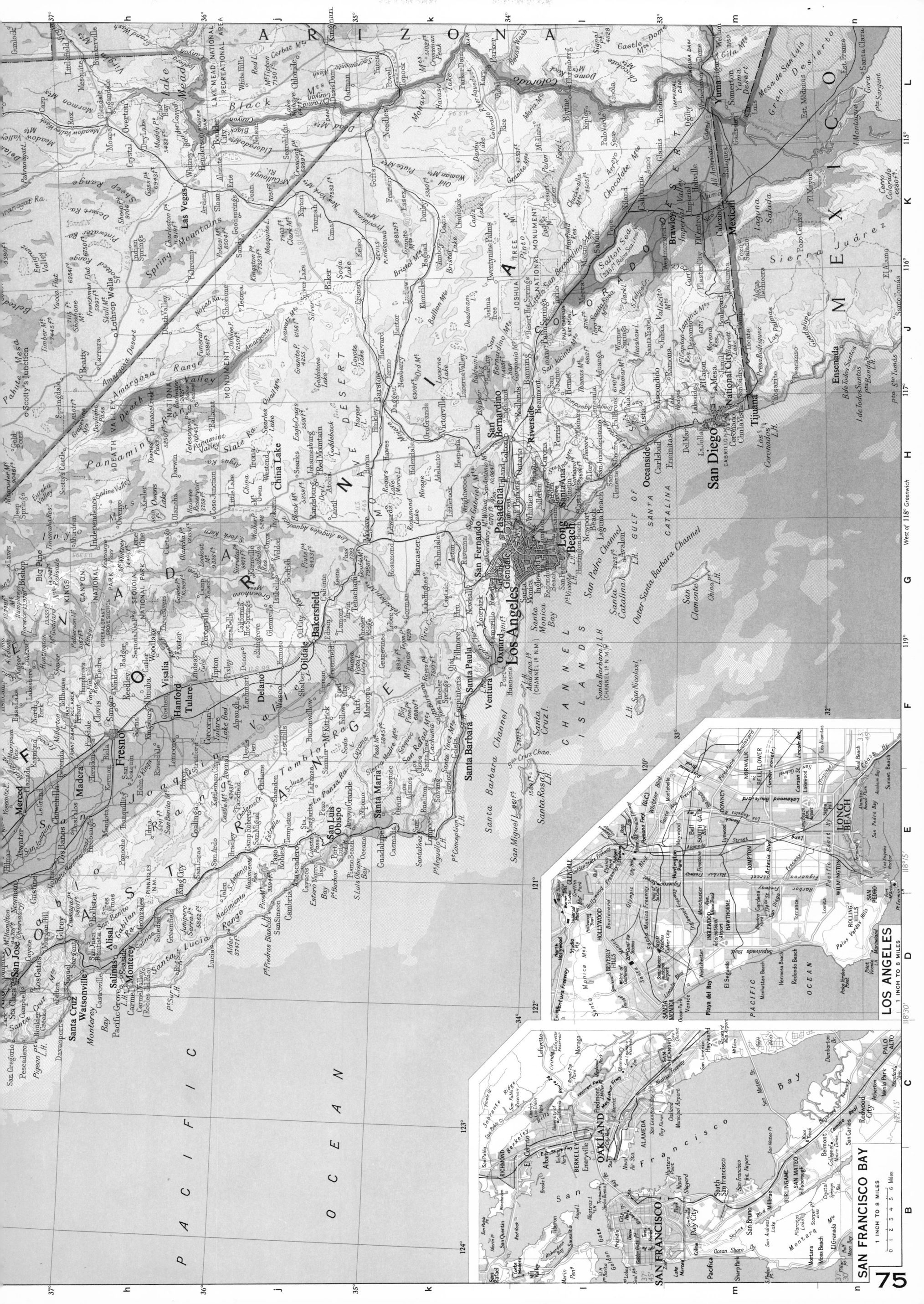

ARIZONA
NEVADA
CALIFORNIA
MEXICO
PACIFIC OCEAN
CHANNEL ISLANDS
MOJAVE DESERT
COLORADO DESERT
San Jose
Merced
Fresno
Visalia
Bakersfield
Santa Barbara
Los Angeles
Pasadena
Long Beach
San Bernardino
San Diego
Las Vegas
Tijuana
Mexicali
Yuma
SAN FRANCISCO BAY
1 INCH TO 8 MILES
LOS ANGELES
1 INCH TO 8 MILES
West of 118° Greenwich

UNITED STATES
ALASKA

SCALE: 1 INCH TO 79 MILES

1 : 5,000,000

40 30 20 10 0 20   40   60   80   100 Statute Miles

Feet 6562   656   0   600   1500   3000   6000   9000   12000 Feet

© JOHN BARTHOLOMEW & SON LTD.

THE GROWTH OF THE UNITED STATES

Dates under state names show entry into Union

- Thirteen original states
- Acquired by conquest during the Revolution and by treaty of 1783
- Louisiana Purchase from France in 1803
- Area ceded to Great Britain, 1818
- Area ceded by Great Britain, 1818
- Acquired by treaty with Spain in 1819
- Independent republic, formerly Mexican, annexed by U.S. in 1845
- Oregon Country, acquired by treaty with Great Britain in 1846
- Mexican Cession of 1848
- Gadsden Purchase from Mexico, 1853

NOTE:
Alaska, purchased from Russia in 1867, and Hawaii, annexed in 1898, were admitted to the Union in 1959. For U.S. Possessions, see pp. 54 and 78–79.

© 1963 BY THE READER'S DIGEST ASSOCIATION, INC.

1 INCH TO 474 MILES
0 100 200 300 400 500 Miles

WASH. 1889 · OREG. 1859 · IDAHO 1890 · MONT. 1889 · N.DAK. 1889 · S.DAK. 1889 · MINN. 1858 · WIS. 1848 · MICH. 1837 · WYO. 1890 · NEBR. 1867 · IOWA 1846 · ILL. 1818 · IND. 1816 · OHIO 1803 · NEV. 1864 · UTAH 1896 · COLO. 1876 · KANS. 1861 · MO. 1821 · KY. 1792 · CALIF. 1850 · ARIZ. 1912 · N. MEX. 1912 · OKLA. 1907 · ARK. 1836 · TENN. 1796 · TEX. 1845 · LA. 1812 · MISS. 1817 · ALA. 1819 · GA. 1788 · FLA. 1845 · N.C. 1789 · S.C. 1788 · VA. 1788 · W.VA. 1863 · MD. 1788 · DEL. 1787 · PA. 1787 · N.J. 1787 · N.Y. 1788 · CONN. 1788 · R.I. 1790 · MASS. 1788 · N.H. 1788 · VT. 1791 · MAINE 1820

Boundary as settled with Great Britain, 1842

CANADA

PACIFIC OCEAN · ATLANTIC OCEAN · GULF OF MEXICO · MEXICO

CONTINUATION OF ALEUTIAN ISLANDS GROUP
ON THE SAME SCALE

GULF OF ALASKA

CANADA

ALEXANDER ARCHIPELAGO

77

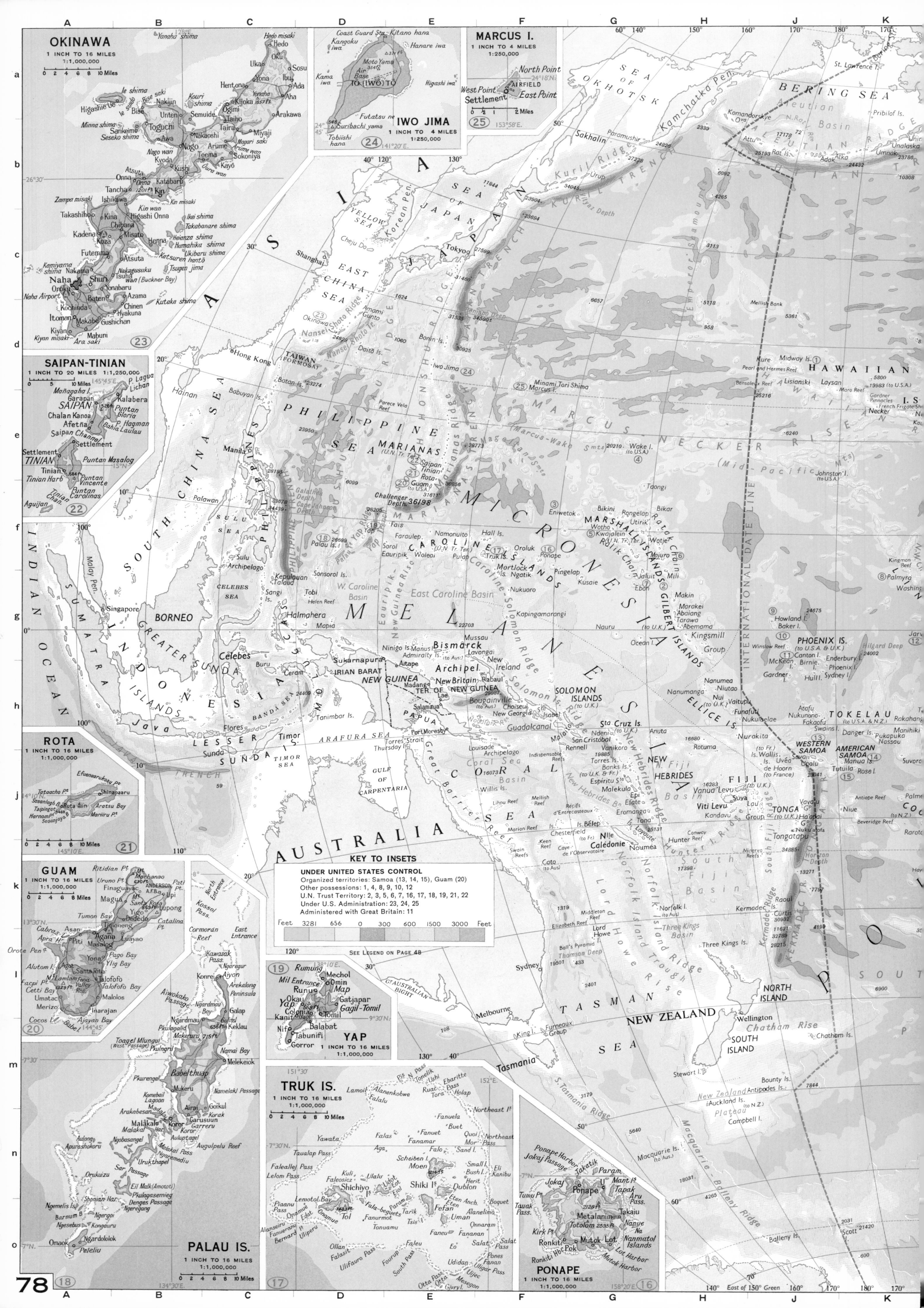
OKINAWA
1 INCH TO 16 MILES
1:1,000,000
IWO JIMA
1 INCH TO 4 MILES
1:250,000
MARCUS I.
1 INCH TO 4 MILES
1:250,000
SAIPAN-TINIAN
1 INCH TO 20 MILES 1:1,250,000
ROTA
1 INCH TO 16 MILES
1:1,000,000
GUAM
1 INCH TO 16 MILES
1:1,000,000
PALAU IS.
1 INCH TO 16 MILES
1:1,000,000
YAP
1 INCH TO 16 MILES
1:1,000,000
TRUK IS.
1 INCH TO 16 MILES
1:1,000,000
PONAPE
1 INCH TO 16 MILES
1:1,000,000
ASIA
SEA OF OKHOTSK
BERING SEA
SEA OF JAPAN
JAPAN
YELLOW SEA
EAST CHINA SEA
SOUTH CHINA SEA
PHILIPPINE SEA
PHILIPPINES
MARIANAS
MICRONESIA
MELANESIA
MARSHALL ISLANDS
CAROLINE ISLANDS
GILBERT ISLANDS
ELLICE IS.
PHOENIX IS.
TOKELAU
HAWAIIAN IS.
INDONESIA
BORNEO
SUMATRA
Java
Celebes
Halmahera
NEW GUINEA
IRIAN BARAT
PAPUA
Bismarck Archipel.
SOLOMON ISLANDS
NEW HEBRIDES
FIJI
TONGA
WESTERN SAMOA
AMERICAN SAMOA
CORAL SEA
TASMAN SEA
AUSTRALIA
NEW ZEALAND
NORTH ISLAND
SOUTH ISLAND
Tasmania
INDIAN OCEAN
INTERNATIONAL DATE LINE
KEY TO INSETS
UNDER UNITED STATES CONTROL
Organized territories: Samoa (13, 14, 15), Guam (20)
Other possessions: 1, 4, 8, 9, 10, 12
U.N. Trust Territory: 2, 3, 5, 6, 7, 16, 17, 18, 19, 21, 22
Under U.S. Administration: 23, 24, 25
Administered with Great Britain: 11
Feet 3281 656 0 300 600 1500 3000 Feet
SEE LEGEND ON PAGE 48

PACIFIC OCEAN
SCALE: 1 INCH TO 632 MILES
1:40,000,000

500 400 300 200 100 0   500   1000 Miles

Feet 26248 22967 19686 16409 13124 9843 6562 3281 Feet

Spot Depths are given in Feet
SEE LEGEND ON PAGE 48
© JOHN BARTHOLOMEW & SON LTD.

MIDWAY IS.
1 INCH TO 4 MILES
1:250,000

Middle Ground
North Breakers
Seaward Roads
Sand Island
Welles Harbor
ANCHORAGE
Eastern I.
177°25'W.
①

ENIWETOK
1 INCH TO 16 MILES
1:1,000,000

Elugelab Lidilbut Bogon
Bogombogo Engebi
Bogallua Mujinkarikku
Biijen Aranit Rojoa
Rujiyoru Arambiru Piirai
Runit
Rigili
Chinieero Joptan
Lagoon Bogen Muti
East Ch. Parry I.
SEAPLANE ANCHORAGE
Southwest Passage
Grinem Libiron
Bogan Igurin
AIRFIELD Eniwetok
South Ch.
11°20'N.
③

MARSHALL IS.
1 INCH TO 158 MILES
1:10,000,000

0 20 40 80 120 Miles

Eniwetok
Bikini
Rongelap
Rongerik
Bikar
Ailinginae
Utirik
Taka
Wotho
Likiep
Jemo
Ailuk
Mejit I.
Kwajalein
Wotje
Ujae
Lae
Erikub
Maloelap
Namu
Jabwot I.
Aur
Ailinglapalap
Majuro
Namorik
Kili I.
Arno
Jaluit
Mili
Ebon

KWAJALEIN
1 INCH TO 39 MILES
1:2,500,000

Ebadon
Mejatto
North Pass
Roi
Oreba
Bigi
Mellu
Gagan
Etcharai
Boggerik
Tabik
Yabbenohr
Nell
Gurer
Onemak
Eniwetak Passow
Eller
Legan
Meck
Mann
Bigej
Ninigi
SEAPLANE ANCHORAGE
Ennylabegan
Ebeye
Missile Range
Kwajalein
⑤

MAJURO
1 INCH TO 16 MILES
1:1,000,000

Jaloklab
Roguron
Erof
Calalin Channel
West Landing
Robokaire
Anemwanot
Majuro
Enigu
Diarrit
Uliga
Settlement
Dalap
AIRFIELD
Majuro
Lagoon
Rairik
Anenelibw
7°N.
171°20'E.
⑥

JALUIT
1 INCH TO 16 MILES
1:1,000,000

Bogenaga
Boggenadick
Jabnoren
Urbett
Ngain
Narmidj
Lijeron
Jinbal
Rua
Medyai
Medyado
Imrodj
Northeast Pass
Kinadyteng
Agidyen
Arlap
Taka
Imieji
West
Jaluit
Imjet
Breakfast I.
Pinglap
Aineman
Bokaljiman
Enybor
Kabbenbock
Southwest Pass.
Aruboe
Jabor
Ali
Elizabeth I.
Menge
Ooa
Southeast Pass
Eneeldak
Jaluit
South Pt.
6°N.
169°30'E.
⑦

WAKE I.
1 INCH TO 8 MILES
1:500,000

0 1 2 3 Miles

Toki Pt.
Flipper Pt.
Peale I.
Kuku Pt.
Heel Pt.
Wilkes I.
Lagoon
19°18'N.
Channel
Settlement
Wake I.
WAKE AIRPORT
Peacock Pt.
166°36'E.
④

PALMYRA I.
1 INCH TO 4 MILES
1:250,000

0 ½ 1 2 Miles

Strawn I.
Cooper I.
Sawle Pt.
Aviation I.
W. Lagoon
AIRFIELD
Eastern I.
Center I.
Portsmouth Pt.
Channel
E. Lagoon
Barren I.
Sand I.
Bird I.
5°52'N.
Penguin Spit
Holei I.
162°5'W.
⑧

BAKER I.
1 INCH TO 4 MILES
1:250,000

0 ½ 1 2 Miles

Landing
Settlement
(Uninhabited)
0°12'N.
176°30'W.
⑩

HOWLAND I.
1 INCH TO 4 MILES
1:250,000

Landing
Settlement
(Uninhabited)
0°48'N.
176°38'W.
⑨

CANTON I.
1 INCH TO 8 MILES
1:500,000

0 1 2 3 4 Miles

CANTON AIRPORT
Northside
DOCK
Boat Channel
Southside
SEAPLANE ANCHORAGE
2°50'S.
Pyramid Pt.
171°40'W.
⑪

JARVIS I.
1 INCH TO 4 MILES
1:250,000

Landing
Settlement
(Uninhabited)
Landing
0°23'S.
160°W.
⑫

SWAINS I.
1 INCH TO 4 MILES
1:250,000

0 ½ 1 2 Miles

FalaAne Pt.
Taulaga Landing
Lagoon
Etena Landing
11°05'S.
171°05'W.
⑬

MANUA IS.
1 INCH TO 16 MILES
1:1,000,000

0 2 4 6 8 10 Miles

Ofu
Sili Olosega
Olosega
Oru
Faleasao
Tau
Maia
Luma
Leusoali'i
Sufaga
14°10'S.
169°30'W.
⑭

TUTUILA
1 INCH TO 16 MILES
1:1,000,000

0 2 4 6 8 10 Miles

Greyhound
Pola I.
Fagasa
Pago Pago
Aua
Alao
Hubner Bay
Leone
Fagatogo
Laulii
Alofau
Amanave
Fanene
Aumi'u
TAFUNA AIRPORT
Pago Pago Harbor
Leone Pt.
Vailoatai
Taputimu
Yaitogi
Steps Pt.
14°20'S.
170°40'W.
⑮

NORTH AMERICA

GULF OF ALASKA
Kodiak
Queen Charlotte Is.
Vancouver I.
Vancouver
San Francisco
Los Angeles
Channel Is.
Guadalupe (to Mex.)
Mendocino Seascarp
Murray Seascarp
Murray Deep
Erben Tmt.
Fieberling Tmt.
Tropic of Cancer
Hawaii
Honolulu
Maui
Kauai
Oahu

CENTRAL AMERICA

GULF OF MEXICO
Mexico
Acapulco Trench
Guatemala Trench
Guatemala Basin
Is. Revilla Gigedo (to Mex.)
Clipperton (to Fr.)
Clarion Fracture Zone
Clipperton Fracture Zone
ALBATROSS PLATEAU
I. del Coco (to Costa Rica)
I. de Maipelo (to Colombia)
CARIBBEAN SEA
Cocos Ridge
Panama
Colon–Ecuador or Carnegie Ridge
Islas Galapagos (to Ecu.)
Isabela
Sta Cruz
Equator

SOUTH AMERICA

SOUTH-EASTERN PACIFIC BASIN
Milne Edwards Deep
Bauer Deep
Krümmel Deep
Bartholomew Deep
Richards Deep
San Félix (to Chile)
San Ambrosio (to Chile)
Más-a-Tierra
Más Afuero
Islas Juan Fernández (to Chile)
Hecule Deep
Santiago
Juan Fernández Ridge
San Félix Ridge
Sala y Gómez
Easter I. (Isla de Pascua)
Tropic of Capricorn
I. de Chiloé
Archipiélago de los Chonos
Wellington
Cape Horn
ATLANTIC OCEAN

POLYNESIA

MARQUESAS (Is. Marquises) (to Fr.)
Nuku Hiva
Hiva Oa
Fatu Hiva
TUAMOTU
Tuamotu Ridge
King George Is.
Disappointment Is.
Fakarava (to Fr.)
Makemo
Hao
SOCIETY IS. (Is. de la Société) (to Fr.)
Tahiti
Papeete
Duke of Gloucester Is.
Actaeon Group
Mururoa (to Fr.)
Mangaréva
Is. Gambier
Oeno
Henderson I. (to U.K.)
Ducie I.
Pitcairn I.
TUBUAI IS.
Rurutu
Tubuai (to Fr.)
Raivavae
Rapa Iti
Ilots de Bass
Austral Ridge
Maria Theresa Reef
Ernest Legouve Reef
Wachusett Shoal
PACIFIC PLATEAU
PACIFIC-ANTARCTIC RIDGE
PACIFIC-ANTARCTIC BASIN
Antarctic Circle
Vostok I.
Caroline I.
Flint
Malden I.
Starbuck
Filippo Reef
Christmas I.
Line Islands Ridge
Motu One
Fenua Ura
Bora Bora
Raiatea
Maupiti
Atiu
Hervey Is.
Is. Maria
Rimatara
L'Orne Bank
Recif Lancaster
Raivavae Recif
President Thiers

North Pacific
Ocean depths / spot depths (scattered numbers)

CANADA

HEIGHTS
IN FEET

12,000

10000

6000

3000

1500

600

SEA LEVEL

3000

DEPTHS
IN FEET

80

CHAMBERLIN TRIMETRIC PROJECTION

SCALE: 1:12,500,000 OR 1 INCH TO 197 MILES
(Approximately)

MAIN HIGHWAYS

RAILWAYS

CANALS

OIL PIPE LINES

SCALE IN MILE

100
200
300
400
500
600
700
800
900
1000
1100
1200
1300
1400
1500
1600
1700
1800
1900
2000

INTERNATIONAL BOUNDARIES
PROVINCE AND STATE BOUNDARIES
SWAMP AND FLOOD AREAS
GLACIERS AND ICECAPS
SPOT HEIGHTS IN FEET △ 2,120 ft.

© JOHN BARTHOLOMEW & SON LTD.

SCALE: 1:12,500,000 OR 1 INCH TO 197 MILES
(Approximately)

Rimming the sea are highlands and lowlands between arcs of mountains. The Canadian

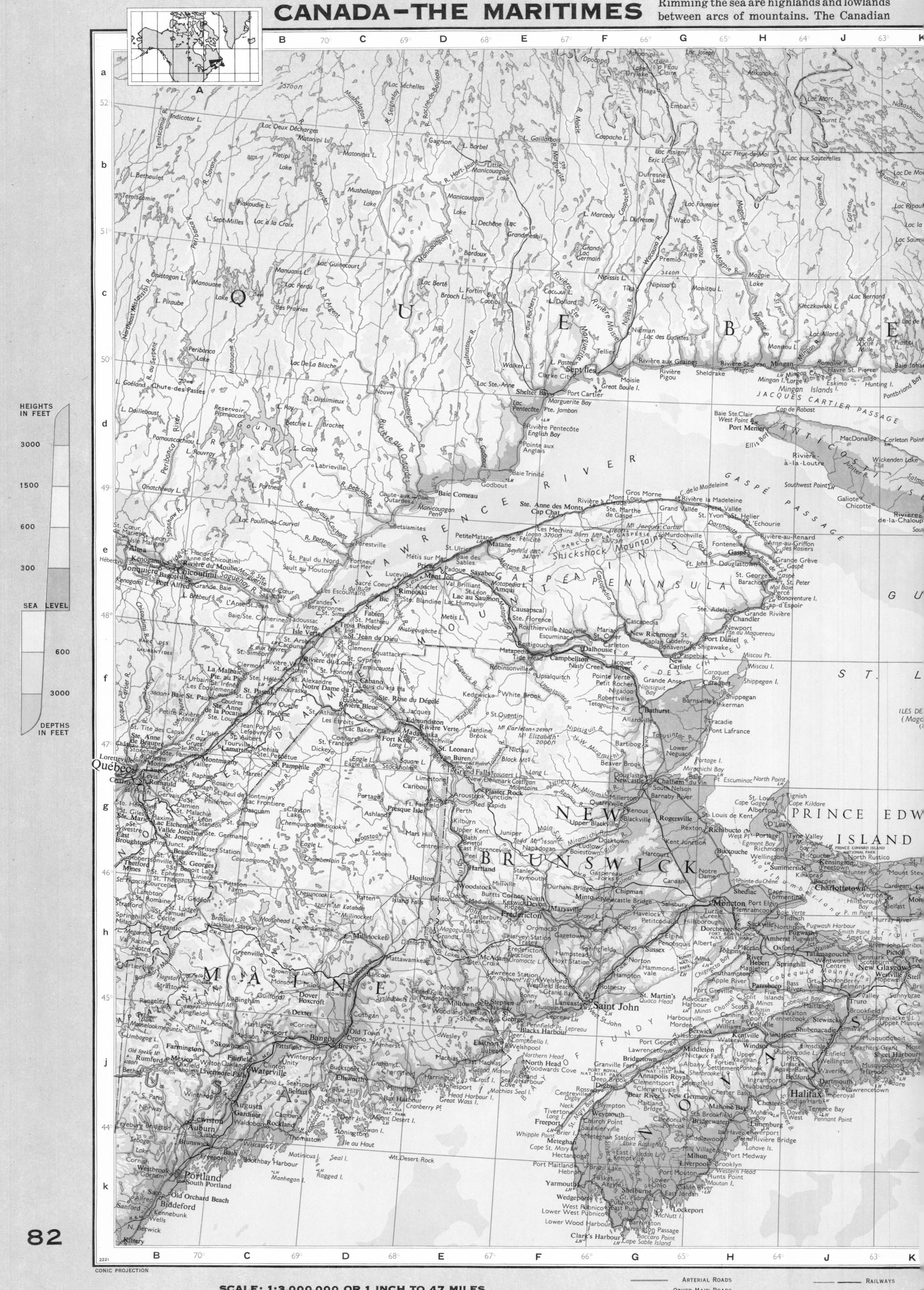

SCALE: 1:3,000,000 OR 1 INCH TO 47 MILES

CONIC PROJECTION

82

LABRADOR

NEWFOUNDLAND

QUEBEC

ATLANTIC OCEAN

LONG RANGE MOUNTAINS

Notre Dame Bay

Bonavista Bay

Corner Brook

Deer Lake

Gander

Grand Falls

Windsor

Buchans

Botwood

St. Anthony

CABOT STRAIT

CAPE BRETON ISLAND

CAPE BRETON NATIONAL PARK

Sydney

Glace Bay

Louisburg

NOVA SCOTIA

Canso

SAINT-PIERRE & MIQUELON (To France)

St. Pierre

PLACENTIA BAY

BURIN PENINSULA

AVALON PENINSULA

St. John's

Placentia

Argentia

GULF OF ST. LAWRENCE

MADELEINE (Islands)

Havre Aubert

St. Paul Island

Cape Ray

Port aux Basques

Stephenville

Port-au-Port Peninsula

ATLANTIC OCEAN

SABLE ISLAND BANK

Sable Island

West Point

East Point

83

SCALE IN MILES

50 — 100 — 150 — 200 — 250 — 300 — 350 — 400 — 450 — 500

INTERNATIONAL BOUNDARIES

PROVINCIAL BOUNDARIES

SWAMP AND FLOOD AREAS

SPOT HEIGHTS IN FEET △ 3700 ft.

SCALE: 1:3,000,000 OR 1 INCH TO 47 MILES

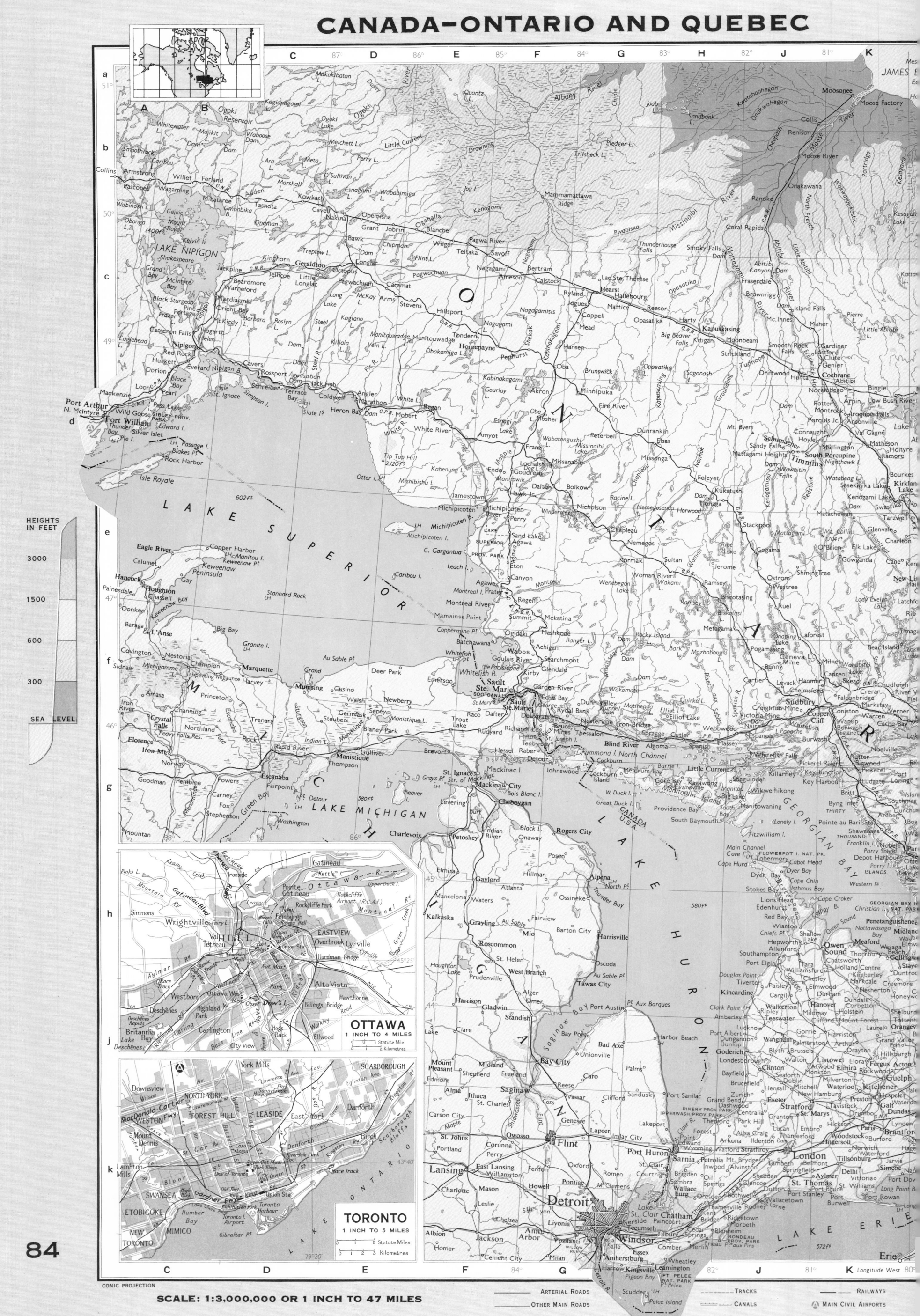

HEIGHTS
IN FEET

3000

1500

600

300

SEA LEVEL

OTTAWA
1 INCH TO 4 MILES

TORONTO
1 INCH TO 5 MILES

84

CONIC PROJECTION

SCALE: 1:3,000,000 OR 1 INCH TO 47 MILES

ARTERIAL ROADS   TRACKS

OTHER MAIN ROADS   RAILWAYS

CANALS   Main Civil Airports

The Great Lakes-St. Lawrence lowlands form the economic heartland of Canada. This region is one of the smallest geographic units in the country, but contains 60 percent of the population. It is probably the most productive area in Canada.

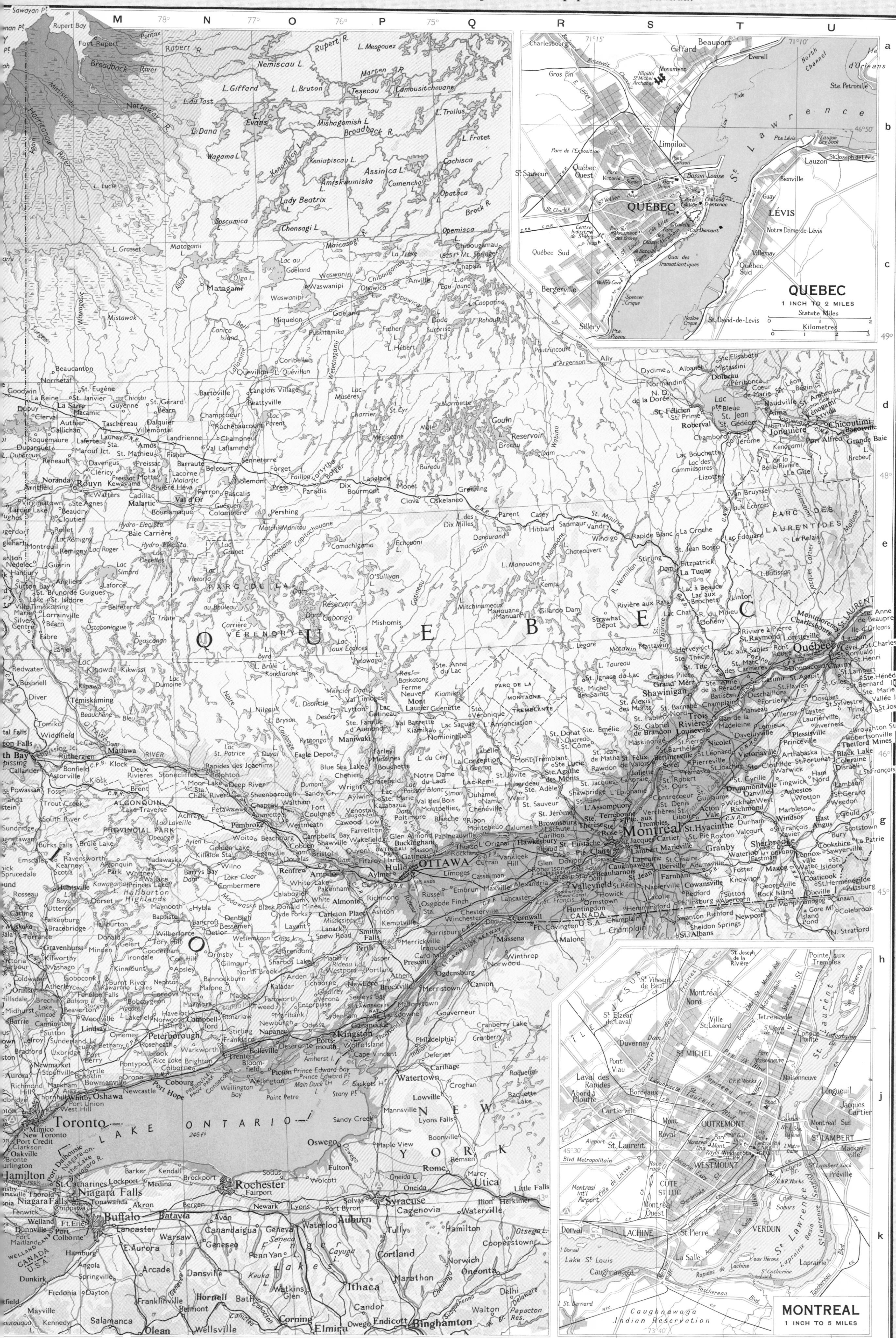

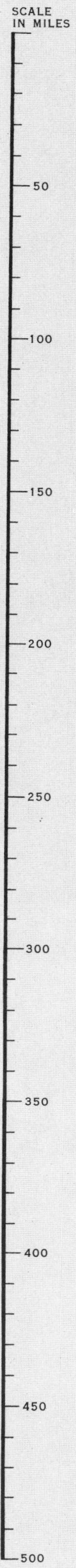

QUEBEC
1 INCH TO 2 MILES
Statute Miles
Kilometres

MONTREAL
1 INCH TO 5 MILES

SCALE
IN MILES

50
100
150
200
250
300
350
400
450
500

INTERNATIONAL BOUNDARIES
PROVINCIAL BOUNDARIES
SWAMP AND FLOOD AREAS
SPOT HEIGHTS IN FEET △ 2,120 Ft.

SCALE: 1:3,000,000 OR 1 INCH TO 47 MILES

Canada's prairies, taking in large areas
of three provinces, were formed by

deposits from the Pre-Cambrian Shield
and from marginal mountains (the

HEIGHTS
IN FEET

9000

6000

3000

1500

600

SEA LEVEL

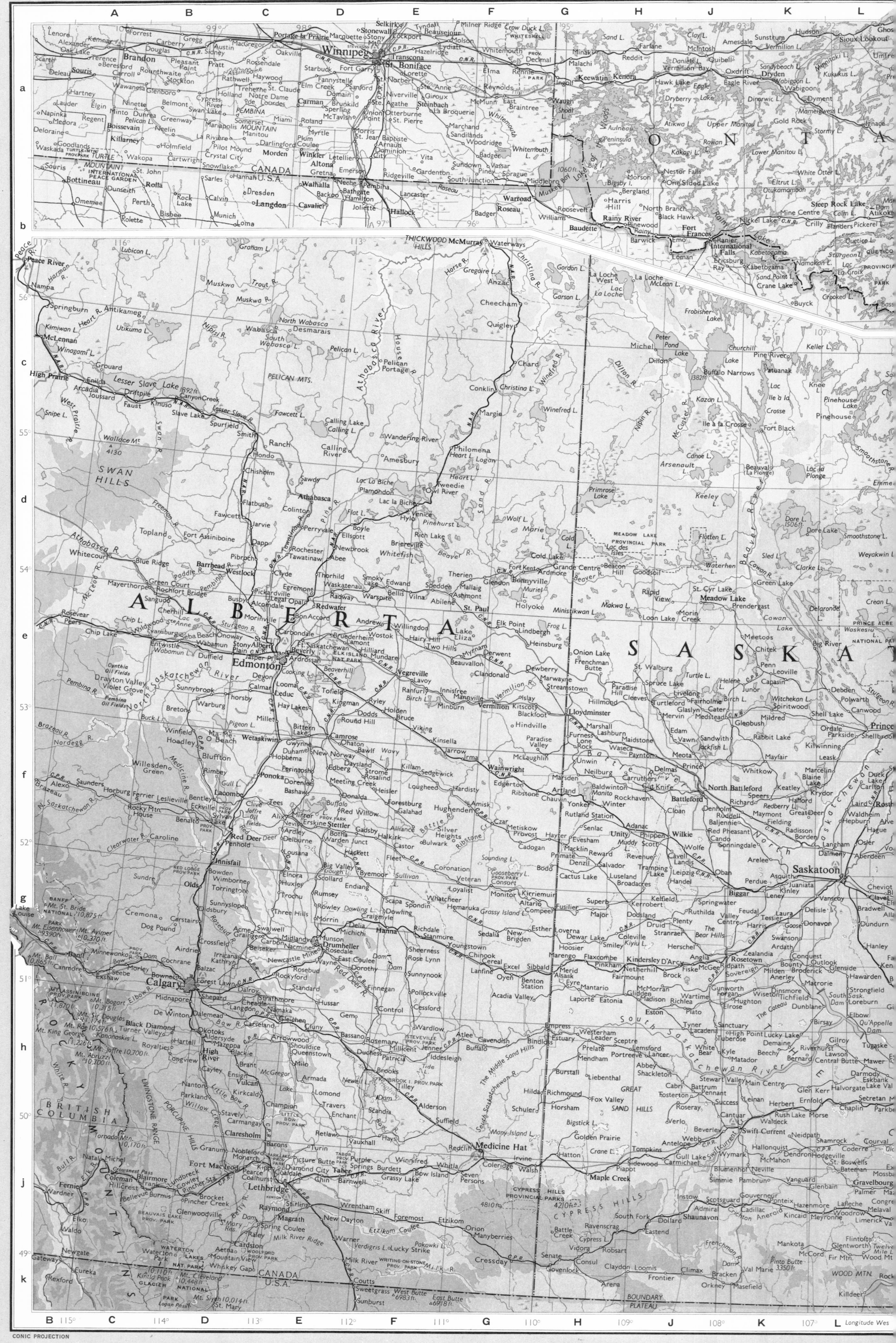

86

CONIC PROJECTION

SCALE: 1:3,000,000 OR 1 INCH TO 47 MILES

ARTERIAL ROADS — — — TRACKS — — — RAILWAYS

OTHER MAIN ROADS — — — CANALS ▲ MAIN CIVIL AIRPORTS

Rockies) laid down in shallow seas. Their sweeping, fertile expanses have made them the breadbasket of

the country for the past half century. They have also recently become a major source of oil and gas.

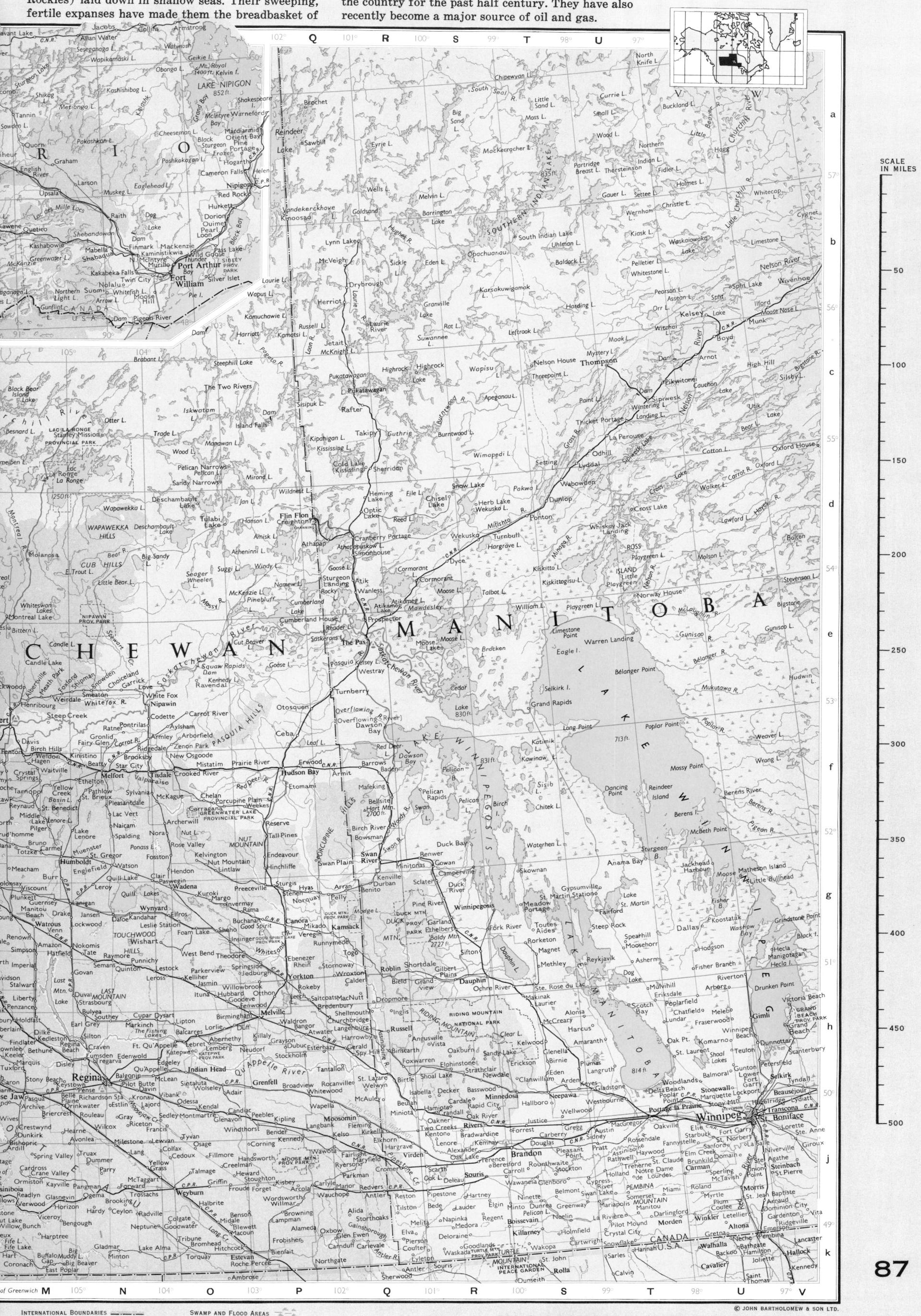

SCALE
IN MILES

© JOHN BARTHOLOMEW & SON LTD.

INTERNATIONAL BOUNDARIES ----

PROVINCIAL BOUNDARIES ----

SWAMP AND FLOOD AREAS

SPOT HEIGHTS IN FEET ▲11,870ft.

SCALE: 1:3,000,000 OR 1 INCH TO 47 MILES

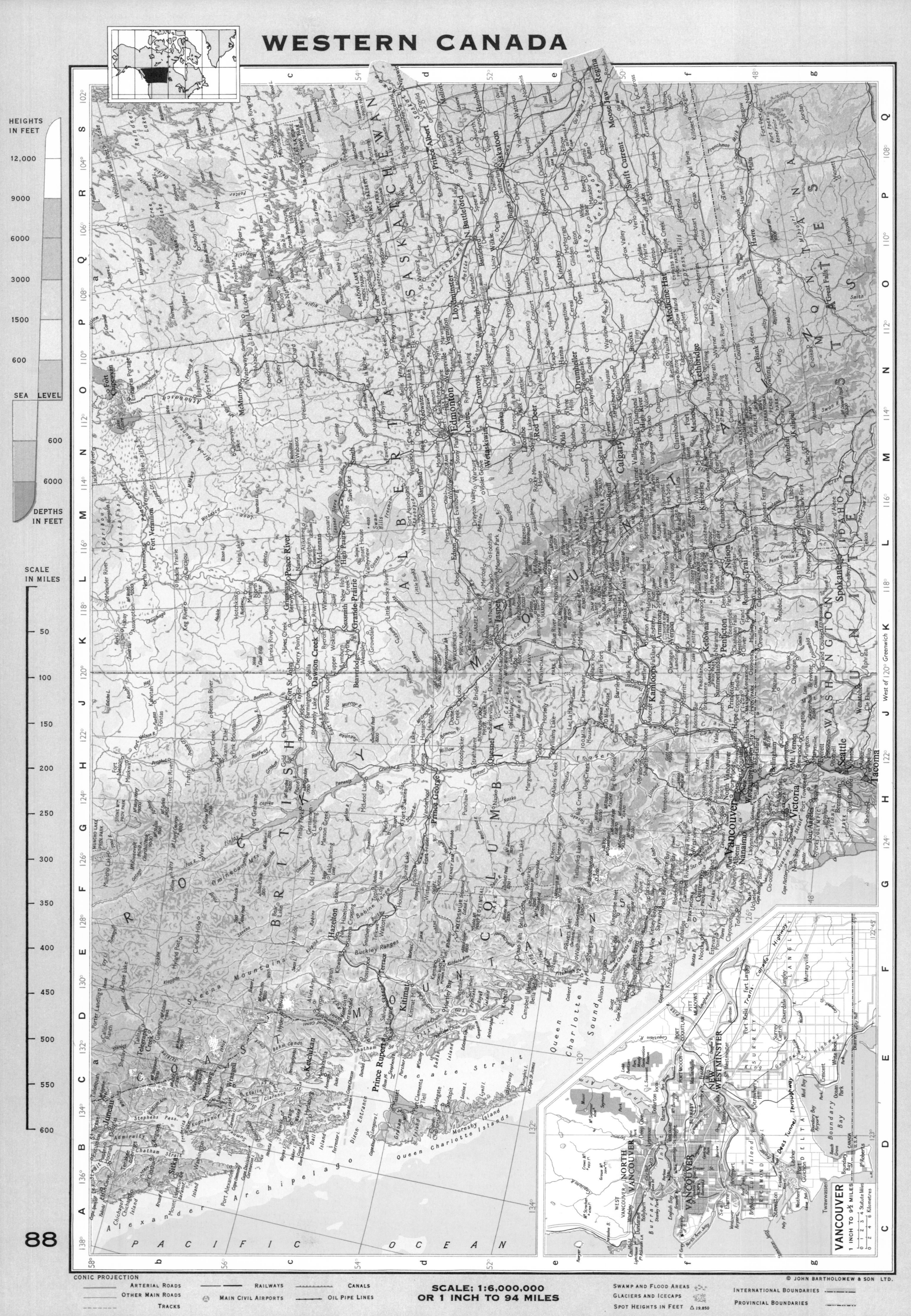

HEIGHTS
IN FEET

12,000

9000

6000

3000

1500

600

SEA LEVEL

600

6000

DEPTHS
IN FEET

SCALE
IN MILES

50

100

150

200

250

300

350

400

450

500

550

600

88

VANCOUVER
1 INCH TO 9½ MILES

CONIC PROJECTION

© JOHN BARTHOLOMEW & SON LTD.

ARTERIAL ROADS
OTHER MAIN ROADS
TRACKS
RAILWAYS
MAIN CIVIL AIRPORTS
CANALS
OIL PIPE LINES

SCALE: 1:6,000,000
OR 1 INCH TO 94 MILES

SWAMP AND FLOOD AREAS
GLACIERS AND ICECAPS
SPOT HEIGHTS IN FEET △ 19,850

INTERNATIONAL BOUNDARIES
PROVINCIAL BOUNDARIES

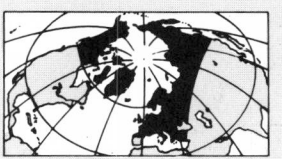

The Asian and North American continents almost meet at the narrow and shallow Bering Strait, only 45 miles across. Between them lies the Arctic Ocean, nearly enclosed and always covered with drifting ice. The high plateau of Greenland is covered with ice up to 11,000 feet thick, yet reaches down to the same latitude as Oslo and Leningrad.

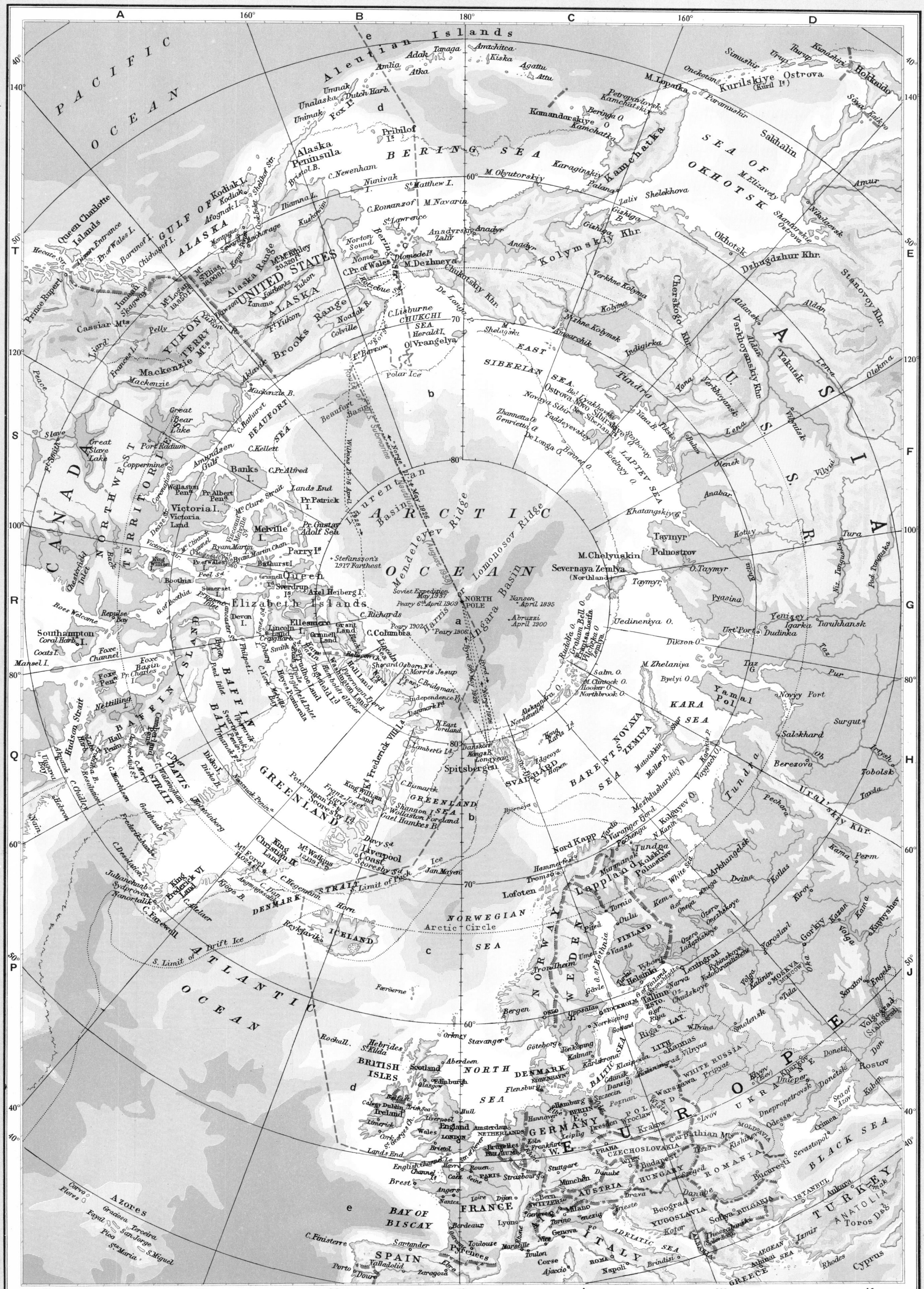

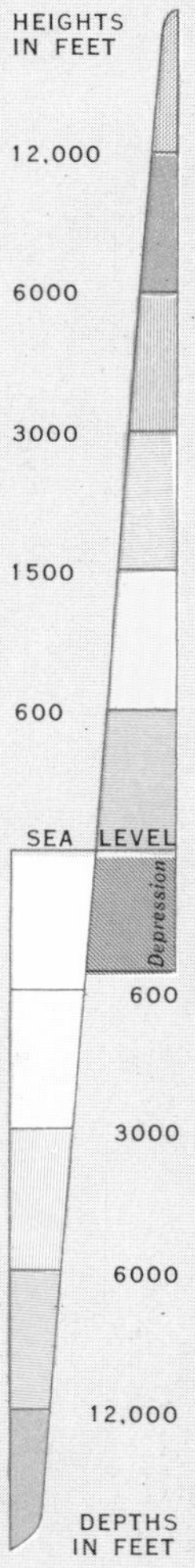

HEIGHTS IN FEET

12,000
6000
3000
1500
600
SEA LEVEL
600
3000
6000
12,000

DEPTHS IN FEET

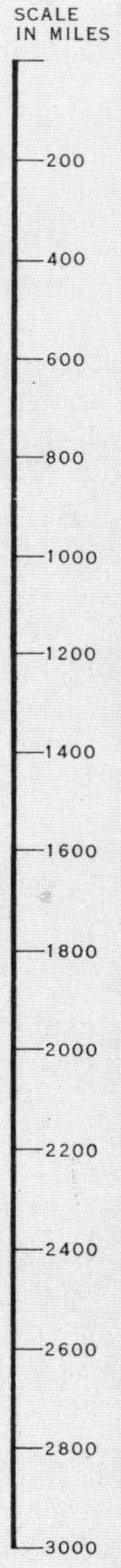

SCALE IN MILES

200
400
600
800
1000
1200
1400
1600
1800
2000
2200
2400
2600
2800
3000

INTERNATIONAL BOUNDARIES

Lambert's Azimuthal Equal-Area Projection
© John Bartholomew & Son Ltd.

SCALE: 1:30,000,000 OR 1 INCH TO 474 MILES
(Approximately)

MEXICO
GUATEMALA, HONDURAS, NICARAGUA, EL SALVADOR, COSTA RICA
(Map Continued on Facing Page)

MEXICO AREA: 759,529 sq. mi. POP: 45,671,000 CAP: Mexico City
GUATEMALA AREA: 42,042 sq. mi. POP: 4,575,000 CAP: Guatemala City
EL SALVADOR AREA: 7722 sq. mi. POP: 3,037,000 CAP: San Salvador
HONDURAS AREA: 43,277 sq. mi. POP: 2,445,000 CAP: Tegucigalpa
NICARAGUA AREA: 53,938 sq. mi. POP: 1,715,000 CAP: Managua
COSTA RICA AREA: 19,575 sq. mi. POP: 1,486,000 CAP: San José

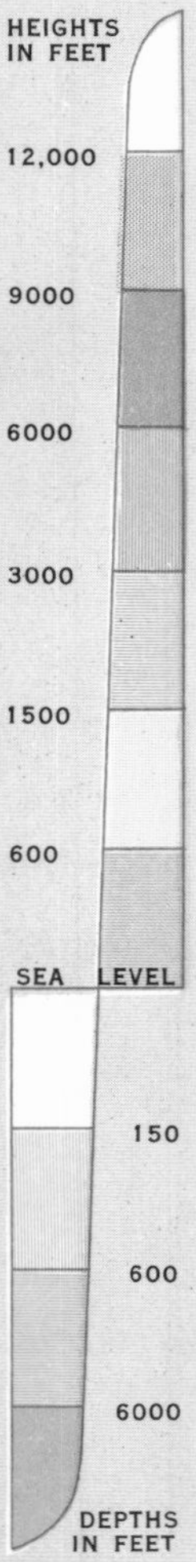

HEIGHTS IN FEET

12,000
9000
6000
3000
1500
600
SEA LEVEL
150
600
6000

DEPTHS IN FEET

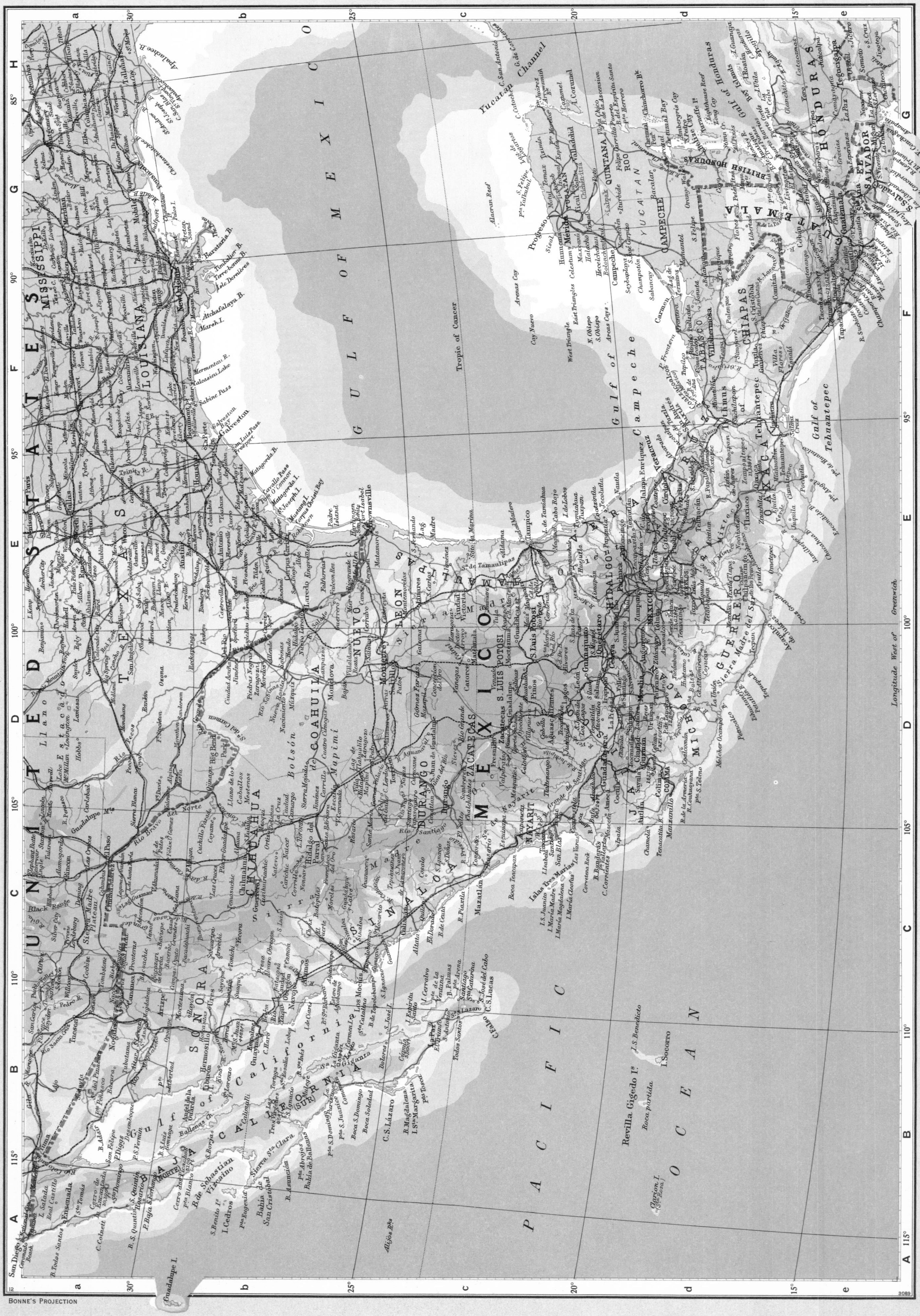

90

BONNE'S PROJECTION

SCALE: 1:10,000,000 OR 1 INCH TO 158 MILES

INTERNATIONAL BOUNDARIES
STATE BOUNDARIES

PANAMA AREA: 29,208 sq. mi. POP: 1,329,000 CAP: Panama City
CUBA AREA: 44,218 sq. mi. POP: 8,033,000 CAP: Havana
JAMAICA AREA: 4232 sq. mi. POP: 1,839,000 CAP: Kingston
HAITI AREA: 10,714 sq. mi. POP: 4,485,000 CAP: Port-au-Prince
DOMINICAN REP. AREA: 18,704 sq. mi. POP: 3,889,000 CAP: Santo Domingo
TRINIDAD AND TOBAGO AREA: 1980 sq. mi. POP: 1,000,000 CAP: Port of Spain

THE CARIBBEAN
WEST INDIES, CUBA, PANAMA, HAITI, DOMINICAN REPUBLIC, JAMAICA, TRINIDAD AND TOBAGO

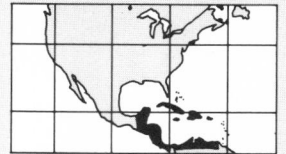

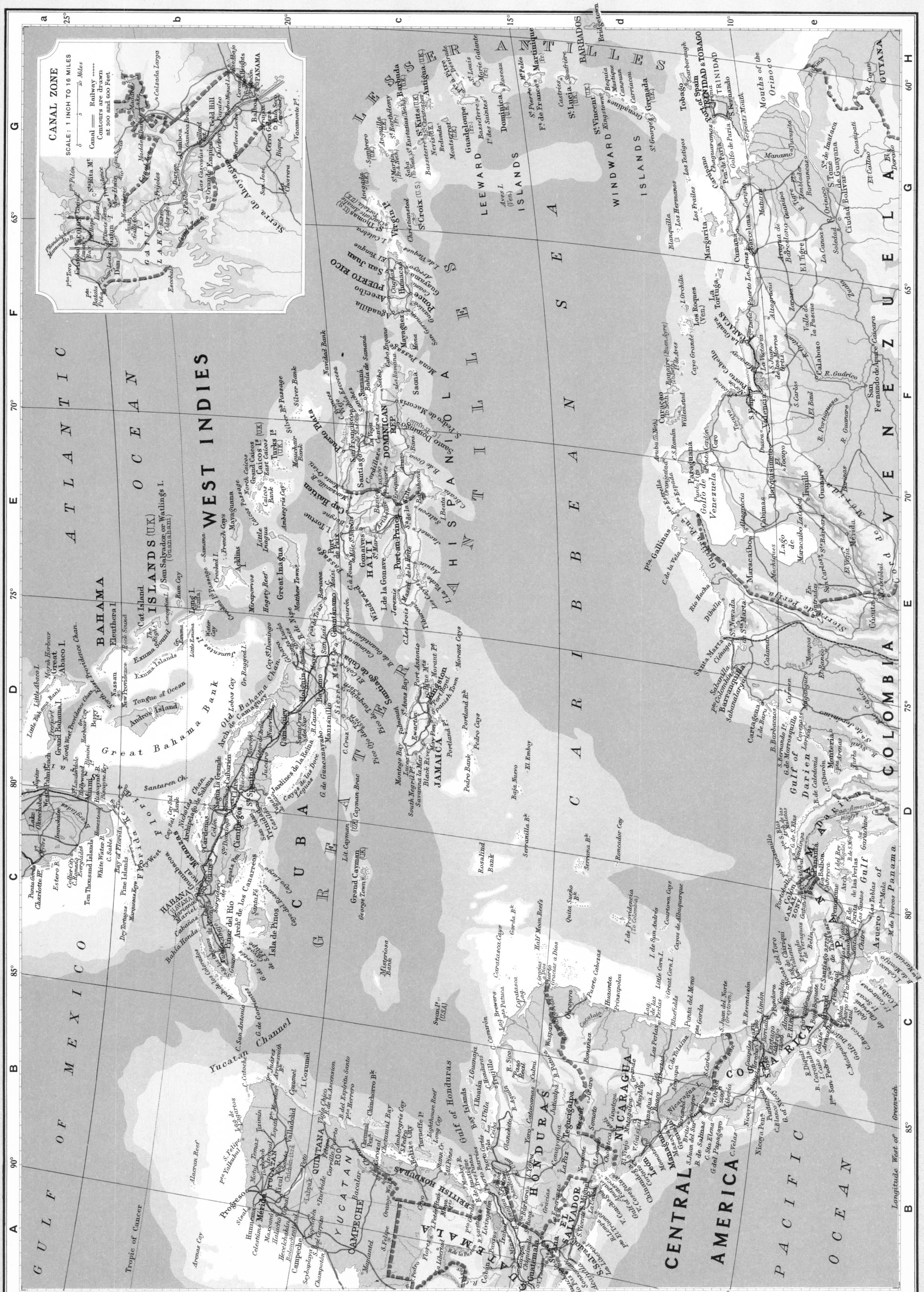

CANAL ZONE
SCALE: 1 INCH TO 16 MILES
Canal ——— Railway ------- Contours are drawn at 300 and 600 Feet.

SCALE IN MILES

100
200
300
400
500
600
700
800
900
1000
1100
1200
1300
1400
1500
1600

MAIN ROADS ———
RAILWAYS -------

SCALE: 1:10,000,000 OR 1 INCH TO 158 MILES

© John Bartholomew & Son Ltd.

91

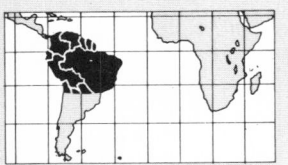

SOUTH AMERICA (NORTH)

BRAZIL, BOLIVIA, PERU, ECUADOR, COLOMBIA, VENEZUELA, GUYANA, SURINAM, FRENCH GUIANA

BRAZIL AREA: *3,286,470 sq. mi.*
POP: *85,655,000* CAP: *Brasília*
BOLIVIA AREA: *424,162 sq. mi.*
POP: *3,801,000* CAPS: *La Paz, Sucre*

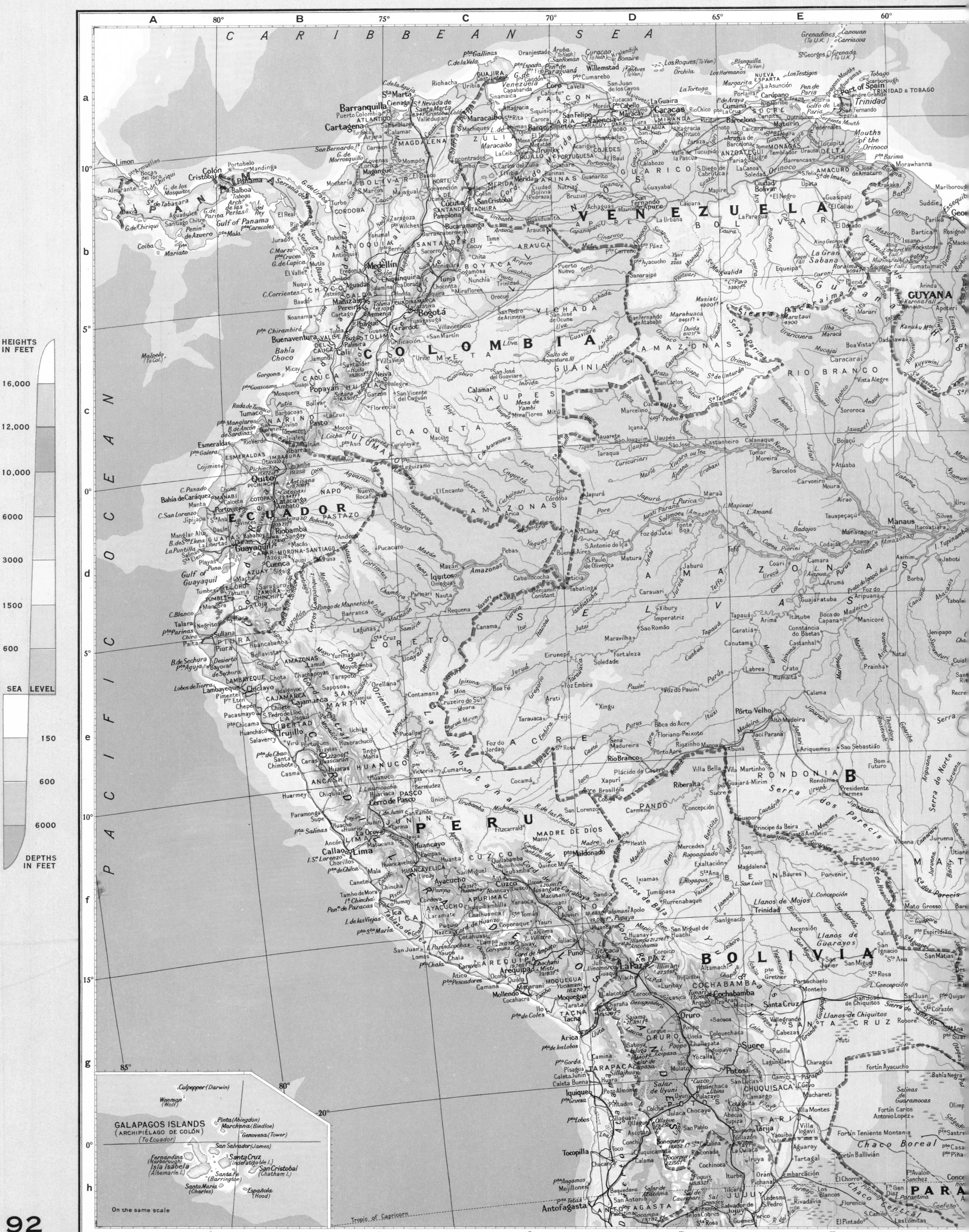
HEIGHTS IN FEET
16,000
12,000
10,000
6000
3000
1500
600
SEA LEVEL
150
600
6000
DEPTHS IN FEET
CARIBBEAN SEA
PACIFIC OCEAN
VENEZUELA
COLOMBIA
ECUADOR
PERU
BOLIVIA
GUYANA
PANAMA
GALAPAGOS ISLANDS (ARCHIPIÉLAGO DE COLÓN) (To Ecuador)
On the same scale
Tropic of Capricorn
LAMBERT'S AZIMUTHAL EQUAL-AREA PROJECTION

SCALE: 1:12,500,000 OR 1 INCH TO 197 MILES
(Approximately)

MAIN ROADS
RAILWAYS

PERU AREA: 496,222 sq. mi.
POP: 12,385,000 CAP: Lima
ECUADOR AREA: 109,483 sq. mi.
POP: 5,508,000 CAP: Quito

COLOMBIA AREA: 439,735 sq. mi.
POP: 18,650,000 CAP: Bogotá
VENEZUELA AREA: 352,143 sq. mi.
POP: 9,352,000 CAP: Caracas

GUYANA AREA: 83,000 sq. mi.
POP: 662,000 CAP: Georgetown
SURINAM AREA: 70,060 sq. mi.
POP: 350,000 CAP: Paramaribo

FRENCH GUIANA
AREA: 35,135 sq. mi.
POP: 37,000 CAP: Cayenne

SCALE IN MILES

SCALE: 1:12,500,000 OR 1 INCH TO 197 MILES
(Approximately)

93

© JOHN BARTHOLOMEW & SON LTD.

INTERNATIONAL BOUNDARIES

STATE AND PROVINCIAL BOUNDARIES

SOUTH AMERICA (SOUTH) ARGENTINA, CHILE, PARAGUAY, URUGUAY

ARGENTINA AREA: *1,072,067 sq. mi.*   **CHILE** AREA: *292,256 sq. mi.*   **PARAGUAY** AREA: *157,047 sq. mi.*   **URUGUAY** AREA: *68,536 sq. mi.*

POP: *23,031,000*   POP: *8,750,000*   POP: *2,161,000*   POP: *2,783,000*

CAP: *Buenos Aires*   CAP: *Santiago*   CAP: *Asunción*   CAP: *Montevideo*

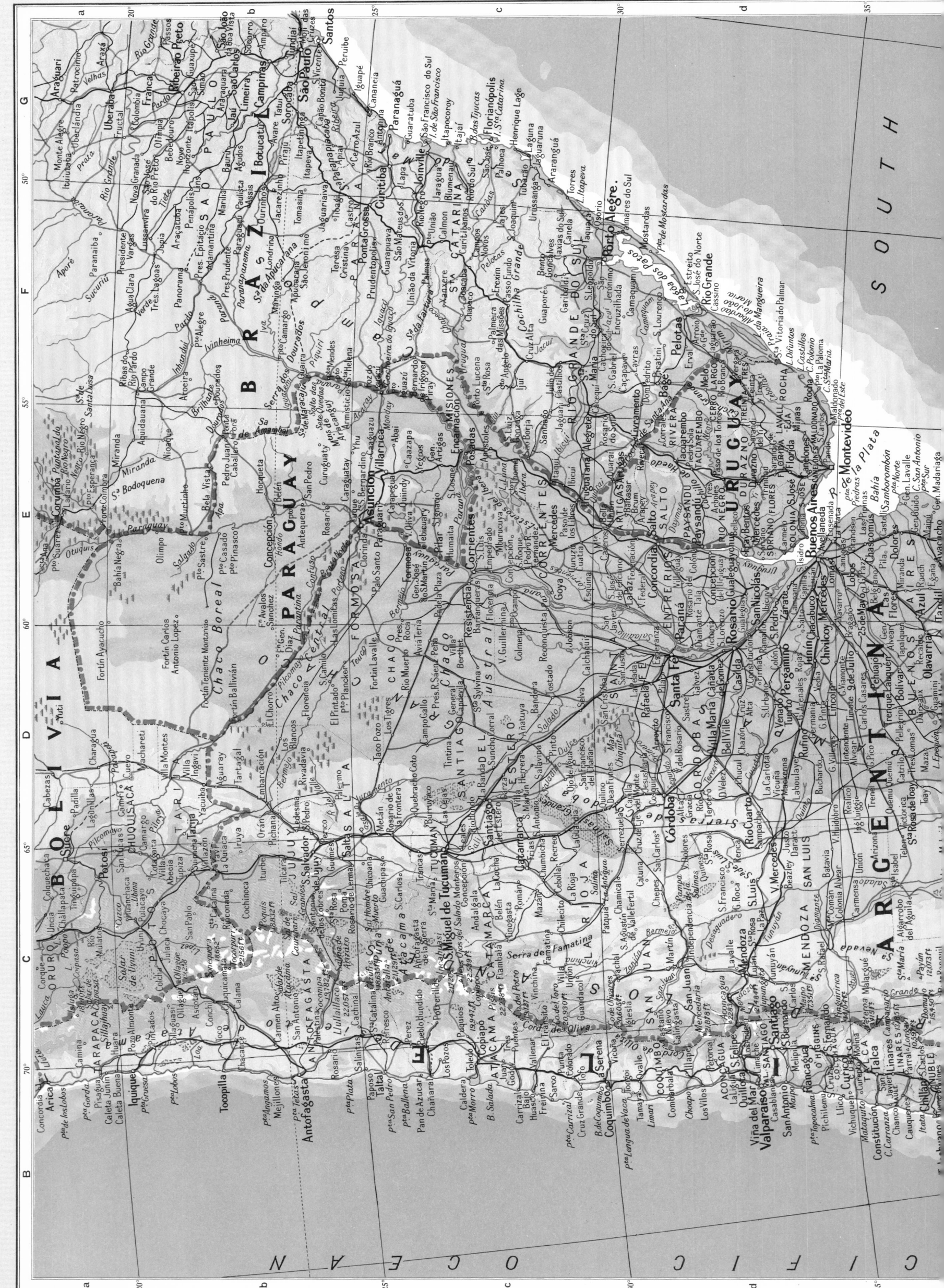

HEIGHTS
IN FEET

16,000
12,000
10,000
6000
3000
1500
600

SEA LEVEL

150
600
6000

DEPTHS
IN FEET

94

LAMBERT'S AZIMUTHAL EQUAL-AREA PROJECTION

SCALE: 1:9,000,000 OR 1 INCH TO 142 MILES

MAIN ROADS

RAILWAYS

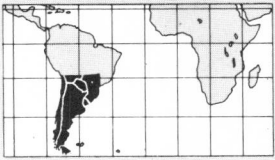

South America, shown here and on the two pages preceding, is the fourth largest continent. It has the second highest mountain range in the world and the longest—the An- des, which follows the western coast for more than 4000 miles. Many of the majestic peaks rise over 20,000 feet. The Amazon River system is the world's largest. The broad Ama- zon basin, with its moist jungles, cuts between the Brazilian and Guiana highlands to meet the great central lowland, which runs south to the fertile pampas of Argentina.

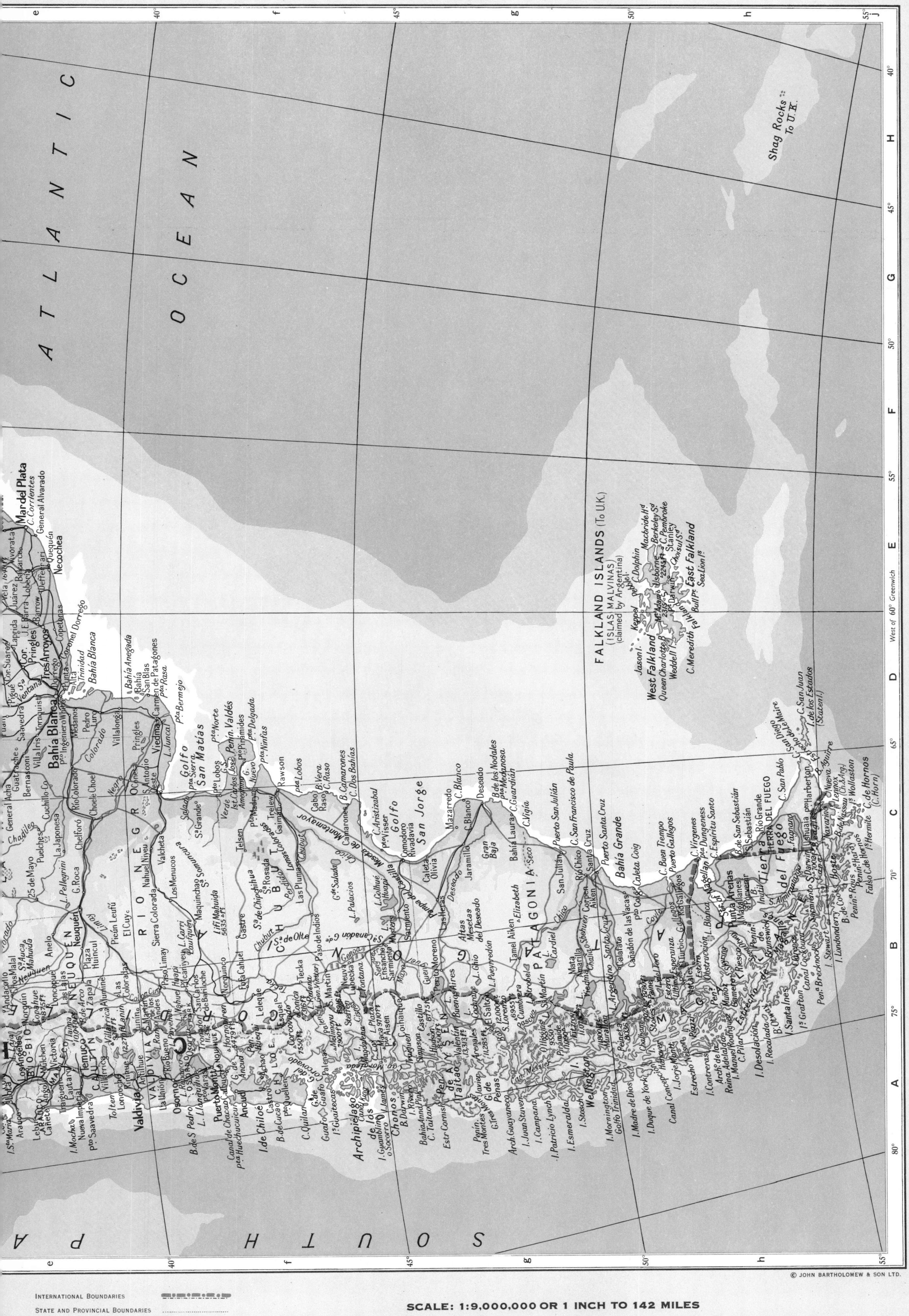

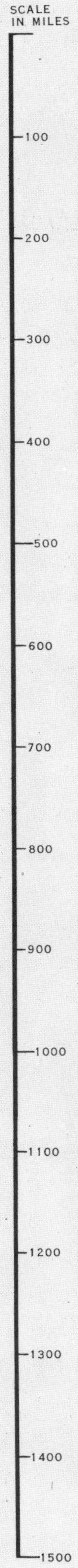

ATLANTIC OCEAN

PACIFIC

SOUTH

FALKLAND ISLANDS (To U.K.)
(ISLAS MALVINAS)
(claimed by Argentina)

West Falkland East Falkland

Shag Rocks
To U.K.

PATAGONIA

TIERRA DEL FUEGO

SCALE
IN MILES

100
200
300
400
500
600
700
800
900
1000
1100
1200
1300
1400
1500

INTERNATIONAL BOUNDARIES
STATE AND PROVINCIAL BOUNDARIES

SCALE: 1:9,000,000 OR 1 INCH TO 142 MILES

© JOHN BARTHOLOMEW & SON LTD.

rivers: the Seine into the English Channel, the Loire and Garonne into the Atlantic, and the Rhône into the Mediterranean. This maritime outlook provides a mild, even climate.

Northwestern France is mainly low-lying. On the eastern border rise the high mountains of the Vosges, the Jura and the Alps (Mont Blanc, 15,771 feet, is the highest peak in Western

Europe). Running southward from the center is the Massif Central, while the Pyrenees in the southwest form a natural barrier between France and Spain. ALGERIA: see page 118.

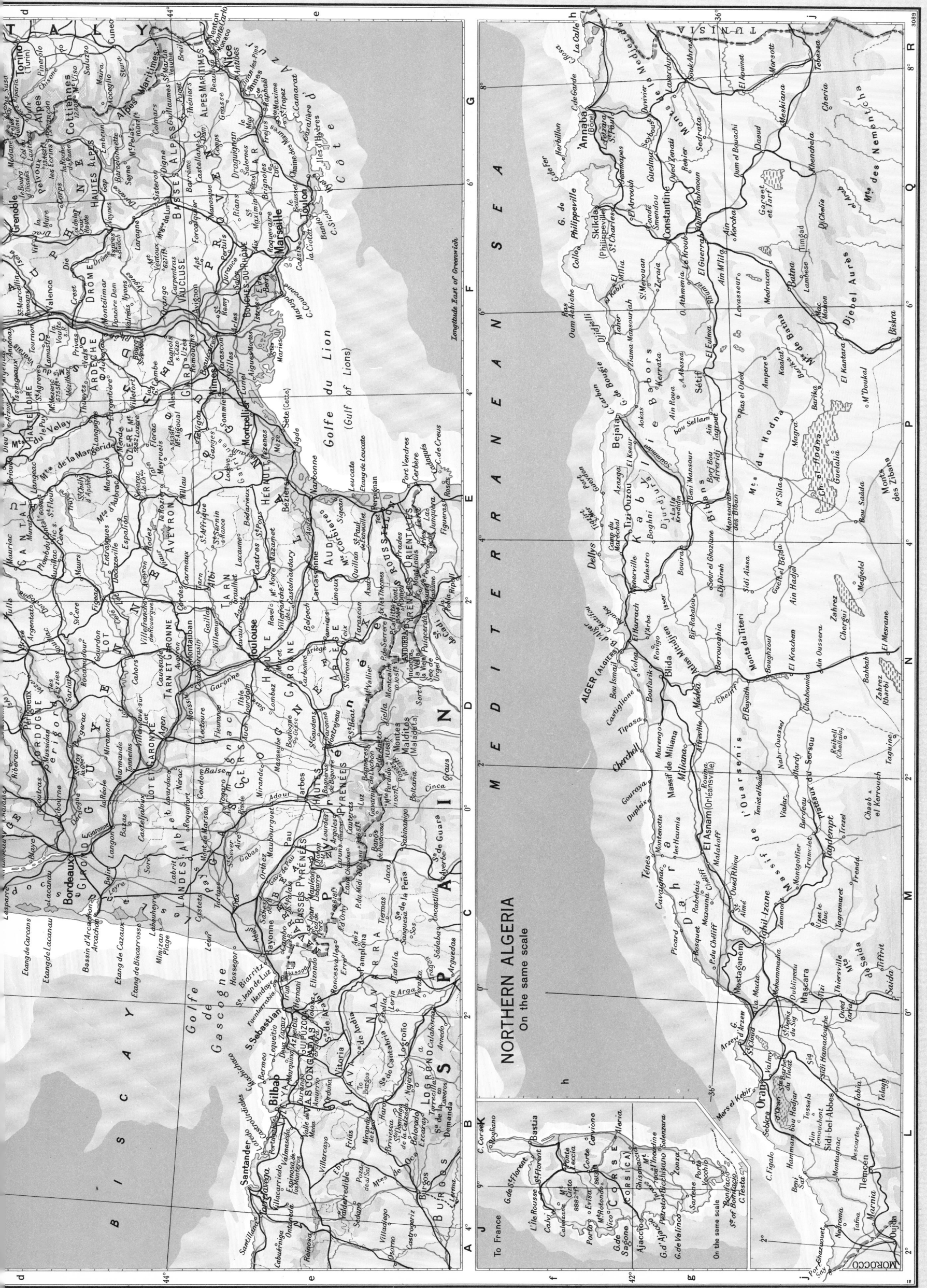

NORTHERN ALGERIA
On the same scale

SCALE IN MILES

109

SCALE: 1:3,000,000 OR 1 INCH TO 47 MILES

ITALY

AREA: *116,303 sq. mi.*
POP: *51,962,000* **CAP:** *Rome*
SAN MARINO **AREA:** *24 sq. mi.*
POP: *18,000* **CAP:** *San Marino*

MALTA **AREA:** *122 sq. mi.*
POP: *317,000* **CAP:** *Valletta*
MONACO **AREA:** *0.58 sq. mi.*
POP: *23,000* **CAP:** *Monte Carlo*

Italy owes its bootlike shape to the Apennines, which reach down its whole length and culminate, across the Straits of Messina, in the island of Sicily. To the north, the Italian Alps encircle

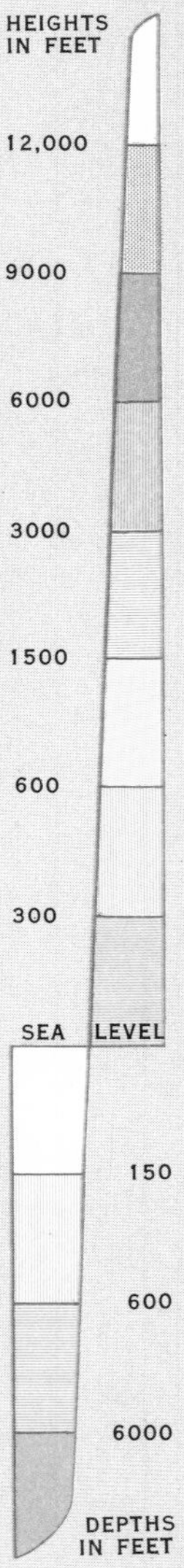

HEIGHTS IN FEET

12,000
9000
6000
3000
1500
600
300
SEA LEVEL
150
600
6000

DEPTHS IN FEET

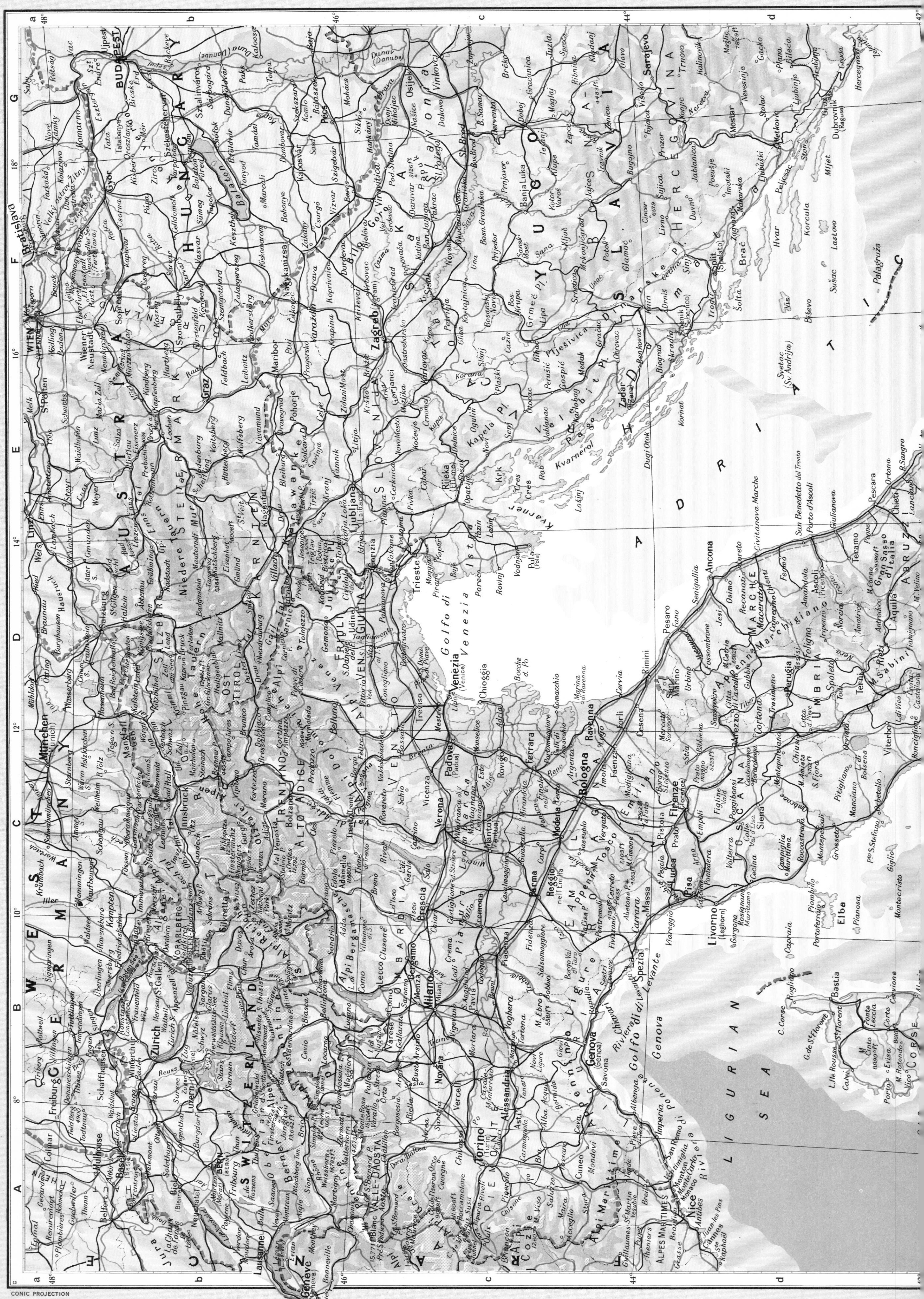

110

CONIC PROJECTION

SCALE: 1:3,000,000 OR 1 INCH TO 47 MILES

MAIN ROADS
RAILWAYS

the peninsula like the head of a mushroom, while east of the Alps are the strange-shaped Dolomites. This mountain barrier makes the country difficult to approach, and the names of the principal passes—the Simplon and St. Gotthard from Switzerland, and the Brenner from Austria — have become household words among travelers all over Europe.

Of the rivers, most of which are unnavigable, the longest is the Po (420 miles), which waters the fertile plain of Lombardy before entering the Adriatic between Venice and Ravenna.

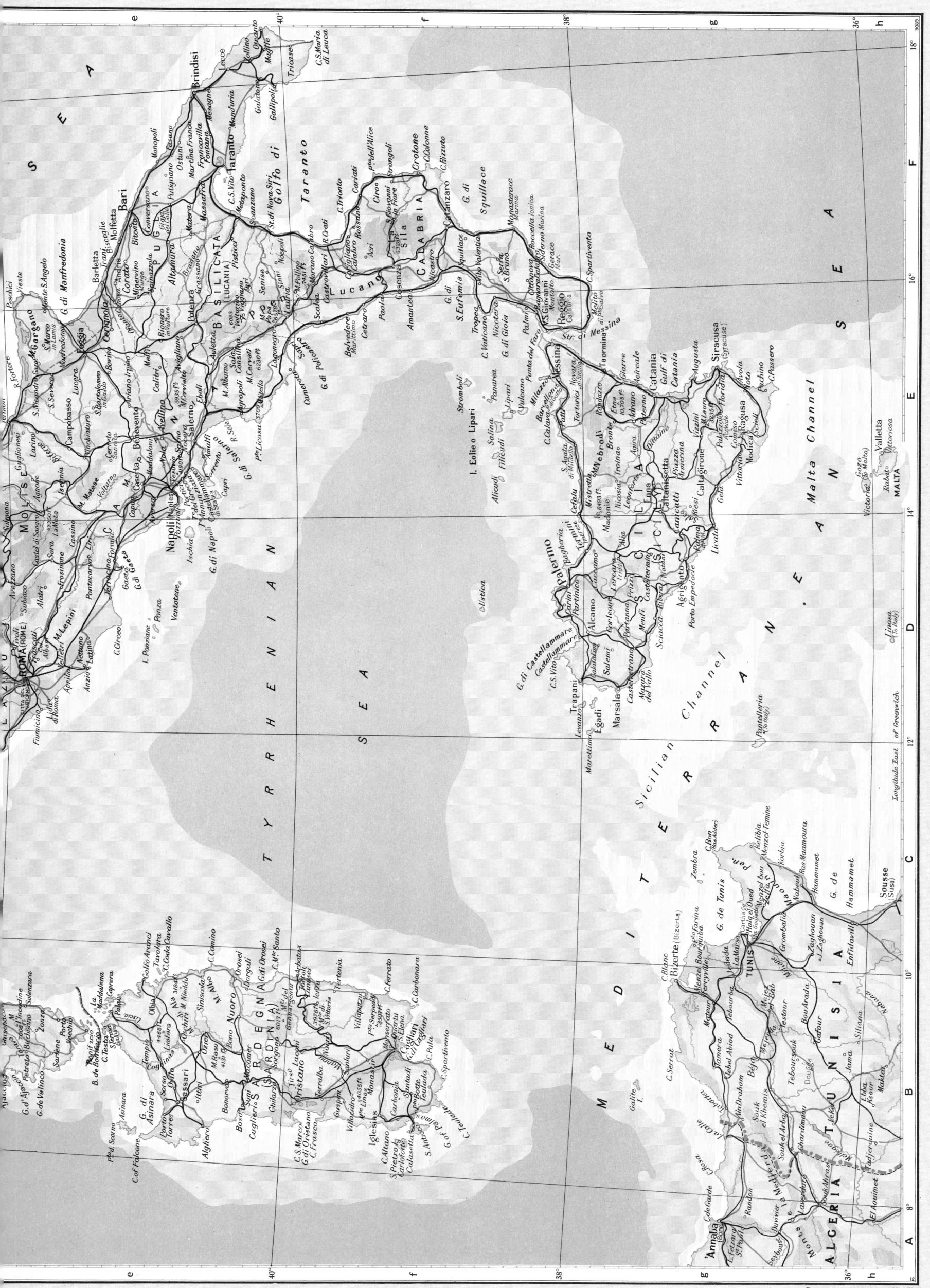

INTERNATIONAL BOUNDARIES

REGIONAL BOUNDARIES

© JOHN BARTHOLOMEW & SON LTD.

SCALE: 1:3,000,000 OR 1 INCH TO 47 MILES

SCALE IN MILES

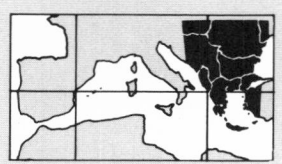

THE BALKANS
ROMANIA, YUGOSLAVIA, BULGARIA, ALBANIA, GREECE

ROMANIA AREA: 91,699 sq. mi.
POP: 19,105,056 CAP: Bucharest
YUGOSLAVIA AREA: 98,766 sq. mi.
POP: 19,958,000 CAP: Belgrade

HEIGHTS IN FEET
6000
3000
1500
600
300
SEA LEVEL
150
600
6000

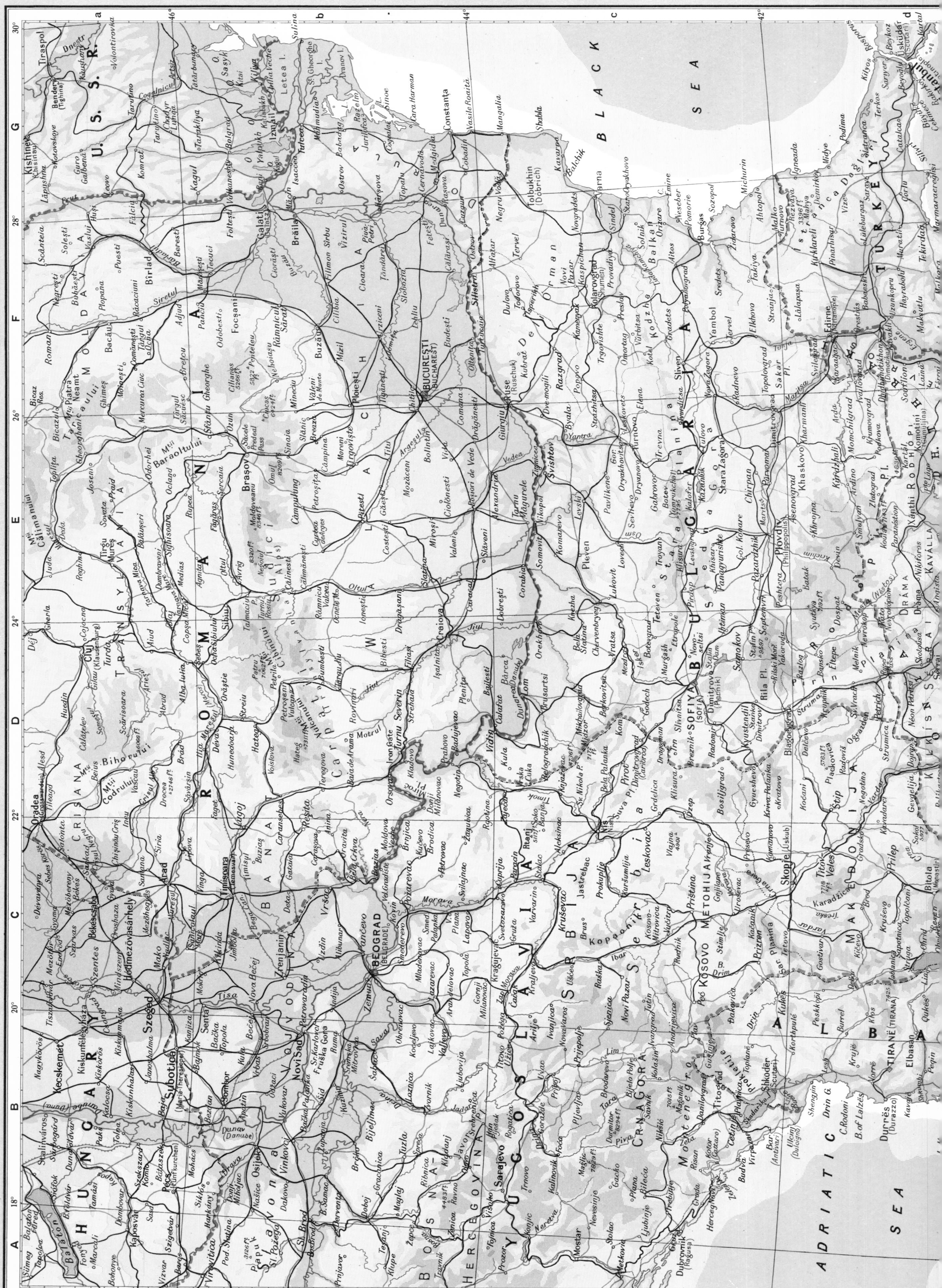

CONIC PROJECTION

SCALE: 1:3,000,000 OR 1 INCH TO 47 MILES

MAIN ROADS
RAILWAYS

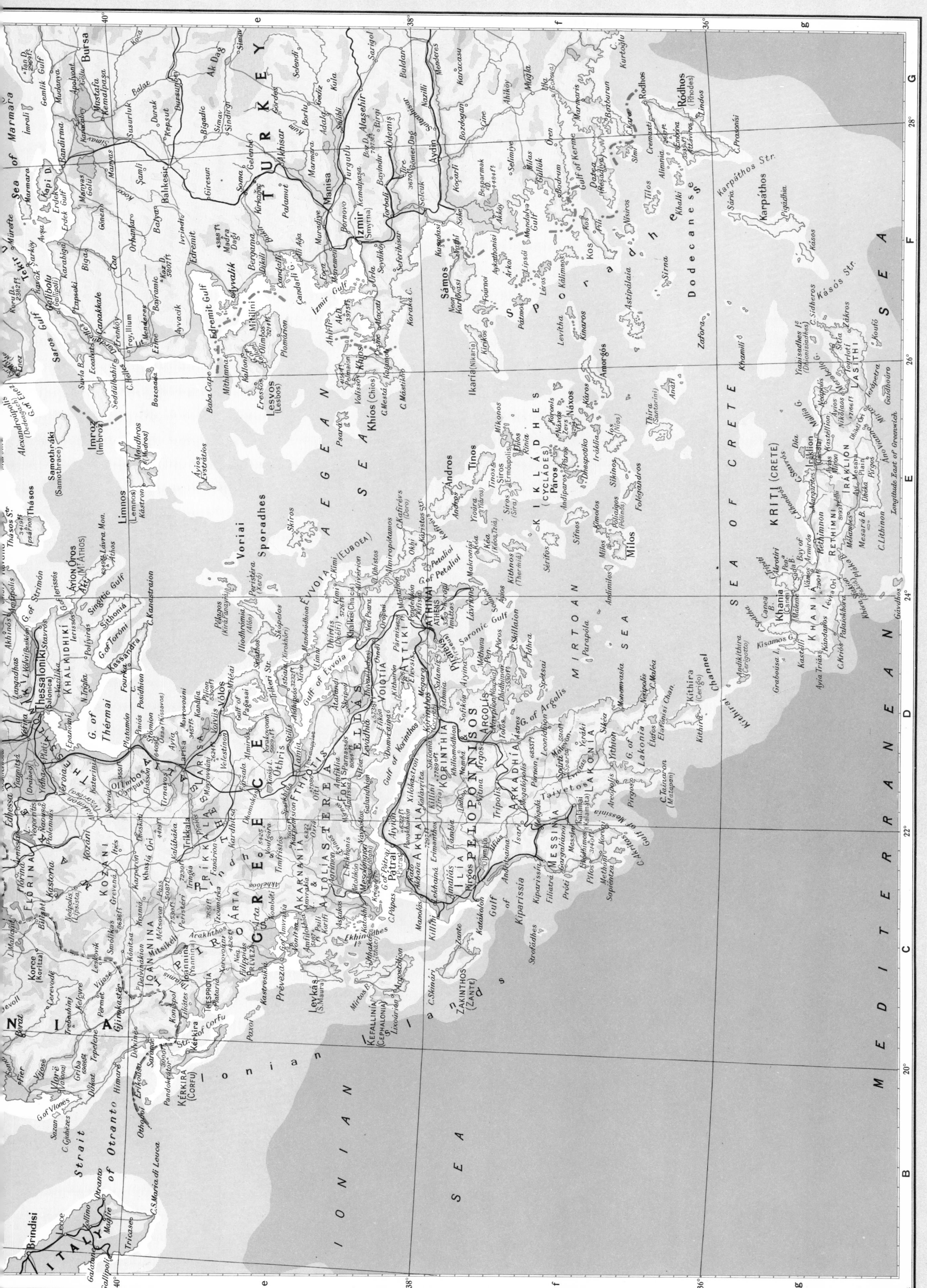

BULGARIA AREA: *42,823 sq. mi.*
POP: *8,258,000* CAP: *Sofia*
ALBANIA AREA: *11,100 sq. mi.*
POP: *1,914,000* CAP: *Tirana*

GREECE AREA: *50,547 sq. mi.*
POP: *8,614,000* CAP: *Athens*
The Balkan peninsula, with its broken coastline and many off-

shore islands, is separated from the rest of Europe by the river Danube (1770 miles long and western Europe's longest river),

which flows eastward from Hungary, through a gorge between the Carpathians and Dinaric Alps, to the Black Sea.

SCALE
IN MILES

50

100

150

200

250

300

350

400

450

500

113

INTERNATIONAL BOUNDARIES
PROVINCIAL BOUNDARIES

SCALE: 1:3,000,000 OR 1 INCH TO 47 MILES

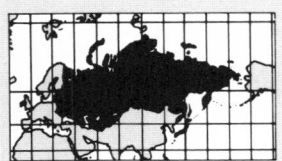

U.S.S.R.
MONGOLIA

SOVIET UNION AREA: *8,649,489 sq. mi.*
POP: *233,105,000* CAP: *Moscow*
MONGOLIA AREA: *604,247 sq. mi.*
POP: *1,140,000* CAP: *Ulan Bator*

The vast area of the U.S.S.R., straddling all Asia and half of Europe, shares its immense boundaries with many countries in both continents. It is divided structurally

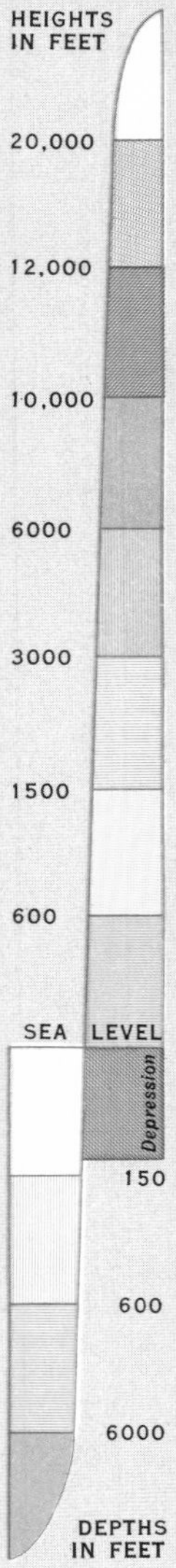

HEIGHTS
IN FEET

20,000
12,000
10,000
6000
3000
1500
600

SEA LEVEL
Depression

150
600
6000

DEPTHS
IN FEET

CONIC PROJECTION

SCALE: 1:17,500,000 OR 1 INCH TO 276 MILES
(Approximately)

———— MAIN ROADS
———— RAILWAYS

into three regions from west to east: two enormous plains, separated by the Urals, and a vast region of hazardous country ending in the remote peninsula of Kamchatka. On the north-south axis there are also three zones. The frozen tundra of the Arctic merges into forests and fertile plains, which end at the borders of the great desert belt stretching from Mongolia to the Caspian. In fact, the U.S.S.R. is hemmed in on three fronts by deserts frozen wastes or mountains.

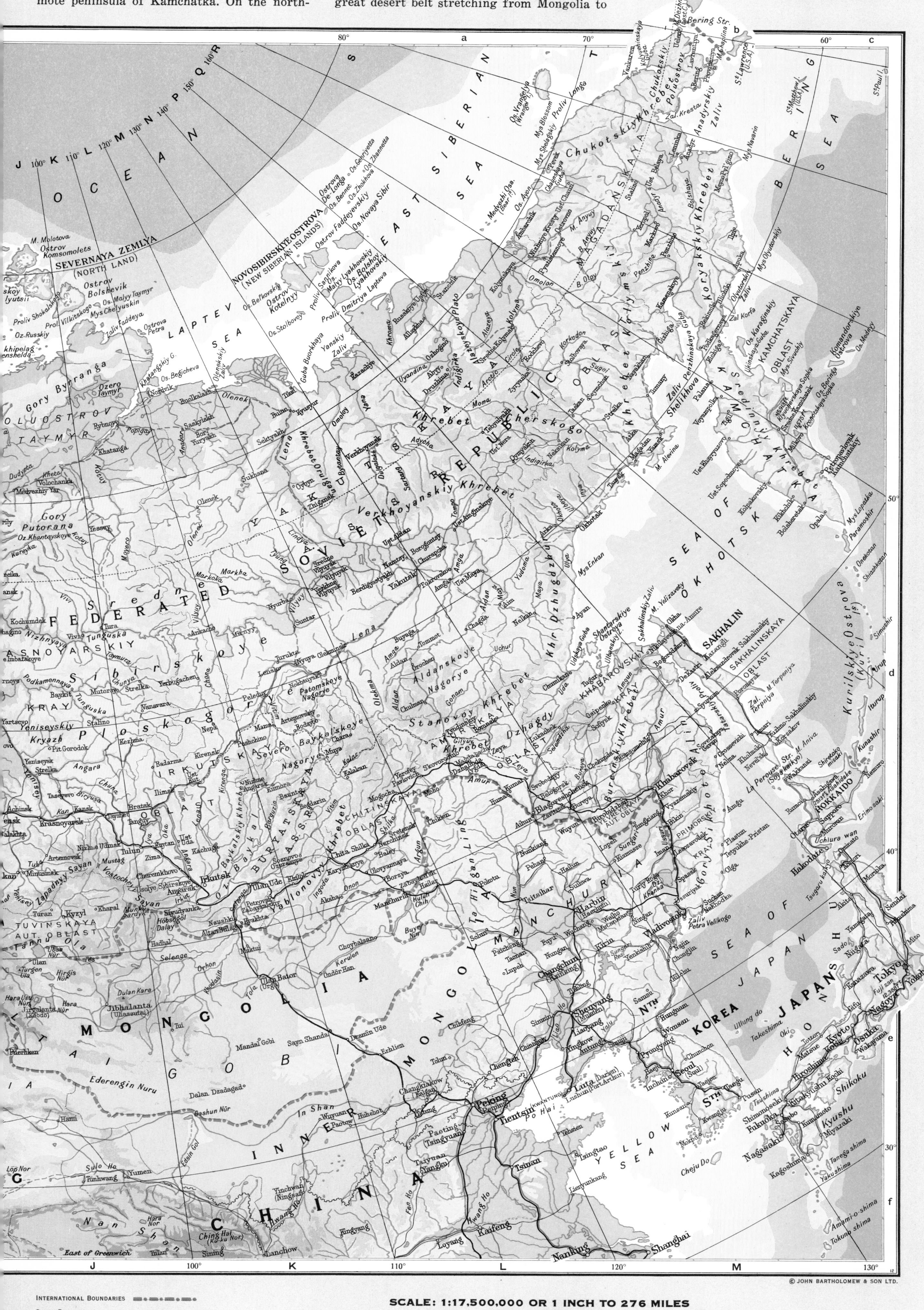

ARCTIC OCEAN

EAST SIBERIAN SEA

LAPTEV SEA

BERING SEA

UNION OF SOVIET SOCIALIST REPUBLICS

RUSSIAN SOVIET FEDERATED SOCIALIST REPUBLIC

YAKUTSKAYA

SEA OF OKHOTSK

KAMCHATKA

SAKHALIN

KHABAROVSKIY KRAY

BURYAT A.S.S.R.

IRKUTSKAYA OBLAST

KRASNOYARSKIY KRAY

TUVINSKAYA AUT. OBLAST

MONGOLIA

INNER MONGOLIA

MANCHURIA

PRIMORSKIY KRAY

SEA OF JAPAN

KOREA

JAPAN

HOKKAIDO

HONSHU

SHIKOKU

KYUSHU

Tokyo

Kyoto

Nagoya

Osaka

Seoul

Pyongyang

Peking

Tientsin

YELLOW SEA

CHINA

Ulan Bator (Urga)

Irkutsk

Vladivostok

Harbin

Mukden

Shanghai

Nanking

SCALE IN MILES

100
200
300
400
500
600
700
800
900
1000
1100
1200
1300
1400
1500
1600
1700
1800
1900
2000
2100
2200
2300
2400
2500
2600
2700
2800
2900
3000

115

© JOHN BARTHOLOMEW & SON LTD.

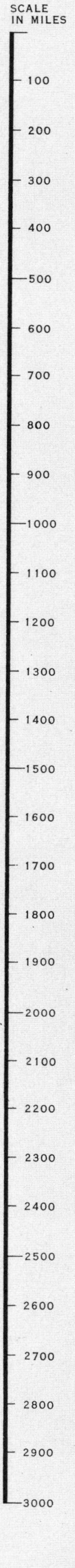

INTERNATIONAL BOUNDARIES
STATE BOUNDARIES

SCALE: 1:17,500,000 OR 1 INCH TO 276 MILES
(Approximately)

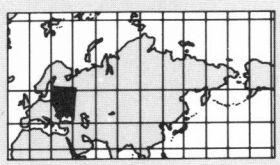

WEST EUROPEAN RUSSIA

The area between the Baltic and the Black Sea is part of the enormous Russian Plain west of the Urals. The low level of this land is indicated by the meandering rivers and the lakes and marshes of the Pripyat region. To the south, the mild undulations of the Ukrainian steppe interrupt the monotony of the northern plain.

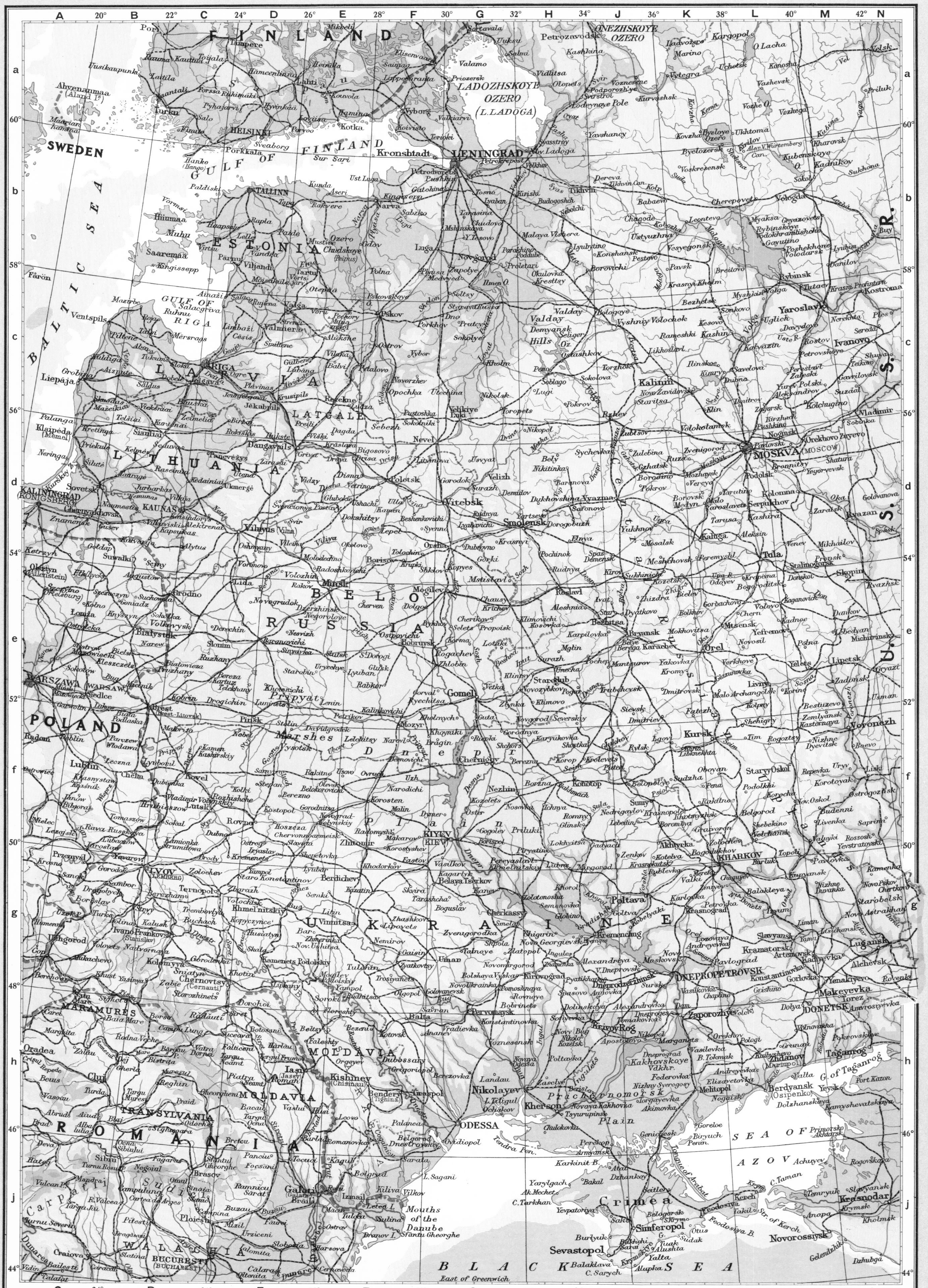

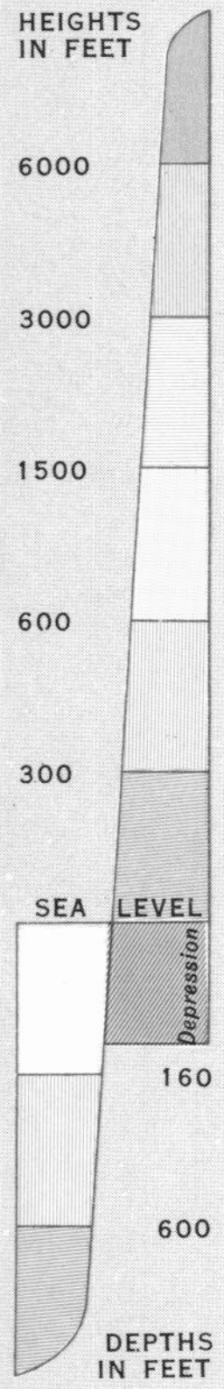

HEIGHTS IN FEET

6000
3000
1500
600
300

SEA LEVEL
Depression

160
600

DEPTHS IN FEET

116

CONIC PROJECTION

© John Bartholomew & Son Ltd.

INTERNATIONAL BOUNDARIES
STATE BOUNDARIES

SCALE: 1:6,000,000 OR 1 INCH TO 94 MILES

VOLGA AND SOUTH URALS

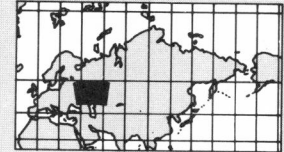

This map shows the highest and the lowest parts of European Russia, from the Urals, up to 5500 feet high, to the northern end of the Caspian, 50 feet below sea level. The two main rivers are the Don and the 2400-mile Volga, which flows through several immense artificial lakes, recently created. A huge, low-lying plain circles the northern end of the Caspian.

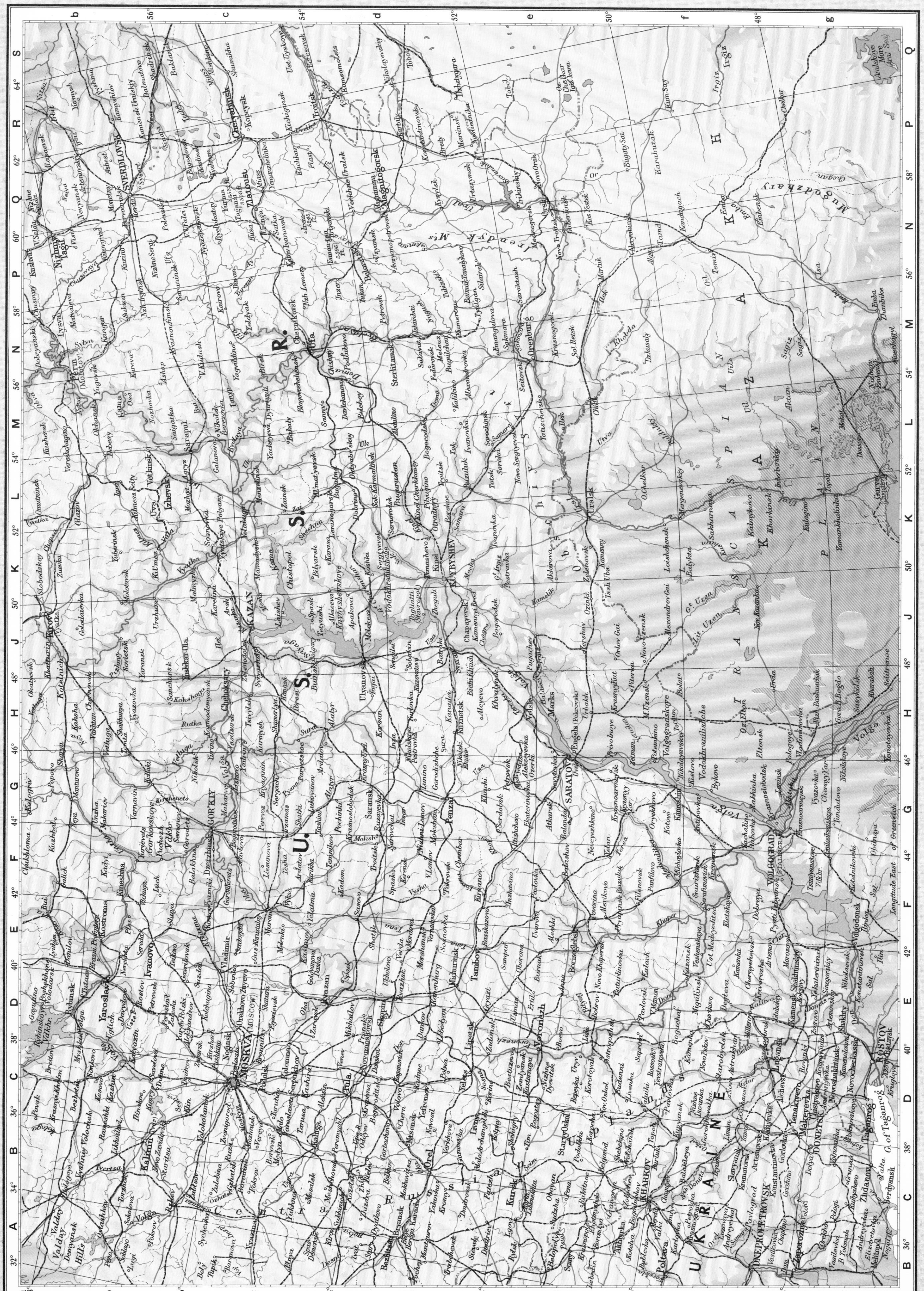

SCALE IN MILES

100 200 300 400 500 600 700 800 900 1000

MAIN ROADS

RAILWAYS

CONIC PROJECTION

SCALE: 1:6,000,000 OR 1 INCH TO 94 MILES

NORTHERN AFRICA

MOROCCO AREA: 171,834 sq. mi. POP: 14,140,000 CAP: Rabat
ALGERIA AREA: 919,590 sq. mi. POP: 12,101,994 CAP: Algiers
TUNISIA AREA: 63,378 sq. mi. POP: 4,457,862 CAP: Tunis
LIBYA AREA: 679,358 sq. mi. POP: 1,738,000 CAPS: Benghazi, Tripoli
U.A.R. (EGYPT) AREA: 386,100 sq. mi. POP: 30,147,000 CAP: Cairo
GAMBIA AREA: 4361 sq. mi. POP: 343,000 CAP: Bathurst

HEIGHTS
IN FEET

12,000
9000
6000
3000
1500
600
SEA LEVEL
Depression
150
600
6000

DEPTHS
IN FEET

118

LAMBERT'S AZIMUTHAL EQUAL-AREA PROJECTION

SCALE: 1:12,500,000 OR 1 INCH TO 197 MILES
(Approximately)

MAIN ROADS
RAILWAYS

NIGER AREA: *489,189 sq. mi.* POP: *3,546,000* CAP: *Niamey*
MALI AREA: *c. 463,947 sq. mi.* POP: *4,745,000* CAP: *Bamako*
UPPER VOLTA AREA: *105,869 sq. mi.* POP: *5,054,000* CAP: *Ouagadougou*
MAURITANIA AREA: *398,841 sq. mi.* POP: *1,070,000* CAP: *Nouakchott*
SENEGAL AREA: *75,750 sq. mi.* POP: *3,580,000* CAP: *Dakar*
GUINEA AREA: *94,925 sq. mi.* POP: *3,702,000* CAP: *Conakry*

SIERRA LEONE AREA: *27,699 sq. mi.* POP: *2,439,000* CAP: *Freetown*
LIBERIA AREA: *43,000 sq. mi.* POP: *1,090,000* CAP: *Monrovia*
IVORY COAST AREA: *124,503 sq. mi.* POP: *3,920,000* CAP: *Abidjan*
GHANA AREA: *92,100 sq. mi.* POP: *8,143,000* CAP: *Accra*
TOGO AREA: *21,853 sq. mi.* POP: *1,724,000* CAP: *Lomé*
DAHOMEY AREA: *43,483 sq. mi.* POP: *2,410,000* CAP: *Porto Novo*

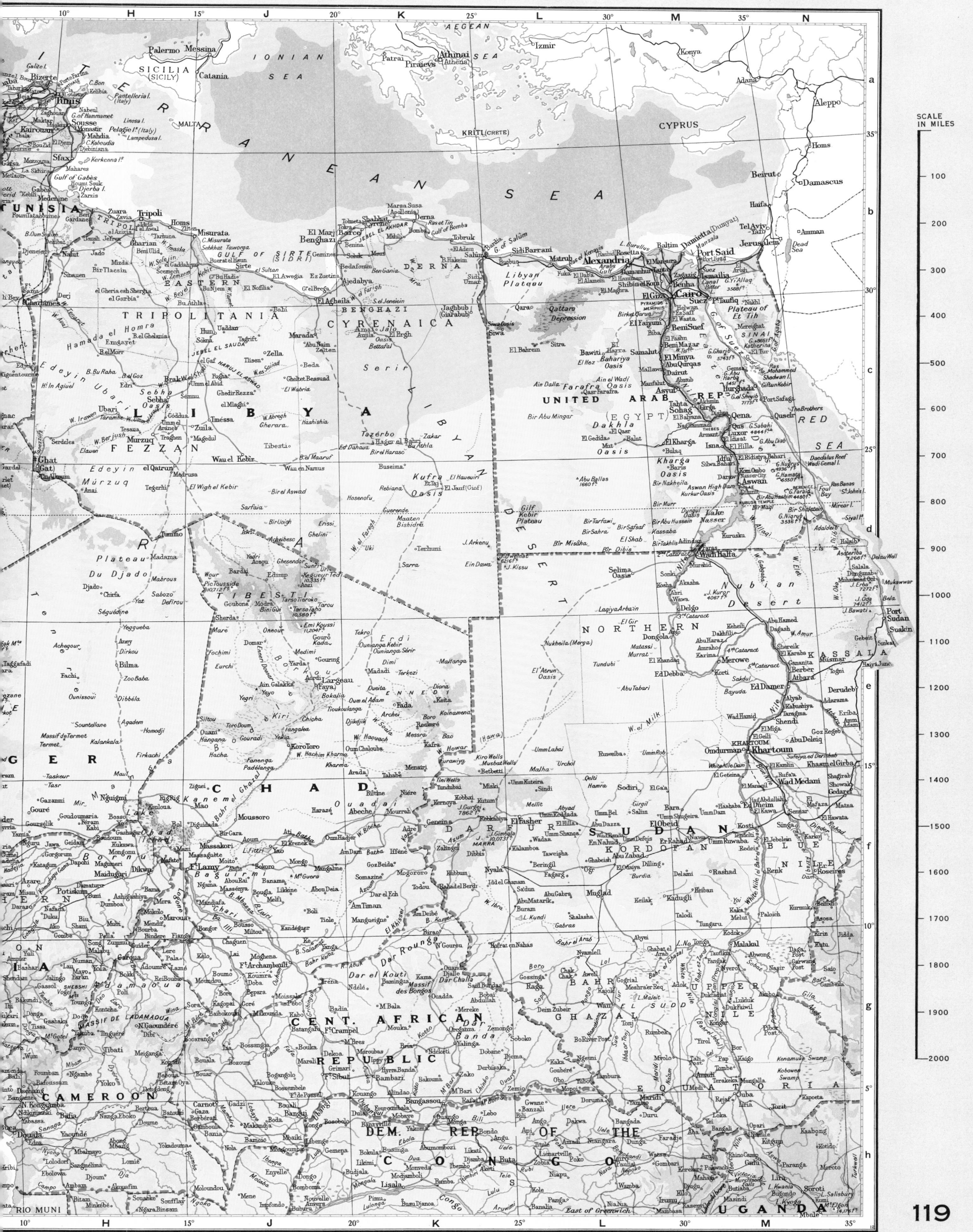

SCALE
IN MILES

119

© JOHN BARTHOLOMEW & SON LTD.

INTERNATIONAL BOUNDARIES
STATE BOUNDARIES

SCALE: 1:12,500,000 OR 1 INCH TO 197 MILES
(Approximately)

CENTRAL AFRICA

NIGERIA AREA: 356,667 sq. mi. POP: 58,600,000 CAP: *Lagos*
CHAD AREA: 495,752 sq. mi. POP: 3,361,000 CAP: *Fort Lamy*
CAMEROON AREA: 183,568 sq. mi. POP: 5,350,000 CAP: *Yaoundé*
CENT. AFRICAN REP. AREA: 240,534 sq. mi. POP: 1,459,000 CAP: *Bangui*
SUDAN AREA: 967,494 sq. mi. POP: 14,355,000 CAP: *Khartoum*
ETHIOPIA AREA: 471,776 sq. mi. POP: 23,000,000 CAP: *Addis Ababa*

HEIGHTS
IN FEET

12,000
9000
6000
3000
1500
600
SEA LEVEL
Depression

150
600
6000
DEPTHS
IN FEET

120

LAMBERT'S AZIMUTHAL EQUAL-AREA PROJECTION

SCALE: 1:12,500,000 OR 1 INCH TO 197 MILES
(Approximately)

MAIN ROADS
RAILWAYS

SOMALI REP. AREA: 246,199 sq. mi. POP: 2,580,000 CAP: Mogadiscio
KENYA AREA: 224,959 sq. mi. POP: 9,948,000 CAP: Nairobi
UGANDA AREA: 91,133 sq. mi. POP: 7,740,000 CAP: Entebbe
TANZANIA AREA: 362,819 sq. mi. POP: 10,717,000 CAP: Dar es Salaam
RWANDA AREA: 10,169 sq. mi. POP: 3,306,000 CAP: Kigali
BURUNDI AREA: 10,747 sq. mi. POP: 3,274,000 CAP: Usumbura

DEM. REP. OF CONGO AREA: 905,562 sq. mi. POP: 15,986,000 CAP: Kinshasa
CONGO REP. AREA: 132,046 sq. mi. POP: 850,000 CAP: Brazzaville
GABON AREA: 103,346 sq. mi. POP: 473,000 CAP: Libreville
ANGOLA AREA: 481,351 sq. mi. POP: 5,225,000 CAP: Luanda
MALAGASY REP. AREA: 226,657 sq. mi. POP: 6,200,000 CAP: Tananarive

MADAGASCAR
(MALAGASY REP.)
On the same scale

INTERNATIONAL BOUNDARIES
STATE BOUNDARIES

SCALE: 1:12,500,000 OR 1 INCH TO 197 MILES
(Approximately)

121

© JOHN BARTHOLOMEW & SON LTD.

SOUTHERN AFRICA

ZAMBIA AREA: *290,584 sq. mi.* POP: *3,881,000* CAP: *Lusaka*
RHODESIA AREA: *150,332 sq. mi.* POP: *4,530,000* CAP: *Salisbury*
MALAWI AREA: *46,066 sq. mi.* POP: *4,042,412* CAP: *Zomba*
SO. WEST AFRICA AREA: *318,259 sq. mi.* POP: *584,000* CAP: *Windhoek*
SOUTH AFRICA AREA: *471,445 sq. mi.* POP: *18,733,000*
CAPS: *Cape Town, Pretoria*

BOTSWANA AREA: *219,915 sq. mi.*
POP: *593,000* CAP: *Gaberones*
MOZAMBIQUE AREA: *302,328 sq. mi.*
POP: *7,040,000* CAP: *Lourenco Marques*
LESOTHO AREA: *11,716 sq. mi.*
POP: *859,058* CAP: *Maseru*

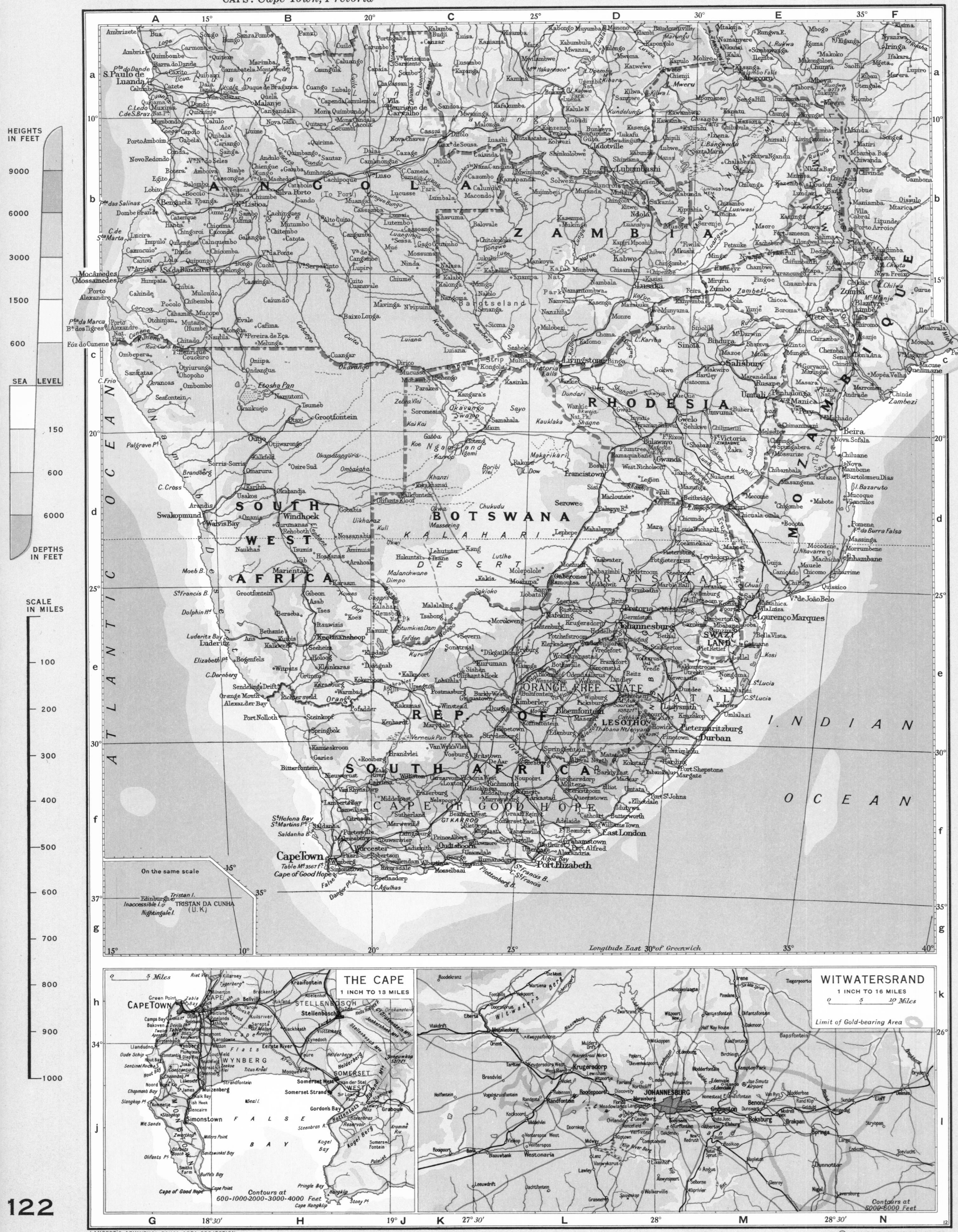

HEIGHTS IN FEET

9000
6000
3000
1500
600
SEA LEVEL
150
600
6000
DEPTHS IN FEET

SCALE IN MILES

100
200
300
400
500
600
700
800
900
1000

122

LAMBERT'S AZIMUTHAL EQUAL-AREA PROJECTION

© JOHN BARTHOLOMEW & SON LTD.

THE CAPE
1 INCH TO 13 MILES

WITWATERSRAND
1 INCH TO 16 MILES
Limit of Gold-bearing Area

SCALE: 1:12,500,000 OR 1 INCH TO 197 MILES
(Approximately)

MAIN ROADS
RAILWAYS

THE LEVANT

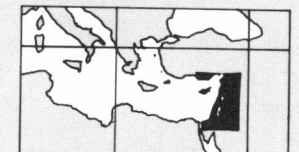

CYPRUS AREA: 3572 sq. mi. POP: 614,000 CAP: *Nicosia*
SYRIA AREA: 71,228 sq. mi. POP: 5,450,000 CAP: *Damascus*
LEBANON AREA: 4015 sq. mi. POP: 2,460,000 CAP: *Beirut*
ISRAEL AREA: 7992 sq. mi. POP: 2,669,000 CAP: *Jerusalem*
JORDAN AREA: 37,737 sq. mi. POP: 2,040,000 CAP: *Amman*

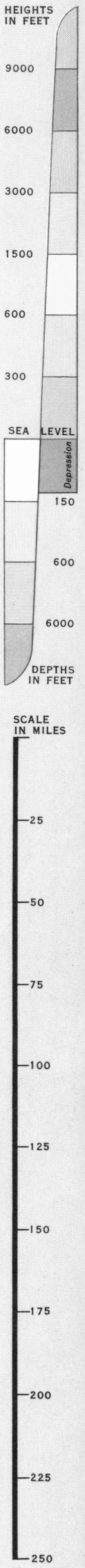

HEIGHTS IN FEET
9000
6000
3000
1500
600
300
SEA LEVEL
Depression
150
600
6000
DEPTHS IN FEET

SCALE IN MILES
25
50
75
100
125
150
175
200
225
250

123

CONIC PROJECTION

© John Bartholomew & Son Ltd.

SCALE: 1:2,500,000 OR 1 INCH TO 39 MILES

INTERNATIONAL BOUNDARIES
STATE BOUNDARIES

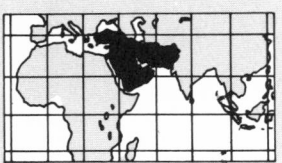

THE MIDDLE EAST
TURKEY, IRAQ, IRAN, AFGHANISTAN, YEMEN, SAUDI ARABIA, SOUTH YEMEN, KUWAIT

SAUDI ARABIA AREA: *829,995 sq. mi.* POP: *6,870,000*
CAP: *Riyadh*
TURKEY AREA: *301,380 sq. mi.* POP: *33,823,000* CAP: *Ankara*
IRAQ AREA: *167,924 sq. mi.* POP: *8,338,000* CAP: *Baghdad*

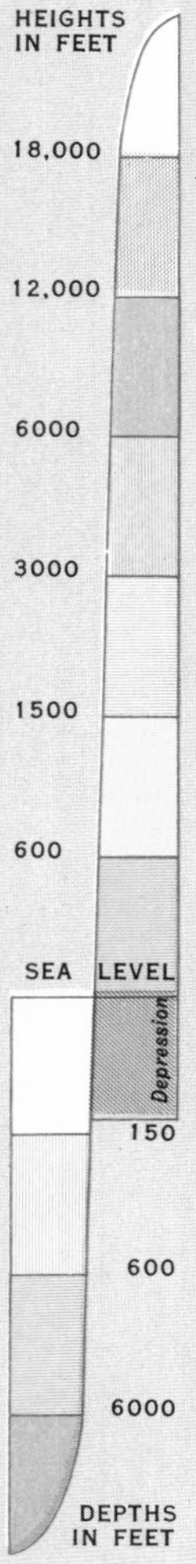

HEIGHTS IN FEET

18,000
12,000
6000
3000
1500
600
SEA LEVEL
Depression
150
600
6000

DEPTHS IN FEET

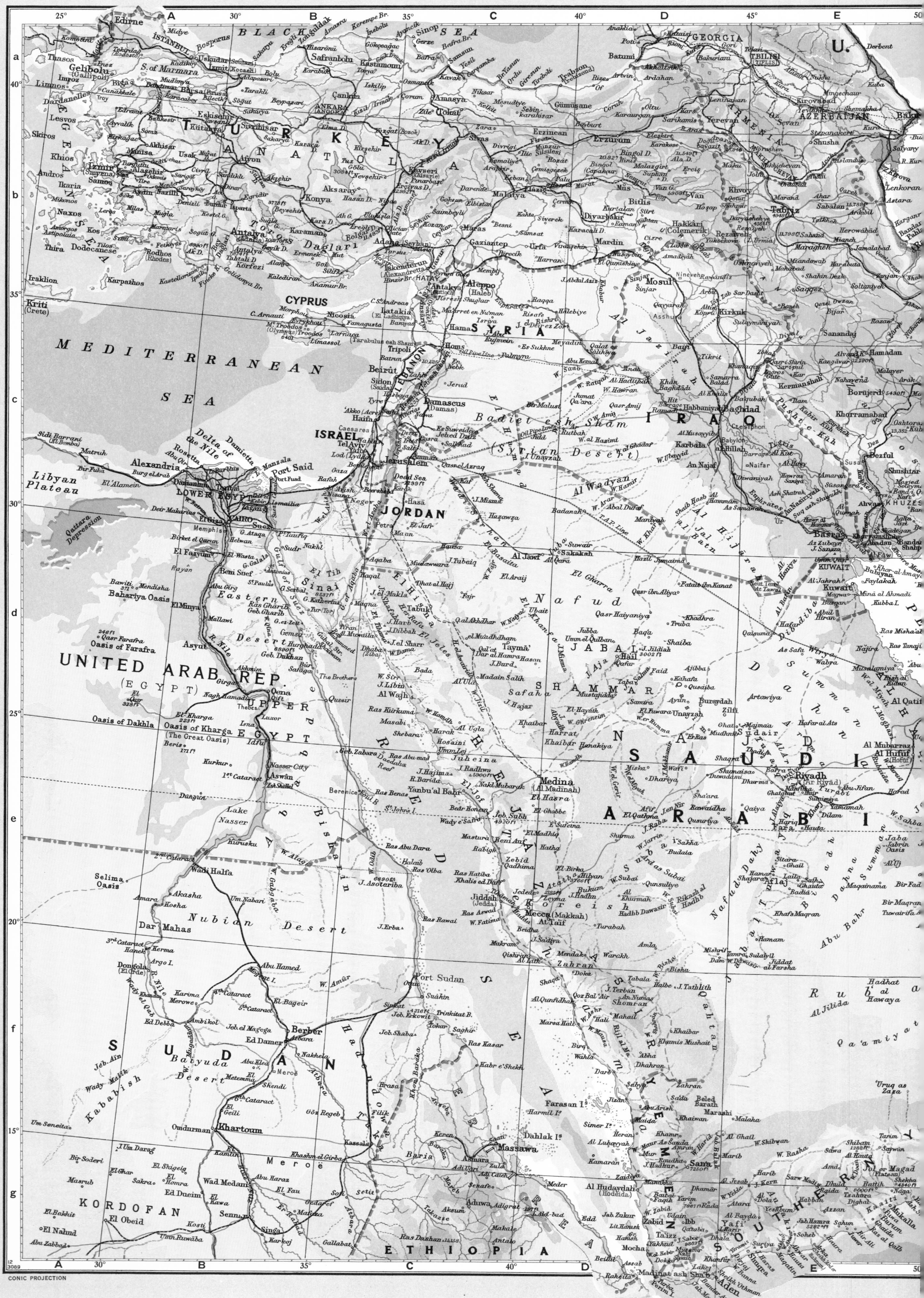

124

3089
3069

CONIC PROJECTION

SCALE: 1:10,000,000 OR 1 INCH TO 158 MILES

MAIN ROADS
RAILWAYS

BLACK SEA

MEDITERRANEAN SEA

TURKEY

CYPRUS

SYRIA

LEBANON

ISRAEL

JORDAN

IRAQ

UNITED ARAB REP. (EGYPT)

UPPER EGYPT

Libyan Plateau

Qattara Depression

Sinai

Nubian Desert

Kordofan

SUDAN

Khartoum

ETHIOPIA

SAUDI ARABIA

Nafud

JABAL SHAMMAR

Riyadh

Mecca (Makkah)

Medina (Al Madinah)

Jiddah (Jedda)

KUWAIT

YEMEN

SOUTH YEMEN

Aden

Sana

GEORGIA

ARMENIA

AZERBAIJAN

U.S.S.R.

Rub' al Khali

Lake Nasser

R. Nile

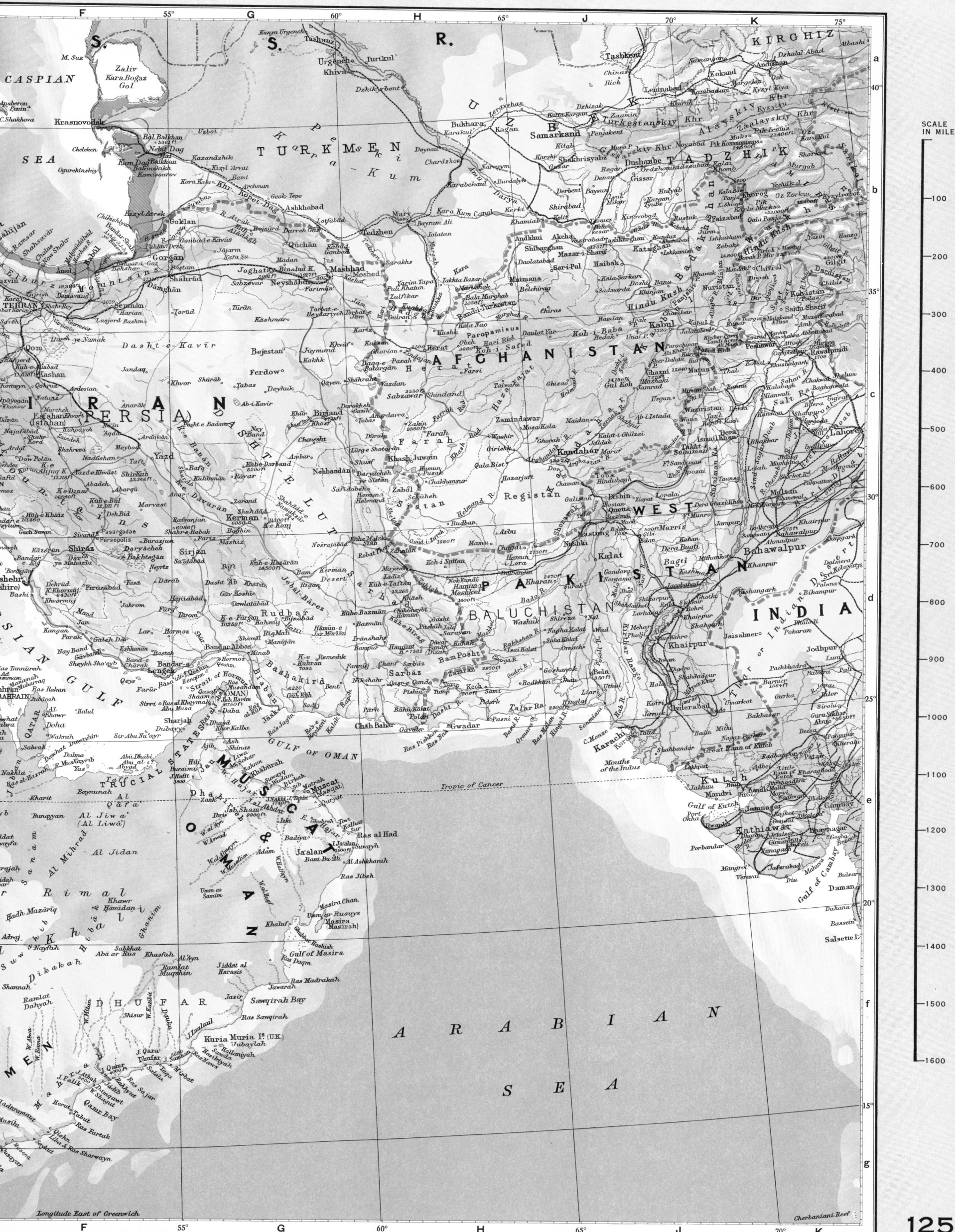

IRAN AREA: 635,326 sq. mi.
POP: 25,139,153 CAP: Tehran
AFGHANISTAN AREA: 249,999 sq. mi.
POP: 15,751,000 CAP: Kabul
BAHRAIN AREA: 231 sq. mi.
POP: 193,000 CAP: Manama

YEMEN AREA: 75,290 sq. mi.
POP: 5,000,000 CAP: San'a
SO. YEMEN AREA: 133,074 sq. mi.
POP: 1,146,000 CAP: Madinat Ash Sha'b
MUSCAT AND OMAN AREA: 82,000 sq. mi.
POP: 565,000 CAP: Muscat

KUWAIT AREA: 6178 sq. mi.
POP: 491,000 CAP: Kuwait City
TRUCIAL STATES AREA: 32,278 sq. mi.
POP: 130,000 CAP: Dubai
QATAR AREA: 4000 sq. mi.
POP: 71,000 CAP: Doha

SCALE IN MILES

125

INTERNATIONAL BOUNDARIES
STATE BOUNDARIES

© JOHN BARTHOLOMEW & SON LTD.

SCALE: 1:10,000,000 OR 1 INCH TO 158 MILES

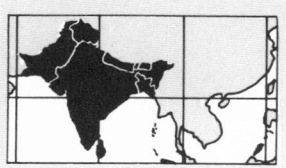

INDIA, PAKISTAN,
CEYLON, BURMA

INDIA AREA: 1,176,251 sq. mi.
POP: 511,115,000 CAP: New Delhi
PAKISTAN AREA: 365,529 sq. mi.
POP: 107,258,000 GOVT: Rawalpindi

CEYLON AREA: 25,332 sq. mi.
POP: 11,500,000 CAP: Colombo
BURMA AREA: 261,789 sq. mi.
POP: 25,246,000 CAP: Rangoon

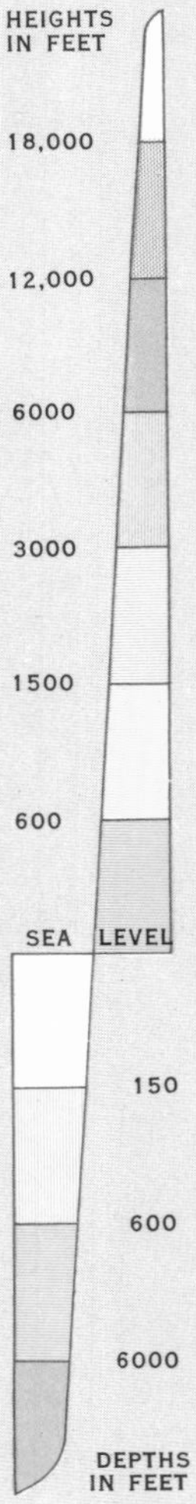

HEIGHTS
IN FEET

18,000
12,000
6000
3000
1500
600
SEA LEVEL

150
600
6000

DEPTHS
IN FEET

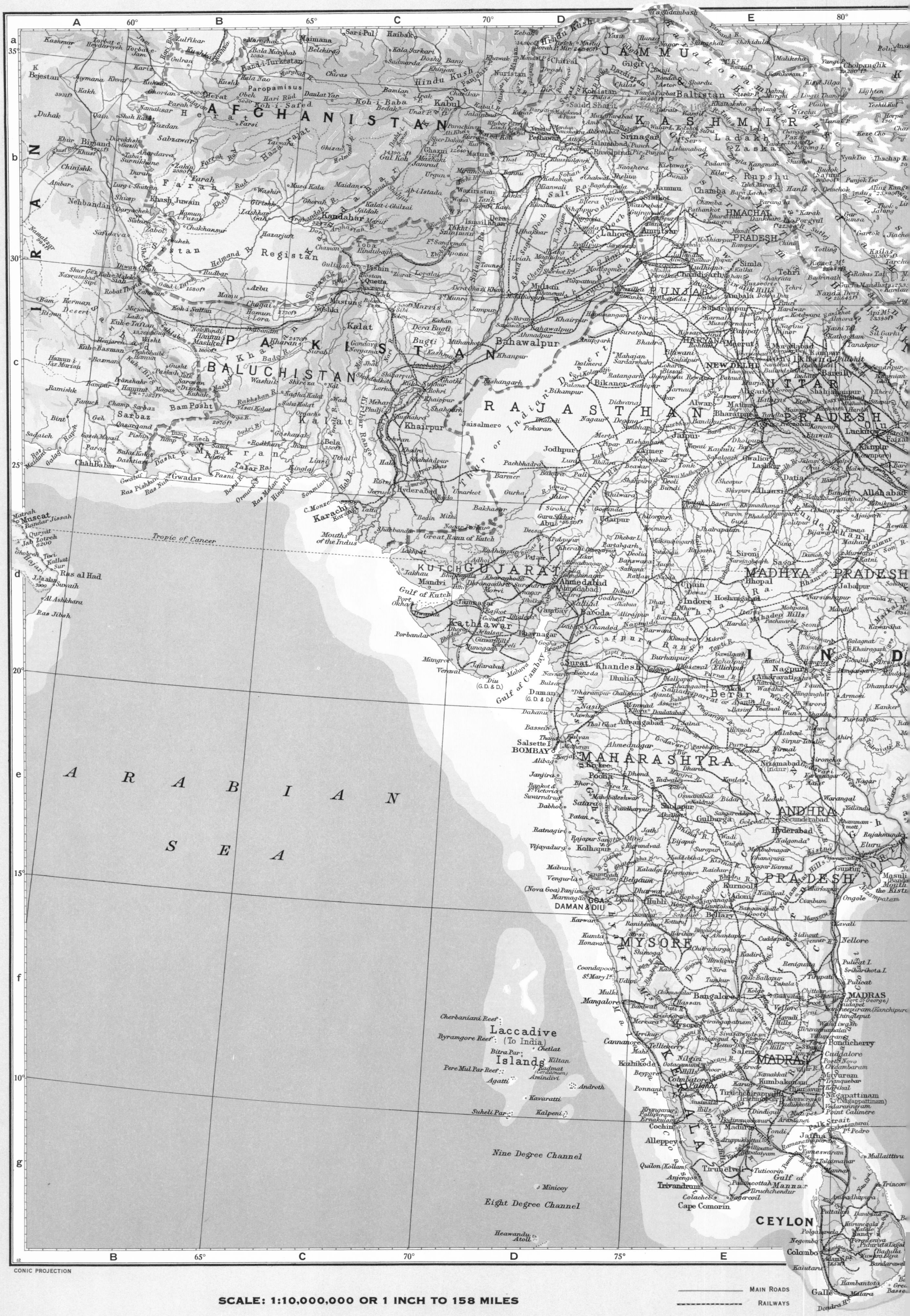

IRAN

AFGHANISTAN

JAMMU

KASHMIR
Ladakh

Hindu Kush
Kabul
Peshawar
Khyber P.

PAKISTAN

BALUCHISTAN

Kalat

Makran
Quetta

Lahore
Amritsar
HIMACHAL PRADESH
Simla
PUNJAB
Ambala
NEW DELHI

Karachi
Hyderabad
Mouths
of the Indus

RAJASTHAN
Bikaner
Jodhpur
Jaipur

UTTAR
PRADESH
Lucknow
Cawnpore
Allahabad

Tropic of Cancer

KUTCH GUJARAT
Ahmadabad
Baroda
KATHIAWAR

MADHYA PRADESH
Bhopal
Indore
Jabalpur
Nagpur

Daman & Diu
Surat

BOMBAY
Poona

MAHARASHTRA
Berar

Hyderabad
ANDHRA
PRADESH

ARABIAN
SEA

Ratnagiri
Kolhapur

MYSORE

GOA
DAMAN & DIU

Bangalore
Mangalore

MADRAS
Pondicherry

Laccadive
(To India)
Islands

Cochin
Trivandrum
Cape Comorin

Nine Degree Channel

Eight Degree Channel

CEYLON
Colombo

126

CONIC PROJECTION

SCALE: 1:10,000,000 OR 1 INCH TO 158 MILES

MAIN ROADS
RAILWAYS

NEPAL AREA: 54,362 sq. mi.
POP: 10,294,000 CAP: Kathmandu
BHUTAN AREA: 18,147 sq. mi.
POP: 750,000 CAP: Thimbu

The Indian peninsula falls into three main regions: the Himalayas, the great plains of the Indus and the Ganges, and the Deccan plateau. The mountains to the north virtually seal off the peninsula from the rest of Asia.

Along the coast, from the Gulf of Cambay down to Cape Comorin, runs the long mountain range of the Western Ghats. The high mountains of Burma are separated by the valley of the Irrawaddy and Sittang rivers.

127

INTERNATIONAL BOUNDARIES
STATE BOUNDARIES

SCALE: 1:10,000,000 OR 1 INCH TO 158 MILES

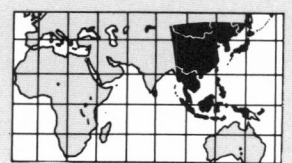

THE FAR EAST

NORTH KOREA, SOUTH KOREA, PHILIPPINES, INDONESIA

NORTH KOREA AREA: 46,540 sq. mi. POP: 12,400,000 CAP: Pyongyang
SOUTH KOREA AREA: 38,004 sq. mi. POP: 29,784,000 CAP: Seoul
PHILIPPINES AREA: 115,830 sq. mi. POP: 34,656,000 CAP: Quezon City

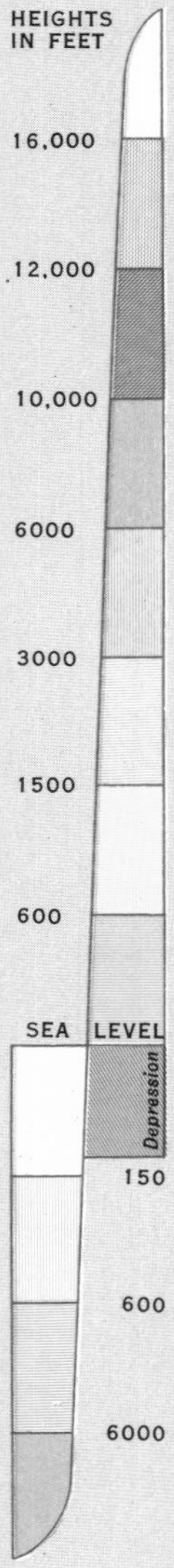

HEIGHTS
IN FEET

16,000
12,000
10,000
6000
3000
1500
600

SEA LEVEL

Depression

150
600
6000

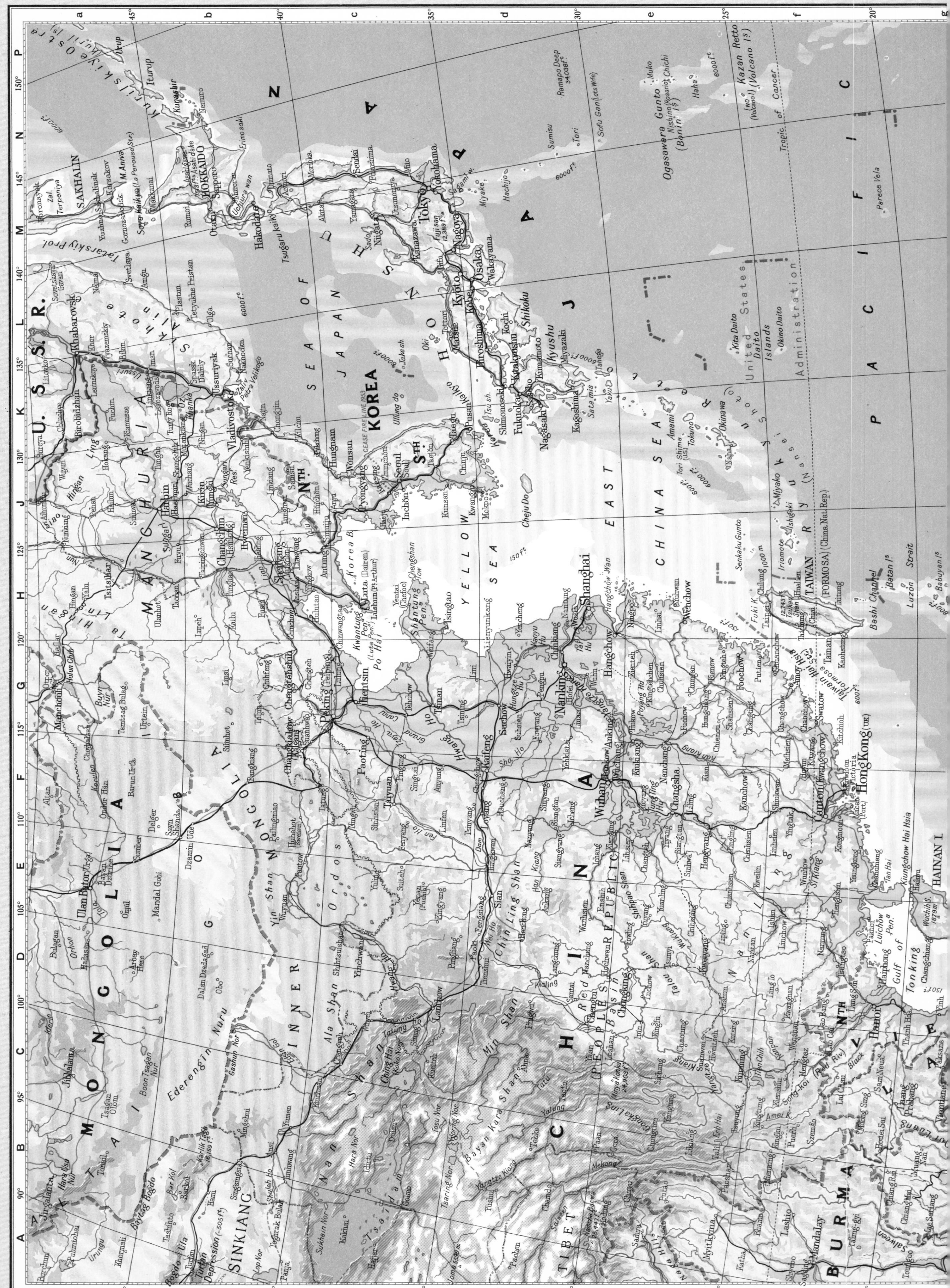

128

BONNE'S PROJECTION

SCALE: 1:15,000,000 OR 1 INCH TO 237 MILES

(Approximately)

MAIN ROADS
RAILWAYS

INDONESIA AREA: *735,268 sq. mi.*
POP: *107,800,000* CAP: *Djakarta*
From the high Tibetan plateau to the deep ocean bed off the Philippines is a drop of nearly 50,000 feet. The shallow seas of the Indonesian Archipelago and the mainly volcanic formation of the mountainous islands curving round Malaya to New Guinea are a marked contrast to the Himalayan fold mountains. The Philippines, comprising some 7000 islands, form the apex of a triangle based on Indonesia and pointing north to the equally mountainous islands of Japan.

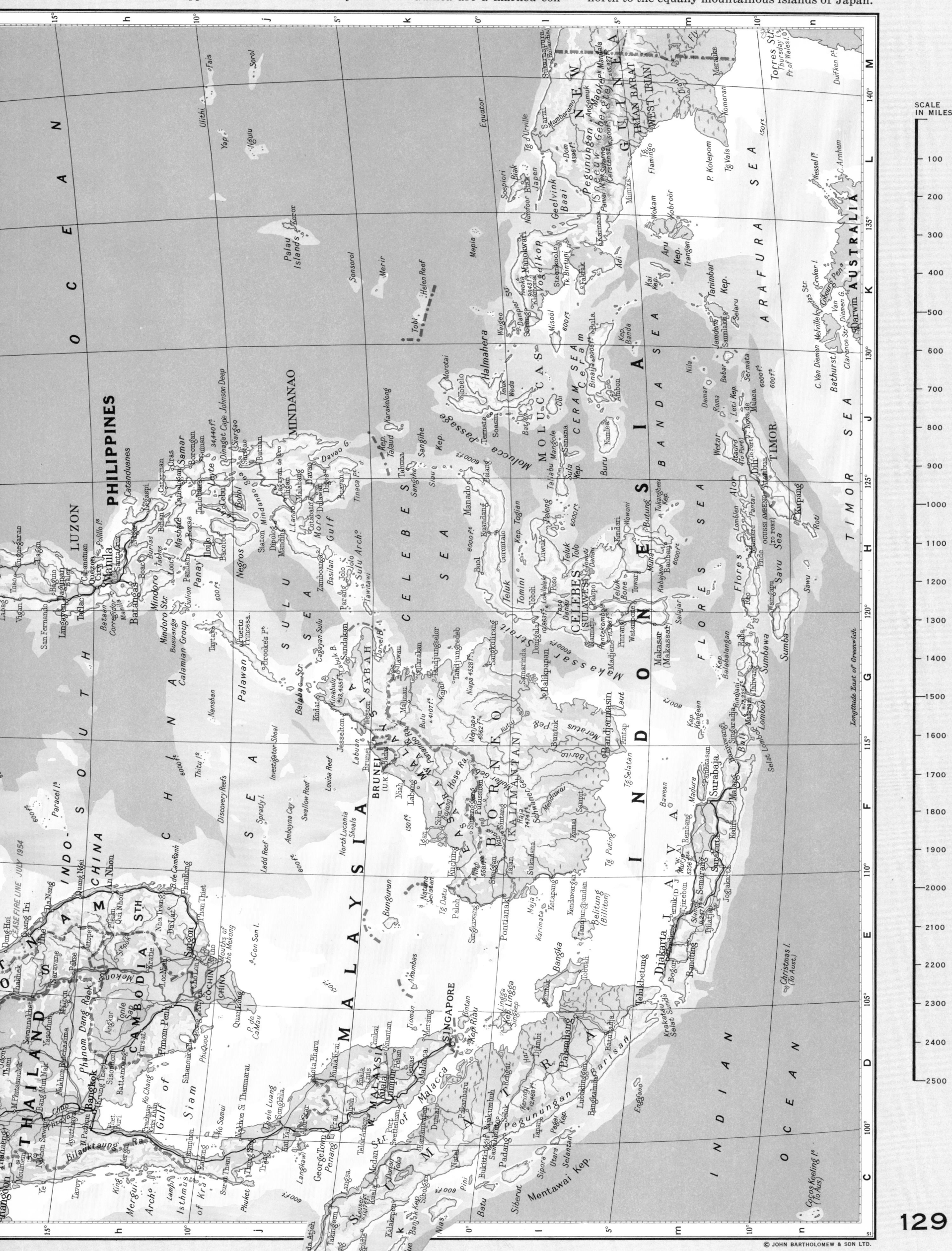

SCALE IN MILES

SCALE: 1:15,000,000 OR 1 INCH TO 237 MILES
(Approximately)

© JOHN BARTHOLOMEW & SON LTD.

129

INTERNATIONAL BOUNDARIES

STATE BOUNDARIES

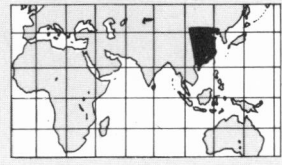

EAST CHINA

COMMUNIST CHINA AREA: *3,691,502* sq. mi. POP: *710,000,000* CAP: *Peking*
NATIONALIST CHINA AREA: *13,885* sq. mi. POP: *13,383,357* CAP: *Taipei*

Though half covered by mountains, China, has the largest population of any country in the world, and also the largest area of fertile land. In the east is a semi-

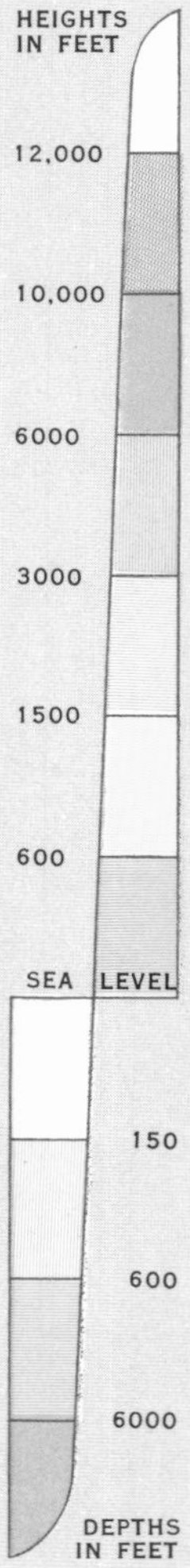

HEIGHTS IN FEET

12,000
10,000
6000
3000
1500
600

SEA LEVEL

150
600
6000

DEPTHS IN FEET

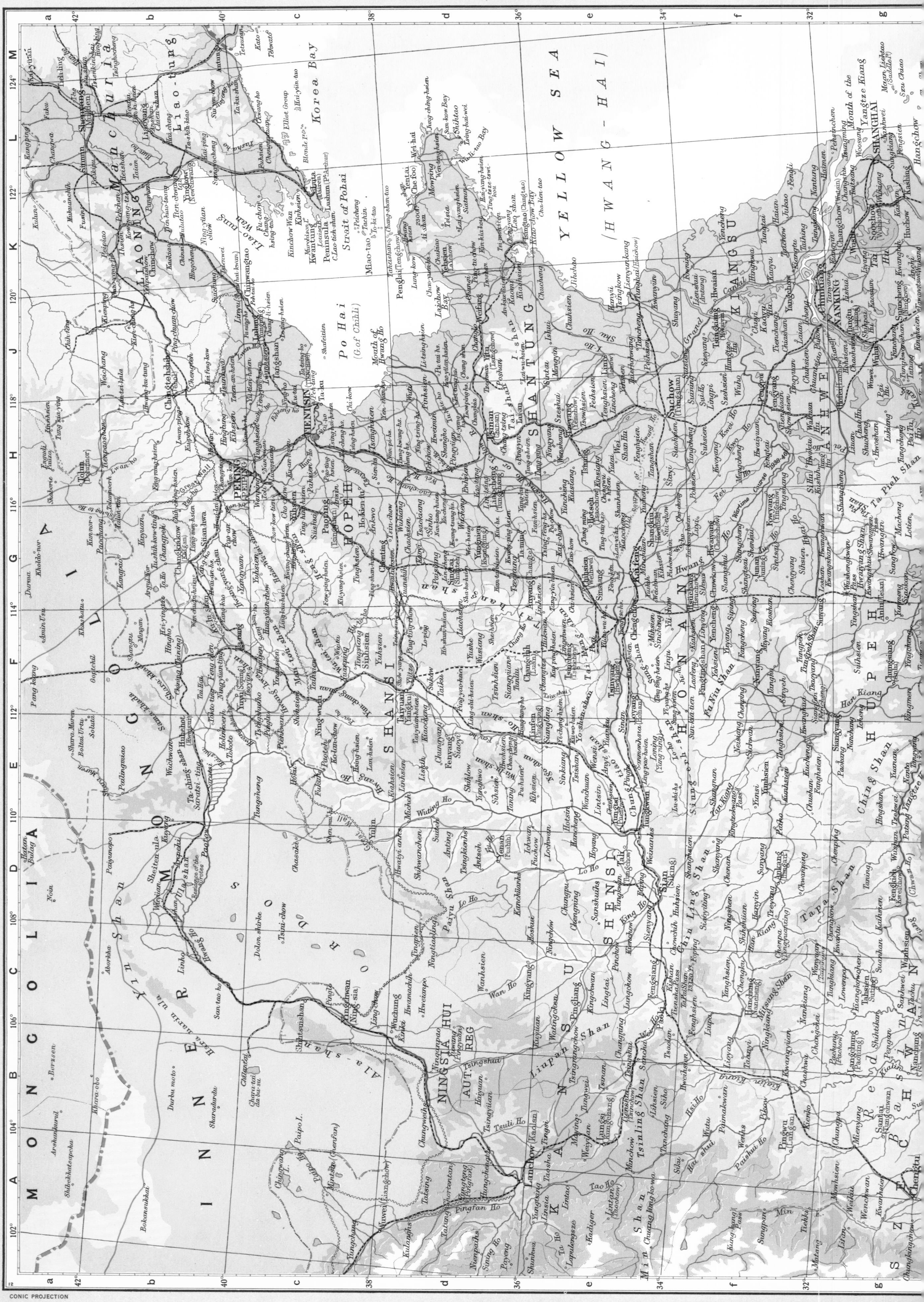

CONIC PROJECTION

SCALE: 1:6,000,000 OR 1 INCH TO 94 MILES

———— MAIN ROADS
- - - - RAILWAYS

circle of low-lying land dotted with lakes, testifying to inadequate river drainage. This area is backed by vast mountain ranges running northeast to Siberia, and cut up by mountainous tracts on a south-east axis reaching down to the coast of Chekiang. Each of the three main rivers, the Hwang Ho (Yellow River), the Yangtze Kiang and the Si Kiang, has a broad, well-watered valley, and together these valleys contain more than two thirds of China's inhabitants. The Gobi Desert covers nearly one third of China's total area.

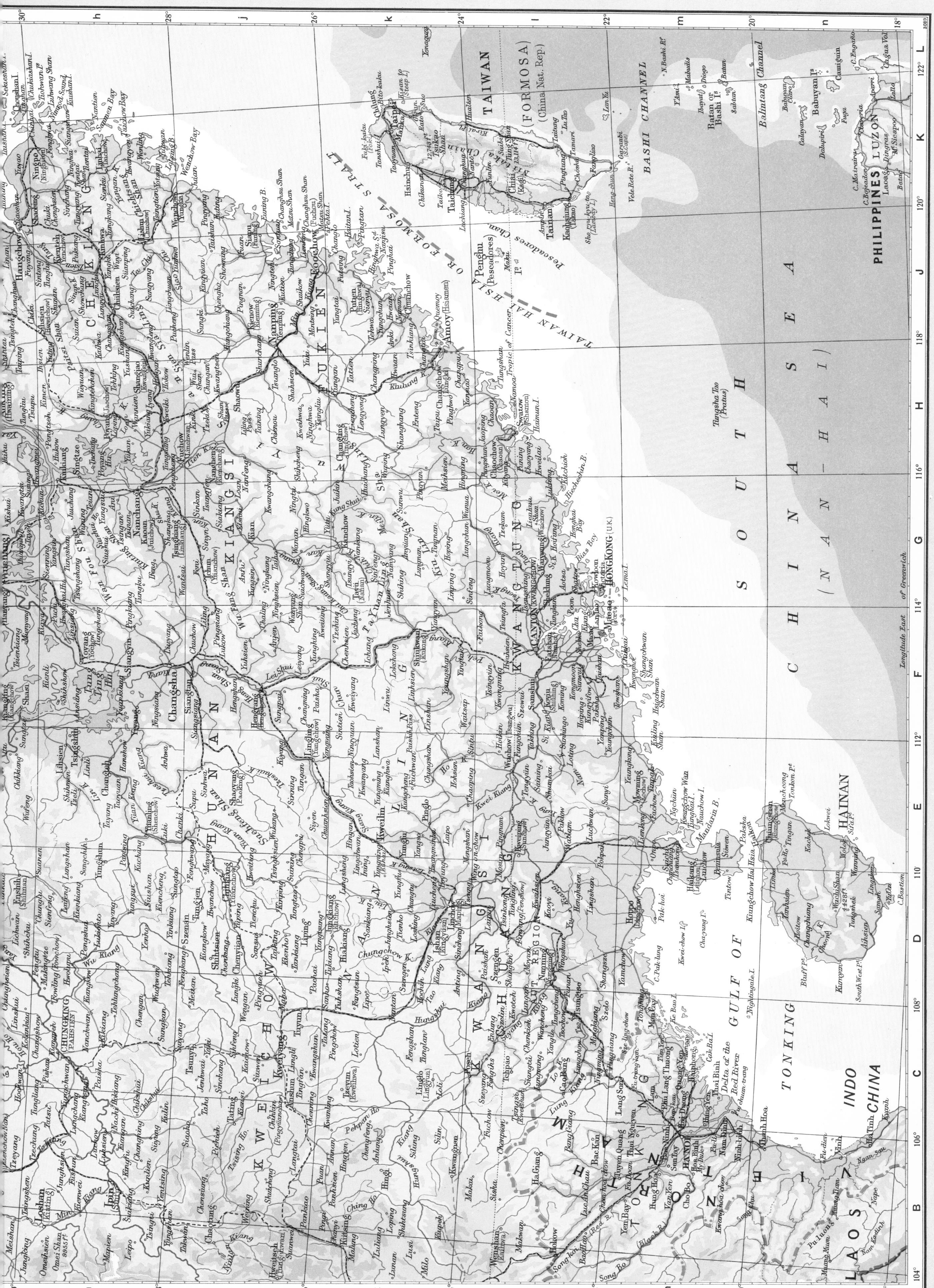

SCALE
IN MILES

INTERNATIONAL BOUNDARIES
PROVINCIAL BOUNDARIES

© JOHN BARTHOLOMEW & SON LTD.

SCALE: 1:6,000,000 OR 1 INCH TO 94 MILES

SOUTHEAST ASIA

THAILAND AREA: *198,455 sq. mi.*
POP: *32,680,000* CAP: *Bangkok*
MALAYSIA AREA: *128,430 sq. mi.*
POP: *9,711,000* CAP: *Kuala Lumpur*

NORTH VIETNAM AREA: *61,293 sq. mi.*
POP: *19,500,000* CAP: *Hanoi*
SOUTH VIETNAM AREA: *65,726 sq. mi.*
POP: *16,543,000* CAP: *Saigon*

LAOS AREA: *91,428 sq. mi.* POP: *2,700,000*
CAPS: *Luang Prabang, Vientiane*
CAMBODIA AREA: *69,898 sq. mi.*
POP: *6,320,000* CAP: *Phnom-Penh*

HEIGHTS
IN FEET

18,000
12,000
6000
3000
1500
600
SEA LEVEL
150
600
6000

DEPTHS
IN FEET

SCALE
IN MILES

100
200
300
400
500
600
700
800
900
1000

132

CONIC PROJECTION

© JOHN BARTHOLOMEW & SON LTD.

3089

SCALE: 1:10,000,000 OR 1 INCH TO 158 MILES

MAIN ROADS
RAILWAYS

Japan consists of a group of four large islands and many smaller ones, stretching from north to south over a thousand miles and separated from China by the shallow Sea of Japan. Off the east coast is the deep Japan Trench. The main island is Honshu, which is approximately the same size as Great Britain.

JAPAN

AREA: *142,771 sq. mi.* **POP:** *99,920,000*
CAP: *Tokyo*
SINGAPORE AREA: *224 sq. mi.*
POP: *1,956,000*

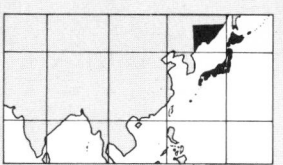

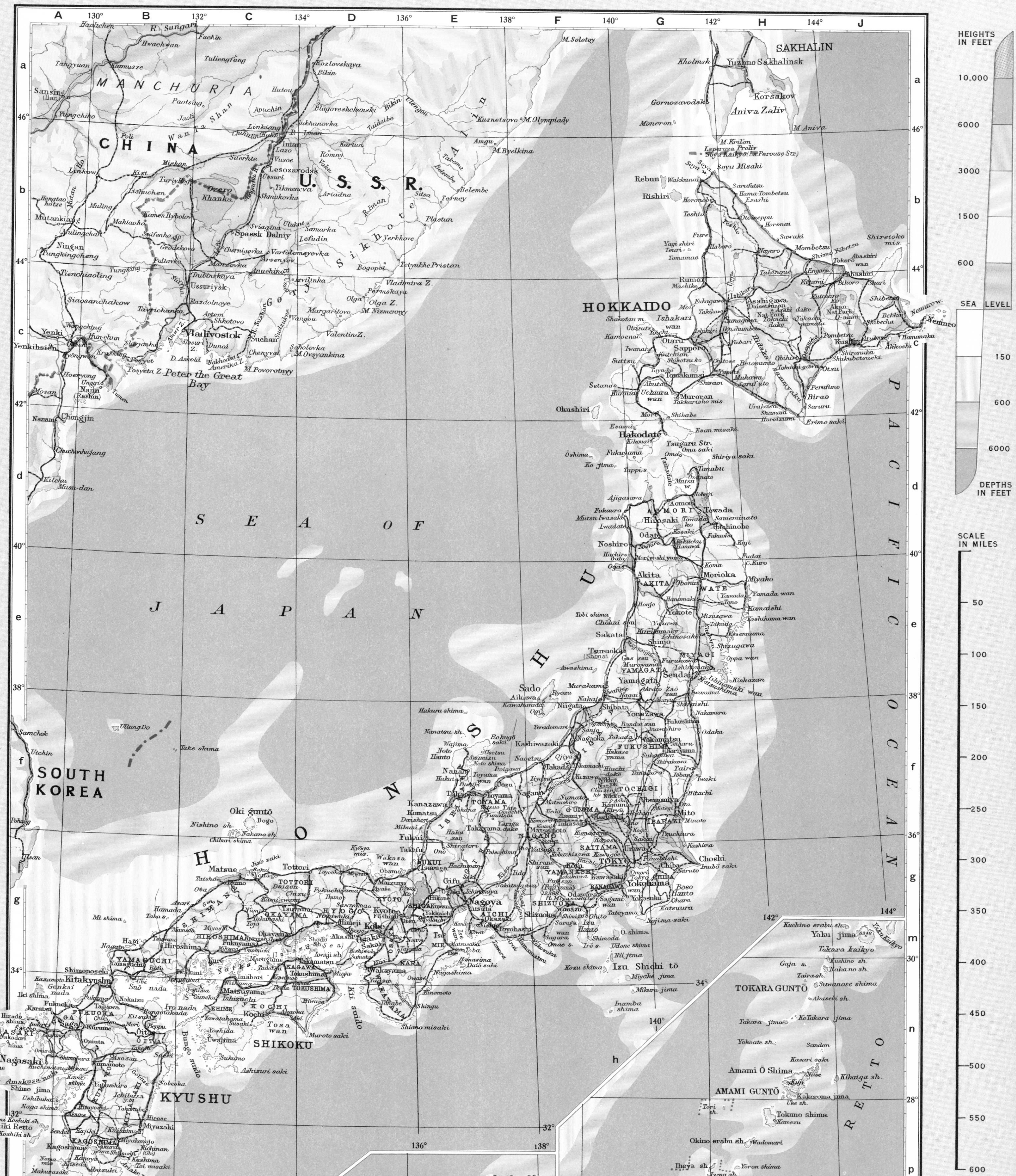

HEIGHTS IN FEET
10,000
6000
3000
1500
600
SEA LEVEL
150
600
6000
DEPTHS IN FEET

SCALE IN MILES
50
100
150
200
250
300
350
400
450
500
550
600

133

CONIC PROJECTION

INTERNATIONAL BOUNDARIES
PROVINCIAL BOUNDARIES

SCALE: 1:6,000,000 OR 1 INCH TO 94 MILES

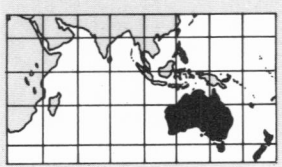

AUSTRALIA AND NEW ZEALAND

AUSTRALIA
AREA: 2,967,909 sq. mi.
POP: 11,540,764 CAP: Canberra
Australia is the largest island in the world. The Great Dividing Range of mountains reaches from Melbourne in the south right up to Cape York peninsula. It divides the fertile coastland from a fertile tableland, which

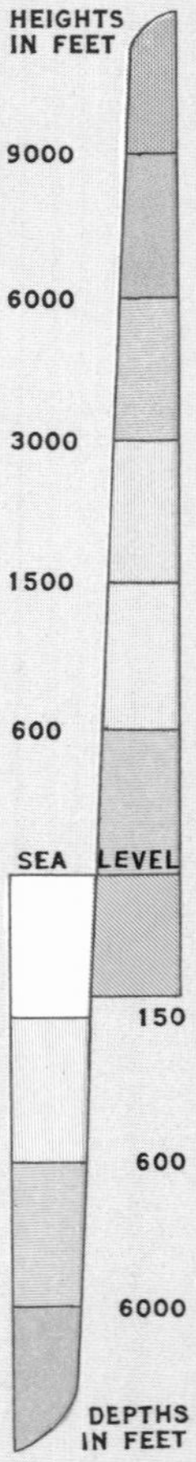

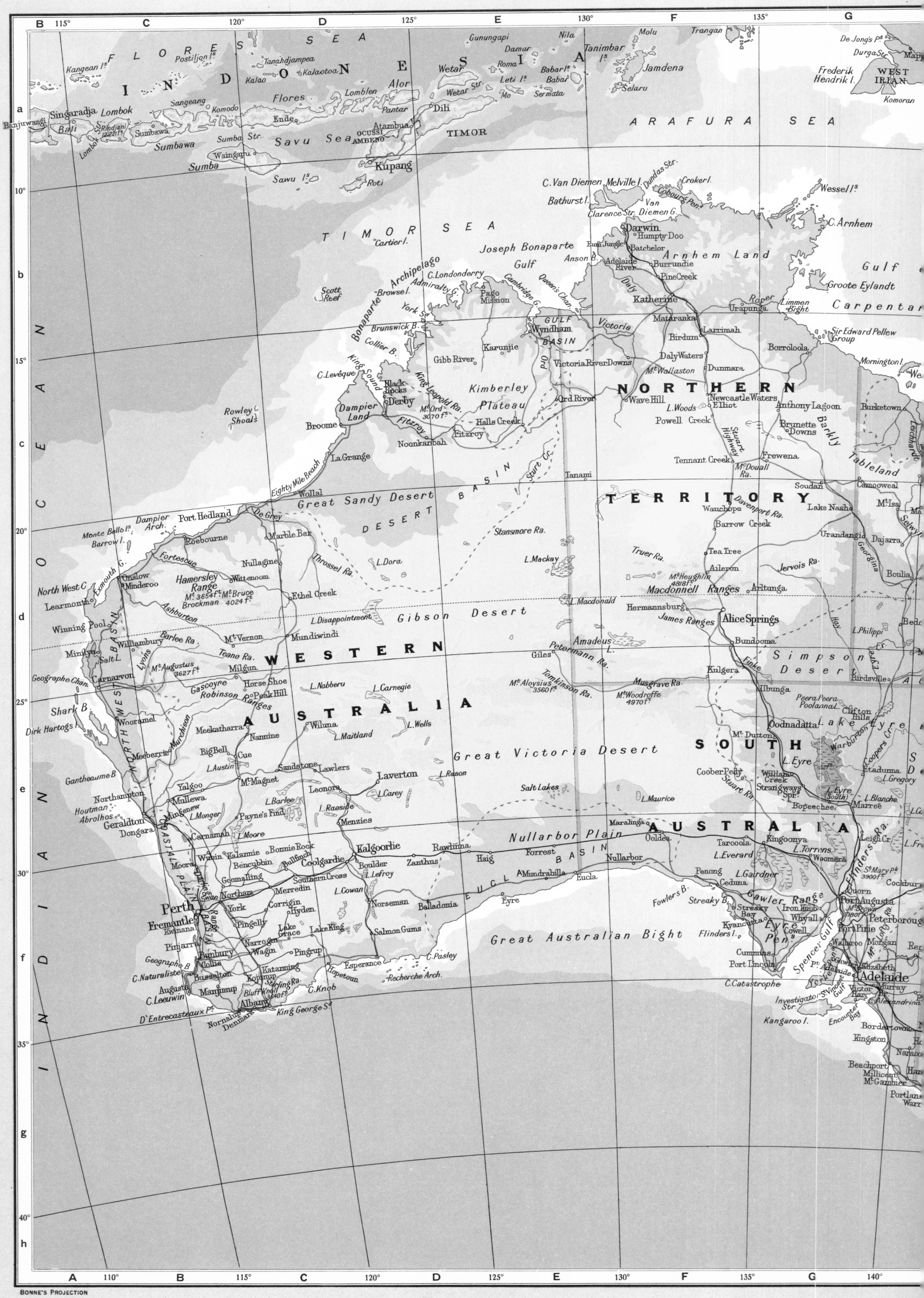

134

BONNE'S PROJECTION

SCALE: 1:12,500,000 OR 1 INCH TO 197 MILES

MAIN ROADS
RAILWAYS
ARTESIAN BASINS

is flanked on the west by an extensive inland plain. The Lake Eyre Basin, partly below sea level, drains the rivers of the eastern plateau. Farther westward, poorly watered plains give way to enormous deserts—and a fertile strip to the extreme southwest.

NEW ZEALAND AREA: 103,740 sq. mi.
POP: 2,676,919 CAP: Wellington

New Zealand includes North Island, South Island and several minor islands. The main islands are mountainous with rich coastal plains.

SCALE IN MILES

NEW ZEALAND

SCALE: 1 INCH TO 118 MILES

0   50   100   150   200

135

© JOHN BARTHOLOMEW & SON LTD.

INTERNATIONAL BOUNDARIES
STATE BOUNDARIES

SCALE: 1:12,500,000 OR 1 INCH TO 197 MILES

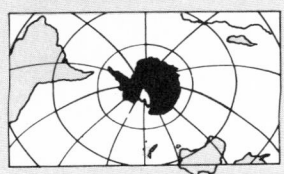

THE ANTARCTIC

The Antarctic comprises those seas and lands around the South Pole within the Antarctic Circle at 66° 33′ S., a total area of about five million square miles. This continent is uniquely isolated, and is covered by an ice cap thousands of feet thick. Much of the rock surface beneath the ice is below sea level. About 35°F. colder than the Arctic, it is uninhabited.

DEPTHS IN FEET

SEA LEVEL
3000
10,000
13,000
16,000
20,000

SCALE IN MILES

200
400
600
800
1000
1200
1400
1600

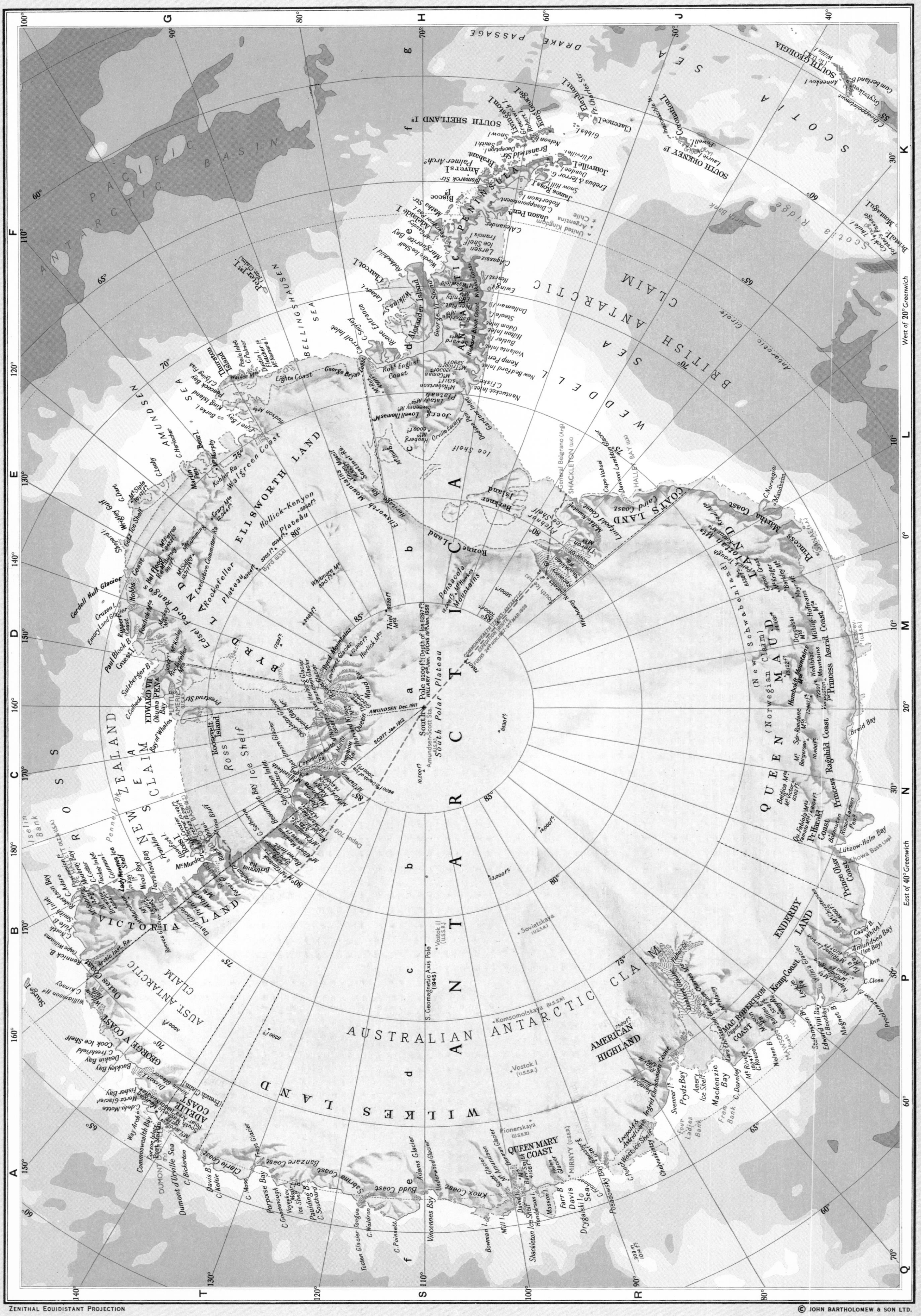

136

ZENITHAL EQUIDISTANT PROJECTION

© JOHN BARTHOLOMEW & SON LTD.

SCALE: 1:20,000,000 OR 1 INCH TO 316 MILES BASES AND STATIONS SHOWN IN RED GLACIERS ICE SHELF

PART THREE

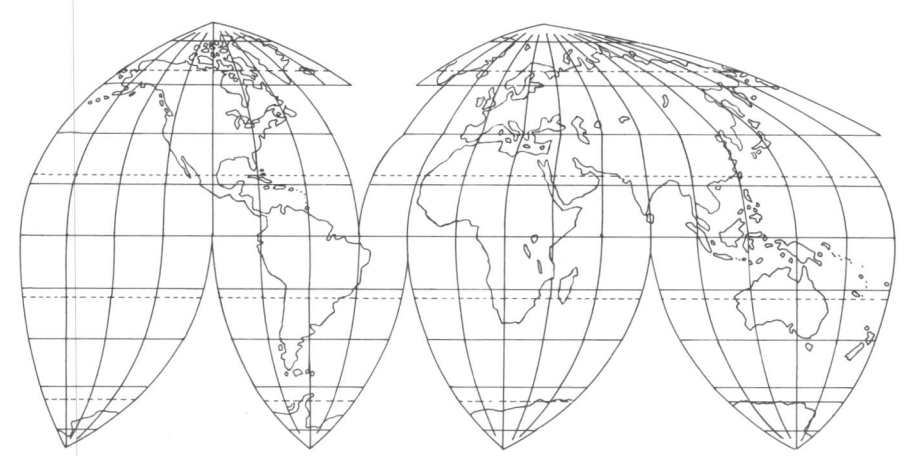

THE WORLD ABOUT US

THE EARTH'S STRUCTURE

OUR PLANET EARTH is about four and a half billion years old. It is customary to imagine the origin of the Earth in a rotating cloud of hot interstellar gas, along with other planets of our Solar System. A highly favored recent explanation indicates a union of cold "dust" materials whose size grew and whose gravitational force increased. The dust, probably born from an exploding star, was made up of all the elements now found on Earth, including certain radioactive elements which provided heat energy. The Earth's interior thus gradually warmed up, and since rock is a poor heat conductor, the temperature in the interior rapidly rose, approaching 7200°F. As the entire planet heated up, lighter mineral elements and gases erupted to the surface, forming the first land, ocean and atmosphere.

Many kinds of rock, of the density and character of granite, became welded together to form the continental "shields" as we know them today.

The Wegener Theory of 1912 states that originally the land was one giant supercontinent, called Pangaea (see opposite page), that fractured into smaller continents which gradually drifted apart.

It has long been thought that an initially hot Earth must be steadily shrinking as it cools. But Einstein's theory of relativity has also provided the idea of an expanding universe. This suggests that a slow reduction in the force of gravity would cause each of the planets to expand. Radioactive heat would provide further expansive energy.

The concept of an expanding Earth would allow the ancient continents to separate slowly without floating on a molten layer. What appears to be a giant crustal split has now been traced for over 40,000 miles, around the entire world (green lines on the map below). It is marked by earthquakes and a ridge of volcanoes, and is opening up at the rate of about one inch per year. The thin oceanic crust itself slowly pushes under the continental shelves. Great fractures (or "fault-lines") mark the borders of many continents and may be traced across the ocean floors (black lines).

The geologic map shows how the land-filled north separated in the direction of the Earth's spin (see red arrow, at the North Pole), leaving an oceanic southern hemisphere. The Antarctic continent remained completely isolated.

Gradually such great forces led to the opening of cracks and hollows in the ancient crust, particularly along the shores of the early continents. The cracks permitted volcanoes to rise from molten chambers in the basaltic crust; then sediment, washed off the land, settled in depressions or trenches on the floor of the sea. Periodically a critical imbalance of weight resulted. Large masses of rock became detached and slid along thrust faults into the trenches. Violent shifting produced great heat in the Earth, melting the rock. Liquids and gases concentrated near the surface further produced light molten "granitic" rock material. These new zones rose to form mountains.

This process of cracking, sedimentation and rising has been repeated many times. The older mountain belts, formed 250 to 500 million years ago (marked in purple), may be traced in each of the continents today, though they have long since worn down. The younger mountain fold belts, formed over the last 200 million years, partly effaced the older ranges and so are more impressive (marked in blue). Deep fractures still cause the eruption of active volcanoes (red dots).

The Earth's crust never becomes quite stable: within the shield, sags have created broad basins. The earliest basins, 200 to 600 million years old, underlie many of the world's great interior plains (solid dark green), as in the American midwest. The younger ones, less than 200 million years of age, are more often in coastal areas (yellow).

The younger mountains follow the margins of the Pacific and separate Eurasia from Africa-India-Australia. These are the principal volcanic and earthquake regions of today (see map). The rim of the Pacific is known as the "Ring of Fire."

DIAGRAMMATIC SECTION THROUGH THE CRUST

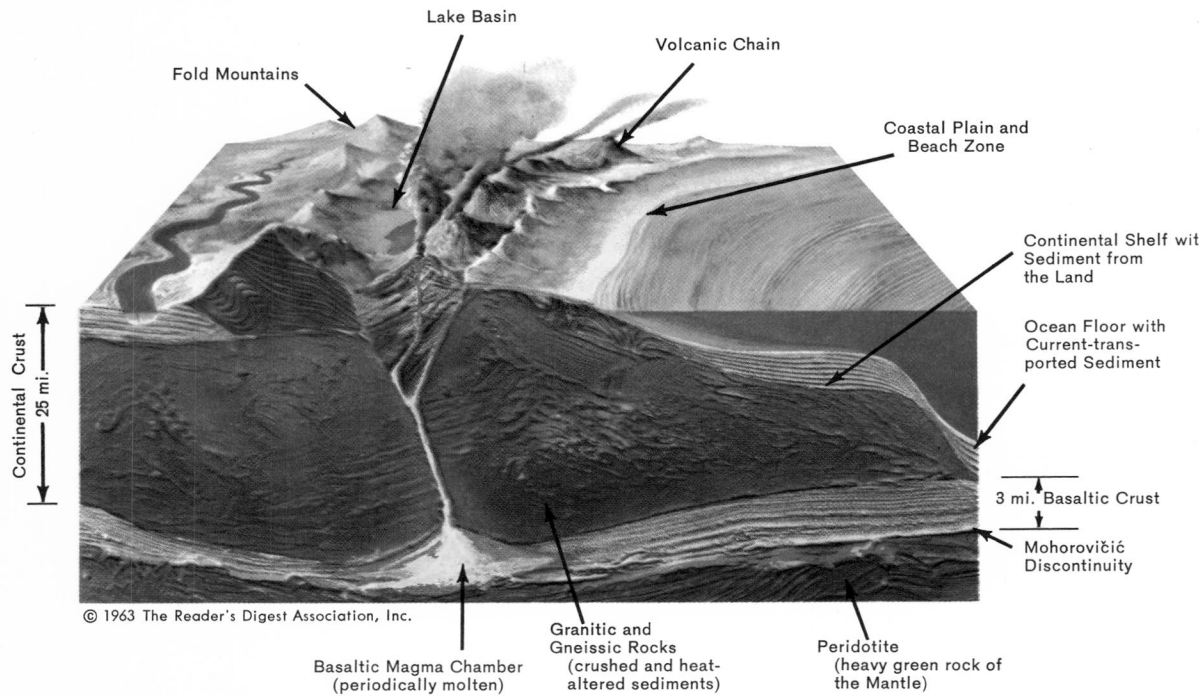

Fold Mountains

Lake Basin

Volcanic Chain

Coastal Plain and Beach Zone

Continental Shelf with Sediment from the Land

Ocean Floor with Current-transported Sediment

Continental Crust 25 mi.

3 mi. Basaltic Crust

Mohorovičić Discontinuity

© 1963 The Reader's Digest Association, Inc.

Basaltic Magma Chamber (periodically molten)

Granitic and Gneissic Rocks (crushed and heat-altered sediments)

Peridotite (heavy green rock of the Mantle)

CROSS SECTION OF THE EARTH

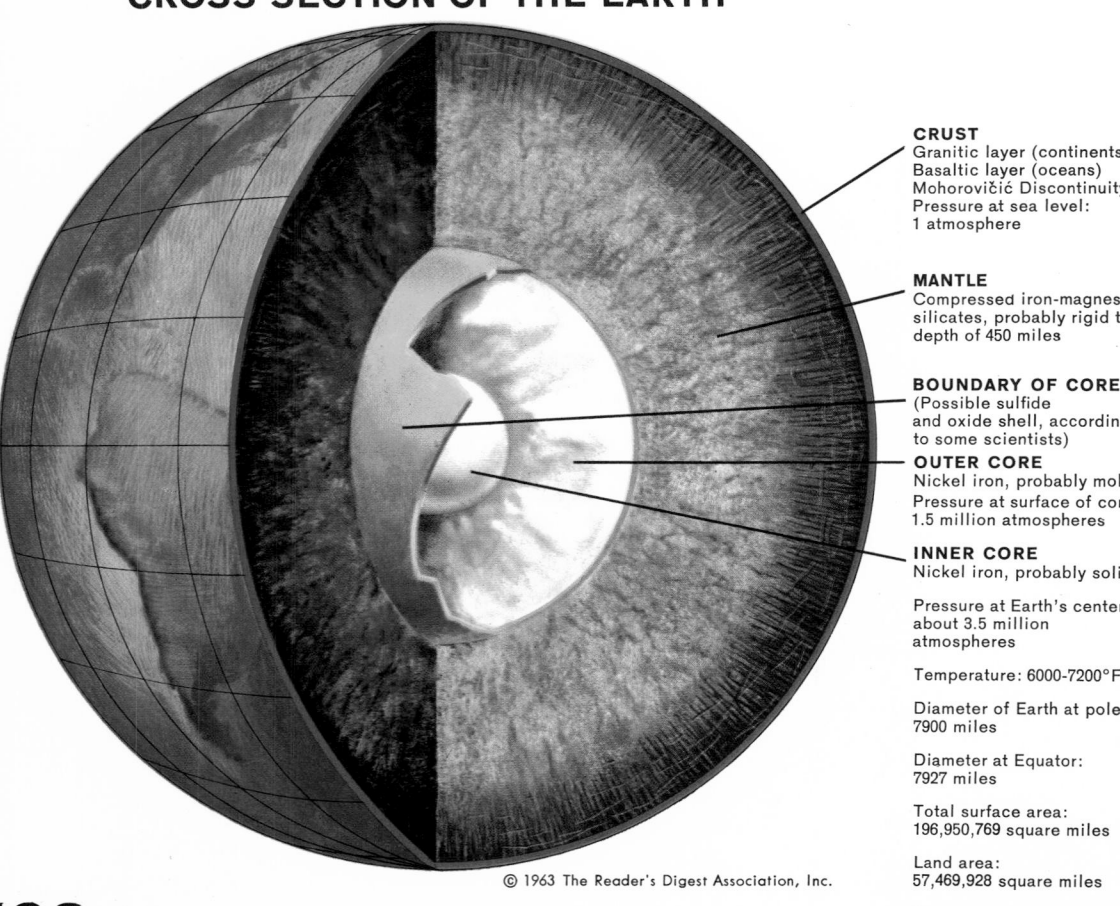

CRUST
Granitic layer (continents)
Basaltic layer (oceans)
Mohorovičić Discontinuity
Pressure at sea level:
1 atmosphere

MANTLE
Compressed iron-magnesium silicates, probably rigid to a depth of 450 miles

BOUNDARY OF CORE
(Possible sulfide and oxide shell, according to some scientists)

OUTER CORE
Nickel iron, probably molten
Pressure at surface of core:
1.5 million atmospheres

INNER CORE
Nickel iron, probably solid

Pressure at Earth's center:
about 3.5 million atmospheres

Temperature: 6000-7200°F.

Diameter of Earth at poles:
7900 miles

Diameter at Equator:
7927 miles

Total surface area:
196,950,769 square miles

Land area:
57,469,928 square miles

Sea area:
139,480,841 square miles

© 1963 The Reader's Digest Association, Inc.

THE EARTH'S INTERIOR

THE CRUST OF THE EARTH under the continents is quite different from that below the ocean. The continental crust is about 20-30 miles thick, made of relatively light materials often called "granitic," as granite is a typical continental rock. The oceanic crust, beneath its layer of water and about 1000 feet of accumulated muddy sediments, is of denser material. It is generally called "basaltic" after the basalt lava so often seen erupting from oceanic island volcanoes. In contrast to the continents, the ocean crust is only about three miles thick.

The interior of the Earth is known mainly from

FORMATION OF CONTINENTS

Alfred Wegener, a German scientist, suggested that the entire land surface of the Earth was once a giant supercontinent, "Pangaea" (some authorities prefer two major land masses: "Laurasia" in the north, "Gondwanaland" in the south). Recent discoveries reveal that geologic formations and fossils coincide where the shores of North America and Europe and Africa were joined, as well as South America and Antarctica and Africa. The separation of continents as we know them is believed to have occurred in Upper Cretaceous times (globe at right), as the present ocean floors do not bear sediment earlier than that of the Cretaceous period, which began about 136 million years ago. By the mid-Tertiary period, the drifting continents looked much as they do today (globe at far right).

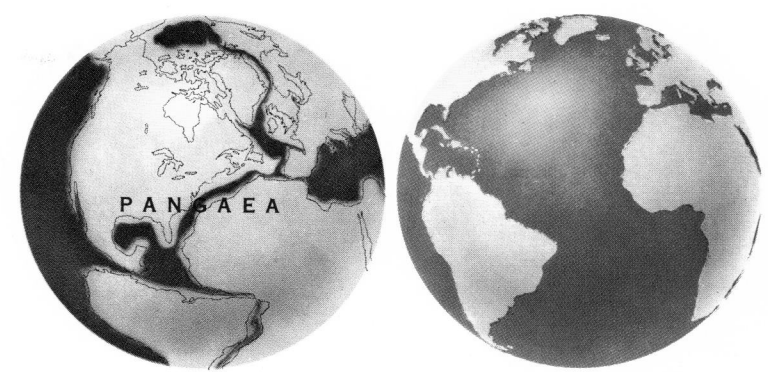

PANGAEA

GEOLOGY OF THE WORLD

☐ SHIELDS, old, stable land masses, consolidated during Pre-Cambrian time (over 600 million years ago)	BELTS OF VOLCANOES active and extinct
☐ FOLD BELTS of Paleozoic Age consolidated 250-500 million years ago	ATOLLS or other coral islands, built on old volcanoes
☐ SEDIMENTARY BASINS of Paleozoic Age	MAJOR CRUSTAL FRACTURES
☐ FOLD BELTS of Mesozoic and Cenozoic Ages, younger than 200 million years	MAJOR OCEANIC TRENCHES (partially filled with sediment)
☐ SEDIMENTARY BASINS of Mesozoic and Cenozoic Ages	MID-OCEAN RIFT and ridges of volcanic material, believed to be the site of oceanic expansion

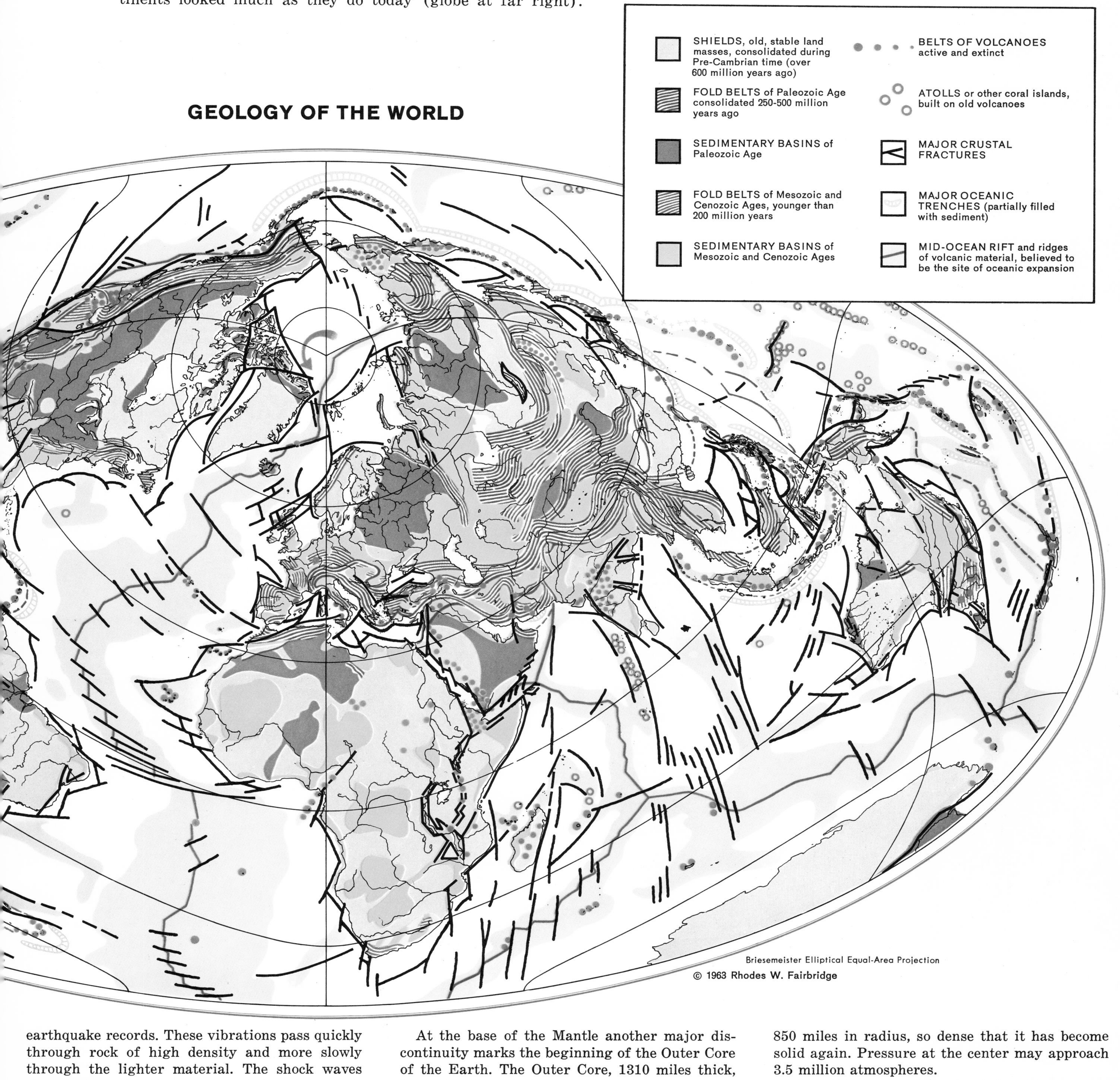

Briesemeister Elliptical Equal-Area Projection

earthquake records. These vibrations pass quickly through rock of high density and more slowly through the lighter material. The shock waves change their direction and speed at certain levels which are known as discontinuities. The first major discontinuity is at the base of the crust. This is named the "Mohorovičić Discontinuity" (Moho for short), after the famous Yugoslav scientist who discovered it. Attempts have been and are being made to drill down to the Moho level. Below it is the Mantle, a deep section which probably consists of a dense greenish rock, "peridotite," to a depth of 1800 miles.

At the base of the Mantle another major discontinuity marks the beginning of the Outer Core of the Earth. The Outer Core, 1310 miles thick, is a "dead" zone for certain earthquake waves, which indicates that it may be liquid. It has been much discussed. Perhaps it is iron with a certain alloy of nickel, resembling a type of meteorite that is believed to have originated at the same time as our Solar System. Such a core in the Earth would be magnetic and would account for the strong magnetic field that prevents the Earth from being dangerously bombarded by cosmic rays.

Beneath the molten layer lies the Inner Core,

850 miles in radius, so dense that it has become solid again. Pressure at the center may approach 3.5 million atmospheres.

The solid nucleus of the Earth is said to possess a momentum of its own, and to spin in the liquid bath of the Outer Core, lagging behind the rotation of the Mantle and the crust of the Earth. From time to time the position of the outer Earth (Mantle and crust) has shifted in relation to the Inner Core, and there has been a reversal in the magnetic field. Magnetic rocks show that the last "flip-over" occurred a million years ago when the North Pole became positive and the South negative.

139

THE AGES OF THE EARTH

OR its first billion and a half years the Earth was probably without life. The Earth's earliest crust may have been volcanic; the most ancient rocks have dominantly greenish colors, an indication of old lavas and their products. The early atmosphere was probably without oxygen, consisting, it is thought, of hydrogen, water vapor, methane and ammonia. Volcanoes gradually contributed more water vapor that condensed to form oceans, along with other gases like carbon dioxide. An atmosphere with oxygen must have evolved at least three billion years ago; in rocks of that age we find fossils of primitive plants which used carbon dioxide and liberated oxygen. Sediments were washed into the ocean, shifting the weight of the crust, producing violent heat changes and creating numerous mountain systems. Widespread ice ages alternated with warmer times.

Bacteria and seaweeds were at first the only forms of plant life. Certain species of algae (*Collenia, Cryptozoon*) fixed lime around themselves, and their extensive fossil remains are found on every continent.

Forms of animal life eventually appeared in the tropical seas—worms, jellyfish, sponges as well as other soft-bodied (invertebrate) forms. Fossil imprints of these are rare, but some were perfectly preserved. The land was apparently lifeless, without soil or plants. All of the above occurred in what geologists call the Pre-Cambrian Era.

Geological time is divided into named periods, each shorter than the one before. The later the stage, the greater its variety of land formations and life, and the more abundant the fossils. The major divisions are the Eras. The first, Pre-Cambrian, including the Proterozoic and Archean, is the time before 580 million years ago, when only primitive soft organisms lived. During the Paleozoic, 225-580 million years ago, fishes and early reptiles became the greatest creatures on Earth, and plants came to clothe the dry land and create soil. The Mesozoic, 65-225 million years ago, produced giant reptiles and primitive mammals on the land. In the Cenozoic, 65 million years ago till the present, mammals became ascendant and, in the last few million years, man's ancestors emerged.

These Eras are in turn subdivided into Periods, as shown in the column on the opposite page.

GEOLOGY OF THE UNITED STATES

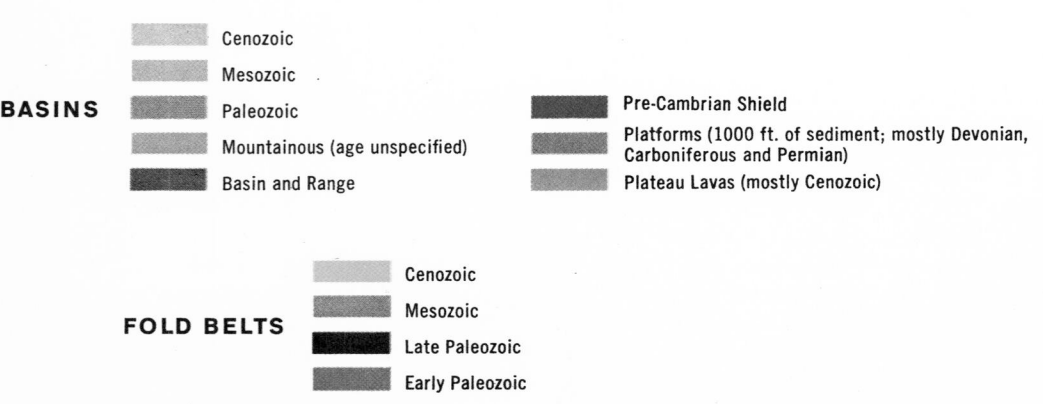

BASINS	
	Cenozoic
	Mesozoic
	Paleozoic
	Mountainous (age unspecified)
	Basin and Range

	Pre-Cambrian Shield
	Platforms (1000 ft. of sediment; mostly Devonian, Carboniferous and Permian)
	Plateau Lavas (mostly Cenozoic)

FOLD BELTS	
	Cenozoic
	Mesozoic
	Late Paleozoic
	Early Paleozoic

PALEOZOIC (Ancient Life)

Cambrian Period (from about 510 to 580 million years ago). The great Pre-Cambrian ice melted. Shallow seas spread across half the land area of the world. Around the borders of the Canadian Shield, the typical rocks laid down were first yellow-red sandstones, then limestones and shales. Great sedimentary basins began to form in the belt from New England to Alabama and in the far west. Climatic conditions were moderately warm.

Lime-secreting plants in the sea, such as *Collenia*, continued to be the only vegetation of which there is evidence. They were restricted to warm, shallow water, where light penetrated. Land was still without life.

Mysterious chemical changes in the seas enabled animals to build skeletons or shells of lime. Advanced groups such as the trilobites (similar to king crabs of today) emerged.

Ordovician Period (from about 450 to 510 million years ago). Shallow seas extended over most of North America, save for some large islands in northern Canada. Climates seem to have remained warm and equable. Over much of the midwest the deposits of the receding seas were limestone or dolomite (magnesium-rich limestone), but in the deep trenches of the east and west coasts thick shales accumulated. Their greatly increased weight began to fold the Earth's crust into mountains from the Carolinas to New England and in the far west.

Plant life was still restricted to the shallow oceans, and widespread limestone suggests the growth of floating algae. Reeflike constructions of algae built up in shallow waters.

In the ocean the ostracoderms—horny-armored, ancestral fish—were the first animals with backbones (vertebrates). Floating

MESOZOIC (Middle Life)

Triassic Period (from about 190 to 225 million years ago). The seas withdrew further, the climate became even drier and the prevailing colors of the rocks were reds, yellows and white, as seen today in the Grand Canyon and Painted Desert. Conditions in the Midwest were similar to the Rocky Mountain area in many ways. The recently formed Appalachians settled; enormous fracture zones produced basins (quickly filled with red-hued sediment) and created volcanoes all along the eastern seaboard.

Arid conditions over much of the Northern Hemisphere discouraged plant life; in southern lands, especially in Africa, India and Australia, a great variety of pines, cycads (similar to the palm) and ferns appeared.

The "Age of Reptiles" dominated most of the Mesozoic Era. Dinosaurs, at first no more than six inches long, appeared in this period. The first mammals—warm-blooded creatures —also very small, evolved from the reptiles. In the insect world the earliest flies and termites arrived.

CENOZOIC (Modern Life)

Eocene Period (from about 37 to 65 million years ago). Late in the Cretaceous Period and continuing in the Eocene, great mountains were emerging from Alaska to South America. Around the margin of the Pacific and from the Alps to Indonesia the present mountain belts began to rise up. Seas remained in the eastern and southern U.S., and interior plains enjoyed a subtropical climate.

On land, flowering plants and deciduous trees dominated, but warm belts permitted tropical species to flourish up to Canada and palms as far north as Greenland.

The giant reptiles became extinct. On land, crocodiles and turtles came and all the groups of insects. A "vacuum" was left by the dinosaurs' eclipse, and an enormous variety of mammals took their place: the pygmy elephant, rhinoceros, dog-sized horse, pig, primitive cattle and the earliest monkey. Life in the sea became much as we know it today.

Oligocene Period (from about 26 to 37 million years ago). Seas retreated slowly from eastern North America and the Gulf coast. In the Rockies massive fracturing helped form interior basins. Sediment from mountain ranges poured out over the great plains in vast alluvial fans. New marine trenches appeared only along the Pacific seaboard, where new deep deposits of sediment were accumulating and mountain-building pressures were rising. Most important for world climate at the end of this period were the new mountains which blocked the former east-west seaways in the Alps, the Middle East and in the Himalayas.

Emergence of broad plains encouraged the spread of extensive grasslands. These favored rapid growth of the grass-eating mammals. The early dog, cat and bear also appeared. A tailless, primitive ape forecast a possible ancestor of man.

far and wide were the graptolites, relatives of the coral. No life on land.

Silurian Period (from about 410 to 450 million years ago). Across the midwest a more distinct pattern of long ridges and broad basins began to emerge. Mountains of both coasts eroded, providing sediments to help fill trenches of the bordering seas.

Vegetation, still leafless, began to evolve further in lakes and swamps—the oldest known fossils are found in Australia. No life known on land. Simple marine invertebrates achieved great variety. Coral reefs grew to a grand scale. Giant-clawed sea scorpions up to nine feet long terrorized the waters.

Devonian Period (from about 360 to 410 million years ago). As Earth's crust sank into basins in the midwest, coral-type reefs formed around them in shallow seas from Iowa to New York. In New England the Cambrian basins became folded, melted, granitized and rose to form the Acadian Mountains. Sediments washed from the existing mountains, forming great deltas, such as are seen today in the Catskills and eastern Pennsylvania.

Vigorous plant life emerged on land everywhere, including horse-tails and ferns, some 40 feet tall. In the Catskill region of New York, fossil trunks of these ancient ferns are over three feet in diameter.

Called the "Age of Fish." Fish evolved rapidly in all modern groups, including early sharks up to 20 feet long. The first amphibians began to exploit favorable land; also spiders, millipedes and wingless insects.

Carboniferous Period (from about 280 to 360 million years ago). The "Great Age of Coal."

The shallow interior seas generally silted up, becoming steamy tropical swamps. Coal seams alternated with layers of sandstones, limestones and shales. In Australia and the Southern Hemisphere in general a great ice age was in progress, and its fluctuations caused frequent rise and fall of sea level, leaving lakes and swamps. The Northern Hemisphere was largely tropical.

Development of great fresh-water swamps favored evolution of tropical tree ferns, horsetails and the earliest conifers (notably pines) up to 100 feet tall. These, when buried, were converted to coal.

Swamps and coastal plains encouraged rapid evolution of amphibians, including a salamander 15 feet long, and the first reptiles. Insects developed wings; giant dragonflies grew to the size of eagles.

Permian Period (from about 225 to 280 million years ago). The seas retreated forever from the midwest, but new basins forming seas developed in the Rocky Mountain area and Texas. Abundant life in warm waters favored the creation of great oilfields. Climate on land in the Northern Hemisphere became more arid, and extensive sand-dune deposits appeared (as in Colorado). The Appalachians reached their greatest height.

During the great ice age of the Southern Hemisphere, strongly marked seasons emerged. Plants adapted to arid and cold conditions, especially deciduous trees, which drop their leaves to withstand frost.

In the ocean many Paleozoic invertebrate types, such as the trilobites and graptolites, died out. On land the reptiles increased slowly, but insects multiplied greatly (lacking natural enemies).

Jurassic Period (from about 136 to 190 million years ago). Often considered by geologists as the ideal "quiet time"; warm seas from the south returned to lap the southern Appalachians, forming the ancestral Gulf of Mexico, and filled many basins in the Rockies. Along the Pacific seaboard the deep Paleozoic trenches gradually filled and pressures began to fold the great Rocky Mountains.

With subtropical conditions returning almost everywhere, land and swamp plants evolved in profusion, including pines, ferns and the cycad with cones which were forerunners of flowers. Some coal swamps developed.

Reptiles reached fantastic dimensions (extremely weak in brain-power), the heavier ones in lakes where their weight (up to 35 tons) could be supported by water. Flying reptiles dominated the air, and swimming reptiles (ichthyosaurs) the ocean. Mammals remained small, no bigger than rats.

Cretaceous Period (from about 65 to 136 million years ago). The "Age of Chalk" began with a general lowering of sea level, probably due to trenches forming in the Mediterranean and around the Pacific. Soon the sea, successively rising and falling, advanced into the interior of America. At its maximum almost 90 percent of the Earth's surface was water-covered. The climate was almost universally temperate to subtropical.

Tropical and subtropical climates favored the development of fleshy-leaved and other deciduous trees—fig, magnolia, poplar and plane. The evolution of insects permitted dissemination of pollen from flowering plants. In temperate belts, vegetation showed a well-marked seasonal control, with growth rings.

Giant reptiles still dominated land, sea and air, but warm-blooded birds were already developing. Mammals remained inconspicuous. A new arrival was the pouched marsupial (ancestor of the kangaroo). By the end of the period, dinosaurs and many other of the earlier animals became totally extinct. Fish were forming in the species familiar today.

Miocene Period (from 7 million to 26 million years ago). Tremendous forces lifted up the Rockies; new local basins were formed by extensive fractures. Marginal seas appeared from New Jersey to the Gulf of Mexico, and on the west coast. Climates became universally warmer and wetter: subtropical in U.S., temperate in Canada. In Eurasia a series of thrusts occurred from the Alps to the Himalayas, and on to the Pacific border.

Favorable climate stimulated deciduous forests (maple, oak, poplar) throughout Europe and North America as well as grasslands on the great North American plains. Coal swamps and tropical forests appeared around the Gulf of Mexico.

Bony fish continued to develop, with sharks 60 feet long. Ducks, pelicans and great penguins appeared. Anthropoid apes were evolving in Africa, Asia and Europe. Elephants, increasing in size, spread from Africa through Siberia to North America.

Pliocene Period (from 2 million to 7 million years ago). Warm humid climates of North America cooled, and present desert areas began to dry. At first, because there were no ice caps, the sea level was over 500 feet above that of today, but continents were assuming their present outlines. The water level fell as the Antarctic Ice Age set in, building its glacial cap, and as the smaller oceanic basins sank and the mountain chains rose.

Oceans gradually cooled. As continents grew drier, grasslands spread out over the great plains in many parts of the world where subtropical plant life had existed.

Giant sharks died out, and many of the species of the ocean became identical to present forms. In contrast, on land the mammals were fast evolving, the horse and giraffe adapting to grasslands. Manlike apes thrived

in forests and also, in open country, a species that walked upright.

Pleistocene Period (started 2 million years ago). The "Great Ice Age," still continuing today, passed through warm and cold cycles of 20,000 to 90,000 years. Continental ice advanced over large tracts of North America and Eurasia. Desert areas expanded during cold periods. Warm periods alternated with cold epochs, and melting ice formed our Great Lakes. Temperatures were then higher than today and wet tropics spread.

Many plants survived in America and Asia by migrating south during the ice ages, but perished in Europe where sea and mountain areas cut them off. Pine forests developed.

Shifting climates forced tremendous migrations upon ancestral man and animals. Modern elephant, horse and cattle evolved. Man-like creatures began to use stones as weapons and tools, marking the dawn of human intelligence.

Holocene Period (started 10,000 years ago). Our present epoch is an interglacial period. At its beginning the sea level rose 350 feet because of the partial melting of glaciers of the Northern Hemisphere, creating the shore-lines that we know today. World climates were cool at first, rising to a peak of warmth 5000 years ago, then cooling again.

With the arrival of warm seasons, trees advanced northward, first pines, later birch and hazel, oak and elder. Forest margins are retreating again in Canada and Siberia.

Paleolithic man attained fire and practical arts at the close of the last ice phase. Then Mesolithic and Neolithic men became farmers and house-builders and learned to domesticate animals. About 5000 B.C. metal-working ushered in the age of cultivated man.

EVOLUTION OF LIFE

GEOLOGICAL DIVISIONS

Holocene — started 10,000 years ago

Pleistocene — started about 2 million years ago

Pliocene — from 2 million to 7 million years ago

Miocene — from 7 million to 26 million years ago

Oligocene — from about 26 to 37 million years ago

Eocene — from about 37 to 65 million years ago

Cretaceous — from about 65 to 136 million years ago

Jurassic — from about 136 to 190 million years ago

Triassic — from about 190 to 225 million years ago

Permian — from about 225 to 280 million years ago

Carboniferous — from about 280 to 360 million years ago

Devonian — from about 360 to 410 million years ago

Silurian — from about 410 to 450 million years ago

Ordovician — from about 450 to 510 million years ago

Cambrian — from about 510 to 580 million years ago

Proterozoic and Archean

© 1963 The Reader's Digest Association, Inc.

FROM THE PRIZED FLINTS of the Stone Age to the uranium ores of the Atomic Age, minerals have contributed vitally to the growth of civilization. Man has long recognized the importance of precious metals and precious stones, and of base metals such as copper, lead and zinc. Tomb paintings made in the Nile Valley nearly 5000 years ago show craftsmen weighing fine metals, smelting mineral ores and carving emeralds into gems.

Rocks are made up of minerals, and minerals themselves are composed of one or more of the 90-odd natural elements in the Earth's crust. While a few elements, such as gold, are found in the pure state, the majority occur in chemical combination with other elements. Thus, oxides are produced when metals combine with oxygen, and sulfides when metals combine

GALENA
Sulfide and chief ore of lead. Lead is used in storage batteries, type metal, paint, pigments, ammunition, solder and as a safety shield with radioactive material. *Missouri*

FLUORITE (FLUORSPAR)
Calcium fluoride. Ornamental stone in Victorian days. Used in steel, ceramic and aluminum industries. *Illinois*

URANIUM MINERALS
Atomic-energy developments are based on uranium. Uranium does not occur uncombined in nature, but is present in over 150 minerals.

SPHALERITE
Sulfide and chief ore of zinc. Zinc is used in die-castings, galvanizing steel and in brasses; the oxide is used in paints, ceramics, rubber and cosmetics. *Sullivan Mine, British Columbia*

ASBESTOS
A group of fire-resistant, fibrous silicate minerals, most of which can be spun into fabrics. *Quebec, Canada*

PITCHBLENDE
Uranium oxides with other components. A variety of uraninite, the most important ore. *Shinkolobwe, Katanga, Congo*

TORBERNITE
Hydrated copper-uranium phosphate. Green plates resemble a mica. *Cornwall, England*

CASSITERITE
Oxide and chief ore of tin. Alloyed with copper, it was the basis of Bronze Age implements. Used in tin plating, solders, bronzes, pewter and type metal. *Malaysia*

TOPAZ
Silicate of fluorine and aluminum. Used as gemstone and in refractories. *Ouro Preto, Brazil*

OLIVINE
Magnesium-iron silicate. A common rock-forming mineral. Peridot and chrysolite are gem varieties. *Zebirget, Egypt*

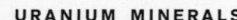
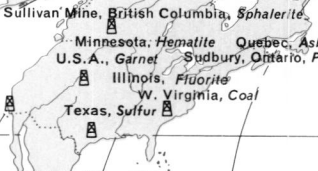

ALUMINA MINERALS
The most abundant metal in the Earth's crust, aluminum does not occur in the free state. Alloys are used in automobiles, airplanes and ships; aluminum in electric transmission lines. Ruby and sapphire are gem varieties of corundum, a natural aluminum oxide.

CORUNDUM
Hardness only exceeded by diamond. Used as an abrasive in grinding optical glass. *Transvaal, South Africa*

SAPPHIRE
Corundum gemstones of whatever color are sapphires with the exception of red (ruby). *Ceylon*

RUBY
"Pigeon-blood" red variety. Large rubies are among the most precious of stones. *Mogok, Burma*

BAUXITE
A rock composed of aluminum oxides. Chief ore of aluminum. Used in making abrasives, refractories, chemicals, high-alumina cement. *Jamaica*

CINNABAR
Sulfide and chief ore of mercury (quicksilver). Used in scientific instruments, detonators, the metal, chemical and electrical industries. *Almaden, Spain*

COPPER MINERALS
Copper and gold were the first metals used by man. Copper is used in the electrical industry, also in bronzes, brasses and other alloys. At least 165 minerals are known to contain copper.

IRON MINERALS
Iron is industry's indispensable metal. Although iron minerals occur abundantly, pure iron is too soft for use, so man learned to harden it by adding carbon. Thus the Iron Age followed the Bronze Age. A moderate amount of carbon produces steel, an excess produces cast iron.

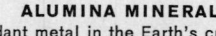

AZURITE
Hydrated copper carbonate. *Katanga, Congo*

CHALCOPYRITE
Copper-iron sulfide. Crystals of chalcopyrite and quartz are shown. Most widespread and important ore of copper. *Zambia*

MALACHITE
Hydrated copper carbonate. An ornamental stone as well as a valuable ore. *Katanga, Congo*

MAGNETITE
Magnetic iron oxide. Crystals show regular octahedral form. Lodestone (leading stone), a variety with magnetic polarity, was used in primitive compasses. *Kiruna, Sweden*

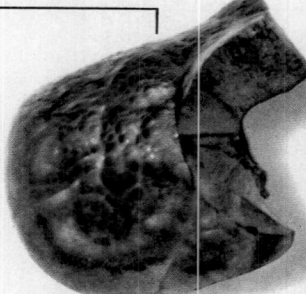

HEMATITE
Oxide of iron. The "kidney-ore" variety is shown. Used as an ornamental stone. *Minnesota*

142

TREASURES

EARTH'S CRUST

with sulfur. Minerals are formed in various ways—for example, by crystallization from molten lava, just as ice crystals form when water freezes, and by crystallization from vapors, as in the formation of sulfur crystals by the cooling of sulfur-bearing gases around active volcanoes.

Some 2000 minerals have been recorded so far. At depths below those of the present deepest mine, we may one day find new minerals that are stable at the high pressures and temperatures nearer the center of the Earth. And the advent of space travel opens up the possibility of the discovery of unknown minerals on other planets.

This small selection of the Earth's minerals shows the variety of their natural forms and colors. Commercially important deposits are indicated on the map.

APATITE
Calcium phosphate. Chief constituent of phosphate rock. Used in manufacture of fertilizers and pesticides.
Kola Peninsula, U.S.S.R.

PENTLANDITE
Nickel-iron sulfide. Used extensively in steels and alloys, nickel is alloyed with copper to make the United States "nickel" and Britain's "silver" coins.
Sudbury, Ontario

BERYLLIUM MINERALS
Beryllium is unusually light and strong and has valuable metallurgical properties. Used in alloys with copper and nickel, also in X-ray tubes. Beryl is the commercial source of beryllium; aquamarine and emerald are varieties with similar composition.

KAOLIN (CHINA CLAY)
Hydrated aluminum silicate. Used in paper, pottery, rubber, chemicals, cosmetics and insecticides.
Cornwall, England

ZIRCON
Zirconium silicate. Besides being a gemstone, zircon in mineral form is used in ceramics. Zirconium metal is used in steel alloys and the chemical and electrical industries.

AQUAMARINE
Sea-green variety.
Minas Gerais, Brazil

BERYL
Can occur in very large crystals up to 25 tons in weight. *Mozambique*

EMERALD
Grass-green, unflawed stones exceeding six carats command high prices. Ranks with diamond and ruby as the most precious stone. *Colombia*

Kola Peninsula, *Apatite*
Kiruna, *Magnetite*
Kingdom: Salt, *Torbernite*
Urals, *Platinum*
Cinnabar
Zebirget, *Olivine*
Korea, *Graphite*
Mogok, *Ruby*
Ceylon, *Sapphire*
Malaysia, *Cassiterite*
Katanga, *Pitchblende, Azurite, Malachite*
Zambia, *Chalcopyrite*
Mozambique, *Beryl*
Transvaal, *Corundum*
Kimberley, *Diamond*
The Rand, *Gold*
New South Wales, *Opal*

CARBON MINERALS
Native crystalline carbon occurs as two important minerals, diamond and graphite. Coals consist largely of noncrystalline carbon. Combination with hydrogen produces the natural hydrocarbons which constitute petroleums and bitumens.

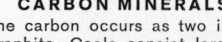

DIAMOND
Hardest known mineral and most valuable gemstone. Photograph shows a crystal in kimberlite. Most diamonds are imperfect and are used in industry, for cutting or abrasive purposes. *Kimberley, South Africa*

COAL
Bituminous coal showing banded structure. Source of many hydrocarbon chemicals.

GRAPHITE
One of the softest minerals. The "lead" in lead pencils. Used in refractory crucibles, electrical equipment, lubricants, pigments and in atomic piles. *Korea*

SULFUR (BRIMSTONE)
Essential to modern industry, used in manufacture of sulfuric acid, paper, and many other chemicals, rubber goods, steel. *Texas*

PLATINUM
Natural platinum usually contains variable amounts of the other platinum-group metals—palladium, iridium, osmium, rhodium and ruthenium. Hardened with some of them, it is used in jewelry and laboratory equipment, the electrical industry, dentistry and anti-corrosive chemical ware. *Urals*

GOLD
Man used gold for decoration from early times. It is hardened by alloying with copper, silver, palladium or nickel for use in jewelry and dentistry.
The Rand, South Africa

SILVER
Specimen carries some milky-white quartz. Used in coinage, plate, jewelry and dentistry and in the electrical, photographic and chemical industries. *Mexico*

SILICA MINERALS
Silicon does not occur uncombined, but its oxide, quartz and the large group of silicates are the most important rock-forming minerals. Silicon is the most abundant element in the Earth's crust after oxygen; it is used in electronic components, ferrous and non-ferrous alloys and for the manufacture of silicones. Chalcedony is a crystalline variety of quartz mixed with opal and other constituents. Precious varieties are shown below.

GARNET
Photograph shows crystal in a metamorphic rock. Garnet is the name of a group of silicates; it is also a semiprecious gemstone. The iron-aluminum garnet, almandine, is used as an abrasive. *U.S.A.*

OPAL
A hydrated non-crystalline form of silica which shows a variegated play of colors or "fire."
New South Wales, Australia

QUARTZ
One of the commonest minerals. High-grade quartz is used for electronic instruments and optical purposes. *Brazil*

VARIETIES OF CHALCEDONY

HALITE (ROCK SALT)
Sodium chloride. Man requires 12 pounds of salt a year. Apart from its use in food seasoning and preserving, salt is chiefly used by the chemical industry.

ONYX
An agate with regular bands in sharply contrasted colors.

CHRYSOPRASE
Apple-green variety colored by nickel oxide.

CARNELIAN
Reddish variety colored by ferric oxide.

AGATE
Grayish variety in which irregular bands conform to shape of original cavity. Easily stained and used for umbrella handles, brooches, etc., also in laboratory equipment.

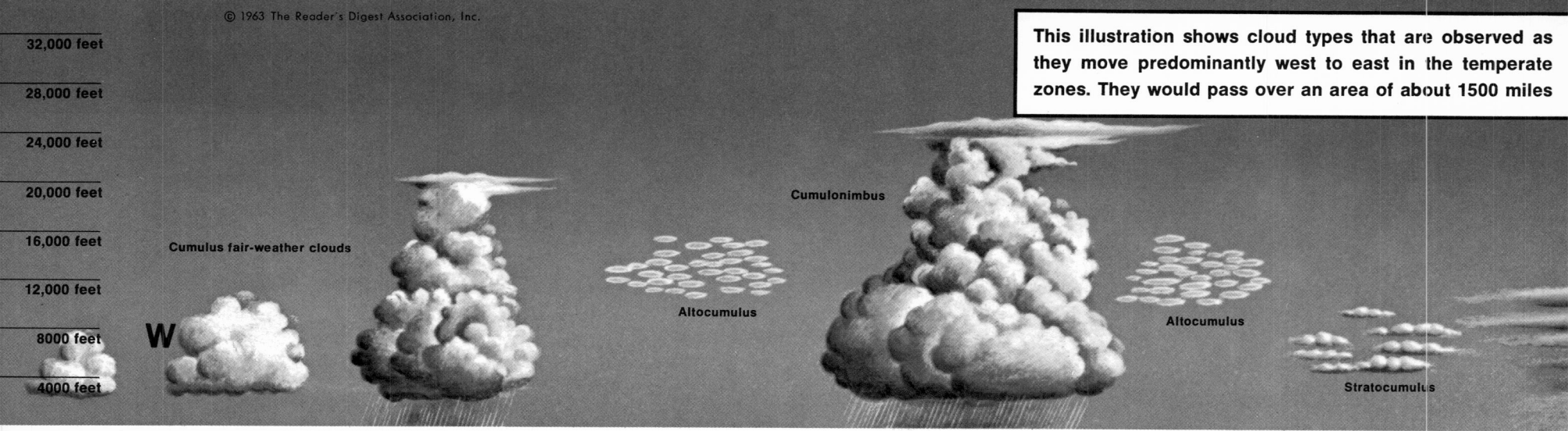

This illustration shows cloud types that are observed as they move predominantly west to east in the temperate zones. They would pass over an area of about 1500 miles

32,000 feet
28,000 feet
24,000 feet
20,000 feet
16,000 feet
12,000 feet
8000 feet
4000 feet

Cumulonimbus

Cumulus fair-weather clouds

Altocumulus

Altocumulus

Stratocumulus

W

INTERMITTENT RAIN SHOWERS   THUNDERSTORMS   ADVANCING COLD FRONT   WARM AIR MASS

PRESSURE ZONES (January)

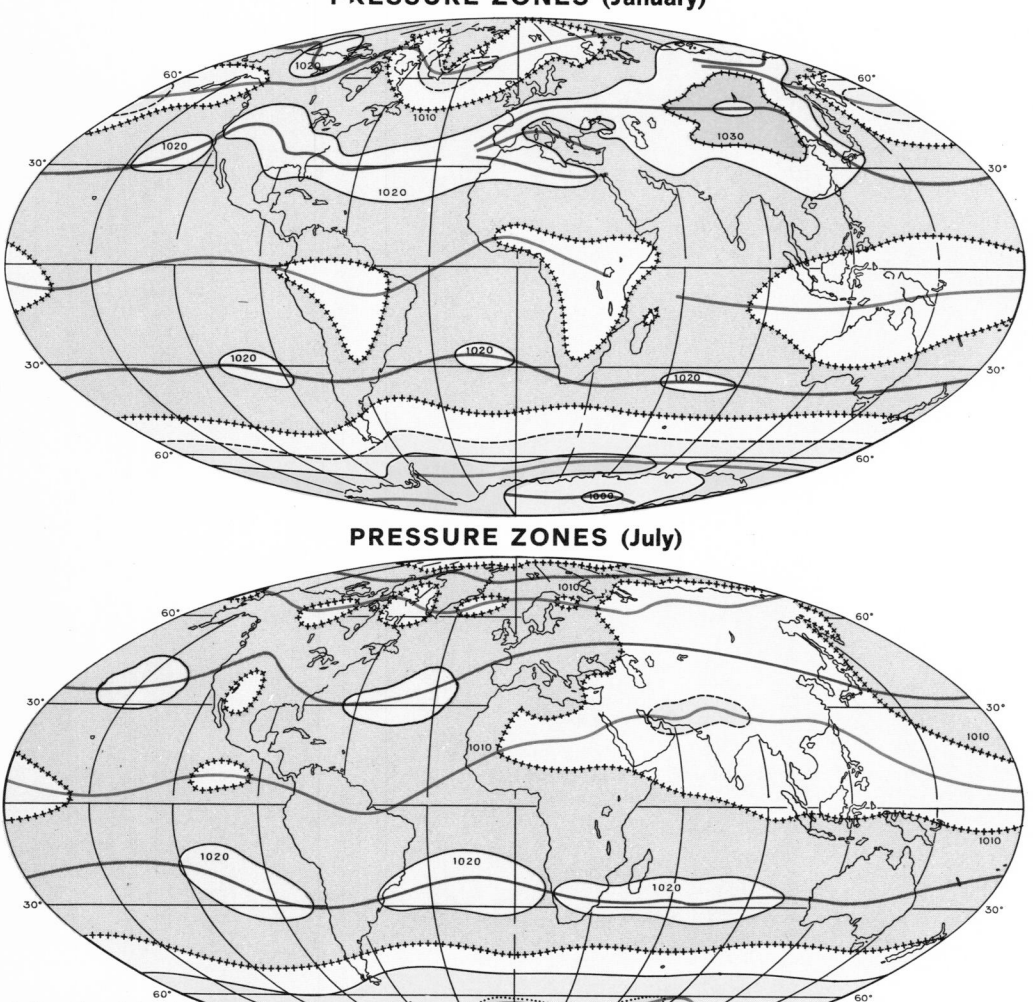

PRESSURE ZONES (July)

Average U.S. pressure at sea level: 1015 millibars
(29.9 inches of barometric pressure)
Yellow and green areas: high-pressure areas

Shades of pink: low-pressure areas
Red lines: join minimum-pressure points of longitude
Blue lines: join maximum-pressure points of longitude

Ice-Cap Blizzards
Canadian Blizzards
Helm Winds
Chinook Winds
For Wi
Mistral Winds
Norther Winds
Levanter Winds
Siroce Wind
Norte Winds
Harmattan Winds
Pampero Winds
Polar Winds

CHART OF TROPICAL CYC

Many local atmospheric phenomena exist which are brought about by particular local conditions. In the low latitudes where there are high temperatures and great humidity, whirling movements may be produced which create violent storms known as tropical cyclones (see circled areas). Then there are the hot dry winds that come from mountains—the Chinook in the Rockies, the Foehn in Switzerland, the Berg Winds in Africa. In contrast are the cold mountain winds—in Europe the Helms,

HOW HOT IS IT?

ARCTIC OCEAN
Arctic Circle
NORTH AMERICA
EUROPE
ASIA
Gobi Desert
Great Western Desert
Mississippi
ATLANTIC
Sahara
Thar Desert
Yangtze
Arabian Desert
PACIFIC OCEAN
AFRICA
Amazon
Equator
SOUTH AMERICA
Congo
INDIAN OCEAN
Atacama Desert
Kalahari Desert
AUSTRALIA
Patagonian Desert
Australian Desert
Equator

WINKEL'S 'TRIPEL' PROJECTION

ALWAYS COLD
WARM SUMMER
    COLD WINTER
HOT SUMMER
    COLD WINTER
COOL SUMMER
    MILD WINTER
HOT SUMMER
    WARM WINTER
ALWAYS HOT

Almost all of our heat comes from the Sun. Therefore the more vertical the Sun's position, the more heat we receive. Air is warmed chiefly by contact with the Earth's surface. The sea both warms and parts with its heat more slowly, so that climates near oceans are more equable than those inland. The highest tempera-tures have been recorded in the Sahara, the lowest in Siberia and the Antarctic.

The heat of the Tropics is somewhat distributed by ocean currents and winds. Thanks to the Gulf Stream and prevailing southeasterly winds, the average tempera-ture of the British Isles is 50°F.; Labra-dor, in the same latitude, averages 32°F.

PATTERNS

THE CLIMATES OF THE WORLD vary mostly according to latitude. Within the Tropics the climate remains fairly stable, but elsewhere climates are seasonal because of the twice-yearly swing of the Sun across the Equator.

From the strength of the winds, we know that the atmosphere has weight; where the atmosphere has piled up, it tends to flow outward on the surface of the Earth, just as water would do, and so becomes a wind. The principal pressure zones on the Earth (see *Pressure Zones* maps) are responsible for a continuous flow of air toward the Equator and toward the Poles, but these flows are not due south or due north, because of the rotation of the Earth. This eastward rotation de-flects winds toward the right in the North-ern Hemisphere and toward the left south of the Equator. As a result, the Trade Winds in the Northern Hemisphere blow from the northeast and the southern Trades from the southeast (see *Dominant Winds* maps). In higher latitudes, how-ever, the winds flow from the west and are known as the Prevailing Westerlies.

The flow of winds is also influenced by the distribution of lands and seas, for in summer temperatures are higher and

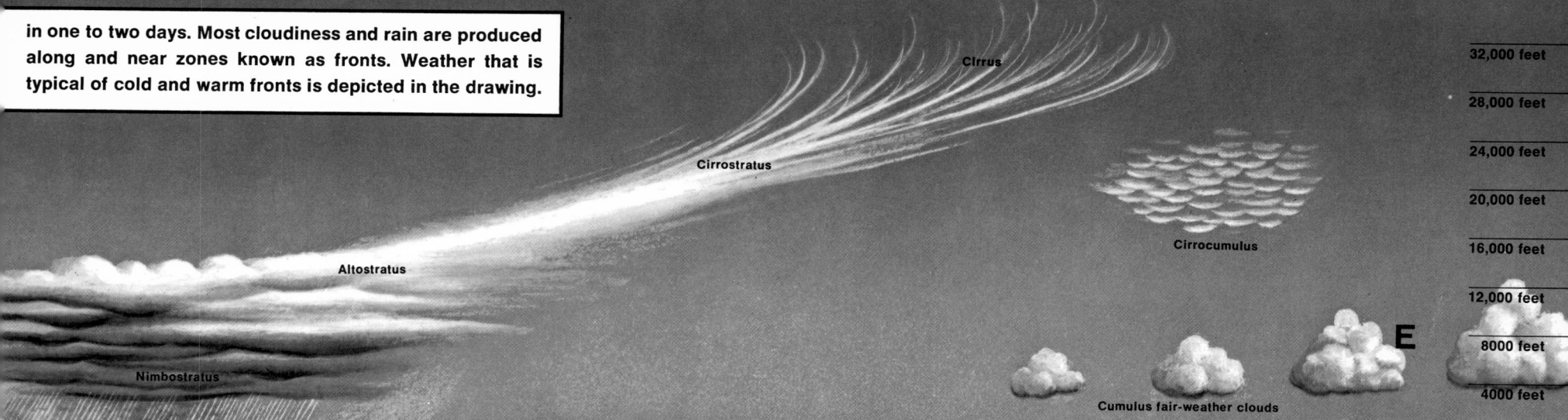

in one to two days. Most cloudiness and rain are produced along and near zones known as fronts. Weather that is typical of cold and warm fronts is depicted in the drawing.

Cirrus

Cirrostratus

Cirrocumulus

Altostratus

E

Nimbostratus

Cumulus fair-weather clouds

32,000 feet
28,000 feet
24,000 feet
20,000 feet
16,000 feet
12,000 feet
8000 feet
4000 feet

PROLONGED WARM-FRONT RAIN   ADVANCING WARM FRONT   COLD AIR MASS

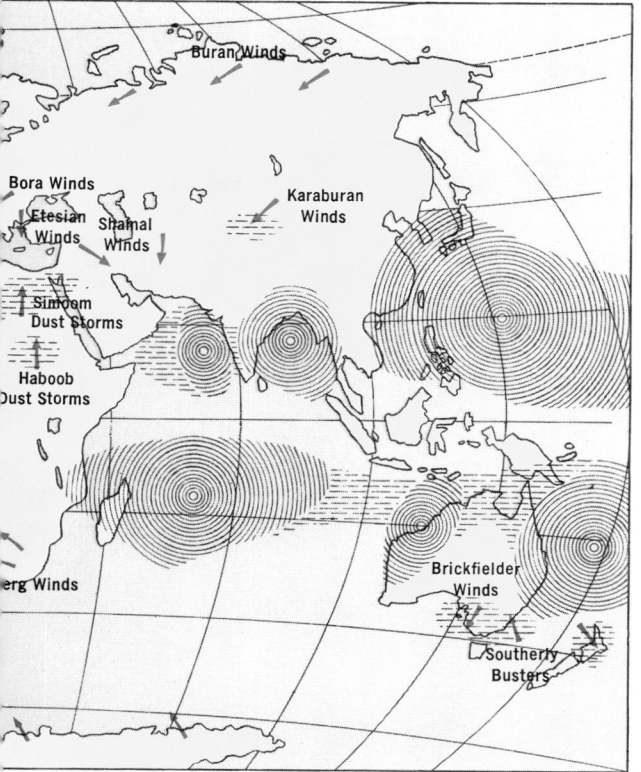

Buran Winds
Bora Winds
Etesian Winds
Shamal Winds
Karaburan Winds
Simoom Dust Storms
Haboob Dust Storms
...erg Winds
Brickfielder Winds
Southerly Busters

...ONES AND LOCAL WINDS

Bora, Mistral, Etesians and Levanters; in Asia the Buran and Karaburan; in the Middle East the Shamal; in South America the Pampero; and in Australia the Southerly Busters. Other cold winds are the American Nortes and Northers. Local winds with snow include blizzards and Polar winds; hot winds originating in desert areas include the African Harmattan, Simoom, Haboob and Sirocco (the latter blowing from North Africa across to Italy) and the Australian Brickfielders.

DOMINANT WINDS (January)

DOMINANT WINDS (July)

© 1963 The Reader's Digest Association, Inc.

→ Northeast and Southeast Trade Winds
→ Monsoons (dry in January, wet in July)
→ Prevailing Westerlies
→ Other major winds
▬ Predominant path of Jet Streams
▬ Boundaries of Trade Winds

...OF CLIMATE

pressures are lower on land, and the reverse is true in winter. In summer the air above the land tends to rise, and surface winds flow in to take its place. This can be seen on a large scale in the Asiatic Monsoons: a wet Monsoon blows in from sea toward land in summer, and a dry Monsoon blows from land toward sea in winter (see *Dominant Winds* maps). On a more local scale onshore breezes develop along coastal areas during daytime hours. At night a reversal may take place as the land cools below the temperature of water.

Although the air moves primarily in a horizontal direction, it tends to rise and sink slowly. As the air rises its moisture is condensed, leading to the formation of clouds and, when conditions are right, to rain or snow. When the air sinks, it is slowly heated and cannot produce either clouds or precipitations, as in the desert regions near the Tropics and in the Polar regions (see *How Wet Is It?*). In temperate zones winds in the upper troposphere—30,000 to 45,000 feet—frequently gather into narrow bands called jet streams. At their cores, jet winds may reach speeds as high as 300 miles per hour on rare occasions. The general direction of the jet is from west to east.

HOW WET IS IT?

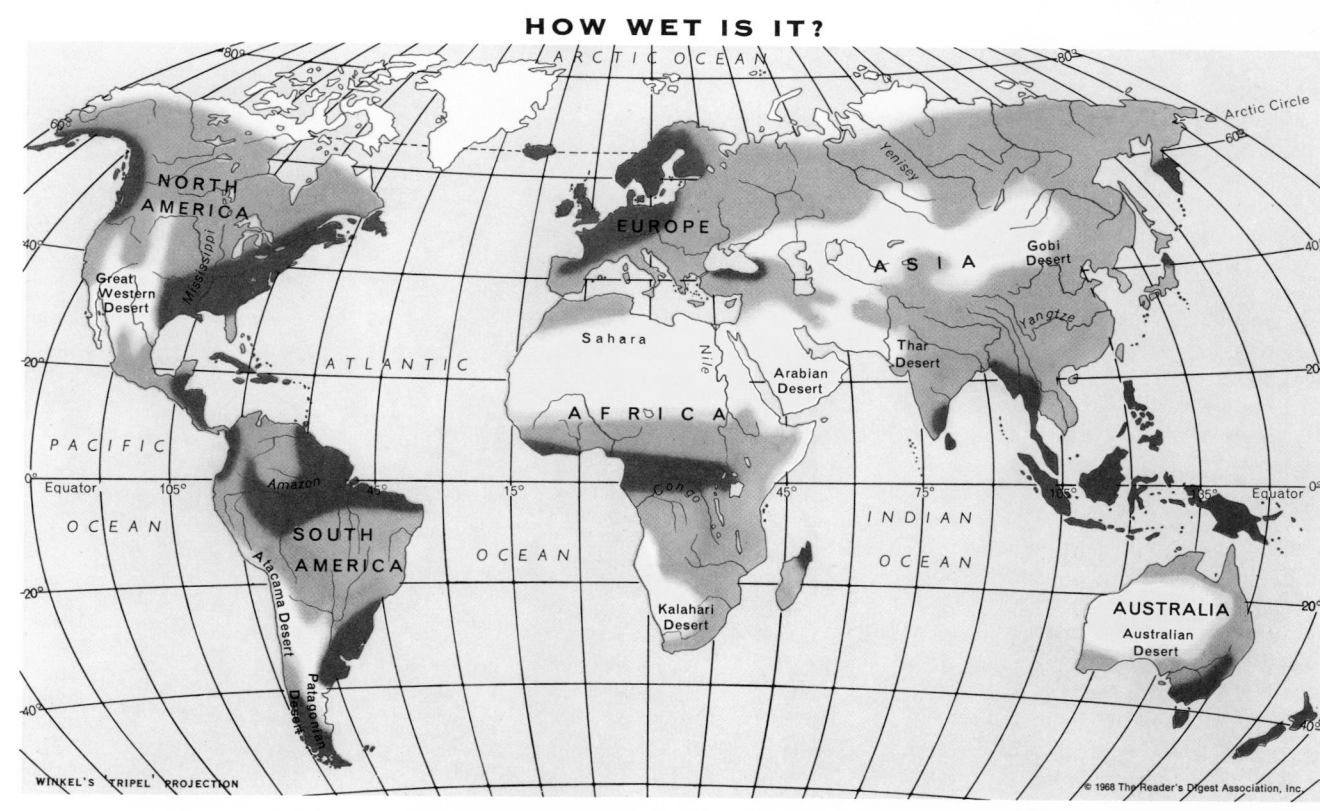

ARCTIC OCEAN
Arctic Circle
NORTH AMERICA
EUROPE
ASIA
Gobi Desert
Great Western Desert
Mississippi
Yenisey
ATLANTIC
Sahara
Nile
Thar Desert
Arabian Desert
Yangtze
PACIFIC OCEAN
AFRICA
Congo
Amazon
Equator
105°
15°
45°
75°
INDIAN OCEAN
Equator 0°
SOUTH AMERICA
OCEAN
Atacama Desert
Kalahari Desert
AUSTRALIA
Australian Desert
Patagonian Desert
WINKEL'S 'TRIPEL' PROJECTION
© 1968 The Reader's Digest Association, Inc.

LIGHT SNOW
SELDOM RAINY
LIGHT SEASONAL RAIN
HEAVY SEASONAL RAIN
RAINFALL IN EVERY MONTH

Air is most likely to be moist over the sea, especially where sea water temperatures are high. The wettest places are in the Tropics and where moist sea air rises on the windward slopes of high mountains. Rainfall belts move northward and southward with the Sun, so that some places, such as the Mediterranean, have most of

their rain in winter, while others, such as Monsoon areas, have more in summer.

The driest areas on Earth are where winds have blown for long distances over heated land, or, more locally, where a range of mountains extracts all the rain on its windward side, leaving what is called a rain shadow on its leeward side.

FRONTIERS OF VEGETATION

ABOUT ONE TENTH of the world's land surface is now under cultivation, little more than one acre per person. The rest, except for areas where nothing grows—such as the permanent ice fields—presents a vast pattern of grassland, woodland, forest and other types of natural vegetation.

This worldwide pattern of vegetation is closely keyed to another pattern—that of climate. Where similar plant cover grows, regardless of continent or hemisphere, a similar climate is usually found.

The world's heaviest and most vigorous growth of natural vegetation is in the rain forests of the tropics. Here thousands of species of trees and other plants flourish in wild, colorful profusion. As there is little seasonal change in this hot moist region, each plant has its own individual time schedule, so that there is continuous shedding of leaves, budding, flowering and fruit bearing.

In contrast are the trees of the seasonal forest (Nos. 3, 4, 5, 6, 13 and 14 on map) which extends from the tropics to the temperate and polar zones, both north and south. These provide the major supply of the world's soft timber—spruce, pine, fir. Trees of the seasonal forest become dormant during part of each year and, in the case of the deciduous species, lose all their leaves in one season.

Twenty percent of our world's land surface is covered by the dry lands we call deserts. Few of them are actually rainless, although some have to wait a year or so between showers. Despite popular belief, a desert is not an endless stretch of sand completely devoid of vegetation. Shrubs and grasses are part of the desert scene, and there are large areas of oasis, some covering hundreds of square miles, where land is extremely fertile.

A region frequently referred to as the cold desert lies far to the north (but not in the Antarctic). This is the tundra, which covers a great strip across Alaska, northern Canada and northern Eurasia. With long cold winters and short cool summers, the climate of the tundra is much too harsh for trees. The natural vegetation is a ground covering of grass, lichens and—sometimes—stunted brush. Similar conditions are found above the tree line in mountain ranges. The limitations that high latitude and high altitude place on vegetation are much alike. In the Rockies of the United States, trees do not grow above 11,000 feet; in Canada few trees grow above the latitude of the Arctic Circle.

Great grasslands stretch across the inland basins of the temperate lands—in the United States and Canada, Australia, Argentina, South Africa and the Soviet Union (Nos. 8 and 9 on map). These have long provided for generations of grazing animals, from buffalo and wild cattle to domesticated cattle and sheep.

Primitive man first demonstrated intelligence by taking direct advantage of the natural vegetation around him, as well as the wildlife it supported. He made use of leaves and wood for fire, and of reeds and saplings to build shelters. He satisfied his appetite first by collecting fruits and nuts, then learned to cultivate wild rice, yams, sugar cane and grains. He tapped trees for their juices and used barks and herbs to treat his ills. The seasonal changes of vegetation and the consequent movements of animal herds caused migrations of hunting tribes. In earliest historic times, areas of rich natural vegetation gave rise to industries such as lumbering and shipbuilding and to the founding of cities such as Tyre.

Man has misused the bounty of Earth's vegetation, too. In prehistoric time great sections of woodland and forest were laid waste by fire. Many of these areas were replaced by grasslands, changing the original pattern of the Earth's vegetation. Little of the "natural" vegetation of the world was left unchanged by primitive man.

Through ignorance and neglect, the land has been scarred and mutilated. Poor farming, including the removal of all trees in large areas, destroyed the natural structure of the soil, reducing it to dust, as in the great Dust Bowl, or creating new man-made deserts. Too often the soil has been washed off unprotected slopes by rain, leaving behind bare unproductive subsoil.

In the areas of yearly crops the maintenance of soil fertility is of the first importance. In North America and parts of South America, Europe, the U.S.S.R., South Africa and Australia, cultivation with machinery is pursued on a grand commercial scale. But in South and East Asia, where good land is scarce and precious and the crops must support some of the densest rural populations in the world, much of the work is done with simple hand tools.

Subsistence farming with crude tools and rudimentary techniques still predominates in many countries of Asia, Africa and Central America. Food is raised largely for home consumption, though some crops, such as cacao, oil palm and peanuts, are grown for sale in local markets.

Areas of shifting cultivation are found near and among the tropical rain forests. Here land is generally cleared indiscriminately for individual needs and, after being wastefully denuded of its fertility by primitive farming methods, is abandoned. Where land in tropical rain forests is successfully cleared and maintained, it is fertile and suitable for such plantation crops as rubber, tobacco, sugar, tea, oil palm and cacao.

Patterns of cultivation vary from country to country according to economic and social development. In the highly developed countries a relatively small number of workers can provide the entire community with enough of the right kinds of food. In the United States, 4,000,000 people (5.3 percent of the working population) are employed in cul-

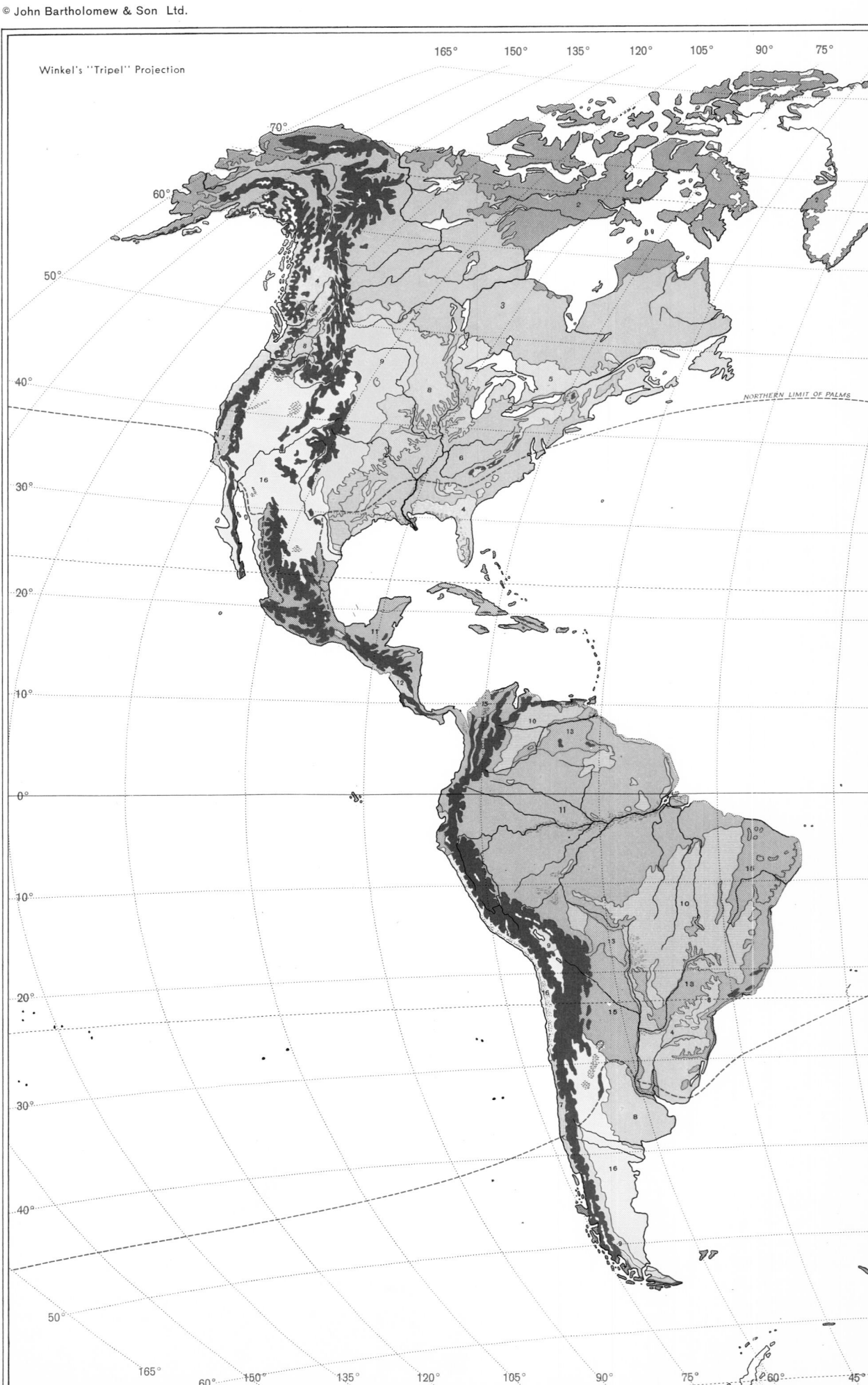

Winkel's "Tripel" Projection

NORTHERN LIMIT OF PALMS

tivation. On the other hand, in India 145,000,000 people (70 percent of the working population) employed in cultivation produce barely enough food for the population of that country.

Scientific and improved technical methods have been constantly applied throughout the world to improve the quality and yield of crops. Irrigation and water conservation in the American west have transformed land once infertile and semi-arid. Cotton is now grown extensively in the irrigated areas of southern California and other parts of the southwest. Forest conservation and reforestation are practiced in many lands, and silviculture, a new type of forest industry in which trees are grown on a crop basis, is vigorously pursued.

By such methods man is not only working to protect natural vegetation and rebuild depleted areas; he is also extending the frontiers of all cultivation. Because of the growing acceptance of scientific agriculture, the raising of food will probably prove no serious problem even in the face of the dramatic population explosion.

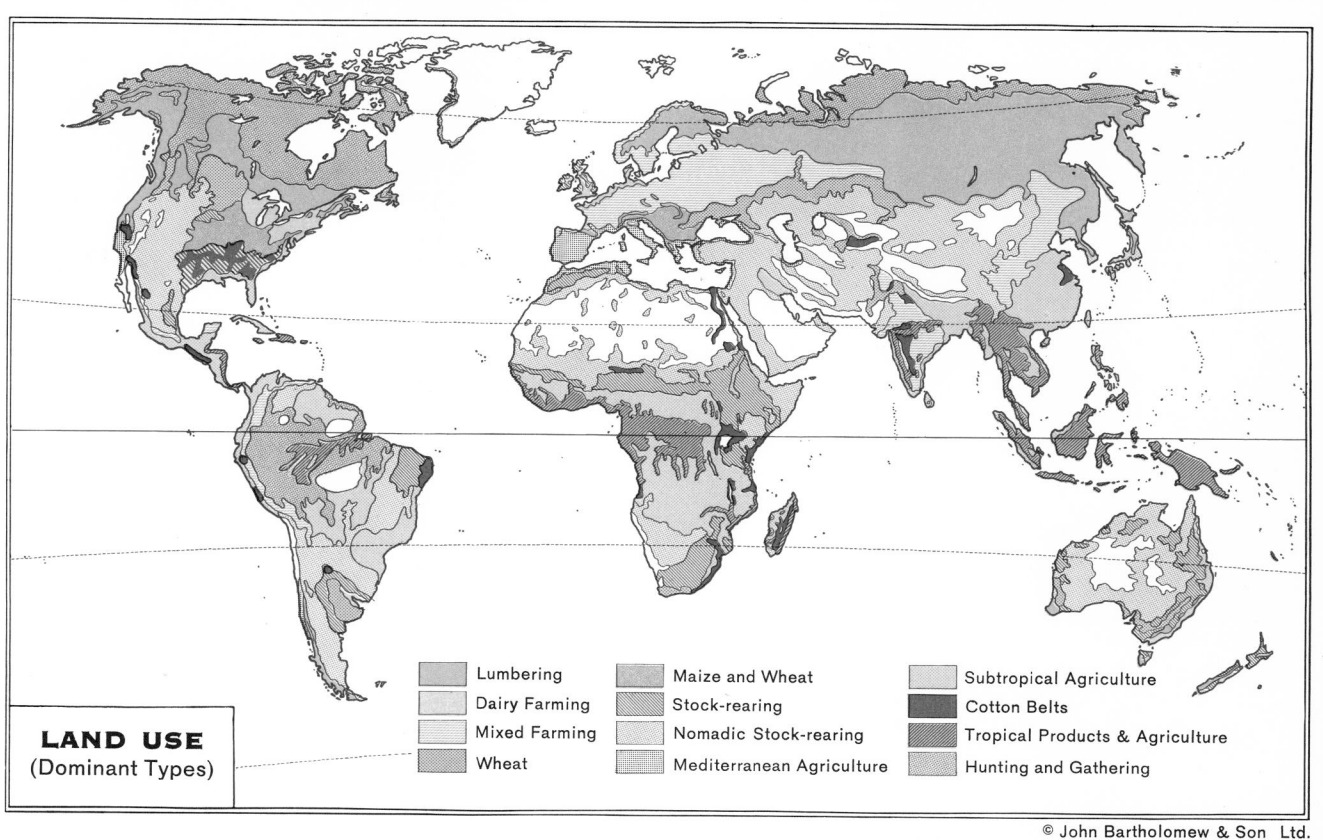

LAND USE
(Dominant Types)
Lumbering
Dairy Farming
Mixed Farming
Wheat
Maize and Wheat
Stock-rearing
Nomadic Stock-rearing
Mediterranean Agriculture
Subtropical Agriculture
Cotton Belts
Tropical Products & Agriculture
Hunting and Gathering

TYPES OF NATURAL VEGETATION
1 Mountain Vegetation
2 Tundra (Moss and Lichen)
3 Northern Forest ("Taiga"—Spruce, Larch)
4 Conifer Forest (Pine)
5 Mixed Forest (Mid-Latitudes) (Broadleaf and Conifer)
6 Broadleaf Forest (Deciduous)
7 Mediterranean Scrub (Citrus, Olive, Agave, etc.)
8 Prairie (Long Grass)
9 Steppe (Short Grass)
10 Savanna (Grass and Scrub)
11 Tropical Rain Forest
12 Monsoon Forest (Moist Deciduous)
13 Dry Tropical Forest (Semi-Deciduous)
14 Subtropical Forest (Broadleaf Evergreen)
15 Dry Tropical Scrub & Thorn Forest
16 Desert Vegetation (Drought-resistant plants)
? Natural Type uncertain
Sand
Stone
Salt
Desert (No Vegetation)
Mangroves
Swamps
SOUTHERN LIMIT OF PALMS
WALLACE'S LINE
WEBER'S LINE

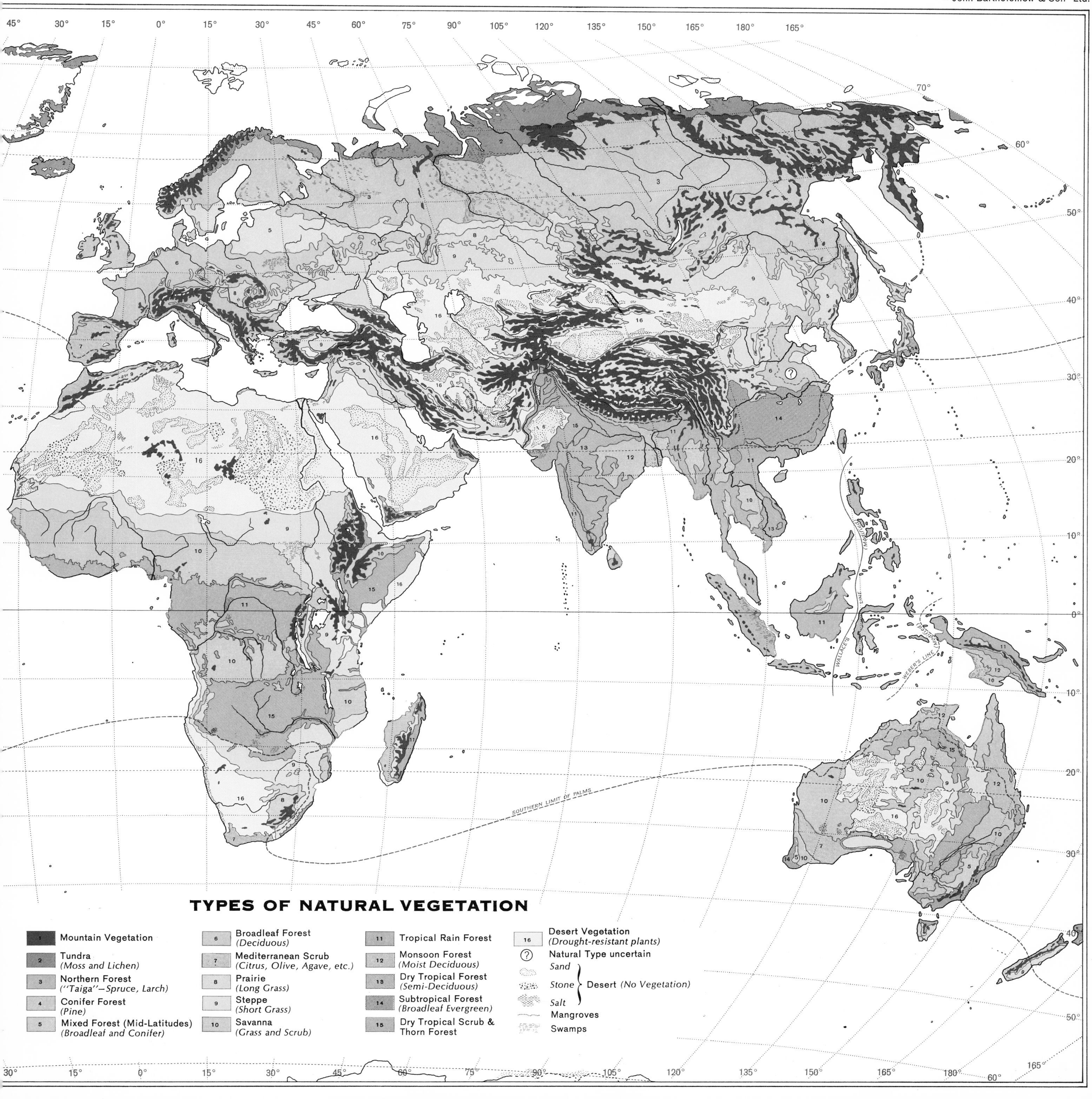

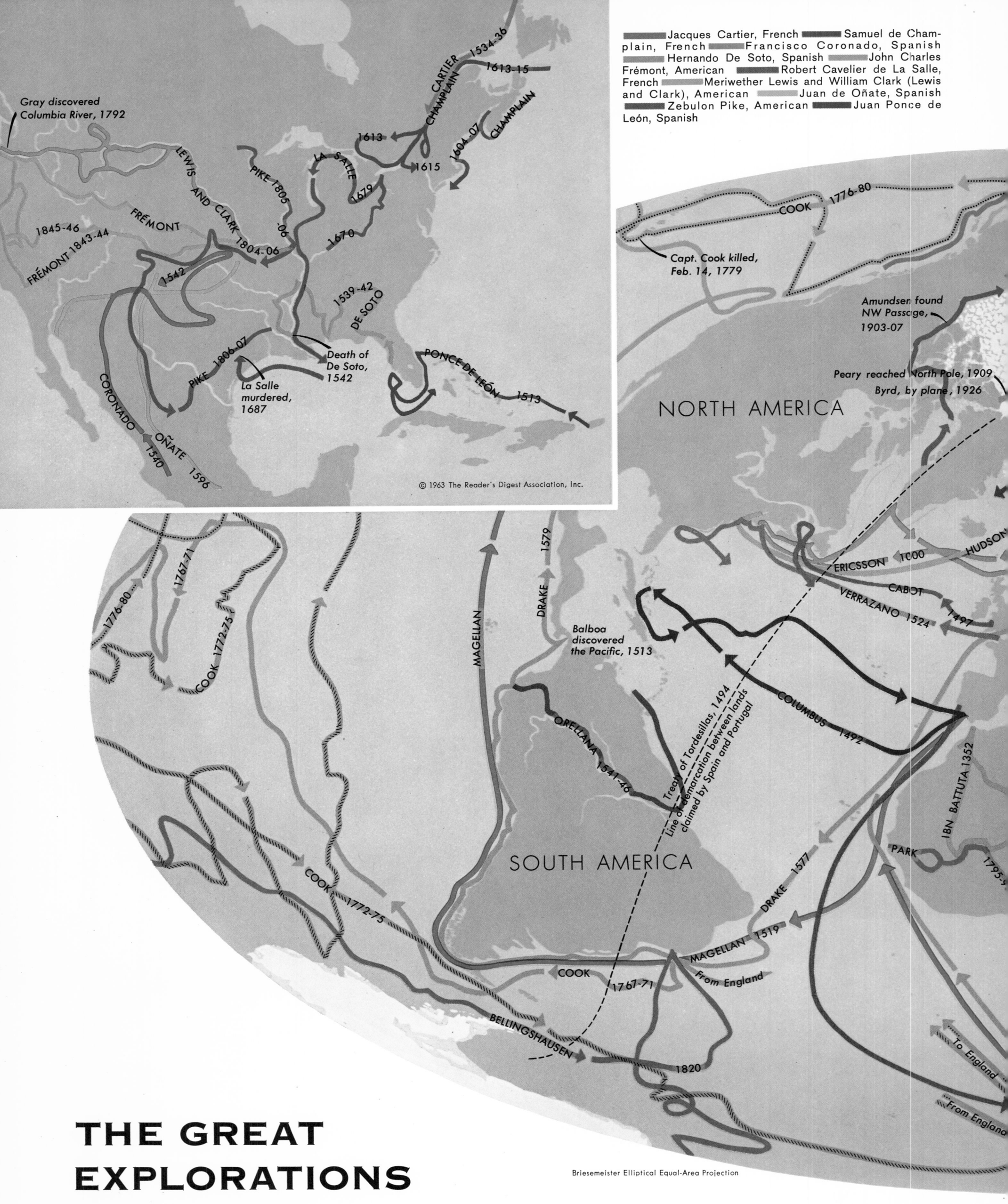

Gray discovered Columbia River, 1792

LEWIS AND CLARK 1804-06
PIKE 1805
1845-46
FRÉMONT
FRÉMONT 1843-44
1542
PIKE 1806-07
CORONADO 1540
OÑATE 1596

CARTIER 1534-36
1613-15
CHAMPLAIN
1604-07 CHAMPLAIN
1613
LA SALLE
1615
1679
1670
1539-42 DE SOTO
Death of De Soto, 1542
La Salle murdered, 1687
PONCE DE LEÓN 1513

COOK 1776-80
Capt. Cook killed, Feb. 14, 1779
Amundsen found NW Passage, 1903-07
Peary reached North Pole, 1909
Byrd, by plane, 1926

NORTH AMERICA

1767-71
1776-80
COOK 1772-75
COOK 1772-75
COOK 1767-71

1579
DRAKE
MAGELLAN
Balboa discovered the Pacific, 1513
ORELLANA 1541-46
Treaty of Tordesillas, 1494
Line of demarcation between lands claimed by Spain and Portugal
COLUMBUS 1492
DRAKE 1577
MAGELLAN 1519
From England
ERICSSON 1000
HUDSON
CABOT 1497
VERRAZANO 1524
IBN BATTUTA 1352
PARK 1795
To England
From England

SOUTH AMERICA

BELLINGSHAUSEN
1820

Briesemeister Elliptical Equal-Area Projection

THE GREAT EXPLORATIONS

MAN'S CURIOSITY and his delight in widening his world — for adventure or gain — have throughout history drawn him to its remotest regions.

As early as 700 B.C., Phoenician traders ventured down the west coast of Africa. Alexander the Great reached India about 330 B.C.; the Greeks and Romans knew the Baltic by the time of Christ; a thousand years later Ericsson, the Norseman, was probably the first European to set foot on North America. In the thirteenth century the Italian Marco Polo, the greatest traveler of his era, made his journeys to the Far East.

But it was in the 1400s that the great Age of Discovery began. Within 30 years all the known oceans were crossed. Columbus voyaged to America in 1492, and Da Gama reached India in 1498. Early in the sixteenth century Balboa discovered the Pacific Ocean, and Magellan's ship sailed around the whole world. In succeeding years many intrepid European explorers, under the flags of many countries, laid claim to land in the Americas and explored some of the New World's mightiest rivers: the St. Lawrence, Mississippi and Amazon.

Then came the Age of Scientific Discovery, an era not yet ended. In the quest for knowledge Captain Cook made three great voyages at the time of the American Revolution.

Exploration by land was slower. It was not till the 1800s that men such as Lewis and Clark, Pike and Frémont opened the American West. The nineteenth century also saw the penetration of Africa by explorers including Nachtigal, Stanley and the remarkable Livingstone. The long-sought Northeast and Northwest Passages through the Arctic seas were found at last — the latter by Amundsen in 1905.

In the early twentieth century the polar regions

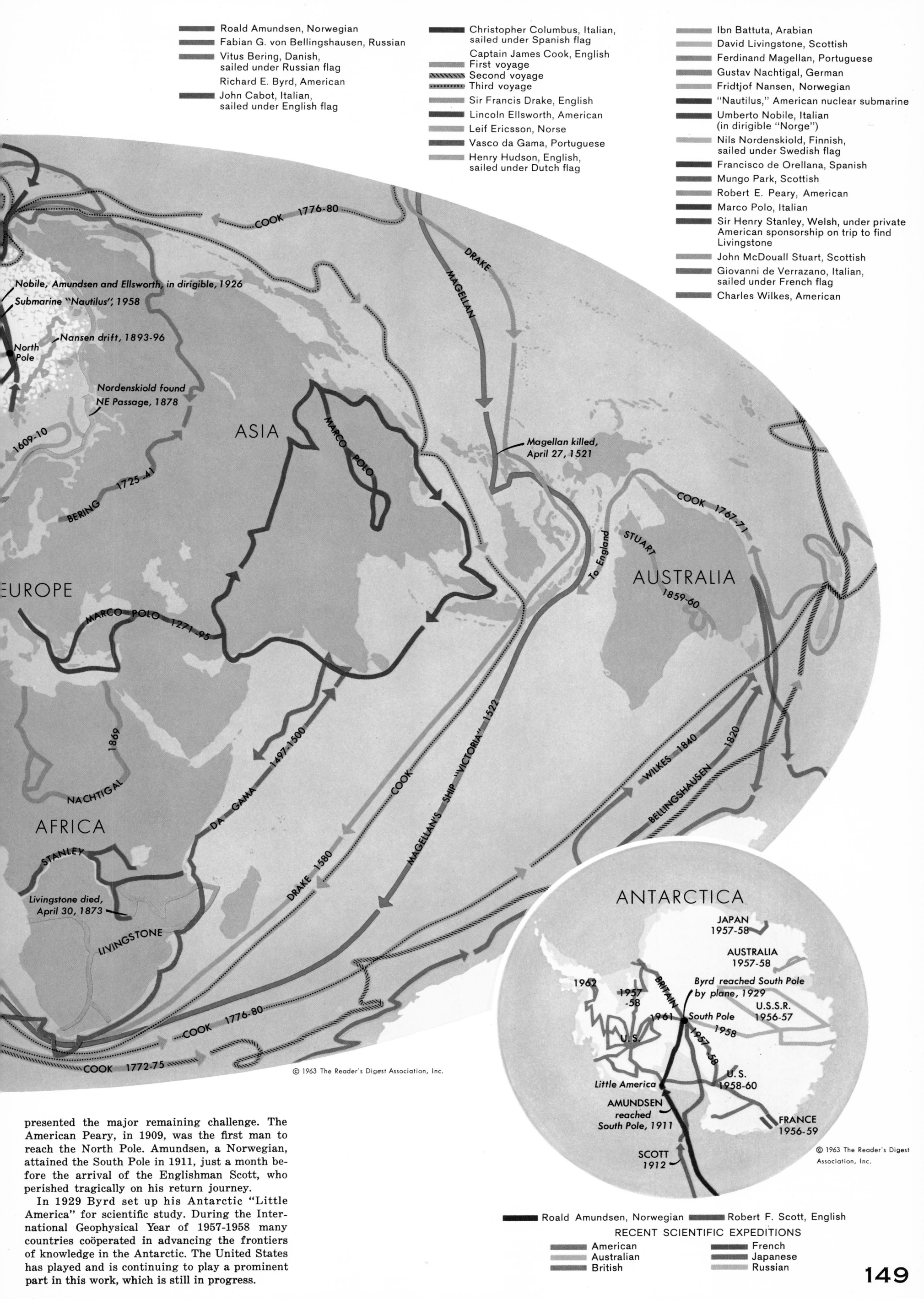

Roald Amundsen, Norwegian
Fabian G. von Bellingshausen, Russian
Vitus Bering, Danish, sailed under Russian flag
Richard E. Byrd, American
John Cabot, Italian, sailed under English flag

Christopher Columbus, Italian, sailed under Spanish flag
Captain James Cook, English
First voyage
Second voyage
Third voyage
Sir Francis Drake, English
Lincoln Ellsworth, American
Leif Ericsson, Norse
Vasco da Gama, Portuguese
Henry Hudson, English, sailed under Dutch flag

Ibn Battuta, Arabian
David Livingstone, Scottish
Ferdinand Magellan, Portuguese
Gustav Nachtigal, German
Fridtjof Nansen, Norwegian
"Nautilus," American nuclear submarine
Umberto Nobile, Italian (in dirigible "Norge")
Nils Nordenskiold, Finnish, sailed under Swedish flag
Francisco de Orellana, Spanish
Mungo Park, Scottish
Robert E. Peary, American
Marco Polo, Italian
Sir Henry Stanley, Welsh, under private American sponsorship on trip to find Livingstone
John McDouall Stuart, Scottish
Giovanni de Verrazano, Italian, sailed under French flag
Charles Wilkes, American

COOK 1776-80

Nobile, Amundsen and Ellsworth, in dirigible, 1926
Submarine "Nautilus", 1958
Nansen drift, 1893-96
North Pole
Nordenskiold found NE Passage, 1878

DRAKE
MAGELLAN

1609-10
BERING 1725-41

ASIA
MARCO POLO

Magellan killed, April 27, 1521

COOK 1767-71

EUROPE
MARCO POLO 1271-95

To England
STUART

AUSTRALIA
1859-60

1869
NACHTIGAL

DA GAMA 1497-1500

COOK

MAGELLAN'S SHIP "VICTORIA" 1522

WILKES 1840

BELLINGSHAUSEN 1820

AFRICA
STANLEY

Livingstone died, April 30, 1873

LIVINGSTONE

DRAKE 1580

COOK 1776-80

COOK 1772-75

© 1963 The Reader's Digest Association, Inc.

ANTARCTICA

JAPAN 1957-58
AUSTRALIA 1957-58
Byrd reached South Pole by plane, 1929
1962
1957-58
BRITAIN
1961
South Pole
1958
U.S.S.R. 1956-57
U.S.
1957-58
Little America
U.S. 1958-60
AMUNDSEN reached South Pole, 1911
FRANCE 1956-59
SCOTT 1912

© 1963 The Reader's Digest Association, Inc.

presented the major remaining challenge. The American Peary, in 1909, was the first man to reach the North Pole. Amundsen, a Norwegian, attained the South Pole in 1911, just a month before the arrival of the Englishman Scott, who perished tragically on his return journey.

In 1929 Byrd set up his Antarctic "Little America" for scientific study. During the International Geophysical Year of 1957-1958 many countries coöperated in advancing the frontiers of knowledge in the Antarctic. The United States has played and is continuing to play a prominent part in this work, which is still in progress.

Roald Amundsen, Norwegian
Robert F. Scott, English
RECENT SCIENTIFIC EXPEDITIONS
American
Australian
British
French
Japanese
Russian

149

2000 A.D.

2 Billion

1 Billion

WORLD POPULATION

THE NUMBER OF PEOPLE who have ever lived on earth probably exceeds 76 billion. Over 3 billion inhabit it today, more than ever before at any one time. Throughout most of history, world population increased very slowly. Poverty, disease and disorder permitted growth from perhaps 300 million people at the beginning of the Christian era to only 550 million by 1650. Then, however, the population doubled in less than two centuries, and by 1930 it had almost doubled again, reaching 2 billion. According to United Nations forecasts, from today's figure it will grow to more than 6 billion by the year 2000. This phenomenal expansion, the result of widespread improvements in food production and increased medical knowledge, is shown on the graph at the right.

1965

1950

MIGRATIONS SINCE 1650 A.D.

1900

1850

© 1963 The Reader's Digest Association, Inc.

1800

1750

1700

MOVEMENTS OF POPULATIONS occur mainly for political, religious and economic reasons. The more important migrations of the past 300 years are shown above. The arrows mark the areas of origin and the destinations but are not intended to indicate the routes.

Europeans to U.S.A. During the 17th century about 500,000 people emigrated from Great Britain to settle principally in New England and Virginia (although some settled in the West Indies). They were followed in the 18th century by three times that number (mainly Irish and Scots). In the 19th century Germans, Italians, Austro-Hungarians and Scandinavians helped to increase the flow. From 1900 to 1920 a total of 14,500,000 from many countries were admitted (1,042,000 in 1907 — a peak for any one year). In the next 30 years the tide slackened (only 5,500,000 were admitted), but from 1951 to 1959 the rate of immigration accelerated to reach a total of 2,250,000.

Europeans to Canada During the 18th century Quebec Province was settled by the French, but later the majority of immigrants to Canada came from Great Britain. Until 1900 settlement was slow, but from 1900 to 1920 about 2,250,000 people entered the country, to be followed by 1,500,000 in the next 30 years. Thereafter immigration greatly increased, with more than 1,500,000 people settling in Canada in the period from 1951 to 1959.

Europeans to South and Central America Spaniards, Portuguese and Italians have predominated among the nearly 20,000,000 Europeans who have migrated to Central and South America during the last three centuries, with Argentina, Brazil and Panama as their principal goals. Immigration was slow until the 1890s, but reached its peak before 1914. From 1900 to 1920 about 3,000,000 settled in Argentina, about 1,500,000 in Brazil.

The Slave Trade Traffic in slaves from West Africa began in the 16th century, reaching its peak in the late 18th and early 19th centuries. About 20,000,000 slaves were taken, chiefly to the tobacco, sugar and coffee plantations of the Caribbean and Brazil. Many, perhaps a million, were moved on to the cotton fields of the southern United States.

Europeans to Africa In the 16th century the French established trading posts in Algeria, but large-scale settlement did not begin there until French rule was established in 1830. Today about 15 percent of the population of this newly independent nation is of European ancestry. Few Europeans settled in Central Africa before 1880, when diamond deposits were discovered in Rhodesia. After that the British (nearly 300,000) settled in Rhodesia and the Belgians in the Congo in large numbers. In East Africa, which received settlers from 1906 on, nearly 100,000 Europeans took up permanent residence, principally in Kenya, Uganda and Tanzania. In South Africa the first Europeans to settle were the Dutch in 1652. By the end of the 18th century emigrants from the British Isles began arriving in great numbers, and in the 19th century the establishment of British rule in Cape Colony was followed by the revolt of the Dutch farmers (Boers) and their Great Trek to the Transvaal. In this century there have been mass movements of South Africans into mining and industrial areas.

Europeans to Australia and New Zealand The first Europeans settled in Australia in 1788, but immigration was slow until the Gold Rush period between 1850 and 1860. After 1860 it slowed down again until the turn of the century. Between 1901 and 1920 about 400,000 emigrated to Australia, principally from the United Kingdom, but since 1945 more than a million people from many European countries have settled in Australia. Emigration to New Zealand has followed much the same pattern but on a smaller scale.

Chinese Migration From the middle of the 19th century onward the Chinese migrated in large numbers, chiefly to Malaya, Burma and the East Indies. In the 1920s there were mass movements to Mongolia, Manchuria and Asiatic Russia. More than 9,500,000 were abroad in 1948, mostly in Asia; more than 100,000 were in the United States.

Jewish Migration Intermittent migrations of Jews from many countries into Palestine took place after the First World War, but since the formation of the State of Israel in 1948 nearly 1.5 million European Jews have arrived.

Internal Migration in the U.S.A. From the end of the 18th century, when pioneers started the movement westward, migration to the west has continued, as well as movement on the Atlantic seaboard to the south. California is now the nation's most populous state. The population of Florida has increased by more than 75 percent. Many Negroes have moved northward from the southern states, and Puerto Ricans have come to the continental U.S. to settle in cities in the eastern states.

Internal Migration in the U.S.S.R. Since 1918 great movements of European Russians to the east of the Urals have taken place. The Second World War accelerated industrial growth beyond the Urals, and a feature of the recent Five Year Plans has been the movement to and the settling of people in Kazakhstan and farther east.

150

1650 A.D.

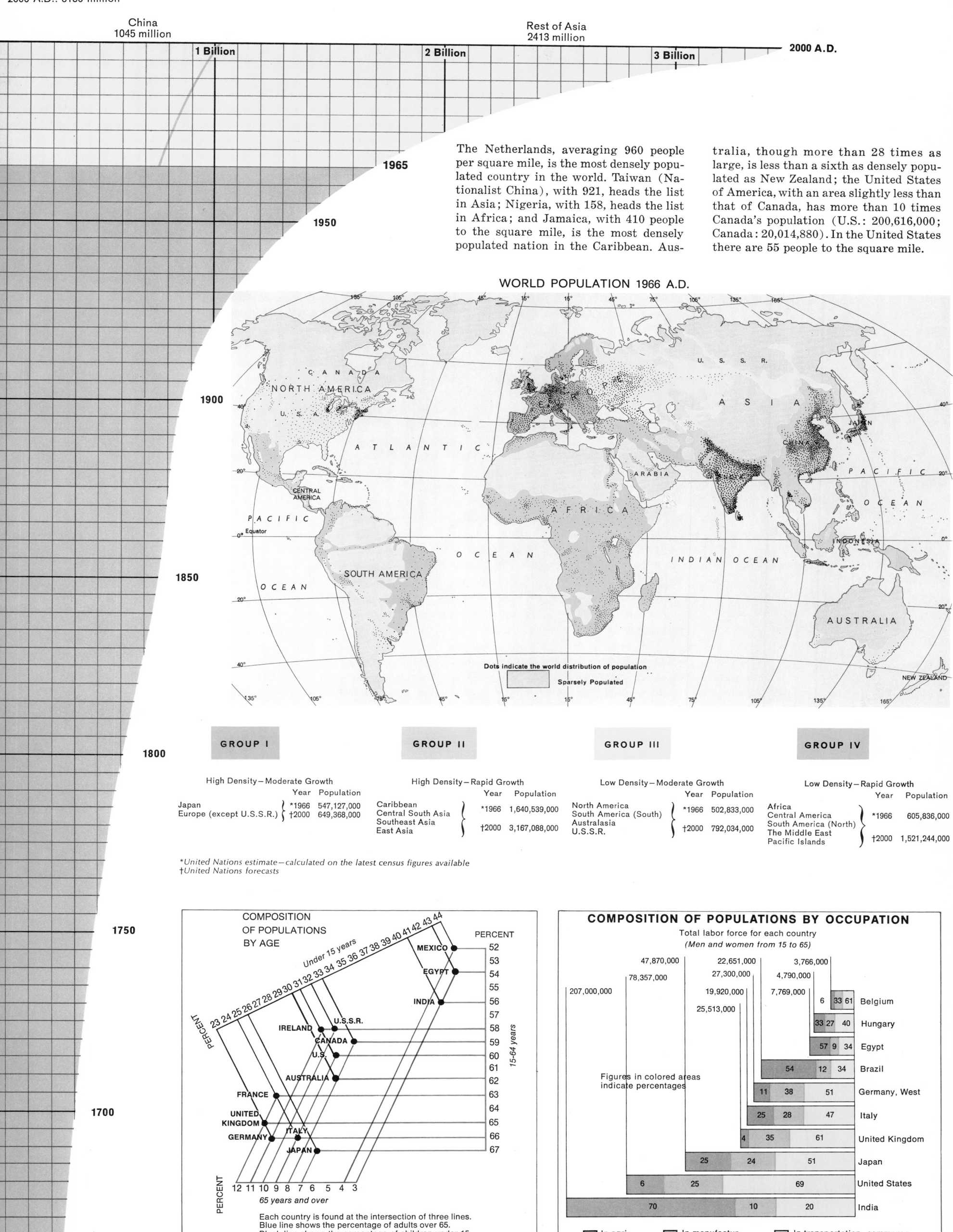

1650 A.D. UNTIL 2000

2000 A.D.: 6130 million

China
1045 million

Rest of Asia
2413 million

1 Billion

2 Billion

3 Billion

2000 A.D.

1965

1950

The Netherlands, averaging 960 people per square mile, is the most densely populated country in the world. Taiwan (Nationalist China), with 921, heads the list in Asia; Nigeria, with 158, heads the list in Africa; and Jamaica, with 410 people to the square mile, is the most densely populated nation in the Caribbean. Australia, though more than 28 times as large, is less than a sixth as densely populated as New Zealand; the United States of America, with an area slightly less than that of Canada, has more than 10 times Canada's population (U.S.: 200,616,000; Canada: 20,014,880). In the United States there are 55 people to the square mile.

WORLD POPULATION 1966 A.D.

Dots indicate the world distribution of population

Sparsely Populated

1900

1850

1800

GROUP I	GROUP II	GROUP III	GROUP IV
High Density—Moderate Growth	**High Density—Rapid Growth**	**Low Density—Moderate Growth**	**Low Density—Rapid Growth**

	Year	Population		Year	Population		Year	Population		Year	Population
Japan	*1966	547,127,000	Caribbean	*1966	1,640,539,000	North America	*1966	502,833,000	Africa	*1966	605,836,000
Europe (except U.S.S.R.)	†2000	649,368,000	Central South Asia	†2000	3,167,088,000	South America (South)	†2000	792,034,000	Central America	†2000	1,521,244,000
			Southeast Asia			Australasia			South America (North)		
			East Asia			U.S.S.R.			The Middle East		
									Pacific Islands		

*United Nations estimate—calculated on the latest census figures available
†United Nations forecasts

COMPOSITION OF POPULATIONS BY AGE

Under 15 years

PERCENT

23 24 25 26 27 28 29 30 31 32 33 34 35 36 37 38 39 40 41 42 43 44

PERCENT

52 53 54 55 56 57 58 59 60 61 62 63 64 65 66 67

15-64 years

MEXICO
EGYPT
INDIA
U.S.S.R.
IRELAND
CANADA
U.S.
AUSTRALIA
FRANCE
UNITED KINGDOM
ITALY
GERMANY
JAPAN

PERCENT

12 11 10 9 8 7 6 5 4 3

65 years and over

Each country is found at the intersection of three lines.
Blue line shows the percentage of adults over 65.
Black line shows the percentage of children under 15.
Red line shows the percentage of adults between 15 and 64.
Total of three figures for each country equals 100%.

© 1968 The Reader's Digest Association, Inc.

COMPOSITION OF POPULATIONS BY OCCUPATION

Total labor force for each country
(Men and women from 15 to 65)

				Year			

47,870,000   22,651,000   3,766,000
78,357,000   27,300,000   4,790,000
19,920,000   7,769,000
207,000,000   25,513,000

Figures in colored areas indicate percentages

	In agriculture	In manufacturing industries	In transportation, commerce, administration and professions
Belgium	6	33	61
Hungary	33	27	40
Egypt	57	9	34
Brazil	54	12	34
Germany, West	11	38	51
Italy	25	28	47
United Kingdom	4	35	61
Japan	25	24	51
United States	6	25	69
India	70	10	20

In agriculture   In manufacturing industries   In transportation, commerce, administration and professions

© 1968 The Reader's Digest Association, Inc.

1750

1700

1650 A.D.

151

FACTS ABOUT THE EARTH

Estimated age . . . at least 4,500,000,000 years
Area . . . . 196,950,769 sq. miles
Land surface . . . . . 57,469,928 sq. miles
Water surface (71% of
    total area) . . . . . 139,480,841 sq. miles

Equatorial circumference . . . . . 24,902 miles
Polar circumference . . . . . . 24,860 miles
Volume of the Earth . 260,000,000,000 cubic miles
Mass or weight . 6,586,242,250,000,000,000,000 tons
Highest point—Mount Everest . . . 29,028 feet

Lowest point—Shores of the Dead Sea,
Israel . . . . 1299 feet below sea level
Greatest ocean depth—
Marianas Trench off
Guam . . . . . . 36,198 feet below sea level

CONTINENTS

	Area (square miles)	Mean Elevation (feet)	Highest Elevation (feet)	Lowest Elevation (feet)	Highest Recorded Temperature	Lowest Recorded Temperature
AFRICA	11,500,000	1900	Mt. Kilimanjaro, Tanzania 19,340	Lake Assal, Fr. Somaliland 492 below sea level	el Azizia, Libya 136.4°F.	Semrir, Morocco −11.4°F.
ANTARCTICA	5,500,000	6000	Vinson Massif 16,863	Sea level	Esperanza, Palmer Peninsula 58.3°F.	Vostok −126.9°F.
ASIA	16,900,000	3000	Mt. Everest, Nepal—Tibet 29,028	Dead Sea, Israel 1299 below sea level	Jacobabad, Pakistan 127.1°F.	Oymyakon, U.S.S.R. −89.9°F.
AUSTRALIA	2,945,000	1000	Mt. Kosciusko, N.S. Wales 7316	Lake Eyre, South Australia 52 below sea level	Cloncurry, Queensland 127.5°F.	Charlotte Pass, N.S. Wales −8°F.
EUROPE	3,700,000	980	Mt. El'brus, U.S.S.R. 18,482	Caspian Sea, U.S.S.R. 92 below sea level	Seville, Spain 122°F.	Ust' Shchugor, U.S.S.R. −67.0°F.
NORTH AMERICA	9,390,000	2000	Mt. McKinley, Alaska 20,320	Death Valley, California 282 below sea level	Death Valley, California 134°F.	Snag, Yukon −81.0°F.
SOUTH AMERICA	6,850,000	1800	Mt. Aconcagua, Argentina 22,834	Valdés Peninsula, Argentina 131 below sea level	Rivadavia, Argentina 120.0°F.	Colonia Sarmiento, Argentina −27.4°F.

HIGHEST MOUNTAINS OF THE WORLD

AFRICA — *Feet*
Kilimanjaro, *Tanzania* . . 19,340
Kenya, *Kenya* 17,058
Margherita, *Congo—Uganda* 16,794
Ras Dashan, *Ethiopia* . . . 15,158
Meru, *Tanzania* 14,977

ANTARCTICA
Vinson Massif 16,863
Elizabeth 14,698
Kirkpatrick 14,600
Markham 14,270
Andrew Jackson 13,747

ASIA — *Feet*
Everest, *Nepal-Tibet* . . . 29,028
K2 (Godwin-Austen)
    Kashmir 28,250
Kangchenjunga, *Nepal-India* 28,146
Makalu, *Tibet—Nepal* . . 27,827
Lhotse, *Nepal* 26,923

EUROPE
El'brus, *U.S.S.R.* . . . 18,482
Shkhara, *U.S.S.R.* . . . 17,059
Dykh-Tau, *U.S.S.R.* . . . 17,054
Kashtan-Tau, *U.S.S.R.* . . 16,877

Dzhangi Tau, *U.S.S.R.* . . 16,565 — *Feet*
Kazbek, *U.S.S.R.* 16,554
Mont Blanc, *France* . . . 15,771
Monte Rosa, *Switzerland* . 15,203
Dom, *Switzerland* . . . 14,912
Weisshorn, *Switzerland* . 14,782

NORTH AMERICA
McKinley, *Alaska, U.S.* . . 20,320
Logan, *Canada* 19,850
Citlaltepetl, *Mexico* . . . 18,700
St. Elias, *Alaska, U.S.* . . 18,008
Popocatepetl, *Mexico* . . . 17,887

Foraker, *Alaska, U.S.* . . . 17,400 — *Feet*
Ixtaccihuatl, *Mexico* . . . 17,343
Lucania, *Canada* 17,150
King, *Canada* 17,130
Blackburn, *Alaska, U.S.* . . 16,523

SOUTH AMERICA
Aconcagua, *Argentina* . . 22,834
Illimani, *Bolivia* 22,579
Bonete, *Argentina* 22,546
Ojos del Salado,
    Argentina-Chile 22,539
Tupungato, *Argentina-Chile* 22,310

GREATEST OCEANS AND SEAS OF THE WORLD

	Area (sq. miles)	Average Depth (feet)	Greatest Depth (feet)
Pacific Ocean . . .	63,985,000	14,040	36,198
Atlantic Ocean . .	31,529,000	12,880	30,180
Indian Ocean . . .	28,357,000	13,000	24,444
Arctic Ocean . . .	5,541,600	4200	17,500
Mediterranean Sea .	1,145,000	4500	15,564
South China Sea . .	895,000	5400	16,456
Bering Sea	878,000	1665	13,420
Caribbean Sea . . .	750,000	8400	23,750
Gulf of Mexico . .	700,000	4700	12,426
Okhotsk, Sea of . .	582,000	3000	12,621
East China Sea . .	480,000	610	8920
Yellow Sea	480,000	160	348
Hudson Bay	472,000	440	846
Japan, Sea of . . .	405,000	4835	13,241
North Sea	221,000	180	2165
Red Sea	178,000	1490	9301
Black Sea	168,000	4300	7362
Baltic Sea	158,000	221	1400

LONGEST RIVERS OF THE WORLD

Miles
Nile, *Africa* 4132
Amazon, *South America* 3900
Mississippi—Missouri—Red Rock, *U.S.A.* 3860
Ob-Irtysh, *Asia* 3461
Yangtze, *China* 3430
Yellow (Hwang Ho), *China* 2903
Congo, *Africa* 2900

Miles
Amur, *Asia* 2802
Lena, *U.S.S.R.* . . . 2653
Mackenzie, *Canada* . . 2635
Mekong, *Asia* 2600
Niger, *Africa* 2590
Yenisey, *U.S.S.R.* . . . 2566
Paraná, *South America* . 2450

Miles
Murray—Darling, *Australia* 2310
Volga, *U.S.S.R.* 2293
Madeira, *South America* . 2060
Indus, *Asia* 1980
Purus, *South America* . . 1900
St. Lawrence, *Canada* . . 1900
Rio Grande, *U.S.A.* . . . 1885

Miles
Brahmaputra, *Asia* . . . 1800
Orinoco, *South America* . 1800
São Francisco, *S. America* 1800
Yukon, *Alaska, U.S.A.* . . 1800
Danube, *Europe* 1770
Salween, *Burma—China* . . 1730
Euphrates, *Asia* 1675

LARGEST LAKES OF THE WORLD

Sq. Miles
Caspian Sea, *U.S.S.R.—Iran (salt)* . 151,123
Superior, *U.S.A.—Canada* 31,820
Victoria, *Africa* 26,828
Aral, *U.S.S.R. (salt)* 26,525
Huron, *U.S.A.—Canada* 23,010
Michigan, *U.S.A.* 22,400
Tanganyika, *Africa* 12,355

Sq. Miles
Baykal, *U.S.S.R.* . . . 12,162
Great Bear, *Canada* . . 12,000
Great Slave, *Canada* . . 11,170
Nyasa, *Africa* 10,900
Erie, *U.S.A.—Canada* . . 9940
Winnipeg, *Canada* . . . 9094
Chad, *Africa* 8000

Sq. Miles
Ontario, *U.S.A.—Canada* . 7540
Ladoga, *U.S.S.R.* 7104
Balkhash, *U.S.S.R.* . . . 6680
Onega, *U.S.S.R.* 3822
Eyre, *Australia (salt)* . . 3700
Rudolf, *Kenya (salt)* . . 3500
Titicaca, *Peru—Bolivia* . . 3261

Sq. Miles
Nicaragua, *Nicaragua* . . 3060
Athabasca, *Canada* . . . 3058
Reindeer, *Canada* 2440
Torrens, *Australia (salt)* . 2400
Koko Nor, *China (salt)* . . 2300
Issyk-Kul', *U.S.S.R.* . . . 2200
Vänern, *Sweden* 2150

PART FOUR

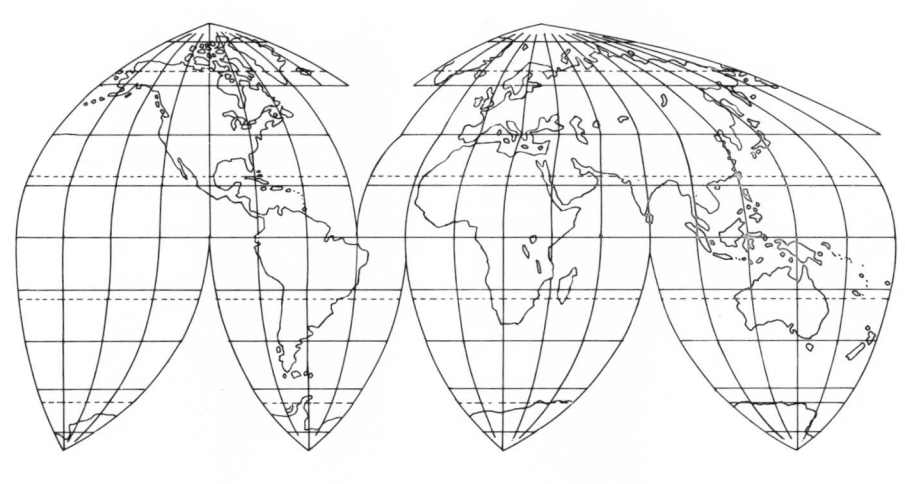

INDEXES

INDEX
TO
THE UNITED STATES
OF AMERICA

LIST OF ABBREVIATIONS

Arch. Archipelago
B. Bay
Batt. Battle
B.C. British Columbia
C. Cape
Can. Canal
Chan. Channel
Cr. Creek
Des. Desert
G. Gulf
Harb. Harbor
Hd. Head
Hist. Historical
I. Island, Isle, Ile
Is. Islands, Isles
L. Lake, Lac
Mil. Military
Mon. Monument
Mt. Mountain, Mount
Nat. National
Pen. Peninsula
Pk. Peak
Plat. Plateau
Prom. Promontory
Pt., Pte. Point, Pointe
R. River
Ra. Range
Res. Reservoir
Sd. Sound
St., Ste. Saint, Sainte
Str. Strait
Val. Valley
Vol. Volcano

(Population figures for towns over 25,000 are from the United States census, 1960; for states, from provisional estimates, United States Census Bureau, July 1, 1967)

Alta Vista, Iowa 61 M a
Alta Vista, Kansas 60 H f
Altavista, Virginia 52 G h
Altha, Florida 54 F g
Altheimer, Arkansas 63 M d
Alto, Texas 65 M d
Alton, California 74 A d
Alton, Illinois (43,047) 57 C l
Alton, Iowa 61 H b
Alton, Kansas 60 F e
Alton, Missouri 61 N h
Alton, New Hampshire 49 D e
Alton, New York 53 K b
Alton, Utah 68 D f
Altona, Illinois 57 C h
Altona, New York 53 N a
Altonah, Utah 68 F c
Altoona, Alabama 54 E c
Altoona, Florida 55 K h
Altoona, Iowa 61 L c
Altoona, Kansas 61 J g
Altoona, Pennsylvania (69,407) 52 H e
Altura, Minnesota 59 P f
Alturas, California 74 E c
Alturas, Florida 55 N f
Altus, Oklahoma 62 D d
Alunite, Nevada 75 L j
Alva, Florida 55 N g
Alva, Kentucky 57 K n
Alva, Oklahoma 62 E b
Alva, Wyoming 67 Q e
Alvarado, Texas 65 K c
Alvin, Illinois 57 F j
Alvin, Texas 65 M f
Alvin, Wisconsin 56 E d
Alvo, Nebraska 60 H d
Alvord, Texas 65 K b
Alvord Des., Oregon 73 M n
Alvord L., Oregon 73 M n
Alvwood, Minnesota 59 M c
Aly, Arkansas 63 K d
Alzada, Montana 67 Q d
Amagansett, New York 51 J d
Amak I., Alaska 76 F j
Amanda, Ohio 52 D f
Amargosa Des., Nevada 75 J h
Amargosa R., California 75 J j
Amargosa Ra., California 75 J h
Amarillo, Texas (137,969) 64 C h
Amasa, Michigan 56 E c
Amatignak I., Alaska 77 N j
Amawalk, New York 50 F c
Amazonia, Missouri 61 K e
Amber, Iowa 61 N b
Amber, Oklahoma 62 F c
Amber, Washington 73 N h
Amber B., Alaska 76 J h
Amberg, Wisconsin 56 F d
Ambler, Pennsylvania 50 C e
Ambler R., Alaska 76 J c
Amboy, California 75 K k
Amboy, Illinois 57 D h
Ambridge, Pennsylvania 52 F e
Ambrose, Georgia 54 H f
Ambrose, North Dakota 58 C b
Ambrose Chan., New Jersey-New York 50 F e
Amchitka I., Alaska 76 M j
Amchitka Pass, Alaska 76 M j
Amedee, California 74 E d
Amelia, Nebraska 60 F b
Amelia, Virginia 52 J h
Amelia I., Florida 55 K g
Amenia, New York 50 F b
American Falls, Idaho 66 H g
American Falls Res., Idaho 66 H g
Americus, Georgia 54 G e
Amery, Wisconsin 56 A d
Ames, Iowa (27,003) 61 L b
Ames, Nebraska 60 H c
Ames, Oklahoma 62 E b
Amesbury, Massachusetts 49 E f
Amesville, Ohio 52 E f
Amherst, Colorado 69 O c
Amherst, Maine 49 G d
Amherst, Massachusetts 49 C f
Amherst, Nebraska 60 E d
Amherst, New Hampshire 49 D f
Amherst, Ohio 52 D d
Amherst, South Dakota 58 J e
Amherst, Texas 64 E a
Amherst, Virginia 52 G h
Amherstdale, West Virginia 52 E h
Amherst Junction, Wisconsin 56 D e
Amidon, North Dakota 58 C d
Amite, Louisiana 63 N h
Amite R., Louisiana 63 N h
Amity, Arkansas 63 K d
Amityville, New York 50 G d
Amlia I., Alaska 77 Q j
Ammon, Idaho 66 J f
Amorita, Oklahoma 62 E b
Amory, Mississippi 63 P e
Amos, California 75 K l
Amphitheater, Arizona 70 G g
Amsterdam, Georgia 54 G g
Amsterdam, Idaho 66 F g
Amsterdam, New York (28,772) 53 M c
Amsterdam, Ohio 52 F e
Amston, Connecticut 51 J b
Amukta Pass, Alaska 77 R j
Amy, Kansas 60 D f
Anacapa Is., California 75 F l
Anacoco, Louisiana 63 K g
Anacoco L., Louisiana 63 K g
Anaconda, Montana 66 H c
Anaconda Ra., Montana 66 G d
Anacortes, Washington 73 H g
Anacostia, District of Columbia 53 Q h
Anadarko, Oklahoma 62 E c
Anaheim, California (104,184) 75 H l
Anaheim B., California 75 F n
Anahuac, Texas 65 N f
Anaktuk, Alaska 76 H a
Anaktuvuk Pass, Alaska 76 M b
Anaktuvuk R., Alaska 76 M b
Analomink, Pennsylvania 50 C c
Anamoose, North Dakota 58 F c
Anamosa, Iowa 61 N b
Anastasia I., Florida 55 K h
Anatone, Washington 73 N j
Anceney, Montana 66 J d
Ancho, New Mexico 71 M f
Anchorage, Alaska (44,237) 76 N f
Anchorage, Kentucky 57 H l
Anchor B., Michigan 56 L g
Anchor Point, Alaska 76 M g
Anclote Keys, Florida 55 M e
Ancram, New York 50 F a
Andale, Kansas 60 G g
Andalusia, Alabama 54 E f
Andalusia, Illinois 57 C h
Anderson, California 74 C d
Anderson, Indiana (49,061) 57 H j
Anderson, Missouri 61 K h
Anderson, South Carolina (41,316) 55 J c
Anderson L., Oregon 73 L n
Anderson Ranch Res., Idaho 66 E f
Andersonville, Georgia 54 G e
Andersonville, Indiana 57 H k
Andes, L., South Dakota 58 H g
Andes, New York 50 D a
Andover, Connecticut 51 J b
Andover, Maine 49 E d
Andover, New Hampshire 49 D e
Andover, New Jersey 50 D d
Andover, New York 52 J c
Andover, Ohio 52 F d
Andover, South Dakota 58 J e
Andreafsky, Alaska 76 F e
Andreafsky R., Alaska 76 F e
Andreanof Is., Alaska 77 O j
Andreas, Pennsylvania 50 B d
Andrew, Iowa 61 O b
Andrew Johnson Nat. Mon., Tennessee 55 J a
Andrews, Indiana 57 H j
Andrews, Nebraska 60 A b
Andrews, North Carolina 54 H b
Andrews, Oregon 73 M n
Andrews, South Carolina 55 M d
Andrews, Texas 64 E c
Andrix, Colorado 69 N f
Andronica I., Alaska 76 G j
Androscoggin R., Maine 49 E d
Aneta, North Dakota 58 J c
Angel I., California 75 B l
Angelica, New York 52 H c
Angelina R., Texas 65 N d
Angels Camp, California 74 E f
Angier, North Carolina 55 N b
Angleton, Texas 65 M f
Angola, Indiana 57 J h
Angola, New York 52 G c
Angola Swamp, North Carolina 55 O c
Angoon, Alaska 77 U h
Angora, Nebraska 60 A c
Angostura Res., South Dakota 58 C g
Angus, Minnesota 59 K b
Aniakchak Vol. Crater, Alaska 76 H h
Aniak R., Alaska 76 H f
Animas, New Mexico 71 J h
Animas Pk., New Mexico 71 J h
Animas R., Colorado 69 J f
Anita, Arizona 70 E d
Anita, Iowa 61 K c
Aniuk R., Alaska 76 J b
Aniwa, Wisconsin 56 D d
Ankeny, Iowa 61 L c
Ann, C., Massachusetts 49 E f
Anna, Illinois 57 D m
Anna, Ohio 52 B e
Anna, Texas 65 L b
Anna Maria, Florida 55 M f
Annandale, Minnesota 59 M e
Annapolis, Maryland 53 K g
Ann Arbor, Michigan (67,340) 57 K g
Annawan, Illinois 57 D h
Annette, Alaska 77 W j
Anniston, Alabama (33,657) 54 F d
Annona, Texas 65 N b
Annville, Pennsylvania 53 K e
Anoka, Minnesota 59 N e
Anoka, Nebraska 60 F b
Anselmo, Nebraska 60 E c
Ansley, Louisiana 63 L f
Ansley, Nebraska 60 E c
Anson, Texas 64 H c
Ansonia, Connecticut 51 G c
Ansonia, Ohio 52 B e
Ansonville, North Carolina 55 L b
Ansted, West Virginia 52 E g
Antelope, Montana 67 Q a
Antelope, Oregon 73 K l
Antelope, Texas 65 J b
Antelope, Utah 68 G c
Antelope Cr., Oregon 73 N n
Antelope I., Utah 68 A g
Antelope Ra., Nevada 74 J e
Antelope Res., Oregon 73 N n
Antero Pk., Colorado 69 K e
Antero Res., Colorado 69 L e
Anthony, Florida 55 J h
Anthony, Kansas 60 F g
Anthony, New Mexico 71 L g
Anthony, Rhode Island 51 K b
Antigo, Wisconsin 56 D d
Antimony, Utah 68 E e
Antioch, California 74 D f
Antioch, Illinois 56 E g
Antioch, Nebraska 60 B b
Antler, North Dakota 58 E b
Antlers, Oklahoma 62 H d
Antoine, Arkansas 63 K d
Anton, Colorado 69 N d
Anton, Texas 64 E b
Antonino, Kansas 60 E f
Antonito, Colorado 69 L f
Antrim, New Hampshire 49 C e
Antrim, Pennsylvania 53 J d
Antwerp, New York 53 L a
Antwerp, Ohio 52 B d
Anvik, Alaska 76 G e
Anvik R., Alaska 76 G e
Anvil Pk., Alaska 76 M j
Anxvasse, Missouri 61 N e
Apache, Arizona 70 H h
Apache, Oklahoma 62 E d
Apache Creek, New Mexico 71 J f
Apache Junction, Arizona 70 F f
Apache L., Arizona 70 F f
Apache Pk., Arizona 70 G h
Apahola, Hawaii 72 B c
Apalachee B., Florida 54 G g
Apalachia Dam, North Carolina 54 G b
Apalachicola, Florida 54 F h
Apalachicola B., Florida 54 G h
Apalachicola R., Florida 54 F g
Apex, North Carolina 55 N b
Apgar, Montana 66 F a
Aphrewn R., Alaska 76 E f
Apishapa R., Colorado 69 M f
Apopka, Florida 55 K j
Apopka, L., Florida 55 K j
Apostle Is., Wisconsin 56 C b
Appalachia, Virginia 52 D j
Appalachian Mts., Pennsylvania, etc. 47 K c
Appleby, Texas 65 N d
Applegate, California 74 E f
Applegate, Oregon 73 G n
Applegate R., Oregon 73 G n
Apple Springs, Texas 65 N d
Appleton, Maine 49 F d
Appleton, Minnesota 59 L e
Appleton, Washington 73 J k
Appleton, Wisconsin (48,411) 56 E e
Appleton City, Missouri 61 K f
Appomattox, Virginia 52 H h
Appomattox Court House Nat. Mon., Virginia 52 H h
Apua Pt., Hawaii 72 E f
Aquarius Mts., Arizona 70 D e
Aquarius Plateau, Utah 68 E f
Aquebogue, New York 51 H d
Aquilla, Texas 65 K d
Arabi, Georgia 54 H f
Arago, C., Oregon 73 F m
Aransas B., Texas 65 K h
Aransas Pass, Texas 65 K h
Arapaho Pk., Colorado 69 L c
Arapahoe, Colorado 69 O e
Arapahoe, Nebraska 60 E d
Arapahoe, Wyoming 67 M g
Arboles, Colorado 69 J f
Arbon, Idaho 66 H g
Arbor Heights, Washington 72 B j
Arbor Vitae, Wisconsin 56 D d
Arbuckle, California 74 C e
Arbuckle, L., Florida 55 N f
Arbuckle Mts., Oklahoma 62 F d
Arbutus, Maryland 53 P f
Arbyrd, Missouri 61 O h
Arcade, New York 52 H c
Arcadia, California (41,005), vicinity of Los Angeles
Arcadia, Florida 55 N f
Arcadia, Indiana 57 G j
Arcadia, Kansas 61 K g
Arcadia, Louisiana 63 L f
Arcadia, Michigan 56 G e
Arcadia, Missouri 61 O g
Arcadia, Nebraska 60 F c
Arcadia, Ohio 52 C d
Arcadia, Oklahoma 62 F c
Arcadia, Rhode Island 51 K b
Arcadia, Wisconsin 56 B e
Arcanum, Ohio 52 B f
Arcata, California 74 A d
Arc Dome, Nevada 74 H f
Archbald, Pennsylvania 53 L d
Archbold, Ohio 52 B d
Archer, Florida 55 J h
Archer City, Texas 65 J b
Arches Nat. Mon., Utah 68 G e
Archie, Missouri 61 K f
Archuleta, New Mexico 71 K c
Arco, Idaho 66 G f
Arco, Minnesota 59 K f
Arcola, Illinois 57 E k
Arcola, Mississippi 63 N e
Arcola, Texas 65 M f
Arctic Lagoon, Alaska 76 D d
Arctic Village, Alaska 77 O b
Arden, Nevada 75 K h
Arden, New York 50 E c
Arden Hills, Minnesota 59 Q h
Ardmore, Oklahoma 62 F d
Ardmore, Pennsylvania 50 C e
Ardmore, South Dakota 58 C g
Ardmore, Tennessee 54 E b
Ardoch, North Dakota 58 J b
Ardsley, New York 50 F d
Arena, New York 50 D a
Arena, Pt., California 74 B f
Arendale, North Carolina 55 M b
Argenta, Montana 66 H d
Argentine, Kansas 61 P a
Argonia, Kansas 60 G g
Argonne, Wisconsin 56 D d
Argora, Idaho 66 H e
Argos, Indiana 57 G h
Arguello, Pt., California 75 E k
Argus Ra., California 75 H j
Argusville, North Dakota 58 J c
Argyle, Georgia 55 J f
Argyle, Michigan 56 L f
Argyle, Minnesota 59 K b
Argyle, Wisconsin 56 D g
Ariel, Washington 73 H k
Arion, Iowa 61 J c
Arikaree R., Colorado 69 O d
Arimo, Idaho 66 H g
Arinosa, Utah 68 C c
Ariton, Alabama 54 F f
Arivaca, Arizona 70 F h
Ariyak R., Alaska 76 L b
Arizona (1,635,000) 113,909 sq. miles 70
Arkabutla L., Mississippi 63 O n
Arkadelphia, Arkansas 63 K d
Arkansas (1,969,000) 53,104 sq. miles 63
Arkansas City, Arkansas 63 M e
Arkansas City, Kansas 60 G g
Arkansas R., Arkansas, etc. 47 H c
Arkport, New York 52 J c
Arkville, New York 50 D a
Arlee, Montana 66 F b
Arling, Idaho 66 D e
Arlington, Arizona 70 E f
Arlington, California 75 H l
Arlington, Colorado 69 N e
Arlington, Florida 55 K g
Arlington, Georgia 54 G f
Arlington, Iowa 61 N b
Arlington, Kansas 60 F g
Arlington, Kentucky 57 D n
Arlington, Maryland 53 P e
Arlington, Massachusetts (49,953) 49 F h
Arlington, Minnesota 59 M f
Arlington, Nebraska 60 H c
Arlington, Ohio 52 C e
Arlington, Oregon 73 K k
Arlington, South Dakota 58 J f
Arlington, Tennessee 54 B b
Arlington, Texas (44,775) 65 M j
Arlington, Vermont 49 B e
Arlington, Virginia (163,401) 53 O h
Arlington, Washington 73 H g
Arlington, Wyoming 67 O h
Arlington Heights, Illinois (27,878) 57 E g
Arlington Res., Missouri 61 M g
Armington, Montana 67 K b
Arminto, Wyoming 67 N f
Armonk, New York 50 F d
Armour, South Dakota 58 H g
Armourdale, North Dakota 58 G b
Armstead, Montana 66 H e
Armstrong, Illinois 57 F j
Armstrong, Iowa 61 K a
Armstrong, Missouri 61 M e
Armstrong, Texas 65 K j
Arnegard, North Dakota 58 C c
Arnett, Oklahoma 62 D b
Arnett, West Virginia 52 E h
Arnia, Kansas 61 K g
Arno, Texas 64 D d
Arnold, California 74 E f
Arnold, Nebraska 60 D c
Arnold, Pennsylvania 52 G e
Arnoldsburg, West Virginia 52 E g
Arnolds Park, Iowa 61 K a
Aroostook R., Maine 49 G b
Aropuk L., Alaska 76 F f
Aroya, Colorado 69 N e
Arp, Texas 65 M c
Arran, Florida 54 G g
Arrey, New Mexico 71 K g
Arriba, Colorado 69 N d
Arrow Cr., Montana 67 L b
Arrow Rock, Missouri 61 M e
Arrow Rock Res., Idaho 66 E f
Arroyo Grande, California 75 E j
Arroyo Hondo, New Mexico 71 M c
Arroyo Seco, California 75 K l
Artas, South Dakota 58 G e
Artesia, California 75 F m
Artesia, Mississippi 63 P e
Artesia, New Mexico 71 N g
Artesian, South Dakota 58 J g
Artesia Wells, Texas 65 H g
Arthur, Illinois 57 E k
Arthur, L., Louisiana 63 L h
Arthur, Nebraska 60 C c
Arthur, North Dakota 58 J c
Arthur City, Texas 65 M b
Arthur Kill, New Jersey 51 J g
Arthursburg, New York 50 F b
Artois, California 74 C e
Arvada, Colorado 69 O h
Arvada, Wyoming 67 O e
Arvin, California 75 G j
Arvonia, Virginia 52 H h
Asbury, Kansas 61 K g
Asbury, New Jersey 50 C d
Asbury Park, New Jersey 50 F e
Asharoken, New York 50 G d
Ashaway, Rhode Island 51 K c
Ashburn, Georgia 54 H f
Ashby, Minnesota 59 L d
Ashby, Nebraska 60 C b
Ashdown, Arkansas 63 J e
Asheboro, North Carolina 55 M b
Asher, Oklahoma 62 G c
Asherton, Texas 65 H g
Asheville, North Carolina (60,192) 55 J b
Ash Flat, Arkansas 63 M b
Ashford, Alabama 54 F f
Ashford, Connecticut 51 J b
Ashford, Washington 73 H j
Ashfork, Arizona 70 E d
Ash Grove, Kansas 60 F e
Ash Grove, Missouri 61 L g
Ashkum, Illinois 57 F j
Ashland, Alabama 54 F d
Ashland, Illinois 57 C k
Ashland, Kansas 60 E g
Ashland, Kentucky (31,283) 57 L l
Ashland, Maine 49 G b
Ashland, Montana 67 O d
Ashland, Mt., Oregon 73 H n
Ashland, Nebraska 60 H c
Ashland, New Hampshire 49 D e
Ashland, New York 50 E a
Ashland, Ohio 52 D e
Ashland, Oregon 73 H n
Ashland, Pennsylvania 53 K e
Ashland, Virginia 52 J h
Ashland, Wisconsin 56 C c
Ashland City, Tennessee 54 D a
Ashley, Illinois 57 D l
Ashley, Michigan 56 J f
Ashley, North Dakota 58 G d
Ashley, Pennsylvania 50 B c
Ashley Falls, Massachusetts 50 G a
Ashmore, Texas 64 E c
Ashokan, New York 50 E b
Ashokan Res., New York 50 E b
Ashtabula, Ohio 52 F d
Ashtabula, L., North Dakota 58 J c
Ashton, Idaho 66 J e
Ashton, Illinois 57 D h
Ashton, Michigan 56 H f
Ashton, Rhode Island 51 L b
Ashton, South Dakota 58 H f
Ashville, Alabama 54 E d
Askin, North Carolina 55 O b
Askov, Minnesota 59 O d
Asotin, Washington 73 N j
Aspen, Colorado 69 K d
Aspen, Wyoming 67 K h
Aspermont, Texas 64 G b
Aspid, Mt., Alaska 76 D k
Aspinwall, Pennsylvania 53 Q a
Assateague I., Virginia 53 L g
Assateague Island Nat. Seashore, Virginia-Maryland 53 L g
Assawompset Pond, Massachusetts 51 M b
Assonet, Massachusetts 51 L b
Assumption, Illinois 57 D k
Astoria, Illinois 57 C j
Astoria, Oregon 73 G j
Astoria, South Dakota 59 K f
Atanik, Alaska 76 H a
Atarque, New Mexico 71 J e
Atascadero, California 75 E j
Atascosa R., Texas 65 J f
Atchafalaya B., Louisiana 63 M j
Atchafalaya R., Louisiana 63 M l
Atchison, Kansas 61 J e
Atchueelingk R., Alaska 76 G e
Atco, Georgia 54 G c
Atco, New Jersey 50 D f
Atglen, Pennsylvania 50 A f
Athelstan, Iowa 61 K d
Athena, Oregon 73 M k
Athens, Alabama 54 E c
Athens, Georgia (31,355) 54 H d
Athens, Illinois 57 D k
Athens, Louisiana 63 K f
Athens, Maine 49 F d
Athens, Michigan 57 H g
Athens, New York 50 F a
Athens, Ohio 52 D f
Athens, Pennsylvania 53 K d
Athens, Tennessee 54 G b
Athens, Texas 65 M c
Athens, Wisconsin 56 C d
Atherton, California 75 C n
Athol, Idaho 66 D b
Athol, Massachusetts 49 C f
Athol, Pennsylvania 50 B e
Atka, Alaska 77 Q j
Atkasuk, Alaska 76 J a
Atkins, Arkansas 63 L c
Atkinson, Illinois 57 C h
Atkinson, Nebraska 60 F b
Atkinson, North Carolina 55 N c
Atlanta, Georgia (487,455) 54 G d
Atlanta, Idaho 66 E f
Atlanta, Illinois 57 D j
Atlanta, Indiana 57 G j
Atlanta, Kansas 60 H g
Atlanta, Michigan 56 J d
Atlanta, Missouri 61 M e
Atlanta, New York 53 J c
Atlanta, Texas 65 N b
Atlantic, Iowa 61 J c
Atlantic, North Carolina 55 P c
Atlantic Beach, New York 50 F d
Atlantic City, New Jersey (59,544) 50 E g
Atlantic City, Wyoming 67 M g
Atlantic Highlands, New Jersey 50 E e
Atlas, Michigan 56 K g
Atmore, Alabama 54 D f
Atoka, Oklahoma 62 G d
Atoka Res., Oklahoma 62 G d
Atolia, California 75 H j
Atomic City, Idaho 66 H f
Atsion, New Jersey 50 D f
Attalla, Alabama 54 E c
Attica, Indiana 57 F j
Attica, Kansas 60 F g
Attica, Michigan 56 K f
Attica, New York 52 H c
Attica, Ohio 52 D d
Attleboro, Massachusetts (27,118) 51 L b
Attoya Bayou, Texas 65 N d
Attu I., Alaska 76 J j
Attu, Alaska 76 J j
Atwater, California 75 E g
Atwater, Minnesota 59 M e
Atwood, Colorado 69 N c
Atwood, Illinois 57 E k
Atwood, Kansas 60 C e
Atwood, New York 50 E b
Atwood Res., Ohio 52 E e
Auau Chan., Hawaii 72 D e
Aubry Cliffs, Arizona 70 E d
Auburn, Alabama 54 F e
Auburn, California 74 D f
Auburn, Illinois 57 D k
Auburn, Indiana 57 H h
Auburn, Kansas 61 J f
Auburn, Kentucky 57 G n
Auburn, Maine 49 E d
Auburn, Massachusetts 51 K a
Auburn, Michigan 56 J f
Auburn, Nebraska 61 J d
Auburn, New Jersey 50 C f
Auburn, New York (35,249) 53 K c
Auburn, Pennsylvania 50 A d
Auburn, Washington 73 H h
Auburndale, Florida 55 N e
Auburndale, Wisconsin 56 D e
Aucilla R., Florida 54 H g
Audenried, Pennsylvania 50 B d
Audubon, Iowa 61 K c
Audubon, New Jersey 50 C f
Au Gres, Michigan 56 K e
Augusta, Arkansas 63 M c
Augusta, Georgia (70,626) 55 J d
Augusta, Illinois 57 C j
Augusta, Kansas 60 H g
Augusta, Kentucky 57 J l
Augusta, Maine 49 F d
Augusta, Michigan 57 H g
Augusta, Montana 66 H b
Augusta, New Jersey 50 D c
Augusta, Wisconsin 56 B e
Augusta Springs, Virginia 52 G g
Augustine I., Alaska 76 L g
Auke Bay, Alaska 77 U g
Aulander, North Carolina 55 O a
Ault, Colorado 69 M c
Aurelia, Iowa 61 J b
Aurora, Colorado (48,548) 69 P h
Aurora, Illinois (63,715) 57 E h
Aurora, Indiana 57 J k
Aurora, Kansas 60 G e
Aurora, Minnesota 59 O c
Aurora, Missouri 61 L h
Aurora, Nebraska 60 F d
Aurora, New York 53 K c
Aurora, North Carolina 55 P b
Aurora, Utah 68 E d
Aurora Lodge, Alaska 77 O d
Ausable Forks, New York 53 N a
Au Sable Pt., Michigan 56 G c
Au Sable Pt., Michigan 56 K e
Au Sable R., Michigan 56 J e
Ausable R., New York 53 N a
Austell, Georgia 54 G d
Austerlitz, New York 50 G a
Austin, Minnesota (27,908) 59 O g
Austin, Montana 66 H c
Austin, Nevada 74 H e
Austin, Oregon 73 M l
Austin, Pennsylvania 52 H d
Austin, Texas (186,545) 65 K e
Austonio, Texas 65 M d
Austwell, Texas 65 L g
Au Train, Michigan 56 G c
Aux Barques, Pt., Michigan 56 G d
Aux Barques, Pt., Michigan 56 L e
Ava, Illinois 57 D m
Ava, Missouri 61 M h
Avalik R., Alaska 76 H a
Avalon, California 75 G l
Avalon, L., New Mexico 71 N g
Avalon, Mississippi 63 N e
Avalon, New Jersey 50 D g
Avalon, Pennsylvania 53 O a
Avard, Oklahoma 62 E b
Avatanak I., Alaska 76 E j
Avawatz Mts., California 75 J j
Avella, Pennsylvania 52 F e
Avenal, California 75 E j
Avery, Idaho 66 E b
Avery, Iowa 61 M c

Avery, *Texas* 65 N b
Avery Island, *Louisiana* 63 M j
Avinger, *Texas* 65 N c
Avis, *Pennsylvania* 53 J d
Avoca, *Iowa* 61 J c
Avoca, *Michigan* 56 L f
Avoca, *New York* 53 J c
Avoca, *Pennsylvania* 50 B c
Avoca, *Texas* 65 H c
Avon, *Colorado* 69 K d
Avon, *Illinois* 57 C j
Avon, *Massachusetts* 51 L a
Avon, *Minnesota* 59 M e
Avon, *Montana* 66 H c
Avon, *North Carolina* 55 P d
Avon, *Ohio* 52 D d
Avon, *South Dakota* 58 H h
Avon by the Sea, *New Jersey* 50 F e
Avondale, *Arizona* 70 E f
Avondale, *Colorado* 69 M e
Avondale, *Missouri* 61 Q a
Avondale, *Pennsylvania* 50 B f
Avondale, *Texas* 65 L h
Avon Lake, *Ohio* 52 D d
Avonmore, *Pennsylvania* 52 G e
Avon Park, *Florida* 55 N f
Awendaw, *South Carolina* 55 M d
Awosting, *New York* 50 E b
Awuna R., *Alaska* 76 J b
Axial, *Colorado* 69 J c
Axson, *Georgia* 55 J f
Axtell, *Kansas* 60 H e
Axton, *Virginia* 52 G j
Aydon, *North Carolina* 55 O b
Ayer, *Massachusetts* 49 D f
Ayers, *Washington* 73 M j
Aylett, *Virginia* 53 J h
Aynor, *South Carolina* 55 M d
Ayr, *Nebraska* 60 F d
Ayr, *North Dakota* 58 J c
Ayrshire, *Iowa* 61 K a
Azalea, *Oregon* 73 G n
Aziscoos L., *Maine* 49 E c
Aztec, *Arizona* 70 D g
Aztec, *New Mexico* 71 K c
Aztec Ruins Nat. Mon., *New Mexico* 71 J c
Babb, *Montana* 66 G a
Babbitt, *Minnesota* 59 P c
Babcock, *Wisconsin* 56 C e
Baboquivari Pk., *Arizona* 70 F h
Babson Park, *Florida* 55 N f
Babylon, *New York* 50 G d
Bacchus, *Utah* 68 B h
Bach, *Michigan* 56 K f
Back Bay, *Virginia* 53 K j
Back River, *New York* 53 L a
Backus, *Minnesota* 59 M d
Baconton, *Georgia* 54 G f
Bad Axe, *Michigan* 56 L f
Baden, *Pennsylvania* 52 F e
Badger, *California* 75 F h
Badger, *Minnesota* 59 K b
Badger Basin, *Wyoming* 67 L e
Badin, *North Carolina* 55 L b
Badin L., *North Carolina* 55 L b
Bad Lands, *North Dakota* 58 C d
Badlands Nat. Mon., *South Dakota* 58 D g
Bad R., *Michigan* 56 J f
Bad R., *South Dakota* 58 F f
Badwater, *California* 75 J h
Baffin B., *Texas* 65 K h
Baird, *Texas* 65 H c
Bagdad, *Arizona* 70 D e
Bagdad, *California* 75 K k
Bagdad, *Kentucky* 57 H l
Baggs, *Wyoming* 67 N h
Bagley, *Minnesota* 59 L c
Bagley, *Wisconsin* 56 B g
Bagley Icefield, *Alaska* 77 Q f
Bagnell Dam, *Missouri* 61 M f
Bailey, *Colorado* 69 L d
Bailey, *North Carolina* 55 N b
Baileyton, *Alabama* 54 E c
Bainbridge, *Georgia* 54 G g
Bainbridge, *Maryland* 50 A f
Bainbridge, *New York* 53 L c
Bainbridge, *Ohio* 52 C f
Bainbridge I., *Washington* 72 B h
Bainville, *Montana* 67 Q a
Baird Inlet, *Alaska* 76 E f
Baird Mts., *Alaska* 76 G c
Bairoil, *Wyoming* 67 N g
Baker, *California* 75 J j
Baker, *Idaho* 66 G d
Baker, *Montana* 67 Q c
Baker, Mt., *Washington* 73 J g
Baker, *Nevada* 74 L e
Baker, *North Dakota* 58 G b
Baker, *Oklahoma* 62 B b
Baker, *Oregon* 73 N l
Baker, *West Virginia* 52 H f
Baker Butte, *Arizona* 70 F e
Baker I., *Alaska* 77 V j
Baker L., *Maine* 49 F b
Bakersfield, *California* (56,848) 75 G j
Bakersfield, *Texas* 64 E e
Bakersfield, *Vermont* 49 C d
Bakersville, *North Carolina* 55 J a
Balaton, *Minnesota* 59 L f
Balch Springs, *Texas* 65 O j
Bald Butte, *Oregon* 73 L m
Bald Eagle, *Minnesota* 59 R h
Bald Eagle L., *Minnesota* 59 R h
Bald Eagle Mt., *Pennsylvania* 52 J e
Bald Knob, *Arkansas* 63 M c
Bald Knob, *West Virginia* 52 E h
Bald Mt., *Idaho* 66 F e
Bald Mt., *Nevada* 75 K g
Baldwin, *Florida* 55 K g
Baldwin, *Kansas* 61 J f
Baldwin, *Michigan* 56 H f
Baldwin, *New York* (30,204), vicinity of New York
Baldwin, *North Dakota* 58 F c
Baldwin, *Pennsylvania* 53 P b
Baldwin, *Wisconsin* 56 A e
Baldwin L., *California* 75 J k
Baldwin Park, *California* (33,951), vicinity of Los Angeles
Baldwin Pen., *Alaska* 76 F c
Baldwin Place, *New York* 50 F c
Baldwinsville, *New York* 53 K b
Baldwinville, *Massachusetts* 49 D f
Baldwyn, *Mississippi* 63 P d
Baldy Pk., *Arizona* 70 H f
Baldy Pk., *New Mexico* 71 M d
Balfour, *North Dakota* 58 F c
Bal Harbor, *Florida* 54 C d
Ballantine, *Montana* 67 M d
Ballarat, *California* 75 H h
Ballard, *Washington* 72 B h
Ball Ground, *Georgia* 54 G c
Ballinger, *Texas* 64 H d
Ballston Spa, *New York* 53 N c
Bally, *Pennsylvania* 50 B e
Balmat, *New York* 53 L a
Balmorhea, *Texas* 64 D e
Balsam Lake, *Wisconsin* 56 A d
Balta, *North Dakota* 58 F b
Baltic, *Connecticut* 51 J b
Baltic, *South Dakota* 59 K g
Baltimore, *Maryland* (939,024) 53 K f
Baltimore, *Ohio* 52 D f
Bamber, *New Jersey* 50 E f
Bamberg, *South Carolina* 55 K d
Banana R., *Florida* 55 O e
Bancroft, *Idaho* 66 J g
Bancroft, *Iowa* 61 K a
Bancroft, *South Dakota* 58 J f
Bandelier Nat. Mon., *New Mexico* 71 L d
Bandera, *Texas* 65 H f
Bandon, *Oregon* 73 F m
Bandy, *Virginia* 52 E h
Bangall, *New York* 50 F b
Bangert, *Missouri* 61 N g
Bangor, *Maine* (38,912) 49 G d
Bangor, *Michigan* 57 G g
Bangor, *Pennsylvania* 50 C d
Bangor, *Washington* 72 A h
Bangor Junction, *Pennsylvania* 50 C d
Bangs, Mt., *Arizona* 70 D c
Bangs, *Texas* 65 H d
Ban I., *Alaska* 76 L g
Banister R., *Virginia* 52 G j
Bankhead L., *Alabama* 54 D d
Banks, *Arkansas* 63 L e
Banks, *Idaho* 66 D e
Banks, *Mississippi* 63 N d
Banks, *Oregon* 73 G k
Banks L., *Washington* 73 L h
Bannack, *Montana* 66 H d
Banning, *California* 75 J l
Bannock Pass, *Montana* 66 G e
Bannock Ra., *Idaho* 66 H g
Bantam, *Connecticut* 50 G b
Bantam L., *Connecticut* 50 G b
Bantry, *North Dakota* 58 F b
Bapchule, *Arizona* 70 F f
Baraboo R., *Wisconsin* 56 D f
Baraga, *Michigan* 56 E c
Baranof, *Alaska* 77 U h
Baranof I., *Alaska* 77 U h
Barataria, *Louisiana* 63 N j
Barataria B., *Louisiana* 63 O j
Barber, *Idaho* 66 D f
Barbers Pt., *Hawaii* 72 C d
Barberton, *Ohio* (33,805) 52 E d
Barberville, *Florida* 55 K h
Barboursville, *Virginia* 52 H g
Barbourville, *Kentucky* 57 K n
Barclay, *Maryland* 50 B g
Barclay, *Nevada* 74 L g
Barco, *North Carolina* 55 P a
Bard, *New Mexico* 71 O d
Bardstown, *Kentucky* 57 H m
Bardwell, *Kentucky* 57 D n
Bardwell, *Texas* 65 L c
Bar Harbor, *Maine* 49 G d
Baring, *Missouri* 61 M d
Baring, *Washington* 73 J h
Barkeyville, *Pennsylvania* 52 G d
Barker, *New York* 52 H b
Barkhamsted Res., *Connecticut* 51 H b
Bark River, *Michigan* 56 F d
Barksdale, *Texas* 64 G f
Barlow, *North Dakota* 58 G c
Barlow Pass, *Oregon* 73 J k
Barnard, *Kansas* 60 F e
Barnard, Mt., *Alaska* 77 T g
Barnard, *South Dakota* 58 H e
Barnegat, *New Jersey* 50 E f
Barnegat B., *New Jersey* 50 E f
Barnes, *Kansas* 60 H e
Barnesboro, *Pennsylvania* 52 H e
Barnes Sd., *Florida* 55 O h
Barneston, *Nebraska* 60 H d
Barnesville, *Georgia* 54 G d
Barnesville, *Minnesota* 59 K d
Barnesville, *Ohio* 52 E e
Barney, *Iowa* 61 K c
Barney Top, *Utah* 68 E f
Barnhart, *Texas* 64 F d
Barnsdall, *Oklahoma* 62 G b
Barnsley, *Pennsylvania* 50 A f
Barnstable, *Massachusetts* 51 N b
Barnstead, *New Hampshire* 49 D e
Barnum, *Minnesota* 59 O d
Barnwell, *South Carolina* 55 K d
Barr, *Colorado* 69 M d
Barraboo, *Wisconsin* 56 D f
Barre, *Massachusetts* 49 C f
Barre, *Vermont* 49 C d
Barren Is., *Alaska* 76 L g
Barren R., *Kentucky* 57 G n
Barrett L., *California* 75 J m
Barrington, *Illinois* 57 E g
Barrington, *Rhode Island* 51 L b
Barr L., *Colorado* 69 P g
Barr Lake, *Colorado* 69 P g
Barro, *Utah* 68 C c
Barron, *Washington* 73 K g
Barron, *Wisconsin* 56 B d
Barronett, *Wisconsin* 56 B d
Barroso, *Texas* 65 J h
Barrow, *Alaska* 76 J a
Barry, *Illinois* 57 B k
Barryton, *Michigan* 56 H f
Barrytown, *New York* 50 F b
Barryville, *New York* 50 D c
Barstow, *California* 75 J k
Barstow, *Texas* 64 D d
Bart, *Pennsylvania* 50 A f
Barter I., *Alaska* 77 Q a
Bartholomew Bayou, *Arkansas* 63 M e
Bartle, *California* 74 D c
Bartles, Mt., *Utah* 68 F d
Bartlesville, *Oklahoma* (27,893) 62 G b
Bartlett, *New Hampshire* 49 D d
Bartlett, *Nebraska* 60 F c
Bartlett Res., *Arizona* 70 F f
Bartlett, *Texas* 65 K e
Bartley, *Nebraska* 60 D d
Barto, *Pennsylvania* 50 B e
Bartolome, C., *Alaska* 77 V j
Barton, *North Dakota* 58 F b
Barton, *Vermont* 49 C d
Barton City, *Michigan* 56 K e
Bartow, *Florida* 55 N f
Bartow, *Georgia* 55 J e
Barwick, *Georgia* 54 H g
Basalt, *Colorado* 69 K d
Basalt, *Idaho* 66 H f
Basalt, *Nevada* 74 G f
Basile, *Louisiana* 63 L h
Basin, *Montana* 66 H c
Basin, *Wyoming* 67 M e
Basinger, *Florida* 55 N f
Baskahegan L., *Maine* 49 H c
Bassett, *Nebraska* 60 E b
Bassett, *Virginia* 52 G j
Bassett Pk., *Arizona* 70 G g
Bassfield, *Mississippi* 63 O g
Bass Lake, *California* 75 F g
Bastonville, *Georgia* 55 J d
Bastrop, *Louisiana* 63 L f
Bastrop, *Texas* 65 K e
Batavia, *Illinois* 57 E h
Batavia, *New York* 52 H b
Batavia, *Ohio* 52 B f
Bates, *Idaho* 66 J f
Bates, *Oregon* 73 M l
Batesburg, *South Carolina* 55 K d
Batesland, *South Dakota* 58 D g
Batesville, *Arkansas* 63 M c
Batesville, *Indiana* 57 H k
Batesville, *Mississippi* 63 O d
Batesville, *Texas* 65 H g
Bath, *Illinois* 57 C j
Bath, *Maine* 49 F e
Bath, *New York* 53 J c
Bath, *North Carolina* 55 P b
Bath, *Pennsylvania* 50 C d
Bath, *South Carolina* 55 K d
Bath, *South Dakota* 58 H e
Bathgate, *North Dakota* 58 J b
Baton Rouge, *Louisiana* (152,419) 63 M h
Batsto, *New Jersey* 50 D f
Battle Cr., *Idaho* 66 D g
Battle Creek, *Michigan* (44,169) 57 H g
Battle Cr., *Montana* 67 L a
Battle Creek, *Nebraska* 60 G c
Battle Ground, *Washington* 73 H k
Battle L., *Alaska* 76 K g
Battle Mountain, *Nevada* 74 J d
Battle Mt., *Nevada* 74 H d
Battleview, *North Dakota* 58 D b
Baudette, *Minnesota* 59 M b
Bauxite, *Arkansas* 63 L d
Bavaria, *Kansas* 60 G f
Baxley, *Georgia* 55 J f
Baxter, *Iowa* 61 L c
Baxter, *Minnesota* 59 M d
Baxter Mt., *Colorado* 69 J d
Baxter Springs, *Kansas* 61 K g
Bayard, *Florida* 55 K g
Bayard, *Iowa* 61 K c
Bayard, *Nebraska* 60 A c
Bayard, *West Virginia* 52 G f
Bayboro, *North Carolina* 55 P b
Bay City, *Michigan* (53,604) 56 K f
Bay City, *Oregon* 73 G k
Bay City, *Texas* 65 M g
Bay City, *Wisconsin* 56 A e
Bay Farm I., *California* 75 C l
Bayfield, *Wisconsin* 56 C c
Bay Minette, *Alabama* 54 D g
Bayonne, *New Jersey* (74,215) 51 K f
Bayou Bodcau Res., *Louisiana* 63 K f
Bayou Cocodrie, *Louisiana* 63 L h
Bayou La Batre, *Alabama* 54 C g
Bayport, *Florida* 55 J j
Bay Port, *Michigan* 56 K f
Bayport, *Minnesota* 59 O f
Bay Ridge, *New York* 51 L g
Bay St. Louis, *Mississippi* 63 O h
Bayshore, *Florida* 55 N g
Bay Shore, *New York* 50 G d
Bayside, *New Jersey* 50 C g
Bay Springs, *Mississippi* 63 O g
Bays R., *Tennessee* 55 J a
Baytown, *Texas* (28,159) 65 N f
Bayview, *Idaho* 66 D b
Bayview, *Maryland* 50 A f
Bayville, *New Jersey* 50 E f
Bayville, *New York* 50 F d
Bazar, *Kansas* 60 H f
Bazine, *Kansas* 60 E f
Beach, *Georgia* 55 J f
Beach, *North Dakota* 58 C d
Beach Haven, *New Jersey* 50 E f
Beach Haven, *Pennsylvania* 50 A c
Beach Haven Inlet, *New Jersey* 50 E f
Beachwood, *New Jersey* 50 E f
Beacon, Mt., *New York* 50 F c
Beacon, *New York* 50 F c
Beacon Falls, *Connecticut* 51 G c
Beacon Hill, *Florida* 54 F h
Beacon Hill, *Washington* 72 B h
Bealeton, *Virginia* 52 J g
Beals Cr., *Texas* 64 F c
Bear, *Idaho* 66 D d
Bear Cr., *Alabama* 54 D c
Bear Cr., *Kansas* 60 C g
Bear Cr., *Wyoming* 67 M g
Bear Cr., *Wyoming* 67 Q h
Bearcreek, *Montana* 67 L d
Bear Creek, *Pennsylvania* 50 B c
Bear Creek, *Wisconsin* 56 E e
Bear Creek Res., *Pennsylvania* 50 B c
Bearden, *Arkansas* 63 L e
Bearden, *Tennessee* 54 G b
Beardsley, *Arizona* 70 E f
Beardsley, *Kansas* 60 C e
Bear L., *Idaho* 66 J g
Bear L., *Utah* 68 E b
Bear Lake, *Michigan* 56 G e
Bear Lodge Mts., *Wyoming* 67 Q e
Bear Mt., *New York* 50 E c
Bearpaw, *Alaska* 76 M d
Bear Paw Mt., *Montana* 67 L a
Bearpen Mt., *New York* 50 E a
Bear R., *Idaho* 66 J g
Bear R., *Wyoming* 67 K h
Bear River City, *Utah* 68 D b
Beardstown, *Illinois* 57 C j
Bearfort Mt., *New Jersey* 50 E c
Bearmouth, *Montana* 66 G c
Bears Ears Pk., *Colorado* 69 J c
Beatrice, *Alabama* 54 D f
Beatrice, *Nebraska* 60 H d
Beattie, *Kansas* 60 H e
Beatty, *Nevada* 75 J h
Beatty, *Oregon* 73 J n
Beattyville, *Kentucky* 57 K m
Beaufort, *North Carolina* 55 P c
Beaufort, *South Carolina* 55 L e
Beaufort Inlet, *North Carolina* 55 P c
Beaufort Lagoon, *Alaska* 77 R b
Beaumont, *California* 75 H l
Beaumont, *Kansas* 60 H g
Beaumont, *Mississippi* 63 P g
Beaumont Place, *Texas* 64 G h
Beaumont, *Texas* (119,175) 65 N e
Beaver, *Alaska* 77 O c
Beaver, *Kansas* 60 F f
Beaver, *Oklahoma* 62 C b
Beaver, *Oregon* 73 G k
Beaver, *Pennsylvania* 52 F e
Beaver, *Utah* 68 D e
Beaver Brook, *New York* 50 D b
Beaver City, *Nebraska* 60 E d
Beaver Cr., *Alaska* 77 O d
Beaver Cr., *Colorado* 69 N d
Beaver Cr., *Idaho* 66 H e
Beaver Cr., *Kansas* 60 C e
Beaver Cr., *Missouri* 61 M h
Beaver Cr., *Montana* 67 Q c
Beaver Cr., *Nebraska* 60 F c
Beaver Cr., *Nebraska* 60 E d
Beaver Cr., *North Dakota* 58 F d
Beaver Cr., *Wyoming* 67 Q f
Beaver Crossing, *Nebraska* 60 G d
Beaver Dam, *Kentucky* 57 G m
Beaver Dam, *Wisconsin* 56 E f
Beaver Falls, *Pennsylvania* 52 F e
Beaverhead R., *Montana* 66 H d
Beaverhead Ra., *Montana* 66 G d
Beaver I., *Michigan* 56 H d
Beaver Kill, *New York* 50 D b
Beaver Kill R., *New York* 50 D b
Beaver L., *Michigan* 56 G c
Beaver Mts., *Alaska* 76 J e
Beaver R., *Utah* 68 C e
Beaver River Flow, *New York* 53 L b
Beaverton, *Michigan* 56 J f
Beaverton, *Oregon* 73 H k
Beavertown, *Pennsylvania* 53 J e
Beaverville, *Illinois* 57 F j
Becharof L., *Alaska* 76 J h
Bechevin B., *Alaska* 76 F j
Bechtelsville, *Pennsylvania* 50 B e
Beckley, *West Virginia* 52 E h
Beckville, *Texas* 65 N c
Beckwourth, *California* 74 E e
Becton, *Texas* 64 F b
Beddington, *Maine* 49 H d
Bedford, *Indiana* 57 G l
Bedford, *Iowa* 61 K d
Bedford, *Kentucky* 57 H l
Bedford, *Ohio* 52 E d
Bedford, *New Hampshire* 49 D f
Bedford, *New York* 50 F c
Bedford, *Pennsylvania* 52 H e
Bedford, *Texas* 65 M j
Bedford, *Virginia* 52 G h
Bedford, *Wyoming* 67 K g
Bedford Hills, *New York* 50 F c
Bee, *Nebraska* 60 G c
Beebe, *Arkansas* 63 M c
Beebe, *South Dakota* 58 G e
Beech Creek, *Kentucky* 57 M m
Beech Creek, *Oregon* 73 L l
Beech Creek, *Pennsylvania* 52 J d
Beecher, *Illinois* 57 F h
Beecher City, *Illinois* 57 E k
Beechey Point, *Alaska* 77 N a
Beech Grove, *Indiana* 57 H k
Beechwood, *Michigan* 56 E c
Beegum, *California* 74 C d
Beekman, *Louisiana* 63 M f
Beeler, *Kansas* 60 D f
Beemer, *Nebraska* 60 H c
Beemerville, *New Jersey* 50 D c
Bee Ridge, *Florida* 55 M f
Beeville, *Texas* 65 K g
Beggs, *Oklahoma* 62 G c
Behm Canal, *Alaska* 77 W j
Bel Air, *Maryland* 53 K f
Belchertown, *Massachusetts* 51 H a
Belden, *California* 74 D d
Belden, *North Dakota* 58 D b
Belding, *Michigan* 56 H f
Belen, *New Mexico* 71 L e
Belfair, *Washington* 73 H h
Belfast, *Maine* 49 F d
Belfast, *Pennsylvania* 50 C d
Belfield, *North Dakota* 58 C d
Belfry, *Montana* 67 L d
Belgium, *Wisconsin* 56 F f
Belgrade, *Nebraska* 60 F c
Belhaven, *North Carolina* 55 P b
Belington, *West Virginia* 52 G f
Belknap, *Iowa* 61 M d
Belknap, *Montana* 66 E b
Belkofski, *Alaska* 76 F j
Bell, *California* 75 E m
Bell, *Florida* 55 J h
Bellaire, *Kansas* 60 F e
Bellaire, *Michigan* 56 H e
Bellaire, *Ohio* 52 F e
Bellaire, *Texas* 64 F j
Belle, *Missouri* 61 N f
Belle, *West Virginia* 52 E g
Belleayre Mt., *New York* 50 D a
Belle Center, *Ohio* 52 C e
Bellflower, *Illinois* 57 E j
Bellefontaine, *Ohio* 52 C e
Bellefonte, *Delaware* 50 B f
Bellefonte, *Pennsylvania* 52 J e
Belle Fourche, *South Dakota* 58 C f
Belle Fourche R., *South Dakota* 58 D f
Belle Fourche R., *Wyoming* 67 P e
Belle Fourche Res., *South Dakota* 58 C f
Belle Glade, *Florida* 55 O g
Belle Mead, *New Jersey* 50 D e
Belle Meade, *Tennessee* 54 E a
Bellemont, *Arizona* 70 F d
Belleplain, *New Jersey* 50 D g
Belle Plaine, *Iowa* 61 M c
Belle Plaine, *Kansas* 60 G g
Belle Plaine, *Minnesota* 59 N f
Belle Rive, *Illinois* 57 E l
Belle Valley, *Ohio* 52 E f
Belleview, *Florida* 55 J h
Belleville, *Illinois* (37,264) 57 C l
Belleville, *Kansas* 60 G e
Belleville, *New Jersey* (35,005) 51 K e
Belleville, *New York* 53 K b
Belleville, *Pennsylvania* 52 J e
Belleville, *West Virginia* 52 E f
Belleville, *Wisconsin* 56 D g
Bellevue, *Idaho* 66 F f
Bellevue, *Iowa* 61 O b
Bellevue, *Michigan* 56 H g
Bellevue, *Ohio* 52 D e
Bellevue, *Pennsylvania* 50 O a
Bellevue, *Texas* 65 J b
Bellevue, *Washington* 72 C h
Bellflower, *California* (45,909) 75 F m
Bellflower, *Missouri* 61 N e
Bell Gardens, *California* (26,467), vicinity of Los Angeles
Bellingham, *Massachusetts* 51 L a
Bellingham, *South Dakota* 59 K e
Bellingham, *Washington* (34,688) 73 H g
Bell Island, *Alaska* 77 W j
Belmont, *California* 75 C m
Belmont, *Texas* 65 K f
Bellota, *California* 74 D f
Bellows Falls, *Vermont* 49 C e
Bellport, *New York* 51 H d
Bell Ranch, *New Mexico* 71 N d
Bells, *Tennessee* 54 B b
Bells, *Texas* 65 L b
Bellville, *Ohio* 52 D e
Bellville, *Texas* 65 L f
Bellvue, *Colorado* 69 L c
Bellwood, *Louisiana* 63 K g
Bellwood, *Nebraska* 60 G c
Bellwood, *Pennsylvania* 52 H e
Belmar, *New Jersey* 50 E e
Belmond, *Iowa* 61 L b
Belmont, *Massachusetts* (28,715) 49 F h
Belmont, *Nevada* 74 J c
Belmont, *New Hampshire* 49 D e
Belmont, *New York* 52 J c
Belmont, *North Carolina* 55 K b
Belmont, *Virginia* 52 J g
Belmont, *Wisconsin* 56 C g
Beloit, *Kansas* 60 F e
Beloit, *Wisconsin* (32,846) 56 D g
Belpre, *Kansas* 60 E g
Belpre, *Ohio* 52 E f
Belt, *Montana* 67 K b
Belted Ra., *Nevada* 75 J g
Belton, *Missouri* 61 K f
Belton, *Montana* 66 G a
Belton, *South Carolina* 55 J c
Belton, *Texas* 65 K d
Beluga L., *Alaska* 76 M f
Belvedere, *Illinois* 57 E g
Belvidere, *Kansas* 60 E g
Belvidere, *Nebraska* 60 G d
Belvidere, *North Carolina* 55 P a
Belvidere, *Pennsylvania* 50 C d
Belvidere, *South Dakota* 58 E g
Belzoni, *Mississippi* 63 N e
Bement, *Illinois* 57 E k
Bemidji, *Minnesota* 59 M c
Bemis, *Tennessee* 54 C b
Bemus Point, *New York* 52 G c
Benavides, *Texas* 65 J h
Ben Avon, *Pennsylvania* 53 O a
Benbrook, *Texas* 65 L j
Benbrook Dam, *Texas* 65 L j
Benbrook Res., *Texas* 65 L k
Benchland, *Montana* 67 K b
Benchley, *Texas* 65 L e
Bend, *Oregon* 73 J l
Bend, *Texas* 65 J d
Bendeleben Mts., *Alaska* 76 F d
Benedict, *Kansas* 61 J g
Benedict, *Maryland* 53 K g
Benedict, *Nebraska* 60 G c
Benedict, *North Dakota* 58 E c
Benevolence, *Georgia* 54 G f
Benezett, *Pennsylvania* 52 H d
Benge, *Washington* 73 M j
Benjamin, *Texas* 65 H b
Benjamin, *Utah* 68 E c
Benjamin L., *Oregon* 73 K m
Benkelman, *Nebraska* 60 C d
Bennet, *Nebraska* 60 H d
Bennett, *Colorado* 69 M d
Bennett, *Iowa* 61 N c
Bennett, *Wisconsin* 56 B c
Bennettsville, *South Carolina* 55 M c
Bennington, *Idaho* 66 J g
Bennington, *Kansas* 60 G e
Bennington, *New Hampshire* 49 D e
Bennington, *Oklahoma* 62 G d
Bennington, *Vermont* 49 B f
Benoit, *Wisconsin* 56 B c
Benson, *Arizona* 70 G h
Benson, *Illinois* 57 D j
Benson, *Louisiana* 63 K g
Benson, *Minnesota* 59 L e
Benson, *North Carolina* 55 N b
Bentley, *Kansas* 60 G g
Bentley, *North Dakota* 58 D d
Bentleyville, *Pennsylvania* 52 G e
Benton, *Alabama* 54 E e
Benton, *Arkansas* 63 L d
Benton, *California* 74 G g
Benton, *Florida* 55 J g
Benton, *Illinois* 57 E l
Benton, *Louisiana* 63 K f
Benton, *Missouri* 61 P g
Benton, *Pennsylvania* 53 K d
Benton, *Wisconsin* 56 C g
Benton Harbor, *Michigan* 57 G g
Bentonia, *Mississippi* 63 N f
Bentonville, *Arkansas* 63 J b
Ben Wheeler, *Texas* 65 M c
Benzonia, *Michigan* 56 G e
Beowawe, *Nevada* 74 J d
Berclair, *Texas* 65 K g
Berea, *Kentucky* 57 J m
Berea, *Nebraska* 60 B b
Berea, *Ohio* 52 E d
Berenda, *California* 75 E g
Beresford, *South Dakota* 59 K g
Bergen, *New York* 52 J b
Bergen, *North Dakota* 58 F b
Bergenfield, *New Jersey* (27,203) 51 L d
Bergholz, *Ohio* 52 F e
Bergland, *Michigan* 56 D c
Bergoo, *West Virginia* 52 F g
Bering Glacier, *Alaska* 77 Q f
Bering L., *Alaska* 77 P f
Bering Sea, *Alaska* 76 E g
Bering Str., *Alaska* 76 C d
Berino, *New Mexico* 71 L g

Berkeley, California (111,268) 75 B l
Berkeley Hills, California 75 B c
Berkeley Springs, West Virginia 52 H f
Berkley, Massachusetts 51 L b
Berkley, Michigan 56 K g
Berkshire Hills, Massachusetts 49 B f
Berlin, Maryland 53 L g
Berlin, New Hampshire 49 D d
Berlin, New Jersey 50 D f
Berlin, North Dakota 58 H d
Berlin, Pennsylvania 52 H f
Berlin, Wisconsin 56 E f
Berlin Res., Ohio 52 F e
Bern, Kansas 61 J e
Bernalillo, New Mexico 71 L d
Bernard, Iowa 61 O b
Bernardino, Arizona 70 H h
Bernardo, New Mexico 71 L e
Bernardsville, New Jersey 50 D d
Berne, Indiana 57 J j
Bernice, Louisiana 63 L f
Bernie, Missouri 61 P h
Bernville, Pennsylvania 50 A e
Berrien Springs, Michigan 57 G g
Berry, Alabama 54 D d
Berry, Kentucky 57 J l
Berry, Maine 49 H d
Berryessa, L., California 74 C f
Berryville, Arkansas 63 K b
Berryville, Virginia 52 H f
Bertha, Minnesota 59 L d
Berthold, North Dakota 58 E b
Berthoud, Colorado 69 L c
Bertram, Texas 65 J e
Bertrand, Nebraska 60 E d
Berwick, Maine 49 E e
Berwick, Pennsylvania 53 K d
Berwyn, Illinois (54,224) 57 A l
Berwyn, Pennsylvania 50 B e
Beryl, Utah 68 C f
Besboro I., Alaska 76 G d
Bessemer, Alabama (33,054) 54 E d
Bessemer, Michigan 56 C c
Bessemer, Pennsylvania 52 F e
Bessemer City, North Carolina 55 K b
Bessie, Oklahoma 62 E c
Bessmay, Texas 65 O e
Best, Texas 64 F d
Beswick, California 74 C c
Bete Grise B., Michigan 56 F b
Bethany, Connecticut 51 H c
Bethany, Missouri 61 K d
Bethany, Oklahoma 62 F c
Bethany Beach, Delaware 53 L g
Bethel, Alaska 76 G f
Bethel, Connecticut 50 G c
Bethel, Delaware 53 L g
Bethel, Minnesota 59 N e
Bethel, Missouri 61 M e
Bethel, New York 50 D b
Bethel, North Carolina 55 O b
Bethel, Ohio 52 B g
Bethel, Oklahoma 63 J d
Bethel, Vermont 49 C e
Bethel Park, Pennsylvania 53 O c
Bethesda, Maryland (56,527) 53 J f
Bethesda, Ohio 52 E e
Bethlehem, Connecticut 50 G b
Bethlehem, New Hampshire 49 D d
Bethlehem, Pennsylvania (75,408) 50 C d
Bethpage, New York 50 G d
Bethpage, Tennessee 54 E a
Bethpage Junction, New York 50 G d
Bethune, Colorado 69 O d
Bethune, South Carolina 55 L c
Betsie, Pt., Michigan 56 G e
Betsy, Michigan 56 H c
Betterton, Maryland 50 A g
Bettie, Texas 65 N c
Bettles, Alaska 76 M c
Bettles Field, Alaska 76 M c
Bettsville, Ohio 52 C d
Beulah, Michigan 56 G e
Beulah, North Dakota 58 E c
Beulah, Oregon 73 M m
Beulah, Wyoming 67 Q e
Beulaville, North Carolina 55 O c
Beverley, Washington 73 L j
Beverly, Kansas 60 G e
Beverly, L., Alaska 76 H g
Beverly, Massachusetts (36,108) 49 E f
Beverly, New Jersey 50 D e
Beverly, Ohio 52 E f
Beverly, West Virginia 52 G g
Beverly Hills, California (30,817) 75 D l
Beverly Park, Washington 73 H h
Bevier, Missouri 61 M e
Bexley, Ohio 52 D f
Bickleton, Washington 73 K k
Bickmore, West Virginia 52 E g
Bicknell, Indiana 57 F l
Bicknell, Utah 68 E e
Biddle, Montana 67 P d
Biddeford, Maine 49 E e
Bidwell, Ohio 52 D g
Bieber, California 74 D c
Bienville, Louisiana 63 L f
Big Arm, Montana 66 F b
Big Baldy Mt., Montana 67 K b
Big Bay, Michigan 56 F c
Big Bear City, California 75 J k
Big Bear Cr., Texas 65 M h
Big Bear L., California 75 H k
Big Belt Mts., Montana 66 J c
Big Bend, California 74 D c
Big Bend, Colorado 69 O e
Big Bend Nat. Park, Texas 64 D f
Big Black Cr., South Carolina 55 L c
Big Black Mt., Virginia 52 D j
Big Black R., Mississippi 63 O e
Big Blue R., Nebraska 60 H d
Big Canyon, Texas 64 E e
Big Chino Wash, Arizona 70 E d
Big Clifty, Kentucky 57 G m
Big Cr., Kansas 60 D f
Big Creek, Idaho 66 E d
Big Creek, West Virginia 52 D g
Big Cypress Swamp, Florida 55 N g
Big Delta, Alaska 77 O d
Big Dry Cr., Montana 67 O b
Big Eau Pleine Res., Wisconsin 56 C e
Big Elk Mt., Idaho 66 J f
Bigelow, Kansas 60 H e
Big Falls, Minnesota 59 N b
Bigfork, Minnesota 59 N c
Bigfork, Montana 66 F a
Big Fossil Cr., Texas 65 L j
Biggers, Arkansas 63 N b
Biggs, California 74 D e
Biggs, Oregon 73 K k
Biggsville, Illinois 57 C j
Big Hatchet Pk., New Mexico 71 J h
Big Hole Battlefield Nat. Mon., Montana 66 G d
Big Hole R., Montana 66 H d
Big Horn, Montana 67 N c
Big Horn Mts., Wyoming 67 N e
Bighorn R., Montana-Wyoming 67 N d
Big I., Arkansas 63 M e
Big Indian, New York 50 E a
Big Island, Virginia 52 G h
Big Koniuji I., Alaska 76 H j
Big L., Maine 49 H c
Big L., Oregon 73 K n
Big Lake, Alaska 76 N c
Big Lake, Texas 64 F d
Biglerville, Pennsylvania 53 J f
Big Lost R., Idaho 66 G f
Big Moose, New York 53 L b
Big Muddy Cr., Montana 67 Q a
Big Muddy R., Illinois 57 D m
Big Pine, California 75 G g
Big Pine, Florida 55 N j
Big Pine L., Minnesota 59 L d
Big Pine Pk., California 75 F k
Big Piney, Wyoming 67 K g
Big Piney R., Missouri 61 M g
Big R., Alaska 76 K e
Big R., California 74 B e
Big Rapids, Michigan 56 H f
Big Rib R., Wisconsin 56 D d
Big Rice L., Minnesota 59 N d
Big Sable Pt., Michigan 56 G e
Big Sage Res., California 74 E c
Big Sandy, Montana 67 K a
Big Sandy, Tennessee 54 C a
Big Sandy, Texas 65 M c
Big Sandy, Wyoming 67 L g
Big Sandy Cr., Colorado 69 M d
Big Sandy Cr., Montana 67 K a
Big Sandy L., Minnesota 59 N d
Big Sandy R., Arizona 70 D e
Big Sandy R., West Virginia 52 D g
Big Sandy Res., Wyoming 67 L g
Big Sioux R., South Dakota 59 K h
Big Smoky Val., Nevada 74 H f
Big Snowy Mt., Montana 67 L c
Big Spring, Texas (31,230) 64 F c
Big Springs, Idaho 66 J e
Big Springs, Nebraska 60 B c
Big Stone City, South Dakota 59 K g
Big Stone Gap, Virginia 52 D j
Big Stone L., Minnesota 59 K e
Big Sur, California 75 D h
Bigtimber, Montana 67 L d
Bigtrails, Wyoming 67 N f
Big Wells, Texas 65 H g
Big Wills Cr., Alabama 54 F c
Big Wood R., Idaho 66 F f
Bijou Hills, South Dakota 58 G g
Bill, Wyoming 67 P f
Billings, Montana (52,851) 67 M d
Billings, New York 50 F b
Billings, Oklahoma 62 F b
Bill Williams Mt., Arizona 70 E d
Bill Williams R., Arizona 70 D e
Biloxi, Mississippi (44,053) 63 P h
Binford, North Dakota 58 H c
Binger, Oklahoma 62 E c
Bingham, Maine 49 F c
Bingham, Michigan 56 H e
Bingham, Nebraska 60 B b
Bingham, New Mexico 71 L f
Bingham Canyon, Utah 68 B j
Binghamton, New York (75,941) 53 L c
Biola, California 75 F h
Bippus, Indiana 57 H j
Birch Cr., Alaska 77 P c
Birch Creek, Alaska 77 P c
Birches, Alaska 76 L d
Birch L., Minnesota 59 P c
Birch Tree, Missouri 61 N h
Birchwood, Minnesota 59 R h
Birchwood, Wisconsin 56 B d
Bird Cape, Alaska 76 M j
Bird City, Kansas 60 C e
Bird I., Alaska 76 H j
Birdsboro, Pennsylvania 50 B e
Birdseye, Indiana 57 G l
Birmingham, Alabama (340,887) 54 E d
Birmingham, Iowa 61 N d
Birmingham, Michigan (25,525) 56 K g
Birmingham, Missouri 61 Q a
Birney, Montana 67 O d
Birthday Pass, Alaska 76 J b
Bisbee, Arizona 70 H h
Bisbee, North Dakota 58 G b
Biscayne B., Florida 54 B e
Biscoe, North Carolina 55 M b
Bishop, California 75 G g
Bishop, Georgia 54 H d
Bishop, Maryland 53 L g
Bishop, Texas 65 K h
Bishop Creek Res., Nevada 74 L c
Bishopville, South Carolina 55 L c
Bismarck, Arkansas 63 K d
Bismarck, Illinois 57 F j
Bismarck, Missouri 61 O g
Bismarck, North Dakota (27,670) 58 F d
Bison, Oklahoma 62 F b
Bison, South Dakota 58 D e
Bistineau, L., Louisiana 63 K f
Bitely, Michigan 56 H f
Bitter Cr., Utah 68 G d
Bitter Cr., Wyoming 67 M h
Bitter Creek, Wyoming 67 M h
Bitter L., South Dakota 58 J e
Bitterroot R., Montana 66 F c
Bitterroot Ra., Idaho 66 G e
Bixby, Missouri 61 N g
Bixby, Oklahoma 62 H c
Blachly, Oregon 73 G l
Black, Alaska 76 E e
Black, Texas 64 B j
Black B., Louisiana 63 O j
Blackbear, California 74 B c
Blackburn, Mt., Alaska 77 Q f
Black Butte, California 74 C e
Black Canyon, Nevada-Arizona 75 L j
Black Canyon of the Gunnison Nat. Mon., Colorado 69 J e
Black Cr., Arizona 70 H d
Black Creek, Wisconsin 56 E e
Black Diamond, Washington 73 H h
Black Dome, mt., New York 50 E a
Blackduck, Minnesota 59 M c
Black Eagle, Montana 66 J b
Blackey, Kentucky 57 K l
Blackfoot, Idaho 66 H f
Blackfoot, Montana 66 H a
Blackfoot R., Idaho 66 J f
Blackfoot R., Montana 66 G c
Blackfoot River Res., Idaho 66 J g
Black Hills, South Dakota 58 C f
Black L., Alaska 76 H h
Black L., Louisiana 63 K f
Black L., Michigan 56 J d
Black L., New York 53 L a
Black L., North Carolina 55 N c
Black Lake, New Mexico 71 M c
Blackleaf, Montana 66 H a
Black Lick, Pennsylvania 52 G e
Black Mesa, Arizona 70 G c
Black Mesa, Arizona 70 E d
Black Mountain, North Carolina 55 J b
Black Mt., California 75 H j
Black Mt., New Mexico 71 J f
Black Mts., Arizona 70 C d
Black Pine Pk., Idaho 66 G g
Black Pk., New Mexico 71 J g
Black R., Alabama 54 D d
Black R., Alaska 77 Q c
Black R., Arizona 70 H f
Black R., Arkansas, etc. 63 M c
Black R., Louisiana 63 M g
Black R., Michigan 56 J d
Black R., Michigan 56 L f
Black R., Mississippi 63 P h
Black R., North Carolina 55 N c
Black R., South Carolina 55 M d
Black R., Wisconsin 56 C e
Black Ra., New Mexico 71 K f
Black Rapids, Alaska 76 P e
Black River, Michigan 56 K e
Black River Falls, Wisconsin 56 C e
Black Rock, Arkansas 63 M b
Black Rock, Utah 68 D e
Black Rock Des., Nevada 74 F d
Blacksburg, South Carolina 55 K b
Blacksburg, Virginia 52 F h
Blackshear, Georgia 55 J f
Blackshear, L., Georgia 54 H f
Black Springs, New Mexico 71 J f
Blackstock, South Carolina 55 K c
Blackstone, Massachusetts 51 K a
Blackstone, Virginia 52 J h
Blackstone R., Rhode Island 51 L b
Blacksville, West Virginia 52 F f
Blackville, South Carolina 55 K d
Blackwater, Missouri 61 L f
Blackwater R., Florida 54 E g
Blackwater R., Missouri 61 L f
Blackwater R., Virginia 53 J h
Blackwell, Oklahoma 62 F b
Blackwell, Texas 64 G c
Black Wolf, Kansas 60 F f
Blackwood Cr., Nebraska 60 C d
Bladen, Georgia 55 K f
Bladen, Nebraska 60 F d
Bladenboro, North Carolina 55 N c
Blain, Pennsylvania 52 J e
Blaine, Kansas 60 H e
Blaine, Washington 73 H g
Blaine, West Virginia 52 G f
Blair, Nebraska 61 H c
Blair, Okahoma 62 D d
Blair, West Virginia 52 E h
Blair, Wisconsin 56 B e
Blair Junction, Nevada 74 H g
Blairsden, California 74 E e
Blairstown, Iowa 61 M c
Blairstown, New Jersey 50 D d
Blairsville, Georgia 54 H c
Blairsville, Pennsylvania 52 G e
Blake I., Washington 72 B h
Blakely, Georgia 54 G f
Blake Pt., Michigan 56 E a
Blakesburg, Iowa 61 M d
Blakeslee, Pennsylvania 50 B c
Blakes Pt., Minnesota 59 S b
Blanca, Colorado 69 L f
Blanca Pk., Colorado 69 L f
Blanchard, Idaho 66 D a
Blanchard, Michigan 56 H f
Blanchard, North Dakota 58 J c
Blanchard, Oklahoma 62 F c
Blanchard, Washington 73 H g
Blanchester, Ohio 52 C f
Blanco, C., Oregon 73 F n
Blanco, New Mexico 71 K c
Blanco, Texas 65 J e
Bland, Virginia 52 E h
Blandford, Massachusetts 51 H a
Blanding, Utah 68 G f
Blandinsville, Illinois 57 C j
Blandon, Pennsylvania 50 B e
Blaney, South Carolina 55 L c
Blaney Park, Michigan 56 H c
Blanket, Texas 65 J d
Blasdell, New York 52 H c
Blawnox, Pennsylvania 53 Q a
Blazon, Wyoming 67 K h
Bleakwood, Texas 65 O e
Bledsoe, Texas 64 E b
Blencoe, Iowa 61 H c
Blessing, Texas 65 L g
Blevins, Arkansas 63 K e
Blewett, Texas 64 G f
Blewett Falls L., North Carolina 55 M b
Bligh I., Alaska 77 O f
Bliss, Idaho 66 F g
Blissfield, Michigan 57 K h
Blitzen, Oregon 73 L n
Block I., Rhode Island 51 K c
Block Island, Rhode Island 51 K c
Block Island Sd., Rhode Island 51 K c
Blomkest, Minnesota 59 M f
Bloodworth I., Maryland 53 K g
Bloom, Colorado 69 N f
Bloomer, Wisconsin 56 B d
Bloomfield, Connecticut 51 H b
Bloomfield, Indiana 57 G k
Bloomfield, Iowa 61 M d
Bloomfield, Kentucky 57 H m
Bloomfield, Missouri 61 P h
Bloomfield, Montana 67 Q b
Bloomfield, Nebraska 60 G b
Bloomfield, New Jersey (51,867) 51 K e
Bloomfield, New Mexico 71 K c
Bloomfield, Vermont 49 D d
Bloomingburg, New York 50 E b
Bloomingdale, New Jersey 50 E d
Blooming Grove, Pennsylvania 50 C c
Blooming Grove, Texas 65 L c
Blooming Prairie, Minnesota 59 N g
Bloomington, Idaho 66 J g
Bloomington, Illinois (36,271) 57 E g
Bloomington, Indiana (31,357) 57 G k
Bloomington, Minnesota (50,498) 59 Q j
Bloomington, Texas 65 L g
Bloomington, Wisconsin 56 C g
Bloomsburg, Pennsylvania 53 K d
Bloomsbury, New Jersey 50 C d
Bloomsdale, Missouri 61 O f
Bloomville, New York 50 D a
Bloomville, Ohio 52 C d
Blossburg, Pennsylvania 53 J d
Blossom, Texas 65 M b
Blountstown, Florida 54 F g
Blowing Rock, North Carolina 55 K a
Bloxom, Virginia 53 L h
Blue Ball, Pennsylvania 50 A e
Blue Bell Knoll, Utah 68 E e
Blue Cr., Idaho 66 D g
Blue Creek, Utah 68 D b
Blue Cypress L., Florida 55 O f
Blue Diamond, Kentucky 57 K m
Blue Earth, Minnesota 59 M g
Blue Earth R., Minnesota 59 M g
Blue Eye, Missouri 61 L h
Bluefield, West Virginia 52 E h
Blue Grass, Iowa 61 O c
Blue Hill, Maine 49 G d
Blue Hill, Nebraska 60 F d
Blue Hill B., Maine 49 G d
Blue I., Illinois 57 F h
Blue Island, Illinois 57 B n
Bluejoint L., Oregon 73 L n
Blue Knob, mt., Pennsylvania 52 H e
Blue L., Utah 68 D d
Blue Lagoon, Florida 54 B d
Blue Lake, California 74 B d
Bluemont, Virginia 52 J f
Blue Mound, Illinois 57 D k
Blue Mountain, Colorado 68 H c
Blue Mountain, Mississippi 63 O d
Blue Mountain Lake, New York 53 M b
Blue Mountain Pass, Oregon 73 N n
Blue Mt., Arkansas 63 K d
Blue Mt., Pennsylvania 53 K e
Blue Mt. Res., Arkansas 63 K c
Blue Mts., Oregon 73 M l
Blue Point, New York 51 G d
Blue R., Arizona 70 H f
Blue R., Colorado 69 K d
Blue R., Missouri 61 P b
Blue R., Oklahoma 62 G d
Blue Rapids, Kansas 60 H e
Blue Ridge, Georgia 54 G c
Blue Ridge L., Georgia 54 G c
Blue River, Oregon 73 H l
Bluestone Res., West Virginia 52 F h
Bluewater, New Mexico 71 K d
Bluff, Utah 68 G f
Bluff City, Kansas 60 G g
Bluff City, Tennessee 55 J a
Bluffdale, Texas 65 J c
Bluff Pt., North Carolina 55 P b
Bluffs, Illinois 57 C k
Bluffton, Arkansas 63 K d
Bluffton, Georgia 54 G f
Bluffton, Indiana 57 H j
Bluffton, Minnesota 59 L d
Bluffton, Ohio 52 C e
Bluffton, South Carolina 55 L e
Blum, Texas 65 K c
Blunt, South Dakota 58 G f
Blunt Point Res., South Dakota 58 F f
Bly, Oregon 73 J n
Blying Sd., Alaska 77 N g
Blythe, California 75 L l
Blythedale, Missouri 61 L d
Blytheville, Arkansas 63 O c
Boardman, Oregon 73 L k
Boardman R., Michigan 56 H e
Boaz, Alabama 54 E c
Boaz, New Mexico 71 O f
Bobrof I., Alaska 77 O j
Boca, California 74 E e
Boca Chica, Florida 55 N j
Boca Grande, Florida 55 M g
Boca Grande Key, Florida 55 N j
Boca Raton, Florida 55 O g
Bode, Iowa 61 K b
Bodega Hd., California 74 B f
Bodfish, California 75 G j
Boelus, Nebraska 60 F c
Boerne, Texas 65 J f
Boeuf R., Arkansas-Louisiana 63 M f
Bogalusa, Louisiana 63 O h
Bogard, Missouri 61 L e
Bogata, Texas 65 M b
Bogoslof I., Alaska 76 C k
Bogue, Kansas 60 E e
Bogue Chitto, Mississippi 63 N g
Bogue Chitto R., Louisiana 63 N h
Bogue Inlet, North Carolina 55 O c
Bois Blanc I., Michigan 56 J d
Boise, Idaho (34,481) 66 D f
Boise City, Oklahoma 62 B c
Boise R., Idaho 66 D f
Bokchito, Oklahoma 62 G d
Bokeelia, Florida 55 M g
Bokoshe, Oklahoma 63 J c
Bolckow, Missouri 61 K d
Bole, Montana 66 H b
Boles, Idaho 66 D d
Boley, Oklahoma 62 G c
Boligee, Alabama 54 C e
Bolivar, Missouri 61 L g
Bolivar, New York 52 H c
Bolivar, Tennessee 54 C b
Bolivar Pen., Texas 65 N f
Bolivia, North Carolina 55 N c
Bolton, North Carolina 55 N c
Bomarton, Texas 65 H b
Bona, Mt., Alaska 77 R f
Bon Air, Virginia 52 J h
Bonanza, Colorado 69 K e
Bonanza, Oregon 73 J n
Bonanza Pk., Washington 73 K g
Bonaparte, Iowa 61 N d
Bonaparte, Mt., Washington 73 L g
Bonasila Dome, mt., Alaska 76 G e
Boncarbo, Colorado 69 M f
Bond, Colorado 69 K d
Bondsville, Massachusetts 51 J a
Bonduel, Wisconsin 56 E e
Bondurant, Wyoming 67 K f
Bone, Idaho 66 J f
Bonesteel, South Dakota 58 H g
Bonetraill, North Dakota 58 C b
Bonham, Texas 65 L b
Bonifay, Florida 54 F g
Bonita, Arizona 70 G g
Bonita, Louisiana 63 M f
Bonita, Pt., California 75 B l
Bonita Springs, Florida 55 N g
Bonner, Montana 66 G c
Bonners Ferry, Idaho 66 D a
Bonner Springs, Kansas 61 K e
Bonne Terre, Missouri 61 O g
Bonneville, Oregon 73 J k
Bonneville, Wyoming 67 M f
Bonneville Dam, Oregon 73 J k
Bonneville Pk., Idaho 66 J g
Bonneville Salt Flats, Utah 68 C c
Bonny Res., Colorado 69 O d
Bono, Arkansas 63 N c
Bon Secour, Alabama 54 D g
Bon Wier, Texas 65 O e
Booker, Texas 64 D g
Boon, Michigan 56 H e
Boone, Colorado 69 M e
Boone, Iowa 61 L b
Boone, North Carolina 55 K a
Boones Mill, Virginia 52 G h
Boonesboro, Maryland 52 J f
Booneville, Arkansas 63 K c
Booneville, California 74 B e
Booneville, Kentucky 57 K m
Booneville, Mississippi 63 P d
Booneville Res., Kentucky 57 K m
Boonton, New Jersey 50 E d
Boonville, Indiana 57 F l
Boonville, Missouri 61 M f
Boonville, New York 53 L b
Boothbay Harbor, Maine 49 F e
Boothton, Alabama 54 E d
Borah Pk., Idaho 66 G e
Bordeaux, Wyoming 67 Q h
Borden, Indiana 57 H l
Bordentown, New Jersey 50 D e
Borger, Texas 64 C h
Borgne, L., Louisiana 63 O h
Borie, Wyoming 67 Q h
Boron, California 75 H j
Borup, Minnesota 59 K c
Boscawen, New Hampshire 49 D e
Bosco, Louisiana 63 L f
Boscobel, Wisconsin 56 C f
Bosler, Wyoming 67 P h
Bosque, New Mexico 71 L e
Bossier City, Louisiana (32,776) 63 K f
Boston, Georgia 54 H g
Boston, Massachusetts (697,197) 49 E f
Boston B., Massachusetts 49 H h
Boston Corners, New York 50 F a
Boston Harb., Massachusetts 49 H j
Boston Mts., Arkansas 63 K c
Boswell, Indiana 57 F j
Boswell, Oklahoma 62 H d
Boswell, Pennsylvania 52 G e
Boswell Res., Oklahoma 62 H d
Bosworth, Missouri 61 L e
Bothell, Washington 72 C g
Botkins, Ohio 52 B e
Botsford, Connecticut 50 G c
Bottineau, North Dakota 58 F b
Boudreau, B., Louisiana 63 O j
Boulder, Colorado (37,718) 69 L c
Boulder, Montana 66 H c
Boulder, Utah 68 E f
Boulder, Wyoming 67 L g
Boulder Canyon, Nevada 75 L h
Boulder City, Nevada 75 L j
Boulder Cr., Idaho 66 D g
Boulder Creek, California 75 C g
Boulevard, California 75 J m
Boundary, Washington 73 N g
Boundary Pk., Nevada 74 G g
Bound Brook, New Jersey 50 D d
Bountiful, Colorado 69 L f
Bountiful, Utah 68 C g
Bourbeuse R., Missouri 61 N f
Bourbon, Indiana 57 G h
Bourbon, Missouri 61 N f
Bourne, Massachusetts 51 M b
Bouse, Arizona 70 D f
Bouse Wash., Arizona 70 C f
Bovill, Idaho 66 D c
Bovina, Texas 64 B j
Bovina Center, New York 50 D a
Bowbells, North Dakota 58 D b
Bowden, Florida 55 K g
Bowdle, South Dakota 98 G e
Bowdoin, L., Montana 67 N a
Bowdon, Alabama 54 F d
Bowdon, North Dakota 58 G c
Bowen, Illinois 57 B j
Bowers, Delaware 50 B g
Bowersville, Ohio 52 C f
Bowery Pk., Idaho 66 F e
Bowie, Arizona 70 H g
Bowie, Colorado 69 J e
Bowie, Texas 65 K b
Bowling Green, Florida 55 N f
Bowling Green, Indiana 57 F k
Bowling Green, Kentucky (28,338) 57 G m
Bowling Green, Missouri 61 N e
Bowling Green, Ohio 52 C d
Bowling Green, Virginia 52 J g
Bowman, Georgia 54 H c
Bowman, North Dakota 58 C d
Bowmansville, Pennsylvania 50 A e
Boyce, Louisiana 63 L g
Boyce, Virginia 52 H f
Boyd, Montana 67 L d
Boyd, Texas 65 K b
Boydton, Virginia 52 H j
Boyer, Iowa 61 J b
Boyero, Colorado 69 N e
Boyer R., Iowa 61 J b
Boyertown, Pennsylvania 50 B e
Boyes, Montana 67 P d
Boykins, Virginia 53 J j
Boyle, Mississippi 63 N e
Boyne City, Michigan 56 J d
Boyne Falls, Michigan 56 J d

Boynton, Missouri 61 L d
Boynton, Oklahoma 62 H c
Boynton Beach, Florida 55 O g
Boysen Res., Wyoming 67 M f
Box Butte Res., Nebraska 60 A b
Box Cr., Wyoming 67 P f
Box Elder, Montana 67 K a
Box Elder, South Dakota 58 C f
Box Elder Cr., Colorado 69 M d
Boxelder Cr., Montana 67 M b
Box Elder Cr., Montana 67 Q d
Bozeman, Montana 67 K d
Bracken, Texas 65 J f
Brackettville, Texas 64 G f
Braddock, North Dakota 58 F d
Braddock, Pennsylvania 53 Q b
Braddyville, Iowa 61 J d
Bradenton, Florida 55 M f
Bradenton Beach, Florida 55 M f
Bradford, Arkansas 63 M c
Bradford, Illinois 57 D h
Bradford, Iowa 61 L b
Bradford, Maine 49 G c
Bradford, New Hampshire 49 C e
Bradford, Ohio 52 B e
Bradford, Pennsylvania 52 H d
Bradford, Rhode Island 51 K c
Bradford, Vermont 49 C d
Bradfordsville, Kentucky 57 H m
Bradley, Arkansas 63 K e
Bradley, California 75 E j
Bradley, Illinois 57 F h
Bradley, New York 50 D b
Bradley, Oklahoma 62 F d
Bradley, South Dakota 58 J e
Bradley Beach, New Jersey 50 F e
Bradley Field, Connecticut 51 H b
Bradleyville, Missouri 61 M h
Bradner, Ohio 52 C d
Bradshaw, Nebraska 60 G d
Bradshaw, Texas 64 H c
Brady, Montana 66 J a
Brady, Nebraska 60 D c
Brady, Texas 65 H d
Brady Glacier, Alaska 77 T g
Braganza, Georgia 55 J f
Bragg City, Missouri 61 P h
Braham, Minnesota 59 N e
Braidwood, Illinois 57 E h
Brainard, Nebraska 60 G c
Brainards, New Jersey 50 C d
Brainerd, Minnesota 59 M d
Braintree, Massachusetts (31,069) 51 L a
Braithwaite, Louisiana 63 O j
Braleys, Massachusetts 51 M b
Braman, Oklahoma 62 F b
Bramley Mt., New York 50 D a
Brampton, North Dakota 58 J e
Bramwell, West Virginia 52 E h
Branch, Michigan 56 G f
Branch, New York 50 E b
Branchport, New York 53 J c
Branchville, New Jersey 50 D c
Branchville, South Carolina 55 L d
Brandenberg, Montana 67 O d
Brandenburg, Kentucky 57 G m
Brandon, Colorado 69 O e
Brandon, Mississippi 63 O f
Brandon, Nebraska 60 C d
Brandon, Vermont 49 B e
Brandon, Wisconsin 56 E f
Brandreth, New York 53 M b
Brandsville, Missouri 61 N h
Brandt, South Dakota 59 K f
Brandy, Virginia 52 J g
Brandywine, Maryland 53 K g
Branford, Connecticut 51 H c
Branford, Florida 55 J h
Branscomb, California 74 B e
Branson, Colorado 69 N f
Branson, Missouri 61 L h
Brantford, North Dakota 58 H c
Brantley, Alabama 54 E f
Brashear, Missouri 61 M d
Brasstown Bald, mt., Georgia 54 H c
Brassua L., Maine 49 E c
Brattleboro, Vermont 49 C f
Brave, Pennsylvania 52 F f
Brawley, California 75 K m
Braymer, Missouri 61 L e
Brays Bayou, Texas 64 F j
Brazil, Indiana 57 F k
Brazonia, Texas 65 M f
Brazos R., Texas 65 M g
Breaux Bridge, Louisiana 63 M h
Breckenridge, Colorado 69 K d
Breckenridge, Michigan 56 J f
Breckenridge, Minnesota 59 K d
Breckenridge, Missouri 61 L e
Breckenridge, Texas 65 J c
Breda, Iowa 61 K b
Breese, Illinois 57 D l
Breien, North Dakota 58 F d
Bremen, Georgia 54 F d
Bremen, Indiana 57 G h
Bremen, Ohio 52 D f
Bremerton, Washington (28,922) 72 A h
Bremner R., Alaska 77 Q f
Bremond, Texas 65 L d
Brenham, Texas 65 L e
Brenner, Montana 66 G e
Brent, Alabama 54 D e
Brentford, South Dakota 58 H e
Brentwood, California 74 D g
Brentwood, New York 50 G d
Brentwood, Pennsylvania 53 P b
Breton I., Louisiana 63 O j
Breton Sd., Louisiana 63 O j
Breton Woods, New Jersey 50 E e
Brevard, North Carolina 55 J b
Brevoort L., Michigan 56 J c
Brevort, Michigan 56 H c
Brewer, Maine 49 G d
Brewerton, New York 53 K b
Brewster, Florida 55 N f
Brewster, Kansas 60 C e
Brewster, Massachusetts 51 N b
Brewster, Nebraska 60 E c
Brewster, New York 50 F c
Brewster, Ohio 52 E e
Brewster, Washington 73 L g
Brewton, Alabama 54 D f
Brian Head, Utah 68 D f
Briarcliff Manor, New York 50 F c
Brice, Texas 64 D j
Briceland, California 74 B d
Bricelyn, Minnesota 59 N g
Brickeys, Arkansas 63 N d
Bridge, Idaho 66 G g
Bridge, Oregon 73 G m
Bridgeboro, Georgia 54 H f
Bridgehampton, New York 51 J d
Bridgeland, Utah 68 F c
Bridgeport, Alabama 54 F c
Bridgeport, California 74 F f
Bridgeport, Connecticut (156,748) 50 G c
Bridgeport, Kansas 60 G f
Bridgeport, Nebraska 60 A c
Bridgeport, New Jersey 50 C f
Bridgeport, Ohio 52 F e
Bridgeport, Oklahoma 62 E c
Bridgeport, Oregon 73 N l
Bridgeport, Pennsylvania 50 C e
Bridgeport, Texas 65 K b
Bridgeport, Washington 73 L h
Bridgeport, West Virginia 52 F f
Bridgeport L., Texas 65 K b
Bridgeport Res., California 74 F f
Bridger, Montana 67 M d
Bridger Pk., Montana 67 K d
Bridger Pk., Wyoming 67 N h
Bridgeton, New Jersey 50 C g
Bridgeton, North Carolina 55 O b
Bridgeville, California 74 B d
Bridgeville, Delaware 53 L g
Bridgeville, Pennsylvania 53 O c
Bridgewater, Connecticut 50 G b
Bridgewater, Maine 49 G b
Bridgewater, Massachusetts 51 L a
Bridgewater, South Dakota 58 J g
Bridgewater, Virginia 52 G g
Bridgman, Michigan 57 G h
Bridgton, Maine 49 E d
Brier Cr., Georgia 55 K d
Brigantine, New Jersey 50 E g
Briggs, Texas 65 K e
Briggsdale, Colorado 69 M c
Brigham City, Utah 68 D b
Bright Angel Point, Arizona 70 E c
Brighton, Colorado 69 P g
Brighton, Florida 55 N f
Brighton, Illinois 57 C k
Brighton, Iowa 61 N c
Brighton, Michigan 56 K g
Brilliant, New Mexico 71 N c
Brillion, Wisconsin 56 E e
Brimfield, Illinois 57 D j
Brimfield, Massachusetts 51 J a
Brinkhaven, Ohio 52 D e
Brinkley, Arkansas 63 M d
Brinsmade, North Dakota 58 G b
Brinson, Georgia 54 G g
Briscoe, Texas 64 D h
Bristol, Colorado 69 O e
Bristol, Connecticut (45,499) 51 H b
Bristol, Florida 54 G g
Bristol, Georgia 55 J f
Bristol, Indiana 57 H h
Bristol, New Hampshire 49 D e
Bristol, Pennsylvania (59,298) 50 D e
Bristol, Rhode Island 51 L b
Bristol, South Dakota 58 J e
Bristol, Tennessee 55 J a
Bristol, Vermont 49 B d
Bristol, Virginia 52 D j
Bristol B., Alaska 76 G h
Bristol L., California 75 K k
Bristol Mts., California 75 K k
Bristol Silver, Nevada 74 L f
Bristow, Oklahoma 62 G c
British Mts., Alaska 77 Q b
Britt, Iowa 61 L a
Britton, Oklahoma 62 F c
Britton, South Dakota 58 J e
Broad, R., South Carolina 55 L e
Broadalbin, New York 53 M b
Broadbent, Oregon 73 F m
Broad Brook, Connecticut 51 H b
Broaddus, Texas 65 N d
Broadland, South Dakota 58 H f
Broad Pass, Alaska 76 N e
Broad R., Georgia 54 H c
Broad R., South Carolina 55 K c
Broadus, Montana 67 P d
Broadview, Montana 67 M c
Broadview, New Mexico 71 O e
Broadwater, Nebraska 60 B c
Broadway, Virginia 52 H g
Brock, Nebraska 61 J d
Brocket, North Dakota 58 H b
Brockport, New York 52 J b
Brocksburg, Nebraska 60 E b
Brockton, Mass. (72,813) 51 L a
Brockton, Montana 67 Q a
Brockway, Montana 67 P b
Brockway, Pennsylvania 52 H d
Brocton, Illinois 57 F k
Brocton, New York 52 G c
Brodhead, Wisconsin 56 D g
Brodnax, Virginia 52 J j
Brogan, Oregon 73 N l
Brokaw, Wisconsin 56 D d
Broken Arrow, Oklahoma 62 H b
Broken Bow, Nebraska 60 E c
Broken Bow, Oklahoma 63 J d
Brompton, Iowa 61 M d
Bronaugh, Missouri 61 K g
Bronson, Florida 55 J h
Bronson, Michigan 57 H h
Bronson, Texas 65 N d
Bronte, Texas 64 G d
Bronxville, New York 51 N d
Brook, Indiana 57 F j
Brooke, Virginia 52 J g
Brookeland, Texas 65 O d
Brooker, Florida 55 J h
Brookfield, Connecticut 50 G c
Brookfield, Massachusetts 51 J a
Brookfield, Missouri 61 L e
Brookfield, Vermont 49 C d
Brookfield, Wisconsin, vicinity of Wauwatosa
Brookhaven, Mississippi 63 N g
Brookhaven, New York 51 H d
Brookings, Oregon 73 F n
Brookings, South Dakota 59 K f
Brookland, Pennsylvania 52 J d
Brooklet, Georgia 55 K e
Brookline, Massachusetts (54,044) 49 F j
Brooklyn, Connecticut 51 K b
Brooklyn, Indiana 57 G k
Brooklyn, Iowa 61 M c
Brooklyn, Maryland 53 Q f
Brooklyn, Michigan 57 J g
Brooklyn, Mississippi 63 O g
Brooklyn, New York 51 L g
Brooklyn, Pennsylvania 53 L d
Brooklyn Center, Minnesota 59 Q h
Brooklyn Park, Minnesota 59 P h
Brookneal, Virginia 52 G j
Brook Park, Minnesota 59 N e
Brookport, Illinois 57 E m
Brooks, L., Alaska 76 J g
Brooks, Maine 49 F d
Brooks, Montana 67 L b
Brooks, Mt., Alaska 76 M e
Brooksburg, New York 50 E a
Brookshire, Texas 65 M f
Brooks I., California 75 B l
Brookside, Texas 64 G j
Brooks Mt., Alaska 76 D d
Brooks Ra., Alaska 76 H b
Brookston, Indiana 57 G j
Brookston, Minnesota 59 O d
Brookston, Texas 65 M b
Brooks Vale, Connecticut 51 H c
Brooksville, Florida 55 J j
Brookton, Maine 49 H c
Brooktondale, New York 53 K c
Brookville, Indiana 57 J k
Brookville, Kansas 60 G f
Brookville, Mississippi 63 P e
Brookville, Pennsylvania 52 G d
Brookwood, Alabama 54 D d
Broomall, Pennsylvania 50 C f
Broomfield, Colorado 69 O g
Brooten, Minnesota 59 L e
Brothers, Oregon 73 K m
Broughton, Illinois 57 E m
Broughton, Kansas 60 G e
Broughton, Pennsylvania 53 P c
Browerville, Minnesota 59 M d
Brown City, Michigan 56 L f
Brownell, Kansas 60 E f
Brownfield, Texas 64 E b
Browning, Missouri 61 L d
Browning, Montana 66 G a
Brownlee, Nebraska 60 D b
Browns, Illinois 57 E l
Brownsboro, Texas 65 M c
Brownsburg, Indiana 57 G k
Browns Mills, New Jersey 50 D f
Brownson, Nebraska 60 A c
Brownstown, Indiana 57 G l
Browns Valley, Minnesota 59 K e
Brownsville, Florida (38,417), vicinity of Pensacola
Brownsville, Indiana 57 J k
Brownsville, Kentucky 57 G m
Brownsville, Oregon 73 H l
Brownsville, Pennsylvania 52 G e
Brownsville, Tennessee 54 B b
Brownsville, Texas (48,040) 65 K k
Brownton, Minnesota 59 M f
Browntown, Wisconsin 56 D g
Brownville, Alabama 54 D d
Brownville, Nebraska 61 J d
Brownville, New York 53 L a
Brownville Junction, Maine 49 F c
Brownwood, L., Texas 65 H d
Brownwood, Texas 65 J d
Broxton, Georgia 55 J f
Bruce, Mississippi 63 O d
Bruce, South Dakota 59 K f
Bruce, Wisconsin 56 B d
Bruce Crossing, Michigan 56 D c
Bruceton, Tennessee 54 C a
Bruceville, Texas 65 K d
Bruin, Pennsylvania 52 G d
Bruin Pt., Utah 68 F d
Brule, Nebraska 60 C c
Brule, Wisconsin 56 B c
Brundage, Texas 65 H g
Brundidge, Alabama 54 F f
Bruneau, Idaho 66 E g
Bruneau R., Idaho 66 E g
Bruni, Texas 65 J h
Bruno, Minnesota 59 O d
Brunswick, Georgia 55 K f
Brunswick, Maine 49 F e
Brunswick, Maryland 52 J f
Brunswick, Missouri 61 L e
Brunswick, Ohio 52 E d
Brush, Colorado 69 N c
Brushton, New York 53 M a
Brushy Mts., North Carolina 55 K a
Brussels, Wisconsin 56 F e
Bruynswick, New York 50 E b
Bryan, Ohio 52 B d
Bryan, Texas (27,542) 65 L e
Bryan, Wyoming 67 L h
Bryant, Arkansas 63 L d
Bryant, California 75 C l
Bryant, Indiana 57 H j
Bryant Cr., Missouri 61 M h
Bryant L., Minnesota 59 P j
Bryant Pond, Maine 49 E d
Bryce Canyon Nat. Park, Utah 68 D f
Bryn Mawr, Pennsylvania 50 C e
Bryn Mawr, Washington 72 C j
Bryson City, North Carolina 54 H b
Bucatunda, Mississippi 63 P g
Buchanan, Georgia 54 F d
Buchanan, Michigan 57 G h
Buchanan, New Mexico 71 N e
Buchanan, North Dakota 58 H c
Buchanan, Virginia 52 G h
Buchanan Dam, Texas 65 J e
Buchanan L., Texas 65 J e
Buchon, Pt., California 75 E j
Buckeye, Arizona 70 E f
Buckeye Lake, Ohio 52 D f
Buckeyestown, Maryland 53 J f
Buckhannon, West Virginia 52 F g
Buckhannon R., West Virginia 52 F f
Buckhead, Georgia 54 G d
Buck Hill Falls, Pennsylvania 50 C c
Buckholts, Texas 65 K e
Buckhorn, Wyoming 67 Q e
Buckingham, Pennsylvania 50 D e
Buckingham, Texas 65 O h
Buckingham, Virginia 52 H h
Buckland, Alaska 76 G d
Buckland R., Alaska 76 G d
Buckley, Illinois 57 E j
Buckley, Michigan 56 H e
Buckley, Washington 73 H h
Bucklin, Kansas 60 E g
Bucklin, Missouri 61 M e
Buck Mountain, Pennsylvania 50 B d
Bucknum, Wyoming 67 O f
Buck Run, Pennsylvania 50 B f
Bucks, California 74 D e
Buckskin Mts., Arizona 70 D e
Bucks Mt., California 74 D e
Bucksport, Maine 49 G d
Bucyrus, North Dakota 58 D d
Bucyrus, Ohio 52 C e
Buda, Texas 65 K e
Buddtown, New Jersey 50 D f
Bude, Mississippi 63 N g
Buellton, California 75 E k
Buena Park, California (46,401) vicinity of Los Angeles
Buena Vista, Georgia 54 G e
Buena Vista, Virginia 52 G h
Buena Vista L., California 75 F j
Bueyeros, New Mexico 71 O d
Buffalo, Kansas 61 J g
Buffalo, Kentucky 57 H m
Buffalo, Minnesota 59 N e
Buffalo, Missouri 61 L g
Buffalo, Montana 67 L c
Buffalo, New York (532,759) 52 H c
Buffalo, North Dakota 58 J d
Buffalo, Oklahoma 62 D b
Buffalo, South Carolina 55 K c
Buffalo, South Dakota 58 C d
Buffalo, Texas 65 L d
Buffalo, West Virginia 52 E g
Buffalo, Wyoming 67 O e
Buffalo Bill Dam, Wyoming 67 L e
Buffalo Bill Res., Wyoming 67 L e
Buffalo Center, Alaska 77 O d
Buffalo Center, Iowa 61 L a
Buffalo Creek, Colorado 69 L d
Buffalo Gap, South Dakota 58 C g
Buffalo L., Texas 64 B j
Buffalo R., Arkansas 63 K c
Buffalo R., Minnesota 59 K d
Buffalo R., Tennessee 54 D b
Buffalo R., Wisconsin 56 B e
Buford, Georgia 54 G c
Buford, North Dakota 58 C b
Buford, Wyoming 67 P h
Buford Res., Georgia 54 G c
Buhl, Idaho 66 F g
Buhl, Minnesota 59 O c
Buldir I., Alaska 76 K j
Bullard, Texas 65 M c
Bull B., South Carolina 55 M e
Bull I., South Carolina 55 M e
Bullion Mts., California 75 J k
Bull Mts., Montana 67 M c
Bulls Gap, Tennessee 54 H a
Bull Shoals L., Missouri-Arkansas 61 M h
Bullville, New York 50 E b
Bully Choop Mt., California 74 C d
Bumble Bee, Arizona 70 E e
Bumping L., Washington 73 J j
Bunceton, Missouri 61 M f
Bunch, Oklahoma 63 J c
Bundicks Cr., Louisiana 63 K h
Bunker, Missouri 61 N g
Bunker Hill, Alaska 76 E d
Bunker Hill, Illinois 57 D k
Bunker Hill, Indiana 57 G j
Bunker Hill, Kansas 60 F f
Bunker Hill, Texas 64 F h
Bunkerville, Nevada 75 L h
Bunkie, Louisiana 63 L h
Bunnell, Florida 55 K h
Buras, Louisiana 63 O j
Burbank, California (90,155) 75 G k
Burchard, Nebraska 60 H d
Burchinal, Iowa 61 L a
Burdett, New York 53 K c
Burgaw, North Carolina 55 O c
Burgdorf, Idaho 66 E d
Burgess Store, Virginia 53 K h
Burien, Washington 72 B j
Burkburnett, Texas 65 J a
Burke, Idaho 66 E b
Burke, South Dakota 58 G g
Burke, Texas 65 N d
Burkesville, Kentucky 57 H n
Burkett, Texas 65 H d
Burkeville, Virginia 52 H h
Burkmere, South Dakota 58 G e
Burleson, Texas 65 K c
Burley, Idaho 66 G g
Burlingame, California 75 B m
Burlingame, Kansas 61 J f
Burlington, Colorado 69 O d
Burlington, Connecticut 51 H b
Burlington, Iowa (32,430) 61 N d
Burlington, Kansas 61 J f
Burlington, New Jersey 50 D e
Burlington, North Carolina (33,199) 55 M a
Burlington, Vermont (35,531) 49 B d
Burlington, Washington 73 H g
Burlington, West Virginia 52 G f
Burlington, Wyoming 67 M e
Burlington Junction, Missouri 61 J d
Burmester, Utah 68 D c
Burnet, Texas 65 J e
Burney, California 74 D d
Burnham, Maine 49 F d
Burnham, Pennsylvania 52 J e
Burns, Colorado 69 K d
Burns, Oregon 73 L m
Burns, Wyoming 67 Q h
Burnside, Kentucky 57 J n
Burnside, New York 50 E c
Burnside, Pennsylvania 52 H e
Burnsville, Mississippi 63 P d
Burnsville, North Carolina 55 J b
Burnsville, West Virginia 52 F g
Burnstad, North Dakota 58 G d
Burntfork, Wyoming 67 L h
Burnt Paw, Alaska 77 Q c
Burnt R., Oregon 73 N l
Burnt Ranch, California 74 B d
Burr Oak, Iowa 61 N a
Burr Oak, Kansas 60 F e
Burr Oak, Michigan 57 H h
Burr Oak Res., Ohio 52 D f
Burro Cr., Arizona 70 D e
Burrton, Kansas 60 G f
Burrwood, Louisiana 63 O j
Burt, Iowa 61 K a
Burt, North Dakota 58 D d
Burt L., Michigan 56 J d
Burton, Nebraska 60 E b
Burton, Texas 65 L e
Burton L., Georgia 54 H c
Burwell, Nebraska 60 E c
Busby, Montana 67 O d
Bushkill, Pennsylvania 50 C c
Bushkill Falls, Pennsylvania 50 C c
Bushland, Texas 64 B h
Bushnell, Florida 55 J j
Bushnell, Illinois 57 C j
Bushnell, Nebraska 60 A c
Bushton, Kansas 60 F f
Bushwick, New York 51 M f
Bussey, Iowa 61 M c
Butler, Alabama 54 C e
Butler, Georgia 54 G e
Butler, Indiana 57 J h
Butler, Kentucky 57 J l
Butler, Missouri 61 K f
Butler, New Jersey 50 E c
Butler, Ohio 52 D e
Butler, Oklahoma 62 D c
Butler, Pennsylvania 52 G e
Butler, South Dakota 58 J e
Butte, Montana (27,877) 66 H d
Butte, Nebraska 60 F b
Butte, North Dakota 58 F c
Butte Falls, Oregon 73 H n
Butte Meadows, California 74 D d
Butter Cr., Oregon 73 L k
Butterfield, Minnesota 59 M g
Butterville, Utah 68 C j
Buttonwillow, California 75 F j
Buttzville, New Jersey 50 D d
Buttzville, North Dakota 58 J d
Buxton, North Carolina 55 P d
Buzzards B., Massachusetts 51 M b
Byars, Oklahoma 62 F d
Byers, Colorado 69 M d
Byers, Texas 65 J a
Byesville, Ohio 52 E f
Byhalia, Mississippi 63 O d
Bynum, Montana 66 H b
Bynum Res., Montana 66 H b
Byram, Mississippi 63 N f
Byromville, Georgia 54 H e
Byron, California 74 D g
Byron, Illinois 57 D g
Byron, Maine 49 E d
Byron, Wyoming 67 M e
Byrson, Texas 65 J b
Caballo, New Mexico 71 K g
Caballo Res., New Mexico 71 K g
Cabery, Illinois 57 E h
Cabezon, New Mexico 71 K d
Cabin Cr., Oklahoma 62 H b
Cabinet Gorge Dam, Idaho 66 D a
Cabinet Mts., Idaho 66 D a
Cable, Wisconsin 56 B c
Cabool, Missouri 61 M g
Cabot, Arkansas 63 M d
Cabrillo Nat. Mon., California 75 H m
Cacapon R., West Virginia 52 H f
Cache, Oklahoma 62 E d
Cache Cr., California 74 C f
Cache R., Arkansas 63 M c
Cacher, Illinois 57 D m
Cachuma Res., California 75 F k
Cactus, Arizona 70 F f
Cactus, Texas 65 H h
Cactus Ra., Nevada 74 J g
Caddo, Oklahoma 62 G d
Caddo, Texas 65 J c
Caddo Lake, Texas 65 N c
Caddo Mills, Texas 65 L b
Caddo R., Arkansas 63 K d
Cades, South Carolina 55 M d
Cadillac, Michigan 56 H e
Cadiz, California 75 K k
Cadiz, Kentucky 57 F n
Cadiz, Ohio 52 F e
Cadiz L., California 75 K k
Cadott, Wisconsin 56 B e
Caesars Head, South Carolina 55 J b
Cahaba R., Alabama 54 D e
Caillou B., Louisiana 63 M j
Cain City, Texas 65 J e
Cainsville, Missouri 61 L d
Cairnbrook, Pennsylvania 52 H e
Cairn Mt., Alaska 76 K f
Cairo, Georgia 54 G g
Cairo, Illinois 57 D m
Cairo, Missouri 61 M e
Cairo, Nebraska 60 F c
Cairo, New York 50 F a
Cairo, Ohio 52 B e
Cairo, West Virginia 52 E f
Calabasas, Arizona 70 G h
Calais, Maine 49 H c
Calamine, Wisconsin 56 C g
Calamus, Iowa 61 O c
Calapooia R., Oregon 73 H l
Calaveras Res., California 74 D g
Calcasieu L., Louisiana 63 K j
Calcasieu R., Louisiana 63 L h
Calder, Idaho 66 D b
Caldwell, Kansas 60 G g
Caldwell, New Jersey 50 E d
Caldwell, Ohio 52 E f
Caldwell, Texas 65 L e
Caledonia, Michigan 56 H g
Caledonia, Minnesota 59 P g
Caledonia, New York 52 J c
Caledonia, Ohio 52 D e
Calera, Alabama 54 E d
Calexico, California 75 K m
Calhan, Colorado 69 M d
Calhoun, Georgia 54 G c
Calhoun, Kentucky 57 F m
Calhoun, Louisiana 63 L f
Calhoun City, Mississippi 63 O e
Calhoun Falls, South Carolina 55 J c
Calhoun, L., Minnesota 59 Q j
Calico Rock, Arkansas 63 L b
Caliente, California 75 G j
Caliente, Nevada 74 L g
Califon, New Jersey 50 D d
California (19,163,000) 158,693 sq. miles 74-75
California, Missouri 61 M f
California, Pennsylvania 52 G e
California City, California 75 B l
California Hot Springs, California 75 G j
Calion, Arkansas 63 L e
Calipatria, California 75 K l
Calispell Pk., Washington 73 N g
Calistoga, California 74 C f
Call, Texas 65 O e
Callab, Virginia 53 K h
Callaghan, Mt., Nevada 74 J e
Callahan, Florida 55 K g
Callao, Missouri 61 M e
Callao, Utah 68 C d
Callaway, Minnesota 59 K d
Callaway, Nebraska 60 E c
Callicoon, New York 50 C b
Callicoon Center, New York 50 D b
Calliham, Texas 65 J g
Calmar, Iowa 61 N a
Caloosahatchee R., Florida 55 N g
Calpet, Wyoming 67 K g
Calpine, California 74 E e
Calumet, Michigan 56 E b
Calumet, Oklahoma 62 E c

Calumet City, *Illinois (25,000),* *vicinity of Chicago*
Calumet Park, *Illinois* 57 C n
Calva, *Arizona* 70 G f
Calvert, *Alabama* 54 C f
Calvert, *Maryland* 50 A f
Calvert, *Texas* 65 L e
Calvert City, *Kentucky* 57 E m
Calverton, *New York* 51 H d
Calverton, *Virginia* 52 J g
Calvin, *North Dakota* 58 H b
Calvin, *Oklahoma* 62 G d
Calypso, *North Carolina* 55 N b
Camanche, *Iowa* 61 O c
Caman I., *Washington* 73 H g
Camargo, *Oklahoma* 62 D b
Camarillo, *California* 75 G k
Camas, *Idaho* 66 H e
Camas, *Washington* 73 H k
Camas Cr., *Idaho* 66 H e
Camas Cr., *Idaho* 66 F f
Camas Valley, *Oregon* 73 G m
Cambray, *New Mexico* 71 K g
Cambria, *California* 75 D j
Cambria, *Wisconsin* 56 D f
Cambridge, *Idaho* 66 D e
Cambridge, *Illinois* 57 C h
Cambridge, *Iowa* 61 L c
Cambridge, *Kansas* 60 H g
Cambridge, *Maryland* 53 K g
Cambridge, *Massachusetts (107,716)* 51 L a
Cambridge, *Minnesota* 59 N e
Cambridge, *Nebraska* 60 D d
Cambridge, *New York* 53 N b
Cambridge, *Ohio* 52 E e
Cambridge City, *Indiana* 57 H k
Cambridge Springs, *Pennsylvania* 52 F d
Camden, *Alabama* 54 D f
Camden, *Arkansas* 63 L e
Camden, *Delaware* 50 B g
Camden, *Maine* 49 F d
Camden, *Michigan* 57 J h
Camden, *New Jersey (117,159)* 50 C f
Camden, *New York* 53 L b
Camden, *South Carolina* 55 L c
Camden, *Tennessee* 54 C a
Camden, *Texas* 65 N e
Camden B., *Alaska* 77 P a
Camden on Gauley, *West Virginia* 52 F g
Camdenton, *Missouri* 61 M g
Cameron, *Arizona* 70 F d
Cameron, *Illinois* 57 C j
Cameron, *Louisiana* 63 K j
Cameron, *Missouri* 61 K e
Cameron, *Montana* 66 J d
Cameron, *New Mexico* 71 O e
Cameron, *New York* 52 J c
Cameron, *North Carolina* 55 M b
Cameron, *Pennsylvania* 52 H d
Cameron, *Texas* 65 L e
Cameron, *West Virginia* 52 F f
Cameron, *Wisconsin* 56 B d
Camilla, *Georgia* 54 G f
Camino, *California* 74 E f
Cammal, *Pennsylvania* 53 J d
Camp Beale, *California* 74 D e
Campbell, *California* 75 C g
Campbell, *Missouri* 61 O h
Campbell, *Nebraska* 60 F d
Campbell, *New York* 53 J c
Campbell, *Ohio* 52 F d
Campbell Hall, *New York* 50 E c
Campbellsburg, *Kentucky* 57 H l
Campbellsport, *Wisconsin* 56 E f
Campbellsville, *Kentucky* 57 H m
Campbellton, *Texas* 65 J g
Camp Crook, *South Dakota* 58 C e
Camp Douglas, *Wisconsin* 56 C f
Camp Hill, *Alabama* 54 F e
Camp Nelson, *California* 75 G h
Campo, *California* 75 J m
Campo, *Colorado* 69 O f
Camp Point, *Illinois* 57 B j
Camp Roberts, *California* 75 E j
Camp San Saba, *Texas* 65 H e
Campti, *Louisiana* 63 K g
Campton, *Kentucky* 57 K m
Campton, *New Hampshire* 49 D e
Camptonville, *California* 74 E e
Camptown, *Pennsylvania* 53 K d
Camp Verde, *Arizona* 70 F e
Camp Wood, *Texas* 64 G f
Canaan, *Connecticut* 50 G a
Canaan, *New Hampshire* 49 D e
Canaan, *Vermont* 49 D d
Canaan Pk., *Utah* 68 E f
Canada Falls Deadwater, *Maine* 49 F c
Canadensis, *Pennsylvania* 50 C c
Canadian, *Texas* 64 D h
Canadian R., *Texas, etc* 64 D h
Canadys, *South Carolina* 55 L d
Canalou, *Missouri* 61 P h
Canal Point, *Florida* 55 O g
Canal Winchester, *Ohio* 52 D f
Canandaigua, *New York* 52 J c
Canandaigua L., *New York* 53 J c
Canarsie, *New York* 51 M g
Canaseraga, *New York* 52 J c
Canaveral, C. See Kennedy, C.
Canby, *California* 74 E c
Canby, *Minnesota* 59 K f
Canby, *Oregon* 73 H k
Candelaria, *Nevada* 74 G f
Candelaria, *Texas* 64 C e
Candle, *Alaska* 76 F d
Candlewood, L., *Connecticut* 50 G b
Cando, *North Dakota* 58 G b
Candor, *New York* 53 K c
Candor, *North Carolina* 55 M b
Caneadea, *New York* 52 H c
Caney, *Kansas* 61 K g
Caney, *Oklahoma* 62 G d
Caneyville, *Kentucky* 57 G m
Canfield, *Arkansas* 63 K e
Canfield, *Ohio* 52 F d
Canisteo, *New York* 52 J c
Cannelton, *Indiana* 57 G m
Canning, *South Dakota* 58 G f
Canning R., *Alaska* 77 O b
Cannon Ball, *North Dakota* 58 F d
Cannonball R., *North Dakota* 58 E d
Cannon Falls, *Minnesota* 59 O f
Cannon R., *Minnesota* 59 O f
Canon City, *Colorado* 69 L e
Canonsburg, *Pennsylvania* 52 F e
Canoochia R., *Georgia* 55 K f
Canova, *South Dakota* 58 J g
Canterbury, *Connecticut* 51 K b
Cantil, *California* 75 H j
Canton, *Connecticut* 51 H b
Canton, *Georgia* 54 G c
Canton, *Illinois* 57 C j
Canton, *Kansas* 60 G f
Canton, *Maine* 49 E d
Canton, *Massachusetts* 51 L a
Canton, *Missouri* 61 N d
Canton, *Montana* 66 J c
Canton, *New Jersey* 50 C g
Canton, *New York* 53 L a
Canton, *North Carolina* 55 J b
Canton, *Ohio (113,631)* 52 E e
Canton, *Oklahoma* 62 E b
Canton, *Pennsylvania* 53 K d
Canton, *South Dakota* 59 K g
Canton, *Texas* 65 M c
Canton Res., *Oklahoma* 62 E b
Cantril, *Iowa* 61 M d
Cantwell, *Alaska* 77 N e
Canute, *Oklahoma* 62 D c
Canutillo, *Texas* 64 A d
Canyon, *Texas* 64 C j
Canyon, *Wyoming* 67 K e
Canyon City, *Oregon* 73 M l
Canyon Cr., *Idaho* 66 E f
Canyon Cr., *Montana* 66 H c
Canyon de Chelly Nat. Mon., *Arizona* 70 H c
Canyon Ferry Dam, *Montana* 66 J c
Canyon L., *Arizona* 70 F f
Canyon R., *New Mexico* 71 K c
Canyonville, *Oregon* 73 G n
Capa, *South Dakota* 58 F f
Cape, *Alaska* 76 C k
Cape Charles, *Virginia* 53 K h
Cape Cod B., *Massachusetts* 51 N b
Cape Cod Can., *Massachusetts* 51 M b
Cape Cod Nat. Seashore, *Massachusetts* 49 F g
Cape Fear R., *North Carolina* 55 N c
Cape Girardeau, *Missouri* 61 P g
Cape Hatteras Nat. Seashore, *North Carolina* 55 P d
Cape I., *South Carolina* 55 M d
Cape Lookout Nat. Seashore, *North Carolina* 55 P c
Cape May, *New Jersey* 50 D g
Cape May Can., *New Jersey* 50 D h
Cape May Court House, *New Jersey* 50 D g
Cape May Point, *New Jersey* 50 D h
Cape Royal, *Arizona* 70 F c
Capeville, *Virginia* 53 K h
Cape Vincent, *New York* 53 K a
Capitan, *New Mexico* 71 M f
Capitan Mts., *New Mexico* 71 M f
Capitol, *Montana* 67 Q d
Capitol Hill, *Washington* 72 B h
Capitol Pk., *Nevada* 74 H c
Capitol Reef Nat. Mon., *Utah* 68 E e
Caprock, *New Mexico* 71 O f
Caprock Mt., *New Mexico* 71 O f
Captain Cook, *Hawaii* 72 E f
Captiva, *Florida* 55 M g
Capulin, *Colorado* 69 K f
Capulin, *New Mexico* 71 O c
Capulin Mountain Nat. Mon., *New Mexico* 71 N c
Carbert, *Montana* 67 P a
Carbon, *Pennsylvania* 50 B d
Carbon, *Texas* 65 J c
Carbondale, *Colorado* 69 J d
Carbondale, *Illinois* 57 D m
Carbondale, *Kansas* 61 J f
Carbondale, *Pennsylvania* 53 L d
Carbon Hill, *Alabama* 54 D d
Cardington, *Ohio* 52 D e
Carey, *Idaho* 66 G f
Carey, *Ohio* 52 C e
Carey, *Texas* 64 D j
Caribou, *Maine* 49 G b
Caribou, *Alaska* 77 P d
Caribou Mt., *Idaho* 66 J f
Caribou R., *Alaska* 76 G j
Carl Blackwell, L., *Oklahoma* 62 F b
Carleton, *Michigan* 57 K g
Carleton, *Nebraska* 60 G d
Carlile, *Wyoming* 67 Q e
Carlin, *Nevada* 74 J d
Carlinville, *Illinois* 57 D k
Carlisle, *Arkansas* 63 M d
Carlisle, *Indiana* 57 F l
Carlisle, *Kentucky* 57 J l
Carlisle, *Pennsylvania* 53 J e
Carlisle, *South Carolina* 55 K c
Carlisle, *Texas* 65 N c
Carlisle I., *Alaska* 77 S h
Carlsbad, *California* 75 H l
Carlsbad, *New Mexico (25,541)* 71 N g
Carlsbad Caverns Nat. Park, *New Mexico* 71 N g
Carlshend, *Michigan* 56 F c
Carlton, *Minnesota* 59 O d
Carlton, *Oregon* 73 G k
Carlton, *Texas* 65 J d
Carlton Pass, *Washington* 73 J j
Carlyle, *Illinois* 57 D l
Carlyle, *Montana* 67 Q c
Carlyle Res., *Illinois* 57 D l
Carmel, *California* 75 D h
Carmel, *Maine* 49 G d
Carmel, *New Jersey* 50 C g
Carmel, *New York* 50 F c
Carmel Valley, *California* 75 D h
Carmen, *Idaho* 66 G d
Carmen, *Oklahoma* 62 E b
Carmi, *Illinois* 57 E l
Carmine, *Texas* 65 L e
Carnegie, *Oklahoma* 62 E c
Carnegie, *Pennsylvania* 53 O b
Carneiro, *Kansas* 60 F f
Carnesville, *Georgia* 54 H c
Carney, *Michigan* 56 F d
Carney, *Oklahoma* 62 G c
Carney L., *Louisiana* 63 L f
Caro, *Alaska* 77 N c
Caro, *Michigan* 56 K f
Carol City, *Florida* 54 B c
Caroleen, *North Carolina* 55 K b
Carolina Beach, *North Carolina* 55 O c
Carp, *Nevada* 75 L g
Carpenter, *Wyoming* 67 Q h
Carpenterville, *Oregon* 73 F n
Carpinteria, *California* 75 F k
Carpio, *North Dakota* 58 E b
Carp Lake, *Michigan* 56 J d
Carr, *Colorado* 69 M c
Carrabelle, *Florida* 54 G h
Carrara, *Nevada* 75 J h
Carriere, *Mississippi* 63 O h
Carriers Mills, *Illinois* 57 E m
Carrington, *North Dakota* 58 G c
Carrizo Cr., *California* 75 J m
Carrizo Cr., *New Mexico* 71 O c
Carrizo Mts., *Arizona* 70 H c
Carrizo Springs, *Texas* 64 H g
Carrizozo, *New Mexico* 71 M f
Carroll, *Iowa* 61 K b
Carroll, *Nebraska* 60 G b
Carrollton, *Alabama* 54 C d
Carrollton, *Georgia* 54 F d
Carrollton, *Illinois* 57 C k
Carrollton, *Kentucky* 57 H l
Carrollton, *Mississippi* 63 O e
Carrollton, *Missouri* 61 L e
Carrollton, *Ohio* 52 E e
Carrollton, *Texas* 65 N h
Carrolltown, *Pennsylvania* 52 H e
Carrollville, *Wisconsin* 56 F g
Carrville, *California* 74 C c
Carson, *California (38,059),* *vicinity of Los Angeles*
Carson, *Iowa* 61 J c
Carson, *North Dakota* 58 E d
Carson, *Washington* 73 J k
Carson City, *Michigan* 56 J f
Carson City, *Nevada* 74 F e
Carson L., *Nevada* 74 G e
Carson R., *Nevada* 74 F e
Carson Sink, *Nevada* 74 G e
Carsonville, *Michigan* 56 L f
Carta Valley, *Texas* 64 G f
Cartago, *California* 75 G h
Carter, *Montana* 67 K b
Carter, *Oklahoma* 62 D c
Carter, *Wyoming* 67 K h
Carteret, *New Jersey* 51 J g
Carterville, *Illinois* 57 D m
Carterville, *Montana* 67 O c
Cartersville, *Georgia* 54 G c
Carthage, *Arkansas* 63 L d
Carthage, *Illinois* 57 B j
Carthage, *Indiana* 57 H k
Carthage, *Mississippi* 63 O f
Carthage, *Missouri* 61 K g
Carthage, *New Mexico* 71 L f
Carthage, *New York* 53 L b
Carthage, *North Carolina* 55 M b
Carthage, *South Dakota* 58 J f
Carthage, *Tennessee* 54 F a
Carthage, *Texas* 65 N c
Cartwright, *North Dakota* 58 C c
Caruthersville, *Missouri* 61 P h
Carver, *Kentucky* 57 K m
Carver, *Massachusetts* 51 M b
Cary, *Mississippi* 63 N f
Cary, *North Carolina* 55 N b
Casa Grande, *Arizona* 70 F g
Casa Grande Nat. Mon., *Arizona* 70 F g
Casapedaga, *Arizona* 76 E d
Casa Piedra, *Texas* 64 C f
Casa View, *Texas* 65 O j
Cascade, *Idaho* 66 D e
Cascade, *Iowa* 61 N b
Cascade, *New Hampshire* 49 D d
Cascade, *Montana* 66 J b
Cascade Res., *Idaho* 66 E e
Cascade Locks, *Oregon* 73 J k
Cascade Pass, *Washington* 73 J g
Cascadia, *Oregon* 73 H l
Casco, *Maine* 49 E e
Casco, *Wisconsin* 56 F e
Casco B., *Maine* 49 E e
Caseville, *Michigan* 56 K f
Casey, *Illinois* 57 F k
Cashion, *Oklahoma* 62 F c
Cashmere, *Washington* 73 K h
Cashton, *Wisconsin* 56 C f
Casmalia, *California* 75 E k
Cason, *Texas* 65 N b
Caspar, *California* 74 B e
Casper, *Wyoming (38,930)* 67 O g
Caspiana, *Louisiana* 63 K f
Cas. Pinckney Nat. Mon., *South Carolina* 55 L e
Cass, *Arkansas* 63 K c
Cass, *West Virginia* 52 G g
Cassa, *Wyoming* 67 Q g
Cass City, *Michigan* 56 K f
Casselton, *North Dakota* 58 J d
Cass L., *Minnesota* 59 M c
Cass Lake, *Minnesota* 59 M c
Cassoday, *Kansas* 60 H f
Cassopolis, *Michigan* 57 H h
Cass R., *Michigan* 56 K f
Cassville, *Missouri* 61 L h
Cassville, *New Jersey* 50 E e
Cassville, *Wisconsin* 56 C g
Castaic, *California* 75 G k
Castell, *Texas* 65 J e
Castella, *California* 74 C c
Castile, *New York* 52 H c
Castillo de San Marcos Nat. Mon., *Florida* 55 K h
Castine, *Maine* 49 G d
Castleberry, *Alabama* 54 D f
Castle Cr., *Idaho* 66 D g
Castle Dale, *Utah* 68 E d
Castle Dome Mts., *Arizona* 70 C f
Castleford, *Idaho* 66 F g
Castle Gate, *Utah* 68 F d
Castle Hayne, *North Carolina* 55 O c
Castle Hot Springs, *Arizona* 70 E f
Castle Mt., *California* 75 E j
Castle Pk., *Idaho* 66 F e
Castle Rock, *Colorado* 69 M d
Castle Rock, *South Dakota* 58 C f
Castle Rock, *Utah* 68 E b
Castle Rock, *Washington* 73 H j
Castle Rock Res., *Wisconsin* 56 D f
Castle Shannon, *Pennsylvania* 53 P c
Castleton, *Utah* 68 G e
Castleton, *Vermont* 49 B e
Castleton on Hudson, *New York* 53 N c
Castlewood, *South Dakota* 59 K f
Castolon, *Texas* 64 D f
Castor, *Louisiana* 63 K f
Castor R., *Louisiana* 63 L f
Castor R., *Missouri* 61 O g
Castorland, *New York* 53 L b
Castro Valley, *California (37,120),* *vicinity of San Francisco*
Castroville, *California* 75 D h
Castroville, *Texas* 65 J f
Caswell, *Alaska* 76 M f
Catahoula L., *Louisiana* 63 L g
Cataouatche, L., *Louisiana* 63 N j
Cataract L., *Indiana* 57 G k
Catarina, *Texas* 65 H g
Catasauqua, *Pennsylvania* 50 C d
Cataula, *Georgia* 54 G e
Catawba, *South Carolina* 55 K c
Catawba, *Wisconsin* 56 C d
Catawba L., *South Carolina* 55 K b
Catawba R., *South Carolina* 55 L c
Catawissa, *Pennsylvania* 53 K e
Cat Creek, *Montana* 67 M b
Catharine, *Kansas* 60 E f
Cathay, *North Dakota* 58 G c
Cathedral Mt., *Texas* 64 D e
Catherine, L., *Arkansas* 63 L d
Catherine, Mt., *Utah* 68 D d
Cathlamet, *Washington* 73 G j
Cathro, *Michigan* 56 K d
Cat I., *Mississippi* 63 O h
Catlettsburg, *Kentucky* 57 L l
Catlin, *Illinois* 57 F j
Cato, *New York* 53 K b
Catoctin Mt., *Maryland* 52 J f
Catonsville, *Maryland (37,372)* 53 P f
Catskill, *New York* 50 F a
Catskill Cr., *New York* 50 F a
Catskill Landing, *New York* 50 F a
Catskill Mts., *New York* 50 E a
Cattaraugus, *New York* 52 H c
Caucomgomoc L., *Maine* 49 F b
Cavalier, *North Dakota* 58 J b
Cave City, *Arkansas* 63 M c
Cave City, *Kentucky* 57 H m
Cavecreek, *Arizona* 70 F f
Cave in Rock, *Illinois* 57 E m
Cave Jo, *Oregon* 73 G n
Cave Spring, *Georgia* 54 F c
Cave Valley, *Nevada* 74 L f
Cavour, *South Dakota* 58 H f
Cawker City, *Kansas* 60 F e
Cayce, *South Carolina* 55 K d
Cayucos, *California* 75 E j
Cayuga, *Indiana* 57 F k
Cayuga, *North Dakota* 58 J d
Cayuga, *Texas* 65 M d
Cayuga L., *New York* 53 K c
Cazenovia, *New York* 53 L c
Cebolla, *New Mexico* 71 L c
Cebollita, *New Mexico* 71 K d
Cecil, *New Jersey* 50 D f
Cecil, *Ohio* 52 B d
Cecil, *Wisconsin* 56 E e
Cecilia, *Kentucky* 57 H m
Cecilton, *Maryland* 50 B g
Cecilville, *California* 74 B c
Cedar, *Kansas* 60 F e
Cedarbluff, *Mississippi* 63 P e
Cedar Bluff, *Virginia* 52 E h
Cedar Bluff Res., *Kansas* 60 E f
Cedar Bluffs, *Kansas* 60 D e
Cedar Bluffs Valley, *Nebraska* 60 H c
Cedar Breaks Nat. Mon., *Utah* 68 D f
Cedar Brook, *New Jersey* 50 D f
Cedarbutte, *South Dakota* 58 E g
Cedar City, *Missouri* 61 M f
Cedar City, *Utah* 68 C f
Cedar Cr., *New Jersey* 50 E f
Cedar Cr., *North Dakota* 58 D d
Cedar Creek, *Texas* 65 K e
Cedar Crest, *Texas* 65 N j
Cedar Falls, *Iowa* 61 M b
Cedar Grove, *New Jersey* 50 E d
Cedar Grove, *West Virginia* 52 E g
Cedar Grove, *Wisconsin* 56 F f
Cedar Grove Res., *New Jersey* 51 K e
Cedar I., *North Carolina* 55 P c
Cedar I., *Virginia* 53 L h
Cedar Key, *Florida* 54 H h
Cedar L., *Texas* 64 E c
Cedar Lake, *Indiana* 57 F h
Cedar Lane, *Texas* 65 M g
Cedar Mts., *Nevada* 74 H f
Cedar Point, *Ohio* 52 C d
Cedar R., *Iowa* 61 M a
Cedar R., *Michigan* 56 J e
Cedar R., *Nebraska* 60 F c
Cedar R., *Washington* 72 C j
Cedar Rapids, *Iowa (92,035)* 61 N c
Cedar Rapids, *Nebraska* 60 F c
Cedar River, *Michigan* 56 F d
Cedar Run, *Pennsylvania* 53 J d
Cedar Springs, *Michigan* 56 H f
Cedartown, *Georgia* 54 F c
Cedar Vale, *Kansas* 60 H g
Cedarville, *California* 74 E c
Cedarville, *New Jersey* 50 C g
Cedarville, *Michigan* 56 J c
Cedarville, *Ohio* 52 C f
Cedarwood, *Colorado* 69 M f
Cedon, *Virginia* 52 J g
Celeste, *Texas* 65 L b
Celina, *Ohio* 52 B e
Celina, *Tennessee* 54 F a
Celina, *Texas* 65 L b
Cement, *Oklahoma* 62 E d
Cement City, *Michigan* 57 J g
Cementon, *Pennsylvania* 50 B d
Centenary, *South Carolina* 55 M c
Centennial, *Wyoming* 67 O h
Centennial Wash, *Arizona* 70 D f
Center, *Colorado* 69 K f
Center, *Missouri* 61 N e
Center, *North Dakota* 58 E c
Center Bridge, *Pennsylvania* 50 D e
Centerburg, *Ohio* 52 D e
Center City, *Minnesota* 59 O e
Center Cross, *Virginia* 53 K h
Centerdale, *Rhode Island* 51 L b
Center Hill, *Florida* 55 K j
Center Hill Res., *Tennessee* 54 F a
Center Line, *Michigan* 57 L h
Center Moriches, *New York* 51 H d
Center Ossipee, *New Hampshire* 49 D e
Center Point, *Texas* 65 H f
Center Square, *Pennsylvania* 50 C e
Centerton, *New Jersey* 50 C f
Center Valley, *Pennsylvania* 50 C d
Centerville, *Alabama* 54 D e
Centerville, *Iowa* 61 M d
Centerville, *Louisiana* 63 M j
Centerville, *Pennsylvania* 52 F e
Centerville, *South Dakota* 59 K g
Centerville, *Tennessee* 54 D b
Centerville, *Texas* 65 M d
Centerville, *Utah* 68 C g
Centerville, *Washington* 73 K k
Centrahoma, *Oklahoma* 62 G d
Central, *Alaska* 77 P d
Central, *New Mexico* 71 J g
Central, *South Carolina* 55 J c
Central, *Utah* 68 C f
Central City, *Colorado* 69 L d
Central City, *Iowa* 61 N b
Central City, *Kentucky* 57 F m
Central City, *Nebraska* 60 F c
Central City, *Pennsylvania* 52 H e
Central City Res., *Iowa* 61 N b
Central Falls, *Rhode Island* 51 L b
Centralia, *Illinois* 57 D l
Centralia, *Kansas* 61 H e
Centralia, *Missouri* 61 M e
Centralia, *Washington* 73 H j
Centralia, *West Virginia* 52 F g
Central Islip, *New York* 50 G d
Central Lake, *Michigan* 56 H d
Central Point, *Oregon* 73 H n
Central Square, *New York* 53 K b
Central Valley, *California* 74 C d
Central Valley, *New York* 50 E c
Central Village, *Connecticut* 51 K b
Centre, *Alabama* 54 F c
Centreville, *Maryland* 50 A g
Centreville, *Michigan* 57 H h
Centreville, *Mississippi* 63 M g
Century, *Florida* 54 D g
Century, *West Virginia* 52 F f
Cerbat Mts., *Arizona* 70 C d
Ceres, *California* 74 D g
Ceres, *New York* 52 H c
Cerillos, *New Mexico* 71 L d
Cerro Gordo, *Illinois* 57 E k
Ceylon, *Minnesota* 59 M g
Chaco Canyon Nat. Mon., *New Mexico* 71 J d
Chacon, C., *Alaska* 77 V j
Chaco R., *New Mexico* 71 J c
Chacra Mesa, *New Mexico* 71 K d
Chadbourn, *North Carolina* 55 N c
Chadds Ford, *Pennsylvania* 50 B f
Chadron, *Nebraska* 60 B b
Chadwick, *Illinois* 57 D g
Chaffee, *Missouri* 61 P g
Chaffee, *New York* 52 H c
Chagrin Falls, *Ohio* 52 E d
Chagulak I., *Alaska* 77 R j
Chain of Rocks Can., *Illinois* 61 P d
Chakachamna L., *Alaska* 76 L f
Chako R., *New Mexico* 71 J c
Chalfant, *Pennsylvania* 53 R b
Chalk Buttes, *Montana* 67 Q d
Chalk Mountain, *Texas* 65 K c
Chalkyitsik, *Alaska* 77 Q c
Challis, *Idaho* 66 F e
Chalmers, *Indiana* 57 G j
Chalmette Nat. Hist. Park, *Louisiana* 63 O j
Chama, *Colorado* 69 L f
Chama, *New Mexico* 71 L c
Chamberlain, *South Dakota* 58 G g
Chamberlain L., *Maine* 49 F b
Chamberlin, Mt., *Alaska* 77 P b
Chambers, *Arizona* 70 H d
Chambers, *Nebraska* 60 F b
Chambersburg, *Pennsylvania* 52 J f
Chambers I., *Wisconsin* 56 F d
Chamita, *New Mexico* 71 L c
Chamita Res., *New Mexico* 71 L c
Chamois, *Missouri* 61 N f
Champaign, *Illinois (49,583)* 57 E j
Champion, *Michigan* 56 F c
Champion Heights, *Ohio* 52 F d
Champlain, *New York* 53 N a
Champlain, *Virginia* 53 J h
Champlain Can., *New York* 53 N b
Champlain, L., *New York-Vermont* 53 N a
Chancellor, *South Dakota* 59 K g
Chandalar, *Alaska* 77 N c
Chandalar L., *Alaska* 77 N c
Chandalar R., *Alaska* 77 O c
Chandeleur Is., *Louisiana* 63 P j
Chandeleur Sd., *Louisiana* 63 O h
Chandler, *Arizona* 70 F f
Chandler, *Oklahoma* 62 G c
Chandler, *Texas* 65 M c
Chandler L., *Alaska* 76 L b
Chandler R., *Alaska* 76 M b
Chandlerville, *Illinois* 57 C j
Chankluit I., *Alaska* 76 H h
Channel Is., *California* 75 F l
Channel Is. Nat. Mons., *California* 75 F l
Channing, *Michigan* 56 F c
Channing, *Texas* 64 B h
Chanute, *Kansas* 61 J g
Chapel Hill, *North Carolina* 55 M b
Chapel Hill, *Tennessee* 54 E b
Chapin, *Illinois* 57 C k
Chaplin, *Connecticut* 51 J b
Chapman, *Alabama* 54 E f
Chapman, *Kansas* 60 G f
Chapman, *Montana* 67 M a
Chapman, *Nebraska* 60 F c
Chapman, *Pennsylvania* 50 B d
Chapman Ranch, *Texas* 65 K h
Chapmanville, *West Virginia* 52 D h
Chappaqua, *New York* 50 F c
Chappaquiddick I., *Massachusetts* 51 N c
Chappell, *Nebraska* 60 B c
Chappell Hill, *Texas* 65 L e
Chaptico, *Maryland* 53 K g
Charbonneau, *North Dakota* 58 C c
Charco, *Texas* 65 K g
Chardon, *Ohio* 52 E d
Chariton, *Iowa* 61 L c
Chariton R., *Missouri-Iowa* 61 M e
Charity I., *Michigan* 56 K e
Charleroi, *Pennsylvania* 52 G e
Charles, C., *Virginia* 53 K h
Charles City, *Iowa* 61 M a
Charles City, *Virginia* 53 J h
Charles R., *Massachusetts* 51 L a
Charleston, *Arkansas* 63 J c
Charleston, *Mississippi* 63 N d
Charleston, *Missouri* 61 P h
Charleston, *Oregon* 73 F m
Charleston, *South Carolina (65,925)* 55 L e
Charleston, *Tennessee* 54 G b
Charleston, *West Virginia (85,796)* 52 E g
Charleston Pk., *Nevada* 75 K h
Charlestown, *Indiana* 57 H l
Charlestown, *Maryland* 50 A f
Charlestown, *New Hampshire* 49 C e
Charlestown, *Rhode Island* 51 K c
Charles Town, *West Virginia* 52 J f

Charleton, *Illinois* 57 E k
Charlevoix, *Michigan* 56 H d
Charlevoix, L., *Michigan* 56 H d
Charley R., *Alaska* 77 Q d
Charlotte, *Iowa* 61 O c
Charlotte, *Michigan* 56 J g
Charlotte, *North Carolina* (201,564) 55 L b
Charlotte, *Texas* 65 J g
Charlotte Harb., *Florida* 55 M g
Charlotte Harbor, *Florida* 55 M g
Charlottesville, *Virginia* (29,427) 52 H h
Charlton City, *Massachusetts* 51 K a
Charter Oak, *Iowa* 61 J b
Chartiers Cr., *Pennsylvania* 53 O b
Chase, *Kansas* 60 F f
Chaseburg, *Wisconsin* 56 B f
Chase City, *Virginia* 52 H j
Chase L., *North Dakota* 58 G d
Chaska, *Minnesota* 59 N f
Chassahowitzka B., *Florida* 55 J j
Chassell, *Michigan* 56 E b
Chatanika, *Alaska* 77 O d
Chatanika R., *Alaska* 77 O d
Chateaugay, *New York* 53 M a
Chatfield, *Minnesota* 59 O g
Chatham, *Alaska* 77 U h
Chatham, *Illinois* 57 D k
Chatham, *Louisiana* 63 L f
Chatham, *Massachusetts* 51 N b
Chatham, *New Jersey* 50 E d
Chatham, *New York* 50 F a
Chatham, *Pennsylvania* 50 B f
Chatham, *Virginia* 52 G j
Chatham Str., *Alaska* 77 U h
Chatom, *Alabama* 54 C f
Chatooga R., *Alabama* 54 F c
Chatsworth, *Georgia* 54 G c
Chatsworth, *Illinois* 57 E j
Chatsworth, *New Jersey* 50 D f
Chattahoochee, *Florida* 54 G g
Chattahoochie R., *Alabama* 54 F f
Chattanooga, *Oklahoma* 62 E d
Chattanooga, *Tennessee* (130,009) 54 F b
Chattaroy, *Washington* 73 N h
Chattaroy, *West Virginia* 52 D h
Chattooga R., *South Carolina* 54 H c
Chatuga L., *North Carolina* 54 H b
Chaubunagungamaug, L., *Massachusetts* 51 K a
Chauekuktuli L., *Alaska* 76 H f
Chaumont, *New York* 53 K a
Chauncey, *Ohio* 52 D f
Chautauqua, *New York* 52 G c
Chautauqua L., *New York* 52 G c
Chavies, *Kentucky* 52 K m
Chazy, *New York* 53 N a
Cheaha Mt., *Alabama* 54 F d
Cheat R., *West Virginia* 52 G f
Cheboygan, *Michigan* 56 J d
Checotah, *Oklahoma* 62 H c
Cheeching, *Alaska* 76 E f
Cheektowaga, *New York* (52,362), vicinity of Buffalo
Cheesman L., *Colorado* 69 L d
Chef Menteur, *Louisiana* 63 O h
Chefornak, *Alaska* 76 E f
Chehalis, *Washington* 73 H j
Chehalis R., *Washington* 73 G j
Chelan, L., *Washington* 73 K g
Chelan, *Washington* 73 K h
Chelan Ra., *Washington* 73 K g
Chelatna L., *Alaska* 76 L e
Chelsea, *Iowa* 61 M c
Chelsea, *Massachusetts* (33,749) 49 G h
Chelsea, *Michigan* 57 J g
Chelsea, *New York* 50 F b
Chelsea, *Oklahoma* 62 H b
Chelsea, *Pennsylvania* 50 B f
Chelsea, *Vermont* 49 C e
Chelyan, *West Virginia* 52 E g
Chemawa, *Oregon* 73 H k
Chemquasabamticook L., *Maine* 49 F b
Chemung R., *New York* 53 K c
Chena Hot Springs, *Alaska* 77 O d
Chenango R., *New York* 53 L c
Chena R., *Alaska* 77 O d
Chenega, *Alaska* 77 N f
Cheney, *Kansas* 60 G g
Cheney, *Washington* 73 N h
Cheneyville, *Louisiana* 63 L g
Chenik, *Alaska* 76 K g
Chenoa, *Illinois* 57 E j
Chepachet, *Rhode Island* 51 K b
Chequamegon B., *Wisconsin* 56 C c
Cheraw, *Colorado* 69 N e
Cheraw, *Mississippi* 63 O g
Cheraw, *South Carolina* 55 M c
Chernabura I., *Alaska* 76 H j
Cherni I., *Alaska* 76 E j
Cherokee, *Alabama* 54 D c
Cherokee, *Iowa* 61 J b
Cherokee, *Oklahoma* 62 E b
Cherokee, *Texas* 65 J d
Cherokee Dam, *Tennessee* 54 H a
Cherokee L., *Tennessee* 54 H a
Cherokee L., *Texas* 65 N c
Cherokees, L. o' the, *Oklahoma* 63 J b
Cherry Creek, *Colorado* 69 P h
Cherry Creek, *Nevada* 74 L e
Cherry Creek, *New York* 52 G c
Cherry Creek, *South Dakota* 58 E f
Cherry Creek Mt., *Nevada* 74 L d
Cherry Creek Res., *Colorado* 69 P j
Cherrydale, *Virginia* 53 O h
Cherryfield, *Maine* 49 H d
Cherry Grove, *New York* 51 G d
Cherry Hill, *Maryland* 50 A f
Cherry Hills Village, *Colo.* 69 O j
Cherryvale, *Kansas* 61 J g
Cherry Valley, *New York* 53 M c
Cherryville, *North Carolina* 55 K b
Chesaning, *Michigan* 56 J f
Chesapeake, *Maryland* 53 L f
Chesapeake, *Ohio* 52 D g
Chesapeake, *Virginia* 53 K j
Chesapeake B., *Maryland* 53 K f
Chesapeake Beach, *Maryland* 53 K g
Chesapeake City, *Maryland* 50 B f
Chesapeake Delaware Can., *Delaware* 50 B f
Cheshire, *Connecticut* 51 H b
Cheshire, *Massachusetts* 49 B f
Chesnee, *South Carolina* 55 K b
Chester, *Arkansas* 63 J c
Chester, *California* 74 D d
Chester, *Connecticut* 51 J c
Chester, *Idaho* 66 J e
Chester, *Illinois* 57 D m
Chester, *Massachusetts* 51 H a
Chester, *Montana* 67 K a
Chester, *Nebraska* 60 G d
Chester, *New Jersey* 50 D d
Chester, *New York* 50 E c
Chester, *Ohio* 52 F e
Chester, *Pennsylvania* (63,658) 50 B f
Chester, *South Carolina* 55 K c
Chester, *Vermont* 49 C e
Chester, *Texas* 65 N e
Chester, *Virginia* 52 J h
Chesterfield, *Connecticut* 51 J c
Chesterfield, *Idaho* 66 J g
Chesterfield, *Illinois* 57 C k
Chesterfield, *New Hampshire* 49 C f
Chesterfield, *South Carolina* 55 L c
Chesterfield, *Utah* 68 C h
Chesterfield, *Virginia* 52 J h
Chesterhill, *Ohio* 52 E f
Chester Pen., *Maryland* 53 K f
Chester R., *Maryland* 50 A g
Chesterton, *Indiana* 57 F h
Chestertown, *Maryland* 50 A g
Chestertown, *New York* 53 N b
Chesterville, *Maryland* 50 A g
Chestnut, *Louisiana* 63 K f
Chestnut Ridge, *Pennsylvania* 52 G e
Chesuncook, *Maine* 49 F b
Chesuncook L., *Maine* 49 F b
Cheswold, *Delaware* 50 B g
Chetek, *Wisconsin* 56 B d
Chetopa, *Kansas* 61 K g
Chevak, *Alaska* 76 E f
Cheverly, *Maryland* 53 R h
Chevreuil, Pt., *Louisiana* 63 M j
Chevy Chase, *Maryland* 53 P g
Chewelah Valley, *Washington* 73 N g
Cheyenne, *Oklahoma* 62 D c
Cheyenne, *Texas* 64 D d
Cheyenne, *Wyoming* (43,505) 67 Q h
Cheyenne Agency, *South Dakota* 58 F e
Cheyenne Bottoms, *Kansas* 60 F f
Cheyenne Pass, *Wyoming* 67 P h
Cheyenne R., *South Dakota* 58 D f
Cheyenne R., *Wyoming* 67 Q f
Cheyenne Wells, *Colorado* 69 O e
Chiachi I., *Alaska* 76 H j
Chibukak Pt., *Alaska* 76 B e
Chicago, *Illinois* (3,550,404) 57 F h
Chicago Heights, *Illinois* (34,331) 57 F h
Chicago R., *Illinois* 57 A k
Chicago Ship Can., *Illinois* 57 E h
Chichagof, *Alaska* 77 T h
Chichagof I., *Alaska* 77 U h
Chichester, *New York* 50 E a
Chickahominy R., *Virginia* 53 J h
Chickaloon, *Alaska* 77 N f
Chickamauga, *Georgia* 54 F c
Chicamauga Dam, *Tennessee* 54 F b
Chickamauga L., *Tennessee* 54 G b
Chickasawhay R., *Mississippi* 63 P g
Chickasha, *Oklahoma* 62 F c
Chicken, *Alaska* 77 R d
Chico, *California* 74 D e
Chico, *Oregon* 73 N k
Chico, *Texas* 65 K b
Chico, *Washington* 72 A h
Chicopee, *Massachusetts* (61,553) 51 H a
Chidester, *Arkansas* 63 K e
Chief Joseph Dam, *Washington* 73 L g
Chiefland, *Florida* 55 J h
Chiftak, *Alaska* 76 E f
Chiginigak, Mt., *Alaska* 76 J h
Chigmit Mts., *Alaska* 76 L f
Chignik, *Alaska* 76 H h
Chignik B., *Alaska* 76 H h
Chignik L., *Alaska* 76 H h
Chikaskia R., *Oklahoma* 62 F b
Chikuminuk L., *Alaska* 76 H f
Chilcoot, *California* 74 E e
Childersburg, *Alabama* 54 E d
Childress, *Texas* 64 D j
Childs, *Arizona* 70 E g
Childs, *Florida* 55 N f
Chilhowee, *Missouri* 61 L f
Chilhowie, *Virginia* 52 E j
Chilikadrotna R., *Alaska* 76 K f
Chilkat R., *Alaska* 77 U g
Chillicothe, *Illinois* 57 D j
Chillicothe, *Missouri* 61 L e
Chillicothe, *Ohio* 52 C f
Chillicothe, *Texas* 65 H a
Chilly, *Idaho* 66 G e
Chilmark, *Massachusetts* 51 M c
Chiloquin, *Oregon* 73 J n
Chilton, *Wisconsin* 56 E e
Chimayo, *New Mexico* 71 M d
Chimney Pk., *New Mexico* 71 M g
China, *Maine* 49 F d
China Grove, *North Carolina* 55 L b
China L., *California* 75 H j
China L., *Maine* 49 F d
China Pt., *California* 75 G m
China Spring, *Texas* 65 K d
Chinati Mts., *Texas* 64 C f
Chincoteague, *Virginia* 53 L h
Chincoteague B., *Virginia* 53 L g
Chiniak, C., *Alaska* 76 L h
Chinitna B., *Alaska* 76 L g
Chinle, *Arizona* 70 H c
Chinle Cr., *Arizona* 70 H c
Chinle Valley, *Arizona* 70 H c
Chino, *Arizona* 70 E d
Chinook, *Montana* 67 L a
Chinook Pass, *Washington* 73 J j
Chino Valley, *Arizona* 70 E e
Chipley, *Georgia* 54 G e
Chipley, *Florida* 54 F g
Chipola R., *Florida* 54 F g
Chippewa Falls, *Wisconsin* 56 B e
Chippewa L., *Wisconsin* 56 B d
Chippewa R., *Minnesota* 59 L e
Chippewa R., *Wisconsin* 56 B e
Chippewa Res., *Wisconsin* 56 B d
Chireno, *Texas* 65 N d
Chiricahua Nat. Mon., *Arizona* 70 H g
Chiricahua Pk., *Arizona* 70 H h
Chirikof I., *Alaska* 76 K j
Chisana, *Alaska* 77 Q e
Chisana Glacier, *Alaska* 77 Q f
Chisana R., *Alaska* 77 R e
Chisholm, *Maine* 49 E d
Chisholm, *Minnesota* 59 O c
Chisos Mts., *Texas* 64 D f
Chispa Cr., *Texas* 64 C e
Chistochina, *Alaska* 77 P e
Chitanana R., *Alaska* 76 L d
Chitina, *Alaska* 77 P f
Chitina R., *Alaska* 77 Q f
Chivington, *Colorado* 69 O e
Chloride, *Arizona* 70 C d
Chocolate Mts., *Arizona* 70 C f
Chocolate Mts., *California* 75 K l
Chocorua, *New Hampshire* 49 D e
Chocowinity, *North Carolina* 55 O b
Choctaw, *Alabama* 54 C e
Choctaw, *Oklahoma* 62 F c
Choctawhatchee B., *Florida* 54 E g
Choctawhatchee R., *Alabama* 54 F f
Choctawhatchee R., *Florida* 54 F g
Chokio, *Minnesota* 59 K e
Cholame, *California* 75 E j
Cholame Cr., *California* 75 E j
Choptank R., *Maryland* 53 L g
Choteau, *Montana* 66 H b
Choteau, *Oklahoma* 62 H b
Chowan R., *North Carolina* 55 P a
Chowchilla, *California* 75 E g
Chowhoctolik, *Alaska* 76 F f
Chowiet I., *Alaska* 76 J h
Chrisman, *Illinois* 57 F k
Christian, *Alaska* 77 P c
Christiana, *Delaware* 50 B f
Christiana, *Pennsylvania* 50 A f
Christiansburg, *Ohio* 52 C e
Christiansburg, *Virginia* 52 F h
Christian Sd., *Alaska* 77 U h
Christina, *Montana* 67 L b
Christine, *Texas* 65 J g
Christopher, *Illinois* 57 D m
Christoval, *Texas* 64 G d
Chromo, *Colorado* 69 K f
Chubbuck, *California* 75 K k
Chuckatuck, *Virginia* 53 K j
Chuckwalla Mts., *California* 75 K l
Chugach Is., *Alaska* 76 M g
Chugach Mts., *Alaska* 77 O f
Chuginadak I., *Alaska* 77 T h
Chugul I., *Alaska* 77 P j
Chugwater, *Wyoming* 67 Q h
Chugwater Cr., *Wyoming* 67 P h
Chuichu, *Arizona* 70 F g
Chuilnuk Mts., *Alaska* 76 J f
Chukchi Sea, *Alaska* 76 C c
Chukfaktoolik, *Alaska* 76 F f
Chula, *Georgia* 54 H f
Chula, *Missouri* 61 L e
Chula, *Virginia* 52 J h
Chula Vista, *California* (42,034) 75 H m
Chulitna, *Alaska* 76 N e
Chulitna R., *Alaska* 76 N e
Chumuckla, *Florida* 54 D g
Chunchula, *Alabama* 54 C g
Church Creek, *Maryland* 53 K g
Church Hill, *Maryland* 50 A g
Church Hill, *Tennessee* 55 J a
Churchill, *Idaho* 66 G g
Churchill L., *Maine* 49 F b
Church Point, *Louisiana* 63 L h
Churchs Ferry, *North Dakota* 58 G b
Churchville, *New York* 52 J b
Churchville, *Virginia* 52 G g
Churdan, *Iowa* 61 K b
Churubusco, *Indiana* 57 H h
Chuska Mts., *New Mexico* 71 J c
Cibecue, *Arizona* 70 G e
Cibola, *Arizona* 70 C f
Cicero, *Illinois* (69,130) 57 B l
Cicero, *Indiana* 57 G j
Cicero, *New York* 53 K b
Cienega, *New Mexico* 71 M g
Cima, *California* 75 K j
Cimarron, *Kansas* 60 D g
Cimarron R., *Kansas* 60 C g
Cimarron R., *Oklahoma* 62 E b
Cincinnati, *Iowa* 61 M d
Cincinnati, *Ohio* (502,550) 52 B f
Cincinnatus, *New York* 53 L c
Cinder R., *Alaska* 76 H h
Circle, *Alaska* 77 Q d
Circle, *Montana* 67 P b
Circle Hot Springs, *Alaska* 76 P d
Circle Pines, *Minnesota* 59 Q h
Circleville, *New York* 50 E c
Circleville, *Ohio* 52 C f
Circleville, *Utah* 68 D e
Cisco, *Illinois* 57 E k
Cisco, *Texas* 65 J c
Cisco, *Utah* 68 G e
Cisne, *Illinois* 57 E l
Cispus Pass, *Washington* 73 J j
Cispus R., *Washington* 73 J j
Cistern, *Texas* 65 K f
Citra, *Florida* 55 J h
Citronelle, *Alabama* 54 C f
City I., *New York* 51 N e
City Point, *Florida* 55 L j
Clackamas R., *Oregon* 73 H k
Claflin, *Kansas* 60 F f
Clagstone, *Idaho* 66 D a
Claire City, *South Dakota* 58 J e
Clairemont, *Texas* 64 G b
Clairton, *Pennsylvania* 52 G e
Clallam Bay, *Washington* 73 F g
Clan Alpine Mts., *Nevada* 74 H e
Clanton, *Alabama* 54 E e
Clapham, *New Mexico* 71 O c
Clara, *Florida* 54 H h
Clara City, *Minnesota* 59 L f
Clare, *Iowa* 61 K b
Clare, *Michigan* 56 J f
Claremont, *New Hampshire* 49 C e
Claremont, *South Dakota* 58 H e
Claremore, *Oklahoma* 62 H b
Clarence, *Iowa* 61 N c
Clarence, *Louisiana* 63 K g
Clarence, *Missouri* 61 M e
Clarence Cannon Res., *Missouri* 61 N e
Clarence Fahnestock Park, *New York* 50 F c
Clarence Str., *Alaska* 77 V j
Clarendon, *Arkansas* 63 M d
Clarendon, *Pennsylvania* 52 G d
Clarendon, *Texas* 64 D j
Clarendon, *Virginia* 53 O h
Clareton, *Wyoming* 67 Q f
Clarinda, *Iowa* 61 J d
Clarington, *Ohio* 52 F f
Clarington, *Pennsylvania* 52 G d
Clarion, *Iowa* 61 L b
Clarion R., *Pennsylvania* 52 G d
Clarita, *Oklahoma* 62 G d
Clark, *Colorado* 69 K c
Clark, L., *Alaska* 76 K f
Clark, *Missouri* 61 M e
Clark, *South Dakota* 58 J f
Clark, *Wyoming* 67 L e
Clark Canyon Res., *Montana* 66 H e
Clarkdale, *Arizona* 70 E e
Clarkfield, *Minnesota* 59 L f
Clark Fork, *Idaho* 66 D a
Clark Fork, *Montana* 66 G c
Clark Fork, *Wyoming* 67 L e
Clark Fork R., *Montana* 66 E b
Clark Hill Dam, *Georgia* 55 J d
Clark Hill Res., *South Carolina-Georgia* 55 J d
Clarkia, *Idaho* 66 D b
Clark L., *California* 75 J l
Clark Mt., *California* 75 J j
Clark Pk., *Colorado* 69 L c
Clarks, *Louisiana* 63 L f
Clarks, *Nebraska* 60 G c
Clarksburg, *New Jersey* 50 E e
Clarksburg, *West Virginia* (28,112) 52 F f
Clarksburg, *Tennessee* 54 C b
Clarksdale, *Mississippi* 63 N d
Clarks Grove, *Minnesota* 59 N g
Clarks Hill, *Indiana* 57 G j
Clarkson, *Nebraska* 60 G c
Clarks Point, *Alaska* 76 H g
Clarkston, *Michigan* 56 K g
Clarkston, *Montana* 66 J c
Clarkston, *Washington* 73 N j
Clarkesville, *Georgia* 54 H c
Clarkesville, *Iowa* 61 M b
Clarksville, *Arkansas* 63 K c
Clarksville, *Maryland* 53 K f
Clarksville, *Michigan* 56 H g
Clarksville, *Missouri* 61 O e
Clarksville, *Tennessee* 54 D a
Clarksville, *Texas* 65 M b
Clarksville, *Virginia* 52 H j
Clarkton, *North Carolina* 55 N c
Clarkwood, *Texas* 65 K h
Clarno, *Oregon* 73 K l
Claryville, *New York* 50 D b
Claude, *Texas* 64 C h
Clauene, *Texas* 64 E b
Claverack, *New York* 50 F a
Clay, *California* 74 D f
Clay, *Kentucky* 57 F m
Clay, *West Virginia* 52 E g
Clay, *Texas* 65 L e
Clay Center, *Kansas* 60 G e
Clay Center, *Nebraska* 60 F d
Clay City, *Illinois* 57 E l
Clay City, *Indiana* 57 F k
Clay City, *Kentucky* 57 K m
Claycomo, *Missouri* 61 Q a
Clayhole Wash, *Arizona* 70 D c
Claymont, *Delaware* 50 B f
Claypool, *Arizona* 70 G f
Clay Springs, *Arizona* 70 G e
Claysville, *Pennsylvania* 52 F e
Clayton, *Alabama* 54 F f
Clayton, *Delaware* 50 B g
Clayton, *Georgia* 54 H c
Clayton, *Idaho* 66 F e
Clayton, *Indiana* 57 G k
Clayton, *Kansas* 60 D e
Clayton, *New Jersey* 50 C f
Clayton, *New Mexico* 71 O c
Clayton, *New York* 53 K a
Clayton, *North Carolina* 55 N b
Clayton, *Oklahoma* 62 H d
Claytor L., *Virginia* 52 F h
Clayville, *New York* 53 L c
Clayville, *Rhode Island* 51 K b
Claxton, *Georgia* 55 K e
Clear Boggy Cr., *Oklahoma* 62 G d
Clearbrook, *Minnesota* 59 L c
Clearco, *West Virginia* 52 F g
Clear Cr., *Arizona* 70 G e
Clear Cr., *Texas* 64 G j
Clear Cr., *Wyoming* 67 O e
Clear Creek, *California* 74 B c
Cleare, C., *Alaska* 76 O g
Clearfield, *Iowa* 61 K d
Clearfield, *Pennsylvania* 52 H d
Clearfield, *Utah* 68 D b
Clear L., *California* 74 C e
Clear L., *Iowa* 61 L a
Clear L., *Louisiana* 63 K f
Clear Lake, *Iowa* 61 L a
Clear Lake, *Minnesota* 59 N e
Clear Lake, *South Dakota* 59 K f
Clear Lake, *Wisconsin* 56 A d
Clear Lake, *Utah* 68 D d
Clear Lake Highlands, *California* 74 C f
Clear Lake Res., *California* 74 D c
Clearmont, *Wyoming* 67 O e
Clearview, *Washington* 72 C g
Clearwater, *Florida* (34,653) 55 M f
Clearwater, *Idaho* 66 E c
Clearwater, *Kansas* 60 G g
Clearwater, *Nebraska* 60 F b
Clearwater Mts., *Idaho* 66 E c
Clearwater R., *Idaho* 66 D c
Clearwater R., *Minnesota* 59 L c
Clearwater Res., *Missouri* 61 O g
Cleburne, *Kansas* 60 H e
Cleburne, *Texas* 65 K c
Cle Elum, *Washington* 73 K h
Cle Elum L., *Washington* 73 J h
Clegg, *Texas* 65 J g
Clemenceau, *Arizona* 70 E e
Clementon, *New Jersey* 50 C f
Clements, *California* 74 D f
Clendenin, *West Virginia* 52 E g
Clendening Res., *Ohio* 52 E e
Cleo Springs, *Oklahoma* 62 E b
Clermont, *Florida* 55 K j
Clermont, *Iowa* 61 N a
Clermont, *New York* 50 F a
Clermont, *Pennsylvania* 52 H d
Cleveland, *Arkansas* 63 L c
Cleveland, *Florida* 55 N g
Cleveland, *Georgia* 54 H c
Cleveland, *Idaho* 66 J g
Cleveland, *Minnesota* 59 N f
Cleveland, *Mississippi* 63 N e
Cleveland, *Montana* 67 L a
Cleveland, Mt., *Alaska* 77 T h
Cleveland, Mt., *Montana* 66 G a
Cleveland, *New York* 53 L b
Cleveland, *North Carolina* 55 L b
Cleveland, *North Dakota* 58 G d
Cleveland, *Ohio* (876,050) 52 E d
Cleveland, *Oklahoma* 62 G b
Cleveland, *South Carolina* 55 J b
Cleveland, *Tennessee* 54 G b
Cleveland, *Texas* 65 M e
Cleveland, *Utah* 68 F d
Cleveland, *Wisconsin* 56 F f
Cleveland Heights, *Ohio* (61,813), vicinity of Cleveland
Clewiston, *Florida* 55 O g
Clichy R., *Tennessee* 54 H a
Clietry R., *Tennessee* 54 H a
Cliff, *New Mexico* 71 J g
Cliffdell, *Washington* 73 J j
Cliff Lake, *Montana* 66 J e
Clifford, *Massachusetts* 51 M b
Clifford, *Michigan* 56 K f
Clifford, *North Dakota* 58 J c
Clifford, *Virginia* 52 G h
Clifford, *Wisconsin* 56 C d
Cliffs, *Idaho* 66 D g
Cliffside, *North Carolina* 55 K b
Cliffside Park, *New Jersey* 51 L e
Clifton, *Arizona* 70 H f
Clifton, *Illinois* 57 F j
Clifton, *Kansas* 60 G e
Clifton, *New Jersey* (82,084) 51 K e
Clifton, *Texas* 65 K d
Clifton, *Wyoming* 67 Q f
Clifton Forge, *Virginia* 52 G h
Climax, *Colorado* 69 K d
Climax, *Georgia* 54 G g
Climax, *Michigan* 57 H g
Climax, *Minnesota* 59 K c
Clinch Mts., *Tennessee-Virginia* 52 D j
Clincho, *Virginia* 52 D h
Clinchport, *Virginia* 52 D j
Clinch R., *Tennessee-Virginia* 54 G b
Cline, *Texas* 64 G f
Clingmans Dome, mt., *Tennessee* 54 H b
Clint, *Texas* 64 A d
Clinton, *Arkansas* 63 L c
Clinton, *Connecticut* 51 H c
Clinton, *Illinois* 57 E j
Clinton, *Indiana* 57 F k
Clinton, *Iowa* (33,589) 61 O c
Clinton, *Louisiana* 63 M h
Clinton, *Maine* 49 F d
Clinton, *Massachusetts* 49 D f
Clinton, *Michigan* 57 K g
Clinton, *Minnesota* 59 K e
Clinton, *Mississippi* 63 N f
Clinton, *Missouri* 61 L f
Clinton, *Montana* 66 G c
Clinton, *New Jersey* 50 D d
Clinton, *New York* 53 L b
Clinton, *North Carolina* 55 N b
Clinton, *Oklahoma* 62 D c
Clinton, *South Carolina* 55 K c
Clinton, *Tennessee* 54 G a
Clinton, *Wisconsin* 56 E g
Clinton Corners, *New York* 50 F b
Clintondale, *New York* 50 E b
Clintonville, *Wisconsin* 56 E e
Clints Well, *Arizona* 70 F e
Clio, *Alabama* 54 F f
Clio, *Iowa* 61 L d
Clio, *Michigan* 56 K f
Clio, *South Carolina* 55 M c
Clive, *Utah* 68 C c
Clontarf, *Minnesota* 59 L e
Cloquet, *Minnesota* 59 O d
Closter, *New Jersey* 50 E d
Cloudcroft, *New Mexico* 71 M g
Cloud Pk., *Wyoming* 67 N e
Cloudy Mt., *Alaska* 76 J e
Clover, *South Carolina* 55 K b
Clover, *Virginia* 52 H j
Cloverdale, *California* 74 B f
Cloverdale, *Indiana* 57 G k
Cloverdale, *New Mexico* 71 J h
Cloverleaf, *Texas* 64 G h
Cloverport, *Kentucky* 57 G m
Clovis, *California* 75 F h
Clovis, *New Mexico* 71 O e
Cluro, *Nevada* 74 J d
Clutier, *Iowa* 61 M b
Clyattville, *Georgia* 54 H g
Clyde, *Kansas* 60 G e
Clyde, *New York* 53 K b
Clyde, *North Dakota* 58 H b
Clyde, *Ohio* 52 D d
Clyde, *Texas* 65 H c
Clyde Park, *Montana* 67 K d
Clyman, *Wisconsin* 56 E f
Clymer, *Pennsylvania* 52 H e
Coahoma, *Texas* 64 F c
Coal City, *Illinois* 57 E h
Coaldale, *Nevada* 74 H f
Coaldale, *Pennsylvania* 50 B d
Coalgate, *Oklahoma* 62 G d
Coal Grove, *Ohio* 52 D g
Coal Hill, *Arkansas* 63 K c
Coalinga, *California* 75 E h
Coalmont, *Colorado* 69 K c
Coalport, *Pennsylvania* 52 H e
Coal R., *West Virginia* 52 E g
Coalton, *Ohio* 52 D f
Coalville, *Utah* 68 E c
Coalwood, *Montana* 67 P d
Coast Ra., *California* 74 B d
Coast Ra., *California* 75 D g
Coatesville, *Pennsylvania* 50 B f
Coats, *Kansas* 60 F g
Coats, *North Carolina* 55 N b
Coatsville, *Missouri* 61 M d
Cobb, I., *Virginia* 53 L h
Cobb, *Wisconsin* 56 C g
Cobble Mountain Res., *Massachusetts* 51 H a
Cobden, *Illinois* 57 D m
Cobleskill, *New York* 53 M c
Cobol, *Alaska* 77 U h
Cobre, *Nevada* 74 L c
Coburg, *Oregon* 73 G l
Coburn, *Pennsylvania* 53 J e
Cochecton, *New York* 50 C b
Cochetopa Pass, *Colorado* 69 K e
Cochise, *Arizona* 70 H g
Cochise Head, mt., *Arizona* 70 H g
Cochituate, *Massachusetts* 51 L a
Cochran, *Georgia* 54 H e
Cochranton, *Pennsylvania* 52 G d
Cochranville, *Pennsylvania* 50 A f
Cockeysville, *Maryland* 53 K f
Cockrell Hill, *Texas* 65 N j
Cocoa, *Florida* 55 O e
Cocoa Beach, *Florida* 55 O e
Cocodrie, *Louisiana* 63 N j
Cocolalla, *Idaho* 66 D a
Coconino Plateau, *Arizona* 70 E d

Coconut Grove, Florida 54 B d
Cod, C., Massachusetts 51 N b
Codell, Kansas 60 E e
Cody, Nebraska 60 C b
Cody, Wyoming 67 L e
Coeburn, Virginia 52 D j
Coeur d'Alene, Idaho 66 D b
Coeur d'Alene L., Idaho 66 D b
Coeur d'Alene R., Idaho 66 D b
Coffee, Georgia 55 J f
Coffee Creek, Montana 67 K b
Coffeen, Illinois 57 D k
Coffee Springs, Alabama 54 F f
Coffeeville, Mississippi 63 O e
Coffeyville, Kansas 61 J g
Coggon, Iowa 61 N b
Cogswell, North Dakota 58 J d
Cohagen, Montana 67 O b
Cohansey Cr., New Jersey 50 C g
Cohasset, Massachusetts 51 M a
Cohocton, New York 52 J c
Cohocton R., New York 53 J c
Cohoes, New York 53 N c
Cohutta, Georgia 54 G c
Coin, Iowa 61 J d
Cokato, Minnesota 59 M e
Cokeburg, Pennsylvania 52 F e
Cokeville, Wyoming 67 K g
Colbert, Washington 73 N h
Colby, Kansas 60 C e
Colby, Wisconsin 56 C e
Colchester, Connecticut 51 J b
Colchester, Illinois 57 C j
Colchester, New York 50 D a
Cold Brook, New York 50 E a
Colden, New York 52 H c
Cold Spring, Minnesota 59 M e
Cold Spring, New Jersey 50 D h
Cold Spring, New York 50 F c
Coldspring, Texas 65 M e
Cold Spring Harbor, New York 50 G d
Coldwater, Kansas 60 E g
Coldwater, Michigan 57 J h
Coldwater, Ohio 52 B e
Coldwater Cr., Texas 64 C g
Coldwater R., Mississippi 63 N d
Colebrook, Connecticut 51 H b
Colebrook, New Hampshire 49 D d
Colebrook River, Connecticut 51 G a
Cole Camp, Missouri 61 L f
Coleen R., Alaska 77 P b
Colegrove, Pennsylvania 52 H d
Coleman, Florida 55 J j
Coleman, Michigan 56 J f
Coleman, Texas 65 H d
Coleraine, Minnesota 59 N c
Coleridge, Nebraska 60 G b
Colesville, New Jersey 50 D c
Coleville, California 74 F f
Colfax, California 74 E e
Colfax, Illinois 57 E j
Colfax, Indiana 57 G j
Colfax, Iowa 61 L c
Colfax, Louisiana 63 L g
Colfax, New Mexico 71 N c
Colfax, Washington 73 N j
Colfax, Wisconsin 56 B d
Collbran, Colorado 69 J d
College, Alaska 77 O d
College Corner, Indiana 57 J k
College Grove, Tennessee 54 E b
College Park, Georgia 54 G d
College Park, Maryland 53 K f
College Place, Washington 73 M j
College Station, Texas 65 L e
Colleyville, Texas 65 M j
Collier City, Florida 55 N h
Collierville, Tennessee 54 B b
Collingswood, New Jersey 50 C f
Collins, Georgia 55 J e
Collins, Mississippi 63 O g
Collins, Missouri 61 L g
Collins, Montana 66 J b
Collins, New York 52 H c
Collinston, Louisiana 63 M f
Collinsville, Alabama 54 F c
Collinsville, Connecticut 51 H b
Collinsville, Illinois 57 D l
Collinsville, Oklahoma 62 H b
Collinwood, Tennessee 54 D b
Collyer, Kansas 60 D e
Colma, California 75 B m
Colmesneil, Texas 65 N e
Colmor, New Mexico 71 N c
Colo, Iowa 61 L b
Cologne, Minnesota 59 N f
Cologne, New Jersey 50 D f
Coloma, Wisconsin 56 D e
Colome, South Dakota 58 G g
Colon, Michigan 57 H h
Colona, Michigan 57 G g
Colonial Beach, Virginia 53 J g
Colonial Heights, Virginia 52 J h
Colonial Nat. Hist. Park, Virginia 53 K h
Colony, Kansas 61 J f
Colora, Maryland 50 A f
Colorado (1,975,000) 104,247 sq. miles 68-69
Colorado City, Texas 64 G c
Colorado Des., California 75 J l
Colorado Nat. Mon., Colorado 68 H d
Colorado Plateau, Arizona 50 F c
Colorado R., California, etc. 46 D d
Colorado R., Texas 65 J d
Colorado Springs, Colorado (70,194) 69 M e
Colquitt, Georgia 54 G f
Colstrip, Montana 67 O d
Coltexo, Texas 64 D h
Colton, California 75 H k
Colton, Maryland 53 K g
Colton, New York 53 M a
Colton, South Dakota 58 J g
Colton, Utah 68 F d
Colton, Washington 73 N j
Colts Neck, New Jersey 50 E e
Columbia, Connecticut 51 J b
Columbia, Florida 55 J g
Columbia, Illinois 57 C l
Columbia, Kentucky 57 H m
Columbia, Louisiana 63 L f
Columbia, Mississippi 63 O g
Columbia, Missouri (36,650) 61 M f
Columbia, New Jersey 50 C d
Columbia, North Carolina 55 P b
Columbia, Pennsylvania 53 K e
Columbia, South Carolina (97,433) 55 L d
Columbia, South Dakota 58 H e
Columbia, Tennessee 54 D b
Columbia, Virginia 52 H h
Columbia City, Indiana 57 H h
Columbia Falls, Maine 49 H d
Columbia Falls, Montana 66 F a
Columbia Glacier, Alaska 77 O f
Columbia Heights, Minnesota 59 Q h
Columbiana, Alabama 54 E d
Columbiana, Ohio 52 F e
Columbia R., Washington 73 L k
Columbia River, Washington 73 K h
Columbia Road Res., South Dakota 58 H e
Columbiaville, New York 50 F a
Columbine, Colorado 69 K c
Columbine, Wyoming 67 O f
Columbus, Georgia (116,779) 54 G e
Columbus, Indiana 57 H k
Columbus, Kansas 61 K g
Columbus, Mississippi 63 P e
Columbus, Montana 67 L d
Columbus, Nebraska 60 G c
Columbus, New Jersey 50 D e
Columbus, New Mexico 71 K h
Columbus, North Dakota 58 D b
Columbus, Ohio (471,316) 52 C f
Columbus, Texas 65 L f
Columbus, Wisconsin 56 D f
Columbus Grove, Ohio 52 C e
Columbus Junction, Iowa 61 N c
Colusa, California 74 D e
Colver, Pennsylvania 52 H e
Colville, Alaska 76 H b
Colville, Washington 73 N g
Colville Bar, Alaska 76 K b
Colville R., Alaska 76 L b
Colville R., Washington 73 N g
Colvos Passage, Washington 72 B j
Colwell, Iowa 61 M a
Comanche, Oklahoma 62 F d
Comanche, Texas 65 J d
Combahee R., South Carolina 55 L e
Combes, Texas 65 K j
Combs, Kentucky 57 K m
Comer, Alabama 54 F e
Comer, Georgia 54 H c
Comertown, Montana 67 Q a
Comfort, Texas 65 J f
Comfrey, Minnesota 59 M f
Comins, Michigan 56 J e
Commerce, Georgia 54 H c
Commerce, Oklahoma 63 J b
Commerce, Texas 65 M b
Commerce Town, Colorado 69 P h
Como, Colorado 69 L d
Como, L., Minnesota 59 Q j
Como, Mississippi 63 O d
Compass, Pennsylvania 50 A e
Comptche, California 74 B e
Compton, California (71,812) 75 E m
Compton, Illinois 57 D h
Comstock, New York 53 N b
Comstock, Texas 64 F f
Conanicut I., Rhode Island 51 L b
Conasauga R., Georgia 54 G c
Conata, South Dakota 58 D g
Concan, Texas 65 H f
Conception, Missouri 61 K d
Conception, Pt., California 75 E k
Conchas, New Mexico 71 N d
Conchas Res., New Mexico 71 N d
Concho, Arizona 70 H e
Concho, Oklahoma 62 F c
Concho R., Texas 64 G d
Concord, California (36,208) 74 D g
Concord, Georgia 54 G d
Concord, Massachusetts, vicinity of Boston
Concord, Michigan 57 J g
Concord, Nebraska 60 H b
Concord, New Hampshire (28,991) 49 D e
Concord, North Carolina 55 L b
Concord, Vermont 49 D d
Concordia, Kansas 60 G e
Concordia, Missouri 61 L f
Concordville, Pennsylvania 50 B f
Concrete, Washington 73 J g
Conda, Idaho 66 J g
Conde, South Dakota 58 H e
Condon, Oregon 73 K k
Conecuh R., Alabama 54 E f
Conejos, Colorado 69 K f
Conemaugh R., Pennsylvania 52 G e
Conesus L., New York 52 J c
Conesville, Iowa 61 N c
Conesville, Ohio 52 E e
Coney Island, New York 51 L g
Confluence, Pennsylvania 52 G f
Confusion Ra., Utah 68 C d
Congaree R., South Carolina 55 L d
Congers, New York 50 F c
Congress, Arizona 70 E e
Congress Heights, Maryland 53 Q h
Conifer, Colorado 69 L d
Conlen, Texas 64 B g
Conneaut, Ohio 52 F d
Conneautville, Pennsylvania 52 F d
Connecticut (2,925,000) 5009 sq. miles 50-51
Connecticut R., Connecticut, etc. 51 J c
Connell, Washington 73 M j
Connellsville, Pennsylvania 52 G e
Connelly, New York 50 E b
Conner, Montana 66 F d
Connersville, Indiana 57 H k
Conover, North Carolina 55 K b
Conover, Wisconsin 56 D c
Conowingo Dam, Maryland 53 K f
Conrad, Montana 66 J a
Conrath, Wisconsin 56 C d
Conroe, Texas 65 M e
Conshohocken, Pennsylvania 50 C e
Constableville, New York 53 L b
Constantine, C., Alaska 76 H g
Constantine, Michigan 57 G g
Constantine Harbor, Alaska 76 M j
Contact, Nevada 74 L c
Continental, Arizona 70 G h
Continental, Ohio 52 B d
Continental Res., Colorado 69 J f
Contoocook, N. H. 49 D e
Contoocook R., N. H. 49 D e
Convent Station, New Jersey 50 E d
Converse, Indiana 57 H j
Converse, Louisiana 63 K g
Convoy, Ohio 52 B e
Conway, Arkansas 63 L c
Conway, Iowa 61 K d
Conway, L., Arkansas 63 L c
Conway, Missouri 61 M g
Conway, New Hampshire 49 D e
Conway, North Carolina 55 O a
Conway, North Dakota 58 J b
Conway, South Carolina 55 M d
Conway, Texas 64 C h
Conway Springs, Kansas 60 G g
Conyers, Georgia 54 G d
Conyngham, Pennsylvania 50 A d
Cook, Minnesota 59 O c
Cook, Mt., Alaska 77 S f
Cook, Nebraska 61 H d
Cooke, Montana 67 L d
Cookeville, Tennessee 54 F a
Cook Inlet, Alaska 76 L g
Cooks, Michigan 56 G d
Cooks Pk., New Mexico 71 K g
Coolee City, Washington 73 L h
Coolee Dam, Washington 73 M g
Cooleemee, North Carolina 55 L b
Coolidge, Arizona 70 F g
Coolidge, Georgia 54 H f
Coolidge, Texas 65 L d
Coolidge Dam, Arizona 70 G f
Coolin, Idaho 66 D a
Coolville, Ohio 52 E f
Coon Rapids, Iowa 61 K c
Coon Rapids, Minnesota 59 Q h
Cooper, Texas 65 M b
Cooper R., South Carolina 55 M e
Coopersburg, Pennsylvania 50 C e
Cooperstown, New York 53 M c
Cooperstown, North Dakota 58 H c
Coopersville, Michigan 56 H f
Coosa R., Alabama 54 F c
Coosawattee R., Georgia 54 G c
Coosawhatchie R., South Carolina 55 K e
Coos Bay, Oregon 73 F m
Copake, New York 50 F a
Copake Falls, New York 50 F a
Copano Bay, Texas 65 K g
Copco, California 74 C c
Cope, Colorado 69 O d
Copeland, Florida 55 N h
Copeland, Idaho 66 D a
Copeland, Kansas 60 D g
Copemash, Michigan 56 H e
Copenhagen, New York 53 L b
Coplay, Pennsylvania 50 B d
Coppell, Texas 65 M h
Copperas Cove, Texas 65 K d
Copper Butte, mt., Washington 73 M g
Copper Center, Alaska 77 P f
Copper Harbor, Michigan 56 F b
Copperhill, Tennessee 54 G c
Copper Hill, New Jersey 50 D e
Copper Mt., Nevada 74 K c
Copper R., Alaska 77 P e
Copperton, Utah 68 B j
Coquille, Oregon 73 F m
Coquille R., Oregon 73 F m
Cora, Wyoming 67 K g
Coral Gables, Florida (34,793) 54 B d
Coralville Res., Iowa 61 N c
Coram, Montana 66 F a
Coram, New York 51 H d
Coraopolis, Pennsylvania 52 F e
Corbett, New York 50 C a
Corbin, Kentucky 57 J n
Corbin City, New Jersey 50 D g
Corcoran, California 75 F h
Cordele, Georgia 54 H f
Cordell, Oklahoma 62 E c
Cordova, Alabama 54 D d
Cordova, Alaska 77 P f
Cordova, Illinois 57 C h
Cordova B., Alaska 77 V j
Cordova Pk., Alaska 77 P f
Corfu, New York 52 H c
Corfu, Washington 73 L j
Corinne, Utah 68 D b
Corinth, Mississippi 63 P d
Corinth, Montana 67 N d
Corinth, New York 53 N b
Corn, Oklahoma 62 E c
Cornelia, Georgia 54 H c
Cornelius, North Carolina 55 L b
Cornell, Illinois 57 E j
Cornell, Wisconsin 56 B d
Cornersville, Tennessee 54 E b
Cornfields, Arizona 70 H d
Corning, Arkansas 63 N b
Corning, California 74 C e
Corning, Iowa 61 K d
Corning, Kansas 61 H e
Corning, Missouri 61 J d
Corning, New York 53 J c
Corning, Ohio 52 D f
Cornish Flat, New Hampshire 49 C e
Cornucopia, Oregon 73 N k
Cornucopia, Wisconsin 56 B b
Cornwall, Connecticut 50 G b
Cornwall, New York 50 E c
Cornwall Bridge, Connecticut 50 G b
Cornwall on the Hudson, New York 50 F c
Corona, California 75 H l
Corona, New Mexico 71 M e
Coronado, California 75 H m
Coronado Beach, Florida 55 L h
Coronation I., Alaska 77 U j
Corpus Christi, L., Texas 65 K g
Corpus Christi, Texas (167,690) 65 K h
Corral, Idaho 66 F f
Correctionville, Iowa 61 J b
Corrigan, Texas 65 N e
Corry, Pennsylvania 52 G d
Corsica, South Dakota 58 H g
Corsicana, Texas 65 L c
Cortaro, Arizona 70 F g
Corte Madero, California 75 B l
Cortez, Colorado 68 H f
Cortez, Nevada 74 J d
Cortez Mts., Nevada 74 J d
Cortland, Nebraska 60 H d
Cortland, New York 53 K c
Cortland, Ohio 52 F d
Corunna, Michigan 56 J g
Corvallis, Montana 66 F c
Corvallis, Oregon 73 G l
Corwin, C., Alaska 76 E g
Corwin, Kansas 60 F g
Corwin Springs, Montana 67 K d
Corwith, Iowa 61 L b
Corydon, Indiana 57 G l
Corydon, Iowa 61 L d
Corydon, Kentucky 57 F m
Corydon, Pennsylvania 52 H d
Coshocton, Ohio 52 E e
Cosmos, Minnesota 59 M f
Coso Junction, California 75 H h
Cost, Texas 65 K f
Costa Mesa, California (37,550) 75 H l
Costello, Pennsylvania 52 H d
Costigan, Maine 49 G c
Costilla, New Mexico 71 M c
Cotati, California 74 C f
Cotopaxi, Colorado 69 L e
Cottage Grove, Oregon 73 G m
Cottageville, South Carolina 55 L e
Cottageville, West Virginia 52 E g
Cotter, Arkansas 63 L b
Cotton, Minnesota 59 O c
Cottondale, Alabama 54 D d
Cottondale, Florida 54 F g
Cotton Plant, Arkansas 63 M d
Cottonport, Louisiana 63 L h
Cotton Valley, Louisiana 63 K f
Cottonwood, Alabama 54 F f
Cottonwood, Arizona 70 F e
Cottonwood, California 74 C d
Cottonwood, Idaho 66 D c
Cottonwood, South Dakota 58 E g
Cottonwood, Texas 65 H c
Cottonwood Cliffs, Arizona 70 D d
Cottonwood Falls, Kansas 60 H f
Cottonwood R., Minnesota 59 M f
Cottonwood Wash., Arizona 70 G d
Cotuit, Massachusetts 51 N b
Cotulla, Texas 65 H g
Couderay, Wisconsin 56 B d
Coudersport, Pennsylvania 52 J d
Cougar, Washington 73 H j
Coulterville, California 74 E g
Coulterville, Illinois 57 D l
Council, Alaska 76 F d
Council, Idaho 66 D e
Council Bluffs, Iowa (55,641) 61 J c
Council Grove, Kansas 60 H f
Council Grove Res., Kansas 60 H f
Countyline, Oklahoma 62 F d
Coupeville, Washington 73 H g
Coupland, Texas 65 K e
Courtenay, North Dakota 58 H c
Courtland, Alabama 54 D c
Courtland, Kansas 60 G e
Courtland, Minnesota 59 M f
Courtland, Virginia 53 J j
Courtney, Texas 65 L e
Coushatta, Louisiana 63 K f
Cove, Arkansas 63 J d
Cove, Oregon 73 N k
Cove, Utah 68 D e
Cove City, North Carolina 55 O b
Covelo, California 74 B e
Cove Mt., Pennsylvania 52 J f
Coventry, Connecticut 51 J b
Coventry, Rhode Island 51 K b
Cove Point, Maryland 53 K g
Covert, Kansas 60 F e
Covert, Michigan 57 G g
Covesville, Virginia 52 H h
Coville, L., Alaska 76 J g
Covington, Georgia 54 H d
Covington, Indiana 57 F j
Covington, Kentucky (60,376) 57 J l
Covington, Louisiana 63 N h
Covington, Michigan 56 E c
Covington, Ohio 52 B e
Covington, Oklahoma 62 F b
Covington, Tennessee 54 B b
Covington, Texas 65 K c
Covington, Virginia 52 F h
Cowan, Tennessee 54 E b
Cowan, Mt., Montana 67 K d
Cowboy Pass, Utah 68 C d
Cow Cr., Washington 73 M h
Cowden, Illinois 57 D k
Cowdrey, Colorado 69 K c
Cowen, West Virginia 52 F g
Coweta, Oklahoma 62 H c
Cow Head L., California 74 E c
Cowles, Nebraska 60 F d
Cowles, New Mexico 71 M d
Cowley, Wyoming 67 M e
Cowlitz Pass, Washington 73 J j
Cowlitz R., Washington 73 H j
Cow Palace, California 75 B m
Compasture R., Virginia 52 G g
Cowpens, South Carolina 55 K b
Cowpens Nat. Batt. Site, South Carolina 55 K b
Coxsackie, New York 50 F a
Coyanesa Draw, Texas 64 D e
Coyle, Oklahoma 62 F c
Coyle, Washington 72 A h
Coyote, California 75 D g
Coyote, New Mexico 71 L c
Coyote, New Mexico 71 M f
Coyote L., California 75 J j
Coyote Pk., Arizona 70 D g
Coyote Pk., California 75 G h
Cozad, Nebraska 60 E d
Crab Cr., Washington 73 M h
Crab Orchard, Kentucky 57 J m
Crab Orchard, Tennessee 54 G b
Crab Orchard L., Illinois 57 D m
Crafton, Pennsylvania 53 O b
Craig, Colorado 69 J c
Craig, Florida 55 O j
Craig, Missouri 61 J d
Craig, Montana 66 J b
Craig, Mt., Alaska 77 R f
Craig, Nebraska 60 H c
Craigmont, Idaho 66 D c
Craigsville, Virginia 52 G g
Cranberry L., New York 53 M a
Cranberry Lake, New York 53 M a
Cranbury, New Jersey 50 D e
Crandall, South Dakota 58 J e
Crandall, Texas 65 L c
Crane, Missouri 61 L h
Crane, Montana 67 Q b
Crane, Oregon 73 M m
Crane, Texas 64 E d
Crane Creek Res., Idaho 66 D e
Cranfills Gap, Texas 65 K d
Cranford, New Jersey (26,424), vicinity of Elizabeth
Crannell, California 74 A c
Cranston, Rhode Island (66,766) 51 L b
Crary, North Dakota 58 H b
Craryville, New York 50 F a
Crater L., Oregon 73 H n
Crater Lake, Oregon 73 H n
Crater Lake Nat. Park, Oregon 73 H n
Crater Pk., California 74 D d
Craters of the Moon Nat. Mon., Idaho 66 G f
Crawford, Florida 55 K g
Crawford, Georgia 54 H d
Crawford, Mississippi 63 P e
Crawford, Nebraska 60 A b
Crawford, Texas 65 K d
Crawford Notch, New Hampshire 49 D d
Crawfordville, Florida 54 G g
Crawfordville, Georgia 55 J d
Crawfordsville, Indiana 57 F j
Crazy Mts., Alaska 77 P d
Crazy Mts., Montana 67 K c
Crazy Pk., Montana 67 K d
Crazy Woman Cr., Wyoming 67 O e
Cream Ridge, New Jersey 50 E e
Creede, Colorado 69 K f
Creedmoor, North Carolina 55 N a
Creekside, Pennsylvania 52 G e
Creighton, Nebraska 60 G b
Crenshaw, Mississippi 63 N d
Cresbard, South Dakota 58 H e
Crescent, Oklahoma 62 F c
Crescent, Oregon 73 J m
Crescent, Utah 68 C j
Crescent Beach, South Carolina 55 N d
Crescent City, California 74 A c
Crescent City, Florida 55 K h
Crescent L., Florida 55 K h
Crescent L., Oregon 73 H m
Crescent L., Washington 73 G g
Crescent Lake, Oregon 73 J m
Crescent Mills, California 74 E d
Crescent Pk., Nevada 75 K j
Cresco, Iowa 61 M a
Cresco, Pennsylvania 50 C c
Cresson, Texas 65 K c
Crested Butte, Colorado 69 K e
Crestline, Nevada 74 L g
Crestline, Ohio 52 D e
Creston, Montana 66 F a
Creston, Iowa 61 K c
Creston, Washington 73 M h
Creston, Wyoming 67 N h
Crestone Pk., Colorado 69 L e
Crestview, Florida 54 E g
Crestview, Tennessee 54 D b
Creswell, North Carolina 55 P b
Creswell, Oregon 73 G m
Crete, Illinois 57 F h
Crete, Nebraska 60 H d
Crete, North Dakota 58 J d
Crewe, Virginia 52 H h
Cridersville, Ohio 52 B e
Chriesman, Texas 65 L e
Crillon, Mt., Alaska 77 T g
Cripple, Alaska 76 J e
Cripple Creek, Colorado 69 L e
Crisfield, Maryland 53 L h
Crittenden, Kentucky 57 J l
Crivitz, Wisconsin 56 E d
Crocker, Missouri 61 M g
Crockett, Texas 65 M d
Crofton, Kentucky 57 F m
Crofton, Nebraska 60 G b
Croghan, New York 53 L b
Crompton, Rhode Island 51 K b
Cromwell, Connecticut 51 H b
Cromwell, Minnesota 59 O d
Crook, Colorado 69 O c
Crook, L., Texas 65 M b
Crooked Cr., Kansas 60 D g
Crooked Cr., Oregon 73 M n
Crooked Creek, Alaska 77 Q d
Crooked L., Florida 55 N f
Crooked L., Minnesota 59 O b
Crooked R., Oregon 73 K l
Crookes Pt., New York 51 K g
Crookston, Minnesota 59 K c
Crookston, Nebraska 60 D b
Croom, Florida 55 J j
Crosby, Minnesota 59 N d
Crosby, Mississippi 63 M g
Crosby, North Dakota 58 C b
Crosby, Texas 65 M f
Crosbyton, Texas 64 F b
Cross City, Florida 54 H h
Crossett, Arkansas 63 M e
Cross Hill, South Carolina 55 K c
Crossing of the Fathers, Utah 68 E f
Cross L., Louisiana 63 K f
Crossman Pk., Arizona 70 C e
Cross Mountain, Colorado 68 H c
Cross Plains, Texas 65 H c
Cross River, New York 50 F c
Cross Sd., Alaska 77 T g
Cross Village, Michigan 56 H d
Crossville, Tennessee 54 F b
Crosswicks, New Jersey 50 D e
Crosswind L., Alaska 77 O e
Croswell, Michigan 56 L f
Crothersville, Indiana 57 H l
Croton Falls, New York 50 F c
Croton Falls Res., New York 50 F c
Croton Lake, New York 50 F c
Croton-on-Hudson, New York 50 F c
Crouch, Idaho 66 D e
Crow Agency, Montana 67 N d
Crow Cr., Colorado 69 M c
Crowder, Mississippi 63 N d
Crowder, Oklahoma 62 H c
Crowell, Texas 65 H b
Crowheart, Wyoming 67 L f
Crowley, Colorado 69 N e
Crowley, L., California 74 G g
Crowley, Louisiana 63 L h
Crowleys Ridge, Arkansas 63 N c
Crown City, Ohio 52 D g
Crown King, Arizona 70 E e
Crown Point, New Mexico 71 J d
Crown Point, New York 53 N b
Crown Pt., Indiana 57 F h
Crow Wing R., Minnesota 59 M d
Croydon, Pennsylvania 50 C e
Crozet, Virginia 52 H g
Crucero, California 75 J j
Crucible, Pennsylvania 52 G f
Cruger, Mississippi 63 N e
Crugers, New York 50 F c
Crump L., Oregon 73 L n
Crumpton, Maryland 50 A g
Crystal, Minnesota 59 P h
Crystal, Nevada 75 L h
Crystal, North Dakota 58 J b
Crystal B., Florida 55 J j
Crystal Beach, Maryland 50 A g
Crystal City, Illinois 57 C l

Crystal City, *Missouri* 61 O f
Crystal City, *Texas* 65 H g
Crystal Falls, *Michigan* 56 E c
Crystal L., *Michigan* 56 G e
Crystal L., *Pennsylvania* 50 B c
Crystal Lake, *Illinois* 57 E g
Crystal Lake, *Iowa* 61 L a
Crystal R., *Colorado* 69 J d
Crystal River, *Florida* 55 J j
Crystal Springs, *Mississippi* 63 N g
Crystal Springs Res., *California* 75 B n
Crystal Valley, *Michigan* 56 G f
Cuba, *Illinois* 57 C j
Cuba, *Kansas* 60 G e
Cuba, *Missouri* 61 N f
Cuba, *New Mexico* 71 L c
Cuba, *New York* 52 H c
Cuba City, *Wisconsin* 56 C g
Cuckoo, *Virginia* 52 J h
Cudahy, *Wisconsin* 56 F g
Cuddeback L., *California* 75 H j
Cuddlesbackville, *New York* 50 D c
Cudjoe Key, *Florida* 55 N j
Cuero, *Texas* 65 K f
Cuervo, *New Mexico* 71 N d
Cuesta Pass, *California* 75 E j
Cuivre R., *Missouri* 61 N e
Culbertson, *Montana* 67 Q a
Culbertson, *Nebraska* 60 D d
Culdesac, *Idaho* 66 D c
Culebra Pk., *Colorado* 69 L f
Cullison, *Kansas* 60 F g
Cullman, *Alabama* 54 E c
Culpeper, *Virginia* 52 H g
Culver, *Indiana* 57 G h
Culver, *Kansas* 60 G f
Culver, *Oregon* 73 J l
Culver City, *California (32,163)* 75 D l
Culver L., *New Jersey* 50 D c
Cumberland, *Iowa* 61 K c
Cumberland, *Kentucky* 57 K l
Cumberland, L., *Kentucky* 57 H n
Cumberland, *Maryland (33,415)* 52 H f
Cumberland, *New Jersey* 50 D g
Cumberland, *Ohio* 52 E f
Cumberland, *Virginia* 52 H h
Cumberland, *Wisconsin* 56 A d
Cumberland City, *Tennessee* 54 D a
Cumberland Gap, *Tennessee* 54 H a
Cumberland I., *Georgia* 55 K g
Cumberland Mts., *Kentucky* 57 K n
Cumberland Plateau, *Tennessee* 54 F b
Cumberland Pt., *Michigan* 56 E a
Cumberland R., *Kentucky* 57 K n
Cumberland R., *Tennessee* 54 D a
Cumberland Res., *Pennsylvania* 52 H f
Cumby, *Texas* 65 M b
Cumming, *Georgia* 54 G c
Cunningham, *Kansas* 60 F g
Cunningham, *Washington* 73 M j
Cummings, *California* 74 B e
Cummings, *North Dakota* 58 J c
Cuprum, *Idaho* 66 D d
Curlew, *Washington* 73 M g
Curlew Is., *Louisiana* 63 P j
Curlew L., *Alaska* 76 F e
Curran, *Michigan* 56 K e
Currant, *Nevada* 74 K f
Current R., *Missouri* 61 N g
Currie, *Minnesota* 59 L f
Currie, *Nevada* 74 L d
Currie, *North Carolina* 55 N c
Currituck, *North Carolina* 55 P a
Currituck Sd., *North Carolina* 55 Q a
Curry, *Alaska* 76 N e
Curryville, *Missouri* 61 N e
Curtin, *Oregon* 73 G m
Curtis, *Louisiana* 63 K f
Curtis, *Michigan* 56 H c
Curtis, *Nebraska* 60 D d
Curtis B., *Maryland* 53 Q f
Curtis Bay, *Maryland* 53 Q g
Curtisville, *Michigan* 56 K e
Curwensville, *Pennsylvania* 52 H e
Cushing, *Minnesota* 59 M d
Cushing, *Oklahoma* 62 G c
Cushing, *Texas* 65 N d
Cushman, *Arkansas* 63 M c
Cushman, *Montana* 67 L c
Cushman, *Oregon* 73 F m
Cushman, Res., *Washington* 73 G h
Cusseta, *Georgia* 54 G e
Cusson, *Minnesota* 59 O b
Custer, *Montana* 67 N c
Custer, *South Dakota* 58 C g
Custer Battlefield Nat. Mon., *Montana* 67 N d
Custer City, *Oklahoma* 62 E c
Cut Bank, *Montana* 66 H a
Cut Bank Cr., *Montana* 66 H a
Cutchogue, *New York* 51 H c
Cuthand Cr., *Texas* 65 M b
Cuthbert, *Georgia* 54 G f
Cuthbert, *South Dakota* 58 H g
Cuthbert, *Texas* 64 F c
Cutler, *California* 75 F h
Cutler, *Maine* 49 H e
Cutler R., *Alaska* 76 H c
Cutoff, *Alaska* 76 J d
Cutter, *Arizona* 70 G f
Cuttyhunk I., *Massachusetts* 51 M c
Cuyahoga Falls, *Ohio (47,922)* 52 E d
Cuyahoga R., *Ohio* 52 E d
Cuyama, *California* 75 F j
Cynthiana, *Kentucky* 57 J l
Cypress, *Illinois* 57 D m
Cypress, *Louisiana* 63 K g
Cypress, *Texas* 65 M f
Cypress Cr., *Texas* 65 M b
Cypress L., *Florida* 55 N e
Dabob B., *Washington* 72 A g
Dacomo, *Oklahoma* 62 E b
Da Costa, *New Jersey* 50 D f
Dade City, *Florida* 55 M e
Dadeville, *Alabama* 54 F e
Dafter, *Michigan* 56 J c
Daggett, *California* 75 H k
Daggett, *Michigan* 56 F d
Dagmar, *Montana* 67 Q a
Dagsboro, *Delaware* 53 L g
Dagus, *Pennsylvania* 52 H d
Dahlgren, *Virginia* 53 J g
Dahlonega, *Georgia* 54 G c
Daingerfield, *Texas* 65 N b
Dairy, *Oregon* 73 J n
Daisetta, *Texas* 65 N e
Daisy, *Washington* 73 M g
Dakota, *Illinois* 56 D g
Dakota, *Minnesota* 59 P g
Dakota City, *Iowa* 61 K b
Dakota City, *Nebraska* 60 H b
Dale, *Indiana* 57 F l
Dale, *Oregon* 73 M l
Dale, *Pennsylvania* 52 H e
Dale, *South Carolina* 55 L e
Dale, *Texas* 65 K f
Dale, *Vermont* 49 B e
Dale Hollow Res., *Tennessee* 54 F a
Daleville, *Indiana* 57 H j
Daleville, *Pennsylvania* 50 B c
Dalgoi I., *Alaska* 76 G j
Dalhart, *Texas* 64 B g
Dalies, *New Mexico* 71 L e
Dall, Mt., *Alaska* 76 L e
Dallas, *Georgia* 54 G d
Dallas, *Oregon* 73 G l
Dallas, *Pennsylvania* 50 A c
Dallas, *Texas (679,684)* 65 L c
Dallas, *Wisconsin* 56 B d
Dallas Center, *Iowa* 61 L c
Dallas City, *Illinois* 57 B j
Dallastown, *Pennsylvania* 53 K f
Dallas Warner Res., *California* 74 E g
Dalles, The, *Oregon* 73 J k
Dall I., *Alaska* 77 V j
Dall L., *Alaska* 76 F f
Dall Mt., *Alaska* 76 N c
Dall R., *Alaska* 76 N c
Dalton, *Georgia* 54 G c
Dalton, *Massachusetts* 49 B f
Dalton, *Nebraska* 60 B c
Dalton, *Pennsylvania* 53 L d
Dalton, *Wisconsin* 56 D f
Daly City, *California (44,791)* 75 B l
Dalzell, *South Dakota* 58 D f
Damar, *Kansas* 60 E e
Damariscotta, *Maine* 49 F d
Damariscotta L., *Maine* 49 F d
Damascus, *Arkansas* 63 L c
Damascus, *Georgia* 54 G f
Damascus, *Maryland* 53 J f
Damascus, *Virginia* 52 E j
Damon, *Texas* 65 M f
Dana, *California* 74 D c
Dana, *Illinois* 57 F k
Dana, *Indiana* 57 E j
Dana, Mt., *California* 74 F g
Dana Vol., *Alaska* 76 G j
Danboro, *Pennsylvania* 50 C e
Danbury, *Connecticut* 50 G c
Danbury, *Nebraska* 60 D d
Danbury, *New Hampshire* 49 D e
Danbury, *Texas* 65 M f
Danbury, *Wisconsin* 56 A c
Danby, *California* 75 K k
Danby, *Vermont* 49 B e
Danby L., *California* 75 K k
Dane, *Wisconsin* 56 D f
Danevang, *Texas* 65 L f
Danforth, *Maine* 49 H c
Dania, *Florida* 55 O g
Daniel, *Wyoming* 67 K g
Danielson, *Connecticut* 51 K b
Danielsville, *Georgia* 54 H c
Danielsville, *Pennsylvania* 50 B d
Dannebrog, *Nebraska* 60 F c
Dannemora, *New York* 53 N a
Danner, *Oregon* 73 N n
Dan R., *North Carolina-Virginia* 55 M a
Dansville, *Michigan* 56 J g
Dansville, *New York* 52 J c
Dante, *Virginia* 52 D j
Danvers, *Illinois* 57 D j
Danvers, *Massachusetts* 49 D f
Danvers, *Minnesota* 59 L e
Danvers, *Montana* 67 L b
Danville, *Arkansas* 63 K c
Danville, *Georgia* 54 H e
Danville, *Illinois (41,856)* 57 F j
Danville, *Indiana* 57 G k
Danville, *Maine* 49 E d
Danville, *Ohio* 52 D e
Danville, *Kentucky* 57 J m
Danville, *Pennsylvania* 53 K e
Danville, *Vermont* 49 C d
Danville, *Virginia (46,577)* 52 G j
Danville, *West Virginia* 52 E g
Danzig, *North Dakota* 58 G d
Daphne, *Alabama* 54 D g
D'Arbonne R., *Louisiana* 63 L f
Darby, *Montana* 66 F c
Darby, *Pennsylvania* 50 F g
Darby Mts., *Alaska* 76 F d
Dardanelle, *Arkansas* 63 K c
Dardanelle, *California* 74 F f
Darien, *Connecticut* 50 G c
Darien, *Georgia* 55 K f
Darlington, *Idaho* 66 G f
Darlington, *Missouri* 61 K d
Darlington, *South Carolina* 55 M c
Darlington, *Wisconsin* 56 C g
Darlow, *Colorado* 69 P g
Darnell, *Louisiana* 63 M f
Darrington, *Washington* 73 J g
Darrouzett, *Texas* 64 D g
Dartmouth, *Massachusetts* 51 L b
Darwin, *California* 75 H h
Dassel, *Minnesota* 59 M e
Date Cr., *Arizona* 70 D e
Dateland, *Arizona* 70 D g
Datil, *New Mexico* 71 K e
Dauphin, *Pennsylvania* 53 K e
Dauphin I., *Alabama* 54 C g
Davenport, *Alaska* 76 J e
Davenport, *California* 75 C g
Davenport, *Florida* 55 N e
Davenport, *Iowa (88,981)* 61 O c
Davenport, *Nebraska* 60 G d
Davenport, *New York* 53 M c
Davenport, *Oklahoma* 62 G c
Davenport, *Washington* 73 M h
David City, *Nebraska* 60 G c
Davids I., *New York* 51 N e
Davidson, *North Carolina* 55 L b
Davidson, *Oklahoma* 62 D d
Davidson, *Texas* 65 H a
Davidson Mts., *Alaska* 77 Q b
Davie, *Florida* 55 O g
Davilla, *Texas* 65 K e
Davis, *California* 74 D f
Davis, *Illinois* 56 D g
Davis, Mt., *Pennsylvania* 52 G f
Davis, *Oklahoma* 62 F d
Davis, *West Virginia* 52 G f
Davisboro, *Georgia* 55 J e
Davis City, *Iowa* 61 L d
Davis Creek, *California* 74 E c
Davis Dam, *Arizona* 70 C d
Davis Mts., *Texas* 64 C e
Davison, *Michigan* 56 K f
Davisville, *Missouri* 61 N g
Davy, *West Virginia* 52 E h
Dawn, *Missouri* 61 L e
Dawn, *Texas* 64 B j
Dawson, *Georgia* 54 G f
Dawson, *Minnesota* 59 K f
Dawson, *New Mexico* 71 N c
Dawson, *North Dakota* 58 G d
Dawson, *Oklahoma* 62 H b
Dawson, *Texas* 65 L d
Dawson Springs, *Kentucky* 57 F m
Dawsonville, *Georgia* 54 G c
Day, *California* 74 D c
Day, *Florida* 54 H g
Daylight Pass, *California* 75 H h
Days Creek, *Oregon* 73 G n
Dayton, *Iowa* 61 K b
Dayton, *New Jersey* 50 D e
Dayton, *New York* 52 H c
Dayton, *Ohio (262,332)* 52 B f
Dayton, *Pennsylvania* 52 G e
Dayton, *Tennessee* 54 F b
Dayton, *Texas* 65 N e
Dayton, *Washington* 73 N j
Dayton, *Wyoming* 67 N e
Daytona Beach, *Florida (37,395)* 55 K h
Dayville, *Oregon* 73 L l
Dazey, *North Dakota* 58 H c
Deacons, *New Jersey* 50 D e
Dead Indian Pk., *Wyoming* 67 L e
Dead L., *Florida* 54 F g
Dead L., *Minnesota* 59 L d
Deadman L., *California* 75 J k
Deadmans B., *Florida* 54 H h
Dead Mts., *California* 75 L k
Dead R., *Maine* 49 E c
Dead R., *Michigan* 56 F c
Deadwood, *South Dakota* 58 C f
Deadwood Res., *Idaho* 66 E e
Deale, *Maryland* 53 K g
Deal Island, *Maryland* 53 L g
Dean, *Iowa* 61 M d
Deansboro, *New York* 53 L c
Dearborn, *Michigan (112,007)* 57 K g
Dearborn, *Missouri* 61 K e
Dearing, *Kansas* 61 J g
Deary, *Idaho* 66 D c
Dease Inlet, *Alaska* 76 K a
Death Val., *California* 75 J h
Death Valley Nat. Mon., *California* 75 H h
Deaver, *Wyoming* 67 M e
Debauch Mt., *Alaska* 76 H d
De Beque, *Colorado* 68 H d
De Berry, *Texas* 65 N c
Deborah, Mt., *Alaska* 77 O e
Deborgia, *Montana* 66 E b
Debruce, *New York* 50 D b
de Cade, L., *Louisiana* 63 N j
Decatur, *Alabama (29,217)* 54 E c
Decatur, *Arkansas* 63 J b
Decatur, *Georgia* 54 G d
Decatur, *Illinois (78,004)* 57 E k
Decatur, *Indiana* 57 J j
Decatur, *Iowa* 61 L d
Decatur, *Michigan* 57 H g
Decatur, *Mississippi* 63 O f
Decatur, *Nebraska* 60 H b
Decatur, *Texas* 65 K b
Decaturville, *Tennessee* 54 C b
Decherd, *Tennessee* 54 E b
Decker, *Indiana* 57 F l
Decker, *Montana* 67 O d
Deckers, *Colorado* 69 L d
Declo, *Idaho* 66 G g
Decorah, *Iowa* 61 N a
Dedham, *Iowa* 61 K c
Dedham, *Massachusetts* 49 F j
Dedrick, *California* 74 B d
Deep Cr., *Idaho* 66 D g
Deep Creek L., *Maryland* 52 G f
Deep Creek Ra., *Utah* 68 C d
Deep Gap., *North Carolina* 55 K a
Deep R., *North Carolina* 55 M b
Deep River, *Connecticut* 51 J c
Deep River, *Iowa* 61 M c
Deep River, *Washington* 73 G j
Deep Springs, *California* 75 H g
Deepwater, *Missouri* 61 L f
Deepwater, *New Jersey* 50 C f
Deepwater Point, *Delaware* 50 B g
Deer, *Arkansas* 63 K c
Deer Cr., *California* 74 D d
Deer Cr., *Nebraska* 60 D d
Deer Cr., *Wyoming* 67 P g
Deer Creek, *Minnesota* 59 L d
Deer Creek, *Oklahoma* 62 F b
Deer Creek Res., *Utah* 68 E c
Deerfield, *Kansas* 60 C g
Deerfield Beach, *Florida* 55 O g
Deerfield Street, *New Jersey* 50 C f
Deer I., *Alaska* 76 F j
Deer I., *Maine* 49 G d
Deering, *Alaska* 76 F c
Deering, *North Dakota* 58 E b
Deer Lake, *Pennsylvania* 50 A d
Deer Lodge, *Montana* 66 H c
Deer Park, *Alabama* 54 C f
Deer Park, *New York* 50 G d
Deer Park, *Washington* 73 N h
Deer River, *Minnesota* 59 N c
Deerton, *Michigan* 56 F c
Deer Trail, *Colorado* 69 M d
Deer Wood, *Minnesota* 59 N d
Deeson, *Mississippi* 63 N d
Deeth, *Nevada* 74 K c
Deferiet, *New York* 53 L a
Defiance, *Iowa* 61 J c
Defiance, *Ohio* 52 B d
De Funiak Springs, *Florida* 54 E g
De Graff, *Minnesota* 59 L e
Degraff, *Ohio* 52 C e
De Gray Res., *Arkansas* 63 K d
De Grey, *South Dakota* 58 G f
De Kalb, *Illinois* 57 E h
De Kalb, *Mississippi* 63 P f
De Kalb, *Texas* 65 N b
De Kalb Junction, *New York* 53 L a
Delacroix, *Louisiana* 63 O j
Delagua, *Colorado* 69 M f
Delake, *Oregon* 73 G l
De Lamar, *Idaho* 66 D f
Delamar, *Nevada* 74 L g
Delamar Mts., *Nevada* 75 L g
De Lancey, *New York* 50 D a
De Land, *Florida* 55 K h
Delano, *California* 75 F j
Delano, *Pennsylvania* 50 A d
Delano Pk., *Utah* 68 D e
Delarof Is., *Alaska* 77 N j
Delavan, *Illinois* 57 D j
Delavan, *Wisconsin* 56 E g
Delaware *(523,000)* 2057 sq. miles 53
Delaware, *New Jersey (31,552)* 50 C d
Delaware, *Ohio* 52 C e
Delaware, *Oklahoma* 62 H b
Delaware B., *Delaware* 50 C g
Delaware B., *New Jersey* 50 C g
Delaware City, *Delaware* 50 B f
Delaware Cr., *Texas* 64 C d
Delaware R., *Delaware, etc.* 50 B g
Delaware R., *Kansas* 61 J e
Delaware Res., *Ohio* 52 C e
Delaware Water Gap, *Pennsylvania* 50 C d
Delcambre, *Louisiana* 63 M j
Delcarbon, *Colorado* 69 M f
De Leon, *Texas* 65 J c
Delevan, *California* 74 C e
Delevan, *New York* 52 H c
Delgada, Pt., *California* 74 A d
Delhi, *Iowa* 61 N b
Delhi, *Louisiana* 63 M f
Delhi, *New York* 50 D a
Delhi, *Oklahoma* 62 D c
Delia, *Kansas* 61 J e
Delight, *Arkansas* 63 K d
Dell, *Arkansas* 63 N c
Dell, *Montana* 66 H e
Delle, *Utah* 68 D c
Dellenbaugh, Mt., *Arizona* 70 D c
Delloma, *California* 74 B d
Dell Rapids, *South Dakota* 59 K g
Dellvale, *Kansas* 60 D e
Del Mar, *California* 75 H m
Delmar, *Iowa* 61 O b
Delmar, *Maryland* 53 L g
Delmont, *New Jersey* 50 D g
Delmont, *South Dakota* 58 H g
Delmues, *Nevada* 74 L g
Del Norte, *Colorado* 69 K f
De Long Mts., *Alaska* 76 F b
Delphi, *Indiana* 57 G j
Delphos, *Kansas* 60 G e
Delphos, *Ohio* 52 B e
Delray Beach, *Florida* 55 O g
Delridge, *Washington* 72 B h
Del Rio, *Texas* 64 G f
Delta, *Colorado* 68 H e
Delta, *Louisiana* 63 N f
Delta, *Missouri* 61 P g
Delta, *Ohio* 52 B d
Delta, *Pennsylvania* 53 K f
Delta, *Utah* 68 D d
Delta Mendota Can., *California* 75 E h
Delta R., *Alaska* 77 O e
Delta Res., *New York* 53 L b
Deltaville, *Virginia* 53 K h
Delton, *Michigan* 56 H g
Del Valle, *Texas* 65 K e
Delwin, *Texas* 64 G b
Demarcation Pt., *Alaska* 77 R b
Deming, *New Mexico* 71 K g
Deming, *Washington* 73 H g
Demopolis, *Alabama* 54 D e
Denali, *Alaska* 76 O e
Denbigh, C., *Alaska* 76 G d
Denham Springs, *Louisiana* 63 N h
Denio, *Oregon* 73 M n
Denison, *Iowa* 61 J b
Denison, Mt., *Alaska* 76 K g
Denison, *Texas* 65 L b
Denison Dam, *Oklahoma* 62 G e
Denmark, *Oregon* 73 F n
Denmark, *South Carolina* 55 K d
Denmark, *Wisconsin* 56 F e
Denning, *New York* 50 E b
Dennis, *Massachusetts* 51 N b
Dennis Port, *Massachusetts* 49 E g
Dennison, *Ohio* 52 E e
Denniston, *Virginia* 52 G j
Dennisville, *New Jersey* 50 D g
Denny, *California* 74 B d
Dennysville, *Maine* 49 H e
Dent, *Idaho* 66 D c
Denton, *Georgia* 55 J f
Denton, *Kentucky* 57 L l
Denton, *Maryland* 53 L g
Denton, *Montana* 67 L b
Denton, *Texas (26,844)* 65 K b
Denver, *Colorado (493,887)* 69 L d
Denver, *Idaho* 66 D d
Denver, *Indiana* 57 G j
Denver, *Iowa* 61 M b
Denver, *New York* 50 D a
Denver, *Pennsylvania* 53 K e
Denver City, *Texas* 64 E c
Denver Harbour, *Texas* 64 G h
Denville, *New Jersey* 50 E d
De Pere, *Wisconsin* 56 E e
Depew, *New York* 52 H c
Depew, *Oklahoma* 62 G c
Deport, *Texas* 65 M b
Deposit, *New York* 53 L c
Depot L., *Maine* 49 F b
Depue, *Illinois* 57 D h
De Queen, *Arkansas* 63 J d
De Quincey, *Louisiana* 63 K h
Derby, *Colorado* 69 P h
Derby, *Connecticut* 51 G c
Derby, *Iowa* 61 L d
Derby, *Kansas* 60 G g
Derby, *Texas* 65 H g
Derby Center, *Vermont* 49 C d
De Ridder, *Louisiana* 63 K h
Dermott, *Arkansas* 63 M e
Derry, *New Hampshire* 49 D f
Derry, *New Mexico* 71 K g
Derry, *Pennsylvania* 52 G e
De Ruyter, *New York* 53 L c
Des Arc, *Arkansas* 63 M d
Des Arc, *Missouri* 61 O g
Desatoya Mts., *Nevada* 74 H e
Descanso, *California* 75 J m
Deschutes R., *Oregon* 73 K k
Desdemona, *Texas* 65 J c
Deseret, *Utah* 68 D d
Deseret Pk., *Utah* 68 D c
Desert Center, *California* 75 K l
Desert Hot Springs, *California* 75 J l
Desert Pk., *Utah* 68 C b
Desert Ra., *Nevada* 75 K h
Desert Val., *Nevada* 74 G c
Desert View, *Arizona* 70 F c
Deshler, *Nebraska* 60 G d
Deshler, *Ohio* 52 C d
De Sinet, *Montana* 66 F c
Des Lacs R., *North Dakota* 58 E b
Desmet, *Idaho* 66 D b
De Smet, *South Dakota* 58 J f
Des Moines, *Iowa (208,982)* 61 L c
Des Moines, *New Mexico* 71 O c
Des Moines R., *Iowa, etc.* 61 K b
De Soto, *Illinois* 57 D m
De Soto, *Kansas* 61 K f
De Soto, *Missouri* 61 O f
De Soto, *Wisconsin* 56 B f
De Soto City, *Florida* 55 N f
Des Plaines, *Illinois (34,886)* 57 F g
Des Sioux, *Missouri* 61 O f
Destin, *Florida* 54 E g
Destruction I., *Washington* 73 F h
Detour, *Michigan* 56 K d
Detour, Pt., *Michigan* 56 G d
Detour Passage, *Michigan* 56 K d
Detroit, *Michigan (1,670,144)* 56 K g
Detroit, *Oregon* 73 H l
Detroit, *Texas* 65 M b
Detroit Lakes, *Minnesota* 59 L d
Detroit R., *Michigan* 57 K g
Detroit Res., *Oregon* 73 H l
De Valls Bluff, *Arkansas* 63 M d
Devereux, *Georgia* 54 H d
De View, Bayou, *Arkansas* 63 M c
Devil Mt., *Alaska* 76 E c
Devil Postpile Nat. Mon., *California* 74 F g
Devils Den, *California* 75 F j
Devils Elbow, *Alaska* 76 K e
Devils Gate, *California* 74 F f
Devils I., *Wisconsin* 56 C b
Devils Kitchen L., *Illinois* 57 E m
Devils L., *North Dakota* 57 H b
Devils L., *Texas* 64 G f
Devils Lake, *North Dakota* 58 H b
Devils Lake Res., *Nevada* 74 K c
Devils Pk., *California* 74 F g
Devils Pk., *Oregon* 73 H n
Devils Playground, *California* 75 K k
Devils R., *Texas* 64 F e
Devils Slide, *Utah* 68 E b
Devils Tower, *Wyoming* 67 Q e
Devils Tower Nat. Mon., *Wyoming* 67 Q e
Devine, *Texas* 65 J f
Devol, *Oklahoma* 62 E d
Devon, *Montana* 66 J a
Dewar, *Oklahoma* 62 H c
Deweese, *Nebraska* 60 F d
Dewey, *Arizona* 70 E e
Dewey, *Oklahoma* 62 H b
Dewey, *South Dakota* 58 C g
Dewey Res., *Kentucky* 57 L m
De Witt, *Arkansas* 63 M d
De Witt, *Iowa* 61 O c
De Witt, *Michigan* 56 J g
De Witt, *Missouri* 61 L e
De Witt, *Nebraska* 60 H d
Dexter, *Arkansas* 63 L d
Dexter, *Iowa* 61 K c
Dexter, *Kansas* 60 H g
Dexter, *Kentucky* 57 E n
Dexter, *Maine* 49 F c
Dexter, *Michigan* 56 K g
Dexter, *Minnesota* 59 O g
Dexter, *Missouri* 61 P h
Dexter, *New Mexico* 71 N f
Dexter, *New York* 53 K a
Dexter, *Texas* 65 L b
Dexter, L., *Florida* 55 K h
Dexterville, *Wisconsin* 56 C e
Dezier, *Alabama* 54 E f
D'Hanis, *Texas* 65 H f
Diablo, Mt., *California* 74 D g
Diablo L., *Washington* 73 J g
Diablo Range, *California* 75 D g
Diagonal, *Iowa* 61 K d
Diamond, *Missouri* 61 K h
Diamond Hd., *Hawaii* 72 C d
Diamond L., *Oregon* 73 H m
Diamond Lake, *Oregon* 73 H m
Diamond Mts., *Nevada* 74 K e
Diamond Pk., *Nevada* 74 K e
Diamond Pk., *Oregon* 73 H m
Diamond Springs, *California* 74 E f
Diamondville, *Wyoming* 67 K h
Diana, *West Virginia* 52 F g
Diboll, *Texas* 65 N d
Dickens, *Nebraska* 60 C d
Dickens, *Texas* 64 G b
Dickey, *Maine* 49 F a
Dickey, *North Dakota* 58 H d
Dickinson, *North Dakota* 58 D d
Dickinson, *Texas* 65 M f
Dickson, *Tennessee* 54 D a
Dickson City, *Pennsylvania* 53 L d
Dido, *Texas* 65 L h
Dierks, *Arkansas* 63 J d
Dieterich, *Illinois* 57 E k
Dietrich, *Idaho* 66 F g
Dighton, *Kansas* 60 D f
Dighton, *Massachusetts* 51 L b
Dighton, *Michigan* 56 H e
Dikeman, *Alaska* 76 J e
Dilia, *New Mexico* 71 M d
Dilkon, *Arizona* 70 G d
Dillay, *Texas* 65 H g
Dill City, *Oklahoma* 62 D c
Diller, *Nebraska* 60 H d
Dillingham, *Alaska* 76 H g
Dillon, *Colorado* 69 K d
Dillon, *Montana* 66 H d
Dillon, *South Carolina* 55 M c
Dillon Res., *Ohio* 52 D e
Dillsburg, *Pennsylvania* 53 K e
Dillwyn, *Virginia* 52 H h
Dimmitt, *Texas* 64 B j
Dimock, *South Dakota* 58 H g
Dingle, *Idaho* 66 J g
Dingmans Ferry, *Pennsylvania* 50 D c
Dinnebito Wash, *Arizona* 70 G c
Dinosaur Nat. Mon., *Utah-Colorado* 68 H c
Dinsdale, *Iowa* 61 M b
Dinsmore, *Florida* 55 K g
Dinuba, *California* 75 F h
Dinwiddie, *Virginia* 52 J h
Dirty Devil R., *Utah* 68 F d
Disappearing I., *Hawaii* 72 C b
Disappointment, C., *Washington* 73 F j
Disautel, *Washington* 73 L g

Discovery Bay, *Washington* 73 H h
Dishkakat, *Alaska* 76 J e
Dishna R., *Alaska* 76 J e
Dismal R., *Nebraska* 60 D c
Dismal Swamp, *Virginia* 53 K j
Disputanta, *Virginia* 52 J h
Disston, *Oregon* 73 H m
District of Columbia (809,000) 67 sq. miles 53 P g
Divernon, *Illinois* 57 D k
Diversion L., *Texas* 65 J b
Divide, *Colorado* 69 L e
Divide, *Montana* 66 H d
Dividing Creek, *New Jersey* 50 C g
Division Pk., *Nevada* 74 F c
Dix, *Nebraska* 60 A c
Dixfield, *Maine* 49 E d
Dixiana, *Alabama* 54 E d
Dixie, *Alabama* 54 E f
Dixie, *Georgia* 54 H g
Dixie, *Idaho* 66 E d
Dixie, *Washington* 73 M j
Dixie Pass, *Oregon* 73 M l
Dixie Valley, *Nevada* 74 G e
Dixmont, *Maine* 49 F d
Dix Mt., *New York* 53 N a
Dixon, *California* 74 D f
Dixon, *Illinois* 57 D h
Dixon, *Iowa* 61 O c
Dixon, *Missouri* 61 M g
Dixon, *Montana* 66 F b
Dixon, *Nebraska* 60 H b
Dixon, *New Mexico* 71 M c
Dixon, *Wyoming* 67 N h
Dixons Mills, *Alabama* 54 D e
Dixonville, *Pennsylvania* 52 G e
Dixville Notch, *New Hampshire* 49 D d
D' Lo, *Mississippi* 63 O g
Dobbin, *Texas* 65 M e
Dobbs Ferry, *New York* 50 F d
Doboy Sd., *Georgia* 55 K f
Dobson, *North Carolina* 55 L a
Doddridge, *Arkansas* 63 K e
Doddridge, *Texas* 65 N b
Dodge, *Nebraska* 60 H c
Dodge, *North Dakota* 58 D c
Dodge Center, *Minnesota* 59 O f
Dodge City, *Kansas* 60 D g
Dodgeville, *Wisconsin* 56 C g
Dodson, *Louisiana* 63 L f
Dodson, *Montana* 67 M a
Dodson, *Texas* 64 D j
Doerun, *Georgia* 54 H f
Doe Run, *Pennsylvania* 50 B f
Dog I., *Florida* 54 G h
Doland, *South Dakota* 58 H f
Dolgeville, *New York* 53 M b
Dolores, *Colorado* 68 H f
Dolores R., *Colorado* 68 H e
Dome, *Arizona* 70 C g
Dome Rock Mts., *Arizona* 70 C f
Domingo, *New Mexico* 71 L d
Dona Ana, *New Mexico* 71 L g
Donaldson, *Arkansas* 63 L d
Donaldson, *Minnesota* 59 K b
Donaldsonville, *Louisiana* 63 M h
Donalsonville, *Georgia* 54 G f
Doncaster, *Maryland* 53 J g
Donelson, *Tennessee* 54 E a
Dongan Hills, *New York* 51 L g
Donie, *Texas* 65 L d
Doniphan, *Missouri* 61 O h
Donken, *Michigan* 56 E c
Donna, *Texas* 65 J j
Donnellson, *Illinois* 57 D k
Donnelly, *Idaho* 66 D e
Donnelly, *Minnesota* 59 K e
Donner Pass, *California* 74 E e
Donner und Blitzen R., *Oregon* 73 M m
Donnybrook, *North Dakota* 58 E b
Donora, *Pennsylvania* 52 G e
Donovan, *Illinois* 57 F j
Don Pedro Res., *California* 74 E g
Doole, *Texas* 65 H d
Dooley, *Montana* 67 Q a
Doonerak, Mt., *Alaska* 76 M c
Door Pen., *Wisconsin* 56 F e
Dora, *Alabama* 54 D d
Dora, *New Mexico* 71 O f
Dora, *Oregon* 73 G m
Doran, *Minnesota* 59 K d
Dorchester, *Nebraska* 60 G d
Dorchester, *Wisconsin* 56 C d
Dorena, *Oregon* 73 H m
Dormont, *Pennsylvania* 53 O b
Dorothy, *New Jersey* 50 D g
Dorrance, *Kansas* 60 F f
Dorrance, *Pennsylvania* 50 A c
Dorris, *California* 74 D c
Dorris Res., *California* 74 E c
Dorset, *Ohio* 52 F d
Dorset, *Vermont* 49 B e
Dos Cabezas, *Arizona* 70 H g
Dos Palos, *California* 75 E h
Dos Rios, *California* 74 B e
Doss, *Texas* 65 H e
Doswell, *Virginia* 53 J h
Dothan, *Alabama* (31,440) 54 F f
Dothan, *Oregon* 73 G n
Dot Lake, *Alaska* 77 P e
Dotsero, *Colorado* 69 K d
Double Bayou, *Texas* 65 N f
Double Mt., *California* 75 G j
Double Pk., *Alaska* 76 L f
Double Springs, *Alabama* 54 D c
Doubletop Mt., *New York* 50 E a
Douds, *Iowa* 61 M d
Dougherty Plain, *Georgia* 54 G f
Douglas, *Alaska* 77 U g
Douglas, *Arizona* 70 H h
Douglas, C., *Alaska* 76 L g
Douglas, *Georgia* 55 J f
Douglas, *Massachusetts* 51 K a
Douglas, *Michigan* 56 G g
Douglas, Mt., *Alaska* 76 L g
Douglas, *Nebraska* 60 H d
Douglas, *North Dakota* 58 E c
Douglas, *Wyoming* 67 P g
Douglas Cr., *Colorado* 68 H d
Douglas Dam, *Tennessee* 54 H b
Douglas L., *Michigan* 56 J d
Douglas L., *Tennessee* 54 H b
Douglass, *Kansas* 60 H g
Douglassville, *Pennsylvania* 50 B e
Douglasville, *Georgia* 54 G d
Dove Creek, *Colorado* 68 H f
Dover, *Arkansas* 63 K c
Dover, *Delaware* 50 B g
Dover, *Florida* 55 M e
Dover, *Georgia* 55 K e
Dover, *Kentucky* 57 J l
Dover, *Massachusetts* 51 L a
Dover, *New Hampshire* 49 D e
Dover, *New Jersey* 50 D d
Dover, *North Carolina* 55 O b
Dover, *Ohio* 52 E e
Dover, *Oklahoma* 62 F c
Dover, *Tennessee* 54 D a
Dover-Foxcroft, *Maine* 49 F c
Dover Furnace, *New York* 50 F b
Dover Plains, *New York* 50 F b
Dowagiac, *Michigan* 57 G h
Downers Grove, *Illinois* 57 F h
Downey, *California* (82,505) 75 D m
Downey, *Idaho* 66 H g
Downieville, *California* 74 E e
Downing, *Missouri* 61 M d
Downingtown, *Pennsylvania* 50 B e
Downs, *Kansas* 60 F e
Downs Mt., *Wyoming* 67 L f
Downstown, *New Jersey* 50 D f
Downsville, *New York* 50 C a
Downsville Dam, *New York* 50 D a
Dows, *Iowa* 61 L b
Doyle, *California* 74 E d
Doyle, *Tennessee* 54 F b
Doylestown, *Pennsylvania* 50 C e
Doyleville, *Colorado* 69 K e
Dracut, *Massachusetts* 49 D f
Drageton, *Utah* 68 F d
Dragoon, *Arizona* 70 G g
Drain, *Oregon* 73 G m
Drake, *Arizona* 70 E d
Drake, *Colorado* 69 L c
Drake, *North Dakota* 58 F c
Drake Pk., *Oregon* 73 K n
Drakes B., *California* 74 C g
Drakesboro, *Kentucky* 57 F m
Drakes Branch, *Virginia* 52 H j
Draper, *Alaska* 77 S g
Draper, *North Carolina* 55 M a
Draper, *South Dakota* 58 F g
Draper, *Utah* 68 C j
Dravosburg, *Pennsylvania* 53 Q c
Drayton, *North Dakota* 58 J b
Dresden, *Kansas* 60 D e
Dresden, *North Dakota* 58 H b
Dresden, *Ohio* 52 E e
Dresden, *Tennessee* 54 C a
Drew, *Mississippi* 63 N e
Drew, *Oregon* 73 H n
Drewsey, *Oregon* 73 M m
Drews Res., *Oregon* 73 K n
Drexel, *Missouri* 61 K f
Drifton, *Florida* 54 H g
Driftwood, *Pennsylvania* 52 H d
Driggs, *Idaho* 66 J f
Dripping Springs, *Texas* 65 J e
Driscoll, *North Dakota* 58 F d
Driscoll, *Texas* 65 K h
Drummond, L., *Virginia* 53 K j
Drummond, *Michigan* 56 K c
Drummond, *Montana* 66 G c
Drummond, *Wisconsin* 56 B c
Drummond I., *Michigan* 56 K c
Drumright, *Oklahoma* 62 G c
Drums, *Pennsylvania* 50 A c
Dryad, *Washington* 73 G j
Dryburg, *Michigan* 56 J c
Dry Cr., *Wyoming* 67 M e
Dryden, *Michigan* 56 K g
Dryden, *New York* 53 K c
Dryden, *Texas* 64 E e
Dry L., *California* 75 H j
Dry L., *Nevada* 74 H e
Dry Lake, *Nevada* 75 L h
Dry Prong, *Louisiana* 63 L g
Dry Tortugas, *Florida* 55 M j
Duane, *New York* 53 M a
Dubach, *Louisiana* 63 L f
Dubakella Mt., *California* 74 B d
Dublin, *Georgia* 55 J e
Dublin, *Indiana* 57 H k
Dublin, *Michigan* 56 H e
Dublin, *Mississippi* 63 N d
Dublin, *Ohio* 52 C e
Dublin, *Pennsylvania* 50 C e
Dublin, *Texas* 65 J c
Dubli R., *Alaska* 76 K d
Dubois, *Idaho* 66 H e
Du Bois, *Nebraska* 61 H d
Du Bois, *Pennsylvania* 52 H d
Dubois, *Wyoming* 67 L f
Dubuque, *Iowa* (56,606) 61 O b
Duchesne, *Utah* 68 F c
Duchesne R., *Utah* 68 F c
Duck Creek, *Wisconsin* 56 E e
Duck Hill, *Mississippi* 63 O e
Duck R., *Tennessee* 54 D b
Ducktown, *Tennessee* 54 G b
Duckwater, *Nevada* 74 K f
Duckwater Pk., *Nevada* 74 K f
Ducor, *California* 75 F j
Dudley, *Georgia* 54 H e
Dudley, *Massachusetts* 51 K a
Dudley, *Missouri* 61 O h
Due West, *South Carolina* 55 J c
Dufur, *Oregon* 73 J k
Dugas, *Arizona* 70 F e
Dugdemona R., *Louisiana* 63 L f
Dugger, *Indiana* 57 F k
Duke, *Oklahoma* 62 D d
Duke I., *Alaska* 77 W j
Dulac, *Louisiana* 63 N j
Dulce, *New Mexico* 71 K c
Dull Center, *Wyoming* 67 Q f
Duluth, *Minnesota* (106,884) 59 O d
Dumas, *Arkansas* 63 M e
Dumas, *Texas* 64 C h
Dumfries, *Virginia* 52 J g
Dumont, *Minnesota* 59 K e
Dumont, *New Jersey* 51 L d
Dumont, *Iowa* 61 L b
Dunbar, *Alaska* 77 N d
Dunbar, *Nebraska* 61 H d
Dunbar, *Oklahoma* 62 H d
Dunbar, *Pennsylvania* 52 G f
Dunbar, *Utah* 68 D c
Dunbar, *West Virginia* 52 E g
Dunbar, *Wisconsin* 56 E d
Duncan, *Arizona* 70 H g
Duncan, *Nebraska* 60 G c
Duncan, *Oklahoma* 62 F d
Duncan, *Wyoming* 67 L f
Duncannon, *Pennsylvania* 53 J e
Duncan Ridge, *Georgia* 54 G c
Duncanville, *Texas* 65 N k
Dundalk, *Maryland* (82,428) vicinity of Baltimore
Dundas, *Ohio* 52 D f
Dundee, *Illinois* 57 E g
Dundee, *Michigan* 57 K h
Dundee, *New York* 53 K c
Dundee, *Texas* 65 J b
Dunedin, *Florida* 55 M e
Dunellen, *New Jersey* 50 E d
Dunken, *New Mexico* 71 M g
Dunkirk, *Indiana* 57 H j
Dunkirk, *Montana* 66 J a
Dunkirk, *New York* 52 G c
Dunlap, *Iowa* 61 J c
Dunlap, *Kansas* 60 H f
Dunlap, *New Mexico* 71 N e
Dunlap, *Tennessee* 54 F b
Dunlap, *Texas* 64 G a
Dunlay, *Texas* 65 J f
Dunmore, *Pennsylvania* 53 L d
Dunn, *North Carolina* 55 N b
Dunn Center, *North Dakota* 58 D c
Dunnell, *Minnesota* 59 M g
Dunnellon, *Florida* 55 J h
Dunnfield, *New Jersey* 50 C d
Dunnigan, *California* 74 D f
Dunning, *Nebraska* 60 D c
Dunphy, *Nevada* 74 J d
Dunraven, *New York* 50 D a
Dunseith, *North Dakota* 58 F b
Dunsmuir, *California* 74 C c
Dupont, *Colorado* 69 P h
Dupont, *Indiana* 57 H l
Dupont, *Pennsylvania* 53 L d
Dupree, *South Dakota* 58 E e
Dupuyer, *Montana* 66 H a
Duquesne, *Arizona* 70 G h
Duquesne, *Pennsylvania* 53 Q c
Du Quoin, *Illinois* 57 D m
Duran, *New Mexico* 71 M e
Durand, *Illinois* 56 D g
Durand, *Michigan* 56 K g
Durand, *Wisconsin* 56 B e
Durango, *Colorado* 69 J f
Durant, *Mississippi* 63 O e
Durant, *Oklahoma* 62 G e
Durbin, *West Virginia* 52 G g
Durham, *California* 74 D e
Durham, *Connecticut* 51 H c
Durham, *Kansas* 60 G f
Durham, *New Hampshire* 49 D e
Durham, *North Carolina* (78,302) 55 N b
Durkee, *Oregon* 73 N l
Duryea, *Pennsylvania* 50 B c
Dushore, *Pennsylvania* 53 K d
Dustin, *Oklahoma* 62 G c
Dutch Harbor, *Alaska* 76 D k
Dutch Mt., *Utah* 68 C c
Dutton, *Montana* 66 J b
Dutton, Mt., *Utah* 68 D e
Duwamish R., *Washington* 72 C j
Duxbury, *Massachusetts* 51 M a
Dwaarkill, *New York* 50 E b
Dwight, *Illinois* 57 E h
Dwight, *Kansas* 60 H f
Dwight, *Nebraska* 60 G c
Dwight, *Virginia* 52 E h
Dwyer, *New Mexico* 71 K g
Dwyer, *Wyoming* 67 Q g
Dyckesville, *Wisconsin* 56 F e
Dyer, *Tennessee* 54 C a
Dyersburg, *Tennessee* 54 B a
Dyersville, *Iowa* 61 N b
Dykemans, *New York* 50 F c
Dyor, *Nevada* 74 G g
Dysart, *Iowa* 61 M b
Eads, *Colorado* 69 O e
Eagar, *Arizona* 70 H e
Eagle, *Alaska* 77 R d
Eagle, *Colorado* 69 K d
Eagle, *Idaho* 66 D f
Eagle, *Nebraska* 60 H d
Eagle, *Wisconsin* 56 E g
Eagle, *Wyoming* 67 M e
Eagle Bend, *Minnesota* 59 L d
Eagle Butte, *South Dakota* 58 E f
Eagle City, *Oklahoma* 62 E c
Eagle Crags, *California* 75 H j
Eagle Grove, *Iowa* 61 L b
Eagle Harbor, *Michigan* 56 E b
Eagle L., *California* 74 E d
Eagle L., *Maine* 49 F b
Eagle L., *Maine* 49 G a
Eagle L., *Minnesota* 59 P h
Eagle Lake, *Florida* 55 N f
Eagle Lake, *Maine* 49 G a
Eagle Lake, *Texas* 65 L f
Eagle Mountain L., *Texas* 65 K c
Eagle Mountain Lake, *Texas* 65 L h
Eagle Mts., *California* 75 K l
Eagle Nest, *New Mexico* 71 M c
Eagle Pass, *Texas* 64 G g
Eagle Point, *Oregon* 73 H n
Eagle R., *Colorado* 69 K d
Eagle R., *Kentucky* 57 J l
Eagle River, *Michigan* 56 E b
Eagle River, *Wisconsin* 56 D d
Eagle Rock, *Virginia* 52 G h
Eagle Summit, *Alaska* 77 O d
Eagle Tail Mts., *Arizona* 70 D f
Eagleton, *Arkansas* 63 J d
Eagletown, *Oklahoma* 63 J d
Eagleville, *California* 74 E c
Eagleville, *Missouri* 61 L d
Eagleville, *Pennsylvania* 50 C e
Eakly, *Oklahoma* 62 E c
Earl, L., *California* 74 A c
Earle, *Arkansas* 63 N c
Earlham, *Iowa* 61 K c
Earlimart, *California* 75 F j
Earling, *Iowa* 61 J c
Earlington, *Kentucky* 57 F m
Earlville, *Illinois* 57 E h
Earlville, *Iowa* 61 N b
Earlville, *Maryland* 50 A g
Earp, *California* 75 L k
Earth, *Texas* 64 E a
Easley, *South Carolina* 55 J c
East Alton, *Illinois* 57 C l
East Aurora, *New York* 52 H c
East B., *Florida* 54 F g
East B., *Louisiana* 63 O j
East B., *Texas* 65 N f
East Bangor, *Pennsylvania* 50 C d
East Bend, *North Carolina* 55 L a
East Berlin, *Connecticut* 51 H b
East Berlin, *Pennsylvania* 53 K f
East Bernard, *Texas* 65 L f
East Bernstadt, *Kentucky* 57 J m
East Boston, *Massachusetts* 49 G h
East Brady, *Pennsylvania* 52 G e
East Branch Clarion River Res., *Pennsylvania* 52 H d
East Branch Res., *Connecticut* 50 G c
East Brewton, *Alabama* 54 D f
East Bridgewater, *Massachusetts* 51 M a
East Brookfield, *Massachusetts* 51 J a
East Butte, *Montana* 66 J a
East C., *Alaska* 76 C e
East Canaan, *Connecticut* 50 G a
East Cape, *Alaska* 76 M j
East Carver, *Massachusetts* 51 M b
Eastchester B., *New York* 51 M e
East Chicago, *Illinois* 57 F h
East Chicago, *Indiana* (57,669) 57 F h
East Cleveland, *Ohio* (37,991), vicinity of Cleveland
East Dallas, *Texas* 65 O j
East Detroit, *Michigan* (45,756) 57 M j
East Dorset, *Vermont* 49 C e
East Douglas, *Massachusetts* 51 K a
East Dubuque, *Illinois* 56 C g
East Ely, *Nevada* 74 L e
Eastern I., *Hawaii* 72 A a
East Fishkill, *New York* 50 F b
Eastford, *Connecticut* 51 J b
East Fort Madison, *Illinois* 57 B j
East Galesburg, *Illinois* 57 C j
Eastgate, *Nevada* 74 H e
East Glacier Park, *Montana* 66 G a
East Granby, *Connecticut* 51 H b
East Greenville, *Pennsylvania* 50 B e
East Greenwich, *Rhode Island* 51 L b
East Haddam, *Connecticut* 51 J c
Eastham, *Massachusetts* 51 N b
East Hampton, *Connecticut* 51 J b
Easthampton, *Massachusetts* 51 H a
East Hampton, *New York* 51 J d
East Hartford, *Connecticut* (43,977) 51 H b
East Hartland, *Connecticut* 51 H b
East Haven, *Connecticut* 51 H c
East Helena, *Montana* 66 J c
East Houston, *Texas* 64 G h
East Islip, *New York* 50 G d
East Jaffrey, *New Hampshire* 49 C f
East Jewitt, *New York* 50 E a
East Jordan, *Michigan* 56 H d
East Killingly, *Connecticut* 51 K b
East L., *Maine* 49 F a
Eastlake, *Colorado* 69 O h
East Lake, *Michigan* 56 G e
Eastland, *Texas* 65 J c
East Lansing, *Michigan* (30,198) 56 J g
East Liberty, *Ohio* 52 C e
East Liberty, *Pennsylvania* 53 Q b
East Liverpool, *Ohio* 52 F e
East Longmeadow, *Massachusetts* 51 H a
East Los Angeles, *California* (104,270), vicinity of Los Angeles
East Lyme, *Connecticut* 51 J c
East Lynn, *West Virginia* 52 D g
East McKeesport, *Pennsylvania* 53 R b
Eastman, *Georgia* 54 H e
East Mauch Chunk, *Pennsylvania* 50 B d
East Meadow, *New York* (46,036), vicinity of New York
East Mill Creek, *Utah* 68 C h
East Millinocket, *Maine* 49 G c
East Millstone, *New Jersey* 50 D d
Eastmont, *Pennsylvania* 53 R b
East New York, *New York* 51 M f
East Nishnabotna R., *Iowa* 61 J c
East Norton, *Massachusetts* 51 L b
East Norwalk, *Connecticut* 50 G c
Easton, *Connecticut* 50 G c
Easton, *Illinois* 57 D j
Easton, *Maryland* 53 K g
Easton, *Massachusetts* 51 L a
Easton, *Minnesota* 59 N g
Easton, *Missouri* 61 K e
Easton, *Pennsylvania* (31,955) 50 C d
Easton, *Washington* 73 J h
East Orange, *New Jersey* (77,259) 51 J f
Eastover, *South Carolina* 55 L d
East Palatka, *Florida* 55 K h
East Palestine, *Ohio* 52 F e
East Park, *New York* 50 F b
East Park Res., *California* 74 C e
East Paterson, *New Jersey* 51 K d
East Peru, *Iowa* 61 L c
East Pittsburgh, *Pennsylvania* 53 R b
East Point, *Georgia* (35,633) 54 G d
East Point, *Kentucky* 57 L m
Eastport, *Maine* 49 H d
Eastport, *New York* 51 H d
East Portal, *Colorado* 69 L d
East Prairie, *Missouri* 61 P h
East Providence, *Rhode Island* (41,955) 51 L b
East R., *New York* 51 M f
East Ra., *Nevada* 74 H d
East Rainelle, *West Virginia* 52 F h
East St. Louis, *Illinois* (87,712) 61 Q d
East Sister Park, *Idaho* 66 E b
East Stroudsburg, *Pennsylvania* 50 C c
East Taunton, *Massachusetts* 51 L b
East Tawas, *Michigan* 56 K c
East Thermopolis, *Wyoming* 67 M f
East Tohopekaliga L., *Florida* 55 N e
East Troy, *Wisconsin* 56 E g
East Verde R., *Arizona* 70 F e
Eastville, *Virginia* 53 L h
East Walden, *New York* 50 E b
East Walker R., *Nevada* 74 F f
East Wareham, *Massachusetts* 51 M b
East Weymouth, *Massachusetts* 51 M a
East White Bluffs, *Washington* 73 L j
East Windham, *New York* 50 E a
East Windsor Hill, *Connecticut* 51 H b
Eaton, *Colorado* 69 M c
Eaton, *Indiana* 57 H j
Eaton, *Ohio* 52 B f
Eaton Rapids, *Michigan* 56 J g
Eatons Neck Point, *New York* 50 G d
Eatonton, *Georgia* 54 H d
Eatontown, *New Jersey* 50 E e
Eatonville, *Washington* 73 H j
Eau Claire, *Michigan* 57 G g
Eau Claire, *South Carolina* 55 K c
Eau Claire, *Wisconsin* (37,987) 56 B e
Eau Claire R., *Wisconsin* 56 B e
Eau Gallie, *Florida* 55 O e
Eben Junction, *Michigan* 56 F c
Ebensburg, *Pennsylvania* 52 H e
Eccles, *West Virginia* 52 E h
Echeta, *Wyoming* 67 P e
Echo, *Minnesota* 59 L f
Echo, *Oregon* 73 L k
Echo, *Utah* 68 E c
Echo Bay, *Nevada* 75 L h
Echo Cliffs, *Arizona* 70 F c
Eckelson, *North Dakota* 58 H d
Eckerman, *Michigan* 56 H c
Eckert, *Texas* 65 J e
Eckley, *Colorado* 69 O c
Eckley, *Pennsylvania* 50 B d
Eckman, *West Virginia* 52 E h
Eclectic, *Alabama* 54 E e
Economy, *Indiana* 57 J k
Ecorse, *Michigan* 57 K k
Ecru, *Mississippi* 63 O d
Edcouch, *Texas* 65 K j
Eddy, *Montana* 66 E b
Eddy, *Texas* 65 K d
Eddyville, *Kentucky* 57 E m
Eddyville, *Iowa* 61 M c
Eddyville, *Nebraska* 60 E c
Eden, *Montana* 66 J b
Eden, Mt., *California* 75 C m
Eden, *New York* 52 H c
Eden, *South Dakota* 58 J e
Eden, *Texas* 65 H d
Eden, *Utah* 68 E b
Eden, *Wisconsin* 56 E f
Eden, *Wyoming* 67 L g
Edenton, *North Carolina* 55 P a
Edenville, *Michigan* 56 J f
Edenville, *New York* 50 E c
Edgar, *Montana* 67 M d
Edgar, *Nebraska* 60 G d
Edgard, *Louisiana* 63 N h
Edgar Springs, *Missouri* 61 N g
Edgartown, *Massachusetts* 51 M c
Edgecliff, *Texas* 65 L j
Edgefield, *South Carolina* 55 K d
Edgeley, *North Dakota* 58 H d
Edgemont, *Arkansas* 63 L c
Edgemont, *South Dakota* 58 C g
Edgerly, *Louisiana* 63 K h
Edgerton, *Minnesota* 59 K g
Edgerton, *Ohio* 52 B d
Edgerton, *Wisconsin* 56 D g
Edgerton, *Wyoming* 67 O f
Edgewater, *Colorado* 69 O h
Edgewater, *Florida* 55 L j
Edgewood, *Illinois* 57 E l
Edgewood, *Maryland* 53 K f
Edgewood, *New Mexico* 71 L d
Edgewood, *New York* 50 E a
Edgewood, *Pennsylvania* 53 Q b
Edgewood, *Texas* 65 M c
Edina, *Minnesota* (28,501) 59 P j
Edina, *Missouri* 61 M d
Edinboro, *Pennsylvania* 52 F d
Edinburg, *Illinois* 57 D k
Edinburg, *Indiana* 57 H k
Edinburg, *Mississippi* 63 O f
Edinburg, *New Jersey* 50 D e
Edinburg, *North Dakota* 58 J b
Edinburg, *Texas* 65 J j
Edinburg, *Virginia* 52 H g
Edison, *California* 75 G j
Edison, *Colorado* 69 M e
Edison, *Georgia* 54 G f
Edison, *New Jersey* (44,799), vicinity of New Brunswick
Edisto Island, *South Carolina* 55 L e
Edisto R., *South Carolina* 55 L d
Edith, *Montana* 66 J c
Edmeston, *New York* 53 L c
Edmond, *Kansas* 60 E e
Edmond, *Oklahoma* 62 F c
Edmonds, *Washington* 72 B g
Edmonton, *Kentucky* 57 H n
Edmore, *Michigan* 56 H f
Edmore, *North Dakota* 58 H b
Edna, *Texas* 65 L g
Edna Bay, *Alaska* 77 V j
Edroy, *Texas* 65 K h
Edson, *Kansas* 60 C e
Edwards, *California* 75 G k
Edwards, *Mississippi* 63 N f
Edwards, *New York* 53 L a
Edwards Plateau, *Texas* 64 G e
Edwardsburg, *Michigan* 57 G g
Edwards R., *Illinois* 57 C h
Edwardsville, *Illinois* 57 C l
Edwardville, *Pennsylvania* 50 A c
Eek, *Alaska* 76 G f
Eek R., *Alaska* 76 G f
Eel R., *California* 74 B d
Eel R., *Indiana* 57 H j
Effie, *Minnesota* 59 N c
Effingham, *Illinois* 57 E k
Effingham, *Kansas* 61 J e
Egan Ra., *Nevada* 74 L e
Egbert, *Wyoming* 67 Q h
Egegik, *Alaska* 76 J g
Egegik B., *Alaska* 76 J g
Egeland, *North Dakota* 58 G b
Eggertsville, *New York* (44,807), vicinity of Buffalo
Egg Harbor, *Wisconsin* 56 F d
Egg Harbor City, *New Jersey* 50 D f
Egg I., *Alaska* 76 G e
Egg Island Pt., *New Jersey* 50 C g
Egmont Key, *Florida* 55 M f
Egypt, *Georgia* 55 K e
Egypt, *Mississippi* 63 P e
Egypt, *Pennsylvania* 50 B d
Egypt, *Texas* 65 L f
Ehren, *Florida* 55 M e
Ehrenberg, *Arizona* 70 C f
Ehrhardt, *South Carolina* 55 K d
Ekalaka, *Montana* 67 Q d
Eklutna, *Alaska* 76 N f
Ekwok, *Alaska* 76 J g
Elaine, *Arkansas* 63 N d
Elam, *Pennsylvania* 50 B f
Eland, *Wisconsin* 56 D e
Elba, *Alabama* 54 E f
Elba, *Idaho* 66 G g
Elba, *Nebraska* 60 F c
Elba, *New York* 52 H b
Elberfield, *Indiana* 57 F l
Elberon, *Iowa* 61 M b
Elbert, Mt., *Colorado* 69 K d
Elbert, *Texas* 65 H b
Elberta, *Michigan* 56 G e
Elberton, *Georgia* 55 J c
Elbow Lake, *Minnesota* 59 K e
Elburz, *Nevada* 74 K d

El Ca UNITED STATES INDEX Farm

El Cajon, California (37,618) 75 J m
El Campo, Texas 65 L f
El Capitan Res., California 75 J m
El Centro, California 75 K m
El Cerrito, California (25,437) 75 B l
Elcho, Wisconsin 56 D d
Elderon, Wisconsin 56 D e
Eldon, Iowa 61 M d
Eldon, Missouri 61 M f
Eldon, Washington 73 G h
Eldora, Iowa 61 L b
Eldora, New Jersey 50 D g
El Dorado, Arkansas (25,292) 63 L e
Eldorado, Illinois 57 E m
El Dorado, Kansas 60 H g
Eldorado, Mt., Washington 73 J g
Eldorado, Oklahoma 62 D d
Eldorado, Texas 64 G e
Eldorado Mts., Nevada 75 L j
Eldorado Springs, Colorado 69 N g
El Dorado Springs, Missouri 61 K g
Eldred, Minnesota 59 K c
Eldred, New York 50 D b
Eldred, Pennsylvania 52 H d
Eldridge, Iowa 61 O c
Eleanor, Washington 73 N h
Eleanor, L., California 74 F f
Electra, Texas 65 J a
Electric Mills, Mississippi 63 P f
Electric Pk., Wyoming 67 K e
Eleele, Hawaii 72 B d
Elephant Butte, New Mexico 71 K f
Elephant Butte Res., New Mexico 71 K f
Elephant Point, Alaska 76 G c
Eleva, Wisconsin 56 B e
Eleven Mile Canyon Res., Colorado 69 L e
Eleven Point R., Missouri 61 N h
Elfin Cove, Alaska 77 T g
Elgin, Arizona 70 G h
Elgin, Illinois (49,447) 57 E g
Elgin, Iowa 61 N b
Elgin, Nebraska 60 F c
Elgin, Nevada 75 L g
Elgin, North Dakota 58 E d
Elgin, Oklahoma 62 E d
Elgin, Oregon 73 N k
Elgin, Texas 65 K e
Elgin, Utah 68 F d
El Granada, California 75 B n
Eli, Nebraska 60 C b
Eliasville, Texas 65 J c
Elida, New Mexico 71 O f
Elim, Alaska 76 F d
Eliot, Maine 49 E e
Elizabeth, Colorado 69 M d
Elizabeth, Illinois 57 C g
Elizabeth, Louisiana 63 L h
Elizabeth, New Jersey (107,698) 50 E d
Elizabeth, Pennsylvania 52 G e
Elizabeth, West Virginia 52 E f
Elizabeth City, North Carolina 55 P a
Elizabeth Is., Massachusetts 51 M c
Elizabeth Mt., Utah 68 F b
Elizabethton, Tennessee 55 J a
Elizabethtown, Indiana 57 H k
Elizabethtown, Kentucky 57 H m
Elizabethtown, New York 53 N a
Elizabethtown, North Carolina 55 N c
Elizabethtown, Pennsylvania 53 K e
Elizabethville, Pennsylvania 53 K e
Elizaville, New York 50 F a
Elk, California 74 B e
Elk, Wyoming 67 K f
Elkader, Iowa 61 N b
Elk Basin, Wyoming 67 M e
Elk City, Idaho 66 E d
Elk City, Kansas 61 J g
Elk City, Oklahoma 62 D c
Elk City Res., Kansas 61 J g
Elk Creek, California 74 C e
Elk Grove, California 74 D f
Elkhart, Indiana (40,274) 57 H h
Elkhart, Kansas 60 C g
Elkhart, Texas 65 M d
Elkhart Lake, Wisconsin 56 F f
Elkhead Mts., Colorado 69 J c
Elk Horn, Iowa 61 J c
Elkhorn, Nebraska 60 H c
Elkhorn, Wisconsin 56 E g
Elkhorn Pk., Montana 66 J c
Elkhorn R., Nebraska 60 F b
Elkin, North Carolina 55 L a
Elkins, New Mexico 71 N f
Elkins, West Virginia 52 G g
Elk L., Michigan 56 H e
Elkland, Pennsylvania (In Tioga County, Pennsylvania) 52 J c
Elkmont, Alabama 54 E c
Elk Mountain, Wyoming 67 O h
Elk Mt., Colorado 69 K c
Elk Mt., Wyoming 67 O h
Elk Mts., Colorado 69 J d
Elk Neck, Maryland 50 A f
Elko, Nevada 74 K d
Elkol, Wyoming 67 K h
Elk Park, Montana 66 H c
Elk Park, North Carolina 55 K a
Elk Point, Montana 67 K c
Elk Point, South Dakota 59 K h
Elk R., Colorado 69 K c
Elk R., Maryland 50 A g
Elk R., Missouri 61 K h
Elk R., Tennessee 54 E b
Elk R., West Virginia 52 E g
Elk Rapids, Michigan 56 H e
Elk River, Idaho 66 D c
Elk River, Minnesota 59 N e
Elk Springs, Colorado 68 H c
Elkton, Florida 55 K h
Elkton, Kentucky 57 F n
Elkton, Maryland 50 B f
Elkton, Minnesota 59 O g
Elkton, Oregon 73 G m
Elkton, South Dakota 59 K f
Elkton, Tennessee 54 E b
Elkton, Virginia 52 H g
Elk Valley, Tennessee 54 G a
Elkville, Illinois 57 D m
Ellamar, Alaska 77 O f
Ellamore, West Virginia 52 F g
Ellaville, Florida 54 H g
Ellaville, Georgia 54 G e
Ellen, Mt., Utah 68 E d
Ellen, Mt., Vermont 49 C d
Ellenburg, New York 53 N a
Ellendale, Delaware 53 L g
Ellendale, Louisiana 63 N j
Ellendale, North Dakota 58 H e
Ellensburg, Washington 73 K h
Ellenton, Florida 55 M f
Ellenville, New York 50 E b
Eller, North Carolina 55 L b
Ellerbe, North Carolina 55 M b
Ellerbee, Florida 55 J g
Ellettsville, Indiana 57 G k
Ellicott City, Maryland 53 K f
Ellicottville, New York 52 H c
Ellijay, Georgia 54 G c
Ellington, Connecticut 51 J b
Ellington, Missouri 61 O g
Ellinwood, Kansas 60 F f
Elliot, Maryland 53 K g
Elliot, South Carolina 55 L c
Elliott, Iowa 61 J c
Elliott, North Dakota 58 J d
Elliott B., Washington 72 B h
Elliott Key, Florida 55 O h
Ellis, Kansas 60 E f
Ellisburg, New York 53 K b
Ellis I., New York 51 L f
Elliston, Montana 66 H c
Elliston, Virginia 52 F h
Ellisville, Mississippi 63 O g
Elloree, South Carolina 55 L d
Ellsinore, Missouri 61 O h
Ellsworth, Kansas 60 F f
Ellsworth, Maine 49 G d
Ellsworth, Minnesota 59 L g
Ellsworth, Nebraska 60 B b
Ellwood City, Pennsylvania 52 F e
Elma, Iowa 61 M a
Elma, Washington 73 G h
Elmaton, Texas 65 L g
Elm City, North Carolina 55 O b
Elm Creek, Nebraska 60 E d
Elmendorf, New Mexico 71 L f
Elmendorf, Texas 65 J f
Elmer, Missouri 61 M e
Elmer, New Jersey 50 C f
Elmer, Oklahoma 62 D d
Elmhurst, Illinois (36,991) 57 F h
Elmhurst, Kansas 61 P b
Elmhurst, Pennsylvania 50 B c
Elmira, California 74 D f
Elmira, Michigan 56 H d
Elmira, New York (46,517) 53 K c
Elm L., South Dakota 58 H e
Elmo, Kansas 60 G f
Elmo, Missouri 61 J d
Elmo, Wyoming 67 O h
Elmont, New York (30,138), vicinity of New York
Elmore, Alabama 54 E e
Elmore, Minnesota 59 M g
Elmore, Ohio 52 C d
Elmore City, Oklahoma 62 F d
El Morro Nat. Mon., New Mexico 71 J e
Elm Mott, Texas 65 K d
Elm Springs, South Dakota 58 D f
Elmwood, Illinois 57 D j
Elmwood, Oklahoma 62 C b
Elmwood, Pennsylvania 50 F h
Elmwood, Wisconsin 56 A e
Elnora, Indiana 57 F l
Eloi B., Louisiana 63 O j
Elora, Tennessee 54 E b
Eloy, Arizona 70 F g
El Paso, Illinois 57 D j
El Paso, Texas (276,687) 64 A d
El Portal, California 74 F g
El Reno, Oklahoma 62 F c
Elridge Glacier, Alaska 76 M e
El Rito, New Mexico 71 L c
Elrod, South Dakota 58 J f
Elrosa, Minnesota 59 M e
Elroy, Wisconsin 56 C f
Elsa, Texas 65 J j
El Sanz, Texas 65 J j
Elsberry, Missouri 61 O e
El Segundo, California 75 D m
Elsie, Nebraska 60 C d
Elsie, Oregon 73 G k
Elsinore, California 75 H l
Elsinore, Utah 68 D e
Elsinore L., California 75 H l
Elsmere, Delaware 53 B f
Elsmere, Nebraska 60 D b
Elsmore, Kansas 61 J g
Elson Lagoon, Alaska 76 J a
Elsworth, Wisconsin 56 A e
Elton, Louisiana 63 L h
Eltopia, Washington 73 M j
El Toro, California 75 H l
El Vado, New Mexico 71 L c
El Vado Res., New Mexico 71 L c
Elverson, Pennsylvania 50 B e
Elwood, Illinois 57 E h
Elwood, Indiana 57 H j
Elwood, Missouri 61 K e
Elwood, Nebraska 60 E d
Elwood, New Jersey 50 D f
Ely, Minnesota 59 P c
Ely, Nevada 74 L e
Elyria, Ohio (43,782) 52 D d
Elysian, Minnesota 59 N f
Embarrass, Minnesota 59 O c
Embarrass R., Illinois 57 E k
Embden, North Dakota 58 J d
Emberly, Nevada 74 K e
Emblem, Wyoming 67 M e
Embreeville, Pennsylvania 50 B f
Emden, Illinois 57 D j
Emerado, North Dakota 58 J c
Emerson, Arkansas 63 K e
Emerson, Iowa 61 J c
Emerson, Michigan 56 H c
Emerson, Nebraska 60 H b
Emery, South Dakota 58 J g
Emeryville, California 75 G l
Emida, Idaho 66 D b
Emigrant, Montana 67 K d
Emigrant Gap, California 74 E e
Emigrant Pass, Nevada 74 J d
Emigrant Pk., Montana 67 K d
Emigrant Val., Nevada 75 K g
Eminence, Kentucky 57 H l
Eminence, Missouri 61 N g
Emlenton, Pennsylvania 52 G d
Emmaus, Pennsylvania 50 B d
Emmaus Junction, Pennsylvania 50 B d
Emmet, Nebraska 60 F b
Emmetsburg, Iowa 61 K a
Emmett, Idaho 66 D f
Emmett, Kansas 61 H e
Emmitsburg, Maryland 53 J f
Emmons, Mt., Utah 68 F c
Emory, Texas 65 M c
Emory Pk., Texas 64 D f
Empire, Georgia 54 H e
Empire, Michigan 56 G e
Empire, Nevada 74 F e
Empire, Oregon 73 F m
Empire Res., Colorado 69 M c
Emporia, Kansas 60 H f
Emporia, Virginia 52 J j
Emporium, Pennsylvania 52 H d
Emrick, North Dakota 58 G c
Encampment, Wyoming 67 O h
Encinal, Texas 65 H g
Encinitas, California 75 H l
Encino, California 75 D l
Encino, New Mexico 71 M e
Encinoso, New Mexico 71 M f
Endeavor, Wisconsin 56 D f
Endee, New Mexico 71 O d
Enderlin, North Dakota 58 J d
Enders Res., Nebraska 60 C d
Endicott, New York 53 K c
Endicott, Washington 73 N j
Endicott Arm, Alaska 77 V h
Endicott Mts., Alaska 76 L c
Enfield, Connecticut (31,464) 51 H b
Enfield, Illinois 57 E l
Enfield, New Hampshire 49 C e
Enfield, North Carolina 55 O a
Engelhard, North Carolina 55 Q b
England, Arkansas 63 M d
Engle, New Mexico 71 L f
Englewood, Colorado (33,398) 69 O j
Englewood, Florida 55 M g
Englewood, Kansas 60 E g
Englewood, New Jersey (26,057) 50 E d
Englewood, Tennessee 54 G b
English, Indiana 57 G l
English Bay, Alaska 76 M g
Englishtown, New Jersey 50 E e
Enid, Montana 67 Q b
Enid, Oklahoma (38,859) 62 F b
Enid L., Mississippi 63 O d
Enning, South Dakota 58 D f
Ennis, Montana 66 J d
Ennis, Texas 65 L c
Ennis L., Montana 66 J d
Eno, Colorado 69 P h
Enochs, Texas 64 E b
Enola, Nebraska 60 G c
Enoree, South Carolina 55 K c
Enoree R., South Carolina 55 K c
Enosburg Falls, Vermont 49 C d
Ensenada, New Mexico 71 L c
Ensign, Kansas 60 D g
Ensign, Michigan 56 G d
Enterprise, Alabama 54 F f
Enterprise, Kansas 60 G f
Enterprise, Mississippi 63 P f
Enterprise, Oregon 73 N k
Enterprise, Utah 68 C f
Entiat, Washington 73 K h
Entiat Mts., Washington 73 K h
Entiat R., Washington 73 K h
Entro, Arizona 70 E e
Enumclaw, Washington 73 J h
Eola, Louisiana 63 L h
Eola, Texas 64 G d
Eolia, Missouri 61 N e
Epes, Alabama 54 C e
Ephraim, Utah 68 E d
Ephraim, Wisconsin 56 F d
Ephrata, Pennsylvania 50 A e
Ephrata, Washington 73 L h
Epiphany, South Dakota 58 J g
Epping, New Hampshire 49 D e
Epping, North Dakota 58 C b
Epsie, Montana 67 P d
Epworth, Iowa 61 O b
Equality, Illinois 57 E m
Equinunk, Pennsylvania 53 L d
Erath, Louisiana 63 L j
Erick, Oklahoma 62 D c
Ericsburg, Minnesota 59 N b
Ericson, Nebraska 60 F c
Erie, Colorado 69 L c
Erie, Illinois 57 C h
Erie, Kansas 61 J g
Erie, L., United States-Canada 47 K b
Erie, Michigan 57 K h
Erie, Nevada 75 K j
Erie, North Dakota 58 J c
Erie, Pennsylvania (138,440) 52 F c
Erin, Tennessee 54 D a
Erlanger, Kentucky 57 J l
Erling, L., Arkansas 63 K e
Erma, New Jersey 50 D h
Ernest Sd., Alaska 77 V j
Eros, Louisiana 63 L f
Errol, New Hampshire 49 D d
Errol I., Louisiana 63 O j
Erskine, Minnesota 59 L c
Erwin, North Carolina 55 N b
Erwin, Tennessee 55 J a
Esbon, Kansas 60 F e
Escalante, Utah 68 E f
Escalante Des., Utah 68 C f
Escalante R., Utah 68 E f
Escambia R., Florida 54 D g
Escanaba, Michigan 56 G d
Escanaba R., Michigan 56 F c
Eschscholtz B., Alaska 76 G c
Escondido, California 75 H l
Eska, Alaska 77 N f
Eskridge, Kansas 61 H f
Esmond, North Dakota 58 G b
Esmond, South Dakota 58 J f
Esopus, New York 50 F b
Espanola, Florida 55 K h
Espanola, New Mexico 71 L d
Esparto, California 74 C f
Espenberg, C., Alaska 76 E c
Esperanza, Texas 64 B d
Esquatzel Coulee R., Washington 73 L j
Essex, California 75 K k
Essex, Connecticut 51 J c
Essex, Iowa 61 J d
Essex, Maryland (35,205), vicinity of Baltimore
Essex, Montana 66 G a
Essex, New York 53 N a
Essex Junction, Vermont 49 B d
Essexville, Michigan 56 K f
Estacada, Oregon 73 H k
Estancia, New Mexico 71 L e
Este, Alaska 77 N d
Estelline, South Dakota 59 K f
Estelline, Texas 64 D j
Estellville, New Jersey 50 D g
Esterbrook, Wyoming 67 P g
Estero, Florida 55 N g
Estero B., Florida 55 N g
Estero B., California 75 D j
Estes Park, Colorado 69 L c
Estherville, Iowa 61 K a
Estill, South Carolina 55 K c
Estrella, Arizona 70 E g
Estrella R., California 75 E j
Ethan, South Dakota 58 H g
Ethel, Louisiana 63 M h
Ethel, Mississippi 63 O e
Ethel, Missouri 61 M e
Ethel, West Virginia 52 E h
Ethelsville, Alabama 54 C d
Ethete, Wyoming 67 M f
Ethridge, Montana 66 H a
Etivluk R., Alaska 76 J b
Etna, California 74 C c
Etna, Maine 49 F d
Etna, Pennsylvania 53 P a
Etna, Utah 68 C b
Etoile, Texas 65 N d
Etolin, C., Alaska 76 D f
Etolin I., Alaska 77 V h
Etolin Str., Alaska 76 E f
Etowah, Tennessee 54 G b
Etowah R., Georgia 54 F c
Etter, Texas 64 C g
Ettersburg, California 74 A d
Ettrick, Wisconsin 56 B e
Eubank, Kentucky 57 J m
Euclid, Minnesota 59 K c
Euclid, Ohio (62,998) 52 E d
Eudora, Arkansas 63 M e
Eufala, Alabama 54 F f
Eufaula, Oklahoma 62 H c
Eufaula Res., Oklahoma 62 H c
Eugene, Oregon (50,977) 73 G l
Euless, Texas 65 M j
Eulonia, Georgia 55 K f
Eunice, Louisiana 63 L h
Eunice, New Mexico 71 O g
Eupora, Mississippi 63 O e
Eureka, Alaska 76 M d
Eureka, California (28,137) 74 A d
Eureka, Illinois 57 D j
Eureka, Kansas 60 H g
Eureka, Montana 66 E a
Eureka, Nevada 74 K e
Eureka, New York 50 E b
Eureka, South Dakota 58 G e
Eureka, Utah 68 D d
Eureka, Washington 73 M j
Eureka Lodge, Alaska 77 O f
Eureka Springs, Arkansas 63 K b
Eureka Val., California 75 H g
Eustace, Texas 65 L c
Eustis, Florida 55 K j
Eustis, Nebraska 60 D d
Eutaw, Alabama 54 D e
Eutawville, South Carolina 55 L d
Eva, Louisiana 63 M g
Eva, Oklahoma 62 B b
Evan, Minnesota 59 M f
Evans, Mt., Colorado 69 L d
Evans, Mt., Montana 66 G c
Evans, Washington 73 N g
Evans City, Pennsylvania 52 F e
Evanston, Illinois (79,283) 57 F g
Evanston, Wyoming 67 K h
Evansville, Illinois 57 D l
Evansville, Indiana (141,543) 57 F m
Evansville, Minnesota 59 L d
Evansville, Wisconsin 56 D g
Evansville, Wyoming 67 O g
Evant, Texas 65 J d
Evart, Michigan 56 H f
Evarts, Kentucky 57 K n
Eveleth, Minnesota 59 O c
Evening Shade, Arkansas 63 M b
Everest, Kansas 61 J e
Everett, Massachusetts (43,544) 49 G h
Everett, Mt., Massachusetts 49 B f
Everett, Pennsylvania 52 H e
Everett, Washington (40,304) 73 H h
Everett City, Georgia 55 K f
Everett Mt., Massachusetts 50 G a
Everglades, Florida 55 N h
Everglades, The, Florida 55 O h
Everglades Nat. Park, Florida 55 O h
Evergreen, Alabama 54 E f
Evergreen, Colorado 69 L d
Evergreen, North Carolina 55 N c
Evergreen Park, Illinois 57 B m
Everman, Texas 65 L k
Ewa, Hawaii 72 C d
Ewan, Washington 73 N h
Ewan L., Alaska 77 O e
Ewing, Kentucky 57 K l
Ewing, Missouri 61 N d
Ewing, Nebraska 60 F b
Ewing, New Jersey (26,628), vicinity of Trenton
Excelsior Mt., California 74 F f
Excelsior Mts., Nevada 74 G f
Excelsior Springs, Missouri 61 K e
Exeland, Wisconsin 56 B d
Exeter, California 75 F h
Exeter, Missouri 61 L h
Exeter, Nebraska 60 G d
Exeter, New Hampshire 49 E f
Exeter, Rhode Island 51 K b
Exira, Iowa 61 K c
Exline, Iowa 61 M d
Exmore, Virginia 53 L h
Eyak, Alaska 77 P f
Eyota, Minnesota 59 O g
Fabens, Texas 64 A d
Fairacres, New Mexico 71 L g
Fairbank, Arizona 70 G h
Fairbank, Iowa 61 M b
Fairbanks, Alaska 77 O d
Fairbanks, Maine 49 E d
Fairbanks, Texas 65 M f
Fair Bluff, North Carolina 55 M c
Fairborn, Ohio 52 B f
Fairburn, Georgia 54 G d
Fairburn, South Dakota 58 C g
Fairbury, Illinois 57 E j
Fairbury, Nebraska 60 G d
Fairchance, Pennsylvania 52 G f
Fairchild, Wisconsin 56 C e
Fairdale, North Dakota 58 H b
Fairfax, Alabama 54 F e
Fairfax, Minnesota 59 M f
Fairfax, Missouri 61 J d
Fairfax, Oklahoma 62 G b
Fairfax, South Carolina 55 K e
Fairfax, South Dakota 58 H g
Fairfax, Vermont 49 B d
Fairfax, Virginia 52 J g
Fairfax, Washington 73 H h
Fairfield, Alabama 54 E d
Fairfield, California 74 C f
Fairfield, Connecticut (46,183) 50 G c
Fairfield, Idaho 66 F f
Fairfield, Illinois 57 E l
Fairfield, Iowa 61 N c
Fairfield, Maine 49 F d
Fairfield, Montana 66 H b
Fairfield, Nebraska 60 F d
Fairfield, North Carolina 55 P b
Fairfield, North Dakota 58 C c
Fairfield, Pennsylvania 52 J f
Fairfield, Texas 65 L d
Fairfield, Vermont 49 C d
Fairfield, Washington 73 N h
Fair Grove, Missouri 61 L g
Fairhaven, Massachusetts 51 M b
Fair Haven, Michigan 56 L g
Fair Haven, New York 53 K b
Fair Haven, Vermont 49 B e
Fairholm, Washington 73 G g
Fairhope, Alabama 54 D g
Fairland, Oklahoma 63 J b
Fair Lawn, New Jersey (36,421) 51 K d
Fairlawn, Massachusetts 51 K a
Fairmont, Minnesota 59 M g
Fairmont, Nebraska 60 G d
Fairmont, North Carolina 55 M c
Fairmont, Oklahoma 62 F b
Fairmont, West Virginia (27,477) 52 G f
Fair Mount, Georgia 54 G c
Fairmount, Indiana 57 H j
Fairmount, Maryland 53 L g
Fairmount, North Dakota 59 K d
Fairoaks, Arkansas 63 M c
Fair Oaks, California 74 D f
Fair Oaks, Indiana 57 F h
Fairplay, Colorado 69 L d
Fair Play, Missouri 61 L g
Fairport, Kansas 60 E e
Fairport, Michigan 56 G d
Fairport, New York 53 J b
Fairport, Virginia 53 K h
Fairport Harbor, Ohio 52 E d
Fairton, New Jersey 50 C g
Fairview, Illinois 57 C j
Fairview, Kansas 61 J e
Fairview, Michigan 56 K e
Fairview, Montana 67 Q b
Fairview, New Jersey 51 L e
Fairview, Oklahoma 62 E b
Fairview, Pennsylvania 52 F c
Fairview, South Dakota 59 K g
Fairview, Utah 68 E d
Fairview, West Virginia 52 F f
Fairway, Kansas 61 P b
Fairweather, Alaska 77 T g
Fairweather, Mt., Alaska 77 T g
Fairylawn, Idaho 66 D g
Faison, North Carolina 55 N b
Faith, South Dakota 58 D e
Falcon, Colorado 69 M e
Falcon Dam, Texas 65 H j
Falconer, New York 52 G c
Falcon Heights, Minnesota 59 Q h
Falcon Res., Texas 65 H j
Falfurrias, Texas 65 J h
Falk, California 74 A d
Falkner, Mississippi 63 P d
Falkner I., Connecticut 51 H c
Falkville, Alabama 54 E c
Fallbrook, California 75 H l
Fall City, Washington 73 J h
Fall Creek, Wisconsin 56 B e
Fall Line Hills, Alabama 54 D d
Fall Line Hills, Georgia 54 H e
Fallon, Montana 67 P c
Fallon, Nevada 74 G e
Fall R., Kansas 61 H g
Fall River, Massachusetts (99,942) 51 L b
Fall River Mills, California 74 D d
Fall River Res., Kansas 60 H g
Falls, Pennsylvania (29,082), vicinity of Scranton
Falls Church, Virginia 52 J g
Falls City, Nebraska 61 J d
Falls City, Oregon 73 G l
Falls City, Texas 65 J g
Falls Creek, Pennsylvania 52 H d
Falls Village, Connecticut 50 G b
Falmouth, Kentucky 57 J l
Falmouth, Massachusetts 51 M b
Falmouth, Michigan 56 H e
Falmouth, Virginia 52 J g
Falmouth Foreside, Maine 49 E e
Falmouth Res., Kentucky 57 K l
False Pass, Alaska 76 F j
False Presque Isle, Michigan 56 K d
Famoso, California 75 F j
Fancy Farm, Kentucky 57 E n
Fannett, Texas 65 N f
Fannin, Mississippi 63 O f
Fannin, Texas 65 K g
Fannsdale, Alabama 54 D e
Fansbaw, Alaska 77 V h
Far, Pte. au, Louisiana 63 M j
Faraker, Mt., Alaska 76 L e
Farallon Is., California 74 B g
Farber, Missouri 61 N e
Farewell, Alaska 76 L e
Fargo, Georgia 55 J g
Fargo, North Dakota (46,662) 59 K d
Fargo, Oklahoma 62 D b
Far Hills, New Jersey 50 D d
Faribault, Minnesota 59 N f
Farista, Colorado 69 L f
Farley, Iowa 61 N b
Farley, New Mexico 71 N c
Farmer, South Dakota 58 J g
Farmer City, Illinois 57 E j
Farmers Branch, Texas 65 N h
Farmersburg, Indiana 57 F k
Farmersburg, Iowa 61 N b
Farmersville, Texas 65 L b
Farmerville, Louisiana 63 L f
Farmingdale, New Jersey 50 E e
Farmingdale, New York 50 G d
Farmingdale, South Dakota 58 D g
Farmington, California 74 E g
Farmington, Connecticut 51 H b
Farmington, Illinois 57 D j
Farmington, Iowa 61 N d
Farmington, Maine 49 E d
Farmington, Minnesota 59 N f
Farmington, Missouri 61 O g
Farmington, New Hampshire 49 D e
Farmington, New Mexico 71 J c

Grafton, Mt., Nevada 74 L f
Grafton, New York 53 N c
Grafton, North Dakota 58 J b
Grafton, Ohio 52 D d
Grafton, West Virginia 52 G f
Grafton, Wisconsin 56 F f
Graham, New York 50 D c
Graham, Texas 65 J b
Graham L., Maine 49 G d
Graham Mt., Arizona 70 H g
Grahamsville, New York 50 D b
Grainfield, Kansas 60 D e
Grainton, Nebraska 60 C d
Granada, Colorado 69 O e
Granbury, Texas 65 K c
Granby, Colorado 69 L c
Granby, Connecticut 51 H b
Granby, L., Colorado 69 L c
Granby, Massachusetts 51 H a
Granby, Missouri 61 K h
Grand B., Louisiana 63 O j
Grand Blanc, Michigan 56 K g
Grand Cane, Louisiana 63 K f
Grand Canyon, town, Arizona 70 E c
Grand Canyon Nat. Mon., Arizona 70 E c
Grand Canyon Nat. Park, Arizona 70 E c
Grand Cheniere, Louisiana 63 L j
Grand Coulee, Washington 73 L h
Grand Coulee Dam, Washington 73 L h
Grande Ronde R., Oregon 73 N k
Grand Falls, Arizona 70 F d
Grandfalls, Texas 64 E d
Grandfather Mt., North Carolina 55 K a
Grandfield, Oklahoma 62 E d
Grand Forks, North Dakota (34,451) 58 J c
Grand Gorge, New York 53 M c
Grand Haven, Michigan 56 G f
Grand I., Louisiana 63 O h
Grand I., Michigan 56 G c
Grandin, Florida 55 K h
Grandin, Missouri 61 O h
Grandin, North Dakota 59 K c
Grand Island, Nebraska (25,742) 60 F d
Grand Isle, Louisiana 63 O j
Grand Isle, Vermont 49 B d
Grand Junction, Colorado 68 H d
Grand Junction, Iowa 61 K b
Grand Junction, Michigan 56 H g
Grand Junction, Tennessee 54 B b
Grand L., Louisiana 63 M j
Grand L., Louisiana 63 L j
Grand L., Maine 49 H c
Grand L., Michigan 56 K d
Grand L., Ohio 52 B e
Grand Lake, Colorado 69 L c
Grand Lake, Louisiana 63 K h
Grand Ledge, Michigan 56 J g
Grand Ls., Maine 49 G b
Grand Manan Chan., Maine 49 H d
Grand Marais, Michigan 56 H c
Grand Marais, Minnesota 59 Q c
Grand Mesa, Colorado 69 J d
Grandon, Wisconsin 56 E d
Grand Pass, Missouri 61 L e
Grand Portage, Minnesota 59 R c
Grand Prairie, Texas (30,386) 65 M j
Grand R., Louisiana 63 M j
Grand R., Michigan 56 H f
Grand R., Missouri 61 K d
Grand R., Ohio 52 E d
Grand R., South Dakota 58 E e
Grand Rapids, Michigan (177,313) 56 H g
Grand Rapids, Minnesota 59 N c
Grand River, Iowa 61 L d
Grand Ronde, Oregon 73 G k
Grand Saline, Texas 65 M c
Grand Seboois L., Maine 49 G b
Grand Terre Is., Louisiana 63 O j
Grand Teton, mt., Wyoming 67 K f
Grand Teton Nat. Park, Wyoming 67 K f
Grand Tower, Illinois 61 P g
Grand Traverse B., Michigan 56 H d
Grand Valley, Colorado 68 H d
Grand View, Idaho 66 D g
Grandview, Texas 65 K c
Grandview, Washington 73 L j
Grandville, Michigan 56 H g
Grand Wash, Arizona 70 D c
Grand Wash Cliffs, Arizona 70 D d
Granger, Missouri 61 N d
Granger, Texas 65 K e
Granger, Utah 68 C h
Granger, Washington 73 K j
Granger, Wyoming 67 L h
Grangeville, Idaho 66 D d
Granite, Oklahoma 62 D d
Granite, Oregon 73 M l
Granite, Wyoming 67 P h
Granite City, Illinois (40,073) 61 Q c
Granite Falls, Minnesota 59 L f
Granite Falls, North Carolina 55 K b
Granite Falls, Washington 73 J g
Granite I., Alaska 76 N g
Granite I., Michigan 56 F c
Granite Mt., Nevada 74 H d
Granite Mts., California 75 K k
Granite Pass, California 75 J j
Granite Pk., Montana 67 L d
Granite Pk., Nevada 74 H c
Granite Pk., Utah 68 C c
Granite Pk., Wyoming 67 M g
Granite Pt., Michigan 56 F c
Granite Ra., Nevada 74 F d
Granite Range, Alaska 77 Q f
Granite Shoals L., Texas 65 J e
Graniteville, New York 51 K g
Graniteville, South Carolina 55 K d
Grannis, Arkansas 63 J d
Grano, North Dakota 58 E b
Gran Quivira Nat. Mon., New Mexico 71 L e
Grant, Florida 55 O f
Grant, Iowa 61 J c
Grant, Michigan 56 H f
Grant, Montana 66 G d
Grant, Mt., Nevada 74 G f
Grant, Mt., Nevada 74 H e
Grant, Nebraska 60 C d
Grant, Oklahoma 62 H e
Grant City, Missouri 61 K d
Grant Creek, Alaska 76 L d
Grantley Harb., Alaska 76 D d
Granton, Wisconsin 56 C e
Grant Ra., Nevada 74 K f
Grants, Alaska 76 M f
Grants, New Mexico 71 K d
Grantsburg, Wisconsin 56 A d
Grantsdale, Montana 66 F c
Grants Pass, Oregon 73 G n
Grantsville, Utah 68 D c
Grantsville, West Virginia 52 E g
Grantville, Georgia 54 G d
Granville, Illinois 57 D h
Granville, Iowa 61 J b
Granville, Massachusetts 51 H a
Granville, New York 53 N b
Granville, North Dakota 58 F b
Granville, Ohio 52 D e
Granville, Pennsylvania 52 J e
Grapeland, Texas 65 M d
Grapevine, California 75 F k
Grapevine, Texas 65 M h
Grapevine Dam, Texas 65 M h
Grapevine Mts., California 75 H h
Grapevine Res., Texas 65 K c
Grass Creek, Wyoming 67 M f
Grass L., Minnesota 59 P j
Grass Lake, California 74 C c
Grassland, Texas 64 F b
Grass R., New York 53 L a
Grassrange, Montana 67 M b
Grass Valley, California 74 D e
Grass Valley, Oregon 73 K k
Grassy Butte, North Dakota 58 C c
Grassy Knob, West Virginia 52 F g
Gratiot, Wisconsin 56 C g
Gratis, Ohio 52 B f
Grave Pk., Idaho 66 F c
Graves, The, Massachusetts 51 M a
Gravette, Arkansas 63 J b
Gravina I., Alaska 77 W j
Gravity, Iowa 61 K d
Grawn, Michigan 56 H e
Gray, Georgia 54 H d
Gray, Maine 49 E e
Gray, Oklahoma 62 C b
Gray Hd., Massachusetts 51 M c
Grayland, Washington 73 F j
Grayling, Michigan 56 J e
Grays, Illinois 56 E g
Grays Harb., Washington 73 F j
Grays L., Idaho 66 J f
Grays Lake Outlet, Idaho 66 J f
Grayson, Kentucky 57 L l
Grayson, Louisiana 63 L f
Grays Pk., Colorado 69 L d
Grays Reef, Michigan 56 H d
Grays River, Washington 73 G j
Grayton Beach, Florida 54 E g
Grayville, Illinois 57 E l
Great B., New Hampshire 49 D e
Great B., New Jersey 50 E f
Great Barrington, Massachusetts 50 G a
Great Basin, Nevada 74 J d
Great Bend, Kansas 60 F f
Great Bend, North Dakota 59 K d
Great Cacapon, West Virginia 52 H f
Great Divide, Colorado 69 J c
Great Egg Harbor Inlet, New Jersey 50 E g
Great Egg Harbor R., New Jersey 50 D g
Great Falls, Montana (55,357) 66 J b
Great Falls, South Carolina 55 L c
Great Falls Dam, Tennessee 54 F b
Great Falls L., Tennessee 54 F b
Great L., North Carolina 55 O c
Great Neck, New York 51 O e
Great Peconic B., New York 51 H d
Great Pond, Maine 49 G d
Great Pt., Massachusetts 49 F g
Great Quittacas Pond, Massachusetts 51 M b
Great Salt L., Utah 68 D b
Great Salt Lake Des., Utah 68 C b
Great Salt Plains Res., Oklahoma 62 E b
Great Salt Pond, Rhode Island 51 K c
Great Sand Dunes Nat. Mon., Colorado 69 L f
Great Sitkin I., Alaska 77 P j
Great Smoky Mts., North Carolina 54 H b
Great Smoky Mts. Nat. Park, Tennessee-North Carolina 54 H b
Great South B., New York 50 G d
Great South Beach, New York 51 H d
Great Wass I., Maine 49 H d
Greeley, Colorado (26,314) 69 M c
Greeley, Nebraska 60 F c
Greeley, Pennsylvania 50 D c
Green, Kansas 60 H e
Greenacres City, Florida 55 O g
Green B., Wisconsin 56 F d
Greenbackville, Maryland 53 L g
Green Bay, Wisconsin (62,888) 56 F e
Greenboro, Vermont 49 C d
Greenbrier R., West Virginia 52 F g
Greenbush, Massachusetts 51 M a
Greenbush, Michigan 56 K e
Greenbush, Minnesota 59 K b
Greencastle, Indiana 57 G k
Greencastle, Pennsylvania 52 J f
Green City, Missouri 61 M d
Green Cove Springs, Florida 55 K h
Green Creek, New Jersey 50 D g
Greendale, New York 50 F a
Greene, Iowa 61 M b
Greene, New York 53 L c
Greene, North Dakota 58 E b
Greene, Rhode Island 51 K b
Greeneville, Tennessee 55 J a
Greenfield, California 75 F j
Greenfield, California 75 D h
Greenfield, Illinois 57 C k
Greenfield, Indiana 57 H k
Greenfield, Iowa 61 K c
Greenfield, Massachusetts 49 C f
Greenfield, Missouri 61 L g
Greenfield, Ohio 52 C f
Greenfield, Oklahoma 62 E c
Greenfield, Pennsylvania 53 P b
Greenfield, Tennessee 54 C a
Greenfield Hill, Connecticut 50 G c
Greenfield Park, New York 50 E b
Green Forest, Arkansas 63 K b
Green Harbor, Massachusetts 51 M a
Greenhorn Mts., California 75 G j
Green I., Alaska 77 O f
Green L., Washington 72 B h
Green L., Wisconsin 56 E f
Green Lake, Texas 65 L g
Green Lake, Wisconsin 56 E f
Greenland, Wisconsin 56 D c
Green Lane, Pennsylvania 50 B e
Greenleaf, Kansas 60 H e
Green Mountain Res., Colorado 69 K d
Green Mts., Vermont 49 C e
Green Mts., Wyoming 67 N g
Greenough, Mt., Alaska 77 R b
Green Pond, South Carolina 55 L e
Greenport, New York 51 J c
Green R., Kentucky 57 F m
Green R., North Carolina 55 J b
Green R., Utah-Wyoming 68 G e
Green River, New York 50 F a
Green River, Utah 68 F d
Green River, Wyoming 67 L h
Greens Bayou, Texas 64 G h
Greensboro, Alabama 54 D e
Greensboro, Florida 54 G g
Greensboro, Georgia 54 H d
Greensboro, Maryland 50 B h
Greensboro, North Carolina (119,574) 55 M a
Greensburg, Indiana 57 H k
Greensburg, Kansas 60 E g
Greensburg, Kentucky 57 H m
Greensburg, Louisiana 63 N h
Greensburg, Pennsylvania 52 G e
Green Spring, West Virginia 52 H f
Green Springs, Ohio 52 C d
Green Swamp, North Carolina 55 N c
Greentop, Missouri 61 M d
Greentown, Indiana 57 H j
Greentown, Pennsylvania 50 C c
Green Tree, Pennsylvania 53 O b
Greenup, Illinois 57 E k
Greenview, California 74 C c
Greenville, Alabama 54 E f
Greenville, California 74 E d
Greenville, Florida 54 H g
Greenville, Illinois 57 D l
Greenville, Kentucky 57 F m
Greenville, Maine 49 F c
Greenville, Michigan 56 H f
Greenville, Mississippi (41,502) 63 M e
Greenville, Missouri 61 O g
Greenville, New Hampshire 49 D f
Greenville, New York 53 M c
Greenville, North Carolina 55 O b
Greenville, Ohio 52 B e
Greenville, Pennsylvania 52 F d
Greenville, South Carolina (66,188) 55 J c
Greenville, Texas 65 L b
Greenville, Virginia 52 G g
Greenway, South Dakota 58 G e
Greenwich, Connecticut (53,793) 50 F c
Greenwich, Kansas 60 G g
Greenwich, New Jersey 50 C g
Greenwich, New York 53 N b
Greenwich, Ohio 52 D d
Greenwich, Utah 68 E e
Greenwood, Arkansas 63 J c
Greenwood, California 74 E f
Greenwood, Delaware 53 L g
Greenwood, Indiana 57 G k
Greenwood, Kentucky 57 J n
Greenwood, Louisiana 63 K f
Greenwood, L., South Carolina 55 K c
Greenwood, Mississippi 63 N e
Greenwood, Nebraska 60 H d
Greenwood, South Carolina 55 J c
Greenwood, South Dakota 58 H h
Greenwood, Washington 72 B h
Greenwood, Wisconsin 56 C e
Greenwood Lake, New York 50 E c
Greenwood Springs, Mississippi 63 P e
Greenwood Village, Colorado 69 O j
Greer, Idaho 66 D c
Greer, South Carolina 55 J c
Greeson, L., Arkansas 63 K d
Greggton, Texas 65 N c
Gregory, South Dakota 58 G g
Grema, Louisiana 63 O j
Grenada, California 74 C c
Grenada, Mississippi 63 O e
Grenada L., Mississippi 63 O e
Grenada Res., Mississippi 63 O e
Grenloch, New Jersey 50 C f
Grenola, Kansas 60 H g
Grenora, North Dakota 58 C b
Grenville, New Mexico 71 O c
Grenville, South Dakota 58 J e
Gresham, Oregon 73 H k
Gretna, Louisiana 62 C f
Gretna, Virginia 52 G j
Greybull, Wyoming 67 M e
Greybull R., Wyoming 67 M e
Greycliff, Montana 67 L d
Grey Eagle, Minnesota 59 M e
Greys R., Wyoming 67 K g
Greystone, Colorado 68 H c
Gridley, California 74 D e
Gridley, Illinois 57 E j
Gridley, Kansas 60 H f
Griffin, Georgia 54 G d
Griffin, L., Florida 55 K j
Griffin Pt., Alaska 77 Q a
Griffithville, Arkansas 63 M c
Grifton, North Carolina 55 O b
Griggstown, New Jersey 50 D e
Griggsville, Illinois 57 C k
Grimes, California 74 D e
Grimes Pass, Idaho 66 E e
Grimville, Pennsylvania 50 B d
Grinnell, Iowa 61 M c
Grinnell, Kansas 60 D e
Grindstone, Maine 49 G c
Griswold, Iowa 61 J c
Groesbeck, Texas 65 L d
Groom, Texas 64 C h
Gross, Florida 55 K g
Grosse Pointe Park, Michigan 57 M j
Grosvenor, L., Alaska 76 K g
Grosvenor, Texas 65 H d
Grosvenor Dale, Connecticut 51 K b
Gros Ventre Ra., Wyoming 67 K f
Groton, Connecticut 51 J c
Groton, Massachusetts 49 D f
Groton, New York 53 K c
Groton, South Dakota 58 H e
Groton, Vermont 49 C d
Grottoes, Virginia 52 H g
Grouse, Idaho 66 G f
Grouse Creek, Utah 68 C b
Grove, Oklahoma 63 J b
Grove City, Ohio 52 C f
Grove City, Pennsylvania 52 F d
Grove Hill, Alabama 54 D f
Groveland, California 74 E g
Grover, Colorado 69 M c
Grover, Wyoming 67 K g
Groves, Texas 65 O f
Groveton, New Hampshire 49 D d
Groveton, Texas 65 M d
Grovetown, Georgia 55 J d
Grovont, Wyoming 67 K f
Growler, Arizona 70 D g
Growler Mts., Arizona 70 D g
Grulla, Texas 65 J j
Grundy Center, Iowa 61 M b
Gruver, Texas 64 C g
Grygla, Minnesota 59 L b
Gu Achi, Arizona 70 F g
Guadalupe, California 75 E k
Guadalupe Mts., New Mexico 71 M g
Guadalupe Pk., Texas 64 C d
Guadalupe R., Texas 65 J f
Gualala, California 74 B f
Guano L., Oregon 73 L n
Guelph, North Dakota 58 H d
Guernsey, Wyoming 67 Q g
Guernsey Res., Wyoming 67 Q g
Guerra, Texas 65 J j
Gueydan, Louisiana 63 L j
Guide Rock, Nebraska 60 F d
Guildhall, Vermont 49 D d
Guilford, Connecticut 51 H c
Guilford, Maine 49 F c
Guilford, Maryland 53 Q e
Guilford College, North Carolina 55 M a
Guilford Courthouse Nat. Mil. Park, North Carolina 55 M a
Guin, Alabama 54 D d
Guinda, California 74 C f
Guion, Arkansas 63 M c
Gu Komelik, Arizona 70 F g
Gulf, North Carolina 55 M b
Gulf Beach, Florida 54 D g
Gulf Outlet, Louisiana 63 O j
Gulfport, Florida 55 M f
Gulfport, Mississippi (30,204) 63 O h
Gulkana, Alaska 77 P e
Gulkana Junction, Alaska 77 P e
Gull I., Michigan 56 H d
Gulliver, Michigan 56 H c
Gull L., Minnesota 59 M d
Gum Spring, Virginia 52 H h
Gunlock, Utah 68 C f
Gunnison, Colorado 69 K e
Gunnison, Utah 68 E d
Gunnison I., Utah 68 D b
Gunnison R., Colorado 68 H e
Gunsight, Montana 66 H a
Gunter, Oregon 73 G m
Gunter, Texas 65 L b
Guntersville, Alabama 54 E c
Guntersville Dam, Alabama 54 E c
Guntersville L., Alabama 54 E c
Guntown, Mississippi 63 P d
Gurdon, Arkansas 63 K e
Gurley, Alabama 54 E c
Gurley, Nebraska 60 B c
Gurnet Pt., Massachusetts 51 M a
Gusher, Utah 68 G c
Gustavus, Alaska 77 U g
Gustine, California 75 D g
Gustine, Texas 65 J d
Guthrie, Kentucky 57 F n
Guthrie, Minnesota 59 M c
Guthrie, North Dakota 58 F b
Guthrie, Oklahoma 62 F c
Guthrie, Texas 64 G b
Guthrie Center, Iowa 61 K c
Guthriesville, Pennsylvania 50 B e
Guttenberg, Iowa 61 N b
Guttenberg, New Jersey 51 L e
Guyandot R., West Virginia 52 D g
Guymon, Oklahoma 62 B b
Guyot Glacier, Alaska 77 R f
Guyton, Georgia 55 K e
Gwendolen, Oregon 73 K k
Gwinn, Michigan 56 F c
Gwinner, North Dakota 58 J d
Gypsum, Colorado 69 K d
Gypsum, Kansas 60 G f
Hachita, New Mexico 71 J h
Hackamore, California 74 D c
Hackberry, Arizona 70 D d
Hackberry, Louisiana 63 K j
Hackberry Cr., Kansas 60 D f
Hackensack, New Jersey (30,521) 50 E d
Hackensack R., New Jersey 50 E c
Hackett, Arkansas 63 J c
Hackettstown, New Jersey 50 D d
Hackleburg, Alabama 54 D c
Hadar, Nebraska 60 G b
Haddam, Connecticut 51 H c
Haddam, Kansas 60 G e
Haddock, Georgia 54 H d
Haddonfield, New Jersey 50 D f
Hadley, Massachusetts 51 H a
Hadweenzic R., Alaska 77 N c
Hagan, Georgia 55 K e
Hageman, Idaho 66 F g
Hagemeister I., Alaska 76 G g
Hagerman, New Mexico 71 N f
Hagerman, New York 51 H d
Hagerstown, Indiana 57 H k
Hagerstown, Maryland (36,660) 52 J f
Hagood, South Carolina 55 L c
Hague, New York 53 N b
Hague, North Dakota 58 G d
Hagues Pk., Colorado 69 L c
Hahira, Georgia 54 H g
Haigler, Nebraska 60 C d
Haiku, Hawaii 72 D e
Hailey, Idaho 66 F f
Haileyville, Oklahoma 62 H d
Haines, Alaska 77 U g
Haines, Oregon 73 N l
Hainesburg, New Jersey 50 C d
Haines City, Florida 55 N e
Haines Falls, New York 50 E a
Hainsville, New Jersey 50 D c
Haivana Nakya, Arizona 70 F g
Haiwee Res., California 75 H h
Hakalau, Hawaii 72 E f
Halawa, C., Hawaii 72 D d
Halcott Center, New York 50 E a
Halcottsville, New York 50 D a
Hale, Colorado 69 O d
Hale, Michigan 56 K e
Hale, Missouri 61 L e
Haleakala Crater, Hawaii 72 D e
Haleakala Nat. Pk., Hawaii 72 D e
Hale Center, Texas 64 F a
Haledon, New Jersey 50 E d
Haleiwa, Hawaii 72 C d
Halena, Hawaii 72 D d
Hales Bar Dam, Tennessee 54 F b
Halethorp, Maryland 53 P f
Haleyville, Alabama 54 D c
Half Moon B., California 75 B n
Halford, Kansas 60 D e
Halfway, Maryland 52 J f
Halfway, Oregon 73 N l
Halfway, Texas 64 F a
Halfway Mt., Alaska 76 K f
Halifax, Massachusetts 51 M b
Halifax, North Carolina 55 O a
Halifax, Pennsylvania 53 K e
Halifax, Virginia 52 H j
Halkett C., Alaska 76 L a
Hall, Montana 66 G c
Hallandale, Florida 54 B c
Halleck, Nevada 74 K d
Haller L., Washington 72 B g
Hallettsville, Texas 65 L f
Halley, Arkansas 63 M e
Hall I., Alaska 76 A f
Halliday, North Dakota 58 D c
Halligan Res., Colorado 69 L c
Hallock, Minnesota 59 K b
Halls, Tennessee 54 B b
Halls Bayou, Texas 64 G h
Hall Station, Colorado 69 N e
Hallstead, Pennsylvania 53 L d
Hall Summit, Louisiana 63 K f
Hallsville, Missouri 61 M e
Hallsville, Texas 65 N c
Hallton, Pennsylvania 52 H d
Halma, Minnesota 59 K b
Halsey, Nebraska 60 D c
Halstad, Minnesota 59 K c
Halstead, Kansas 60 G f
Haltom City, Texas 65 L j
Hamar, North Dakota 58 H c
Hamberg, North Dakota 58 G c
Hambone, California 74 D c
Hamburg, Arkansas 63 M e
Hamburg, California 74 B c
Hamburg, Connecticut 51 J c
Hamburg, Iowa 61 J d
Hamburg, New Jersey 50 D c
Hamburg, New York 52 H c
Hamburg, Pennsylvania 50 A d
Hamden, Connecticut (41,056) 51 H c
Hamden, New York 50 D a
Hamden, Ohio 52 D f
Hamer, Idaho 66 H f
Hamilton, Alabama 54 D c
Hamilton, Alaska 76 F e
Hamilton, Colorado 69 J c
Hamilton, Georgia 54 G e
Hamilton, Illinois 57 B j
Hamilton, Indiana 57 J h
Hamilton, Kansas 61 H g
Hamilton, L., Arkansas 63 K d
Hamilton, Maryland 53 Q e
Hamilton, Michigan 56 H g
Hamilton, Missouri 61 K e
Hamilton, Montana 66 F c
Hamilton, Mt., Nevada 74 K c
Hamilton, New York 53 L c
Hamilton, North Dakota 58 J b
Hamilton, Ohio (72,354) 52 B f
Hamilton, Oregon 73 L l
Hamilton, Pennsylvania 52 J e
Hamilton, Texas 65 J d
Hamilton, Washington 73 J g
Hamilton City, California 74 C e
Hamilton Dome, Wyoming 67 M f
Hamler, Ohio 52 C d
Hamlet, Indiana 57 G h
Hamlet, Nebraska 60 C d
Hamlet, North Carolina 55 M c
Hamlin, New York 52 J b
Hamlin, West Virginia 52 D g
Hamlin, Texas 64 G c
Hamlin L., Michigan 56 G e
Hammett, Idaho 66 E g
Hammon, Oklahoma 62 D c
Hammond, Illinois 57 E k
Hammond, Indiana (111,698) 57 F h
Hammond, Louisiana 63 N h
Hammond, Montana 67 Q d
Hammond, New York 53 L a
Hammond, Oregon 73 G j
Hammond, Wisconsin 56 A d
Hammond B., Michigan 56 J d
Hammondsport, New York 53 J c
Hammonton, California 74 D e
Hammonton, New Jersey 50 D f
Hamorton, Pennsylvania 50 B f
Hampden, Massachusetts 51 J a
Hampden, North Dakota 58 H b
Hampden Highlands, Maine 49 G d
Hampstead, Maryland 53 K f
Hampstead, North Carolina 55 O c
Hampton, Arkansas 63 L e
Hampton, Connecticut 51 J b
Hampton, Florida 55 J h
Hampton, Georgia 54 G d
Hampton, Iowa 61 L b
Hampton, Nebraska 60 G d
Hampton, New Hampshire 49 E f
Hampton, New Jersey 50 D d
Hampton, Oregon 73 K m
Hampton, South Carolina 55 K e
Hampton, Virginia (89,258) 53 K h
Hampton, Wyoming 67 K h
Hampton Bays, New York 51 H d
Hams Fork, Wyoming 67 K g
Hamtramck, Michigan (34,137) 57 L j
Hana, Hawaii 72 D e
Hanale, Hawaii 72 B c
Hanamanioa, C., Hawaii 72 D e
Hanamaulu, Hawaii 72 B d
Hanapepe, Hawaii 72 B d
Hanceville, Alabama 54 E c
Hancock, L., Florida 55 N f

Hancock, Maine 49 G d
Hancock, Maryland 52 H f
Hancock, Michigan 56 E b
Hancock, Minnesota 59 L e
Hancock, New York 53 L d
Hancock, Wisconsin 56 D e
Hancocks Bridge, New Jersey 50 C f
Handley, Texas 65 K c
Hanford, California 75 F h
Hanford, Maine 49 G b
Hanford, Washington 73 L j
Hanging Rock, Ohio 52 D g
Hangman Cr., Washington 73 N h
Hankinson, North Dakota 58 J d
Hanksville, Utah 68 F d
Hanley Falls, Minnesota 59 L f
Hanna, Utah 68 F c
Hanna, Wyoming 67 O h
Hannaford, North Dakota 58 H c
Hannah, North Dakota 58 H b
Hannibal, Missouri 61 N e
Hannibal, Wisconsin 56 C d
Hannover, North Dakota 58 E c
Hanover, Connecticut 51 J b
Hanover, Kansas 60 H e
Hanover, Massachusetts 51 M a
Hanover, Minnesota 59 N e
Hanover, Montana 67 L b
Hanover, New Hampshire 49 C e
Hanover, Pennsylvania 53 J f
Hansboro, North Dakota 58 G b
Hanson, Massachusetts 51 M a
Happy, Texas 64 C j
Happy Camp, California 74 B c
Harahan, Louisiana 62 B f
Harbor, Oregon 73 F n
Harbor Beach, Michigan 56 L f
Harbor I., Washington 72 B h
Harbor Springs, Michigan 56 J d
Harcuvar Mts., Arizona 70 D e
Hardee, Mississippi 63 N f
Hardeeville, South Carolina 55 K e
Hardesty, Oklahoma 62 B b
Hardin, Illinois 57 C k
Hardin, Missouri 61 L e
Hardin, Montana 67 N d
Harding, Minnesota 59 M d
Harding Icefield, Alaska 76 M f
Hardinsburg, Kentucky 57 G m
Hardman, Oregon 73 L k
Hardwick, Minnesota 59 K g
Hardwick, Vermont 49 C d
Hardy, Arkansas 63 M b
Hardy, Montana 66 J b
Hardy Res., Michigan 56 H f
Hargill, Texas 65 J j
Harkers Island, North Carolina 55 P c
Harlan, Iowa 61 J c
Harlan, Kansas 60 F e
Harlan, Kentucky 57 K n
Harlan County Res., Nebraska 60 E d
Harlem, Georgia 55 J d
Harlem, Montana 67 M a
Harlemville, New York 50 F a
Harleysville, Pennsylvania 50 C e
Harleyville, South Carolina 55 L d
Harlingen, Texas (41,207) 65 K j
Harlow, North Dakota 58 G b
Harlowton, Montana 67 L c
Harman, West Virginia 52 G g
Harmarville, Pennsylvania 53 Q a
Harmersville, New Jersey 50 C g
Harmon, Oklahoma 62 D b
Harmony, Maine 49 F d
Harmony, Minnesota 59 O g
Harmony, New Jersey 50 C d
Harmony, Rhode Island 51 K b
Harney, L., Florida 55 K j
Harney, Oregon 73 M m
Harney Basin, Oregon 73 L m
Harney (Dry) L., Oregon 73 L m
Harney Pk., South Dakota 58 C g
Harpath R., Tennessee 54 D a
Harper, Kansas 60 F g
Harper, Mt., Alaska 77 Q d
Harper, Oregon 73 N m
Harper, Texas 65 H e
Harper, Washington 72 B j
Harper Bend, Alaska 76 M d
Harper L., California 75 H j
Harpers Ferry, West Virginia 52 J f
Harpster, Idaho 66 E d
Harquahala Mts., Arizona 70 D f
Harrah, Oklahoma 62 F c
Harrell, Arkansas 63 L e
Harriet, L., Minnesota 59 Q j
Harrietta, Michigan 56 H e
Harriman, New York 50 E c
Harriman, Tennessee 54 G b
Harrington, Delaware 50 B h
Harrington, Maine 49 H d
Harrington, Washington 73 M h
Harris, California 74 B d
Harris, L., Florida 55 K j
Harris, Missouri 61 L d
Harrisburg, Arkansas 63 N c
Harrisburg, Illinois 57 E m
Harrisburg, Nebraska 60 A c
Harrisburg, Ohio 52 C f
Harrisburg, Oregon 73 G l
Harrisburg, Pennsylvania (79,697) 53 J e
Harrisburg, South Dakota 59 K g
Harrison, Arkansas 63 K b
Harrison, Georgia 55 J e
Harrison, Idaho 66 D b
Harrison, Michigan 56 J e
Harrison, Montana 66 J d
Harrison, Nebraska 60 A b
Harrison, New Jersey 51 K f
Harrison, New York 50 F d
Harrison, South Dakota 58 H g
Harrison B., Alaska 76 L a
Harrisonburg, Louisiana 63 M g
Harrisonburg, Virginia 52 H g
Harrisonville, New Jersey 50 C f
Harrisonville, Missouri 61 K f
Harrisville, Michigan 56 K e
Harrisville, New York 53 L a
Harrisville, Rhode Island 51 K b
Harrisville, West Virginia 52 E f
Harrodsburg, Indiana 57 G k
Harrodsburg, Kentucky 57 J m
Harrold, South Dakota 58 G f
Harrold, Texas 65 H a
Harrow, Pennsylvania 50 C e
Harry Strunk L., Nebraska 60 D d
Hart, Michigan 56 G f
Hart, Texas 64 B j
Hartford, Alabama 54 F f
Hartford, Arkansas 63 J c
Hartford, Connecticut (162,178) 51 H b
Hartford, Kansas 61 J f
Hartford, Kentucky 57 F m
Hartford, Michigan 57 G g
Hartford, Ohio 52 D e
Hartford, Tennessee 54 H b
Hartford, Wisconsin 56 E f
Hartford City, Indiana 57 H j
Hartington, Nebraska 60 G b
Hart I., New York 51 N e
Hart L., Oregon 73 L n
Hartland, Maine 49 F d
Hartley, Iowa 61 J a
Hartley, Texas 64 B h
Hartline, Washington 73 L h
Hartly, Delaware 50 B g
Hartman, Colorado 69 O e
Hart Mt., Oregon 73 L n
Hartsel, Colorado 69 L d
Hartselle, Alabama 54 E c
Hartshorne, Oklahoma 62 H d
Hartsville, South Carolina 55 L c
Hartsville, Tennessee 54 E a
Hartville, Missouri 61 M g
Hartville, Wyoming 67 Q g
Hartwell, Georgia 55 J c
Hartwell Reservoir, South Carolina 55 J c
Hartwood, New York 50 D c
Harvard, California 75 J k
Harvard, Idaho 66 D c
Harvard, Illinois 56 E g
Harvard, Mt., Colorado 69 K e
Harvard, Nebraska 60 F d
Harvard Glacier, Alaska 77 O f
Harvey, Illinois (29,071) 57 F h
Harvey, Iowa 61 M c
Harvey, Louisiana 62 C f
Harvey, North Dakota 58 F c
Harvey Mt., California 74 D d
Harveyville, Kansas 61 J f
Harviell, Missouri 61 O h
Harwich, Massachusetts 51 N b
Harwich Port, Massachusetts 51 N b
Harwinton, Connecticut 51 G b
Harwood, Texas 65 K f
Haskell, Arkansas 63 L d
Haskell, Oklahoma 62 H c
Haskell, Texas 65 H b
Haslet, Texas 65 L h
Hassayampa R., Arizona 70 E f
Hastings, Florida 55 K h
Hastings, Iowa 61 J c
Hastings, Michigan 56 H g
Hastings, Minnesota 59 O f
Hastings, Nebraska 60 F d
Hastings, Oklahoma 62 E d
Hastings, Pennsylvania 52 H e
Hastings-on-Hudson, New York 50 F d
Hasty, Colorado 69 O e
Haswell, Colorado 69 N e
Hatboro, Pennsylvania 53 L e
Hatch, New Mexico 71 K g
Hatch, Utah 68 D f
Hatchel, Texas 64 G d
Hatchie R., Tennessee 54 B b
Hatchville, Massachusetts 51 M b
Hat Creek, California 74 D d
Hat Creek, Wyoming 67 Q g
Hatfield, Arkansas 63 J d
Hatfield, Minnesota 59 K g
Hatfield, Pennsylvania 50 C e
Hathaway, Montana 67 O c
Hatteras, Cape, North Carolina 55 P d
Hatteras, North Carolina 55 P d
Hatteras Inlet, North Carolina 55 P d
Hattiesburg, Mississippi (34,989) 63 O g
Hatton, North Dakota 58 J c
Hatton, Washington 73 M j
Haugen, Wisconsin 56 B d
Haughton, Louisiana 63 K f
Haulover Beach Park, Florida 54 C c
Hauser Lake Dam, Montana 66 J c
Hauula, Hawaii 72 C d
Havana, Arkansas 63 K c
Havana, Florida 54 G g
Havana, Illinois 57 C j
Havana, Kansas 61 J g
Havana, North Dakota 58 J e
Havasu L., California 75 L k
Havelock, North Carolina 55 P c
Havelock, North Dakota 58 D d
Haven, Kansas 60 G g
Haven, New York 50 D b
Havensville, Kansas 61 H e
Haverhill, Massachusetts (46,346) 49 E f
Haverhill, New Hampshire 49 C d
Haverstraw, New York 50 F c
Haviland, Kansas 60 E g
Haviland, Ohio 52 B d
Havre, Montana 67 L a
Havre de Grace, Maryland 50 A f
Hawaii (741,000) 6424 sq. miles 72
Hawaii, I., Hawaii 72 E f
Hawaii Volcanoes Nat. Pk., Hawaii 72 E f
Hawarden, Iowa 60 H b
Hawes, California 75 H k
Hawesville, Kentucky 57 G m
Hawi, Hawaii 72 E e
Hawk Chan., Florida 55 O j
Hawk Inlet, Alaska 77 U g
Hawkins Pk., Utah 68 C f
Hawkinsville, Georgia 54 H e
Hawk Point, Missouri 61 N f
Hawks, Michigan 56 K d
Hawk Springs, Wyoming 67 Q h
Hawley, Colorado 69 N f
Hawley, Minnesota 59 K d
Hawley, Pennsylvania 53 L d
Hawley, Texas 65 H c
Haworth, Oklahoma 63 J e
Haw R., North Carolina 55 M b
Hawthorn, Florida 55 J h
Hawthorne, California (33,035) 75 D m
Hawthorne, Nevada 74 G f
Hawthorne, New Jersey 50 E d
Hawthorne, Wisconsin 56 B c
Hawthorne Place, Texas 64 F h
Hay, Washington 73 N j
Haybro, Colorado 69 K c
Haycock, Alaska 76 G d
Hayden, Arizona 70 G f
Hayden, Colorado 69 J c
Hayden L., Idaho 66 D b
Hayes, Louisiana 63 L h
Hayes, Mt., Alaska 77 O e
Hayes, South Dakota 58 E f
Hayes Center, Nebraska 60 C d
Hayes Glaciers, Alaska 76 L f
Hayesville, North Carolina 54 H b
Hayfield, Minnesota 59 O g
Hayfield Res., California 75 K l
Hayfork, California 74 B d
Haylow, Georgia 55 J g
Haymarket, Virginia 52 J g
Haynes, North Dakota 58 D e
Haynesville, Louisiana 63 K f
Haynesville, Maine 49 G c
Hayneville, Alabama 54 E e
Hay R., Wisconsin 56 B d
Hays, Kansas 60 E f
Hays, Montana 67 M a
Hays, Pennsylvania 53 Q b
Hay Springs, Nebraska 60 B b
Haystack Mt., Nevada 74 K c
Haystack Pk., Utah 68 C d
Hayti, Missouri 61 P h
Hayti, South Dakota 58 J f
Hayward, California (72,700) 75 C m
Hayward, Minnesota 59 N g
Hayward, Oklahoma 62 F b
Hayward, Wisconsin 56 B c
Haxby, Montana 67 O b
Haxtun, Colorado 69 O c
Hazard, Kentucky 57 K m
Hazardville, Connecticut 51 H b
Hazel, Kentucky 57 E n
Hazel, Minnesota 59 K b
Hazel, South Dakota 58 J f
Hazel Park, Michigan (25,631) 57 L j
Hazelton, Kansas 60 F g
Hazelton, North Dakota 58 F d
Hazelton, Pennsylvania 50 B d
Hazelwood, Pennsylvania 53 P b
Hazen, Arkansas 63 M d
Hazen, Nevada 74 G e
Hazen, North Dakota 58 E c
Hazen B., Alaska 76 E f
Hazewood, North Carolina 55 J b
Hazlehurst, Georgia 55 J f
Hazlehurst, Mississippi 63 N g
Hazleton, Pennsylvania (32,056) 53 L e
Headland, Alabama 54 F f
Head of Westport, Massachusetts 51 L b
Headquarters, Idaho 66 E c
Heads, The, Oregon 73 F n
Heafford Junction, Wisconsin 56 D d
Healdsburg, California 74 C f
Healdton, Oklahoma 62 F d
Healy, Alaska 76 N e
Healy, Kansas 60 D f
Healy L., Alaska 77 P e
Healy R., Alaska 77 P d
Hearne, Texas 65 L e
Hearst, California 74 B e
Heart L., Wyoming 67 K e
Heart R., North Dakota 58 D d
Heartwell, Nebraska 60 F d
Heath Springs, South Carolina 55 L c
Heathsville, Virginia 53 K h
Heavener, Oklahoma 63 J d
Hebbronville, Texas 65 J h
Heber, Arizona 70 G e
Heber, Utah 68 E c
Heber Springs, Arkansas 63 L c
Hebgen L., Montana 66 J e
Hebo, Oregon 73 G k
Hebron, Connecticut 51 J b
Hebron, Colorado 69 K c
Hebron, Illinois 56 E g
Hebron, Indiana 57 F h
Hebron, Mt., California 74 C c
Hebron, Nebraska 60 G d
Hebron, North Dakota 58 D d
Hebron, Ohio 52 D f
Hebronville, Massachusetts 51 L b
Heceta Hd., Oregon 73 F l
Heceta I., Alaska 77 V j
Hecla, South Dakota 58 H e
Hector, California 75 J k
Hector, Minnesota 59 M f
Hedgesville, Montana 67 L c
Hedgesville, West Virginia 52 H f
Hedley, Texas 64 D j
Hedrick, Iowa 61 M c
Heflin, Alabama 54 F d
Heidelberg, Kentucky 57 J m
Heidelberg, Mississippi 63 P g
Heidelberg, Pennsylvania 53 O b
Heights, The, Michigan 56 J e
Heimdal, North Dakota 58 G e
Heine Creek, Alaska 77 N d
Heislerville, New Jersey 50 D g
Helen, Georgia 54 H c
Helen, Mt., Nevada 75 J g
Helena, Alabama 54 E d
Helena, Arkansas 63 N d
Helena, California 74 B d
Helena, Georgia 55 J e
Helena, Montana 66 H c
Helena, Oklahoma 62 E b
Helendale, California 75 H k
Hells Canyon, Idaho 66 D d
Helm, California 75 E h
Helmville, Montana 66 H c
Helotes, Texas 65 J f
Helper, Utah 68 F d
Heltonville, Indiana 57 G l
Hemet, California 75 J l
Hemingford, Nebraska 60 A b
Hemingway, South Carolina 55 M d
Hemlock Res., Connecticut 50 G c
Hemphill, Texas 65 O d
Hempstead, New York (34,641) 50 F d
Hempstead, Texas 65 L e
Henderson, Colorado 69 P h
Henderson, Kentucky 57 F m
Henderson, Maryland 50 B g
Henderson, Nevada 75 L h
Henderson, New York 53 K b
Henderson, North Carolina 55 N a
Henderson, Tennessee 54 C b
Henderson, Texas 65 N c
Henderson, West Virginia 52 D g
Hendersonville, North Carolina 55 J b
Hendricks, Minnesota 59 K f
Hendricks, West Virginia 52 G f
Henefer, Utah 68 E b
Henleyville, California 74 C e
Henlopen, C., Delaware 53 L g
Henly, Texas 65 J e
Hennepin, Illinois 57 D h
Hennessey, Oklahoma 62 F b
Henniker, New Hampshire 49 D e
Henning, Illinois 57 F j
Henning, Minnesota 59 L d
Henning, Tennessee 54 B b
Henrietta, Texas 65 J b
Henrieville, Utah 68 E f
Henry, C., Virginia 53 L j
Henry, Idaho 66 J g
Henry, Illinois 57 D h
Henry, Mt., Montana 66 E a
Henryetta, Oklahoma 62 G c
Henry L., Montana 66 J e
Henry Mts., Utah 68 E d
Henryville, Indiana 57 H l
Henryville, Pennsylvania 50 C c
Henshaw, Kentucky 57 E m
Henshaw L., California 75 J l
Hensonville, New York 50 E a
Hephzibah, Georgia 55 J d
Heppner, Oregon 73 L k
Herbert I., Alaska 77 S j
Herd, Oklahoma 62 G b
Hereford, Colorado 69 M c
Hereford, Pennsylvania 50 B e
Hereford, Texas 64 B j
Hereford Inlet, New Jersey 50 D g
Herington, Kansas 60 H f
Herkimer, New York 53 M b
Herman, Michigan 56 E c
Herman, Minnesota 59 K e
Herman, Nebraska 60 H c
Hermanas, New Mexico 71 K h
Hermann, Missouri 61 N f
Hermansville, Michigan 56 F d
Hermanville, Mississippi 63 N g
Hermes Reef, Hawaii 72 A a
Hermiston, Oregon 73 L k
Hermitage, Arkansas 63 L e
Hermits Rest, Arizona 70 E c
Hermleigh, Texas 64 G c
Hermosa, South Dakota 58 C g
Hermosa Beach, California 75 D m
Hernando, Florida 55 J j
Hernando, Mississippi 63 O d
Herndon, California 75 E h
Herndon, Iowa 61 K c
Herndon, Kansas 60 D e
Herndon, Kentucky 57 F n
Herndon, Pennsylvania 53 K e
Herndon, Virginia 52 J f
Herndon, West Virginia 52 E h
Heron, Montana 66 E a
Heron L., Minnesota 59 L g
Heron Lake, Minnesota 59 L g
Herreid, South Dakota 58 F e
Herrick, South Dakota 58 G g
Herrin, Illinois 57 D m
Herrington L., Kentucky 57 J m
Herscher, Illinois 57 E h
Hersey, Michigan 56 H f
Hershey, Pennsylvania 53 K e
Hertford, North Carolina 55 P a
Hesper, North Dakota 58 G c
Hesperia, California 75 H k
Hesperia, Michigan 56 G f
Hesperus, Colorado 68 H f
Hesperus Pk., Colorado 68 H f
Hess Cr., Alaska 76 N d
Hessel, Michigan 56 J c
Hesston, Kansas 60 G f
Hetch Hetchy Res., California 74 F g
Hetherton, Michigan 56 J d
Hettinger, North Dakota 58 D d
Heuvelton, New York 53 L a
Hewitt, New Jersey 50 E c
Hewlett Point, New York 51 O e
Hext, Texas 65 H e
Heyburn, Idaho 66 G g
Heyburn Res., Oklahoma 62 G c
Hialeah, Florida (66,972) 54 B d
Hialeah Gardens, Florida 54 A d
Hialeah Park, Florida 54 B d
Hiawassee, Georgia 54 H c
Hiawatha, Kansas 61 J e
Hiawatha, Utah 68 F d
Hiawatha L., Minnesota 59 Q j
Hibbing, Minnesota 59 N c
Hibernia, New Jersey 50 E d
Hickewan, Arizona 70 E g
Hickman, Kentucky 57 D n
Hickman, Nebraska 60 H d
Hickman, New Mexico 71 K e
Hickman Mills, Missouri 61 P b
Hickok, Kansas 60 C g
Hickory, L., North Carolina 55 K b
Hickory, Mississippi 63 O f
Hickory, North Carolina 55 K b
Hickory Run State Park, Pennsylvania 50 B c
Hickory Valley, Tennessee 54 B b
Hicks, Texas 65 L h
Hicksville, New York (50,405) 50 G d
Hicksville, Ohio 52 B d
Hico, Texas 65 J d
Higbee, Missouri 61 M e
Higganum, Connecticut 51 H b
Higgins, Texas 64 D g
Higgins L., Michigan 56 J e
Higginsville, Missouri 61 L e
Highbee, Colorado 69 N f
High Bridge, New Jersey 50 D d
Highcliff, Wisconsin 56 E e
High Desert, Oregon 73 K m
High Falls, New York 50 E b
High Falls Res., Wisconsin 56 E d
High I., Michigan 56 H d
High Island, Texas 65 N f
Highland, California 75 H k
Highland, Illinois 57 D l
Highland, Kansas 61 J e
Highland, New York 50 F b
Highland, Wisconsin 56 C f
Highland Falls, New York 50 E c
Highland Heights, Texas 64 F h
Highland L., Connecticut 51 H b
Highland Mills, New York 50 E c
Highland Park, Illinois (25,532) 57 F g
Highland Park, Michigan (38,063) 57 L j
Highland Park, Texas 65 N j
Highland Pk., California 74 F f
Highland Pk., Nevada 74 L g
Highland Pt., Florida 55 N h
Highlands, New Jersey 50 F e
Highlands, North Carolina 54 H b
Highlands, Texas 65 M f
Highland Springs, Virginia 53 J h
Highlandtown, Maryland 53 Q f
Highmore, South Dakota 58 G f
High Point, North Carolina (62,063) 55 M b
High Point State Park, New Jersey 50 D c
High Rock, North Carolina 55 L b
High Rock L., North Carolina 55 L b
High Springs, Florida 55 J h
Hightstown, New Jersey 50 D e
Highwood, Illinois 57 E g
Highwood, Montana 67 K b
Hiko, Nevada 74 K g
Hiland, Wyoming 67 N f
Hildebrand, Oregon 73 J n
Hildreth, Nebraska 60 E d
Hilger, Montana 67 L b
Hill, Montana 66 J a
Hill, New Hampshire 49 D e
Hilland, South Dakota 58 E f
Hillburn, New York 50 E c
Hill Cr., Utah 68 G d
Hill City, Idaho 66 E f
Hill City, Kansas 60 E e
Hill City, Minnesota 59 N d
Hill City, South Dakota 58 C g
Hillhead, South Dakota 58 J e
Hilliard, Florida 55 K g
Hillman, Michigan 56 K d
Hillman, Minnesota 59 N d
Hillrose, Colorado 69 N c
Hills, Iowa 61 N c
Hills, Minnesota 59 K g
Hillsboro, Georgia 54 H d
Hillsboro, Illinois 57 D k
Hillsboro, Iowa 61 N d
Hillsboro, Kansas 60 G f
Hillsboro, Missouri 61 O f
Hillsboro, New Hampshire 49 D e
Hillsboro, New Mexico 71 K g
Hillsboro, North Carolina 55 M a
Hillsboro, North Dakota 58 J c
Hillsboro, Ohio 52 C f
Hillsboro, Oregon 73 H k
Hillsboro, Texas 65 K c
Hillsboro, West Virginia 52 F g
Hillsboro, Wisconsin 56 C f
Hillsboro Canal, Florida 55 O g
Hillsborough, California 75 B m
Hillsdale, Michigan 57 J h
Hillsdale, New York 50 G a
Hillsdale, Wyoming 67 Q h
Hillside, Arizona 70 E e
Hillside, Colorado 69 L e
Hillside, New Jersey 51 J f
Hillsview, South Dakota 58 G e
Hillsville, Massachusetts 51 J a
Hillsville, Virginia 52 F j
Hilltonia, Georgia 55 K e
Hillview, Illinois 57 C k
Hilmar, California 75 E g
Hilo, Hawaii (25,966) 72 E f
Hilolo, Florida 55 O f
Hilton, New York 52 J b
Hilton Head I., South Carolina 55 L e
Hilts, California 74 C c
Himes, Wyoming 67 M e
Hinchinbrook Entrance, Alaska 77 O f
Hinchinbrook I., Alaska 77 O f
Hinckley, Minnesota 59 O d
Hinckley, Utah 68 D d
Hinckley Res., New York 53 M b
Hindes, Texas 65 J g
Hinesville, Georgia 55 K f
Hingham, Montana 67 K a
Hinesburg, Vermont 49 B d
Hinkley, California 75 H k
Hinsdale, Illinois 57 F h
Hinsdale, Massachusetts 49 C f
Hinsdale, Montana 67 N a
Hinsdale, New Hampshire 49 C f
Hinsdale, New York 52 H c
Hinton, Oklahoma 62 E c
Hinton, West Virginia 52 F h
Hiram, Maine 49 E e
Hisle, South Dakota 58 E g
Hitchcock, Oklahoma 62 E c
Hitchcock, South Dakota 58 H f
Hitchcock, Texas 65 M f
Hitchita, Oklahoma 62 H c
Hite, Utah 68 F f
Hither Hills State Park, New York 51 J c
Hiwassee Dam, North Carolina 54 G b
Hiwassee L., North Carolina 54 G b
Hiwassee R., Tennessee 54 G b
Hoagland, Nebraska 60 D c
Hoback Pk., Wyoming 67 K f
Hoback R., Wyoming 67 K f
Hobart, Indiana 57 F h
Hobart, Oklahoma 62 D c
Hobbs, New Mexico 71 O g
Hobbs Island, Alabama 54 E c
Hobe Sound, Florida 55 O f
Hobgood, North Carolina 55 O a
Hoboken, Georgia 55 J f
Hoboken, New Jersey (48,441) 50 E d
Hobson, Montana 67 L c
Hobucken, North Carolina 55 P b
Hochatown, Oklahoma 63 J d
Hochheim, Texas 65 K f
Hockingport, Ohio 52 E f
Hocking R., Ohio 52 D f
Hockley, Texas 65 M e
Hodge, Louisiana 63 L f
Hodgenville, Kentucky 57 H m
Hodges, L., California 75 H m
Hodges, Montana 67 Q c
Hodges, South Carolina 55 J c
Hodzana R., Alaska 77 N c
Hoehne, Colorado 69 M f
Hoffman, Minnesota 59 L e
Hoffman, North Carolina 55 M b
Hoffman I., New York 51 L g
Hogan Res., California 74 E f
Hogansville, Georgia 54 G d
Hogatzu R., Alaska 76 K c
Hogback Mt., Montana 66 H e
Hogeland, Montana 67 M a
Hog I., Michigan 56 H d
Hog I., Virginia 53 L h
Hog River, Alaska 76 K c
Hohenwald, Tennessee 54 D b
Hohokus, New Jersey 50 E c

Hoho UNITED STATES INDEX Isla

Hoholitna R., Alaska 76 J f
Hoh R., Washington 73 F h
Hoisington, Kansas 60 F f
Hokah, Minnesota 59 P g
Holbrook, Arizona 70 G e
Holbrook, Idaho 66 H g
Holbrook, Massachusetts 51 L a
Holbrook, Nebraska 60 D d
Holcombe, Wisconsin 56 B d
Holden, Massachusetts 49 D f
Holden, Missouri 61 L f
Holden, Utah 68 D d
Holden, West Virginia 52 D h
Holdenville, Oklahoma 62 G c
Holdingford, Minnesota 59 M e
Holdrege, Nebraska 60 E d
Holgate, Ohio 52 B d
Holikachuk, Alaska 76 H e
Holitna R., Alaska 76 J f
Holladay, Utah 68 C h
Holland, Massachusetts 51 J a
Holland, Michigan 56 G g
Holland, Minnesota 59 K f
Holland, New York 52 H c
Holland, Oregon 73 G n
Holland, Texas 65 K e
Hollandale, Mississippi 63 N e
Holley, New York 52 H b
Holliday, Kansas 61 O a
Holliday, Texas 65 J b
Hollidaysburg, Pennsylvania 52 H e
Hollis, New York 51 N f
Hollister, California 75 D h
Hollister, Idaho 66 F g
Hollister, Missouri 61 L h
Hollister, Oklahoma 62 E d
Holliston, Massachusetts 51 L a
Holloway, Louisiana 63 L g
Hollowville, New York 50 F a
Holly, Colorado 69 O e
Holly, Michigan 56 K g
Holly Bluff, Mississippi 63 N f
Holly Grove, Arkansas 63 M d
Holly Hill, Florida 55 K h
Holly Hill, South Carolina 55 L d
Holly Ridge, North Carolina 55 O c
Holly Springs, Mississippi 63 O d
Hollywood, California 75 D l
Hollywood, Florida (35,237) 54 B c
Hollywood, Maryland 53 K g
Hollywood, Washington 72 C g
Holman, New Mexico 71 M c
Holmen, Wisconsin 56 B f
Holmes, Mt., Wyoming 67 K e
Holmes, New York 50 F c
Holmwood, Louisiana 63 K h
Holopaw, Florida 55 N e
Holstein, Iowa 61 J b
Holstein, Nebraska 60 F d
Holston Mt., Tennessee 55 J a
Holston R., Tennessee-Virginia 54 H a
Holt, Alabama 54 D d
Holt, Florida 54 E g
Holt, Michigan 56 J g
Holt, Minnesota 59 K b
Holt Cr., Nebraska 60 E b
Holter L., Montana 66 J c
Holton, Indiana 57 H k
Holton, Kansas 61 J e
Holton, Michigan 56 H f
Holtville, California 75 K m
Holvaloa, Hawaii 72 E f
Holy Cross, Alaska 76 H e
Holy Cross, Mt. of the, Colorado 69 K d
Holyoke, Colorado 69 O c
Holyoke, Massachusetts (52,689) 51 H a
Holyrood, Kansas 60 F f
Homedale, Idaho 66 D f
Homeland, Georgia 55 J g
Homer, Alaska 76 M g
Homer, Illinois 57 F j
Homer, Louisiana 63 K f
Homer, Michigan 57 J g
Homer, New York 53 K c
Homer City, Pennsylvania 52 G e
Homerville, Georgia 55 J f
Homestead, Florida 55 O h
Homestead, Iowa 61 N c
Homestead, Montana 67 Q a
Homestead, Oklahoma 62 E b
Homestead, Oregon 73 O k
Homestead, Pennsylvania 53 Q b
Homestead Nat. Mon., Nebraska 60 H d
Homewood, Alabama 54 E d
Hominy, Oklahoma 62 G b
Hominy R., Oklahoma 62 G b
Homochitto R., Mississippi 63 M g
Homosassa, Florida 55 J j
Homosassa Is., Florida 55 J j
Honcut, California 74 D e
Hondo, New Mexico 71 M f
Hondo, Texas 65 H f
Honea Path, South Carolina 55 J c
Honesdale, Pennsylvania 53 L d
Honey Brook, Pennsylvania 50 B e
Honeydew, California 74 A d
Honeyford, North Dakota 58 J b
Honey Grove, Texas 65 M b
Honey Island, Texas 65 N e
Honey L., California 74 E d
Honokaa, Hawaii 72 E e
Honokahua, Hawaii 72 D e
Honokokau, Hawaii 72 D d
Honolulu, Hawaii (294,194) 72 C d
Honomu, Hawaii 72 E f
Honuapo, Hawaii 72 E f
Hood, Mt., Oregon 73 J k
Hood Bay, Alaska 77 U h
Hood Can., Washington 72 A h
Hood River, Oregon 73 J k
Hoodsport, Washington 73 G h
Hookena, Hawaii 72 E f
Hooker, Oklahoma 62 B b
Hooks, Texas 65 N b
Hookset, New Hampshire 49 D e
Hoolehua, Hawaii 72 D d
Hoonah, Alaska 77 U g
Hoopa, California 74 B c
Hooper, Colorado 69 L f
Hooper, Nebraska 60 H c
Hooper, Utah 68 D b
Hooper, Washington 73 M j
Hooper B., Alaska 76 D f
Hooper Bay, Alaska 76 D f
Hooper I., Maryland 53 K g
Hoopeston, Illinois 57 F j
Hoople, North Dakota 58 J b
Hoosick Falls, New York 53 N c
Hoover, South Dakota 58 C e
Hoover Dam, Nevada-Arizona 75 L h
Hoover Res., Ohio 52 D e
Hooversville, Pennsylvania 52 H e
Hopatcong, L., New Jersey 50 D d
Hopatcong, New Jersey 50 D d
Hop Bottom, Pennsylvania 53 L d
Hope, Alaska 76 N f
Hope, Arizona 70 D f
Hope, Arkansas 63 K e
Hope, Indiana 57 H k
Hope, Kansas 60 G f
Hope, Maryland 53 A g
Hope, New Jersey 50 D d
Hope, New Mexico 71 N g
Hope, North Dakota 58 J c
Hope, Rhode Island 51 K b
Hopedale, Massachusetts 51 K a
Hope Mills, North Carolina 55 N c
Hope Valley, Rhode Island 51 K b
Hope Villa, Louisiana 63 M h
Hopewell, New Jersey 50 D e
Hopewell, Pennsylvania 52 H e
Hopewell, Virginia 53 J h
Hopewell Junction, New York 50 F b
Hopi Buttes, Arizona 70 G d
Hopkins, Michigan 56 H g
Hopkins, Minnesota 59 P j
Hopkins, Missouri 61 K d
Hopkinsville, Kentucky 57 F n
Hopkinton, Massachusetts 51 K a
Hopkinton, Rhode Island 51 K c
Hopland, California 74 B f
Hopwood, Pennsylvania 52 G f
Hoquiam, Washington 73 G j
Horace, Kansas 60 C f
Horatio, Arkansas 63 J e
Hords Creek Res., Texas 65 H d
Horicon, Wisconsin 56 E f
Hornbeck, Louisiana 63 K g
Hornbrook, California 74 C c
Hornell, New York 52 J c
Hornerstown, New Jersey 50 D e
Hornersville, Missouri 61 O h
Horn I., Mississippi 63 P h
Horn Mts., Alaska 76 H f
Hornsby, Tennessee 54 C b
Horse Branch, Kentucky 57 G m
Horse Cave, Kentucky 57 H m
Horse Cr., Colorado 69 N e
Horse Cr., Missouri 61 L g
Horse Cr., Wyoming 67 Q h
Horse Creek, Wyoming 67 P h
Horsehead L., North Dakota 58 G c
Horseheads, New York 53 K c
Horse L., California 74 E d
Horseneck Beach, Massachusetts 51 M b
Horseshoe, Florida 54 H h
Horse Shoe Bend, Idaho 66 D f
Horseshoe L., Illinois 61 Q d
Horseshoe Res., Arizona 70 F e
Horse Springs, New Mexico 71 J f
Horsham, Pennsylvania 50 C e
Hortense, Georgia 55 K f
Horton, Kansas 61 J e
Horton, New York 50 C b
Hortonville, New York 50 C b
Hosford, Florida 54 G g
Hoskins, Nebraska 60 G b
Hosmer, South Dakota 58 G e
Hosta Butte, New Mexico 71 J d
Hotchkiss, Colorado 69 J e
Hot Creek Ra., Nevada 74 J f
Hotham Inlet, Alaska 76 F c
Hot Springs, Arkansas (28,337), vicinity of Little Rock
Hot Springs, Montana 66 F b
Hot Springs, North Carolina 55 J b
Hot Springs, South Dakota 58 C g
Hot Springs, Texas 64 D f
Hot Springs, Virginia 52 G h
Hot Springs Nat. Park, Arkansas 63 K d
Hot Sulphur Springs, Colorado 69 K c
Hot Wells, Texas 64 B d
Hough, Oklahoma 62 B b
Houghton, Michigan 56 E b
Houghton, New York 52 H c
Houghton, South Dakota 58 H e
Houghton L., Michigan 56 J e
Houlka, Mississippi 63 O d
Houlton, Maine 49 H b
Houma, Louisiana 63 N j
Housatonic, Massachusetts 50 G a
Housatonic R., Connecticut 50 G c
Housatonic R., Massachusetts 50 G a
House, New Mexico 71 O e
House Ra., Utah 68 C d
Houston, Delaware 50 B h
Houston, L., Texas 65 M e
Houston, Minnesota 59 P g
Houston, Mississippi 63 O e
Houston, Missouri 61 N g
Houston, Texas (938,219) 65 M f
Houston Heights, Texas 64 F h
Houstonia, Missouri 61 L f
Houston R., Louisiana 63 K h
Houtzdale, Pennsylvania 52 H e
Hoven, North Dakota 58 G e
Hovenweep Nat. Mon., Utah 68 G f
Hovland, Minnesota 59 R c
Howard, Kansas 60 H g
Howard, Ohio 52 D e
Howard, Pennsylvania 52 J d
Howard, South Dakota 58 J f
Howard City, Michigan 56 H f
Howard Cr., Texas 64 F e
Howard Lake, Minnesota 59 M e
Howard Pass, Alaska 76 J b
Howards Grove, Wisconsin 56 F f
Howe, Idaho 66 G f
Howe, Indiana 57 H h
Howe, Oklahoma 63 J d
Howe, Texas 65 L b
Howell, Michigan 56 K g
Howell, Utah 68 D b
Howells, Nebraska 60 G c
Howells, New York 50 E c
Howes, South Dakota 58 D f
Howland, Maine 49 G c
Hoxie, Arkansas 63 N b
Hoxie, Kansas 60 D e
Hoyleton, Illinois 57 D l
Hoyt, Kansas 61 J e
Hoyt Pk., Utah 68 E c
Hualalei Mt., Hawaii 72 E f
Hualpai Mts., Arizona 70 D e
Hubbard, Iowa 61 L b
Hubbard, Texas 65 L d
Hubbard L., Michigan 56 K e
Hubbard Lake, Michigan 56 K e
Hubbell, Nebraska 60 G d
Hudson, Colorado 69 M c
Hudson, Florida 55 M e
Hudson, Illinois 57 D j
Hudson, Indiana 57 H h
Hudson, Iowa 61 M b
Hudson, Kansas 60 F f
Hudson, Michigan 57 J h
Hudson, New Hampshire 49 D f
Hudson, New York 50 F a
Hudson, Ohio 52 E d
Hudson, South Dakota 59 K g
Hudson, Wisconsin 56 A d
Hudson, Wyoming 67 M g
Hudson Falls, New York 53 N b
Hudson Highlands, New York 50 E c
Hudson R., New York 50 F c
Hudsonville, Michigan 56 H g
Hueco Mts., Texas 64 A d
Huerfano R., Colorado 69 M e
Huff, North Dakota 58 F d
Huffton, South Dakota 58 H e
Huggins I., Alaska 76 K d
Hugh Butler L., Nebraska 60 D d
Hughes, Alaska 76 L c
Hughes, Arkansas 63 N d
Hughes Springs, Texas 65 N c
Hughesville, Missouri 61 L f
Hughsonville, New York 50 F b
Hugo, Colorado 69 N d
Hugo, Minnesota 59 N e
Hugo, Oklahoma 62 H d
Hugo, Oregon 73 G n
Hugo Res., Oklahoma 62 H d
Hugoton, Kansas 60 C g
Huguenot, New York 50 D c
Hulah, Oklahoma 62 G b
Hulah Res., Oklahoma 62 G b
Hulett, Wyoming 67 Q e
Hull, Illinois 57 B k
Hull, Iowa 61 H a
Hull, Massachusetts 51 M a
Hull, North Dakota 58 F d
Hull, Texas 65 N e
Humansville, Missouri 61 L g
Humbird, Wisconsin 56 C e
Humble, Texas 65 M f
Humble City, New Mexico 71 O g
Humboldt, Arizona 70 E e
Humboldt, Illinois 57 E k
Humboldt, Iowa 61 K b
Humboldt, Kansas 61 J g
Humboldt, Nebraska 61 J d
Humboldt, Nevada 74 G d
Humboldt, Tennessee 54 C b
Humboldt B., California 74 A d
Humboldt L., Nevada 74 G e
Humboldt R., Nevada 74 K d
Humboldt Ra., Nevada 74 G d
Humboldt Salt Marsh, Nevada 74 H e
Hume, Virginia 52 H g
Humeston, Iowa 61 L d
Hummelstown, Pennsylvania 53 K e
Humphrey, Arkansas 63 M d
Humphrey, Idaho 66 H e
Humphrey, Nebraska 60 G c
Humphrey, Washington 73 J h
Humphreys, California 75 F h
Humphreys, Missouri 61 L d
Humphreys, Mt., California 75 G g
Humphreys Pk., Arizona 70 F d
Humphreysville, New York 50 F a
Humptulips, Washington 73 G h
Hungerford, Texas 65 L f
Hungry Horse Dam, Montana 66 F a
Hungry Horse Res., Montana 66 G a
Hunnewell, Missouri 61 N e
Hunt, Texas 65 H e
Hunter, Arkansas 63 M c
Hunter, Kansas 60 F e
Hunter, Mt., Alaska 76 M e
Hunter, Mt., New York 50 E a
Hunter, New York 50 E a
Hunter, North Dakota 58 J c
Hunter, Oklahoma 62 F b
Hunter, Texas 65 J f
Hunters, Washington 73 M g
Hunters Point, California 75 B m
Hunterstown, Indiana 57 H h
Huntersville, North Carolina 55 L b
Huntersville, West Virginia 52 F g
Huntingburg, Indiana 57 F l
Huntingdon, Pennsylvania 52 J e
Huntingdon, Tennessee 54 C a
Hunting I., South Carolina 55 L e
Huntington, Indiana 57 H j
Huntington, Massachusetts 51 H a
Huntington, New York 50 G d
Huntington, Oregon 73 N l
Huntington, Texas 65 N d
Huntington, Utah 68 F d
Huntington, West Virginia (83,627) 52 D g
Huntington B., New York 50 G d
Huntington Beach, California 75 G l
Huntington L., California 75 F g
Huntington Park, California (29,920) 75 E l
Huntley, Montana 67 M d
Huntley, Nebraska 60 E d
Huntley, Wyoming 67 Q h
Hunts Mt., Wyoming 67 N e
Huntsville, Alabama (72,365) 54 E c
Huntsville, Arkansas 63 K b
Huntsville, Missouri 61 M e
Huntsville, Texas 65 M e
Huntsville, Utah 68 E b
Hurdland, Missouri 61 M d
Hurdsfield, North Dakota 58 G c
Hurley, Mississippi 63 P h
Hurley, New Mexico 71 J g
Hurley, New York 50 E b
Hurley, South Dakota 58 J g
Hurley, Wisconsin 56 C c
Hurleyville, New York 50 D b
Hurlock, Maryland 53 L g
Huron, California 75 E h
Huron, Kansas 61 J e
Huron, L., United States-Canada 47 K b
Huron, Ohio 52 D d
Huron, South Dakota 58 H f
Huron B., Michigan 56 E b
Huron City, Michigan 56 L e
Huron Mts., Michigan 56 F c
Hurricane, Utah 68 C f
Hurricane, West Virginia 52 D g
Hurricane Cr., Georgia 55 J f
Hurricane Mills, Tennessee 54 D b
Hurst, Texas 65 M j
Hurtsboro, Alabama 54 F e
Huslia, Alaska 76 J d
Huslia R., Alaska 76 J d
Huson, Montana 66 F b
Hutch, Mt., Arizona 70 F e
Hutchins, Texas 65 O k
Hutchinson, Kansas (37,574) 60 G f
Hutchinson, Minnesota 59 M f
Hutchinsons I., Florida 55 O f
Hutsonville, Illinois 57 F k
Huttig, Arkansas 63 L e
Hutto, Texas 65 K e
Huttonsville, West Virginia 52 F g
Huxley, Iowa 61 L c
Huxley, Mt., Alaska 77 R f
Hyalite Peak, Montana 67 K d
Hyampom, California 74 B d
Hyannis, Massachusetts 51 N b
Hyannis, Nebraska 60 C b
Hyannis Port, Massachusetts 51 N b
Hyatt Res., Oregon 73 H n
Hyattsville, Maryland 53 Q g
Hyattville, Wyoming 67 N e
Hybart, Alabama 54 D f
Hydaburg, Alaska 77 V j
Hyden, Kentucky 57 K m
Hyde Park, New York 50 E b
Hyder, Alaska 77 W j
Hyder, Arizona 70 D f
Hydro, Oklahoma 62 E c
Hye, Texas 65 J e
Hygiene, Colorado 69 L c
Hylton Res., Nevada 74 K d
Hyman, Texas 64 F c
Hymera, Indiana 57 F k
Hyndman, Pennsylvania 52 H f
Hyndman Pk., Idaho 66 F f
Hyner, Pennsylvania 52 J d
Hyrum, Utah 68 E b
Hysham, Montana 67 N c
Iaeger, West Virginia 52 E h
Iamonia, L., Florida 54 G g
Iatan, Texas 64 F c
Iatt, L., Louisiana 63 L g
Ibapah, Utah 68 C c
Iberia, Missouri 61 M f
Iceberg Canyon, Nevada-Arizona 75 L h
Ice Harbor Dam, Washington 73 M j
Icy B., Alaska 77 R g
Icy C., Alaska 76 F a
Icy Pt., Alaska 77 T g
Icy Str., Alaska 77 U g
Ida, Louisiana 63 K f
Ida, Michigan 57 K h
Idabel, Oklahoma 63 J e
Ida Grove, Iowa 61 J b
Idaho (699,000) 83,557 sq. miles 66
Idaho City, Idaho 66 E f
Idaho Falls, Idaho (33,161) 66 H f
Idaho Springs, Colorado 69 L d
Idalia, Colorado 69 O d
Idalou, Texas 64 F b
Idanha, Oregon 73 H l
Ideal, Georgia 54 G e
Iditarod, Alaska 76 H e
Iditarod R., Alaska 76 H e
Idlewild. See John F. Kennedy International Airport
Idria, California 75 E h
Igitkin I., Alaska 77 P j
Igiugig, Alaska 76 J g
Igloo, South Dakota 58 C g
Ignacio, Colorado 69 J f
Igo, California 74 C d
Igvak, C., Alaska 76 K h
Ikatan, Alaska 76 F j
Ikolik, C., Alaska 76 K h
Ikpikpuk R., Alaska 76 K a
Ilak I., Alaska 77 N j
Iliamna, Alaska 76 K g
Iliamna L., Alaska 76 K g
Iliamna Vol., Alaska 76 L f
Iliff, Colorado 69 N c
Ilion, New York 53 L b
Ilio Pt., Hawaii 72 D d
Ilivit Mts., Alaska 76 G e
Illinois (10,894,000) 56,400 sq. miles 56-57
Illinois & Mississippi Can., Illinois 57 D h
Illinois R., Illinois 57 D j
Illinois R., Oklahoma 63 J b
Illinois R., Oregon 73 G n
Illiopolis, Illinois 57 D k
Illmo, Missouri 61 P g
Ilnik, Alaska 76 H h
Ilwaco, Washington 73 F j
Imbler, Oregon 73 N k
Imboden, Arkansas 63 M b
Imlay, Nevada 74 G d
Imlay, South Dakota 58 D g
Imlay City, Michigan 56 K f
Immaha, Oregon 73 O k
Immaha R., Oregon 73 O k
Immokalee, Florida 55 N g
Imogene, Iowa 61 J d
Imperial, California 75 K m
Imperial, Nebraska 60 C d
Imperial, Texas 64 E d
Imperial Dam, California 75 L m
Imperial Val., California 75 K m
Imuruk Basin, Alaska 76 D d
Imuruk L., Alaska 76 F d
Inadale, Texas 64 G c
Inanudak B., Alaska 76 C k
Inchelium, Washington 73 M g
Independence, California 75 G h
Independence, Iowa 61 N b
Independence, Kansas 61 J g
Independence, Louisiana 63 N h
Independence, Missouri (62,328) 61 K e
Independence, Oregon 73 G l
Independence, Virginia 52 E j
Independence, Wisconsin 56 B e
Independence Mts., Nevada 74 J c
Index, Washington 73 J h
Indiahoma, Oklahoma 62 E d
Indiana (4,999,000) 36,291 sq. miles 57
Indiana, Pennsylvania 52 G e
Indianapolis, Indiana (476,258) 57 G k
Indian Cr., Kansas 61 P b
Indian Head, Maryland 53 J g
Indian L., Michigan 56 G c
Indian L., New York 53 M b
Indian L., Ohio 52 C e
Indian Mills, New Jersey 50 D f
Indian Mt., Wyoming 67 K g
Indianola, Iowa 61 L c
Indianola, Mississippi 63 N e
Indianola, Nebraska 60 D d
Indianola, Oklahoma 62 H c
Indianola, Washington 72 B g
Indian Pk., Utah 68 C e
Indian Pk., Wyoming 67 L e
Indian R., Florida 55 L j
Indian R., Michigan 56 G c
Indian R., New York 53 L a
Indian River, Michigan 56 J d
Indian River City, Florida 55 L j
Indian Springs, Nevada 75 K h
Indian Town, Florida 55 O f
Indian Valley, Idaho 66 D e
Indian Village, Missouri 61 P b
Indian Wells, Arizona 68 F h
Indio, California 75 J l
Indrio, Florida 55 O f
Industry, Illinois 57 C j
Industry, Texas 65 L f
Inez, Texas 65 L g
Ingalls, Indiana 57 H k
Ingalls, Kansas 60 D g
Ingalls, Michigan 56 F d
Ingalls, Mt., California 74 E e
Ingersoll, Oklahoma 62 E b
Ingleside, Maryland 50 A g
Ingleside, Texas 65 K h
Inglewood, California (63,390) 75 D m
Inglutalik R., Alaska 76 G d
Ingomar, Montana 67 N c
Ingot, California 74 C d
Ingram, Pennsylvania 50 O b
Ingram, Texas 65 H e
Ingram, Wisconsin 56 C d
Iniakuk R., Alaska 76 L c
Inka, Kansas 60 F g
Inkom, Idaho 66 H g
Inkster, Michigan (39,097), vicinity of Detroit
Inkster, North Dakota 58 J b
Inland L., Alaska 76 H c
Inman, Nebraska 60 F b
Inman, New York 53 M a
Inman, South Carolina 55 J b
Inner Grove, Minnesota 59 R j
Innoko R., Alaska 76 H e
Inola, Oklahoma 62 H b
Intake, Montana 67 Q b
Interior, South Dakota 58 E g
Interlachen, Florida 55 K h
International Falls, Minnesota 59 N b
Inverness, Florida 55 J j
Inverness, Montana 67 K a
Inwood, California 74 D d
Inyan Kara Cr., Wyoming 67 Q e
Inyokern, California 75 G j
Inyo Mts., California 75 G g
Iola, Kansas 61 J g
Iola, Texas 65 L e
Iona, Idaho 66 J f
Iona, Minnesota 59 L g
Iona, South Dakota 58 G g
Ione, Nevada 74 H f
Ione, Oregon 73 L k
Ione, Washington 73 N g
Ionia, Iowa 61 M a
Ionia, Michigan 56 H g
Ionia, Missouri 61 L f
Iowa (2,753,000) 56,290 sq. miles 60-61
Iowa, Louisiana 63 K h
Iowa City, Iowa (33,443) 61 N c
Iowa Falls, Iowa 61 L b
Iowa Park, Texas 65 J b
Iowa R., Iowa 61 M c
Ipava, Illinois 57 C j
Ipewik, Alaska 76 E b
Ipswich, Massachusetts 49 E f
Ipswich, South Dakota 58 G e
Iraan, Texas 64 F e
Irasburg, Vermont 49 C d
Iredell, Texas 65 K d
Ireland, Texas 65 K d
Irene, South Dakota 58 J g
Ireton, Iowa 60 H b
Irma, Wisconsin 56 D d
Irmo, South Carolina 55 K c
Iron Canyon Res., California 74 C d
Iron City, Tennessee 54 D b
Iron Creek, Alaska 76 E d
Irondale, Missouri 61 O g
Irondale, Ohio 52 F e
Iron Mt., Michigan 56 E d
Iron Mt., Oregon 73 F n
Iron Mt., Utah 68 C f
Iron Nation, South Dakota 58 G f
Iron Ridge, Wisconsin 56 E f
Iron River, Michigan 56 E c
Iron River, Wisconsin 56 B c
Irons, Michigan 56 H e
Ironside, Oregon 73 N l
Iron Springs, Utah 68 C f
Ironton, Michigan 56 H d
Ironton, Missouri 61 O g
Ironton, Ohio 52 D g
Ironwood, Michigan 56 D c
Iroquois, South Dakota 58 J f
Iroquois R., Illinois 57 F j
Irvine, Kentucky 57 K m
Irving, Kansas 60 H e
Irving, Texas (43,985) 65 L c
Irvington, Kentucky 57 G m
Irvington, New Jersey (59,379) 51 J f
Irvington, New York 50 F c
Irvington, Virginia 53 K h
Irvona, Pennsylvania 52 H e
Irwin, Idaho 66 J f
Irwin, Iowa 61 J c
Irwin, Nebraska 60 C b
Irwinton, Georgia 54 H e
Isabel, Kansas 60 F g
Isabel, South Dakota 58 E e
Isabella, California 75 G j
Isabella, Minnesota 59 P c
Isabella Res., California 75 G j
Isabelle, Pt., Michigan 56 F b
Isbell, Alabama 54 D c
Ishpeming, Michigan 56 F c
Islamorada, Florida 55 O j

Isla UNITED STATES INDEX Key L

Island, *Kentucky* 57 F m
Island Beach, *New Jersey* 50 E f
Island City, *Oregon* 73 N k
Island Falls, *Maine* 49 G b
Island Heights, *New Jersey* 50 E f
Island Mountain, *California* 74 B d
Island Park, *Idaho* 66 J e
Island Park Res., *Idaho* 66 J e
Island Pond, *Vermont* 49 D d
Isle, *Minnesota* 59 N d
Isle au Haut, I., *Maine* 49 G d
Isle aux Pêches, *Michigan* 57 M k
Isle of Hope, *Georgia* 55 K f
Isle Royale, I., *Michigan* 56 E a
Isle Royale Nat. Pk., *Michigan* 56 E a
Islesboro, *Maine* 49 F d
Isles Dernieres, *Louisiana* 63 N j
Isleta, *New Mexico* 71 L e
Isleton, *California* 74 D f
Islip, *New York* 50 G d
Ismay, *Montana* 67 Q c
Isola, *Mississippi* 63 N e
Isoline, *Tennessee* 54 F a
Issaquah, *Washington* 72 C h
Istokpoga, L., *Florida* 55 N f
Italy, *Texas* 65 L c
Itasca, L., *Minnesota* 59 L c
Itasca, *Texas* 65 K c
Itasca State Park, *Minnesota* 59 L c
Ithaca, *Michigan* 56 J f
Ithaca, *New York* (28,799) 53 K c
Itkilik R., *Alaska* 76 M b
Itta Bena, *Mississippi* 63 N e
Itulilik, *Alaska* 76 J f
Iuka, *Illinois* 57 E l
Iva, *South Carolina* 55 J c
Ivanhoe, *Minnesota* 59 K f
Ivanhoe, *Virginia* 52 F j
Ivanpah, *California* 75 K j
Ivesdale, *Illinois* 57 E k
Ivishak R., *Alaska* 77 N b
Ivor, *Virginia* 53 K j
Ivoryton, *Connecticut* 51 J c
Ivydale, *West Virginia* 52 E g
Izaviknek R., *Alaska* 76 F f
Izigan, C., *Alaska* 76 D k
Jacinto City, *Texas* 64 G h
Jackman, *Maine* 49 E c
Jack Mt., *Pennsylvania* 52 J e
Jack Mt., *Washington* 73 K g
Jacksboro, *Tennessee* 54 G a
Jacksboro, *Texas* 65 J b
Jackson, *Alabama* 54 D f
Jackson, *California* 74 E f
Jackson, *Georgia* 54 H d
Jackson, *Kentucky* 57 K m
Jackson, L., *Florida* 54 G g
Jackson, *Louisiana* 63 M h
Jackson, *Michigan* (50,720) 57 J g
Jackson, *Minnesota* 59 L g
Jackson, *Mississippi* (144,422) 63 N f
Jackson, *Missouri* 61 P g
Jackson, *Montana* 66 G d
Jackson, *North Carolina* 55 O a
Jackson, *Ohio* 52 D f
Jackson, *South Carolina* 55 K d
Jackson, *Tennessee* (34,376) 54 C b
Jackson, *Wyoming* 67 K f
Jackson Center, *Ohio* 52 C e
Jackson Gulch Res., *Colorado* 68 H f
Jackson Heights, *New York* 51 M f
Jackson L., *Georgia* 54 H d
Jackson L., *Wyoming* 67 K f
Jackson Mts., *Nevada* 74 G c
Jacksonport, *Wisconsin* 56 F e
Jackson Prairie, *Mississippi* 63 O f
Jackson Res., *Colorado* 69 M c
Jackson R., *Virginia* 52 G g
Jacksonville, *Alabama* 54 F d
Jacksonville, *Arkansas* 63 L d
Jacksonville, *Florida* (201,030) 55 K g
Jacksonville, *Illinois* 57 D k
Jacksonville, *Missouri* 61 M e
Jacksonville, *North Carolina* 55 O c
Jacksonville, *Texas* 65 M d
Jacksonville Beach, *Florida* 55 K g
Jack Wade, *Alaska* 77 R d
Jacob Lake, *Arizona* 70 E c
Jacobstown, *New Jersey* 50 D e
Jacumba, *California* 75 J m
Jadito Canyon, *Arizona* 70 G d
Jago R., *Alaska* 77 Q b
Jal, *New Mexico* 71 O g
Jamaica, *New York* 50 F d
Jamaica, *Vermont* 49 C e
Jamaica B., *New York* 51 M g
James, L., *North Carolina* 55 K b
Jamesburg, *New Jersey* 50 E e
James City, *Pennsylvania* 52 H d
Jameson, *Missouri* 61 L d
Jamesport, *Missouri* 61 L e
Jamesport, *New York* 51 H d
James R., *Missouri* 61 L h
James R., *North-South Dakota* 58 J g
James R., *Virginia* 53 K h
Jamestown, *Indiana* 57 G k
Jamestown, *Kansas* 60 G e
Jamestown, *Michigan* 56 H g
Jamestown, *New York* (41,818) 52 G c
Jamestown, *North Dakota* 58 H d
Jamestown, *Ohio* 52 C f
Jamestown, *Pennsylvania* 52 F d
Jamestown, *Rhode Island* 51 L b
Jamestown, *South Carolina* 55 M d
Jamestown, *Tennessee* 54 G a
Jamestown Nat. Hist. Site, *Virginia* 53 K h
Jamestown Res., *North Dakota* 58 H c
Jamesville, *New York* 53 K c
Jamesville, *North Carolina* 55 P b
Jamieson, *Oregon* 73 N l
Jamison, *Nebraska* 60 E b
Jamul, *California* 75 J m
Jane Lew, *West Virginia* 52 F f
Janesville, *California* 74 E d
Janesville, *Iowa* 61 M b
Janesville, *Minnesota* 59 N f
Janesville, *Wisconsin* (35,164) 56 D g
Jansen, *Nebraska* 60 G d
Jansen Kill, *New York* 50 F a
Jarbridge, *Nevada* 74 K c
Jarbridge R., *Idaho* 66 E g
Jaroso, *Colorado* 69 L f
Jarratt, *Virginia* 52 J j
Jarrell, *Texas* 65 K e
Jasonville, *Indiana* 57 F k
Jasper, *Alabama* 54 D d
Jasper, *Arkansas* 63 K c
Jasper, *Colorado* 69 K f
Jasper, *Florida* 55 J g
Jasper, *Georgia* 54 G c
Jasper, *Indiana* 57 G l
Jasper, *Michigan* 57 J h
Jasper, *Minnesota* 59 K g
Jasper, *Missouri* 61 K g
Jasper, *New York* 52 J c
Jasper, *Tennessee* 54 F b
Jasper, *Texas* 65 O e
Jay, *Oklahoma* 63 J b
Jay Em, *Wyoming* 67 Q g
Jayton, *Texas* 64 G b
Jean, *Nevada* 75 K j
Jean, *Texas* 65 J b
Jeanerette, *Louisiana* 63 M j
Jeannette, *Pennsylvania* 52 G e
Jeddo, *Michigan* 56 L f
Jeffers, *Minnesota* 59 L f
Jefferson, *Colorado* 69 L d
Jefferson, *Georgia* 54 H c
Jefferson, *Iowa* 61 K b
Jefferson, *Maryland* 52 J f
Jefferson, Mt., *Nevada* 74 J f
Jefferson, Mt., *Oregon* 73 J l
Jefferson, *Ohio* 52 F d
Jefferson, *Oklahoma* 62 F b
Jefferson, *Oregon* 73 H l
Jefferson, *South Dakota* 59 K h
Jefferson, *Texas* 65 N c
Jefferson, *Wisconsin* 56 E f
Jefferson City, *Missouri* (28,228) 61 M f
Jefferson City, *Montana* 66 H c
Jefferson City, *Tennessee* 54 H a
Jefferson Island, *Montana* 66 J d
Jeffersontown, *Kentucky* 57 H l
Jeffersonville, *Georgia* 54 H e
Jeffersonville, *New York* 50 D b
Jeffersonville, *Ohio* 52 C f
Jeffersonville, *Vermont* 49 C d
Jekyll I., *Georgia* 55 K f
Jellico, *Tennessee* 54 G a
Jelly, *California* 74 C d
Jemez Pueblo, *New Mexico* 71 L d
Jemez R., *New Mexico* 71 L d
Jemez Springs, *New Mexico* 71 L d
Jena, *Louisiana* 63 L g
Jenkinjones, *West Virginia* 52 E h
Jenkins, *Minnesota* 59 M d
Jenkins, *New Jersey* 50 D f
Jenkintown, *Pennsylvania* 50 C e
Jenner, *California* 74 B f
Jennings, *Florida* 54 H g
Jennings, *Kansas* 60 D e
Jennings, *Louisiana* 63 L h
Jennings, *Montana* 66 E a
Jennings, *Oklahoma* 62 G b
Jennyjump Mt., *New Jersey* 50 D d
Jensen, *Utah* 68 G c
Jensen Beach, *Florida* 55 O f
Jerome, *Arizona* 70 E e
Jerome, *Idaho* 66 F g
Jersey City, *New Jersey* (276,101) 50 E d
Jersey Shore, *Pennsylvania* 52 J d
Jersey Village, *Texas* 64 E h
Jerseyville, *Illinois* 57 C k
Jessamine Creek Res., *Kentucky* 57 J m
Jessie, *North Dakota* 58 H c
Jessup, L., *Florida* 55 K j
Jesup, *Georgia* 55 K f
Jesup, *Iowa* 61 M b
Jet, *Oklahoma* 62 E b
Jetersville, *Virginia* 52 H h
Jetmore, *Kansas* 60 E f
Jewel Cave Nat. Mon., *South Dakota* 58 C g
Jewell, *Iowa* 61 L b
Jewell, *Kansas* 60 F e
Jewell, *Oregon* 73 G k
Jewett, *Illinois* 57 E k
Jewett, *New York* 50 E a
Jewett, *Ohio* 52 F e
Jewett, *Texas* 65 L d
Jewitt City, *Connecticut* 51 K b
Jiggs, *Nevada* 74 K d
Jim R., *Alaska* 76 M c
Jim Thorpe, *Pennsylvania* 50 B d
Joanna, *Pennsylvania* 50 B e
Joaquin, *Texas* 65 N d
Job Pk., *Nevada* 74 G e
Jobstown, *New Jersey* 50 D e
Joes, *Colorado* 69 O d
Joffre, *New Mexico* 71 M e
Johannesburg, *California* 75 H j
Johannesburg, *Michigan* 56 J e
John Day, *Oregon* 73 M l
John Day Dam, *Oregon* 73 K k
John Day R., *Oregon* 73 K k
John F. Kennedy International Airport, *New York* 51 N g
John F. Kennedy Space Center, *Florida* 55 O e
John H. Kerr Res., *Virginia* 52 H j
John Martin Res., *Colorado* 69 O e
John R., *Alaska* 76 L c
John Redmond Res., *Kansas* 61 J f
Johnson, *Kansas* 60 C g
Johnson, *Nebraska* 61 H d
Johnson, *New York* 50 E c
Johnsonburg, *Pennsylvania* 52 H d
Johnson City, *New York* 53 L c
Johnson City, *Tennessee* (31,187) 55 J a
Johnson City, *Texas* 65 J e
Johnson Creek, *Wisconsin* 56 E f
Johnsonville, *South Carolina* 55 M d
Johnston, *South Carolina* 55 K d
Johnston City, *Illinois* 57 E m
Johnstown, *Nebraska* 60 D b
Johnstown, *New York* 53 M b
Johnstown, *Ohio* 52 D e
Johnstown, *Pennsylvania* (53,949) 52 H e
Joiner, *Arkansas* 63 N c
Joliet, *Illinois* (66,780) 57 E h
Joliet, *Montana* 67 L d
Joliette, *North Dakota* 58 J b
Jolley, *Iowa* 61 K b
Jolon, *California* 75 D j
Jones, *Oklahoma* 62 F c
Jones Beach State Park, *New York* 50 G d
Jonesboro, *Arkansas* 63 N c
Jonesboro, *Georgia* 54 G d
Jonesboro, *Illinois* 57 D m
Jonesboro, *Louisiana* 63 L f
Jonesboro, *Maine* 49 H d
Jonesboro, *North Carolina* 55 M b
Jonesboro, *Tennessee* 55 J a
Jonesboro, *Texas* 65 K d
Jones Is., *Alaska* 76 N a
Jonesport, *Maine* 49 H d
Jonestown, *Mississippi* 63 N d
Jonesville, *Alaska* 76 N f
Jonesville, *Indiana* 57 H k
Jonesville, *Louisiana* 63 M g
Jonesville, *Michigan* 57 J g
Jonesville, *South Carolina* 55 K c
Jonesville, *Virginia* 52 C j
Joplin, *Missouri* (38,958) 61 K g
Joplin, *Montana* 67 K a
Joppa, *Illinois* 57 E m
Jordan, *Minnesota* 59 N f
Jordan, *Montana* 67 O b
Jordan, *New York* 53 K b
Jordan L., *Alabama* 54 E e
Jordan R., *Oregon* 73 N n
Jordan R., *Utah* 68 C j
Jordan Valley, *Oregon* 73 N n
Jornada del Muerto, mts., *New Mexico* 71 K f
Joseph, *Idaho* 66 D d
Joseph, *Oregon* 73 N k
Joseph City, *Arizona* 70 G e
Joseph R., *Oregon* 73 N k
Joshua, *Texas* 65 K c
Joshua Tree, *California* 75 J k
Joshua Tree Nat. Mon., *California* 75 J k
Jourdanton, *Texas* 65 J g
Jualin, *Alaska* 77 U g
Juan, *Texas* 65 J j
Juan de Fuca, Str. of, *United States-Canada* 73 F g
Juanita, *Washington* 72 C h
Jubilee Pass, *California* 75 J j
Jud, *North Dakota* 58 H d
Juda, *Wisconsin* 56 D g
Judith, Pt., *Rhode Island* 51 L c
Judith Basin, *Montana* 67 K b
Judith Gap, *Montana* 67 L c
Judith R., *Montana* 67 L b
Judson, *North Dakota* 58 E d
Julesburg, *Colorado* 69 O c
Juliaetta, *Idaho* 66 D c
Julian, *California* 75 J l
Julius, *Alaska* 76 N d
Junction, *Texas* 65 H e
Junction, *Utah* 68 D e
Junction City, *Arkansas* 63 L e
Junction City, *Georgia* 54 G e
Junction City, *Kansas* 60 H e
Junction City, *Kentucky* 57 J m
Junction City, *Oregon* 73 G l
Junction City, *Wisconsin* 56 C e
Juneau, *Alaska* 77 U g
Juneau, *Wisconsin* 56 E f
June in Winter, L., *Florida* 55 N f
June L., *California* 74 F g
Jungo, *Nevada* 74 G d
Juniata, *Nebraska* 60 F d
Juniata R., *Pennsylvania* 53 J e
Junior, *West Virginia* 52 G g
Junior L., *Maine* 49 G c
Juniper Mts., *Arizona* 70 D d
Junipero Serra Pk., *California* 75 D h
Junjik R., *Alaska* 77 O b
Juno, *Texas* 64 F e
Juntura, *Oregon* 73 M m
Jupiter, *Florida* 55 O g
Justiceburg, *Texas* 64 F b
Justin, *Texas* 65 K b
Kaalualu, *Hawaii* 72 E f
Kabetogama, *Minnesota* 59 N b
Kabetogama L., *Minnesota* 59 N b
Kachemak B., *Alaska* 76 M g
Kachess L., *Washington* 73 J h
Kadoka, *South Dakota* 58 E g
Kaea, C., *Hawaii* 72 D e
Kaena Pt., I. of Lanai, *Hawaii* 72 D e
Kaena Pt., I. of Oahu, *Hawaii* 72 C d
Kagalaska I., *Alaska* 77 P j
Kagamil I., *Alaska* 77 T h
Kagati L., *Alaska* 76 G g
Kaguyak, *Alaska* 76 L h
Kahala Pt., *Hawaii* 72 B c
Kahaluu, *Hawaii* 72 C d
Kahiltna Glacier, *Alaska* 76 M e
Kahlotus, *Washington* 73 M j
Kahoka, *Missouri* 61 N d
Kahoolawe, I., *Hawaii* 72 D e
Kahua, *Hawaii* 72 E e
Kahuku, *Hawaii* 72 C d
Kahuku Pt., *Hawaii* 72 C d
Kahului *Hawaii* 72 D e
Kaibab Cr., *Arizona* 70 E c
Kaibib Plateau, *Arizona* 70 E c
Kaibito Plateau, *Arizona* 70 F c
Kailua, *Hawaii* 72 D f
Kailua-Lanikai, *Hawaii* (25,622) 72 C d
Kainaliu, *Hawaii* 72 E f
Kaiparowits Plateau, *Utah* 68 E f
Kaiser Pk., *California* 75 F g
Kaiwi Chan., *Hawaii* 72 C d
Kaiyuh Mts., *Alaska* 76 H e
Kaka, *Arizona* 70 E g
Kaka Pt., *Hawaii* 72 D e
Kakatovik, *Alaska* 77 Q a
Kake, *Alaska* 77 V h
Kakhonak, *Alaska* 76 K g
Kakhonak L., *Alaska* 76 K g
Ka Lae (South C.), *Hawaii* 72 E f
Kalalau, *Hawaii* 72 B c
Kalama, *Washington* 73 H j
Kalama R., *Washington* 73 H j
Kalamazoo, *Michigan* (82,089) 57 H g
Kalamazoo R., *Michigan* 56 H g
Kalaupapa, *Hawaii* 72 D d
Kalawao (Leper Colony), *Hawaii* 72 D d
Kaleva, *Michigan* 56 G e
Kalgary, *Texas* 64 F b
Kalgin I., *Alaska* 76 M f
Kalida, *Ohio* 52 B e
Kalispell, *Montana* 66 F a
Kalkaska, *Michigan* 56 H e
Kalona, *Iowa* 61 N c
Kaloni Chan., *Hawaii* 72 D e
Kalska, *Alaska* 76 G f
Kaltag, *Alaska* 76 H d
Kamakou, Mt., *Hawaii* 72 D d
Kamalino, *Hawaii* 72 A d
Kamalo, *Hawaii* 72 D d
Kamas, *Utah* 68 E c
Kamela, *Oregon* 73 M k
Kamiah, *Idaho* 66 E c
Kamishak B., *Alaska* 76 K g
Kamrar, *Iowa* 61 L b
Kanab, *Utah* 68 D f
Kanaga I., *Alaska* 77 O j
Kanakanak, *Alaska* 76 H g
Kanarraville, *Utah* 68 C f
Kanatak, *Alaska* 76 K h
Kanawha, *Iowa* 61 L b
Kanawha, *Texas* 65 M b
Kanawha R., *West Virginia* 52 D g
Kandik R., *Alaska* 77 R d
Kane, *Illinois* 57 C k
Kane, *Pennsylvania* 52 H d
Kane, *Wyoming* 67 M e
Kanektok R., *Alaska* 76 G g
Kaneohe, *Hawaii* 72 C d
Kangik, *Alaska* 76 H a
Kankakee, *Illinois* (27,666) 57 F h
Kankakee R., *Illinois* 57 E h
Kannapolis, *North Carolina* (34,647) 55 L b
Kanona, *Kansas* 60 D e
Kanopolis, *Kansas* 60 F f
Kanorado, *Colorado* 69 O d
Kanorado, *Kansas* 60 C e
Kanosh, *Utah* 68 D e
Kansas (2,275,000) 82,264 sq. miles 60-61
Kansas, *Illinois* 57 F k
Kansas, *Oklahoma* 63 J b
Kansas City, *Kansas* (121,901) 61 K e
Kansas City, *Missouri* (475,539) 61 K e
Kansas R., *Kansas* 61 J e
Kantishna, *Alaska* 76 M e
Kantishna R., *Alaska* 76 M d
Kanuti R., *Alaska* 76 M c
Kapaa, *Hawaii* 72 B c
Kapaau-Halaula, *Hawaii* 72 E e
Kaplan, *Louisiana* 63 L j
Kapoho, *Hawaii* 72 E f
Karlsruhe, *North Dakota* 58 F b
Karlstad, *Minnesota* 59 K b
Karluk, *Alaska* 76 K h
Karluk L., *Alaska* 76 K h
Karnack, *Texas* 65 N c
Karnak, *Illinois* 57 E m
Karnes City, *Texas* 65 K g
Karthaus, *Pennsylvania* 52 H d
Karval, *Colorado* 69 N e
Kasatochi I., *Alaska* 77 P j
Kasegaluk Lagoon, *Alaska* 76 F a
Kashega, *Alaska* 76 D k
Kashegelok, *Alaska* 76 J f
Kasiglook, *Alaska* 76 F f
Kasilof, *Alaska* 76 M f
Kaskaskia R., *Illinois* 57 D k
Kasson, *Minnesota* 59 O f
Katahdin, Mt., *Maine* 49 G c
Katakturak R., *Alaska* 77 P b
Katalla, *Alaska* 77 P f
Kateel R., *Alaska* 76 H d
Kathleen, *Florida* 55 M e
Kathryn, *North Dakota* 58 H d
Katmai, Mt., *Alaska* 76 K g
Katmai B., *Alaska* 76 K h
Katmai Nat. Mon., *Alaska* 76 K g
Katonah, *New York* 50 F c
Kauai, I., *Hawaii* 72 B d
Kauai Chan., *Hawaii* 72 B d
Kau Des., *Hawaii* 72 E f
Kaufman, *Texas* 65 L c
Kau I., *Alaska* 77 U h
Kauiki Hd., *Hawaii* 72 D e
Kaukauna, *Wisconsin* 56 E e
Kaula, I., *Hawaii* 72 D b
Kauluoa Pt., *Hawaii* 72 E f
Kaumakani, *Hawaii* 72 B d
Kaunakakai, *Hawaii* 72 D d
Kauna Pt., *Hawaii* 72 E f
Kavalga I., *Alaska* 77 N j
Kavik R., *Alaska* 77 O b
Kawaihae, *Hawaii* 72 E e
Kawaihoa Pt., *Hawaii* 72 A d
Kawaikini, Mt., *Hawaii* 72 B c
Kaw City, *Oklahoma* 62 G b
Kaweah R., *California* 75 F h
Kawich Ra., *Nevada* 74 J g
Kayak I., *Alaska* 77 P g
Kaycee, *Wyoming* 67 O f
Kayenta, *Arizona* 70 G c
Kayford, *West Virginia* 52 E g
Kaysville, *Utah* 68 E b
Keaau, *Hawaii* 72 E f
Keahole Pt., *Hawaii* 72 D f
Kealaikahiki Chan., *Hawaii* 72 D e
Kealaikahiki Pt., *Hawaii* 72 D e
Kealakekua, *Hawaii* 72 E f
Kealia, I. of Hawaii, *Hawaii* 72 E f
Kealia, I. of Kauai, *Hawaii* 72 B c
Keams Canyon, *Arizona* 70 G d
Keamuku, *Hawaii* 72 E f
Keansburg, *New Jersey* 50 E e
Kearns, *Utah* 68 B j
Kearny, *New Jersey* (37,472) 51 K f
Kearsarge Pass, *California* 75 G h
Keetchie, *Louisiana* 63 K f
Keating, *Oregon* 73 N l
Keating, *Pennsylvania* 52 H d
Keatons Beach, *Florida* 54 H h
Keddie, *California* 74 E d
Kedron, *Arkansas* 63 L d
Keeler, *California* 75 H h
Keene, *California* 75 G j
Keene, *New Hampshire* 49 C f
Keene, *New York* 53 N a
Keener, *Alabama* 54 F c
Keensburg, *Colorado* 69 M c
Keeseville, *New York* 53 N a
Keewatin, *Minnesota* 59 N c
Keithsburg, *Illinois* 57 C h
Keithville, *Louisiana* 63 K f
Kekaha, *Hawaii* 72 B d
Kelford, *North Carolina* 55 O a
Kelim, *Colorado* 69 M c
Keller, *Texas* 65 M h
Keller, *Virginia* 53 L h
Keller, *Washington* 73 M g
Kellerton, *Iowa* 61 K d
Kellettville, *Pennsylvania* 52 G d
Kelleys I., *Ohio* 52 D d
Kelliher, *Minnesota* 59 M c
Kellogg, *Idaho* 66 D b
Kellogg, *Iowa* 61 M c
Kelly, *Kentucky* 57 F n
Kelly, *Louisiana* 63 L g
Kelly, *Wyoming* 67 K f
Kelly R., *Alaska* 76 F b
Kelseyville, *California* 74 C f
Kelso, *California* 75 K j
Kelso, *North Dakota* 58 J c
Kelso, *Washington* 73 H j
Kelton, *Utah* 68 C b
Keltys, *Texas* 65 N d
Kelvin, *Arizona* 70 G f
Kemblesville, *Pennsylvania* 50 B f
Kemmerer, *Wyoming* 67 K h
Kemp, *Texas* 65 L c
Kemp, L., *Texas* 65 H b
Kempner, *Texas* 65 K d
Kempton, *Illinois* 57 E j
Kempton, *North Dakota* 58 J c
Kenai, *Alaska* 76 M f
Kenai L., *Alaska* 66 N f
Kenai Mts., *Alaska* 76 M g
Kenai Pen., *Alaska* 66 N f
Kenansville, *Florida* 55 O f
Kenbridge, *Virginia* 52 H j
Kendall, *Florida* 54 A e
Kendall, *Kansas* 60 C g
Kendall, *New York* 52 H b
Kendallville, *Indiana* 57 H h
Kendrick, *Idaho* 66 D c
Kendrick Pk., *Arizona* 70 F d
Kenedy, *Texas* 65 K g
Kenefick, *Oklahoma* 62 G d
Kenel, *South Dakota* 58 F e
Kenesaw, *Nebraska* 60 F d
Kenibuna L., *Alaska* 76 L f
Kenly, *North Carolina* 55 N b
Kenmare, *North Dakota* 58 E b
Kenmore, *Washington* 72 B g
Kenna, *New Mexico* 71 O f
Kenna, *West Virginia* 52 E g
Kennebago L., *Maine* 49 E c
Kennebec, *South Dakota* 58 G g
Kennebec R., *Maine* 49 F d
Kennebunk, *Maine* 49 E e
Kennebunkport, *Maine* 49 E e
Kennedy, C., *Florida* 55 L j
Kennedy, *Minnesota* 59 K b
Kennedy, *Nebraska* 60 D b
Kennedy, *New York* 52 G c
Kennedyville, *Maryland* 50 A g
Kennendale, *Texas* 65 L k
Kenner, *Louisiana* 62 A e
Kennesaw Mountain Nat. Batt. Park, *Georgia* 54 G d
Kennett, *Missouri* 61 O h
Kennett Square, *Pennsylvania* 50 B f
Kennewick, *Washington* 73 L j
Kenney, *Illinois* 57 D j
Kenney, *Texas* 65 L e
Kennydale, *Washington* 72 C h
Keno, *Oregon* 73 J n
Kenosha, *Wisconsin* (67,899) 56 F g
Kenova, *West Virginia* 57 L l
Kenoza Lake, *New York* 50 D b
Kensal, *North Dakota* 58 H c
Kensett, *Arkansas* 63 M c
Kensett, *Iowa* 61 L a
Kensico Res., *New York* 50 F c
Kensington, *Connecticut* 51 H b
Kensington, *Kansas* 60 E e
Kent, *Connecticut* 50 G b
Kent, *Iowa* 61 K d
Kent, *Minnesota* 59 K d
Kent, *Ohio* 52 E d
Kent, *Oregon* 73 K k
Kent, *Texas* 64 C d
Kent, *Washington* 73 H h
Kent City, *Michigan* 56 H f
Kent Cliffs, *New York* 50 F c
Kent Dam, *Rhode Island* 51 K b
Kentland, *Indiana* 57 F j
Kenton, *Delaware* 50 B g
Kenton, *Michigan* 56 E c
Kenton, *Ohio* 52 C e
Kenton, *Oklahoma* 62 B c
Kenton, *Tennessee* 54 B a
Kentucky (3,191,000) 40,395 sq. miles 57
Kentucky Dam, *Kentucky* 57 E n
Kentucky L., *Ky.-Tenn.* 54 C a
Kentucky R., *Kentucky* 57 J l
Kentwood, *Louisiana* 63 N h
Kenyon, *Minnesota* 59 O f
Kenyonville, *Connecticut* 51 J b
Keokea, *Hawaii* 72 D e
Keokuk, *Iowa* 61 N d
Keota, *Colorado* 69 M c
Keota, *Iowa* 61 N c
Keoto, *Oklahoma* 63 J c
Kerby, *Oregon* 73 G n
Kerens, *Texas* 65 L c
Kerhonkson, *New York* 50 E b
Kerkhoven, *Minnesota* 59 L e
Kerman, *California* 75 E h
Kermit, *Texas* 64 D d
Kermit, *West Virginia* 52 D h
Kernersville, *North Carolina* 55 L a
Kern R., *California* 75 G j
Kernville, *California* 75 G j
Kerr, L., *Florida* 55 K h
Kerrick, *Texas* 64 B g
Kerrs Creek, *Virginia* 52 G h
Kerrville, *Tennessee* 54 B b
Kerrville, *Texas* 65 H e
Kershaw, *South Carolina* 55 L c
Kersey, *Colorado* 69 M c
Keshena, *Wisconsin* 56 E e
Ketchikan, *Alaska* 77 W j
Ketchum, *Idaho* 66 F f
Ketchum, *Oklahoma* 62 H b
Ketchum Mt., *Texas* 64 F d
Ketik R., *Alaska* 76 H b
Kettering, *Ohio* (54,462), vicinity of Dayton
Kettle Cr., *Pennsylvania* 52 J d
Kettle Falls, *Washington* 73 M g
Kettleman City, *California* 75 E h
Kettle R., *Minnesota* 59 O d
Kettle R., *Washington* 73 M g
Kettle River Ra., *Washington* 73 M g
Keuka L., *New York* 53 J c
Kevil, *Kentucky* 57 E m
Kevin, *Montana* 66 J a
Kewanee, *Illinois* 57 D h
Kewanee, *Mississippi* 63 P f
Kewanna, *Indiana* 57 G h
Keweenaw B., *Michigan* 56 E c
Keweenaw Bay, *Michigan* 56 E c
Keweenaw Pen., *Michigan* 56 F b
Keweenaw Pt., *Michigan* 56 F b
Keyaluvik, *Alaska* 76 E f
Keyapaha, *South Dakota* 58 F g
Keya Paha R., *South Dakota* 58 F g
Key Biscayne, *Florida* 54 C e
Keyes, *Oklahoma* 62 A b
Keyesport, *Illinois* 57 D l
Keyhole Res., *Wyoming* 67 Q e
Key Largo, *Florida* 55 O h

Lonerock, Oregon 73 L k
Lone Rock, Wisconsin 56 C f
Lonesome Lake Res., Montana 67 K a
Lonetree, Wyoming 67 K h
Lonetree Res., North Dakota 58 F c
Lone Wolf, Oklahoma 62 D d
Long, Alaska 76 K d
Long B., South Carolina 55 N d
Long Beach, California (344,168) 75 G l
Long Beach, Mississippi 63 O h
Long Beach, New York (26,473) 50 F d
Long Beach I., New Jersey 50 E f
Longboat Key, Florida 55 M f
Long Branch, New Jersey (26,228) 50 F e
Long Cr., North Dakota 58 C b
Long Creek, Oregon 73 L l
Longdale, Oklahoma 62 E b
Long Eddy, New York 53 L d
Long Falls Dam, Maine 49 E c
Longfellow, Texas 64 E e
Longford, Kansas 60 G e
Long Hill, Connecticut 50 G c
Longhurst, North Carolina 55 N a
Long I., Massachusetts 49 H j
Long I., New York 50 F d
Long Island, Kansas 60 E e
Long Island City, New York 51 M f
Long Island Sd., New York-Connecticut 50 G d
Long L., Alaska 76 K f
Long L., Maine 49 G a
Long L., Michigan 56 H e
Long L., Michigan 56 K d
Long L., Minnesota 59 M d
Long L., New York 53 M a
Long L., North Dakota 58 F d
Long L., Washington 72 A j
Long Lake, New York 53 M b
Long Lake, Wisconsin 56 E d
Long Lake Res., Washington 73 L h
Longmeadow, Massachusetts 51 H a
Longmont, Colorado 69 L c
Long Pine, Nebraska 60 E b
Long Point, Illinois 57 E h
Long Pond, Massachusetts 51 L b
Long Prairie, Minnesota 59 M e
Long Prairie R., Minnesota 59 M d
Longs, South Carolina 55 N d
Longs Pk., Colorado 69 L c
Long Tom Res., Idaho 66 E f
Longton, Kansas 61 H g
Longtown, Missouri 61 P g
Long Valley, New Jersey 50 D d
Longvalley, South Dakota 58 E g
Long Valley Res., California 74 G g
Longview, Texas (40,050) 65 N c
Longview, Washington 73 H j
Longville, Louisiana 63 K h
Longwood, Florida 55 K j
Longwood, Mississippi 63 M e
Longworth, Texas 64 G c
Lonoke, Arkansas 63 M d
Lonsdale, Minnesota 59 N f
Lonsdale, Rhode Island 51 L b
Loogootee, Indiana 57 G l
Lookeba, Oklahoma 62 E c
Lookingglass R., Michigan 56 J g
Lookout, California 74 D c
Lookout, C., North Carolina 55 P c
Lookout Pt., Michigan 56 K e
Lookout Mt., Alaska 76 H e
Lookout Mt., California 75 G h
Lookout Mt., Georgia 54 F c
Lookout Mt., New Mexico 71 J d
Lookout Pass, Montana 66 E b
Lookout Point Res., Oregon 73 H m
Lookout Ridge, Alaska 76 H b
Lookout Shoals L., North Carolina 55 K b
Loomis, Nebraska 60 E d
Loomis, Washington 73 L g
Loon L., Maine 49 F b
Loosahatchie R., Tennessee 54 B b
Lorain, Ohio (68,932) 52 D d
Loraine, Illinois 57 B j
Loraine, North Dakota 58 E b
Loraine, Texas 64 G c
Lordsburg, New Mexico 71 J g
Lords Valley, Pennsylvania 50 C c
Lorena, Texas 65 K d
Lorenzo, Idaho 66 J f
Lorenzo, Nebraska 60 A c
Lorenzo, Texas 64 F b
Loretta, Wisconsin 56 C d
Loretto, Kentucky 57 H m
Loretto, Tennessee 54 D b
Lorimor, Iowa 61 K c
Loring, Montana 67 N a
Loris, South Carolina 55 N c
Lorraine, Kansas 60 F f
Los Alamitos, California 75 F m
Los Alamos, California 75 E k
Los Alamos, New Mexico 71 L d
Los Angeles, California (2,479,015) 75 G k
Los Angeles, Texas 65 H g
Los Angeles Harb., California 75 E n
Los Banos, California 75 E g
Los Ebanos, Texas 65 J j
Los Fresnos, Texas 65 K j
Los Gatos, California 75 D g
Los Indios, Texas 65 K j
Los Lunas, New Mexico 71 L e
Los Molinos, California 74 C d
Los Olivos, California 75 E k
Lost Cabin, Wyoming 67 N f
Lost City, West Virginia 52 H g
Lost Cr., Wyoming 67 M g
Lost Hills, California 75 F j
Lostine, Oregon 73 N k
Lost L., Louisiana 63 M j
Lost Nation, Iowa 61 O c
Lost River, West Virginia 52 H g
Lost River Ra., Idaho 66 G e
Lost Springs, Kansas 60 H f
Lost Springs, Wyoming 67 Q g
Lost Trail Pass, Montana 66 G d
Lostwood, North Dakota 58 D b
Lothair, Montana 66 J a
Lott, Texas 65 K d
Lotts Cr., Georgia 55 K e
Lotus, Idaho 66 D b
Lotus, Illinois 57 E j
Louann, Arkansas 63 L e
Loudon, New Hampshire 49 D e
Loudon, Tennessee 54 G b
Loudonville, Ohio 52 D e
Louin, Mississippi 63 O f
Louisa, Kentucky 57 L l
Louisa, Virginia 52 H g
Louisburg, Kansas 61 K f
Louisburg, North Carolina 55 N a
Louise, L., Alaska 77 O e
Louise, Texas 65 L f
Louisiana (3,660,000) 48,523 sq. miles 63
Louisiana, Missouri 61 N e
Louisiana Pt., Texas-Louisiana 65 O f
Louisville, Alabama 54 F f
Louisville, Colorado 69 O g
Louisville, Georgia 55 J d
Louisville, Kentucky (390,639) 57 H l
Louisville, Mississippi 63 O e
Louisville, Nebraska 61 H d
Louisville, Ohio 52 E e
Loup City, Nebraska 60 F c
Loup R., Nebraska 60 F c
Louviers, Colorado 69 M d
Lovelady, Texas 65 M d
Loveland, Colorado 69 L c
Loveland, Ohio 52 B f
Loveland Pass, Colorado 69 L d
Lovell, Wyoming 67 M e
Lovells, Michigan 56 J e
Lovelock, Nevada 74 G d
Lovenia, Mt., Utah 68 F c
Love Point, Maryland 53 K f
Lovett, Florida 54 H g
Lovilia, Iowa 61 M c
Loving, New Mexico 71 N g
Loving, Texas 65 J b
Lovingston, Virginia 52 H h
Lovington, Illinois 57 E k
Lovington, New Mexico 71 O g
Low, Utah 68 C c
Lowden, Iowa 61 N c
Low Des., Oregon 73 K m
Lowell, Arizona 70 H h
Lowell, Arkansas 63 J b
Lowell, Idaho 66 E c
Lowell, Indiana 57 F h
Lowell, Massachusetts (92,107) 49 D f
Lowell, Michigan 56 H g
Lowell, Ohio 52 E f
Lowell, Oregon 73 H m
Lowell, L., Idaho 66 D f
Lower Brule, South Dakota 58 G f
Lower Falls, Wyoming 67 K e
Lower Granite Gorge, Arizona 70 D d
Lower Klamath L., California 74 D c
Lower L., California 74 E c
Lower Lake, California 74 C f
Lower New York B., New York 51 L g
Lower Paia, Hawaii 72 D e
Lower Red L., Minnesota 59 L c
Lower Red Rock Ls., Montana 66 J e
Lowes, Kentucky 57 E n
Lowman, Idaho 66 E e
Lowndesboro, Alabama 54 E e
Lowry City, Missouri 61 L f
Lowrys, South Carolina 55 K c
Lowville, New York 53 L b
Loxley, Alabama 54 D g
Loyal, Wisconsin 56 C e
Loyal Heights, Washington 72 B h
Loyall, Kentucky 57 K n
Loyalsock Cr., Pennsylvania 53 K d
Loyalton, California 74 E e
Loyalton, South Dakota 58 G e
Lualualei, Hawaii 72 C d
Lubbock, Texas (128,691) 64 F b
Lubec, Maine 49 H e
Lublin, Wisconsin 56 C d
Lucas, Iowa 61 L c
Lucas, Kansas 60 F e
Lucas, Ohio 52 D e
Lucca, North Dakota 58 J d
Lucedale, Mississippi 63 P h
Lucerne, California 74 C e
Lucerne, Missouri 61 L d
Lucerne, Washington 73 K g
Lucerne, Wyoming 67 M f
Lucerne L., California 75 J k
Lucerne Valley, California 75 J k
Lucher, Louisiana 63 N h
Lucia, California 75 D h
Lucile, Idaho 66 D d
Lucin, Utah 68 C b
Lucinda, Pennsylvania 52 G d
Luck, Wisconsin 56 A d
Lucky Peak Res., Idaho 66 E f
Lucy, New Mexico 71 M e
Ludden, North Dakota 58 H d
Ludell, Kansas 60 D e
Ludington, Michigan 56 G f
Ludlow, California 75 J k
Ludlow, Colorado 69 M f
Ludlow, Illinois 57 E j
Ludlow, Massachusetts 51 J a
Ludlow, Pennsylvania 52 H d
Ludlow, South Dakota 58 C e
Ludlow, Vermont 49 C e
Ludowici, Georgia 55 K f
Lueders, Texas 65 H c
Lufkin, Texas 65 N d
Luka, Mississippi 63 P d
Lula, Georgia 54 H c
Lula, Mississippi 63 N d
Luling, Louisiana 63 N j
Luling, Texas 65 K f
Lulu, Florida 55 J g
Lumber City, Georgia 55 J f
Lumber City, Pennsylvania 52 H e
Lumberport, West Virginia 52 F f
Lumber R., North Carolina 55 M c
Lumberton, Mississippi 63 O g
Lumberton, New Mexico 71 L c
Lumberton, North Carolina 55 M c
Lumpkin, Georgia 54 G e
Luna, New Mexico 71 J f
Lund, Nevada 74 K f
Lund, Utah 68 C e
Lunenburg, Vermont 49 D d
Luning, Nevada 74 G f
Lupus, Missouri 61 M f
Luray, Kansas 60 F e
Luray, Virginia 52 H g
Lure, L., North Carolina 55 J b
Lurton, Arkansas 63 K c
Lusk, Wyoming 67 Q g
Lustre, Montana 67 P a
Lutesville, Missouri 61 P g
Luther, Iowa 61 L c
Luther, Oklahoma 62 F c
Lutie, Texas 64 D h
Luttrell, Tennessee 54 H a
Lutz, Florida 55 M e
Luverne, Alabama 54 E f
Luverne, Iowa 61 K b
Luverne, Minnesota 59 K g
Luverne, North Dakota 58 J c
Luxapalila R., Alabama 54 D d
Luxemburg, Iowa 61 N b
Luzerne, Michigan 56 J e
Luzerne, New York 53 N b
Luzerne, Pennsylvania 53 B c
Lybrook, New Mexico 71 K c
Lycan, Colorado 69 O f
Lydia, South Carolina 55 L c
Lyell, Mt., California 74 F g
Lyerly, Georgia 54 F c
Lyford, Texas 65 K j
Lykens, Pennsylvania 53 K e
Lyle, Minnesota 59 O g
Lyle, Washington 73 J k
Lyles, Tennessee 54 D b
Lyman, Mississippi 63 O h
Lyman, Oklahoma 62 G b
Lyman, South Carolina 55 J c
Lyman, Nebraska 60 A c
Lyman, Wyoming 67 K h
Lyme, New Hampshire 49 C e
Lyn, Indiana 57 J j
Lynch, Kentucky 57 L n
Lynch, Maryland 50 A g
Lynch, Nebraska 60 F b
Lynchburg, Ohio 52 C f
Lynchburg, Tennessee 54 E b
Lynchburg, Virginia (54,790) 52 G h
Lynches R., South Carolina 55 M d
Lynchville, Maine 49 E d
Lyndell, Pennsylvania 50 B e
Lynden, Washington 73 H g
Lyndhurst, New Jersey 51 K e
Lyndon, Kansas 61 J f
Lyndon, Vermont 49 C d
Lyndonville, New York 52 H b
Lyndonville, Vermont 49 C d
Lynn, Alabama 54 D c
Lynn, Massachusetts (94,478) 49 H g
Lynn, Utah 68 C b
Lynn Can., Alaska 77 U g
Lynndyl, Utah 68 D d
Lynn Harb., Massachusetts 49 H h
Lynn Haven, Florida 54 F g
Lynnport, Pennsylvania 50 B d
Lynnville, Iowa 61 M c
Lynnville, Tennessee 54 D b
Lynwood, California (31,614) 75 E m
Lyon Manor, Michigan 56 J e
Lyon Mountain, New York 53 N a
Lyons, Colorado 69 L c
Lyons, Georgia 55 J e
Lyons, Indiana 57 F l
Lyons, Kansas 60 F f
Lyons, Michigan 56 J g
Lyons, Nebraska 60 H c
Lyons, New York 53 J b
Lyons, Ohio 52 B d
Lyons, Oregon 73 H l
Lyons, Pennsylvania 50 B e
Lyons, South Dakota 59 K g
Lyons, Texas 65 L e
Lyons, Wisconsin 56 E g
Lyons Falls, New York 53 L b
Lysite, Wyoming 67 N f
Lytle, Texas 65 J f
Lytton, California 74 C f
Maalaea, Hawaii 72 D e
Maalaea B., Hawaii 72 D e
Mabank, Texas 65 L c
Mabel, Minnesota 59 P g
Maben, West Virginia 52 E h
Mabton, Washington 73 K j
McAdoo, Texas 64 F b
McAlester, L., Oklahoma 62 H c
McAlester, Oklahoma 62 H d
McAlister, New Mexico 71 O e
McAllen, Texas (32,728) 65 J j
McAllister, Montana 66 J d
McAlpin, Florida 55 J g
McArthur, California 74 D c
McArthur, Ohio 52 D f
Macatawa, Michigan 56 G g
McBain, Michigan 56 H e
McBaine, Missouri 61 M f
McBean, Georgia 55 K d
McBee, South Carolina 55 L c
McCall, Idaho 66 D e
McCamey, Texas 64 E d
McCammon, Idaho 66 H g
McCanna, North Dakota 58 J b
McCarthy, Alaska 77 Q f
McCleary, Washington 73 G h
Maccleny, Florida 55 J g
McClellanville, South Carolina 55 M d
McCloud, California 74 C c
McCloud R., California 74 C c
McClure, L., California 74 E g
McClure, Ohio 52 C d
McClure, Pennsylvania 53 J e
McClure, Virginia 52 D h
McCluskey, North Dakota 58 F c
McColl, South Carolina 55 M c
McComb, Mississippi 63 N g
McComb, Ohio 52 C d
Macomb, Oklahoma 62 F c
McConaughy, L., Nebraska 60 C c
McConnellsburg, Pennsylvania 52 H f
McConnelsville, Ohio 52 E f
McCook, Nebraska 60 D d
McCool, Mississippi 63 O e
McCool Junction, Nebraska 60 G d
McCormick, South Carolina 55 J d
McCoy, Colorado 69 K d
McCracken, Kansas 60 E f
McCredie, Missouri 61 N f
McCrory, Arkansas 63 M c
McCullough, Alabama 54 D f
McCullough Ridge, Nevada 75 K j
McCurtain, Oklahoma 63 J c
McDade, Texas 65 K e
McDavid, Florida 54 D g
McDermitt, Nevada 74 H c
McDermitt, Oregon 73 N n
McDermott, Ohio 52 C g
Macdoel, California 74 C c
McDonald, Kansas 60 C e
McDonald, L., Montana 66 G a
McDonald, Pennsylvania 52 F e
McDonald Pk., California 74 E d
McDonald Pk., Montana 66 G b
McDonough, Georgia 54 G d
McDowell Pk., Arizona 70 F f
Macedon, New York 52 J b
Macedonia, Iowa 61 J c
Macedonia Brook State Park, Connecticut 50 G b
McEwen, Oregon 73 M l
McEwen, Tennessee 54 D a
McFadden, Wyoming 67 O h
McFall, Missouri 61 K d
McFarland, Kansas 60 H e
McGaffey, New Mexico 71 J d
McGehee, Arkansas 63 M e
McGill, Nevada 74 L e
McGrath, Alaska 76 K e
McGrath, Minnesota 59 N d
McGraw, New York 53 K c
McGregor, Michigan 56 L f
McGregor, Minnesota 59 N d
McGregor, Texas 65 K d
McGrew, Nebraska 60 A c
McGuire, Mt., Idaho 66 F d
Machen, Georgia 54 H d
McHenry, Illinois 56 E g
McHenry, Mississippi 63 O h
McHenry, North Dakota 58 H c
Machias, Maine 49 H d
Machias B., Maine 49 H d
Machias R., Maine 49 G b
Machias Seal I., Maine 49 H d
McIntire, Iowa 61 M a
McIntosh, Minnesota 59 L c
McIntosh, South Dakota 58 E e
Mack, Colorado 68 H d
Mackay, Idaho 66 G f
Mackay Res., Idaho 66 G f
McKeesport, Pennsylvania (45,489) 53 Q c
McKees' Rocks, Pennsylvania 53 O a
McKenzie, Alabama 54 E f
McKenzie, North Dakota 58 F d
McKenzie, Tennessee 54 C a
McKenzie Bridge, Oregon 73 H l
McKenzie Pass, Oregon 73 H l
McKenzie R., Oregon 73 H l
Mackinac, Str. of, Michigan 56 J d
Mackinac Island, Michigan 56 J d
Mackinaw, Illinois 57 D j
Mackinaw City, Michigan 56 J d
Mackinaw R., Illinois 57 D j
McKinley, Mt., Alaska 76 M e
McKinley Park, Alaska 77 N e
McKinney, Kentucky 57 J m
McKinney, L., Kansas 60 C f
McKinney, Texas 65 L b
McKinnon, Tennessee 54 D a
McKittrick, California 75 F j
Macksburg, Ohio 52 E f
Macks Inn, Idaho 66 J e
Macksville, Kansas 60 F g
McLain, Mississippi 63 P g
MacLaren R., Alaska 77 O e
McLaughlin, South Dakota 58 F e
McLean, Illinois 57 D j
McLean, Texas 64 D h
McLean, Virginia 53 J g
McLeansboro, Illinois 57 E l
McLeod, North Dakota 58 J d
McLoughlin, Mt., Oregon 73 H n
McLouth, Kansas 61 J e
McMechen, West Virginia 52 F e
McMichaels, Pennsylvania 50 C c
McMillan, L., New Mexico 71 N g
McMillan, Michigan 56 H c
McMinnville, Oregon 73 G k
McMinnville, Tennessee 54 F b
McMurray, Washington 73 H g
McNair, Mississippi 63 M g
McNary, Arizona 70 H e
McNary, Texas 64 B d
McNary Dam, Oregon 73 L k
McNeal, Arizona 70 H h
McNeil, Arkansas 63 K e
McNeil, Texas 65 K e
McNeill, Mississippi 63 O h
Macomb, Illinois 57 C j
Macon, Georgia (69,764) 54 H e
Macon, Illinois 57 E k
Macon, Mississippi 63 P e
Macon, Missouri 61 M e
Macon, Nebraska 60 F d
Macon Bayou, Louisiana 63 M f
McPherson, Kansas 60 G f
McRae, Georgia 55 J e
McRoberts, Kentucky 57 L m
Macungie, Pennsylvania 53 L e
McVeigh, Kentucky 57 L m
McVille, North Dakota 58 H c
Macwahoc, Maine 49 G c
McWilliams, Alabama 54 D f
Madalin, New York 50 F a
Maddock, North Dakota 58 G c
Madelia, Minnesota 59 M f
Madeline, California 74 E c
Madeline I., Wisconsin 56 C c
Madera, California 75 E h
Madera, Mt., Texas 64 E e
Madera, Pennsylvania 52 H e
Madill, Oklahoma 62 G d
Madison, Alabama 54 E c
Madison, Arkansas 63 N c
Madison, Connecticut 51 H c
Madison, Florida 54 H g
Madison, Georgia 54 H d
Madison, Illinois 61 Q d
Madison, Indiana 57 H l
Madison, Kansas 60 H f
Madison, Maine 49 F d
Madison, Minnesota 59 K e
Madison, Missouri 61 M e
Madison, Nebraska 60 G c
Madison, New Jersey 50 E d
Madison, North Carolina 55 M a
Madison, Ohio 52 E d
Madison, South Dakota 58 J f
Madison, Tennessee 54 E a
Madison, Virginia 52 H g
Madison, West Virginia 52 E g
Madison, Wisconsin (126,706) 56 D f
Madison Heights, Michigan (33,343), vicinity of Detroit
Madison Heights, Virginia 52 G h
Madison Junction, Wyoming 67 K e
Madison R., Montana 66 J d
Madison Ra., Montana 66 J d
Madisonville, Kentucky 57 F m
Madisonville, Louisiana 63 N h
Madisonville, Tennessee 54 G b
Madisonville, Texas 65 M e
Madoc, Montana 67 P a
Mad R., California 74 B d
Madras, Oregon 73 J l
Madre Mt., New Mexico 71 K e
Madrid, Iowa 61 L c
Madrid, Nebraska 60 C d
Madrid, New Mexico 71 L d
Madrid, New York 53 L a
Maeser, Utah 68 G c
Magazine Mt., Arkansas 63 K c
Magdalena, New Mexico 71 K e
Magee, Colorado 69 P h
Magee, Mississippi 63 O g
Mageik Vol., Alaska 76 K g
Magic Res., Idaho 66 F f
Magma, Arizona 70 F f
Magna, Utah 68 B h
Magnet, Nebraska 60 G b
Magnolia, Arkansas 63 K e
Magnolia, Delaware 50 B g
Magnolia, Minnesota 59 K g
Magnolia, Mississippi 63 N g
Magnolia, North Carolina 55 N c
Magnolia, Texas 65 M e
Magnolia Bluff, Washington 72 B h
Magnum, Oklahoma 62 D d
Magruder Mt., Nevada 75 H g
Mahaffy, Pennsylvania 52 H e
Mahanoy City, Pennsylvania 50 A d
Mahaska, Kansas 60 G e
Mahnomen, Minnesota 59 L c
Mahogany Pk., Nevada 74 F c
Mahomet, Illinois 57 E j
Mahopac, New York 50 F c
Mahopac Falls, New York 50 F c
Mahto, South Dakota 58 F e
Maiden, North Carolina 55 K b
Maiden Cr., Pennsylvania 50 B d
Maiden Rock, Wisconsin 56 A e
Maine (973,000) 33,215 sq. miles 49
Maine, Arizona 70 F d
Maine, New York 53 K c
Maineville, Ohio 52 B f
Main Pt., Louisiana 63 O j
Maitland, Missouri 61 J d
Makapala, Hawaii 72 E e
Makapuu Pt., Hawaii 72 C d
Makawao, Hawaii 72 D e
Makoti, North Dakota 58 E c
Makushin B., Alaska 76 D k
Makushin Vol., Alaska 76 D k
Malabar, Florida 55 O e
Malad City, Idaho 66 H g
Malaga, New Jersey 50 C f
Malaga, New Mexico 71 N g
Malaga, Washington 73 K h
Malakoff, Texas 65 L c
Malaspina Glacier, Alaska 77 R g
Malcom, Iowa 61 M c
Malden, Massachusetts (57,676) 49 G h
Malden, Missouri 61 P h
Malden, Washington 73 N h
Malden, West Virginia 52 E g
Malheur, Oregon 73 N l
Malheur L., Oregon 73 M m
Malheur R., Oregon 73 N m
Malin, Oregon 73 J n
Maljamar, New Mexico 71 O g
Mallard, Iowa 61 K b
Mallory, West Virginia 52 E h
Malone, Florida 54 F g
Malone, New York 53 M a
Malone, Texas 65 L d
Maloney Res., Nebraska 60 D c
Malott, Washington 73 L g
Malpais, New Mexico 71 K h
Malta, Colorado 69 K d
Malta, Idaho 66 G g
Malta, Montana 67 N a
Malta, Ohio 52 E f
Maltby, Washington 72 C g
Malvern, Arkansas 63 L d
Malvern, Iowa 61 J c
Malvern, Ohio 52 E e
Malvern, Pennsylvania 50 B e
Mamakating, New York 50 E b
Mamaroneck, New York 50 F d
Mammoth, Arizona 70 G g
Mammoth, West Virginia 52 E g
Mammoth Cave, Kentucky 57 G m
Mammoth Cave Nat. Park, Kentucky 57 G m
Mammoth Hot Springs, Wyoming 67 K e
Mammoth Spring, Arkansas 63 M b
Mamou, Louisiana 63 L h
Mamtou, New York 50 F c
Man, West Virginia 52 E h
Mana, Hawaii 72 B c
Manahawkin, New Jersey 50 E f
Manakin, Virginia 52 J h
Manasquan, New Jersey 50 E e
Manasquan R., New Jersey 50 E e
Manassa, Colorado 69 L f
Manassas, Virginia 53 J g
Manatawny, Pennsylvania 50 B e
Manawa, Wisconsin 56 D e
Manayunk, Pennsylvania 50 F f
Mancelona, Michigan 56 H e
Manchaug, Massachusetts 51 K a
Manchaug Pond, Massachusetts 51 K a
Manchester, California 75 D m
Manchester, Connecticut (42,102) 51 H b
Manchester, Georgia 54 G e
Manchester, Illinois 57 C k
Manchester, Iowa 61 N b
Manchester, Kansas 60 G e
Manchester, Kentucky 57 K m
Manchester, Michigan 57 K g
Manchester, New Hampshire (88,282) 49 D f
Manchester, New York 53 J c
Manchester, Ohio 52 C g
Manchester, Oklahoma 62 E b
Manchester, Pennsylvania 53 K e
Manchester, Tennessee 54 E b
Manchester, Vermont 49 B e
Manchester, Washington 72 B h
Manchester Bridge, New York 50 F b
Mancos R., Colorado 68 H f
Mandan, North Dakota 58 E d
Manderfield, Utah 68 D e
Manderson, Wyoming 67 N e
Mandeville, Louisiana 63 N h
Manfred, North Dakota 58 G c
Mangas, New Mexico 71 J e
Mangham, Louisiana 63 M f
Mangum, Oklahoma 62 D d
Manhan R., Massachusetts 51 H a
Manhattan, Illinois 57 F h

Manhattan, *Kansas* 60 H e
Manhattan, *Montana* 66 J d
Manhattan, *Nevada* 74 H f
Manhattan, *New York* 50 F d
Manhattan Beach, *California* (33,934) 75 D m
Manhattan I., *New York* 51 M e
Manila, *Arkansas* 63 N c
Manila, *Utah* 68 G c
Manilla, *Iowa* 61 J c
Manistee, *Michigan* 56 G e
Manistee R., *Michigan* 56 H e
Manistique, *Michigan* 56 G d
Manistique L., *Michigan* 56 H c
Manistique R., *Michigan* 56 G c
Manito, *Illinois* 57 D j
Manitou, *Oklahoma* 62 E d
Manitou I., *Michigan* 56 F b
Manitou Springs, *Colorado* 69 L e
Manitowoc, *Wisconsin* (32,275) 56 F e
Mankato, *Kansas* 60 F e
Mankato, *Minnesota* 59 N f
Mankins, *Texas* 65 J b
Manley Hot Springs, *Alaska* 76 M d
Manlius, *New York* 53 L b
Manly, *Iowa* 61 L a
Manning, *Arkansas* 63 L d
Manning, *Iowa* 61 J c
Manning, *North Dakota* 58 D c
Manning, *South Carolina* 55 L d
Manning, *Texas* 65 N d
Mannington, *West Virginia* 52 F f
Manns Harbor, *North Carolina* 55 Q b
Mannsville, *New York* 53 K b
Manokotak, *Alaska* 76 H g
Manor, *Georgia* 55 J f
Manor, *Texas* 65 K e
Manorville, *New York* 51 H d
Mansfield, *Arkansas* 63 J c
Mansfield, *Georgia* 54 H d
Mansfield, *Illinois* 57 E j
Mansfield, *Louisiana* 63 K f
Mansfield, *Massachusetts* 51 L a
Mansfield, *Missouri* 61 M g
Mansfield, Mt., *Vermont* 49 C d
Mansfield, *Ohio* (47,325) 52 D e
Mansfield, *Pennsylvania* 53 K d
Mansfield, *South Dakota* 58 H e
Mansfield, *Texas* 65 K c
Mansfield, *Washington* 73 L h
Manson, *Iowa* 61 K b
Manson, *Washington* 73 K h
Mansura, *Louisiana* 63 L g
Manteca, *California* 74 D g
Mantee, *Mississippi* 63 O e
Manteno, *Illinois* 57 F h
Manteo, *North Carolina* 55 P d
Manter, *Kansas* 60 C g
Manti, *Utah* 68 E d
Mantoloking, *New Jersey* 50 E e
Manton, *California* 74 D d
Manton, *Michigan* 56 H e
Mantua, *New Jersey* 50 C f
Mantua, *Ohio* 52 E d
Manuelito, *New Mexico* 71 J d
Manvel, *North Dakota* 58 J b
Manville, *New Jersey* 50 D d
Manville, *Rhode Island* 51 L b
Manville, *Wyoming* 67 Q g
Many, *Louisiana* 63 K g
Manzano, *New Mexico* 71 L e
Manzanola, *Colorado* 69 N e
Manzano Mts., *New Mexico* 71 L e
Maple Heights, *Ohio* (31,667), vicinity of Cleveland
Maple Island, *Minnesota* 59 N g
Mapleleaf, *Washington* 72 B h
Maple Park, *Missouri* 61 Q a
Maple R., *Iowa* 61 J b
Maple R., *Michigan* 56 J f
Maple Shade, *New Jersey* 50 D f
Maplesville, *Alabama* 54 E e
Mapleton, *Iowa* 61 J b
Mapleton, *Maine* 49 G b
Mapleton, *Minnesota* 59 N g
Mapleton, *Oregon* 73 G l
Maple Valley, *Washington* 73 H h
Maple View, *New York* 53 K b
Maplewood, *Minnesota* 59 R h
Maplewood, *New Jersey* 51 J f
Maplewood, *Washington* 72 C j
Maquoketa, *Iowa* 61 O b
Maquoketa R., *Iowa* 61 O b
Maquon, *Illinois* 57 D j
Marais des Cygnes R., *Kansas* 61 K f
Marana, *Arizona* 70 F g
Marathon, *Iowa* 61 K b
Marathon, *New York* 53 K c
Marathon, *Texas* 64 D e
Marathon, *Wisconsin* 56 C e
Maravillas Cr., *Texas* 64 D f
Marble, *Colorado* 69 J d
Marble, *Washington* 73 N g
Marble Canyon, *Arizona* 70 F c
Marble City, *Oklahoma* 63 J c
Marble Falls, *Texas* 65 J e
Marblehead, *Illinois* 57 B k
Marblehead, *Massachusetts* 49 E f
Marblehead, *Ohio* 52 D d
Marble Rock, *Iowa* 61 M b
Marbleton, *Wyoming* 67 K g
Marbury, *Maryland* 53 J g
Marceline, *Missouri* 61 M e
Marcella, *Arkansas* 63 M c
Marcellus, *Michigan* 57 H g
Marcellus, *Washington* 73 M h
Marco, *Florida* 55 N h
Marco, *Indiana* 57 F l
Marcola, *Oregon* 73 H l
Marcus, *Iowa* 61 J b
Marcus, *Washington* 73 M g
Marcus Baker, Mt., *Alaska* 77 O f
Marcus Hook, *Pennsylvania* 50 C f
Marcy, Mt., *New York* 53 M a
Marcy, *New York* 53 L b
Marengo, *Illinois* 57 E g
Marengo, *Indiana* 57 G l
Marengo, *Iowa* 61 M c
Marengo, *Ohio* 52 D e
Marengo, *Washington* 73 M h
Marengo, *Wisconsin* 56 C c
Marenisco, *Michigan* 56 D c
Margaret, *Texas* 65 H a
Margaretville, *New York* 50 D a
Margate City, *New Jersey* 50 E g
Margie, *Minnesota* 59 N b
Margrethe, L., *Michigan* 56 J e
Maria, *Texas* 64 C e
Maria Mts., *California* 75 L h
Marian, L., *South Carolina* 55 L d
Marianna, *Arkansas* 63 N d
Marianna, *Florida* 54 F g
Marias Pass, *Montana* 66 G a
Marias R., *Montana* 66 H a
Maribel, *Wisconsin* 56 F e
Maricopa, *Arizona* 70 E f
Maricopa, *California* 75 F j
Maricopa Mts., *Arizona* 70 E f
Marienthal, *Kansas* 60 C f
Marienville, *Pennsylvania* 52 G d
Marietta, *Georgia* (25,565) 54 G d
Marietta, *Ohio* 52 E f
Marietta, *Oklahoma* 62 F e
Marietta, *Pennsylvania* 53 K e
Marietta, *South Carolina* 55 J b
Marine, *Illinois* 57 D l
Marine City, *Michigan* 56 L g
Marineland, *Florida* 55 K h
Marinette, *Wisconsin* 56 F d
Maringouin, *Louisiana* 63 M h
Marin Is., *California* 75 B k
Marin Pen., *California* 75 B l
Marion, *Alabama* 54 D e
Marion, *Arkansas* 63 N c
Marion, *Illinois* 57 E m
Marion, *Indiana* (37,854) 57 H j
Marion, *Iowa* 61 N b
Marion, *Kansas* 60 G f
Marion, *Kentucky* 57 E m
Marion, *Louisiana* 63 L f
Marion, *Maine* 49 H e
Marion, *Massachusetts* 51 M b
Marion, *Michigan* 56 H e
Marion, *Mississippi* 63 P f
Marion, *Montana* 66 F a
Marion, *Nebraska* 60 D d
Marion, *North Carolina* 55 J b
Marion, *North Dakota* 58 H d
Marion, *Ohio* (37,079) 52 C e
Marion, *South Carolina* 55 M c
Marion, *South Dakota* 58 J g
Marion, *Texas* 65 J f
Marion, *Virginia* 52 E j
Marion, *Wisconsin* 56 E e
Marion Junction, *Alabama* 54 D e
Marion Res., *Kansas* 60 G f
Marionville, *Missouri* 61 L g
Mariposa, *California* 75 F g
Mariposa R., *California* 75 E g
Mariposa Res., *California* 75 F g
Marissa, *Illinois* 57 D l
Marked Tree, *Arkansas* 63 N c
Markesan, *Wisconsin* 56 E f
Markham, *Texas* 65 L g
Markham, *Virginia* 52 J g
Markham, *Washington* 73 G j
Markham Ferry Res., *Oklahoma* 62 H b
Markleville, *California* 74 F f
Marks, *Mississippi* 63 N d
Marksboro, *New Jersey* 50 D d
Marksville, *Louisiana* 63 L g
Markville, *Minnesota* 59 O d
Marland, *Oklahoma* 62 F b
Marlboro, *Massachusetts* 49 D f
Marlboro, *New Jersey* 50 E e
Marlboro, *New Hampshire* 49 C f
Marlboro, *New York* 50 F b
Marlborough, *Connecticut* 51 J b
Marlborough, *Missouri* 61 P b
Marlette, *Michigan* 56 K f
Marlin, *Texas* 65 L d
Marlinton, *West Virginia* 52 F g
Marlow, *New Hampshire* 49 C e
Marlow, *Oklahoma* 62 F d
Marlton, *New Jersey* 50 D f
Marmaduke, *Arkansas* 63 N b
Marmarth, *North Dakota* 58 C d
Marmet, *West Virginia* 52 E g
Marmot B., *Alaska* 76 L g
Marmot I., *Alaska* 76 L g
Marne, *Michigan* 56 H f
Maroa, *Illinois* 57 E j
Maro Reef, *Hawaii* 72 B a
Marquand, *Missouri* 61 O g
Marquesas Keys, *Florida* 55 M j
Marquette, *Iowa* 61 N a
Marquette, *Kansas* 60 G f
Marquette, *Michigan* 56 F c
Marquette, *Nebraska* 60 F c
Marquez, *New Mexico* 71 K d
Marquez, *Texas* 65 L d
Marrero, *Louisiana* 62 B f
Mars, *Pennsylvania* 52 G e
Marseilles, *Illinois* 57 E h
Marseilles, *Ohio* 52 C e
Marsh, *Montana* 67 Q c
Marshall, *Alaska* 76 F f
Marshall, *Arkansas* 63 L c
Marshall, *Colorado* 69 N g
Marshall, *Illinois* 57 F k
Marshall, *Michigan* 57 J g
Marshall, *Minnesota* 59 L f
Marshall, *Missouri* 61 L e
Marshall, *North Carolina* 55 J b
Marshall, *North Dakota* 58 D c
Marshall, *Oklahoma* 62 F b
Marshall, *Texas* 65 N c
Marshall, *Virginia* 52 J g
Marshall, *Wyoming* 67 P g
Marshalls Cr., *Pennsylvania* 50 C c
Marshallton, *Delaware* 50 B f
Marshallton, *Pennsylvania* 50 B f
Marshalltown, *Iowa* 61 L b
Marshfield, *Massachusetts* 51 M a
Marshfield, *Missouri* 61 M g
Marshfield, *Wisconsin* 56 C e
Marshfield Hills, *Massachusetts* 51 M a
Mars Hill, *Maine* 49 G b
Marsh Hill, *Pennsylvania* 53 K d
Marsh I., *Louisiana* 63 L j
Marsh Pk., *Utah* 68 G c
Marshville, *North Carolina* 55 L c
Marsing, *Idaho* 66 D f
Marsland, *Nebraska* 60 A b
Marston, *Wyoming* 67 L h
Marston Res., *Colorado* 69 O j
Mart, *Texas* 65 L d
Martensdale, *Iowa* 61 L c
Marthasville, *Missouri* 61 N f
Martha's Vineyard, *Massachusetts* 51 M c
Martin, *Alaska* 77 N f
Martin, *Kentucky* 57 L m
Martin, *Michigan* 56 H g
Martin, *South Dakota* 58 E g
Martin, *Tennessee* 54 C a
Martindale, *Texas* 65 K f
Martindale Depot, *New York* 50 F a
Martinez, *California* 74 C f
Martin L., *Alabama* 54 F e
Martin Pt., *Alaska* 77 Q a
Martinsburg, *Missouri* 61 N e
Martinsburg, *New York* 53 L b
Martinsburg, *Ohio* 52 D e
Martinsburg, *Pennsylvania* 52 H e
Martinsburg, *West Virginia* 52 H f
Martins Creek, *Pennsylvania* 50 C d
Martins Creek Junction, *Pennsylvania* 50 C d
Martinsdale, *Montana* 67 K c
Martins Ferry, *Ohio* 52 F e
Martinsville, *Illinois* 57 F k
Martinsville, *Indiana* 57 G k
Martinsville, *Virginia* 52 G j
Marvell, *Arkansas* 63 N d
Marvin, *South Dakota* 59 K e
Marvine, *Colorado* 69 J c
Marvine, Mt., *Utah* 68 E e
Mary, L., *Mississippi* 63 M g
Marydel, *Maryland* 50 B g
Maryland (3,685,000) 10,577 sq. miles 52-53
Maryneal, *Texas* 64 G c
Marys R., *Nevada* 74 K c
Marysvale, *Utah* 68 D e
Marysville, *California* 74 D e
Marysville, *Idaho* 66 J e
Marysville, *Kansas* 60 H e
Marysville, *Michigan* 56 L g
Marysville, *Ohio* 52 C e
Marysville, *Washington* 73 H g
Maryville, *Missouri* 61 K d
Maryville, *Tennessee* 54 H b
Masardis, *Maine* 49 G b
Masaryktown, *Florida* 55 J j
Mascot, *Nebraska* 60 E d
Mascot, *Tennessee* 54 H a
Mascoutah, *Illinois* 57 D l
Mashpee, *Massachusetts* 51 N b
Mason, *Illinois* 57 E l
Mason, *Ohio* 52 B f
Mason, *Michigan* 56 J g
Mason, *Nevada* 74 F f
Mason, *South Dakota* 58 C e
Mason, *Tennessee* 54 B b
Mason, *Texas* 65 H e
Mason, *West Virginia* 52 E g
Mason, *Wisconsin* 56 B c
Mason, *Wyoming* 67 K g
Mason City, *Illinois* 57 D j
Mason City, *Iowa* (30,642) 61 L a
Mason City, *Nebraska* 60 E c
Masontown, *Pennsylvania* 52 G f
Masontown, *West Virginia* 52 G f
Mass, *Michigan* 56 E c
Massachusetts (5,421,000) 8257 sq. miles 49
Massachusetts B., *Massachusetts* 51 M a
Massacre L., *Nevada* 74 F c
Massadona, *Colorado* 68 H c
Massanutten Mt., *Virginia* 52 H g
Massapequa, *New York* (32,900), vicinity of New York City
Massaponax, *Virginia* 52 J g
Massena, *Iowa* 61 K c
Massena, *New York* 53 M a
Massey, *Maryland* 50 B g
Massies Mill, *Virginia* 52 G h
Massillon, *Ohio* (31,236) 52 E e
Mastic Beach, *New York* 51 H d
Matador, *Texas* 64 G a
Matagorda, *Texas* 65 M g
Matagorda B., *Texas* 65 L g
Matagorda I., *Texas* 65 L g
Matagorda Pen., *Texas* 65 M g
Matamoras, *Pennsylvania* 50 D c
Matanuska, *Alaska* 77 N f
Matanuska R., *Alaska* 77 N f
Matanzas Inlet, *Florida* 55 K h
Matawan, *New Jersey* 50 E e
Matewan, *West Virginia* 52 D h
Matfield Green, *Kansas* 60 H f
Mather, *California* 74 F g
Mather, *Pennsylvania* 52 F f
Matherville, *Illinois* 57 C h
Matheson, *Colorado* 69 N d
Mathews, *Alabama* 54 E e
Mathews, *Virginia* 53 K h
Mathis, *Texas* 65 K g
Mathiston, *Mississippi* 63 O e
Matinicus I., *Maine* 49 G e
Matlock, *Washington* 73 G h
Matoaka, *West Virginia* 52 E h
Mattamuskeet L., *North Carolina* 55 P b
Mattapoisett, *Massachusetts* 51 M b
Mattaponi R., *Virginia* 53 K h
Mattawamkeag, *Maine* 49 G c
Matterhorn, *Nevada* 74 K c
Matterhorn, *Oregon* 73 N k
Matthie, *Arizona* 70 E e
Mattituck, *New York* 51 H d
Mattole R., *California* 74 A d
Mattoon, *Illinois* 57 E k
Mattoon, *Kentucky* 57 E m
Mattoon, *Wisconsin* 56 D d
Matunuck, *Rhode Island* 51 K c
Maud, *Oklahoma* 62 G c
Maud, *Texas* 65 N b
Maudlow, *Montana* 66 J c
Maugansville, *Maryland* 52 J f
Maui, I., *Hawaii* 72 D e
Maukport, *Indiana* 57 G l
Maumee, *Ohio* 52 C d
Maumee B., *Michigan* 57 K h
Maumee B., *Ohio* 52 C d
Maumee R., *Ohio* 52 C d
Maumelle, L., *Arkansas* 63 L d
Mauna Kea, mt., *Hawaii* 72 E f
Maunaloa, *Hawaii* 72 D d
Mauna Loa, mt., *Hawaii* 72 E f
Mauneluk R., *Alaska* 76 J c
Maupin, *Oregon* 73 J k
Maurepas, L., *Louisiana* 63 N h
Maurice R., *New Jersey* 50 C g
Mauricetown, *New Jersey* 50 C g
Mauriceville, *Texas* 65 O e
Maurine, *South Dakota* 58 D e
Mauston, *Wisconsin* 56 C f
Mawah, *New Jersey* 50 E c
Max, *Nebraska* 60 C d
Max, *North Dakota* 58 E c
Maxbass, *North Dakota* 58 E b
Maxeys, *Georgia* 54 H d
Max Meadows, *Virginia* 52 F j
Maxton, *North Carolina* 55 M c
Maxville, *Florida* 55 J g
Maxville, *Montana* 66 G c
Maxwell, *California* 74 C e
Maxwell, *Iowa* 61 L c
Maxwell, *Nebraska* 60 D c
Maxwell, *New Mexico* 71 N c
May, C., *New Jersey* 50 D g
May, *Idaho* 66 G e
May, *Oklahoma* 62 D b
May, *Texas* 65 J d
Maybee, *Michigan* 57 K g
Maybell, *Colorado* 68 H c
Maybrook, *New York* 50 E c
Maydelle, *Texas* 65 M d
Mayer, *Arizona* 70 E e
Mayesville, *South Carolina* 55 L d
Mayetta, *Kansas* 61 J e
Mayfield, *Idaho* 66 E f
Mayfield, *Oklahoma* 62 D c
Mayfield, *Pennsylvania* 53 L d
Mayfield, *Utah* 68 E d
Mayfield Cr., *Kentucky* 57 E n
Mayflower, *Arkansas* 63 L d
Mayhew, *Mississippi* 63 P e
Mayhill, *New Mexico* 71 M g
Mayland, *Tennessee* 54 F a
Maynard, *Iowa* 61 N b
Mayo, *Florida* 54 H g
Mayo, *Maryland* 53 K g
Mayodan, *North Carolina* 55 M a
Mayport, *Florida* 55 K g
Mays Landing, *New Jersey* 50 D g
Maysville, *Georgia* 54 H c
Maysville, *Kentucky* 57 K l
Maysville, *Missouri* 61 K e
Maysville, *North Carolina* 55 O c
Maysville, *Oklahoma* 62 F d
Mayville, *Michigan* 56 K f
Mayville, *New York* 52 G c
Mayville, *North Dakota* 58 J c
Mayville, *Oregon* 73 K k
Mayville, *Wisconsin* 56 E f
Maywood, *California* 75 E m
Maywood, *Illinois* (27,330), vicinity of Chicago
Maywood, *Nebraska* 60 D d
Maza, *North Dakota* 58 G b
Mazama, *Washington* 73 K g
Mazatzal Pk., *Arizona* 70 F e
Mazomanie, *Wisconsin* 56 D f
Mazon, *Illinois* 57 E h
Meacham, *Oregon* 73 M k
Meacham Airport, *Texas* 65 L j
Mead, L., *Nevada* 75 L h
Mead, *Washington* 73 N h
Meade, *Kansas* 60 D g
Meade Pk., *Idaho* 66 J g
Meade R., *Alaska* 76 J a
Meade River, *Alaska* 76 J a
Meadow, *South Dakota* 58 D e
Meadow, *Texas* 64 E b
Meadow, *Utah* 68 D e
Meadow Bridge, *West Virginia* 52 F h
Meadowbrook, *Texas* 65 M j
Meadow Creek, *West Virginia* 52 F h
Meadowdale, *Washington* 72 B g
Meadowdale, *Wyoming* 67 Q g
Meadowlands, *Minnesota* 59 O c
Meadows, *Idaho* 66 D e
Meadow Valley Mts., *Nevada* 75 L g
Meadow Valley Wash, *Nevada* 75 L h
Meadville, *Mississippi* 63 N g
Meadville, *Missouri* 61 L e
Meadville, *Nebraska* 60 E b
Meadville, *Pennsylvania* 52 F d
Meares, C., *Oregon* 73 G k
Mears, *Michigan* 56 G f
Mebane, *North Carolina* 55 M a
Mecca, *California* 75 J l
Mechanic Falls, *Maine* 49 E d
Mechanicsburg, *Ohio* 52 C e
Mechanicsburg, *Pennsylvania* 53 J e
Mechanics Grove, *Pennsylvania* 50 A f
Mechanicsville, *Maryland* 53 K g
Mechanicville, *New York* 53 N c
Mechant Caillou L., *Louisiana* 63 N j
Meckesville, *Pennsylvania* 50 B d
Mecosta, *Michigan* 56 H f
Medaryville, *Indiana* 57 G h
Meddybemps L., *Maine* 49 H c
Medfield, *Massachusetts* 51 L a
Medford, *Massachusetts* (64,971) 49 G h
Medford, *New Jersey* 50 D f
Medford, *Oklahoma* 62 F b
Medford, *Oregon* 73 H n
Medford, *Wisconsin* 56 C d
Medford Station, *New York* 51 H d
Medfra, *Alaska* 76 K e
Media, *Pennsylvania* 50 C f
Mediapolis, *Iowa* 61 N c
Medical Lake, *Washington* 73 N h
Medicine Bow, *Wyoming* 67 O h
Medicine Bow Mts., *Wyoming-Colorado* 67 O h
Medicine Bow Pk., *Wyoming* 67 O h
Medicine Bow R., *Wyoming* 67 O h
Medicine L., *California* 74 D c
Medicine L., *Minnesota* 59 P h
Medicine L., *Montana* 67 Q a
Medicine Lake, *Montana* 67 Q a
Medicine Lodge, *Kansas* 60 F g
Medicine Lodge R., *Kansas* 60 F g
Medicine Mound, *Texas* 65 H a
Medicine Rocks, *Montana* 67 Q c
Medina, *New York* 52 H b
Medina, *North Dakota* 58 G d
Medina, *Ohio* 52 E d
Medina, *Tennessee* 54 C b
Medina, *Texas* 65 H f
Medina, *Washington* 72 C h
Medina L., *Texas* 65 J f
Medina R., *Texas* 65 H f
Medon, *Tennessee* 54 C b
Medora, *Illinois* 57 C k
Medora, *Kansas* 60 G f
Medora, *North Dakota* 58 C d
Medway, *Maine* 49 G c
Medway, *Massachusetts* 51 L a
Meeker, *Colorado* 69 J c
Meeker, *Oklahoma* 62 G c
Meeteetse, *Wyoming* 67 M e
Megargel, *Texas* 65 J b
Meggett, *South Carolina* 55 L e
Megler, *Washington* 73 G j
Meherrin, *Virginia* 53 H h
Meherrin R., *Virginia* 52 H j
Meigs, *Georgia* 54 G f
Mekinock, *North Dakota* 58 J b
Mekoryuk, *Alaska* 76 D f
Melba, *Idaho* 66 D f
Melbourne, *Florida* 54 O e
Melbourne, *Iowa* 61 L c
Melbourne Beach, *Florida* 55 O e
Melcher, *Iowa* 61 L c
Meldrim, *Georgia* 55 K e
Melfa, *Virginia* 53 L h
Mellen, *Wisconsin* 56 C c
Mellenville, *New York* 50 F a
Mellette, *South Dakota* 58 H e
Mellwood, *Arkansas* 63 N d
Melones Res., *California* 74 E g
Melozitna, *Alaska* 76 K d
Melrose, *Idaho* 66 D c
Melrose, *Massachusetts* (29,619) 49 G g
Melrose, *Minnesota* 59 M e
Melrose, *Montana* 66 H d
Melrose, *New Mexico* 71 O e
Melrose, *Oregon* 73 G m
Melrose, *Wisconsin* 56 B e
Melstone, *Montana* 67 N c
Melstrand, *Michigan* 56 G c
Melvern, *Kansas* 61 J f
Melville, *Louisiana* 63 M h
Melville, *Montana* 67 L c
Melville, *New York* 50 G d
Melvin, *Texas* 65 H d
Melvindale, *Michigan* 57 K k
Melvine, *Tennessee* 54 F b
Memphis, *Missouri* 61 M d
Memphis, *Tennessee* (497,524) 54 A b
Memphis, *Texas* 64 D j
Mena, *Arkansas* 63 J d
Menahga, *Minnesota* 59 L d
Menard, *Montana* 66 J d
Menard, *Texas* 65 H e
Menasha, *Wisconsin* 56 E e
Mendenhall, C., *Alaska* 76 D g
Mendenhall, *Mississippi* 63 O g
Mendenhall Glacier, *Alaska* 77 U g
Mendham, *New Jersey* 50 D d
Mendocino, *California* 74 B e
Mendocino, C., *California* 74 A d
Mendon, *Massachusetts* 51 K a
Mendon, *Michigan* 57 H g
Mendon, *Ohio* 52 B e
Mendota, *California* 75 E h
Mendota, *Illinois* 57 D h
Mendota, L., *Wisconsin* 56 D f
Mendota, *Minnesota* 59 R j
Mendota, *Texas* 64 D h
Mendota Heights, *Minnesota* 59 R j
Menlo, *Georgia* 54 F c
Menlo, *Iowa* 61 K c
Menlo, *Kansas* 60 D e
Menlo Park, *California* (26,957) 75 C n
Menno, *South Dakota* 58 J g
Meno, *Oklahoma* 62 E b
Menominee, *Michigan* 56 F d
Menominee R., *Michigan* 56 F d
Menomonee Falls, *Wisconsin* 56 E f
Menomonie, *Wisconsin* 56 B e
Mentanontli R., *Alaska* 76 L c
Mentasta Mts., *Alaska* 77 Q e
Mentasta Village, *Alaska* 77 P e
Mentone, *Indiana* 57 G h
Mentone, *Texas* 64 D d
Mentor, *Minnesota* 59 K c
Mentor, *Ohio* 52 E d
Meramec Park, *Missouri* 61 O f
Merced, *California* 75 E g
Merced, L. de la, *California* 75 B m
Mercedes, *Texas* 65 K j
Merced R., *California* 75 E g
Mercer, *Missouri* 61 L d
Mercer, *North Dakota* 58 F c
Mercer, *Pennsylvania* 52 F d
Mercer, *Tennessee* 54 B b
Mercer, *Washington* 72 C h
Mercer, *Wisconsin* 56 C c
Mercer I., *Washington* 72 C h
Mercersburg, *Pennsylvania* 52 H f
Mercur, *Utah* 68 D c
Mercury, *Texas* 65 H d
Meredith, *New Hampshire* 49 D e
Meredosia, *Illinois* 57 C k
Meriden, *Connecticut* (51,850) 51 H b
Meriden, *Kansas* 61 J e
Meriden, *New Hampshire* 49 C e
Meriden, *Wyoming* 67 Q h
Meridian, *California* 74 D e
Meridian, *Idaho* 66 D f
Meridian, *Mississippi* (49,374) 63 P f
Meridian, *New York* 53 K b
Meridian, *Texas* 65 K d
Merino, *Colorado* 69 N c
Meriwether Lewis Nat. Mon., *Tennessee* 54 D b
Merkel, *Texas* 64 G c
Merlin, *Oregon* 73 G n
Mermentau, *Louisiana* 63 L h
Mermentau R., *Louisiana* 63 L j
Merna, *Nebraska* 60 E c
Merna, *Wyoming* 67 K g
Merriam, *Kansas* 61 P b
Merricourt, *North Dakota* 58 H d
Merrill, *Iowa* 60 H b
Merrill, *Michigan* 56 J f
Merrill, *Mississippi* 63 P h
Merrill, *Oregon* 73 J n
Merrill, *Wisconsin* 56 D d
Merrillan, *Wisconsin* 56 C e
Merrimac, *Wisconsin* 56 D f
Merrimack R., *New Hampshire* 49 D e
Merriman, *Nebraska* 60 C b
Merriman Dam, *New York* 50 E b
Merritt, L., *California* 75 C l
Merritt I., *Florida* 55 L j
Merritt Res., *Nebraska* 60 D b
Mer Rouge, *Louisiana* 63 M f
Merryville, *Louisiana* 63 K h
Mertzon, *Texas* 64 G d
Merwin, L., *Washington* 73 H k
Mesa, *Arizona* (33,772) 70 F f
Mesa, *Idaho* 66 D e
Mesa, *New Mexico* 71 N f
Mesabi Ra., *Minnesota* 59 N c
Mesa Mt., *Alaska* 76 K f
Mesa Verde Nat. Park, *Colorado* 68 H f
Mescal, *Arizona* 70 G h
Mescalero, *New Mexico* 71 M f
Mesick, *Michigan* 56 H e
Mesilla, *New Mexico* 71 L g

Moro, *Arkansas* 63 N d
Moro, *Oregon* 73 K k
Morocco, *Indiana* 57 F j
Moroni, *Utah* 68 E d
Morral, *Ohio* 52 C e
Morrice, *Michigan* 56 J g
Morrill, *Kansas* 61 J e
Morrill, *Nebraska* 60 A c
Morrilton, *Arkansas* 63 L c
Morris, *Connecticut* 50 G b
Morris, *Illinois* 57 E h
Morris, *Minnesota* 59 L e
Morris, *New York* 53 L c
Morris, *Oklahoma* 62 H c
Morris, *Pennsylvania* 53 J d
Morris I., *South Carolina* 55 M e
Morrison, *Colorado* 69 N j
Morrison, *Illinois* 57 D h
Morrison, *Oklahoma* 62 G b
Morrison, *Tennessee* 54 F b
Morrisonville, *Illinois* 57 D k
Morris Plains, *New Jersey* 50 D d
Morris Run, *Pennsylvania* 53 K d
Morriston, *Florida* 55 J h
Morristown, *Arizona* 70 E f
Morristown, *Minnesota* 59 N f
Morristown, *New Jersey* 50 D d
Morristown, *New York* 53 L a
Morristown, *South Dakota* 58 E e
Morristown, *Tennessee* 54 H a
Morristown Nat. Hist. Park, *New Jersey* 50 D d
Morrisville, *New York* 53 L c
Morrisville, *Pennsylvania* 50 D e
Morrisville, *Vermont* 49 C d
Morrisville, *Virginia* 52 J g
Morro Bay, *California* 75 E j
Morrow, *Louisiana* 63 L h
Morrow, *Ohio* 52 B f
Morse, *Louisiana* 63 L h
Morse, *Texas* 64 C g
Morse Res., *Indiana* 57 G j
Mortmar, *California* 75 K l
Morton, *Illinois* 57 D j
Morton, *Minnesota* 59 M f
Morton, *Mississippi* 63 O f
Morton, *Texas* 64 E b
Morton, *Washington* 73 H j
Morton Grove, *Illinois, vicinity of Chicago*
Mortons Gap, *Kentucky* 57 F m
Morven, *Georgia* 54 H g
Morven, *North Carolina* 55 L c
Morzhovoi B., *Alaska* 76 F j
Mosby, *Montana* 67 N b
Moscow, *Idaho* 66 D c
Moscow, *Kansas* 60 C g
Moscow, *Missouri* 61 O f
Moscow, *Ohio* 52 B g
Moscow, *Pennsylvania* 50 B c
Moscow, *Tennessee* 54 B b
Moselem Springs, *Pennsylvania* 50 B d
Moseley, *Virginia* 52 J h
Moselle, *Mississippi* 63 O g
Moses, Mt., *Nevada* 74 H d
Moses, *New Mexico* 71 O c
Moses Coulee, *Washington* 73 L h
Moses Coulee R., *Washington* 73 L h
Moses L., *Washington* 73 L h
Moses Lake, *Washington* 73 L h
Moses Point, *Alaska* 76 F d
Mosheim, *Tennessee* 55 J a
Moskee, *Wyoming* 67 Q e
Mosmee, *Wisconsin* 56 D e
Mosquero, *New Mexico* 71 N d
Mosquite Creek Res., *Ohio* 52 F d
Mosquito Lagoon, *Florida* 55 L j
Moss Beach, *California* 75 B n
Moss Pt., *Mississippi* 63 P h
Mossy Head, *Florida* 54 E g
Mossyrock, *Washington* 73 H j
Mother Goose L., *Alaska* 76 J h
Motley, *Minnesota* 59 M d
Motoqua, *Utah* 68 C f
Mott, *North Dakota* 58 D d
Moulton, *Alabama* 54 D c
Moulton, *Idaho* 66 G g
Moulton, *Iowa* 61 M d
Moulton, *Texas* 65 K f
Moultrie, *Georgia* 54 H f
Moultrie, L., *South Carolina* 55 L d
Mound Bayou, *Mississippi* 63 N e
Mound City, *Illinois* 57 D m
Mound City, *Kansas* 61 K f
Mound City, *Missouri* 61 J d
Mound City, *South Dakota* 58 F e
Mound City Nat. Mon., *Ohio* 52 D f
Mound Ridge, *Kansas* 60 G f
Mounds, *Illinois* 57 D m
Mounds, *Oklahoma* 62 G c
Mounds View, *Minnesota* 59 Q h
Moundsville, *West Virginia* 52 F f
Mound Valley, *Kansas* 61 J g
Moundville, *Alabama* 54 D e
Mountain, *North Dakota* 58 J b
Mountain, *West Virginia* 52 F f
Mountain, *Wisconsin* 56 E d
Mountainair, *New Mexico* 71 L e
Mountain City, *Nevada* 74 K c
Mountain City, *Tennessee* 55 K a
Mountain Creek L., *Texas* 65 N j
Mountain Dale, *New York* 50 E b
Mountain Grove, *Missouri* 61 M g
Mountain Home, *Arkansas* 63 L b
Mountain Home, *Idaho* 66 E f
Mountainhome, *Pennsylvania* 50 C c
Mountain Home, *Texas* 65 H e
Mountain Home, *Utah* 68 F c
Mountain Island L., *North Carolina* 55 L b
Mountain Lake, *Minnesota* 59 L g
Mountain Lakes, *New Jersey* 50 E d
Mountain Park, *Oklahoma* 62 E d
Mountain Pine, *Arkansas* 63 K d
Mountaintop, *Pennsylvania* 50 B c
Mountain View, *Arkansas* 63 L c
Mountain View, *California (30,889), vicinity of San Francisco*
Mountain View, *Hawaii* 72 E f
Mountain View, *Missouri* 61 N h
Mountain View, *Oklahoma* 62 E c
Mountainview, *Wyoming* 67 K h
Mountain Village, *Alaska* 76 F e
Mountainville, *New York* 50 E c
Mount Airy, *Maryland* 53 J f
Mount Airy, *North Carolina* 55 L a
Mount Angel, *Oregon* 73 H k
Mount Auburn, *Illinois* 57 D k
Mount Ayr, *Iowa* 61 K d
Mount Calm, *Texas* 65 L d
Mount Calvary, *Wisconsin* 56 E f
Mount Carmel, *Connecticut* 51 H c
Mount Carmel, *Illinois* 57 E l
Mount Carmel, *Pennsylvania* 53 K e
Mount Carmel, *South Carolina* 55 J c
Mount Carmel, *Utah* 68 D f
Mount Carroll, *Illinois* 57 D g
Mount Clare, *Nebraska* 60 F d
Mount Clare, *West Virginia* 52 F f
Mount Clemens, *Michigan* 56 L g
Mount Dell Res., *Utah* 68 D h
Mount Desert I., *Maine* 49 G d
Mount Desert Rock, *Maine* 49 G e
Mount Dora, *Florida* 55 K j
Mount Dora, *New Mexico* 71 O c
Mount Edgecombe, *Alaska* 77 U h
Mount Enterprise, *Texas* 65 N d
Mount Gilead, *North Carolina* 55 L b
Mount Gilead, *Ohio* 52 D e
Mount Harris, *Colorado* 69 J c
Mount Hays, *Maryland* 53 R f
Mount Holly, *New Jersey* 50 D e
Mount Holly Springs, *Pennsylvania* 52 J e
Mount Hope, *Kansas* 60 G g
Mount Hope, *New Jersey* 50 D d
Mount Hope, *West Virginia* 52 E h
Mount Hope B., *Rhode Island* 51 L b
Mount Horeb, *Wisconsin* 56 D f
Mount Ida, *Arkansas* 63 K d
Mount Idaho, *Idaho* 66 D d
Mount Jackson, *Virginia* 52 H g
Mount Jewett, *Pennsylvania* 52 H d
Mount Joy, *Pennsylvania* 53 K e
Mount Kisco, *New York* 50 F c
Mount Laurel, *New Jersey* 50 D f
Mount Lebanon, *Pennsylvania (35,361)* 53 O b
Mount Lena, *Utah* 68 G c
Mount McKinley Nat. Park, *Alaska* 76 M e
Mount Meadows Res., *California* 74 E d
Mount Moriah, *Missouri* 61 L d
Mount Morris, *Illinois* 57 D g
Mount Morris, *New York* 52 J c
Mount Morris Res., *New York* 52 J c
Mount Olive, *Illinois* 57 D k
Mount Olive, *Mississippi* 63 O g
Mount Olive, *North Carolina* 55 N b
Mount Oliver, *Pennsylvania* 53 P b
Mount Orab, *Ohio* 52 B f
Mount Owen, *California* 75 H j
Mount Penn, *Pennsylvania* 50 B e
Mount Pleasant, *Iowa* 61 N d
Mount Pleasant, *Michigan* 56 J f
Mount Pleasant, *Pennsylvania* 52 G e
Mount Pleasant, *South Carolina* 55 M e
Mount Pleasant, *Tennessee* 54 D b
Mount Pleasant, *Texas* 65 N b
Mount Pleasant, *Utah* 68 E d
Mount Pocono, *Pennsylvania* 50 C c
Mount Prospect, *Illinois, vicinity of Chicago*
Mount Pulaski, *Illinois* 57 D j
Mount Rainier, *Maryland* 53 Q g
Mount Rainier Nat. Park, *Washington* 73 J j
Mount Riga, *New York* 50 F b
Mount Riley, *New Mexico* 71 K h
Mount Royal, *New Jersey* 50 C f
Mount Rushmore Nat. Memorial, *South Dakota* 58 C g
Mount Savage, *Maryland* 52 G f
Mount Selman, *Texas* 65 M c
Mount Shasta, *California* 74 C c
Mount Sterling, *Illinois* 57 C k
Mount Sterling, *Ohio* 52 C f
Mount Storm, *West Virginia* 52 G f
Mount Trumbull, *Arizona* 70 D c
Mount Union, *Iowa* 61 N c
Mount Union, *Pennsylvania* 52 J e
Mount Vernon, *Alabama* 54 D f
Mount Vernon, *Arkansas* 63 L c
Mount Vernon, *Georgia* 55 J e
Mount Vernon, *Illinois* 57 D l
Mount Vernon, *Indiana* 57 F m
Mount Vernon, *Iowa* 61 N c
Mount Vernon, *Kentucky* 57 J m
Mount Vernon, *Missouri* 61 L g
Mount Vernon, *New York (76,010)* 51 N d
Mount Vernon, *Ohio* 52 D e
Mount Vernon, *Oregon* 73 L l
Mount Vernon, *South Dakota* 58 H g
Mount Vernon, *Texas* 65 M b
Mount Vernon, *Virginia* 53 J g
Mount Vernon, *Washington* 73 H g
Mount Victory, *Ohio* 52 C e
Mount View, *Washington* 72 B j
Mount Washington, *Maryland* 53 P e
Mount Washington, *Massachusetts* 50 G a
Mount Willing, *Alabama* 54 E e
Mount Wilson Res., *California* 75 H k
Mount Zion, *Illinois* 57 E k
Mount Zion, *Iowa* 61 N d
Mouse R., *North Dakota* 58 E b
Moville, *Iowa* 61 H b
Moweaqua, *Illinois* 57 E k
Mowich, *Oregon* 73 J m
Moxee City, *Washington* 73 K j
Moyie Springs, *Idaho* 66 D a
Mud Butte, *South Dakota* 58 D e
Mud Cr., *Nebraska* 60 E c
Muddy Boggy Cr., *Oklahoma* 62 G d
Muddy Cr., *Wyoming* 67 N h
Muddy Cr., *Wyoming* 67 O g
Muddy Cr., *Wyoming* 67 K h
Muddy Cr., *Wyoming* 67 M f
Muddy Creek, *Utah* 68 E e
Muddy Gap, *Wyoming* 67 N g
Muddy Pk., *Nevada* 75 L h
Mud Flat, *Nevada* 74 F d
Mud L., *Idaho* 66 H f
Mud L., *Montana* 67 L a
Mud L., *Nevada* 74 H g
Mud L., *Nevada* 74 F c
Mud Lake Res., *South Dakota* 58 H e
Muenster, *Texas* 65 K b
Muhlenburg, *Pennsylvania* 50 A c
Muir, *Michigan* 56 J f
Muir Glacier, *Alaska* 77 T g
Muir Woods Nat. Mon., *California* 74 C g
Mukwonago, *Wisconsin* 56 E g
Mulberry, *Arkansas* 63 J c
Mulberry, *Florida* 55 N f
Mulberry, *Indiana* 57 G j
Mulberry, *Kansas* 61 K g
Mulberry Grove, *Illinois* 57 D l
Mulberry R., *Arkansas* 63 K c
Mulchatna R., *Alaska* 76 K f
Muldoon, *Idaho* 66 G f
Mule Cr., *Texas* 64 E e
Mule Creek, *New Mexico* 71 J f
Mule Creek, *Wyoming* 67 Q f
Muleshoe, *Texas* 64 E a
Mulgrave Hills, *Alaska* 76 F c
Mulhall, *Oklahoma* 62 F b
Mullan, *Idaho* 66 E b
Mullen, *Nebraska* 60 C b
Mullen, *Texas* 65 J d
Mullens, *West Virginia* 52 E h
Mullet Key, *Florida* 55 M f
Mullett L., *Michigan* 56 J d
Mullica Hill, *New Jersey* 50 C f
Mullica R., *New Jersey* 50 D f
Mullins, *South Carolina* 55 M c
Mullinville, *Kansas* 60 E g
Mulvane, *Kansas* 60 G g
Mumford, *Texas* 65 L e
Mumtrak, *Alaska* 76 G g
Muncie, *Indiana (68,603)* 57 H j
Muncie, *Kansas* 61 O a
Muncy, *Pennsylvania* 53 K d
Munday, *Texas* 65 H b
Munden, *Kansas* 60 G e
Munfordville, *Kentucky* 57 H m
Munger, *Michigan* 56 K f
Mungerville, *Texas* 64 E c
Munhall, *Pennsylvania* 53 Q b
Munich, *North Dakota* 58 H b
Munising, *Michigan* 56 G c
Munson, *Florida* 54 D g
Munuscong L., *Michigan* 56 J c
Murdo, *South Dakota* 58 F g
Murdock, *Florida* 55 M f
Murdock, *Nebraska* 60 H d
Murfreesboro, *Arkansas* 63 K d
Murfreesboro, *North Carolina* 55 O a
Murfreesboro, *Tennessee* 54 E b
Muroc L. See Rogers L., *California* 75 H k
Murphy, *Idaho* 66 D f
Murphy, *North Carolina* 54 G b
Murphy, *Oregon* 73 G n
Murphys, *California* 74 E f
Murphysboro, *Illinois* 57 D m
Murray, *Iowa* 61 L c
Murray, *Kentucky* 57 E n
Murray, L., *Oklahoma* 62 F d
Murray, L., *South Carolina* 55 K c
Murray, *Nebraska* 61 J d
Murray, *Utah* 68 C h
Murray City, *Ohio* 52 D f
Murrayville, *Illinois* 57 C k
Murrells Inlet, *South Carolina* 55 M d
Murtaugh, *Idaho* 66 F g
Murvaul Res., *Texas* 65 N c
Muscatine, *Iowa* 61 N c
Muscle Shoals, *Alabama* 54 D c
Muscoda, *Wisconsin* 56 C f
Musconetcong R., *New Jersey* 50 D d
Muscongus B., *Maine* 49 F e
Muskeg B., *Minnesota* 59 L b
Muskeget Chan., *Massachusetts* 51 N c
Muskeget I., *Massachusetts* 51 N c
Muskegon, *Michigan (46,485)* 56 G f
Muskegon Heights, *Michigan* 56 G f
Muskegon R., *Michigan* 56 H f
Muskingum R., *Ohio* 52 E f
Muskogee, *Oklahoma (38,059)* 62 H c
Muskrat Cr., *Wyoming* 67 N f
Music Mt., *Arizona* 70 D d
Musinia Pk., *Utah* 68 E d
Musselshell, *Montana* 67 M c
Musselshell R., *Montana* 67 N c
Mustang, *Oklahoma* 62 F c
Mustang Creek, *Texas* 64 E c
Mustang I., *Texas* 65 K h
Mustinka, *Minnesota* 59 K e
Mutual, *Oklahoma* 62 D b
Muzon, C., *Alaska* 77 V j
Myakka, *Florida* 55 M f
Myakka City, *Florida* 55 M f
Myakka R., *Florida* 55 M f
Myers Chuck, *Alaska* 77 V j
Myerstown, *Pennsylvania* 53 K e
Mykawa, *Texas* 64 G j
Mylo, *North Dakota* 58 G b
Myra, *Texas* 65 K b
Myricks, *Massachusetts* 51 L b
Myrtle, *Idaho* 66 D c
Myrtle, *Mississippi* 63 O d
Myrtle Beach, *South Carolina* 55 N d
Myrtle Creek, *Oregon* 73 G m
Myrtle Point, *Oregon* 73 F m
Mystic, *Connecticut* 51 K c
Mystic, *Georgia* 54 H f
Mystic, *Iowa* 61 M d
Mystic, *South Dakota* 58 C f
Mytkof I., *Alaska* 77 V h
Myton, *Utah* 68 F c
Naalehu, *Hawaii* 72 E f
Nabesna, *Alaska* 77 Q e
Nabesna Glacier, *Alaska* 77 Q f
Nabesna R., *Alaska* 77 Q e
Nabesna Village, *Alaska* 77 Q e
Naches, *Washington* 73 K j
Naches Pass, *Washington* 73 J h
Naches R., *Washington* 73 K j
Nacimiento R., *California* 75 D j
Nacimiento Res., *California* 75 D j
Nacogdoches, *Texas* 65 N d
Nada, *Utah* 68 C e
Nadeau, *Michigan* 56 F d
Nadine, *Pennsylvania* 53 Q a
Naf, *Idaho* 66 G g
Nagai I., *Alaska* 76 G j
Nahant, *Massachusetts* 49 H h
Nahcotta, *Washington* 73 F j
Nahma, *Michigan* 56 G d
Nahunta, *Georgia* 55 K f
Nakchamik I., *Alaska* 76 J h
Naked I., *Alaska* 77 O f
Naknek, *Alaska* 76 J g
Naknek L., *Alaska* 76 J g
Nallen, *West Virginia* 52 F g
Namekagon R., *Michigan* 56 B c
Nampa, *Idaho* 66 D f
Nanakuli, *Hawaii* 72 C d
Nantahala L., *North Carolina* 54 H b
Nantasket Beach, *Massachusetts* 51 M a
Nanticoke, *Pennsylvania* 50 B c
Nanticoke R., *Maryland* 53 L g
Nantucket I., *Massachusetts* 51 N c
Nantucket Sd., *Massachusetts* 51 N b
Nanty Glo, *Pennsylvania* 52 H e
Nanuet, *New York* 50 E c
Nanushuk R., *Alaska* 76 M b
Naomi Pk., *Utah* 68 E b
Napa, *California* 74 C f
Napaiskak, *Alaska* 76 G f
Napamute, *Alaska* 76 H f
Napanoch, *New York* 50 E b
Napavine, *Washington* 73 H j
Napeague B., *New York* 51 J c
Napeague Beach, *New York* 51 K c
Naperville, *Illinois* 57 E h
Napier, *Missouri* 61 J d
Naples, *Florida* 55 N g
Naples, *New York* 53 J c
Naples, *Texas* 65 N b
Napoleon, *Indiana* 57 H k
Napoleon, *North Dakota* 58 G d
Napoleon, *Ohio* 52 B d
Napoleonville, *Louisiana* 63 M j
Naponee, *Nebraska* 60 E d
Napoopoo, *Hawaii* 72 E f
Nappanee, *Indiana* 57 H h
Napton, *Missouri* 61 L e
Naranja, *Florida* 55 O h
Nara Visa, *New Mexico* 71 O d
Narberth, *Pennsylvania* 50 A a
Narka, *Kansas* 60 G e
Narragansett B., *Rhode Island* 51 L b
Narragansett Pier, *Rhode Island* 51 L c
Narrows, *Oregon* 73 M m
Narrows, The, *New York* 51 L g
Narrows, *Virginia* 52 F h
Narrowsburg, *New York* 50 C b
Nash, *Oklahoma* 62 E b
Nash, *Texas* 65 N b
Nashawena, *Massachusetts* 51 M c
Nash Harbor, *Alaska* 76 D f
Nashua, *Iowa* 61 M b
Nashua, *Missouri* 61 K e
Nashua, *Montana* 67 O a
Nashua, *New Hampshire (39,096)* 49 D f
Nashville, *Arkansas* 63 K e
Nashville, *Georgia* 54 H f
Nashville, *Illinois* 57 D l
Nashville, *Indiana* 57 G k
Nashville, *Kansas* 60 F g
Nashville, *Michigan* 56 H g
Nashville, *North Carolina* 55 N b
Nashville, *Ohio* 52 D e
Nashville, *Tennessee (170,874)* 54 E a
Nashville Basin, *Tennessee* 54 E b
Nashwauk, *Minnesota* 59 N c
Nassau, *New York* 53 N c
Nassau, *South Dakota* 59 K e
Nassau Sd., *Florida* 55 K g
Nassawadox, *Virginia* 53 L h
Natalia, *Texas* 65 J f
Natchez, *Mississippi* 63 M g
Natchitoches, *Louisiana* 63 K g
Nathrop, *Colorado* 69 K e
Natick, *Massachusetts (28,831)* 51 L a
Natick, *Rhode Island* 51 L b
Nation, *Alaska* 77 R d
National City, *California (32,771)* 75 J m
Nation R., *Alaska* 77 R d
Natoma, *Kansas* 60 E e
Natrona, *Wyoming* 67 O f
Natural Bridge, *New York* 53 L a
Natural Bridge, *Virginia* 52 G h
Natural Bridges Nat. Mon., *Utah* 68 F f
Natural Dam L., *Texas* 64 F c
Naturita, *Colorado* 68 H e
Natuvukti L., *Alaska* 76 K c
Naubinway, *Michigan* 56 H c
Naugatuck, *Connecticut* 50 G c
Naushon I., *Massachusetts* 51 M b
Nauvoo, *Alabama* 54 D d
Nauvoo, *Illinois* 57 B j
Navajo, *Arizona* 70 H d
Navajo L., *Utah* 68 D f
Navajo Mt., *Utah* 68 F f
Navajo Nat. Mon., *Arizona* 70 G c
Navajo Point, *Arizona* 70 F c
Navajo Res., *Colorado-New Mexico* 71 K c
Navarre, *Ohio* 52 E e
Navarro, *California* 74 B e
Navarro R., *California* 74 B e
Navasota, *Texas* 65 L e
Navasota R., *Texas* 65 L e
Navesink, *New Jersey* 50 E e
Navidad R., *Texas* 65 L f
Navy Town, *Alaska* 76 J j
Naylor, *Georgia* 54 H g
Naylor, *Missouri* 61 O h
Nazareth, *Pennsylvania* 50 C d
Nazareth, *Texas* 64 B j
Neah Bay, *Washington* 73 F g
Neal, *Kansas* 61 H g
Near Is., *Alaska* 76 J j
Nebo, Mt., *Utah* 68 E d
Nebraska *(1,435,000)* 77,227 sq. miles 60-61
Nebraska City, *Nebraska* 61 J d
Necedah, *Wisconsin* 56 C e
Neche, *North Dakota* 58 J b
Neches, *Texas* 65 M d
Neches R., *Texas* 65 N e
Necker I., *Hawaii* 72 D b
Nederland, *Colorado* 69 L d
Nederland, *Texas* 65 N f
Needham, *Massachusetts (25,793)* 49 F j
Needle Mt., *Wyoming* 67 L e
Needles, *California* 75 L k
Needmore, *Georgia* 55 J g
Needmore, *Texas* 64 E a
Needville, *Texas* 65 M f
Neely, *Idaho* 66 H g
Neelyville, *Missouri* 61 O h
Neenah, *Wisconsin* 56 E e
Nee Res., *Colorado* 69 O e
Neeses, *South Carolina* 55 K d
Neffs, *Pennsylvania* 50 B d
Negaunee, *Michigan* 56 F c
Negro Mt., *Maryland* 52 G f
Nehalem, *Oregon* 73 G k
Nehalem R., *Oregon* 73 G k
Neihart, *Montana* 67 K c
Neillsville, *Wisconsin* 56 C e
Neilton, *Washington* 73 G h
Nekoma, *North Dakota* 58 H b
Nekoosa, *Wisconsin* 56 D e
Neligh, *Nebraska* 60 F b
Nelson, *Arizona* 70 D d
Nelson, *California* 74 D e
Nelson, *Missouri* 61 L f
Nelson, *Nebraska* 60 F d
Nelson, *Nevada* 75 L j
Nelson, *North Carolina* 55 N b
Nelson, *Pennsylvania* 53 J d
Nelson, *Wisconsin* 56 A e
Nelson I., *Alaska* 76 E f
Nelson Res., *Montana* 67 N a
Nelsonville, *New York* 50 F c
Nelsonville, *Ohio* 52 D f
Nemadji R., *Minnesota* 59 O d
Nemaha, *Nebraska* 61 J d
Nenana, *Alaska* 76 N d
Nenana R., *Alaska* 76 N d
Nenzel, *Nebraska* 60 C b
Neodesha, *Kansas* 61 J g
Neodesha Res., *Kansas* 61 J g
Neoga, *Illinois* 57 E k
Neola, *Iowa* 61 J c
Neola, *Utah* 68 F c
Neopit, *Wisconsin* 56 E e
Neosho, *Missouri* 61 K h
Neosho, *Wisconsin* 56 E f
Neosho Dam, *Oklahoma* 62 H b
Neosho R., *Kansas* 61 J g
Nepaug Res., *Connecticut* 51 H b
Nephi, *Utah* 68 E d
Neptune Beach, *Florida* 55 K g
Neragon I., *Alaska* 76 D f
Nerka, L., *Alaska* 76 H g
Nescopeck, *Pennsylvania* 50 A c
Neshaminy, *Pennsylvania* 50 C e
Neshaminy Cr., *Pennsylvania* 50 C e
Neshkoro, *Wisconsin* 56 D f
Neshoba, *Mississippi* 63 O f
Nespelem, *Washington* 73 M g
Nesquehoning, *Pennsylvania* 50 B d
Ness City, *Kansas* 60 E f
Nestoria, *Michigan* 56 E c
Netawaka, *Kansas* 61 H e
Netcong, *New Jersey* 50 D d
Nett L., *Minnesota* 59 N b
Nettleton, *Arkansas* 63 N c
Nettleton, *Mississippi* 63 P d
Neuse R., *North Carolina* 55 O b
Neuville, *Texas* 65 N d
Neva, *Wisconsin* 56 D d
Nevada *(444,000)* 110,540 sq. miles 74-75
Nevada, *Iowa* 61 L b
Nevada, *Missouri* 61 K g
Nevada, *Texas* 65 L b
Nevada City, *California* 74 E e
Neva Shoal, *Hawaii* 72 B a
Neversink, *New York* 50 D b
Neversink R., *New York* 50 D b
Neversink Res., *New York* 50 D b
Nevils, *Georgia* 55 K e
Nevis, *Minnesota* 59 M d
Newagen, *Maine* 49 F e
New Albany, *Indiana (37,812)* 57 H l
New Albany, *Mississippi* 63 O d
New Albany, *Pennsylvania* 53 K d
New Albin, *Iowa* 61 N a
Newald, *Wisconsin* 56 E d
Newark, *Arkansas* 63 M c
Newark, *California* 74 C g
Newark, *Delaware* 50 B f
Newark, *Illinois* 57 E h
Newark, *Nebraska* 60 F d
Newark, *New Jersey (405,220)* 50 E d
Newark, *New York* 53 J b
Newark, *Ohio (41,790)* 52 D e
Newark B., *New Jersey* 51 K f
Newark Valley, *New York* 53 K c
New Athens, *Illinois* 57 D l
New Auburn, *Wisconsin* 56 B d
New Augusta, *Mississippi* 63 O g
Newaygo, *Michigan* 56 H f
New Baltimore, *Michigan* 56 L g
New Baltimore, *Pennsylvania* 52 H f
New Bedford, *Massachusetts (102,477)* 51 L b
Newberg, *Oregon* 73 H k
New Berlin, *Illinois* 57 C k
New Berlin, *New York* 53 L c
New Berlinville, *Pennsylvania* 50 B e
Newbern, *Alabama* 54 D e
New Bern, *North Carolina* 55 O b
Newbern, *Tennessee* 54 B a
Newberry, *California* 75 J k
Newberry, *Florida* 55 J h
Newberry, *Indiana* 57 F l
Newberry, *South Carolina* 55 K c
New Bethlehem, *Pennsylvania* 52 G d
New Bloomfield, *Missouri* 61 M f
Newbold, *Wisconsin* 56 D d
New Boston, *Illinois* 57 C h
New Boston, *Massachusetts* 51 G a
New Boston, *Texas* 65 N b
New Braunfels, *Texas* 65 J f
New Bremen, *Ohio* 52 B e
New Brighton, *Minnesota* 59 Q h
New Brighton, *New York* 51 K g
New Britain, *Connecticut (82,201)* 51 H b
New Brockton, *Alabama* 54 F f
New Brunswick, *New Jersey (40,139)* 50 E e
New Buffalo, *Michigan* 57 G h
Newburg, *Iowa* 61 M c
Newburg, *Missouri* 61 N g
Newburg, *Pennsylvania* 52 J e
Newburg, *West Virginia* 52 G f
Newburgh, *Indiana* 57 F m
Newburgh, *New York (30,979)* 50 E c
Newburgh Junction, *New York* 50 E c
Newburyport, *Massachusetts* 49 E f
New Canaan, *Connecticut* 50 G c

New Canton, *Illinois* 57 B k
New Carlisle, *Ohio* 52 B f
Newcastle, *California* 74 D f
New Castle, *Colorado* 69 J d
New Castle, *Delaware* 50 B f
New Castle, *Indiana* 57 H k
New Castle, *Kentucky* 57 H l
Newcastle, *Nebraska* 60 H b
Newcastle, *Oklahoma* 62 F c
New Castle, *Pennsylvania* *(44,790)* 52 F e
New Castle, *Texas* 65 J b
Newcastle, *Utah* 68 C f
New Castle, *Virginia* 52 F h
Newcastle, *Wyoming* 67 Q f
New City, *New York* 50 F c
Newcomb, *New Mexico* 71 J c
Newcomerstown, *Ohio* 52 E e
New Concord, *Ohio* 52 E e
New Croton Res., *New York* 50 F c
Newdale, *Idaho* 66 J f
New Dorp, *New York* 51 K g
New Edinburg, *Arkansas* 63 L e
New Egypt, *New Jersey* 50 D e
Newell, *Georgia* 55 J g
Newell, *Iowa* 61 J b
Newell, *North Carolina* 55 L b
Newell, *South Dakota* 58 C f
New Ellenton, *South Carolina* 55 K d
Newellton, *Louisiana* 63 M f
New England, *North Dakota* 58 D d
Newenham, C., *Alaska* 76 F g
Newent, *Connecticut* 51 J b
New Era, *Michigan* 56 G f
New Eshota Nat. Mon., *Georgia* 54 G c
New Fairfield, *Connecticut* 50 G c
Newfane, *New York* 52 H b
Newfane, *Vermont* 49 C e
Newfield, *Maine* 49 E e
Newfield, *New Jersey* 50 D f
New Florence, *Missouri* 61 N f
Newfolden, *Minnesota* 59 K b
Newfoundland, *New Jersey* 50 E c
Newfoundland, *Pennsylvania* 50 C c
New Franklin, *Missouri* 61 M e
New Freedom, *Pennsylvania* 53 K f
New Glarus, *Wisconsin* 56 D g
New Gloucester, *Maine* 49 E e
New Gretna, *New Jersey* 50 E f
New Gulf, *Texas* 65 M f
Newhalem, *Washington* 73 J g
Newhalen, *Alaska* 76 K g
Newhall, *California* 75 G k
New Hamburg, *New York* 50 F b
New Hamilton, *Alaska* 76 F e
New Hampshire *(685,000)* 9304 sq. miles 49
New Hampton, *Iowa* 61 M a
New Hampton, *Missouri* 61 K d
New Hampton, *New York* 50 E c
New Harbor, *Maine* 49 F e
New Harmony, *Indiana* 57 F l
New Hartford, *Connecticut* 51 H b
New Haven, *Connecticut* *(152,048)* 51 H c
New Haven, *Indiana* 57 H h
New Haven, *Missouri* 61 N f
New Haven, *West Virginia* 52 E g
New Haven, *Wyoming* 67 Q e
New Holland, *Illinois* 57 D j
New Holland, *Pennsylvania* 50 A e
New Holstein, *Wisconsin* 56 E f
Newhope, *Arkansas* 63 K d
New Hope, *Minnesota* 59 P h
New Hope, *Pennsylvania* 50 D e
New Iberia, *Louisiana* *(29,062)* 63 M j
Newington, *Connecticut* 51 H b
Newington, *Georgia* 55 K e
New Jersey *(7,004,000)* 7836 sq. miles 50
New Kensington, *Pennsylvania* 52 G e
New Kent, *Virginia* 53 K h
Newkirk, *New Mexico* 71 N d
Newkirk, *Oklahoma* 62 F b
New Knock Hock, *Alaska* 76 E e
New L., *North Carolina* 55 P b
New Leipzig, *North Dakota* 58 E d
New Lexington, *Ohio* 52 D f
Newlin, *Texas* 64 D j
New Lisbon, *Wisconsin* 56 C f
New London, *Connecticut* *(34,182)* 51 J c
New London, *Iowa* 61 N d
New London, *Minnesota* 59 M e
New London, *Missouri* 61 N e
New London, *Ohio* 52 D d
New London, *Pennsylvania* 50 B f
New London, *Wisconsin* 56 E e
New Madrid, *Missouri* 61 P h
Newman, *California* 75 D g
Newman, *Illinois* 57 F k
Newman, *New Mexico* 71 L g
Newman Grove, *Nebraska* 60 G c
New Market, *Alabama* 54 E c
New Market, *Iowa* 61 K d
Newmarket, *New Hampshire* 49 E e
New Market, *Virginia* 52 H g
New Marlborough, *Massachusetts* 50 G a
New Marshfield, *Ohio* 52 D f
New Martinsville, *West Virginia* 52 F f
New Matamoras, *Ohio* 52 E f
New Meadows, *Idaho* 66 D e
New Mexico *(1,003,000)* 121,666 sq. miles 71
New Miami, *Ohio* 52 B f
New Milford, *Connecticut* 50 G b
New Milford, *New Jersey* 51 L d
New Milford, *New York* 50 E c
New Milford, *Pennsylvania* 53 L d
New Moore, *Texas* 64 E b
Newnan, *Georgia* 54 G d
Newnan L., *Florida* 55 J h
New Orleans, *Louisiana* *(627,525)* 63 N h
New Oxford, *Pennsylvania* 52 J f
New Paltz, *New York* 50 E b
New Paris, *Ohio* 52 B f
New Pekin, *Indiana* 57 G l
New Philadelphia, *Ohio* 52 E e
New Pine Creek, *Oregon* 73 K n
New Plymouth, *Idaho* 66 D f
Newport, *Arkansas* 63 M c
Newport, *Delaware* 50 B f
Newport, *Indiana* 57 F k
Newport, *Kentucky (30,070)* 57 J l
Newport, *Maine* 49 F d
Newport, *Michigan* 57 K h
Newport, *Minnesota* 59 R j
Newport, *Nebraska* 60 E b
Newport, *New Hampshire* 49 C e
Newport, *New Jersey* 50 C g
Newport, *North Carolina* 55 P c
Newport, *Oregon* 73 F l
Newport, *Pennsylvania* 53 J e
Newport, *Rhode Island* *(47,049)* 51 L b
Newport, *Tennessee* 54 H b
Newport, *Texas* 65 J b
Newport, *Vermont* 49 C d
Newport, *Washington* 73 N g
Newport B., *Rhode Island* 51 L c
Newport Beach, *California* *(26,564)* 75 H l
Newport News, *Virginia* *(113,662)* 53 K j
New Port Richey, *Florida* 55 M e
New Prague, *Minnesota* 59 N f
New Preston, *Connecticut* 50 G b
New R., *California* 75 K m
New R., *Florida* 55 J h
New R., *Virginia, etc.* 52 F j
New Raymer, *Colorado* 69 N c
New Richland, *Minnesota* 59 N g
New Richmond, *Ohio* 52 B g
New Richmond, *Wisconsin* 56 A d
New Ringgold, *Pennsylvania* 50 A d
New River, *Tennessee* 54 G a
New River Inlet, *North Carolina* 55 O c
New Roads, *Louisiana* 63 M h
New Rochelle, *New York* *(76,812)* 51 N d
New Rockford, *North Dakota* 58 G c
New Ross, *Indiana* 57 G k
Newry, *Maine* 49 E d
Newry, *Pennsylvania* 52 H e
New Salem, *North Dakota* 58 E d
New Salem, *Pennsylvania* 52 G f
New Sharon, *Iowa* 61 M c
New Smyrna Beach, *Florida* 55 L h
New Straitsville, *Ohio* 52 D f
New Stuyahok, *Alaska* 76 J g
New Tazewell, *Tennessee* 54 H a
Newton, *Alabama* 54 F f
Newton, *Illinois* 57 E l
Newton, *Iowa* 61 L c
Newton, *Kansas* 60 G f
Newton, *Massachusetts* *(92,384)* 49 F h
Newton, *Mississippi* 63 O f
Newton, *New Jersey* 50 D c
Newton, *North Carolina* 55 K b
Newton, *Pennsylvania* 52 J e
Newton, *Texas* 65 O e
Newton, *Utah* 68 D b
Newton Falls, *New York* 53 L a
Newton Falls, *Ohio* 52 F d
Newton Grove, *North Carolina* 55 N b
Newton Res., *Utah* 68 E b
Newtown, *Connecticut* 50 G c
Newtown, *Missouri* 61 L d
Newtown, *North Dakota* 58 D b
Newtown, *Pennsylvania* 50 C e
Newtown, *Virginia* 52 J h
Newtown Square, *Pennsylvania* 50 B f
New Tripoli, *Pennsylvania* 50 B d
New Ulm, *Minnesota* 59 M f
New Ulm, *Texas* 65 L f
New Underwood, *South Dakota* 58 D f
Newville, *Alabama* 54 F f
Newville, *California* 74 C e
Newville, *Pennsylvania* 52 J e
New Virginia, *Iowa* 61 L c
New Washington, *Ohio* 52 D e
New Waverly, *Texas* 65 M e
New Windsor, *Maryland* 53 J f
New Windsor, *New York* 50 E c
New Year L., *Nevada* 74 F c
New York *(18,335,000)* 49,576 sq. miles 52-53
New York, *New York* *(7,781,984)* 51 F d
New York International Airport. *See* John F. Kennedy International Airport
New York Mts., *California* 75 K j
Ney, *Ohio* 52 B d
Nezperce, *Idaho* 66 D c
Nezpique R., *Louisiana* 63 L h
Niagara, *North Dakota* 58 H b
Niagara, *Wisconsin* 56 E d
Niagara Falls, *New York* *(102,394)* 52 H b
Niagara R., *New York* 52 H b
Niangua R., *Missouri* 61 M g
Niantic, *Connecticut* 51 J c
Niarada, *Montana* 66 F b
Nibbe, *Montana* 67 M c
Nicatous L., *Maine* 49 G c
Nice, *California* 74 C e
Niceville, *Florida* 54 E g
Nicholasville, *Kentucky* 57 J m
Nicholls, *Georgia* 55 J f
Nichols, *Connecticut* 50 G c
Nichols, *Iowa* 61 N c
Nichols, *Minnesota* 59 Q j
Nichols, *New York* 53 K c
Nicholson, *Pennsylvania* 53 L d
Nicholville, *New York* 53 M a
Nickerson, *Kansas* 60 F f
Nicolet Neebish I., *Michigan* 56 J c
Nicollet, *Minnesota* 59 M f
Nielsville, *Minnesota* 59 K c
Nighthawk, *Washington* 73 L g
Nigtmute, *Alaska* 76 E f
Nigu R., *Alaska* 76 J b
Nihoa, I., *Hawaii* 72 D b
Niihau, I., *Hawaii* 72 A d
Nikabuna Ls., *Alaska* 76 K f
Nikishka No. 2, *Alaska* 76 M f
Nikolai, *Alaska* 76 K e
Nikolski, *Alaska* 77 T h
Niland, *California* 75 K l
Niles, *California* 74 D g
Niles, *Illinois, vicinity of Chicago*
Niles, *Kansas* 60 G f
Niles, *Michigan* 57 G g
Niles, *Ohio* 52 F d
Nilikluguk, *Alaska* 76 E f
Nimrod, *Montana* 66 G c
Nimrod Res., *Arkansas* 63 K d
Ninemile, *Alaska* 77 W h
Ninemile Cr., *Minnesota* 59 Q j
Ninemile Pk., *Nevada* 74 J e
Nine Point Mesa, *Texas* 64 D f
Ninety Six, *South Carolina* 55 J c
Nineveh, *Pennsylvania* 52 F f
Ninigret Pond, *Rhode Island* 51 K c
Ninilchik, *Alaska* 76 M f
Ninneka, *Oklahoma* 62 F d
Ninnescah R., *Kansas* 60 G g
Ninock, *Louisiana* 63 K f
Ninole, *Hawaii* 72 E f
Niobe, *New York* 52 G c
Niobrara, *Nebraska* 60 F b
Niobrara R., *Nebraska* 60 E b
Niota, *Tennessee* 54 G b
Nipomo, *California* 75 E j
Nipton, *California* 75 K j
Nirvana, *Michigan* 56 H f
Nishlik L., *Alaska* 76 H f
Nisland, *South Dakota* 58 C f
Nisqually R., *Washington* 73 H j
Nitro, *West Virginia* 52 E g
Nivloc, *Nevada* 74 H g
Nixon, *Nevada* 74 F e
Nixon, *Texas* 65 K f
Nizina, *Alaska* 77 Q f
Nizina R., *Alaska* 77 Q f
Nizki I., *Alaska* 76 K j
Noank, *Connecticut* 51 K c
Noatak, *Alaska* 76 F c
Noatak R., *Alaska* 76 F c
Noble, *Illinois* 57 E l
Noble, *Oklahoma* 62 F c
Noble Lake, *Arkansas* 63 M d
Noblesville, *Indiana* 57 G j
Nobska Pt., *Massachusetts* 51 M b
Nocona, *Texas* 65 K b
Nodaway, *Iowa* 61 K d
Nodaway R., *Iowa* 61 K c
Node, *Wyoming* 67 Q g
Noel, *Missouri* 61 K h
Nogales, *Arizona* 70 G h
Nogamut, *Alaska* 76 J f
Nokomis, *Illinois* 57 D k
Nokomis, L., *Minnesota* 59 Q j
Nolan, *North Dakota* 58 J c
Nolan, *Texas* 64 G c
Nolichucky Dam, *Tennessee* 55 J a
Nolichucky R., *Tennessee* 55 J a
Noma, *Florida* 54 F g
No Mans Land, *Massachusetts* 51 M c
Nome, *Alaska* 76 E d
Nome, *North Dakota* 58 J d
Nondalton, *Alaska* 76 K g
Nonvianuk L., *Alaska* 76 K g
Noonan, *North Dakota* 58 C b
Noorvik, *Alaska* 76 G c
Nooseneck, *Rhode Island* 51 K b
Nopah Ra., *California* 75 J h
Noquebay, L., *Wisconsin* 56 F d
Nora, *Nebraska* 60 G d
Nora Springs, *Iowa* 61 L a
Norbeck, *South Dakota* 58 G e
Norborne, *Missouri* 61 L e
Norcatur, *Kansas* 60 D e
Norcross, *Georgia* 54 G d
Nordheim, *Texas* 65 K g
Nordman, *Idaho* 66 D a
Nordon, *Nebraska* 60 D b
Norfolk, *Arkansas* 63 L b
Norfolk, *Connecticut* 50 G b
Norfolk, *Massachusetts* 51 L a
Norfolk, *Nebraska* 60 G b
Norfolk, *New York* 53 L a
Norfolk, *Virginia (304,869)* 53 K j
Norfolk L., *Arkansas* 63 L b
Norias, *Texas* 65 K j
Norlina, *North Carolina* 55 N a
Normal, *Pennsylvania* 50 B d
Norman, *Arkansas* 63 K d
Norman, *Nebraska* 60 F d
Norman, *Oklahoma* *(33,412)* 62 F c
Normandy, *Tennessee* 54 E b
Normangee, *Texas* 65 L d
Normanna, *Texas* 65 K g
Norphlet, *Arkansas* 63 L e
Norridgewock, *Maine* 49 F d
Norris, *Illinois* 57 C j
Norris, *Montana* 66 J d
Norris, *South Dakota* 58 E g
Norris, *Tennessee* 54 G a
Norris, *Wyoming* 67 K e
Norris City, *Illinois* 57 E m
Norris Dam, *Tennessee* 54 G a
Norris L., *Tennessee* 54 H a
Norristown, *Pennsylvania* *(38,925)* 50 C e
North, *South Carolina* 55 K d
North Adams, *Massachusetts* 49 B f
North Adams, *Michigan* 57 J h
Northampton, *Massachusetts* *(30,058)* 51 H a
Northampton, *Pennsylvania* 50 B d
Northampton Banks, *Hawaii* 72 B a
North Anna R., *Virginia* 52 J h
North Anson, *Maine* 49 E d
North Arlington, *New Jersey* 51 K e
North Attleboro, *Massachusetts* 51 L b
North Augusta, *South Carolina* 55 K d
North Baltimore, *Ohio* 52 C d
North Bend, *Nebraska* 60 H c
North Bend, *Oregon* 73 F m
North Bennington, *Vermont* 49 B f
North Bergen, *New Jersey* *(42,387)* 51 L e
North Berwick, *Maine* 49 E e
North Bessemer, *Pennsylvania* 53 R a
Northboro, *Iowa* 61 J d
Northboro, *Massachusetts* 51 K a
North Branch, *Michigan* 56 K f
North Branch, *Minnesota* 59 O e
North Branch, *New Jersey* 50 D d
North Branford, *Connecticut* 51 H c
Northbridge, *Massachusetts* 51 K a
North Brookfield, *Massachusetts* 51 J a
North C., *Alaska* 77 Q j
North Canadian R., *Oklahoma* 62 B c
North Canton, *Ohio* 52 E e
North Carolina *(5,027,000)* 52,712 sq. miles 54-55
North Carver, *Massachusetts* 51 M b
North Charleston, *South Carolina* 55 L e
North Chicago, *Illinois* 57 F g
North Collins, *New York* 52 H c
North Concho R., *Texas* 64 F d
North Conway, *New Hampshire* 49 D d
North Cove, *Washington* 73 F j
North Creek, *New York* 53 M b
North Dakota *(639,000)* 70,665 sq. miles 58-59
North Dallas, *Texas* 65 N j
North Dighton, *Massachusetts* 51 L b
North East, *Maryland* 50 A f
North East, *Pennsylvania* 52 G c
Northeast C., *Alaska* 76 C e
Northeast Cape Fear R., *North Carolina* 55 O c
Northeast Harbor, *Maine* 49 G d
North Easton, *Massachusetts* 51 L a
North English, *Iowa* 61 M c
Northern Heights, *Missouri* 61 P a
Northfield, *Massachusetts* 49 C f
Northfield, *Minnesota* 59 N f
Northfield, *New Jersey* 50 D g
Northfield, *Vermont* 49 C d
North Fond du Lac, *Wisconsin* 56 E f
Northford, *Connecticut* 51 H c
North Fork, *California* 75 F g
North Fork, *Idaho* 66 G d
North Fork, *Nevada* 74 K c
North Fox I., *Michigan* 56 H d
North Fox R., *Texas* 64 D h
North Freedom, *Wisconsin* 56 D f
North Fryburg, *Maine* 49 E d
North Germantown, *New York* 50 F a
North Grosvenor Dale, *Connecticut* 51 J b
North Guilford, *Connecticut* 51 H c
North Haven, *Connecticut* 51 H c
North Haven, *New York* 51 J c
North I., *Hawaii* 72 A a
North I., *South Carolina* 55 M d
North Judson, *Indiana* 57 G h
North Kansas City, *Missouri* 61 P a
North Kingsville, *Ohio* 52 F d
Northland, *Michigan* 56 F c
North Laramie R., *Wyoming* 67 P g
North Liberty, *Indiana* 57 G h
North Little Rock, *Arkansas* *(58,032)* 63 L d
North Loup, *Nebraska* 60 F c
North Loup R., *Nebraska* 60 F c
North Madison, *Connecticut* 51 H c
North Mam Pk., *Colorado* 69 J d
North Manchester, *Indiana* 57 H h
North Manitou I., *Michigan* 56 G d
North Miami, *Florida* *(28,708)* 54 B d
North Miami Beach, *Florida* 54 B c
Northmoor, *Missouri* 61 P a
North Muskegon, *Michigan* 56 G f
North New River Canal, *Florida* 55 O g
North Ogden, *Utah* 68 E b
Northome, *Minnesota* 59 M c
North Palisade, *California* 75 G g
North Pelham, *New York* 51 N d
North Plainfield, *New Jersey* 50 E d
North Platte, *Nebraska* 60 D c
North Platte R., *Nebraska, etc.* 60 B c
North Pleasanton, *Texas* 65 J g
Northport, *Alabama* 54 D d
Northport, *Michigan* 56 H d
Northport, *Nebraska* 60 A c
Northport, *New York* 50 G d
Northport, *Washington* 73 N g
North Powder, *Oregon* 73 N k
North Prairie, *Wisconsin* 56 E g
North Pt., *Louisiana* 63 O j
North Pt., *Michigan* 56 K d
North R., *Washington* 73 G j
North Richland Hills, *Texas* 65 M j
North St. Paul, *Minnesota* 59 R h
North Salt Lake, *Utah* 68 C h
North San Juan, *California* 74 D e
North Santiam R., *Oregon* 73 H l
North Shadydale, *Texas* 64 G h
North Shoshone Pk., *Nevada* 74 H e
North Side, *Pennsylvania* 53 P b
North Skunk R., *Iowa* 61 M c
North Spencer, *Massachusetts* 51 J a
North Star, *Ohio* 52 B e
North Stonington, *Connecticut* 51 K c
North Stratford, *New Hampshire* 49 D d
North Syracuse, *New York* 53 K b
North Tarrytown, *New York* 50 F c
North Tisbury, *Massachusetts* 51 M c
North Tonawanda, *New York (34,757)* 52 H b
North Troy, *Vermont* 49 C d
North Truchas Pk., *New Mexico* 71 M a
North Truro, *Massachusetts* 51 N a
North Umpqua R., *Oregon* 73 H m
North Vernon, *Indiana* 57 H k
Northville, *Connecticut* 50 G b
Northville, *New York* 53 M b
Northville, *South Dakota* 58 H e
North Wales, *Pennsylvania* 50 C e
Northway, *Alaska* 77 R e
Northway Junction, *Alaska* 77 R e
North Wilkesboro, *North Carolina* 55 K a
North Windham, *Connecticut* 51 J b
Northwood, *Iowa* 61 L a
Northwood, *North Dakota* 58 J c
North Woodstock, *New Hampshire* 49 D d
North Zulch, *Texas* 65 L e
Norton, *Kansas* 60 E e
Norton, *Massachusetts* 51 L b
Norton, *Virginia* 52 D j
Norton B., *Alaska* 76 G d
Norton Res., *Massachusetts* 51 L b
Norton Sd., *Alaska* 76 E e
Nortonville, *Kansas* 61 J e
Nortonville, *North Dakota* 58 H d
Norutak L., *Alaska* 76 K c
Norwalk, *California* *(88,739)* 75 F m
Norwalk, *Connecticut* *(67,775)* 50 G c
Norwalk, *Iowa* 61 L c
Norwalk, *Michigan* 56 G e
Norwalk, *Ohio* 52 D d
Norwalk, *Wisconsin* 56 C f
Norway, *Iowa* 61 N c
Norway, *Maine* 49 E d
Norway, *Michigan* 56 F d
Norway, *South Carolina* 55 K d
Norwell, *Massachusetts* 51 M a
Norwich, *Connecticut* *(38,506)* 51 J b
Norwich, *Kansas* 60 G g
Norwich, *New York* 53 L c
Norwich, *North Dakota* 58 E b
Norwichtown, *Connecticut* 51 J b
Norwood, *Florida* 54 B c
Norwood, *Massachusetts* 51 L a
Norwood, *Minnesota* 59 M f
Norwood, *New York* 53 M a
Norwood, *North Carolina* 55 L b
Norwood, *Ohio (34,580), vicinity of Cincinnati*
Notasulga, *Alabama* 54 F e
Notch Pk., *Utah* 68 C d
Noti, *Oregon* 73 G l
Nottely L., *Georgia* 54 G c
Nottingham, *Pennsylvania* 50 A f
Nottoway R., *Virginia* 52 J j
Notus, *Idaho* 66 D f
Novato, *California* 74 C f
Novelty, *Missouri* 61 M d
Novice, *Texas* 65 H d
Novinger, *Missouri* 61 M d
Nowata, *Oklahoma* 62 H b
Nowitna, *Alaska* 76 K d
Nowlin, *South Dakota* 58 E f
Nowood Cr., *Wyoming* 67 N e
Noxapater, *Mississippi* 63 O f
Noxen, *Pennsylvania* 53 K d
Noxon, *Montana* 66 E b
Noxon Res., *Montana* 66 E b
Noxubee R., *Mississippi* 63 P e
Noyes I., *Alaska* 77 V j
Noyo, *California* 74 B e
Nubieber, *California* 74 D c
Nueces R., *Texas* 65 K g
Nuka I., *Alaska* 76 M g
Nulato, *Alaska* 76 H d
Nunachuak, *Alaska* 76 J g
Nunapitchuk, *Alaska* 76 F f
Nunavakanuk I., *Alaska* 76 E f
Nunavak Anukslak L., *Alaska* 76 F f
Nunavakpak L., *Alaska* 76 F f
Nunavaugaluk, L., *Alaska* 76 H g
Nunda, *New York* 52 J c
Nunivak I., *Alaska* 76 E g
Nunn, *Colorado* 69 M c
Nunnelly, *Tennessee* 54 D b
Nuremburg, *Pennsylvania* 50 A d
Nushagak B., *Alaska* 76 H g
Nushagak Pen., *Alaska* 76 H g
Nushagak R., *Alaska* 76 J f
Nutley, *New Jersey (29,513)* 50 E d
Nutt, *New Mexico* 71 K g
Nutzotin Mts., *Alaska* 77 Q e
Nuu, *Hawaii* 72 D e
Nuyakuk, L., *Alaska* 76 H g
Nuyakuk R., *Alaska* 76 J g
Nyac, *Alaska* 76 H f
Nyack, *Montana* 66 G a
Nyack, *New York* 50 F c
Nyssa, *Oregon* 73 O m
Oacoma, *South Dakota* 58 G g
Oahe Dam, *South Dakota* 58 F f
Oahe Res., *South Dakota* 58 F e
Oahu, I., *Hawaii* 72 C d
Oak Beach, *New York* 50 G d
Oak Bluffs, *Massachusetts* 51 M c
Oakboro, *North Carolina* 55 L b
Oak City, *North Carolina* 55 O b
Oak City, *Utah* 68 D d
Oak Cliff, *Texas* 65 N j
Oak Creek, *Colorado* 69 K c
Oakdale, *California* 74 E g
Oakdale, *Louisiana* 63 L h
Oakdale, *Nebraska* 60 G b
Oakes, *North Dakota* 58 H d
Oakesdale, *Washington* 73 N h
Oakfield, *Wisconsin* 56 E f
Oakford, *Illinois* 57 D j
Oak Forest, *Texas* 64 F h
Oak Grove, *Louisiana* 63 M f
Oak Harbor, *Ohio* 52 C d
Oak Hill, *Florida* 55 L j
Oak Hill, *Kansas* 60 G e
Oak Hill, *Ohio* 52 D g
Oak Hill, *West Virginia* 52 E h
Oak I., *Wisconsin* 56 C c
Oakland, *California (367,548)* 75 C l
Oakland, *Illinois* 57 E k
Oakland, *Iowa* 61 J c
Oakland, *Maine* 49 F d
Oakland, *Maryland* 52 G f
Oakland, *Mississippi* 63 O d
Oakland, *Nebraska* 60 H c
Oakland, *Oregon* 73 G m
Oakland, *Pennsylvania* 53 P b
Oakland, *Rhode Island* 51 K b
Oakland, *Tennessee* 54 B b
Oakland, *Texas* 65 L f
Oakland City, *Indiana* 57 F l
Oakland Park, *Florida* 55 O g
Oak Lane, *Pennsylvania* 50 G f
Oaklawn, *Illinois (27,471)* 57 B n
Oakley, *California* 74 D g
Oakley, *Idaho* 66 G g
Oakley, *Kansas* 60 D e
Oakley, *Michigan* 56 J f
Oakman, *Georgia* 54 G c
Oakmont, *Pennsylvania* 52 G e
Oakpark, *Georgia* 55 J e
Oak Park, *Illinois (61,093)* 57 A l
Oak Park, *Michigan (36,632)* 57 K j
Oak R., *Arizona* 70 F e
Oak Ridge, *Louisiana* 63 M f
Oak Ridge, *Missouri* 61 P g
Oakridge, *Oregon* 73 H m
Oak Ridge, *Tennessee* *(27,169)* 54 G a
Oakville, *Connecticut* 50 G b
Oakville, *Texas* 65 J g
Oakwood, *Illinois* 57 F j
Oakwood, *Missouri* 61 P a
Oakwood, *Ohio* 52 B d
Oakwood, *Oklahoma* 62 E c
Oakwood, *Texas* 65 M d
Oasis, *California* 75 H g
Oasis, *Nevada* 74 L c
Oatman, *Arizona* 70 C d
Obar, *New Mexico* 71 O d
Oberlin, *Kansas* 60 D e
Oberlin, *Louisiana* 63 L h
Oberlin, *Ohio* 52 D d
Oberon, *North Dakota* 58 G c
Obey R., *Tennessee* 54 F a
Obion, *Tennessee* 54 B a
Obion R., *Tennessee* 54 B a
Oblong, *Illinois* 57 E l

Plainview, New York (27,710), vicinity of New York City
Plainview, Texas 64 F a
Plainville, Connecticut 51 H b
Plainville, Illinois 57 B k
Plainville, Kansas 60 E e
Plainville, Massachusetts 51 L a
Plainwell, Michigan 56 H g
Planada, California 75 E g
Plankinton, South Dakota 58 H g
Plano, Illinois 57 E h
Plano, Texas 65 L b
Plant City, Florida 55 M e
Plantersville, Alabama 54 E e
Plantsville, Connecticut 51 H b
Plaquemine, Louisiana 63 M h
Plaster City, California 75 J m
Platina, California 74 C d
Platinum, Alaska 76 G g
Plato, Missouri 61 M g
Platt Nat. Park, Oklahoma 62 G d
Platte, South Dakota 58 H g
Platte Center, Nebraska 60 G c
Platte City, Missouri 61 K e
Platte Mt., Colorado 69 L d
Platte R., Nebraska, etc. 46 F b
Platteville, Colorado 69 M c
Platteville, Wisconsin 56 C g
Plattsburg, Missouri 61 K e
Plattsburg, New York 53 N a
Plattsmouth, Nebraska 61 J c
Playa del Rey, California 75 D m
Playas L., New Mexico 71 J h
Plaza, North Dakota 58 E b
Pleasant, L., Arizona 70 E f
Pleasant B., Massachusetts 51 N b
Pleasant City, Ohio 52 E f
Pleasant Gap, Pennsylvania 52 J e
Pleasant Grove, Utah 68 E c
Pleasant Hill, Illinois 57 C k
Pleasant Hill, Louisiana 63 K g
Pleasant Hill, Missouri 61 K f
Pleasant Hill, Ohio 52 B e
Pleasant Hill Res., Ohio 52 D e
Pleasant Hills, Pennsylvania 53 P c
Pleasant L., Minnesota 59 R h
Pleasanton, California 74 D g
Pleasanton, Kansas 61 K f
Pleasanton, Nebraska 60 E d
Pleasanton, Texas 65 J g
Pleasant Plains, Arkansas 63 M c
Pleasant Plains, New Jersey 50 E e
Pleasant Plains, New York 50 F b
Pleasant Valley, New York 50 F b
Pleasant Valley, Oregon 73 N l
Pleasant View, Washington 73 M j
Pleasantville, Iowa 61 L c
Pleasantville, New Jersey 50 D g
Pleasantville, New York 50 F c
Pleasantville, Pennsylvania 52 G d
Pleasureville, Kentucky 57 H l
Plentywood, Montana 67 Q a
Plevna, Montana 67 Q c
Plover, Iowa 61 K b
Plover, Wisconsin 56 D e
Plover Is., Alaska 76 K a
Plover R., Wisconsin 56 D e
Plum City, Wisconsin 56 A e
Plum I., New York 51 J c
Plummer, Idaho 66 D b
Plummer, Minnesota 59 K c
Plummer, Mt., Alaska 76 H f
Plummerville, Arkansas 63 L c
Plush, Oregon 73 L n
Plymouth, California 74 E f
Plymouth, Connecticut 51 G b
Plymouth, Illinois 57 C j
Plymouth, Indiana 57 G h
Plymouth, Iowa 61 L a
Plymouth, Massachusetts 51 M b
Plymouth, Minnesota 59 P h
Plymouth, Nebraska 60 H d
Plymouth, New Hampshire 49 D e
Plymouth, North Carolina 55 P b
Plymouth, Ohio 52 D e
Plymouth, Pennsylvania 50 A c
Plymouth, Utah 68 D b
Plymouth, Vermont 49 C e
Plymouth, Wisconsin 56 E f
Plymouth B., Massachusetts 51 M b
Plympton, Massachusetts 51 M b
Pocahontas, Arkansas 63 M b
Pocahontas, Iowa 61 K b
Pocahontas, Virginia 52 E h
Pocasset, Massachusetts 51 M b
Pocasset, Oklahoma 62 E c
Pocatalico R., West Virginia 52 E g
Pocatello, Idaho (28,534) 66 H g
Pocomoke City, Maryland 53 L g
Pocomoke R., Maryland 53 L g
Pocomoke Sd., Virginia 53 L h
Pocono L., Pennsylvania 50 C c
Pocono Lake, Pennsylvania 50 B c
Pocono Mts., Pennsylvania 50 C c
Pocono Pines, Pennsylvania 50 C c
Podunk, Massachusetts 51 J a
Poe Reef, Michigan 56 J d
Pogromni Vol., Alaska 76 E j
Pohakuloa, Hawaii 72 E f
Poinsett, L., Florida 55 O e
Point Barre, Louisiana 63 M h
Pointblank, Texas 65 M e
Point Comfort, Texas 65 L g
Pointe a la Hache, Louisiana 63 O j
Pointe Chicot I., Louisiana 63 O j
Pointers, New Jersey 50 C f
Point Ewen, New York 53 M d
Point Harbor, North Carolina 55 Q a
Point Hope, Alaska 76 D b
Point Judith Pond, Rhode Island 51 L c
Point Lay, Alaska 76 F b
Point Lookout, Maryland 53 K g
Point Marion, Pennsylvania 52 G f
Point of Rocks, Maryland 52 J f
Point of Rocks, Wyoming 67 M h
Point Pleasant, New Jersey 50 E e
Point Pleasant, Pennsylvania 50 C e
Point Pleasant, West Virginia 52 D g
Point Reyes Nat. Seashore, California 75 B f
Poison Cr., Wyoming 67 N f
Pojoaque, New Mexico 71 M d
Poko Mt., Alaska 76 F b
Polacca, Arizona 70 G d
Polacca Wash, Arizona 70 G d
Poland, New York 53 L b
Polar, Wisconsin 56 E d
Polaris, Montana 66 G d
Polk, Nebraska 60 G c
Polk, Pennsylvania 52 G d
Polk City, Florida 55 N e
Pollard, Arkansas 63 N b
Pollock, Idaho 66 D d
Pollock, Louisiana 63 L g
Pollock, South Dakota 58 F e
Pollocksville, North Carolina 55 O b
Polo, Illinois 57 D h
Polo, Missouri 61 K e
Polpis, Massachusetts 51 N c
Polson, Montana 66 F b
Polvadera, New Mexico 71 K e
Polychrome Pass, Alaska 76 N e
Pomaria, South Carolina 55 K c
Pomerene, Arizona 70 G g
Pomeroy, Iowa 61 K b
Pomeroy, Ohio 52 D f
Pomeroy, Washington 73 N j
Pomfret, Connecticut 51 K b
Pomfret Center, Connecticut 51 K b
Pomme de Terre R., Minnesota 59 L e
Pomme de Terre R., Missouri 61 L g
Pomme de Terre Res., Missouri 61 L g
Pomona, California (67,157) 75 H k
Pomona, Kansas 61 J f
Pomona, Missouri 61 N h
Pomona, New Jersey 50 D g
Pomona, New York 50 E c
Pompano Beach, Florida 55 O g
Pompey, New York 53 L c
Pompeys Pillar, Montana 67 N d
Pompton Lakes, New Jersey 50 E c
Ponca, Nebraska 60 H b
Ponca City, Oklahoma 62 F b
Ponce de Leon, Florida 54 F g
Ponce de Leon B., Florida 55 N h
Ponce de Leon Inlet, Florida 55 L h
Ponchatoula, Louisiana 63 N h
Pond Creek, Oklahoma 62 F b
Pond Eddy, Pennsylvania 50 D c
Ponder, Texas 65 K b
Pondosa, California 74 D c
Pondosa, Oregon 73 N k
Ponemah, Minnesota 59 M b
Poneto, Indiana 57 H j
Pontchartrain, L., Louisiana 63 N h
Ponte Vedra Beach, Florida 55 L h
Pontiac, Illinois 57 E j
Pontiac, Michigan (82,233) 56 K g
Pontotoc, Mississippi 63 O d
Pontotoc, Texas 65 J e
Pony, Montana 66 J d
Pooler, Georgia 55 K e
Poolesville, Maryland 53 J f
Poolville, Texas 65 K c
Poorman, Alaska 76 K d
Pope, California 75 K l
Pope, Mississippi 63 O d
Popejoy, Iowa 61 L b
Popham Beach, Maine 49 F e
Poplar, Montana 67 P a
Poplar, Wisconsin 56 B c
Poplar Bluff, Missouri 61 O h
Poplar R., Minnesota 59 L c
Poplar R., Montana 67 P a
Poplarville, Mississippi 63 O h
Popof Is., Alaska 76 G j
Poquoson, Virginia 53 K h
Porcupine Cr., Montana 67 O a
Porcupine Mts., Michigan 56 D c
Porcupine R., Alaska 77 Q c
Portage, Alaska 77 N f
Portage, Maine 49 G b
Portage, Missouri 61 L d
Portage, Montana 66 J b
Portage, Pennsylvania 52 H e
Portage, Utah 68 D b
Portage, Wisconsin 56 D f
Portage R., Ohio 52 C d
Portageville, Missouri 61 P h
Portageville, New York 52 H c
Portal, Arizona 70 H h
Portal, Georgia 55 K e
Portales, New Mexico 71 O e
Port Alexander, Alaska 77 U h
Port Allegany, Pennsylvania 52 H d
Port Allen, Louisiana 63 M h
Port Angeles, Washington 73 G g
Port Aransas, Texas 65 K h
Port Arthur, Texas (66,676) 65 O f
Port Austin, Michigan 56 L e
Port Blakely, Washington 72 B h
Port Bolivar, Texas 65 N f
Port Byron, Illinois 57 C h
Port Byron, New York 53 K b
Port Carbon, Pennsylvania 50 A d
Port Chester, New York 50 F d
Port Chilkoot, Alaska 77 U g
Port Clarence, Alaska 76 D d
Port Clinton, Ohio 52 D d
Port Clyde, Maine 49 F e
Port Deposit, Maryland 50 A f
Porte des Morts, Wisconsin 56 G d
Port Elizabeth, New Jersey 50 D g
Porter, Minnesota 59 K f
Porter, Nebraska 60 A b
Porter, Oklahoma 62 H c
Porterdale, Georgia 54 H d
Porterfield, Wisconsin 56 F d
Porters Lake, Pennsylvania 50 C c
Porterville, California 75 G h
Port Ewen, New York 50 F b
Port Gamble, Washington 72 A g
Port Gibson, Mississippi 63 M g
Port Graham, Alaska 76 M g
Port Heiden, Alaska 76 H h
Port Henry, New York 53 N a
Porthill, Idaho 66 D a
Port Hope, Michigan 56 L f
Port Hueneme, California 75 F k
Port Huron, Michigan (36,084) 56 L g
Portis, Kansas 60 F e
Port Isabel, Texas 65 K j
Port Jefferson, New York 51 G d
Port Jervis, New York 50 D c
Portland, Colorado 69 L e
Portland, Connecticut 51 H b
Portland, Indiana 57 J j
Portland, Maine (72,566) 49 E e
Portland, Michigan 56 J g
Portland, North Dakota 58 J c
Portland, Oregon (372,676) 73 H k
Portland, Pennsylvania 50 C d
Portland, Tennessee 54 E a
Portland, Texas 65 K h
Portland Can., Alaska 77 W j
Port Lavaca, Texas 65 L g
Port Leyden, New York 54 L b
Port Madison, Washington 72 B h
Port Madison Indian Reservation, Washington 72 B g
Port Mansfield, Texas 65 K j
Port Matilda, Pennsylvania 52 J e
Port Mayaca, Florida 55 O g
Port Moller, Alaska 76 G j
Port Murray, New Jersey 50 D d
Port Neches, Texas 65 O f
Port Nellie Juan, Alaska 77 N f
Portneuf, Idaho 66 H g
Portneuf R., Idaho 66 H g
Portneuf Res., Idaho 66 J g
Port Norris, New Jersey 50 C g
Port O'Brian, Alaska 76 L h
Port O'Connor, Texas 65 L g
Portola, California 74 E e
Port Orange, Florida 55 K h
Port Orchard, Washington 72 A h
Port Orchard R., Washington 72 A h
Port Orford, Oregon 73 F n
Port Penn, Delaware 50 B f
Port Richmond, New York 51 K g
Port Richmond, Pennsylvania 50 G g
Port Roberts, Washington 73 G g
Port Royal, South Carolina 55 L e
Port Royal, Virginia 52 J g
Port Royal Sd., South Carolina 55 L e
Port St. Joe, Florida 54 F h
Port Sanilac, Michigan 56 L f
Port San Luis, California 75 E j
Portsmouth, Iowa 61 J c
Portsmouth, New Hampshire (25,833) 49 E e
Portsmouth, North Carolina 55 P b
Portsmouth, Ohio (33,637) 52 C g
Portsmouth, Rhode Island 51 L b
Portsmouth, Virginia (144,773) 53 K j
Port Sulphur, Louisiana 63 O j
Port Tampa, Florida 55 M f
Port Townsend, Washington 73 H g
Portville, New York 52 H c
Port Vue, Pennsylvania 53 Q c
Port Washington, New York 50 F d
Port Washington, Wisconsin 56 F f
Port Wentworth, Georgia 55 K e
Port Wing, Wisconsin 56 B c
Porum, Oklahoma 62 H c
Porvenir, Texas 64 C e
Posen, Michigan 56 K d
Poseyville, Indiana 57 F l
Possum Kingdom L., Texas 65 J c
Post, Oregon 73 K l
Post, Texas 64 F b
Post Falls, Idaho 66 D b
Postville, Iowa 61 N a
Potagannissing B., Michigan 56 K c
Poteau, Oklahoma 63 J c
Poteau R., Oklahoma 63 J d
Poteet, Texas 65 J f
Poth, Texas 65 J f
Potholes Res., Washington 73 L h
Potlatch, Idaho 66 D c
Potlatch R., Idaho 66 D c
Potomac, Montana 66 G c
Potomac R., Virginia 53 K g
Potomac R., West Virginia 52 H f
Potosi, Missouri 61 O g
Potosi Mt., Nevada 75 K j
Potsdam, New York 53 M a
Potter, Nebraska 60 A c
Pottersville, New Jersey 50 D d
Potter Valley, California 74 B e
Potterville, Michigan 56 J g
Potts, Nevada 74 J e
Pottsboro, Texas 65 L b
Potts Camp, Mississippi 63 O d
Pottstown, Pennsylvania (26,144) 50 B e
Pottsville, Pennsylvania 50 A d
Pottsville, Texas 65 J d
Potwin, Kansas 60 G g
Poughkeepsie, N. Y. (38,330) 50 F b
Poughquag, New York 50 F b
Poulsbo, Washington 72 A g
Poultney, Vermont 49 B e
Pound, Wisconsin 56 E d
Pound Ridge, New York 50 F c
Powderhorn, Colorado 69 J e
Powder R., Montana 67 P d
Powder R., Oregon 73 N l
Powder R., Wyoming 67 O e
Powder River, Wyoming 67 O f
Powderville, Montana 67 P d
Powell, Arizona 70 C e
Powell, L., Utah 68 F f
Powell, Mt., Colorado 69 K d
Powell, South Dakota 58 E f
Powell, Wisconsin 56 D c
Powell, Wyoming 67 M e
Powell Butte, Oregon 73 K l
Powell Mt., Nevada 74 G f
Powell R., Tennessee 54 H a
Powellton, West Virginia 52 E g
Power, Montana 66 J b
Powers, Michigan 56 F d
Powers, Oregon 73 F n
Powers Lake, North Dakota 58 D b
Powersville, Missouri 61 L d
Powhatan, Louisiana 63 K g
Powhatan, Virginia 52 J h
Powhatan Point, Ohio 52 F f
Powhattan, Kansas 61 J e
Pownal, Vermont 49 B f
Poyen, Arkansas 63 L d
Poygan, L., Wisconsin 56 E e
Pozo, California 75 E j
Prague, Oklahoma 62 G c
Prairie, Idaho 66 E f
Prairie City, Illinois 57 C j
Prairie City, Oregon 73 M i
Prairie Dog Cr., Kansas 60 D e
Prairie Dog Town Fork, Oklahoma-Texas 62 D d
Prairie du Chien, Wisconsin 56 B f
Prairie du Sac, Wisconsin 56 D f
Prairie Grove, Arkansas 63 J c
Prairie Hill, Texas 65 L d
Prairie Lea, Texas 65 K f
Prairieton, Indiana 57 F k
Prairie View, Kansas 60 E e
Prairie Village, Kansas (25,356) 61 P b
Prairieville, Louisiana 63 N h
Praise, Kentucky 57 L m
Pratt, Kansas 60 F g
Prattsville, New York 50 E a
Prattville, Alabama 54 E e
Premont, Texas 65 J h
Prentice, Wisconsin 56 C d
Prentiss, Mississippi 63 O g
Presa Rodriguez, California 75 J m
Prescott, Arizona 70 E e
Prescott, Arkansas 63 K e
Prescott, Iowa 61 K c
Prescott, Michigan 56 K e
Prescott, Washington 73 M j
Prescott, Wisconsin 56 A e
Presho, South Dakota 58 F g
Presidio, California 75 B l
Presidio, Texas 64 C f
Presque Isle, Maine 49 G b
Presque Isle, Michigan 56 K d
Presque Isle Pt., Michigan 56 F c
Preston, California 74 B f
Preston, Connecticut 51 K b
Preston, Georgia 54 G e
Preston, Idaho 66 J g
Preston, Iowa 61 O b
Preston, Kansas 60 F g
Preston, Maryland 53 L g
Preston, Minnesota 59 O g
Preston, Missouri 61 L g
Preston, Nevada 74 K f
Preston, Oklahoma 62 H c
Prestonburg, Kentucky 57 L m
Preston Hollow, Texas 65 N j
Prettyboy Res., Maryland 53 K f
Pretty Prairie, Kansas 60 F g
Prewitt, New Mexico 71 J d
Prewitt Res., Colorado 69 N c
Pribilof Is., Alaska 76 B h
Price, Maryland 50 A g
Price, North Dakota 58 F c
Price, Utah 68 F d
Price Creek, Colorado 68 H c
Price R., Utah 68 F d
Pricetown, Pennsylvania 50 B e
Prichard, Alabama (47,371) 54 C g
Priddy, Texas 65 J d
Priest L., Idaho 66 D a
Priest Rapids, Washington 73 L j
Priest Rapids Res., Washington 73 L j
Priest River, Idaho 66 D a
Primghar, Iowa 61 J a
Prince Frederick, Maryland 53 K g
Prince of Wales I., Alaska 77 V j
Prince of Wales, C., Alaska 76 C d
Princess Anne, Maryland 53 L g
Princeton, California 74 D e
Princeton, Illinois 57 D h
Princeton, Indiana 57 F l
Princeton, Iowa 61 O c
Princeton, Maine 49 H c
Princeton, Michigan 56 F c
Princeton, Minnesota 59 N e
Princeton, Missouri 61 L d
Princeton, New Jersey 50 D e
Princeton, North Carolina 55 N b
Princeton, West Virginia 52 E h
Princeton, Wisconsin 56 D f
Princeton Junction, New Jersey 50 D e
Princeville, Illinois 57 D j
Prince William Sd., Alaska 77 O f
Prineville, Oregon 73 K l
Pringle, South Dakota 58 C g
Pringle, Texas 64 C h
Pritchard, Idaho 66 E b
Pritchett, Colorado 69 O f
Proctor, Colorado 69 O c
Proctor, Texas 65 J d
Proctor, Vermont 49 B e
Proctorsville, Vermont 49 C e
Progresso, New Mexico 71 M e
Promise City, Iowa 61 L d
Promised Land, Pennsylvania 50 C c
Promontory, Utah 68 D b
Pronto, Nevada 74 G d
Prophetstown, Illinois 57 D h
Prospect, New York 53 L b
Prospect, Ohio 52 C e
Prospect, Oregon 73 H n
Prospect, Pennsylvania 52 F e
Prospect Park, Pennsylvania 50 C f
Prospect Plains, New Jersey 50 E e
Prosper, Oregon 73 F m
Prosperity, South Carolina 55 K c
Prosser, Nebraska 60 F d
Prosser, Washington 73 L j
Protection, Kansas 60 E g
Protivin, Iowa 61 M a
Provencal, Louisiana 63 K g
Providence, Kentucky 57 F m
Providence, L., Alaska 76 J h
Providence, Maryland 50 A f
Providence, North Carolina 55 N a
Providence, Rhode Island (207,498) 51 K b
Providence, Utah 68 E b
Providence Mts., California 75 K k
Provincetown, Massachusetts 51 N a
Provo, South Dakota 58 C g
Provo, Utah (36,047) 68 E c
Prudence I., Rhode Island 51 L b
Prudenville, Michigan 56 J e
Pryor, Montana 67 M d
Pryor, Oklahoma 62 H b
Pryor Cr., Montana 67 M d
Puako, Hawaii 72 E f
Puale B., Alaska 76 K h
Puckaway L., Wisconsin 56 E f
Puckett, Mississippi 63 O f
Pueblo, Colorado (91,181) 69 M e
Pueblo, New Mexico 71 L d
Pueblo Bonito, New Mexico 71 K c
Pueblo Mts., Oregon 73 M n
Puerco R., Arizona 70 H e
Puget Sd., Washington 73 H h
Pughtown, Pennsylvania 50 B e
Puhi, Hawaii 72 B d
Pukwana, South Dakota 58 G g
Pulaski, Iowa 61 M d
Pulaski, New York 53 K b
Pulaski, Tennessee 54 D b
Pulaski, Virginia 52 F h
Pulaski, Wisconsin 56 E e
Pullman, Washington 73 N j
Pumphrey, Maryland 53 P g
Pumpkin Cr., Montana 67 P d
Pumpkin Cr., Nebraska 60 A c
Pumpville, Texas 64 F f
Pungo L., North Carolina 55 P b
Pungo R., North Carolina 55 P b
Punta, New Mexico 71 L e
Punta de Aqua R., Texas 64 B h
Punta Gorda, California 74 A d
Punta Gorda, Florida 55 M g
Punta Rassa, Florida 55 N g
Punuk Is., Alaska 76 C e
Punxsutawney, Pennsylvania 52 H e
Purcell, Oklahoma 62 F c
Purcell Mt., Alaska 76 J c
Purcell Ra., Montana 66 E a
Purcellville, Virginia 52 J f
Purdin, Missouri 61 L e
Purdum, Nebraska 60 D b
Purdy, Missouri 61 L h
Purdys, New York 50 F c
Purgatoire R., Colorado 69 N f
Purgatory, Alaska 77 N c
Purling, New York 50 F a
Purvis, Mississippi 63 O g
Puryear, Tennessee 54 C a
Pushaw L., Maine 49 G d
Putah Cr., California 74 C f
Putnam, Connecticut 51 K b
Putnam, Oklahoma 62 E c
Putnam, Texas 65 H c
Putnam Junction, New York 50 F c
Putnam Lake, New York 50 F c
Putney, Georgia 54 G f
Putney, South Dakota 58 H e
Putney, Vermont 49 C f
Puuanahulu, Hawaii 72 E f
Puukolii, Hawaii 72 D e
Puuwai, Hawaii 72 A d
Puyallup, Washington 73 H h
Pyatt, Arkansas 63 L b
Pye Is., Alaska 76 M g
Pymatuning Res., Pennsylvania 52 F d
Pyote, Texas 64 D d
Pyramid, Nevada 74 F d
Pyramid Canyon, Arizona-Nevada 70 C d
Pyramid L., Nevada 74 F d
Pyramid Pk., Colorado 69 J c
Pyramid Pt., Michigan 56 H e
Pyramid Ra., Nevada 74 F e
Quabbin Res., Massachusetts 51 J a
Quaboag R., Massachusetts 51 J a
Quaboin Res., Massachusetts 49 C f
Quail Mts., California 75 J j
Quakertown, New Jersey 50 D d
Quakertown, Pennsylvania 50 C e
Quanah, Texas 65 H a
Quantico, Virginia 52 J g
Quarryville, New York 50 F a
Quarryville, Pennsylvania 50 A f
Quartzite Mt., Nevada 74 J g
Quartz Mt., Nevada 74 H e
Quartz Mt., Washington 73 M g
Quartzsite, Arizona 70 C f
Quasqueton, Iowa 61 N b
Quay, New Mexico 71 O e
Quealy, Wyoming 67 K h
Queen Anne, Maryland 50 A h
Queen City, Missouri 61 M d
Queen City, Texas 65 N b
Queens, New York 50 F d
Queenstown, Maryland 53 K g
Queets, Washington 73 F h
Queets R., Washington 73 G h
Quemado, New Mexico 71 J e
Quemado, Texas 64 G g
Quenemo, Kansas 61 J f
Quentin, Mississippi 63 N g
Questa, New Mexico 71 M c
Queue de Tortue R., Louisiana 63 L h
Quijotoa, Arizona 70 E g
Quilcene, Washington 73 H h
Quinault, Washington 73 G h
Quinault R., Washington 73 F h
Quincy, California 74 E e
Quincy, Florida 54 G g
Quincy, Illinois (43,793) 57 B k
Quincy, Kentucky 57 K l
Quincy, Massachusetts (87,409) 49 H j
Quincy, Michigan 57 H h
Quincy, Ohio 52 C e
Quincy, Oregon 73 G j
Quincy, Washington 73 L h
Quincy B., Massachusetts 49 H j
Quinebaug R., Massachusetts 51 J a
Quinhagak, Alaska 76 G g
Quinlan, Texas 65 L c
Quinn, South Dakota 58 D g
Quinn Canyon Ra., Nevada 74 K g
Quinn R., Nevada 74 H c
Quinn River Crossing, Nevada 74 G c
Quinter, Kansas 60 D e
Quinton, New Jersey 50 C f
Quinton, Oklahoma 62 H c
Quinwood, West Virginia 52 F g
Quitaque, Texas 64 C j
Quitman, Arkansas 63 L c
Quitman, Georgia 54 H g
Quitman, Louisiana 63 L f
Quitman, Mississippi 63 P f
Quitman, Texas 65 M c
Quivero, Arizona 70 E d
Quivira L., Kansas 61 O a
Quogue, New York 51 H d
Quonochontaug, Rhode Island 51 K c
Rabbit Cr., South Dakota 58 D e
Rabbit Ears Pass, Colorado 69 K c
Raber, Michigan 56 J c
Rabun, L., Georgia 54 H c
Raccoon Cr., Ohio 52 D g
Raccoon Pt., Louisiana 63 M j
Raccoon R., Iowa 61 K c
Raceland, Kentucky 57 L l
Raceland, Louisiana 63 N j
Race Pt., Massachusetts 51 N a
Racepond, Georgia 55 J f
Race Track, Montana 66 H c
Rachal, Texas 65 J j
Racine, Wisconsin (89,144) 56 F g
Raco, Michigan 56 J c
Radcliffe, Iowa 61 L b
Radford, Virginia 52 F h
Radisson, Wisconsin 56 B d
Radium, Colorado 69 K d
Radium, Minnesota 59 K b
Raeford, North Carolina 55 M c
Raft R., Idaho 66 G g
Raft River Mts., Utah 68 C b
Ragged I., Maine 49 G e
Ragland, Alabama 54 E d
Ragland, New Mexico 71 O e
Rago, Kansas 60 F g
Rahway, New Jersey (27,699) 50 E d
Railroad City, Alaska 76 H e
Railroad Pass, Nevada 74 H e
Railroad Val., Nevada 74 K f

Rain UNITED STATES INDEX Rock

Rainbow Bridge Nat. Mon., *Utah* 68 F f
Rainbow Park Beach, *Illinois* 57 C m
Rainier, *Oregon* 73 H j
Rainier, *Washington* 73 H j
Rainier, Mt., *Washington* 73 J j
Rainrock, *Oregon* 73 G l
Rainsburg, *Pennsylvania* 52 H f
Rainy Pass, *Alaska* 76 L e
Rainy Pass, *Washington* 73 K g
Rainy Pass Lodge, *Alaska* 76 L e
Rainy R., *Michigan* 56 J d
Rainy R., *Minnesota* 59 M b
Raita Bank, *Hawaii* 72 C a
Rake, *Iowa* 61 L a
Raleigh, *Mississippi* 63 O f
Raleigh, *North Carolina* (93,931) 55 N b
Raleigh, *North Dakota* 58 E d
Raleigh B., *North Carolina* 55 P c
Ralls, *Texas* 64 F b
Ralph, *Michigan* 56 F c
Ralph, *South Dakota* 58 C e
Ralston, *Nebraska* 61 H c
Ralston, *Oklahoma* 62 G b
Ralston, *Pennsylvania* 53 K d
Ralston, *Washington* 73 M j
Ralston, *Wyoming* 67 M e
Ralston Res., *Colorado* 69 N h
Ramah, *Colorado* 69 M d
Ramah, *New Mexico* 71 J d
Ramapo, *New York* 50 E c
Ramapo Mt., *New Jersey* 50 E c
Ramapo R., *New Jersey* 50 E c
Ramer, *Alabama* 54 E e
Ramirez, *Texas* 65 J h
Ramirito, *Texas* 65 J j
Ramona, *California* 75 J l
Ramona, *Michigan* 56 H f
Ramona, *Oklahoma* 62 H b
Ramona, *South Dakota* 58 J f
Rampart, *Alaska* 76 M d
Ramseur, *North Carolina* 55 M b
Ramsey, *Illinois* 57 D k
Ramsey, *New Jersey* 50 E c
Ranchester, *Wyoming* 67 N e
Ranchos de Taos, *New Mexico* 71 M c
Rancocas Cr., *New Jersey* 50 D e
Rand, *Colorado* 69 K c
Randado, *Texas* 65 J h
Randall, *Iowa* 61 L b
Randall, *Kansas* 60 F e
Randall, *Minnesota* 59 M d
Randle, *Washington* 73 J j
Randleman, *North Carolina* 55 M b
Randlett, *Oklahoma* 62 E d
Randlett, *Utah* 68 G c
Randolph, *Iowa* 61 J d
Randolph, *Kansas* 60 H e
Randolph, *Maine* 49 F d
Randolph, *Massachusetts* 51 L a
Randolph, *Mississippi* 63 O d
Randolph, *Missouri* 61 Q a
Randolph, *Nebraska* 60 G b
Randolph, *New York* 52 H c
Randolph, *Utah* 68 E b
Randolph, *Vermont* 49 C e
Randolph, *Wisconsin* 56 E f
Random Lake, *Wisconsin* 56 F f
Randsburg, *California* 75 H j
Range, *Alabama* 54 D f
Rangeley, *Maine* 49 E c
Rangeley L., *Maine* 49 E d
Rangely, *Colorado* 68 H c
Ranger, *Texas* 65 J c
Ranger, *West Virginia* 52 D g
Ranier, *Minnesota* 59 N b
Rankin, *Illinois* 57 F j
Rankin, *Pennsylvania* 53 Q b
Rankin, *Texas* 64 F d
Ransom, *Illinois* 57 E h
Ransom, *Kansas* 60 E f
Ranson, *West Virginia* 52 J f
Rantoul, *Illinois* 57 E j
Rapelje, *Montana* 67 L d
Raphine, *Virginia* 52 G h
Rapidan, *Virginia* 52 H g
Rapidan R., *Virginia* 52 J g
Rapid City, *South Dakota* (42,399) 58 C f
Rapid R., *Alaska* 77 R c
Rapid R., *Minnesota* 59 M b
Rapid River, *Michigan* 56 F d
Rappahannock R., *Virginia* 52 J g
Raquette L., *New York* 53 M b
Raquette Lake, *New York* 53 M b
Raquette R., *New York* 53 M a
Raritan, *New Jersey* 50 D d
Raritan R., *New Jersey* 50 E d
Raspberry I., *Alaska* 76 L g
Ratcliff, *Arkansas* 63 K c
Ratcliff, *Texas* 65 M d
Rathdrum, *Idaho* 66 D b
Rat I., *Alaska* 76 M j
Rat Is., *Alaska* 76 L j
Raton, *New Mexico* 71 N c
Raton Pass, *Colorado* 69 M f
Rattan, *Oklahoma* 62 H d
Rattlesnake Buttes, *Colorado* 69 M f
Rattlesnake Cr., *Kansas* 60 E g
Rattlesnake Cr., *Oregon* 73 N n
Rattlesnake Ra., *Wyoming* 67 N g
Ratz, Mt., *Alaska* 77 V h
Raubsville, *Pennsylvania* 50 C d
Raunt, The, *New York* 51 N g
Rauschs, *Pennsylvania* 50 A d
Ravalli, *Montana* 66 F b
Raven, *Virginia* 52 E h
Ravena, *New York* 53 N c
Ravena Gardens, *Missouri* 61 Q a
Ravendale, *California* 74 E d
Ravenna, *California* 75 G k
Ravenna, *Kentucky* 57 J m
Ravenna, *Nebraska* 60 F c
Ravenna, *Ohio* 52 E d
Ravenswood, *West Virginia* 52 E g
Ravia, *Oklahoma* 62 G d
Rawlins, *Wyoming* 67 N h
Rawson, *Ohio* 52 C e
Ray, *Arizona* 70 G f
Ray, *Minnesota* 59 N b
Ray, *North Dakota* 58 C b
Ray City, *Georgia* 54 H f
Raymond, *California* 75 F g
Raymond, *Illinois* 57 D k
Raymond, *Mississippi* 63 N f
Raymond, *Montana* 67 Q a
Raymond, *New Hampshire* 49 D f
Raymond, *South Dakota* 58 J f
Raymond, *Washington* 73 G j
Raymondville, *Texas* 65 K j
Ray Mts., *Alaska* 76 L d
Rayne, *Louisiana* 63 L h
Raynesford, *Montana* 67 K b
Raynham, *Massachusetts* 51 L b
Rayo, *New Mexico* 71 L e
Ray R., *Alaska* 76 M d
Raytown, *Missouri* 61 Q b
Rayville, *Louisiana* 63 M f
Rea, *Missouri* 61 K d
Reader, *Arkansas* 63 K e
Reading, *Kansas* 61 J f
Reading, *Michigan* 57 J h
Reading, *Minnesota* 59 L g
Reading, *Pennsylvania* (98,177) 50 B e
Readington, *New Jersey* 50 D d
Readsboro, *Vermont* 49 C f
Readstown, *Wisconsin* 56 C f
Reagan, *Texas* 65 L d
Realitos, *Texas* 65 J h
Reamstown, *Pennsylvania* 50 A e
Reardan, *Washington* 73 N h
Reaville, *New Jersey* 50 D e
Rebecca, *Georgia* 54 H f
Rebel Creek, *Nevada* 74 H c
Recluse, *Wyoming* 67 P e
Rector, *Arkansas* 63 N b
Red Bank, *New Jersey* 50 E e
Red Bay, *Alabama* 54 C c
Redbay, *Florida* 54 F g
Red Bluff, *California* 74 C d
Red Bluff Res., *Texas* 64 D d
Red Boiling Springs, *Tennessee* 54 F a
Red Bud, *Illinois* 57 C l
Red Butte, *Arizona* 70 E d
Red Buttes, *Wyoming* 67 P h
Redby, *Minnesota* 59 M c
Red Cliff, *Colorado* 69 K d
Red Cloud, *Nebraska* 60 F d
Red Cr., *Wyoming* 67 M h
Red Creek, *New York* 53 K b
Reddell, *Louisiana* 63 L g
Reddick, *Florida* 55 J h
Redding, *California* 74 C d
Redding, *Connecticut* 50 G c
Red Elm, *South Dakota* 58 E e
Redfield, *Arkansas* 63 L d
Redfield, *Iowa* 61 K c
Redfield, *South Dakota* 58 H f
Redfish L., *Idaho* 66 E e
Redford, *Texas* 64 C f
Redgranite, *Wisconsin* 56 E e
Red Hills, *Alabama* 54 E f
Red Hills, *South Carolina* 55 L c
Red Hook, *New York* 50 F b
Red House, *Nevada* 74 H c
Redig, *South Dakota* 58 C e
Redington, *Arizona* 70 G g
Redington, *Nebraska* 60 A c
Red Key, *Indiana* 57 H j
Red L., *Arizona* 70 C d
Red Lake, *Arizona* 70 E d
Red Lake Falls, *Minnesota* 59 K c
Red Lake R., *Minnesota* 59 L b
Redlands, *California* (26,829) 75 H k
Red Lion, *New Jersey* 50 D f
Red Lion, *Pennsylvania* 53 K f
Red Lodge, *Montana* 67 L d
Redmon, *Illinois* 57 F k
Redmond, *Oregon* 73 J l
Redmond, *Utah* 68 E d
Redmond, *Washington* 72 C h
Red Mountain, *California* 75 H j
Red Mountain, *Tennessee* 54 G a
Red Mt., *California* 74 B c
Red Oak, *Iowa* 61 J c
Red Oak, *Oklahoma* 62 H d
Red Oak, *Texas* 65 L c
Redondo Beach, *California* (46,986) 75 D m
Redoubt Vol., *Alaska* 76 L f
Red R., *Louisiana, etc.* 47 H d
Red R., *North Dakota* 59 K c
Red R., *Tennessee* 54 D a
Red River Hot Springs, *Idaho* 66 E d
Redrock, *Arizona* 70 F g
Red Rock, *California* 75 B l
Red Rock, *New Mexico* 71 J g
Red Rock, *Oklahoma* 62 F b
Red Rock, *Texas* 65 K f
Red Springs, *North Carolina* 55 M c
Redstone, *Montana* 67 Q a
Redwater, *Texas* 65 N b
Redwater Cr., *Montana* 67 P b
Red Willow Cr., *Colorado* 69 O c
Red Willow Cr., *Nebraska* 60 C d
Red Wing, *Minnesota* 59 O f
Redwood City, *California* (46,290) 75 C n
Redwood Falls, *Minnesota* 59 L f
Redwood R., *Minnesota* 59 K f
Redwood Valley, *California* 74 B e
Reed City, *Michigan* 56 H f
Reeder, *North Dakota* 58 D d
Reedpoint, *Montana* 67 L d
Reedley, *California* 75 F h
Reedsburg, *Wisconsin* 56 D f
Reeds Pk., *New Mexico* 71 K f
Reedsport, *Oregon* 73 F m
Reedsville, *West Virginia* 52 E f
Reedy, *West Virginia* 52 E g
Reedy R., *South Carolina* 55 J c
Ree Heights, *South Dakota* 58 G f
Reelfoot L., *Tennessee* 54 B a
Reese, *Michigan* 56 K f
Reese R., *Nevada* 74 H d
Reform, *Alabama* 54 C d
Refugio, *Texas* 65 K g
Regan, *North Dakota* 58 F c
Regent, *North Dakota* 58 D d
Rehoboth, *Massachusetts* 51 L b
Rehoboth B., *Delaware* 53 L g
Rehoboth Beach, *Delaware* 53 L g
Reichle, *Montana* 66 H d
Reidsville, *Georgia* 55 J e
Reidsville, *North Carolina* 55 M a
Reiley Pk., *Arizona* 70 G g
Reinbeck, *Iowa* 61 M b
Reinholds, *Pennsylvania* 50 A e
Reistertown, *Maryland* 53 K f
Reklaw, *Texas* 65 N d
Relee, *Georgia* 55 J f
Reliance, *South Dakota* 58 G g
Reliance, *Wyoming* 67 L h
Remer, *Minnesota* 59 N c
Remington, *Indiana* 57 F j
Remington, *Virginia* 52 J g
Remote, *Oregon* 73 G m
Remsen, *Iowa* 61 J b
Remsen, *New York* 53 L b
Remus, *Michigan* 56 H f
Renick, *West Virginia* 52 F h
Reno, L., *Minnesota* 59 L e
Reno, *Nevada* (51,470) 74 F e
Renovo, *Pennsylvania* 52 J d
Rensselaer, *Indiana* 57 F j
Rensselaer, *New York* 53 N c
Rensselaerville, *New York* 53 M c
Renton, *Washington* 72 C j
Renville, *Minnesota* 59 L f
Renwick, *Iowa* 61 L b
Repton, *Alabama* 54 D f
Republic, *Kansas* 60 G e
Republic, *Michigan* 56 E c
Republic, *Ohio* 52 C d
Republic, *Washington* 73 M g
Republican R., *Nebraska* 60 D d
Requa, *California* 74 A c
Reseda, *California* 75 G k
Reserve, *Louisiana* 63 N h
Reserve, *Montana* 67 Q a
Reserve, *New Mexico* 71 J f
Reshanau L., *Minnesota* 59 R h
Retrop, *Oklahoma* 62 D c
Reva, *South Dakota* 58 C e
Reveille Pk., *Nevada* 74 J g
Revere, *Massachusetts* (40,080) 49 H h
Revere Beach, *Massachusetts* 49 H h
Revillagigedo I., *Alaska* 77 W j
Revillo, *South Dakota* 59 K e
Rew, *Pennsylvania* 52 H d
Rewey, *Wisconsin* 56 C g
Rex, *Alaska* 76 N d
Rexburg, *Idaho* 66 J f
Rexford, *Montana* 66 E a
Reydon, *Oklahoma* 62 D c
Reyes Pk., *California* 75 F k
Reyes, Pt., *California* 74 B g
Reyes, Pt., Nat. Seashore, *California* 75 B f
Reynolds, *Georgia* 54 G e
Reynolds, *Idaho* 66 D f
Reynolds, *Illinois* 57 C h
Reynolds, *Indiana* 57 F j
Reynolds, *Nebraska* 60 G d
Reynoldsville, *Pennsylvania* 52 H d
Rhame, *North Dakota* 58 C d
Rhedhiss L., *North Carolina* 55 K b
Rhine, *Georgia* 54 H f
Rhinebeck, *New York* 50 F b
Rhinecliff, *New York* 50 F b
Rhinelander, *Wisconsin* 56 D d
Rhode I., *Rhode Island* 51 L b
Rhode Island (901,000) 1214 sq. miles 51
Rhodell, *West Virginia* 52 E h
Rhodes, *Michigan* 56 J f
Rhome, *Texas* 65 K b
Rib Lake, *Wisconsin* 56 C d
Rib Mt., *Wisconsin* 56 D e
Ricardo, *Texas* 65 K h
Rice, *California* 75 L k
Rice, *Minnesota* 59 M e
Rice, *Texas* 65 L c
Riceboro, *Georgia* 55 K f
Rice L., *Minnesota* 59 Q h
Rice Lake, *Wisconsin* 56 B d
Riceville, *Iowa* 61 M a
Richard City, *Tennessee* 54 F b
Richards, *Missouri* 61 K g
Richardson, *Alaska* 77 O d
Richardson, *Texas* 65 O h
Richardson B., *California* 75 B l
Richardson Ls., *Maine* 49 E d
Richardton, *North Dakota* 58 D d
Richboro, *Pennsylvania* 50 C e
Richburg, *New York* 52 H c
Richey, *Montana* 67 P b
Richfield, *Idaho* 66 F f
Richfield, *Kansas* 60 C g
Richfield, *Minnesota* (42,523) 59 Q j
Richfield, *Utah* 68 D e
Richfield Springs, *New York* 53 M c
Richford, *New York* 53 K c
Richford, *Vermont* 49 C d
Richgrove, *California* 75 F j
Rich Hill, *Missouri* 61 K f
Richland, *Georgia* 54 G e
Richland, *Michigan* 56 H g
Richland, *Missouri* 61 M g
Richland, *Montana* 67 O a
Richland, *New Jersey* 50 D f
Richland, *Oregon* 73 N l
Richland, *Texas* 65 L d
Richland, *Washington* 73 L j
Richland Balsam, Mt., *North Carolina* 55 J b
Richland Center, *Wisconsin* 56 C f
Richland Cr., *Texas* 65 L d
Richland Hills, *Texas* 65 M j
Richland Res., *Missouri* 61 M g
Richlands, *North Carolina* 55 O c
Richlands, *Virginia* 52 E h
Richland Springs, *Texas* 65 J d
Richlandtown, *Pennsylvania* 50 C e
Richmond, *California* (71,854) 75 B k
Richmond, *Indiana* (44,149) 57 J k
Richmond, *Kansas* 61 J f
Richmond, *Kentucky* 57 J m
Richmond, *Maine* 49 F d
Richmond, *Minnesota* 59 M e
Richmond, *Missouri* 61 L e
Richmond, *Oregon* 73 L l
Richmond, *Texas* 65 M f
Richmond, *Utah* 68 E b
Richmond, *Vermont* 49 B d
Richmond, *Virginia* (219,958) 52 J h
Richmond Beach, *Washington* 72 B g
Richmond Highlands, *Washington* 72 B g
Richmond Hill, *Georgia* 55 K f
Richmondville, *New York* 53 M c
Rich Mt., *Arkansas* 63 J d
Richton, *Mississippi* 63 P g
Richville, *Minnesota* 59 L d
Richwood, *Ohio* 52 C e
Richwood, *West Virginia* 52 F g
Richwood, *Wisconsin* 56 E f
Richwoods, *Missouri* 61 O f
Rico, *Colorado* 68 H f
Riddle, *Idaho* 66 D g
Riddle, *Oregon* 73 G n
Ridge, *Montana* 67 Q d
Ridgedale, *Idaho* 66 H g
Ridge Farm, *Illinois* 57 F k
Ridgefield, *Connecticut* 50 G c
Ridgefield, *New Jersey* 51 L e
Ridgefield Park, *New Jersey* 51 L e
Ridgeland, *Mississippi* 63 N f
Ridgeland, *South Carolina* 55 K e
Ridgeland, *Wisconsin* 56 B d
Ridgelea, *Texas* 65 L j
Ridgeley, *West Virginia* 52 H f
Ridgely, *Maryland* 50 A h
Ridge Spring, *South Carolina* 55 K d
Ridgeview, *South Dakota* 58 F e
Ridgeville, *Indiana* 57 H j
Ridgeville, *South Carolina* 55 L d
Ridgeway, *Missouri* 61 L d
Ridgeway, *Montana* 67 Q d
Ridgeway, *South Carolina* 55 L c
Ridgeway, *Wisconsin* 56 C f
Ridgewood, *New Jersey* (25,391) 50 E d
Ridgley, *Tennessee* 54 B a
Ridgway, *Colorado* 69 J e
Ridgway, *Illinois* 57 E m
Ridgway, *Pennsylvania* 52 H d
Riegelsville, *Pennsylvania* 50 C d
Rienzi, *Mississippi* 63 P d
Rifle, *Colorado* 69 J d
Rifle R., *Michigan* 56 J e
Rifton, *New York* 50 E b
Rigby, *Idaho* 66 J f
Riggins, *Idaho* 66 D d
Riggston, *Illinois* 57 C k
Rikers I., *New York* 51 M e
Riley, *Indiana* 57 F k
Riley, *Kansas* 60 H e
Riley, *New Mexico* 71 K e
Riley, *Oregon* 73 L m
Rimersburg, *Pennsylvania* 52 G d
Rincon, *New Mexico* 71 L g
Ringling, *Montana* 67 K c
Ringling, *Oklahoma* 62 F d
Ringgold, *Louisiana* 63 K f
Ringgold, *Nebraska* 60 D c
Ringgold, *Texas* 65 K b
Ringoes, *New Jersey* 50 D e
Ringold, *Oklahoma* 62 H d
Ringsted, *Iowa* 61 K a
Ringwood, *New Jersey* 50 E c
Ringwood, *Oklahoma* 62 E b
Rio, *Illinois* 57 C h
Rio, *Louisiana* 63 O h
Rio, *New York* 50 D c
Rio, *Wisconsin* 56 D f
Rio Chama, *New Mexico* 71 L c
Rio Felix, *New Mexico* 71 N f
Rio Grande, *New Jersey* 50 D g
Rio Grande City, *Texas* 65 J j
Rio Grande R., *United States-Mexico* 46 G e
Rio Grande Res., *Colorado* 69 J f
Rio Hondo, *New Mexico* 71 N f
Rio Hondo, *Texas* 65 K j
Rio Linda, *California* 74 D f
Riomedina, *Texas* 65 J f
Rio Penasco, *New Mexico* 71 N g
Rio Puerco, *New Mexico* 71 K d
Rio Res., *New York* 50 D c
Rio Salado, *New Mexico* 71 K e
Rio San Jose, *New Mexico* 71 K e
Rio Tinto, *Nevada* 74 J c
Riovista, *Texas* 65 K c
Riparia, *Washington* 73 M j
Ripley, *California* 75 L l
Ripley, *Mississippi* 63 P d
Ripley, *New York* 52 G c
Ripley, *Ohio* 52 C g
Ripley, *Oklahoma* 62 G b
Ripley, *Tennessee* 54 B b
Ripley, *West Virginia* 52 E g
Ripon, *California* 74 D g
Ripon, *Wisconsin* 56 E f
Rippey, *Iowa* 61 K c
Rising Fawn, *Georgia* 54 F c
Rising Star, *Texas* 65 J c
Rising Sun, *Indiana* 57 J l
Rising Sun, *Maryland* 50 A f
Rising Sun, *Ohio* 52 C d
Rison, *Arkansas* 63 L e
Rita, *Pennsylvania* 50 B c
Ritter, Mt., *California* 74 F g
Ritter, *Oregon* 73 L l
Rittman, *Ohio* 52 E e
Ritzville, *Washington* 73 M h
Riverbank Res., *California* 74 E g
Riverdale, *California* 75 F h
Riverdale, *New Jersey* 50 E c
Riverdale, *Kansas* 60 G g
Riverdale, *Montana* 66 J b
Riverdale, *Nebraska* 60 E d
Riverdale, *North Dakota* 58 E c
River Edge, *New Jersey* 51 L d
River Falls, *Alabama* 54 E f
River Falls, *Wisconsin* 56 A e
Riverhead, *New York* 51 H d
River Oaks, Fort Worth, *Texas* 65 L j
River Oaks, Houston, *Texas* 64 F j
River Point, *Rhode Island* 51 L b
River Rouge, *Michigan* 57 K k
Riverside, *California* (84,332) 75 H l
Riverside, *Maryland* 53 J g
Riverside, *Michigan* 57 M k
Riverside, *New Jersey* 50 D e
Riverside, *Oregon* 73 M m
Riverside, *Rhode Island* 51 L b
Riverside, *Texas* 65 M e
Riverside, *Utah* 68 D b
Riverside, *Wyoming* 67 O h
Riverside Res., *Colorado* 69 M c
Riverton, *Illinois* 57 D k
Riverton, *Iowa* 61 J d
Riverton, *Nebraska* 60 F d
Riverton, *New Jersey* 50 D e
Riverton, *Virginia* 52 H g
Riverton, *Wyoming* 67 M f
Riverton Heights, *Washington* 72 B j
Rivervale, *Arkansas* 63 N c
Riverview, *Nebraska* 60 E b
Rives, *Tennessee* 54 B a
Rives Junction, *Michigan* 56 J g
Rivesville, *West Virginia* 52 F f
Riviera, *Texas* 65 K h
Riviera Beach, *Florida* 55 O g
Roachdale, *Indiana* 57 G k
Road Forks, *New Mexico* 71 J g
Roan Cliffs, *Utah* 68 G d
Roan Cr., *Colorado* 68 H d
Roan Mt., *North Carolina* 55 J a
Roanoke, *Alabama* 54 F d
Roanoke, *Illinois* 57 D j
Roanoke, *Indiana* 57 H j
Roanoke, *Texas* 65 K b
Roanoke, *Virginia* (97,110) 52 G h
Roanoke I., *North Carolina* 55 P d
Roanoke R., *North Carolina* 55 O a
Roanoke R., *Virginia* 52 G h
Roanoke Rapids, *North Carolina* 55 O a
Roan Plateau, *Colorado-Utah* 68 G d
Roans Prairie, *Texas* 65 M e
Roaring Branch, *Pennsylvania* 53 K d
Roaring Gap, *North Carolina* 55 L a
Roaring Springs, *Texas* 64 G b
Robberson, *Texas* 65 J j
Robbins, *North Carolina* 55 M b
Robbinsdale, *Minnesota* 59 P h
Robbinsville, *New Jersey* 50 D e
Robbinsville, *North Carolina* 54 H b
Robeline, *Louisiana* 63 K g
Robersonville, *North Carolina* 55 O b
Roberta, *Georgia* 54 G e
Robert Lee, *Texas* 64 G d
Roberts, *Idaho* 66 H f
Roberts, *Montana* 67 L d
Roberts, *Oregon* 73 K l
Roberts Creek Mt., *Nevada* 74 J e
Robertsdale, *Alabama* 54 D g
Roberts Mt., *Wyoming* 67 L f
Robertson, *Wyoming* 67 K h
Robesonia, *Pennsylvania* 50 A e
Robin, *Idaho* 66 H g
Robinette, *Oregon* 73 N l
Robinson, *Illinois* 57 F k
Robinson, *North Dakota* 58 G c
Robinson Mts., *Alaska* 77 Q f
Robles del Rio, *California* 75 D h
Robles Pass, *Arizona* 70 F g
Robles Ranch, *Arizona* 70 F g
Robstown, *Texas* 65 K h
Roby, *Texas* 64 G c
Rochdale, *Massachusetts* 51 K a
Rochelle, *Florida* 55 J h
Rochelle, *Georgia* 54 H f
Rochelle, *Illinois* 57 D h
Rochelle, *Louisiana* 63 L g
Rochelle, *Texas* 65 H d
Rocheport, *Missouri* 61 M f
Rochester, *Illinois* 57 D k
Rochester, *Indiana* 57 G h
Rochester, *Massachusetts* 51 M b
Rochester, *Michigan* 56 K g
Rochester, *Minnesota* (40,663) 59 O f
Rochester, *New Hampshire* 49 D e
Rochester, *New York* (318,611) 53 J b
Rochester, *Ohio* 52 D d
Rochester, *Pennsylvania* 52 F e
Rochester, *Texas* 65 H b
Rochester, *Washington* 73 G j
Rochester Res., *Iowa* 61 N c
Rochford, *South Dakota* 58 C f
Rock, *Kansas* 60 H g
Rock, *Massachusetts* 51 M b
Rock, *Michigan* 56 F c
Rockaway, *New Jersey* 50 D d
Rockaway Beach, *New York* 51 M g
Rockaway Inlet, *New York* 51 M g
Rockaway Park, *New York* 50 F d
Rock City, *New York* 50 F b
Rock Cr., *Montana* 66 G c
Rock Cr., *Montana* 67 N a
Rock Cr., *Oregon* 73 K k
Rock Cr., *Wyoming* 67 O h
Rockcreek, *Idaho* 66 F g
Rock Creek, *Ohio* 52 F d
Rock Creek, *Oregon* 73 K k
Rockdale, *Texas* 65 L e
Rocket Launching, *New Mexico* 71 L g
Rockfall, *Connecticut* 51 H b
Rock Falls, *Illinois* 57 D h
Rockfish, *Virginia* 52 H h
Rockford, *Alabama* 54 E e
Rockford, *Idaho* 66 H f
Rockford, *Illinois* (126,706) 57 D g
Rockford, *Michigan* 56 H f
Rockford, *Minnesota* 59 N e
Rockford, *Ohio* 52 B e
Rockford, *Washington* 73 N h
Rockham, *South Dakota* 58 H f
Rock Harbor, *Michigan* 56 E a
Rock Hill, *South Carolina* (29,404) 55 K c
Rockingham, *North Carolina* 55 M c
Rock Island, *Illinois* (51,863) 57 C h
Rock Island, *Texas* 65 L f
Rock Island, *Washington* 73 K h
Rock Island Dam, *Washington* 73 K h
Rock L., *Washington* 73 N h
Rocklake, *North Dakota* 58 G b
Rockland, *Connecticut* 51 H c
Rockland, *Idaho* 66 H g
Rockland, *Maine* 49 F d
Rockland, *Massachusetts* 51 M a
Rockland, *Michigan* 56 D c
Rockland, *New York* 50 D b
Rockland, *Texas* 65 N d
Rockland Lake, *New York* 50 F c
Rockland Res., *Texas* 65 N d
Rocklyn, *Washington* 73 M h
Rockmart, *Georgia* 54 F c
Rock Point, *Maryland* 53 K g
Rockport, *California* 74 B e
Rockport, *Illinois* 57 B k
Rockport, *Indiana* 57 F m
Rockport, *Maine* 49 F d
Rockport, *Massachusetts* 49 E f
Rockport, *Missouri* 61 J d
Rockport, *Texas* 65 K g
Rockport, *Washington* 73 J g
Rock R., *Illinois* 57 D h
Rock R., *Iowa* 60 H a
Rock R., *South Carolina* 55 J c
Rock R., *Wisconsin* 56 E f
Rock Rapids, *Iowa* 61 H a
Rock River, *Wyoming* 67 P h
Rock Springs, *Arizona* 70 E e
Rock Springs, *Montana* 67 O c
Rocksprings, *Texas* 64 G e
Rock Springs, *Wyoming* 67 L h
Rockton, *Illinois* 56 D g
Rock Valley, *Iowa* 60 H a
Rockville, *Connecticut* 51 H b
Rockville, *Indiana* 57 F k
Rockville, *Maryland* (26,090) 53 J f
Rockville, *South Carolina* 55 L e
Rockville, *Oregon* 73 N m
Rockville, *Utah* 68 C f
Rockville Centre, *New York* (26,355) 50 F d
Rockwall, *Texas* 65 L c
Rockwell, *Iowa* 61 L b
Rockwell, *North Carolina* 55 L b

Rock UNITED STATES INDEX Sand

Rockwell City, Iowa 61 K b
Rockwood, Colorado 69 J f
Rockwood, Maine 49 F c
Rockwood, Pennsylvania 52 G f
Rockwood, Tennessee 54 G b
Rockwood, Texas 65 H d
Rocky, Oklahoma 62 D c
Rocky Bar, Idaho 66 E f
Rocky Ford, Colorado 69 N e
Rocky Ford, Georgia 55 K e
Rockyford, South Dakota 58 D g
Rocky Ford Res., Ohio 52 C f
Rocky Grove, Pennsylvania 52 G d
Rocky Hill, Connecticut 51 H b
Rocky Hill, New Jersey 50 D e
Rocky Mount, North Carolina (32,147) 55 O b
Rocky Mount, Virginia 52 G j
Rocky Mount Nat. Park, Colorado 69 L c
Rocky Mt., Montana 66 H b
Rocky Mts., Colorado, etc. 46 E c
See also individual ranges
Rocky Point, New York 51 H d
Rockypoint, Wyoming 67 P e
Rocky Pt., Alaska 76 F d
Rocky R., North Carolina 55 L b
Rocky River, Ohio 52 E d
Rocliff R., New York 50 F a
Rodanthe, North Carolina 55 P d
Rodeo, New Mexico 71 J h
Rodessa, Louisiana 63 J f
Rodessa, Texas 65 N c
Rodgers Forge, Maryland 53 Q e
Rodi, Pennsylvania 53 R b
Rodney, C., Alaska 76 D d
Roe, Arkansas 63 M d
Roebling, New Jersey 50 D e
Roeland Park, Kansas 61 P a
Roff, Oklahoma 62 G d
Roganville, Texas 65 O e
Rogers, Arkansas 63 J b
Rogers, North Dakota 58 H c
Rogers, Texas 65 K e
Rogers City, Michigan 56 K d
Rogers L., California 75 H k
Rogerson, Idaho 66 F g
Rogersville, Alabama 54 D c
Rogersville, Missouri 61 L g
Rogersville, Tennessee 54 H a
Roggen, Colorado 69 M c
Rogue R., Oregon 73 F n
Rogue River, Oregon 73 G n
Rohwer, Arkansas 63 M e
Roland, Arkansas 63 L d
Roland, Iowa 61 L b
Roland, L., Maryland 53 P e
Rolette, North Dakota 58 G b
Rolfe, Iowa 61 K b
Rolfe, Pennsylvania 52 H d
Roll, Arizona 70 D g
Rolla, Kansas 60 C g
Rolla, Missouri 61 N g
Rolla, North Dakota 58 G b
Rollingbay, Washington 72 B h
Rolling Fork, Mississippi 63 N f
Rollins, Montana 66 F b
Romain, C., South Carolina 55 M d
Roma-Los Saenz, Texas 65 H j
Romano, C., Florida 55 N h
Romanzof, C., Alaska 76 D f
Romanzof Mts., Alaska 77 Q b
Rome, Georgia (32,226) 54 F c
Rome, New York (51,646) 53 L b
Rome, Oregon 73 N n
Rome, Pennsylvania 53 K d
Rome, Tennessee 54 E a
Romeo, Colorado 69 K f
Romeo, Michigan 56 L g
Romero, Texas 64 B h
Romeroville, New Mexico 71 M d
Romney, West Virginia 52 H f
Romulus, Michigan 57 K g
Ronan, Montana 66 F b
Ronceverte, West Virginia 52 F h
Rondout Cr., New York 50 E b
Rondout Res., New York 50 E b
Ronkonkoma, New York 50 G d
Roodhouse, Illinois 57 C k
Roosevelt, Arizona 70 F f
Roosevelt, Minnesota 59 L b
Roosevelt, Oklahoma 62 D d
Roosevelt, Texas 64 G e
Roosevelt, Utah 68 F c
Roosevelt, Washington 73 K k
Roosevelt Dam, Arizona 70 F f
Rootok I., Alaska 76 E j
Root R., Minnesota 59 P g
Roper, North Carolina 55 P b
Ropes Creek, Maryland 53 K g
Ropesville, Texas 64 E b
Rosalia, Kansas 60 H g
Rosalia, Washington 73 N h
Rosamond, California 75 G k
Rosamond L., California 75 G k
Rosanky, Texas 65 K f
Rosarito, California 75 H m
Roscoe, Illinois 56 D g
Roscoe, Montana 67 L d
Roscoe, New York 50 D b
Roscoe, South Dakota 58 G e
Roscoe, Texas 64 G c
Roscommon, Michigan 56 J e
Rose, Mt., Nevada 74 F e
Rose, Nebraska 60 E b
Roseau, Minnesota 59 L b
Roseau R., Minnesota 59 K b
Roseberry, Idaho 66 D e
Roseboro, North Carolina 55 N c
Rosebud, Missouri 61 N f
Rosebud, Montana 67 O c
Rosebud, New Mexico 71 O d
Rosebud, South Dakota 58 F g
Rosebud, Texas 65 L d
Rosebud Cr., Montana 67 O d
Rosebud Mts., Montana 67 N d
Roseburg, Oregon 73 G m
Rosebush, Michigan 56 J f
Rose City, Michigan 56 J e
Rose Creek, Nevada 74 H d
Rose Creek Mts., Utah 68 C b
Rosedale, Indiana 57 F k
Rosedale, Mississippi 63 N e
Rose Hill, Iowa 61 M c
Rose Hill, North Carolina 55 N c
Roseland, Louisiana 63 N h
Roselle, New Jersey 50 E d
Rosemount, Minnesota 59 N f
Rosenberg, Texas 65 M f
Rosendale, Missouri 61 K d
Rosendale, New York 50 E b
Rosenhayn, New Jersey 50 C g
Rosepine, Louisiana 63 K h
Roseton, New York 50 F b
Rosette, Utah 68 C b
Roseville, California 74 D f
Roseville, Illinois 57 C j
Roseville, Michigan (50,195), vicinity of Detroit
Roseville, Minnesota 59 Q h
Roseville, Ohio 52 D f
Roseworth, Idaho 66 F g
Rosharon, Texas 65 M f
Rosholt, South Dakota 59 K e
Rosholt, Wisconsin 56 D e
Rosiclare, Illinois 57 E m
Roskruge Mts., Arizona 70 F g
Roslyn, New York 50 F d
Roslyn, South Dakota 58 J e
Roslyn, Washington 73 K h
Ross, North Dakota 58 D b
Ross, Wyoming 67 P f
Ross City, Texas 64 F c
Rosser, Texas 65 L c
Rossiter, Pennsylvania 52 H e
Ross L., Washington 73 J g
Rosslyn, Texas 64 F h
Rosston, Oklahoma 62 D b
Rossview Res., Tennessee 54 D a
Rossville, Georgia 54 F c
Rossville, Illinois 57 F j
Rossville, Kansas 61 J e
Rossville, New York 51 K g
Roswell, Georgia 54 G c
Roswell, New Mexico (39,593) 71 N f
Rotan, Texas 64 G c
Rothbury, Michigan 56 G f
Rothsay, Minnesota 59 K d
Rough R., Kentucky 57 G m
Rough River Res., Kentucky 57 G m
Roulette, Pennsylvania 52 H d
Roundabout Mt., Alaska 76 J d
Round Butte, Montana 66 F b
Round I., Alaska 76 H g
Round Mountain, Nevada 74 H f
Round Mountain, Texas 65 J e
Round Pond, Maine 49 F e
Round Rock, Texas 65 K e
Round Spring, Missouri 61 N g
Roundup, Montana 67 M c
Rouse, Colorado 69 M f
Rouses Point, New York 53 N a
Rouseville, Pennsylvania 52 G d
Rowan, Iowa 61 L b
Rowe, New Mexico 71 M d
Rowena, Texas 64 G d
Rowesville, South Carolina 55 L d
Rowland, Minnesota 59 P j
Rowland, Nevada 74 K c
Rowland, North Carolina 55 M c
Rowland, Pennsylvania 50 C c
Rowlesburg, West Virginia 56 G f
Rowood, Arizona 70 E g
Rox, Nevada 75 L h
Roxboro, North Carolina 55 N a
Roxburg, New Jersey 50 C d
Roxbury, Connecticut 50 G b
Roxbury, Massachusetts 49 G j
Roxbury, New York 50 D a
Roxbury, Vermont 49 C d
Roxie, Mississippi 63 M g
Roxton, Texas 65 M b
Roy, Montana 67 M b
Roy, New Mexico 71 N d
Roy, Washington 73 H h
Royal, Nebraska 60 F b
Royal Center, Indiana 57 G j
Royal Oak, Michigan (80,612) 56 K g
Royal Palm Hammock, Florida 55 N h
Royal Palm Ranger Station, Florida 55 O h
Royalty, Texas 64 E d
Royersford, Pennsylvania 50 B e
Royse City, Texas 65 L c
Royston, Georgia 54 H c
Rozel, Kansas 60 E f
Rozet, Wyoming 67 P e
Rubicon R., California 74 E f
Ruby, Alaska 76 K d
Ruby, Arizona 70 F h
Ruby, New York 50 F a
Ruby, Washington 73 N g
Ruby Dome, Nevada 74 K d
Ruby L., Nevada 74 K d
Ruby Mts., Nevada 74 K d
Ruby R., Montana 66 H d
Ruby Valley, Nevada 74 K d
Ruch, Oregon 73 G n
Rude R., Alaska 77 P f
Rudyard, Michigan 56 J c
Rudyard, Montana 67 K a
Ruffin, South Carolina 55 L d
Rufus Woods L., Washington 73 L g
Rugby, North Dakota 58 G b
Ruidosa, Texas 64 C e
Ruidoso, New Mexico 71 M f
Rule, Texas 64 H b
Ruleton, Kansas 60 C e
Ruleville, Mississippi 63 N e
Rulo, Nebraska 61 J d
Rumford, Maine 49 E d
Rumson, New Jersey 50 F e
Runge, Texas 65 K g
Runnells, Iowa 61 L c
Runnemede, New Jersey 50 C f
Running Water Cr., Texas 64 B j
Rupert, Idaho 66 G g
Rupert, Vermont 49 B e
Rupert, West Virginia 52 F h
Rural Hall, North Carolina 55 L a
Rural Retreat, Virginia 52 E j
Rush, Colorado 69 M e
Rush Center, Kansas 60 E f
Rush City, Minnesota 59 O e
Rush Cr., Colorado 69 N e
Rushford, Minnesota 59 P g
Rushford, New York 52 H c
Rush Springs, Oklahoma 62 F d
Rushville, Illinois 57 C j
Rushville, Indiana 57 H k
Rushville, Nebraska 60 B b
Rusk, Texas 65 M d
Ruskin, Florida 55 M f
Ruso, North Dakota 58 F c
Russell, Iowa 61 L d
Russell, Kansas 60 F f
Russell, Kentucky 57 L l
Russell, Massachusetts 51 H a
Russell, Minnesota 59 L f
Russell, Mt., Alaska 76 L e
Russell, New York 53 L a
Russell, Pennsylvania 52 G d
Russell Springs, Kentucky 57 H m
Russellville, Alabama 54 D c
Russellville, Arkansas 63 K c
Russellville, Missouri 61 M f
Russellville, Ohio 52 C g
Russellville, Pennsylvania 50 A f
Russels Point, Ohio 52 C e
Russelville, Kentucky 57 G n
Russian Mission, Alaska 76 G f
Russian Mts., Alaska 76 H f
Rustburg, Virginia 52 H j
Ruston, Louisiana 63 L f
Ruth, California 74 B d
Ruth, Nevada 74 K e
Rutherford, New Jersey 50 E d
Rutherfordton, North Carolina 55 K b
Ruther Glen, Virginia 52 J h
Ruth Glacier, Alaska 76 M e
Ruthsburg, Maryland 50 A g
Ruthton, Minnesota 59 K f
Ruthven, Iowa 61 K a
Rutland, Illinois 57 D j
Rutland, North Dakota 58 J d
Rutland, Ohio 52 D f
Rutland, Vermont 49 C e
Rutledge, Minnesota 59 O d
Rutledge, Missouri 61 M d
Ryan, Iowa 61 N b
Ryan, Oklahoma 62 F d
Ryan Park, Wyoming 67 O h
Ryan Pk., Idaho 66 F f
Ryder, North Dakota 58 E c
Ryderwood, Washington 73 G j
Rye, Colorado 69 M f
Rye, New Hampshire 49 E e
Rye, New York 50 F d
Rye, Texas 65 N e
Ryegate, Montana 67 L c
Rye Patch, Nevada 74 G d
Rye Patch Res., Nevada 74 G d
Sabak, C., Alaska 76 J j
Sabetha, Kansas 61 J e
Sabina, Ohio 52 C f
Sabinal, Texas 65 H f
Sabine, Texas 65 O f
Sabine L., Louisiana 63 K j
Sabine L., Texas 65 O f
Sabine R., Louisiana 63 K g
Sabine R., Texas 65 N c
Sable, C., Florida 55 N h
Sabraton, West Virginia 52 G f
Sabula, Iowa 61 O b
Sacandaga R., New York 53 M b
Sacandaga Res., New York 53 M b
Sacaton, Arizona 70 F f
Sac City, Iowa 61 J b
Sachem Hd., Connecticut 51 H c
Sachse, Texas 65 O h
Sackets Harbor, New York 53 K b
Saco, Maine 49 E e
Saco, Montana 67 N a
Sac Osage, L., Missouri 61 L f
Sac R., Missouri 61 L g
Sacramento, California (191,667) 74 D f
Sacramento Mts., New Mexico 71 M f
Sacramento R., California 74 D f
Sacramento Val., California 74 C e
Sacramento Wash, Arizona 70 C d
Saddle Mt., Oregon 73 F n
Saddle Mt., Wyoming 67 L e
Sadieville, Kentucky 57 J l
Sadlerochit R., Alaska 77 P b
Safety Harbor, Florida 55 M e
Safford, Alabama 54 D e
Safford, Arizona 70 H g
Sagamore, Pennsylvania 52 G e
Sagaponack, New York 51 J c
Sagavanirkok R., Alaska 77 N b
Sag Chan., Illinois 57 B n
Sage, Wyoming 67 K h
Sage Cr., Montana 67 K a
Sage Cr., Wyoming 67 N h
Sagerton, Texas 64 H b
Sag Harbor, New York 51 J d
Sagigik I., Alaska 77 Q j
Saginaw, Michigan (98,265) 56 K f
Saginaw, Texas 65 L j
Saginaw B., Michigan 56 K f
Sagola, Michigan 56 F c
Saguache, Colorado 69 K e
Saguaro L., Arizona 70 F f
Saguaro Nat. Mon., Arizona 70 G g
Sahuarita, Arizona 70 G h
Sailor Cr., Idaho 66 E g
St. Albans, New York 51 N f
St. Albans, Vermont 49 C d
St. Albans, West Virginia 52 E g
St. Andrew, Florida 54 F g
St. Andrew B., Florida 54 F g
St. Andrew Sd., Georgia 55 K g
St. Ann, Nebraska 60 D d
St. Anne, Illinois 57 F h
St. Ansgar, Iowa 61 M a
St. Anthony, Idaho 66 J f
St. Anthony, Minnesota 59 Q h
St. Augustine, Florida 55 K h
St. Benedict, Iowa 61 K a
St. Bernice, Indiana 57 F k
St. Catherine, L., Louisiana 63 O h
St. Catherines I., Georgia 55 K f
St. Catherines Sd., Georgia 55 K f
St. Charles, Idaho 66 J g
St. Charles, Illinois 57 E h
St. Charles, Michigan 56 J f
St. Charles, Minnesota 59 O g
St. Charles, Missouri 61 O f
St. Clair, L., Michigan 56 L g
St. Clair, Michigan 56 L g
St. Clair, Minnesota 59 N f
St. Clair, Missouri 61 O f
St. Clair, Pennsylvania 50 A d
St. Clair R., Michigan 56 L g
St. Clair Shores, Michigan (76,657), vicinity of Detroit
St. Cloud, Florida 55 N e
St. Cloud, Minnesota (33,815) 59 M e
St. Croix R., Maine 49 H c
St. Croix R., Wisconsin 56 A d
St. David, Illinois 57 C j
St. Edward, Nebraska 60 G c
Ste. Genevieve, Missouri 61 O g
St. Elias, C., Alaska 77 P g
St. Elias, Mt., Alaska 77 R f
St. Elmo, Illinois 57 E k
Ste. Marie, Illinois 57 E l
St. Francis, Kansas 60 C e
St. Francis, Maine 49 G a
St. Francis R., Maine 49 F a
St. Francis R., Missouri 61 O h
St. Francisville, Illinois 57 E l
St. Francisville, Louisiana 63 M h
St. Francois Mts., Missouri 61 O g
St. Froid L., Maine 49 G b
St. Gabriel, Louisiana 63 M h
St. George, Alaska 76 D h
St. George, Georgia 55 J g
St. George, New York 51 L g
St. George, Pt., California 74 A c
St. George, South Carolina 55 L d
St. George, Utah 68 C f
St. George I., Alaska 76 C h
St. George I., Florida 54 G h
St. Georges, Delaware 50 B f
St. Helen, Michigan 56 J e
St. Helena, California 74 C f
St. Helena I., Michigan 56 J d
St. Helena Sd., South Carolina 55 L e
St. Helens, Mt., Washington 73 H j
St. Helens, Oregon 73 H k
St. Hilaire, Minnesota 59 K b
St. Ignace, Michigan 56 J d
St. Ignatius, Montana 66 F b
St. James, Michigan 56 H d
St. James, Minnesota 59 M f
St. James, Missouri 61 N f
St. James, New York 50 G d
St. James City, Florida 55 M g
St. Jo, Texas 65 K b
St. Joe, Arkansas 63 L b
St. Joe, Idaho 66 D b
St. Joe, Indiana 57 J h
St. Joe R., Idaho 66 E b
St. John, Kansas 60 F f
St. John, North Dakota 58 G b
St. John, Utah 68 D c
St. John, Washington 73 N h
St. John R., Maine 49 F b
St. Johns, Arizona 70 H e
St. Johns, Michigan 56 J f
St. Johns, Pennsylvania 50 A c
St. Johnsbury, Vermont 49 C d
St. Johns R., Florida 55 K g
St. Johnsville, New York 53 M b
St. Joseph, Louisiana 63 M g
St. Joseph, Michigan 57 G g
St. Joseph, Missouri (79,673) 61 K e
St. Joseph B., Florida 54 F h
St. Joseph I., Texas 65 L h
St. Joseph R., Michigan 57 G g
St. Josephs, New York 50 D b
St. Landry, Louisiana 63 L h
St. Lawrence I., Alaska 76 B e
St. Lawrence R., New York 53 L a
St. Lawrence Seaway, United States-Canada 47 M b
St. Louis, Michigan 56 J f
St. Louis, Missouri (750,026) 61 O f
St. Louis Park, Minnesota (43,310) 59 P j
St. Louis R., Minnesota 59 O c
St. Louisville, Ohio 52 D e
St. Lucie Canal, Florida 55 O f
St. Lucie Inlet, Florida 55 O f
St. Lucie R., Florida 55 O f
St. Maries, Idaho 66 D b
St. Marks, Florida 54 G g
St. Martin B., Michigan 56 J d
St. Martin I., Michigan 56 G d
St. Martinville, Louisiana 63 M h
St. Mary L., Montana 66 G a
St. Marys, Alaska 76 F e
St. Marys, Georgia 55 K g
St. Marys, Kansas 61 H e
St. Marys, Missouri 61 P g
St. Marys, Ohio 52 B e
St. Marys, Pennsylvania 52 H d
St. Marys, West Virginia 52 E f
St. Marys B., Michigan 56 J c
St. Marys City, Maryland 53 K g
St. Marys R., Florida 55 K g
St. Marys R., Indiana 57 J j
St. Mathews, South Carolina 55 L d
St. Matthew I., Alaska 76 A f
St. Meinrad, Indiana 57 G l
St. Michael, Alaska 76 F e
St. Michael, Nebraska 60 F c
St. Michaels, Arizona 70 H d
St. Michaels, Maryland 53 K g
St. Onge, South Dakota 58 C f
St. Paris, Ohio 52 C e
St. Paul, Alaska 76 B h
St. Paul, Arkansas 63 K c
St. Paul, Indiana 57 H k
St. Paul, Kansas 61 J g
St. Paul, Minnesota (313,411) 59 N e
St. Paul, Nebraska 60 F c
St. Paul, South Carolina 55 L d
St. Paul, Virginia 52 D j
St. Paul I., Alaska 76 B h
St. Pauls, North Carolina 55 M c
St. Peter, Illinois 57 E l
St. Peter, Minnesota 59 M f
St. Peters, Pennsylvania 50 B e
St. Petersburg, Florida (181,298) 55 M f
St. Regis, Montana 66 E b
St. Regis Falls, New York 53 M a
St. Regis R., New York 53 M a
St. Simons, Georgia 55 K f
St. Simons I., Georgia 55 K f
St. Stephen, South Carolina 55 M d
St. Stephens, Wyoming 67 M g
St. Terese, Alaska 77 U g
St. Thomas, North Dakota 58 J b
St. Vincent I., Florida 54 F h
St. Vital Pt., Michigan 56 J d
St. Vrain, New Mexico 71 O e
St. Xavier, Montana 67 N d
Sakakawea, L., North Dakota 58 D c
Sakatonchee R., Mississippi 63 P e
Sakonnet Pt., Rhode Island 51 L c
Sakonnet R., Rhode Island 51 L b
Salado, Texas 65 K e
Salamanca, New York 52 H c
Salamonie R., Indiana 57 H j
Salcha, Alaska 77 O d
Sale City, Georgia 54 G f
Sale Creek, Tennessee 54 F b
Salem, Alabama 54 F e
Salem, Arkansas 63 M b
Salem, Connecticut 51 J c
Salem, Florida 54 H h
Salem, Illinois 57 E l
Salem, Indiana 57 G l
Salem, Massachusetts (39,211) 49 D f
Salem, Missouri 61 N g
Salem, New Jersey 50 C f
Salem, New Mexico 71 K g
Salem, New York 53 N b
Salem, Ohio 52 F e
Salem, Oregon (49,142) 73 G l
Salem, South Carolina 55 J c
Salem, South Dakota 58 J g
Salem, Virginia 52 F h
Salem, West Virginia 52 L f
Salem, Wisconsin 56 E g
Salem Depot, New Hampshire 49 D f
Salem R., New Jersey 50 C f
Salerno, Florida 55 O f
Salida, Colorado 69 K e
Salina, Kansas (43,202) 60 G f
Salina, Oklahoma 62 H b
Salina, Utah 68 E e
Salinas, California (28,957) 75 D h
Salinas Pk., New Mexico 71 L f
Salinas R., California 75 D h
Saline, Michigan 57 K g
Saline Bayou R., Louisiana 63 L f
Saline L., Louisiana 63 L g
Saline R., Arkansas 63 L e
Saline R., Illinois 57 E m
Saline R., Kansas 60 E e
Saline Val., California 75 H h
Salineville, Ohio 52 F e
Salisbury, Connecticut 50 G b
Salisbury, Maryland 53 L g
Salisbury, Missouri 61 M e
Salisbury, Mt., Alaska 77 O b
Salisbury, North Carolina 55 L b
Salisbury, Pennsylvania 52 H f
Salisbury, Vermont 49 B e
Salisbury Sd., Alaska 77 U h
Salkehatchie R., South Carolina 55 K e
Salley, South Carolina 55 K d
Sallisaw, Oklahoma 63 J c
Salmon, Alaska 77 Q c
Salmon, Idaho 66 G d
Salmon Bank, Hawaii 72 A a
Salmon Creek Res., Idaho 66 F g
Salmon Falls, Idaho 66 E g
Salmon Falls Cr., Idaho 66 F g
Salmon Mt., California 74 B c
Salmon R., Idaho 66 D d
Salmon Res., New York 53 L b
Salmon River Mts., Idaho 66 E e
Salol, Minnesota 59 L b
Salome, Arizona 70 D f
Salt, Colorado 69 J d
Saltair, Utah 68 B h
Saltaire, New York 50 G d
Salt Basin, Texas 64 B d
Salt Cr., Illinois 57 D j
Salt Cr., Ohio 52 D f
Salt Cr., Wyoming 67 O f
Salt Draw, Texas 64 C d
Salt Flat, Texas 64 B d
Salt Gap, Texas 65 H d
Saltillo, Pennsylvania 52 J e
Saltillo, Tennessee 54 C b
Salt L., Texas 64 C d
Salt L., Utah 68 D d
Salt Lake City, Utah (189,454) 68 E c
Salt Lick, Kentucky 57 K l
Salton, California 75 K l
Salton Sea, California 75 K l
Salt Point, New York 50 F b
Salt R., Arizona 70 G f
Salt R., Kentucky 57 H m
Salt R., Missouri 61 N e
Salt R., Wyoming 67 K f
Salt River Ra., Wyoming 67 K g
Saltville, Virginia 52 E j
Salt Wells, Nevada 74 G e
Saluda, South Carolina 55 K d
Saluda R., South Carolina 55 J c
Salus, Arkansas 63 K c
Salvador, L., Louisiana 63 N j
Salvation Cr., Utah 68 E e
Salyersville, Kentucky 57 K m
Sam, Idaho 66 J f
Samalga I., Alaska 77 T h
Samaria, Idaho 66 H g
Sam Creek, Alaska 77 Q d
Sammamish, L., Washington 72 C h
Samoa, California 74 A d
Sam Rayburn Res., Texas 65 N d
Samson, Alabama 54 E f
Samsonville, New York 50 E b
Sams Point, New York 50 E b
San Acacia, New Mexico 71 L e
Sanak I., Alaska 76 F j
San Andreas, California 74 E f
San Andreas L., California 75 B m
San Andres Mts., New Mexico 71 L g
San Angelo, Texas (58,815) 64 G d
San Antonio, Florida 55 M e
San Antonio, New Mexico 71 L f
San Antonio, Texas (587,718) 65 J f
San Antonio B., Texas 65 L g
San Antonio Mt., California 75 H k
San Antonio Mt., Texas 64 B d
San Antonio R., California 75 D j
San Antonio R., Texas 65 K g
San Ardo, California 75 E h
Sanatorium, Texas 64 G d
San Augustine, Texas 65 N d
San Benito, Texas 65 K j
San Benito Mt., California 75 E h
San Benito R., California 75 D h
San Bernardino, California (91,922) 75 H k
San Bernardino Mts., California 75 J k
San Bernard R., Texas 65 M f
San Blas, C., Florida 54 F h
San Blas, Florida 54 F g
Sanborn, Iowa 61 J a
Sanborn, Minnesota 59 L f
Sanborn, North Dakota 58 H d
Sanbornville, New Hampshire 49 D e
San Bruno, California (29,063) 75 B m
San Carlos, Arizona 70 G f
San Carlos, California 75 C n
San Carlos L., Arizona 70 G f
Sanchez Res., Colorado 69 L f
San Clemente, California 75 H l
San Clemente I., California 75 G m
San Cristobal Wash, Arizona 70 D g
Sand, Massachusetts 50 G a
Sand Arroyo R., Colorado 69 O f
Sanders, Arizona 70 H d
Sanders, Idaho 66 D b
Sanders, Montana 67 N c
Sanderson, Florida 55 J g

Shell Cr., *Wyoming* 67 N e
Shelley, *Idaho* 66 H f
Shell Lake, *Wisconsin* 56 B d
Shellman, *Georgia* 54 G f
Shell Mt., *California* 74 B d
Shell R., *Minnesota* 59 L d
Shell Rock, *Iowa* 61 M b
Shellrock R., *Iowa* 61 M b
Shellsburg, *Iowa* 61 N b
Shelter Cove, *California* 74 A d
Shelter I., *New York* 51 J c
Shelter Island, *New York* 51 J c
Shelton, *Connecticut* 50 G c
Shelton, *Nebraska* 60 F d
Shelton, *Washington* 73 G h
Shemya I., *Alaska* 76 K j
Shenandoah, *Iowa* 61 J d
Shenandoah, *Pennsylvania* 53 K e
Shenandoah, *Virginia* 52 H g
Shenandoah Junction, *West Virginia* 52 J f
Shenandoah Mts., *West Virginia* 52 G g
Shenandoah Nat. Park, *Virginia* 52 H g
Shenandoah R., *Virginia* 52 J f
Shenango R., *Pennsylvania* 52 F d
Shepherd, *Michigan* 56 J f
Shepherd, *Montana* 67 M d
Shepherd, *Texas* 65 M e
Shepherdstown, *West Virginia* 52 J f
Shepherdsville, *Kentucky* 57 H m
Sheppton, *Pennsylvania* 50 A d
Sherborn, *Massachusetts* 51 L a
Sherburne, *New York* 53 L c
Sheridan, *Arkansas* 63 L d
Sheridan, *Colorado* 69 O j
Sheridan, *Indiana* 57 G j
Sheridan, *Michigan* 56 H f
Sheridan, *Montana* 66 H d
Sheridan, Mt., *Wyoming* 67 K e
Sheridan, *Oregon* 73 G k
Sheridan, *Wyoming* 67 O e
Sheridan Lake, *Colorado* 69 O e
Sherman, *Connecticut* 50 G b
Sherman, *Mississippi* 63 P d
Sherman, *New York* 52 G c
Sherman, *Texas* 65 L b
Sherman Mills, *Maine* 49 G c
Sherman Mt., *Nevada* 74 K d
Sherman Pk., *Idaho* 66 J g
Sherman Res., *Nebraska* 60 F c
Sherrill, *New York* 53 L b
Sherwood, *North Dakota* 58 E b
Sherwood, *Texas* 64 G d
Shetek, L., *Minnesota* 59 L f
Shevlin, *Minnesota* 59 L c
Sheyenne, *North Dakota* 58 G c
Sheyenne R., *North Dakota* 58 J d
Shiawassee R., *Michigan* 56 J f
Shickley, *Nebraska* 60 G d
Shickshinny, *Pennsylvania* 53 K d
Shidler, *Oklahoma* 62 G b
Shields, *Kansas* 60 D f
Shields, *North Dakota* 58 E d
Shillington, *Pennsylvania* 53 L e
Shiloh, *New Jersey* 50 C g
Shilo Nat. Mil. Park, *Tennessee* 54 C b
Shine, *Washington* 72 A g
Shiner, *Texas* 65 K f
Shinglehouse, *Pennsylvania* 52 H d
Shingleton, *Michigan* 56 G c
Shingletown, *California* 74 D d
Shinnecock B., *New York* 51 H d
Shinnston, *West Virginia* 52 F f
Ship Bottom, *New Jersey* 50 E f
Ship I., *Mississippi* 63 P h
Shippensburg, *Pennsylvania* 52 J e
Ship Rock, *New Mexico* 71 J c
Ship Rock, mt., *New Mexico* 71 J c
Shirley, *Arkansas* 63 L c
Shirley, *Indiana* 57 H k
Shirley, *New Jersey* 50 C f
Shishaldin Vol., *Alaska* 76 F j
Shishmaref, *Alaska* 76 D c
Shishmaref Inlet, *Alaska* 76 E c
Shivwits Plateau, *Arizona* 70 D c
Shoal R., *Florida* 54 E g
Shoals, *Indiana* 57 G l
Shoemakersville, *Pennsylvania* 50 B d
Shohola Cr., *Pennsylvania* 50 C c
Shorehan, *New York* 51 H d
Shorewood, *Wisconsin* 56 F f
Short Creek, *Arizona* 60 D c
Shorter, *Alabama* 54 F e
Shortsville, *New York* 52 J c
Shoshone, *California* 75 J j
Shoshone, *Idaho* 66 F g
Shoshone Cavern Nat. Mon., *Wyoming* 67 L e
Shoshone Falls, *Idaho* 66 F g
Shoshone L., *Wyoming* 67 K e
Shoshone Mt., *Nevada* 75 J h
Shoshone Mts., *Nevada* 74 H f
Shoshoni, *Wyoming* 67 M f
Shoulder Mt., *Alaska* 77 Q c
Shoup, *Idaho* 66 F d
Shovel Lake, *Minnesota* 59 N d
Show Low, *Arizona* 70 G e
Shreve, *Ohio* 52 E e
Shreveport, *Louisiana* (164,372) 63 K f
Shrewsbury, *Louisiana* 62 B e
Shrewsbury, *Massachusetts* 51 K a
Shrub Oak, *New York* 50 F c
Shubelik Mts., *Alaska* 77 P b
Shubert, *Nebraska* 61 J d
Shubuta, *Mississippi* 63 P g
Shuksan, Mt., *Washington* 73 J g
Shuksan, *Washington* 73 J g
Shullsburg, *Wisconsin* 56 C g
Shumagin Is., *Alaska* 76 G j
Shuman House, *Alaska* 77 Q c
Shumla, *Texas* 64 F f
Shumway, *Arizona* 70 G e
Shungilak, *Alaska* 76 J c
Shuqualak, *Mississippi* 63 P f
Shuyak I., *Alaska* 76 L g
Shuyak Str., *Alaska* 76 L g
Siasconset, *Massachusetts* 51 N c
Sibley, *Illinois* 57 E j
Sibley, *Iowa* 61 J a
Sibley, *Louisiana* 63 K f
Sicily Island, *Louisiana* 63 M g
Sidell, *Illinois* 57 F k
Sidnaw, *Michigan* 56 E c
Sidney, *Illinois* 57 E j
Sidney, *Iowa* 61 J d
Sidney, *Montana* 67 Q b
Sidney, *Nebraska* 60 B c
Sidney, *New York* 53 L c
Sidney, *Ohio* 52 B e
Sidney Lanier, L., *Georgia* 54 G c
Siegersville, *Pennsylvania* 50 B d
Sierra Blanca, mt., *New Mexico* 71 M f
Sierra Blanca, mt., *Texas* 64 B d
Sierra Blanca, *Texas* 64 B d
Sierra Buttes, *California* 74 E e
Sierra Diablo, mt., *Texas* 64 C d
Sierra Estrella, *Arizona* 70 E f
Sierra Madre, mts., *California* 75 E k
Sierra Nevada, mts., *California* 75 G g
Sierra Pinta, *Arizona* 70 D g
Sierra Vieja, mts., *Texas* 64 C e
Sierraville, *California* 74 E e
Sigel, *Illinois* 57 E k
Sigel, *Pennsylvania* 52 G d
Signal, *Arizona* 70 D e
Signal Hill, *California* 75 E m
Signal Mountain, *Tennessee* 54 F b
Signal Pk., *Arizona* 70 C f
Sigourney, *Iowa* 61 M c
Sigurd, *Utah* 68 E e
Sikes, *Louisiana* 63 L f
Sikeston, *Missouri* 61 P h
Siknik C., *Alaska* 76 B e
Silas, *Alabama* 54 C f
Siler City, *North Carolina* 55 M b
Silesia, *Montana* 67 M d
Silica, *Minnesota* 59 N c
Siloam Springs, *Arkansas* 63 J b
Silsbee, *Texas* 65 N e
Siluria, *Alabama* 54 E d
Silver Bay, *Minnesota* 59 P c
Silver Beach, *Massachusetts* 51 M b
Silverbell, *Arizona* 70 F g
Silverbow, *Montana* 66 H d
Silver City, *Idaho* 66 D f
Silver City, *Mississippi* 63 N e
Silver City, *New Mexico* 71 J g
Silver City, *Utah* 68 D d
Silver Cr., *Oregon* 73 L m
Silver Creek, *Mississippi* 63 N g
Silver Creek, *Nebraska* 60 G c
Silver Creek, *New York* 52 G c
Silver Crown, *Wyoming* 67 P h
Silverdale, *Kansas* 60 H g
Silverdale, *Washington* 72 A h
Silver L., *California* 75 J j
Silver L., *Massachusetts* 51 M a
Silver L., *Michigan* 56 F c
Silver L., *Oregon* 73 K m
Silver L., *Oregon* 73 L m
Silver Lake, *California* 75 J j
Silver Lake, *Oregon* 73 J m
Silvernails, *New York* 50 F a
Silverpeak, *Nevada* 74 H g
Silver Peak Ra., *Nevada* 74 H g
Silver Spring, *Maryland* (66,348) 53 J f
Silver Springs, *New York* 52 H c
Silver Star, *Montana* 66 H d
Silverton, *Colorado* 69 J f
Silverton, *New Jersey* 50 E e
Silverton, *Oregon* 73 H k
Silverton, *Texas* 64 C j
Silverton, *Washington* 73 J g
Silvertown, *Georgia* 54 G e
Silvies R., *Oregon* 73 L m
Simeon, *Nebraska* 60 D b
Simeonof I., *Alaska* 76 H j
Simla, *Colorado* 69 M d
Simmesport, *Louisiana* 63 M h
Simmler, *California* 75 F j
Simmons, *Texas* 65 J g
Simms, *Montana* 66 J b
Simms, *Texas* 65 N b
Simon, *Nevada* 74 H f
Simpson, *Kansas* 60 G e
Simpson, *Minnesota* 59 O g
Simpson, *Montana* 67 K a
Simpson Park Mts., *Nevada* 74 J e
Simpsonville, *South Carolina* 55 J c
Sims, *California* 74 C c
Simsbury, *Connecticut* 51 H b
Sinai, *South Dakota* 58 J f
Sinaru, *Alaska* 76 J a
Sinclair, *Wyoming* 67 N h
Sinclair L., *Georgia* 54 H d
Sinclairville, *New York* 52 G c
Singac, *New Jersey* 50 E d
Singer, *Louisiana* 63 K h
Singleton, *Texas* 65 M e
Sinking Spring, *Ohio* 52 C f
Sinnemahoning, *Pennsylvania* 52 J d
Sinton, *Texas* 65 K g
Sioux Center, *Iowa* 60 H b
Sioux City, *Iowa* (89,159) 60 H b
Sioux Falls, *South Dakota* (65,466) 59 K g
Sioux Rapids, *Iowa* 61 K b
Sipsey, *Alabama* 54 D d
Sipsey R., *Alabama* 54 D d
Siren, *Wisconsin* 56 A d
Sirretta Pk., *California* 75 G j
Siskiwit B., *Michigan* 56 E a
Siskiyou, *Oregon* 73 H n
Siskiyou Mts., *California* 74 B c
Sisquoc, *California* 75 E k
Sisquoc R., *California* 75 F k
Sisseton, *South Dakota* 58 J e
Sisterdale, *Texas* 65 J f
Sisters, *Oregon* 73 J l
Sisters, The, mts., *Alaska* 76 G e
Sistersville, *West Virginia* 52 F f
Sitka, *Alaska* 77 U h
Sitka, *Kansas* 60 E g
Sitkalidak I., *Alaska* 76 L h
Sitkinak I., *Alaska* 76 L h
Sitkinak Str., *Alaska* 76 L h
Sitkum, *Oregon* 73 G m
Sixes, *Oregon* 73 F n
Six Mile L., *Louisiana* 63 M j
Siyeh, Mt., *Montana* 66 G a
Skagway, *Alaska* 77 U g
Skamania, *Washington* 73 H k
Skandia, *Michigan* 56 F c
Skaneateles, *New York* 53 K c
Skaneateles L., *New York* 53 K c
Skanee, *Michigan* 56 E b
Skanit R., *Washington* 73 J g
Skellytown, *Texas* 64 C h
Skiatook, *Oklahoma* 62 G b
Skidaway I., *Georgia* 55 K f
Skidmore, *Maryland* 53 K f
Skidmore, *Texas* 65 K g
Skilak I., *Alaska* 76 M f
Skillet R., *Illinois* 57 E l
Skokie, *Illinois* (59,364) 57 A k
Skowhegan, *Maine* 49 F d
Skull Mt., *Nevada* 75 J h
Skull Valley, *Arizona* 70 E e
Skuna R., *Mississippi* 63 O e
Skunk R., *Iowa* 61 M c
Skwentna, *Alaska* 76 M f
Skwentna R., *Alaska* 76 L f
Skykomish, *Washington* 73 J h
Skytop, *Pennsylvania* 50 C c
Slagle, *Louisiana* 63 K g
Slana, *Alaska* 77 P e
Slatedale, *Pennsylvania* 50 B d
Slateford, *Pennsylvania* 50 C d
Slater, *Colorado* 69 J c
Slater, *Missouri* 61 L e
Slater, *Wyoming* 67 Q h
Slate Ra., *California* 75 H j
Slatersville, *Rhode Island* 51 K b
Slate Springs, *Mississippi* 63 O e
Slatington, *Pennsylvania* 50 B d
Slaton, *Texas* 64 F b
Slatyfork, *West Virginia* 52 F g
Slaughter, *Louisiana* 63 M h
Slayton, *Minnesota* 59 L g
Sledge I., *Alaska* 76 D d
Sleeping Bear Pt., *Michigan* 56 G e
Sleepy Eye, *Minnesota* 59 M f
Sleetmute, *Alaska* 76 J f
Slidell, *Louisiana* 63 O h
Slidell, *Texas* 65 K b
Slide Mt., *New York* 50 E a
Sligo, *Pennsylvania* 52 G d
Slinger, *Wisconsin* 56 E f
Slippery Rock, *Pennsylvania* 52 F d
Sloan, *Iowa* 60 H b
Sloan, *Montana* 66 F b
Sloan, *Nevada* 75 K j
Sloat, *California* 74 E e
Sloatsburg, *New York* 50 E c
Slocombe, *Alabama* 54 F f
Smackover, *Arkansas* 63 L e
Small, *Idaho* 66 H e
Small Pt., *Maine* 49 F e
Smethport, *Pennsylvania* 52 H d
Smiley, *Texas* 65 K f
Smith, *Nevada* 74 F f
Smith B., *Alaska* 76 K a
Smithboro, *Illinois* 57 D l
Smithburg, *New Jersey* 50 E e
Smith Center, *Kansas* 60 F e
Smithfield, *Nebraska* 60 E d
Smithfield, *North Carolina* 55 N b
Smithfield, *Pennsylvania* 52 G f
Smithfield, *Rhode Island* 51 K b
Smithfield, *Texas* 65 M j
Smithfield, *Utah* 68 E b
Smithfield, *Virginia* 53 K h
Smithfield, *West Virginia* 52 F f
Smith I., *Maryland* 53 L g
Smith I., *North Carolina* 55 O d
Smith I., *Washington* 73 H g
Smith I., *Virginia* 53 L h
Smith Pk., *Idaho* 66 D a
Smith R., *California* 74 A c
Smith R., *Montana* 66 J b
Smith R., *Virginia* 52 G j
Smith River, *California* 74 A c
Smiths Ferry, *Idaho* 66 D e
Smiths Grove, *Kentucky* 57 G m
Smithton, *Missouri* 61 L f
Smithtown, *New York* 50 G d
Smithtown B., *New York* 50 G d
Smithtown Branch, *New York* 50 G d
Smithville, *Georgia* 54 G f
Smithville, *Missouri* 61 K e
Smithville, *New Jersey* 50 E f
Smithville, *Oklahoma* 63 J d
Smithville, *Tennessee* 54 F b
Smithville, *Texas* 65 K f
Smithville, *West Virginia* 52 E f
Smithwick, *South Dakota* 58 C g
Smoke Creek Des., *Nevada* 74 F d
Smoke Hole, *West Virginia* 52 G g
Smoking Water Cr., *Nebraska* 60 C d
Smoky Hill R., *Kansas* 60 F f
Smoky Hills, *Kansas* 60 E e
Smoot, *Wyoming* 67 K g
Smyer, *Texas* 64 E b
Smyrna, *Delaware* 50 B g
Smyrna, *Georgia* 54 G d
Smyrna, *New York* 53 L c
Smyrna, *Tennessee* 54 E b
Smyrna Mills, *Maine* 49 G b
Smyrna R., *Delaware* 50 B g
Snake R., *Washington, etc.* 46 C a
Snake Ra., *Nevada* 74 L e
Snake River, *Washington* 73 M j
Snake River, *Wyoming* 67 K e
Snake River Canyon (Hell's Canyon), *Idaho* 66 D d
Snake River Plain, *Idaho* 66 G f
Sneads, *Florida* 54 G g
Snelling, *California* 74 E g
Snipatuit Pond, *Massachusetts* 51 M b
Snohomish, *Washington* 73 H h
Snoqualmie, *Washington* 73 J h
Snoqualmie Pass, *Washington* 73 J h
Snoqualmie R., *Washington* 72 C g
Snover, *Michigan* 56 L f
Snowcap Mt., *Alaska* 76 L f
Snowden, *California* 74 B c
Snowflake, *Arizona* 70 G e
Snow Hill, *Maryland* 53 L g
Snow Hill, *North Carolina* 55 O b
Snow Lake, *Arkansas* 63 M d
Snowmass Pk., *Colorado* 69 K d
Snow Shoe, *Pennsylvania* 52 J d
Snowshoe Pk., *Montana* 66 E a
Snowville, *Utah* 68 D b
Snow Water L., *Nevada* 74 K d
Snyder, *Nebraska* 60 H c
Snyder, *Oklahoma* 62 E d
Snyder, *Texas* 64 G c
Snyders, *Pennsylvania* 50 B d
Snydersville, *Pennsylvania* 50 C d
Soap Lake, *Washington* 73 L h
Sobrante Ridge, *California* 75 C k
Social Circle, *Georgia* 54 H d
Society Hill, *South Carolina* 55 M c
Socorro, *New Mexico* 71 L e
Socorro, *Texas* 64 A d
Soda L., *California* 75 J j
Soda Lake, *California* 75 K j
Soda Springs, *Idaho* 66 J g
Sodaville, *Nevada* 74 G f
Soddy, *Tennessee* 54 F b
Sodus, *New York* 53 J b
Sodus Point, *New York* 53 K b
Sofia, *New Mexico* 71 O c
Solano, *New Mexico* 71 N d
Soldier, *Iowa* 61 J c
Soldier, *Kansas* 61 J e
Soldier, *Kentucky* 57 K l
Soldier R., *Iowa* 61 J c
Soldier Summit, *Utah* 68 E d
Soledad, *California* 75 D h
Soleduck R., *Washington* 73 F g
Solomon, *Alaska* 76 E d
Solomon, *Arizona* 70 H g
Solomon, *Kansas* 60 G f
Solomon R., *Kansas* 60 F e
Solon, *Iowa* 61 N c
Solon, *Ohio* 52 E d
Solon Springs, *Wisconsin* 56 B c
Solvang, *California* 75 E k
Solvay, *New York* 53 K b
Sombrero Key, *Florida* 55 N j
Somerdale, *New Jersey* 50 C f
Somers, *Connecticut* 51 J b
Somers, *Iowa* 61 K b
Somers, *Montana* 66 F a
Somers, *New York* 50 F c
Somers, *Wisconsin* 56 F g
Somerset, *Colorado* 69 J e
Somerset, *Kentucky* 57 J m
Somerset, *Massachusetts* 51 L b
Somerset, *Ohio* 52 D f
Somerset, *Pennsylvania* 52 G e
Somerset, *Texas* 65 J f
Somerset Res., *Vermont* 49 B e
Somers Point, *New Jersey* 50 D g
Somersworth, *New Hampshire* 49 D e
Somerton, *Arizona* 70 C g
Somerville, *Massachusetts* (94,697) 49 G h
Somerville, *New Jersey* 50 D d
Somerville, *Tennessee* 54 B b
Somerville, *Texas* 65 L e
Somesbar, *California* 74 B c
Somonauk, *Illinois* 57 E h
Sonama Ra., *Nevada* 74 H d
Sondheimer, *Louisiana* 63 M f
Sonestown, *Pennsylvania* 53 K d
Sonnette, *Montana* 67 P d
Sonoita, *Arizona* 70 G h
Sonoma, *California* 74 C f
Sonoma Pk., *Nevada* 74 H d
Sonora, *Arizona* 70 F f
Sonora, *California* 74 E f
Sonora, *Texas* 64 G e
Sonora Pk., *California* 74 F f
Sonyea, *New York* 52 J c
Sopchoppy, *Florida* 54 G g
Soper, *Oklahoma* 62 H d
Soperton, *Georgia* 55 J e
Soquel, *California* 75 D h
Sorrento, *Louisiana* 63 N h
Sorrento, *Maine* 49 G d
Sorum, *South Dakota* 58 D e
Soso, *Mississippi* 63 O g
Souderton, *Pennsylvania* 50 C e
Souris, *North Dakota* 58 F b
Sourlake, *Texas* 65 N e
Sourland Mts., *New Jersey* 50 D e
Southam, *North Dakota* 58 H b
South Amboy, *New Jersey* 50 E e
Southampton, *Massachusetts* 51 H a
Southampton, *New York* 51 J d
South Anna R., *Virginia* 52 J h
Southard, *New Jersey* 50 E e
South Attleboro, *Massachusetts* 51 L b
South Baldy, mt., *New Mexico* 71 K f
South Bass I., *Ohio* 52 D d
South Bay, *Florida* 55 O g
South Beloit, *Illinois* 56 D g
South Bend, *Indiana* (132,445) 57 G h
South Bend, *Texas* 65 J b
South Bend, *Washington* 73 G j
South Berwick, *Maine* 49 E e
South Boardman, *Michigan* 56 H e
Southboro, *Massachusetts* 51 K a
South Boston, *Virginia* 52 H j
South Branch, *Michigan* 56 K e
Southbridge, *Massachusetts* 51 J a
Southbury, *Connecticut* 50 G c
South Canon, *Colorado* 69 L e
South Carolina (2,603,000) 31,055 sq. miles 54-55
South Carver, *Massachusetts* 51 M b
South Chan., *Michigan* 56 J d
South Charleston, *Ohio* 52 C f
South Charleston, *West Virginia* 52 E g
South China, *Maine* 49 F d
South Colton, *New York* 53 M a
South Coventry, *Connecticut* 51 J b
South Dakota (674,000) 77,047 sq. miles 58-59
South Dallas, *Texas* 65 N j
South Dartmouth, *Massachusetts* 51 M b
South Dayton, *New York* 52 G c
South Deerfield, *Massachusetts* 49 C f
Southeast C., *Alaska* 76 C e
Southeast I., *Hawaii* 72 A a
Southeast Pt., *Louisiana* 63 O j
South Egremont, *Massachusetts* 50 G a
South English, *Iowa* 61 M c
Southern Cross, *Montana* 66 G c
Southern Pines, *North Carolina* 55 M b
South Euclid, *Ohio* (27,569), vicinity of Cleveland
South Fabius R., *Missouri* 61 N e
South Fallsburg, *New York* 50 D b
Southfield, *Massachusetts* 50 G a
Southfield, *Michigan* (31,501), vicinity of Detroit
Southfields, *New York* 50 E c
Southford, *Connecticut* 50 G c
South Fork, *California* 74 B d
South Fork, *Colorado* 69 K f
South Fork, *Pennsylvania* 52 H e
South Fork, *Wyoming* 67 O f
South Foster, *Rhode Island* 51 K b
South Fox I., *Michigan* 56 H d
South Fulton, *Tennessee* 54 C a
South Gate, *California* (53,831) 75 E m
South Gifford, *Missouri* 61 M d
South Haven, *Kansas* 60 G g
South Haven, *Michigan* 56 G g
South Hill, *Virginia* 52 H j
South Holston L., *Tennessee* 55 J a
South Houston, *Texas* 64 G j
South Huntington, *New York* 50 G d
Southington, *Connecticut* 51 H b
South Jordan, *Utah* 68 C j
South Kenosha, *Wisconsin* 56 F g
South Kortright, *New York* 50 D a
South Glastonbury, *Connecticut* 51 H b
South Grand R., *Missouri* 61 K f
South Hadley, *Massachusetts* 51 H a
South Hadley Falls, *Massachusetts* 51 H a
Southlake, *Texas* 65 M h
Southland, *Texas* 64 F b
South Loup R., *Nebraska* 60 E c
South Lyon, *Michigan* 56 K g
South Manchester, *Connecticut* 51 H b
South Manitou I., *Michigan* 56 G d
South Miami, *Florida* 54 B d
South Millbrook, *New York* 50 F b
South Mills, *North Carolina* 55 P a
South Milwaukee, *Wisconsin* 56 F g
Southmost, *Texas* 65 K k
South Mt., *Pennsylvania* 53 J e
South Naknek, *Alaska* 76 J g
South Newport, *Georgia* 55 K f
South Norwalk, *Connecticut* 50 G c
Southold, *New York* 51 J c
South Orange, *New Jersey* 51 J f
South Orleans, *Massachusetts* 51 N b
South Otselic, *New York* 53 L c
South Paris, *Maine* 49 E d
South Park, *Kansas* 61 P a
South Parkersburg, *West Virginia* 52 E f
South Pass, *Wyoming* 67 M g
South Pass City, *Wyoming* 67 M g
South Pekin, *Illinois* 57 D j
Southern Pine Hills, *Alabama* 54 C f
South Pittsburg, *Tennessee* 54 F b
South Platte, *Colorado* 69 L d
South Platte R., *Colorado* 69 O c
Southport, *Connecticut* 50 G c
Southport, *Indiana* 57 G k
Southport, *North Carolina* 55 N d
South Portland, *Maine* 49 E e
South Pt., *Louisiana* 63 O j
South R., *North Carolina* 55 N c
South Range, *Michigan* 56 E b
South Rita, *New Mexico* 71 J g
South River, *New Jersey* 50 E e
South St. Paul, *Minnesota* 59 R j
South Salt Lake, *Utah* 68 C h
South San Francisco, *California* (39,418) 75 B m
South San Gabriel, *California* (26,213), vicinity of Los Angeles
South Santiam R., *Oregon* 73 H l
South Seaville, *New Jersey* 50 D g
South Side, *Pennsylvania* 53 P b
South Sioux City, *Nebraska* 60 H b
South Sioux Falls, *South Dakota* 59 K g
South Sterling, *Pennsylvania* 50 C c
South Superior, *Wyoming* 67 M h
South Tent, *Utah* 68 E d
South Torrington, *Wyoming* 67 Q g
South Truro, *Massachusetts* 51 N b
South Umpqua R., *Oregon* 73 H m
South Vineland, *New Jersey* 50 C g
Southwest C., *Alaska* 76 B e
Southwest Pt., *Louisiana* 63 O j
South Whitley, *Indiana* 57 H h
Southwick, *Massachusetts* 51 H a
South Wilkes-Barre, *Pennsylvania* 50 B c
South Williamsport, *Pennsylvania* 53 K d
South Wilmington, *Illinois* 57 E h
South Windham, *Maine* 49 E e
South Windsor, *Connecticut* 51 H b
South Yadkin R., *North Carolina* 55 L b
Spalding, *Idaho* 66 D c
Spalding, *Nebraska* 60 F c
Spangle, *Washington* 73 N h
Spangler, *Pennsylvania* 52 H e
Spanish Fork City, *Utah* 68 E c
Spanish Pks., *Colorado* 69 L f
Sparkill, *New York* 50 F c
Sparkman, *Arkansas* 63 L e
Sparks, *Georgia* 54 H f
Sparks, *Nebraska* 60 D b
Sparks, *Nevada* 74 F e
Sparks, *Oklahoma* 62 G c
Sparland, *Illinois* 57 D h
Sparr, *Michigan* 56 J d
Sparrow Bush, *New York* 50 D c
Sparta, *Georgia* 55 J d
Sparta, *Illinois* 57 D l
Sparta, *Michigan* 56 H f
Sparta, *Missouri* 61 L h
Sparta, *New Jersey* 50 D c
Sparta, *North Carolina* 55 K a
Sparta, *Oregon* 73 N l
Sparta, *Tennessee* 54 F b
Sparta, *Wisconsin* 56 C f
Spartanburg, *South Carolina* (44,352) 55 K c
Spartansburg, *Pennsylvania* 52 G d
Spavinaw L., Upper, *Oklahoma* 63 J b
Speaks, *Texas* 65 L f
Spearfish, *South Dakota* 58 C f
Spearman, *Texas* 64 C g
Spearville, *Kansas* 60 E g
Speculator, *New York* 53 M b
Speer, *Oklahoma* 62 H d
Speer, *Wyoming* 67 Q h
Spencer, C., *Alaska* 77 T g
Spencer, *Idaho* 66 H e
Spencer, *Indiana* 57 G k
Spencer, *Iowa* 61 J a
Spencer, *Massachusetts* 51 J a
Spencer, *Nebraska* 60 F b
Spencer, *New York* 53 K c
Spencer, Pt., *Alaska* 76 D d
Spencer, *South Dakota* 58 J g
Spencer, *West Virginia* 52 E g
Spencer, *Wisconsin* 56 C e
Spencer L., *Maine* 49 E c
Spencerport, *New York* 52 J b
Spencertown, *New York* 50 G a
Spencerville, *Ohio* 52 B e
Sperryville, *Virginia* 52 H g

Spes UNITED STATES INDEX Tabo

Spesutie I., *Maryland* 50 A g
Spikard, *Missouri* 61 L d
Spike Mt., *Alaska* 77 R c
Spindale, *North Carolina* 55 K b
Spirit L., *Iowa* 61 J a
Spirit L., *Washington* 73 H j
Spirit Lake, *Idaho* 66 D b
Spirit Lake, *Iowa* 61 J a
Spirit Lake, *Washington* 73 H j
Spiritwood, *North Dakota* 58 H d
Spiro, *Oklahoma* 63 J c
Splendora, *Texas* 65 M e
Split Pk., *Nevada* 74 G c
Split Rock, *Wyoming* 67 N g
Spofford, *Texas* 64 G f
Spokane, *Washington* (181,608) 73 N h
Spokane R., *Washington* 73 N h
Spooner, *Wisconsin* 56 B d
Spooner Res., *California* 74 E c
Spoon R., *Illinois* 57 C j
Spotswood, *New Jersey* 50 E e
Spotted Horse, *Wyoming* 67 P e
Spotted Ra., *Nevada* 75 K h
Sprague, *Alabama* 54 E e
Sprague, *Washington* 73 N h
Sprague, *Wisconsin* 56 C e
Sprague L., *Washington* 73 M h
Sprague River, *Oregon* 73 J n
Spray, *North Carolina* 55 M a
Spray, *Oregon* 73 L l
Spring, *Texas* 65 M e
Spring B., *Utah* 68 D b
Springboro, *Pennsylvania* 52 F d
Spring Branch, *Texas* 64 F h
Spring Brook, *North Dakota* 58 C b
Spring City, *Pennsylvania* 50 B e
Spring City, *Tennessee* 54 G b
Spring City, *Utah* 68 E d
Spring Cr., *Nebraska* 60 C d
Springdale, *Arkansas* 63 J b
Springdale, *Montana* 67 K d
Springdale, *Nevada* 75 J g
Springdale, *Utah* 68 D f
Springdale, *Washington* 73 N g
Springer, *New Mexico* 71 N c
Springer, *Oklahoma* 62 F d
Springerville, *Arizona* 70 H e
Springfield, *Colorado* 69 O f
Springfield, *Georgia* 55 K e
Springfield, *Idaho* 66 H f
Springfield, *Illinois* (83,271) 57 D k
Springfield, *Kentucky* 57 H m
Springfield, L., *Illinois* 57 D k
Springfield, *Massachusetts* (174,463) 51 H a
Springfield, *Minnesota* 59 L f
Springfield, *Missouri* (95,865) 61 L g
Springfield, *Ohio* (82,723) 52 C f
Springfield, *Oregon* 73 H l
Springfield, *Pennsylvania* (26,733), vicinity of Philadelphia
Springfield, *South Carolina* 55 K d
Springfield, *South Dakota* 58 J h
Springfield, *Tennessee* 54 E a
Springfield, *Vermont* 49 C e
Spring Glen, *New York* 50 E b
Spring Green, *Wisconsin* 56 C f
Spring Grove, *Minnesota* 59 P g
Spring Grove, *Pennsylvania* 53 K f
Springhill, *Louisiana* 63 K f
Spring Hill, *Tennessee* 54 E b
Spring Hope, *North Carolina* 55 N b
Spring Lake, *Michigan* 56 G f
Spring Lake, *New Jersey* 50 E e
Springlake, *Texas* 64 E a
Spring Lake Park, *Minnesota* 59 Q h
Spring Mts., *Nevada* 75 K h
Spring R., *Arkansas* 63 M b
Spring R., *Oklahoma* 63 J b
Springs, *New York* 51 J c
Springton Res., *Pennsylvania* 50 B f
Springtown, *Pennsylvania* 50 C d
Springtown, *Texas* 65 K c
Springvale, *Maine* 49 E e
Spring Valley, *Minnesota* 59 O g
Spring Valley, *New York* 50 E c
Springview, *Nebraska* 60 E b
Springville, *Alabama* 54 E d
Springville, *New York* 52 H c
Springville, *Utah* 68 E c
Springwater, *New York* 52 J c
Spruce, *Michigan* 56 K e
Spruce Knob, *West Virginia* 52 G g
Spruce Mt., *Nevada* 74 L d
Spruce Pine, *North Carolina* 55 J b
Spruceton, *New York* 50 E a
Spry, *Utah* 68 D f
Spur, *Texas* 64 G b
Spurger, *Texas* 65 N e
Spur Lake, *New Mexico* 71 J f
Spurr, Mt., *Alaska* 76 L f
Squam L., *New Hampshire* 49 D e
Squantum, *Massachusetts* 49 H j
Squapan L., *Maine* 49 G b
Square Butte, *Montana* 67 K b
Square L., *Maine* 49 G a
Squaw Lake, *Minnesota* 59 M c
Squibnocket Pt., *Massachusetts* 51 M c
Squirrel R., *Alaska* 76 G c
Squirrel R., *Alaska* 77 Q d
Staatsburg, *New York* 50 F b
Stabler, *Washington* 73 J k
Stacy, *California* 74 E d
Stacy, *North Carolina* 55 P c
Stafford, *Connecticut* 51 J b
Stafford, *Kansas* 60 F b
Stafford, *Nebraska* 60 F b
Stafford, *Texas* 64 E j
Stafford, *Virginia* 52 J g
Stafford Springs, *Connecticut* 51 J b
Stalwart, *Michigan* 56 J c
Stamford, *Connecticut* (92,713) 50 F c
Stamford, *New York* 53 M c
Stamford, *South Dakota* 58 E g
Stamford, *Texas* 65 H c
Stampede, *Washington* 73 J h
Stamping Ground, *Kentucky* 57 J l
Stamps, *Arkansas* 63 K e
Stanardsville, *Virginia* 52 H g
Stanberry, *Missouri* 61 K d
Standard, *Arizona* 70 G e
Standish, *Michigan* 56 K f
Standley L., *Colorado* 69 O h
Standrod, *Utah* 68 C b
Stanfield, *Oregon* 73 L k
Stanford, *Indiana* 57 G k
Stanford, *Kentucky* 57 J m
Stanford, *Montana* 67 K b
Stanfordville, *New York* 50 F b
Stanhope, *New Jersey* 50 D d
Stanislaus R., *California* 74 E g
Stanley, *Idaho* 66 F e
Stanley, *New Mexico* 71 M d
Stanley, *North Carolina* 55 K b
Stanley, *North Dakota* 58 D b
Stanley, *Oklahoma* 62 H d
Stanley, *Virginia* 52 H g
Stanley, *Wisconsin* 56 C e
Stannard Rock, *Michigan* 56 F b
Stanton, *Iowa* 61 J d
Stanton, *Kentucky* 57 K m
Stanton, *Michigan* 56 H f
Stanton, *Nebraska* 60 G c
Stanton, *North Dakota* 58 E c
Stanton, *Tennessee* 54 B b
Stanton, *Texas* 64 F c
Stanwood, *Michigan* 56 H f
Stanwood, *Washington* 73 H g
Staples, *Minnesota* 59 M d
Stapleton, *Alabama* 54 D g
Stapleton, *Georgia* 55 J d
Stapleton, *Nebraska* 60 D c
Stapleton, *New York* 51 L g
Star, *Mississippi* 63 N f
Star, *North Carolina* 55 M b
Star, *Texas* 65 J d
Starbuck, *Minnesota* 59 L e
Starbuck, *Washington* 73 M j
Star City, *Arkansas* 63 M e
Star City, *Indiana* 57 G j
Star City, *West Virginia* 52 F f
Stark, *Arizona* 70 G h
Stark, *Montana* 66 F b
Stark, *New Hampshire* 49 D d
Starke, *Florida* 55 J h
Starkey, *Idaho* 66 D e
Starkey, *Oregon* 73 M k
Starks, *Louisiana* 63 K h
Starkville, *Colorado* 69 M f
Starkville, *Mississippi* 63 P e
Starkweather, *North Dakota* 58 H b
Starlake, *Wisconsin* 56 D c
Star Pk., *Nevada* 74 G d
Starr, *Maryland* 50 A h
State Center, *Iowa* 61 L b
State College, *Pennsylvania* 52 J e
State Line, *Mississippi* 63 P g
State Line, *New York* 50 G b
Staten I., *New York* 51 K g
Statesboro, *Georgia* 55 K e
Statesville, *North Carolina* 55 L b
Stauffer, *Oregon* 73 K m
Staunton, *Illinois* 57 D k
Staunton, *Virginia* 52 G g
Stayton, *Oregon* 73 H l
Steamboat, *Nevada* 74 F e
Steamboat Springs, *Colorado* 69 K c
Stearns, *Kentucky* 57 J n
Stebbins, *Alaska* 76 F e
Steel Creek, *Alaska* 77 R d
Steele, *Alabama* 54 E d
Steele, *Missouri* 61 P h
Steele, *North Dakota* 58 G d
Steele City, *Nebraska* 60 G d
Steele Valley, *Illinois* 57 D l
Steelton, *Pennsylvania* 53 K e
Steelville, *Missouri* 61 N g
Steens Mt., *Oregon* 73 M n
Stegall, *Nebraska* 60 A c
Steger, *Illinois* 57 F h
Steinauer, *Nebraska* 60 H d
Steinhatchee, *Florida* 54 H h
Steins, *New Mexico* 71 J g
Steliekin, *Washington* 73 K g
Stella, *Nebraska* 61 J d
Stella, *North Carolina* 55 O c
Steller, Mt., *Alaska* 77 Q f
Stem, *North Carolina* 55 N a
Stemplersville, *Pennsylvania* 50 B d
Stephen, *Minnesota* 59 K b
Stephens, *Arkansas* 63 K e
Stephens City, *Virginia* 52 H f
Stephenson, *Michigan* 56 F d
Stephens Pass, *Alaska* 77 V h
Stephenville, *Texas* 65 J c
Stepovak B., *Alaska* 76 H j
Steptoe, *Nevada* 74 L e
Sterley, *Texas* 64 F a
Sterling, *Alaska* 76 M f
Sterling, *Colorado* 69 O d
Sterling, *Connecticut* 51 K b
Sterling, *Illinois* 57 D h
Sterling, *Kansas* 60 F f
Sterling, *Michigan* 56 J e
Sterling, Mt., *Kentucky* 57 K l
Sterling, *Nebraska* 60 H d
Sterling, *North Dakota* 58 F d
Sterling, *Oklahoma* 62 E d
Sterling, *Pennsylvania* 50 C c
Sterling, *Utah* 68 E d
Sterling City, *Texas* 64 G d
Sterling Landing, *Alaska* 76 K e
Sterling Res., *Colorado* 69 N c
Steuben, *Michigan* 56 G c
Steuben, *Wisconsin* 56 C f
Steubenville, *Ohio* (32,495) 52 F e
Stevenson, *Alabama* 54 F c
Stevenson, *Washington* 73 J k
Stevens Pt., *Wisconsin* 56 D e
Stevens Village, *Alaska* 76 N c
Stevensville, *Michigan* 57 G g
Stevensville, *Montana* 66 F c
Steward, *Illinois* 57 E h
Stewardson, *Illinois* 57 E k
Stewart, *Minnesota* 59 M f
Stewart, *Nevada* 74 F e
Stewartstown, *Pennsylvania* 53 K f
Stewartsville, *Missouri* 61 K e
Stewartsville, *New Jersey* 50 C d
Stewartville, *Minnesota* 59 O g
Stibnite, *Idaho* 66 E e
Stickney, *South Dakota* 58 H g
Stigler, *Oklahoma* 62 H c
Stikine Str., *Alaska* 77 V h
Stiles, *Texas* 64 F d
Stilesville, *Indiana* 57 G k
Stillman Valley, *Illinois* 57 D g
Still Pond, *Maryland* 50 A g
Stillwater, *Minnesota* 59 O e
Stillwater, *Nevada* 74 G e
Stillwater, *New Jersey* 50 D c
Stillwater, *Oklahoma* 62 F b
Stillwater, *Wisconsin* 56 A d
Stillwater R., *Montana* 66 F a
Stillwater Ra., *Nevada* 74 G e
Stilwell, *Oklahoma* 63 J c
Stimson, Mt., *Montana* 66 G a
Stinnett, *Texas* 64 C h
Stirling City, *California* 74 D e
Stirum, *North Dakota* 58 J d
Stissing, *New York* 50 F b
Stites, *Idaho* 66 E c
Stitzer, *Wisconsin* 56 C g
Stockbridge, *Massachusetts* 50 G a
Stockbridge, *Michigan* 56 J g
Stockdale, *Ohio* 52 D g
Stockdale, *Texas* 65 K f
Stockertown, *Pennsylvania* 50 C d
Stockett, *Montana* 66 J b
Stockham, *Nebraska* 60 G d
Stockholm, *Maine* 49 G a
Stockholm, *New Jersey* 50 E c
Stockport, *New York* 50 F a
Stockport, *Ohio* 52 E f
Stockton, *Alabama* 54 D g
Stockton, *California* (86,321) 74 D g
Stockton, *Illinois* 56 C g
Stockton, *Kansas* 60 E e
Stockton, *Maryland* 53 L g
Stockton, *Missouri* 61 L g
Stockton, *New Jersey* 50 D e
Stockton, *Utah* 68 D c
Stockton I., *Wisconsin* 56 C c
Stockton Is., *Alaska* 77 O a
Stockton Springs, *Maine* 49 G d
Stockville, *Nebraska* 60 D d
Stoddard, *Wisconsin* 56 B f
Stokesdale, *North Carolina* 55 M a
Stone, *Idaho* 66 H g
Stoneboro, *Pennsylvania* 52 F d
Stone City, *Colorado* 69 M e
Stone Corral L., *Oregon* 73 L n
Stoneham, *Colorado* 69 N c
Stone Harbor, *New Jersey* 50 D g
Stone Lake, *Wisconsin* 56 B d
Stone Mountain, *Georgia* 54 G d
Stone Ridge, *New York* 50 E b
Stonersville, *Pennsylvania* 50 B e
Stones River Nat. Mil. Park, *Tennessee* 54 E b
Stoneville, *Massachusetts* 51 K a
Stonewall, *Mississippi* 63 P f
Stonewall, *Oklahoma* 62 G d
Stonewall, *Texas* 65 J e
Stonington, *Colorado* 69 O f
Stonington, *Connecticut* 51 K c
Stonington, *Illinois* 57 D k
Stonington, *Maine* 49 G d
Stony Brook, *New York* 50 G d
Stony Creek, *Connecticut* 51 H c
Stony Creek, *Virginia* 52 J j
Stonyford, *California* 74 C e
Stony Point, *New York* 50 E c
Stony Point, *North Carolina* 55 K b
Stony Pt., *New York* 53 K b
Stony R., *Alaska* 76 K f
Stony River, *Alaska* 76 J f
Storm L., *Iowa* 61 J b
Storm Lake, *Iowa* 61 J b
Stormville, *New York* 50 F b
Storrs, *Connecticut* 51 J b
Story, *Wyoming* 67 O e
Story City, *Iowa* 61 L b
Stottville, *New York* 50 F a
Stoughton, *Massachusetts* 51 L a
Stoughton, *Wisconsin* 56 D g
Stoutsville, *Ohio* 52 D f
Stover, *Missouri* 61 M f
Stowe, *Pennsylvania* 53 O a
Stowe, *Vermont* 49 C d
Stowell, *Texas* 65 N f
Strafford, *Missouri* 61 L g
Straight Cliffs, *Utah* 68 E f
Strang, *Nebraska* 60 G d
Strasburg, *Colorado* 69 M d
Strasburg, *Illinois* 57 E k
Strasburg, *North Dakota* 58 F d
Strasburg, *Ohio* 52 E e
Strasburg, *Pennsylvania* 50 A f
Strasburg, *Virginia* 52 H g
Stratford, *California* 75 F h
Stratford, *Connecticut* (45,012) 50 G c
Stratford, *Iowa* 61 L b
Stratford, *New Hampshire* 49 D d
Stratford, *Oklahoma* 62 G d
Stratford, *South Dakota* 58 H e
Stratford, *Texas* 64 B g
Stratford, *Wisconsin* 56 C e
Stratford Pt., *Connecticut* 51 G c
Strathmere, *New Jersey* 50 D g
Stratton, *Colorado* 69 O d
Stratton, *Maine* 49 E c
Stratton, *Nebraska* 60 C d
Strauss, *New Mexico* 71 L h
Strausstown, *Pennsylvania* 50 A d
Straw, *Montana* 67 L c
Strawberry, *Arkansas* 63 M b
Strawberry, *Nevada* 74 K e
Strawberry Mt., *Oregon* 73 M l
Strawberry Point, *Iowa* 61 N b
Strawberry R., *Utah* 68 F c
Strawberry Res., *Utah* 68 E c
Strawn, *Illinois* 57 E j
Strawn, *Texas* 65 J c
Streator, *Illinois* 57 E h
Streeter, *North Dakota* 58 G d
Streeter, *Texas* 65 H e
Streetman, *Texas* 65 L d
Striker Creek Res., *Texas* 65 N d
Stringer, *Mississippi* 63 O g
Stringtown, *Oklahoma* 62 G d
Stromsburg, *Nebraska* 60 G c
Stroner, *Wyoming* 67 P e
Strong, *Arkansas* 63 L e
Strong, *Maine* 49 E d
Strong, *Mississippi* 63 P e
Strong City, *Kansas* 60 H f
Strong City, *Oklahoma* 62 D c
Stronghurst, *Illinois* 57 C j
Strongs, *Michigan* 56 J c
Strongsville, *Ohio* 52 E d
Strother, *South Carolina* 55 K c
Stroud, *Oklahoma* 62 G c
Stroudsburg, *Pennsylvania* 50 C d
Strum, *Wisconsin* 56 B e
Struthers, *Ohio* 52 F d
Stryker, *Montana* 66 F a
Stryker, *Ohio* 52 B d
Stuart, *Florida* 55 O f
Stuart, *Iowa* 61 K c
Stuart, Mt., *Washington* 73 K h
Stuart, *Nebraska* 60 E b
Stuart, *Oklahoma* 62 G d
Stuart, *Virginia* 52 F j
Stuart I., *Alaska* 76 F e
Studio City, *California* 75 D l
Stumpy Point, *North Carolina* 55 Q b
Sturbridge, *Massachusetts* 51 J a
Sturgeon, *Missouri* 61 M e
Sturgeon B., *Michigan* 56 H d
Sturgeon Bay, *Wisconsin* 56 F e
Sturgeon Bay Can., *Wisconsin* 56 F e
Sturgeon R., *Michigan* 56 G c
Sturgis, *Kentucky* 57 F m
Sturgis, *Michigan* 57 H h
Sturgis, *Mississippi* 63 O e
Sturgis, *Oklahoma* 62 A a
Sturgis, *South Dakota* 58 C f
Sturtevant, *Wisconsin* 56 E g
Stuttgart, *Arkansas* 63 M d
Stuttgart, *Kansas* 60 E e
Stuyvesant Falls, *New York* 50 F a
Suamico, *Wisconsin* 56 E e
Sublett, *Idaho* 66 G g
Sublette, *Illinois* 57 D h
Sublette, *Kansas* 60 D g
Sublime, *Texas* 65 L f
Success, *Missouri* 61 M g
Sucia I., *Washington* 73 H g
Sucker Cr., *Oregon* 73 N m
Suckling, C., *Alaska* 77 Q e
Sudan, *Texas* 64 E a
Sudbury Res., *Massachusetts* 51 K a
Suemez I., *Alaska* 77 V j
Sue Pk., *Texas* 64 D f
Suffern, *New York* 50 E c
Suffield, *Connecticut* 51 H b
Suffolk, *Montana* 67 L b
Suffolk, *Virginia* 53 K j
Sugar, *Idaho* 66 J f
Sugar City, *Colorado* 69 N e
Sugar Creek, *Missouri* 61 Q a
Sugar Grove, *Pennsylvania* 52 G d
Sugar Grove, *Virginia* 52 E j
Sugar I., *Michigan* 56 J c
Sugar Land, *Texas* 65 M f
Sugar Loaf, *New York* 50 E c
Sugarloaf Key, *Florida* 55 N j
Sugar R., *Wisconsin* 56 D g
Suiattle Pass, *Washington* 73 J g
Suitland, *Maryland* 53 K g
Sula, *Montana* 66 G d
Sulatna R., *Alaska* 76 K d
Sulligent, *Alabama* 54 C d
Sullivan, *Illinois* 57 E k
Sullivan, *Indiana* 57 F k
Sullivan, *Missouri* 61 N f
Sully, *Iowa* 61 M c
Sulphur, *Louisiana* 63 K h
Sulphur, *Montana* 67 K c
Sulphur, *Nevada* 74 G d
Sulphur, *Oklahoma* 62 G d
Sulphurdale, *Utah* 68 D e
Sulphur R., *Arkansas* 63 K e
Sulphur Springs, *Texas* 65 M b
Sulphur Springs Cr., *Texas* 64 F c
Sultan, *Washington* 73 J h
Sulukna R., *Alaska* 76 K e
Sulzer, Mt., *Alaska* 77 R f
Sumas, *Washington* 73 H g
Sumatra, *Florida* 54 G g
Sumatra, *Montana* 67 N c
Sumiton, *Alabama* 54 D d
Summerfield, *Kansas* 60 H e
Summerfield, *Ohio* 52 E f
Summerfield, *Texas* 64 B j
Summer I., *Michigan* 56 G d
Summer L., *Oregon* 73 K n
Summer Lake, *Oregon* 73 K n
Summer Shade, *Kentucky* 57 H n
Summer Str., *Alaska* 77 V h
Summersville, *Missouri* 61 N g
Summersville, *West Virginia* 52 F g
Summerton, *South Carolina* 55 L d
Summertown, *Georgia* 55 J e
Summerville, *Georgia* 54 F c
Summerville, *Pennsylvania* 52 G d
Summerville, *South Carolina* 55 L d
Summit, *Alaska* 76 N e
Summit, *California* 75 H k
Summit, *Mississippi* 63 N g
Summit, *Montana* 66 G a
Summit, *New Jersey* 50 E d
Summit, *New Mexico* 71 J g
Summit, *Oregon* 73 G l
Summit, *South Dakota* 59 K e
Summit, *Utah* 68 D f
Summit City, *Michigan* 56 H e
Summithill, *Pennsylvania* 50 B d
Summit L., *Alaska* 77 P e
Summit L., *Nevada* 74 F c
Summit Mt., *Nevada* 74 J e
Summit Pk., *Colorado* 69 K f
Summitville, *Colorado* 69 K f
Summitville, *Indiana* 57 H j
Summitville, *New York* 50 E b
Summitville, *Tennessee* 54 F b
Sumner, *Illinois* 57 E l
Sumner, *Missouri* 61 L e
Sumner, *Iowa* 61 M b
Sumpter, *Oregon* 73 M l
Sumrall, *Mississippi* 63 O g
Sumter, *South Carolina* 55 L d
Sunbeam, *Colorado* 68 H c
Sunbeam, *Idaho* 66 F e
Sunbright, *Tennessee* 54 G a
Sunburst, *Montana* 66 J a
Sunbury, *North Carolina* 55 P a
Sunbury, *Ohio* 52 D e
Sunbury, *Pennsylvania* 53 K e
Sun City, *Kansas* 60 F g
Suncook, *New Hampshire* 49 D e
Sundance, *Wyoming* 67 Q e
Sunderland, *Massachusetts* 49 C f
Sundown, *New York* 50 E b
Sundown, *Texas* 64 E b
Sunfield, *Michigan* 56 J g
Sunflower, *Mississippi* 63 N e
Sunflower R., *Mississippi* 63 N e
Sunglow, *Arizona* 70 H h
Sunman, *Indiana* 57 H k
Sunniland, *Florida* 55 N g
Sunny Isles, *Florida* 54 C c
Sunnyside, *Nevada* 74 K f
Sunny Side, *Texas* 64 F j
Sunnyside, *Utah* 68 F d
Sunnyside, *Washington* 73 L j
Sunnyvale, *California* (52,898), vicinity of San Francisco
Sun Prairie, *Wisconsin* 56 D f
Sun R., *Montana* 66 H b
Sunray, *Texas* 64 C g
Sunrise, *Alaska* 76 N f
Sunrise, *Arizona* 70 G d
Sunrise, *Wyoming* 67 Q g
Sun River, *Montana* 66 J b
Sunset, *Louisiana* 63 L h
Sunset, *Texas* 65 K b
Sunset Beach, *California* 75 F n
Sunset Crater Nat. Mon., *Arizona* 70 F d
Sunshine, *Arizona* 70 F d
Sunshine, *Wyoming* 67 L e
Suntrana, *Alaska* 77 N e
Sunup Plateau, *Arizona* 70 D d
Supai, *Arizona* 70 E c
Superior, *Arizona* 70 F f
Superior, *Colorado* 69 N g
Superior, L., *United States-Canada* 47 J a
Superior, *Montana* 66 F b
Superior, *Nebraska* 60 F d
Superior, *Wisconsin* (33,563) 56 A b
Superior, *Wyoming* 67 M h
Suplee, *Oregon* 73 L l
Suplee, *Pennsylvania* 50 B e
Suquamish, *Washington* 72 B h
Sur, Pt., *California* 75 D h
Surf, *California* 75 E k
Surf City, *New Jersey* 50 E f
Surfside, *Florida* 54 C d
Surfside, *Massachusetts* 51 N c
Suring, *Wisconsin* 56 E d
Surprise, *Nebraska* 60 G c
Surrency, *Georgia* 55 J f
Surrey, *North Dakota* 58 E b
Surry, *Virginia* 53 K h
Survey Pass, *Alaska* 76 K c
Susan R., *California* 74 E d
Susanville, *California* 74 E d
Susanville, *Oregon* 73 M l
Susitna, *Alaska* 76 M f
Susitna L., *Alaska* 77 O e
Susitna R., *Alaska* 76 M e
Susquehanna, *Pennsylvania* 53 L d
Susquehanna R., *New York* 53 L c
Susquehanna R., *Pennsylvania* 53 K e
Sussex, *New Jersey* 50 D c
Sussex, *Wyoming* 67 O f
Susulatna R., *Alaska* 76 K e
Sutcliffe, *Nevada* 74 F e
Sutherland, *Iowa* 61 J b
Sutherland, *Nebraska* 60 C c
Sutherland Res., *Nebraska* 60 C c
Sutherlin, *Oregon* 73 G m
Sutter Creek, *California* 74 E f
Sutton, *Massachusetts* 51 K a
Sutton, *Nebraska* 60 G d
Sutton, *North Dakota* 58 H c
Sutton Res., *West Virginia* 52 F g
Sutwik I., *Alaska* 76 J h
Suwannee, *Florida* 54 H h
Suwannee R., *Florida* 54 H h
Suwannee R., *Georgia* 55 J g
Suwannee Sd., *Florida* 54 H h
Suwanoochee Cr., *Georgia* 55 J g
Svensen, *Oregon* 73 G j
Swainsboro, *Georgia* 55 J e
Swallows, *Colorado* 69 M e
Swan L., *Montana* 66 G b
Swan L., *South Dakota* 58 G e
Swan L., *Utah* 68 D d
Swan Lake, *Montana* 66 G b
Swan Lake, *New York* 50 D b
Swannanoa, *North Carolina* 55 J b
Swanquarter, *North Carolina* 55 P b
Swan R., *Montana* 66 G b
Swan River, *Minnesota* 59 N c
Swansboro, *North Carolina* 55 O c
Swansea, *Arizona* 70 D e
Swansea, *Massachusetts* 51 L b
Swansea, *South Carolina* 55 K d
Swans I., *Maine* 49 G d
Swanson Res., *Nebraska* 60 C d
Swanton, *Nebraska* 60 G d
Swanton, *Ohio* 52 C d
Swanton, *Vermont* 49 B d
Swan Valley, *Idaho* 66 J f
Swanville, *Minnesota* 59 M e
Swarthmore, *Pennsylvania* 50 C f
Swartswood, *New Jersey* 50 D c
Swasey Pk., *Utah* 68 C d
Swea City, *Iowa* 61 K a
Swedesboro, *New Jersey* 50 C f
Sweeny, *Texas* 65 M f
Sweet, *Idaho* 66 D f
Sweetgrass, *Montana* 66 J a
Sweet Home, *Arkansas* 63 L d
Sweet Home, *Oregon* 73 H l
Sweet Home, *Texas* 65 L f
Sweet Springs, *Missouri* 61 L f
Sweet Valley, *Pennsylvania* 50 A c
Sweetwater, *Oklahoma* 62 D c
Sweetwater, *Tennessee* 54 G b
Sweetwater, *Texas* 64 G c
Sweetwater R., *Wyoming* 67 M g
Swenson, *Texas* 64 G b
Swifton, *Arkansas* 63 M c
Swift R., *Alaska* 76 K f
Swift R., *Maine* 49 E d
Swift Res., *Washington* 73 H j
Swiftwater, *Pennsylvania* 50 C c
Swinburne I., *New York* 51 L g
Swinging Bridge Res., *New York* 50 D b
Swink, *Colorado* 69 N e
Swissvale, *Pennsylvania* 53 Q b
Sybille Cr., *Wyoming* 67 P h
Sycamore, *Alabama* 54 E d
Sycamore, *Illinois* 57 E h
Sycamore, *Ohio* 52 C e
Sycamore, *South Carolina* 55 K d
Sykeston, *North Dakota* 58 G c
Sykesville, *Maryland* 53 K f
Sykesville, *Pennsylvania* 52 H d
Sylacauga, *Alabama* 54 E d
Sylamore, *Arkansas* 63 L c
Sylva, *North Carolina* 54 H b
Sylvan, *Pennsylvania* 52 H f
Sylvan Grove, *Kansas* 60 F e
Sylvania, *Georgia* 55 K e
Sylvania, *Ohio* 52 C d
Sylvan Pass, *Wyoming* 67 L e
Sylvester, *Georgia* 54 H f
Sylvester, *Texas* 64 G c
Sylvia, *Kansas* 60 F g
Syosset, *New York* 50 G d
Syracuse, *Indiana* 57 H h
Syracuse, *Kansas* 60 C g
Syracuse, *Nebraska* 60 H d
Syracuse, *New York* (216,038) 53 K b
Syracuse, *Utah* 68 D b
Sysladobsis L., *Maine* 49 G c
Tabernacle, *New Jersey* 50 D f
Tabiona, *Utah* 68 F c
Table Mt., *Alaska* 77 Q b
Tablerock Res., *Missouri* 61 L h
Tabor, *Iowa* 61 J d
Tabor, *South Dakota* 58 J h
Tabor City, *North Carolina* 55 N c

Tacna, Arizona 70 D g
Tacoma, Washington (147,979) 73 H h
Tafoya, New Mexico 71 N c
Taft, California 75 F j
Taft, Oklahoma 62 H c
Taft, Texas 65 K h
Tafton, Pennsylvania 50 C c
Taftville, Connecticut 51 J b
Tagagawik R., Alaska 76 H d
Tagalak I., Alaska 77 P j
Tagus, North Dakota 58 E b
Tahlequah, Oklahoma 63 J c
Tahoe, L., California-Nevada 74 E e
Tahoe City, California 74 E e
Tahoe Valley, California 74 E f
Tahoka, Texas 64 F b
Taholah, Washington 73 F h
Tahquamenon Falls, Michigan 56 H c
Tahquamenon R., Michigan 56 H c
Taiban, New Mexico 71 O e
Tailings Pond, Utah 68 B h
Tajique, New Mexico 71 L e
Takilma, Oregon 73 G n
Takoma Park, Maryland 53 Q g
Takotna, Alaska 76 J e
Takslesluk, Alaska 76 F f
Taku Harbor, Alaska 77 V g
Talala, Oklahoma 62 H b
Talbot I., Florida 55 K g
Talbotton, Georgia 54 G e
Talco, Texas 65 M b
Talcott, West Virginia 52 F h
Talent, Oregon 73 H n
Talihina, Oklahoma 62 H d
Talkeetna, Alaska 76 N e
Talkeetna Mts., Alaska 77 N e
Talkeetna R., Alaska 77 N e
Talladega, Alabama 54 E d
Tallahala R., Mississippi 63 O g
Tallahassee, Florida (48,174) 54 G g
Tallahatchie R., Mississippi 63 N d
Tallapoosa, Georgia 54 F d
Tallapoosa R., Alabama 54 E e
Tallassee, Alabama 54 F e
Tallula, Illinois 57 D k
Tallulah, Louisiana 63 M f
Talmage, California 74 B e
Talmage, Kansas 60 G e
Talmage, Nebraska 61 H d
Taloga, Oklahoma 62 E b
Talpa, New Mexico 71 M c
Talpa, Texas 65 H d
Talquin, L., Florida 54 G g
Tama, Iowa 61 M c
Tamaqua, Pennsylvania 50 B d
Tamarack, Idaho 66 D e
Tamarack, Minnesota 59 N d
Tamarack Landing, Alaska 76 K d
Tamaroa, Illinois 57 D l
Tamiami Can., Florida 55 N h
Tamms, Illinois 57 D m
Tampa, Florida (274,970) 55 M f
Tampa, Kansas 60 G f
Tampa B., Florida 55 M f
Tampico, Illinois 57 D h
Tampico, Montana 67 O a
Tamworth, New Hampshire 49 D e
Tanacross, Alaska 77 Q e
Tanada L., Alaska 77 Q e
Tanadak I., Alaska 77 R j
Tanaga I., Alaska 77 N j
Tanaga Pass, Alaska 77 N j
Tanak, C., Alaska 76 C k
Tanalian Point, Alaska 76 K f
Tanana, Alaska 76 M d
Tanana R., Alaska 77 P e
Tana R., Alaska 77 Q f
Taneytown, Maryland 53 J f
Tangipahoa R., Louisiana 63 N h
Tanglewood, Texas 65 L e
Tankersly, Texas 64 G d
Tannersville, New York 50 E a
Tannersville, Pennsylvania 50 C c
Tanque, Arizona 70 H g
Tanunak, Alaska 76 E f
Taopi, Minnesota 59 O g
Taos, New Mexico 71 M c
Tappahannock, Virginia 53 K h
Tappan, New York 50 F c
Tappan Res., Ohio 52 E e
Tappen, North Dakota 58 G d
Tarboro, North Carolina 55 O b
Tarentum, Pennsylvania 52 G e
Tarheel, North Carolina 55 N c
Tariffville, Connecticut 51 H b
Tarkinsville, Alabama 54 E c
Tarkio, Missouri 61 J d
Tarkio, Montana 66 F b
Tarpley, Texas 65 H f
Tarpon Springs, Florida 55 M e
Tar R., North Carolina 55 N a
Tarrant City, Alabama 54 E d
Tarryall, Colorado 69 L d
Tarryall R., Colorado 69 L d
Tarrytown, Georgia 55 J e
Tarrytown, New York 50 F c
Tasco, Kansas 60 D e
Tascosa, Texas 64 B h
Tatamy, Pennsylvania 50 C d
Tate, Georgia 54 G c
Tatitlek, Alaska 77 O f
Tatlawiksuk R., Alaska 76 K e
Tatman Mt., Wyoming 67 M e
Tatna, L., Alaska 76 K f
Tatum, New Mexico 71 O f
Tatum, Texas 65 N c
Tatums, Oklahoma 62 F d
Taum Sauk Mt., Missouri 61 O g
Taunton, Massachusetts (41,132) 51 L b
Taunton R., Massachusetts 51 L b
Tavares, Florida 55 K j
Tavernier, Florida 55 O h
Tawas B., Michigan 56 K e
Tawas City, Michigan 56 K e
Taylor, Alaska 76 E d
Taylor, Arizona 70 G e
Taylor, Arkansas 63 K e
Taylor, Mississippi 63 O d
Taylor, Missouri 61 N e
Taylor, Mt., New Mexico 71 K d
Taylor, Nebraska 60 E c
Taylor, Texas 65 K e
Taylor, Washington 73 J h
Taylor, Wisconsin 56 B e
Taylor Mts., Alaska 76 J f
Taylor Park Res., Colorado 69 K e
Taylor Ridge, Georgia 54 F c
Taylors, South Carolina 55 J c
Taylors Bridge, Delaware 50 B g
Taylor Springs, New Mexico 71 N c
Taylorsville, Kentucky 57 H l
Taylorsville, Mississippi 63 O g
Taylorsville, North Carolina 55 K b
Taylorsville, Ohio 52 E f
Taylorsville, Utah 68 C h
Taylorville, Illinois 57 D k
Tazewell, Virginia 52 E h
Tazimina Ls., Alaska 76 K g
Tazlina L., Alaska 77 O f
Tazlina R., Alaska 77 P e
Tchula, Mississippi 63 N e
Tea, South Dakota 59 K g
Teague, New Mexico 71 O g
Teague, Texas 65 L d
Teaneck, New Jersey (42,085) 51 L e
Teapot Dome, mt., Wyoming 67 O f
Tecolote, Lincoln County, New Mexico 71 M e
Tecolote, San Miguel County, New Mexico 71 M d
Tecoma, Nevada 74 L c
Tecopa, California 75 J j
Tecumseh, Michigan 57 K g
Tecumseh, Missouri 61 M h
Tecumseh, Nebraska 60 H d
Tecumseh, Oklahoma 62 G c
Tehachapi, California 75 G j
Tehachapi Mts., California 75 G k
Tehama, California 74 C d
Tejon Pass, California 75 G k
Tekamah, Nebraska 60 H c
Tekoa, Washington 73 N h
Tekonsha, Michigan 57 J g
Telaguana, L., Alaska 76 L f
Telephone, Texas 65 L b
Telescope Pk., California 75 H h
Tell, Texas 64 D j
Tell City, Indiana 57 G m
Teller, Alaska 76 D d
Tellico Plains, Tennessee 54 G b
Telluride, Colorado 69 J f
Telocaset, Oregon 73 N k
Teman, Virginia 52 J h
Temblor Ra., California 75 E j
Temecula, California 75 H l
Tempe, Arizona 70 F f
Temperance, Michigan 57 K h
Temple, Maine 49 E d
Temple, Michigan 56 J e
Temple, Oklahoma 62 E d
Temple, Pennsylvania 50 B e
Temple, Texas (30,419) 65 K d
Temple City, California (31,838), vicinity of Los Angeles
Templeton, California 75 E j
Templeton, Pennsylvania 52 G e
Templeville, Maryland 50 B g
Temvik, North Dakota 58 F d
Tenabo, Mt., Nevada 74 J d
Tenabo, Nevada 74 J d
Tenafly, New Jersey 51 M d
Tenaha, Texas 65 N d
Tenakee Springs, Alaska 77 U h
Tendoy, Idaho 66 G e
Ten Hills, Maryland 53 P f
Tenino, Washington 73 H j
Tenkiller Ferry Res., Oklahoma 63 J c
Tenmile R., New York 50 F b
Ten Mile River, New York 50 D b
Tennanah Lake, New York 50 D b
Tennant, California 74 D c
Tennent, New Jersey 50 E e
Tennessee (3,888,000) 42,244 sq. miles 54-55
Tennessee Pass, Colorado 69 K d
Tennessee R., Alabama 54 E c
Tennessee R., Tennessee, etc. 47 J d
Tennille, Georgia 55 J e
Tennyson, Texas 64 G d
Tensas R., Louisiana 63 M f
Tensaw R., Alabama 54 D g
Tensed, Idaho 66 D b
Ten Sleep, Wyoming 67 N e
Tenstrike, Minnesota 59 M c
Ten Thousand Is., Florida 55 N h
Tercio, Colorado 69 M f
Terlingua, Texas 64 D f
Terlingua Cr., Texas 64 D f
Terminal I., California 75 E n
Termo, California 74 E d
Tern I., Hawaii 72 C b
Terra Alta, West Virginia 52 G f
Terra Bella, California 75 G j
Terrace, Pennsylvania 53 Q b
Terral, Oklahoma 62 F e
Terrebonne, Oregon 73 J l
Terrebonne B., Louisiana 63 N j
Terre Haute, Indiana (72,500) 57 F k
Terre Hill, Pennsylvania 50 A e
Terrell, Texas 65 L c
Terreton, Idaho 66 H f
Terry, Mississippi 63 N f
Terry, Montana 67 P c
Terryville, Connecticut 51 G b
Tescott, Kansas 60 G e
Teshekpuk L., Alaska 76 L a
Tesnus, Texas 64 E e
Tesuque, New Mexico 71 L d
Tetlin, Alaska 77 Q e
Tetlin Junction, Alaska 77 Q e
Tetlin L., Alaska 77 Q e
Tetonia, Idaho 66 J f
Teton R., Montana 66 J b
Teton Ra., Wyoming 67 K f
Texarkana, Arkansas 63 K e
Texarkana, L., Texas 65 N b
Texarkana, Texas (30,218) 65 N b
Texas (10,873,000) 267,339 sq. miles 64-65
Texas City, Texas (32,065) 65 N f
Texico, New Mexico 71 O e
Texline, Texas 64 B g
Texola, Oklahoma 62 D c
Texon, Texas 64 F d
Thackerville, Oklahoma 62 F e
Thalman, Georgia 55 K f
Thames R., Connecticut 51 J c
Thane, Alaska 77 U g
Thatcher, Arizona 70 H g
Thatcher, Colorado 69 M f
Thatcher, Idaho 66 J g
Thackerville, Texas 65 K b
Thayer, Missouri 61 N h
Thayne, Wyoming 67 K g
Theba, Arizona 70 E g
Thebes, Illinois 57 D m
Thedford, Nebraska 60 D b
Thelma, Georgia 55 J g
Theodore, Alabama 54 C g
Theodore Roosevelt L., Arizona 70 F f
Theodore Roosevelt Nat. Mem. Park, North Dakota 58 C c
Theresa, New York 53 L a
Theresa, Wisconsin 56 E f
Theriot, Louisiana 63 N j
Thermo, Utah 68 C e
Thermopolis, Wyoming 67 M f
Thibodaux, Louisiana 63 N j
Thief R., Minnesota 59 K b
Thief River Falls, Minnesota 59 K b
Thief Valley Res., Oregon 73 N k
Thielsen, Mt., Oregon 73 H m
Thiensville, Wisconsin 56 F f
Thistle, Utah 68 E d
Thoeny, Montana 67 O a
Thomas, L. J. B., Texas 64 F c
Thomas, Oklahoma 62 E c
Thomas, West Virginia 52 G f
Thomas A. Edison, L., California 75 F g
Thomas Mt., California 75 J l
Thomaston, Alabama 54 D e
Thomaston, Connecticut 50 G b
Thomaston, Georgia 54 G e
Thomaston, Maine 49 F d
Thomaston, Texas 65 K g
Thomastown, Mississippi 63 O f
Thomasville, Alabama 54 D f
Thomasville, Georgia 54 H g
Thomasville, Missouri 61 N h
Thomasville, North Carolina 55 L b
Thompson, Connecticut 51 K b
Thompson, Iowa 61 L a
Thompson, Michigan 56 G d
Thompson, North Dakota 58 J c
Thompson, Pennsylvania 53 L d
Thompson, Utah 68 G e
Thompson Falls, Montana 66 E b
Thompson Pass, Alaska 77 P f
Thompson R., Missouri 61 L d
Thompsons, Texas 65 M f
Thompsonville, Connecticut 51 H a
Thompsonville, Michigan 56 H e
Thomson, Georgia 55 J d
Thomson, Illinois 57 C h
Thoreau, New Mexico 71 J d
Thornapple R., Michigan 56 H g
Thornburg, Pennsylvania 53 O b
Thornburg, Virginia 52 J g
Thorndale, Texas 65 K e
Thorndike, Massachusetts 51 J a
Thorne, Nevada 74 G f
Thornhurst, Pennsylvania 50 B c
Thornton, Arkansas 63 L e
Thornton, Colorado 69 O h
Thornton, Iowa 61 L b
Thornton, Texas 65 L d
Thornton, Washington 73 N h
Thorntown, Indiana 57 G j
Thorp, Washington 73 K h
Thorp, Wisconsin 56 C e
Thousand Is., New York 53 K a
Thousand Lake Mt., Utah 68 E e
Thousand Spring Cr., Nevada 74 L c
Thousand Springs, Idaho 66 F g
Thrall, Texas 65 K e
Thrall, Washington 73 K j
Three Bridges, New Jersey 50 D d
Three Creek, Idaho 66 E g
Three Forks, Montana 66 J d
Three Islands Res., Tennessee 54 D a
Three Lakes, Wisconsin 56 D d
Three Oaks, Michigan 57 G h
Three Rivers, California 75 G h
Three Rivers, Massachusetts 51 J a
Three Rivers, Michigan 57 H h
Three Rivers, New Mexico 71 L f
Three Rivers, Texas 65 J g
Three Sisters, Mts., Oregon 73 J l
Throckmorton, Texas 65 H b
Thumb, Wyoming 67 K e
Thunder B., Michigan 56 K e
Thunder Butte Cr., South Dakota 58 D e
Thunder Mt., Alaska 76 G b
Thurlow, Montana 67 O c
Thurlow Dam, Alabama 54 F e
Thurmont, Maryland 52 J f
Tiber Res., Montana 66 J a
Tiburon, California 75 B l
Ticonderoga, New York 53 N b
Tidewater, Oregon 73 G l
Tidioute, Pennsylvania 52 G d
Tiekel, Alaska 77 P f
Tierra Amarilla, New Mexico 71 L c
Tie Siding, Wyoming 67 P h
Tieton, Washington 73 K j
Tieton Res., Washington 73 J j
Tiffany Mt., Washington 73 L g
Tiffin, Iowa 61 N c
Tiffin, Ohio 52 C d
Tifton, Georgia 54 H f
Tigalda I., Alaska 76 E j
Tigara, Alaska 76 D b
Tigard, Oregon 73 H k
Tiger, Washington 73 N g
Tiger R., South Carolina 55 K c
Tigerton, Wisconsin 56 D e
Tignall, Georgia 55 J d
Tijeras, New Mexico 71 L d
Tikchik L., Alaska 76 H f
Tikikluk, Alaska 76 J a
Tilden, Illinois 57 D l
Tilden, Nebraska 60 G b
Tilden, Texas 65 J g
Tilford, South Dakota 58 C f
Tillamook, Oregon 73 G k
Tillamook Rock, Oregon 73 F k
Tillery, L., North Carolina 55 L b
Tillman, South Carolina 55 K e
Tilton, Georgia 54 G c
Tilton, Illinois 57 F j
Tilton, New Hampshire 49 D e
Timbalier B., Louisiana 63 N j
Timbalier I., Louisiana 63 N j
Timber, Oregon 73 G k
Timberlake, North Carolina 55 N a
Timber Lake, South Dakota 58 E e
Timber Mt., Nevada 75 J g
Timmonsville, South Carolina 55 M c
Timpahute Ra., Nevada 74 K g
Timpanogos Cave Nat Mon., Utah 68 E c
Timpie, Utah 68 D c
Timpson Center, Texas 65 N d
Tindall, Idaho 66 E g
Tinemaha Res., California 75 G g
Tingley, Iowa 61 K d
Tingmerkpuk Mt., Alaska 76 F b
Tinsman, Arkansas 63 L e
Tintah, Minnesota 59 K d
Tioga, Louisiana 63 L g
Tioga, North Dakota 58 D b
Tioga, Pennsylvania 53 J d
Tioga, Texas 65 L b
Tioga, West Virginia 52 F g
Tioga Pass, California 74 F g
Tioga R., Pennsylvania 53 J d
Tionesta, California 74 D c
Tionesta, Pennsylvania 52 G d
Tionesta Creek Res., Pennsylvania 52 G d
Tioughnioga R., New York 53 K c
Tipp City, Ohio 52 B f
Tippecanoe, Indiana 57 G h
Tippecanoe R., Indiana 57 G j
Tippo, Mississippi 63 N e
Tipton, California 75 F h
Tipton, Indiana 57 G j
Tipton, Iowa 61 N c
Tipton, Kansas 60 F e
Tipton, Missouri 61 M f
Tipton, Mt., Arizona 70 C d
Tipton, Oklahoma 62 D d
Tipton, Wyoming 67 M h
Tiptonville, Tennessee 54 B a
Tiptop, Virginia 52 E h
Tiro, Ohio 52 D e
Tishomingo, Mississippi 63 P d
Tishomingo, Oklahoma 62 G d
Tiskilwa, Illinois 57 D h
Titaluk R., Alaska 76 K b
Titna, Alaska 76 L d
Titonka, Iowa 61 K a
Tittabawassee R., Michigan 56 J f
Titusville, Florida 55 L j
Titusville, Pennsylvania 52 G d
Tiverton, Rhode Island 51 L b
Tivoli, New York 50 F a
Tivoli, Texas 65 L g
Toano, Virginia 53 K h
Toano Ra., Nevada 74 L d
Tobar, Nevada 74 L d
Tobias, Nebraska 60 G d
Tobin, Mt., Nevada 74 H d
Tobyhanna, Pennsylvania 50 C c
Tobyhanna State Park, Pennsylvania 50 C c
Toccoa, Georgia 54 H c
Tofti, Minnesota 59 Q c
Tofty, Alaska 76 M d
Togiak, Alaska 76 G g
Togiak B., Alaska 76 G g
Togiak L., Alaska 76 H g
Togiak R., Alaska 76 G g
Tohakum Pk., Nevada 74 F d
Tohatchi, New Mexico 71 J d
Tohopekaliga L., Florida 55 N e
Toimi, Minnesota 59 P c
Toivola, Michigan 56 E c
Toiyabe Ra., Nevada 74 H e
Tokewanna Pk., Utah 68 F c
Tokio, North Dakota 58 H c
Tokio, Texas 64 E b
Tok Junction, Alaska 77 Q e
Toklat, Alaska 76 M d
Toklat R., Alaska 76 M e
Tolar, New Mexico 71 O e
Tolar, Texas 65 K c
Toledo, Illinois 57 E k
Toledo, Iowa 61 M b
Toledo, Ohio (318,003) 52 C d
Toledo, Oregon 73 G l
Toledo, Washington 73 H j
Toledo Bend Res., Texas-Louisiana 65 O d
Tolland, Connecticut 51 J b
Tolland, Massachusetts 51 G a
Tolleson, Arizona 70 E f
Tolley, North Dakota 58 E b
Tollhouse, California 75 F g
Tolono, Illinois 57 E k
Tolovana R., Alaska 76 N d
Toltec, Arizona 70 F g
Toluca, Illinois 57 D h
Tomah, Wisconsin 56 C f
Tomahawk, Wisconsin 56 D d
Tomball, Texas 65 M e
Tombigbee R., Mississippi-Alabama 54 C f
Tombstone, Arizona 70 G h
Tompkins Center, Michigan 56 J g
Tompkins Cove, New York 50 E c
Tompkinsville, Kentucky 57 H n
Toms R., New Jersey 50 E e
Toms River, New Jersey 50 E f
Tom White, Mt., Alaska 77 P f
Tonalea, Arizona 70 G c
Tonasket, Washington 73 L g
Tonawanda, New York (83,771) 52 H b
Tonganoxie, Kansas 61 J e
Tongue R., Montana 67 P c
Tongue R. Res., Montana 67 O d
Tonica, Illinois 57 D h
Tonkawa, Oklahoma 62 F b
Tonki C., Alaska 76 L g
Tonopah, Nevada 74 H f
Tonsina, Alaska 77 P f
Tonto Basin, Arizona 70 F f
Tonzona R., Alaska 76 L e
Tooele, Utah 68 D c
Toolik R., Alaska 76 N b
Topagaruk R., Alaska 76 J a
Topawa, Arizona 70 F h
Topaz L., California 74 F f
Topeka, Indiana 57 H h
Topeka, Kansas (119,484) 61 J e
Topock, Arizona 70 C e
Toponas, Colorado 69 K c
Toppenish, Washington 73 K j
Topsfield, Maine 49 H c
Topsham, Maine 49 E e
Topton, Pennsylvania 50 B d
Toquerville, Utah 68 C f
Toquima Ra., Nevada 74 H f
Torbert, Mt., Alaska 76 L f
Torch L., Michigan 56 H e
Tornillo, Texas 64 A d
Toronto, Kansas 61 J g
Toronto, Ohio 52 F e
Toronto Res., Kansas 61 J g
Toronto Res., New York 50 D b
Toro Pk., California 75 J l
Torrance, California (100,991) 75 D m
Torrey, Utah 68 E e
Torrington, Connecticut (30,045) 50 G b
Torrington, Wyoming 67 Q g
Toston, Montana 66 J c
Tottenville, New York 50 F d
Touchet, Washington 73 M j
Touchet R., Washington 73 M j
Toughkenamon, Pennsylvania 50 B f
Toulon, Illinois 57 D h
Toulon, Nevada 74 G d
Toulumne, California 74 E g
Toutle, Washington 73 H j
Towanda, Illinois 57 E j
Towanda, Kansas 60 G g
Towanda, Pennsylvania 53 K d
Tower, Minnesota 59 O c
Tower City, North Dakota 58 J d
Tower City, Pennsylvania 53 K e
Tower Falls, Wyoming 67 K e
Tower Hill, Illinois 57 E k
Towner, Colorado 69 O e
Towner, North Dakota 58 F b
Towners, New York 50 F c
Townes Pass, California 75 H h
Townley, Alabama 54 D d
Town Point, Maryland 50 B g
Townsend, Delaware 50 B g
Townsend, Georgia 55 K f
Townsend, Montana 66 J c
Townsend, Tennessee 54 H b
Townsend, Wisconsin 56 E d
Townville, Pennsylvania 52 G d
Towson, Maryland 53 K f
Toyah, Texas 64 D d
Toyah L., Texas 64 D d
Tozitna R., Alaska 76 M d
Tracy, California 74 D g
Tracy, Iowa 61 M c
Tracy, Minnesota 59 L f
Tracy City, Tennessee 54 F b
Tracyton, Washington 72 A h
Traders I., Alaska 76 J d
Tradewater R., Kentucky 57 F m
Traer, Iowa 61 M b
Traer, Kansas 60 D e
Trafford, Alabama 54 E d
Trafford, L., Florida 55 N g
Trail, Oregon 73 H n
Trail City, South Dakota 58 F e
Tralake, Mississippi 63 N e
Tranquility, California 75 E h
Trappe, Maryland 53 K g
Trappe, Pennsylvania 50 B e
Trapper Pk., Montana 66 F d
Trappers Lake, Colorado 69 J d
Traskwood, Arkansas 63 L d
Traunik, Michigan 56 G c
Travellers Rest, South Carolina 55 J c
Traverse City, Michigan 56 H e
Traverse L., South Dakota 59 K e
Traverse Mts., Utah 68 D j
Traverse Pk., Alaska 76 H d
Travis, L., Texas 65 J e
Travis, New York 51 K g
Trawick, Texas 65 N d
Treadwell, New York 50 C a
Treasure I., California 75 B l
Treat, Alaska 76 J c
Trechado, New Mexico 71 J e
Trego, Montana 66 F a
Trego, Nevada 74 F d
Trego, Wisconsin 56 B d
Trementina, New Mexico 71 N d
Tremont, Illinois 57 D j
Tremont, Mississippi 63 P d
Tremont, Pennsylvania 53 K e
Tremonton, Utah 68 D b
Trempealeau, Wisconsin 56 B e
Trempealeau R., Wisconsin 56 B e
Tremper, Mt., New York 50 E a
Trenary, Michigan 56 G c
Trent, North Carolina 55 O b
Trent, Texas 64 G c
Trenton, Florida 55 J h
Trenton, Michigan 57 K g
Trenton, Missouri 61 L d
Trenton, Nebraska 60 C d
Trenton, New Jersey (114,167) 50 D e
Trenton, New York 53 L b
Trenton, North Dakota 58 C b
Trenton, Ohio 52 B f
Trenton, South Carolina 55 K d
Trenton, Tennessee 54 C b
Tres Lagunas, New Mexico 71 J e
Tres Piedras, New Mexico 71 M c
Tres Pinos, California 75 D h
Trexler, Pennsylvania 50 B d
Trexlertown, Pennsylvania 50 B d
Triangle, Idaho 66 D g
Tribune, Kansas 60 C f
Trident Pk., Nevada 74 G c
Trilby, Florida 55 J j
Trimont, Minnesota 59 M g
Trinchere, Colorado 69 M f
Trinidad, California 74 A c
Trinidad, Colorado 69 M f
Trinidad, Washington 73 K h
Trinity, Texas 65 M e
Trinity Center, California 74 C c
Trinity Is., Alaska 76 K h
Trinity R., California 74 B d
Trinity R., Texas 65 N e
Trinity Ra., Nevada 74 G d
Trinity Res., California 74 C d
Trion, Georgia 54 F c
Tripoli, Iowa 61 M b
Tripp, South Dakota 58 H g
Trona, California 75 H j
Tropic, Utah 68 D f
Trosky, Minnesota 59 K g
Trotters, North Dakota 58 C c
Troublesome, Colorado 69 K c
Troup, Texas 65 M c
Trousdale, Kansas 60 E g
Trout, Louisiana 63 L g
Trout Cr., Arizona 70 D d
Trout Cr., Oregon 73 K l
Trout Creek, Michigan 56 D c
Trout Creek, Montana 66 E b
Trout Creek, Utah 68 C d
Trout L., Wisconsin 56 D c
Trout Lake, Michigan 56 J c
Trout Pk., Wyoming 67 L e
Trout Run, Pennsylvania 53 K d
Troutville, Pennsylvania 52 H d
Troutville, Virginia 52 F h
Troy, Alabama 54 F f
Troy, Idaho 66 D c
Troy, Indiana 57 G l

West Cote Blanche B., Louisiana 63 M j
West Covina, California (50,645) 75 G k
West Coxsackie, New York 50 F a
West Creek, New Jersey 50 E f
West Dallas, Texas 65 N j
West De Pere, Wisconsin 56 E e
West Des Moines, Iowa 61 L c
Westend, California 75 H j
West End, Louisiana 62 C e
West End, North Carolina 55 M b
West End, Pennsylvania 53 O b
Westerly, Rhode Island 51 K c
Western, Nebraska 60 G d
Westernport, Maryland 52 G f
Westfall, Kansas 60 F f
Westfall, Oregon 73 N m
West Falmouth, Massachusetts 51 M b
Westfield, Illinois 57 F k
Westfield, Massachusetts (26,302) 51 H a
Westfield, New Jersey (31,447) 50 E d
Westfield, New York 52 G c
Westfield, Pennsylvania 52 J d
Westfield, Wisconsin 56 D f
Westfield R., Massachusetts 51 H a
Westford, Connecticut 51 J b
West Fork, Arkansas 63 J c
West Fork, Montana 67 P a
West Frankfort, Illinois 57 E m
West Granville, Massachusetts 51 H a
West Green, Georgia 55 J f
West Greenwich Center, Rhode Island 51 K b
West Grove, Pennsylvania 50 B f
West Hamlin, West Virginia 52 D g
Westhampton, New York 51 H d
Westhampton Beach, New York 53 O e
West Hartford, Connecticut (62,382) 51 H b
West Hartland, Connecticut 51 H b
West Haven, Connecticut (43,002) 51 H c
West Haverstraw, New York 50 E c
West Helena, Arkansas 63 N d
Westhoff, Texas 65 K f
West Hollywood, California (28,870), vicinity of Los Angeles
Westhope, North Dakota 58 E b
West Hurley, New York 50 E b
West Jefferson, North Carolina 55 K a
West Jefferson, Ohio 52 C f
West Jordan, Utah 68 C j
West Kill, New York 50 E a
West Kingston, Rhode Island 51 K c
West L., Nevada 74 F c
West Lafayette, Indiana 57 E j
West La Fayette, Ohio 52 E e
Westlake, Oregon 73 F m
West Leyden, New York 53 L b
West Liberty, Iowa 61 N c
West Liberty, Kentucky 57 K m
West Liberty, Ohio 52 C e
West Liberty, Pennsylvania 53 P b
West Little Owyhee R., Oregon 73 N n
West Long Branch, New Jersey 50 E e
West Manchester, Ohio 52 B f
West Memphis, Arkansas 63 N c
West Miami, Florida 54 B d
West Middlesex, Pennsylvania 52 F d
West Mifflin, Pennsylvania (27,289), vicinity of Pittsburgh
West Milford, New Jersey 50 E c
West Milton, Ohio 52 B f
Westminster, California (25,750), vicinity of Los Angeles
Westminster, Colorado 69 O h
Westminster, Maryland 53 K f
Westminster, South Carolina 54 H c
Westminster, Vermont 49 C e
West Monroe, Louisiana 63 L f
Westmorland, California 75 K l
Westmoreland, Kansas 60 H e
Westmoreland, New Hampshire 49 C e
Westmoreland, Tennessee 54 E a
West Nanticoke, Pennsylvania 50 A c
West New York, New Jersey (35,547) 51 L e
West Nishnabotna R., Iowa 61 J c
West Nueces R., Texas 64 G f
West Okoboji L., Iowa 61 J a
West Olive, Michigan 56 G g
Weston, Connecticut 50 G c
Weston, Idaho 66 H g
Weston, Michigan 57 J h
Weston, Missouri 61 K e
Weston, Nebraska 60 H c
Weston, Ohio 52 C d
Weston, Oregon 73 M k
Weston, West Virginia 52 F f
Weston, Wyoming 67 P e
West Orange, New Jersey (39,895) 51 J e
Westover, Texas 65 H b
West Palm Beach, Florida (56,208) 55 O g
West Paris, Maine 49 E d
West Petersburg, Alaska 77 V h
Westphalia, Indiana 57 F l
Westphalia, Kansas 61 J f
West Pike, Pennsylvania 52 J d
West Pittston, Pennsylvania 50 B c
West Plains, Missouri 61 N h
West Point, California 74 E f
West Point, Georgia 54 F e
Westpoint, Indiana 57 F j
West Point, Iowa 61 N d
West Point, Kentucky 57 H m
West Point, Mississippi 63 P e
West Point, mt., Alaska 77 P d
West Point, Nebraska 60 H c
West Point, New York 50 E c
West Point, Virginia 53 K h
Westport, California 74 B e
Westport, Connecticut 50 G c
Westport, Indiana 57 H k
Westport, New York 53 N a
Westport, Oregon 73 G j
Westport, South Dakota 58 H e
Westport, Tennessee 54 C b
Westport, Washington 73 F j
West Portal, New Jersey 50 C d
West Reading, Pennsylvania 50 A e
West Roxbury, Massachusetts 49 F j
West Rutland, Vermont 49 C e
West St. Paul, Minnesota 59 R j
West Salem, Illinois 57 E l
West Salem, Ohio 52 D e
West Salem, Wisconsin 56 B f
West Saugerties, New York 50 E a
West Seattle, Washington 72 B h
West Shokan, New York 50 E b
Westside, Iowa 61 J b
West Side, Oregon 73 K n
West Springfield, Massachusetts 51 H a
West Stewartstown, New Hampshire 49 D d
West Stockbridge, Massachusetts 50 G a
West Suffield, Connecticut 51 H b
West Tisbury, Massachusetts 51 M c
Westtown, New York 50 D c
West Trenton, New Jersey 50 D e
West Union, Illinois 57 F k
West Union, Iowa 61 M b
West Union, Ohio 52 C g
West Union, West Virginia 52 F f
West Unity, Ohio 52 B d
West University Place, Texas 64 F j
West View, Pennsylvania 53 O a
Westville, Florida 54 F g
Westville, Illinois 57 F j
Westville, Indiana 57 G h
Westville, New Jersey 50 C f
Westville, Oklahoma 63 J c
West Virginia (1,798,000) 24,181 sq. miles 52
West Walker R., Nevada 74 F f
West Warren, Massachusetts 51 J a
West Warwick, Rhode Island 51 K b
Westwater, Utah 68 G d
Westwego, Louisiana 62 B f
West Winfield, New York 53 L c
Westwood, California 74 E d
Westwood, Massachusetts 51 L a
Westwood, New Jersey 50 E d
Westworth, Texas 65 L j
West Yellowstone, Montana 66 J e
Wethersfield, Connecticut 51 H b
Wetmore, Colorado 69 L e
Wetmore, Texas 65 J f
Wet Mts., Colorado 69 L e
Wetonka, South Dakota 58 H e
Wetumpka, Alabama 54 E e
Wetumka, Oklahoma 62 G c
Wever, Iowa 61 N d
Wevertown, New York 53 M b
Wevok, Alaska 76 E b
Wewahitchka, Florida 54 F g
Wewoka, Oklahoma 62 G c
Weyauwega, Wisconsin 56 D e
Weyerhauser, Wisconsin 56 B d
Weymouth, Massachusetts (48,177) 51 M a
Whale B., Alaska 77 U h
Whalebone C., Alaska 76 D k
Whaleyville, Virginia 53 K j
Wharton, New Jersey 50 D d
Wharton, Pennsylvania 52 J d
Wharton, Texas 65 L f
What Cheer, Iowa 61 M c
Whatcom, L., Washington 73 H g
Whatley, Alabama 54 D f
Wheatfield, Indiana 57 F h
Wheatland, California 74 D e
Wheatland, Iowa 61 O c
Wheatland, Wyoming 67 Q g
Wheatland Res., Wyoming 67 P h
Wheatley, Arkansas 63 M d
Wheaton, Illinois 57 F h
Wheaton, Kansas 60 H e
Wheaton, Maryland (54,635), vicinity of Washington, D.C.
Wheaton, Minnesota 59 K e
Wheaton, Missouri 61 K h
Wheat Ridge, Colorado 69 O h
Wheeler, Kansas 60 C e
Wheeler, Oregon 73 G k
Wheeler, Texas 64 D h
Wheeler, Wisconsin 56 B d
Wheeler Dam, Alabama 54 D c
Wheeler L., Alabama 54 D c
Wheeler Pk., Nevada 74 L f
Wheeler Pk., New Mexico 71 M c
Wheeler Ridge, California 75 G j
Wheelersburg, Ohio 52 D g
Wheeler Springs, California 75 F k
Wheeling, West Virginia (53,400) 52 F e
Wheelock, North Dakota 58 C b
Wheelwright, Kentucky 57 L m
Whidbey I., Washington 73 H g
Whigham, Georgia 54 G g
Whipholt, Minnesota 59 M c
Whippany, New Jersey 50 E d
Whistler, Alabama 54 C g
Whitakers, North Carolina 55 O a
White, South Dakota 59 K f
White Bear L., Minnesota 59 R h
White Bear Lake, Minnesota 59 R h
White Bird, Idaho 66 D d
White Bluff, Tennessee 54 D a
White Bluffs, Washington 73 L j
White Butte, South Dakota 58 D e
White Castle, Louisiana 63 M h
White City, Florida 54 F h
White City, Florida 55 O f
White City, Kansas 60 H f
White City, New Mexico 71 N g
White Cloud, Kansas 61 J e
White Cloud, Michigan 56 H f
White Deer, Texas 64 C h
White Earth, North Dakota 58 D b
Whiteface, Texas 64 E b
Whiteface Mt., New York 53 M a
Whitefield, New Hampshire 49 D d
Whitefish, Montana 66 F a
Whitefish B., Michigan 56 J c
Whitefish Bay, Wisconsin 56 F f
Whitefish L., Alaska 76 K f
Whitefish L., Alaska 76 H f
Whitefish L., Minnesota 59 M d
Whitefish L., Montana 66 F a
Whitefish Pt., Michigan 56 J c
Whitefish R., Michigan 56 G c
Whitefish Ra., Montana 66 F a
Whiteflat, Texas 64 G a
White Hall, Illinois 57 C k
Whitehall, Michigan 56 G f
Whitehall, Montana 66 H d
Whitehall, New York 53 N b
Whitehall, Pennsylvania 53 P c
Whitehall, Wisconsin 56 B e
Whitehall Res., Massachusetts 51 K a
White Haven, Pennsylvania 50 B c
White Hills, Alaska 76 N b
White Hills, Arizona 70 C d
White Horse, California 74 D c
White Horse Beach, Massachusetts 51 M b
White Horse Pass, Nevada 74 L d
White House Station, New Jersey 50 D d
White L., Louisiana 63 L j
White L., Michigan 56 G f
White Lake, New York 50 D b
White Lake, South Dakota 58 H g
White Lake, Wisconsin 56 E d
Whiteland, Indiana 57 G k
Whitelocks Crossing, South Dakota 58 F e
White Mountain, Alaska 76 F d
White Mts., Alaska 77 O d
White Mts., California 74 G g
White Mts., New Hampshire 49 D d
White Oak, Pennsylvania 53 R c
White Oak Cr., Texas 65 M b
White Oak L., Arkansas 63 K e
White Oak Swamp, North Carolina 55 O c
White Owl, South Dakota 58 D f
White Pass, Washington 73 J j
White Pigeon, Michigan 57 H h
White Pine, Michigan 56 D c
Whitepine, Montana 66 E b
White Pine, Tennessee 54 H a
White Pine Ra., Nevada 74 K e
White Plains, New York (50,485) 50 F d
White Plains, North Carolina 55 L a
Whiteport, New York 50 E b
White R., Arizona 70 G f
White R., Arkansas 63 M d
White R., Indiana 57 G k
White R., Michigan 56 G f
White R., Nevada 74 K f
White R., South Dakota 58 F g
White R., Texas 64 F b
White R., Utah-Colorado 68 G d
White R., Vermont 49 C e
White R., Washington 73 J h
White R., Wisconsin 56 C c
Whiteriver, Arizona 70 G f
White River, South Dakota 58 F g
White River Junction, Vermont 49 C e
White River Val., Nevada 74 K f
White Rock, Nevada 74 J c
White Rock, Texas 65 O j
White Rock Cr., Kansas 60 F e
White Rock L., Texas 65 O j
White Rock Pk., Nevada 74 L f
White Salmon, Washington 73 J k
White Sands Nat. Mon., New Mexico 71 L g
Whitesboro, New York 53 L b
Whitesboro, Texas 65 L b
Whitesburg, Georgia 54 G d
Whitesburg, Kentucky 57 L m
White Settlement, Texas 65 L j
Whiteson, Oregon 73 G k
White Springs, Florida 55 J g
White Springs, Montana 66 J c
Whitestone, New York 51 N e
White Sulphur Springs, New York 50 D b
White Sulphur Springs, West Virginia 52 F h
Whitesville, Kentucky 57 G m
Whitesville, New Jersey 50 E e
Whitesville, New York 52 J c
Whitesville, West Virginia 52 E h
White Swan, Washington 73 K j
Whitetail, Montana 67 P a
Whiteville, North Carolina 55 N c
Whiteville, Tennessee 54 B b
Whitewater, Montana 67 N a
Whitewater, New Mexico 71 J g
Whitewater, Wisconsin 56 E g
Whitewater B., Florida 55 N h
Whitewater R., Indiana 57 H k
Whitewood, L., South Dakota 58 J f
Whitewood, South Dakota 58 C f
Whitewright, Texas 65 L b
Whiting, Iowa 61 H b
Whiting, Kansas 61 J e
Whiting, Maine 49 H e
Whiting, New Jersey 50 E f
Whitingham Res., Vermont 49 B f
Whitinsville, Massachusetts 51 K a
Whitlash, Montana 66 J a
Whitley City, Kentucky 57 J n
Whitman, Massachusetts 51 M a
Whitman, Nebraska 60 C b
Whitman, North Dakota 58 H b
Whitman Nat. Mon., Washington 73 M j
Whitmire, South Carolina 55 K c
Whitney, L., Texas 65 K d
Whitney, Mt., California 75 G h
Whitney, Nebraska 60 A b
Whitney, Nevada 75 L h
Whitney, Oregon 73 M l
Whitney, Texas 65 K d
Whitsett, Texas 65 J g
Whitt, Texas 65 J c
Whittaker, West Virginia 52 F f
Whittemore, Iowa 61 K a
Whittemore, Michigan 56 K e
Whittier, Alaska 77 N f
Whittier, California (33,663) 75 G l
Whitwell, Tennessee 54 F b
Wibaux, Montana 67 Q c
Wichita, Kansas (254,698) 60 G g
Wichita Falls, Texas (101,724) 65 J b
Wichita Mts., Oklahoma 62 E d
Wichita R., Texas 65 J a
Wickatunk, New Jersey 50 E e
Wickenburg, Arizona 70 E f
Wickersham, Washington 73 H g
Wickett, Texas 64 D d
Wickford, Rhode Island 51 L b
Wickiup Res., Oregon 73 J m
Wickliffe, Kentucky 57 D n
Wide B., Alaska 76 J h
Widen, West Virginia 52 F g
Wien L., Alaska 76 M d
Wiergate, Texas 65 O d
Wiggins, Colorado 69 M c
Wiggins, Mississippi 63 O h
Wikieup, Arizona 70 D e
Wilber, Nebraska 60 H d
Wilborn, Montana 66 H c
Wilbraham, Massachusetts 51 J a
Wilbur, Oregon 73 G m
Wilbur, Washington 73 M h
Wilbur Dam, Tennessee 55 J a
Wilburton, Oklahoma 62 H d
Wilcox, Missouri 61 K d
Wilcox, Nebraska 60 E d
Wilcox, Pennsylvania 52 H d
Wildcat Pk., Nevada 74 J e
Wilder, Tennessee 54 F a
Wildersville, Tennessee 54 C b
Wild Horse Res., Nevada 74 K c
Wild L., Alaska 76 M c
Wildorado, Texas 64 B h
Wild Rice R., Minnesota 59 K c
Wild Rice R., North Dakota 59 K d
Wildrose, North Dakota 58 C b
Wild Rose, Wisconsin 56 D e
Wildwood, Florida 55 J j
Wildwood, New Jersey 50 D h
Wiley, Colorado 69 O e
Wilkes-Barre, Pennsylvania (63,551) 50 B c
Wilkesboro, North Carolina 55 K a
Wilkinsburg, Pennsylvania (30,066) 53 Q b
Willacoochee, Georgia 54 H f
Willaha, Arizona 70 E d
Willamette R., Oregon 73 G k
Willapa B., Washington 73 F j
Willapa R., Washington 73 G j
Willard, Colorado 69 N c
Willard, Montana 67 Q c
Willard, New Mexico 71 L e
Willard, Ohio 52 D d
Willard, Utah 68 D b
Willards, Maryland 53 L g
Willcox, Arizona 70 H g
Williams, Arizona 70 E d
Williams, California 74 C e
Williams, Indiana 57 G l
Williams, Iowa 61 L b
Williams, Minnesota 59 M b
Williams Bay, Wisconsin 56 E g
Williamsbridge, New York 51 N e
Williamsburg, Iowa 61 M c
Williamsburg, Kentucky 57 J n
Williamsburg, Massachusetts 49 C f
Williamsburg, New York 51 M f
Williamsburg, Ohio 52 B f
Williamsburg, Pennsylvania 52 H e
Williamsburg, Virginia 53 K h
Williamson, Iowa 61 L c
Williamson, New York 53 J b
Williamson, West Virginia 52 D h
Williamsport, Indiana 57 F j
Williamsport, Maryland 52 J f
Williamsport, Pennsylvania (41,967) 53 J d
Williamston, Michigan 56 J g
Williamston, North Carolina 55 O b
Williamston, South Carolina 55 J c
Williamstown, Kentucky 57 J l
Williamstown, Massachusetts 49 B f
Williamstown, New Jersey 50 D f
Williamstown, Vermont 49 C d
Williamstown, West Virginia 52 E f
Williamsville, Missouri 61 O h
Willimantic, Connecticut 51 J b
Willimantic R., Connecticut 51 J b
Willington, Connecticut 51 J b
Willis, Texas 65 M e
Willis, Virginia 52 F j
Williston, Florida 55 J h
Williston, North Dakota 58 C b
Williston, South Carolina 55 K d
Willisville, Illinois 57 D m
Willits, California 74 B e
Willmar, Minnesota 59 L e
Willoughby, L., Vermont 49 D d
Willoughby, Ohio 52 E d
Willow, Alaska 76 M f
Willow, New York 50 E a
Willow, Oklahoma 62 D c
Willow Bend, Texas 64 F j
Willow City, North Dakota 58 F b
Willow Cr., California 74 E d
Willow Cr., Oregon 73 N l
Willow Cr., Oregon 73 L k
Willow Cr., Utah 68 G d
Willow Cr., Wyoming 67 K h
Willow Creek, Alaska 77 P f
Willow Creek, California 74 B d
Willowemoc, New York 50 D b
Willowemoc Cr., New York 50 D b
Willow Grove, Pennsylvania 50 C e
Willow Lake, South Dakota 58 J f
Willowranch, California 74 E c
Willow Res., Wisconsin 56 D d
Willow River, Minnesota 59 O d
Willow Run, Michigan 57 K g
Willows, California 74 C e
Willow Springs, Missouri 61 N h
Willsboro, New York 53 N a
Wills Creek Res., Ohio 52 E e
Wills Point, Texas 65 L c
Wilmer, Alabama 54 C g
Wilmette, Illinois (28,268) 57 F g
Wilmington, California 75 E n
Wilmington, Delaware (95,827) 50 B f
Wilmington, Illinois 57 E h
Wilmington, North Carolina (44,013) 55 O c
Wilmington, Ohio 52 C f
Wilmington, Vermont 49 B f
Wilmont, Minnesota 59 L g
Wilmore, Kansas 60 E g
Wilmore, Kentucky 57 J m
Wilmot, Arkansas 63 M e
Wilmot, Ohio 52 E e
Wilsall, Montana 67 K c
Wilson, Arkansas 63 N c
Wilson, Kansas 60 F f
Wilson, Louisiana 63 M h
Wilson, Mt., Colorado 68 H f
Wilson, Mt., Nevada 74 L f
Wilson, New York 52 H b
Wilson, North Carolina (28,753) 55 O b
Wilson, Oklahoma 62 F d
Wilson, Pennsylvania 50 C d
Wilson, Texas 64 F b
Wilson, Wyoming 67 K f
Wilson Cr., Washington 73 L h
Wilsoncreek, Washington 73 L h
Wilson Creek Ra., Nevada 74 L f
Wilson Dam, Alabama 54 D c
Wilson Junction, Colorado 69 O e
Wilson L., Alabama 54 D c
Wilson Res., Kansas 60 F f
Wilsonville, Nebraska 60 D d
Wilton, Arkansas 63 J e
Wilton, Connecticut 50 G c
Wilton, Iowa 61 N c
Wilton, Maine 49 E d
Wilton, New Hampshire 49 D f
Wilton, North Dakota 58 F c
Wilton, Wisconsin 56 C f
Wimauma, Florida 55 M f
Wimbledon, North Dakota 58 H c
Wimico, L., Florida 54 F h
Winamac, Indiana 57 G h
Winchell, Texas 65 H d
Winchendon, Massachusetts 49 D f
Winchester, Idaho 66 D c
Winchester, Illinois 57 C k
Winchester, Indiana 57 J j
Winchester, Kentucky 57 J m
Winchester, Massachusetts 49 F g
Winchester, New Hampshire 49 C f
Winchester, Ohio 52 C g
Winchester, Tennessee 54 E b
Winchester, Texas 65 K e
Winchester, Virginia 52 H f
Winchester Bay, Oregon 73 F m
Winchester Center, Connecticut 50 G b
Windam, Montana 67 K b
Windber, Pennsylvania 52 H e
Wind Cave Nat. Park, South Dakota 58 C g
Winder, Georgia 54 H d
Windfall, Indiana 57 H j
Wind Gap, Pennsylvania 50 C d
Windham, Alaska 77 V h
Windham, Connecticut 51 J b
Windham, New York 50 E a
Winding Stair Mts., Oklahoma 63 J d
Windmill Pt., Virginia 53 K h
Windom, Kansas 60 G f
Windom, Minnesota 59 L g
Windom Pk., Colorado 69 J f
Wind Pt., Wisconsin 56 F g
Wind R., Wyoming 67 M f
Wind River, Wyoming 67 M g
Wind River Ra., Wyoming 67 L f
Windsor, Colorado 69 M c
Windsor, Connecticut 51 H b
Windsor, Illinois 57 E k
Windsor, Massachusetts 49 C f
Windsor, Michigan 57 L k
Windsor, Missouri 61 L f
Windsor, New York 53 L c
Windsor, North Carolina 55 P a
Windsor, South Carolina 55 K d
Windsor, Vermont 49 C e
Windsor, Virginia 53 K j
Windsor Heights, West Virginia 52 F e
Windsor Locks, Connecticut 51 H b
Windthorst, Texas 65 J b
Windy, Alaska 77 N e
Winegars, Michigan 56 J f
Winehaven, California 75 B k
Winesap, Washington 73 K h
Winfield, Alabama 54 D d
Winfield, Iowa 61 N c
Winfield, Kansas 60 H g
Winfield, Texas 65 M b
Winifred, Montana 67 L b
Winifred, South Dakota 58 J g
Wing, North Dakota 58 F c
Wingate, Indiana 57 F j
Wingate, New Mexico 71 J d
Wingdale, New York 50 F b
Wingo, Kentucky 57 E n
Wink, Texas 64 D d
Winkelman, Arizona 70 G g
Winlock, Washington 73 H j
Winn, Maine 49 G c
Winn, Michigan 56 J f
Winnebago, L., Wisconsin 56 E e
Winnebago, Minnesota 59 M g
Winnebago, Nebraska 60 H b
Winneconne, Wisconsin 56 E e
Winnemucca, Nevada 74 H d
Winnemucca L., Nevada 74 F d
Winner, South Dakota 58 G g
Winnetka, Illinois 57 F g
Winnetoon, Nebraska 60 G b
Winnett, Montana 67 M b
Winnfield, Louisiana 63 L g
Winnibigoshish L., Minnesota 59 N c
Winnie, Texas 65 N f
Winnipesaukee, L., New Hampshire 49 D e
Winnsboro, Louisiana 63 M f
Winnsboro, South Carolina 55 K c
Winnsboro, Texas 65 M c
Winnwood, Missouri 61 Q a
Winokur, Georgia 55 J f
Winona, Arizona 70 F d
Winona, Kansas 60 C e
Winona, L., Arkansas 63 L d
Winona, Michigan 56 D c
Winona, Minnesota 59 P f
Winona, Mississippi 63 O e
Winona, Missouri 61 N g
Winona, Texas 65 M c
Winona, Washington 73 N j
Winooski, Vermont 49 B d
Winooski R., Vermont 49 C d
Winside, Nebraska 60 G b
Winslow, Arizona 70 G d
Winslow, Arkansas 63 J c
Winslow, Indiana 57 F l
Winslow, Maine 49 F d
Winslow, Washington 72 B h
Winsor Dam, Massachusetts 51 J a
Winsper, Idaho 66 H e
Winstead, Connecticut 51 G b
Winston, Montana 66 J c
Winston, New Mexico 71 K f
Winston-Salem, North Carolina (111,135) 55 L a
Winter Garden, Florida 55 K j
Winterhaven, California 75 L m
Winter Haven, Florida 55 N e
Winter Park, Colorado 69 L d
Winter Park, Florida 55 K j
Winters, California 74 C f
Winters, Texas 64 H d
Wintersburg, Arizona 70 E f
Winterset, Iowa 61 K c
Wintersport, Maine 49 G d
Winterton, New York 50 E b
Winthrop, Maine 49 F d
Winthrop, Massachusetts 49 H h

Winthrop, Minnesota 59 M f
Winthrop, New York 53 M a
Winthrop, Washington 73 K g
Winthrop Harbor, Illinois 56 F g
Winton, Minnesota 59 P c
Winton, North Carolina 55 P a
Winton, Pennsylvania 53 L d
Winton, Washington 73 K h
Winton, Wyoming 67 L h
Winyah B., South Carolina 55 M d
Wiota, Iowa 61 K c
Wirt, Minnesota 59 N c
Wiscasset, Maine 49 F d
Wisconsin (4,188,000) 56,154 sq. miles 56
Wisconsin, L., Wisconsin 56 D f
Wisconsin Dells, Wisconsin 56 D f
Wisconsin R., Wisconsin 56 C f
Wisconsin Rapids, Wisconsin 56 D e
Wisdom, Montana 66 G d
Wise, Virginia 52 D h
Wiseman, Alaska 76 M c
Wise River, Montana 66 H d
Wishek, North Dakota 58 G d
Wishram, Washington 73 K k
Wisner, Louisiana 63 M g
Wisner, Nebraska 60 H c
Wisner, New York 50 E c
Wissota L., Wisconsin 56 B e
Wister, Oklahoma 63 J d
Wister Res., Oklahoma 63 J d
Witherbee, New York 53 N a
Witherspoon, Mt., Alaska 77 O f
Withington, Mt., New Mexico 71 K f
Withlacoochie R., Florida 54 H g
Withrow, Washington 73 L h
Witt, Illinois 57 D k
Witten, South Dakota 58 F g
Wittenberg, Wisconsin 56 D e
Wittmann, Arizona 70 E f
Woburn, Massachusetts (31,214), vicinity of Boston
Wofford, Kentucky 57 J n
Wolbach, Nebraska 60 F c
Wolcott, Colorado 69 K d
Wolcott, Connecticut 51 H b
Wolcott, Kansas 61 O a
Wolcott, New York 53 K b
Wolfeboro, New Hampshire 49 D e
Wolfe City, Texas 65 L b
Wolf Cr., Texas 64 D g
Wolf Creek, Montana 66 H b
Wolf Creek, Oregon 73 G n
Wolf Creek Dam, Kentucky 57 H n
Wolf Creek Pass, Colorado 69 K f
Wolfforth, Texas 64 F b
Wolf Hole, Arizona 70 D c
Wolf L., Illinois 57 D n
Wolf Mts., Montana 67 N d
Wolford, North Dakota 58 G b
Wolf Point, Montana 67 P a
Wolf R., Mississippi 63 O h
Wolf R., Tennessee 54 B b
Wolf R., Wisconsin 56 E d
Wolsey, South Dakota 58 H f
Wolverine, Michigan 56 J d
Wolverton, Minnesota 59 K d
Womelsdorf, Pennsylvania 50 A e
Wonder, Oregon 73 G n
Wonder L., Alaska 76 M e
Wood, Mt., Montana 67 L d
Wood, South Dakota 58 F g
Wood, Pennsylvania 52 H e
Woodbine, Georgia 55 K g
Woodbine, Iowa 61 J c
Woodbine, Kansas 60 H f
Woodbine, Kentucky 57 J n
Woodbine, New Jersey 50 D g
Woodbine, Tennessee 54 E a
Woodbourne, New York 50 D b
Woodbridge, Connecticut 51 G c
Woodbridge, New Jersey (78,846) 50 E d
Woodbridge, Virginia 52 J g
Woodburn, Iowa 61 L d
Woodburn, Kentucky 57 G n
Woodburn, Oregon 73 H k
Woodbury, Connecticut 50 G b
Woodbury, Georgia 54 G e
Woodbury, New Jersey 50 C f
Woodbury, Tennessee 54 E b
Woodchopper, Alaska 77 Q d
Woodcliff, Georgia 55 K e
Woodfords, California 74 F f
Woodhaven, New York 51 N f
Woodhull, Illinois 57 C h
Woodhull, New York 52 J c
Woodinville, Washington 72 C g
Woodlake, California 75 F h
Wood Lake, Nebraska 60 D b
Woodland, California 74 D f
Woodland, Illinois 57 F j
Woodland, Maine 49 H c
Woodland, Pennsylvania 52 H d
Woodland, Washington 73 H k
Woodland Hills, Texas 65 N k
Woodland Park, Colorado 69 L e
Woodlawn, Illinois 57 D l
Woodlawn, Maryland 53 P e
Wood R., Alaska 77 O d
Woodridge, New York 50 D b
Wood River, Illinois 57 C l
Wood River, Nebraska 60 F d
Wood River Junction, Rhode Island 51 K c
Woodrow, Colorado 69 N d
Woodrow, Texas 64 F b
Woodruff, Arizona 70 H e
Woodruff, Kansas 60 E e
Woodruff, South Carolina 55 J c
Woodruff, Utah 68 E b
Woodsboro, Texas 65 K g
Woods Cross, Utah 68 C g
Woodsfield, Ohio 52 E f
Woods Hole, Massachusetts 51 M b
Woodside, Delaware 50 B g
Woodside, Utah 68 F d
Woodson, Arkansas 63 L d
Woodson, Illinois 57 C k
Woodson, Texas 65 H b
Woodstock, Connecticut 51 J b
Woodstock, Illinois 56 E g
Woodstock, New York 50 E a
Woodstock, Vermont 49 C e
Woodstock, Virginia 52 H g
Woodston, Kansas 60 E e
Woodstown, New Jersey 50 C f
Woodsville, New Hampshire 49 D d
Woodville, Alabama 54 E c
Woodville, Florida 54 G g
Woodville, Mississippi 63 M g
Woodville, Ohio 52 C d
Woodville, Texas 65 N e
Woodward, Oklahoma 62 D b
Woodward Res., California 74 E g
Woodworth, Louisiana 63 L g
Woodworth, North Dakota 58 G c
Woody Island, Alaska 76 L h
Wooldridge, Missouri 61 M f
Woolsey, Nevada 74 G d
Woonsocket, Rhode Island (47,080) 51 L b
Woonsocket, South Dakota 58 H f
Wooster, Ohio 52 E e
Worcester, Massachusetts (186,587) 51 K a
Worcester, New York 53 M c
Worden, Illinois 57 D l
Worden, Montana 67 M d
Worden, Oregon 73 J n
Worland, Wyoming 67 N e
Worth, Missouri 61 K d
Wortham, Texas 65 L d
Worthington, Indiana 57 F k
Worthington, Minnesota 59 L g
Worthington, Missouri 61 M d
Worthington, Ohio 52 D e
Worthville, Kentucky 57 H l
Worton, Maryland 50 A g
Wounded Knee, South Dakota 58 D g
Wrangell, Alaska 77 V h
Wrangell, C., Alaska 76 J j
Wrangell, Mt., Alaska 77 Q f
Wrangell I., Alaska 77 V h
Wrangell Mts., Alaska 77 Q f
Wray, Colorado 69 O c
Wren, Oregon 73 G l
Wrens, Georgia 55 J d
Wrentham, Massachusetts 51 L a
Wright, Kansas 60 E g
Wright Bros. Nat. Memorial, North Carolina 55 P c
Wright City, Oklahoma 62 H d
Wrightson, Mt., Arizona 70 G h
Wrightstown, New Jersey 50 D e
Wrightsville, Georgia 55 J e
Wrightsville, Pennsylvania 53 K e
Wrightsville Beach, North Carolina 55 O c
Wrightwood, California 75 H k
Wulik R., Alaska 76 F c
Wupatki Nat. Mon., Arizona 70 F d
Wursboro, New York 50 E b
Wurtsboro, New York 53 M d
Wyaconda R., Missouri 61 N d
Wyandotte, Michigan (43,519) 57 K g
Wyarno, Wyoming 67 O e
Wyatt, Missouri 61 P h
Wyeville, Wisconsin 56 C e
Wylie, Texas 65 L b
Wyman Dam, Maine 49 F c
Wymer, Washington 73 K j
Wymore, Nebraska 60 H d
Wyndmere, North Dakota 58 J d
Wynne, Arkansas 63 N c
Wynnewood, Oklahoma 62 F d
Wynona, Oklahoma 62 G b
Wynot, Nebraska 60 G b
Wyocena, Wisconsin 56 D f
Wyodak, Wyoming 67 P e
Wyola, Montana 67 N d
Wyoming (315,000) 97,914 sq. miles 67
Wyoming, Delaware 50 B g
Wyoming, Illinois 57 D h
Wyoming, Michigan (45,829), vicinity of Grand Rapids
Wyoming, Minnesota 59 N e
Wyoming, New York 52 J c
Wyoming, Pennsylvania 50 B c
Wyoming, Rhode Island 51 K b
Wyoming Pk., Wyoming 67 K g
Wyoming R., Wyoming 67 K g
Wytheville, Virginia 52 E j
Xenia, Illinois 57 E l
Xenia, Ohio 52 C f
Yaak, Montana 66 E a
Yaak R., Montana 66 E a
Yachats, Oregon 73 F l
Yacolt, Washington 73 H k
Yadkin R., North Carolina 55 K a
Yadkinville, North Carolina 55 L a
Yakak, C., Alaska 77 O j
Yakataga, Alaska 77 Q f
Yakima, Washington (43,284) 73 K j
Yakima R., Washington 73 L j
Yakobi I., Alaska 77 T h
Yakt, Montana 66 F a
Yakutat, Alaska 77 S g
Yakutat B., Alaska 77 R g
Yale, Illinois 57 E k
Yale, Iowa 61 K c
Yale, Michigan 56 L f
Yale, Oklahoma 62 G b
Yale, South Dakota 58 H f
Yale L., Washington 73 H k
Yalesville, Connecticut 51 H c
Yalobusha R., Mississippi 63 O e
Yamato, Florida 55 O g
Yampa, Colorado 69 K c
Yampa R., Colorado 68 H c
Yamsay Mt., Oregon 73 J n
Yancey, Texas 65 H f
Yanceyville, North Carolina 55 M a
Yankton, South Dakota 58 J h
Yantic, Connecticut 51 J b
Yaphank, New York 51 H d
Yaquina Hd., Oregon 73 F l
Yardley, Pennsylvania 50 D e
Yardville, New Jersey 50 D e
Yarmouth, Maine 49 E e
Yarmouth, Massachusetts 51 N b
Yarnell, Arizona 70 E e
Yates, New Mexico 71 O c
Yatesboro, Pennsylvania 52 G e
Yates Center, Kansas 61 J g
Yauhannah, South Carolina 55 M d
Yava, Arizona 70 E e
Yazoo City, Mississippi 63 N f
Yazoo R., Mississippi 63 N f
Yegua Cr., Texas 65 K e
Yellow Medicine R., Minnesota 59 L f
Yellow Pine, Idaho 66 E e
Yellow R., Florida-Alabama 54 E f
Yellow R., Wisconsin 56 C e
Yellow Springs, Ohio 52 C f
Yellowstone L., Wyoming 67 K e
Yellowstone Nat. Park, Wyoming 67 K e
Yellowstone R., Montana, etc. 67 Q b
Yellowtail Res., Montana 67 M d
Yellville, Arkansas 63 L b
Yemassee, South Carolina 55 L e
Yentna R., Alaska 76 M e
Yerba Buena I., California 75 B l
Yermo, California 75 J k
Yerrington, Nevada 74 F f
Yeso, New Mexico 71 N e
Yoakum, Texas 65 K f
Yocemento, Kansas 60 E f
Yocona R., Mississippi 63 O d
Yoder, Colorado 69 M e
Yoder, Wyoming 67 Q h
Yokena, Mississippi 63 N f
Yoncalla, Oregon 73 G m
Yonkers, New York (190,634) 51 M d
Yonkers Res., Oklahoma 62 H b
York, Alabama 54 C e
York, Montana 66 J c
York, Nebraska 60 G d
York, North Dakota 58 G b
York, Pennsylvania (54,504) 53 K f
York, South Carolina 55 K c
York Mts., Alaska 76 D d
York R., Virginia 53 K h
York Springs, Pennsylvania 53 J e
Yorktown, New Jersey 50 C f
Yorktown, Texas 65 K g
Yorktown, Virginia 53 K h
Yorktown Heights, New York 50 F c
York Village, Maine 49 E e
Yorkville, Illinois 57 E h
Yosemite Falls, California 74 F g
Yosemite L., California 75 E g
Yosemite Lodge, California 74 F g
Yosemite Nat. Park, California 74 F g
Yost, Utah 68 C b
Young, Arizona 70 G e
Youngs, L., Washington 72 C j
Youngstown, Florida 54 F g
Youngstown, New York 52 H b
Youngstown, Ohio (166,689) 52 F d
Youngsville, Louisiana 63 L h
Youngsville, New Mexico 71 L c
Youngsville, North Carolina 55 N a
Youngsville, Pennsylvania 52 G d
Youngwood, Pennsylvania 52 G e
Younts Pk., Wyoming 67 K f
Yountville, California 74 C f
Ypsilanti, Michigan 57 K g
Yreka, California 74 C c
Ysleta, Texas 64 A d
Yuba City, California 74 D e
Yuba R., California 74 D e
Yucca, Arizona 70 C e
Yucca Flat, Nevada 75 J g
Yucca House Nat. Mon., Colorado 68 H f
Yukon, Florida 55 K g
Yukon, Oklahoma 62 F c
Yukon Delta, Alaska 76 E e
Yukon R., Alaska 76 G e
Yuko R., Alaska 76 J d
Yulan, New York 50 D b
Yulee, Florida 55 K g
Yuma, Arizona 70 C g
Yuma, Colorado 69 O c
Yuma Des., Arizona 70 C g
Yunaska I., Alaska 77 S j
Yutan, Nebraska 60 H c
Zachary, Louisiana 63 M h
Zahl, North Dakota 58 C b
Zalesky, Ohio 52 D f
Zalma, Missouri 61 O g
Zamora, California 74 D f
Zane Hills, Alaska 76 J c
Zanesville, Ohio (39,077) 52 D f
Zap, North Dakota 58 E c
Zapata, Texas 65 H j
Zarembo I., Alaska 77 V h
Zavalla, Texas 65 N d
Zearing, Iowa 61 L b
Zebulon, North Carolina 55 N b
Zeeland, Michigan 56 G g
Zeeland, North Dakota 58 G e
Zehner, Pennsylvania 50 B c
Zehners, Pennsylvania 50 B d
Zeigler, Illinois 57 D m
Zelienople, Pennsylvania 52 F e
Zell, South Dakota 58 H f
Zenda, Kansas 60 F g
Zenia, California 74 B d
Zeona, South Dakota 58 D e
Zephyr, Texas 65 J d
Zephyrhills, Florida 55 M e
Zero, Montana 67 P c
Zieglerville, Pennsylvania 50 B e
Zimmerman, Minnesota 59 N e
Zion, Illinois 56 F g
Zion, Maryland 50 A f
Zion Canyon, Utah 68 D f
Zion Grove, Pennsylvania 50 A d
Zion Nat. Park, Utah 68 D f
Zionsville, Indiana 57 G k
Zirkel, Mt., Colorado 69 K c
Zitziana R., Alaska 76 M d
Zoar L., Connecticut 50 G c
Zolfo Springs, Florida 55 N f
Zortman, Montana 67 M b
Zuber, Florida 55 J h
Zumbro Falls, Minnesota 59 O f
Zumbro R., Minnesota 59 O f
Zumbrota, Minnesota 59 O f
Zumwalt, Oregon 73 O k
Zuni, New Mexico 71 J d
Zuni Mts., New Mexico 71 J d
Zuni R., Arizona 70 H e
Zurich, Kansas 60 E e
Zurich, Montana 67 L a
Zwolle, Louisiana 63 K g

INDEX TO THE WORLD

(EXCEPT U.S.A.)

LIST OF ABBREVIATIONS

Afghan. Afghanistan
Afr. Africa
Alg. Algeria
Alta. Alberta (Canada)
Antarc. Antarctica
Arch., Archipel. Archipelago, Archipel
Argent. Argentina
Atl. Oc. Atlantic Ocean
Aust. Australia
Aut. Autonomous
Azerbai. Azerbaijan (Azerbaydzhanskaya)
B. Bay, Bahía, Baie, Bucht
Baluch. Baluchistan
B.C., etc. British Columbia (Canada)
Belg. Belgium, Belgian
Bol. Bolivia
Br. Bridge
Br., Brit., British
Bulg. Bulgaria
C. Cape, Cabo, Cap
Can. Canal
Cap. Capital
Car. Caroline
Cel. Celebes
Cent. Central
Ch. China
Chan. Channel
Co. County
Col. Colony
Colomb. Colombia
Cord. Cordillera (Mountains)
Cr. Creek
Czech. Czechoslovakia
Den. Denmark
Dep. Department
Des. Desert
Dist. District
Div. Division
Dom. Dominican
E. East, Eastern
Ecua. Ecuador
E.I. East Indies
Eng. England
Erit. Eritrea
Ethio. Ethiopia
Fd. Fiord, Fjord
Fed. Dist. Federal District
Fr. French, France
G. Gulf, Golfe, Golfo, Guba
Geb. Gebirge (Mountains)
Ger. Germany
G.F. Goldfield
Grp. Group
Gt. Great
Guat. Guatemala
Harb. Harbor, Harbour
Hd. Head
Hisp. Hispaniola
Hist. Historical
Hond. Honduras
Hung. Hungary
I. Island, Islet, Ile, Ilet, Isle
Ind. Res. Indian Reservation
Indon. Indonesia
Internat. International
Is. Islands, Isles, Iles
It. Italian, Italy
Iv. Cst. Ivory Coast
Jeb. Jebel (Mountain)
Junc. Junction
Kan. Kanal (Canal)
Kazakh. Kazakhstan (Kazakhskaya)
Kep. Kepulauan (Islands)
Kirgiz. Kirgizia (Kirgizskaya S.S.R.)
L. Lake, Loch, Lough, Lago, Lac, Lagoon, Lagôa
Ld. Land
Leb. Lebanon
Lit. Little
Lith. Lithuania
Lr. Lower
Lt. Ho. Light House
Mal. Rep. Malagasy Republic
Man. Manitoba (Canada)
Maur. Mauritania
Medit. Mediterranean
Me., Mex. Mexico
Mong. Mongolia
Mozamb. Mozambique
Mt. Mountain, Mount, Mont, Monte
N. North, Northern, New
Nat. National
N.B., etc. New Brunswick (Canada)
Neth., etc. Netherlands
Nfd., etc. Newfoundland (Canada)
Nic. Nicaragua
N. Ire. Northern Ireland
N.S. Nova Scotia (Canada)
N.-W. Terr., etc. North-West Territories (Canada)
N.Z., etc. New Zealand
O., Os. Ostrov (Island)
Ont. Ontario
Oc. Ocean
Ova. Ostrova (Islands)
Oz. Ozero (Lake)
Pac. Pacific
Pak. Pakistan
Pan. Panama
Para. Paraguay
Pass. Passage
P.E.I., etc. Prince Edward Island (Canada)
Pen. Peninsula
Phil. Philippines
Pk. Peak, Park
Plat. Plateau
Pol. Poluostrov (Peninsula)
Port. Portuguese, Portugal
Princip. Principality
Prom. Promontory
Prot. Protectorate
Prov. Province, Provincial
Pt., Pte. Point, Pointe
Pta. Punta (Point)
Pto. Puerto
Que. Quebec (Canada)
R. River, Río, Rivière
Ra. Range
Reg. Region
Rom. Romania
S. South, Southern, San, Santo
Sa. Serra, Sierra
Sard. Sardinia
Sask. Saskatchewan (Canada)
Scot. Scotland
Sd. Sound
Set. Settlement
Sol. Solomon
Som. Somaliland, Somali
Sp. Spanish, Spain
St., Ste., Sta. Saint, Sainte, Santa
Sta. Station
Str. Strait
Swed. Sweden
Switz. Switzerland
Tadzhik. Tadzhikistan (Tadzhikskaya)
Tan. Tanzania
Terr. Territory, Territories
Trucial St. Trucial States
Turkmen. Turkmenistan (Turkmenskaya)
U.A.R. United Arab Republic
Ukr. Ukraine
Up. Upper
U.S.A. United States of America
Uzbek., Uzb. Uzbekistan (Uzbekskaya)
U.S.S.R. Union of Soviet Socialist Republics
Val. Valley
Vdkhr. Vodokhranilishche (Reservoir)
Venez. Venezuela
Viet. Vietnam
Vol. Volcano
W. West, Western
W.I. West Indies
Yugosl. Yugoslavia

Aach **Ajax**

Aachen, *Germany* 104 A c
Aalborg, *Denmark* 103 D h
Aalen, *Germany* 104 D d
Aalestrup, *Denmark* 103 C h
Aalsmeer, *Netherlands* 100 C b
Aalst. *See* Alost
Aalten, *Netherlands* 100 E c
Aarau, *Switzerland* 101 D a
Aarberg, *Switzerland* 101 C a
Aarburg, *Switzerland* 101 C a
Aardenburg, *Netherlands* 100 B c
Aare, R., *Switzerland* 101 C a
Aargau, canton, *Switzerland* 101 D a
Aarhus, *Denmark* 103 D h
Aars, *Denmark* 103 C h
Aarschot, *Belgium* 100 C d
Aba, *Congo* 121 G d
Abacaxis R., *Brazil* 92 F e
Abaco I., Gt., *Bahama Is.* 91 D a
Abaco I., Lit., *Bahama Is* 91 D a
Abadan, *Iran* 124 E c
Abadeh, *Iran* 125 F c
Abaete, *Brazil* 93 H d
Abaiang, I., *Gilbert Is.* 78 H g
Abakan, *U.S.S.R.* 115 J c
Abal Dufaf, *Saudi Arabia* 124 D c
Abancay, *Peru* 92 C f
Abarqu, *Iran* 125 F c
Abashiri & B., *Japan* 133 J b
Abau, *Papua* 135 J b
Abaya L., *Ethiopia* 121 H c
Abbeville, *France* 108 D a
Abbey, *Saskatchewan* 86 J h
Abbotsford, *Br. Columbia* 88 H f
Abbottabad, *Pakistan* 126 D b
Abdul Aziz, Jebel, *Syria* 124 D b
Abdulino, *U.S.S.R.* 117 L d
Abéché, *Chad* 119 K f
Abee, *Alberta* 86 E d
Abeele, *Belgium* 100 A d
Abelessa, *Algeria* 118 F d
Abemama, I., *Gilbert Is.* 78 H g
Abengourou, *Ivory Coast* 118 E g
Abeokuta, *Nigeria* 118 F g
Aberaeron, *Wales* 99 E h
Abercorn, *Quebec* 85 S g
Aberdare, *Wales* 99 E j
Aberdeen, *Saskatchewan* 86 L f
Aberdeen & co., *Scotland* 98 F c
Aberfeldy, *Scotland* 98 E d
Aberfoyle, *Scotland* 98 E d
Abergavenny, *Wales* 99 E j
Abernethy, *Manitoba* 87 O h
Aberystwyth, *Wales* 99 E h
Abha, *Saudi Arabia* 98 D f
Abidjan, *Ivory Coast* 118 E g
Abilene, *Alberta* 87 F d
Ab-i-Istada L., *Afghanistan* 125 J c
Abisko, *Sweden* 102 H b
Abitibi, *Ontario* 84 K c
Abitibi Canyon Dam, *Ont.* 84 J c
Abitibi L., *Ontario* 84 K d
Abitibi R., Little, *Ontario* 84 J b
Abitibi R., *Ontario* 84 J b
Abomey, *Dahomey* 118 F g
Abord à Plouffe, *Quebec* 85 Q j
Abound, *Saskatchewan* 87 M h
Abraham, Plains of, *Quebec* 85 S c
Abrantes, *Portugal* 106 A c
Abrud, *Romania* 112 D a
Abruzzi, dep., *Italy* 110 D d
Abruzzi, Mt., *Br. Columbia* 86 B h
Abtenau, *Austria* 104 E e
Abu, *India* 126 D d
Abu al Abyad, *Trucial States* 125 F e
Abu Arish, *Saudi Arabia* 124 D f
Abu Bahr, *Saudi Arabia* 124 E e
Abu Deleiq, *Sudan* 119 M e
Abu Dhabi, *Trucial States* 125 F e
Abu ed Duhur, *Syria* 123 F b
Abu el Jurdhan, *Jordan* 123 D g
Abu Jifan, *Saudi Arabia* 124 E e
Abu Kemal, *Syria* 124 D c
Abumombozi, *Congo* 120 E d
Abunã, *Brazil* 92 D e
Abu Qurqas, *Egypt* 119 M c
Abuta, *Japan* 133 G c
Abut Hd., *New Zealand* 135 Q l
Abuya Myeda, Mt., *Ethiopia* 121 H b
Abu Zabad, *Sudan* 119 L f
Abyei, *Sudan* 119 L g
Åbyn, *Sweden* 102 J d
Abyy, *U.S.S.R.* 115 P b
Acadia Valley, *Alberta* 86 G g
Acajutla, *Salvador* 91 B d
Acámbaro, *Mexico* 90 D c
Acaponeta, *Mexico* 90 C c
Acapulco, *Mexico* 90 D d
Acará & R., *Brazil* 93 H d
Acarigua, *Venezuela* 92 D b
Acatlán, *Mexico* 90 E d
Accra, *Ghana* 118 E g
Achaguas, *Venezuela* 92 D b
Achao, *Chile* 95 B f
Acheninni L., *Saskatchewan* 87 P d
Achigan, *Ontario* 84 F f
Achill I., *Eire* 99 A g
Achinsk, *U.S.S.R.* 115 J c
Achray, *Ontario* 85 N g
Acklins, I., *Bahamas Is.* 91 E b
Acme, *Alberta* 86 D g
Aconcagua, Mt., *Argentina* 94 C d
Açores, Is., *Atlantic Ocean* 118 B a
Acorizal, *Brazil* 93 F g
Acoyapa, *Nicaragua* 91 B d
Acre, *Israel* 123 D e
Actaeon Grp., *Tuamotu Archipelago* 79 N j
Acton, *Ontario* 84 K j
Acton Vale, *Quebec* 85 S g
Açú & R., *Brazil* 93 K e
Ada, *Okinawa* 78 C a
Adair, *Manitoba* 87 O h
Adak, I., *Aleutian Is.* 78 J b
Adalia. *See* Antalya
Adam, *Muscat & Oman* 125 G e
Adama, *Ethiopia* 121 H c
Adamant Mt., *Br. Columbia* 88 L e
Adamello, Mt., *Italy* 110 C b
Adam's Bridge, *India-Ceylon* 126 E g
Adams Glacier, *Antarctica* 136 S e
Adams L., *Br. Columbia* 88 K e
Adam's Pk., *Ceylon* 126 F g
Adamsville, *Quebec* 85 S g
Adana, *Turkey* 124 C b
Adanac, *Saskatchewan* 86 H f
Adapazari, *Turkey* 124 B a
Adare, C., *Antarctica* 136 B d
Adare, *Eire* 99 B h
Adavale, *Australia* 135 H e
Addis Ababa, *Ethiopia* 121 H c
Addis Derra, *Ethiopia* 121 H b
Adelaer, C., *Greenland* 89 P c
Adelaide, *Australia* 135 G f
Adelaide, I., *Antarctica* 136 H e
Adelaide, Pt., *Australia* 134 G f
Adelaide, *South Africa* 122 D f
Adelaide River, *Australia* 134 G f
Adelboden, *Switzerland* 101 C b
Ademuz, *Spain* 107 E b
Aden, G. of, *Africa-Arabia* 121 K b
Aden, *S. Yemen* 124 E g
Adh Dhahiriya, *Jordan* 123 C f
Adhoi, *India* 126 D d
Adhra, *Syria* 123 E d
Adi, I., *W. Irian* 129 K l
Adi Kaie, *Ethiopia* 121 H b
Adilabad, *India* 126 E e
Adi Ugri, *Ethiopia* 121 H b
Adjuntas, *Puerto Rico* 54 C h
Adlavik Is., *Labrador* 81 O g
Admiral, *Saskatchewan* 86 J j
Admiralty G., *Australia* 134 E b
Admiralty Inlet, *N.-W. Terr.* 81 L c
Admiralty Is., *Pacific Ocean* 78 E g
Adolfo Alşina, *Argentina* 94 D e
Adoni, *India* 126 E e
Adoumré, *Cameroon* 119 H g
Adour R., *France* 109 C e
Adra, *Spain* 106 D d
Adraj, *Saudi Arabia* 125 F e
Adrano, *Sicily* 111 E g
Adrar, *Algeria* 118 E c
Adria, *Italy* 110 D c
Adriatic Sea, *Italy, etc.* 110 E d
Aduwa, *Ethiopia* 121 H b
Advocate Harbour, *Nova Scotia* 82 H h
Aegean Sea, *Greece* 113 E e
Aeltre, *Belgium* 100 B c
Ærösköbing, *Denmark* 103 D j
Aesch, *Switzerland* 101 C a
Aetna, *Alberta* 86 D j
Afetña, *Saipan-Tinian Is.* 78 A e
Afferden, *Netherlands* 100 E c
Affuá, *Brazil* 93 G d
Afghanistan, *Asia* 125 H c
Afif, *Saudi Arabia* 124 D e
Afogados de Ingazeira, *Brazil* 93 K e
Afono B., *Tutuila I.* 79 U o
Africa 118-122
Afrin, *Syria* 123 E a
Afula, *Israel* 123 D e
Afyon, *Turkey* 124 B b
Aga, *Truk Is.* 78 D n
Agab Workei, *Ethiopia* 121 H b
Agadès, *Niger* 118 G e
Agadir, *Morocco* 118 D b
Again, R., *Quebec* 85 L b
Agana, *Guam* 78 B l
Agartala, *India* 127 H d
Agassiz, *Br. Columbia* 88 J f
Agassiz, C., *Antarctica* 136 H e
Agat, *Guam* 78 A l
Agawa, *Ontario* 84 F e
Agawa, R., *Ontario* 84 F e
Agde, *France* 109 E e
Agen, *France* 109 D d
Agiabampo, *Mexico* 90 C b
Agidyen, *Jaluit I.* 79 U h
Agira, *Sicily* 111 E g
Agnébilékrou, *Ivory Coast* 118 E g
Agnes L., *Ontario* 87 L b
Agno, *Switzerland* 101 D c
Agordat, *Ethiopia* 121 H a
Agram. *See* Zagreb
Agrigento, *Sicily* 111 D g
Agrínion, *Greece* 113 C e
Agropoli, *Italy* 111 E e
Agryz, *U.S.S.R.* 117 L b
Agua Clara, *Brazil* 93 G h
Aguadas, *Colombia* 92 B b
Aguadilla, *Puerto Rico* 91 F c
Aguadulce, *Panama* 91 C e
Aguanish, *Quebec* 83 K c
Aguanus R., *Quebec* 83 K c
Agua Prieta, *Mexico* 90 C a
Aguaray, *Argentina* 94 D b
Aguasabon Dam, *Ontario* 84 C d
Aguascalientes, *Mexico* 90 D c
Agudo, *Spain* 106 C c
Agudos, *Brazil* 93 H h
Aguijan, *Saipan-Tinian Is.* 78 A f
Águila, Pta., *Puerto Rico* 54 B j
Aguilar, *Spain* 106 C d
Aguilar de Campos, *Spain* 106 C a
Águilas, *Spain* 107 E d
Aguirre, B., *Argentina* 95 C j
Agujereada, Pta., *Puerto Rico* 54 B h
Agulhas C., *South Africa* 122 C f
Agusta, *Australia* 134 C f
Aha, *Okinawa* 78 C a
Ahar, *Iran* 124 E b
Ahmadnegar, *India* 126 D e
Ahmedabad, *India* 126 D d
Ahtopol, *Bulgaria* 112 F c
Ahuachapán, *Salvador* 91 A d
Ahualulco, *Mexico* 90 D c
Ahuntsic, *Quebec* 85 R j
Ahus, *Sweden* 103 F j
Ahvaz, *Iran* 124 E c
Ahvenanmaa, *Finland* 103 H f
Ahwar, *S. Yemen* 124 E g
Ai, *Jaluit I.* 79 T j
Aibonito, *Puerto Rico* 54 C h
Aigle, L. à l', *Quebec* 82 G b
Aigle, *Switzerland* 101 B b
Aihunkiu, *China* 128 J a
Aijal, *India* 127 H d
Aikawa, *Japan* 133 F e
Aileron, *Australia* 134 F d
Ailinginae I., *Marshall Is.* 79 S a
Ailinglapalap I., *Marshall Is.* 79 T c
Ailsa Craig, *Ontario* 84 J j
Aim, *U.S.S.R.* 115 N c
Aimores, *Brazil* 93 J g
Ain, dep., *France* 108 F c
Aineman, *Jaluit I.* 79 U j
Aïn Galakka, *Chad* 118 J e
Aïn Safra, *Mauritania* 118 C e
Ainslie, L., C. Breton I., *Nova Scotia* 83 L g
Airai, *Palau Is.* 78 B m
Airdrie, *Alberta* 86 C g
Aire, *France* 109 C e
Aire, R., *England* 99 G g
Air Force I., *N.-W. Terr* 81 M d
Airolo, *Switzerland* 101 D b
Aishihik & L., *Yukon* 77 T f
Aisne, dep., *France* 108 E b
Aiun, El, *Sp. Sahara* 118 C c
Aiwokako Passage, *Palau Is.* 78 B l
Aix, *France* 109 F e
Aix-la-Chapelle. *See* Aachen
Aiyansh, *Br. Columbia* 88 L c
Aiyina I., *Greece* 113 D f
Aiyion, *Greece* 113 C e
Aiyon, I., *Palau Is.* 78 C l
Aizpute, Latvia, *U.S.S.R.* 103 J h
Ajaccio & G. d', *Corsica* 111 B e
Ajaigarh, *India* 126 F d
Ajanta, *India* 126 E d
Ajanta Ra. *See* Sahiadriparvat
Ajax, *Ontario* 85 L j

Ajayan B., *Guam* 78 A m
Ajib, *Muscat & Oman* 125 G e
Ajibba, *Saudi Arabia* 124 D d
Ajigasawa, *Japan* 133 G d
Ajlun, *Jordan* 123 D e
Ajmer, *India* 126 D c
Ajoewa, *Surinam* 93 F c
Akalkot, *India* 126 E e
Akan Nat. Park, *Japan* 133 H c
Akanthou, *Cyprus* 123 B b
Akaoka, *Japan* 133 C h
Akarnania & Aitolía, *Greece* 113 C e
Akaroa, *New Zealand* 135 Q l
Akashi, *Japan* 133 D g
Akcha, *Afghanistan* 125 J b
Akhdhar, Jeb., *Muscat & Oman* 125 G e
Akhisar, *Turkey* 124 A b
Akhterin, *Syria* 123 F a
Akhtyrka, Ukraine, *U.S.S.R.* 116 J f
Akimiski I., James B., *North-West Territories* 81 L g
Akita, *Japan* 133 G e
Akkrum, *Netherlands* 100 D a
Ako, *Nigeria* 120 C b
Akola, *India* 126 E d
Akpatok I., *N.-W. Terr* 81 N e
Akra, Jebel el, *Turkey* 123 D b
Akron, *Ontario* 84 F d
Akrotiri Pen., *Crete* 113 E g
Aksaray, *Turkey* 124 B b
Aksehir, *Turkey* 124 B b
Aksha, *U.S.S.R.* 115 L c
Āksi, Estonia, *U.S.S.R* 103 M g
Akti, *Greece* 113 E d
Aktyubinsk, Kazakh., *U.S.S.R.* 114 E c
Akure, *Nigeria* 118 G g
Akureyri, *Iceland* 102 Wm
Akyab, *Burma* 127 H d
Akzhal, Kazakh., *U.S.S.R.* 114 H d
Alaejos, *Spain* 106 C b
Alagoas, *Brazil* 93 K e
Alagoinhas, *Brazil* 93 K f
Alagón, *Spain* 107 E b
Alaja, *Syria* 123 D b
Alajuela, *Costa Rica* 91 C d
Alam, *Ethiopia* 121 H c
Alameda, *Saskatchewan* 87 P j
Alamos, *Mexico* 90 C b
Åland. See Ahvenanmaa
Ålands Hav, *Sweden-Finland* 103 H g
Alanelimo, *Truk Is.* 78 F o
Alanseiru, *Truk Is.* 78 C o
Alao, *Tutuila I.* 79 U o
Alapayevsk, *U.S.S.R* 117 Q b
Alasehir, *Turkey* 124 A b
Ala Shan, *China* 128 D c
Al Ashkharah, *Muscat & Oman* 125 G e
Alaska Highway, *Alaska-Canada* 88 H b
Alatyr, *U.S.S.R.* 117 H c
Alavus, *Finland* 102 K e
Al 'Ayn, *Muscat & Oman* 125 G f
Alayskiy Khrebet, Kirgiz., *U.S.S.R.* 114 G e
Alazeyskoye Plat., *U.S.S.R* 114 P b
Albacete, *Spain* 107 E c
Alba de Tormes, *Spain* 106 C b
Albaida, *Spain* 107 E c
Alba Iulia, *Romania* 112 D a
Albanel, *Quebec* 85 S d
Albania, *S. Europe* 112 C d
Albany, *Australia* 134 C f
Albany, *Nova Scotia* 82 G j
Albany R., *Ontario* 84 F b
Albarracin, *Spain* 107 E b
Albergaria-a-Velha, *Portugal* 106 A b
Alberique, *Spain* 107 E c
Alberni, Vancouver I., *British Columbia* 88 G f
Albert, *New Brunswick* 82 H h
Alberta, Mt., *Alberta* 88 L d
Alberta, prov., *Canada* 80 H g
Albert Edward Mt., *Papua* 135 J a
Albert L., *Congo* 121 G d
Albert Markham, Mt., *Antarctica* 136 A b
Alberton, *Prince Edward I.* 82 H g
Albertville, *Congo* 121 F f
Albertville, *France* 108 G d
Albertville, *Saskatchewan* 87 M e
Albi, *France* 109 E e
Albina, *Surinam* 93 G b
Albocácer, *Spain* 107 E b
Albreda, *Br. Columbia* 88 K d
Albufeira, *Portugal* 106 A d
Albuñol, *Spain* 106 D d
Albuquerque, *Spain* 106 B c
Albury, *Australia* 135 J g
Alcacer do Sal, *Portugal* 106 A c
Alcala de Chisvert, *Spain* 107 F b
Alcalá de Henares, *Spain* 106 D b
Alcamo, *Sicily* 111 D g
Alcañices, *Spain* 106 B b
Alcañiz, *Spain* 107 E b
Alcântara, *Brazil* 93 J d
Alcántara, *Spain* 106 B c
Alcantarilla, *Spain* 107 E d
Alcaraz, *Spain* 107 D c
Alcázar de San Juan, *Spain* 106 D c
Alchevsk, Ukraine, *U.S.S.R* 116 L g
Alcira, *Spain* 107 E c
Alcobaça, *Portugal* 106 A c
Alcolea del Pinar, *Spain* 107 D b
Alcomdale, *Alberta* 86 D e
Alcoutim, *Portugal* 106 B d
Alcoy, *Spain* 107 E c
Alcuhemas, *Morocco* 118 E a
Aldabra Is., *Indian Ocean* 121 K a
Aldama, Chihuahua, *Mexico* 90 C b
Aldama, Tamaulipas, *Mexico* 90 E c
Aldan & R., *U.S.S.R.* 115 M c
Aldeburgh, *England* 99 J h
Alderney, I., *Channel Is.* 99 A k
Aldershot, *England* 99 G j
Alderson, *Alberta* 86 F h
Aldersyde, *Alberta* 86 D h
Al Dola, *S. Yemen* 124 E g
Alegrete, *Brazil* 94 E c
Aleih, *Lebanon* 123 D d
Aleksandra Ostrova, *Arctic Ocean* 89 K a
Aleksandrov, *U.S.S.R.* 116 L c
Aleksandrovsk Sakhalinskiy, *U.S.S.R.* 115 P c
Alekseyevka, Kazakh., *U.S.S.R.* 114 G c
Alekseyevka, *U.S.S.R.* 117 H d
Alençon, *France* 108 D b
Alenquer, *Brazil* 93 G d
Alenquer, *Portugal* 106 A c
Aleppo, *Syria* 123 F a
Alert, *N.-W. Terr.* 81 N a
Alert Bay, *Br. Columbia* 88 F e
Alès, *France* 109 F d
Aleshki, *U.S.S.R.* 117 E e
Alessandria, *Italy* 110 B c
Ålesund, *Norway* 102 B e
Aletschhorn, Mt., *Switz.* 101 C b
Alexander, C., *Antarctica* 136 H e
Alexander, *Manitoba* 87 R j
Alexander I., *Antarctica* 136 H d
Alexandra, *New Zealand* 135 P m
Alexandretta. See Iskenderun
Alexandria, *Br. Columbia* 88 H d
Alexandria, *Egypt* 119 L b
Alexandria, *Ontario* 85 Q g
Alexandrina, L., *Australia* 134 G g
Alexandroúpolis, *Greece* 113 E d
Alexikovo, *U.S.S.R.* 117 F e
Alexis B., *Labrador* 81 O g
Alexis Creek, *Br. Columbia* 88 H d
Alexis R., *Labrador* 83 P a
Alexo, *Alberta* 86 B f
Aleysk, *U.S.S.R.* 114 H c
Alfaro, *Spain* 107 E a
Al Fāw, *Iraq* 124 E d
Alga, Kazakh., *U.S.S.R.* 114 E d
Ålgård, *Norway* 103 A g
Al Garrobo del Aquila, *Argentina* 94 C e
Algauer Alpen, *Austria, etc.* 104 D e
Algeciras, *Spain* 106 C d
Alger (Algiers), *Algeria* 109 N f
Algeria, *N.-W. Africa* 118 E b
Al Ghail, *Yemen* 124 E f
Alghero, *Sardinia* 111 B e
Algoa B., *South Africa* 122 D f
Algoma, *Ontario* 84 H f
Algonquin Park, *Ontario* 85 M g
Algonquin Prov. Park, *Ont.* 85 M g
Alguada Reef, *Burma* 127 H e
Alhama de Granada, *Spain* 106 D d
Al Hasa, *Saudi Arabia* 124 E d
Al Hauta, *S. Yemen* 124 E f
Al Hayy, *Iraq* 124 E c
Alhucemas I., *Spain* 106 D e
Alia, *Sicily* 111 D g
Aliaga, *Spain* 107 E b
Alibag, *India* 126 D e
Alicante, *Spain* 107 E c
Alice Arm, *Br. Columbia* 88 E c
Alice Springs, *Australia* 134 F d
Alicudi, I., *Italy* 111 E f
Alida, *Saskatchewan* 87 Q j
Aligarh, *India* 126 E c
Ali Khel, *Afghanistan* 125 J c
Alimnia, I., *Greece* 113 F f
Aling Kangri, *Tibet* 126 F b
Alingsås, *Sweden* 103 E h
Alirajpur, *India* 126 D d
Al Ittihad, *South Arabia* 124 D g
Alivérion, *Greece* 113 E e
Alix, *Alberta* 86 D f
Al Jawf, *Saudi Arabia* 124 C d
Al Jesab, *Saudi Arabia* 124 E f
Aljustrel, *Portugal* 106 A d
Alken, *Belgium* 100 D d
Alkmar, *Netherlands* 100 C b
Al Kut, *Iraq* 124 E c
Allahabad, *India* 126 F c
Allan, *Saskatchewan* 86 L g
Allanmyo, *Burma* 127 J e
Allan Water, *Ontario* 87 N a
Allard, L., *Quebec* 82 J c
Allard, R., *Quebec* 85 N c
Allardville, *N.B.* 82 G f
Allariz, *Spain* 106 B a
Allaykha, *U.S.S.R.* 115 P a
Alle, *Belgium* 100 C e
Allenby Bridge, *Jordan* 123 D f
Allenford, *Ontario* 84 J h
Allen L., *Eire* 99 B f
Alleppey, *India* 126 E g
Alliance, *Alberta* 86 F f
Allier, dep., *France* 108 E c
Allier, R., *France* 108 E d
Allison Harbour, *British Columbia* 88 F e
Alliston, *Ontario* 84 L h
Alloa, *Scotland* 98 E d
All Pines, *Br. Honduras* 91 B c
Al Luhaygah, *Yemen* 124 D f
Allumette I., *Quebec* 85 N g
Ally, *Quebec* 85 R c
Alma, *New Brunswick* 82 H h
Alma, *Quebec* 85 T d
Alma Ata, Kazakh., *U.S.S.R.* 114 G d
Almadén, *Spain* 106 C c
Almagro, *Spain* 106 D c
Almansa, *Spain* 107 E c
Alma Pk., *Br. Columbia* 88 F b
Almazán, *Spain* 107 D b
Almeirim, *Brazil* 93 G d
Almeirim, *Portugal* 106 A c
Almelo, *Netherlands* 100 E b
Almeria & Gulf, *Spain* 107 D d
Al'met'yevsk, *U.S.S.R.* 117 L c
Almirante, *Panama* 91 C e
Almiropótamos, *Greece* 113 E e
Almirós, *Greece* 113 D e
Almodôvar, *Portugal* 106 B d
Almodóvar, *Spain* 106 C c
Almonte, *Ontario* 85 O g
Almora, *India* 126 E c
Almorox, *Spain* 106 C b
Almudebar, *Spain* 107 E a
Almunia de Doña Godina, La, *Spain* 107 E b
Al Musayyib, *Iraq* 124 D c
Al Muwailha, *Saudi Arabia* 124 C d
Alness, *Scotland* 98 E c
Alnwick, *England* 98 F e
Alocén, *Spain* 107 D b
Alofau, *Tutuila I.* 79 U o
Aloja, Latvia, *U.S.S.R.* 103 L h
Alon, *Burma* 127 J d
Alón. See Iliodhrómia, I.
Alonsa, *Manitoba* 87 T h
Alor, I., *Indonesia* 129 H m
Alora, *Spain* 106 C d
Alor Star, *Malaysia* 132 C e
Alost, *Belgium* 100 C d
Aloysius, Mt., *Australia* 134 E e
Alpes-Maritimes, dep., *Fr.* 109 G e
Alphen, *Netherlands* 100 C b
Alps, Mts., *Cent. Europe* 97 J g
Al Qara, *Saudi Arabia* 124 D d
Al Qayyara, *Iraq* 124 D b
Al Qunfidhah, *Saudi Arabia* 124 D f
Al Qurnah, *Iraq* 124 E c
Alright I., Madeleine Is., *Quebec* 83 L f
Als, I., *Denmark* 103 C j
Alsask, *Saskatchewan* 86 H g
Alsten, *Norway* 102 E d
Alston, *England* 99 F f
Alšvanga, Latvia, *U.S.S.R.* 103 J h
Alta Gracia, *Argentina* 94 D d
Altagracia, *Venezuela* 92 C a
Altagracia de Orituco, *Venezuela* 92 D b
Altai, Mts., *Central Asia* 114 H c
Altamachi, *Bolivia* 92 D g
Altamura, *Italy* 111 F e
Altan Bulag, *Mongolia* 115 K c
Altar, *Mexico* 90 B a
Altario, *Alberta* 86 G g
Altata, *Mexico* 90 C c
Altayskiy Kray, *U.S.S.R.* 114 H c
Altdorf, *Switzerland* 101 D b
Altea, *Spain* 107 F c
Altenburg, *Germany* 104 E c
Altin Koprü, *Iraq* 124 D b
Altmark, *Germany* 104 D b
Alto-Adige, *Italy* 110 C b
Alto Araguaia, *Brazil* 93 G g
Alto Longa, *Brazil* 93 J e
Alto Madeira, *Brazil* 92 E e
Alto Molocue, *Mozambique* 121 H h
Altona, *Germany* 104 C b
Altona, *Manitoba* 87 U j
Altstätten, *Switzerland* 101 E a
Al Ugla, *Saudi Arabia* 124 C d
Al 'Uj, *Saudi Arabia* 124 E e
Alūksne, Latvia, *U.S.S.R.* 103 M h
Alula, *Somali Republic* 103 L b
Aluminé, *Argentina* 95 B e
Alupka, *U.S.S.R.* 116 J j
Alushta, *U.S.S.R.* 116 J j
Alvarado, *Mexico* 90 E d
Alvear, *Argentina* 94 D e
Alvena, *Saskatchewan* 87 L f
Alvesta, *Sweden* 103 F h
Älvho, *Sweden* 103 F f
Alvinston, *Ontario* 84 J k
Alvito, *Portugal* 106 A c
Al Wajh, *Saudi Arabia* 124 C d
Alwar, *India* 126 E c
Alyab, *Sudan* 119 M e
Alytus, Lithuania, *U.S.S.R.* 102 L j
Amadeus L., *Australia* 134 E d
Amadi, *Sudan* 119 M g
Amadiyah, *Iraq* 124 D b
Amadjuak L., *N.-W. Terr.* 81 M d
Amakusa Nada, *Japan* 133 A h
Amal, *Libya* 119 K c
Åmål, *Sweden* 103 E g
Amalfi, *Italy* 111 E e
Amaliás, *Greece* 113 C f
Amami Gunto, *Japan* 133 N n
Amaná, L., *Brazil* 92 E d
Amanalco, *Mexico* 90 D d
Amanave, *Tutuila I.* 79 T o
Amantea, *Italy* 111 F f
Amapá, *Brazil* 93 G c
Amapala, *Honduras* 93 B d
Amarah, *Iraq* 124 E c
Amarante, *Brazil* 93 J e
Amaranth, *Manitoba* 87 T h
Amarapura, *Burma* 127 J d
Amaravti, *India* 126 E d
Amargosa, *Brazil* 93 K f
Amasra, *Turkey* 124 B a
Amasya, *Turkey* 124 C a
Amatique, G. de, *Guatemala* 90 G d
Amatitlán, *Guatemala* 90 F e
Amazon, Mouths of the, *Brazil* 93 H c
Amazon, R., *Brazil* 93 G d
Amazon, *Saskatchewan* 87 M g
Amb, *Pakistan* 126 D b
Ambala, *India* 126 E b
Ambalavoa, *Mal. Rep.* 121 N l
Ambam, *Cameroon* 120 C d
Ambar, *Iran* 125 G c
Ambarchik, *U.S.S.R.* 115 R b
Ambato, *Ecuador* 92 B d
Ambato-Boéni, *Mal. Rep.* 121 N k
Amberg, *Germany* 104 D d
Ambergris Cay, *Bahama Is.* 91 E b
Ambergris Cay, *Brit. Hond.* 91 B c
Ambérieu, *France* 108 F c
Amberley, *Ontario* 84 J h
Ambert, *France* 108 E d
Ambikapur, *India* 127 F d
Ambilobe, *Mal. Rep.* 121 N j
Ambition, Mt., *British Columbia* 88 D b
Amblève, *Belgium* 100 E d
Ambohimahasoa, *Mal. Rep.* 121 N l
Ambon, I., *Indonesia* 129 J l
Ambositra, *Mal. Rep.* 121 N l
Ambriz, *Angola* 120 C f
Ambrizete, *Angola* 120 C f
Amd, *Aden* 124 E f
Amderma, *U.S.S.R.* 114 F b
Ameca, *Mexico* 90 D c
Ameland I., *Netherlands* 100 D a
American Highland, *Antarctica* 136 R d
Amerongen, *Netherlands* 100 D b
Amersfoort, *Netherlands* 100 D b
Amery Ice Shelf, *Antarctica* 136 Q e
Amesbury, *Alberta* 86 E c
Amescale, *Ontario* 86 J a
Ameson, *Ontario* 84 F c
Amfiklia, *Greece* 113 D e
Amfilokhia, *Greece* 113 C e
Amga & R., *U.S.S.R.* 115 N b
Amgu, *U.S.S.R.* 115 N d
Amherst, *Burma* 127 J e
Amherst, *Nova Scotia* 82 H h
Amherstburg, *Ontario* 84 G k
Amherst I., Madeleine Is., *Quebec* 83 L f
Amherst I., *Ontario* 85 O h
Amiens, *France* 108 E b
Amindivi, I., *India* 126 D f
Amingaon, *India* 127 H c
Aminuis, *S.W. Africa* 122 B d
Amirante Is., *Indian Ocean* 121 K a
Amisk, *Alberta* 86 F f
Amisk L., *Saskatchewan* 87 P d
Amiskwumiska L., *Quebec* 85 O b
Amla, *Saudi Arabia* 124 D e
Amlwch, *Wales* 99 E g
Amm Adam, *Sudan* 119 N e
Amman, *Jordan* 123 D f
Amol, *Iran* 125 F b
Amorgós, I., *Greece* 113 E f
Amos, *Quebec* 85 M d
Amototi. See Eil Malk
Amoy, *China* 131 J k
Amparo, *Brazil* 93 H h
Amqui, *Quebec* 82 E e
Amraho, *Sudan* 119 M e
Amran, *Yemen* 124 D f
Amreli, *India* 126 D d
Amriswil, *Switzerland* 101 E a
Amritsar, *India* 126 E b
Amstelveen, *Netherlands* 100 C b
Amsterdam, *Netherlands* 100 C b
Am Timan, *Chad* 119 K f
Amu Darya, Turkmen., *U.S.S.R.* 114 F d
Amund Ringnes I., *North-West Territories* 81 K b
Amundsen, Mt., *Antarctica* 136 S e
Amundsen B. (Ice B.) *Antarctica* 136 P e
Amundsen G., *N.-W. Terr.* 80 G c
Amundsen Glacier, *Antarc.* 136 D b
Amundsen Sea, *Antarctica* 136 F d
Amur, R., *U.S.S.R.-China* 115 M c
Amurskaya Oblast, *U.S.S.R.* 115 M c
Amyot, *Ontario* 84 F d
Amyun, *Lebanon* 123 D c
An, *Burma* 127 H e
Anabta, *Jordan* 123 D e
Anadyr & R., *U.S.S.R.* 115 S b
Anadyrskiy Zaliv, *U.S.S.R* 115 T b
Anáfi, I., *Greece* 113 E f
Anah, *Iraq* 124 D c
Anahim Lake, *Br. Columbia* 88 G d
Anai, *Libya* 119 H d
Anaimalai Hills, *India* 126 E f
Anakapalle, *India* 127 F e
Analalava, *Mal. Rep.* 121 N j
Anamã, *Brazil* 92 E d
Anama Bay, *Manitoba* 87 T g
Anambas Is., *Indonesia* 132 D f
Anamizu, *Japan* 133 E f
Anantapur, *India* 126 E f
Anápolis, *Brazil* 93 H g
Anar, *Iran* 125 G c
Anarak, *Iran* 125 F c
Anardarra, *Afghanistan* 125 H c
Anasco, *Puerto Rico* 54 B h
Anatolia, *Turkey* 124 B b
Añatuya, *Argentina* 94 D c
Anchuras, *Spain* 106 C c
Ancienne Lorette, airport, *Quebec* 85 T f
Ancohuma, Mt., *Bolivia* 92 D g
Ancon, B. de, *Colombia* 92 B c
Ancón, *Peru* 92 B f
Ancona, *Italy* 110 D d
Ancud, *Chile* 95 B f
Andacollo, *Argentina* 95 B e
Andalgala, *Argentina* 94 C c
Åndalsnes, *Norway* 102 B e
Andaman Is. & Str., *Bay of Bengal* 127 H f
Andaman Sea, *Bay of Bengal* 127 H f
Andeer, *Switzerland* 101 E b
Andelfingen, *Switzerland* 101 D a
Andenne, *Belgium* 100 D d
Andermatt, *Switzerland* 101 D b
Andes, Cord. de los, *South America* 94 C c
Andevoranto, *Mal. Rep* 121 N k
And Fd., *Norway* 102 G b
Andhra Pradesh, *India* 126 E e
Andikíthira I., *Greece* 113 D g
Andímilos, I., *Greece* 113 E f
Andíparos, I., *Greece* 113 E f
Andizhan, Uzbek., *U.S.S.R.* 114 G d
Andkhui, *Afghanistan* 125 J b
Andoas, *Ecuador* 92 B d
Andorra & rep., *Pyrenees* 107 F a
Andover, *New Brunswick* 82 E g
Andöy, *Norway* 102 F b
Andrade, *Mozambique* 122 F c
Andreas, C., *Cyprus* 123 C b
Andrelândia, *Brazil* 93 J h
Andrew, *Alberta* 86 E e
Andreyevka, Ukraine, *U.S.S.R.* 116 J g
Andria, *Italy* 111 F e
Andriba, *Mal. Rep.* 121 N k
Andritsaina, *Greece* 113 C f
Andros, I., *Greece* 113 E f
Ándros I., *Bahama Is.* 91 D b
Anegada, B., *Argentina* 95 D f
Anegada, I., *Virgin Is.* 91 G c
Anelo, *Argentina* 95 C e
Anemwanot, *Majuro Is* 79 U f
Anenelibw, *Majuro Is.* 79 U g
Anerley, *Saskatchewan* 86 K g
Aneroid, *Saskatchewan* 86 K j
Aney, *Niger* 119 H e
Anfa, *Lebanon* 123 D c
Angangueo, *Mexico* 90 D d
Angara Basin, *Arctic Ocean* 89 L a
Angel de la Guarda, I., *Mex.* 90 B b
Angel Fall, *Venezuela* 92 E b
Angelholm, *Sweden* 103 E h
Angelm, Mt., *New Zealand* 135 P m
Angemuk Mt., *New Guinea* 129 L l
Angers, *France* 108 C c
Angikuni L., *N.-W. Terr* 81 K e
Angkor, *Cambodia* 132 C d
Angler, *Ontario* 84 D d
Anglesey, *Wales* 99 E g
Anglia, *Saskatchewan* 86 J g
Angliers, *Quebec* 85 L e
Angol, *Chile* 95 B e
Angola, *W. Africa* 120 D g
Angontsy, *Mal. Rep.* 121 P k
Angora. See Ankara
Angoulême, *France* 108 D d
Angoumois, prov., *France* 108 D d
Angra, *Brazil* 93 J h
Anguilla, I., *Leeward Is.* 91 G c
Anguille, C. & Mts., *Newfoundland* 83 N f
Angul, *India* 127 G d
Angus, co. *Scotland* 98 E d
Angus, *Ontario* 84 L h
Angusville, *Manitoba* 87 Q h
Anholt, I., *Denmark* 103 D h
An-hui. See Anhwei
Anhwei, prov., *China* 130 H f
Anina, *Romania* 112 C b
Anjengo, *India* 126 E g
Anjou, prov., *France* 108 C c
Anjouan I., *Comores, Arch. des* 121 J g
Anjozorobe, *Mal. Rep.* 121 N k
Ankacho, *U.S.S.R.* 115 K b
Ankang, *China* 130 D f
Ankara, *Turkey* 124 B a
Anking. See Hwaining
Ankober, *Ethiopia* 121 H c
Ankwo, *China* 130 G c
Anlier, *Belgium* 100 D e
Anlu, *China* 130 F g
Anlu. See Chungsiang
Anna, *U.S.S.R.* 117 E e
Annaba (Bône), *Algeria* 109 Q h
Annacis I., *Br. Columbia* 88 E g
Annai, *Guyana* 92 F c
An Najaf, *Iraq* 124 D c
Annam, *Vietnam* 132 D c
Annan, *Scotland* 98 E e
Annapolis R., *Nova Scotia* 82 G j
Annapolis Royal, *Nova S.* 82 G j
An Nasjriyah, *Iraq* 124 E c
Ann C., *Antarctica* 136 P e
Annecy & L. d', *France* 108 G d
Annenkov I., *Antarctica* 136 K g
Annieopsquotch Mts., *Newfoundland* 83 P e
Annobón I., *Gulf of Guinea* 120 B e
Annonay, *France* 109 F d
An Numas, *Saudi Arabia* 124 D f
Anole, *Somali Republic* 121 J e
Áno Viannos, *Crete* 113 E g
Anpehi, *China* 130 D b
Ansariya, Jebel el, *Syria* 123 E b
Ansbach, *Germany* 104 D d
Anse-au-Griffon, *Quebec* 82 H e
Anse au Loup, *Labrador* 83 Q b
Anshan, *China* 128 H b
Anshun, *China* 131 B j
Ansi, *China* 128 C b
Ansin, *China* 130 G c
Anson, B., *Australia* 134 E b
Ansongo, *Mali* 118 F e
Ansonville, *Ontario* 84 K d
Anta, *Peru* 92 C f
Antakya (Antioch), *Turkey* 123 E a
Antalo, *Ethiopia* 121 H b
Antalya, G. of, *Turkey* 124 B b
Antalya, *Turkey* 124 B b
Antarctica 136
Antarctic Basin, *Antarctica* 136 F f
Antelope, *Saskatchewan* 86 J h
Antequera, *Paraguay* 94 E b
Antequera, *Spain* 106 C d
Anthony Lagoon, *Australia* 134 G c
Antibes, *France* 109 G e
Anticosti I., *Quebec* 82 J d
Antigonish, *Nova Scotia* 83 K h
Antigua, I., *Leeward Is.* 91 G c
Antilhue, *Chile* 95 B e
Antilla, *Cuba* 91 D b
Antilles, Greater, *W. I.* 91 D c
Antilles, Lesser, *West Indies* 91 G c
Antioch. See Antakya
Antiope Reef, *Cook Is.* 78 K j
Antioquia, *Colombia* 92 B b
Antipodes Is., *Pacific Islands* 78 J m
Antivari. See Bar
Antler, *Saskatchewan* 87 Q j
Antler R., *Man.-Sask.* 87 Q j
Antofagasta, *Chile* 94 B b
Antofagasta de la S., *Arg* 94 C c
Antofalla, Mt., *Argentina* 94 C c
Antoing, *Belgium* 100 B d
Antongil, B. d', *Mal. Rep.* 121 N k
Antrain, *France* 108 C b
Antrim & co., *N. Ireland* 99 C f
Antrim Hills, *N. Ireland* 98 C e
Antsirabe, *Mal. Rep.* 121 N k
Antsirane, *Mal. Rep.* 121 N j
Antsla, Estonia, *U.S.S.R.* 103 M h
Antung, *China* 130 M b
Antwerp. See Antwerpen
Antwerpen & prov., *Belg.* 100 C c
Anupgarh, *India* 126 D c
Anuradhapura, *Ceylon* 126 F g
Anuta, I., *New Hebrides* 78 H j
Anver I., *Antarctica* 136 H f
Anvers. See Antwerpen
Anville, *Quebec* 85 P c
Anyang, *China* 130 G d
Anyi, *China* 130 E e
Anykščiai, Lithuania, *U.S.S.R.* 103 L j
Anyox, *Br. Columbia* 88 E c
Anzac, *Alberta* 88 O b
Anzhero Sudzhensh, *U.S.S.R.* 114 H c
Anzio, *Italy* 111 D e
Aoa B., *Tutuila I.* 79 U o
Aoloau, *Tutuila I* 79 T o
Aomori, *Japan* 103 G d
Aosta, *Italy* 110 A c
Aoudèras, *Niger* 118 G e
Apakova, *U.S.S.R.* 117 J c
Aparri, *Philippines* 129 H g
Apatin, *Yugoslavia* 112 B b
Apatity, *U.S.S.R.* 117 C b
Ape, Latvia, *U.S.S.R.* 103 M h
Apeldoorn, *Netherlands* 100 D b
Apenganau L., *Manitoba* 87 S c
Apennines, Mts., *Italy* 97 K h
Api, *Nepal* 126 F c
Api, Mt., *Nepal* 126 F c
Apiai, *Brazil* 94 G b
Apodi, *Brazil* 93 K e
Apolo, *Bolivia* 92 D f
Apostoles, *Argentina* 94 E c
Apoteri, *Guyana* 92 F c
Apozai, *Pakistan* 126 C b
Appenzell & canton, *Switz.* 101 E a
Applecross, *Scotland* 98 D c
Apple River, *Nova Scotia* 82 H h
Apra Harb., *Guam* 78 A l
Apsley, *Ontario* 85 M h
Apt, *France* 111 F e
Apurashokoru, *Palau Is.* 78 A n
Aqaba, *Jordan* 123 D h
Aqarbat, *Syria* 123 F b
'Aqda, *Iran* 125 F c
Aqiq, *Sudan* 121 H a
Aqraba, *Jordan* 123 D e
Aquidauana, *Brazil* 93 F h
Aquila, L', *Italy* 110 D d
Aquin, *Haiti* 91 E c
Arabia, Saudi. See Saudi Arabia
Arabian L., *Quebec* 83 N c
Arabian Sea, *S. Asia* 126 B e
Aracaju, *Brazil* 93 K f
Aracatí, *Brazil* 93 K d
Aracruz, *Brazil* 93 K h
Araçuaí, *Brazil* 93 J g
Arad, *Romania* 112 C a
Arada, *Chad* 119 K e
Arafura Sea, *Indonesia-Australia* 134 F a
Araguacema, *Brazil* 93 H e

Aragua de Barcelona, Venez. 92 E b
Araguaia, R., Brazil 93 H e
Araguari, Brazil 93 H g
Arak, Iran 124 E c
Arakabesan, Palau Is. 78 B n
Arakaka, Guyana 92 F b
Arakan. See Myohaung
Arakan Yoma, Burma 127 H d
Arakawa, Okinawa 78 C a
Araks, R., Iran, etc. 114 D e
Ara L., Ontario 84 C b
Aral Sea. See Aral'skoye More
Aral'sk, Kazakh., U.S.S.R. 114 F d
Aral'skoye More (Aral Sea), Kazakh.-Uzb., U.S.S.R. 114 E d
Aramac, Australia 135 J d
Arambiru, Eniwetok 79 S c
Aranda de Duero, Spain 106 D b
Arani, Bolivia 92 D g
Aran Is., Eire 99 A g
Aranit, Eniwetok 79 S c
Aranjuez, Spain 106 D b
Aranya, Thailand 132 C d
Arapey, Uruguay 94 E d
Arapkir, Turkey 124 C b
Araranguá, Brazil 94 G c
Ararat, Australia 135 H g
Ararat, Mt., Turkey 124 D b
Ara saki, Okinawa 78 A d
Aratsu B., Rota I. 78 A j
Araty, Brazil 92 C e
Arauca, Colombia 92 C b
Arauco, Chile 95 B e
Aravalli Ra., India 126 D c
Araxá, Brazil 94 G a
Arbai Khere, Mongolia 128 D a
Arbatax, Sardinia 111 B f
Arbil, Iraq 124 D b
Arboga, Sweden 103 F g
Arbois, France 108 F c
Arbon, Switzerland 101 E a
Arborfield, Saskatchewan 87 O e
Arborg, Manitoba 87 U h
Arbroath, Scotland 98 F d
Arcadia, Alberta 86 A c
Arcen, Netherlands 100 E c
Archerwill, Saskatchewan 87 O f
Archidona, Spain 106 C d
Archive, Saskatchewan 87 M h
Arcola, Saskatchewan 87 P j
Arcot, India 126 E f
Arctic Bay, N.-W Terr 81 L c
Arctic Ocean 89
Ardabil, Iran 124 E b
Ardahan, Turkey 124 D a
Ardakan, Iran 125 F c
Ardal, Iran 125 F c
Årdal, Norway 103 B f
Ardath, Saskatchewan 86 K g
Ardatov, U.S.S.R. 117 F c
Ardbeg, Ontario 84 K g
Ardèche, dep., France 109 F d
Arden, Manitoba 86 S h
Arden, Ontario 85 O h
Ardennes, dep., France 108 F b
Ardennes Mts., Belgium, etc. 108 F a
Ardestan, Iran 125 F c
Ardez, Switzerland 101 F b
Ardglass, N. Ireland 99 D f
Ardill, Saskatchewan 87 M j
Ardino, Bulgaria 112 E d
Ardley, Alberta 86 D f
Ardmore, Alberta 86 G d
Ardrishaig, Scotland 98 D e
Ardrossan, Alberta 86 D e
Ardrossan, Scotland 98 D e
Ardud, Romania 105 K e
Arecibo, Puerto Rico 54 C h
Areia Branco, Brazil 93 K d
Arekalong Pen., Palau Is. 78 C l
Arelee, Saskatchewan 86 K f
Arena, Saskatchewan 86 H j
Arenales, Argentina 94 D d
Arenales, Mt., Chile 95 B g
Arenas, Pta., Puerto Rico 54 D h
Arenas de San Pedro, Spain 106 C b
Arendal, Norway 103 C g
Arenys de Mar, Spain 107 G b
Arequipa, Peru 92 C g
Areré, Brazil 93 G d
Arévalo, Spain 106 C b
Arezzo, Italy 110 C d
Argenson, L. d', Quebec 85 R c
Argent, R. à l', Quebec 82 C c
Argenta, Br. Columbia 88 L e
Argentan, France 108 C b
Argentat, France 109 D d
Argentia, Newfoundland 83 S f
Argentina, S. America 94-95
Argentino, L., Argentina 95 B h
Argent-sur-Sauldre, France 108 E c
Argo, Sudan 119 M e
Argolis, G. of, Greece 113 D f
Argonne, France 108 F b
Argos, Greece 113 D f
Arguedas, Spain 107 E a
Argungu, Nigeria 118 F f
Argun R., U.S.S.R.-Manchuria 115 L c
Argyle, Nova Scotia 82 G k
Argyll, co., Scotland 98 D d
Ariake Wan, Japan 133 B j
Ariano Irpino, Italy 111 E e
Arica, Chile 94 B a
Arica, Colombia 92 C d
Arichat, C. Breton I., N.S. 83 M h
Ariège, dep., France 109 D e
Arilje, Yugoslavia 112 C c
Arima, Brazil 92 E e
Arinda, Guyana 92 F c
Ario, Mexico 90 D d
Aripuanã, Brazil 92 E e
Ariquemes, Brazil 92 E e
Arisaig, Scotland 98 D d
Aristazabal I., Br. Columbia 88 E d
Arivechi, Mexico 90 C b
Ariza, Spain 107 D b
Arizona, Argentina 94 C e
Arizpe, Mexico 90 B a
Arka, S. Yemen 124 E g
Arka, U.S.S.R. 115 P b
Arkadhia, Greece 113 D f
Arkhangel'sk, U.S.S.R. 114 D b
Arklow, Eire 99 C h
Árkoi, I., Greece 113 F f
Arkona, Ontario 84 J j
Arlap, Jaluit I. 79 T h
Arles, France 109 F e
Arlon, Belgium 100 D e
Arltunga, Australia 134 G d
Armada, Alberta 86 E h
Armagh, Quebec 82 B g
Armagh & co., N. Ireland 99 C f
Armavir, U.S.S.R. 117 D d
Armenia, Colombia 92 B c
Armenia, U.S.S.R. 124 D a
Armentières, France 108 E a
Armidale, Australia 135 K f
Armirós, B. of, Crete 113 E g
Armit, Saskatchewan 87 Q f
Armley, Saskatchewan 87 N e
Armori, India 126 F d
Arms, Ontario 84 D c
Armstrong, Br. Columbia 88 K e
Armstrong, Ontario 87 O a
Armyanskaya, U.S.S.R. 114 D d
Arnaud, Manitoba 87 U j
Arnaud, R., Quebec 81 M f
Arnauti, C., Cyprus 123 A b
Arnhem, C., Australia 134 G b
Arnhem, Netherlands 100 D c
Arnhem Ld., Australia 134 F b
Arni, India 126 E f
Árnissa, Greece 113 C d
Arno, I., Marshall Is 79 U c
Arno, R., Italy 110 C d
Arnot, Manitoba 87 V c
Arnöy, Norway 102 J a
Arnprior, Ontario 85 O g
Arnsberg, Germany 104 C c
Arnstadt, Germany 104 D c
Arnstein, Ontario 84 L g
Arntfield, Quebec 85 L d
Aroe Eiln. See Aru Kep
Arolla, Switzerland 101 C b
Aroostock Junc., N.B. 82 E g
Arosa, Switzerland 101 E b
Arpin, Ontario 84 K d
Arrah, India 127 F c
Arraias, Brazil 93 H f
Arran, Saskatchewan 87 Q g
Arrandale, Br. Columbia 88 E c
Arran I., Scotland 98 D e
Arras, France 108 E a
Arroba, Spain 106 C c
Arromanches, France 108 C b
Arronches, Portugal 106 B c
Arrow, L., Eire 99 B f
Arrowhead, Br. Columbia 88 L e
Arrow L., Lower, British Columbia 88 K f
Arrow L., Ontario 87 N b
Arrow L., Upper, British Columbia 88 L e
Arrow Park, Br. Columbia 88 K e
Arrowtown, New Zealand 135 P m
Arrowwood, Alberta 86 D h
Arroyito, Argentina 94 D d
Arroyo, Puerto Rico 54 C j
Arsenault L., Sask. 86 J c
Arsk, U.S.S.R. 117 J b
Árta, Greece 113 C e
Artawiya, Saudi Arabia 124 E d
Artemovsk, Ukraine, U.S.S.R. 116 K g
Artemovsk, U.S.S.R. 115 J c
Artemovskiy, U.S.S.R. 115 L c
Artemovskiy, U.S.S.R. 117 Q b
Artenay, France 108 D b
Arthabaska, Quebec 85 T f
Arthur, Ontario 84 K j
Arthur Pass, New Zealand 135 Q l
Artibonite, R., Haiti 91 E c
Artigas, Uruguay 94 E d
Artland, Saskatchewan 86 H f
Artois, prov., France 108 E a
Artvin, Turkey 124 D a
Aru, Congo 121 G d
Aruanã, Brazil 93 G f
Aruba, I., Caribbean 91 F d
Aruboe, Jaluit I. 79 T j
Aru Kep., Indonesia 129 K m
Arumá, Brazil 92 E d
Arume wan, Okinawa 78 C b
Aru Passage, Ponape I. 78 G o
Aruppukkottai, India 126 E g
Arusha, Tanzania 121 H e
Aru Tso, Tibet 127 F b
Arvida, Quebec 85 T d
Arvika, Sweden 103 E g
Arzamas, U.S.S.R. 117 F c
Arzew, Algeria 118 E a
Arzua, Spain 106 A a
Aš, Czechoslovakia 104 E c
Asahigawa, Japan 133 H c
Asan, Guam 78 A l
Åsarna, Sweden 102 F e
Asbestos, Quebec 85 T g
Ascensión, B. de la, Mexico 90 G d
Ascensión, Bolivia 92 E g
Ascensión I., Atlantic Ocean 120 A g
Asch, Belgium 100 D c
Aschaffenburg, Germany 104 C d
Ascoli, Italy 110 D d
Ascona, Switzerland 101 D b
Ascotán, Chile 94 C b
Aseda, Sweden 103 F h
Åsele, Sweden 102 G d
Åsen, Sweden 103 E f
Asenovgrad, Bulgaria 112 E d
Ash, Muscat & Oman 125 G e
Ashburton, New Zealand 135 Q l
Ashburton, R., Australia 134 C d
Ashcroft, Br. Columbia 88 J e
Ashdod, Israel 123 C f
Ashern, Manitoba 87 T g
Ashkhabad, Turkmen., U.S.S.R. 114 E e
Ashmont, Alberta 86 F d
Ashqelon, Israel 123 C f
Ash Shihr, S. Yemen 124 E g
Ashton, Ontario 85 O g
Ashuanipi, L., Quebec 81 N g
Ashuapmuchuan, R., Quebec 85 R c
Ashūrādehye Bozorg, Iran 125 F b
Asinara, I. & G. di, Sardinia 111 B e
Asino, U.S.S.R. 114 H c
Asir, Saudi Arabia 124 D f
Askersund, Sweden 103 F g
Askvoll, Norway 103 A f
Aslandus, Iran 124 E b
Asmara, Ethiopia 121 H a
Aspern, Austria 105 G d
Aspinaje, Brazil 93 H f
Aspiring, Mt., New Zealand 135 P m
Aspres-sur-Buëch, France 109 F d
Aspro, C., Cyprus 123 A c
Aspy B., C. Breton I., N.S. 83 M g
Asquith, Saskatchewan 86 K f
Assab, Ethiopia 121 J b
As Safa, Saudi Arabia 124 E d
Assal, L., Fr. Somaliland 121 J b
Assam, India 127 H c
As Sauda, Yemen 124 D f
Assaye, India 126 E d
Assche, Belgium 100 C d
Assean L., Manitoba 87 V b
Assen, Netherlands 100 E a
Asshur, Iraq 124 D b
Assigny, L., Quebec 82 G b
Assiniboia, Saskatchewan 87 M j
Assiniboine, Mt., British Columbia-Alberta 88 M e
Assiniboine R., Manitoba-Saskatchewan 87 T j
Assinica L., Quebec 85 P b
Assisi, Italy 110 D d
Assumar, Portugal 106 B c
Assumption, Alberta 88 K a
Asten, Netherlands 100 D c
Asti, Italy 110 B c
Astipálaia, I., Greece 113 F f
Astorga, Spain 106 B a
Astorville, Ontario 85 L f
Astrakhan, U.S.S.R. 114 D d
Asträsk, Sweden 102 H d
Astros, Greece 113 D f
Astudillo, Spain 106 C a
Asunción, Paraguay 94 E c
Aswan, Egypt 119 M d
Aswan High Dam, Egypt 119 M d
Asyût, Egypt 119 M c
Atacama Des., Chile 94 C b
Atafu, I., Pacific Ocean 78 J h
Atakpame, Togo 118 F g
Atalaia, Brazil 93 K e
Atalèh, Somali Rep. 121 K d
Atalándi, Greece 113 D e
Atambua, Timor I., Indon. 129 H m
Atar, Mauritania 118 C d
Atara, Yemen 124 E g
Ataran, R., Burma 127 J e
Atasu, Kazakh., U.S.S.R. 117 G d
Atauba, Brazil 92 E d
Atbara, Sudan 119 M e
Atbasar, Kazakh., U.S.S.R 114 F c
Ateca, Spain 107 E b
Ath, Belgium 100 B d
Athabasca, Alberta 86 D d
Athabasca, L., Alberta-Sask. 80 J f
Athabasca, R., Alberta 88 O b
Athapap, Manitoba 87 Q d
Athapapuskow L., Man. 87 Q d
Athboy, Eire 99 C g
Athenry, Eire 99 B g
Athens, Greece 113 D f
Athens, Ontario 85 P h
Atherley, Ontario 85 L h
Atherton, Australia 135 H c
Atherton Plat., Australia 135 H c
Athínai. See Athens
Athlone, Eire 99 B g
Athna, Cyprus 123 B b
Athy, Eire 99 C h
Atico, Peru 92 C g
Aticonipi L., Quebec 83 N b
Atienza, Spain 106 D b
Atik, Manitoba 87 Q d
Atikameg, Alberta 86 B c
Atikameg L., Manitoba 87 Q d
Atikokan, Ontario 86 L b
Atikonak L., Labrador 82 H a
Atikwa L., Ontario 86 J j
Atiu, I., Cook Is. 79 L j
Atka, I., Aleutian Is. 78 J b
Atka, U.S.S.R. 115 Q b
Atkarsk, U.S.S.R. 117 G e
Atkinson, Pt., Br. Columbia 88 C f
Atlee, Alberta 86 G h
Atlin & L., Br. Columbia 77 V g
Atlit, Israel 123 C e
Atnarko, Br. Columbia 88 G d
Atsuta, Japan 133 E g
Atsuta, Okinawa 78 B b
Atsuta, Okinawa 78 B c
Attawapiskat, Ontario 81 L g
Attawapiskat, R., Ontario 81 L g
Attiki, Greece 113 D e
Attu, I., Aleutian Is. 78 H b
Atukesi, Japan 133 J c
Atulom I., Guam 78 A l
Atupi, Brazil 93 G c
Atwater, Saskatchewan 87 P h
Atwood, Ontario 84 J j
Aua, Tutuila I. 79 U o
Auati Paraná, Brazil 92 D d
Aube, dep., France 108 F b
Aubel, Belgium 100 D d
Aubenas, France 109 F d
Aubonne, Switzerland 101 B b
Aubusson, France 108 E d
Auce, Latvia, U.S.S.R. 103 K h
Auch, France 109 D e
Auckland, New Zealand 135 R k
Auckland Is., Pacific Ocean 78 H m
Aude, dep., France 109 E e
Audegle, Somali Republic 121 J d
Auden, Ontario 84 C b
Audenarde, Belgium 100 B d
Audierne, B. d', France 108 A c
Aufa, Lebanon 123 D f
Augathella, Australia 135 J e
Augsburg, Germany 104 D d
Augulpelu Reef, Palau Is. 78 C n
Augusta, Sicily 111 E g
Augustów, Poland 105 K b
Augustus, Mt., Australia 134 C d
Auletta, Italy 111 E e
Aulneau Pen., Ontario 86 H a
Aulong, Palau Is. 78 A n
Aunis, prov., France 108 C c
Aunu'u, Tutuila I. 79 U o
Aur, I., Marshall Is. 79 U b
Aura, Finland 103 K f
Aurangabad, India 126 D e
Auray, France 108 B c
Aurillac, France 109 E d
Aurora, Ontario 85 L j
Aus, S.W. Africa 122 B e
Austin, L., Australia 134 C e
Australia 134-135
Australian Alps, Australia 135 J g
Australian Claim, Antarctica 136 A d
Austria, Central Europe 104 F e
Auteuil, L. d', Quebec 83 L c
Authier, Quebec 85 M d
Autlán, Mexico 90 D d
Autse. See Auce
Autun, France 108 F c
Auvergne, prov., France 109 E d
Auxerre, France 108 E c
Aux Sources, Mt., Lesotho 122 D e
Ava, Burma 127 J d
Avallon, France 108 E c
Avalon Pen., Newfoundland 83 T f
Avanoas, S.W. Africa 122 A c
Avaré, Brazil 93 H h
Avaviken, Sweden 102 H d
Aveiro, Brazil 93 G d
Aveiro, Portugal 106 A b
Avelghem, Belgium 100 B d
Avellanada, Argentina 94 E d
Avellino, Italy 111 E e
Avenir, French Guiana 93 G c
Averöy, Norway 102 B e
Aversa, Italy 111 E e
Avesnes, France 108 E a
Avesta, Sweden 103 G f
Aveyron, dep., France 109 E d
Avezzano, Italy 111 D e
Aviá Teria, Argentina 94 D c
Aviation I., Palmyra I. 79 U k
Aviemore, Scotland 98 E c
Avigliano, Italy 111 E e
Avignon, France 109 F e
Ávila, Spain 106 C b
Aviz, Portugal 106 B c
Avola, Br. Columbia 88 K e
Avola, Sicily 111 E g
Avonlea, Saskatchewan 87 M h
Avranches, France 108 C b
Awa, Okinawa 78 B b
Awaji Shima, Japan 133 D g
Awe, L., Scotland 98 D d
Awusa, L., Ethiopia 121 H c
Axat, France 109 E e
Axel, Netherlands 100 B c
Axel Heiberg Glacier, Antarctica 136 D b
Axel Heiberg I., N.-W. Terr. 81 K a
Axinim, Brazil 92 F d
Axios, R. See Vardar, R.
Axminster, England 99 E k
Ayabaca, Peru 92 B d
Ayacucho, Argentina 94 E e
Ayacucho, Peru 92 C f
Ayaguz, Kazakh., U.S.S.R. 114 H d
Ayamonte, Spain 106 B d
Ayan, U.S.S.R. 115 N c
Ayancik, Turkey 124 B a
Ayaviri, Peru 92 C f
Aydin, Turkey 124 A b
Ayerbe, Spain 107 E a
Ayia, Greece 113 D e
Ayion Oros, Greece 113 E d
Áyios Evstrátios, Greece 113 E e
Aykathonisi, Greece 113 F f
Aylen L., Ontario 85 N g
Aylesbury, England 99 G j
Aylesbury, Saskatchewan 87 M h
Aylesford, Nova Scotia 82 H h
Aylmer, Mt., Alberta 86 B g
Aylmer, Ontario 84 K k
Aylmer, Quebec 85 P g
Aylsham, Saskatchewan 87 O e
Aylwin, Quebec 85 O g
Ayon, Ostrov, U.S.S.R. 115 R a
Ayora, Spain 107 E c
Ayr, Australia 135 J c
Ayr & R., Scotland 98 D e
Ayr, co., Scotland 98 D e
Ayun, Saudi Arabia 124 D d
Ayutla, Guatemala 90 F e
Ayutla, Mexico 90 E d
Ayvalik, Turkey 124 A b
Aywaille, Belgium 100 D d
Azaila, Spain 107 E b
Azama, Okinawa 78 B c
Azamgarh, India 127 F c
Azare, Nigeria 119 H f
Azaz, Syria 123 F a
Azerbaijan. See Azerbaydzhanskaya
Azerbaydzhanskaya, U.S.S.R. 114 D d
Azogues, Ecuador 92 B d
Azores Is., Atlantic Ocean 118 A a
Azov, Sea of, U.S.S.R. 116 K j
Azpeitia, Spain 109 B e
Azua, Dom. Rep. 91 E c
Azuaga, Spain 106 C c
Azufre, Mt., Chile 94 C c
Azul, Argentina 95 E e
Azzan, S. Yemen 124 E g
Az Zubayr, Iraq 124 E c
Baalbek, Lebanon 123 E c
Baarle Nassau, Netherlands 100 C c
Baarn, Netherlands 100 D b
Babahoya, Ecuador 92 B d
Babar, I., Indonesia 129 J m
Babati, Tanzania 121 H e
Babe I., Guam 78 A l
Bab el Mandeb, Red Sea 121 J b
Babelthuap, Palau Is. 78 B m
Babenna, Syria 123 E b
Babine, Br. Columbia 88 F c
Babine, R., Br. Columbia 88 F c
Babine L., Br. Columbia 88 G c
Babine Ra., Br. Columbia 88 F c
Babol, Iran 125 F b
Babura, Nigeria 120 B b
Babuyan Is., Philippines 128 H g
Babylon, Iraq 124 D c
Bacabal, Brazil 93 F e
Bacadehuachi, Mexico 90 C b
Bacalar, Mexico 90 G d
Bacău, Romania 112 F a
Baccaro Pt., Nova Scotia 82 G k
Bacerac, Mexico 90 C a
Bache Pen., N.-W. Terr. 81 M b
Bačka Topola, Yugoslavia 112 B b
Bäckefors, Sweden 103 E g
Backergunge, East Pakistan 127 H d
Bac Lieu, S. Vietnam 132 D e
Bac-Ninh, N. Vietnam 132 D b
Bacoachic, Mexico 90 C a
Bacolod, Philippines 129 H h
Bada, Saudi Arabia 124 C d
Badajos, Brazil 93 H d
Badajoz, Spain 106 B c
Badalona, Spain 107 G b
Badarma, U.S.S.R. 115 K c
Badas, Brunei 129 F k
Baddeck, C. Breton I., N.S. 83 M g
Baden, Germany 104 C d
Baden, Manitoba 87 Q f
Baden, Switzerland 101 D a
Baden-Baden, Germany 104 C d
Badger, Manitoba 86 F a
Badger, Newfoundland 83 Q e
Badia, Saudi Arabia 124 E e
Badin, Pakistan 126 C d
Bad Ischl, Austria 104 E e
Badiya, Muscat & Oman 125 G e
Bad Kissingen, Germany 104 D c
Badon, Senegal 118 C f
Badrinath, India 126 E b
Baduen, Somali Republic 121 K c
Badulla, Ceylon 126 F g
Baelen, Belgium 100 D c
Baena, Spain 106 C d
Baerle-Duc, Belgium 100 C c
Baetas, Brazil 92 E e
Baffin B., Greenland-Canada 81 M c
Baffin I., N.-W. Terr. 81 L c
Bafia, Cameroon 119 H h
Bafoulabé, Mali 118 C f
Baf'q, Iran 125 G c
Bafra, Turkey 124 C a
Bafra Br., Turkey 124 C a
Baft, Iran 125 G d
Bafwasende, Congo 120 F d
Bagata, Congo 120 D e
Bagawala, India 126 D b
Bagé, Brazil 94 F d
Baghdad, Iraq 124 D c
Baghin, Iran 125 G c
Bagnara Calabra, Italy 111 E f
Bagnols-sur-Cèze, France 109 F d
Bagotville, Quebec 82 B e
Baguio, Philippines 129 H g
Bahaar-i-Gaz, Iran 125 F b
Bahama I., Grand, Bahama Is. 91 D a
Bahama Is., West Indies 91 D b
Baheri, India 126 D c
Bahía. See Salvador
Bahía Blanca, Argentina 95 D e
Bahía Choco, Colombia 92 B c
Bahía de Caráquez, Ecuador 92 A d
Bahia Laulau, Saipan-Tinian Is 78 B e
Bahía Laura, Argentina 95 C g
Bahía Negra, Paraguay 92 E g
Bahrain I., Persian Gulf 125 F d
Bahret el Ateibe, Syria 123 E d
Bahret el Hijane, Syria 123 E d
Bahret Homs, Syria 123 E c
Bahu Kalat, Iran 125 H d
Baiao, Brazil 93 H d
Baibokoum, Chad 119 J g
Baie Carrière, Quebec 85 N e
Baie Comeau, Quebec 82 D d
Baie-du-Milieu, Quebec 83 P b
Baie du Vin, New Brunswick 82 G f
Baie Johan Beetz, Quebec 82 K c
Baie Ste. Catherine, Quebec 82 C e
Baie Ste. Clair, Anticosti I., Quebec 82 H d
Baie St. Paul, Quebec 82 B f
Baie-Trinité, Quebec 82 E d
Baie Verte, Newfoundland 83 Q d
Baiji, Iraq 124 D c
Baile-Átha-Cliath. See Dublin
Bailen, Spain 106 D c
Baillie Hamilton I., North-West Territories 81 K b
Baillieu Pk., Antarctica 136 Q e
Baimak Tanalykovo, U.S.S.R. 117 N d
Bairnsdale, Australia 135 J g
Baital Faqih, Yemen 124 D g
Baixo Longa, Angola 122 B c
Baja, Hungary 112 B a
Baja California, state, Mex. 90 B b
Baján, Mexico 90 D b
Bajmok, Yugoslavia 112 B b
Bakal, U.S.S.R. 116 H j
Bakaly, U.S.S.R. 117 L c
Bakel, Senegal 118 C f
Baker Foreland, N.-W. Terr. 81 K e
Baker I., Pacific Ocean 78 J g
Baker L., N.-W. Terr. 81 K e
Baker Lake, N.-W. Terr 81 K e
Bakhasar, India 126 D d
Baklansk, U.S.S.R. 117 S c
Bako, Ethiopia 121 H c
Bakonyerdo, Hungary 105 G e
Baksa Duar, India 127 H c
Baku, Azerbai., U.S.S.R. 114 D d
Bala, Ontario 85 L g
Bala, Wales 99 E h
Balabac Str., Philippines 129 G j
Balabat, Yap I. 78 D m
Balagnat, India 126 F d
Balakhta, U.S.S.R. 115 J c
Balaklava, U.S.S.R. 116 H j
Balakleya, Ukraine, U.S.S.R. 116 K g
Balama, Mozambique 121 H g
Bala Murghab, Afghanistan 125 H b
Balancán, Mexico 90 F d
Balaquer, Spain 107 F b
Balashov, U.S.S.R. 117 F e
Balasore, India 127 G d
Balat, Egypt 119 L c
Balaton, L., Hungary 105 G e
Balazote, Spain 107 D c
Balboa, Panama 89 D e
Balbriggan, Eire 99 C g
Balcarce, Argentina 95 E e
Balcarres, Saskatchewan 87 O h
Balchik, Bulgaria 112 G c
Balclutha, New Zealand 135 P m
Baldock L., Manitoba 87 T b
Baldwinton, Saskatchewan 86 H f
Baldy Mt., Manitoba 87 R g
Baleares, Is., Medit. Sea 107 G c
Balearic Is. See Baleares
Baler, Philippines 129 H g
Balestrand, Norway 103 B f
Baley, U.S.S.R. 115 L c
Balfour, Br. Columbia 88 L f
Balgonie, Saskatchewan 87 N h
Bali, I., Indonesia 129 F m
Balikesir, Turkey 124 A b
Balikpapan, Borneo 129 G l
Baljennie, Saskatchewan 86 K f
Balk, Netherlands 100 D b
Balkans, The, Europe 112
Balkhash & Oz., Kazakh., U.S.S.R. 114 G d
Ball, Mt., Alberta 86 B h
Ballachulish, Scotland 98 D d
Balladonia, Australia 134 D f
Ballaghaderreen, Eire 99 B g
Ballantrae, Scotland 98 D e
Ballantyne Str., N.-W. Terr. 86 H b
Ballarat, Australia 135 H g
Ballater, Scotland 98 E c
Ballé, Mali 118 D e
Ballenas, B. de, Mexico 90 B b
Ballenas Channel, Mexico 90 B b
Balleny Is., Antarctica 136 B e
Ballina, Eire 99 A f
Ballinasloe, Eire 99 B g
Ballinrobe, Eire 99 A g
Ballinskelligs B., Eire 99 A j

Ball's Pyramid, Tasman Sea 78 G l
Ballycastle, N. Ireland 98 C e
Ballymahon, Eire 99 B g
Ballymena, N. Ireland 99 C f
Ballymoney, N. Ireland 98 C e
Ballyshannon, Eire 99 B f
Balmoral, Manitoba 87 U h
Balombo, Angola 120 C g
Balotra, India 126 D c
Balranald, Australia 135 H f
Balsaa, Brazil 93 H e
Balsam L., Ontario 85 M h
Balta, Ukraine, U.S.S.R. 116 F h
Baltanás, Spain 106 C b
Baltasar Brum, Uruguay 94 E d
Baltic Sea, N.-W. Europe 103
Baltim, Egypt 119 M b
Baltimore, Eire 99 A j
Baltistan, Kashmir 126 E a
Baltiysk, U.S.S.R. 103 H j
Baluchistan, Pakistan 126 B c
Balzac, Alberta 86 D g
Bam, Iran 125 G d
Bama, Nigeria 119 H f
Bamako, Mali 118 D f
Bambari, Cent. Afr. Rep 119 K g
Bamberg, Germany 104 D d
Bambuí, Brazil 93 H h
Bamenda, Cameroon 119 G g
Bamfield, Br. Columbia 88 G f
Bamian, Afghanistan 125 J c
Bampton, England 99 E k
Bampur, Iran 125 H d
Bam Tso, Tibet 127 D c
Banat, Romania 112 C b
Banayyan, Saudi Arabia 125 F e
Banbury, England 99 G h
Banchory, Scotland 98 F c
Bancroft, Ontario 88 N g
Bancroft, Zambia 122 D b
Banda Beila, Somali Republic 121 L c
Banda Sea, Indonesia 129 J m
Bandar Abbas, Iran 125 G d
Bandarawela, Ceylon 126 F g
Bandar e Deylam, Iran 125 F c
Bandar e Lengeh, Iran 125 F d
Bandar e Pahlavi, Iran 124 E b
Bandar e Rig, Iran 125 F d
Bandar e Shapur, Iran 124 E c
Bandar Shah, Iran 125 F b
Bandera, Argentina 94 D c
Banderas, B., Mexico 90 C c
Bandiagara, Mali 118 E f
Bandikui, India 126 E c
Band-i-Qir, Iran 124 E c
Bandirma, Turkey 124 A a
Bandjarmasin, Borneo 129 F l
Bandol, France 109 F e
Bandon, Eire 99 B j
Bandung, Java 129 E m
Baneh, Iran 124 E b
Banes, Cuba 91 D b
Banff, Alberta 88 M e
Banff & co., Scotland 98 F c
Banff Nat. Park, Alberta 88 L e
Bangada, Congo 121 F d
Bangalore, India 126 E f
Banganga R., India 126 E c
Bangassou, Cent. Afr. Rep. 119 K h
Bangka, I., Indonesia 129 E l
Bangkok, Bight of, Thailand 132 C d
Bangkok, Thailand 129 D h
Bang Mun Nak, Thailand 129 D g
Bangor, N. Ireland 99 D f
Bangor, Saskatchewan 87 P h
Bangor, Wales 99 E g
Bang Saphan Yai, Thailand 132 B d
Bangui, Cent. Afr. Rep. 119 J h
Bangweulu L., Zambia 121 G g
Ban Houei Sai, Laos 132 C b
Bania, Cent. Afr. Rep. 120 D d
Bani Bu 'Ali, Muscat & Oman 125 G e
Banica, Dom. Rep. 91 E c
Baniyas, Syria 123 D b
Baniyas, Syria 123 D d
Banjak Kep., Indonesia 129 C k
Banja Luka, Yugoslavia 110 F c
Banji, India 126 D a
Banjuwangi, Java 129 F m
Banki, India 127 G d
Banks I., Australia 135 H b
Banks I., Br. Columbia 88 D d
Banks I., N.-W. Terr. 89 G c
Banks I., Pacific Ocean 78 G j
Banks Pen., New Zealand 135 Q l
Banks Str., Tasmania 135 J h
Bankura, India 127 G d
Banningville. See Bundundu
Bannockburn, Ontario 83 N h
Bann R., N. Ireland 99 C f
Bañolas, Spain 107 G a
Baños de Montemayor, Spain 106 B b
Banova Jaruga, Yugoslavia 110 F c
Ban-pot, Thailand 132 B c
Bansda, India 126 D d
Banswara, India 126 D d
Ban Thakham, Thailand 132 B e
Ban tha U, Thailand 132 C c
Bantry & B., Eire 99 A j
Banu, Afghanistan 125 J b
Banyo, Cameroon 119 H g
Banzare Coast, Antarctica 136 T e
Banzyville, Congo 120 E d
Bapaume, France 108 E a
Baptiste, Ontario 85 M g
Baq'a, Saudi Arabia 124 D d
Ba'quba, Iraq 124 D c
Bar, Yugoslavia 112 B c
Bara, Sudan 119 M f
Barabinsk, U.S.S.R. 114 G c
Barachois, Quebec 82 H e
Baracoa, Cuba 91 E b
Barad, Syria 123 F b
Barahona, Dom. Rep. 107 D b
Barahona, Spain 91 E c
Barail Ra., India 127 H c
Barak, R., India 127 H d
Bara Lacha Pass, Kashmir 126 E b
Baranovichi, U.S.S.R. 116 E e
Baranów Sandomierski, Poland 105 J c
Barbacena, Brazil 93 J h
Barbacoas, Colombia 92 B c
Barbadillo del Mercada, Sp. 106 D a
Barbados, I., Windward Is. 91 H d
Barbara L., Ontario 84 C c
Barbastro, Spain 107 F a
Barbel, L., Quebec 82 D b
Barbezieux, France 108 C d
Barbuda, I., Leeward Is. 91 G c
Barca d'Alva, Portugal 106 B b
Barcaldine, Australia 135 J d
Barcarrota, Spain 106 B c
Barce. See Marj, el
Barcellona Pozza di Gotto, Sicily 111 E f
Barcelona, Spain 107 G b
Barcelona, Venezuela 92 E a
Barceloneta, Puerto Rico 54 C h
Barcelonnette, France 109 G d
Barcelos, Brazil 92 E d
Barcelos, Portugal 106 A b
Barco de Avila, el, Spain 106 C b
Barcoo, R., Australia 135 H d
Bardera, Somali Republic 121 J d
Bardia, Libya 119 L b
Bardoux, L., Quebec 82 E b
Bardsey, I., Wales 99 D h
Bareilly, India 126 E c
Barentsöya, I., Arctic Ocean 114 B a
Barents Sea, Arctic Ocean 114 B a
Bargal, Somali Republic 121 L b
Barge Bay, Labrador 83 Q b
Barhaj, India 127 F c
Bari, India 126 E c
Bari, Italy 111 F e
Bari Doab, Pakistan 126 D b
Barinas, Venezuela 92 C b
Barisal, East Pakistan 127 G d
Barito, R., Borneo 129 F l
Barkald, Norway 103 D f
Barkerville, Br. Columbia 88 J d
Bark L., Ontario 84 H f
Barkley Mt., Antarctica 136 M d
Barkly Tableland, Australia 134 G c
Bârlad, Romania 112 F a
Bar-le-Duc, France 108 F b
Barlee L., Australia 135 C e
Barlee Ra., Australia 135 C d
Barletta, Italy 111 F e
Barmer, India 126 D c
Barmouth, Wales 99 E h
Barnaby River, N.B. 82 G g
Barnard Castle, England 99 F f
Barnaul, U.S.S.R. 114 H c
Barne Inlet, Antarctica 136 A b
Barnes Icecap, N.-W. Terr. 81 M c
Barnet, Br. Columbia 88 D f
Barneveld, Netherlands 100 D b
Barn Mt., Quebec 82 F e
Barnsley, England 99 G g
Barnstaple, England 99 E j
Barnum B., Palau Is. 78 A o
Barnwell, Alberta 86 E j
Baroda, India 126 D d
Barons, Alberta 86 D j
Barotseland, Zambia 122 C c
Barpeta, India 127 H c
Barquinha, Portugal 106 A c
Barquisimeto, Venezuela 92 D a
Barra, Brazil 93 J f
Barra, I., Scotland 98 C d
Barra, Saudi Arabia 124 E e
Barra, Sd. of, Scotland 98 B c
Barrackpore, India 127 G d
Barra do Bugres, Brazil 92 F f
Barra do Corda, Brazil 93 H e
Barra do Pirai, Brazil 93 J h
Barra Hd., Scotland 98 B d
Barra Mansa, Brazil 93 J h
Bâran, Somali Republic 121 K b
Barranca, Peru 92 B d
Barranca Bermeja, Colombia 92 C b
Barrancas, Venezuela 92 E b
Barrancos, Portugal 106 B c
Barranqueras, Argentina 94 E c
Barranquilla, Colombia 92 C a
Barraute, Quebec 85 N d
Barreiras, Brazil 93 J f
Barreirinha, Brazil 93 F d
Barreirinhas, Brazil 93 J d
Barreiro, Portugal 106 A c
Barreiros, Brazil 93 K e
Barrême, France 109 G e
Barren I., Palmyra I. 79 U k
Barrhead, Alberta 86 C d
Barrie, Ontario 85 L h
Barrie I., Ontario 84 H f
Barrière, Br. Columbia 88 J e
Barrier I., Great, N.Z. 135 R k
Barrier I., Little, N.Z. 135 R k
Barrington, Mt., Australia 135 K f
Barrington, Nova Scotia 82 G k
Barrington L., Manitoba 87 R a
Barrington Passage, N.S 82 G k
Barringun, Australia 135 J e
Barrow, Argentina 95 D e
Barrow, England 99 E f
Barrow Creek, Australia 134 F d
Barrow R., Eire 99 C h
Barrows, Manitoba 87 Q f
Barrow Str., N.-W. Terr. 81 K c
Barr Smith, Mt., Antarctica 136 R e
Barry, Wales 99 E j
Barrys Bay, Ontario 85 N g
Barsaloi, Kenya 121 H d
Barsi, India 126 E e
Bar-sur-Aube, France 108 F b
Bar-sur-Seine, France 108 F b
Bartibog, New Brunswick 82 G f
Bartica, Guyana 92 F b
Bartle Frere Mt., Australia 135 H c
Bartlett's Harbour, Newfoundland 83 P c
Bartoville, Quebec 85 N d
Baruva, India 127 F e
Barvaux, Belgium 100 D d
Barwani, India 126 E d
Barwick, Ontario 80 H b
Barwon, R., Australia 135 J e
Basel (Basle), Switzerland 101 C a
Baselland, canton, Switz. 101 C a
Bashaw, Alberta 86 E f
Bashi, Iran 125 F d
Bashi Chan., Phil.-Taiwan 131 K m
Bashkirskaya, U.S.S.R. 114 E c
Basilan, I., Philippines 129 H j
Basilicata, reg., Italy 111 E e
Basingstoke, England 99 G j
Basin L., Saskatchewan 87 M f
Baskatong Res., Quebec 85 P f
Basle. See Basel
Båsmo, Norway 102 F c
Basongo, Congo 120 E e
Basra, Iraq 124 E c
Bas-Rhin, dep., France 108 G b
Bassac, Laos 132 D d
Bassano, Alberta 86 E h
Bassein, Burma 127 H e
Bassein, India 126 D e
Basses, Gt. & Lit., Ceylon 126 F g
Basses-Alpes, dep., France 109 G d
Basses-Pyrénées, dep., Fr. 109 C e
Basse Terre, Leeward Is. 91 G c
Bassevelde, Belgium 100 B c
Bass River, Nova Scotia 82 J h
Bass Str., Australia 135 J g
Basswood, Manitoba 87 R h
Basswood L., Minn.-Ont. 86 L b
Båstad, Sweden 103 E h
Bastak, Iran 125 F d
Baştam, Iran 125 G b
Bastia, Corsica 110 B d
Bastille, L., Quebec 82 L b
Bastogne, Belgium 100 D e
Basutoland. See Lesotho
Bata, Rio Muni, Sp. Guinea 120 B d
Bataan, Philippines 129 H h
Batacosta, Mexico 90 C b
Batalha, Portugal 106 A c
Batangas, Philippines 129 H h
Batan Is., Philippines 128 H f
Batavia, Argentina 94 C d
Batavia. See Djakarta
Bataysk, U.S.S.R. 117 D g
Batchawana, Ontario 84 F f
Batchelor, Australia 134 F b
Bateman, Saskatchewan 86 L j
Baten, Okinawa 78 A c
Batenburg, Netherlands 100 D c
Bath, England 99 F j
Bath, New Brunswick 82 E g
Bathurst, Australia 135 J f
Bathurst, Gambia 118 B f
Bathurst, New Brunswick 82 G f
Bathurst I., Australia 134 E b
Bathurst I., N.-W. Terr. 80 J b
Batie, Upper Volta 118 E g
Batiscan, L., Quebec 85 T e
Batiscan, Quebec 85 S f
Batjan, I., Indonesia 129 J l
Batna, Algeria 118 G a
Batoche, Saskatchewan 87 L f
Batopilas, Mexico 90 C b
Batraki, U.S.S.R. 117 J d
Batrun, Lebanon 123 D c
Battambang, Cambodia 132 C d
Batterbee Mts., Antarctica 136 H d
Batticaloa, Ceylon 126 F g
Battice, Belgium 100 D d
Battih, S. Yemen 124 E f
Battle Creek, Saskatchewan 86 H j
Battleford, Saskatchewan 86 J f
Battle Harbour, Labrador 83 R a
Battle R., Alberta 86 F f
Battrum, Saskatchewan 86 J h
Batu, Indonesia 129 C l
Batumi, U.S.S.R. 114 D d
Baturadja, Sumatra 129 D l
Baturite, Brazil 93 K d
Baubau, Celebes 129 H m
Bauchi, Nigeria 119 G f
Baud, India 127 F d
Baudó, Colombia 92 B b
Baudouinville, Congo 121 F f
Bauge, France 108 C c
Bauld, C., Newfoundland 83 R b
Baunt, U.S.S.R. 115 L c
Baures, Bolivia 92 E f
Baurú, Brazil 94 G b
Baús, Brazil 93 G g
Bauska, Latvia, U.S.S.R. 103 L h
Bautzen, Germany 104 F c
Bavaria. See Bayern
Bavispe, Mexico 90 C a
Baweah, I., Indonesia 129 F m
Bawiti, Egypt 119 L c
Bawk, Ontario 84 D c
Bawku, Ghana 118 E f
Bawlf, Alberta 86 E f
Bayamo, Cuba 91 D b
Bayamón, Puerto Rico 54 C h
Bayan Aul, Kazakh., U.S.S.R. 114 G c
Bayan Dzurihe, Mongolia 128 E a
Bayan Kara Shan, China 128 C d
Bay Bulls, Newfoundland 83 T f
Bayburt, Turkey 124 D a
Baydaratskaya B., U.S.S.R. 114 F a
Bay de Verde, Nfd. 83 T e
Bay du Nord, Nfd. 83 R f
Bayern, Germany 104 D d
Bayeux, France 108 C b
Bayfield, Ontario 84 J j
Bayfield I., Quebec 83 O b
Bayfield Mt., Quebec 82 F e
Bayir, Jordan 123 E g
Bay Is., Honduras 91 B c
Baykal, Oz., U.S.S.R. 115 K c
Baykit, U.S.S.R. 115 J b
Baykonur, Kazakh., U.S.S.R. 114 F d
Bay L'Argent, Nfd. 83 S f
Bayona, Spain 106 A a
Bayonne, France 109 C e
Bayovar, Peru 92 A e
Bay Pt., Br. Columbia 88 F e
Bayram Ali, Turkmen., U.S.S.R. 114 F e
Bayreuth, Germany 104 D d
Bayrischer Wald, Germany 104 E d
Bay Roberts, Newfoundland 83 T f
Bays, L. of, Ontario 85 L g
Baysville, Ontario 85 L g
Baytag Bogdo, China 128 B b
Baza, Sa. de, Spain 107 D d
Bazaruto, I., Mozambique 122 F d
Bazas, France 109 C d
Bazias, Romania 112 C b
Bazin, R., Quebec 85 Q e
Bazman, Iran 125 H d
Beachburg, Ontario 85 O g
Beach Grove, Br. Columbia 88 D g
Beachport, Australia 134 G g
Beachy Head, England 99 H k
Beacon Hill, Saskatchewan 86 H d
Beale, C., Vancouver I., British Columbia 88 G f
Beal Ra., Australia 135 H e
Beamsville, Ontario 85 L j
Beardmore, Ontario 84 C c
Beardmore Gl., Antarctica 136 B b
Bear Head, Anticosti I., Quebec 83 K d
Bear Hills, The, Sask. 86 J g
Bear I., Antarctica 136 F d
Bear I., James B., N.-W.Terr. 81 L g
Bear Is. See Medvezhi Osa.
Bear Island, Ontario 84 K f
Bear L., Manitoba 87 V c
Bear Lake, Br. Columbia 88 F b
Béarn, prov., France 109 C e
Béarn, Quebec 85 L e
Béarn, Quebec 85 M d
Bear River, Nova Scotia 82 G j
Bearskin Lake, Ontario 81 K g
Beata, I., Dom. Rep. 91 E c
Beatenberg, Switzerland 101 C b
Beatton R., Br. Columbia 88 J b
Beatton River, Br. Columbia 88 J b
Beatty, Saskatchewan 87 N f
Beattyville, Quebec 85 N d
Beaucanton, Quebec 85 L c
Beauceville, Quebec 82 B g
Beauchêne, L., Quebec 85 M f
Beaudry, Quebec 85 L d
Beaufort Basin, Arctic Ocean 89 A b
Beaufort I., Antarctica 136 B c
Beaufort Sea, North-West Territories, etc. 86 E c
Beaufort West, S. Africa 122 C f
Beaugency, France 108 D c
Beauharnois, Quebec 85 R g
Beauharnois Power Can., Quebec 85 Q g
Beauly, Scotland 98 D c
Beaumont, Belgium 100 C d
Beaumont, France 108 E b
Beaumont, Newfoundland 83 R d
Beaumont B., Antarctica 136 B b
Beaune, France 108 F c
Beauport, Quebec 85 T a
Beauraing, Belgium 100 C d
Beauséjour, Manitoba 87 V h
Beauvais, France 108 E b
Beauvais Lake Prov. Park, Alberta 86 C j
Beauval, Saskatchewan 86 K c
Beauvallon, Alberta 86 F e
Beauvoir-sur-Mer, France 108 B c
Beaver Bank, Nova Scotia 82 J j
Beaver Brook, New Brunswick 82 G j
Beaverdell, Br. Columbia 88 K f
Beaverhill L., Alberta 86 E e
Beaver Island L., Quebec 83 O b
Beaverlodge, Alberta 88 K c
Beavermouth, Br. Columbia 88 L e
Beaver R., Alberta 86 F d
Beaver R., Saskatchewan 86 K d
Beaverton, Ontario 85 L h
Beawar, India 126 D c
Beazley, Argentina 94 C d
Bebedouro, Brazil 93 H h
Bečej, Yugoslavia 112 B b
Becerrea, Spain 106 B a
Bechuanaland. See Botswana, Republic of
Becleau, Romania 105 L e
Bedak, Afghanistan 125 J c
Bédar, Spain 107 E d
Bede, Manitoba 87 R j
Bedford, Nova Scotia 82 J j
Bedford, Quebec 85 S g
Bedford & co., England 99 G h
Bedourie, Australia 134 G d
Bedretto, Switzerland 101 D b
Bedr Honein, Saudi Arabia 124 E c
Bedzin, Poland 105 H c
Beechwood Hydro-Electric Sta., New Brunswick 82 E f
Beechy, Saskatchewan 86 K h
Beek, Netherlands 100 D c
Beek, Netherlands 100 D d
Beekbergen, Netherlands 100 D b
Beeringen, Belgium 100 D c
Beerlegem, Belgium 100 B d
Beer Menuha, Israel 123 D g
Beernem, Belgium 100 B c
Beers, Netherlands 100 D c
Beersheba, Israel 123 C f
Befale, Congo 120 E d
Befandriana, Mal. Rep. 121 N k
Bega, Australia 135 K g
Bégin, Quebec 85 T d
Behbehan, Iran 125 F c
Beho, Belgium 100 D d
Beidha, Saudi Arabia 124 C e
Beilen, Netherlands 100 E b
Beilul, Ethiopia 121 J b
Beinwil, Switzerland 101 D a
Beira, Mozambique 122 F c
Beirût (Beyrouth), Lebanon 123 D d
Beiseker, Alberta 86 D g
Beitbridge, Rhodesia 122 E d
Beit-et-Din, Lebanon 123 D d
Beius, Romania 112 D a
Beja, Portugal 106 B c
Bejaia (Bougie), Algeria 109 P h
Béjar, Spain 106 C b
Bejestan, Iran 125 G c
Bejucal, Cuba 91 C b
Békéscsaba, Hungary 105 J e
Bela, Pakistan 126 C c
Beland, Celebes 129 H k
Bélanger Pt., Manitoba 87 U e
Bélanger R., Manitoba 87 U e
Bela Palanka, Yugoslavia 112 D c
Belaya Tserkov, Ukraine, U.S.S.R. 116 G g
Belcher Chan., N.-W. Terr. 81 K b
Belcher Is., Hudson Bay, North-West Territories 81 M f
Belcher Is., North, Hudson Bay, N.-W. Terr. 81 M f
Belchirag, Afghanistan 125 J b
Belchite, Spain 107 E b
Belcourt, Quebec 85 N d
Belebey, U.S.S.R. 117 M c
Belém, Mexico 90 B b
Belém, Brazil 93 H d
Belén, Argentina 94 C c
Belén, Panama 91 C e
Bélep, Is., Coral Sea 78 G j
Belfast, Prince Edward I. 82 K g
Belfast & L., N. Ireland 99 D f
Belfeld, Netherlands 100 E c
Belford, England 98 F e
Belfort, France 108 G c
Belgaum, India 126 D e
Belgica Mts., Antarctica 136 N d
Belgium, Central Europe 100 B d
Belgorod, U.S.S.R. 116 K f
Belgorod Dnestrovskiy, Ukraine, U.S.S.R. 116 G h
Belgrade. See Beograd
Belgrano, Argentina 94 E e
Belin, France 109 C d
Belitung, I., Indonesia 129 E l
Belize City, British Honduras 91 B c
Bell, R., Quebec 85 N c
Bella Bella, Br. Columbia 88 E d
Bellac, France 108 D c
Bella Coola, Br. Columbia 88 F d
Bellary, India 126 E e
Bellavista, Peru 92 B e
Bellburns, Newfoundland 83 P c
Belle B., Newfoundland 83 R f
Belle Ile, France 108 B c
Belle Isle, Newfoundland 83 R b
Belle Isle, Str. of, Labrador-Newfoundland 83 Q b
Belle Isle Landing, Belle Isle, Nfd. 83 R b
Bellême, France 108 D b
Belleoram, Newfoundland 83 R f
Belle Plain, Saskatchewan 87 M h
Belle-Rivière, L. de la, Quebec 85 T d
Belleterre, Quebec 85 M e
Belleville, France 108 F c
Belleville, Ontario 85 N h
Bellevue, Alberta 86 C j
Belley, France 108 F d
Belle Yella, Liberia 118 C g
Bell I., Harbour Main, Nfd. 83 T f
Bell I., White B., Nfd. 83 R c
Bellingham, England 98 F e
Bellinghausen Sea, Antarc. 136 G c
Bellinzona, Switzerland 101 E b
Bellis, Alberta 86 E d
Bell Pen., N.-W. Territories 81 L e
Bellsite, Manitoba 87 Q f
Belluno, Italy 110 D b
Bell Ville, Argentina 94 D d
Belly R., Alberta 86 D j
Belmez, Spain 106 C c
Belmont, Manitoba 87 S j
Belmont, Nova Scotia 82 J h
Belmont, Ontario 84 J k
Belmonte, Brazil 93 K g
Belmonte, Portugal 106 B b
Belmonte, Spain 107 D c
Belmullet, Eire 99 A f
Belo Horizonte, Brazil 93 J g
Belomorsk, U.S.S.R. 114 C b
Belopol'ye, Ukraine, U.S.S.R. 116 J f
Belorado, Spain 106 D a
Beloretsk, U.S.S.R. 117 P d
Belorussia, U.S.S.R. 116 E e
Belostok. See Bialystok
Beloye More, U.S.S.R. 114 C b
Beloye Oz., U.S.S.R. 116 K a
Belp, Switzerland 101 C b
Belt, Lille, Denmark 103 C j
Belt, Store, Denmark 103 D j
Belterra, Brazil 93 G d
Belvedere Marittimo, Italy 111 E f
Belver, Portugal 106 B c
Belyy, Os., U.S.S.R. 114 F a
Benalla, Australia 135 J g
Benalto, Alberta 86 C f
Benares. See Varanasi
Benavente, Spain 106 C b
Benbecula, I., Scotland 98 C c
Bencubbin, Australia 134 C f
Ben Dearg, Scotland 98 D c
Bender, Saskatchewan 87 P h
Bendery, Moldavia, U.S.S.R. 116 F h
Bendigo, Australia 135 H g
Benevento, Italy 111 E e
Bengal, B. of, India, etc. 127 G e
Bengal, East, E. Pakistan 127 G c
Bengal, West, India 127 F d
Ben Gardane, Tunisia 119 H b
Benghazi, Libya 119 K b
Bengough, Saskatchewan 87 M j
Benguela, Angola 120 C g
Benha, Egypt 119 M b
Ben Hope, Scotland 98 D b
Beni, R., Bolivia 92 D f
Beni Abbès, Algeria 118 E b
Benicarlo, Spain 107 F b
Beni Mazar, Egypt 119 M c
Benin, Bight of, W. Africa 118 F h
Benin City, Nigeria 118 G g
Beni Saf, Algeria 118 E a
Beni Suef, Egypt 119 M c
Benito, Manitoba 87 Q g
Benito, Rio Muni, Spanish Guinea 120 B d
Benjamin Constant, Brazil 92 C d
Benkovac, Yugoslavia 110 E c
Ben Lomond, Australia 135 K e
Ben Macdhui, Scotland 98 E c
Ben More Assynt, Scotland 98 D b
Ben Nevis, Scotland 98 D d
Benny, Ontario 84 J f
Benson, Saskatchewan 87 O j
Bent, Iran 125 G d
Bentinck I., Burma 127 J f
Bentley, Alberta 86 C f
Bento Goncalves, Brazil 94 F c
Benton, New Brunswick 82 E g
Benton Station, Alberta 86 G g
Benue R., Nigeria 119 G g
Benwee Hd., Eire 99 A f
Ben Wyvis, Scotland 98 D c
Beograd, Yugoslavia 112 C b
Beowa R., India 126 E c
Beppu, Japan 133 B h
Berar, India 126 E d
Berat, Albania 113 B d
Berber, Sudan 119 M e
Berbera, Somali Republic 121 K b
Berberati, Cent. Afr. Rep. 119 J h
Berchtesgaden, Germany 104 E e
Berdichev, Ukraine, U.S.S.R. 116 F g
Berdigyastyakh, U.S.S.R. 115 M b
Berdyansk, Ukraine, U.S.S.R. 116 K h
Berens, I., Manitoba 87 U f
Berens R., Manitoba 87 V f
Berens River, Manitoba 87 V f
Beresford, Manitoba 87 R j
Beresti, Romania 112 F a
Berezniki, U.S.S.R. 114 E c
Berezovo, U.S.S.R. 114 F b
Berg, Norway 102 G b
Berga, Spain 107 F a
Bergamo, Italy 110 B c
Bergen, Germany 104 C b
Bergen, Germany 104 E a
Bergen, Norway 103 A f
Bergen-op-Zoom, Netherlands 100 C c
Bergerac, France 109 D d
Bergersen Mt., Antarctica 136 N d
Bergerville, dist., Quebec 85 R c
Bergisch Gladbach, Germany 104 B c
Bergland, Ontario 86 H a
Bergün, Switzerland 101 E b
Berhampur, India 127 G d
Bering, U.S.S.R. 115 T b
Bering Sea, Asia-America 78 J a
Bering Str., Asia-America 78 K a
Berislavl, Ukraine, U.S.S.R 116 H h
Berjeik, Netherlands 100 D c

Berkåk, Norway 102 D e
Berkeley, C., N.-W. Terr. 80 J c
Berkner I., Antarctica 136 J c
Berkovitsa, Bulgaria 112 D c
Berkshire, co., England 99 G j
Berland, R., Alberta 88 L c
Berlin, Germany 104 E b
Berlinguet Inlet, N.-W. Terr. 81 L c
Bermillo de Savago, Spain 106 B b
Bermuda Is., Atlantic Oc. 43
Bern & canton, Switzerland 101 C b
Bernard, L., Quebec 82 J c
Bernard, Saskatchewan 86 K h
Bernard Is., Truk Is. 78 C o
Bernasconi, Argentina 95 D e
Bernay, France 108 D b
Bernburg, Germany 104 D c
Berne. See Bern
Berneau, Belgium 100 D d
Berneck, Switzerland 101 E a
Berner Alpen, Switzerland 101 C b
Bernier B., N.-W. Terr. 81 L c
Bernina, Passo del, Switzerland 101 E b
Beromunster. See Münster
Berri, prov., France 108 E c
Berry Is., Bahama Is. 91 D a
Bersillies, Belgium 100 C d
Berté, L., Quebec 82 D c
Berthierville, Quebec 85 R f
Bertoua, Cameroon 119 H h
Bertraghboy B., Eire 99 A g
Bertram, Ontario 84 F c
Bertrix, Belgium 100 D e
Beru, I., Gilbert Is. 78 H j
Berwick, co., Scotland 98 F e
Berwick, Nova Scotia 82 H h
Berwick-upon-Tweed, England 98 F e
Berwyn, Alberta 88 L b
Berwyn Mts., Wales 99 E h
Berzee, Belgium 100 C d
Besançon, France 108 G c
Beskidy Zachodnie, Mts., Central Europe 105 H d
Besnard L., Saskatchewan 87 M c
Besni, Turkey 124 C b
Bessemer, Ontario 85 N g
Best, Netherlands 100 D c
Betanzos, Spain 106 A a
Betbetti, Sudan 119 K e
Betchie, L., Quebec 82 C d
Bethanie, S.W. Africa 122 B e
Bethany, Ontario 85 M h
Bethlehem, Jordan 123 D f
Bethlehem, South Africa 122 D e
Bethoulet, L., Quebec 82 A b
Bethune, Saskatchewan 87 M h
Betling Sib, India 127 H d
Betsiamites, Quebec 82 C e
Betsiamites R., Quebec 82 C d
Bettiah, India 127 F c
Beugen, Netherlands 100 D c
Beulah, Manitoba 87 Q h
Beveland, Noord, I., Netherlands 100 B c
Beveland, Zuid, I., Netherlands 100 B c
Beveren, Belgium 100 C c
Beveridge Reef, Cook Is. 78 K j
Beverley, Saskatchewan 86 J h
Beverloo, Belgium 100 D c
Beverly, Alberta 86 D e
Beverst, Belgium 100 D d
Bex, Switzerland 101 C b
Beyla, Guinea 118 D g
Beypazari, Turkey 124 B a
Beypore, India 126 E f
Beysehir, Turkey 124 B b
Beyt Guvrin, Israel 123 C f
Beyt Shean, Israel 123 D e
Bezdán, Yugoslavia 112 B b
Bezhitsa, U.S.S.R. 116 H e
Béziers, France 109 E e
Bhadra, India 127 D c
Bhagalpur, India 127 G c
Bhakkar, Pakistan 126 D b
Bhamo, Burma 127 J d
Bhandara, India 126 E d
Bhannis, Lebanon 123 D d
Bhanrer Ra., India 126 E d
Bhatgaon, Nepal 127 G c
Bhavnagar, India 126 D d
Bhawani Patna, India 127 F e
Bhera, Pakistan 126 D b
Bhilwara, India 126 D c
Bhima, R., India 126 E e
Bhir (Bir), India 126 E e
Bhiwani, India 126 E c
Bhong Chu, R., Tibet 127 G c
Bhopal, India 126 E d
Bhuj, India 126 C d
Bhusawal, India 126 E d
Bhutan, Himalayas 127 H c
Biafra, Bight of, W. Africa 120 B d
Biak, I., W. Irian 129 L l
Białogard, Poland 105 G a
Białowieza, Poland 105 K b
Białystok, Poland 105 K b
Bianche, L., Australia 134 G e
Biarritz, France 109 C e
Biberach, Germany 104 C d
Bic, I. du, Quebec 82 D e
Bic, Quebec 82 D e
Biche, L. la, Alberta 82 E d
Bickerton, C., Antarctica 136 T e
Bida, Nigeria 118 G g
Bidar, India 126 E e
Bideford & B., England 99 E j
Biel, Switzerland 101 C a
Bield, Manitoba 82 Q g
Bielefeld, Germany 104 C b
Bieler See, Switzerland 101 C a
Bielsk, Poland 105 K b
Bienfait, Saskatchewan 82 P j
Bienne. See Biel
Bienville, L., Quebec 81 M f
Bienville, Quebec 85 T b
Bière, Switzerland 101 B b
Bietschhorn, Mt., Switz. 101 C b
Biga, Turkey 124 A a
Big B., New Zealand 135 P m
Big Bar Creek, Br. Columbia 88 H e
Big Beaver, Saskatchewan 87 M j
Big Beaver Falls, Ontario 84 H c
Big Beaver House, Ontario 81 L g
Big Bell, Australia 134 C e
Big Caotibi L., Quebec 82 E c
Big Creek, Br. Columbia 88 H e
Bigej, Kwajalein Is. 79 U e
Biggar, Saskatchewan 86 K f
Bight, The, Bahama Is. 91 D b
Bigi, Kwajalein Is. 79 T e
Big I., N.-W. Territories 81 M e
Big I., Ontario 86 G a
Big Lake, Ontario 84 H g
Big Muddy L., Saskatchewan 87 M j
Bignasco, Switzerland 101 D b
Bignona, Senegal 118 B f
Big Pond, Cape Breton I. 83 M h
Big River, Saskatchewan 86 K e
Big Sandy L., Saskatchewan 87 N d
Bigsby I., Ontario 86 H a
Bigstick L., Saskatchewan 86 H h
Bigstone L., Manitoba 87 W e
Bigstone R., Manitoba 87 W c
Big Trout L., Ontario 81 L g
Big Valley, Alberta 86 E f
Bigwood, Ontario 84 K f
Bihac, Yugoslavia 110 E c
Bihar, India 127 G d
Bihar, state, India 127 G d
Biharamulo, Tanzania 121 G e
Bihorului, Mts., Romania 112 D a
Biijiri, Eniwetok 79 S c
Bijagós, Archipel. of Portuguese Guinea 118 B f
Bijapur, India 126 E e
Bijar, Iran 124 E b
Bijawar, India 126 E d
Bijeljina, Yugoslavia 112 B b
Bijnabad, Iran 125 G d
Bijnor, India 126 E c
Bikampur, India 126 D c
Bikaner, India 126 D c
Bikar, I., Marshall Is. 79 G f
Bikin, U.S.S.R. 115 N d
Bikini I., Marshall Is. 78 G f
Bikoro, Congo 120 D e
Bilaspur, India 127 F d
Bilauktaung Ra., Burma-Thailand 129 C h
Bilbao, Spain 106 D a
Bileća, Yugoslavia 112 B c
Bilecik, Turkey 124 A a
Bilé Karpaty, Czech. 105 G d
Bilin, Burma 127 J e
Bilisht, Albania 113 C d
Billabong, R. See Moulmein
Billee, Eniwetok 79 R c
Billings Bridge, Ontario 84 D j
Billiton, I. See Belitung
Bilma, Niger 119 H e
Biloela, Australia 135 J d
Bilo Goro, Yugoslavia 110 F c
Bilsen, Belgium 100 D d
Bilta, Norway 102 J b
Bilthoven, Netherlands 100 D b
Bilugyun, I., Burma 127 J e
Bilyarsk, U.S.S.R. 117 K c
Bimbe, Angola 120 D g
Bimlipatam, India 127 F e
Bina, India 126 E d
Binaija, Mt., Ceram I., Indonesia 129 J l
Binalud, Mt., Iran 125 G b
Binche, Belgium 100 C d
Bindloss, Alberta 86 G h
Bindura, Rhodesia 122 E c
Binefar, Spain 107 F b
Binga, Rhodesia 122 D c
Bingen, Germany 104 B d
Bingerville, Ivory Coast 118 E g
Bingle, Ontario 84 K d
Bingol, Turkey 124 D b
Binh Dinh, S. Vietnam 132 D d
Binn, Switzerland 101 D b
Binscarth, Manitoba 87 Q h
Bintan, I., Indonesia 129 D k
Bint Jubeil, Lebanon 123 D d
Bir Ali, S. Yemen 124 E g
Birao, Japan 133 H c
Birch Cliff, Ontario 84 E k
Birch Hills, Saskatchewan 87 M e
Birch I., Manitoba 87 S f
Birch L., Alberta 86 F e
Birch L., Saskatchewan 86 J e
Birch Mts., Alberta 88 N b
Birch R., Alberta 88 N a
Birch River, Manitoba 87 Q f
Birchwood, New Zealand 135 P m
Bird, Manitoba 80 K f
Bird Cove, Newfoundland 83 Q b
Bird I., Palmyra I. 79 U k
Bird Rocks Lt. Ho., Madeleine Is., Quebec 83 L f
Birdsville, Australia 134 G e
Birdum, Australia 134 F c
Birecik, Turkey 124 C b
Birein, Syria 123 E b
Bir Fadhil, Saudi Arabia 124 E e
Bir Gara, Chad 119 J f
Birhan, Mt., Ethiopia 121 H b
Bir Ilacsin, Libya 119 H b
Birjand, Iran 125 G c
Birkah, Muscat & Oman 125 G e
Birkenhead, England 99 E g
Bir Malusi, Iraq 124 C c
Bir Maqran, Saudi Arabia 124 E e
Birmingham, England 99 F h
Birmingham, Saskatchewan 87 P h
Birnie, Manitoba 87 S h
Birnie I., Phoenix Is. 78 J g
Birni-n-Kebbi, Nigeria 118 F f
Birni-n' Konni, Niger 118 G f
Birobidzhan, U.S.S.R. 115 N d
Biroo. See Hiro
Birq, Saudi Arabia 124 D f
Birr, Eire 99 B g
Birsay, Saskatchewan 86 L g
Birsk, U.S.S.R. 117 M c
Birtle, Manitoba 87 Q h
Biryusa R., U.S.S.R. 115 J c
Biržai (Birzhay), Lithuania, U.S.S.R. 103 L h
Bisbal, La, Spain 107 G b
Biscay, B. of, France-Spain 97 F g
Bischofszell, Switzerland 101 E a
Biscoe, Is., Antarctica 136 H e
Biscotasing, Ontario 84 H e
Bise saki, Okinawa 78 B a
Bisha, Saudi Arabia 124 D e
Bishnath, India 127 H c
Bishop Auckland, England 99 F f
Bishopric, Saskatchewan 87 M h
Bishop's Falls, Newfoundland 83 R d
Bishops Stortford, England 99 H j
Bishri, Jebel el, Syria 124 C b
Bisisthal, Switzerland 101 D b
Biskia, Ethiopia 121 H a
Biskotasi L., Ontario 84 H e
Bismarck Arch., Pacific Oc. 78 E g
Bismarck Str., Antarctica 136 H f
Bison L., Alberta 88 L b
Bissau, India 126 E c
Bissau, Port. Guinea 118 B f
Bitlis, Turkey 124 D b
Bitola, Yugoslavia 112 C d
Bitonto, Italy 111 F e
Bitterfeld, Germany 104 E c
Bittern L., Saskatchewan 87 M e
Bittern Lake, Alberta 86 D e
Bitumount, Alberta 88 O b
Bivio, Switzerland 101 E b
Biwa Ko, Japan 133 D g
Biysk, U.S.S.R. 114 H c
Bizerte, Tunisia 119 G a
Bjelovar, Yugoslavia 110 F c
Björkö, Sweden 103 H g
Bjorli, Norway 102 C e
Björna, Sweden 102 H e
Björnör, Norway 102 D d
Björnöya, I., Barents Sea 114 A a
Blache, L. de la, Quebec 82 C c
Blackall, Australia 135 J d
Black B., Ontario 84 B d
Black Bear Island L., Sask. 87 M c
Black Birch L., Saskatchewan 88 Q b
Blackburn, England 99 F g
Black Coast, Antarctica 136 H d
Black Diamond, Alberta 86 C h
Black Dome, pk., British Columbia 88 F d
Black Donald Mines, Ontario 85 O g
Blackdown Hills, England 99 E k
Blackfoot, Alberta 86 G e
Black Hawk, Ontario 86 H b
Blackhead B., Newfoundland 83 T e
Black I., Antarctica 136 B c
Black I., Manitoba 87 V g
Blackie, Alberta 86 D h
Black Isle, Scotland 98 E c
Black Lake, Quebec 85 T f
Black Mts., New Brunswick 82 E f
Black Mts., Wales 99 E j
Black Pines, Br. Columbia 88 J e
Black Pool, Br. Columbia 88 J e
Blackpool, England 99 E g
Black Rocks, Quebec 83 N c
Black Sea, Europe-Asia 114 C d
Blacks Harbour, N.B. 82 F h
Blacksod B., Eire 99 A f
Black Sturgeon, L., Ontario 84 B c
Black Sugar Loaf, Mt., Australia 135 K f
Blackville, New Brunswick 82 G g
Black Volta R., Ghana 118 E g
Blackwater R., Eire 99 B h
Bladworth, Saskatchewan 86 L g
Blagoevgrad, Bulgaria 112 D c
Blagoveshchensk, U.S.S.R. 115 M c
Blagoveshchensk, U.S.S.R. 117 M c
Blaine Lake, Saskatchewan 86 L f
Blair Atholl, Scotland 98 E d
Blairgowrie, Scotland 98 E d
Blairmore, Alberta 86 C j
Blaj, Romania 112 D a
Blanc, C., Mauritania 118 B d
Blanc, Mt., France-Italy 108 G d
Blanca, B., Argentina 95 D e
Blanche, L., Australia 135 G e
Blanche, Ontario 84 E b
Blanche, Quebec 85 P g
Blanco, Pico, Costa Rica 91 C e
Blanc Sablon, Quebec 83 P b
Blandford, England 59 F k
Blanes, Spain 107 G b
Blangpidie, Sumatra 129 C k
Blangy, France 108 D b
Blankenberge, Belgium 100 B c
Blantyre, Malawi 121 H h
Blaregnies, Belgium 100 B d
Blaton, Belgium 100 B d
Blaye, France 109 C d
Blazowa, Poland 105 K d
Bleharies, Belgium 100 B d
Blenheim, New Zealand 135 Q l
Blenheim, Ontario 84 J k
Bleu, L., Quebec 85 M f
Blewett, Saskatchewan 87 O j
Blida, Algeria 118 F a
Blind River, Ontario 84 H f
Blitta, Togo 118 F g
Block B., Antarctica 136 D c
Bloedel, Vancouver I., British Columbia 88 G e
Bloemfontein, South Africa 122 D e
Blois, France 108 D c
Blokzijl, Netherlands 100 E b
Bloody Foreland, Eire 98 B e
Bloomfield, Ontario 85 N j
Blucher, Saskatchewan 86 L f
Blueberry R., Br. Columbia 88 J b
Bluefields, Nicaragua 91 C d
Blue Hills of Coteau, Newfoundland 83 O f
Blue Mt., India 127 H d
Blue Mts., Australia 135 K f
Blue Mts., Jamaica 91 D c
Blue Ridge, Alberta 86 B d
Blue River, Br. Columbia 88 K d
Blue Sea Lake, Quebec 85 O f
Blue Stack Mts., Eire 99 B f
Bluff, New Zealand 135 P m
Bluff Knoll, Australia 134 C f
Bluffton, Alberta 86 C f
Blumenau, Brazil 94 G c
Blumenhof, Saskatchewan 86 K h
Blyth, England 98 G e
Blyth, Ontario 84 J j
Bo, Sierra Leone 118 C g
Boac, Philippines 129 H h
Boaco, Nicaragua 91 B d
Bôa Fé, Brazil 92 C e
Boakview, Ontario 84 K g
Bôa Vista, Brazil 92 E c
Bobcaygeon, Ontario 85 M h
Bobo Dioulasso, Upper Volta 118 E f
Bobolice, Poland 105 G b
Bobrov, U.S.S.R. 117 E e
Bobruysk, Belorussia, U.S.S.R. 116 F e
Bôca do Acre, Brazil 92 D e
Bôca do Copana, Brazil 92 E e
Bocas del Toro, Panama 91 C e
Bochart, Quebec 85 R c
Bochnia, Poland 105 J d
Bocholt, Belgium 100 D c
Bocholt, Germany 104 B c
Bochum, Germany 104 B c
Bocota, Mozambique 122 E d
Bodaybo, U.S.S.R. 115 L c
Boden, Sweden 102 J d
Boden See, Switzerland-Germany 101 E a
Boderg L., Eire 99 B g
Bodmin & Moors, England 99 D k
Bodo, Alberta 86 G f
Bodö, Norway 102 F c
Boende, Congo 120 E e
Boertange, Netherlands 100 E a
Bogallua, Eniwetok 79 R c
Bogandé, Upper Volta 118 E f
Bogart, Mt., Alberta 86 B h
Bogbonga, Congo 120 D d
Bogdarin, U.S.S.R. 115 L c
Bogdo Ula, China 128 A b
Bogenaga, Jaluit I. 79 T g
Boggenadick, Jaluit I. 79 T g
Boggeragh Mts., Eire 99 A h
Boggerik, Kwajalein Is. 79 U e
Bogombogo, Eniwetok 79 R c
Bogong, Mt., Australia 135 J g
Bogor, Java 129 E m
Bogorodsk, U.S.S.R. 117 J d
Bogorodskoye, U.S.S.R. 115 P c
Bogotá, Colombia 92 C c
Bogotol, U.S.S.R. 114 H c
Bogra, E. Pakistan 127 G d
Boguet, Truk Is. 78 F o
Boharm, Saskatchewan 87 M h
Bohemia, Czechoslovakia 104 E d
Böhmer Wald, Germany-Czechoslovakia 104 E d
Bohol, I., Philippines 129 H j
Boiaçu, Brazil 92 E d
Boiestown, New Brunswick 82 F g
Boigu, I., Aust. 135 H a
Boim, Brazil 93 F d
Boisdale, Cape Breton I. 83 M g
Bois-le-Duc. See 's Hertogenbosch
Boissevain, Manitoba 87 R j
Bojnurd, Iran 125 G b
Bokalijman, Jaluit I. 79 T j
Boké, Guinea 118 C f
Bokki, Cameroon 119 H g
Bokn Fd., Norway 103 A g
Bokoro, Chad 119 J f
Bolan, Pakistan 126 C c
Bolangir, India 127 F d
Bolan Pass, Pakistan 126 C c
Bolbec, France 108 D b
Bole, Ghana 118 E g
Bölebyn, Sweden 102 J d
Bolger, Quebec 85 O d
Bolgrad, Ukraine, U.S.S.R. 116 F j
Bolintin, Romania 112 E b
Bolívar, Argentina 94 D e
Bolívar, Colombia 92 B c
Bolivia, S. America 92 D g
Bolkow, Ontario 84 G d
Bollon, Australia 135 J e
Bollstabruk, Sweden 102 G e
Bolmen, L., Sweden 103 E h
Bolobo, Congo 120 D e
Bologna, Italy 110 C c
Bologoye, U.S.S.R. 116 J c
Bolomba, Congo 120 D d
Bolotnoye, U.S.S.R. 114 H c
Bolsena, L. di, Italy 110 C d
Bolshevik, Ostrov, U.S.S.R. 115 K a
Bolshoy Lyakhovskiy, Ostrov, U.S.S.R. 115 P a
Boltana, Spain 107 F a
Bolton, England 97 F g
Bolton, Ontario 85 L j
Bolton L., Manitoba 87 W d
Bolu, Turkey 124 B a
Bolzano, Italy 110 C b
Bomal, Belgium 100 D d
Bomba & G. of, Libya 119 K b
Bombala, Australia 135 J g
Bombarral, Portugal 106 A c
Bombay, India 126 D e
Bom Futoro, Brazil 92 E f
Bomhus, Sweden 103 G f
Bom Jesus, Brazil 93 J e
Bömlo, I., Norway 103 A g
Bomnak, U.S.S.R. 115 M c
Bon Accord, Alberta 86 D e
Bonaduz, Switzerland 101 E b
Bonaire I., Neth. Antilles 92 D a
Bonanza, Nicaragua 91 C d
Bonarlaw, Ontario 85 N h
Bonaventure, Quebec 82 G e
Bonaventure I., Quebec 82 H e
Bonavista & B., Nfd. 83 T e
Bondo, Congo 120 E d
Bône. See Annaba
Bone, G. of, Celebes 79 H l
Boney River Sta., New Brunswick 82 F h
Bonfield, Ontario 85 L f
Bongor, Chad 119 J f
Bonheur, Ontario 87 L a
Bonifacio & B. de, Corsica 111 B e
Bonin Is., Pacific Ocean 78 E d
Bonn, Germany 104 B c
Bonne Bay, Newfoundland 83 P d
Bonne Espérance, Quebec 83 P b
Bonneval, France 108 D b
Bonnie Rock, Australia 134 C f
Bonny, France 108 E c
Bonny, Nigeria 118 G h
Bonny River, New Brunswick 82 F h
Bonnyville, Alberta 86 G d
Bonom Mhai, Mts., South Vietnam 132 D d
Boom, Belgium 100 C c
Boon Tsagan Nur, Mongolia 128 C a
Boothby, C., Antarctica 136 P e
Boothia, G. of, N.-W. Terr. 81 L d
Boothia Pen., N.-W. Terr. 81 K c
Bopeechee, Australia 134 G e
Boquerón, Cuba 91 D c
Boquete, Panama 91 C e
Bora Bora, Society Is. 79 L j
Boramo, Somali Republic 121 J c
Borås, Sweden 103 E h
Borba, Brazil 92 F d
Bordeaux, France 109 C d
Bordeaux, Quebec 85 R j
Borden, Saskatchewan 86 K f
Borden I., N.-W. Terr. 80 H b
Borden Pen., N.-W. Terr. 81 L c
Bordertown, Australia 134 H g
Borga, Sweden 102 F d
Börge Fjell, Norway 102 E d
Borger, Netherlands 100 E b
Borgholm, Sweden 103 G h
Borgne, Haiti 91 E c
Borisoglebsk, U.S.S.R. 117 E e
Borisov, Belorussia, U.S.S.R. 116 F d
Bo River Post, Sudan 119 L g
Borja, Spain 107 E b
Borjas Blancas, Spain 107 F b
Borkum, I., Germany 104 B b
Borlänge, Sweden 103 F f
Borneo, Indonesia 129 F k
Bornholm, I., Denmark 103 F j
Borodino, U.S.S.R. 116 J d
Borogontsy, U.S.S.R. 115 N b
Borongan, Philippines 129 J h
Borovichi, U.S.S.R. 116 H b
Borroloola, Australia 134 G c
Borskoye, U.S.S.R. 117 K d
Borūjerd, Iran 124 E c
Bor Yuryakh, U.S.S.R. 115 L a
Borzya, U.S.S.R. 115 L c
Bosaso, Somali Republic 121 K b
Bosco, Switzerland 101 D b
Bosiljgrad, Yugoslavia 112 D c
Boskoop, Netherlands 100 C b
Bosna-Hercegovina, Yugosl. 112 A b
Bosobolo, Congo 120 D d
Bosoli, Botswana 122 D d
Bōso Pen., Japan 133 G g
Bosporus, Turkey 124 A a
Bosso, Niger 119 H f
Bostan, Pakistan 126 C b
Boston, England 99 H h
Boston Bar, Br. Columbia 88 J f
Boswarlos, Newfoundland 83 O e
Boswell, Br. Columbia 88 L f
Botera, Angola 120 C g
Botha, Alberta 86 E f
Bothaville, West Africa 122 D e
Bothnia, G. of, North-West Europe 103 H f
Bothwell, Ontario 84 J k
Botswana, Republic of, Southern Africa 122 C d
Botucatu, Brazil 93 H h
Botwood, Newfoundland 83 R d
Bouaké, Ivory Coast 118 E g
Bouar, Cent. Afr. Rep. 119 J g
Bou Arfa, Morocco 118 E b
Boucher, L., Quebec 83 N b
Boucherville, Is., Quebec 85 T h
Bouches-du-Rhône, dep., France 109 F e
Bouchette, Quebec 85 P f
Bou Djébéha, Mali 118 E e
Boudoukou, Ivory Coast 118 E g
Boudry, Switzerland 101 B b
Bougainville, I., Solomon Is. 78 F h
Bougaroun C., Algeria 118 G a
Bougie. See Bejaia
Bougouni, Mali 118 D f
Bouillon, Belgium 100 D e
Boulain, L., Quebec 83 L c
Boulder, Australia 134 D f
Bouleau, L. au, Quebec 85 N e
Boulia, Australia 134 G d
Boulogne, France 108 D a
Bouna, Ivory Coast 118 E g
Boundary B., Br. Columbia 88 D g
Boundary Bay, dist., Vancouver 88 D g
Boundary Bay Airport, British Columbia 88 D g
Boundary Mts., Maine-Quebec 82 B h
Boundary Plat., Montana-Saskatchewan 86 J j
Bounty, Saskatchewan 86 K g
Bounty Is., Pacific Ocean 78 J m
Bourbonnais, prov., France 108 E c
Bourem, Mali 118 E e
Bourg, France 108 F c
Bourg-Argental, France 109 F d
Bourges, France 108 E c
Bourget, L. du, France 108 F d
Bourg-Léopold, Belgium 100 D c
Bourgogne, prov., France 108 F c
Bourg-St. Pierre, Switz. 101 C c
Bourke, Australia 135 J f
Bourkes, Ontario 84 K d
Bourlamaque, Quebec 85 N d
Bourmont, Quebec 85 P d
Bourne, C., N.-W. Terr. 80 K a
Bournemouth, England 99 F k
Bovigny, Belgium 100 D d
Bovino, Italy 111 E e
Bowden, Alberta 86 C g
Bowen, Australia 135 J c
Bowen I., Br. Columbia 88 H f
Bow Island, Alberta 86 F j
Bowman B., N.-W. Terr. 81 M d
Bowman I., Antarctica 136 S e
Bowmanville, Ontario 85 M j
Bowness, Alberta 86 C g
Bow R., Alberta 86 D h
Bowron Lake Prov. Park, British Columbia 88 J d
Bowron R., Br. Columbia 88 J d
Bowser L., Br. Columbia 88 E b
Bowsman, Manitoba 87 Q f
Bowyer I., Br. Columbia 88 C e
Boxholm, Sweden 103 F g
Boxmeer, Netherlands 100 D c
Boxtel, Netherlands 100 D c
Boyd, Manitoba 87 V c
Boyd's Cove, Newfoundland 83 S d
Boyle, Alberta 86 E d
Boylston, Nova Scotia 83 L h
Boyne, R., Eire 99 C g
Bozok. See Yozgat
Bozoum, Cent. Afr. Rep. 119 J g
Bra, Italy 110 A c
Brabant, Noord, prov., Netherlands 100 D c
Brabant, prov., Belgium 100 C d
Brabant I., Antarctica 136 H f
Brabant L., Saskatchewan 87 O b
Brac, I., Yugoslavia 110 F d
Bracadale L., Scotland 98 C c
Bracebridge, Ontario 85 L g
Bräcke, Sweden 102 F e
Bracken, Saskatchewan 86 J j
Bracken L., Manitoba 87 S e
Brád, Romania 112 D a
Bradford, England 99 F g
Bradford, Ontario 85 L h
Bradore Bay, Quebec 85 P b
Bradore Hills, Quebec 85 P b
Bradwardine, Manitoba 87 R j
Bradwell, Saskatchewan 86 L g
Braemar, Scotland 98 E d
Braga, Portugal 106 A b
Bragado, Argentina 94 D e
Bragança, Portugal 106 B b
Bragança Paulista, Brazil 93 H h
Brahmanbaria, E. Pakistan 127 H d
Brahmaputra R., India 127 F c

Campina Grande, *Brazil* 93 K e
Campinas, *Brazil* 93 H h
Campoalegre, *Colombia* 92 B c
Campobasso, *Italy* 111 E e
Campobello I., *New Brunswick* 82 F j
Campo Belo, *Brazil* 93 H h
Campo Formosa, *Brazil* 93 J f
Campo Gallo, *Argentina* 94 D c
Campo Grande, *Brazil* 93 G h
Campo Maior, *Brazil* 93 J d
Campo Maior, *Portugal* 106 B c
Campos, *Brazil* 93 J h
Campos Novos, *Brazil* 94 F c
Campos Sales, *Brazil* 93 J e
Campulung, *Romania* 112 E b
Cam Ranh, B., *S. Vietnam* 132 D d
Camrose, *Alberta* 86 E e
Camuy, *Puerto Rico* 54 C h
Canaan, *New Brunswick* 82 G g
Canaan R., *New Brunswick* 82 G h
Canada, *North America* 80-81
Canada Bay, *Newfoundland* 83 Q c
Cañada de Gómez, *Argent.* 94 D d
Cañadón de las Vacas, *Argentina* 95 C h
Canakkale, *Turkey* 124 A a
Canal Flats, *Br. Columbia* 88 M e
Canama, *Brazil* 92 C e
Cananea, *Mexico* 90 B a
Cananeia, *Brazil* 94 G c
Cañar, *Ecuador* 92 B d
Canarias, Islas, *Atlantic Oc.* 118 B c
Canarreos, Arch. de los, *Cuba* 91 C b
Canary Is. *See* Canarias
Canas, *Portugal* 106 B b
Canatlán, *Mexico* 90 D c
Cañaveral, *Spain* 106 B c
Cañaveras, *Spain* 107 D b
Canavieiras, *Brazil* 93 K g
Canberra, *Australia* 135 J g
Candasnos, *Spain* 107 E b
Candia. *See* Iráklion
Candiac, *Manitoba* 87 O h
Candle L., *Saskatchewan* 87 M e
Candle Lake, *Saskatchewan* 87 M e
Cando, *Saskatchewan* 86 J f
Cane, *Ontario* 84 K e
Canea. *See* Khania
Canella, *Brazil* 94 F c
Canelones, *Uruguay* 94 E d
Cañete, *Chile* 95 B e
Cañete, *Peru* 92 B f
Cañete, *Spain* 107 E b
Cangamba, *Angola* 120 D g
Cangandala, *Angola* 120 D f
Cangas, *Spain* 106 B a
Canguaretama, *Brazil* 93 L e
Canha, *Portugal* 106 A c
Canica Island, *Quebec* 85 N c
Canicatti, *Sicily* 111 D g
Canim L., *Br. Columbia* 88 J e
Canindé, R., *Brazil* 93 J e
Çankiri, *Turkey* 124 B a
Canmore, *Alberta* 86 B g
Canna, I., *Scotland* 98 C c
Cannanore, *India* 126 E f
Cannes, *France* 109 G e
Canning, *Nova Scotia* 82 H h
Cannington, *Ontario* 85 L h
Canoe, L., *Saskatchewan* 86 J c
Canoe Passage, *Br. Columbia* 88 C d
Canoe R., *Br. Columbia* 88 K d
Canora, *Saskatchewan* 87 P g
Canosa, *Italy* 111 F e
Canso, C., *Nova Scotia* 83 M h
Canso, *Nova Scotia* 83 M h
Canso, Str. of, *Nova Scotia* 83 L h
Cantabrica, *Spain* 106 C a
Cantal, dep., *France* 109 E d
Cantanhede, *Portugal* 106 A b
Cantaur, *Saskatchewan* 86 J h
Canterbury, *England* 99 H j
Canterbury Bight, *New Zealand* 135 Q m
Canterbury Plains, *New Zealand* 135 Q m
Canterbury Sta., *N.B.* 82 E h
Can Tho, *S. Vietnam* 132 D e
Canton, *China* 131 F l
Canton I., *Phoenix Is.* 78 J g
Canuelas, *Argentina* 94 E e
Canutama, *Brazil* 92 E e
Canwood, *Saskatchewan* 86 L e
Canyon, *Ontario* 84 F e
Canyon Creek, *Alberta* 86 B c
Caopacho L., *Quebec* 82 F a
Caopacho R., *Quebec* 82 F b
Caopatina, L., *Quebec* 85 Q c
Capabarida, *Venezuela* 92 C a
Capakçur. *See* Bingol
Capana, *Brazil* 92 E e
Capão Bonito, *Brazil* 94 G b
Capassin, *Saskatchewan* 86 K e
Cap Chat, *Quebec* 82 F d
Cap de la Madeleine, *Quebec* 85 S f
Cap-d'Espoir, *New Brunswick* 82 H e
Cape Barren I., *Tasmania* 135 J h
Cape Breton Highlands Nat. Park, *C. Breton I., Nova Scotia* 83 M g
Cape Breton I., *Nova Scotia* 83 N g
Cape Broyle, *Newfoundland* 83 T f
Cape Charles, *Labrador* 83 R a
Cape Clear, *Eire* 99 A j
Cape Coast, *Ghana* 118 E g
Cape Dorset, *N.-W. Terr* 81 M e
Cape Dyer, *N.-W. Terr.* 81 N d
Cape Hopes Advance, *Quebec* 81 N e
Cape La Hune, *Nfd.* 83 Q f
Capelinha, *Brazil* 93 J g
Capelle, La, *France* 108 E b
Cape Province, *South Africa* 122 C f
Cape Race, *Newfoundland* 83 T g
Cape Ray, *Newfoundland* 83 N f
Cape Sable I., *Nova Scotia* 82 G k
Cape St. Mary Lt. Ho., *Nova Scotia* 82 F j
Cape Tormentine, *N.B.* 82 J g
Cape Town, *South Africa* 122 B f
Cape Verde Is., *Atlantic Oc.* 118 B h
Cape York Pen., *Australia* 135 H b
Cap Haïtien, *Haiti* 91 E c
Capica, *Italy* 111 E e
Capilano R., *Br. Columbia* 88 D f
Capilla, *Argentina* 94 E d
Capilla del Monte, *Argentina* 94 D d
Capim, *Brazil* 93 H d
Capitachouane, R., *Quebec* 85 O e
Caplan, *Quebec* 82 G e
Capraia, I., *Italy* 110 B d
Capreol, *Ontario* 84 K f
Caprera, I., *Sardinia* 111 B e
Capri, I., *Italy* 111 E e
Capricorn Chan., *Australia* 135 K d
Caprivi Strip, *S.W. Africa* 122 C c
Capstick, *Cape Breton I.* 83 M g
Caquetá, R., *Colombia* 92 B c
Caquetá, R., *Venezuela* 92 C d
Carabaya, Cord. de, *Peru* 92 C f
Caracaraí, *Brazil* 92 E c
Caracas, *Venezuela* 92 D a
Caracol, *Brazil* 93 J e
Caraguatay, *Paraguay* 94 E b
Caramat, *Ontario* 84 D c
Caransebes, *Romania* 112 D b
Carapegua, *Paraguay* 94 E c
Caraquet & B., *N.B.* 82 H f
Caras, *Peru* 92 B e
Caratasca L., *Honduras* 91 C c
Caratinga, *Brazil* 93 J g
Carauari, *Brazil* 92 D d
Caravaca, *Spain* 107 D c
Caravelas, *Brazil* 93 K g
Caraveli, *Peru* 92 C g
Carballino, *Spain* 106 A a
Carballo, *Spain* 106 A a
Carberry, *Manitoba* 87 S j
Carbon, *Alberta* 86 D g
Carbonara, C., *Sardinia* 111 B f
Carbondale, *Alberta* 86 D e
Carbonear, *Newfoundland* 83 T f
Carcajou, *Alberta* 88 L b
Carcassonne, *France* 109 E e
Carcross, *Yukon* 77 U f
Cardamom Hills, *India* 126 E g
Cárdenas, *Cuba* 91 C b
Cárdenas, *Mexico* 90 E c
Cardiel, L., *Argentina* 95 B g
Cardiff, *Wales* 99 E j
Cardigan, co., *Wales* 99 E h
Cardigan, *Prince Edward I.* 82 K g
Cardigan & B., *Wales* 99 D h
Cardigan B., *Prince Edward I.* 82 K g
Cardona, *Spain* 107 F b
Cardross, *Saskatchewan* 87 M j
Cardston, *Alberta* 86 D j
Cardwell, *Australia* 135 J c
Carey, L., *Australia* 134 D e
Cargill, *Ontario* 84 J h
Carhaix, *France* 108 B b
Carhué. *See* Adolfo Alsina
Caribbean Sea, *West Indies, etc.* 91 D d
Cariboo Mts., *Br. Columbia* 88 J d
Caribou, L., *Ontario* 84 A b
Caribou, *Manitoba* 81 K f
Caribou Hide, *Br. Columbia* 88 F b
Caribou I., *Nova Scotia* 82 K h
Caribou I., *Ontario* 84 E e
Caribou Mts., *Alberta* 88 M a
Caribrod. *See* Dimitrovgrad
Carichic, *Mexico* 90 C b
Carievale, *Saskatchewan* 87 Q j
Carillon, *Quebec* 85 Q g
Cariñena, *Spain* 107 E b
Carinhanha, *Brazil* 93 J f
Caripito, *Venezuela* 92 E a
Cariús, *Brazil* 93 K e
Carlet, *Spain* 107 E c
Carleton, Mt., *New Brunswick* 82 F f
Carleton, *Quebec* 82 F e
Carleton Place, *Ontario* 85 O g
Carleton Pt., *Anticosti I., Quebec* 82 K d
Carlingford L., *Eire* 99 D g
Carlington, *Ontario* 84 C j
Carlisle, *England* 99 F f
Carlos Casares, *Argentina* 94 D e
Carlow & co., *Eire* 99 C h
Carlton, *Saskatchewan* 86 L f
Carlyle, *Saskatchewan* 87 P j
Carmacks, *Yukon* 77 T e
Carman, *Manitoba* 87 U j
Carmangay, *Alberta* 86 D h
Carmanville, *Newfoundland* 83 S d
Carmarthen & co., *Wales* 99 E j
Carmarthen B., *Wales* 99 D j
Carmaux, *France* 109 E d
Carmel, Mt., *Israel* 123 D e
Carmel, *Saskatchewan* 87 M f
Carmelo, *Uruguay* 94 E d
Carmen, *Bolivia* 92 D f
Carmen, *Colombia* 92 B b
Carmen, *Mexico* 90 F d
Carmen Alto, *Chile* 94 C b
Carmen de Patagones, *Argentina* 95 D f
Carmen I., *Mexico* 90 B b
Carmensa, *Argentina* 94 C e
Carmichael, *Saskatchewan* 86 J h
Carmona, *Angola* 120 D f
Carmona, *Spain* 106 C d
Carnamah, *Australia* 134 C e
Carnarvon, *Australia* 134 B d
Carnarvon, *South Africa* 122 C f
Carndonagh, *Eire* 98 C e
Carnduff, *Saskatchewan* 87 Q j
Carnegie, L., *Australia* 134 D e
Carnot, *Cent. Afr. Rep* 119 J h
Carnsore Pt., *Eire* 99 C h
Carolina, *Brazil* 93 H e
Carolina, *Puerto Rico* 54 D h
Carolina, *South Africa* 122 E e
Caroline, *Alberta* 86 C f
Caroline I., *Pacific Ocean* 79 M h
Caroline Is., *Pacific Ocean* 78 E f
Caron, *Saskatchewan* 87 M h
Caroní, R., *Venezuela* 92 E b
Carora, *Venezuela* 92 C a
Carp, *Ontario* 85 O g
Carpathian Mts., *Cent. Eur.* 97 N f
Carpatii Sudici, *Romania* 112 D b
Carpentaria, G. of, *Australia* 134 G b
Carp L., *Br. Columbia* 88 H c
Carragana, *Saskatchewan* 87 O f
Carrara, *Italy* 110 C c
Carreño, *Spain* 106 C a
Carrickmacross, *Eire* 99 C g
Carrick-on-Shannon, *Eire* 99 B g
Carrick-on-Suir, *Eire* 99 C h
Carrière, L., *Quebec* 85 N e
Carrión de los Condes, *Spain* 106 C a
Carroll, *Manitoba* 87 R j
Carroll Inlet, *Antarctica* 136 G d
Carrot R., *Manitoba* 87 V d
Carrot R., *Saskatchewan* 87 N e
Carrot River, *Saskatchewan* 87 O e
Carrowmore L., *Eire* 99 A f
Carruthers, *Saskatchewan* 86 H f
Carsamba, *Turkey* 124 C a
Carseland, *Alberta* 86 D h
Carstairs, *Alberta* 86 C g
Carstairs, *Scotland* 98 E e
Carstensz, Mt., *W. Irian* 129 L l
Carswell L., *Saskatchewan* 88 P a
Cartagena, *Colombia* 92 B a
Cartagena, *Spain* 107 E d
Cartago, *Colombia* 92 B c
Cartago, *Costa Rica* 91 C e
Cartaxo, *Portugal* 106 A c
Cartaya, *Spain* 106 B d
Carteret, *France* 108 C b
Cartier, *Ontario* 84 J f
Cartierville, *Quebec* 85 R j
Cartierville Airport, *Quebec* 85 Q j
Cartwright, *Labrador* 81 O g
Cartwright, *Manitoba* 87 S j
Carúpano, *Venezuela* 92 E a
Carutaperá, *Brazil* 93 H d
Carvoeiro, *Brazil* 92 E d
Casablanca, *Chile* 94 B d
Casablanca, *Morocco* 118 D b
Casaccia, *Switzerland* 101 E b
Casapedia, *Quebec* 82 G e
Casapedia R., *Quebec* 82 F e
Casas Grandes, *Mexico* 90 C a
Casas Ibañez, *Spain* 107 E c
Cascade, *Br. Columbia* 88 K f
Cascade Mts., *Canada-U.S.A.* 88 J f
Cascade Pt., *New Zealand* 135 P l
Cascais, *Portugal* 106 A c
Caserta, *Italy* 111 E e
Casey B., *Antarctica* 136 P e
Casey, *Quebec* 85 Q e
Casey Ra., *Antarctica* 136 Q e
Cashel, *Eire* 99 B h
Casilda, *Argentina* 94 D d
Casilda, *Cuba* 91 D b
Casino, *Australia* 135 K e
Casma, *Peru* 92 B e
Caspe, *Spain* 107 E b
Caspian Sea, *Europe-Asia* 114 E e
Cassai, *Angola* 120 E g
Cassamba, *Angola* 120 E g
Cassel, *France* 108 E a
Casselman, *Ontario* 85 P g
Cassiar Mts., *Br. Columbia* 80 F e
Cassino, *Brazil* 94 F d
Cassino, *Italy* 111 D e
Cassiparé, *Brazil* 93 G c
Cassis, *France* 109 F e
Cassou, *Upper Volta* 118 E f
Castanhal, *Brazil* 92 E e
Castanheiro, *Brazil* 92 D d
Castaño, *Argentina* 94 C d
Castasegna, *Switzerland* 101 E b
Casteljaloux, *France* 109 C d
Castellammare & G. di, *Sicily* 111 D f
Castellammare di Stabia, *Italy* 111 E e
Castellane, *France* 109 G e
Castellar de Santiago, *Spain* 106 D c
Castelli, *Argentina* 94 E e
Castellón de la Plana, *Spain* 107 E c
Castellote, *Spain* 107 E b
Castelnaudary, *France* 109 E e
Castelo Branco, *Portugal* 106 B c
Castelo de Vide, *Portugal* 106 B c
Castelsarrasin, *France* 109 D e
Castelvetrano, *Sicily* 111 D g
Casterle, *Belgium* 100 C c
Castets, *France* 109 C e
Castilletes, *Colombia* 92 C a
Castillo, Mt., *Chile* 95 B g
Castlebar, *Eire* 99 A g
Castle Douglas, *Scotland* 99 E f
Castlegar, *Br. Columbia* 88 L f
Castlerea, *Eire* 99 B g
Castlereagh, R., *Australia* 135 J f
Castor, *Alberta* 86 F f
Castres, *France* 109 E e
Castro, *Brazil* 94 F b
Castro, *Chile* 95 B f
Castro Marin, *Portugal* 106 B d
Castropol, *Spain* 106 B a
Castrovillari, *Italy* 111 F f
Castuera, *Spain* 106 C c
Catabola, *Angola* 120 D g
Catalina, *Newfoundland* 83 T e
Catalina Pt., *Guam* 78 B k
Catamaran, *Tasmania* 135 J h
Catamarca, *Argentina* 94 C c
Catanduanes, I., *Philippines* 129 H h
Catania & G. di, *Sicily* 111 E g
Catanzaro, *Italy* 111 F f
Catarman, *Philippines* 129 H h
Catastrophe, C., *Australia* 134 G g
Catbalogan, *Philippines* 129 H h
Cateau, Le, *France* 108 E a
Cater, *Saskatchewan* 86 J e
Cat I., *Bahama Is.* 91 D b
Cat Lake, *Ontario* 81 K g
Cato, I., *Coral Sea* 78 F k
Catorce, *Mexico* 90 D c
Catriló, *Argentina* 94 D e
Catuna, *Argentina* 94 C d
Cauchon L., *Manitoba* 87 V c
Caughnawaga, *Quebec* 85 R g
Caughnawaga Ind. Res., *Quebec* 85 R k
Caulfeild, *Br. Columbia* 88 C f
Caungula, *Angola* 120 D f
Cauquenes, *Chile* 94 B e
Causapscal, *Quebec* 82 E e
Cauto, R., *Cuba* 91 D b
Cauvery R., *India* 126 E f
Cavalcante, *Brazil* 93 H f
Cavan & co., *Eire* 99 C g
Cavell, *Ontario* 84 C b
Cavell, *Saskatchewan* 86 J f
Cavendish, *Alberta* 86 G h
Cavergno, *Switzerland* 101 D b
Cavers, *Ontario* 84 C d
Caviana, I., *Brazil* 93 G c
Cawnpore. *See* Kanpur
Cawood, *Quebec* 85 O g
Caxias, *Brazil* 92 C d
Caxias, *Brazil* 93 J d
Caxias do Sul, *Brazil* 94 F c
Cayambe, *Ecuador* 92 B c
Cayenne, *French Guiana* 93 G c
Cayes, Les, *Haiti* 91 E c
Cayey, *Puerto Rico* 54 C h
Cayley, *Alberta* 86 D h
Cayman Is., *W. Indies* 91 C c
Cayo, *British Honduras* 91 B c
Cayuga, *Ontario* 84 L k
Cazage, *Angola* 120 E g
Cazalla de la Sierra, *Spain* 106 C d
Cazin, *Yugoslavia* 110 E c
Cazorla, *Spain* 106 D d
Ceanannus Mór. *See* Kells
Ceará. *See* Fortaleza
Ceará Mirim, *Brazil* 93 K e
Ceba, *Saskatchewan* 87 P e
Cebaco, I., *Panama* 91 C e
Cebollar, *Argentina* 94 C c
Cebollera, Sa., *Spain* 107 D b
Cebu, *Philippines* 129 H h
Ceclavín, *Spain* 106 B c
Cedar L., *Manitoba* 87 R e
Cedar Springs, *Ontario* 84 H k
Cedoux, *Manitoba* 87 O j
Cedral, *Mexico* 90 D c
Cedros, I., *Mexico* 90 A b
Ceduna, *Australia* 134 F f
Cefalu, *Sicily* 111 E f
Cegled, *Hungary* 105 H e
Cehegin, *Spain* 107 E c
Ceiba, *Puerto Rico* 54 D h
Cejal, *Colombia* 92 D c
Celanova, *Spain* 106 B a
Celaya, *Mexico* 90 D c
Celebes, I., *Indonesia* 129 G l
Celebes Sea, *Indonesia* 129 H k
Celje, *Yugoslavia* 110 E b
Cella, *Spain* 107 E b
Celle, *Germany* 104 C b
Celles, *Belgium* 100 B d
Çemişgezek, *Turkey* 124 C b
Cenis, Mt., *France* 110 A c
Center L., *Palmyra I.* 79 U k
Central, Cord., *Dom. Rep.* 91 E c
Central, Cord., *Peru* 92 B e
Central African Republic, *Central Africa* 119 J g
Central America 91 B d
Central Butte, *Saskatchewan* 86 L h
Centralia, *Ontario* 84 J f
Centreville, *New Brunswick* 82 E g
Centreville, *Nova Scotia* 82 F j
Cephalonia. *See* Kefallinía
Ceram I., *Indonesia* 129 J l
Ceram Sea, *Indonesia* 129 J l
Cereal, *Alberta* 86 G g
Cerf, L. du, *Quebec* 85 P f
Cerignola, *Italy* 111 E e
Cerigo. *See* Kíthira I.
Cerigotto. *See* Andikíthira
Cerknica, *Yugoslavia* 110 E c
Çermik, *Turkey* 124 C b
Cernauti. *See* Chernovtsy
Cerralvo, I., *Mexico* 90 C c
Cerralvo, *Mexico* 90 E b
Cerreto Sannita, *Italy* 111 E e
Cerro de Pasco, *Peru* 92 B f
Cerro de Punta, Mt., *Puerto Rico* 54 C h
Cervera de Pisuerga, *Spain* 106 C a
Cesena, *Italy* 110 D c
Cēsis, *Latvia, U.S.S.R.* 103 L h
Česká Lipa, *Czechoslovakia* 104 F c
Česke Budějovice, *Czech.* 104 F d
Cessford, *Alberta* 86 F g
Cessnock, *Australia* 135 K f
Cetinje, *Yugoslavia* 112 B c
Cetraro, *Italy* 111 E f
Cette. *See* Sete
Cetti B., *Guam* 78 A l
Ceuta, B. de, *Mexico* 90 C c
Ceuta, *N. Africa* 118 D a
Cévennes, *France* 109 E e
Cevio, *Switzerland* 101 D b
Ceylon, I., *Indian Ocean* 126 F g
Ceylon, *Saskatchewan* 87 N j
Chablis, *France* 108 E c
Chacabuco, *Argentina* 94 D d
Chacance, *Chile* 94 C b
Chachapoyas, *Peru* 92 B e
Chachwengsao, *Thailand* 132 C d
Chad (Tchad), *Cent. Africa* 119 J f
Chad (Tchad) L., *Chad* 119 H f
Chagai, *Pakistan* 126 B c
Chagda, *U.S.S.R.* 115 N c
Chagny, *France* 108 F c
Chagode, *U.S.S.R.* 116 J b
Chaguaramas, *Trinidad* 92 E a
Chāh Bahār, *Iran* 125 H d
Chaibassa, *India* 127 G d
Chaise Dieu, *France* 109 E d
Chakansur, *Afghanistan* 125 H c
Chakrata, *India* 126 E b
Chaksam, *Tibet* 127 H c
Chakwal, *Pakistan* 126 D b
Chala, *Peru* 92 C g
Chalan Kanoa, *Saipan-Tinian Is.* 78 A e
Chalchihuites, *Mexico* 90 D c
Chalcis. *See* Khalkís
Chaleur, B. de, *Quebec-New Brunswick* 82 H e
Chalham, I., *Chile* 95 C h
Chalhuanca, *Peru* 92 C f
Chaling, *China* 131 F j
Chalisgaon, *India* 126 D d
Chalk River, *Ontario* 85 N f
Chalky Inlet, *New Zealand* 135 P m
Challapata, *Bolivia* 92 D g
Challenger Mts., *N.-W. Terr.* 81 L a
Châlons-sur-Marne, *France* 108 F b
Châlons-sur-Saône, *France* 108 F c
Chalus, *France* 108 D d
Chalus, *Iran* 125 F b
Cham, *Germany* 104 E d
Chaman, *Pakistan* 126 C b
Chamba, *Tanzania* 121 H g
Chambal R., *India* 126 E c
Chamberlain, *Saskatchewan* 87 M h
Chambéry, *France* 108 F d
Chambica, *Brazil* 93 H e
Chambord, *Quebec* 85 S d
Chamdo, *China* 128 C d
Chamical, *Argentina* 94 C d
Chamo, L., *Ethiopia* 121 H c
Chamonix, *France* 108 G d
Champa, *India* 126 E b
Champagne, prov., *France* 108 E b
Champcoeur, *Quebec* 85 N d
Champerico, *Guatemala* 90 F e
Champion, *Alberta* 86 D h
Champion, *Belgium* 100 D d
Champlain, *Quebec* 85 S f
Champlitte, *France* 108 F c
Champneuf, *Quebec* 85 N d
Chamusca, *Portugal* 106 A c
Chanchiang, *China* 131 E m
Chanchiang, *Hainan I., China* 131 D n
Chan-ching. *See* Tsamkong
Chanco, *Chile* 94 B e
Chancy, *Switzerland* 101 A b
Chanda, *India* 126 E d
Chandler, *Quebec* 82 H e
Chandod, *India* 126 D d
Chandpur, *East Pakistan* 127 H d
Chanf, *Iran* 125 H d
Chang-chia-k'on. *See* Changkiakow
Changchih, *China* 130 F d
Changchow, *China* 131 H k
Changchow, *China* 130 K g
Changchun, *China* 128 J b
Change Island, *Newfoundland* 83 S d
Changhsu Shan, *China* 131 K j
Changhsu Shan, I., *China* 131 K j
Changhua, *Taiwan* 131 K k
Changkiakow, *China* 130 G b
Changlang, *Kashmir* 126 E b
Changlo, *China* 130 J d
Changpeh, *China* 130 G b
Changping, *China* 130 H b
Changpu, *China* 131 H k
Changsha, *China* 131 F h
Changshan, *China* 131 J h
Changte. *See* Anyang
Changteh, *China* 131 E h
Changting, *China* 131 H k
Changyeh, *China* 128 D c
Channel, *Newfoundland* 83 N f
Channel Is., *English Channel* 99 A l
Channing, airfield, *Man.* 87 Q d
Chantada, *Spain* 106 B a
Chanthaburi, *Thailand* 132 C d
Chantilly, *France* 108 E b
Chany, Oz., *U.S.S.R.* 114 G c
Chao Phraya, R., *Thailand* 129 D g
Chaoan, *China* 131 H l
Chaochow, *China* 131 H l
Chao Hu, *China* 130 H g
Chaotung, *China* 131 A j
Chapais, *Quebec* 85 Q c
Chapala, L., *Mexico* 90 D c
Chapayevsk, *U.S.S.R.* 117 J d
Chapeau, *Quebec* 85 N g
Chapelle, L. de la, *Quebec* 83 L c
Chapleau, *Ontario* 84 G e
Chapleau, R., *Ontario* 84 G d
Chaplin, *Saskatchewan* 86 L h
Chapman, Mt., *Br. Columbia* 88 K e
Chaput Hughes, *Ontario* 84 K d
Char, *Mauritania* 118 C d
Chara, *U.S.S.R.* 115 L c
Charagua, *Bolivia* 92 E g
Charaña, *Bolivia* 92 D g
Charco Azul B., *Panama* 91 C e
Charcot, I., *Antarctica* 136 H e
Chard, *Alberta* 88 O c
Chardzhou, *Turkmen., U.S.S.R.* 114 F e
Charente, dep., *France* 108 D d
Charente, R., *France* 108 C d
Charente-Maritime, dep., *France* 108 C d
Charikar, *Afghanistan* 125 J c
Chari R., *Chad* 119 J f
Charité, La, *France* 108 E c
Charleroi, *Belgium* 100 C d
Charlesbourg, *Quebec* 85 R a
Charles I., *N.-W. Terr* 81 M e
Charleville, *Australia* 135 J e
Charleville, *Eire* 99 B h
Charleville, *France* 108 F b
Charlie Lake, *Br. Columbia* 88 J b
Charlotte Amalie, *Virgin Is.* 54 E h
Charlotte L., *Br. Columbia* 88 G d
Charlottenburg, *Germany* 104 E b
Charlottetown, *Prince Edward I.* 82 J g
Charlton, *Australia* 135 H g
Charlton, *Ontario* 84 K e
Charlton I., James Bay, *North-West Territories* 81 M g
Charmey, *Switzerland* 101 C b
Charny, *Quebec* 82 A g
Charolles, *France* 108 F c
Charskiy, *Kazakh., U.S.S.R.* 117 H d
Charters Towers, *Australia* 135 J d
Charterville, *Quebec* 82 A h
Chartres, *France* 108 D b
Chartreuse, *France* 108 F d
Charvonnex, *France* 101 B c
Chascomús, *Argentina* 94 E e
Chase, *Br. Columbia* 88 O k
Chasm, *Br. Columbia* 88 J e
Chasseneuil, *France* 108 D d
Châteaubriant, *France* 108 C c
Château Chinon, *France* 108 E c
Châteauchinon, *France* 108 C c
Château-du-Loir, *France* 108 D c
Châteaudun, *France* 108 D b
Château Gontier, *France* 108 C c
Château-la-Vallière, *France* 108 D c
Châteaulin, *France* 108 A b
Châteauneuf-en-Thymerais, *France* 108 D b
Châteaurenault, *France* 108 D c
Château Richer, *Quebec* 82 A f
Châteauroux, *France* 108 D c
Château Salins, *France* 108 G b
Château Thierry, *France* 108 E b
Châteauvert, L., *Quebec* 85 R e
Châteauvillain, *France* 108 F b
Châtelet, *Belgium* 100 C d
Châtellerault, *France* 108 D c
Châtel-St. Denis, *Switzerland* 101 B b
Chatfield, *Manitoba* 87 U h
Chatham, *England* 99 H j
Chatham, *New Brunswick* 82 G f
Chatham, *Ontario* 84 H k
Chatham Is., *Pacific Ocean* 78 J m
Chatham Sd., *Br. Columbia* 88 D c
Cha Thing Phra, *Thailand* 132 C e
Châtillon-sur-Seine, *France* 108 F c
Chatra, *India* 127 F d
Chatrapur, *India* 127 G e
Châtre, La, *France* 108 E c
Chatsworth, *Ontario* 84 K h
Chaudière Falls, *Quebec* 84 C h
Chau-doc, *S. Vietnam* 132 C d
Chaumont-en-Bassigny, *France* 108 F b
Chaunskaya Guba, *U.S.S.R.* 115 R b
Chauvin, *Alberta* 86 G f
Chaux-de-Fonds, La, *Switzerland* 101 B a
Chaves, *Brazil* 93 H d
Chaves, *Portugal* 106 B b
Chayu, *Tibet* 128 C e
Chazón, *Argentina* 94 D d

Convención, *Colombia* 92 C b
Conway, *Wales* 99 E g
Conway Reef, *Pacific Ocean* 78 H j
Coober Pedy, *Australia* 134 F e
Cooch Behar, *India* 127 G b
Cook, B. de, *Chile* 95 B j
Cook, C., *Vancouver I., British Columbia* 88 F e
Cook, Mt., *New Zealand* 135 Q l
Cook Deep, *Pacific Ocean* 78 C f
Cook I., *Antarctica* 136 K g
Cook Ice Shelf, *Antarctica* 136 A e
Cooking L., *Alberta* 86 D e
Cook Is., *Pacific Ocean* 78 K j
Cook's Harbour, *Newfoundland* 83 R b
Cookshire, *Quebec* 85 T g
Cook's Passage, *Australia* 135 J b
Cookstown, *Ontario* 85 L h
Cook Str., *New Zealand* 135 R l
Cooktown, *Australia* 135 J c
Coolgardie, *Australia* 134 D f
Cooma, *Australia* 135 J g
Coonamble, *Australia* 135 J f
Coondiwindi, *Australia* 135 K e
Coonor, *India* 126 E f
Cooper I., *Palmyra I.* 79 U k
Cooper Mt., *Br. Columbia* 88 L e
Coopers Cr., *Australia* 134 G e
Cooroy, *Australia* 135 K e
Cootamundra, *Australia* 135 J f
Cootehill, *Eire* 99 C f
Copenhagen, *Denmark* 103 E j
Copetonas, *Argentina* 95 D e
Copiapó, *Chile* 94 B c
Coporaque, *Peru* 92 C f
Coppell, *Ontario* 84 G f
Copper Cliff, *Ontario* 84 J c
Coppermine, *N.-W. Terr.* 80 H d
Coppermine Pt., *Ontario* 84 F f
Copper Mountain, *B. C.* 88 J f
Coppet, *Switzerland* 101 B b
Coquilhatville. *See* Mbandaka
Coquimbo & B. de, *Chile* 94 B c
Coquitlam R., *Br. Columbia* 88 E f
Corabia, *Romania* 112 E c
Coraçoes, *Brazil* 93 H h
Coral Harbour, *North-West Territories* 81 L e
Coral Rapids, *Ontario* 84 J b
Coral Sea, *Australia* 78 F j
Corato, *Italy* 111 F e
Corbetton, *Ontario* 84 K h
Corbin Hd., *Newfoundland* 83 R g
Corcaigh. *See* Cork
Corcovado, G. del, *Chile* 95 B f
Corcovado, Mt., *Chile* 95 B f
Corcubíon, *Spain* 106 A a
Córdoba, *Mexico* 90 E d
Córdoba, *Spain* 106 C d
Córdoba & Sa. de, *Argentina* 94 D d
Córdova, *Peru* 92 C f
Cordova Mines, *Ontario* 85 N h
Corfu, Str. of, *Greece* 113 C e
Corfu (Kérkira) I., *Greece* 113 B e
Coria, *Spain* 106 B b
Corigliano Calabro, *Italy* 111 F f
Coringa, *India* 127 F e
Corinth (Korinthos), *Greece* 113 D f
Corinto, *Brazil* 93 J g
Corinto, *Nicaragua* 91 B d
Cork & co., *Eire* 99 B j
Cork Harb., *Eire* 99 B j
Corleone, *Sicily* 111 D g
Cormack, Mt., *Newfoundland* 83 R g
Cormack, *Newfoundland* 83 P d
Cormier, L., *Quebec* 83 L b
Cormoran Reef, *Palau Is.* 78 B l
Cormorant & L., *Manitoba* 87 R d
Cormorant Pt., *Anticosti I., Quebec* 83 L d
Corner Brook, *Nfd.* 83 P e
Corning, *Saskatchewan* 87 P j
Cornwall, co., *England* 99 D k
Cornwall & I., *Ontario* 85 Q g
Cornwall I., *N.-W. Terr.* 81 K b
Cornwallis I., *N.-W. Terr* 81 K b
Coro, *Venezuela* 92 D a
Coroata, *Brazil* 93 J d
Corocoro, *Bolivia* 92 D g
Coroico, *Bolivia* 92 D g
Coromandel Ra, *N. Zealand* 135 R k
Coronach, *Saskatchewan* 87 M j
Coronada, B., *Costa Rica* 91 C e
Coronation, *Alberta* 86 F f
Coronation G., *N.-W. Terr.* 80 H d
Coronation I., *Antarctica* 136 J g
Coronel, *Chile* 95 B e
Coronel Pringles, *Argentina* 95 D e
Coronel Suarez, *Argentina* 95 D e
Coronie, *Surinam* 93 F b
Coropuna, Mt., *Peru* 92 C g
Corozal, *Brit. Honduras* 91 B c
Corpen Aiken, *Argentina* 95 C g
Corque, *Bolivia* 92 D g
Corrales, *Uruguay* 94 E d
Corralitos, *Mexico* 90 C a
Corregidor, I., *Philippines* 129 H h
Corrèze, dep., *France* 109 D d
Corribelle, *Quebec* 85 O c
Corrib L., *Eire* 99 A g
Corrientes, *Argentina* 94 E c
Corrientes, C., *Argentina* 95 E e
Corrientes, C., *Mexico* 90 C c
Corrigin, *Australia* 134 C f
Corse. *See* Corsica
Corsewall Pt., *Scotland* 98 D e
Corsica (Corse), I., *France* 110 B d
Cortés, G. de, *Cuba* 91 C b
Cortessem, *Belgium* 100 D d
Cortona, *Italy* 110 D d
Coruche, *Portugal* 106 A c
Coruh, R., *Turkey* 124 D a
Çorum, *Turkey* 124 C a
Corumbá, *Brazil* 94 E a
Corunna. *See* La Coruña
Corwen, *Wales* 99 E h
Cosalo, *Mexico* 90 C c
Coscurita, *Spain* 107 D b
Coseguina, Vol., *Nicaragua* 91 B d
Cosenza, *Italy* 111 F f
Cosquin, *Argentina* 94 D d
Cossonay, *Switzerland* 101 B b
Costa Rica, *Central America* 91 C d
Costebelle, L., *Quebec* 83 K c
Costermansville. *See* Bukavu
Costigan Mts., *New Brunswick* 82 E g
Cotabato, *Philippines* 129 H j
Cotagaita, *Bolivia* 92 D h
Cotahuasi, *Peru* 92 C g
Côteau, The, plat., *Sask.* 86 K g
Côteau Station, *Quebec* 85 Q g
Côte d'Azur, *France* 109 G e
Côte-d'Or., dep., *France* 108 F c
Côtes-du-Nord, dep., *France* 108 B b
Côte St. Luc, *Quebec* 85 R j
Cotonou, *Dahomey* 118 F g
Cotswold Hills, *England* 99 F j
Cottbus, *Germany* 104 F c
Cottel I., *Newfoundland* 83 T e
Cotter, C., *Antarctica* 136 B d
Cottica, *Surinam* 93 G c
Cotton L., *Manitoba* 87 V c
Couckelaere, *Belgium* 100 A c
Coudres, I. aux, *Quebec* 82 B f
Coulman I., *Antarctica* 136 B d
Coulonge, R., *Quebec* 85 O f
Coulter, *Manitoba* 87 Q j
Coupe, C., *Miquelon I., Atlantic Ocean* 83 Q g
Courantyne, R., *Guyana, etc.* 93 F c
Courcelles, *Quebec* 82 B h
Couronne C., *France* 109 F e
Courtenay, *Vancouver I., British Columbia* 88 G f
Courtmacsherry, *Eire* 99 B j
Courtrai, *Belgium* 100 B d
Courtright, *Ontario* 84 H k
Court St. Étienne, *Belgium* 100 C d
Courval, *Saskatchewan* 86 L h
Couta Magalhães, *Brazil* 93 H e
Couterne, *France* 108 C b
Couthuin, *Belgium* 100 D d
Coutts, *Alberta* 86 F j
Couvin, *Belgium* 100 C d
Cove I., *Ontario* 84 J g
Covenas, *Colombia* 92 B b
Coventry, *England* 99 F h
Covilhã, *Portugal* 106 B b
Cowan, L., *Australia* 134 D f
Cowan, *Manitoba* 87 R f
Cowan L., *Saskatchewan* 86 K d
Cowan R., *Saskatchewan* 86 K d
Cowansville, *Quebec* 85 S g
Cowdenbeath, *Scotland* 98 E d
Cowell, *Australia* 134 G f
Cowes, *Isle of Wight, England* 99 G k
Cow Head, *Newfoundland* 83 P d
Cowley, *Alberta* 86 D j
Cowra, *Australia* 135 J f
Coxipi L., *Quebec* 83 O b
Cox's Bazar, *E. Pakistan* 127 H d
Cox's Cove, *Newfoundland* 83 O d
Coxyde, *Belgium* 100 A c
Coyame, *Mexico* 90 C b
Coyuca, *Mexico* 90 D d
Cozumel, I., *Mexico* 90 G c
Cozumel, *Mexico* 90 G c
Cracow (Krakow), *Poland* 105 H c
Craigmyle, *Alberta* 86 E g
Craik, *Saskatchewan* 87 M g
Craiova, *Romania* 112 D b
Cranberry Portage, *Manitoba* 87 Q d
Cranbrook, *Br. Columbia* 88 M f
Crandall, *Manitoba* 87 R h
Crane L., *Saskatchewan* 86 H h
Crane Valley, *Saskatchewan* 87 M j
Crans, *Switzerland* 101 C b
Crary Mts., *Antarctica* 136 F c
Crateus, *Brazil* 93 J e
Crato, *Brazil* 92 E e
Crato, *Brazil* 93 K e
Craven, *Saskatchewan* 87 N h
Crean L., *Saskatchewan* 86 L d
Cree, R., *Saskatchewan* 88 Q a
Cree L., *Saskatchewan* 88 Q b
Cree Lake, *Saskatchewan* 88 Q b
Creelman, *Manitoba* 87 O j
Creemore, *Ontario* 84 K h
Creighton, *Saskatchewan* 87 P d
Creighton Mine, *Ontario* 84 J f
Cremona, *Alberta* 86 C g
Cremona, *Italy* 110 C c
Creporí, R., *Brazil* 93 F e
Crerar, *Ontario* 84 K f
Cres, I., *Yugoslavia* 110 E c
Crescent, *Br. Columbia* 88 E g
Cressday, *Alberta* 86 G j
Cresta, *Switzerland* 101 E b
Creston, *Br. Columbia* 88 L f
Crestwynd, *Saskatchewan* 87 M h
Crete, Sea of, *Greece* 113 E g
Crete (Kríti), I., *Greece* 113 E g
Creuse, dep., *France* 108 D c
Crewe, *England* 99 F g
Crichton, *Saskatchewan* 86 K j
Crieff, *Scotland* 98 E d
Crilly, *Ontario* 86 K b
Crimea (Krym), *U.S.S.R.* 116 H j
Crimmitschau, *Germany* 104 E c
Crisana, *Romania* 112 C a
Cristóbal, *Panama* 91 D e
Cristóbal Colón, *Venezuela* 92 C a
CrnaGora, *Yugoslavia* 112 B c
Croisic, Le, *France* 108 B c
Croix, L. à la, *Quebec* 82 B b
Croker, C., *Ontario* 84 K h
Croker I., *Australia* 134 F b
Cromarty, *Scotland* 98 E c
Cromer, *England* 99 H h
Cromer, *Manitoba* 87 Q j
Cromwell, *New Zealand* 135 P m
Crooked I., *Bahama Is.* 91 E b
Crooked Island Pass, *Bahama Is.* 91 E b
Crooked L., *Newfoundland* 83 Q e
Crooked R., *Br. Columbia* 88 H c
Crooked River, *Sask.* 87 O f
Croque, *Newfoundland* 83 R b
Cross Fell, *England* 99 F f
Crossfield, *Alberta* 86 C g
Cross L., *Manitoba* 87 U b
Cross L., *Ontario* 85 O h
Cross Lake, *Manitoba* 87 U d
Crossley, Mt., *New Zealand* 135 Q l
Crotone, *Italy* 111 F f
Crow Duck L., *Manitoba* 86 G a
Crown Mt., *Br. Columbia* 88 D e
Crown Prince Frederik I., *North-West Territories* 81 L d
Crowsnest Pass, *Alberta-Br. Columbia* 86 C j
Croydon, *Australia* 135 H c
Croydon, *England* 99 G j
Crozier, C., *Antarctica* 136 B c
Crozier Chan., *N.-W. Terr.* 80 H b
Cruyshautem, *Belgium* 100 B d
Cruz Alta, *Argentina* 94 D d
Cruz Alta, *Brazil* 94 F c
Cruz Bay, *Virgin Is.* 54 E h
Cruz del Eje, *Argentina* 94 D d
Cruzeiro do Sul, *Brazil* 92 C e
Cruzen I., *Antarctica* 136 D d
Cruz Grande, *Chile* 94 B c
Cruz Grande, *Mexico* 90 E d
Cry L., *Br. Columbia* 88 E a
Crysdale, Mt., *Br. Columbia* 88 H c
Crystal City, *Manitoba* 87 T j
Crystal Falls, *Ontario* 84 L f
Crystal Springs, *Sask.* 87 M f
Cuangar, *Angola* 122 B c
Cuango, *Angola* 120 D f
Cuanza R., *Angola* 120 C f
Cuatro Ciénegas, *Mexico* 90 D b
Cuba, I., *West Indies* 91 C b
Cuba, *Portugal* 106 B c
Cub Hills, *Saskatchewan* 87 N d
Cuchi, *Angola* 120 D g
Cuchillo-Co, *Argentina* 95 D e
Cuchillo Parado, *Mexico* 90 C b
Cúcuta, *Colombia* 92 C b
Cuddalore, *India* 126 E f
Cuddapah, *India* 126 E f
Cudworth, *Saskatchewan* 87 M f
Cue, *Australia* 134 C e
Cuéllar, *Spain* 106 C b
Cuenca, *Ecuador* 92 B d
Cuenca, *Spain* 107 D b
Cuencame, *Mexico* 90 D c
Cuernavaca, *Mexico* 90 E d
Cuevo, *Bolivia* 92 E h
Cuff L., *Quebec* 83 N b
Cuglieri, *Sardinia* 111 B e
Cuiabá, *Brazil* 93 F g
Cuiabá, *Brazil* 92 F e
Cuicuina, *Nicaragua* 91 C d
Cuillin Hills, *Scotland* 98 C c
Cuiña, P. de, *Spain* 106 B a
Cuito Cuanavale, *Angola* 122 B c
Culcairn, *Australia* 135 J g
Culebra, I., *West Indies* 91 F c
Culgoa, R., *Australia* 135 J e
Culiacán, *Mexico* 90 C c
Cullera, *Spain* 107 E c
Cully, *Switzerland* 101 B b
Culmi, *Honduras* 91 B c
Cumá, B. de, *Brazil* 93 J d
Cumaná, *Venezuela* 92 E a
Cumaria, *Peru* 92 C e
Cumberland, co., *England* 99 E f
Cumberland, *Vancouver I., British Columbia* 88 G f
Cumberland B., *Antarctica* 136 K g
Cumberland House, *Sask.* 87 P e
Cumberland L., *Sask.* 87 P d
Cumberland Pen., *North-West Territories* 81 N d
Cumberland Sd., *N.-W. Terr.* 81 N d
Cumbrian Mts., *England* 99 E f
Cumbum, *India* 126 E e
Cumming, Mt., *Antarctica* 136 E c
Cummins, *Australia* 134 G f
Cumpas, *Mexico* 90 C a
Cunene R., *Angola* 122 A c
Cuneo, *Italy* 110 A c
Cunnamulla, *Australia* 135 J e
Cupar, *Saskatchewan* 87 N h
Cupar, *Scotland* 98 E d
Cuprija, *Yugoslavia* 112 C c
Cura, *Venezuela* 92 D a
Curaçá, *Brazil* 93 K e
Curaçao, I., *Caribbean Sea* 92 D a
Curaglia, *Switzerland* 101 D b
Curiapo, *Venezuela* 92 E b
Curicó, *Chile* 94 B d
Curiplaya, *Colombia* 92 C c
Curitiba, *Brazil* 94 G c
Curitibanos, *Brazil* 94 F c
Curlew Pt., *Quebec* 83 L c
Curling, *Newfoundland* 83 O e
Currais Novos, *Brazil* 93 K e
Curralinho, *Brazil* 93 H d
Curran, *Ontario* 85 Q g
Currie L., *Manitoba* 87 U a
Curtis, I., *Pacific Ocean* 78 J k
Curuá, R., *Brazil* 93 G e
Curuai, L. Gde do, *Brazil* 93 F d
Curuçá, *Brazil* 93 H d
Curuzú Cuatia, *Argentina* 94 E c
Curzon Islets, *Antarctica* 136 A e
Cutbank, R., *Alberta* 88 K c
Cut Beaver L., *Saskatchewan* 87 P e
Cut Knife, *Saskatchewan* 86 J f
Cutler, *Ontario* 84 H f
Cuttack, *India* 127 G d
Cuxhaven, *Germany* 104 C b
Cuzco, *Peru* 92 C f
Cyclādes (Kiklādhes), Is., *Greece* 113 E f
Cygnet L., *Manitoba* 87 W b
Cynthia Oil Fields, *Alberta* 86 B e
Cypress Hills, *Saskatchewan* 86 H j
Cypress Hills Prov. Parks, *Alberta-Saskatchewan* 86 G j
Cypress L., *Saskatchewan* 86 H j
Cypress River, *Manitoba* 87 S j
Cyprus, I., *Medit. Sea* 123 B b
Cyrenaica, *Libya* 119 K c
Cyrene (Shahhat), *Cyrenaica* 119 K b
Cyrus Field B., *N.-W. Terr.* 81 N e
Cyrville, *Ontario* 84 E h
Czar, *Alberta* 86 G f
Czarnków, *Poland* 105 G b
Czechoslovakia, *Central Europe* 97 L f
Czersk, *Poland* 105 G b
Czestochowa, *Poland* 105 H c
Człopa, *Poland* 105 G b
Daaquam, *Quebec* 82 B g
Daba, *Muscat & Oman* 125 G d
Dabakala, *Ivory Coast* 118 E g
Dabaro, *Somali Republic* 121 K c
Dabeiba, *Colombia* 92 B b
Dabhoi, *India* 126 D d
Dabie, *Poland* 104 F b
Dabola, *Guinea* 118 C f
Dabrowa Górnicza, *Poland* 105 H c
Dacca, *East Pakistan* 127 H d
Dadanawa, *Guyana* 92 F c
Daedalus Reef, *Red Sea* 124 C e
Dafoe, *Saskatchewan* 87 N g
Dagana, *Senegal* 118 B e
Dagarita, *Somali Republic* 121 J b
Dagash, *Sudan* 119 M e
Dagda, *Latvia, U.S.S.R.* 103 M h
Dagupan, *Philippines* 129 H g
Dahlak Arch., *Ethiopia* 121 J a
Dahni Murghi, *Kashmir* 126 E a
Dahomey, *W. Africa* 118 F g
Dailleboust, L., *Quebec* 82 A d
Daimiel, *Spain* 106 D c
Daireaux, *Argentina* 94 D e
Dairen. *See* Luta
Dairut, *Egypt* 119 M c
Daisetsuzan Nat. Pk., *Japan* 133 H c
Daishoji, *Japan* 133 E f
Daito Is., *Pacific Ocean* 78 D d
Dajarra, *Australia* 134 G d
Dakar, *Senegal* 118 B f
Dakovica, *Yugoslavia* 112 C c
Dal, *Norway* 103 D f
Dala, *Angola* 120 E g
Dal Älv, *Sweden* 103 G f
Dalan Dszadagad, *Mongolia* 128 D b
Dalap, *Majuro Is.* 79 U g
Dalat, *S. Vietnam* 132 D d
Dalbandin, *Pakistan* 126 B c
Dalbo Sjön, *Sweden* 103 E g
Dalby, *Australia* 135 K e
Dalby, *Sweden* 103 E f
Dalemead, *Alberta* 86 D h
Dalen, *Netherlands* 100 E b
Dalen, *Norway* 103 B g
Dalhousie, *New Brunswick* 82 F e
Dallas, *Manitoba* 87 U g
Dalmacio Velez, *Argentina* 94 D d
Dalmatia, *Yugoslavia* 110 E d
Dalmatovo, *U.S.S.R.* 117 R b
Dalmeny, *Saskatchewan* 86 L f
Dalmira, *India* 126 D c
Daloa, *Ivory Coast* 118 D g
Dalquier, *Quebec* 85 M d
Dalroy, *Alberta* 86 D g
Dalrymple, Mt., *Australia* 135 J d
Dalton, *Ontario* 84 F d
Daltonganj, *India* 127 F d
Daly, R., *Australia* 134 F b
Daly L., *Saskatchewan* 88 R b
Daly Waters, *Australia* 134 F c
Dam, *Surinam* 93 G c
Daman, *India* 126 D d
Damanhur, *Egypt* 119 M b
Damar, I., *Indonesia* 129 J m
Damascus (Damas), *Syria* 124 C c
Damāvand, Mt., *Iran* 125 F b
Dambacha, *Ethiopia* 121 H b
Dambe, *Angola* 120 D f
Damghan, *Iran* 125 F b
Damietta, *Egypt* 119 M b
Damiya, *Jordan* 123 D e
Dammam, Ad, *Saudi Arabia* 125 F d
Damoh, *India* 126 E d
Dampier Arch., *Australia* 134 C d
Dampier Land, *Australia* 134 D c
Dampier Str., *Indonesia* 129 K l
Damqawt, *S. Yemen* 125 F f
Dan, C., *Greenland* 89 N c
Dana, L., *Quebec* 85 N b
Dana, *Saskatchewan* 87 M f
Da Nang, *S. Vietnam* 132 D c
Dancing Point, *Manitoba* 87 T f
Dandenong, *Australia* 135 H g
Danforth, *Ontario* 84 E k
Danger Is., *Pacific Ocean* 78 K h
Danger Pt., *S. Africa* 122 B f
Daniels' Cove, *Newfoundland* 83 P c
Daniels L., *Ontario* 86 J a
Danilov, *U.S.S.R.* 116 M b
Dankaz, *Ethiopia* 120 H b
Dankhar, *Kashmir* 126 E b
Dannevirke, *New Zealand* 135 R l
Danube, R., *Cent. Europe* 97 M g
Danville, *Quebec* 85 S g
Danzig, G. of, *Poland* 105 H a
Danzig (Gdansk), *Poland* 105 H a
Daolatabad, *Afghanistan* 125 J b
Dapp, *Alberta* 86 D d
Daqq e Patargan, L., *Afghanistan-Iran* 125 H c
Daran, *Iran* 125 F c
Daraw, *Egypt* 119 M d
Darb, *Saudi Arabia* 124 D f
Darbhanga, *India* 127 G c
D'Arcy, *Saskatchewan* 86 J g
Dardanelles, *Turkey* 124 A b
Dar el Baida, El. *See* Casablanca
Darende, *Turkey* 124 C b
Dar-es-Salaam, *Tanzania* 121 H f
Dargai, *Pakistan* 126 D b
Dargaon, *India* 127 F d
Dargaville, *New Zealand* 135 Q j
Dariyah, *Saudi Arabia* 124 E e
Darjeeling, *India* 127 G c
Darke Lane Prov. Park, *British Columbia* 88 K f
Darling, R., *Australia* 135 H f
Darling Downs, *Australia* 135 J e
Darlingford, *Manitoba* 87 T j
Darling Pen., *N.-W. Terr.* 81 M b
Darling Ra., *Australia* 134 C f
Darlington, *England* 99 F f
Darłowo, *Poland* 105 G a
Darmody, *Saskatchewan* 86 L h
Darmstadt, *Germany* 104 C d
Darnley, C., *Antarctica* 136 Q e
Daroca, *Spain* 107 E b
Darreh Gaz, *Iran* 125 G b
Dart, C., *Antarctica* 136 E d
Dart, R., *England* 99 E k
Dartmoor, *England* 99 E k
Dartmouth, *England* 99 E k
Dartmouth, *Nova Scotia* 82 J j
Dartmouth R., *Quebec* 82 H d
Daru, I., *Papua* 135 H a
Daruvar, *Yugoslavia* 110 F c
Darwin, *Australia* 134 F b
Darwin, Mt., *Antarctica* 136 A a
Darwin, Mt., *Chile* 95 C h
Darwin, Mt., *Rhodesia* 122 E c
Daryācheh e Baktegān, L., *Iran* 125 F d
Daryācheh-ye-Rezā'iyeh, *Iran* 124 E b
Dasht, R., *Pakistan* 126 B c
Dasht Ab, *Iran* 125 G d
Dashwood, *Ontario* 84 J j
Datia, *India* 126 E c
Daugava (Dvina), R., *Latvia, U.S.S.R.* 103 L h
Daugavpils, *Latvia, U.S.S.R.* 103 M j
Daulatabad, *India* 126 E d
Daulat Yar, *Afghanistan* 125 J c
Daule, *Ecuador* 92 A d
Dauphin, *Manitoba* 87 R g
Dauphiné, prov., *France* 109 F d
Dauphin L., *Manitoba* 87 S g
Davao & G., *Philippines* 129 J j
Daveluyville, *Quebec* 85 S f
Davengus, *Quebec* 85 M d
Davenport Ra., *Australia* 134 F d
David, *Panama* 91 C e
David Glacier, *Antarctica* 136 A c
David I., *Antarctica* 136 R e
Davidson, *Saskatchewan* 87 M g
Davignab, *S.W. Africa* 122 B e
Davin, *Saskatchewan* 87 N h
Davin L., *Saskatchewan* 88 S b
Davis, *Saskatchewan* 87 M e
Davis B., *Antarctica* 136 T e
Davis Inlet, *Labrador* 81 N f
Davis Str., *Greenland-Canada* 81 O d
Davos Dorf, *Switzerland* 101 E b
Davos Platz, *Switzerland* 101 E b
Dawna Ra., *Burma, etc.* 127 J e
Dawson, Mt., *Br. Columbia* 88 L e
Dawson, R., *Australia* 135 J e
Dawson, *Yukon* 80 F e
Dawson B., *Manitoba* 87 R f
Dawson Bay, *Manitoba* 87 Q e
Dawson Creek, *British Columbia* 88 J c
Dawson-Lambton Glacier, *Antarctica* 136 K c
Dax, *France* 109 C e
Daysland, *Alberta* 86 E f
De Aar, *South Africa* 122 C f
Dead Sea, *Jordan-Israel* 123 D f
Deakin B., *Antarctica* 136 A e
Deal, *England* 99 H j
Dean Chan., *Br. Columbia* 88 F d
Dean Funes, *Argentina* 94 D d
Dean R., *Br. Columbia* 88 G d
Dease L., *Br. Columbia* 88 D a
Deauville, *France* 108 C b
Debar, *Yugoslavia* 112 C d
Debden, *Saskatchewan* 86 L e
Debec, *New Brunswick* 82 E g
Debesy, *U.S.S.R.* 117 L b
Debica, *Poland* 105 J c
Deblin, *Poland* 105 J c
Debno, *Poland* 104 F b
Debra Markos, *Ethiopia* 121 H b
Debrecen, *Hungary* 105 J e
Deccan, *India* 126 E f
Decelles, L., *Quebec* 85 M e
Deception, I., *S. Shetlands* 136 H f
Dechêne, L., *Quebec* 82 E b
Decimal, *Manitoba* 86 G a
Děčín, *Czechoslovakia* 104 F c
Decize, *France* 108 E c
Decker, *Manitoba* 87 R h
Dedeagach. *See* Alexandroúpolis
Dededo, *Guam* 78 B k
Dédougou, *Upper Volta* 118 E f
Dedza, *Malawi* 121 G g
Deep Brook, *Nova Scotia* 82 G j
Deep Cove, *Br. Columbia* 88 D f
Deep River, *Ontario* 85 N f
Dee R., *Scotland* 98 F c
Dee R., *Wales* 99 E g
Deer I., *New Brunswick* 82 F j
Deer Lake, *Newfoundland* 83 P d
Deerlyck, *Belgium* 100 B d
Deer Park, *Br. Columbia* 88 K f
Deesa, *India* 126 D a
Defferrari, *Argentina* 95 E e
Degana, *India* 126 D c
Degerfors, *Sweden* 102 H d
De Grey, R., *Australia* 134 C d
Deh Bid, *Iran* 125 F c
Deh Dehdez, *Iran* 125 F c
Dehrud, *Iran* 125 F d
Deim Zubeir, *Sudan* 119 L g
Deir Abu Said, *Jordan* 123 D e
Deir 'Ali, *Syria* 123 E d
Deir Atiye, *Syria* 123 E c
Deir ez Zor, *Syria* 124 C b
Deir Hafir, *Syria* 123 F a
Deir Shemil, *Syria* 123 E b
Déj, *Romania* 105 K e
De Kastri, *U.S.S.R.* 115 P c
Delaronde L., *Saskatchewan* 86 L d
Delburne, *Alberta* 86 D f
Delden, *Netherlands* 100 E b
Deleau, *Manitoba* 87 R j
Deleitosa, *Spain* 106 C c
De Lemmer, *Netherlands* 100 D b
Delémont, *Switzerland* 101 C a
Delfshaven, *Netherlands* 100 C c
Delft, *Netherlands* 100 C b
Delfzijl, *Netherlands* 100 E a
Delger, *Mongolia* 128 F a
Delgo, *Sudan* 119 M d
Delhi, *India* 126 E c
Delhi, *Ontario* 84 K k
Delia, *Alberta* 86 E g
Delisle, *Saskatchewan* 86 K g
Dellys, *Algeria* 118 F a
Delmas, *Saskatchewan* 86 J f
Delmenhorst, *Germany* 104 C b
Deloraine, *Manitoba* 87 R j
Delta, co., *Br. Columbia* 88 D g
Delta Beach, *Manitoba* 87 T h
Demaine, *Saskatchewan* 86 K h
Demanda, Sa. de la, *Spain* 106 D a
Demchok, *Tibet* 126 E b
Demmin, *Germany* 104 E b
Denbigh, *Ontario* 85 N g
Denbigh & co., *Wales* 99 E g
Denderleeuw, *Belgium* 100 C d
Dendermonde, *Belgium* 100 C c
Dendi, Mt., *Ethiopia* 121 H c
Dendron, *Saskatchewan* 86 K h
Denekamp, *Netherlands* 100 E b
Denges Passage, *Palau Is.* 78 B o
Den Helder, *Netherlands* 100 C b
Denholm, *Saskatchewan* 86 J f
Denia, *Spain* 107 F c
Deniau, *Quebec* 82 C f
Deniliquin, *Australia* 135 J g
Denizli, *Turkey* 124 A b
Denman Glacier, *Antarctica* 136 S e
Denmark, *Nova Scotia* 82 J h
Denmark, *W. Europe* 103 C j
Denmark Str., *Greenland, etc.* 89 N c
Den Oever, *Netherlands* 106 D b
Dent Blanche, Mt., *Switzerland* 101 C b
D'Entrecasteaux Is., *Papua* 135 K a
D'Entrecasteaux Pt., *Australia* 134 C f
Denzil, *Saskatchewan* 86 H f
Deobhog, *India* 127 F d
Deogarh, *India* 127 F d
Deoghar, *India* 127 G d
Deoli, *India* 126 E c
Deolia, *India* 126 D d
De Panne, *Belgium* 100 A c

Eddies Cove West, Newfoundland 83 P c
Eddrachillis B., Scotland 98 D b
Ed Dueim, Sudan 119 M f
Ede, Netherlands 100 D b
Edebäck, Sweden 103 E f
Eden, Manitoba 87 S h
Edenburg, South Africa 122 D e
Edendale, New Zealand 135 B g
Edenderry, Eire 99 C g
Edenhurst, Ontario 84 J h
Eden L., Manitoba 87 R b
Eden R., England 99 F f
Edenwold, Saskatchewan 87 N h
Ederengin Nuru, Mongolia 128 C b
Edgeley, Saskatchewan 87 O h
Edgell I., N.-W. Territories 81 N e
Edgeöya, I., Arctic Ocean 114 B a
Edgerton, Alberta 86 G f
Edgewood, Br. Columbia 88 K f
Édhessa, Greece 113 D d
Edievale, New Zealand 135 P m
Edinburgh, Scotland 98 E e
Edirne, Turkey 124 A a
Edith Cavell, Mt., Alberta 88 L d
Edmonton, Alberta 86 D e
Edmundston, New Brunswick 82 D f
Edom, Jordan 123 D g
Edremit, Turkey 124 A b
Edsele, Sweden 102 G e
Edsin Gol, China 128 D b
Edson, Alberta 88 L d
Edwand, Alberta 86 E d
Edward I., Ontario 84 B d
Edward L., Congo 121 F e
Edward VII Pen., Antarctica 136 C c
Edward VIII B., Antarctica 136 P e
Edziza, Mt., Br. Columbia 88 D b
Eecke, Belgium 100 B d
Eeklo (Eecloo), Belgium 100 B c
Efate, I., New Hebrides 78 G j
Eferding, Austria 104 E d
Efuenaarukosu Pt., Rota I 78 A h
Egadi Is., Sicily 111 D g
Egaña, Argentina 94 E e
Eganville, Ontario 85 N g
Eger, Hungary 105 J e
Eger. See Cheb
Egersund, Norway 103 B g
Eggenfelden, Germany 104 E d
Eghezee, Belgium 100 C d
Eglinton I., N.-W. Terr. 80 H b
Egmont, C., New Zealand 135 Q k
Egmont, Mt., New Zealand 135 Q k
Egmont B., Prince Edward I. 82 H g
Egremont, Alberta 86 D d
Egridir, Turkey 124 B b
Egypt. See United Arab Republic
Eibergen, Netherlands 100 E b
Eichstätt, Germany 104 D d
Eide, Norway 103 B f
Eidsvoll, Norway 103 D f
Eifel, Mts., Germany 104 B c
Eigg, I., Scotland 98 C d
Eights Coast, Antarctica 136 G d
Eighty Mile Beach, Australia 134 D c
Eil, Somali Republic 121 K c
Eilat, Israel 123 C h
Eil Malk, Palau Is. 78 B n
Eindhoven, Netherlands 100 D c
Ein Yahav, Israel 123 D g
Eiol, I., Truk Is. 78 E n
Eire. See Ireland, Rep. of
Eirunepé, Brazil 92 C e
Eisden, Netherlands 100 D d
Eisenach, Germany 104 D c
Eisenerz, Austria 104 F e
Eisenhower, Mt., Alberta 86 B g
Eisleben, Germany 104 D c
Ejutla, Mexico 90 E d
Ekaterinoslav. See Dnepropetrovsk
Eketahana, New Zealand 135 R l
Ekhinádhes Is., Greece 113 C e
Eksjö, Sweden 103 F h
Ekträsk, Sweden 102 H d
Ekwan, R., Ontario 81 L g
El Abde, Lebanon 123 D c
Elafónisi Chan., Greece 113 D f
Élafos I., Greece 113 D f
El Agheila, Libya 119 J b
El 'Aina, Jordan 123 D g
El Alamein, Egypt 119 L b
El Asnam (Orléansville), Algeria 109 M g
Elassón, Greece 113 D e
El Auja. See Nizana
Elâzig, Turkey 124 C b
Elba, I., Italy 110 C d
El Bab, Syria 123 F a
El Bahluiye, Syria 123 D b
El Banco, Colombia 92 C b
El Barco de Valdeorras, Spain 106 B a
Elbasan, Albania 112 C d
El Baul, Venezuela 92 D b
El Bayadh, Algeria 109 N j
Elbe R., Germany 104 D b
Elbeuf, France 108 D b
Elbing. See Elblag
El-Birka, Saudi Arabia 124 D e
Elbistan, Turkey 124 C b
Elblag, Poland 105 H a
Elbow, Saskatchewan 87 L g
Elbow R., Alberta 86 C h
El Br'aij, Syria 123 E c
El'brus, Mt., U.S.S.R. 114 D d
Elburg, Netherlands 100 D b
Elburz Mts., Iran 125 F b
El Callao, Venezuela 92 E b
El Cardón, Venezuela 92 C a
Elche, Spain 107 E c
El Chorro, Argentina 94 D b
El Cuy, Argentina 95 C e
El Dab, Somali Republic 121 K c
El Diwân, Egypt 119 M d
El Donfar, Somali Republic 121 K b
El Dorado, Mexico 90 C c
El Dorado, Venezuela 92 E b
Eldoret, Kenya 121 H d
El Encanto, Colombia 92 C d
Elephant I., Antarctica 136 J g
El Ergh, Libya 119 K c
Eleşkirt, Turkey 124 D b
Eleuthera I., Bahama Is. 91 D a
Elewyt, Belgium 100 C d
El Faiyum, Egypt 119 M c
El Fasher, Sudan 119 L f
El Ferrol del Caudillo, Spain 106 A a
Elfros, Saskatchewan 87 O g
El Fuwara, Saudi Arabia 124 D d
Elgena, Ethiopia 121 H a
El Geteina, Sudan 119 M f
Elgg, Switzerland 101 D a
El Ghobbe, Saudi Arabia 124 C e
Elgin, Manitoba 87 R j
Elgin, New Brunswick 82 G h
Elgin, Scotland 98 E c
El Giof. See Al Jawf
El Giza, Egypt 119 M b
El Goléa, Algeria 118 F b
Elgon, Mt., Uganda 121 G d
El Hamra, Syria 123 F b
El Hamrat, Syria 123 E c
El Harrach, Algeria 109 N g
El-Hayath, Saudi Arabia 124 D d
El Hijane, Syria 123 E d
El Hilla, Sudan 119 L f
Elie, Manitoba 87 U j
Elisabethville. See Lubumbashi
Elista, U.S.S.R. 114 D d
Elizabeth, Australia 134 G f
Elizabeth, Mt., Antarctica 136 B b
Elizabeth, Mt., Argentina 95 C g
Elizabeth, Mt., New Brunswick 82 F f
Elizabeth I., Jaluit I. 79 T j
Elizavetgrad. See Kirovograd
Elizondo, Spain 107 E a
El Jafr, Jordan 123 E g
El Jauf, Libya 119 K d
Elk, Poland 105 K b
El Kharga, Egypt 119 M c
Elkhorn, Manitoba 87 Q j
El Khushniye, Syria 123 D d
Elk Island Nat. Park, Alberta 86 E e
Elk Lake, Ontario 84 K e
Elko, Br. Columbia 88 M f
Elk Point, Alberta 86 G e
Elk R., Br. Columbia 88 M f
El Lādhiqīya. See Latakia
Ellás, Greece 113 D e
Ellef Ringnes I., North-West Territories 80 J b
Eller I., Kwajalein Is. 79 U e
Ellesmere, L., New Zealand 135 Q l
Ellesmere I., North-West Territories 81 L b
Ellezelles, Belgium 100 B d
Ellichpur, India 126 E d
Elliot, Australia 134 F c
Elliot, South Africa 122 D f
Elliot Group, China 130 L c
Elliot L., Ontario 84 H f
Elliot Lake, Ontario 84 H f
Ellis B., Anticosti I., Quebec 82 H d
Elliston, Newfoundland 83 T e
Ellora, India 126 E d
Ellscott, Alberta 86 E d
Ellsworth Land, Antarctica 136 F c
Ellsworth Mts., Antarctica 136 G b
Elm, Switzerland 101 E b
Elma, Manitoba 86 F a
El Ma'arra, Syria 123 E a
Elma Dagh, Turkey 124 B b
El Madhiq, Saudi Arabia 121 C e
El Mansura, Egypt 119 M b
El Mazar, Jordan 123 D f
El Mazra'a, Jordan 123 D f
Elm Creek, Manitoba 87 U j
El Meget, Somali Republic 121 K d
El Menzil, Jordan 123 E f
El Minya, Egypt 119 M c
Elmira, Ontario 84 K j
Elmira, Prince Edward I 83 K g
El Molar, Spain 106 D b
Elmsdale, Nova Scotia 82 J j
Elmsvale, Nova Scotia 82 J h
El Muwaqqar, Jordan 123 E f
Elmvale, Ontario 84 L h
Elmwood, Ontario 84 J h
El Negro, Venezuela 92 E b
Elnora, Alberta 86 D g
El Obeid, Sudan 119 M f
El Odaiya, Sudan 119 L f
Elora, Ontario 84 K j
El Pardo, Spain 106 D b
Elphinstone, Manitoba 84 R h
Elphinstone I., Burma 127 J f
El Pintado, Argentina 94 D b
El Portugues, Peru 92 B e
El Puente del Arzobispo, Spain 106 C c
El Qadmus, Syria 123 E b
El Qanawat, Syria 123 E e
El Qaryatein, Syria 123 F c
El Qathma, Saudi Arabia 124 D e
El Qatrana, Jordan 123 E f
El Qatrun, Libya 119 H d
El Quds esh Sherif. See Jerusalem
El Quneitrea, Syria 123 D d
El Quseir, Syria 123 E c
El Quweira, Jordan 123 D h
Elrose, Saskatchewan 86 J g
El Salto, Mexico 90 C c
El Salvador, Cent. America 91 B d
Elsas, Ontario 84 H d
Elsenborn, Belgium 100 E d
Elsloo, Netherlands 100 D d
Elsona, Br. Columbia 88 D f
Elspeet, Netherlands 100 D b
Elst, Netherlands 100 D c
Elsterwerda, Germany 104 E c
Elstow, Saskatchewan 87 L g
El Temblador, Venezuela 91 G e
Eltham, New Zealand 135 R k
El Tigre, Venezuela 92 E b
El Toro, Spain 107 E b
El Tránsito, Chile 94 B c
Eltrut L., Ontario 86 K a
Elugelab, I., Eniwetok 79 R c
Eluru, India 126 F e
Elva, Manitoba 87 Q j
El Valle, Colombia 92 B b
Elvas, Portugal 106 B c
El Vigía, Venezuela 92 C b
Elvira, C., N.-W. Territories 80 J c
Ely, England 99 H h
El Yunque, Mt., Puerto Rico 54 D h
Emangulova, U.S.S.R. 117 M d
Emba R., Kazakh., U.S.S.R. 114 E d
Embar, Labrador 82 G a
Embarcación, Argentina 92 E g
Embarras Portage, Alberta 88 O a
Embóna, Greece 113 F f
Embro, Ontario 84 K j
Embrun, France 109 G d
Embrun, Ontario 85 P g
Emden, Germany 104 B b
Emerald, Australia 135 J d
Emerald I., N.-W. Territories 80 H b
Emerson, Manitoba 87 U j
Emgayet, Libya 119 H c
Emidj, I., Jaluit I. 79 U j
Emilia-Romagna, reg., Italy 100 C c
Emmaste, Estonia, U.S.S.R. 103 K g
Emmeline L., Saskatchewan 86 L c
Emmen, Netherlands 100 E b
Emo, Ontario 86 J b
Emory Land Glacier, Antarctica 136 D c
Empalme, Mexico 90 B b
Empedrado, Argentina 94 E c
Empress, Alberta 86 G h
Emptinne, Belgium 100 D d
Ems, Germany 104 B c
Emsdale, Ontario 85 L g
Enard B., Scotland 98 D b
Encantada, Cerro de, Mexico 90 A a
Encarnación, Paraguay 94 E c
Enchant, Alberta 86 E h
Encontrados, Venezuela 92 C b
Encounter B., Australia 134 G g
Encruzilhada, Brazil 94 F d
Endako, Br. Columbia 88 G c
Ende, Flores I., Indonesia 129 H m
Endeavour, Saskatchewan 87 P f
Enderbury I., Phoenix Is. 78 J g
Enderby, Br. Columbia 88 M e
Enderby Ld., Antarctica 136 P d
Endo, Ontario 84 F d
Eneeldak, Jaluit I. 79 T j
Enez, G. of, Greece 113 E d
Enez, Turkey 124 A a
Enfield, Nova Scotia 82 J j
Engaño, C., Philippines 129 H g
Engebi, I., Eniwetok 79 R b
Engelberg, Switzerland 101 D b
Engels, U.S.S.R. 117 H e
Enggaño, I., Indonesia 129 D m
Enghien, Belgium 100 C d
England, Great Britain 99 F h
Englee, Newfoundland 83 Q c
Englefield, Saskatchewan 87 N j
Englehart, Ontario 84 L e
Englewood, Vancouver I., British Columbia 88 F e
English B., Br. Columbia 88 C f
English B., Quebec 82 E d
English Bazar, India 127 G c
English Chan., France-England 97 G f
English Harbour West, Newfoundland 83 R f
English River, Ontario 87 M a
Enigu, I., Majuro Is. 79 U f
Enilda, Alberta 86 A c
Eniwetok, I., Marshall Is. 78 F f
Enkhuizen, Netherlands 100 D b
Enköping, Sweden 103 G g
Enna, Sicily 111 E g
En Nahud, Sudan 119 L f
En Naqura, Lebanon 123 D d
En Nebk, Syria 123 E c
Ennell L., Eire 99 C g
Ennis, Eire 99 B h
Enniscorthy, Eire 99 C h
Enniskillen, N. Ireland 99 B f
Ennistimon, Eire 99 A h
Enns, Austria 104 F d
Enns, R., Austria 104 F e
Ennylabegan, Kwajalein Is. 79 U e
Enontekiö, Finland 102 K b
Enriquillo, L., Dom. Rep. 91 E c
Ensanche Sarmiento, Argentina 95 B g
Enschede, Netherlands 100 E b
Ensenada, Argentina 94 E d
Ensenada, Mexico 90 A a
Ensenadao, Puerto Rico 54 C j
Enshih, China 131 D g
Ensign, Alberta 86 D h
Entebbe, Uganda 121 G e
Enterprise, Ontario 85 O h
Entraygues, France 109 E d
Entrée, I. d', Madeleine Is., Quebec 83 L f
Entre Rios, Brazil 93 K f
Entre Rios, Brazil 93 G e
Entwistle, Alberta 86 C b
Enybor, I., Jaluit I. 79 T j
Eo, I., Truk Is. 78 E o
Eolie, Isole, Italy 111 E f
Epe, Netherlands 100 D b
Épernay, France 108 E b
Epi, I., New Hebrides 78 G j
Episkopi & B., Cyprus 123 A c
Epping, England 99 H j
Equatorial Guinea, W. Africa 120 C d
Equiepa, Venezuela 92 E b
Erciş, Turkey 124 D b
Erciyas Dag, Mt., Turkey 124 C b
Erd, Hungary 105 H e
Erebus, Mt., Antarctica 136 B c
Erebus Gulf, Antarctica 136 J f
Ereğli, Turkey 124 B a
Erepecú, L., Brazil 93 F d
Eressós, Greece 113 E e
Erexim, Brazil 94 F c
Erfurt, Germany 104 D c
Erh Hai, China 128 D e
Erhlien, China 115 L d
Ericht L., Scotland 98 E d
Eric L., Quebec 82 G b
Erieau, Ontario 84 J k
Eriha, Syria 123 E b
Eriksdale, Manitoba 87 T h
Erikson, Manitoba 87 S h
Erikub Is., Marshall Is. 79 U b
Erin, Ontario 84 K j
Eritrea, prov., Ethiopia 121 H a
Erlach, Switzerland 101 C a
Erlangen, Germany 104 D d
Erlenbach, Switzerland 101 C d
Ermelo, Netherlands 100 D b
Ermenek, Turkey 124 B b
Ernakulam, India 126 E f
Ernée, France 108 C b
Erne L., N. Ireland 99 B f
Erne L., Upper, N. Ireland 99 B f
Ernfold, Saskatchewan 86 L h
Eroj, I., Majuro Is. 79 T f
Eromanga, I., New Hebrides 78 J g
Erquelinnes, Belgium 100 C d
Er Rabba, Jordan 123 D f
Er Rahad, Sudan 119 M f
Er Rastan, Syria 123 E c
Errigal, Eire 98 B e
Erris Hd., Eire 99 A f
Er Rumman, Jordan 123 D e
Erskine, Alberta 86 E f
Erval, Brazil 94 F d
Erwood, Saskatchewan 87 P f
Erz Geb., Mts., Germany 104 E c
Erzincan, Turkey 124 C b
Erzurum, Turkey 124 D b
Erżviljkas, Lithuania, U.S.S.R. 103 K j
Esash, Japan 133 H b
Esbjerg, Denmark 103 C j
Escada, Brazil 93 K e
Escala, La, Spain 107 G a
Escalón, Mexico 90 D b
Escaut, R., Belgium 100 C c
Esch, Luxembourg 104 A d
Escholzmatt, Switzerland 101 C b
Escravos, R., Nigeria 118 F g
Escudo de Veraguas, Panama 91 C e
Escuinapa, Mexico 90 C c
Escuintla, Guatemala 90 F e
Escuminac, Pt., New Brunswick 82 H f
Escuminac, Quebec 82 F e
Esfahan, Iran 125 F c
Eshowe, South Africa 122 E e
Eskbank, Saskatchewan 86 L h
Eskilstuna, Sweden 103 G g
Eskimo I., Quebec 82 J c
Eskimo Point, N.-W. Terr 81 K e
Eskişehir, Turkey 124 B b
Esla, R., Spain 106 C b
Eslöv, Sweden 103 E j
Esmeralda, I., Chile 95 A g
Esmeraldas, Ecuador 92 B c
Esnagami L., Ontario 84 D b
Esnagi L., Ontario 84 F d
Espalion, France 109 E d
Espanola, Ontario 84 J f
Esperance, Australia 134 D f
Esperanza, Argentina 94 D d
Espiel, Spain 106 C c
Espinho, Portugal 106 A b
Espinosa de los Monteros, Spain 106 D a
Espírito Santo, Brazil 93 J g
Espíritu Santo, B. del, Mexico 90 G d
Espíritu Santo, C., Argentina 95 C h
Espíritu Santo, I., Mexico 90 B c
Espíritu Santo, I., New Hebrides 78 G j
Espoir, B. d', Newfoundland 83 R f
Esquel, Argentina 95 B f
Esquimalt, Vancouver I., British Columbia 88 H f
Esquina, Argentina 94 E c
Es Sa'an, Syria 123 F b
Es Salt, Jordan 123 D e
Es Samra, Jordan 123 E e
Es Sanamein, Syria 123 E d
Essaouira. See Mogador
Esse Älv, Finland 102 K e
Essen, Belgium 100 C c
Essen, Germany 104 B c
Essequibo, R., Guyana 92 F b
Essex, co., England 99 H j
Essex, Ontario 84 H k
Esslingen, Germany 104 C d
Es Sukhne, Syria 124 C c
Es Suweidīya, Syria 123 E e
Est, Lac de l', Quebec 82 C f
Estados, I. de los, Argentina 95 D h
Estaire. See Burwash
Estância, Brazil 93 K f
Estavayer, Switzerland 101 B b
Estcourt, South Africa 122 D e
Este, Pta., Puerto Rico 54 D h
Esteli, Nicaragua 91 B d
Esterhazy, Saskatchewan 87 P h
Esternay, France 108 E b
Estevan, Saskatchewan 87 O j
Estevan Group, Br. Columbia 88 E d
Estevan Point, Br. Columbia 88 F f
Esther, Alberta 86 G g
Estlin, Saskatchewan 87 N h
Eston, Saskatchewan 86 J g
Estonia, U.S.S.R. 103 L g
Estoril, Portugal 106 A c
Estreito, Brazil 94 F d
Estremoz, Portugal 106 B c
Estrondo, Sa. do, Brazil 93 H e
Estuary, Saskatchewan 86 H h
Etadunna, Australia 134 G e
Etah, Greenland 89 Q b
Etah, India 126 E c
Etalle, Belgium 100 D e
Etamamiou, R., Quebec 83 N b
Etamamu, Quebec 83 N c
Etamamu R., Quebec 83 N c
Étampes, France 108 E b
Étang-du-Nord, Madeleine Is., Quebec 83 L f
Étaples, France 108 D a
Etawah, India 126 E c
Etawney L., Manitoba 87 V a
Eten, I., Truk Is. 78 E o
Eten, Peru 92 B e
Etena, I., Swains I. 79 R o
Eten Anchorage, Truk Is. 78 E n
Eternity Ra., Antarctica 136 H d
Ethe, Belgium 100 D e
Ethelbert, Manitoba 87 R g
Ethel Creek, Australia 134 D d
Ethelton, Saskatchewan 87 N f
Ethiopia, E. Africa 121 H c
Étivaz, L', Switzerland 101 C b
Etive L., Scotland 98 D d
Etna, Mt., Sicily 111 E g
Etobicoke, Ontario 84 C k
Etomami, Saskatchewan 87 P f
Eton, Ontario 84 F e
Ettelbrück, Luxembourg 104 B d
Etten, Netherlands 100 C c
Etzikom, Alberta 86 F j
Etzikom Coulee, R., Alberta 86 F j
Euboea. See Évvoia, I.
Eucla, Australia 134 E f
Eudistes, L. des, Quebec 82 G c
Eugmö, Finland 102 K e
Eupen, Belgium 100 E d
Euphrates, R., Iraq, etc. 124 E c
Eure, dep., France 108 D b
Eure-et-Loir, dep., France 108 D b
Eureka, N.-W. Territories 81 L a
Eureka River, Alberta 88 K b
Eureka Sd., N.-W. Territories 81 L b
Europe 96-97
Eursinge, Netherlands 100 E b
Eutin, Germany 104 D a
Eutsuk, L., Br. Columbia 88 F c
Evale, Angola 122 B c
Evans, C., N.-W. Territories 81 L a
Evans, L., Quebec 81 M g
Evans, L., Quebec 85 O b
Evans, Mt., Alberta 88 K d
Evansburg, Alberta 86 C e
Evans Str., N.-W. Territories 81 L e
Evansville, Ontario 84 H g
Évaux, France 108 E c
Everard, L., Australia 134 F f
Everard, Ontario 84 B d
Everell, Quebec 85 T a
Everest, Mt., Nepal-Tibet 127 G c
Evergem, Belgium 100 B c
Evesham, England 99 F h
Evesham, Saskatchewan 86 H f
Évian, France 108 G c
Evijärvi, Finland 102 K e
Evje, Norway 103 B g
Evolène, Switzerland 101 C b
Evora, Portugal 106 B c
Évreux, France 108 D b
Evros, Greece 113 F d
Evrykhou, Cyprus 123 A b
Évvoia, G. of, Greece 113 D e
Évvoia, I., Greece 113 D e
Ewarton, Jamaica 91 D c
Ewe L., Scotland 98 D c
Ewing I., Antarctica 136 H e
Exaltación, Bolivia 92 D f
Excel, Alberta 86 G g
Executive Committee Ra., Antarctica 136 E c
Exeter, England 99 E k
Exeter, Ontario 84 J j
Exloo, Netherlands 100 E b
Exmoor, England 99 E j
Exmouth, England 99 E k
Exmouth G., Australia 134 B d
Expanse, Saskatchewan 87 M j
Expedition Ra., Australia 135 J d
Exploits R., Newfoundland 83 R e
Exshaw, Alberta 86 B g
Exuma Is., Bahama Is. 91 D b
Exuma Sd., Bahama Is. 91 D b
Eyasi, L., Tanzania 121 G e
Eyebrow, Saskatchewan 86 L h
Eyemouth, Scotland 98 F e
Eymoutiers, France 108 D d
Eyre, Australia 134 E f
Eyre, L., Australia 134 G e
Eyre, Saskatchewan 86 H g
Eyre Cr., Australia 134 G e
Eyre Pen., Australia 134 G f
Eyrie L., Manitoba 87 R a
Eyzies, Les, France 109 D d
Ezcaray, Spain 109 B b
Faaborg, Denmark 103 D j
Fabre, Quebec 85 L e
Facatativa, Colombia 92 C c
Facpi Pt., Guam 78 A l
Fada, Chad 119 K e
Fadan'Gourma, UpperVolta 118 F f
Faddeyevskiy, Ostrov, U.S.S.R. 115 P a
Faenza, Italy 110 C c
Færöerne, Is., Atlantic Oc. 89 M c
Faeroes. See Færöerne
Fafa, Mali 118 F e
Faga'itua, Tutuila I. 79 U o
Făgăras, Romania 112 E b
Fagarg, Sudan 119 L f
Fagasa, Tutuila I. 79 T o
Fagatogo, Tutuila I 79 U o
Fagerli, Norway 102 F c
Fagernes, Norway 103 C f
Fagnano, L., Argentina 95 C h
Faid, Saudi Arabia 124 D d
Faido, Switzerland 101 D b
Faifo, S. Vietnam 132 D c
Faillon, L., Quebec 85 O d
Fairford, Manitoba 87 T g
Fair Head, N. Ireland 98 C e
Fairholme, Saskatchewan 86 J e
Fair I., Scotland 98 F a
Fairlie, New Zealand 135 Q m
Fairlight, Saskatchewan 87 Q j
Fairmont Hot Springs, British Columbia 88 M e
Fairmount, Saskatchewan 86 H g
Fair Ness, C., N.-W. Terr. 81 M e
Fairview, Alberta 88 K b
Fairy Glen, Saskatchewan 87 N e
Faiza, India 126 F c
Faizabad, Afghanistan 125 K b
Fajardo, Puerto Rico 54 D h
Fajr, Saudi Arabia 124 C d
Fakaofu, I., Tokelau Is. 78 J h
Fakarava, I., Tuamotu Arch. 79 M j
Fak Fak, W. Irian 129 K l
Fakiya, Bulgaria 112 F c
Fala Ane Pt., Swains I. 79 Q o
Fala-beguets I., Truk Is. 78 D o
Falalu I., Truk Is. 78 D m
Falam, Burma 127 H d
Falama, Guinea 118 D f
Falas, I., Truk Is. 78 E n
Falasit, I., Truk Is. 78 D o
Fâlciu, Romania 112 G a
Falconbridge, Ontario 84 K g
Falcone, C. of, Sardinia 111 B e
Falealej Pass, Truk Is. 78 D n
Faleasao I., Manua Is. 79 S o
Faleniu I., Tutuila I. 79 T o
Falkenberg, Sweden 103 E h
Falkenburg, Ontario 85 L f
Falkirk, Scotland 98 E e
Falkland, Br. Columbia 88 K e
Falkland Is., S. Atlantic Ocean 95 D h
Falkland Sd., Falkland Is. 95 D h
Falköping, Sweden 103 E g
Falmagne, Belgium 100 C d
Falmouth, England 99 D k
Falmouth, Jamaica 91 D c
Falo, I., Truk Is. 78 E n
False B., South Africa 122 B f
False Point, India 127 G d
Falset, Spain 107 F b
Falso, C., Mexico 90 B c
Falster, I., Denmark 103 D j
Falun, Sweden 103 F f
Famagusta & B., Cyprus 123 B b
Famatina, Argentina 94 C c
Fanan, I., Truk Is. 78 F o
Fananan, I., Truk Is. 78 E o
Faneu, I., Truk Is. 78 E o
Fannich L., Scotland 98 D c

Fanning, I., *Pacific Ocean* 78 K g
Fannīy, *Iran* 125 G d
Fanny Bay, *Br. Columbia* 88 G f
Fannystelle, *Manitoba* 87 U j
Fanö, I., *Denmark* 103 C j
Fanö Bugt, *Denmark* 103 C j
Fanuela, I., *Truk Is.* 78 E n
Fanuet, I., *Truk Is.* 78 E n
Faradje, *Congo* 121 F d
Farafangana, *Mal. Rep.* 121 N l
Farah, *Afghanistan* 125 H c
Farajah, *Saudi Arabia* 125 F e
Faranah, *Guinea* 118 C f
Faranlep, I., *Caroline Is.* 78 E f
Farasan Is., *Red Sea* 124 D f
Farewell, C., *New Zealand* 135 Q l
Farewell C., *Greenland* 89 P d
Faridkot, *India* 126 E b
Faridpur, *India* 127 G d
Farīman, *Iran* 125 G b
Farlane, *Ontario* 86 H a
Farley, *Quebec* 85 O f
Farmington, *Br. Columbia* 88 J c
Farne Is., *England* 98 F e
Farnes, *Norway* 103 B f
Farnham, Mt., *Br. Columbia* 88 L e
Farnham, *Quebec* 85 S g
Faro, *Brazil* 93 F d
Faro, *Portugal* 106 B d
Fårön, I., *Sweden* 103 H h
Farr B. Davis Sea, *Antarctica* 136 R e
Farrellton, *Quebec* 85 P g
Farrerdale, *Saskatchewan* 87 M g
Farrukhabad, *India* 126 E c
Fársala, *Greece* 113 D e
Farsi, *Afghanistan* 125 H c
Farsund, *Norway* 103 B g
Fasā, *Iran* 125 F d
Fatait ibn Kanat, *Saudi Arabia* 124 D d
Fatehgarh, *India* 126 E c
Fatehpur, *India* 126 D c
Father, *Alberta* 88 L c
Father L., *Quebec* 85 P c
Fatmomakke, *Sweden* 102 F d
Fatshan. *See* Namhoi
Fatu Hiva, I., *Marquesas Is.* 79 N h
Fauquier, *Br. Columbia* 88 L f
Faust, *Alberta* 86 B c
Fawcett, *Alberta* 86 C d
Fawcett L., *Alberta* 86 D c
Fawn, R., *Ontario* 81 L g
Faxaflói, *Iceland* 102 U m
Faya. *See* Largeau
Fazilka, *India* 126 D b
Feale R., *Eire* 99 A h
Fécamp, *France* 108 D b
Federación, *Argentina* 94 E d
Fefan, I., *Truk Is.* 78 E o
Fehmarn, I., *Germany* 104 D a
Feify. *See* Faifo
Feijó, *Brazil* 92 C e
Feira de Santana, *Brazil* 93 K f
Feldbach, *Austria* 105 F e
Feldkirch, *Austria* 104 C e
Felipe Carrillo Puerto, *Mexico* 90 G d
Félix U Gómez, *Mexico* 90 C a
Femund, L., *Norway* 102 D e
Fena Valley Res., *Guam* 78 A l
Fenelon Falls, *Ontario* 85 M h
Feng chên, *China* 130 F b
Fenghsien, *China* 130 H e
Fenghwang, *China* 131 D j
Fengkieh, *China* 130 D g
Fengsiang, *China* 130 C e
Fengyang, *China* 130 H f
Fenton, *Saskatchewan* 87 M e
Fenua Ura, I., *Society Is.* 79 L j
Fenwick, *Ontario* 85 L j
Fenwood, *Saskatchewan* 87 O g
Fenyang, *China* 130 E d
Feodosiya & B., *U.S.S.R.* 116 J j
Ferdow, *Iran* 125 G c
Fergus, *Ontario* 84 K j
Fergusson I., *Papua* 135 K a
Ferintosh, *Alberta* 86 E f
Ferland, *Ontario* 84 B b
Fermanagh, co., *N. Ireland* 99 B f
Ferme Neuve, *Quebec* 85 P f
Fermoy, *Eire* 99 B h
Fernando Poo, I., *Equatorial Guinea* 120 B d
Fernie, *Br. Columbia* 88 M f
Ferrara, *Italy* 110 C c
Ferrar Glacier, *Antarctica* 136 A c
Ferrato C., *Sardinia* 111 B f
Ferreira do Zezere, *Portugal* 106 A c
Ferreira Gomes, *Brazil* 93 G c
Ferrier, *Alberta* 86 C f
Ferolle Pt., *Newfoundland* 83 P b
Ferru, L., *Quebec* 83 N b
Ferryland, *Newfoundland* 83 T f
Fès, *Morocco* 118 D b
Fethard, *Eire* 99 B h
Fethiye, *Turkey* 124 A b
Fetlar I., *Shetland* 98 J a
Feu, L. du, *Quebec* 83 M c
Feudal, *Saskatchewan* 86 K g
Fez. *See* Fès
Fiambalá, *Argentina* 94 C c
Ficalho, *Portugal* 106 B d
Fichtel Geb., *Germany* 104 D c
Fideris, *Switzerland* 101 E b
Fidler L., *Manitoba* 87 V a
Field, *Ontario* 84 K f
Fielding, *Saskatchewan* 86 K f
Fier, *Albania* 113 B d
Fiesch, *Switzerland* 101 D b
Fife, co., *Scotland* 98 E d
Fife L., *Saskatchewan* 87 M j
Fife Lake, *Saskatchewan* 87 M j
Fife Ness, *Scotland* 98 F d
Figeac, *France* 109 E d
Figline Vald, *Italy* 110 C d
Figueira de Castelo Rodrigo, *Portugal* 106 B d
Figueras, *Spain* 107 G a
Figuig, *Morocco* 118 E b
Fiji Is., *Pacific Ocean* 78 H j
Filakovo, *Czechoslovakia* 105 H d
Filchner, C., *Antarctica* 136 R e
Filchner Ice Shelf, *Antarctica* 136 K c
File L., *Manitoba* 87 R d
Filiátes, *Greece* 113 C e
Filicudi, I., *Italy* 111 E f
Filipów, *Poland* 105 K a
Filippo Reef, *Line Is.* 79 L h
Filisur, *Switzerland* 101 E b
Fillmore, *Manitoba* 87 O j
Filonovsk, *U.S.S.R.* 117 F e
Finch, *Ontario* 85 P g
Findhorn R., *Scotland* 98 E c
Findlater, *Saskatchewan* 87 M h
Findlay, Mt., *Br. Columbia* 88 L e
Finhaut, *Switzerland* 101 B b
Finistère, dep., *France* 108 A b
Finisterre, C., *Spain* 106 A a
Finke, *Australia* 134 F e
Finke, R., *Australia* 134 F e
Finland, G. of, *North-West Europe* 103 L g
Finland, *North Europe* 102 L e
Finlay Forks, *Br. Columbia* 88 H c
Finlay R., *Br. Columbia* 88 G b
Finmark, *Ontario* 87 N b
Finnegan, *Alberta* 86 E g
Finschhafen, *New Guinea* 135 J a
Finspång, *Sweden* 103 F g
Finsteraarhorn, *Switzerland* 101 D b
Fintona, *N. Ireland* 99 C f
Fionnay, *Switzerland* 101 C b
Fiq, *Syria* 123 D e
Firat, R., *Turkey* 124 C b
Firebag R., *Alberta* 88 O b
Firenze (Florence), *Italy* 110 C d
Fire River, *Ontario* 84 G d
Firmat, *Argentina* 94 D d
Fir Mountain, *Saskatchewan* 86 L j
Firozabad, *India* 126 E c
Firūzābad, *Iran* 125 F d
Fisher, *Quebec* 85 N d
Fisher B., *Antarctica* 136 A e
Fisher B., *Manitoba* 87 U g
Fisher Branch, *Manitoba* 87 U g
Fisher Glacier, *Antarctica* 136 Q d
Fisher Str., *N.-W. Terr.* 81 L e
Fishguard, *Wales* 99 D j
Fish Hoek, *S. Africa* 122 G j
Fishing Ls., The, *Sask.* 87 N h
Fiske, C., *Antarctica* 136 J d
Fiske, *Saskatchewan* 86 J g
Fitful Hd., *Shetland* 98 H b
Fitzcarrald, *Peru* 92 C f
Fitzhugh Sd., *Br. Columbia* 88 F e
Fitzpatrick, *Quebec* 85 S e
Fitzroy, *Australia* 134 E c
Fitzroy, R., *Australia* 135 J d
Fitzroy, R., *Australia* 134 D c
Fitzroy Harbour, *Ontario* 85 O g
Fitzwilliam I., *Ontario* 84 J g
Fiume. *See* Rijeka
Five Islands, *Nova Scotia* 82 H h
Fjällåsen, *Sweden* 102 J c
Flamborough Hd., *England* 99 G f
Flamingo B., *W. Irian* 129 L m
Flanders, *Ontario* 86 L b
Flanders. *See* Vlaanderen
Flat Bay, *Newfoundland* 83 O e
Flatbush, *Alberta* 86 C d
Flat I., *Quebec* 83 O c
Flat L., *Alberta* 86 E d
Flattery, C., *Australia* 135 J b
Flaxcombe, *Saskatchewan* 86 H g
Flèche, La, *France* 108 C c
Fleet, *Alberta* 86 F f
Fleetwood, *England* 99 E g
Flekkefjord, *Norway* 103 B g
Fleming, *Saskatchewan* 87 Q h
Flensburg, *Germany* 104 C a
Flers, *France* 108 C b
Flesherton, *Ontario* 84 K h
Fletcher Is., *Antarctica* 136 G d
Fleurance, *France* 109 D e
Fleur de Lys, *Newfoundland* 83 Q c
Fleur-de-Mai, L., *Labrador* 82 H b
Fleurier, *Switzerland* 101 B d
Fleuru, *Belgium* 100 C d
Flims, *Switzerland* 101 E b
Flinders I., *Australia* 134 F f
Flinders I., *Tasmania* 135 J g
Flinders R., *Australia* 135 H c
Flinders Ra., *Australia* 134 G f
Flin Flon, *Manitoba* 87 Q d
Flint & co., *Wales* 99 E g
Flint I., *Pacific Ocean* 79 L h
Flint L., *Ontario* 84 E c
Flintoft, *Saskatchewan* 86 L j
Flipper Pt., *Wake I.* 79 S d
Flisa, *Norway* 103 E f
Flood Ra., *Antarctica* 136 E c
Florac, *France* 109 E d
Floreffe, *Belgium* 100 C d
Florence. *See* Firenze
Florencia, *Argentina* 94 E c
Florencia, *Argentina* 94 D b
Florencia, *Colombia* 92 B c
Florennes, *Belgium* 100 C d
Florenville, *Belgium* 100 D e
Flores, *Guatemala* 90 F d
Flores, I., *Atlantic Ocean* 118 A a
Flores I., Vancouver I., *British Columbia* 88 F f
Flores I. & Sea, *Indonesia* 129 H m
Floriano, *Brazil* 93 J e
Floriano Peixoto, *Brazil* 92 D e
Florianópolis, *Brazil* 94 G c
Florida, *Uruguay* 94 E d
Floridia, *Sicily* 111 E g
Flórina, *Greece* 113 C d
Flörö, *Norway* 102 A f
Flotten L., *Saskatchewan* 86 J d
Flowerpot I. Nat. Park, *Ontario* 84 J g
Flower's Cove, *Nfd.* 83 Q b
Flüelen, *Switzerland* 101 D b
Flushing. *See* Vlissingen
Fly, R., *Papua-W. Irian* 135 H a
Flying Fish, C., *Antarctica* 136 F d
Foam Lake, *Saskatchewan* 87 O g
Foča, *Yugoslavia* 112 B c
Focşani, *Romania* 112 F b
Fofa Cahuel, *Argentina* 95 B f
Foggia, *Italy* 111 E e
Fogo & I., *Newfoundland* 83 S d
Föhr, I., *Germany* 104 C a
Foix & prov., *France* 109 D e
Fokis, *Greece* 113 D e
Folda, Fd., *Norway* 102 F c
Folégandros, I., *Greece* 113 E f
Foleyet, *Ontario* 84 H d
Foley I., *N.-W. Territories* 81 M d
Foligno, *Italy* 110 D d
Folkestone, *England* 99 H j
Follega, *Netherlands* 100 D b
Fonsagrada, *Spain* 106 B a
Fonseca, G. of, *Honduras* 91 B d
Fontaine, *Belgium* 100 C d
Fontainebleau, *France* 108 E b
Fontana, L., *Argentina* 95 B f
Fontas, *Br. Columbia* 88 J a
Fontas, R., *Br. Columbia* 88 J a
Fontenay-le-Comte, *France* 108 C c
Fonteneau, L., *Quebec* 83 L b
Fontenelle, *Quebec* 82 H e
Foochow, *China* 131 J j
Foothills, *Alberta* 88 L d
Forbes, *Australia* 135 J f
Forbes, Mt., *Alberta* 88 L e
Forcados, *Nigeria* 118 G g
Forcalquier, *France* 109 F e
Förde, *Norway* 103 A f
Fordlândia, *Brazil* 93 F d
Ford Ranges, *Antarctica* 136 D c
Forel, Mt., *Greenland* 89 N c
Foremost, *Alberta* 86 F j
Forest, *Ontario* 84 H j
Forestburg, *Alberta* 86 E f
Forest Hill, *Ontario* 84 C j
Forest Lawn, *Alberta* 86 D g
Forestville, *Quebec* 82 C e
Forfar, *Scotland* 98 F d
Forgan, *Saskatchewan* 86 K g
Forget, *Quebec* 85 O d
Forget, *Saskatchewan* 87 P j
Fork River, *Manitoba* 87 S g
Forli, *Italy* 110 D c
Formentera I., *Balearic Is.* 107 F c
Formia, *Italy* 111 D e
Formiga, *Brazil* 93 H h
Formosa, *Argentina* 94 E c
Formosa, *Brazil* 93 H g
Formosa. *See* Taiwan, I.
Fornos d'Algôdres, *Portugal* 106 B b
Forres, *Scotland* 98 E c
Forrest, *Australia* 134 E f
Forrest, *Manitoba* 87 S j
Forrest L., *Saskatchewan* 88 P b
Forsa, *Sweden* 103 G f
Forsayth, *Australia* 135 H c
Forsnäs, *Sweden* 102 H c
Forssa, *Finland* 103 K f
Forster's Passage, *Antarctica* 136 K g
Forsythe, *Quebec* 85 O d
Fort Albany, *Ontario* 81 L g
Fortaleza, Acre, *Brazil* 92 D e
Fortaleza, *Brazil* 93 K d
Fort Ann Nat. Hist. Park, *Nova Scotia* 82 G j
Fort Archambault, *Chad* 118 J g
Fort Assiniboine, *Alberta* 88 M c
Fort Augustus, *Scotland* 98 D c
Fort Beaufort, *South Africa* 122 D f
Fort Beauséjour Nat. Hist. Park, *Nova Scotia* 82 H h
Fort Black, *Saskatchewan* 86 K c
Fort Chimo, *Quebec* 81 N f
Fort Chipewyan, *Alberta* 88 O a
Fort Coulonge, *Quebec* 85 O g
Fort Crampel, *Cent. Afr. Rep.* 119 J g
Fort Dauphin, *Mal. Rep.* 121 N m
Forteau, *Labrador* 83 Q b
Fort Erie, *Ontario* 85 M k
Fortescue, R., *Australia* 134 C d
Fort Flatters, *Algeria* 118 G c
Fort Frances, *Ontario* 86 J b
Fort Fraser, *Br. Columbia* 88 G c
Fort Garry, *Manitoba* 87 U j
Fort George, *Quebec* 81 M g
Fort Gouraud, *Mauritania* 118 C d
Fort Graham, *Br. Columbia* 88 G b
Forth, Firth of, *Scotland* 98 F d
Fort Henrique, *S.W. Africa* 122 A c
Fort Hertz, *Burma* 127 J f
Fort Hope, *Ontario* 81 L g
Forth R., *Scotland* 98 E d
Fortierville, *Quebec* 85 S f
Forties Settlement, *N.S.* 82 H j
Fortin, L., *Quebec* 82 E c
Fortín Avalos Sánchez, *Paraguay* 94 D b
Fortín Ayacucho, *Paraguay* 92 E g
Fortin Ballivian, *Paraguay* 92 E g
Fortín General Díaz, *Para.* 94 D b
Fortín López, *Paraguay* 94 D b
Fortín Teniente Montania, *Paraguay* 94 D b
Fort Jameson, *Zambia* 121 G g
Fort Johnston, *Malawi* 121 H g
Fort Kent, *Alberta* 86 G d
Fort Lallemand, *Algeria* 118 G b
Fort Lamy, *Chad* 119 J f
Fort Langley, *Br. Columbia* 88 F f
Fort Laperrine. *See* Tamanrasset
Fort Liard, *N.-W. Territories* 86 M e
Fort MacKay, *Alberta* 80 S g
Fort McKenzie, *Quebec* 81 N f
Fort Macleod, *Alberta* 86 D j
Fort McPherson, *N.-W. Terr.* 80 F d
Fort Munro, *W. Pakistan* 126 C c
Fort Nelson, *Br. Columbia* 88 H a
Fort Nelson R., *Br. Columbia* 88 H a
Fort Polignac, *Algeria* 118 G c
Fort Portal, *Uganda* 121 G d
Fort Providence, *N.-W. Terr.* 80 H e
Fort Qu'Appelle, *Sask.* 87 O h
Fortress of Louisbourg Nat. Hist. Pk., C. Breton I., *Nova Scotia* 83 M h
Fortrose, *Scotland* 98 E c
Fort-Rupert, *Quebec* 81 M g
Fort Saint, *Algeria* 119 G b
Fort St. George. *See* Madras
Fort St. James, *Br. Columbia* 88 G c
Fort St. John, *Br. Columbia* 88 J b
Fort Sandeman, *Pakistan* 126 C b
Fort Saskatchewan, *Alberta* 86 D e
Fort Selkirk, *Yukon* 77 T e
Fort Severn, *Ontario* 81 L f
Fort Sibut, *Cent. Afr. Rep.* 119 J g
Fortuna, *Spain* 107 E c
Fortuna Ledge. *See* Marshall
Fortune & B., *Newfoundland* 83 R f
Fort Vermilion, *Alberta* 88 M a
Fort Victoria, *Rhodesia* 122 E d
Fort White, *Burma* 127 H d
Fort William, *Ontario* 87 O b
Fort William, *Scotland* 98 D d
Forty Mile, *Yukon* 77 R d
Forville, *Belgium* 100 C d
Forward, *Saskatchewan* 87 N j
Fosheim Pen., *N.-W. Terr.* 81 L b
Fosse, *Belgium* 100 C d
Fossmill, *Ontario* 85 L f
Fosston, *Saskatchewan* 87 O f
Foster, *Quebec* 85 S g
Foster Ls., *Saskatchewan* 88 R b
Foster R., *Saskatchewan* 88 R b
Fosterton, *Saskatchewan* 86 J h
Fougères, *France* 108 C b
Foul, I., *Burma* 127 H e
Foula, I., *Scotland* 98 H a
Foul B., *Egypt* 119 N d
Foulness, I., *England* 99 H j
Foulwind, C., *New Zealand* 135 Q l
Fourchu, C. Breton I., *N.S.* 83 M h
Fournel, L., *Quebec* 83 P b
Fournier, L., *Quebec* 82 G b
Foúrnoi, Is., *Greece* 113 F f
Fourup, I., *Truk Is.* 78 E o
Foveaux Strait, *New Zealand* 135 P m
Fowchow. *See* Fowling
Fowlers B., *Australia* 134 F f
Fowling, *China* 131 C h
Fowning, *China* 130 J f
Fowyang, *China* 130 G f
Fox, R., *Manitoba* 81 K f
Fox Bay, Anticosti I., *Quebec* 83 L d
Foxe Basin, *N.-W. Territories* 81 L d
Foxe Chan., *N.-W. Territories* 81 L d
Foxe Pen., *N.-W. Territories* 81 M e
Foxford, *Saskatchewan* 87 M e
Fox Harbour, *Labrador* 83 R a
Fox Pt., *Anticosti I., Quebec* 83 L d
Fox R., *Br. Columbia* 88 G b
Foxton, *New Zealand* 135 R l
Fox Valley, *Saskatchewan* 86 H h
Foxwarren, *Manitoba* 87 Q h
Foyle L., *N. Ireland* 98 C e
Foynes, *Eire* 99 A h
Foz do Aripuana, *Brazil* 92 E e
Foz do Cunene, *Angola* 122 A c
Foz do Jordão, *Brazil* 92 C e
Foz do Jutaí, *Brazil* 92 D d
Foz do Pauiní, *Brazil* 92 D e
Foz Embira, *Brazil* 92 C e
Fraire, *Belgium* 100 C d
Frameries, *Belgium* 100 B d
Franca, *Brazil* 93 H h
Francavilla Fontana, *Italy* 111 F e
France, *W. Europe* 108-109
Franceville, *Gabon* 120 C e
Franche-Comté, prov., *France* 108 G c
Francis, *Manitoba* 87 O h
Francis Harbour, *Labrador* 83 R a
Francis I., *Antarctica* 136 H e
Francistown, *Botswana* 122 D d
François, *Newfoundland* 83 Q f
François L., *Br. Columbia* 88 G c
Frank, *Alberta* 86 C j
Frankford, *Ontario* 85 N h
Frankfurt-am-Main, *Germany* 104 C c
Frankfurt-an-der-Oder, *Germany* 104 F b
Fränkischer Jura, *Germany* 104 D d
Franklin, Dist. of, *North-West Territories* 80 H c
Franklin, I., *Antarctica* 136 B c
Franklin, *Tasmania* 135 J h
Franklin I., *Ontario* 84 K g
Franklin Str., *N.-W. Terr.* 81 K c
Franklyn, Mt., *New Zealand* 135 Q l
Frantsa Iosifa, Zemlya, *Arctic Ocean* 114 D a
Franz, *Ontario* 84 F d
Franz Josef Fd., *Greenland* 89 N b
Franz Josef Land. *See* Frantsa Iosifa, Zemlya
Fraser, R., *Br. Columbia* 88 K d
Fraserburg, *South Africa* 122 C f
Fraserburgh, *Scotland* 98 F c
Fraserdale, *Ontario* 84 J c
Fraser Mills, *Br. Columbia* 88 E f
Fraserwood, *Manitoba* 87 U h
Frasnes, *Belgium* 100 B d
Frater, *Ontario* 84 F e
Frauenfeld, *Switzerland* 101 D a
Fray Bentos, *Uruguay* 94 E d
Frazer L., *Ontario* 84 B c
Fredericia, *Denmark* 103 C j
Frederick House, R., *Ontario* 84 J c
Fredericton, *New Brunswick* 82 F h
Fredericton Junc., *New Brunswick* 82 F h
Frederik Hendrik I. *See* Kolepom
Frederikshaab, *Greenland* 89 P c
Frederikshavn, *Denmark* 103 D h
Fredonia, *Colombia* 92 B b
Fredrika, *Sweden* 102 H d
Fredrikstad, *Norway* 103 D g
Freeman R., *Alberta* 86 B d
Freeport, *Bahama Is.* 91 D a
Freeport, *Nova Scotia* 82 F j
Freetown, *Prince Edward I.* 82 J g
Freetown, *Sierra Leone* 118 C g
Fregenal de la Sierra, *Spain* 106 B c
Fréhel C., *France* 108 B b
Freiberg, *Germany* 104 E c
Freiburg, *Germany* 104 B d
Freirina, *Chile* 94 B c
Freistadt, *Austria* 104 F d
Freital, *Germany* 104 E c
Freixiel, *Portugal* 106 B b
Freixo, *Portugal* 106 B b
Fremantle, *Australia* 134 C f
French Guiana, *S. America* 93 G c
Frenchman Butte, *Sask.* 86 H e
Frenchman's Cove, *Newfoundland* 83 O d
French Somaliland, *E. Africa* 121 J b
Fresco, *Ivory Coast* 118 D g
Freshfield, C., *Antarctica* 136 A e
Freshwater, *Newfoundland* 83 T f
Fresnillo, *Mexico* 90 D c
Frewena, *Australia* 134 G c
Frias, *Spain* 106 D a
Fribourg & canton, *Switzerland* 101 C b
Fridtjof Nansen Mt., *Antarctica* 136 C a
Friedland, *Germany* 104 E b
Friesische Is., Nord, *Germany* 103 C j
Friesische Is., Ost, *Germany* 104 A b
Friesland, prov., *Neth.* 100 D a
Frio, C., *S.W. Africa* 122 A c
Friuli-Venezia Giulia, reg., *Italy* 110 D b
Frizzleton, Cape Breton I., *Nova Scotia* 83 L g
Frobisher, *Saskatchewan* 87 P j
Frobisher B., *N.-W. Terr.* 81 N e
Frobisher Bay, *N.-W. Terr.* 81 N e
Frobisher L., *Saskatchewan* 88 P b
Frog L., *Alberta* 86 G e
Fro Havet, *Norway* 102 C e
Frome, *England* 99 F j
Frome, L., *Australia* 134 H f
Fronteira, *Portugal* 106 B c
Frontera, *Mexico* 90 F d
Fronteras, *Mexico* 90 C a
Frontier, *Saskatchewan* 86 J j
Fronton de la Brea, *Puerto Rico* 54 C j
Frosinone, *Italy* 111 D e
Frost Glacier, *Antarctica* 136 T e
Frotet, L., *Quebec* 85 Q b
Froude, *Saskatchewan* 87 O j
Fröya, *Norway* 102 C e
Frunze, *Kirgiz., U.S.S.R.* 114 G d
Frutigen, *Switzerland* 101 C b
Frutuoso, *Brazil* 92 E f
Frýdek, *Czechoslovakia* 105 G c
Fthiótis, *Greece* 113 D e
Fuchin, *China* 128 K a
Fu-chou. *See* Foochow
Fuchow. *See* Linchwan
Fu-chow, *China* 130 K c
Fuente-Alamo de Murcia, *Spain* 107 E d
Fuente del Arco, *Spain* 106 C c
Fuentes de Onoro, *Spain* 106 B b
Fuertaventura I., *Canary Is.* 118 C c
Fuerte, El, *Mexico* 90 C b
Fuerte, R., *Mexico* 90 C b
Fujiyama (Fuji san), *Japan* 133 F g
Fukien, prov., *China* 131 H j
Fuki Kaku, *Taiwan* 128 H e
Fukui, *Japan* 133 E f
Fukuoka, *Japan* 133 B h
Fukushima, *Japan* 133 G f
Fukuyama, *Japan* 133 G d
Fukuyama, *Japan* 133 C g
Fulda, R., *Germany* 104 C c
Funafuti, I., *Ellice Is.* 78 H h
Funchal, *Madeira I.* 118 B b
Fundão, *Portugal* 106 B b
Fundy, B. of, *Canada* 82 G j
Fundy Nat. Park, *New Brunswick* 82 G h
Fünen. *See* Fyn
Fünfkurchen. *See* Pécs
Funing. *See* Siapu
Funk I., *Newfoundland* 83 T d
Fure, *Japan* 133 G b
Furg, *Iran* 125 G d
Furneaux Grp., *Tasmania* 135 J h
Furnes. *See* Veurne
Furness, *Saskatchewan* 86 H e
Furqlus, *Syria* 123 F c
Fürth, *Germany* 104 D d
Furue. *See* Kanoya
Furukawa, *Japan* 133 G e
Fury & Hecla Str., *North-West Territories* 81 L d
Fusagasugá, *Colombia* 92 C c
Fushih, *China* 130 D d
Fushimi, *Japan* 133 D g
Fu-shun, *China* 130 L b
Fusilier, *Saskatchewan* 86 H g
Fusin, *China* 130 K a
Fusio, *Switzerland* 101 D b
Futatsu ne, I., *Iwo Jima* 78 D a
Futemma, I., *Okinawa* 78 A c
Futiga, I., *Tutuila I.* 79 U o
Fuwa, *S. Yemen* 124 E g
Fuyu, *China* 128 H a
Fyn, *Denmark* 103 D j
Fyne L., *Scotland* 98 D d
Fyzabad. *See* Faizabad
Gabarouse, Cape Breton I., *Nova Scotia* 83 M h
Gabarouse B., C. Breton I., *Nova Scotia* 83 M h
Gaberones, *Botswana* 122 D d
Gabès & G. of, *Tunisia* 119 H b
Gąbin, *Poland* 105 H b
Gable Mt., *Br. Columbia* 88 F d
Gabon, *Central Africa* 120 C e
Gabrovo, *Bulgaria* 112 E c
Gach Saran, *Iran* 125 F c
Gadag, *India* 126 E e
Gadsby, *Alberta* 86 E f
Gael Hamkes B., *Greenland* 89 M b
Găeşti, *Romania* 112 E b
Gaeta & G. di, *Italy* 111 D e
Gafsa, *Tunisia* 119 G b
Gagan, I., *Kwajalein Is.* 79 U e
Gage, C., *Prince Edward I.* 82 H g
Gagetown, *New Brunswick* 82 F h
Gagil-Tomil, I., *Yap I.* 78 D l
Gagnon, L., *Quebec* 85 P f
Gagnon, *Quebec* 82 D b
Gaillac, *France* 109 D e
Gaillarbois, L., *Quebec* 82 E a
Gaima, *Papua* 135 H a
Gaimán, *Argentina* 95 C f
Gainsborough, *England* 99 G g
Gainsborough, *Saskatchewan* 87 Q j
Gairdner, L., *Australia* 134 G f
Gairloch, *Scotland* 98 D c
Galag. *See* Kalak
Galahad, *Alberta* 86 F f
Galangue, *Angola* 120 D g
Galap, I., *Palau Is.* 78 C l
Galápagos Is., *Pacific Ocean* 79 R h
Galashiels, *Scotland* 98 F e
Galathea B., *Nicobar Is.* 127 H g
Galati, *Romania* 112 G b
Galatz. *See* Galati
Galcaio, *Somali Republic* 121 K c
Galch Dar, *Iran* 125 F d
Galdhopiggen, Mt., *Norway* 103 C f
Galeana, *Mexico* 90 C a
Galeana, *Mexico* 90 E c
Galiano I., *Br. Columbia* 88 H f
Galich, *U.S.S.R.* 117 F a
Galilee, L., *Australia* 135 J d
Galilee, Sea of. *See* Tiberias L.
Galiote, Anticosti I., *Quebec* 82 J d
Galissonnière, L. la, *Que.* 82 K b
Galle, *Ceylon* 126 F g
Gallegos R., *Argentina* 95 B h
Gallet, L., *Quebec* 83 O b
Gallichan, *Quebec* 85 L d
Gallipoli, *Italy* 111 F e
Gallipoli. *See* Gelibolu
Gällivare, *Sweden* 102 J c
Galloway, Mull of, *Scotland* 99 D f
Galt, *Ontario* 84 K j
Galtee Mts., *Eire* 99 B h
Galvez, *Argentina* 94 D d
Galway B., *Eire* 99 A g
Galway (Gaillimh), *Eire* 99 A g
Gambaga, *Ghana* 118 E f
Gambia, The & R., *N.W. Africa* 118 B f
Gambier, Is., *Pacific Ocean* 79 N k
Gambier Mt., *Australia* 134 H g
Gambo, *Newfoundland* 83 S e
Gams, *Switzerland* 101 E a
Gananoque, *Ontario* 85 O h
Gand, *Belgium* 100 B c

Gandak R., *India* 127 F c
Gandava, *Pakistan* 126 C c
Gander, L., *Newfoundland* 83 S e
Gander & airport, *Newfoundland* 83 S e
Gander Bay South, *Newfoundland* 83 S d
Gander R., *Newfoundland* 83 R e
Gandesa, *Spain* 106 F b
Gandia, *Spain* 107 E c
Ganga. See Ganges
Gangaw, *Burma* 127 H d
Ganges (Ganga), R., *India* 127 G d
Gangtok, *India* 127 G c
Ganjam, *India* 127 G e
Gannat, *France* 108 E c
Gantheaume B., *Australia* 134 B e
Gao, *Mali* 118 E e
Gaoual, *Guinea* 118 C f
Garachiné, *Panama* 91 D e
Gara L., *Eire* 99 B g
Garanhuns, *Brazil* 93 K e
Garapan, I., *Saipan-Tinian Is.* 78 A e
Garba Tula, *Kenya* 121 H d
Gard, dep., *France* 109 F d
Garda, L. di, *Italy* 110 C c
Gardafui, C., *Somali Rep.* 121 L b
Garden River, *Ontario* 84 F f
Gardenton, *Manitoba* 87 V j
Gardiner, *Ontario* 84 J c
Gardner Inlet, *Antarctica* 136 H c
Gardó, *Somali Republic* 121 K c
Gardula, *Ethiopia* 121 H c
Gargantua, C., *Ontario* 84 E e
Gar Gunsa, *Tibet* 126 F b
Garibaldi, *Brazil* 94 F c
Garibaldi, *Br. Columbia* 88 H f
Garibaldi Prov. Park, *British Columbia* 88 H e
Garies, *South Africa* 122 B f
Garissa, *Kenya* 121 H e
Garland, *Manitoba* 87 R g
Garm, *Tadzhik., U.S.S.R.* 114 G e
Garmsar, *Iran* 125 F b
Garneau R., *Quebec* 82 J b
Garnet B., *N.-W. Territories* 81 M d
Garo Hills, *India* 127 H c
Garonne, R., *France* 109 D e
Garoua, *Cameroon* 119 H g
Garraway, *Liberia* 118 D h
Garreru, I., *Palau Is.* 78 C n
Garrick, *Saskatchewan* 87 N e
Garrovillas, *Spain* 106 B c
Garsen, *Kenya* 119 J e
Garson L., *Alberta* 86 G b
Gartok, *Tibet* 126 F b
Garupá & R., *Brazil* 93 G d
Garusuun, I., *Palau Is.* 78 B n
Garza, *Argentina* 94 D c
Garzón, *Colombia* 92 B c
Gasan Kuli, *Turkmen., U.S.S.R.* 114 E e
Gascogne, G. de, *France-Spain* 109 B e
Gascogne, prov., *France* 109 D e
Gascoyne, R., *Australia* 134 C e
Gasht, *Iran* 125 H d
Gaspé, C., *Quebec* 82 H e
Gaspé & B. de, *Quebec* 82 H e
Gaspé Passage, *Quebec-New Brunswick* 82 H d
Gaspé Pen., *Quebec* 82 E e
Gaspereau Forks, *New Brunswick* 82 G g
Gaspésie, Parc de la, *Que.* 82 F e
Gasselte, *Netherlands* 100 E b
Gastre, *Argentina* 95 C f
Gata, C., *Cyprus* 123 B c
Gata, *Spain* 106 B b
Gataga, R., *Br. Columbia* 88 F a
Gateshead, *England* 98 F f
Gat (Ghat), *Libya* 119 H d
Gatineau, *Quebec* 85 P g
Gatineau, R., *Quebec* 85 P e
Gatineau Park, *Quebec* 85 P g
Gatjapar, I., *Yap I.* 78 D l
Gatooma, *Rhodesia* 122 D c
Gatun L., *Panama* 91 C e
Gaud-i-Zirreh, *Afghanistan* 125 H d
Gaudreault, L., *Quebec* 83 K c
Gaudry, Mt., *Antarctica* 136 H e
Gauer L., *Manitoba* 87 U a
Gauhati, *India* 127 H c
Gauporé, *Brazil* 92 E f
Gaurihar, *India* 126 F c
Gaussberg Mt., *Antarctica* 136 R e
Gavāter, *Iran* 125 H d
Gāvbandī, *Iran* 125 F d
Gavdhos, I., *Crete* 113 E g
Gavião, *Portugal* 106 B c
Gāv Koshi, *Iran* 125 G d
Gävle, *Sweden* 103 G f
Gävle Bukten, *Sweden* 103 G f
Gawler, *Australia* 134 G f
Gawler Ra., *Australia* 135 G f
Gaya, *Niger* 118 F f
Gayaza, *Uganda* 121 G e
Gaza, *Cent. Afr. Rep.* 119 J h
Gaza, *West Asia* 123 C f
Gazi Antep, *Turkey* 124 C b
Gazik, *Iran* 125 H c
Gdansk, *Poland* 105 H a
Gdynia, *Poland* 105 H a
Gebeit, *Sudan* 119 N e
Gedaref, *Sudan* 119 N f
Gedinne, *Belgium* 100 C e
Geel, *Belgium* 100 C c
Geelong, *Australia* 135 H g
Geelvink B., *W. Irian* 129 L l
Geeraardsbergen. See Grammont
Gegnon, L., *Quebec* 85 P f
Geikie, I., *Ontario* 84 B b
Geikie, R., *Saskatchewan* 88 R b
Gela, *Sicily* 111 E g
Gelderland, *Netherlands* 100 D b
Geldrop, *Netherlands* 100 D c
Gelert, *Ontario* 85 M h
Gelib, *Somali Republic* 121 J d
Gelibolu, *Turkey* 124 A a
Gelinden, *Belgium* 100 D d
Gellinam, I., *Kwajalein Is.* 79 U e
Gelsenkirchen, *Germany* 104 B c
Gem, *Alberta* 86 E h
Gemas, *Malaysia* 132 C f
Gembloux, *Belgium* 100 C d
Gemena, *Congo* 120 D d
Gemert, *Netherlands* 100 D c
Gemmenich, *Belgium* 100 D d
Gemmi Pass, *Switzerland* 101 C b
Genappe, *Belgium* 100 C d
Gendringen, *Netherlands* 100 E c
Geneina, *Sudan* 119 K f
Genemuiden, *Netherlands* 100 E b
General Acha, *Argentina* 95 D e
General Alvarado, *Argentina* 95 E e
General Alvear, *Argentina* 94 D e
General Capdevila, *Argentina* 94 D c
General Carneiro, *Brazil* 93 G g
General Guido, *Argentina* 94 E e
General José de San Martín, *Argentina* 94 E c
General La Madrid, *Argentina* 95 D e
General Lavalle, *Argentina* 94 E e
General Madariaga, *Argentina* 94 E e
General Pico, *Argentina* 94 D e
General Pinto, *Argentina* 94 D d
General Roca, *Argentina* 95 C e
General Viamonte, *Argentina* 94 D e
General Villegas, *Argentina* 94 D e
Geneva, L. of. See Léman, Lac
Geneva (Genève), *Switz.* 101 B b
Geneva L. Mine, *Ontario* 85 J f
Genève. See Geneva
Genier, *Ontario* 84 K c
Genkai Nada, *Japan* 133 A h
Gennargentu, Mt. del, *Sardinia* 111 B e
Gennep, *Netherlands* 100 D c
Genoa (Genova), *Italy* 110 B c
Genova, G. di, *Italy* 110 B c
Genova. See Genoa
Gent. See Gand
Geographe B., *Australia* 134 C f
Geographe Chan., *Australia* 134 B d
Georga Zemlya, *Arctic Oc.* 114 D a
George, L., *Ontario* 84 F f
George B., *Nova Scotia* 83 L h
George L., *Australia* 135 J g
George Sd., *New Zealand* 135 P m
Georgetown, *Australia* 135 H c
Georgetown, *Guyana* 92 F b
George Town, *Gr. Cayman, West Indies* 91 C c
Georgetown, *Ontario* 84 L j
George Town, *Penang I., Malaysia* 132 C e
Georgetown, *Prince Edward I.* 82 K g
George V Coast, *Antarctica* 136 A e
Georgeville, *Quebec* 85 S g
George VI Sd., *Antarctica* 136 H d
Georgia, Str. of, *British Columbia* 88 G f
Georgian B., *Ontario* 84 J g
Georgian Bay Is. Nat. Park, *Ontario* 84 K h
Georgina, R., *Australia* 135 G d
Georgiyevka, *Kazakh., U.S.S.R.* 117 H d
Georgiyevsk, *U.S.S.R.* 114 D d
Gera, *Germany* 104 E c
Geraardsbergen, *Belgium* 100 B d
Gerald, *Saskatchewan* 87 Q h
Geraldton, *Australia* 134 B e
Geraldton, *Ontario* 84 D c
Gérgal, *Spain* 107 D d
Germain, Grand L., *Quebec* 82 F b
Germania, *Argentina* 94 D d
Germansen Landing, *British Columbia* 88 G c
Germany, *Central Europe* 104 C c
Gerona, *Spain* 107 G a
Gers, dep., *France* 109 D e
Gerze, *Turkey* 124 C a
Getafe, *Spain* 106 D b
Gethsémani, *Quebec* 83 M c
Getz Ice Shelf, *Antarctica* 136 E d
Gevar. See Yuksekova
Gevgelija, *Yugoslavia* 112 D d
Ghabaghib, *Syria* 123 E d
Ghadames, *Libya* 119 G b
Ghaghara, R., *India* 126 F c
Ghaida, *S. Yemen* 124 E g
Ghail, *Saudi Arabia* 124 E e
Ghana, *West Africa* 118 E g
Ghantur, *Syria* 123 F c
Gharandal, *Jordan* 123 D g
Ghardaïa, *Algeria* 118 F b
Gharian, *Libya* 119 H b
Ghat, *Saudi Arabia* 124 E d
Ghatghat, *Saudi Arabia* 124 E e
Ghats, Eastern, *India* 126 F e
Ghats, Western, *India* 126 D e
Ghauta, *Saudi Arabia* 124 E e
Ghazaouet, *Algeria* 109 L j
Ghazi Khan, *India* 126 D b
Ghazir, *Lebanon* 123 D c
Ghazni, *Afghanistan* 125 J c
Gheorgheni, *Romania* 112 E a
Ghislenghien, *Belgium* 100 B d
Ghizao, *Afghanistan* 125 J c
Ghorak, *Afghanistan* 125 J c
Ghorian, *Afghanistan* 125 H c
Ghost Mt., *Br. Columbia* 88 L d
Ghost River, *Ontario* 86 L a
Ghotki, *Pakistan* 126 C c
Ghubreh, *Muscat & Oman* 125 G e
Giarre, *Sicily* 111 E g
Gibara, *Cuba* 91 D b
Gibbs I., *Antarctica* 136 J f
Gibeon, *S.W. Africa* 122 B e
Gibraltar, Str. of, *Spain* 106 C e
Gibraltar (Brit.), *Spain* 106 C d
Gibraltar Point, *Ontario* 84 D k
Gibson Desert, *Australia* 134 D d
Gibsons, *Br. Columbia* 88 H f
Gien, *France* 108 E c
Giessen, *Germany* 104 C c
Giffard, *Quebec* 85 T a
Gifhorn, *Germany* 104 D b
Gifu, *Japan* 133 E g
Giganta, La, *Mexico* 90 B b
Gijón, *Spain* 106 C a
Gilardo Dam, *Quebec* 85 R e
Gilau, *Romania* 112 D a
Gilbert, R., *Australia* 135 H c
Gilbert Is., *Pacific Ocean* 78 H j
Gilbert Mt., *Br. Columbia* 88 G e
Gilberton, *Australia* 135 H c
Gilbert Plains, *Manitoba* 87 R g
Gilbués, *Brazil* 93 J e
Gilgit & R., *Kashmir* 126 D a
Gil I., *Br. Columbia* 88 E d
Gillam, *Manitoba* 81 K f
Gilmour, *Ontario* 85 N h
Gilroy, *Saskatchewan* 86 L h
Gimel, *Switzerland* 101 B b
Gimli, *Manitoba* 87 V h
Ginir, *Ethiopia* 121 J c
Ginzo, *Spain* 106 B a
Gioia, G. di, *Italy* 111 E f
Giornico, *Switzerland* 101 D b
Girardot, *Colombia* 92 C c
Girdle Ness, *Scotland* 98 F c
Giresun, *Turkey* 124 C a
Girga, *Egypt* 119 M c
Giridih, *India* 127 G d
Girishk, *Afghanistan* 125 H c
Gironde, dep., *France* 109 C d
Gironde, R., *France* 108 C d
Giroux, *Manitoba* 87 V j
Girvan & R., *Scotland* 98 D e
Girvin, *Saskatchewan* 87 M g
Gisborne, *New Zealand* 135 S k
Gisburn L., *Newfoundland* 83 S f
Giscome, *Br. Columbia* 88 H c
Gisenyi, *Rwanda* 121 F e
Gisors, *France* 108 D b
Giswil, *Switzerland* 101 D b
Gitch, Mt., *Ethiopia* 121 H b
Giurgiu, *Romania* 112 E c
Givry, *Belgium* 100 C d
Givry I., *Truk Is.* 78 E o
Gizhiga, *U.S.S.R.* 115 R b
Giżycko, *Poland* 105 J a
Gjinokaster, *Albania* 113 C d
Gjövik, *Norway* 103 D f
Glabbeek, *Belgium* 100 C d
Glace Bay, *C. Breton I., Nova Scotia* 83 N g
Glacier, *Br. Columbia* 88 L e
Glacier Nat. Park, *B.C.* 88 K e
Glacier Str., *North-West Territories* 81 M b
Gladmar, *Saskatchewan* 87 N j
Gladstone, *Australia* 135 K d
Gladstone, *Manitoba* 87 T h
Glamoc, *Yugoslavia* 110 F c
Glamorgan, *Wales* 99 E j
Glärnisch, Mt., *Switzerland* 101 D b
Glarus & canton, *Switzerland* 101 E a
Glasgow, *Scotland* 98 E e
Glaslyn, *Saskatchewan* 86 J e
Glasnevin, *Saskatchewan* 87 M j
Glauchau, *Germany* 104 E c
Glazov, *U.S.S.R.* 117 L a
Gleichen, *Alberta* 86 D h
Glen Affric, *Scotland* 98 D c
Glen Almond, *Quebec* 85 P g
Glenavon, *Manitoba* 87 O h
Glenbain, *Saskatchewan* 86 K j
Glenboro, *Manitoba* 87 S j
Glenburnie, *Newfoundland* 83 P d
Glenbush, *Saskatchewan* 86 K e
Glencoe, *Ontario* 84 J k
Glendale, *Ontario* 84 F f
Glendale Cove, *British Columbia* 88 G e
Glendon, *Alberta* 86 F d
Glenella, *Manitoba* 87 S h
Glen Ewen, *Saskatchewan* 87 P j
Glen Garry, *Scotland* 98 E d
Glenhope, *New Zealand* 135 Q l
Glen Innes, *Australia* 135 K e
Glen Kerr, *Saskatchewan* 86 K h
Glenora, *Br. Columbia* 88 D b
Glen Robertson, *Ontario* 85 Q g
Glenside, *Saskatchewan* 86 L g
Glenties, *Eire* 99 B f
Glentworth, *Saskatchewan* 86 L j
Glenvale, *Ontario* 84 K e
Glenwood, *Newfoundland* 83 S e
Glenwoodville, *Alberta* 86 D j
Gletsch, *Switzerland* 101 D b
Glidden, *Saskatchewan* 86 H g
Glittertind, Mt., *Norway* 103 C f
Gliwice, *Poland* 105 H c
Glogau. See Glogów
Glogów, *Poland* 105 G c
Gloppen, *Norway* 102 B f
Gloria, *Brazil* 93 K e
Gloucester & co., *England* 99 F j
Glover I., *Newfoundland* 83 P e
Glovertown, *Newfoundland* 83 S e
Glukhov, *Ukraine, U.S.S.R.* 116 H f
Gmünd, *Austria* 104 E e
Gmünd, *Germany* 104 C d
Gmunden, *Austria* 104 E e
Gniezno, *Poland* 105 G b
Goa, *India* 126 D e
Goalpara, *India* 127 H c
Gobabis, *S.W. Africa* 122 B d
Gobi, Des., *E. Asia* 115 K d
Gockel Crest, *Antarctica* 136 L d
Godavari, R., *India* 126 E e
Godbout & R., *Quebec* 82 E d
Godech, *Bulgaria* 112 D c
Goderich, *Ontario* 84 J j
Godfrey, *Ontario* 85 O h
Godhra, *India* 126 D d
God's L., *Manitoba* 81 K g
Godthåb, *Greenland* 81 O e
Godwin Austen. See K2
Goeland, L. au, *Quebec* 85 O c
Goeland, L., *Quebec* 82 A d
Goeland, *Quebec* 85 O c
Goes, *Netherlands* 100 B c
Gogama, *Ontario* 84 J e
Gog Magog Hills, *England* 99 H h
Gogrial, *Sudan* 119 L g
Goiânia, *Brazil* 93 H g
Goias, *Brazil* 93 H f
Goikul, I., *Palau Is.* 78 B m
Goirle, *Netherlands* 100 D c
Gökçeağac, *Turkey* 124 B a
Goksun, *Turkey* 124 C b
Golaghat, *India* 127 H c
Gol'chikha, *U.S.S.R.* 114 H a
Golconda, *India* 126 E e
Gołdap, *Poland* 105 K a
Gold Bar, *Br. Columbia* 88 H b
Goldboro, *Nova Scotia* 83 L h
Golden, *Br. Columbia* 88 L e
Golden B., *New Zealand* 135 Q l
Golden Lake, *Ontario* 85 N g
Golden Prairie, *Sask.* 86 H h
Goldenville, *Nova Scotia* 83 K h
Gold Rock, *Ontario* 86 K a
Goldsand L., *Manitoba* 87 Q a
Goleniow, *Poland* 104 F b
Golfito, *Costa Rica* 91 C e
Golmo, *China* 128 C c
Goltva, *Ukraine, U.S.S.R.* 116 H g
Gomal Pass, *Pakistan* 126 C b
Gombe, *Nigeria* 119 H f
Gomel', *Belorussia, U.S.S.R.* 116 G e
Gomera, I., *Canary Is.* 118 B c
Gómez Fariás, *Mexico* 90 D c
Gómez Palacio, *Mexico* 90 D b
Gonaïves, *Haiti* 91 E c
Gonave, I. de la, *Haiti* 91 E c
Gonbad-e-Kavus, *Iran* 125 G b
Gondal, *India* 126 D d
Gondia, *India* 126 F d
Gondo, *Switzerland* 101 D b
Gönen, *Turkey* 113 F d
Gongka Ling, *China* 128 D e
Goniądz, *Poland* 105 K b
Goodenough I., *Papua* 135 K a
Gooderham, *Ontario* 85 M h
Goodeve, *Saskatchewan* 87 O g
Good Hope, C. of, *South Africa* 122 B f
Good Hope, Mt., *B.C.* 88 G e
Good Hope, *N.-W. Terr.* 80 G d
Goodlands, *Manitoba* 87 R j
Goodsir, Mt., *Br. Columbia* 88 L e
Goodsoil, *Saskatchewan* 86 H d
Good Spirit L., *Saskatchewan* 87 P g
Good Spirit Lake Prov. Park, *Saskatchewan* 87 P g
Goodwater, *Saskatchewan* 87 O j
Goodwin, *Ontario* 85 L d
Goole, *England* 99 G g
Goomalling, *Australia* 134 C f
Goor, *Netherlands* 100 E b
Goose Bay, *Labrador* 81 N g
Gooseberry Lake Prov. Park, *Alberta* 86 G f
Goose Cove, *Newfoundland* 83 R b
Goose L., *Manitoba* 87 Q d
Goose L., *Saskatchewan* 86 K g
Goose L., *Saskatchewan* 87 P e
Goose R., *Alberta* 88 L c
Gopalpur, *India* 127 F e
Göppingen, *Germany* 104 C d
Gor, *Spain* 106 D d
Gora, *China* 128 C e
Gorakhpur, *India* 127 F c
Gordola, *Switzerland* 101 D b
Gordon L., *Alberta* 86 G b
Gordonvale, *Australia* 135 J c
Goré, *Chad* 119 J g
Gore, *Ethiopia* 121 H c
Gore, *New Zealand* 135 P m
Gore Bay, *Ontario* 84 H g
Gorey, *Eire* 99 C h
Gorgan, *Iran* 125 F b
Gorgona, I., *Italy* 110 B d
Gorinchem, *Netherlands* 100 C c
Gorizia, *Italy* 110 D c
Gor'kiy, *U.S.S.R.* 117 G b
Gorlice, *Poland* 105 J d
Görlitz, *Germany* 104 F c
Gorlovka, *Ukraine, U.S.S.R.* 116 L g
Gorodetz, *U.S.S.R.* 117 F b
Gorodishche, *U.S.S.R.* 117 G d
Gorodnitsa, *Ukraine, U.S.S.R.* 116 E f
Gorontalo, *Celebes* 129 H k
Gorrahei, *Ethiopia* 121 J c
Gorrie, *Ontario* 84 J j
Gorror, I., *Yap I.* 78 D m
Gorsel, *Netherlands* 100 E b
Gorzów (Wielkopolski), *Poland* 104 F b
Gosaint han, Mt., *Nepal-Tibet* 127 G c
Göschenen, *Switzerland* 101 D b
Goshanak, *Pakistan* 126 B c
Gospić, *Yugoslavia* 110 E c
Gosport, *England* 99 G k
Gossau, *Switzerland* 101 E a
Gosselies, *Belgium* 100 C d
Gossen, *Norway* 102 B e
Gostivar, *Yugoslavia* 112 C d
Göta Älv, *Sweden* 103 E g
Göteborg, *Sweden* 103 D h
Gotha, *Germany* 104 D c
Gothenburg. See Göteborg
Gotland, I., *Sweden* 103 H h
Goto Retto, *Japan* 133 A h
Gotska Sandön, *Sweden* 103 H g
Göttingen, *Germany* 104 C c
Gott Pk., *Br. Columbia* 88 H e
Gottwaldov, *Czechoslovakia* 105 G d
Gouda, *Netherlands* 100 C b
Goudreau, *Ontario* 84 F d
Goudswaard, *Netherlands* 100 C c
Gough L., *Alberta* 86 E f
Gouin Res., *Quebec* 85 Q d
Goulais River, *Ontario* 84 F f
Goulburn, *Australia* 135 J f
Gould, *Quebec* 85 T g
Goundam, *Mali* 118 E e
Gouré, *Niger* 119 H f
Gourlay L., *Ontario* 84 F d
Gournay, *France* 108 D b
Gouverneur, *Saskatchewan* 86 K j
Govan, *Saskatchewan* 87 N g
Govenlock, *Saskatchewan* 86 H j
Governor L., *Nova Scotia* 82 K h
Gowganda, *Ontario* 84 K e
Gowna L., *Eire* 99 B g
Goya, *Argentina* 94 E c
Goyelle, L., *Quebec* 83 M c
Gozo, I. (Brit.), *Malta* 111 E g
Graaf Reinet, *South Africa* 122 C f
Grabow, *Poland* 105 H c
Gračac, *Yugoslavia* 111 E c
Gracefield, *Quebec* 85 O f
Gracias, *Honduras* 91 B d
Gracias a Dios, *Nicaragua* 91 C d
Gradets, *Bulgaria* 112 F c
Grado, *Spain* 106 B a
Grafton, *Australia* 135 K e
Grafton, Is., *Chile* 95 B h
Graham, *Ontario* 87 M a
Graham Bell, I., *Arctic Oc.* 114 F a
Graham I., *Br. Columbia* 88 C d
Graham I., *N.-W. Territories* 81 K b
Graham L., *Alberta* 86 C b
Graham R., *Br. Columbia* 88 H b
Grahamstown, *South Africa* 122 D f
Grainger, *Alberta* 86 D g
Grajewo, *Poland* 105 K b
Grammont, *Belgium* 100 B d
Grampian Mts., *Scotland* 98 D d
Gramsbergen, *Netherlands* 100 E b
Granada, *Nicaragua* 91 B d
Granada, *Spain* 106 D d
Granby, *Quebec* 85 S g
Gran Canaria, I., *Canary Is.* 118 B c
Gran Chaco, *Argentina* 94 D c
Grand, R., *Ontario* 84 K j
Grand Bank, *Newfoundland* 83 R f
Grand Bassa. See Buchanan
Grand Bassam, *Ivory Coast* 118 E g
Grand Bay, *New Brunswick* 82 F h
Grand Beach, *Manitoba* 87 V h
Grand Beach Prov. Park, *Manitoba* 87 V h
Grand Bend, *Ontario* 84 J j
Grand Bruit, *Newfoundland* 83 O f
Grand Can., *China* 128 G c
Grand Cayman, I., *West Indies* 91 C c
Grande, B., *Argentina* 95 C h
Grande, Rio, *Brazil* 93 G g
Grande Anse, *New Brunswick* 82 G f
Grande Baie, *Quebec* 82 B e
Grande Centre, *Alberta* 86 G d
Grande Comore, I., *Archipel des Comores* 121 J g
Grande de Santigao, R., *Mexico* 90 D c
Grand Falls, *Labrador* 81 N g
Grande Grève, *Quebec* 82 H e
Grande Prairie, *Alberta* 88 K c
Grande Rivière, *Quebec* 82 H e
Grande-Rivière, La, *Quebec* 81 M g
Grandes Bergeronnes, *Quebec* 82 C e
Grandes Piles, *Quebec* 85 S f
Grand Étang, *C. Breton I., Nova Scotia* 83 L g
Grand Falls, *Labrador* 81 N g
Grand Falls, *New Brunswick* 82 E f
Grand Falls, *Newfoundland* 83 R e
Grand Falls L., *Maine-New Brunswick* 82 E h
Grand Forks, *Br. Columbia* 88 K f
Grand Harbour, *N.B.* 82 F j
Grand L., *New Brunswick* 82 F h
Grand L., *Newfoundland* 83 P d
Grand Lahou, *Ivory Coast* 118 D g
Grand Manan I., *N.B.* 82 F j
Grand' Mère, *Quebec* 85 S f
Grandmesnil, L., *Quebec* 82 E b
Grand Mt., *Br. Columbia* 88 L e
Grandois, *Newfoundland* 83 R b
Grandola, *Portugal* 106 A c
Grand Rapids, *Manitoba* 87 S e
Grandrieu, *Belgium* 100 C d
Grand River, *C. Breton I., Nova Scotia* 83 M h
Grand Ruisseau, *Madeleine Is., Quebec* 83 L f
Grandson, *Switzerland* 101 B b
Grand Vallée, *Quebec* 82 G d
Grand Valley, *Ontario* 84 K j
Grandview, *Manitoba* 87 R g
Grane, *Norway* 102 E d
Granet, L., *Quebec* 85 N e
Granite Bay, *Br. Columbia* 88 G e
Granja, *Brazil* 93 J d
Grankulla, *Finland* 103 L f
Granollers, *Spain* 107 G b
Granön, *Sweden* 102 H d
Grant, *Ontario* 84 D b
Grantham, *England* 99 G h
Grant Ld., *Arctic Ocean* 89 Q a
Granton, *Ontario* 84 J j
Grantown-on-Spey, *Scotland* 98 E c
Granum, *Alberta* 86 D j
Granville Ferry, *Nova Scotia* 82 G j
Granville L., *Manitoba* 87 R b
Graskop, *South Africa* 122 E d
Gräsö, *Sweden* 103 H f
Grassano, *Italy* 111 F e
Grasse, *France* 109 G e
Grasset, L., *Quebec* 85 M c
Grassier, *Switzerland* 101 B b
Grass R., *Manitoba* 87 T c
Grassy Island L., *Alberta* 86 G g
Grassy Lake, *Alberta* 86 F j
Grate's Cove, *Newfoundland* 83 T e
Graubünden, canton, *Switzerland* 101 E b
Graus, *Spain* 107 F a
Gravarne, *Sweden* 103 D g
Grave, *Netherlands* 100 D c
Gravelbourg, *Saskatchewan* 86 L j
's Gravenhage. See Hague, The
Gravenhurst, *Ontario* 85 L h
's Gravenzande, *Neth.* 100 C b
Gray, *France* 108 F c
Gray, *Saskatchewan* 87 N h
Grayson, *Saskatchewan* 87 P h
Grayson L., *Ontario* 84 A b
Graz, *Austria* 105 F e
Great Australian Bight, *Australia* 134 E f
Great Barrier Reef, *Australia* 135 R k
Great Bear L., *N.-W. Terr.* 80 G d
Great Bernard, *Quebec* 85 T f
Great Blasket I., *Eire* 99 A h
Great Boule I., *Quebec* 82 F c
Great Burnt L., *Nfd.* 83 Q e
Great Colinet I., *Nfd.* 83 T g
Great Deer, *Saskatchewan* 86 K f
Great Dividing Ra., *Australia* 135 J d
Greater Sunda Is., *Indonesia* 78 B g
Great Geysir, *Iceland* 102 V m
Great Harbour Deep, *Newfoundland* 83 Q c
Great Lake. See Tonle Sap
Great North East Passage, *New Guinea* 135 H a
Great Pubnico L., *N. S.* 82 G k
Great Sandy Des., *Australia* 134 D d
Great Sandy I. (Fraser I.), *Australia* 135 K e
Great Slave L., *N.-W. Terr.* 80 H e
Great Snow Mt., *B. C.* 88 G b
Great Torrington, *England* 99 E k
Great Victoria Des., *Australia* 134 E e
Great Village, *Nova Scotia* 82 J h
Great Whale R., *Quebec* 81 M f
Great Whale River, *Quebec* 81 M f
Great Yarmouth, *England* 99 J k
Grebbestad, *Sweden* 103 D g
Greco, C., *Cyprus* 123 C c
Greece, *S. Europe* 113 C e
Greely Fd., *N.-W. Territories* 81 L a
Green Court, *Alberta* 86 B d
Green Cr., *Ontario* 84 E h
Green I., *Newfoundland* 83 Q b
Green I., *New Zealand* 135 Q m
Greening, *Quebec* 85 Q d
Green L., *Br. Columbia* 88 J e
Green Lake, *Saskatchewan* 86 K d
Greenland, *N. Atlantic* 89 P b
Greenland Sea, *Greenland* 89 M b
Greenly I., *Quebec* 83 P b
Greenock, *Scotland* 98 D e
Green R., *New Brunswick* 82 D f
Greenspond, *Newfoundland* 83 T d
Greenville, *Liberia* 118 D g

Greenwater L., *Ontario* 87 M b
Greenwater Lake Prov. Park, *Saskatchewan* 87 O f
Greenway, *Manitoba* 87 S j
Greenwich, *England* 99 H j
Greenwich I., *Antarctica* 136 H f
Gregg, *Manitoba* 87 S j
Gregoire L., *Alberta* 86 F b
Gregory, L., *Australia* 134 G e
Gregory Ra., *Australia* 135 H c
Greifen See, *Switzerland* 101 D a
Greifswald, *Germany* 104 E a
Grein, *Austria* 104 F d
Greiz, *Germany* 104 E c
Grenaa, *Denmark* 103 D h
Grenada, I., *Windward Is.* 91 G d
Grenadines, Is., *Windward Is.* 91 G d
Grenchen, *Switzerland* 101 C a
Grenfell, *Saskatchewan* 87 P h
Grenoble, *France* 109 F d
Grenville, C., *Australia* 135 H b
Grenville, Mt., *B.C.* 88 G e
Grenville Chan., *B.C.* 88 E d
Gretna, *Manitoba* 87 U j
Grevelingen, *Netherlands* 100 C c
Grevená, *Greece* 113 C d
Grey, Pt., *Br. Columbia* 88 C f
Greyhound Pt., *Tutuila I.* 79 T o
Grey Is., *Newfoundland* 83 R c
Grey Islands Harbour, *Newfoundland* 83 R c
Greymouth, *New Zealand* 135 Q l
Grey R., *Newfoundland* 83 Q e
Grey Ra., *Australia* 135 H e
Greystones, *Eire* 99 C g
Greytown, *New Zealand* 135 R l
Greytown. See San Juan del Norte
Griesalp, *Switzerland* 101 C b
Griffin, *Manitoba* 87 O j
Griffith, *Australia* 135 J f
Griffith I., *N.-W. Terr.* 81 K c
Grim C., *Tasmania* 135 H h
Grimsby, *England* 99 G g
Grimsby, *Ontario* 85 L j
Grimshaw, *Alberta* 88 L b
Grimstad, *Norway* 103 C g
Grindelwald, *Switzerland* 101 D b
Grindstone I., *Madeleine Is., Quebec* 83 L f
Grindstone Pt., cape, *Manitoba* 87 V g
Grinem, I., *Eniwetok* 79 R d
Grinnell Ld., *Arctic Ocean* 89 Q a
Grinnell Pen., *N.-W. Terr.* 81 K b
Griquatown, *South Africa* 122 C e
Griquet, *Newfoundland* 83 R b
Grise Fiord, *N.-W. Terr.* 81 L b
Grīva, *Latvia, U.S.S.R.* 103 M j
Groais I., *Newfoundland* 83 Q c
Grobina, *Latvia, U.S.S.R.* 103 J h
Gröbming, *Austria* 104 E e
Grodno, *Belorussia, U.S.S.R.* 116 C e
Grodzisk, *Poland* 105 G b
Groenlo, *Netherlands* 100 E b
Groix, I. de, *France* 108 B c
Groningen & prov., *Netherlands* 100 E a
Gronlid, *Saskatchewan* 87 N e
Grono, *Switzerland* 101 E b
Groote Eylandt, *Australia* 134 G b
Grootfontein, *S.W. Africa* 122 B c
Groot Natuna I. See Bunguran Kep.
Gros Morne, pk., *Newfoundland* 83 P d
Gros Morne, *Quebec* 82 G d
Gros Pate, pk., *Newfoundland* 83 P c
Gros Pin, *Quebec* 85 R b
Grosse I., *Madeleine Is., Quebec* 83 L f
Grossevichi, *U.S.S.R.* 115 N d
Gross Glockner, *Austria* 104 E e
Grosswardein. See Oradea
Grouard, *Alberta* 86 A c
Groundhog, R., *Ontario* 84 H d
Grouse Mt., *Br. Columbia* 88 D e
Grovedale, *Alberta* 88 K c
Grozynyy, *U.S.S.R.* 114 D d
Grüau, *S.W. Africa* 122 B e
Grudziądz, *Poland* 105 H b
Grues, I. aux, *Quebec* 82 B f
Grüsch, *Switzerland* 101 E b
Gruz, *Yugoslavia* 112 B c
Gruzinskaya, *U.S.S.R.* 114 D d
Grybów, *Poland* 105 J d
Grytviken, *Antarctica* 136 K g
Gsteig, *Switzerland* 101 C b
Guabito, *Panama* 91 C e
Guacanayabo, G. de, *Cuba* 91 D b
Guachipas, *Argentina* 94 C c
Guadalajara, *Mexico* 90 D c
Guadalajara, *Spain* 106 D b
Guadalcanal, I., *Solomon Is.* 78 F h
Guadalcanal, *Spain* 106 C c
Guadalcazar, *Mexico* 90 D c
Guadalquivir, R., *Spain* 106 C d
Guadalupe, *Mexico* 90 D c
Guadalupe I., *Mexico* 90 A b
Guadalupe-y-Calvo, *Mexico* 90 C b
Guadarrama, Sa. de, *Spain* 106 D b
Guadarrama, *Spain* 106 C b
Guadeloupe, I., *Leeward Is.* 91 G c
Guadiana, R., *Spain* 106 B c
Guadix, *Spain* 106 D d
Guafo & G. de, *Chile* 95 B f
Guaitecas, Is., *Chile* 95 B f
Guajará, R., *Brazil* 93 G d
Guajará Mirim, *Brazil* 92 D f
Guajaratuba, *Brazil* 92 E e
Gualeguaychú, *Argentina* 94 E d
Guam, I., *Pacific Ocean* 78 A k
Guamá, *Brazil* 93 H d
Guamini, *Argentina* 94 D e
Guamo, *Colombia* 92 C c
Guanabacoa, *Cuba* 91 C b
Guanaceví, *Mexico* 90 C b
Guanahani. See San Salvador
Guanajuato, *Mexico* 90 D c
Guanare, *Venezuela* 92 D b
Guanarito, *Venezuela* 92 D b
Guandacol, *Argentina* 94 C c
Guane, *Cuba* 91 C b
Guanica, *Puerto Rico* 91 F c
Guanta. See Puerto La Cruz
Guantánamo, *Cuba* 91 D b
Guapi, *Colombia* 92 B c
Guapiles, *Costa Rica* 91 C d
Guaporé, *Brazil* 94 F c
Guaporé, R., *Brazil-Bolivia* 92 E f
Guaporé (Rondonia), *Brazil* 92 E f
Guaqui, *Bolivia* 92 D g
Guarapuava, *Brazil* 94 F c
Guarda, *Portugal* 106 B b
Guasdualito, *Venezuela* 92 C b
Guasipati, *Venezuela* 92 E b
Guatemala, *C. America* 90 F e
Guatemala, *Guatemala* 90 F e
Guatrache, *Argentina* 95 D e
Guaviare, R., *Colombia* 92 D c
Guaxupé, *Brazil* 94 G b
Guay, *Quebec* 85 T b
Guayabal, *Venezuela* 92 D b
Guayama, *Puerto Rico* 54 C j
Guayaquil, *Ecuador* 92 B d
Guaymas, *Mexico* 90 B b
Guben, *Germany* 104 F c
Gubin. See Guben
Gudiyatam, *India* 126 E f
Guéguen, L., *Quebec* 85 N d
Guelma, *Algeria* 118 G a
Guelph, *Ontario* 84 K j
Güemes, *Argentina* 94 C b
Guenette, *Quebec* 85 P f
Guéret, *France* 108 D c
Guerin, *Quebec* 85 L e
Guernsey, I., *Channel Is.* 108 B b
Guernsey, *Saskatchewan* 87 M g
Guerrero, *Mexico* 90 C b
Guerrero, state, *Mexico* 90 D d
Guerrero, *Tamaulipas, Mex.* 90 E b
Guest I., *Antarctica* 136 D c
Guiana Highlands, *S. America* 92 E c
Guija, *Mozambique* 122 E d
Guildford, *England* 99 G j
Guillaumes, *France* 109 G d
Guimarães, *Brazil* 93 J d
Guimarães, *Portugal* 106 A b
Guinea, *West Africa* 118 C f
Guinea, Equatorial, *West Africa* 120 B d
Guinea, G. of, *N.-W. Africa* 120 A d
Guinecourt, L., *Quebec* 82 C c
Güines, *Cuba* 91 C b
Guingamp, *France* 108 B b
Güira de Melena, *Cuba* 91 C b
Guiria, *Venezuela* 92 E a
Guisanbourg, *French Guiana* 93 G c
Guise, *France* 108 E b
Guisisil, Vol., *Nicaragua* 91 B d
Gujranwala, *Pakistan* 126 D b
Gujrat, *Pakistan* 126 D b
Gulbarga, *India* 126 E e
Gulbene, *Latvia, U.S.S.R.* 103 M h
Gulistan, *Pakistan* 126 C b
Gulitel, I., *Palau Is.* 78 C l
Gul Koh, *Afghanistan* 125 J c
Gull I., *Alberta* 86 D f
Gull Lake, *Saskatchewan* 86 J h
Gulpen, *Netherlands* 100 D d
Gulran, *Afghanistan* 125 H b
Gulu, *Uganda* 121 G d
Gumel, *Nigeria* 119 G f
Gummersbach, *Germany* 104 B c
Gümüljina. See Komotini
Gümüsane, *Turkey* 124 C a
Gunchu, *Japan* 133 C h
Gunisao L., *Manitoba* 87 V e
Gunisao R., *Manitoba* 87 U e
Gunnedah, *Australia* 135 K f
Guntakal, *India* 126 E e
Gunton, *Manitoba* 87 U h
Guntur, *India* 126 F e
Gunworth, *Saskatchewan* 86 J g
Gurer, I., *Marshall Is.* 79 T e
Gurgl, *Austria* 104 D e
Gurha, *India* 126 D c
Gurla Mandhata, Mt., *Tibet* 126 F b
Gurnigel, *Switzerland* 101 C b
Gursköy, *Norway* 102 A e
Guru, *Tibet* 127 G c
Gurupá, *Brazil* 93 G d
Gurupá, Is., *Brazil* 93 G d
Gurupí, B. do, *Brazil* 93 H d
Gurupí, R., *Brazil* 93 H d
Guru Sikhar, *India* 126 D d
Guryev, *Kazakh., U.S.S.R.* 114 E d
Gusev, *U.S.S.R.* 103 K j
Gushichan, *Okinawa* 78 A d
Guspini, *Sardinia* 111 B f
Güstrow, *Germany* 104 E b
Guthrie L., *Manitoba* 87 R c
Guttannen, *Switzerland* 101 D b
Guyana (British Guiana) *S. America* 92 F c
Guyenne, prov., *France* 109 D d
Guyenne, *Quebec* 85 M d
Guysborough, *Nova Scotia* 83 L h
Guzmán, *Mexico* 90 D d
Gwa, *Burma* 127 H e
Gwadar, *Iran* 125 H e
Gwadar, *Pakistan* 126 B c
Gwalior, *India* 126 E c
Gwanda, *Rhodesia* 122 D d
Gweebarra B., *Eire* 99 B f
Gwelo, *Rhodesia* 122 D c
Gwynne, *Alberta* 86 D f
Gyangtse, *Tibet* 127 G c
Gydanskiy Pol., *U.S.S.R.* 114 G a
Gympie, *Australia* 135 K e
Györ, *Hungary* 105 G e
Gypsumville, *Manitoba* 87 T g
Gyula, *Hungary* 105 J e
Gzhatsk, *U.S.S.R.* 116 J d
Haag, Mt., *Antarctica* 136 H e
Haag, *Switzerland* 101 E a
Haaksbergen, *Netherlands* 100 E b
Ha'apai Group, *Tonga Is.* 78 J j
Haarlem, *Netherlands* 100 C b
Haast R., *New Zealand* 135 P l
Habana. See Havana
Habay, *Alberta* 88 K a
Habban, *S. Yemen* 124 E g
Habbaniyah, *Iraq* 124 D c
Habigang, *E. Pakistan* 127 H d
Haboro, *Japan* 133 G b
Hachinohe, *Japan* 133 G d
Hachuman, *Japan* 133 E g
Hackett, *Alberta* 86 E f
Hadason, *Mongolia* 128 D a
Hadda, *Saudi Arabia* 124 C e
Haddington, *Scotland* 98 F e
Hadera, *Israel* 123 C e
Haderslev, *Denmark* 103 C j
Hadhal, *Mongolia* 115 K c
Hadhramaut, *South Arabia* 124 E f
Hadjin. See Saimbeyli
Hadley B., *N.-W. Territories* 80 J c
Hadlow Crique, B., *Quebec* 83 R j
Haecht, *Belgium* 100 C d
Haeju, *N. Korea* 128 J c
Haelen, *Belgium* 100 D d
Haerhpin. See Pinkiang
Hafar, *Saudi Arabia* 124 E d
Hafar al Ats, *Saudi Arabia* 124 E d
Haffe. See Babenna
Hafford, *Saskatchewan* 86 K f
Hafnarfjördhur, *Iceland* 102 V m
Hagen, *Germany* 104 B c
Hagen, *Saskatchewan* 87 M f
Hageri, *Estonia, U.S.S.R.* 103 L g
Hagersville, *Ontario* 84 K k
Hagi, *Japan* 133 B g
Hague, C. de la, *France* 108 C b
Hague, *Saskatchewan* 86 L f
Hague, The ('s Gravenhage), *Netherlands* 100 C b
Ha Ha Bay, *Quebec* 83 O c
Haibak, *Afghanistan* 125 J b
Hai cheng, *China* 130 L b
Haichow. See Tunghai
Haidar Pasha. See Kadiköy
Haifa, *Israel* 123 C e
Haig, *Australia* 134 E f
Haig Lake, *Alberta* 88 L b
Haikang, *China* 131 E m
Haikou, *Hainan I., China* 131 E m
Hail, *Saudi Arabia* 124 D d
Hailar, *China* 128 G a
Haileybury, *Ontario* 85 L e
Hailun, *China* 128 J a
Hailuoto, *Finland* 102 L d
Hainan I., *China* 131 E n
Hainan Str., *China* 131 D m
Hainaut, prov., *Belgium* 100 B d
Haines Junction, *Yukon* 77 T c
Haiphong, *N. Vietnam* 132 D b
Hair, *Saudi Arabia* 124 E e
Hairy Hill, *Alberta* 86 F e
Haiten I., *China* 131 J k
Haiti, *West Indies* 91 E c
Hajdúböszörmény, *Hungary* 105 J e
Hajima, Jebel, *Saudi Arabia* 124 C e
Hajjar, *China* 128 B c
Haka, *Burma* 127 H d
Hakkâri, *Turkey* 124 D b
Hakodate, *Japan* 133 G d
Hal, *Belgium* 100 C d
Hala, *Pakistan* 126 C c
Halacho, *Mexico* 90 F c
Halaib, *Sudan* 124 C e
Halba, *Lebanon* 123 E c
Halbe, *Saudi Arabia* 124 D f
Halberstadt, *Germany* 104 D c
Halbrite, *Saskatchewan* 87 O j
Halcyon Hot Springs, *British Columbia* 88 K e
Halden, *Norway* 103 D g
Haleb. See Aleppo
Halebiye, *Syria* 124 C b
Halfway, R., *Br. Columbia* 88 H b
Hali, *Saudi Arabia* 124 D f
Haliburton, *Ontario* 85 M g
Haliburton Highlands, reg., *Ontario* 85 M g
Halifax, *England* 99 F g
Halifax, *Nova Scotia* 82 J j
Halifax B., *Australia* 135 J c
Halkirk, *Alberta* 86 E f
Hall, *Germany* 104 C d
Hallboro, *Manitoba* 87 S h
Halle, *Germany* 104 E c
Halle. See Hal
Hallebourg, *Ontario* 84 G c
Hallein, *Austria* 104 E e
Hall Is., *Caroline Is.* 78 F f
Halliste, *Estonia, U.S.S.R.* 103 L g
Hall Lake, *N.-W. Territories* 81 L d
Hall Ld., *Greenland* 89 P a
Hällnäs, *Sweden* 102 H d
Hallonquist, *Saskatchewan* 86 K h
Hall Pen., *N.-W. Territories* 81 N e
Halls Creek, *Australia* 134 E c
Hallstavik, *Sweden* 103 H f
Hallviken, *Sweden* 102 F e
Halmahera, I., *Indonesia* 129 J k
Halmstad, *Sweden* 103 E h
Halsa, *Norway* 102 C e
Hälsingborg, *Sweden* 103 E h
Halvorgate, *Saskatchewan* 86 L h
Halys, C. See Bafra Br.
Hama, *Syria* 123 E b
Hamada, *Japan* 133 C g
Hamadan, *Iran* 124 E c
Hamahika, *Okinawa* 78 B c
Hamam, *Saudi Arabia* 124 E e
Hamamatsu, *Japan* 133 E g
Hamar, *Norway* 103 D f
Hamar, *Saudi Arabia* 124 E e
Hambantota, *Ceylon* 126 F g
Hamber Prov. Park, *British Columbia* 88 K d
Ham Bluff, *Virgin Is.* 54 E j
Hamburg, *Germany* 104 D b
Hamdanīya, *Syria* 123 E b
Hämeenlinna, *Finland* 103 L f
Hameln, *Germany* 104 C b
Hamersley Ra., *Australia* 134 C d
Hami, *S. Yemen* 124 E g
Hamidan, *Saudi Arabia* 125 F e
Hamidiya, *Syria* 123 D c
Hamilton, *Australia* 134 H g
Hamilton, *New Zealand* 135 R k
Hamilton, *Ontario* 85 L j
Hamilton, R., *Labrador* 81 N g
Hamilton, *Scotland* 98 E e
Hamilton Inlet, *Labrador* 81 O g
Hamina, *Finland* 103 M f
Hamiota, *Manitoba* 87 R h
Hamirpai, *India* 126 E c
Hamm, *Germany* 104 B c
Hammān, *Iraq* 124 D c
Hamme, *Belgium* 100 C c
Hammerdal, *Sweden* 102 F e
Hammerfest, *Norway* 102 K a
Hammondvale, *New Brunswick* 82 G h
Ham Nord, *Quebec* 85 T g
Hamont, *Belgium* 100 D c
Hampden, *Newfoundland* 83 Q d
Hampden, *New Zealand* 135 Q l
Hampshire, co., *England* 99 G j
Hampstead, *New Brunswick* 82 F h
Hampton, *New Brunswick* 82 G h
Hamun-i-Helmand, *Iran-Afghanistan* 125 H c
Hamun-i-Puzak, *Afghanistan* 125 H c
Han, *Belgium* 100 D d
Hanakiya, *Saudi Arabia* 124 D d
Hanare iwa, *Iwo Jima* 78 E a
Hanau, *Germany* 104 C c
Hanbury, *Ontario* 85 L e
Hanchung, *China* 130 C f
Handegg, *Switzerland* 101 D b
Handel, *Saskatchewan* 86 J f
Handeni, *Tanzania* 121 H f
Handsworth, *Saskatchewan* 87 P j
Hangchow, *China* 131 K g
Hangchow B., *China* 130 K g
Han Kiang, *China* 128 E d
Hankö & Fd., *Finland* 103 K g
Hankow (Wuhan), *China* 130 G g
Hanle, *Kashmir* 126 E b
Hanley, *Saskatchewan* 86 L g
Hanmer, *New Zealand* 135 Q l
Hanmer, *Ontario* 84 K f
Hanna, *Alberta* 86 F g
Hannah B., *Ontario* 84 L a
Hannover, *Germany* 104 C b
Hannut, *Belgium* 100 D d
Hanö Bukten, *Sweden* 103 F j
Hanoi, *N. Vietnam* 132 D b
Hanover, I., *Chile* 95 B h
Hanover, *Ontario* 84 J h
Hansard, *Br. Columbia* 88 J c
Hansen, *Ontario* 84 F c
Hans Lollik Is., *Virgin Is.* 54 E h
Hanson L., *Saskatchewan* 87 P d
Hansweert, *Netherlands* 100 C c
Hantsport, *Nova Scotia* 82 H h
Hanyang, *China* 131 G g
Hanyin, *China* 130 D f
Hao, I., *Tuamotu Arch.* 79 N j
Haparanda, *Sweden* 102 L d
Haqal, *Saudi Arabia* 124 B d
Haqrayot, *Israel* 123 C e
Harak, *Saudi Arabia* 124 C d
Harar, *Ethiopia* 121 J c
Harardera, *Somali Republic* 121 K d
Hara Usu Nur, *Mongolia* 128 B a
Harbin. See Pinkiang
Harbour Breton, *Nfd.* 83 R f
Harbour Buffett, *Nfd.* 83 S f
Harbour Grace, *Nfd.* 83 T f
Harbour Mille, *Nfd.* 83 S f
Harbourville, *Nova Scotia* 82 H h
Harburg, *Germany* 104 C b
Harcourt, *New Brunswick* 82 G g
Harcus, *Manitoba* 87 T h
Harda, *India* 126 E d
Hardanger Fd., *Norway* 103 B f
Hardangerfjell, *Norway* 103 B f
Hardenberg, *Netherlands* 100 E b
Harderwijk, *Netherlands* 100 D b
Harding, *South Africa* 122 E f
Harding L., *Manitoba* 87 T b
Hardisty, *Alberta* 86 F f
Hardwar, *India* 126 E c
Hardy, Pen., *Chile* 95 C j
Hardy, *Saskatchewan* 87 N j
Hare B., *Newfoundland* 83 R b
Hare Bay, *Newfoundland* 83 S e
Hareidland, *Norway* 102 A e
Hargeisa, *Somali Republic* 121 J c
Hargrave, *Manitoba* 87 Q j
Hargrave L., *Manitoba* 87 S d
Hari, R., *Sumatra* 129 D l
Harian, *Iran* 125 F b
Harib, *Saudi Arabia* 124 E f
Harihar, *India* 126 E f
Harim, *Syria* 123 E a
Hariq, *Saudi Arabia* 124 E e
Harishpur, *India* 127 G d
Harlebeke, *Belgium* 100 B d
Harlingen, *Netherlands* 100 D a
Harmanli. See Kharmanli
Harmon R., *Alberta* 86 A b
Harnom Pt., *Rota I.* 78 A j
Härnösand, *Sweden* 102 G e
Harper, *Liberia* 118 D h
Harper Cr., *Alberta* 88 M a
Harptree, *Saskatchewan* 87 M j
Harran, *Turkey* 124 C b
Harricanaw R., *Quebec* 85 L b
Harrington Harbour, *Quebec* 83 N c
Harriott L., *Saskatchewan* 87 P b
Harris, *Saskatchewan* 86 K g
Harris & Sd. of, *Scotland* 98 C c
Harris Hill, *Ontario* 86 H b
Harrison, C., *Labrador* 81 O g
Harrison L., *Br. Columbia* 88 J f
Harris Ridge, *Arctic Ocean* 89 P a
Harriston, *Ontario* 84 K j
Harrogate, *England* 99 F g
Harrow, *Ontario* 84 H k
Harrowby, *Manitoba* 87 Q h
Har Sagī, *Israel* 123 C g
Hârşova, *Romania* 112 F b
Harspränget, *Sweden* 102 J c
Harstad, *Norway* 102 G b
Hart, *Saskatchewan* 87 M j
Hartell, *Alberta* 86 C h
Hart-Jaune R., *Quebec* 82 D b
Hartland, *New Brunswick* 82 E g
Hartlepool, *England* 99 G f
Hartley Bay, *Br. Columbia* 88 E d
Hart Mt., *Manitoba* 87 Q f
Hartney, *Manitoba* 87 R j
Harty, *Ontario* 84 H c
Harvey Station, *N.B.* 82 F h
Harwich, *England* 99 H j
Harz, Mts., *Germany* 104 D c
Hasā, *Jordan* 123 D g
Hasan D., *Turkey* 124 B b
Hasbaya, *Lebanon* 123 D d
Hassan, *India* 126 E f
Hassel Sd., *N.-W. Terr.* 81 K b
Hasselt, *Belgium* 100 D d
Hasselt, *Netherlands* 100 E b
Hastiere, *Belgium* 100 C d
Hastings, *England* 99 H k
Hastings, *New Zealand* 135 R k
Hastings, *Ontario* 85 N h
Hatay, *Turkey* 124 C b
Hateg, *Romania* 112 D b
Hatfield, *Saskatchewan* 87 M g
Hatha, *Saudi Arabia* 124 D e
Hathras, *India* 126 E c
Hatillo, *Puerto Rico* 54 C h
Ha-tinh, *N. Vietnam* 132 D c
Hatton, *Saskatchewan* 86 H h
Hatvan, *Hungary* 105 H e
Hat Yai, *Thailand* 129 D j
Hauberg Mts., *Antarctica* 136 H c
Haugesund, *Norway* 103 A g
Haukipudas, *Finland* 102 L d
Hauki vesi, *Finland* 102 N e
Haura, *S. Yemen* 124 E g
Hauraki Gulf, *New Zealand* 135 R k
Hauroko, L., *New Zealand* 135 P m
Hausa, *Jordan* 123 F h
Hausstock, Mt., *Switzerland* 101 E b
Hauta, *Saudi Arabia* 124 E e
Hauta, *S. Yemen* 124 E g
Haut Atlas, Mts., *Morocco* 118 D b
Haute-Garonne, dep., *France* 109 D e
Haute-Loire, dep., *France* 109 E d
Haute-Marne, dep., *France* 108 F b
Hautes-Alpes, dep., *France* 109 G d
Haute-Saône, dep., *France* 108 G c
Haute-Savoie, dep., *France* 108 G c
Hautes-Pyrénées, dep., *France* 109 D e
Haute-Vienne, dep., *France* 108 D d
Haut-Rhin, dep., *France* 108 G c
Havana (Habana), *Cuba* 91 C b
Havelange, *Belgium* 100 D d
Havelland, *Germany* 104 E b
Havelock, *New Brunswick* 82 G h
Havelock, *Ontario* 85 N h
Havelock I., *Andaman Is.* 127 H f
Haverfordwest, *Wales* 99 D j
Havre, *Belgium* 100 C d
Havre Aubert, *Madeleine Is., Quebec* 83 L f
Havre Boucher, *Nova Scotia* 83 L h
Havre St. Pierre, *Quebec* 82 J c
Hawarden, *Saskatchewan* 86 L g
Hawea, L., *New Zealand* 135 P m
Hawera, *New Zealand* 135 R k
Hawick, *Scotland* 98 F e
Hawke B., *New Zealand* 135 R k
Hawkes, Mt., *Antarctica* 136 J b
Hawkesbury, *Ontario* 85 Q g
Hawk Junction, *Ontario* 84 F d
Hawk Lake, *Ontario* 86 H a
Hawr al Hammar, *Iraq* 124 E c
Hawr Saniya, *Iraq* 124 E c
Hay, *Australia* 135 H f
Hay, R., *Alberta-Br. Columbia* 88 J a
Hayes Pen., *Greenland* 89 Q b
Hayes R., *Manitoba* 87 V d
Hay L., *Alberta* 88 K a
Hay Lakes, *Alberta* 86 D e
Hay River, *N.-W. Terr.* 80 H e
Hays, *Alberta* 86 F h
Hayter, *Alberta* 86 G f
Haywood, *Manitoba* 87 T j
Hazara Highlands, *Afghanistan* 125 H c
Hazaribagh, *India* 127 G d
Hazarjuft, *Afghanistan* 125 H c
Hazawza, *Saudi Arabia* 124 C c
Hazelridge, *Manitoba* 87 V j
Hazelton, *Br. Columbia* 88 F c
Hazen L., *N.-W. Territories* 81 N a
Hazenmore, *Saskatchewan* 86 K j
Hazen Str., *N.-W. Terr.* 80 H b
Hazeva, *Israel* 123 D g
Hazil, *Saudi Arabia* 124 D d
Hearne, *Saskatchewan* 87 M h
Hearst, *Ontario* 84 G c
Hearst I., *Antarctica* 136 H e
Heart L., *Alberta* 86 F d
Heart R., *Alberta* 86 A c
Heart's Content, *Nfd.* 83 T f
Heart's Delight, *Nfd.* 83 T f
Heath Pt., *Anticosti Is., Que.* 83 L d
Hébert, L., *Quebec* 85 P c
Hébertville, *Quebec* 85 T d
Hebrides, Outer, *Scotland* 98 B c
Hebron, *Jordan* 123 D f
Hebron, *Labrador* 81 N f
Hebron, *Nova Scotia* 82 F k
Hecate Str., *Br. Columbia* 88 D d
Hecelchakán, *Mexico* 90 F c
Hechingen, *Germany* 104 C d
Hechtel, *Belgium* 100 D c
Hecla & Griper B., *North-West Territories* 80 H b
Hecla & I., *Manitoba* 81 V g
Hectanooga, *Nova Scotia* 82 F j
Hector, Mt., *Alberta* 88 L e
Hede, *Sweden* 102 E e
Hedemora, *Sweden* 103 F f
Hedley, *Br. Columbia* 88 J f
Hedo, I., *Okinawa* 78 C a
Hedo misaki, *Okinawa* 78 C a
Heel Pt., *Wake I.* 79 S d
Heemstede, *Netherlands* 100 C b
Heer, *Netherlands* 100 D d
Heerenveen, *Netherlands* 100 D b
Heerlen, *Netherlands* 100 D d
Heffley, *Br. Columbia* 88 J e
Hegemann, C., *Greenland* 89 N c
Heianza shima, *Okinawa* 78 B c
Heide, *Germany* 104 C a
Heidelberg, *Germany* 104 C d
Heidelberg, *South Africa* 122 D e
Heiden, *Switzerland* 101 E a
Heijen, *Netherlands* 100 D c
Heilbronn, *Germany* 104 C d
Heinola, *Finland* 103 M f
Heinsburg, *Alberta* 86 G e
Heisler, *Alberta* 86 E f
Heist, *Belgium* 100 B c
Hekla, Mt., *Iceland* 102 W n
Helchteren, *Belgium* 100 D c
Helder, Den, *Netherlands* 100 C b
Hélène L., *Saskatchewan* 86 J e
Helen Glacier, *Antarctica* 136 R e
Helen L., *Ontario* 84 B c
Helensburgh, *Scotland* 98 D d
Helensville, *New Zealand* 135 R k
Helgoland, I., *Germany* 104 B a
Helgoländer Bucht, *Germany* 104 B a
Hellin, *Spain* 107 E c
Helmand Des., *Afghanistan* 125 H c
Helmand R., *Afghanistan* 125 H c
Helme, *Estonia, U.S.S.R.* 103 L h
Helmond, *Netherlands* 100 D c
Helmsdale, *Scotland* 98 E b
Helsingfors. See Helsinki
Helsingör, *Denmark* 103 E h
Helsinki, *Finland* 103 L f
Helston, *England* 99 D k
Hemaruka, *Alberta* 86 F g
Hemelum, *Netherlands* 100 D b
Heming Lake, *Manitoba* 87 Q d
Hemmingford, *Quebec* 85 R g
Hemnes, *Norway* 102 E c
Hemse, *Sweden* 102 H h
Hendaye, *France* 109 C e
Henderson I., *Antarctica* 136 R e
Henderson I., *Pacific Ocean* 79 O k
Hendon, *Saskatchewan* 87 O f
Hengam, I., *Iran* 125 G d
Hengchow. See Hengyang
Hengelo, *Netherlands* 100 E b
Henghsien, *China* 131 D l
Hengshan, *China* 131 F j
Hengyang, *China* 131 F j
Henley Harbour, *Labrador* 83 R b
Henley-on-Thames, *England* 99 G j

Hennebont, France 108 B c
Henri, Mt., Br. Columbia 88 G b
Henribourg, Saskatchewan 87 M e
Henrietta Maria, C., Ontario 81 L f
Henrique de Carvalho, Angola 120 E f
Henry Kater Pen., North-West Territories 81 N d
Hensall, Ontario 84 J j
Hentona, I., Okinawa 78 C a
Henzada, Burma 127 J e
Hepburn, Saskatchewan 86 L f
Hepworth, Ontario 84 J h
Heran, Yemen 124 D f
Herat, Afghanistan 125 H c
Herau. See Herowabad
Hérault, dep., France 109 E e
Herbert, Saskatchewan 86 K h
Herbertville, Quebec 82 A e
Herbesthal, Belgium 100 E d
Herb Lake, Manitoba 87 S d
Hercegnovi, Yugoslavia 112 B c
Herchmer, Manitoba 81 K f
Heredia, Costa Rica 91 C d
Hereford & co., England 99 F h
Herford, Germany 104 C b
Herinnes, Belgium 100 C d
Heriot. See Edievale
Heriot Bay, Br. Columbia 88 G e
Herisau, Switzerland 101 E a
Herit, I., Truk Is. 78 F n
Heritage Ra., Antarctica 136 H b
Herlacher, C., Antarctica 136 F d
Herma Ness, Shetland 98 J a
Hermil, Lebanon 123 E c
Hermitage, Newfoundland 83 R f
Hermitage B., Newfoundland 83 Q f
Hermite, Is., Chile 95 C j
Hermon, Mt. See Jesh Sheikh
Hermosillo, Mexico 90 B b
Herning, Denmark 103 C h
Héron, Belgium 100 D d
Heron Bay, Ontario 84 D d
Heron I., Australia 135 K d
Hérons, I. aux, Quebec 85 S k
Herowabad, Iran 124 E b
Herräng, Sweden 103 H f
Herrera, Argentina 94 D c
Herrera di Pisuerga, Spain 106 C a
Herring Neck, Nfd. 83 S d
Herriot, Manitoba 87 Q b
Herschel, Saskatchewan 86 J g
Herselt, Belgium 100 C c
Hertford & co., England 99 G j
's Hertogenbosch, Netherlands 100 D c
Herval. See Joacaba
Hervás, Spain 106 C b
Hervé, Belgium 100 D d
Hervey B., Australia 135 K d
Hervey Is., Cook Is. 79 L j
Hervey Junction, Quebec 85 S f
Herzberg, Germany 104 E c
Herzliya, Israel 123 C e
Herzogenbuchsee, Switzerland 101 C a
Hesdin, France 108 E a
Hespeler, Ontario 84 K j
Heught, Mt., Australia 134 F d
Heusden, Netherlands 100 D c
Hève, C. de la, France 108 D b
Heward, Manitoba 87 O j
Hexham, England 98 F f
Hiakiang, China 131 D k
Hickman's Harbour, Nfd. 83 T e
Hickson, Ontario 84 K j
Hidalgo, Mexico 90 E b
Hidalgo, state, Mexico 90 E c
Hieflau, Austria 104 F e
Hierro, I., Canary Is. 118 B c
Higashie Ue, I., Okinawa 78 A a
Higashi iwa, Iwo Jima 78 E a
Higashi Onna, Okinawa 78 B c
High Hill L., Manitoba 87 W c
Highland, Ontario 84 C j
High Point, Saskatchewan 86 K h
High Prairie, Alberta 88 L c
High River, Alberta 86 D h
Highrock & L., Manitoba 87 R c
Highrock L., Saskatchewan 88 R b
Higuro, Pta., Puerto Rico 54 B h
Hiimeji, Japan 133 D g
Hiiumaa, Estonia, U.S.S.R 103 K g
Hijar, Spain 107 E b
Hijaz, Saudi Arabia 124 C e
Hikone, Japan 133 E g
Hikurangi, Mt., New Zealand 135 S k
Hikurangi, New Zealand 135 R j
Hilda, Alberta 86 G h
Hildesheim, Germany 104 C b
Hillah, al, Iraq 124 D c
Hillcrest, Alberta 86 C j
Hilliard, Alberta 86 E e
Hillmond, Saskatchewan 86 H e
Hillsborough, New Brunswick 82 H h
Hillsborough B., Prince Edward I. 82 J g
Hillsburgh, Ontario 84 K j
Hillsdale, Ontario 85 L h
Hillsport, Ontario 84 E c
Hillston, Australia 135 J f
Hilton Beach, Ontario 84 G f
Hilton Inlet, Antarctica 136 J d
Hilversum, Netherlands 100 D b
Hilyan, Saudi Arabia 124 D e
Himachal Pradesh, India 126 E b
Himalaya Mts., India, etc. 126 E b
Himanka, Finland 102 K d
Himare, Albania 113 B d
Hinchcliffe, Saskatchewan 87 P f
Hindeloopen, Netherlands 100 D b
Hinds Hill, pk., Nfd. 83 Q d
Hindubagh, Pakistan 126 C b
Hindu Kush, Mts., Afghanistan-Pakistan 126 C a
Hindupur, India 126 E f
Hindville, Alberta 86 G e
Hines Creek, Alberta 88 K b
Hingan, China 128 H a
Hingan. See Ankang
Hinganghat, India 126 E d
Hingho, China 130 F b
Hinghwa, China 130 J f
Hinghwa. See Putien
Hingi, China 131 B k
Hinglaj, Pakistan 126 C c
Hingoli, India 126 E e
Hingol R., Pakistan 126 C c
Hinis, Turkey 124 D b
Hinnöy, Norway 102 F b
Hinton, Alberta 88 L d
Hiro. See Birao
Hirosaki, Japan 133 G d
Hiroshima, Japan 133 C g
Hisarönü, Turkey 124 B a
Hisban, Jordan 123 D f
Hispaniola, I., West Indies 91 E c
Hissar, India 126 E c
Hissmofors, Sweden 102 F e
Hisya, Syria 123 E c
Hit, Iraq 124 D c
Hitchcock, Saskatchewan 87 O j
Hitra, Norway 102 C e
Hivaoa, I., Marquesas Is. 79 N h
Hiwasa, Japan 133 D h
Hjälmaren, L., Sweden 103 F g
Hjörring, Denmark 103 C h
Hkamti, Burma 127 J c
Hoadley, Alberta 86 C f
Hobart, Tasmania 135 J h
Hobbema, Alberta 86 D f
Hobbs Coast, Antarctica 136 E c
Hoboken, Belgium 100 C c
Hobro, Denmark 103 C h
Hobsogol, Mongolia 115 K c
Hochwan, China 131 C g
Hodeida, Yemen 124 D g
Hodges Hill, pk., Nfd. 83 R d
Hodgeville, Saskatchewan 86 L h
Hodgson, Manitoba 87 U g
Hódmezövásárhely, Hungary 105 J e
Hoek van Holland, Netherlands 100 C c
Hoey, Saskatchewan 87 M f
Hof, Germany 104 D c
Hofei, China 130 H g
Hofs Jökull, Iceland 102 Wm
Hofuf, Saudi Arabia 124 E d
Höganäs, Sweden 103 E h
Hogarth, Ontario 84 B c
Hogg L., Manitoba 87 V a
Hogs Back, Ontario 84 D j
Hohe Tauern, Austria 104 E e
Hohsien, China 131 E k
Hokianga Harb., New Zealand 135 Q j
Ho-kien-fu, China 130 H c
Hokitika, New Zealand 135 Q l
Hokkaido I., Japan 133 G c
Holap, I., Truk Is. 78 E m
Holbæk, Denmark 103 D j
Holberg, British Columbia 88 E e
Holden, Alberta 86 E e
Holdfast, Saskatchewan 87 M h
Holei, I., Palmyra I. 79 U k
Holguín, Cuba 91 D b
Holinkoerh, China 130 E b
Holland, Manitoba 87 T j
Holland, Noord, prov., Netherlands 100 C b
Holland, Zuid, prov., Netherlands 100 C b
Holland Centre, Ontario 84 K h
Hollandia. See Sukarnapura
Hollange, Belgium 100 D e
Hollick-Kenyon Plateau, Antarctica 136 F c
Hollogne, Belgium 100 D d
Hollow Crique, Quebec 85 S c
Hollyburn, Br. Columbia 88 C f
Holmes L., Manitoba 87 V a
Holmestrand, Norway 103 D g
Holmfield, Manitoba 87 S j
Holmsund, Sweden 102 J e
Holstebro, Denmark 103 C h
Holstein, Germany 104 C b
Holstein, Ontario 84 K h
Holsteinsborg, Greenland 89 P c
Holten, Netherlands 100 E b
Holtyre, Ontario 84 K d
Holwerd, Netherlands 100 D a
Holyhead, Wales 99 D g
Holy I., England 98 F e
Holy I., Wales 99 D g
Holyoke, Alberta 86 G d
Holyrood, Newfoundland 83 T f
Home B., N.-W. Territories 81 N d
Homfray Str., Andaman Is. 127 H f
Hommelvik, Norway 102 D e
Homs, Libya 119 H b
Homs, Syria 123 E c
Honan, prov., China 130 F e
Honan. See Loyang
Honda, B., Cuba 91 C b
Honda, Colombia 92 C b
Hondo, Alberta 86 C c
Hondo, Mexico 90 D b
Honduras, C., Honduras 91 B c
Honduras, Cent. America 91 B d
Honduras, G. of, Brit. Hond. 91 B c
Hönefoss, Norway 103 D f
Honeywood, Ontario 84 K h
Honfleur, France 108 D b
Honghai B., China 131 G l
Hong Kong (Brit.), China 131 G l
Honshu I., Japan 133 C g
Hoofdplaat, Netherlands 100 B c
Hooger Smilde, Netherlands 100 E b
Hoogeveen, Netherlands 100 E b
Hoogezand, Netherlands 100 E a
Hooghalen, Netherlands 100 E b
Hooghly, India 127 G d
Hooghly R., India 127 G e
Hook Hd., Eire 99 C h
Hooping Harbour, Nfd. 83 Q c
Hoorn, Netherlands 100 D b
Hoorn Is., Pacific Ocean 78 J j
Hoosier, Saskatchewan 86 H g
Hope, Br. Columbia 88 J f
Hopedale, Labrador 81 N f
Hopeh, prov., China 130 G c
Hopen, I., Barents Sea 114 B a
Hopes Advance C., Quebec 82 N e
Hopetoun, Australia 134 D f
Hope Town, Andaman Is. 127 H f
Hopetown, South Africa 122 C e
Hopewell, Nova Scotia 82 K h
Hopewell Is., N.-W. Terr. 81 M f
Hoppo, China 131 D m
Horaždovice, Czechoslovakia 104 E d
Horburg, Alberta 86 B f
Horcasitas, Mexico 90 B b
Horgen, Switzerland 101 D a
Horizon, Saskatchewan 87 M j
Horka, Germany 104 F c
Horlick Mts., Antarctica 136 F a
Hormoz, Iran 125 F d
Hormoz I., Iran 125 G d
Hormuz, Str. of, Saudi Arabia-Iran 125 G d
Horn, Austria 105 F d
Horn, C. See Hornos, C. de
Horn, Iceland 102 U l
Hornavan, Sweden 102 G c
Hörnefors, Sweden 102 H e
Hornepayne, Ontario 84 F c
Hornopiren, Mt., Chile 95 B f
Hornos, C. de, Chile 95 C j
Hornsea, England 99 G g
Horo, Netherlands 100 D c
Horonobe, Japan 133 G b
Horqueta, Paraguay 94 E b
Horsefly, Br. Columbia 88 J d
Horse Is., Newfoundland 83 R c
Horse Islands, Newfoundland 83 R c
Horsens, Denmark 103 C j
Horse R., Alberta 86 F b
Horse Shoe, Australia 134 C e
Horseshoe Bay, Br. Columbia 88 C e
Horsham, Australia 134 H g
Horsham, England 99 G j
Horsham, Saskatchewan 86 H h
Horšovský Týn, Czechoslovakia 104 E d
Horst, Netherlands 100 E c
Horten, Norway 103 D g
Horwood L., Ontario 84 H d
Hoşap, Turkey 124 D b
Hose Ra., Sarawak 129 F k
Hoshangabad, India 126 E d
Hoshiarpur, India 126 E b
Hospel, India 126 E e
Hospenthal, Switzerland 101 D b
Hossegor, France 109 C e
Hoste, I., Chile 95 C j
Hosur, India 126 E f
Hotagen, Sweden 102 E e
Hotchkiss, Alberta 88 L b
Hotseh, China 130 G e
Hotton, Belgium 100 D d
Houdelaincourt, France 108 F b
Houffalize, Belgium 100 D d
Hourn L., Scotland 98 D c
House Harbour, Madeleine Is., Quebec 83 L f
House R., Alberta 86 E c
Houston, Br. Columbia 88 F c
Houten, Netherlands 100 D b
Houtman Abrolhos, Australia 134 B e
Howe Sd., Br. Columbia 88 H f
Howick, Quebec 85 R g
Howick, South Africa 122 E e
Howland I., Pacific Ocean 79 T l
Howley, Newfoundland 83 P d
Howser, Br. Columbia 88 L e
Hoyes, Spain 106 B b
Hoy I., Orkney 98 E b
Hoyle, Ontario 84 J d
Hoyt Station, New Brunswick 82 F h
Hoyun, China 128 F f
Hozat, Turkey 124 C b
Hrubieszów, Poland 105 K c
Hsawnghsup. See Thaungdut
Hsenwi, Burma 127 J d
Hsiachwan Shan, China 131 F m
Hsiamen. See Amoy
Hsi-an. See Sian
Hsi-ch'ang. See Sichang
Hsinchu, Taiwan 131 K k
Hsi-ning. See Sining
Hsinking. See Changchun
Hsipaw, Burma 127 J d
Hsüchang, China 130 F f
Hsuchow. See Hsüchang
Huachi, Bolivia 92 D g
Huacho, Peru 92 B f
Huachuacho, Peru 92 B e
Hualgayoc, Peru 92 B e
Hualien, Taiwan 131 K l
Huanay, Bolivia 92 D g
Huancabamba, Peru 92 B e
Huancane, Peru 92 D g
Huancavelica, Peru 92 B f
Huancayo, Peru 92 B f
Huanchaca, Bolivia 92 D h
Huanchaco, Peru 92 B e
Huanta, Peru 92 C f
Huánuco, Peru 92 B e
Huaonta, Nicaragua 91 C d
Huara, Chile 94 C a
Huaras, Peru 92 B e
Huariaca, Peru 92 B f
Huario, Peru 92 B f
Huarmey, Peru 92 B f
Huascarán, Mt., Peru 92 B e
Huasco, Chile 94 B c
Huatusco. See Coatepec
Huaylas, Peru 92 B e
Hubbard, Nova Scotia 82 H j
Hubbard, Saskatchewan 87 O g
Huberdeau, Quebec 85 Q g
Hubli, India 126 E e
Hubner B., Tutuila I. 79 T o
Huddersfield, England 99 F g
Hudiksvall, Sweden 103 G f
Hudson, Ontario 86 K a
Hudson B., Canada 81 L f
Hudson Bay, Saskatchewan 87 P f
Hudson Hope, Br. Columbia 88 J b
Hudson Mts., Antarctica 136 G d
Hudson Str., Canada 81 M e
Hudwin L., Manitoba 87 W e
Hue, S. Vietnam 132 D c
Huedin, Romania 112 D a
Huehuetenango, Guatemala 90 F d
Huejutla, Mexico 90 E c
Huelva, Spain 106 B d
Huereal Overa, Spain 107 E d
Huete, Spain 107 D b
Hughenden, Alberta 86 F f
Hughenden, Australia 135 H d
Hughes R., Manitoba 86 R b
Hughton, Saskatchewan 86 K g
Huhehot, China 130 E b
Hüichŏn, Korea 128 J b
Hukawng Valley, Burma 127 J c
Hukow, China 128 G e
Hukuntsi, Botswana 122 C d
Hula L., Israel 123 D d
Hulin. See Linkiang
Hull, England 99 G g
Hull, Quebec 85 P g
Hull Glacier, Antarctica 136 D d
Hull I., Phoenix Is. 78 J h
Hulst, Netherlands 100 C c
Hulun. See Hailar
Hulun Chih, China 128 G a
Hulutao, China 128 H b
Huma, China 115 M c
Humacao, Puerto Rico 54 D h
Humaitá, Brazil 92 E e
Humaitá, Paraguay 94 E c
Humansdorp, South Africa 122 C f
Humay, Peru 92 B f
Humbe. See Mutano
Humber B., Ontario 84 C k
Humbermouth, Newfoundland 83 P e
Humber R., England 99 H g
Humboldt, Saskatchewan 87 M f
Humboldt Glacier, Greenland 89 Q b
Humboldt Mts., Antarctica 136 M d
Humenné, Czechoslovakia 105 J d
Hume Res., Australia 135 J g
Hun, Libya 118 J c
Húna-flói, Iceland 102 V m
Hunan, prov., China 131 E j
Hundred Mile House, British Columbia 88 J e
Hungary, Central Europe 97 M g
Hungchiang, China 131 J j
Hungnam, N. Korea 128 J c
Hungtze Hu, China 130 J f
Hunsrück, Mts., Germany 104 B d
Hunta, Ontario 84 J c
Hunter I., Br. Columbia 88 E e
Hunter I., Pacific Ocean 78 H j
Hunter Is., Tasmania 135 H h
Hunters River, Prince Edward I. 82 J g
Hunting I., Quebec 82 J c
Huntingdon, England 99 G h
Huntingdon, Quebec 85 Q g
Huntingdon & Peterborough co., England 99 G h
Huntly, New Zealand 135 R k
Huntly, Scotland 98 F c
Hunts Point, Nova Scotia 82 H k
Huntsville, Ontario 85 L g
Hunucma, Mexico 90 F c
Hun-yüan-chow, China 130 F c
Hunza, Kashmir 126 D a
Huon Pen., New Guinea 135 J a
Hupeh, prov., China 130 F g
Hurd C., Ontario 84 J g
Hurdman Bridge, Ontario 84 D h
Hurghada, Egypt 119 M c
Hurkeet, Ontario 84 B d
Huronia, reg., Ontario 84 L h
Huskvarna, Sweden 103 F h
Hussar, Alberta 86 E g
Husum, Germany 104 C a
Hüttenberg, Austria 104 F e
Hutton, Br. Columbia 88 J c
Huttwil, Switzerland 101 C a
Huxley, Alberta 86 D g
Huy, Belgium 100 D d
Hvar, I., Yugoslavia 110 F d
Hwahsien, China 131 F l
Hwaian, China 130 J f
Hwaijen, China 130 F c
Hwaiking. See Tsinyang
Hwaining, China 131 H g
Hwaiyang, China 130 G f
Hwaiyn. See Tsingkiang
Hwangchow. See Hwangkang
Hwang-Hai. See Yellow Sea
Hwang Ho, China 128 G c
Hwang Ho, Mouth of, China 130 J c
Hwanghsien, China 130 K d
Hwangkang, China 130 G g
Hweichow. See Sihsien
Hweimin, China 130 H d
Hweinan, China 128 J b
Hweitseh, China 131 A j
Hwohsien, China 130 E d
Hyakuna, I., Okinawa 78 B d
Hyas, Saskatchewan 87 P g
Hybla, Ontario 85 N g
Hyden, Australia 134 C f
Hyderabad, India 126 E e
Hyderabad, Pakistan 126 C c
Hyères, France 109 G e
Hyères, Is. d', France 109 G e
Hyland Post, Br. Columbia 88 E b
Hylo, Alberta 86 E d
Hyogo, Japan 133 D g
Hyrynsalmi, Finland 102 N d
Hythe, Alberta 88 K c
Hythe, England 99 H j
Iaşi, Romania 116 E h
Iauarete, Colombia 92 D c
Ibadan, Nigeria 118 F g
Ibagué, Colombia 92 B c
Ibarra, Ecuador 92 B c
Ibb, Yemen 124 D g
Ibembo, Congo 120 E d
Iberville, Quebec 85 R g
Ibiapaba, Sa. da, Brazil 93 J d
Ibicuí, Brazil 94 E c
Ibiza I., Balearic Is. 107 F c
Ibresi, U.S.S.R. 117 H c
Ibri, Muscat & Oman 125 G e
Ibu, I., Okinawa 78 C a
Ibwe Munyama, Zambia 122 D c
Ica, Peru 92 B f
Içá, R., Brazil 92 D d
Içana, Brazil 92 D c
Içel, Turkey 124 B b
Iceland, I., North Atlantic Ocean 102 Wm
Ichang, China 130 E g
Icheng, China 130 F g
Ichow. See Lini
Ichun, China 131 G j
Idah, Nigeria 118 G g
Iddesleigh, Alberta 86 F h
Ideles, Algeria 118 G d
Idfu, Egypt 119 M d
Idhra, I., Greece 113 D f
Idirtu, China 128 C c
Idlib, Syria 123 E b
Idutywa, South Africa 122 D f
Ieper, Belgium 100 A d
Ierissós, G. of, Greece 113 D d
Ie shima, Okinawa 78 B a
Ifakara, Tanzania 121 H f
Iférouane, Niger 118 G e
Ifni, N.-W. Africa 118 C c
Igan, Sarawak 129 F k
Igarapé Miri, Brazil 93 H d
Igarka, U.S.S.R. 114 H b
Ighil-Izane, Algeria 109 M j
Iglesias, Sardinia 111 B f
Igli, Algeria 118 E b
Igloolik, N.-W. Territories 81 L d
Ignace, Ontario 86 L a
Igoma, Tanzania 121 G f
Igra, U.S.S.R. 117 L b
Iguacú & R., Brazil 94 F c
Iguala, Mexico 90 E d
Iguapé, Brazil 94 G b
Iguatú, Brazil 93 K e
Igumira, Tanzania 121 G f
Igurin, I., Eniwetok 79 R d
Ihosy, Mal. Rep. 121 N l
Ihtiman, Bulgaria 112 D c
Iida, Japan 133 E g
Iisalmi, Finland 102 M e
Ijebu-Ode, Nigeria 118 F g
IJselmonde, Netherlands 100 C c
IJselmuiden, Netherlands 100 D b
IJselstein, Netherlands 100 D b
IJssel Meer, Netherlands 100 D b
IJssel R., Netherlands 100 E b
Ijui, Brazil 94 F c
Ijzendijke, Netherlands 100 B c
Ikaría, I., Greece 113 F f
Ikei shima, Okinawa 78 B c
Ikisu, Tanzania 121 G e
Ikla, Estonia, U.S.S.R. 103 L h
Ikushumbet, Japan 133 G c
Ilagan, Philippines 129 H g
Ilam, Iran 124 E c
Ilanz, Switzerland 101 E b
Iława, Poland 105 H b
Iławka, Poland 105 J a
Ilbunga, Australia 134 G e
Ilderton, Ontario 84 J j
Ile à la Crosse, L., Sask. 86 K b
Ile à la Crosse, Saskatchewan 86 K c
Ile-de-France, prov., France 108 E b
Ile Mayotte, I., Archipel des Comores 121 K g
Ilford, Manitoba 87 W b
Ilfracombe, England 99 E j
Ilhavo, Portugal 106 A b
Ilhéus, Brazil 93 K f
Ili, Kazakh., U.S.S.R. 114 G d
Ilia, Greece 113 C f
Ilic, Turkey 124 C b
Ilich, Kazakh., U.S.S.R. 114 F d
Iligan, Philippines 129 H j
Ilikotu. See Ankang
Ilimsk, U.S.S.R. 115 K c
Iliodhrómia, I., Greece 113 D e
Illapel, Chile 94 B d
Ille-et-Vilaine, dep., France 108 C b
Illescas, Spain 106 D b
Illimani, Mt., Bolivia 92 D g
Illora, Spain 106 D d
Il'men', Oz., U.S.S.R. 116 G b
Ilo, Peru 92 C g
Iloilo, Philippines 129 H h
Ilorin, Nigeria 118 F g
Ilots de Bass, Tubuai Is. 79 M k
Ilpi, U.S.S.R. 115 S b
Imabari, Japan 133 C g
Iman, U.S.S.R. 115 N d
Imandra, Oz., U.S.S.R. 114 C b
Imerimandroso, Mal. Rep. 121 N k
Imi, Ethiopia 121 J c
Imieji Anchorage, Jaluit I. 79 U j
Immendingen, Germany 104 C e
Imperatriz, Brazil 92 D e
Imperatriz, Brazil 93 H e
Imperia, Italy 110 B d
Imperial, Saskatchewan 87 M g
Imperoyal, Nova Scotia 82 J j
Imphal, India 127 H d
Imrodj, I., Jaluit I. 79 T h
Imroz, I., Turkey 124 A a
Imtan, Syria 123 E e
Inaccessible Is., Antarctica 136 J f
Inagua, Gt., I., Bahama Is. 91 E b
Inagua, Lit., I., Bahama Is. 91 E b
Inarajan, Guam 78 A l
Inari & L., Finland 102 M b
Inchkeith, Scotland 98 E d
Inchŏn, S. Korea 128 J c
Incourt, Belgium 100 C d
Indaal, L., Scotland 98 C e
Indals Älv, Sweden 102 G e
Indaw, Burma 127 J d
Indawgyi L., Burma 127 J c
Independencia, Argentina 94 C d
India, S. Asia 126-127
Indian Arm, inlet, British Columbia 88 D f
Indian Brook, Cape Breton I., Nova Scotia 83 M g
Indian Des. See Thar
Indian Harbour, Labrador 83 O g
Indian Harbour, Nova Scotia 82 J j
Indian Head, Manitoba 87 O h
Indian Head, Saskatchewan 80 J g
Indian L., Northern, Man. 87 U a
Indian L., Southern, Man. 87 T a
Indicator L., Quebec 82 A b
Indiga, U.S.S.R. 114 D b
Indigirka, R., U.S.S.R 115 P b
Indispensable Reefs, Coral Sea 78 F j
Indonesia, S.-E. Asia 129 F l
Indore, India 126 E d
Indre, dep., France 108 D c
Indre-et-Loire, dep., France 108 N k
Indur (Nizamabad), India 126 E e
Indus, R., Pakistan, etc. 126 C d
Inebolu, Turkey 124 B a
Ingelmunster, Belgium 100 B d
Ingenika, R., Br. Columbia 88 G b
Ingersoll, Ontario 84 K j
Ingham, Australia 135 J c
Inglefield Inlet, Greenland 89 Q b
Inglefield Ld., Greenland 89 Q b
Ingleside, Ontario 85 R b
Inglis, Manitoba 87 Q h
Ing Luiggi, Argentina 94 D e
Ingolf, Ontario 86 G a
Ingolstadt, Germany 104 D d
Ingonish, C. Breton I., N. S. 83 M g
Ingramport, Nova Scotia 82 H j
Ingrid Christensen Coast, Antarctica 136 R e
Inhambane, Mozambique 122 F d
Inírida, R., Colombia 92 D c
Inishark I., Eire 99 A g
Inishbofin, I., Eire 99 A g
Inishkea I., Eire 99 A f
Inishman, I., Eire 99 A g
Inishmore, I., Eire 99 A g
Inishmurray, I., Eire 99 B f
Inishtrahull, Eire 98 C e
Inishturk, I., Eire 99 A g
Injune, Australia 135 J e
Inkerman, New Brunswick 82 H f
Innertkirchen, Switzerland 101 D b
Innisfail, Alberta 86 D f
Innisfail, Australia 135 J c
Innisfree, Alberta 86 F e
Innsbruck, Austria 104 D e
Inoucdjouac, Quebec 81 R e

Inowrocław, Poland 105 H b
Inquisivi, Bolivia 92 D g
Ins, Switzerland 101 C a
In Salah, Algeria 118 F c
Insar, U.S.S.R. 117 G d
Insein, Burma 127 J e
In Shan. See Yin Shan
Insinger, Saskatchewan 87 O g
Insterburg. See Chernyakhovsk
Instow, Saskatchewan 86 J j
Intelewa, Surinam 93 F c
Interlaken, Switzerland 101 C b
International Peace Garden, Canada-U.S.A. 87 R k
Interview I., Andaman Is. 127 H f
Intragna, Switzerland 101 D b
Inutil, B., Chile 95 C h
Inuvik, N.-W. Territories 80 F d
Inveraray, Scotland 98 D d
Invercargill, New Zealand 135 P m
Inverell, Australia 135 K e
Invermay, Saskatchewan 87 O g
Invermere, Br. Columbia 88 L e
Inverness, C. Breton I., Nova Scotia 83 L g
Inverness, Quebec 85 T f
Inverness & co., Scotland 98 E c
Inverurie, Scotland 98 F c
Investigator Str., Australia 134 G g
Inwood, Ontario 84 J k
Inyati, Rhodesia 122 D c
Inza, U.S.S.R. 117 H d
Inzer, U.S.S.R. 117 N c
Ioánnina, Greece 113 C e
Ioco, Br. Columbia 88 E f
Iona, C. Breton I., N.S. 83 M h
Iona I., Scotland 98 C d
Ionian Is., Greece 113 B e
Ionian Sea, Italy, etc. 97 M j
Ionishkis, Lithuania, U.S.S.R. 103 K h
Ios, I., Greece 113 E f
Ipala, Mexico 90 C c
Ipameri, Brazil 93 H g
Ipen. See Ypres
Ipiales, Colombia 90 B c
Ipin, China 131 B h
Ipiros, Greece 113 C e
Ipoh, Malaysia 132 C f
Ipperwash Prov. Park, Ont. 84 J j
Ippy, Cent. Afr. Republic 119 K g
Ipswich, Australia 135 K e
Ipswich, England 99 H h
Ipú, Brazil 93 J d
Iquique, Chile 94 B b
Iquitos, Peru 92 C d
Iracoubo, French Guiana 93 G b
Iráklia, I., Greece 113 E f
Iráklion, Crete 113 E g
Iran (Persia), Asia 125 F c
Irapa, Venezuela 92 E a
Irapuato, Mexico 90 D c
Iraq, W. Asia 124 D c
Irazú, Vol., Costa Rica 91 C d
Irbid, Jordan 123 D e
Irbit, U.S.S.R. 117 R b
Ireland, Rep. of (Eire), British Isles 99 B g
Irendyk Khr., U.S.S.R. 117 N e
Irgiz, Kazakh., U.S.S.R. 114 F d
Irian Barat. See West Irian
Irikinskiy, U.S.S.R. 117 P e
Iringa, Tanzania 121 H f
Irish Sea, British Isles 99 D g
Irkutsk, U.S.S.R. 115 K c
Irkutskaya Oblast, U.S.S.R. 115 K c
Irma, Alberta 86 F f
Iron Bridge, Ontario 84 G f
Irondale, Ontario 85 M h
Iron Knob, Australia 134 G f
Iroquois Dam, Ontario 85 P b
Iroquois Falls, Ontario 84 K d
Irrawaddy, Burma 127 H e
Irrawaddy, R., Burma 127 H e
Irricana, Alberta 86 D g
Irtysh, R., U.S.S.R. 114 F c
Irumu, Congo 121 F d
Irvine, Alberta 86 G j
Isa, Mt., Australia 134 G d
Isaac L., Br. Columbia 88 J d
Isaacs Harbour, Nova Scotia 83 L h
Isabela I., Galápagos Is. 79 R g
Isabella, Manitoba 87 R h
Isabella, Puerto Rico 54 B h
Isabel Segundo, Puerto Rico 54 D h
Isaccea, Romania 112 G b
Isachsen, C., N.-W. Terr 80 J b
Isachsen, N.-W. Terr. 80 J b
Isafjördhur, Iceland 102 U l
Isai Kalat, Pakistan 126 B c
Isangi, Congo 120 E d
Isari, Greece 113 D f
Ischia, I., Italy 111 D e
Ise, Japan 133 E g
Ise B., Japan 133 E g
Iseghem, Belgium 100 B d
Iseltwald, Switzerland 101 C b
Isère, dep. & R., France 109 F d
Isernia, Italy 111 E e
Isfandaqeh. See Gav Koshī
Isha Baidao, Somali Rep 121 J d
Ishan, China 131 D k
Ishikari, Japan 133 H c
Ishikawa, I., Okinawa 78 B b
Ishim, U.S.S.R. 114 F c
Ishimbai, U.S.S.R. 117 N d
Ishinomaki B., Japan 133 G e
Ishkamish, Afghanistan 125 J b
Ishkanan, Iran 125 F d
Ishkasham, Afghanistan 125 K b
Isil Kul, U.S.S.R. 114 G c
Isiolo, Kenya 121 H d
Isisford, Australia 135 H d
Iskenderun, Turkey 124 C b
Iskilip, Turkey 124 B a
Iskitim, U.S.S.R. 114 H c
Iskut, R., Br. Columbia 88 D b
Iskwatam L., Saskatchewan 87 O c
Islamabad, Pakistan 126 D b
Island Falls, Ontario 84 J c
Island Falls, Saskatchewan 87 P c
Island L., Manitoba 81 K g
Island L., Newfoundland 83 Q e
Island L., Ontario 84 K g
Islands, B. of, Newfoundland 83 O d
Islands, B. of, New Zealand 135 R j
Islay, Alberta 86 G e
Islay I., Scotland 99 C e
Isle aux Morts, Nfd. 83 O f
Isle Maligne, Quebec 82 A e
Isle of Man, British Isles 99 E f
Isles, L. des, Saskatchewan 86 H d
Isle Verte, Quebec 82 C e
Ismailia, Egypt 119 M b
Ismail Khan, India 126 D b
Isna, Egypt 119 M c
Isoka, Zambia 121 G g
Isparta, Turkey 124 B b
Israel, W. Asia 123 C e
Isriya, Syria 123 F b
Issoudun, France 108 D c
Issyk Kul, Oz., Kirgiz., U.S.S.R. 114 G d
Istanbul, Turkey 124 A a
Isthmus B., Ontario 84 J g
Istmina, Colombia 92 B b
Istra, Yugoslavia 110 D c
Itabaiana, Brazil 93 K e
Itacare, Brazil 93 K f
Itacoatiara, Brazil 92 F d
Itaeté, Brazil 93 J f
Itaituba, Brazil 93 F d
Itajaí, Brazil 94 G c
Itajuí, Brazil 93 H f
Italy, Central Europe 110-111
Itapaci, Brazil 93 H f
Itapajé, Brazil 93 K d
Itapecurú-mirim, Brazil 93 J d
Itapemirim, Cachoeiro de, Brazil 93 J h
Itapetininga, Brazil 93 H h
Itapeva, Brazil 93 H h
Itaqüi, Brazil 94 E c
Itarsi, India 126 E d
Itatube, Brazil 92 E e
Itaúna, Brazil 93 J h
Itéa, Greece 113 D e
Itháci. See Ithaká
Ithaká, Greece 113 C e
Itiés, Greece 113 C d
Itoman, I., Okinawa 78 A d
Ituaçú, Brazil 93 J f
Itubera, Brazil 93 K f
Itula, Congo 121 F e
Ituna, Saskatchewan 87 O g
Iturbe, Argentina 94 C b
Iturup, I., Kuril Is. 89 D e
Ivailovgrad, Bulgaria 112 F d
Ivanhoe, Australia 135 H f
Ivanhoe, R., Ontario 84 H d
Ivanic Grad, Yugoslavia 110 F c
Ivano-Frankovsk (Stanislav), Ukraine, U.S.S.R. 116 D g
Ivanovka, U.S.S.R. 117 K d
Ivanovo, U.S.S.R. 116 M c
Ivdel, U.S.S.R. 114 F b
Iviza I. See Ibiza
Ivory Coast, West Africa 118 D g
Iwakuni, Japan 133 C g
Iwaniska, Poland 105 J c
Iwo Jima, Pacific Ocean 78 E d
Ixiamas, Bolivia 92 D f
Ixtla, Mexico 90 E d
Ixtlán de Juárez, Mexico 90 E d
Iyang, China 131 H h
Iyella Ra., New Zealand 135 Q l
Iyo Nada, Japan 133 B h
Izabal & L., Guatemala 90 G d
Izegem (Iseghem), Belgium 100 B d
Izhevsk, U.S.S.R. 117 L b
Izhma & R., U.S.S.R. 114 E b
Izki, Muscat & Oman 125 G e
Izmail, Ukraine, U.S.S.R 116 F j
Izmir, Turkey 124 A b
Izmit, Turkey 124 A a
Izra, Syria 123 E e
Iztapa, Guatemala 90 F e
Izu Pen., Japan 133 F g
Izu Shichito, Japan 133 F g
Izyum, Ukraine, U.S.S.R. 116 K g
Jääski. See Svetogorsk
Jabalpur, India 126 F d
Jabbeke, Belgium 100 B c
Jabbul, Syria 123 F a
Jablonec, Czechoslovakia 104 F c
Jabnoren, Jaluit I. 79 T g
Jabor, Jaluit I. 79 U j
Jaboti, Brazil 92 F d
Jabrin Oasis, Saudi Arabia 124 E e
Jaburú, Brazil 92 D d
Jabwot I., Marshall Is 79 T c
Jaca, Spain 107 E a
Jacarezinho, Brazil 93 H h
Jachal, Argentina 94 C d
Jaci Paraná, Brazil 92 E e
Jack Fish, Ontario 84 D d
Jackfish L., Saskatchewan 86 J e
Jackhead Harbour, Manitoba 87 U g
Jack Lane B., Labrador 81 N f
Jackpine, Ontario 84 C c
Jackson B., New Zealand 135 P l
Jackson Bay, Br. Columbia 88 G e
Jackson's Arm, Newfoundland 83 Q d
Jacmel, Haiti 91 E c
Jacobabad, Pakistan 126 C c
Jacobina, Brazil 93 J f
Jacobs, Ontario 87 N a
Jacques Cartier, Mt., Quebec 82 G d
Jacques Cartier, Quebec 85 R g
Jacques Cartier, R., Quebec 85 T e
Jacques Cartier Pass, Quebec 82 H c
Jacquet, R., New Brunswick 82 F f
Jade Mines, Burma 127 J c
Jadib, S. Yemen 125 F f
Jadida, El. See Mazagan
Jadotville, Congo 120 F g
Jaén, Spain 106 D d
Jafarabad, India 126 D d
Jaffa. See Tel Aviv-Yafo
Jaffna, Ceylon 126 E g
Jaghbub, Libya 119 K c
Jaguarão, Brazil 94 F d
Jaguari, Brazil 94 F c
Jaguariaiva, Brazil 93 H h
Jaguaruna, Brazil 94 G c
Jahra, Kuwait 124 E d
Jahrom, Iran 125 F d
Jaicós, Brazil 93 J e
Jaipur, India 126 E c
Jaisalmer, India 126 D c
Jajarm, Iran 125 G b
Jajpur, India 127 G d
Jakarta. See Djakarta
Jäkkvik, Sweden 102 G c
Jakobi, Estonia, U.S.S.R. 103 M g
Jakobshavn, Greenland 81 O d
Jalalabad, Afghanistan 126 C b
Jalapa, Nicaragua 91 E d
Jalapa Enriquez, Mexico 90 E d
Jalasjärvi, Finland 102 K e
Jaldak, Afghanistan 125 J c
Jalgaon, India 126 E d
Jalisco, state, Mexico 90 D d
Jaloklab, Majuro Is. 79 T f
Jalor, India 126 D c
Jalpaiguri, India 127 G c
Jalq, Iran 125 H d
Jaluit, I., Marshall Is. 78 H g
Jaluit Lagoon, Jaluit I. 79 T h
Jam, Iran 125 F d
Jamaica, I., West Indies 91 D c
Jamaja, Estonia, U.S.S.R. 103 K g
Jamalabad, Iran 124 E b
Jamalpur, India 127 G c
Jambon, Pt., Quebec 82 F d
Jamdena, I., Indonesia 129 K m
James B., Ontario 81 L g
James Ras., Australia 134 F d
James Ross I., Antarctica 136 J f
Jamestown. See Wawa
Jamiltepec, Mexico 90 E d
Jammer Bugt, Denmark 103 C h
Jammu, Kashmir 126 E b
Jamnagar, India 126 D d
Jamrad, Afghanistan 125 J c
Jamrao, Pakistan 126 C c
Jämsä, Finland 103 L f
Jamshedpur, India 127 G d
Jamundi, Colombia 92 B c
Jandaq, Iran 125 F c
Janjira, India 126 D e
Jan L., Saskatchewan 87 P d
Jan Mayen I., Arctic Ocean 114 A a
Janos, Mexico 90 C a
Jansen, Saskatchewan 87 N g
Jansenville, South Africa 122 C f
Januária, Brazil 93 J g
Janze, France 108 C c
Jaora, India 126 E d
Japan & Sea of, E. Asia 133
Japen, I., W. Irian 129 L l
Japtan I., Eniwetok 79 S c
Japurá, Brazil 92 D d
Japvo Mt., India 127 H c
Jaragua, Brazil 93 H g
Jaragua, Brazil 94 G c
Jaramillo, Argentina 95 C g
Jarandilla, Spain 106 C b
Jaranwala, India 126 D b
Jardim, Brazil 93 K e
Jardine Brook, New Brunswick 82 E f
Jardines de la Reina, Cuba 91 D b
Jarí, R., Brazil 93 G c
Jarji, Nigeria 118 G f
Jarocin, Poland 105 G c
Jaromer, Czechoslovakia 105 F c
Jaroslaw, Poland 105 K c
Järpen, Sweden 102 E e
Jarrow, Alberta 86 F f
Jarvie, Alberta 86 D d
Jarvis, Ontario 84 K k
Jarvis I., Pacific Ocean 78 K g
Järvsö, Sweden 103 G f
Jashpurnagar, India 127 F d
Jask, Iran 125 G d
Jasmin, Saskatchewan 87 O g
Jason I., Falkland Is. 95 D h
Jason Pen., Antarctica 136 J e
Jasper, Alberta 88 K d
Jasper, Ontario 85 P h
Jasper Nat. Park, Alberta 88 K d
Jasper Place, Alberta 86 D e
Jassy. See Iaşi
Jastrowie, Poland 105 G b
Jaszberény, Hungary 105 H e
Jataí, Brazil 93 G g
Jath, India 126 E e
Jativa, Spain 107 E c
Jatobá, Brazil 93 H d
Jaú, Brazil 93 H h
Jauche, Belgium 100 C d
Jauf. See Al Jawf
Jauja, Peru 92 B f
Jaumave, Mexico 90 E c
Jaunpur, India 127 F c
Jauuperí, Brazil 92 E c
Java, I., Indonesia 129 E m
Javarí, R., Peru-Brazil 92 C e
Javier, I., Chile 95 B g
Jawa, Nigeria 119 H f
Jayuya, Puerto Rico 54 C h
Jazir, Muscat & Oman 125 G f
Jebba, Nigeria 118 F g
Jebel Abiod, Tunisia 111 B g
Jeble, Syria 123 D b
Jech Doab, Pakistan 126 D b
Jedburgh, Saskatchewan 87 P g
Jedburgh, Scotland 98 F e
Jedede, Saudi Arabia 125 D e
Jēkabpils, Latvia, U.S.S.R. 103 L h
Jelgava (Yelgava), Latvia, U.S.S.R. 103 K h
Jellicoe, Ontario 84 C c
Jelsava, Czechoslovakia 105 J d
Jemeppe, Belgium 100 C d
Jemmapes, Algeria 109 Q h
Jemo I., Marshall Is. 79 T a
Jemseg, New Brunswick 82 F h
Jena, Germany 104 D c
Jenin, Jordan 123 D e
Jenipapo, Brazil 92 F e
Jenner, Alberta 86 F h
Jens Munk I., N.-W. Terr 81 L d
Jeorg Plat., Antarctica 136 H c
Jeppo, Finland 102 K e
Jerablus, Syria 123 F a
Jerash, Jordan 123 D e
Jérémie, Haiti 91 E c
Jeremoabo, Brazil 93 K f
Jerez de la Frontera, Spain 106 B d
Jericho, Australia 135 J d
Jericho, Jordan 123 D f
Jerome, Ontario 84 H e
Jerruck, Pakistan 126 C c
Jersey, I., Channel Is. 108 B b
Jerusalem, Israel-Jordan 123 D f
Jervis I., New Guinea 135 H a
Jervis Inlet, Br. Columbia 88 H e
Jervois Ra., Australia 134 G d
Jesselton, Sabah 129 G j
Jessore, E. Pakistan 127 G d
Jésus, Ile, Quebec 85 Q h
Jetait, Manitoba 87 Q b
Jetalsar, India 126 D d
Jeypore, India 127 F e
Jezzin, Lebanon 123 D d
Jhabua, India 126 D d
Jhal, Pakistan 126 C c
Jhalrapatan, India 126 E d
Jhang Maghiana, Pakistan 126 D b
Jhansi, India 126 E c
Jhelum, Pakistan 126 D b
Jhelum R., Pakistan 126 D b
Jhesh Sheikh, Syria 123 D d
Jhudo, Pakistan 126 C c
Jhunjhunu, India 126 E c
Jiachan, Tibet 126 F b
Jibhalanta, Mongolia 115 J d
Jicaro, Nicaragua 91 B d
Jičin, Czechoslovakia 104 F c
Jidd, Iraq 124 C c
Jiddah, Saudi Arabia 124 C e
Jiggitai L., Tibet 127 G a
Jihlava, Czechoslovakia 105 F d
Jildiah, Jebel, Saudi Arabia 124 D d
Jimena de la Frontera, Spain 106 C d
Jiménez, Mexico 90 D b
Jimma, Ethiopia 121 H c
Jinbal, Jaluit I. 79 T h
Jinotega, Nicaragua 91 B d
Jipijapa, Ecuador 92 A d
Jirgalanta, Mongolia 115 J d
Jishah, Saudi Arabia 124 E d
Jisr esh Shughur, Syria 123 E b
Jiul R., Romania 112 D b
Jiza, Jordan 123 D f
Jizan, Saudi Arabia 124 D f
Joab L., Ontario 84 G a
Joacaba, Brazil 94 F c
João Pessoa, Brazil 93 L e
Jobrin, Ontario 84 D b
Jobson, Argentina 94 D c
Jodhpur, India 126 D c
Joe Batt's Arm, Nfd. 83 S d
Joensuu, Finland 102 N e
Jofane, Mozambique 122 E d
Joffre, Mt., Br. Columbia 88 M e
Joffre Oil Fields, Alberta 84 E b
Joggins, Nova Scotia 82 H h
Jogjakarta, Indonesia 129 F m
Jog L., Ontario 84 E b
Jogues, Ontario 84 G c
Johannesburg, South Africa 122 D e
Johan Pen., N.-W. Terr. 81 M b
John C., Nova Scotia 82 J h
John o' Groats, Scotland 98 E b
Johnstone Str., Br. Columbia 88 F e
Johnston I., Pacific Ocean 78 J e
Johore Bahru, Malaysia 132 C f
Joinville, Brazil 94 G c
Joinville, France 108 F b
Joinville I., Antarctica 136 J f
Jokaj, I., Ponape I. 78 F n
Jokaj Passage, Ponape I. 78 F n
Jokkmökk, Sweden 102 H c
Joliette, Quebec 85 R f
Jolo & I., Philippines 129 H j
Jol Plat., Saudi Arabia 124 E f
Jonava, Lithuania, U.S.S.R. 103 L j
Jones Sd., N.-W. Territories 81 L b
Jönköping, Sweden 103 F h
Jonquière, Quebec 85 T d
Jonuta, Mexico 90 F d
Jordan, R., Israel-Jordan 123 D e
Jordan, W. Asia 124 C c
Jordan L., Nova Scotia 82 G j
Jorhat, India 127 H c
Jorge Montt, I., Chile 95 B h
Joseph, L., Labrador 81 N h
Joseph, L., Ontario 84 L h
Joseph Bonaparte Gulf, Australia 134 E b
Joseph Pt., Anticosti I., Quebec 83 K d
Jotunheimen, Norway 103 C f
Joussard, Alberta 86 B c
Joux, L. de, Switzerland 101 B b
Jowai, India 127 H c
Juan Fernández, Is., Pac. Oc. 79 R m
Juan Gallegos I., Canal Zone 91 F b
Juaniata, Saskatchewan 86 K f
Juan-les-Pins, France 109 G e
Juan Stuven, I., Chile 95 A g
Juárez, Argentina 95 E e
Juba, Sudan 119 M h
Juba R., Somali Republic 121 J d
Jubba, Saudi Arabia 124 D d
Jubbulpore. See Jabalpur
Jubeil, Lebanon 123 D c
Jubilee L., Newfoundland 83 R e
Jucaro, Cuba 91 D b
Juchitán, Mexico 90 E d
Jude I., Newfoundland 83 S f
Judeidat el Wadi, Syria 123 E d
Judenburg, Austria 104 F e
Judique, C. Breton I., Nova Scotia 83 L h
Jugoslavia. See Yugoslavia
Juian, China 131 K j
Juichow. See Kaoan
Juist, I., Germany 104 B b
Juiz de Fóra, Brazil 93 J h
Jujuy, Argentina 94 C b
Jukao, China 130 K f
Jukkasjarvi, Sweden 102 J c
Julaca, Bolivia 92 D h
Juli, Peru 92 D g
Juliaca, Peru 92 C g
Julia Creek, Australia 135 H d
Julianehaab, Greenland 89 P d
Julio de Castilhos, Brazil 94 F c
Jumaima, Iraq 124 D d
Jumet, Belgium 100 C d
Jumilla, Spain 107 E c
Jumin. See Juymand
Jumoo Mt., Br. Columbia 88 L e
Junagarh, India 126 D d
Junan, China 130 G f
Juncos, Puerto Rico 54 D h
Jundah, Australia 135 H d
Jundiaí, Brazil 93 H h
Junee, Australia 135 J f
Jungfrau, Mt., Switzerland 101 C b
Jungfraujoch, Switzerland 101 C b
Jungkiang, China 131 D k
Junín, Argentina 95 B e
Junín, Argentina 94 D d
Junín, Chile 94 B a
Junin, Peru 92 B f
Junina, R., India 126 E c
Juning. See Junan
Juniper, New Brunswick 82 E g
Juniye, Lebanon 123 D d
Junor, Saskatchewan 86 K e
Junsele, Sweden 102 G e
Juo Järvi, Finland 102 N e
Jupia, Brazil 93 G h
Jupiter R., Anticosti I., Quebec 82 J d
Juquila, Mexico 90 E d
Jura, dep., France 108 F c
Jura, Mts., France-Switzerland 108 G c
Juradó, Colombia 92 B b
Jura I. & Sd. of, Scotland 98 D d
Jurbarkas, Lithuania, U.S.S.R. 103 K j
Jurf ed Darawish, Jordan 123 D g
Jüri (Yüri), Estonia, U.S.S.R. 103 L g
Jurm, Afghanistan 125 K b
Juruá, R., Brazil 92 D d
Juruena & R., Brazil 92 F f
Jurutí, Brazil 93 F d
Jusiye, Syria 123 E c
Jussy, Switzerland 101 B b
Justice, Manitoba 87 S h
Justo Daract, Argentina 94 C d
Juticalpa, Honduras 91 B d
Jutland. See Jylland
Juuka, Finland 102 N e
Juwain, Afghanistan 125 H c
Juwarah, Muscat & Oman 125 G f
Juwer, S. Yemen 124 E g
Juxtlahuaco, Mexico 90 E d
Juymand, Iran 125 G c
Jylland, Denmark 103 C h
Jylland, Syd, Denmark 103 C j
Jyväskylä, Finland 102 L e
K2 (Godwin Austen), Mt., Kashmir 126 E a
Kabajana, I., Indonesia 129 H m
Kabala, Sierra Leone 118 C g
Kabale, Uganda 121 G e
Kabba, Nigeria 118 G g
Kåbbenbock, Jaluit I. 79 T j
Kabenung L., Ontario 84 E d
Kabinakagami, R., Ontario 84 F c
Kabinakagami L., Ontario 84 F d
Kabinda, Congo 120 E f
Kabongo, Congo 120 F f
Kabul & R., Afghanistan 125 J c
Kabunda, Congo 121 F g
Kabwe, Zambia 122 D b
Kačanik, Yugoslavia 112 C c
Kachiry, Kazakh., U.S.S.R. 114 G c
Kachkar, U.S.S.R. 117 Q c
Kachuga, U.S.S.R. 115 K c
Kadena, I., Okinawa 78 A c
Kadiger, China 130 A c
Kadiköy, Turkey 124 A a
Kadiri, India 124 E f
Kadiyevka, Ukraine, U.S.S.R. 116 L g
Kadom, U.S.S.R. 117 F c
Kadugli, Sudan 119 L f
Kaduna, Nigeria 118 G f
Kadur, India 126 E f
Kadyi, U.S.S.R. 117 F b
Kaegudeck L., Newfoundland 83 R e
Kaesong, N. Korea 128 J c
Kaf, Saudi Arabia 124 C c
Kafakumba, Congo 120 E f
Kafanchan, Nigeria 118 G g
Kafra, Chad 119 K e
Kafr Behum, Syria 123 E b
Kafrun, Syria 123 E c
Kagan, Uzbek., U.S.S.R 114 F e
Kagawong, Ontario 84 H h
Kagi. See Chiai
Kagianagami L., Ontario 84 C b
Kagiano L., Ontario 84 D c
Kagoshima, Japan 133 B j
Kagoshima B., Japan 133 A j
Kagul, Moldavia, U.S.S.R. 116 F j
Kahafa, Saudi Arabia 124 D d
Kahama, Tanzania 119 G e
Kahan, India 126 C c
Kahntah, Br. Columbia 88 J a
Kahnuj, Iran 125 G d
Kahta, Turkey 124 C b
Kahutara Pt., New Zealand 135 S k
Kaiama, Nigeria 118 F g
Kaiapoi, New Zealand 135 Q l
Kaiashk, R., Ontario 87 O a
Kai-chow, China 130 G e
Kaieteur Fall, Guyana 92 E b
Kai fêng, China 130 G e
Kaigo, Sudan 119 M g
Kaihwa. See Wenshan
Kai-Kep, Indonesia 129 K m
Kaikohe, New Zealand 135 Q j
Kaikoura, New Zealand 135 Q l
Kaikoura Ra., New Zealand 135 Q l
Kailas Ra., India-Tibet 126 E a
Kaimana, W. Irian 129 K l
Kaimanawa Mts., New Zealand 135 R k
Kaimur Ra., India 126 F d
Kaipara Harb., New Zealand 135 Q k
Kaira, India 126 D d
Kairouan, Tunisia 119 H a
Kairovo, U.S.S.R. 117 N c
Kaisarie. See Kayseri
Kaiserlautern, Germany 104 B d
Kaitaia, New Zealand 135 Q j
Kaitangata, New Zealand 135 P m
Kai-yüan, China 130 M a
Kajaani, Finland 102 M d
Kajiado, Kenya 121 H e
Kajiki, Japan 133 B j
Kakabeka Falls, Ontario 87 N b
Kakagi L., Ontario 86 J a
Kakamari, Uganda 121 G d
Kakamega, Kenya 121 G d
Kakhk, Iran 125 G c
Kakhovskoye Vdkhr., Ukraine, U.S.S.R. 116 J h
Kakia, Botswana 122 C d
Kaksha, U.S.S.R. 117 H a
Kakwa, R., Alberta 88 K c
Kalábáka, Greece 113 C e
Kalabera, I., Saipan-Tinian Is. 78 B e
Kala Bist. See Qala Bist
Kalabo, Zambia 122 C c
Kalach, U.S.S.R. 117 E e
Kaladar, Ontario 85 N h
Kalahari Des., Botswana 122 C d
Kalajoki, Finland 102 K d
Kalak, Iran 125 G d
Kalakan, U.S.S.R. 115 L c
Kalakepen, Sumatra 129 C k
Kalámai, Greece 113 D f
Kalamáta. See Kalámai
Kala Nao, Afghanistan 125 H c
Kalangali, Tanzania 121 G f
Kalannie, Australia 134 C f
Kalarnian Ghat, India 126 F c
Kala Sarkari, Afghanistan 125 J b
Kalat, Pakistan 126 C c
Kalat-i-Ghilzai, Afghanistan 125 J c
Kalaw, Burma 127 J d
Kale, Burma 127 H d
Kaledran, Turkey 124 B b
Kalewa, Burma 127 H d

Kalgan. See Changkiakow
Kalgoorlie, Australia 134 D f
Kalhat, Muscat & Oman 125 G e
Kalikino, U.S.S.R. 117 M d
Kalimnos, I., Greece 113 F f
Kalingapatnam, India 127 F e
Kalinin, U.S.S.R. 116 J c
Kaliningrad, U.S.S.R. 103 J j
Kalisz, Poland 105 H c
Kaliua, Tanzania 121 G f
Kalix Älv, Sweden 102 J c
Kalixfors, Sweden 102 J c
Kalkfeld, S.W. Africa 122 B d
Kalkfontein, Botswana 122 C d
Kalkwerk, S.W. Africa 122 B e
Kallaste, Estonia, U.S.S.R. 103 M g
Kallavesi, Finland 102 M e
Kalloni, Greece 113 F e
Kall Sjön, Sweden 102 E e
Kalmar, Sweden 103 F h
Kalmar Sund, Sweden 103 G h
Kalmykovo, Kazakh., U.S.S.R. 114 E d
Kalocsa, Hungary 105 H e
Kalokhorio, Cyprus 123 A b
Kalone Pk., Br. Columbia 88 F d
Kaluga, U.S.S.R. 116 K d
Kalule, Congo 120 F f
Kalundborg, Denmark 103 D j
Kalundu, Zambia 121 F g
Kalutara, Ceylon 126 E g
Kalvarija, Lithuania, U.S.S.R. 103 K j
Kalyan, India 126 D e
Kalvazin, U.S.S.R. 116 K c
Kama, R., U.S.S.R. 114 E b
Kamalampaka, Tanzania 121 G f
Kamaran, I., Red Sea 124 D f
Kamatsi, Saskatchewan 87 P b
Kamchatka, U.S.S.R. 115 R c
Kamchatskaya Oblast, U.S.S.R. 115 R c
Kamen, U.S.S.R. 114 H c
Kamenets Podolskiy, Ukraine, U.S.S.R. 116 E g
Kamenskoye, U.S.S.R. 115 R b
Kamensk Shakhtinski, U.S.S.R. 117 E f
Kamensk Ural'skiy, U.S.S.R. 117 Q b
Kamet, Mt., India 126 E b
Kami Iwani, Japan 133 C g
Kamina, Congo 120 E f
Kaminak L., N.-W. Terr. 81 K e
Kaministikwia, Ontario 87 N b
Kaminuriak L., N.-W. Terr. 81 K e
Kamiyama shima, Okinawa 78 A c
Kam Keut, Laos 132 C c
Kamloops, Br. Columbia 88 J e
Kamloops L., Br. Columbia 88 J e
Kamnik, Yugoslavia 110 E b
Kamouraska, Quebec 82 C f
Kampa Dzong, Tibet 127 G c
Kampala, Uganda 121 G d
Kampen, Netherlands 100 D b
Kampot, Cambodia 132 C d
Kamptee, India 126 E d
Kamsack, Saskatchewan 87 Q g
Kamuchawie L., Saskatchewan 87 P b
Kamyshin, U.S.S.R. 117 G e
Kamyshlov, U.S.S.R. 117 R b
Kanaaupscow & R., Quebec 81 M g
Kananaskis L., Alberta 86 B h
Kanayama. See Hachuman
Kanazawa, Japan 133 E f
Kanchanaburi, Thailand 132 B d
Kancheepuram, India 126 E f
Kanchow, China 131 G k
Kandahar, Afghanistan 125 J c
Kandahar, Saskatchewan 87 N g
Kandalaksha, U.S.S.R. 114 C b
Kandava, Latvia, U.S.S.R. 103 K h
Kandavu, I., Fiji Is. 78 H j
Kandla, India 125 K e
Kandole, Congo 120 E e
Kandy, Ceylon 126 F g
Kane Basin, Greenland 89 Q b
Kanev, Ukraine, U.S.S.R. 116 G g
Kang, Botswana 122 C d
Kangan, Iran 125 F d
Kangar, Malaysia 132 C e
Kangaroo I., Australia 134 F g
Kangāvar, Iran 124 E c
Kangchenjunga, Mt.,Nepal 127 G c
Kangeeak Pt., N.-W. Terr 81 N d
Kangmar, Kashmir 126 E b
Kango, Gabon 120 C d
Kangoku iwa, Iwo Jima 78 D a
Kangpao, China 130 G b
Kangra, India 126 E b
Kangsa R., E. Pakistan 127 H c
Kani, Burma 127 H d
Kaniama, Congo 120 E f
Kaniapiskau R., Quebec 81 N f
Kaniapiskau L., Quebec 81 N g
Kanibadam, Tadzhik., U.S.S.R. 125 K a
Kanif, Yap I. 78 C l
Kankan, Guinea 118 D f
Kanker, India 126 F d
Kankesanturai, Ceylon 126 E g
Kan Kiang, China 128 G e
Kannauj, India 126 E c
Kannus, Finland 102 K e
Kano, Nigeria 118 G f
Kanoya, Japan 133 B j
Kanpur, India 126 F c
Kansk, U.S.S.R. 115 J c
Kansu, prov., China 130 A e
Kantchari, Upper Volta 118 F f
Kanturk, Eire 99 B h
Kanuma, Japan 133 F f
Kanye, Botswana 122 D e
Kaoan, China 131 G h
Kaocheng, China 130 G e
Kaohsiung, Taiwan 131 K l
Kaolack, Senegal 118 B f
Kaolan. See Lanchow
Kao Lu-ang, Mt., Thailand 132 B e
Kaomi, China 130 J d
Kaoyi, China 130 G d
Kaoyu, China 130 J f
Kaoyu Hu, China 130 J f
Kapal. See Taldy Kurgan
Kapaus, R., Borneo 129 F k
Kapfenberg, Austria 105 F e
Kapiri Mposhi, Zambia 121 F g
Kapiskau, Ontario 81 L g
Kapoeta, Sudan 119 M h
Kaposvár, Hungary 112 A a
Kapsabet, Kenya 121 H d
Kapsukas, Lithuania, U.S.S.R. 103 K j
Kapurthala, India 126 E b
Kapuskasing, Ontario 84 H c
Kapuskasing, R., Ontario 84 H d
Kar, Iran 124 E c
Kara, U.S.S.R. 114 F b
Kara Bogaz Gol, Turkmen., U.S.S.R. 114 E d
Karabuk, Turkey 124 B a
Karabuta, Iran 124 E b
Karacabey, Turkey 124 A a
Karaca Dagh, Turkey 124 B b
Karachev, U.S.S.R. 116 J e
Karachi, Pakistan 126 C d
Karaganda, Kazakh., U.S.S.R. 114 G d
Karaginskiy Os., U.S.S.R. 115 R c
Karaj, Iran 125 F b
Karak, Jordan 123 D f
Karak, Tibet 126 E b
Kara Kalpakskaya, Uzbek., U.S.S.R. 114 E d
Karakelong, I., Indonesia 129 J k
Karakoram Ra., Kashmir 126 D b
Karakose, Turkey 124 D b
Kara Kum, Turkmen., U.S.S.R. 114 E e
Kara Kum Can., Turkmen., U.S.S.R. 125 H b
Karaman, Turkey 124 B b
Karamea Bight, New Zealand 135 Q l
Karapiro, L., New Zealand 135 R k
Karasa, U.S.S.R. 117 K c
Karasburg, S.W. Africa 122 B e
Kara Sea, U.S.S.R. 114 G a
Karasjok, Norway 102 L b
Karatina, Kenya 121 H e
Karatsu, Japan 133 A h
Karaul, U.S.S.R. 114 H a
Karaurgan, Turkey 124 D a
Kardam, Tibet 126 F b
Kardhítsa, Greece 113 C e
Karelskaya A.S.S.R., U.S.S.R. 114 C b
Karenni, Burma 127 J e
Karesuando, Sweden 102 K b
Karganrud, Iran 124 E b
Kargil, Kashmir 126 E b
Kargopol, U.S.S.R. 116 L a
Kariba & L., Rhodesia 122 D c
Karibib, S.W. Africa 122 B d
Karikal, India 126 E f
Karimata, I., Indonesia 129 E l
Karin, Somali Republic 121 K b
Karind. See Kar
Karis, Finland 103 K f
Kariz, Iran 125 H c
Karkaralinsk, U.S.S.R. 114 G d
Karkkila, Finland 103 L f
Karlik Tagh, China 128 B b
Karl Marx Stadt, Germany 104 E c
Karlovac, Yugoslavia 110 E c
Karlovy Vary, Czechoslovakia 104 E c
Karlsbad. See Karlovy Vary
Karlsborg, Sweden 103 F g
Karlshamn, Sweden 103 F h
Karlskrona, Sweden 103 F h
Karlsruhe, Germany 104 C d
Karlstad, Sweden 103 E g
Karmöy, I., Norway 103 A g
Karnal, India 126 E c
Karnten, prov., Austria 104 E e
Karona Fall, Guyana 92 F c
Karora, Sudan 121 H a
Karpáthos, I. & Str., Greece 113 F g
Karperón, Greece 113 C e
Karroo, Great, S. Africa 122 C f
Kars, Turkey 124 D a
Karsakpay, Kazakh., U.S.S.R. 114 F d
Karsakuwigamak, L., Manitoba 87 S b
Kärsämäki, Finland 102 L e
Kārsava, Latvia, U.S.S.R. 103 M h
Karshi, Uzbek., U.S.S.R. 114 F e
Karstula, Finland 102 L e
Karsun, U.S.S.R. 117 H c
Kartaly, U.S.S.R. 117 Q d
Karungi, Sweden 102 K c
Karungu, Kenya 121 G e
Karunki, Finland 102 L c
Karur, India 126 E f
Karvina, Czechoslovakia 105 H d
Karwar, India 126 D f
Karymskoye, U.S.S.R. 115 L c
Kasai R., Congo 120 D e
Kasama, Zambia 121 G g
Kasanga, Tanzania 121 G f
Kasempa, Zambia 120 F g
Kasenga, Congo 121 F g
Kasenga, Zambia 122 D c
Kashabowie, Ontario 87 M b
Kashan, Iran 125 F c
Kashgar, China 114 G e
Kashing, China 131 K g
Kashira, U.S.S.R. 116 L d
Kashishibog L., Ontario 87 N a
Kashiwazaki, Japan 133 F f
Kāshmar, Iran 125 G b
Kashmir, S. Asia 126 E b
Kashmor, Pakistan 126 C c
Kasimov, U.S.S.R. 117 E e
Kasinka, Botswana 122 C c
Kaskinen, Finland 102 J e
Kas Kong, Cambodia 132 C d
Kaslo, Br. Columbia 88 L f
Kasongo, Congo 120 F e
Kásos, I., Greece 113 F g
Kásos Str., Crete 113 F g
Kaspichan, Bulgaria 112 F c
Kas Rong, Cambodia 132 C d
Kassala, Sudan 121 H a
Kassandra, Greece 113 D d
Kassel, Germany 104 C c
Kastamonu, Turkey 124 B a
Kastélli, Crete 113 D g
Kastéllion, Crete 113 E g
Kastoria, Greece 113 C d
Kastrosikiá, Greece 113 C e
Kasulu, Tanzania 121 G e
Kasungu, Malawi 121 G g
Kasur, Pakistan 126 D b
Katabaru, I., Okinawa 78 B b
Katákolon, Greece 113 C f
Katanga, prov., Congo 120 E g
Katangli, U.S.S.R. 115 P c
Katanning, Australia 134 C f
Katav Ivanovsk, U.S.S.R. 117 P c
Katepwe, Saskatchewan 87 O h
Katepwe Prov. Park, Sask. 87 O h
Katerini, Greece 113 D d
Kates Needle, Mt., B.C. 88 C b
Katha, Burma 127 J d
Katherine, Australia 134 F b
Kathgodam, India 126 E c
Kathiawar, India 126 D d
Kathmandu, Nepal 127 G c
Kathryn, Alberta 86 D g
Katihar, India 127 G c
Katimik L., Manitoba 87 S f
Katni, India 126 F d
Kato Akhaia, Greece 113 C e
Katol, India 126 E d
Káto Nevrokópion, Greece 112 D d
Katoomba, Australia 135 K f
Katowice (Stalinogród), Poland 105 H c
Katrine, L., Scotland 98 D d
Katrineholm, Sweden 103 G g
Katsina, Nigeria 118 G f
Katsuren hantō, Okinawa 78 B c
Kattawagami L., Ontario 84 K c
Kattegat, Sweden-Denmark 103 D h
Kattowitz. See Katowice
Katwewe, Congo 121 F f
Katwijk-aan-Zee, Netherlands 100 C b
Kaufbeuren, Germany 104 D e
Kauhava, Finland 102 K e
Kaula I., Palmyra I. 79 U k
Kaunas, Lithuania, U.S.S.R. 103 K j
Kauriya, India 127 F d
Kautokeino, Norway 102 K b
Kavak, Turkey 124 C a
Kavali, India 126 E f
Kavālla, Greece 113 E d
Kavālla, prov., Greece 112 E d
Kavkaz Bolshoi & Maly, Mts., U.S.S.R. 114 D d
Kaw, French Guiana 93 G c
Kawactha Lakes, Ontario 85 M h
Kawagama L., Ontario 85 M g
Kawambwa, Zambia 121 F f
Kawanoe, Japan 133 C g
Kawardha, India 126 F d
Kawasaki, Japan 133 F g
Kawasak Passage, Palau Is. 78 C h
Kawene, Ontario 87 L a
Kawerau, New Zealand 135 R k
Kawhia, New Zealand 135 R k
Kawinaw L., Manitoba 87 S f
Kawkareik, Burma 127 J e
Kayes, Mali 118 C f
Kay Is., Antarctica 136 B d
Kayo, Okinawa 78 C b
Kayseri, Turkey 124 C b
Kayshyadoris, Lithuania, U.S.S.R. 103 L j
Kayville, Saskatchewan 87 M j
Kazabazua, Quebec 85 O g
Kazach'ye, U.S.S.R. 115 N a
Kazakhskaya, U.S.S.R. 114 F d
Kazakhstan. See Kazakhskaya
Kazalinsk, Kazakh., U.S.S.R. 114 F d
Kazan, U.S.S.R. 117 J c
Kazan L., Saskatchewan 86 J c
Kazanlŭk, Bulgaria 112 E c
Kazan R., N.-W. Territories 81 K e
Kazérun, Iran 125 F d
Kazvin. See Qazvin
Kdyne, Czechoslovakia 104 E d
Kéa, I., Greece 113 E f
Kearney, Ontario 85 L g
Keatley, Saskatchewan 86 K f
Keban Maden, Turkey 124 C b
Ke-bao I., N. Vietnam 132 D b
Kecskemét, Hungary 105 H e
Kedainiai, Lithuania, U.S.S.R. 103 K j
Kedgwick & R., N.B. 82 E f
Kediri, Indonesia 129 F m
Kedleston, Saskatchewan 87 M h
Keefers, Br. Columbia 88 J e
Keeler, Saskatchewan 87 M h
Keeley L., Saskatchewan 86 J d
Keels, Newfoundland 83 T e
Keely L., Saskatchewan 88 P c
Keetmanshoop, S.W. Africa 122 B e
Keewatin, Dist. of, North-West Territories 81 K e
Keewatin, Ontario 86 H a
Kefallinía, Greece 113 C e
Kegashka L., Quebec 83 L c
Kegaska, Quebec 83 L c
Keg River, Alberta 88 L b
Kegueur Tedi, Libya 119 J d
Keila, Estonia, U.S.S.R. 103 L g
Keita, Chad 119 K e
Keitele, Finland 102 M e
Keith, Scotland 98 F c
Keithley Creek, Br. Columbia 88 J d
Kekertuk, N.-W. Territories 81 N d
Keklau, Palau Is. 78 C m
Kelcyre, Albania 113 C d
Keller L., Saskatchewan 86 L b
Kellet, C., N.-W. Territories 80 G c
Kelliher, Saskatchewan 87 O g
Kelloselka, Finland 102 N c
Kells, Eire 99 C g
Kelme, Lithuania, U.S.S.R. 103 K j
Kelowna, Br. Columbia 88 K f
Kelsey, Manitoba 87 V b
Kelsey Bay, Vancouver I., British Columbia 88 G e
Kelsey L., Manitoba 87 Q e
Kelso, Saskatchewan 87 Q j
Kelso, Scotland 98 F e
Keltie, C., Antarctica 136 T e
Kelvington, Saskatchewan 87 O f
Kelvin I., Nipigon L., Ont. 84 B c
Kelwood, Manitoba 87 S h
Kem, U.S.S.R.-Finland 114 C b
Ké-Macina, Mali 118 D f
Kemano, Br. Columbia 88 F d
Kemel Paşa, Turkey 124 A b
Kemerovo, U.S.S.R. 114 H c
Kemi, Finland 102 L d
Kemijärvi, Finland 102 M c
Kemi Joki, Finland 102 L c
Kemnay, Manitoba 87 R j
Kempele, Finland 102 L d
Kemp Ld., Antarctica 136 P e
Kemp Pen., Antarctica 136 J d
Kempsey, Australia 135 K f
Kempt, L., Quebec 85 Q e
Kempten, Germany 104 D e
Kemptville, Ontario 85 P g
Kenabeek, Ontario 84 L e
Kenaston, Saskatchewan 86 L g
Kendal, England 99 F f
Kendal, Saskatchewan 87 O h
Kendall, C., N.-W. Terr. 81 L e
Kendari, Celebes 129 H l
Kendawangan, Borneo 129 F l
Kenema, Sierra Leone 118 C g
Kenge, Congo 120 D e
Keng-tung, Burma 127 J d
Kenhardt, South Africa 122 C e
Keniapiscau L., Quebec 85 O b
Kenitra. See Mina Hassan Tani
Kenmare & R., Eire 99 A j
Kennedy, Saskatchewan 87 P h
Kennedy Chan., N.-W. Terr.-Greenland 81 N a
Kennedy L., Quebec 83 O b
Kennedy, Mt., Alaska-Yukon 77 S f
Kennetcook, Nova Scotia 82 J h
Kenney Dam, Br. Columbia 88 G d
Kenogami, L., Quebec 85 T d
Kenogami, Quebec 85 T d
Kenogami, R., Ontario 84 E b
Kenogami Lake, Ontario 84 K d
Kenogamissi L., Ontario 84 J d
Kenonisca L., Quebec 85 O b
Kenora, Ontario 86 H a
Kensington, Prince Edward I. 82 J g
Kent, co., England 99 H j
Kent Bridge, Ontario 84 H k
Kent Junction, New Brunswick 82 G g
Kenton, Manitoba 87 R j
Kentville, Nova Scotia 82 H h
Kenville, Manitoba 87 Q g
Kenya, E. Africa 121 H d
Kenya, Mt., Kenya 121 H e
Keonjhar, India 127 G d
Kéos Tziá. See Kéa I.
Kep. Lingga, Sumatra 129 D l
Keppel, I., Falkland Is. 95 D h
Kerala, state, India 126 E f
Kerang, Australia 135 H g
Kerava, Finland 103 L f
Kerch, U.S.S.R. 116 K j
Kerchoual, Mali 118 F e
Kerema, Papua 135 J a
Keremeos, Br. Columbia 88 K f
Keren, Ethiopia 121 H a
Kericho, Kenya 121 H e
Kerintji, Mt., Sumatra 129 D l
Kerkenbosch. See Zuidwolde
Kerkenna Is., Tunisia 119 H b
Kerki, Turkmen., U.S.S.R. 114 F e
Kérkira & I., Greece 113 B e
Kerkrade, Netherlands 100 D d
Kermadec Is., Pacific Ocean 78 J k
Kerman, Iran 125 G c
Kerman Des., Iran 125 G d
Kermanshah, Iran 124 E c
Kerrobert, Saskatchewan 86 H g
Kerry, co., Eire 99 A h
Kerulen R., Mongolia 128 F a
Kerzers, Switzerland 101 C b
Kesagami, R., Ontario 84 K b
Kesagami L., Ontario 84 K b
Kesteren, Netherlands 100 D c
Kestilä, Finland 102 M d
Keswick, England 99 E f
Keswick Ridge, New Brunswick 82 F h
Keszthely, Hungary 105 G e
Ketapang, Borneo 129 E l
Ketrzyn, Poland 105 J a
Kettering, England 99 G h
Kettle I., Quebec 84 D h
Kettlestone B., Quebec 81 M e
Kewagama, Quebec 85 M d
Keyes, Manitoba 87 S h
Key Harbour, Ontario 84 K g
Key Junction, Ontario 84 K g
Key L., Eire 99 B f
Keystown, Saskatchewan 87 M h
Kezhma, U.S.S.R. 115 K c
Khaapsalu, Estonia, U.S.S.R. 103 K g
Khabab, Syria 123 E d
Khabarovsk, U.S.S.R. 115 N d
Khabarovskiy Kroy, U.S.S.R. 115 N c
Khaburah, Muscat & Oman 125 G e
Khadhra, Saudi Arabia 124 D d
Khadro, Pakistan 126 C c
Khafs Maqran, Saudi Arabia 124 E e
Khaibar, Saudi Arabia 124 C d
Khairagarh, India 126 F d
Khairpur, Pakistan 126 C c
Khaitaksho, Kashmir 126 E b
Khaiwan, Yemen 124 D f
Khalis-ed-Daff, Saudi Arabia 124 C e
Khalki, I, Greece 113 F f
Khalkidhki, Greece 113 D d
Khalkís, Greece 113 D e
Khal-Mer-Sede. See Tazovskoye
Khalturin, U.S.S.R. 117 J a
Khaluf, Saudi Arabia 125 G e
Khamadhana, India 126 E c
Khamgaon, India 126 E d
Khamiab, Afghanistan 125 J b
Khamis, Mushait, Saudi Arabia 124 D f
Khamr, Yemen 124 D f
Khanabad, Afghanistan 125 J b
Khanaqin, Iraq 124 E c
Khān Baghdādī, Iraq 124 D c
Khandwa, India 126 E d
Khan-ez-Zebib, Jordan 123 E f
Khanfar, S. Yemen 124 E g
Khanh-hoa, S. Vietnam 132 D d
Khaniá, Crete 113 D g
Khanka, Oz., U.S.S.R. 115 N d
Khan Sheikhun, Syria 123 E b
Khan Tengri. See Pobedy, Mt.
Khanty Mansiysk, U.S.S.R. 114 F b
Khanu. See Kahnuj
Khan Yunis, Egypt 123 C f
Kharaghoda, India 126 D d
Kharan, Pakistan 126 C c
Kharkov, Ukraine, U.S.S.R. 116 K g
Kharmanli, Bulgaria 112 E d
Kharovsk, U.S.S.R. 116 M b
Khartoum, Sudan 119 M e
Khasfah, Saudi Arabia 125 F f
Khash, Afghanistan 125 H c
Khasi Hills, India 127 H c
Khaskovo, Bulgaria 112 E d
Khasmel Girba, Sudan 119 N f
Khatanga, U.S.S.R. 115 K a
Khatangskiy Guba, Russia 115 L a
Khawak Pk., Afghanistan 126 D a
Kheralu, India 126 D d
Kheri, India 126 F c
Kherson, Ukraine, U.S.S.R. 116 H h
Khilok, U.S.S.R. 115 L c
Khinis. See Hinis
Khinjan, Afghanistan 126 C a
Khíos & I., Greece 113 F e
Khisfin, Syria 123 D e
Khiuma, Os. See Hiiumaa
Khiva, Uzbek., U.S.S.R. 114 F d
Khmel'nitskiy, Ukraine, U.S.S.R. 116 E g
Kholm, U.S.S.R. 116 G c
Kholmsk, U.S.S.R. 115 P d
Khomeyn, Iran 125 F c
Khong, Laos 132 D d
Khor, U.S.S.R. 115 N d
Khor-al-Amaya, Iraq 124 E d
Khóra Sfakion, Crete 112 E g
Khormali, China 128 A a
Khorramabad, Iran 124 E c
Khorramshahr, Iran 124 E c
Khotan, China 114 G e
Khrisoúpolis, Greece 112 E d
Khrojna, Bulgaria 112 E d
Khunsar, Iran 125 F c
Khur, Iran 125 G c
Khur. See Khvor
Khurmah, Saudi Arabia 124 D e
Khusf, Iran 125 G c
Khvaf, Iran 125 H c
Khvalynsk, U.S.S.R. 117 J d
Khvor, Iran 125 F c
Khvoy, Iran 124 D b
Khyber Pass, Pakistan 126 D b
Kiambi, Congo 121 F f
Kiamika, L., Quebec 85 P f
Kiamiki, Quebec 85 P f
Kiamusze, China 128 K a
Kian, China 131 G j
Kiangchow. See Kiangling
Kiangling, China 131 F g
Kiangpeh, China 131 C h
Kiangsi, prov., China 131 G j
Kiangsu, prov., China 130 J f
Kiangtu, China 130 J f
Kiangyin, China 130 K g
Kianto Järvi, Finland 102 N d
Kiao-chow B., China 130 K e
Kiaohsien, China 130 K d
Kiask L., Manitoba 87 U b
Kiating. See Loshan
Kibangula, Congo 120 F e
Kibombo, Congo 120 F e
Kibondo, Tanzania 121 G e
Kičevo, Yugoslavia 112 C d
Kichiga, U.S.S.R. 115 R c
Kichiginsk, U.S.S.R. 117 Q c
Kicking Horse Pass, British Columbia 88 L e
Kidal, Mali 118 F e
Kidderminster, England 99 F h
Kidnappers, C., N. Zealand 135 R k
Kidodi, Tanzania 121 H f
Kiel, Germany 104 D a
Kielce, Poland 105 J c
Kieldrecht, Belgium 100 C c
Kieler Bucht, Germany 104 D a
Kiel (Nord-Ostsee) Kan., Germany 104 C a
Kienchang. See Nancheng
Kiencheng, China 131 D h
Kienko, China 130 B f
Kienning, China 131 H j
Kienning. See Kienow
Kienow, China 131 J j
Kienping, China 130 J b
Kienshui, China 128 D f
Kienteh, China 131 J h
Kiev (Kiyev), Ukraine, U.S.S.R. 116 G f
Kiffa, Mauritania 118 C e
Kigali, Rwanda 121 G e
Kiganga, Tanzania 121 G f
Kigoma, Tanzania 121 F e
Kihsien, China 130 H b
Kii Chan, Japan 133 D h
Kijabe, Kenya 121 H e
Kijoka, I., Okinawa 78 C a
Kikhchik, U.S.S.R. 115 Q c
Kikinda, Yugoslavia 112 C b
Kikládhes, Is., Greece 113 E f
Kikori & R., Papua 135 H a
Kikuyu, Kenya 121 H e
Kikwissi, L., Quebec 85 M f
Kikwit, Congo 120 D f
Kilburn, New Brunswick 82 E g
Kilchu, N. Korea 128 J b
Kildala Arm, Br. Columbia 88 F d
Kildare, C., Prince Edward I. 82 J g
Kildare & co., Eire 99 C g
Kildonan, Br. Columbia 88 G f
Kilifi, Kenya 121 H e
Kili I., Marshall Is. 79 T c
Kilimanjaro, Mt., Tan. 121 H e
Kilindini, Kenya 121 H e
Kilkee, Eire 99 A h
Kilkenny & co., Eire 99 C h
Kilkieran B., Eire 99 A g
Kilkís, Greece 113 D d
Kilkís, prov., Greece 112 D d
Killala, Ontario 84 D c
Killala B., Eire 99 A f
Killaloe, Eire 99 B h
Killaloe Station, Ontario 85 N g
Killaly, Saskatchewan 87 P h
Killam, Alberta 86 F f
Killarney, Eire 99 A h
Killarney, Manitoba 87 S j
Killarney, Ontario 84 J g
Killary Harb., Eire 99 A g
Killdeer, Saskatchewan 86 L j
Killin, Scotland 98 E d
Killíni, Greece 113 C f
Killybegs, Eire 99 B f
Kilmarnock, Scotland 98 D e
Kil'mez, U.S.S.R. 117 K b
Kilosa, Tanzania 121 H f
Kilrush, Eire 99 A h
Kilwa Kivinje, Tanzania 121 H f
Kilwinning, Saskatchewan 86 L e
Kilworthy, Ontario 85 L h
Kima, Congo 120 F e
Kimberley, Br. Columbia 88 M f
Kimberley, Ontario 84 K h
Kimberley, South Africa 122 C e
Kimi, Greece 113 E e
Kimito, Finland 103 K f
Kimiwan L., Alberta 86 A c
Kimolos, I., Greece 113 E f
Kimvula, Congo 122 D f
Kin, I., Okinawa 78 B b
Kina, I., Okinawa 78 A c
Kinabulu, Mt., Sabah 129 G j
Kinadyeng, Jaluit I. 79 T h
Kinbrace, Scotland 98 E b
Kinbrook Island Prov. Park, Alberta 86 F h
Kincaid, Saskatchewan 86 K j
Kincardine, co., Scotland 98 F d

Kincardine, Ontario 84 J h
Kinchow Wan, China 130 K c
Kincolith, Br. Columbia 88 E c
Kindat, Burma 127 H d
Kindersley, Saskatchewan 86 H g
Kindia, Guinea 118 C f
Kindu-Port Empain, Congo 120 F e
Kinel', U.S.S.R. 117 K d
Kinel' Cherkkassy, U.S.S.R. 117 K d
Kineshma, U.S.S.R. 117 F b
Kingaroy, Australia 135 K e
King Christian I., N.-W. Terr. 80 J b
King Christian IX Ld., Greenland 89 N c
Kingcome Inlet, Br. Columbia 88 F e
King Edward VIII Fall, Guyana 92 F b
King Frederick VI Land, Greenland 89 P c
King Frederick VIII Land, Greenland 89 N b
Kingfu, China 128 D e
King George, Mt., British Columbia 88 M e
King George I, I., South Shetlands 136 H f
King George Is., Hudson B., North-West Territories 81 M f
King George Sd., Australia 134 C g
King George VI Falls, Guyana 92 E b
Kinghorn, Ontario 84 C c
King I., Antarctica 136 F d
King I., Br. Columbia 88 F d
King I., Burma 127 J f
King I., Tasmania 135 H g
Kingisepp, U.S.S.R. 103 N g
Kingku, China 128 D f
King Leopold Ra., Australia 134 E c
Kingman, Alberta 86 E e
Kingmen, China 130 F g
Kingoonya, Australia 134 G f
Kingsbridge, England 99 E k
Kingscourt, Eire 99 C g
King's Lynn, England 99 H h
King Sound, Australia 134 D c
Kingsport, Nova Scotia 82 H h
Kingston, Australia 134 H g
Kingston, Jamaica 91 D c
Kingston, New Zealand 135 P m
Kingston, Ontario 85 O h
Kingston-on-Thames, England 99 G j
Kingsussie, Scotland 98 E c
Kingsville, Ontario 84 H k
Kingtung, China 128 D f
Kingushi, Congo 120 D f
King William Ld., Greenland 89 N b
Kingyang, China 130 C d
Kingyüan. See Ishan
Kinhsien, China 130 K c
Kinhwa, China 131 J h
Kinistino, Saskatchewan 87 M f
Kinki, China 130 C d
Kinkora, Prince Edward I. 82 J g
Kinleith, New Zealand 135 R k
Kinley, Saskatchewan 86 K f
Kin misari, Okinawa 78 B b
Kinmount, Ontario 85 M h
Kinnaird, Br. Columbia 88 L f
Kino, Mexico 90 B b
Kinoosao, Saskatchewan 87 P a
Kinross & co., Scotland 98 E d
Kinsale, Eire 99 B j
Kinsale, Old Hd. of, Eire 99 B j
Kinsella, Alberta 86 F e
Kinsey, C., Antarctica 136 A e
Kinshasa (Léopoldville), Congo 120 D e
Kintap, Borneo 129 G l
Kintyre, Mull of, Scotland 98 D e
Kintyre, Scotland 98 D e
Kinuso, Alberta 86 B c
Kin wan, Okinawa 78 B b
Kinyangiri, Tanzania 121 G e
Kiosk, Ontario 85 M f
Kipanigan L., Manitoba-Saskatchewan 87 Q c
Kiparissía, G. of, Greece 113 C f
Kiparissía, Greece 113 C f
Kipawa, L., Quebec 85 M f
Kipawa, Quebec 85 M f
Kipini, Kenya 121 J e
Kipling, Saskatchewan 87 P h
Kipp, Alberta 86 E j
Kirby, Ontario 84 F f
Kirchberg, Switzerland 101 C a
Kirensk, U.S.S.R. 115 K c
Kirgizia. See Kirgizskaya
Kirgizskaya S.S.R., U.S.S.R. 114 G d
Kiri, Congo 120 D e
Kirin, China 128 J b
Kirit, Somali Republic 121 K c
Kiriwina, I., Papua 135 K a
Kiriwini Is. See Trobriand Is.
Kirkağaç, Turkey 124 A b
Kirkby Lonsdale, England 99 F f
Kirkcaldy, Alberta 86 D h
Kirkcaldy, Scotland 98 E d
Kirkcudbright & co., Scotland 98 E e
Kirkee, India 126 D e
Kirkella, Manitoba 87 Q h
Kirkenes, Norway 102 N a
Kirkland I., Br. Columbia 88 D g
Kirkland Lake, Ontario 84 K d
Kirkliston Ra., New Zealand 135 Q m
Kirkpatrick, Mt., Antarctica 136 A b
Kirk Pt., Ponape I. 78 F o
Kirkuk, Iraq 124 D b
Kirkwall, Orkney 98 F b
Kirov, U.S.S.R. 116 J d
Kirov, U.S.S.R. 117 J a
Kirovgrad, U.S.S.R. 117 P b
Kirovograd, Ukraine, U.S.S.R. 116 H g
Kirovsk, U.S.S.R. 114 C b
Kirriemuir, Alberta 86 G g
Kirriemuir, Scotland 98 E d
Kirsanov, U.S.S.R. 117 F d
Kirsehir, Turkey 124 B b
Kirthar Ra., Pakistan 126 C c
Kirun. See Chilung
Kiruna, Sweden 102 J c
Kiryū, Japan 133 F f
Kisamba, Congo 120 E f
Kisangani, Congo 120 F d
Kisbér, Hungary 105 H e
Kisbey, Saskatchewan 87 P j
Kishan, China 130 C e
Kishanganj, India 126 G c
Kishangarh, India 126 D c
Kishi, Nigeria 118 F g
Kishinev, Moldavia, U.S.S.R. 116 F h
Kisii, Kenya 121 G e
Kisiju, Tanzania 121 H f
Kiskittogisu L., Manitoba 87 T d
Kiskitto L., Manitoba 87 T d
Kiskunfélégyháza, Hungary 105 H e
Kismayu. See Chisimaio
Kispest, Hungary 105 H e
Kispiox, R., Br. Columbia 88 E c
Kissaraing I., Burma 127 J f
Kissidougou, Guinea 118 C g
Kississing. See Cold Lake
Kistawar, India 126 E b
Kistna R., India 126 E e
Kisujszállás, Hungary 105 J e
Kisumu, Kenya 121 G e
Kisvárda, Hungary 105 K d
Kiswe, Syria 123 E d
Kita, Mali 118 D f
Kitab, Uzbek., U.S.S.R. 114 F e
Kitakyushu, Japan 128 K d
Kitale, Kenya 121 H d
Kitano hana, Iwo Jima 78 E a
Kitchener, Ontario 84 K j
Kitchioh, China 131 G l
Kitgum, Uganda 121 G d
Kithira, I., Greece 113 D f
Kíthirai Chan., Greece 113 D g
Kithnos, I., Greece 113 E f
Kitigan, Ontario 84 H c
Kitimat, Br. Columbia 88 E d
Kitimat Mill, Br. Columbia 88 E d
Kitscoty, Alberta 86 G e
Kittila, Finland 102 L c
Kitui, Kenya 121 H e
Kitwanga, Br. Columbia 88 F c
Kityang, China 131 H l
Kitzbühel, Austria 104 E e
Kitzingen, Germany 104 D d
Kiuchuan, China 128 C c
Kiukiang, China 131 H h
Kiumbi, Congo 120 F f
Kiungchow Str. See Hainan Str.
Kiuruvesi, Finland 102 M e
Kivi Järvi, Finland 102 L e
Kivu L., Congo 121 F e
Kivu Nat. Park, Congo 121 F e
Kiwai I., Papua 135 H a
Kiyan, Okinawa 78 A d
Kiyan misaki, Okinawa 78 A d
Kiyiu L., Saskatchewan 86 J g
Kiyma, Kazakh., U.S.S.R. 114 F c
Kizel, U.S.S.R. 114 E c
Kizil Irmak, Turkey 124 B a
Kizyl Arvat, Turkmen., U.S.S.R. 114 E e
Kizyl Jilga, Kashmir 126 E a
Kjerringöy, Norway 102 F c
Kjöge B., Greenland 89 N c
Kladanj, Yugoslavia 112 B b
Kladno, Czechoslovakia 104 F c
Klagenfurt, Austria 104 E e
Klaipeda (Memel), Lithuania, U.S.S.R 103 J j
Klamona, W. Irian 129 K l
Klang, Malaysia 132 C f
Klappan R., Br. Columbia 88 E b
Klar Älv, Sweden 102 E f
Klausenburg. See Cluj
Kleczkowski L., Quebec 82 J c
Kleena Kleene, Br. Columbia 88 G e
Klemtu, Br. Columbia 88 E d
Klerksdorp, South Africa 122 D e
Kleszczele, Poland 105 K b
Klimpfjall, Sweden 102 F d
Klinaklini, R., Br. Columbia 88 G e
Klisura, Bulgaria 112 E c
Kliuchi, U.S.S.R. 117 G d
Ključ, Yugoslavia 110 F c
Klock, Ontario 85 M f
Klodawa, Poland 105 H b
Klofta, Norway 103 D f
Klomnice, Poland 105 H c
Kloosterzande, Netherlands 100 C c
Klosters, Switzerland 101 E b
Kluirja, India 126 E c
Klundert, Netherlands 100 C c
Klyuchyevskaya Sopka, U.S.S.R. 115 R c
Knee L., Saskatchewan 86 K c
Knewstubb L., Br. Columbia 88 G d
Knight Inlet, Br. Columbia 88 F e
Knighton, Wales 99 E h
Knin, Yugoslavia 110 F c
Knob, C., Australia 134 C f
Knockmealdown Mts., Eire 99 B h
Knokke, Belgium 100 B c
Knowlton, Quebec 85 S g
Knox, C., Graham I., B.C 88 C c
Knox Coast, Antarctica 136 S e
Knysna, South Africa 122 C f
Knyszyn, Poland 105 K b
Kobarid, Yugoslavia 110 D b
Kobe, Japan 133 D g
København (Copenhagen), Denmark 103 D j
Koblenz, Germany 104 B c
Kobrin, Belorussia, U.S.S.R. 116 D e
Kobroör, !., Indonesia 129 K m
Kocaeli. See Izmit
Kočani, Yugoslavia 112 D d
Kočevje, Yugoslavia 110 E c
Ko Chang, Thailand 132 C d
Kochi, Japan 133 C h
Koch I., N.-W. Territories 81 M d
Kochinda, I., Okinawa 78 A d
Kochiu, China 130 K d
Kochow. See Mowming
Kochumdek, U.S.S.R. 115 J b
Koffiefontein, South Africa 122 D e
Koforidua, Ghana 118 E g
Kofu, Japan 133 F g
Kohat, India 126 D b
Kohima, India 127 H c
Kohler Ra., Antarctica 136 F c
Kojonup, Australia 134 C f
Kokand, Uzbek., U.S.S.R. 125 K a
Kokanee Glacier Prov. Park, British Columbia 88 L f
Kokchetav, Kazakh., U.S.S.R. 114 F c
Kokhtla Yarva, Estonia, U.S.S.R. 103 M g
Kokkola, Finland 102 K e
Kokoda, Papua 135 J a
Kokoshili Ra., Tibet 127 F a
Kokpekty, Kazakh., U.S.S.R. 114 H d
Koksoak, R., Quebec 81 N f
Kokstad, South Africa 122 D f
Kokura, Japan 133 B h
Ko Kut, Thailand 132 C d
Ko-lan-chow, China 130 E c
Kolar, India 126 E f
Kolari, Finland 102 K c
Kolarovgrad, Bulgaria 112 F c
Kolberg. See Kolobrzeg
Kolda, Senegal 118 B f
Kolding, Denmark 103 C j
Kole, Belgian Congo 120 F d
Kolepom, I., W. Irian 129 L m
Kolguyev Ostrov, U.S.S.R. 114 D b
Kolhapur, India 126 D e
Kolin, Czechoslovakia 104 F c
Kolkas Rags, Latvia, U.S.S.R. 103 K h
Köln (Cologne), Germany 104 B c
Kolno, Poland 105 J b
Koło, Poland 105 H b
Kolo, Tanzania 121 H e
Kołobrzeg, Poland 105 F a
Kologriv, U.S.S.R. 117 G a
Kolokani, Mali 118 D f
Kolomna, U.S.S.R. 116 L d
Kolomyya, Ukraine, U.S.S.R. 116 D g
Kolossia, Kenya 121 H d
Kolpakovskiy, U.S.S.R. 115 Q c
Kolpashevo, U.S.S.R. 114 H c
Kolwezi, Congo 120 F g
Kolyma, R., U.S.S.R. 115 Q b
Kolymskiy, Khrebet, U.S.S.R. 115 Q b
Komandorskiye Ova., U.S.S.R. 115 R c
Komariya, Ceylon 126 F g
Komarno, Czechoslovakia 105 H e
Komarno, Manitoba 87 U h
Komatsu, Japan 133 E f
Komebail Lagoon, Palau Is. 78 B m
Komi, U.S.S.R. 114 E b
Kommunisma Pk., Tadzhik., U.S.S.R. 114 G e
Komoran, I., W. Irian 129 L m
Komotini, Greece 112 E d
Kompong Cham, Cambodia 132 D d
Kompong Chhnang, Camb. 132 C d
Kompong-thom, Cambodia 132 C d
Komsomolets, Kazakh., U.S.S.R. 117 R d
Komsomolets Ostrov, U.S.S.R. 115 J a
Komsomolsk, U.S.S.R. 115 N c
Kondiaronk L., Quebec 85 O f
Kondinskoe, U.S.S.R. 114 F b
Kondoa, Tanzania 121 H e
Kong, Ivory Coast 118 E g
Kongauru, Palau Is. 78 A o
Kong Karl's Land, Arctic Ocean 114 B a
Kongmoon, China 131 F l
Kongor, Sudan 119 M g
Kongsberg, Norway 103 C g
Kongsmoen, Norway 102 E d
Kongsvinger, Norway 103 E f
Kongwa, Tanzania 121 H f
Königsberg. See Kaliningrad
Königshütte. See Chorzow
Konispol, Albania 113 C e
Konjic, Yugoslavia 112 A c
Konotop, Ukraine, U.S.S.R. 116 H f
Konrei, Palau Is. 78 C l
Konstantinovka, Ukraine, U.S.S.R. 116 K g
Konstantinovsk, U.S.S.R. 117 E g
Konstanz, Germany 104 C e
Kontiomäki, Finland 102 N d
Konya, Turkey 124 B b
Konza, Kenya 121 H e
Koostatak, Manitoba 87 U g
Kootenay L., Br. Columbia 88 L f
Kootenay Nat. Park, British Columbia 88 L e
Kootenay R., Br. Columbia 88 L f
Kootwijk, Netherlands 100 D b
Kopervik, Norway 103 A g
Kopeysk, U.S.S.R. 117 Q c
Köping, Sweden 103 F g
Kopparberg, Sweden 103 F g
Koppigen, Switzerland 101 C a
Koprivnica, Yugoslavia 110 F b
Korak, Palau Is. 78 C n
Korangi, Pakistan 125 J e
Korçë, Albania 113 C d
Korčula, I., Yugoslavia 110 F d
Korea, N., E. Asia 128 J b
Korea, S., E. Asia 128 J c
Korea B., Korea 128 H c
Korea Kaikyo, Korea 128 J d
Korinthía & Argolís, Greece 113 D f
Kórinthos, G. of, Greece 113 D e
Kórinthos, Greece 113 D f
Koritza. See Korçë
Kormak, Ontario 84 H e
Kormakiti, C., Cyprus 123 A b
Kornat, I., Yugoslavia 110 E d
Korneuburg, Austria 105 G d
Korogwe, Tanzania 121 H f
Koror, Palau Is. 78 B n
Koror Auluptagel, Palau Is. 78 B n
Körös, Hungary 112 C a
Korosten, Ukraine, U.S.S.R. 116 F f
Koro-Toro, Chad 119 J e
Korpo, Finland 103 J f
Korsakov, U.S.S.R. 115 P d
Korsnas, Finland 102 J e
Korsnes, Norway 102 G b
Kortgem, Netherlands 100 B c
Korthpulé, Albania 112 B d
Korti, Sudan 119 M e
Kortrijk. See Courtrai
Koryakskiy Khrebet, U.S.S.R. 115 R b
Kos, I., Greece 113 F f
Koscierzyna, Poland 105 G a
Kosha, Sudan 119 M d
Koshchagyl, Kazakh., U.S.S.R. 114 E d
Koshiki Retto, Japan 133 A j
Koshki, U.S.S.R. 117 K c
Košice, Czechoslovakia 105 J d
Kosima, Kuwait 124 E d
Koskaecodde L., Newfoundland 83 R f
Koslan, U.S.S.R. 114 D b
Köslin. See Koszalin
Kosovo Metohija, Yugoslavia 112 C c
Kossol Pass, Palau Is. 78 C k
Kostainica, Yugoslavia 110 F c
Kosti, Sudan 119 M f
Kostino, U.S.S.R. 114 H b
Kostroma, U.S.S.R. 116 M c
Koszalin, Poland 105 G b
Kota Bharu, Malaysia 132 C e
Kotah, India 126 E c
Kota Kota, Malawi 121 G g
Kota Tinggi, Malaysia 132 C f
Kotawara, India 126 E c
Kotcho, R., Br. Columbia 88 J a
Kotcho L., Br. Columbia 88 J a
Kotel, Bulgaria 112 F c
Kotelnich, U.S.S.R. 117 J a
Kotelnyy, Ostrov, U.S.S.R. 115 N a
Köthen, Germany 104 D c
Kotido, Uganda 121 G d
Kotka, Finland 103 M f
Kotlas, U.S.S.R. 114 D b
Kotonkoro, Nigeria 118 G f
Kotri, Pakistan 126 C c
Kottas Mts., Antarctica 136 L d
Kotturu, India 126 E f
Kouango, Cent. Afr. Rep. 119 K g
Koudougou, Upper Volta 118 E f
Koulikoro, Mali 118 D f
Koundé, Cent. Afr. Rep. 119 H g
Kouri shima, Okinawa 78 B a
Kourou, French Guiana 93 G b
Koutiala, Mali 118 D f
Kouvola, Finland 103 M f
Kovel', Ukraine, U.S.S.R. 116 D f
Kovno. See Kaunas
Kovrov, U.S.S.R. 117 E b
Kowkash, Ontario 84 C b
Kowloon, China 131 G l
Koyiu, China 131 F l
Koza, Okinawa 78 A c
Kozan, Turkey 124 C b
Kozáni, Greece 113 C d
Kozhikode (Calicut), India 126 E f
Kra & Isthmus of, Thailand 132 B d
Krabi, Thailand 132 B e
Kragerö, Norway 103 C g
Kragujevac, Yugoslavia 112 C b
Krakatau, I., Indonesia 129 E m
Kraków, Poland 105 H c
Kramatorsk, Ukraine, U.S.S.R. 116 K g
Kranj, Yugoslavia 110 E b
Kranystaw, Poland 105 K c
Krapina, Yugoslavia 110 E b
Krasino, Novaya Zemlya, U.S.S.R. 114 E a
Krasnobród, Poland 105 K c
Krasnodar, U.S.S.R. 114 C d
Krasnograd, Ukraine, U.S.S.R. 116 J g
Krasnoufimsk, U.S.S.R. 117 N b
Krasnovishersk, U.S.S.R. 114 E b
Krasnovodsk, Turkmen., U.S.S.R. 114 E d
Krasnoyarsk, U.S.S.R. 115 J c
Krasnoyarskiy Kroy, U.S.S.R. 115 J b
Krasnyi Kholm, U.S.S.R 116 K b
Krasnyi Uzel, U.S.S.R. 117 G c
Krasny Kut, U.S.S.R. 117 H e
Krasnyy Yar, U.S.S.R. 117 G e
Kratie, Cambodia 132 D d
Kraul Mts, Antarctica 136 L d
Krefeld, Germany 104 B c
Kremenchug, Ukraine, U.S.S.R. 116 H g
Kremensk, U.S.S.R. 117 F f
Krems, Austria 105 F d
Kretinga, Lithuania, U.S.S.R. 103 J j
Kreuzlingen, Switzerland 101 E a
Kribi, Cameroon 119 G h
Krimml, Austria 104 E e
Krishnanagar, India 127 G d
Krishnaraja Res., India 126 E f
Kristiansand, Norway 103 C g
Kristianstad, Sweden 103 F h
Kristiansund, Norway 102 B e
Kristiinankaupunki, Finland 102 J e
Kristinehamn, Sweden 103 F g
Kríti, I. See Crete
Kriva Palanka, Yugoslavia 112 D c
Krivoy Rog, Ukraine, U.S.S.R. 116 H h
Krizevči, Yugoslavia 110 F b
Krk, I., Yugoslavia 110 E c
Krnov, Czechoslovakia 105 G c
Kroken, Norway 102 F d
Kroměříz, Czechoslovakia 105 G d
Kronau, Saskatchewan 87 N h
Kronoby, Finland 102 K e
Kronshtadt, U.S.S.R. 116 F a
Kroonstad, South Africa 122 D e
Kropotkin, U.S.S.R. 114 D d
Krotoszyn, Poland 105 G c
Krško, Yugoslavia 110 E c
Krüger, Mt., Antarctica 136 L d
Krugerdorf, Ontario 84 L e
Krugersdorp, South Africa 122 D e
Krujë, Albania 112 B d
Krumbach, Germany 104 D d
Krumlov, Czechoslovakia 104 F d
Krung Thep, Thailand 132 C d
Krupnik, Bulgaria 112 D d
Kruševac, Yugoslavia 112 C c
Kruševo, Yugoslavia 112 C d
Krustpils, Latvia, U.S.S.R. 103 L h
Krydor, Saskatchewan 86 K f
Krzyz, Poland 105 G b
Ksabi, Algeria 118 E c
Ksar El Boukhari, Algeria 118 F a
Ksar-el-Kebir, Morocco 118 D b
Ktima, Cyprus 123 A c
Kuala, Sumatra 129 C k
Kuala Kangsar, Malaysia 132 C f
Kuala Klawang, Malaysia 132 C f
Kuala Krai, Malaysia 129 D j
Kuala Lipis, Malaysia 132 C f
Kuala Lumpur, Malaysia 132 C f
Kuandang, Celebes 129 H k
Kuang-chow. See Canton
Kuang-hsi. See Kwangsi
Kuang-tung. See Kwangtung
Kuantan, Malaysia 129 D k
Kub, S.W. Africa 122 B d
Kucha, China 114 H d
Kuching, Sarawak 129 F k
Kuchow. See Jungkiang
Kudat, Sabah 129 G j
Kudymkar, U.S.S.R. 114 E c
Kuei-chou. See Fengkieh
Kuei-lin. See Kweilin
Kueiteh, China 128 D c
Kuhak, Iran 125 H d
Kuh Banan, Iran 125 G c
Kuh-e-Bul, Iran 125 F c
Kuh Furgan, Iran 125 G d
Kuh-i-Dinar, Iran 125 F c
Kuhmo, Finland 102 N d
Kuhpayeh, Iran 125 F c
Kuhrud. See Qohoud
Kuhsan, Afghanistan 125 H c
Kuibis, S.W. Africa 122 B e
Kuikang, China 131 H h
Kuilenburg, Netherlands 100 D c
Kuinre, Netherlands 100 D b
Kui Nua, Thailand 132 B d
Kukatush, Ontario 84 H d
Kukawa, Nigeria 119 H f
Kukës, Albania 112 C c
Kukong, China 131 F k
Kukukus L., Ontario 86 L a
Kuku Pt., Wake I. 79 S d
Kuldīga, Latvia, U.S.S.R. 103 K h
Kuldja, China 114 H d
Kuldo, Br. Columbia 88 F c
Kulgera, Australia 134 F e
Kulhakangri Mt., Tibet 127 H c
Kuli, Truk Is. 78 D d
Kuljn, China 131 B h
Kulmbach, Germany 104 D c
Kulunda, U.S.S.R. 114 G c
Kumai, Borneo 129 F l
Kumamoto, Japan 133 B h
Kumara, New Zealand 135 Q l
Kumara, U.S.S.R. 115 M c
Kumasi, Ghana 118 E g
Kumbakonam, India 126 E f
Kumora, U.S.S.R. 115 L c
Kumta, India 126 D f
Kunar, India 126 D b
Kunda, Estonia, U.S.S.R. 103 M g
Kundar, India 126 C b
Kunduz, Afghanistan 125 J b
Kungchang. See Lungsi
Kunghit I., Queen Charlotte Is., British Columbia 88 D d
Kungnang, India 127 H d
Kungrad, Uzbek., U.S.S.R. 114 E d
Kungur, U.S.S.R. 117 N b
Kunhsien, China 130 E f
Kunlun Mts., China-Tibet 127 F a
Kunming, China 128 D e
Kunsan, S. Korea 128 J c
Kuopio, Finland 102 M e
Kupang, Timor I. 129 H n
Kupa R., Yugoslavia 110 E c
Kupiškis, Lithuania, U.S.S.R. 103 L j
Kupyansk, Ukraine, U.S.S.R. 116 K g
Kure, Japan 133 C g
Kureika, U.S.S.R. 114 H b
Kurgan, U.S.S.R 114 F c
Kuria Muria Is., Arabian Sea 125 G f
Kuril'skiye Ostrova (Kuril Is.), U.S.S.R. 115 P d
Kurnool, India 126 E e
Kuroki, Saskatchewan 87 O g
Kurow, New Zealand 135 Q m
Kurskiy Zaliv, U.S.S.R. 103 J j
Kursky, U.S.S.R. 116 K f
Kurtalan, Turkey 124 D b
Kuru, Finland 103 K f
Kuruman, South Africa 122 C e
Kurume, Japan 133 B h
Kurunegala, Ceylon 126 F g
Kusa, U.S.S.R. 117 P c
Kusaie, I., Caroline Is. 78 G g
Kushersk, U.S.S.R. 117 M a
Kushi, Okinawa 78 B b
Kushima, Japan 133 B j
Kushiro, Japan 133 J c
Kushk, Afghanistan 125 H c
Kushka, Turkmen., U.S.S.R. 114 F e
Kushva, U.S.S.R. 117 P a
Kustanay, Kazakh., U.S.S.R. 114 F c
Kütahya, Turkey 124 A b
Kutai R., Borneo 129 G k
Kutaka shima, Okinawa 78 B c
Kut-al-Hai. See Al Hayy
Kutaradja, Sumatra 129 C j
Kutch, Gt. Rann of, India 126 C d
Kutch & G. of, India 126 C d
Kutchian, Japan 133 G c
Kutina, Yugoslavia 110 F c
Kutno, Poland 105 H b
Kütsing, China 131 A k
Kutu, Ethiopia 121 G c
Kutum, Sudan 119 K f
Kuusamo, Finland 102 N d
Kuusjärvi, Finland 102 N e
Kuwait & state, Persian Gulf 124 E d
Kuyang, China 130 E b
Kuybyshev, U.S.S.R. 117 K d
Kuybyshev, U.S.S.R. 114 G c
Kuybyshevskoye Vdkhr., U.S.S.R. 117 J c
Kuytan, U.S.S.R. 115 K c
Kuzhbal, U.S.S.R. 117 G a
Kuzino, U.S.S.R. 117 P b
Kuzmin, Yugoslavia 112 B b
Kuznetsk, U.S.S.R. 117 H d
Kuzovatovo, U.S.S.R. 117 H d
Kvalöy, N., Norway 102 H a
Kvalöy, S., Norway 102 H b
Kvarken, Östra, chan., Swed. 102 J e
Kvarner, G. of, Yugoslavia 110 E c
Kvarnerolo, G. of, Yugoslavia 110 E c
Kvesmenes, Norway 102 J b
Kwajalein, Is., Marshall Is. 78 G f
Kwajalein Lagoon, Kwajalein Is. 79 T e
Kwakhnani, Botswana 122 C d
Kwakoegron, Surinam 93 F b
Kwangchang, China 131 H j
Kwangchow Wan, China 131 E m
Kwangnan, China 131 B k
Kwangping. See Yungnien
Kwangshun, China 131 C j
Kwangsi, prov., China 131 C l
Kwangsin. See Shangjao
Kwangtung, prov., China 131 F l
Kwantung Pen., China 130 K c
Kwania L., Uganda 121 G d
Kwataboahegan, R., Ontario 84 J a
Kweichih, China 131 H g
Kweichow, prov., China 131 B j
Kweichow. See Fengkieh
Kweihwa. See Huhehot
Kweihwa. See Tzeyun
Kweiki, China 131 H h
Kweilin, China 131 E k
Kweiping, China 131 E l
Kweisui. See Huhehot
Kweiteh. See Shangkiu
Kweiyang, China 131 C j
Kweiyang, China 131 F k
Kwi-chu. See Phu Qui
Kwidzyń, Poland 105 H b
Kwitao, Burma 127 J c
Kwoka, Mt., W. Irian 129 K l
Kyakhta, U.S.S.R. 115 K c
Kyancutta, Australia 135 G f
Kyangin, Burma 127 J e

Liant, C., *Thailand* 132 C d
Liaocheng, *China* 130 H d
Liaohsien, *China* 130 F d
Liao R., *China* 128 H b
Liaoyang, *China* 130 L b
Liaoyang, *China* 130 L b
Liari, *Pakistan* 126 C c
Liberec, *Czechoslovakia* 104 F c
Liberia, *Costa Rica* 91 B d
Liberia, *W. Africa* 118 C g
Liberty, *Saskatchewan* 87 M g
Lib I., *Marshall Is.* 79 S b
Libiron, I., *Eniwetok* 79 R d
Libnan, Jebel, *Lebanon* 123 D c
Libourne, *France* 109 C d
Libreville, *Gabon* 120 B d
Libya, *N. Africa* 119 H c
Licata, *Sicily* 111 D g
Lichan, I., *Saipan-Tinian Is.* 78 B d
Licheng. *See* Tsinan
Lichfield, *England* 99 F h
Lida, *Belorussia, U.S.S.R.* 116 D e
Lida-di-Roma, *Italy* 111 D e
Liddes, *Switzerland* 101 C c
Lidilbut, I., *Eniwetok* 79 R b
Lidköping, *Sweden* 103 E g
Lidzbark, *Poland* 105 J a
Liebenthal, *Saskatchewan* 86 H h
Liechtenstein, *Europe* 101 E a
Liège & prov., *Belgium* 100 D d
Liegnitz. *See* Legnica
Lieksa, *Finland* 102 P e
Lienkong, *China* 131 J j
Lienyunkang, *China* 130 J e
Lienz, *Austria* 104 E e
Liepāja, *Latvia, U.S.S.R.* 103 J h
Lier, *Belgium* 100 C c
Lierneux, *Belgium* 100 D d
Liestal, *Switzerland* 101 C a
Lièvre, R. du, *Quebec* 85 P g
Lièvres, I. aux, *Quebec* 82 C f
Ligure, Appennino, Mts., *Italy* 110 B c
Liguria, reg., *Italy* 110 B c
Ligurian Sea, *Italy* 110 B d
Lihou Reef, *Coral Sea* 78 F j
Lihsien, *China* 131 E h
Lijeron, I., *Jaluit I.* 79 T h
Likely, *Br. Columbia* 88 J d
Likiang, *China* 128 D e
Likiep, I., *Marshall Is.* 79 T b
Likimi, *Congo* 120 E d
Liling, *China* 131 F j
Lilla Edet, *Sweden* 103 E g
Lille, *Belgium* 100 C c
Lille, *France* 108 E a
Lillehammer, *Norway* 103 D f
Lillesand, *Norway* 103 C g
Lillian L., *Quebec* 83 L b
Lillo, *Belgium* 100 C c
Lillo, *Spain* 106 D c
Lillooet, *Br. Columbia* 88 J e
Lillooet R., *Br. Columbia* 88 H e
Lilongwe, *Malawi* 121 G g
Lima, *Peru* 92 B f
Limache, *Chile* 94 B d
Limassol, *Cyprus* 123 B c
Limay, R., *Argentina* 95 C e
Limay Mahuida, *Argentina* 94 C e
Limbazi, *Latvia, U.S.S.R.* 103 L h
Limbourg, *Belgium* 100 D d
Limburg, *Germany* 104 C c
Limburg, prov., *Belgium* 100 D d
Limchow. *See* Hoppo
Limeira, *Brazil* 93 H h
Limerick, *Saskatchewan* 86 L j
Limerick (Luimneach), *Eire* 99 B h
Limes, *Belgium* 100 D e
Limestone L., *Manitoba* 87 W b
Limestone Pt., *Manitoba* 87 T e
Lim Fd., *Denmark* 103 C h
Limmavady, *N. Ireland* 98 C e
Limmen, *Netherlands* 100 C b
Limmen Bight, *Australia* 134 G b
Limni, *Greece* 113 D e
Limnos, I., *Greece* 113 E e
Limoges, *France* 108 D d
Limoges, *Ontario* 85 P g
Limoilou, *Quebec* 85 S b
Limón, *Costa Rica* 91 C d
Limousin, prov., *France* 108 D d
Limoux, *France* 109 E e
Limpopo R., *Mozambique, etc.* 122 E d
Linares, *Chile* 94 B e
Linares, *Mexico* 90 E c
Linares, *Spain* 106 D c
Lincheng, *China* 130 H e
Linchwan, *China* 131 H j
Lincoln, *Argentina* 94 D d
Lincoln, *England* 99 G g
Lincoln & co., *England* 99 G g
Lincoln Sea, *Arctic Ocean* 89 P a
Lincolnville, *Nova Scotia* 83 L h
Lincoln Wolds, *England* 99 G g
Lindau, *Germany* 104 C e
Lindbergh, *Alberta* 86 G e
Lindesay, Mt., *Australia* 135 K e
Lindesnes, *Norway* 103 B h
Lindi, *Tanzania* 121 H f
Lindley, *South Africa* 122 D e
Lindos, *Greece* 113 G f
Lindsay, *Ontario* 85 M h
Lindsey, *England* 99 G g
Line Is., *Pacific Ocean* 78 K g
Linfen, *China* 128 F c
Lingchwan, *China* 131 E k
Lingen, *Germany* 104 B b
Lingga, I., R. au Arch., *Indonesia* 129 E l
Lingling, *China* 128 F e
Linguère, *Senegal* 118 B e
Lingyun, *China* 131 C k
Linhai, *China* 129 H e
Linhares, *Brazil* 93 J g
Linho, *China* 130 C b
Linhsien, *China* 131 F k
Lini, *China* 128 G c
Linière, *Quebec* 82 B g
Linkiang, *China* 128 J b
Linkiang. *See* Tsingkiang
Linköping, *Sweden* 103 F g
Linkuva, *Lithuania, U.S.S.R.* 103 K h
Linnhe L., *Scotland* 98 D d
Linosa, I., *Medit. Sea* 111 D h
Linping, *China* 131 G k
Lins, *Brazil* 94 G b
Linsi, *China* 128 G b
Lintan. *See* Kadiger
Linth, R., *Switzerland* 101 E b
Linthal, *Switzerland* 101 D b
Lintlaw, *Saskatchewan* 87 O f
Linton Junction, *Quebec* 85 S e
Linyu, *China* 130 J b
Linz, *Austria* 104 F d
Lion, G. du, *France* 109 F e
Lions Head, *Ontario* 84 J h
Lio Porgyul, *Tibet* 126 E b
Liouesso, *Congo* 120 D d
Lipa, *Yugoslavia* 110 F c
Lipari, Is. (Eolie, Isole), *Italy* 111 E f
Lipetsk, *U.S.S.R.* 116 L e
Liping, *China* 131 D j
Lipovets, *Ukraine, U.S.S.R* 116 F g
Lippstadt, *Germany* 104 C c
Lipsói, I., *Greece* 113 F f
Lipton, *Saskatchewan* 87 O h
Lira, *Uganda* 121 G d
Lircay, *Peru* 92 C f
Liria, *Spain* 107 E c
Lisala, *Congo* 120 E d
Lisboa. *See* Lisbon
Lisbon, *Portugal* 106 A c
Lisburn, *N. Ireland* 99 C f
Liscannor B., *Eire* 99 A h
Liscomb, *Nova Scotia* 83 K h
Lisdoonvarna, *Eire* 99 A g
Lishih, *China* 130 E d
Lishui, *China* 131 J h
Lisieux, *France* 108 D b
Lisieux, *Saskatchewan* 87 M j
Liski, *U.S.S.R.* 117 D e
L'Isle, *Switzerland* 101 B b
L'Islet, *Quebec* 82 B f
Lismore, *Australia* 135 K e
Lismore, *Eire* 99 B h
Lismore, *Nova Scotia* 83 K h
Listowel, *Eire* 99 A h
Listowel, *Ontario* 84 K j
Lith, Al, *Saudi Arabia* 124 D e
Lithgow, *Australia* 135 K f
Líthinon, C., *Crete* 113 E g
Lithuania, *U.S.S.R.* 103 K j
Litoměrice, *Czechoslovakia* 104 F c
Little America, *Antarctica* 136 C c
Little Anitibi L., *Ontario* 84 K c
Little Barrier I., *New Zealand* 135 R k
Little Bay Islands, *Nfd.* 83 R d
Little Bear L., *Saskatchewan* 87 N d
Little Beaver R., *Manitoba* 87 V a
Little Bow Prov. Park, *Alberta* 86 E h
Little Bow R., *Alberta* 86 D h
Little Bullhead, *Manitoba* 87 V g
Little Burnt Bay, *Nfd.* 83 R d
Little Chicago, *N.-W. Terr.* 80 F d
Little Current, *Ontario* 84 J f
Little Current, R., *Ontario* 84 D b
Little Harbour Deep, *Nfd.* 83 Q c
Little Longlac, *Ontario* 84 D c
Little Manicougan L., *Quebec* 82 E b
Little Playgreen L., *Manitoba* 87 U d
Little R., *Newfoundland* 83 P f
Little River. *See* St. Andrews
Liuan, *China* 128 G d
Liuchow, *China* 128 E f
Liupan Shan, *China* 130 B e
Liusvaara, *U.S.S.R.* 102 P e
Livelong, *Saskatchewan* 86 J e
Liverpool, *Australia* 135 K f
Liverpool, C., *N.-W. Terr.* 81 M c
Liverpool, *Nova Scotia* 82 H j
Liverpool & B., *England* 99 E g
Liverpool Coast, *Greenland* 89 N b
Liverpool Ra., *Australia* 135 J f
Livingston, *Guatemala* 91 B c
Livingston, I., *S. Shetlands* 136 H f
Livingstone, *Zambia* 122 D c
Livingstonia, *Malawi* 122 E b
Livingston Ra., *Alberta* 86 C h
Livno, *Yugoslavia* 110 F d
Livny, *U.S.S.R.* 116 K e
Livo Joki, *Finland* 102 M d
Livorno (Leghorn), *Italy* 110 C d
Livramento, *Brazil* 94 E d
Liwa, *Muscat & Oman* 125 G e
Liwale, *Tanzania* 121 H f
Liyepaya, *Latvia, U.S.S.R.* 103 J h
Lizard Pt., *England* 99 D l
Lizotte, *Quebec* 85 S d
Ljubljana, *Yugoslavia* 110 E b
Ljubuški, *Yugoslavia* 110 F d
Ljungdalen, *Sweden* 102 E e
Ljusdal, *Sweden* 103 G f
Llandovery, *Wales* 99 E j
Llandrindod Wells, *Wales* 99 E h
Llandudno, *Wales* 99 E g
Llanelli, *Wales* 99 E j
Llanes, *Spain* 106 C a
Llangollen, *Wales* 99 E h
Llanguihue, L., *Chile* 95 B f
Llerena, *Spain* 106 B c
Llico, *Chile* 94 B d
Lloyd George, Mt. & ra., *British Columbia* 88 G b
Lloyd L., *Saskatchewan* 88 P b
Lloydminster, *Alberta-Saskatchewan* 86 H e
Lluchmayor, *Balearic Is* 107 G c
Loango, *Congo* 120 C e
Lobbes, *Belgium* 100 C d
Lobería, *Argentina* 95 E e
Lobito, *Angola* 120 C g
Lobos, *Argentina* 94 E e
Lobstick L., *Labrador* 81 N g
Locarno, *Switzerland* 101 D b
Lochaber Mines, *Nova Scotia* 83 K h
Lochalsh, Kyle of, *Scotland* 98 D c
Lochalsh, *Ontario* 84 F d
Lochem, *Netherlands* 100 E b
Lochinver, *Scotland* 98 D b
Lochnagar, *Scotland* 98 E d
Lochy L., *Scotland* 98 D d
Lockeport, *Nova Scotia* 82 G k
Lockerbie, *Scotland* 98 E e
Lockport, *Manitoba* 87 U h
Lockwood, *Saskatchewan* 87 N g
Loc Ninh, *S. Vietnam* 129 E h
Lodeynoye Pole, *U.S.S.R.* 116 H a
Lodhran, *Pakistan* 126 D c
Lödingen, *Norway* 102 F b
Lodwar, *Kenya* 121 H d
Łódź, *Poland* 105 H c
Loenen, *Netherlands* 100 E b
Loewoek (Luwuk), *Celebes* 129 H l
Lofer, *Austria* 104 E e
Lofoten Is., *Norway* 102 E c
Lofty Ra., *Australia* 134 G f
Logan, Mt., *Quebec* 82 F e
Logan L., *Alberta* 86 F c
Logone R., *Cameroon-Chad* 120 C b
Logrono, *Spain* 107 D a
Lohardaga, *India* 127 F d
Loharu, *India* 126 E c
Loikaw, *Burma* 127 J e
Loir, R., *France* 108 C c
Loire, dep., *France* 108 E d
Loire, R., *France* 108 D c
Loire-Atlantique, dep., *France* 108 C c
Loiret, dep., *France* 108 E c
Loiret, R., *Quebec* 85 R b
Loir-et-Cher, dep., *France* 108 D c
Loja, *Ecuador* 92 B d
Loja, *Spain* 106 C d
Loka, *Sudan* 119 M h
Lokeren, *Belgium* 100 C c
Lokka, *Finland* 102 M c
Lökken, *Denmark* 103 C h
Lökken, *Norway* 102 C e
Loko, *Nigeria* 118 G g
Loks Land, *N.-W. Terr.* 81 N e
Lola, *Angola* 120 C g
Lolland, *Denmark* 103 D j
Lom, *Bulgaria* 112 D c
Lomas, *Argentina* 94 E d
Lomas, *Peru* 92 C g
Lombardia, reg., *Italy* 110 B c
Lomblem, I., *Indonesia* 129 H m
Lombok, I. & Str., *Indonesia* 129 G m
Lomé, *Togo* 118 F g
Lomela, *Congo* 120 E e
Lomié, *Cameroon* 119 H h
Lommel, *Belgium* 100 D c
Lomond, *Alberta* 86 E h
Lomond, Loch, C. Breton I., *Nova Scotia* 83 M h
Lomond, Loch, *Scotland* 98 D d
Lomond, *Newfoundland* 83 P d
Łomza, *Poland* 105 K b
Loncoché, *Chile* 95 B e
Loncopué, *Argentina* 95 B e
Londesborough, *Ontario* 84 J j
Londiani, *Kenya* 121 H e
London, *England* 99 G j
London, *Ontario* 84 J k
Londonderry, C., *Australia* 134 E b
Londonderry, I., *Chile* 95 B j
Londonderry, *Nova Scotia* 82 J h
Londonderry & co., *N. Ire.* 98 C f
Lonely I., *Ontario* 84 J g
Lone Rock, *Saskatchewan* 86 H e
Long, L., *New Brunswick* 82 F f
Long, L., *Scotland* 98 D d
Longa, *Brazil* 93 J e
Longchamps, *Belgium* 100 D d
Long Cr., *Saskatchewan* 87 O j
Longford & co., *Eire* 99 B g
Long Harbour, *Nfd.* 83 T f
Long I., *Bahama Is.* 91 D b
Long I., Hudson Bay, *North-West Territories* 81 M g
Long I., *Nova Scotia* 82 F j
Long L., *Ontario* 84 D c
Longlac, *Ontario* 84 D c
Long Point, *Manitoba* 87 T e
Long Point B., *Ontario* 84 K k
Long Pond, *Newfoundland* 83 T f
Long Pt., *Ontario* 84 K k
Long Range Mts., *Newfoundland* 83 P d
Longreach, *Australia* 135 H d
Long Sault, *Ontario* 85 S b
Long Sault Dam, *Ontario* 85 S b
Longtown, *England* 98 F e
Longué, *France* 108 C c
Longue Pointe, *Quebec* 85 T h
Longueuil, *Quebec* 85 T j
Longuyon, *France* 108 F b
Longview, *Alberta* 86 C h
Longwy, *France* 108 F b
Long-Xuyen, *S. Vietnam* 132 D d
Lonneker, *Netherlands* 100 E b
Lons-le-Saunier, *France* 108 F c
Looc, *Philippines* 129 H h
Loochristi, *Belgium* 100 B c
Looe, *England* 99 E k
Loolmalasin, Mt., *Tanzania* 119 H e
Looma, *Alberta* 86 D e
Loomis, *Saskatchewan* 86 J j
Loon, *Ontario* 84 B d
Loon, R., *Alberta* 88 M b
Loon Bay, *Newfoundland* 83 S d
Loon Lake, *Saskatchewan* 86 H d
Loon R., *Manitoba* 87 Q b
Loop Hd., *Eire* 99 A h
Loos, *Br. Columbia* 88 J d
Lopez C., *Gabon* 120 B e
Lopez I., *Canal Zone* 91 G a
Lopik, *Netherlands* 100 C c
Lop Nor, *China* 128 B b
Lopphavet, *Norway* 102 J a
Lora Hamun, *Pakistan* 126 B c
Loralai, *Pakistan* 126 C b
Lorca, *Spain* 107 E d
Lord Howe I., *Pacific Ocean* 78 G l
Lord Mayor B., *N.-W. Terr.* 81 K d
Loreburn, *Saskatchewan* 86 L j
Lorena, *Brazil* 93 J h
Loreto, *Brazil* 93 H e
Loreto, *Mexico* 90 B b
Lorette, *Manitoba* 87 V j
Loretteville, *Quebec* 85 T f
Lorica, *Colombia* 92 B b
Lorient, *France* 108 B c
L'Original, *Ontario* 85 Q g
Lorlie, *Manitoba* 87 O h
Lorn, Firth of, *Scotland* 98 D d
L'Orne Bank, *Pacific Ocean* 79 L k
Lörrach, *Germany* 104 B e
Lorraine, prov., *France* 108 F b
Lorrainville, *Quebec* 85 L e
Los Andes, *Chile* 94 B d
Los Angeles, *Chile* 95 B e
Los Blancos, *Argentina* 94 D b
Loshan, *China* 131 A h
Lošinj, I., *Yugoslavia* 110 E c
Los Lamentos. *See* Félix U Gómez
Los Menucos, *Argentina* 95 C f
Los Pozos, *Chile* 94 B c
Los Santos, *Panama* 91 C e
Los Santos de Maimona, *Spain* 106 B c
Lossiemouth, *Scotland* 98 E c
Los Teques, *Venezuela* 92 D a
Los Tigres, *Argentina* 94 D c
Los Vilos, *Chile* 94 B d
Lot, dep., *France* 109 D d
Lot, I., *Ponape I.* 78 G o
Lot, R., *France* 109 D d
Lota, *Chile* 95 B e
Lot-et-Garonne, dep., *France* 109 D d
Lot Harb., *Ponape I.* 78 G o
Lottigna, *Switzerland* 101 D b
Loudéac, *France* 108 B b
Loudima, *Congo* 120 C e
Loudon, *Malawi* 121 G g
Loudun, *France* 108 D c
Louga, *Senegal* 118 B e
Loughborough, *England* 99 G h
Loughborough's I., *Burma* 127 J f
Lougheed, *Alberta* 86 F f
Lougheed I., *N.-W. Terr.* 80 J b
Loughrea, *Eire* 99 B g
Louhans, *France* 108 F c
Louisburg, C. Breton I., *Nova Scotia* 83 N h
Louisdale, C. Breton I., *Nova Scotia* 83 L h
Louise, L., *Alberta* 88 L e
Louise I., *Br. Columbia* 88 D d
Louiseville, *Quebec* 85 S f
Louisiade Arch., *Papua* 135 K b
Louis Trichardt, *S. Africa* 122 D d
Louis XIV, Pte., *Quebec* 81 M g
Loulé, *Portugal* 106 A d
Lourdes, *France* 109 C e
Lourdes, *Newfoundland* 83 N e
Lourenço Marques, *Mozambique* 122 E e
Louriçal, *Portugal* 106 A b
Lourinhã, *Portugal* 106 A c
Lousana, *Alberta* 86 D f
Louth, *Australia* 135 J f
Louth, co., *Eire* 99 C g
Louth, *England* 99 H g
Louvain, *Belgium* 100 C d
Louveigne, *Belgium* 100 D d
Louviers, *France* 108 D b
Lövanger, *Sweden* 102 J d
Love, *Saskatchewan* 87 N e
Loverna, *Saskatchewan* 86 H g
Loviisa, *Finland* 103 M f
Lövlid, *Sweden* 102 G d
Low, C., *N.-W. Territories* 81 L e
Low, *Quebec* 85 P g
Lowa, *Congo* 120 F e
Low Bush River, *Ontario* 84 K d
Lower Fort Garry, *Manitoba* 87 U h
Lower Hutt, *New Zealand* 135 R l
Lower Island Cove, *Newfoundland* 83 T f
Lower Neguac, *New Brunswick* 82 G f
Lower Ohio, *Nova Scotia* 82 G k
Lower Savage Is., *N.-W. Terr.* 81 N e
Lower West Pubnico, *Nova Scotia* 82 G k
Lower Wood Harbour, *Nova Scotia* 82 G k
Lowestoft, *England* 99 J h
Łowicz, *Poland* 105 H b
Lowther I., *N.-W. Terr.* 81 K c
Loyalist, *Alberta* 86 F g
Loyalty Is., *Pacific Ocean* 78 G j
Loyang, *China* 130 F e
Loyung, *China* 131 D k
Lozère, dep., *France* 109 E d
Loznica, *Yugoslavia* 112 B b
Luan. *See* Changchih
Luang Prabang, *Laos* 132 C c
Luarca, *Spain* 106 B a
Luashi, *Congo* 120 E g
Luayao, I., *Guam* 78 B l
Lubaczów, *Poland* 105 K c
Lubāna, *Latvia, U.S.S.R.* 103 M h
Lubartów, *Poland* 105 K c
Lübben, *Germany* 104 E c
Lübeck, *Germany* 104 D b
Lübecker B., *Germany* 104 D a
Lubefu, *Congo* 120 E e
Lubicon L., *Alberta* 86 B b
Lubin, *Poland* 105 G c
Lublin, *Poland* 105 K c
Lubliniec, *Poland* 105 H c
Lubuklinggau, *Sumatra* 129 D l
Lubumbashi (Elisabethville), *Congo* 122 D b
Luc, Le, *France* 109 G e
Lucala, *Angola* 120 D f
Lucan, *Ontario* 84 J j
Lucania. *See* Basilicata
Lucca, *Italy* 110 C d
Lucea, *Jamaica* 91 D c
Luce B., *Scotland* 99 D f
Lucena, *Spain* 106 C d
Lučenec, *Czechoslovakia* 105 H d
Lucera, *Italy* 111 E e
Lucerne (Luzern), *Switzerland* 101 D a
Luceville, *Quebec* 82 D e
Luch, *U.S.S.R.* 117 F b
Luchenya, *Malawi* 121 H h
Luchow, *China* 131 B h
Luchow (Hofei), *China* 130 H g
Lucie, L., *Quebec* 85 M b
Luckau, *Germany* 104 E c
Luckenwalde, *Germany* 104 E b
Lucknow, *India* 126 F c
Lucknow, *Ontario* 84 J j
Lucky Lake, *Saskatchewan* 86 K h
Lucky Strike, *Alberta* 86 F j
Luçon, *France* 108 C c
Lüderitz, *S.W. Africa* 122 A e
Ludgate, *Ontario* 84 K g
Ludhiana, *India* 126 E b
Ludlow, *England* 99 F h
Ludlow, *New Brunswick* 82 F g
Ludvika, *Sweden* 103 F f
Ludwigshafen, *Germany* 104 C d
Ludwigslust, *Germany* 104 D b
Ludza, *Latvia, U.S.S.R.* 103 M h
Luebo, *Congo* 120 E f
Luga, *U.S.S.R.* 116 F b
Lugano & L. di, *Switzerland* 101 D b
Lugansk, *Ukraine, U.S.S.R.* 116 L g
Lugh Ferrandi, *Somali Rep.* 121 J d
Lugo, *Spain* 106 B a
Lugoj, *Romania* 112 C b
Lugovay, Kazakh., *U.S.S.R.* 114 G d
Luhit R., *India* 127 J c
Luhsien. *See* Luchow
Luhwang Shan, I., *China* 131 L h
Luichow Pen., *China* 128 E f
Luime, *Angola* 120 D g
Luitpold Coast, *Antarctica* 136 K c
Luján, *Argentina* 94 E d
Luján, *Argentina* 94 C d
Lukachek, *U.S.S.R.* 122 N c
Lukala, *Congo* 120 C f
Lukovit, *Bulgaria* 112 E c
Lukoyanov, *U.S.S.R.* 117 G c
Lukula, *Congo* 120 C f
Lukulu, *Zambia* 122 C b
Luleå, *Sweden* 102 K d
Lule Älv, *Sweden* 102 J c
Luluabourg, *Congo* 120 E f
Lulu I., *Br. Columbia* 88 D g
Lulung, *China* 130 J c
Luma, I., *Manua Is.* 79 S o
Lumbres, *France* 108 E a
Lummen, *Belgium* 100 D d
Lumsden, *Newfoundland* 83 T d
Lumsden, *New Zealand* 135 P m
Lumsden, *Saskatchewan* 87 N h
Lund, *Sweden* 103 E j
Lundar, *Manitoba* 87 T h
Lundbreck, *Alberta* 86 C j
Lundy I., *England* 99 D j
Lüneburg, *Germany* 104 D b
Lunel, *France* 109 F e
Lunenburg, *Nova Scotia* 82 H j
Lunéville, *France* 108 G b
Lungan. *See* Pingwu
Lungki, *China* 131 H k
Lungnan, *China* 131 G k
Lungsi, *China* 130 B e
Lungyen, *China* 131 H k
Luni, *India* 126 D c
Lunino, *U.S.S.R.* 117 G d
Lunz, *Austria* 104 F e
Lupeh, *China* 128 H b
Lupiro, *Tanzania* 121 H f
Lupkow, *Poland* 105 K d
Lupong, I., *Guam* 78 B k
Luputa, *Congo* 120 E f
Luque, *Paraguay* 94 E c
Luquillo, *Puerto Rico* 54 D h
Lurgan, *N. Ireland* 99 C f
Luribay, *Bolivia* 92 D g
Luröy, *Norway* 102 E c
Lusaka, *Zambia* 122 D c
Lusambo, *Congo* 120 E e
Lusambo, *Congo* 120 E f
Luscar, *Alberta* 88 L d
Luseland, *Saskatchewan* 86 H f
Lushai Hills. *See* Mizo Hills
Lushnjë, *Albania* 113 B d
Lushun, *China* 130 K c
Lussanvira, *Brazil* 93 G h
Luta, *China* 130 K c
Lut Des., *Iran* 125 G c
Lutembo, *Angola* 120 E g
Luton, *England* 99 G j
Lutsk, *Ukraine, U.S.S.R.* 116 D f
Luttre, *Belgium* 100 C d
Lützow-Holm B., *Antarctica* 136 N d
Luvia, *Finland* 103 J f
Luwuk (Loewoek), *Celebes* 129 H l
Luxembourg, prov., *Belgium* 108 F b
Luxembourg & Grand Duchy, *N.-W. Europe* 100 E e
Luxeuil, *France* 108 G c
Luxor, *Egypt* 119 M c
Luzern & canton, *Switzerland* 101 D a
Luziânia, *Brazil* 93 H g
Luzilândia, *Brazil* 93 J d
Luzon, I., *Philippines* 129 H g
Luzon Str., *Philippines* 128 H f
Luzy, *France* 108 E c
Lvov, *Ukraine, U.S.S.R.* 116 D g
Lwanhsien, *China* 130 J c
Lwan-ping, *China* 130 H b
Lyall Ra., *New Zealand* 135 P m
Lybster, *Scotland* 98 E b
Lycksele, *Sweden* 102 H d
Lydavénai, Lithuania, *U.S.S.R.* 103 K j
Lydda, *Israel* 123 C f
Lyddal, *Manitoba* 87 T c
Lydenburg, *South Africa* 122 E e
Lydiatt, *Manitoba* 87 V j
Lyell I., Queen Charlotte Is., *British Columbia* 88 D d
Lyleton, *Manitoba* 87 Q j
Lymburn, *Alberta* 88 K c
Lyme B., *England* 99 F k
Lyme Regis, *England* 99 F k
Lynden, *Ontario* 84 K j
Lynn Lake, *Manitoba* 87 Q b
Lynnmour, *Br. Columbia* 88 D f
Lynton, *England* 99 E j
Lyon, *France* 108 F d
Lyonnais, prov., *France* 108 E d
Lyons, R., *Australia* 134 C d
Lys, R., *Belgium, etc.* 100 B d
Łyse, *Poland* 105 J b
Lysekil, *Sweden* 103 D g
Lyss, *Switzerland* 101 C a
Lyster, *Quebec* 85 T f
Lysva, *U.S.S.R.* 117 N a
Lyttelton, C., *Antarctica* 136 B b
Lyttelton, *New Zealand* 135 Q l
Lytton, *Br. Columbia* 88 J e
Lytton, *Quebec* 85 O f
Ma'an, *Jordan* 123 D g
Maarheeze, *Netherlands* 100 D c
Maarianhamina. *See* Mariehamn
Ma'arret en Numan, *Syria* 123 E b
Maas, R., *Netherlands* 100 D c
Maasbree, *Netherlands* 100 E c
Maaseik, *Belgium* 100 D c
Ma'asir. *See* Hazawza
Maassluis, *Netherlands* 100 C c
Maastricht, *Netherlands* 100 D d
Mabella, *Ontario* 87 N b
Maberly, *Ontario* 85 O h
Mabote, *Mozambique* 122 E d
Mabou, C. Breton I., *N.S.* 83 L g
Mabrouk, *Mali* 118 E e
Mabuki, *Tanzania* 121 G e
Mabuni I., *Okinawa* 78 A d
McAdam, *New Brunswick* 82 E h
Macaé, *Brazil* 93 J h
Macaíba, *Brazil* 93 K e
Macamic, *Quebec* 85 L d
Macao (Port.), *China* 131 F l
Macapá, *Brazil* 93 G c
Macas, *Ecuador* 92 B d
Macau, *Brazil* 93 K e
Macaúba, *Brazil* 93 G f
McAuley, *Manitoba* 87 Q h
McBeth Pt., *Manitoba* 87 U f
McBride, *Br. Columbia* 88 J d
Maccan, *Nova Scotia* 82 H h
Macclesfield, *England* 99 F g
Maccles L., *Newfoundland* 83 S e
M'Clintock, C., *N.-W. Terr.* 81 M a
McClintock, Mt., *Antarctica* 136 A c
M'Clintock B., *N.-W. Terr.* 81 M a
McClintock Chan., *North-West Territories* 80 J c

McCluer G., New Guinea 129 K l
McClure C., N.-W. Terr. 80 H c
McClure Str., N.-W. Terr. 80 H c
McCord, Saskatchewan 86 L j
McCreary, Manitoba 87 S h
Macculloch, C., N.-W. Terr. 81 M c
McCusker R., Sask. 86 J c
Macdiarmid, Ontario 84 B c
MacDonald, Anticosti I., Quebec 82 J d
Macdonald, L., Australia 134 E d
Macdonnell Ras., Australia 134 F d
McDouall Ra., Australia 134 F c
Macdougall L., N.-W. Terr. 81 K d
Mace, Ontario 84 L d
Maceió, Brazil 93 K e
Macerata, Italy 110 D d
Macey, Mt., Antarctica 136 Q d
McGee, Saskatchewan 86 J g
Macgillycuddy's Reeks, Eire 99 A j
McGregor, Manitoba 87 T j
McGregor L., Alberta 86 E h
McGregor R., Br. Columbia 88 J c
McGregor Ra., Australia 135 H e
Mach, Pakistan 126 C c
Machala, Ecuador 92 B d
Machanao Mt., Guam 78 B k
Macharetí, Bolivia 92 E h
Machias Seal I., Maine-New Brunswick 82 E j
Machicha, Mozambique 122 F d
Machiques, Venezuela 92 C a
Măcin, Romania 112 G b
McInnes, Ontario 84 J c
McIntosh, Ontario 86 J a
McIntyre B., Ontario 84 B c
McKague, Saskatchewan 87 O f
Mackay, Australia 135 J d
Mackay, L., Australia 134 E d
McKay L., Ontario 84 D c
Mackay Mts., Antarctica 136 D c
McKay R., Alberta 88 N b
Mackayville, Quebec 85 T j
McKean I., Phoenix Is. 78 J g
Mackenna, Argentina 94 D d
Mackenzie, Guyana 92 F b
Mackenzie, Dist. of, North-West Territories 80 J c
Mackenzie, Ontario 84 B d
Mackenzie B., Antarctica 136 Q e
Mackenzie B., Yukon 80 F d
Mackenzie King I., N.-W. Terr. 80 H b
McKenzie L., Ontario 87 L b
McKenzie L., Saskatchewan 87 P d
Mackenzie Mts., Yukon-N.-W. Terr. 80 F e
Mackenzie Plains, New Zealand 135 Q m
Mackenzie R., N.-W. Terr. 80 G e
McKerracher L., Manitoba 87 S a
McKinley Pk., Antarctica 136 D c
McKirdy, Ontario 84 B c
Macklin, Saskatchewan 86 H f
McKnight L., Manitoba 87 Q b
McLaughlin, Alberta 86 G f
McLaughlin R., Manitoba 87 U e
McLean, Manitoba 87 N h
McLean L., Saskatchewan 86 H b
McLennan, Alberta 88 L c
McLeod Lake, B. C. 88 H c
McLeod R., Alberta 86 B e
Macloutsie, Botswana 122 D d
MacMahon, Algeria 118 F c
McMahon, Saskatchewan 86 K h
Macmillan Ra., Yukon 80 F e
McMorran, Saskatchewan 86 J g
McMunn, Manitoba 86 F a
McMurdo Sd., Antarctica 136 B c
McMurphy, Br. Columbia 88 K e
McMurray, Alberta 88 O b
McNamara I., Antarctica 136 G d
McNutt, Saskatchewan 87 Q g
McNutt I., Nova Scotia 82 G k
Macomer, Sardinia 111 B e
Macon, Belgium 100 C d
Mâcon, France 108 F c
Macoun, Saskatchewan 87 O j
Macoun L., Saskatchewan 88 S b
Macouria, Fr. Guiana 93 G c
Macpherson Ra., Australia 135 K e
Macquarie, R., Australia 135 J f
Macquarie Harb., Tasmania 135 J h
MacRobertson Coast, Antarctica 136 Q e
Macroom, Eire 99 B j
Macrorie, Saskatchewan 86 K g
McTaggart, Saskatchewan 87 N j
McTavish, Manitoba 87 U j
MacTier, Ontario 85 L g
Macuje, Colombia 92 C c
Macusani, Peru 92 C f
McVeigh, Manitoba 87 Q b
McWatters, Quebec 85 M d
Madaba, Jordan 123 D f
Madadi, Chad 119 K e
Madagascar, I. See Mal. Rep.
Madain Salih, Saudi Arabia 124 C d
Madalai, I., Palau Is. 78 B n
Madame I., C. Breton I., N.S. 83 M h
Madan, Iran 125 G b
Madang, New Guinea 78 E h
Madaripur, E. Pakistan 127 H d
Madawaska, Ontario 85 N g
Madawaska R., Ontario 85 N g
Madawaska R., Quebec-New Brunswick 82 D f
Madeira, Is., Atlantic Oc. 118 B b
Madeira, R., Brazil 92 E e
Madeleine, C. de la, Quebec 82 G d
Madeleine, Is. de la, Quebec 82 K f
Madge, L., Saskatchewan 87 Q g
Madhopur, India 126 E c
Madhya Pradesh, India 126 E d
Madigan Nunatak, Antarc. 136 A e
Madinat Ash Sha'b, S. Yemen 124 D g
Madison, Saskatchewan 86 J g
Madoc, Ontario 85 N h
Madona, Latvia, U.S.S.R. 103 M h
Madras, India 126 F f
Madre, Sa., Mexico 90 C b
Madre Austral, L. de la, Mexico 90 E c
Madre de Dios, I., Chile 95 A h
Madre de Dios, R., Peru-Bolivia 92 D f
Madre del Sur, Sa., Mexico 90 D d
Madrid, Spain 106 D b
Madridejos, Spain 106 D c
Madura, I., Indonesia 129 F m
Madurai, India 126 E g
Maebashi, Japan 133 F f
Maestra, Sa., Cuba 91 D b
Maevatanana, Mal. Rep. 121 L k
Mafeking, Manitoba 87 Q f
Mafeking, South Africa 122 D e
Mafia I., Tanzania 121 H f
Mafra, Portugal 106 A c
Mafraq, Jordan 123 E e
Magadan, U.S.S.R. 115 Q c
Magadi & L., Kenya 121 H e
Magadino, Switzerland 101 D b
Magad Plat. See Jol Plat.
Magaguadavic L., New Brunswick 82 E h
Magallanes, & Estrecho de, Chile 95 B h
Magangué, Colombia 92 C b
Magari saki, Okinawa 78 C b
Magas. See Panāh
Magaz, Spain 106 C b
Magburaka, Sierra Leone 118 C g
Magdagachi, U.S.S.R. 115 M c
Magdala, Ethiopia 121 H b
Magdalena, B., Mexico 90 B c
Magdalena, Bolivia 92 E f
Magdalena, I., Chile 95 B f
Magdalena, Mexico 90 B a
Magdalena, R., Colombia 92 C b
Magdalena, R., Mexico 90 B a
Magdalen Is. See Madeleine, Is. de la
Magdanskaya Oblast, U.S.S.R. 115 R b
Magdeburg, Germany 104 D b
Magellan, Str. of, Chile 95 C h
Mageröya, Norway 102 M a
Maggia, Switzerland 101 D b
Maggiore, L., Italy 110 B b
Maghang Tsangpo R., Tibet 127 G c
Maghara, Mt., Egypt 123 B g
Magherafelt, N. Ireland 99 C f
Maglaj, Yugoslavia 112 B b
Maglie, Italy 111 G e
Magnet, Manitoba 87 S g
Magnetawan, Ontario 85 L g
Magnet B., Antarctica 136 P e
Magnetic I., Australia 135 J c
Magnetic Pole, N., North-West Territories 80 J c
Magnitogorsk, U.S.S.R. 117 P d
Magog, Quebec 85 S g
Magosol, Mexico 90 E c
Magpie, Quebec 82 H c
Magpie L., Quebec 82 H c
Magpie R., Ontario 84 F d
Magpie R., Quebec 82 H c
Magpie R., West, Quebec 82 G b
Magrath, Alberta 86 E j
Magua, I., Guam 78 B k
Maguse River, N.-W. Terr. 81 K e
Magwe, Burma 127 J d
Mahabad, Iran 124 E b
Mahabaleshwar, India 126 D e
Mahaddei Uen, Somali Rep. 121 K d
Mahadeo Hills, India 126 E d
Mahail, Saudi Arabia 124 D f
Mahajamba, B. de, Mal. Rep. 121 N k
Mahalapye, Botswana 122 D d
Mahallat, Iran 125 F c
Mahanadi R., India 127 F d
Mahanoro, Mal. Rep. 121 N k
Mahbubnagar, India 126 E e
Mahdia, Tunisia 119 H a
Mahe, India 126 E f
Mahendragiri, Mt., India 127 F e
Maher, Ontario 84 J c
Mahia Pen., New Zealand 135 S k
Mahmed-Hussein-magala. See Shahsavar
Mahmudabad, Iran 125 F b
Mahone Bay, Nova Scotia 82 H j
Mahua, Mozambique 121 H g
Mahuva, India 126 D d
Maiã, I., Manua Is. 79 S o
Maicasagi R., Quebec 85 O c
Maida, Yemen 124 D f
Maidan, Afghanistan 125 J c
Maidstone, England 99 H j
Maidstone, Saskatchewan 86 H e
Maiduguri, Nigeria 119 H f
Maienfeld, Switzerland 101 E a
Maihar, India 126 F d
Maikal Ra., India 126 F d
Maikop, U.S.S.R. 114 D d
Maillardville, Br. Columbia 88 E f
Maimana, Afghanistan 125 H b
Main-à-Dieu, C. Breton I., Nova Scotia 83 N h
Main Barrier Ra., Australia 135 H f
Main Brook, Newfoundland 83 Q b
Main Centre, Saskatchewan 86 K h
Main Chan., Ontario 84 J g
Main Duck I., Ontario 85 O j
Maine, prov., France 108 C b
Maine-et-Loire, dep., France 108 C c
Maing Kaing, Burma 127 J d
Maingkwan, Burma 127 J c
Mainpuri, India 126 E c
Main R., Germany 104 C d
Main Topsail, pk., Nfd. 85 Q d
Mainz, Germany 104 C d
Maipo, Mt., Argentina 94 C d
Maipú, Argentina 94 E e
Maiquetía, Venezuela 92 D a
Maisonneuve, Quebec 85 S j
Maissin, Belgium 100 D e
Mait & I., Somali Republic 121 K b
Maitland, Australia 135 K f
Maitland, L., Australia 134 D e
Maitland, Nova Scotia 82 J h
Maitland Bridge, Nova Scotia 82 G j
Maíz, Mexico 90 E c
Maizuru, Japan 133 D g
Maja, I., Indonesia 129 E l
Majagual, Colombia 92 C b
Majmaa, Saudi Arabia 124 E d
Major, Saskatchewan 86 H g
Majorca (Mallorca), Balearic Is. 107 G c
Majunga, Mal. Rep. 121 N k
Majuro, Is., Marshall Is. 79 U g
Majuro Lagoon, Majuro Is. 79 U g
Makabe, I., Okinawa 78 A d
Makale, Ethiopia 121 H b
Makania, Tanzania 121 H e
Makariev, U.S.S.R. 117 F b
Makarvey, U.S.S.R. 117 G b
Makassar, Celebes 129 G m
Makassar Str., Indonesia 129 G l
Makedhonia, Greece 113 C d
Makemo, I., Tuamotu Arch. 79 M j
Makeruru, I., Palau Is. 78 B n
Makeyevka, Ukraine, U.S.S.R. 116 K g
Makhach Kala, U.S.S.R. 114 D d
Makhai, China 128 B c
Makin, I., Gilbert Is. 78 H g
Makinak, Manitoba 86 S h
Makindu, Kenya 121 H e
Makinson Inlet, N.-W. Terr. 81 M b
Makkinga, Netherlands 100 E b
Makkovik, Labrador 81 O f
Makla, Jeb. el, Saudi Arabia 124 C d
Makó, Hungary 112 C a
Makokibatan L., Ontario 84 C a
Makongolosi, Tanzania 121 G f
Makorako, Mt., New Zealand 135 R k
Makram, Saudi Arabia 124 C e
Makri, India 126 F e
Makri. See Fethiye
Maksamaa, Finland 102 K e
Maksmo. See Maksamaa
Maku, Iran 124 D b
Makum, India 127 J c
Makurdi, Nigeria 118 G g
Makwa L., Saskatchewan 86 H d
Makwiro, Rhodesia 122 E c
Malá, Peru 92 B f
Malabang, Philippines 129 H j
Malabar Coast, India 126 D f
Malabu, Nigeria 119 H g
Malacca, Malaysia 129 D k
Malacca, Str. of, Sumatra-Malaysia 129 D k
Malachi, Ontario 86 G a
Maladeta, Mt., Spain 107 F a
Málaga, Spain 106 C d
Malagasy Rep. (Madagascar), I., Indian Ocean 121 N l
Malaita, Solomon Is. 78 F h
Malakal, I., Palau Is. 78 B n
Malakal, Sudan 119 M g
Malakal Harb., Palau Is. 78 B n
Malakal Pass, Palau Is. 78 B n
Malakand & Pass, Pakistan 126 D b
Malån, Sweden 102 H d
Malang, Java 129 F m
Malanje, Angola 120 D f
Mälaren, L., Sweden 103 G g
Malargüé, Argentina 94 C e
Malartic, L., Quebec 85 M d
Malartic, Quebec 85 M d
Malaspina Str., Br. Columbia 88 G f
Malathia, Kenya 121 H e
Malatya, Turkey 120 C b
Malawi (Nyasaland), East Africa 121 G g
Malaya. See Malaysia
Malayer, Iran 124 E c
Malaysia, South-East Asia 129 D j
Malazgirt, Turkey 124 D b
Mal B., Quebec 82 H e
Malbaie R., Quebec 82 B f
Malbork, Poland 105 H a
Malchow, Germany 104 E b
Malda, India 127 G c
Maldegem, Belgium 100 B c
Malden I., Pacific Ocean 79 L h
Maldon, England 99 H j
Maldonado, Uruguay 94 F d
Maléa, C., Greece 113 D f
Malé Karpaty, Czech. 105 G d
Malekula, I., New Hebrides 78 G j
Máleme, Crete 113 D g
Malesherbes, France 108 E b
Mali, W. Africa 118 E e
Malignant Cove, Nova Scotia 83 K h
Maliksha, India 126 E a
Malinau, Borneo 129 G k
Malindi, Kenya 121 J e
Malines, Belgium 100 C c
Malin Hd., Eire 98 C e
Malkangiri, India 127 F e
Malko Tŭrnovo, Bulgaria 112 F d
Mallaig, Alberta 86 F d
Mallaig, Scotland 98 D c
Mállia G., Crete 113 E g
Mallorca. See Majorca
Mallorytown, Ontario 85 P h
Mallow, Eire 99 B h
Malmberget, Sweden 102 J c
Malmédy, Belgium 100 E d
Malmesbury, England 99 F j
Malmö, Sweden 103 E j
Malmyzh, U.S.S.R. 117 K b
Maloelap, I., Marshall Is. 79 U b
Maloggia, Switzerland 101 E b
Malolos, I., Guam 78 A l
Malombe L., Malawi 121 H g
Malone, Ontario 85 N h
Malonga, Congo 120 E g
Malpelo I., Pacific Ocean 79 S g
Malpeque B., Prince Edward I. 82 J g
Malta, I., Mediterranean Sea 111 E h
Malta Chan., Medit. Sea 111 E g
Malters, Switzerland 101 D a
Malton, airport, Ontario 85 L j
Malton, England 99 G f
Malung, Sweden 103 E f
Malvaglia, Switzerland 101 D b
Malvan, India 126 D e
Malvern Hills, England 99 F h
Malvinas, Islas. See Falkland Is.
Malwa, India 126 F c
Mama, U.S.S.R. 115 L c
Mamainse Point, Ontario 84 F e
Mamantel, Mexico 90 F d
Mambasa, Congo 121 F d
Mameigweiss L., Ontario 86 L a
Ma-me-o Beach, Alberta 86 D f
Mammamattawa, Ontario 84 F b
Mamonal, Colombia 92 B a
Mamou, Guinea 118 C f
Mampoko, Congo 120 D d
Mamu, Afghanistan 125 H d
Mamudju, Celebes 129 G l
Man, I. of, Irish Sea 99 E f
Man, Ivory Coast 118 D g
Manacapurú, Brazil 92 E d
Manacor, Balearic Is. 107 G c
Manado, Celebes 129 H k
Mañagaha, I., Saipan-Tinian Is. 78 A d
Managua, Nicaragua 91 B d
Managua L., Nicaragua 91 B d
Manakha, Yemen 124 D f
Manamah, Bahrein I. 124 F d
Mananjary, Mal. Rep. 121 N l
Manantenina, Mal. Rep. 121 N l
Manapouri L., New Zealand 135 P m
Manasarowar, L., Tibet 126 F b
Manati, Puerto Rico 54 C h
Manaus, Brazil 92 E d
Manawan L., Saskatchewan 87 O c
Manche, dep., France 108 C b
Manchester, England 99 F g
Manchouli, China 128 G a
Manchuria, China 128 H a
Mancora, Peru 92 A d
Manda. See Mbamba Bay
Mandal, Norway 103 B g
Mandalay, Burma 127 J d
Mandal Gobi, Mongolia 128 E a
Mandarin B., China 131 E m
Mander, Netherlands 100 E b
Mandera, Kenya 121 J d
Mandi, India 126 E b
Mandih, Philippines 129 H j
Mandla, India 126 F d
Mandritsara, Mal. Rep. 121 N k
Mandvi, India 126 C d
Manfredonia, G. di, Italy 111 F e
Manfuha, Saudi Arabia 124 E e
Mangaia, I., Cook Is. 78 K j
Mangaldai, India 127 H c
Mangalme, Chad 119 J f
Mangalore, India 126 D f
Mangaréva, I., Tuamotu Arch. 79 N k
Mangfall Geb., Germany 104 D e
Manglaralto, Ecuador 92 A d
Mangrol, India 126 D d
Mangualde, Portugal 106 B b
Mangueira, L. da, Brazil 94 F d
Manhay, Belgium 100 D d
Manhuaça, Brazil 93 J h
Manicoré, Brazil 92 E e
Manicouagan L., Quebec 82 D b
Manicouagan Pen. & R., Quebec 82 D d
Manifold, C., Australia 135 K d
Manigotan, Manitoba 87 V g
Manihiki, I., Pacific Ocean 78 K h
Manikpur, E. Pakistan 126 F c
Manila, Philippines 129 H h
Manipur (Imphal), India 127 H c
Manisa, Turkey 124 A b
Manitoba, L., Manitoba 87 T h
Manitoba, prov., Canada 80 J f
Manito L., Saskatchewan 86 H f
Manitou, Manitoba 87 T j
Manitou Beach, Sask. 87 M g
Manitou L., Lower, Ontario 86 K a
Manitou L., Ontario 84 J g
Manitou L., Quebec 82 J c
Manitou L., Upper, Ontario 86 J a
Manitoulin I., Ontario 84 H g
Manitou R., Quebec 82 G b
Manitouwadge, Ontario 84 E c
Manitouwadge L., Ontario 84 E c
Manitowaning, Ontario 84 J g
Manitowik L., Ontario 84 F d
Maniwaki, Quebec 85 P f
Maniyah, Iraq 124 D c
Manizales, Colombia 92 B b
Manja, Mal. Rep. 121 M l
Manjimup, Australia 134 C f
Manka, Taiwan 131 K k
Mankota, Saskatchewan 86 K j
Manlleu, Spain 107 G a
Manmad, India 126 D d
Mann, I., Kwajalein Is. 79 U e
Mannar, Ceylon 126 E g
Mannar, G. of, India 126 E g
Mannargudi, India 126 E f
Mannheim, Germany 104 C d
Manning, Alberta 88 L b
Manning Prov. Park, British Columbia 88 J f
Mannville, Alberta 86 F e
Manoa, Bolivia 92 D e
Manokwari, W. Irian 129 K l
Manono, Congo 120 F f
Manor, Saskatchewan 87 P j
Manosque, France 109 F e
Manouane, R., Quebec 85 Q e
Manouane L. & R., Quebec 82 B c
Manresa, Spain 107 F b
Mansa, Zambia 122 D b
Manseau, Quebec 85 T f
Mansel I., N.-W. Territories 81 L e
Mansfield, England 99 G g
Mansi, Burma 127 J d
Mansilla de Las Mulas, Spain 106 C a
Manson Creek, Br. Columbia 88 G c
Manta, Ecuador 92 A d
Mantario, Saskatchewan 86 H g
Mant I., Ponape I. 78 G n
Mantova. See Mantua
Mantua, Italy 110 C c
Manú, Peru 92 C f
Manua Is., American Samoa 78 K j
Manuan, Quebec 85 Q e
Manuanis L., Quebec 82 B c
Manuel Rodriguez, I., Chile 95 B h
Manujan, Iran 125 G d
Manukau Harb., N. Zealand 135 R k
Manus I., Admiralty Is. 78 E g
Manyberries, Alberta 86 G j
Many Island L., Alberta 86 G h
Manyoni, Tanzania 121 G f
Manzala L., Egypt 119 M b
Manzanares, Spain 106 D c
Manzanillo, Cuba 91 D b
Manzanillo, Mexico 90 D d
Manzanillo, Pta., Panama 91 D e
Manzini, Swaziland 122 E e
Mao, Chad 119 J f
Map, I., Yap I. 78 D l
Mapia Is., Pacific Ocean 78 D g
Mapimí, Mexico 90 D b
Mapire, Venezuela 92 E b
Maple Creek, Saskatchewan 86 H j
Maqainama, Saudi Arabia 124 E e
Maqatin, S. Yemen 124 E g
Maqna, Saudi Arabia 124 B d
Maquela do Zombo, Angola 120 D f
Maquereau, Pte. au, cape, Quebec 82 H e
Maquinchao, Argentina 95 C f
Mara, South Africa 122 D d
Maraã, Brazil 92 D d
Marabá, Brazil 93 H e
Maracá, I. de, Brazil 93 G c
Maracaçumé, Brazil 93 H d
Maracaibo, L. de, Venezuela 92 C b
Maracaibo, Venezuela 92 C a
Maracanã, Brazil 93 H d
Maracay, Venezuela 92 D a
Marada, Libya 119 J c
Maradi, Niger 118 G f
Maragheh, Iran 124 E b
Maragogi, Brazil 93 K e
Marajó, Brazil 93 H d
Marakei, I., Gilbert Is 78 H g
Marakwet, Kenya 121 H d
Maralinga, Australia 134 F f
Maramures, Romania 105 K e
Marand, Iran 124 E b
Maranguape, Brazil 93 K d
Marañon, R., Peru 92 B d
Maras, Turkey 124 C b
Marathon, Ontario 84 D d
Maraú, Brazil 93 K f
Maravilha, Brazil 92 D e
Marbella, Spain 106 C d
Marble Bar, Australia 134 C d
Marbleton, Quebec 85 T g
Marc, L., Labrador 82 J a
Marceau L., Quebec 82 F b
Marcelin, Saskatchewan 86 L f
Marcelino, Brazil 92 D c
Marchand, Manitoba 86 F a
Marche, Belgium 100 D d
Marche, reg., Italy 110 D d
Marchena, Spain 106 C d
Marchin, Belgium 100 D d
Mar Chiquita, Argentina 94 D d
Marcus I., Pacific Ocean 78 F d
Mardan, Pakistan 126 D b
Mar del Plata, Argentina 95 E e
Mardin, Turkey 124 D b
Marechal Deodoro. See Alagoas
Maree, L., Scotland 98 D c
Mareeba, Australia 135 J c
Marengo, Saskatchewan 86 H g
Marganets, Ukraine, U.S.S.R. 116 J h
Margaree Harbour, Cape Breton I., Nova Scotia 83 L g
Margaret Bay, Br. Columbia 88 F e
Margarita, I., Venezuela 92 E a
Margarites, Crete 113 E g
Margate, England 99 H j
Margie, Alberta 88 O c
Margo, Saskatchewan 87 O g
Marguerite, Br. Columbia 88 H d
Marguerite B., Antarctica 136 H e
Marguerite B., Quebec 82 F d
Maria, Quebec 82 F e
Maria I., Tabuai Is. 79 L j
Marianao, Cuba 91 C b
Marianas, Is., Pacific Ocean 78 E e
Marianske Lázně. See Marienbad
Mariapolis, Manitoba 87 T j
Maria van Diemen, C., New Zealand 135 Q j
Marib, Yemen 124 D f
Maribor, Yugoslavia 110 E b
Maridi, Sudan 119 L h
Mariefred, Sweden 103 G g
Marie Galante, I., Leeward Is. 91 G c
Mariehamn, Finland 103 H f
Marie L., Alberta 86 G d
Marienbad (Marianske Lázně), Czechoslovakia 104 E d
Marienberg, Netherlands 100 E b
Marienbourg, Belgium 100 C d
Marienburg. See Malbork
Mariental, S.W. Africa 122 B d
Mariestad, Sweden 103 E g
Marieville, Quebec 85 R g
Mariiru Pt., Rota I. 78 A j
Marina Fall, Guyana 92 F b
Marinha Grande, Portugal 106 A c
Maritsa R., Bulgaria, etc. 112 E d
Mariyampole. See Kapsukas
Mariyskaya A.S.S.R., U.S.S.R. 114 D c
Marj, el, Libya 119 K b
Marjamaa, Estonia, U.S.S.R. 103 L g
Markala, Mali 118 D f
Markapur, India 126 E e
Markdale, Ontario 84 K h
Markelo, Netherlands 100 E b
Marken, I., Netherlands 100 D b
Market Drayton, England 99 F h
Market Harborough, England 99 G h
Markham, L., Tibet 127 F a
Markham, Mt., Antarctica 136 A b
Markham, Ontario 85 L j
Markinch, Saskatchewan 87 N h
Markovo, U.S.S.R. 115 S b
Marks, U.S.S.R. 117 H e
Markstay, Ontario 84 K f
Marlbank, Ontario 85 N h
Marlborough, Guyana 92 F b
Marmagão, India 126 D e
Marmande, France 109 D d
Marmara, Sea of, Turkey 124 A a
Marmaris, Turkey 124 A b
Marmion L., Ontario 86 L a
Marmora, Ontario 85 N h
Marne, dep., France 108 F b
Maroua, Cameroon 119 H f
Marouf Junction, Quebec 85 L d
Marouini, R., Fr. Guiana 93 G c
Marquesas Is., Pacific Ocean 79 N h
Marquette, Manitoba 87 U h
Marquina, Spain 107 D a
Marquis, Saskatchewan 87 M h
Marrakech. See Marrakesh
Marrakesh, Morocco 118 D b
Marree, Australia 134 G e
Marris, India 126 C c
Marsabit, Kenya 121 H d
Marsa Hali, Saudi Arabia 124 D f
Marsala, Sicily 111 D g
Marsden, Saskatchewan 86 H f
Marseille, France 109 F e
Marshall, Saskatchewan 85 H e
Marshall Is., Pacific Ocean 78 G f
Marshall L., Ontario 84 C b
Marsh Harbour, Bahama Is. 91 D a
Marstrand, Sweden 103 D h
Marsum, Netherlands 100 D a
Martaban, Burma 127 J e
Martaban, G. of, Burma 127 J e
Martelange, Belgium 100 D e
Marten R., Quebec 85 P a
Martigny Ville, Switzerland 101 C b
Martina, Switzerland 101 F b
Martinho, Brazil 93 F e
Martinique I., Windward Is. 91 G d
Martin Pen., Antarctica 136 F d
Marton, New Zealand 135 R l
Martos, Spain 106 D d
Maruf, Afghanistan 125 J c
Marugame, Japan 133 C g
Marum, Netherlands 100 E a
Marvejols, France 109 E d
Marwayne, Alberta 86 G e
Mary, Turkmen., U.S.S.R. 114 F e
Maryborough, Australia 135 H g

Maryborough, Australia 135 K e
Maryborough. See Portlaoise
Marydale, South Africa 122 C e
Maryfield, Saskatchewan 87 Q j
Mary Henry, Mt., British Columbia 88 G a
Mary Kathleen, Australia 135 H d
Maryport, England 99 E f
Mary's Harbour, Labrador 83 R a
Marystown, Newfoundland 83 R f
Marysville, New Brunswick 82 F h
Más Afuera, I., Pacific Oc. 79 R m
Masaka, Uganda 121 G e
Masalog, I., Guam 78 B l
Masangena, Mozambique 122 E d
Masara, Mozambique 122 E c
Masasi, Tanzania 121 H g
Más-á-Tierra, Juan Fernández Is. 79 R m
Masaya, Nicaragua 91 B d
Masbate, I., Philippines 129 H h
Mascara, Algeria 119 F a
Masefau B., Tutuila I. 79 U o
Masefield, Saskatchewan 86 K j
Masères, L., Quebec 85 P d
Maseru, Lesotho 122 D e
Mashaki, Afghanistan 125 J c
Mashhad, Iran 125 G b
Mashkode, Ontario 84 F e
Mashkol, Hamun-i-, Pakistan 126 B c
Masi-Manimba, Congo 120 D e
Masindi, Uganda 121 G d
Masira, G. of, Saudi Arabia 125 G f
Masira Chan., Saudi Arabia 125 G e
Masira I., Muscat & Oman 125 G e
Masjed Soleyman, Iran 124 E c
Maskinongé, Quebec 85 R f
Mask L., Eire 99 A g
Masoala C., Mal. Rep. 119 P k
Mason Creek, Br. Columbia 88 H b
Masöy, Norway 102 L a
Massa, Italy 110 C c
Massafra, Italy 111 F e
Massakori, Chad 119 J f
Massapê, Brazil 93 J d
Massawa, Ethiopia 121 H a
Massénya, Chad 119 J f
Masset, Graham I., British Columbia 88 C d
Masset Inlet, Queen Charlotte Is., British Columbia 88 C d
Masseube, France 109 D e
Massey, Ontario 84 H f
Massinga, Mozambique 122 F d
Masson, Quebec 85 P g
Masson I., Antarctica 136 R e
Masson Ra., Antarctica 136 R e
Masterton, New Zealand 135 R l
Mastuf, W. Pakistan 126 D a
Mastung, Pakistan 126 C c
Mastura, Saudi Arabia 124 C e
Masulipatnam, India 126 F e
Masyaf, Syria 123 E b
Mata Amarilla, Argentina 95 B g
Matachewan, Ontario 84 K e
Matador, Saskatchewan 86 K h
Matafao, Tutuila I. 79 U o
Matagalpa, Nicaragua 91 B d
Matagami, Quebec 85 N c
Matagami L., Quebec 85 N c
Matale, Ceylon 120 F g
Matam, Senegal 118 C e
Matamoros, Mexico 90 D b
Matamoros, Mexico 90 E b
Matamoros, Mexico 90 E d
Matane & R., Quebec 82 E e
Matanzas, Cuba 91 C b
Matapedia, Quebec 82 F f
Matapedia L. & R., Quebec 82 E e
Matapozuelos, Spain 106 C b
Matara, Ceylon 126 F g
Mataram, Lombok I., Indon. 129 G m
Mataranka, Australia 134 F b
Mataró, Spain 107 G b
Matatiele, South Africa 122 D f
Matauale, Brazil 93 G c
Mataura, New Zealand 135 P m
Matawai, New Zealand 135 R k
Matawin, R., Quebec 85 R f
Matchi-Manitou, L., Quebec 85 N e
Matehuala, Mexico 90 D c
Matera, Italy 111 F e
Mátészalka, Hungary 105 K e
Mateur, Tunisia 119 G a
Matfors, Sweden 102 G e
Matha Str., Antarctica 136 H e
Matheson, Ontario 84 K d
Matheson Island, Manitoba 87 V g
Mathura, India 126 E c
Matiara, India 127 G c
Matinenda L., Ontario 84 G f
Matlock, England 99 F g
Matna, Sudan 119 N f
Mato Grosso, Brazil 92 F f
Matonipi L., Quebec 82 C b
Matonipis L., Quebec 82 C b
Matrah, Muscat & Oman 129 G e
Matruh, Egypt 119 L b
Matsue, Japan 133 C g
Matsumoto, Japan 133 F f
Matsushima, Japan 133 G e
Matsuyama, Japan 133 C h
Mattagami, R., Ontario 84 H b
Mattagami Heights, Ontario 84 J d
Mattagami L., Ontario 84 J e
Mattawa, Ontario 85 M f
Mattawin, Quebec 85 S f
Matterhorn, Mt., Switzerland-Italy 101 C c
Matthew Town, Bahama Is. 91 E b
Mattice, Ontario 84 G c
Matucana, Peru 92 B f
Matun, Afghanistan 125 J c
Matu One, Society Is. 79 L j
Matura, Brazil 92 D d
Maturín, Venezuela 92 E b
Matvaieva, U.S.S.R. 117 N b
Mau, India 126 E c
Maubeuge, France 108 E a
Maubin, Burma 127 J e
Maubourguet, France 109 D e
Maudheim, Antarctica 136 L d
Mauele, Mozambique 122 E d
Maués, Brazil 93 F d
Mauléon Licharre, France 109 C e
Maurice, L., Australia 134 F e
Mauritania, W. Africa 118 C d
Mauritius, I., Indian Ocean 121 L a
Maurs, France 109 E d
Maury B., Antarctica 136 T e
Mawdesley L., Manitoba 87 R d
Mawer, Saskatchewan 86 L h
Mawk Mai, Burma 127 J d
Mawlaik, Burma 127 H d
Maxcanú, Mexico 90 G c
Maxstone, Saskatchewan 86 L j
Maxville, Ontario 85 Q g
May, I. of, Scotland 98 F d
Mayaguana I., Bahamas Is. 91 E b
Mayagüez, Puerto Rico 54 B h
Mayari, Cuba 91 D b
Mayen, Germany 104 B c
Mayenne, dep., France 108 C b
Mayerthorpe, Alberta 88 M d
Mayfair, Saskatchewan 86 K e
Maymont, Saskatchewan 86 K f
Maymyo, Burma 127 J d
Maynooth, Ontario 85 N g
Mayno Pyl'gino, U.S.S.R. 115 S b
Mayo, co., Eire 99 A g
Mayoumba, Gabon 120 C e
Mayr Mt., Antarctica 136 M d
Mayuram, India 126 E f
Maza, Argentina 94 D e
Mazabuka, Zambia 122 D c
Mazagan, Morocco 118 D b
Mazagão, Brazil 93 G d
Mazamet, France 109 E e
Mazán, Argentina 94 C c
Mazán, Peru 92 C d
Mazapil, Mexico 90 D c
Mazara del Vallo, Sicily 111 D g
Mazaredo, Argentina 95 C g
Mazar-i-Sharif, Afghanistan 125 J b
Mazarrón, Spain 107 E d
Mazatenango, Guatemala 90 F e
Mazatlán, Mexico 90 C c
Mažeikiai, Lithuania, U.S.S.R. 103 K h
Mazenod, Saskatchewan 86 L j
Mazeppa, Alberta 86 D h
Mbabane, Swaziland 122 E e
Mbale, Uganda 121 G d
Mbamba Bay, Tanzania 121 G g
Mbana Bay, Tanzania 121 G l
Mbandaka, Congo 120 D d
Mbarangandu, Tanzania 121 H g
Mbarara, Uganda 121 G e
Mbeya, Tanzania 121 G f
Meacham, Saskatchewan 87 M f
Mead, Ontario 84 G c
Meadow Lake, Sask. 86 J d
Meadow Lake Prov. Park, Saskatchewan 86 H d
Meadow Portage, Manitoba 87 S g
Meaford, Ontario 84 K h
Meaghers Grant, Nova Scotia 82 J j
Mealy Mts., Labrador 81 O g
Meander River, Alberta 88 L a
Meath, co., Eire 99 C g
Meath Park, Saskatchewan 87 M e
Mecatina I., Gt., Quebec 83 O c
Mecatina I., Little, Quebec 83 N c
Mecca, Saudi Arabia 124 C e
Mechelen, Belgium 100 D d
Mechelen. See Malines
Mécheria, Algeria 118 E b
Mechol, Yap I. 78 D l
Meck, Kwajalein Is. 79 U e
Medak, India 126 E e
Medak, Yugoslavia 110 E c
Medan, Sumatra 129 C k
Médanos, Argentina 95 D e
Medellín, Colombia 92 B b
Medemblik, Netherlands 100 D b
Médenine, Tunisia 119 H b
Meder, Ethiopia 121 J b
Medgidia, Romania 112 G b
Medias, Romania 112 E a
Medicine Hat, Alberta 86 G h
Medicine R., Alberta 86 C f
Medina, Saudi Arabia 124 C e
Medinaceli, Spain 107 D b
Medina del Campo, Spain 106 C b
Medina de Rioseco, Spain 106 C b
Medina Sidonia, Spain 106 C d
Médine, Mali 118 C f
Mediterranean Sea, Southern Europe, etc 97 J j
Mednogorsk, U.S.S.R. 117 N e
Medora, Manitoba 87 R j
Medstead, Saskatchewan 86 J e
Meductic, New Brunswick 82 E g
Medvezhegorsk, U.S.S.R. 114 C b
Medvezhi Osa., U.S.S.R. 115 R a
Medvezhiy Ova., U.S.S.R. 115 R a
Medyado, Jaluit I. 79 U h
Medyai, Jaluit I. 79 U h
Meekatharra, Australia 134 C e
Meelpaeg L., Newfoundland 83 Q e
Meenin. See Menin
Meerle, Belgium 100 C c
Meerlo, Netherlands 100 E c
Meersburg, Germany 104 C e
Meersen, Netherlands 100 D d
Meerut, India 126 E c
Meeting Creek, Alberta 86 E f
Meetoos, Saskatchewan 86 K e
Meeuwen, Belgium 100 D c
Mega, Ethiopia 121 H d
Megalópolis, Greece 113 D f
Mégantic & L., Quebec 82 B h
Mégara, Greece 113 D e
Megiddo, Israel 123 D e
Mégiscane, L., Quebec 85 P d
Mehar, Pakistan 126 C c
Mehin, Syria 123 F c
Meighen I., N.-W. Terr. 81 K a
Meihsien, China 131 H k
Meikle, R., Alberta 88 K b
Meiktila, Burma 127 J d
Meiningen, Germany 104 D c
Meiringen, Switzerland 101 D b
Meissen, Germany 104 E c
Meitene, Latvia, U.S.S.R. 103 K h
Mejato, Kwajalein Is. 79 T e
Mejillones, Chile 94 B b
Mejit, I., Marshall Is. 79 U a
Mekatina, Ontario 84 F e
Meknès Morocco 118 D b
Mekong, R., Cambodia, etc. 132 D d
Melanesia, Pacific Ocean 78 E g
Melaval, Saskatchewan 86 L j
Melbourne, Australia 135 J g
Melchett L., Ontario 84 D b
Melchor Ocampo, Mexico 90 D d
Meldrum Bay, Ontario 84 G g
Meleb, Manitoba 87 U h
Melekeiok, Palau Is. 78 C m
Melfi, Italy 111 E e
Melfort, Saskatchewan 87 N f
Meligalá, Greece 113 C f
Melilla, Morocco 118 E a
Melipilla, Chile 94 B d
Melita, Manitoba 87 Q j
Melitopol, Ukraine, U.S.S.R 116 J h
Melk, Austria 104 F d
Melle, France 108 C c
Mellier, Belgium 100 D e
Mellingen, Switzerland 101 D a
Mellish Reef, Coral Sea 78 F j
Mellu, Kwajalein Is. 79 U e
Melo, Uruguay 94 F d
Melona, Israel 123 D e
Melreux, Belgium 100 D d
Melrose, Nova Scotia 83 K h
Melton Mowbray, England 99 G h
Melun, France 108 E b
Melut, Sudan 119 M f
Melville, C., Australia 135 H b
Melville, L., Labrador 81 O g
Melville, Saskatchewan 87 P h
Melville B., Greenland 89 Q b
Melville I., Australia 134 F b
Melville I., N.-W. Terr. 81 H b
Melville Pen., N.-W. Terr. 81 L d
Melvin L., Eire-N. Ireland 99 B f
Melvin L., Manitoba 87 R a
Memba & B., Mozambique 121 J g
Membij, Syria 123 F a
Memel. See Klaipeda
Memphrémagog, L., Quebec-Vermont 85 T g
Memramcook, N. B. 82 H g
Menairi, Chad 119 K e
Menai Str., Wales 99 E g
Ménaka, Mali 118 F e
Menaskwagama, L., Quebec 83 L b
Mendak, Saudi Arabia 124 D e
Mendawai, R., Borneo 129 F l
Mende, France 109 E d
Mendebo Mts., Ethiopia 121 H c
Mendeleyer Ridge, Arctic Ocean 89 S a
Menderes, R., Turkey 124 A b
Mendham, Saskatchewan 86 H h
Mendip Hills, England 99 F j
Mendoza, Argentina 94 C d
Mendrisio, Switzerland 101 D c
Menfi, Sicily 111 D g
Meng Chai Nat, Thailand 132 C c
Meng Chumporn. See Chumporn
Menge, Jaluit I. 79 T j
Meng Fang, Thailand 132 B c
Meng Khemmarat, Thailand 132 D c
Meng Krabin. See Aranya
Meng Kuwi. See Kui Nua
Meng Phree, Thailand 132 B c
Meng Thoen, Thailand 132 B c
Mengtsz, China 128 D f
Meng Uthen. See Ban tha U
Menin, Belgium 100 B d
Menindee, Australia 133 H f
Menjapa, Mt., Borneo 129 G k
Menorca. See Minorca
Mentawai Is., Indonesia 129 C l
Menton, France 109 G e
Menzel Bourguiba, Tunisia 111 B g
Menzelinsk, U.S.S.R. 117 L c
Menzies, Australia 134 D e
Me'ono, Israel 123 D e
Meoqui, Mexico 90 C b
Meota, Saskatchewan 86 J e
Me-ping, R., Thailand 132 B c
Meppel, Netherlands 100 E b
Merabello G., Crete 113 E g
Merano, Italy 110 C b
Merasheen & I., Nfd. 83 S f
Meratus Peg, Borneo 129 G l
Merauke, W. Irian 129 M m
Merca, Somali Republic 121 J d
Mercara, India 126 E f
Mercedaria, Mt., Argentina 94 B d
Mercedes, Argentina 94 E d
Mercedes, Argentina 94 E c
Mercedes, Bolivia 92 D f
Mercedes, Uruguay 94 E d
Merchtem, Belgium 100 C d
Mercier Dam, Quebec 85 P f
Mercoal, Alberta 88 L d
Mercury Is. (Iles d'Haussez), New Zealand 135 R k
Mercy, C., N.-W. Terr. 81 N e
Mercy B., N.-W. Terr. 80 G c
Meredith, C., Falkland Is. 95 D h
Meregh, Somali Republic 121 K d
Mergentheim, Germany 104 C d
Mergui, Burma 127 J f
Mergui Arch., Burma 127 J f
Merid, Saskatchewan 86 H g
Mérida, Mexico 90 G c
Mérida, Spain 106 B c
Mérida & Cord. do, Venezuela 92 C b
Merioneth, co., Wales 99 E h
Merizo, Guam 78 A l
Merj Uyun, Lebanon 123 D d
Merlin, Ontario 84 H k
Merowe, Sudan 119 M e
Merredin, Australia 134 C f
Merrickville, Ontario 85 P h
Merritt, Br. Columbia 88 J e
Mersey, R., England 99 F g
Mersin, Turkey 124 B b
Mersing, Malaysia 129 D k
Mersis, Somali Republic 121 K d
Mersrags, Latvia, U.S.S.R. 103 K h
Merta, India 126 D c
Merthyr Tydfil, Wales 99 E j
Mertola, Portugal 106 B d
Mertz Glacier, Antarctica 136 A e
Meru, Kenya 121 H d
Meru, Mt., Tanzania 121 H e
Mervin, Saskatchewan 86 J e
Merxplas, Belgium 100 C c
Merzig, W. Germany 104 B d
Mesagne, Italy 111 F e
Mesakonan Pt., Quebec 85 L a
Mesará B., Crete 113 E g
Mesegon, Truk Is. 78 E o
Mesgouez, L., Quebec 85 P a
Meshchovsk, U.S.S.R. 116 J d
Meshghara, Lebanon 123 D d
Mesilinka, R., Br. Columbia 88 G b
Meskene, Syria 123 F a
Mesmiye, Syria 123 E d
Mesocco, Switzerland 101 E b
Mesolóngion, Greece 113 C e
Messancy, Belgium 100 D e
Messina, Sicily 111 E f
Messina, Str. di, Italy 111 E f
Messines, Belgium 100 A d
Messines, Quebec 85 O f
Messinía, G. of, Greece 113 D f
Messinía, Greece 113 C f
Mesudiye, Turkey 124 C a
Metagama, Ontario 84 J e
Meta L., Ontario 84 C b
Metalanim, Ponape I. 78 G o
Metán, Argentina 94 D c
Metangula, Mozambique 121 G g
Meta Pond, Newfoundland 83 S e
Meteghan, Nova Scotia 82 F j
Meteghan Sta., Nova Scotia 82 F j
Méthana Pen., Greece 113 D f
Methil, Scotland 98 E d
Methley, Manitoba 87 S g
Methven, New Zealand 135 Q l
Metionga L., Ontario 87 N a
Metis Beach, Quebec 82 E e
Metiskow, Alberta 86 G f
Metis L., Quebec 82 E e
Metkovic, Yugoslavia 112 A c
Metlika, Yugoslavia 110 E c
Metorica, Mozambique 121 H g
Métsovon, Greece 113 C e
Mettet, Belgium 100 C d
Mettlen, Switzerland 101 C b
Mettur Dam, India 126 E f
Metulla, Israel 123 D d
Metz, France 108 G b
Meulebeke, Belgium 100 B d
Meurthe-et-Moselle, dep., France 108 G b
Meuse, dep. & R., France 108 F b
Meuse R., Belgium 100 D d
Méxcala & R., Mexico 90 E d
Mexiana, I., Brazil 93 H d
Méxicali, Mexico 90 A a
Mexico, Cent. America 90 D c
Mexico, G. of, Mexico, etc 90 F b
México, Mexico 90 E d
Meyadin, Syria 124 D b
Meybod, Iran 125 F c
Meymac, France 108 E d
Meyronne, Saskatchewan 86 L j
Mèze, France 109 E e
Mezen', U.S.S.R. 114 D b
Mézières, France 108 F b
Mezöberemy Békés, Hungary 105 J e
Mezökövesd, Hungary 105 J e
Mezötúr, Hungary 105 J e
Mezquitic, Mexico 90 D c
Mgori, Tanzania 121 G e
Mhow, India 126 E d
Miahuatlán, Mexico 90 E d
Miajadas, Spain 106 C c
Miami, Manitoba 87 T j
Miandowab, Iraq 124 E b
Miandrívazo, Mal. Rep. 121 N k
Mianeh, Iran 124 E b
Miao-tao, I., China 130 K c
Miass, U.S.S.R. 117 Q c
Miastko, Poland 105 G a
Mica Creek, dam site, British Columbia 88 K d
Micay, Colombia 92 B c
Michailovsk, U.S.S.R. 117 L d
Micheh, China 130 E d
Michel, Br. Columbia 88 M f
Michel, Saskatchewan 86 H b
Michichi, Alberta 86 E g
Michikamau L., Labrador 81 N g
Michipicoten, Ontario 84 F e
Michipicoten B., Ontario 84 E e
Michipicoten I., Ontario 84 E e
Michipicoten R., Ontario 84 F e
Michoacan, state, Mexico 90 D d
Michurinsk, U.S.S.R. 117 E d
Micronesia, Pacific Ocean 78 F f
Midale, Saskatchewan 87 O j
Middelburg, Netherlands 100 B c
Middelburg, South Africa 122 D e
Middelharnis, Netherlands 100 C c
Middelkerke, Belgium 100 A c
Middlebro, Manitoba 86 F a
Middle Ground, Midway Is. 79 P b
Middle Lake, Saskatchewan 87 M f
Middle Ridge, Newfoundland 83 R e
Middlesbrough, England 99 G f
Middleton, England 99 F f
Middleton, Nova Scotia 82 G j
Middleton Reef, Tasman Sea 78 G k
Middlewood, Nova Scotia 82 H j
Midhurst, Ontario 85 L h
Midland, Ontario 84 L h
Midlandvale, Alberta 86 E g
Midlothian, co., Scotland 98 E e
Midnapore, Alberta 86 C h
Midnapore, India 127 G d
Midway, Br. Columbia 88 K f
Midway Is., Pacific Ocean 79 P b
Midye, Turkey 124 A a
Miécourt, Switzerland 101 C a
Miedzyrzec, Poland 105 K c
Mienning, China 128 D f
Mienyang, China 131 F g
Mienyang, China 130 B g
Mier, Mexico 90 E b
Mieres, Spain 106 C a
Migdal Gad. See Ashqelon
Mikado, Saskatchewan 87 P g
Mikhaylovgrad, Bulgaria 112 D c
Mikhaylovka, U.S.S.R. 117 F e
Mikkeli, Finland 103 M f
Mikkwa R., Alberta 88 M b
Mikonos I., Greece 113 E f
Milan, Quebec 82 A h
Milan. See Milano
Milano, Italy 110 B c
Milas, Turkey 124 A b
Milazzo, Sicily 111 E f
Milden, Saskatchewan 86 K g
Mildmay, Ontario 85 J h
Mildred, Saskatchewan 86 K e
Mildura, Australia 135 H f
Miléai, Greece 113 D e
Mil Entrance, Yap I. 78 D l
Miles, Australia 135 K e
Milestone, Saskatchewan 87 N j
Milford Haven, Wales 99 D j
Milford Sound, New Zealand 135 P m
Milgun, Australia 134 C e
Mili, Is., Marshall Is. 78 H g
Miliana, Algeria 118 F a
Milkovo, U.S.S.R. 115 Q c
Milk River, Alberta 86 E j
Milk River Ridge, Alberta 86 E j
Mill, Netherlands 100 D c
Millau, France 109 E d
Millbrook, Ontario 85 M h
Mille Lacs, L. des, Ontario 87 M b
Millerovo, U.S.S.R. 117 E f
Millerton, New Brunswick 82 G g
Millertown, Newfoundland 83 Q e
Millet, Alberta 86 D e
Mill I., Antarctica 136 S e
Mill I., N.-W. Territories 81 M e
Millicent, Alberta 86 F h
Millicent, Australia 134 H g
Milltown, New Brunswick 82 E h
Mill Village, Nova Scotia 82 H j
Millville, New Brunswick 82 E g
Milne B., Papua 135 K b
Milner Ridge, Manitoba 86 F a
Milnet, Ontario 84 K f
Milo, Alberta 86 E h
Milos, I., Greece 113 E f
Milparinka, Australia 135 H e
Milton, New Zealand 135 P m
Milton, Nova Scotia 82 H j
Milton, Ontario 84 L j
Miltown Malbay, Eire 99 A h
Milverton, Ontario 84 K j
Mimico, Ontario 85 L j
Mimika, W. Irian 129 L l
Mina al Ahmadī, Kuwait 124 E d
Minab, Iran 125 G d
Minago R., Manitoba 87 T d
Mina Hassan Tani, Morocco 118 D b
Minaki, Ontario 86 G a
Minas, Uruguay 94 E d
Minas Basin & Chan., Nova Scotia 82 H h
Minas de Riotinto, Spain 106 B d
Minas Novas, Brazil 93 J g
Minataree, Ontario 84 B b
Minatitlán, Mexico 90 F d
Minbu, Burma 127 H d
Minburn, Alberta 86 F e
Minch, Little, Scotland 98 C c
Minch, North, Scotland 98 C b
Mindanao, I., Philippines 129 J j
Minden, Germany 104 C b
Minden, Ontario 85 M h
Mindoro, I. & Str., Philippines 129 H h
Mine Centre, Ontario 86 K b
Mîneciu, Romania 112 F b
Mine Hd., Eire 99 B j
Minehead, England 99 E j
Minerva Reefs, Pacific Ocean 78 J k
Minga, Zambia 121 G g
Mingan, Quebec 82 H c
Mingan Chan. & Is., Quebec 82 H c
Mingan I., Quebec 82 H c
Mingan R., Quebec 82 J c
Mingechaur, Azerbai., U.S.S.R. 124 E a
Mingenew, Australia 134 C e
Mingin, Burma 127 H d
Minglanilla, Spain 107 E c
Mingoyo, Tanzania 121 H g
Mingshui, China 128 C b
Minhla, Burma 127 J e
Minicoy, I., India 126 D g
Minilya, Australia 134 B d
Miniota, Manitoba 87 Q h
Minipi L., Labrador 83 L a
Ministikwan L., Sask. 86 H d
Minitonas, Manitoba 87 Q f
Minna, Nigeria 118 G g
Minna Bluff, Antarctica 136 B c
Minna shima, Okinawa 78 A b
Minnedosa, Manitoba 87 S h
Minnewanka, L., Alberta 86 B g
Minnik, Syria 123 F a
Minnipuka, Ontario 84 G d
Minnitaki L., Ontario 86 K a
Miño (Minho), R., Spain-Portugal 106 A a
Miño, Spain 106 A a
Minorca (Menorca), I., Balearic Is. 107 H b
Min Shan, China 130 A e
Minsk, Belorussia, U.S.S.R. 116 E e
Minsk Mazowiecki, Poland 105 J b
Minto, L., Quebec 81 M f
Minto, Manitoba 87 R j
Minto, New Brunswick 82 F g
Minto Hd., N.-W. Territories 80 J c
Minton, Saskatchewan 87 N j
Minusinsk, U.S.S.R. 115 J c
Minya Konka, China 128 D e
Miquelon, Grande I., Atlantic Ocean 83 Q f
Miquelon, Quebec 85 O c
Miracema do Norte, Brazil 93 H e
Mirador, Brazil 93 J e
Miraflores, Colombia 92 C b
Mira Gut, C. Breton I., Nova Scotia 83 N g
Miraj, India 126 D e
Mirambeau, France 109 C d
Miramichi B., New Brunswick 82 G f
Miramichi R., Little S.W., New Brunswick 82 F g
Miramichi R., Main S.W., New Brunswick 82 F g
Miramichi R., N.W., N.B. 82 F f
Miramont, France 109 D d
Miram Shah, Pakistan 126 C b
Miranda, Argentina 94 E e
Miranda, Brazil 93 F h
Miranda. See Bonanza
Miranda de Ebro, Spain 106 D a
Miranda do Corvo, Portugal 106 A b
Miranda do Douro, Portugal 106 B b
Mirande, France 109 D e
Mirandela, Portugal 106 B b
Mirandilla, Spain 106 B c
Mirbat, Muscat & Oman 125 F f
Mirdum, Netherlands 100 D b
Mirebeau, France 108 D c
Mirim, L., Brazil 94 F d
Mirjaveh, Iran 125 H d
Mirnoye, U.S.S.R. 114 H b
Mirond L., Saskatchewan 87 P c
Mirosi, Romania 112 E b
Mirpur Khas, Pakistan 126 C c
Mirror, Alberta 86 D f
Mirtoan Sea, Greece 113 D f
Mirtos, Crete 113 E g
Mirt Padam, India 127 J c
Misato, Okinawa 78 B c
Miscouche, Prince Edward I. 82 J g
Miscou I., New Brunswick 82 H f
Miscou Pt., New Brunswick 82 H e
Mishibishu L., Ontario 84 E d
Mishomis, Quebec 85 P e
Mishrif, Saudi Arabia 124 D e
Misis, Turkey 124 C b
Miska, Saudi Arabia 124 D e
Miskolc, Hungary 105 J d
Misoöl, I., W. Irian 129 K l
Missanabie, Ontario 84 F d

Missinaibi L., *Ontario* 84 G d
Missinaibi R., *Ontario* 84 H b
Mission City, *Br. Columbia* 88 H f
Missisicabi, R., *Quebec* 85 L a
Mississagi, R., *Ontario* 84 G f
Mississippi L., *Ontario* 85 O g
Missolónghin.
See Mesolóngion
Missonga, *Ontario* 84 H d
Mistanipisipou R., *Quebec* 83 K b
Mistassibi R., N.E., *Quebec* 82 A c
Mistassibi R., *Quebec* 85 S c
Mistassini, L., *Quebec* 81 M g
Mistassini, *Quebec* 85 S d
Mistatim, *Saskatchewan* 87 O f
Mistawak L., *Quebec* 85 M c
Mistigougèche L., *Quebec* 82 D e
Mistretta, *Sicily* 111 E g
Misurata, *Libya* 119 J b
Mitala Maria, *Uganda* 121 G d
Mitchell, *Australia* 135 J e
Mitchell, *Ontario* 84 J j
Mitchell R., *Australia* 135 H c
Mitchell River, *Australia* 135 H c
Mitchelstown, *Eire* 99 B h
Mitchinamecus, L., *Quebec* 85 P e
Mithi, *Pakistan* 126 C d
Mithimna, *Greece* 113 F e
Mitilíni, *Lesbos, Greece* 113 F e
Mitishto R., *Manitoba* 87 S d
Mito, *Japan* 133 G f
Mitre Pk., *New Zealand* 135 P m
Mittelmark, *Germany* 104 E b
Mitú, *Colombia* 92 D c
Mitumba Mts., *Congo* 121 F e
Mitzic, *Gabon* 120 C d
Miyaji, *Okinawa* 78 C b
Miyako, *Japan* 133 H e
Miyandowab, *Iran* 124 E b
Miyazaki, *Japan* 133 B j
Mizda, *Libya* 119 H b
Mizen Hd., *Eire* 99 A j
Mizil, *Romania* 112 F b
Mizo Hills, *India* 127 H d
Mizque, *Bolivia* 92 D g
Mjölby, *Sweden* 103 F g
Mjosa, L., *Norway* 103 D f
Mladá Boleslav, *Czech.* 104 F c
Mlanje, Mt., *Malawi* 121 H h
Mława, *Poland* 105 J b
Mljet, I., *Yugoslavia* 110 F d
Mo, *Norway* 102 F c
Moak L., *Manitoba* 87 U c
Mo Ångsåg, *Sweden* 102 H e
Moberly Lake, *Br. Columbia* 88 J c
Mobert, *Ontario* 84 E d
Mocajuba, *Brazil* 93 H d
Moçambique, *Mozambique* 121 J h
Mocâmedes, *Angola* 120 C h
Mocha, *Yemen* 124 D g
Mochudi, *Botswana* 122 D d
Mocimboa-de-Praia, *Mozambique* 121 J g
Mocoa, *Colombia* 92 B c
Mocorito, *Mexico* 90 C b
Moctezuma, *Mexico* 90 D c
Moctezuma, *Mexico* 90 C b
Mocuba, *Mozambique* 122 F c
Mocuburi, *Mozambique* 121 H g
Modane, *France* 109 G d
Modave, *Belgium* 100 D d
Modena, *Italy* 110 C c
Modica, *Sicily* 111 E g
Modjamboli, *Congo* 120 E d
Mo-duc, *S. Vietnam* 132 D d
Modung, *China* 128 C e
Moen, *Truk Is.* 78 E n
Moengo, *Surinam* 93 G b
Mofa, *Ethiopia* 121 J b
Moffat, *Scotland* 98 E e
Mogadiscio (Mogadishu), *Somali Republic* 121 K d
Mogadishu. See Mogadiscio
Mogador, *Morocco* 118 D b
Mogadouro, *Portugal* 106 B b
Mogar, *Ethiopia* 121 H c
Mogaung, *Burma* 127 J c
Mogilev, *Belorussia, U.S.S.R.* 116 G e
Mogilev Podol'skiy, *Ukraine, U.S.S.R.* 116 E g
Mogocha, *U.S.S.R.* 115 L c
Mogochin, *U.S.S.R.* 114 H c
Mogok, *Burma* 127 J d
Mogu, *Ethiopia* 121 J d
Moguer, *Spain* 106 B d
Mohács, *Hungary* 112 B b
Mohammedia, *Algeria* 118 F a
Moheli I., *Comores Arch* 121 J g
Moho, *China* 115 M c
Mohoro, *Tanzania* 121 H f
Moirang, *India* 127 H d
Moisie & R., *Quebec* 82 F c
Moissac, *France* 109 D d
Moji, *Brazil* 93 H h
Mojikit L., *Ontario* 84 B b
Moju & R., *Brazil* 93 H d
Mokai, *New Zealand* 135 R k
Mokau R., *New Zealand* 135 R k
Mokolo, *Cameroon* 119 H f
Mokpo, *S. Korea* 128 J d
Mokshany, *U.S.S.R.* 117 G d
Mol, *Belgium* 100 D c
Molanosa, *Saskatchewan* 87 M d
Moldava, *Czechoslovakia* 105 J d
Moldavia, *Romania* 112 F a
Moldavia, *U.S.S.R.* 116 F h
Molde & Fd., *Norway* 102 B e
Moldova Veche, *Romania* 112 C b
Molepolole, *Botswana* 122 D d
Môle St. Nicolas, *Haiti* 91 E c
Molfetta, *Italy* 111 F e
Molina, *Chile* 94 B e
Molina, *Spain* 107 E c
Molina, *Spain* 107 E b
Moliro, *Congo* 121 G f
Mollendo, *Peru* 92 C g
Mollis, *Switzerland* 101 E a
Mollosund, *Sweden* 103 D g
Molndal, *Sweden* 103 E h
Molotov. See Perm
Molotovsk, *U.S.S.R.* 114 C b
Molotovsk, *U.S.S.R.* 117 J b
Molson, *Manitoba* 86 E a
Molson L., *Manitoba* 87 V d
Moltke Nunatak, *Antarctica* 136 K c
Molucca Pass, *Indonesia* 129 J k
Moluccas, Is., *Indonesia* 129 J l
Moma, *Mozambique* 121 H h
Mombasa, *Kenya* 121 H e
Mombetsu, *Japan* 133 H b
Momchilgrad, *Bulgaria* 112 E d
Momeik. See Mong-mit
Momignies, *Belgium* 100 C d
Momotombo, *Nicaragua* 91 B d
Mompós, *Colombia* 92 C b
Mön, I., *Denmark* 103 E j
Mona, I., *Puerto Rico* 54 B h
Monå Fd., *Finland* 102 K e
Monach I., *Scotland* 98 B c
Monaco, *S. Europe* 109 G e
Monadhliath Mts., *Scotland* 98 E c
Monaghan & co., *Eire* 99 C f
Mona Pass, *West Indies* 91 F c
Monarch, *Alberta* 86 D j
Monarch Mt., *Br. Columbia* 88 G e
Monashee Mts., *British Columbia* 80 H g
Monasterace Marina, *Italy* 111 F f
Monastir, *Sardinia* 111 B f
Monastir, *Tunisia* 119 H a
Monbuey, *Spain* 106 B a
Monchique, *Portugal* 106 A d
Monclova, *Mexico* 90 D b
Moncton, *New Brunswick* 82 H g
Mondoñedo, *Spain* 106 B a
Mondul, *Tanzania* 121 H e
Monemvasia, *Greece* 113 D f
Monet, *Quebec* 85 P d
Monetny, *U.S.S.R.* 117 Q b
Moneva, *Spain* 107 E b
Monforte, *Portugal* 106 B c
Monga, *Congo* 120 E d
Mongalla, *Sudan* 119 M g
Monger, L., *Australia* 134 C e
Möng-Hsu, *Burma* 127 J d
Monghyr, *India* 127 G c
Möng Kiang. See Mong Yai
Möng Kung, *Burma* 127 J d
Mong-mit, *Burma* 127 J d
Mongo, *Chad* 119 J f
Mongolia, *East Asia* 115 J d
Mongolia, Inner, *China* 115 K d
Mongonu, *Nigeria* 119 H f
Mongoumba, *Cent. Afr. Rep.* 119 J h
Möng-pai, *Burma* 127 J e
Möng Pan, *Burma* 127 J d
Möng Pawn, *Burma* 127 J d
Möng-Sit, *Burma* 127 J d
Mongu, *Zambia* 122 C c
Mong Yai, *Burma* 127 J d
Moniquira, *Colombia* 92 C b
Monitor, *Alberta* 86 G g
Monkey Bay, *Malawi* 122 E b
Monkira, *Australia* 134 H d
Monkton, *Ontario* 84 J j
Monmouth, Mt., *British Columbia* 88 H e
Monmouth & co., *Wales* 99 F j
Monnikendam, *Netherlands* 100 D b
Monopoli, *Italy* 111 F e
Monovar, *Spain* 107 E c
Monreal del Campo, *Spain* 107 E b
Monrovia, *Liberia* 118 C g
Mons, *Belgium* 100 B d
Monsanto, *Portugal* 106 B b
Monserrato, *Sardinia* 111 B f
Monster, *Netherlands* 100 C b
Mönsterås, *Sweden* 103 G h
Mont, *Belgium* 100 D d
Montagne Tremblante, Parc de la, *Quebec* 85 Q f
Montagny, *Quebec* 82 B g
Montague, *Prince Edward I.* 82 K g
Montague I., *Antarctica* 136 K g
Montaigu, *Belgium* 100 C d
Montalbán, *Spain* 107 E b
Montánchez, *Spain* 106 B c
Montargis, *France* 108 E c
Montauban, *France* 109 D d
Montbard, *France* 108 F c
Montblanch, *Spain* 107 F b
Montbrison, *France* 108 F d
Montcevelles, L., *Quebec* 83 M b
Montcornet, *France* 108 F b
Mont de Marsan, *France* 109 C e
Montdidier, *France* 108 E b
Mont Dore, Le, *France* 108 E d
Monte Alegre, *Brazil* 93 G d
Monte Alegre, *Brazil* 93 H g
Montebello, *Quebec* 85 Q g
Monte Carlo, *Monaco* 109 G e
Monte Carmelo, *Brazil* 93 H g
Monte Caseros, *Argentina* 94 E d
Monte Comán, *Argentina* 94 C d
Monte Cristi, *Dom. Rep.* 91 E c
Montecristo, I., *Italy* 110 C d
Montefrío, *Spain* 106 C d
Montego Bay, *Jamaica* 91 D c
Montélimar, *France* 109 F d
Montemorelos, *Mexico* 90 E b
Montenegro, *Yugoslavia* 112 B c
Montereau, *France* 108 E b
Montería, *Colombia* 92 B b
Montero, *Bolivia* 92 E g
Monteros, *Argentina* 94 C c
Monterrey, *Mexico* 90 D b
Monte Sant' Angelo, *Italy* 111 E e
Montes Claros, *Brazil* 93 J g
Montevideo, *Uruguay* 94 E d
Montfort-sur-Meu, *France* 108 B b
Montgomery, *Pakistan* 126 D b
Montgomery & co., *Wales* 99 E h
Monthey, *Switzerland* 101 B b
Montijo, B. de, *Panama* 91 C e
Montilla, *Spain* 106 C d
Mont Joli, *Quebec* 82 D e
Mont Laurier, *Quebec* 85 P f
Mont Louis, *Quebec* 82 G d
Montluçon, *France* 108 E c
Montmagny, *Quebec* 82 B g
Montmartre, *Saskatchewan* 87 O h
Montmédy, *France* 108 F b
Montmirail, *France* 108 E b
Montmorency, *Quebec* 82 A g
Montmorency R., *Quebec* 82 A f
Montoro, *Spain* 106 C c
Montpellier, *France* 109 E e
Montpellier, *Quebec* 85 P g
Montreal, L., *Ontario* 84 F e
Montreal, *Quebec* 85 R g
Montreal, R., *Ontario* 84 K e
Montreal I., *Ontario* 84 F e
Montreal L. & R., *Sask.* 87 M d
Montreal Lake, *Saskatchewan* 87 M d
Montréal Nord, *Montreal, Quebec* 85 R h
Montréal Ouest, *Montreal, Quebec* 85 R k
Montreal River, *Ontario* 84 F e
Montréal Sud, *Montreal, Quebec* 85 T j
Montrejeau, *France* 109 D e
Montreuil, *France* 108 D a
Montreuil, *Quebec* 85 L e
Montreuil Bellay, *France* 108 C c
Montreux, *Switzerland* 101 B b
Montrock, *Ontario* 84 K d
Montrose, *Scotland* 98 F d
Mont Royal, dist., *Montreal* 85 R j
Monts, Pte. des, *Quebec* 81 N h
Mont-St.-Jean, *Belgium* 100 C d
Mont-St.-Michel & B., *France* 108 C b
Montserrat, I., *Leeward Is.* 91 G c
Mont Tremblant, *Quebec* 85 Q f
Monywa, *Burma* 127 J d
Monza, *Italy* 110 B c
Monze, *Zambia* 122 D c
Monzón, *Spain* 107 F b
Moonbeam, *Ontario* 84 H c
Moora, *Australia* 134 C f
Moore, L., *Australia* 134 C e
Moore's Mills, *New Brunswick* 82 E h
Moorfoot Hills, *Scotland* 98 E e
Moor Lake Sta., *Ontario* 85 N f
Moorsel, *Belgium* 100 C d
Moorslede, *Belgium* 100 B d
Moose Factory, *Ontario* 84 K a
Moose Hill, *Ontario* 87 N b
Moosehorn, *Manitoba* 87 T g
Moose I., *Manitoba* 87 U g
Moose Jaw, *Saskatchewan* 87 M h
Moosejaw Cr., *Saskatchewan* 87 N h
Moose Lake, *Manitoba* 87 R e
Moose Mt. Prov. Park, *Saskatchewan* 87 P j
Moose Nose L., *Manitoba* 87 W b
Moose R., *Ontario* 84 J b
Moose River, *Ontario* 84 J b
Moosomin, *Saskatchewan* 87 Q h
Moosonee, *Ontario* 84 K a
Mopti, *Mali* 118 E f
Moquegua, *Peru* 92 C g
Mor, *Truk Is.* 78 E n
Mora, *Cameroon* 119 H f
Mora, *Ethiopia* 121 H b
Mora, *Portugal* 106 A c
Mora, *Spain* 106 D c
Mora, *Sweden* 102 F f
Moradabad, *India* 126 E c
Mora de Rubielos, *Spain* 107 E b
Moramanga, *Mal. Rep.* 121 N k
Morano Calabro, *Italy* 111 F f
Morar L., *Scotland* 98 D d
Morat. See Murten
Moratalla, *Spain* 107 E c
Morava, *Czechoslovakia* 105 G d
Morava R., *Yugoslavia* 112 C b
Moravska Trebova, *Czechoslovakia* 105 G d
Morawhanna, *Guyana* 92 F b
Moray, co., *Scotland* 98 E c
Moray Firth, *Scotland* 98 E c
Morbihan, dep., *France* 108 B c
Morbihan, L. De, *Quebec* 82 K b
Morden, *Manitoba* 87 T j
Morden, *Nova Scotia* 82 H h
Mordova, *U.S.S.R.* 117 E d
Mordovskaya, *U.S.S.R.* 114 D c
Morecambe & B., *England* 99 F f
Moreda, *Spain* 106 D d
Moree, *Australia* 135 J e
Moreira, *Brazil* 92 E d
Mörel, *Switzerland* 101 D b
Morelia, *Mexico* 90 D d
Morella, *Spain* 107 E b
Morelos, *Mexico* 90 D b
Morelos, *Mexico* 90 C b
Morelos, state, *Mexico* 90 E d
Morena, Sa., *Spain* 106 C c
Moreni, *Romania* 112 E b
Moresby I., *Br. Columbia* 88 C d
Moreton B., *Australia* 135 K e
Morez, *France* 108 G c
Morgan, *Australia* 134 G f
Morgat, *France* 108 A b
Morges, *Switzerland* 101 B b
Morgins, *Switzerland* 101 B b
Moriani, *India* 127 H c
Morice L., *Br. Columbia* 88 F c
Morin Creek, *Saskatchewan* 86 J d
Morinville, *Alberta* 86 D e
Morioka, *Japan* 133 G e
Morisset Station, *Quebec* 82 B g
Morlaix, *France* 108 B b
Morley, *Alberta* 86 C g
Mornington, I., *Chile* 95 A g
Mornington I., *Australia* 134 G c
Morobe, *New Guinea* 135 J a
Morocco, *N.-W. Africa* 118 D b
Moro G., *Philippines* 129 H j
Morogoro, *Tanzania* 121 H f
Morokwen, *South Africa* 122 C e
Morón, *Cuba* 91 D b
Morona, *Ecuador* 92 B d
Morondava, *Mal. Rep.* 121 M l
Morón de la Frontera, *Spain* 106 C d
Morotai, I., *Indonesia* 129 J k
Moroto, *Uganda* 121 G d
Morpeth, *England* 98 F e
Morpeth, *Ontario* 84 J k
Morphou & B., *Cyprus* 123 A b
Morrin, *Alberta* 86 E g
Morrinhos, *Brazil* 93 H g
Morrinsville, *New Zealand* 135 R k
Morris, *Manitoba* 87 U j
Morrisburg, *Ontario* 85 P h
Morris Jesup, C., *Arctic Oc.* 89 N a
Morrosquillo, G. de, *Colombia* 92 B b
Mors, *Denmark* 103 C h
Morse, *Saskatchewan* 86 K h
Morshansk, *U.S.S.R.* 117 E d
Morson, *Ontario* 86 H a
Mortagne, *France* 108 D b
Mortagua, *Portugal* 106 A b
Mortain, *France* 108 C b
Mortlach, *Saskatchewan* 87 L h
Mortlock Is., *Pacific Ocean* 78 F f
Morven, *Australia* 135 J e
Morvi, *India* 126 D d
Moscow (Moskva), *U.S.S.R.* 116 K d
Mose, C., *Antarctica* 136 T e
Moselle, dep., *France* 108 G b
Moselle, R., *France* 108 G b
Mosera, I. See Masira I.
Mosers River, *Nova Scotia* 83 K j
Mosgiel, *New Zealand* 135 Q m
Mosher, *Ontario* 84 F d
Moshupa, *Botswana* 122 D d
Mosjöen, *Norway* 102 E d
Moskenesöy, *Norway* 102 E c
Moskva. See Moscow
Mosonmagyarovar, *Hungary* 108 G e
Mosqueiro, *Brazil* 93 H d
Mosquera, *Colombia* 92 B c
Moss, *Norway* 103 D g
Mossâmedes, *Angola* 122 A c
Mossbank, *Saskatchewan* 87 M j
Mosselbaai, *South Africa* 122 C f
Mossendjo, *Congo* 120 C e
Moss L., *Manitoba* 87 T a
Mossoró, *Brazil* 93 K e
Mossuma, *Angola* 120 E g
Mossurize, *Mozambique* 122 E d
Mossy Pt., *Manitoba* 87 U f
Mossy R., *Saskatchewan* 87 O d
Most, *Czechoslovakia* 104 E c
Mostaganem, *Algeria* 118 F a
Mostar, *Yugoslavia* 112 A c
Mostardas, *Brazil* 94 F d
Mostoos Hills, *Saskatchewan* 88 P c
Mosul, *Iraq* 124 D b
Mota del Marqués, *Spain* 106 C b
Motala, *Sweden* 103 F g
Motatán, *Venezuela* 92 C b
Motherwell, *Scotland* 98 E e
Môtier, *Switzerland* 101 C b
Môtiers, *Switzerland* 101 B b
Motihari, *India* 127 G c
Motôt, *Switzerland* 101 C b
Moto Yama, *Iwo Jima* 78 D a
Motril, *Spain* 106 D d
Motte, C. de la, *Antarctica* 136 A e
Motueka, *New Zealand* 135 Q l
Motul, *Mexico* 90 G c
Moubray B., *Antarctica* 136 B d
Moudhros, *Greece* 113 E e
Moudon, *Switzerland* 101 B b
Mouila, *Gabon* 120 C e
Mould Bay, *North-West Territories* 80 H b
Moulins, *France* 108 E c
Moulmein, *Burma* 127 J e
Moulouya R., *Morocco* 118 E b
Mountain Park, *Alberta* 88 L d
Mountain View, *Alberta* 86 D j
Mount Assiniboine Prov. Park, *Alberta* 86 B h
Mount Bellew, *Eire* 99 B g
Mount Brydges, *Ontario* 84 J k
Mount Carmel, *Nfd.* 83 T f
Mount Dennis, *Ontario* 84 C k
Mount Dutton, *Australia* 135 G e
Mount Forest, *Ontario* 84 K j
Mount Gambier, *Australia* 135 H g
Mount Lofty Ra., *Australia* 135 G f
Mount Magnet, *Australia* 134 C e
Mount Morgan, *Australia* 135 K d
Mount Revelstoke Nat. Park, *British Columbia* 88 K e
Mounts B., *England* 99 D k
Mount Stewart, *Prince Edward I.* 82 K g
Mount Uniacke, *Nova Scotia* 82 J j
Mount Vernon, *Australia* 134 C d
Moura, *Brazil* 92 E d
Moura, *Portugal* 106 B c
Mourão, *Portugal* 106 B c
Mourne Mts., *N. Ireland* 99 C f
Moussoro, *Chad* 119 J f
Moutier, *Switzerland* 101 C a
Mouton I., *Nova Scotia* 82 H k
Mowming, *China* 131 E m
Mowping, *China* 130 K d
Moyale, *Kenya* 121 H d
Moyie, *British Columbia* 88 M f
Moyobamba, *Peru* 92 B e
Mozambique, *Southern Africa* 122 E d
Mozambique, *Mozambique* 121 J h
Mozhabong L., *Ontario* 84 H f
Mozhga, *U.S.S.R.* 117 L b
Mozyr, *Belorussia, U.S.S.R.* 116 F e
Mpanda, *Tanzania* 121 G f
Mporokoso, *Zambia* 121 G f
Mstislavl, *Belorussia, U.S.S.R.* 116 G d
Mtakuja, *Tanzania* 121 G f
Mtito Andei, *Kenya* 121 H e
Mtoko, *Rhodesia* 122 E c
Mtsensk, *U.S.S.R.* 116 K e
Mu, R., *Burma* 127 J d
Muádhdham, el, *Saudi Arabia* 124 C d
Muang Chaiya, *Thailand* 132 B e
Muang Nan, *Thailand* 132 C c
Muang Palien, *Thailand* 132 B e
Mubarraz, *Saudi Arabia* 124 E d
Mubende, *Uganda* 121 G d
Muchinga Mts., *Zambia* 121 G g
Mucuri, *Brazil* 93 K g
Mudanya, *Turkey* 124 A a
Mudawwara, *Jordan* 123 D h
Mud B., *British Columbia* 88 E g
Muddus Järvi, *Finland* 102 M b
Muddy L., *Saskatchewan* 86 H f
Mudgee, *Australia* 135 J f
Mudhnib, *Saudi Arabia* 124 D d
Mudjatik, R., *Saskatchewan* 88 Q b
Mueda, *Mozambique* 121 H g
Muenster, *Saskatchewan* 87 N f
Muggendorf, *Germany* 104 D d
Mugía, *Spain* 106 A a
Muğla, *Turkey* 124 A b
Muglad, *Sudan* 119 L f
Muhammadabad. See Darreh Gaz
Muharraq, *Persian Gulf* 125 F d
Mühldorf, *Germany* 104 E d
Mühlehorn, *Switzerland* 101 E a
Mühlig-Hofmann Mts., *Antarctica* 136 M d
Muhu, *Estonia, U.S.S.R.* 103 K g
Muinak, *Uzbek., U.S.S.R.* 114 E d
Muine Bheag, *Eire* 99 C h
Mujinkarikku, *Eniwetok* 79 S b
Mukalla, *S. Yemen* 124 E g
Mukdahan, *Thailand* 132 C c
Mukden. See Shenyang
Mukeru, *Palau Is.* 78 B m
Mukhtuya, *U.S.S.R.* 115 L b
Mukhu Väin, *Estonia, U.S.S.R.* 102 K g
Muktinath, *Nepal* 127 F c
Mukutawa R., *Manitoba* 87 U e
Mula, *Spain* 107 E c
Mulchen, *Chile* 95 B e
Mulege, *Mexico* 90 B b
Mulgrave, *Nova Scotia* 83 L h
Mülhausen, *Germany* 104 D c
Mülheim, *Germany* 104 B c
Mulhouse, *France* 108 G c
Mulki, *India* 126 D f
Mullaittivu, *Ceylon* 126 F g
Muller Geb., Mts., *Borneo* 129 F k
Mullewa, *Australia* 134 C e
Müllheim, *Switzerland* 101 E a
Mull I., *Scotland* 98 D d
Mullingar, *Eire* 99 C g
Multan, *Pakistan* 126 D b
Multia, *Finland* 102 L e
Mulvihill, *Manitoba* 87 T h
Mumbondo, *Angola* 120 C g
Mumbwa, *Zambia* 120 F g
Muna, I., *Indonesia* 129 H m
München. See Munich
München Gladbach, *Germany* 104 B c
Muncho Lake, *British Columbia* 88 G a
Muncho Lake Prov. Park, *British Columbia* 88 G a
Mundare, *Alberta* 86 E e
Mundiwindi, *Australia* 134 D d
Mundo Novo, *Brazil* 93 J f
Mundrabilla, *Australia* 134 E f
Mungari, *Mozambique* 122 E c
Munich (München), *Germany* 104 D d
Muniesa, *Spain* 107 E b
Munk, *Manitoba* 87 W c
Munkfors, *Sweden* 103 E g
Munnerstadt, *Germany* 104 D c
Muñoz Gamero, Pen., *Chile* 95 B h
Munson, *Alberta* 86 E g
Münster, *Germany* 104 B c
Munster, prov., *Eire* 99 A h
Münster, *Switzerland* 101 F b
Münster, *Switzerland* 101 D b
Münster, *Switzerland* 101 D a
Muntok, *Bangka I., Indonesia* 129 E l
Muong Attopeu, *Laos* 132 D d
Muong Borikone, *Laos* 132 C c
Muong Saravane, *Laos* 132 D c
Muonio, R., *Sweden-Finland* 102 K c
Muonionalusta, *Sweden* 102 K c
Muotathal, *Switzerland* 101 D b
Mur, *Yemen* 124 D f
Murakami, *Japan* 133 F e
Murang'a, *Kenya* 121 H e
Murat, R., *Turkey* 124 D b
Murat Dagh, *Turkey* 124 A b
Murayama, *Japan* 133 G e
Murça, *Portugal* 106 B b
Murcheh Khur, *Iran* 125 F c
Murchison, Mt., *Antarctica* 136 B d
Murchison, R., *Australia* 134 C e
Murchison Falls, *Uganda* 121 G d
Murcia, *Spain* 107 E d
Murdochville, *Quebec* 82 G e
Muresul (Maros), R., *Romania* 112 C a
Murgon, *Australia* 135 K e
Muri, *Switzerland* 101 D a
Muriae, *Brazil* 93 J h
Murias de Paredes, *Spain* 106 B a
Muriel L., *Alberta* 86 G d
Murillo, *Ontario* 87 O b
Müritz See, *Germany* 104 E b
Murjo, Mt., *Java* 129 F m
Murmansk, *U.S.S.R.* 114 C b
Murom, *U.S.S.R.* 117 F c
Muroran, *Japan* 133 G c
Muros, *Spain* 106 A a
Murphy, Mt., *Antarctica* 136 F d
Murray, R., *Australia* 135 J g
Murray Bridge, *Australia* 134 G g
Murray Harbour, *Prince Edward I.* 82 K g
Murray Head, *Prince Edward I.* 82 K h
Murray R., *Br. Columbia* 88 J c
Murray River, *Prince Edward I.* 82 K h
Murrayville, *Br. Columbia* 88 F g
Mürren, *Switzerland* 101 C b
Murrumbidgee, R., *Australia* 135 J f
Mursir. See Ash
Murten & See, *Switzerland* 101 C b
Murtle L., *Br. Columbia* 88 K d
Mururoa I., *Tuamotu Arch.* 79 M k
Murwara, *India* 126 F d
Murzuq, *Libya* 119 H c
Muş, *Turkey* 124 D b
Musa Kala, *Afghanistan* 125 H c
Musalamiya, *Saudi Arabia* 124 E d
Muscat, *Muscat & Oman* 125 G e
Muscat & Oman, *Arabian Peninsula* 125 G e
Musemir, *S. Yemen* 124 D g
Musgrave, *Australia* 135 H b
Musgrave Ra., *Australia* 134 F e
Musgravetown, *Nfd.* 83 T e
Mushalagan L., *Quebec* 82 C b
Mushalagan R., *Quebec* 82 C a
Mushie, *Congo* 120 D e
Muskeg L., *Ontario* 87 N a
Muskoka L., *Ontario* 85 L g
Muskwa, *Br. Columbia* 88 H a
Muskwa, L., *Alberta* 86 C b
Muskwa R., *Alberta* 86 C b
Musmar, *Sudan* 119 N e
Musoma, *Tanzania* 121 G e
Musquanus L., *Quebec* 83 L c
Musquaro, L., *Quebec* 83 L c
Musquaro, *Quebec* 83 L c
Musquash, *New Brunswick* 83 F h
Musquodoboit, *Nova Scotia* 82 J h
Musquodoboit Harb., *Nova Scotia* 83 J j
Mussau, I., *Pacific Ocean* 78 E g
Mussidan, *France* 109 D d
Mustahil, *Ethiopia* 121 J c
Mustajidda, *Saudi Arabia* 124 D d
Mustang, *Nepal* 127 F c
Musters, L., *Argentina* 95 C g
Muswellbrook, *Australia* 135 K f
Mut, *Egypt* 119 L c
Mut, *Turkey* 124 B b
Mutanda, *Zambia* 120 F g
Mutano, *Angola* 122 A c
Muti, *Eniwetok* 79 S c
Mutok, *Ponape I.* 78 G o
Mutok Harb., *Ponape I* 78 G o
Mutoray, *U.S.S.R.* 115 K b
Mutsu B., *Japan* 133 G d
Mutton Bay, *Quebec* 83 N c
Mutton I., *Eire* 99 A h
Mutumbo, *Angola* 120 D g
Mutupet, *India* 126 E f
Muwale, *Tanzania* 121 G f
Muy, Le, *France* 109 G e
Muya, *Japan* 133 D g
Muya, *U.S.S.R.* 115 L c

Muy Muy, Nicaragua 91 B d
Muzaffarabad, Kashmir 126 D b
Muzaffargarh, Pakistan 126 D b
Muzaffarnagar, India 127 F c
Muzaffarpur, India 127 F c
Muzhi, U.S.S.R. 114 F b
Múzquiz, Mexico 90 D b
Mwanza, Tanzania 121 G e
Mweelrea, Eire 99 A g
Mweru L., Congo 121 F f
Mwinilunga, Zambia 120 E g
Myadaung, Burma 127 J d
Myanaung, Burma 127 J e
Myaungmya, Burma 127 J e
Myebon, Burma 127 H d
Myingyan, Burma 127 J d
Myinmolettka, Mt., Burma 127 J f
Myitkyina, Burma 127 J c
Myjava, Czechoslovakia 105 G d
Mymensingh, East Pakistan 127 H d
Myohaung, Burma 127 H d
Myrdal, Norway 103 B f
Myrnam, Alberta 86 F e
Myrtle, Manitoba 87 U j
Myrtle, Ontario 85 M h
Myslowice, Poland 105 H c
Mysore, India 126 E f
Mystery L., Manitoba 87 U c
My Tho, S. Vietnam 129 E h
Myzakyula, Estonia, U.S.S.R. 103 L g
Mziha, Tanzania 121 H f
Mzimba, Malawi 121 G g
Na, Ponape I. 78 G o
Naantali, Finland 103 K f
Naarden, Netherlands 100 D b
Naas, Eire 99 C g
Nabatiya, Lebanon 123 D d
Nabberu, L., Australia 134 D e
Nabisipi R., Quebec 83 K c
Nablus, Jordan 123 D e
Nacaome, Honduras 91 B d
Nacimiento, Mexico 90 D b
Nacmine, Alberta 86 E g
Nacozari de Garcia, Mexico 90 C a
Nadiad, India 126 D d
Næröy, Norway 102 D d
Næstved, Denmark 103 D j
Nafels, Switzerland 101 E a
Naft, Iran 124 E c
Nafud Des., Saudi Arabia 124 C d
Naga, Philippines 129 H h
Naga, S. Yemen 124 E g
Nagagami, Ontario 84 F c
Nagagami, R., Ontario 84 F c
Nagagami L., Ontario 84 E c
Nagagamisis L., Ontario 84 F c
Naga Hills, India 127 H c
Nagalama, Uganda 121 G d
Nagaland, India 132 A a
Nagano, Japan 133 F f
Nagaoka, Japan 133 F f
Nagapattinam, India 126 E f
Nagar, Kashmir 126 D a
Nagar Karnul, India 126 E e
Nagar Parkar, India 126 D d
Nagasaki, Japan 133 A h
Nagato, Japan 133 B g
Nagaur, India 126 D c
Nagda, India 126 E d
Nagercoil, India 126 E g
Nagha Kalat, Pakistan 126 C c
Nagina, India 126 E c
Nago, Okinawa 78 B b
Nagoya, Japan 133 E g
Nago wan, Okinawa 78 B b
Nagpur, India 126 E d
Nagu, Finland 103 J f
Naguabo, Puerto Rico 54 D h
Nagykanizsa, Hungary 105 G e
Naha, Japan 133 M p
Naha, Okinawa 78 A c
Nahael Niyeu, Argentina 95 C f
Nahan, India 126 E b
Nahariya, Israel 123 D d
Nahavendi, Iran 124 E e
Naicam, Saskatchewan 87 N f
Naifar, Iraq 124 E c
Nain, Iran 125 F c
Nain, Labrador 81 N f
Naini Tal, India 126 E c
Nain Sing Ra., Tibet 126 F b
Nairn, Ontario 84 J f
Nairn & co., Scotland 98 E c
Nairobi, Kenya 121 H e
Naisecho, Kenya 121 H d
Naivasha & L., Kenya 121 H e
Najd, Saudi Arabia 124 D d
Najera, Spain 107 D a
Najin, N. Korea 128 K b
Najira, Saudi Arabia 124 E d
Nakagusuku, Okinawa 78 B c
Nakajo, Japan 133 F e
Nakama, Okinawa 78 A c
Nakaoshi, Okinawa 78 B b
Nakatsu, Japan 133 B h
Nakfa, Ethiopia 121 H a
Nakhichevan, U.S.S.R. 114 D e
Nakhla, Saudi Arabia 125 F e
Nakhon Pathom, Thailand 132 C d
Nakhon Phanom, Thailand 132 C c
Nakhon Ratchasima, Thailand 132 C d
Nakhon Sawan, Thailand 132 C c
Nakhon Si Thammarat, Thailand 132 C e
Nakijin, Okinawa 78 B a
Nakina, Ontario 84 D b
Nakl Mubarak, Saudi Arabia 124 C b
Nakuru, Kenya 121 H e
Nakusp, Br. Columbia 88 L e
Nalgonda, India 126 E e
Nallamalai Hills, India 126 E e
Nalusa, Zambia 120 E g
Nalut, Libya 119 H b
Namai, B., Palau Is. 78 C m
Namaka, Alberta 86 D h
Namangan, Uzbek., U.S.S.R. 114 G d
Namarik I., Marshall Is 79 T c
Namasagali, Uganda 121 G d
Namatail, Mozambique 121 H h
Nambala, Zambia 120 F h
Namcha Barwa, China 128 C e
Nam-dinh, N. Vietnam 132 D b
Namelakl Passage, Palau Is. 78 C m
Namew L., Saskatchewan 87 P d
Namhoi, China 131 F l
Namib Des., S.W. Africa 122 A d
Namlea, I., Indonesia 129 J l
Namling Dzong, Tibet 127 G c
Nam Mao R. See Shweli R.
Namonuito, Is., Carolina Is. 78 E f
Namorona, Mal. Rep. 121 N l
Nampa, Alberta 88 L b
Nampula, Mozambique 121 H h
Namsen R., Norway 102 E d
Namsos, Norway 102 D d
Nams Vatn, Norway 102 E d
Namtsy, U.S.S.R. 115 M b
Namtu, Burma 127 J d
Namu, Br. Columbia 88 F e
Namu I., Marshall Is. 79 T b
Namur, Quebec 85 Q g
Namur & prov., Belgium 100 C d
Namur L., Alberta 88 N b
Namutoni, S.W. Africa 122 B c
Namwala, Zambia 122 D c
Namyang. China 131 G k
Nanaimo, Vancouver I., British Columbia 88 H f
Nana Kru, Liberia 118 D h
Nanan. See Tayü
Nanao, Japan 133 E f
Nanchang, China 131 G h
Nancheng, China 131 H j
Nancheng. See Hanchung
Nan-ching. See Nanking
Nanchung, China 130 C g
Nancy, France 108 G b
Nanda Devi, Mt., India 126 E b
Nanded, India 126 E e
Nanga Parbat, Kashmir 126 D a
Nanjangud, India 126 E f
Nanking, China 130 J g
Nanmatol Is., Ponape I. 78 G o
Nannine, Australia 134 C e
Nanning, China 131 D l
Nanortalik, Greenland 89 P d
Nanping, China 131 J j
Nanripo, Mozambique 121 H g
Nansei Shoto. See Ryukyu Retto
Nansen Sd., N.-W. Terr. 81 K a
Nan Shan, China 124 C c
Nantais, L., Quebec 81 M e
Nantan, China 131 C k
Nantes, France 108 C c
Nanton, Alberta 86 D h
Nantucket Inlet, Antarctica 136 J d
Nantung, China 130 K f
Nanue, Ponape I. 78 G o
Nanumanga, I., Ellice Is 78 H h
Nanumea, I., Ellice Is. 78 H h
Nanuque, Brazil 93 J g
Nanyang, China 130 F f
Nanyuki, Kenya 121 H d
Naococane L., Quebec 81 M g
Naoetsu, Japan 133 F f
Naoshera, Kashmir 126 D b
Napadogan, New Brunswick 82 F g
Napanee, Ontario 85 O h
Napas, U.S.S.R. 114 H c
Napetipi R., Quebec 83 O b
Napier, New Zealand 135 R k
Napier Mts., Antarctica 136 P e
Napierville, Quebec 85 R g
Napinka, Manitoba 87 R j
Naples (Napoli), Italy 111 D e
Napoli, G. di, Italy 111 D e
Napoli. See Naples
Naqb Ashtar, Jordan 123 D g
Nara, Japan 133 D g
Nara, Mali 118 D e
Naracoorte, Australia 134 H g
Naramata, Br. Columbia 88 K f
Narathiwat, Thailand 132 C e
Narayanganj, E. Pakistan 127 H d
Narbonne, France 109 E e
Nares Ld., Greenland 89 P a
Nares Str., Canada-Greenland 81 M b
Narino, Colombia 92 B c
Nari R., Pakistan 126 C c
Narken, Sweden 102 K c
Narmada R., India 126 D d
Narmidj, Jaluit I. 79 T h
Narnaul, India 126 E c
Narok, Kenya 121 H e
Narovchat, U.S.S.R. 117 F d
Narrabri, Australia 135 J f
Narranderra, Australia 135 J f
Narrogin, Australia 134 C f
Narsimhapur, India 126 E d
Narsinghgarh, India 126 E d
Narva, Estonia, U.S.S.R 103 N g
Narva Laht, Estonia, U.S.S.R. 103 M g
Narvik, Norway 102 G b
Naryan Mar, U.S.S.R 114 E b
Narykary, U.S.S.R. 114 F b
Narym, U.S.S.R. 114 H c
Naryn, Kirgiz., U.S.S.R. 114 H c
Narynkol, Kazakh., U.S.S.R. 117 H d
Naseby, New Zealand 135 Q m
Nash Creek, New Brunswick 82 F f
Nasi Järvi, Finland 103 K f
Nasian, Ghana 118 E g
Nasik, India 126 D d
Nasirabad, India 126 D c
Nassau, Bahama Is. 91 D a
Nassau, B. de, Chile 95 C j
Nassau, I., Pacific Ocean 78 K h
Nasser L., Egypt 119 M d
Nässjö, Sweden 103 F h
Nass R., Br. Columbia 88 E c
Nastapoka Is., N.-W. Terr. 81 M f
Nata, Panama 91 C e
Natal, Br. Columbia 86 C j
Natal, Brazil 92 E e
Natal, Brazil 93 K e
Natal, prov., South Africa 122 E e
Natal, Sumatra 129 C k
Natashquan, Quebec 83 L c
Natashquan R., Labrador-Quebec 82 K a
Nation R., Br. Columbia 88 G c
Natiskotek B., Anticosti I., Quebec 83 K d
Natividade, Brazil 93 H f
Natron L., Tanzania 121 H e
Nattavaara, Sweden 102 J c
Natuna Besar. See Bunguran Is.
Natuna Selatan, I., Indonesia 129 E k
Naturaliste, C., Australia 134 B f
Naudville, Quebec 85 T d
Naujoji Vilnia, Lithuania, U.S.S.R. 103 L j
Naukhas, S. W. Africa 122 B d
Naumburg, Germany 104 D c
Nauplia. See Navplion
Naur, Jordan 123 D f
Nauru, I., Pacific Ocean 78 G g
Naushahro, Pakistan 126 C c
Naushki, U.S.S.R. 115 K c
Nauta, Peru 92 C d
Nautla, Mexico 90 E c
Nava del Rey, Spain 106 C b
Navalcarnero, Spain 106 C b
Navalmoral, Spain 106 C c
Navan, Eire 99 C g
Navarino, I., Chile 95 C j
Navarre, prov., France 109 C e
Navarro, Argentina 94 E e
Navojoa, Mexico 90 C b
Navplion, Greece 113 D f
Navrongo, Ghana 118 E f
Navsari, India 126 D d
Nawa, Syria 123 E e
Nawai, India 126 E c
Náxos, I., Greece 113 E f
Nayakhan, U.S.S.R. 115 Q b
Nayarit, Sa. de, Mexico 90 D c
Nayarit, state, Mexico 90 C c
Nay Band, Iran 125 F d
Nayfah, Saudi Arabia 125 F f
Nayoro, Japan 133 H b
Nazaré da Mata, Brazil 93 K e
Nazareth, Israel 123 D e
Nazas, Mexico 90 D b
Nazca, Peru 92 C f
Naze, The. See Lindesnes
Nazilli, Turkey 124 A b
Nazimovo, U.S.S.R. 115 J c
Nazko, British Columbia 88 H d
Nazko, R., Br. Columbia 88 H d
Ncheu, Malawi 121 G g
Ndala, Tanzania 121 G e
Ndeni, I., Santa Cruz Is 78 G h
Ndjolé, Gabon 120 C e
Ndola, Zambia 121 F g
Neagh L., N. Ireland 99 C f
Neápolis, Crete 113 E g
Neath, Wales 99 E j
Nebikon, Switzerland 101 C a
Nebit-Dag, Turkmen., U.S.S.R. 114 E e
Nechako, R., Br. Columbia 88 G d
Neckar, R., Germany 104 C d
Necochea, Argentina 95 E e
Nedelec, Quebec 85 L e
Nederweert, Netherlands 100 D c
Neede, Netherlands 100 E b
Needles, The, England 99 F k
Neelin, Manitoba 87 S j
Neemuch, India 126 D d
Neepawa, Manitoba 87 S h
Neergaard L., N.-W. Terr. 81 L c
Neerpelt, Belgium 100 D c
Negev, Israel 123 C g
Negombo, Ceylon 126 E g
Negrais, C., Burma 127 H e
Negra Pt., Philippines 129 H g
Negritos, Peru 92 A d
Negro, R., Argentina 95 D e
Negro, R., Brazil 92 E d
Negro, R., Uruguay 94 E d
Negros, I., Philippines 129 H j
Negru Vodă, Romania 112 G c
Nehbandān, Iran 125 H c
Neidpath, Saskatchewan 86 K h
Neilburg, Saskatchewan 86 H f
Neils Harbour, Cape Breton I., Nova Scotia 83 M g
Neisse. See Nysa
Neiva, Colombia 92 B c
Neksö, Bornholm I., Denmark 103 F j
Nelkan, U.S.S.R. 115 N c
Nell, Kwajalein Is. 79 T e
Nellore, India 124 F f
Nelma, U.S.S.R. 115 N d
Nelson, Br. Columbia 88 L f
Nelson, New Zealand 135 Q l
Nelson, R., Manitoba 81 K f
Nelson Forks, Br. Columbia 80 G f
Nelson House, Manitoba 87 T c
Nelson I., Antarctica 136 J f
Néma, Mauritania 118 D e
Neman, U.S.S.R. 103 K j
Nemegos, Ontario 84 G e
Nemegosenda L., Ontario 84 G d
Nemeiben L., Saskatchewan 87 M c
Nemiscau, Quebec 81 M g
Nemiscau L., Quebec 85 O a
Nemours. See Ghazaouet
Nemours, France 108 E b
Nemunas, R., Lithuania, U.S.S.R. 103 K j
Nemuro, Japan 133 J c
Nemuro B., Japan 133 J c
Nenagh, Eire 99 B h
Nendeln, Liechtenstein 101 E a
Nene R., England 99 G h
Neópolis, Brazil 93 K f
Nepa, U.S.S.R. 115 K c
Nepal, Asia 127 F c
Nephton, Ontario 85 N h
Neptune, Saskatchewan 87 N j
Nérac, France 109 D d
Nerchinsk, U.S.S.R. 115 L c
Neringa, Lithuania, U.S.S.R. 103 J j
Nerpio, Spain 107 D c
Nes, U.S.S.R. 114 D b
Nesle, L., Quebec 83 N c
Nesna, Norway 102 E c
Nesset, Norway 102 C e
Ness L., Scotland 98 E c
Nesslau, Switzerland 101 E a
Nesterville, Ontario 84 G f
Nesthorn, Mt., Switzerland 101 C b
Nestor Falls, Ontario 86 H a
Nesttun, Norway 103 A f
Netanya, Israel 123 C e
Netherhill, Saskatchewan 86 H g
Netherlands, W. Europe 100 C b
Nettilling L., N.-W. Terr. 81 M d
Nettuno, Italy 111 D e
Neubrandenburg, Germany 104 E b
Neuburg, Germany 104 D d
Neuchâtel, L. de, Switzerland 101 B b
Neuchâtel & canton, Switzerland 101 B a
Neudorf, Saskatchewan 87 P h
Neufchâteau, Belgium 100 D e
Neufchâteau, France 108 F b
Neufchâtel, France 108 D b
Neufelden, Austria 104 E d
Neuhausen, Switzerland 101 D a
Neumünster, Germany 104 C a
Neunkirch, Switzerland 101 D a
Neuquén, Argentina 95 C e
Neusiedler See, Austria 105 G e
Neuss, Germany 104 B c
Neustadt, Germany 104 D a
Neustettin. See Szczecinek
Neustrelitz, Germany 104 E b
Neu Ulm, Germany 104 D d
Neuve Église. See Nieuwkerke
Neuveville, Switzerland 101 C a
Neuwerk, I., Germany 104 C b
Nevada, Sa., Mts., Spain 106 D d
Nevel, U.S.S.R. 116 F c
Nevel'sk, U.S.S.R. 115 P d
Nevers, France 108 E c
Nevesinje, Yugoslavia 112 B c
Neveyezhkino, U.S.S.R. 117 G e
Neville, Saskatchewan 86 K j
Nevis, Alberta 86 D f
Nevis, I., Leeward Is. 91 G c
Nevşehir, Turkey 124 B b
Nevyansk, U.S.S.R. 117 Q b
New Amsterdam, Guyana 93 F b
Newark, England 99 G g
New Bedford Inlet, Antarctica 136 J d
Newboro, Ontario 85 O h
New Brigden, Alberta 86 G g
New Britain, Bismarck Arch. 78 E h
Newbrook, Alberta 86 E d
New Brunswick, prov., Canada 81 N h
Newburgh, Ontario 85 O h
New Burnt Cove, Newfoundland 83 T e
Newbury, England 99 G j
New Caledonia, Pacific Oc. 78 G j
New Carlisle, Quebec 82 G f
Newcastle, Australia 135 K f
Newcastle, New Brunswick 82 G f
Newcastle, N. Ireland 99 C f
Newcastle, Ontario 85 M j
Newcastle, South Africa 122 D e
Newcastle Bridge, New Brunswick 82 F g
Newcastle Emlyn, Wales 99 D h
Newcastle Mine, Alberta 86 E g
Newcastle-under-Lyme, England 99 F g
Newcastle-upon-Tyne, England 99 F e
Newcastle Waters, Australia 134 F c
Newchwang. See Yingkow
Newdale, Manitoba 87 R h
New Dayton, Alberta 86 E j
New Delhi, India 126 E c
New Denmark, New Brunswick 82 E g
New Edinburgh, dist., Ottawa 84 D h
Newell L., Alberta 86 E h
New England Ra., Australia 135 K f
New Fish Creek, Alberta 88 L c
New Forest, England 99 F k
Newfoundland, I. of, Canada 81 O h
Newfoundland, prov., Canada 81 N f
New Galloway, Scotland 98 E e
Newgate, Br. Columbia 86 B j
New Georgia, I., Solomon Is. 78 F h
New Germany, Nova Scotia 82 H j
New Glasgow, Nova Scotia 82 K h
New Guinea, Pacific Ocean 78 D h
New Hamburg, Ontario 84 K j
Newhaven, England 99 H k
New Hazelton, Br. Columbia 88 F c
New Hebrides, Is., Pacific Ocean 78 G j
New Ireland, Bismarck Arch. 78 F h
New Liskeard, Ontario 85 L e
Newman's Cove, Newfoundland 83 T e
Newmarket, Eire 99 B h
Newmarket, England 99 H h
Newmarket, Ontario 85 L h
New Norfolk, Tasmania 135 J h
New Norway, Alberta 86 E f
New Osgoode, Saskatchewan 87 O f
New Plymouth, New Zealand 135 Q k
Newport, Isle of Wight, England 99 G k
Newport, Quebec 82 H e
Newport, Wales 99 F j
New Providence, I., Bahama Is. 91 D b
Newquay, England 99 D k
New Quebec Crater, Quebec 81 M e
New Richmond, Quebec 82 G e
New Ross, Eire 99 C h
Newry, N. Ireland 99 C f
New Schwabenland, Antarctica 136 M d
New Siberian Islands. See Novosibirskiye Ostrova
New South Wales, state, Australia 135 J f
Newton Abbott, England 99 E k
Newton Stewart, Scotland 99 E f
New Toronto, Ontario 85 L j
Newtown, Newfoundland 83 T d
Newtown, Wales 99 E h
Newtownards, N. Ireland 99 D f
New Waterford, C. Breton I., Nova Scotia 83 M g
New Westminster, British Columbia 88 H f
New World I., Newfoundland 83 S d
New Zealand 135
New Zealand Claim, Antarctica 136 C c
Nexö. See Neksö
Neya, U.S.S.R. 117 H a
Neyriz, Iran 125 F d
Neyshābūr, Iran 125 G b
Nezhin, Ukraine, U.S.S.R 116 G f
Ngain, Jaluit I. 79 T h
Nganglaring Tso, Tibet 127 F b
N'Gaoundéré, Cameroon 119 H g
Ngardmau, Palau Is. 78 B m
Ngardmau B., Palau Is. 78 C l
Ngardololok, Palau Is. 78 A o
Ngaregur, Palau Is. 78 C l
Ngaremediu, Palau Is. 78 B n
Ngatapa, New Zealand 135 R k
Ngatik, I., Caroline Is. 78 F g
Ngauruhoe, Mt., New Zealand 135 R k
Ngemelis Is., Palau Is 78 A o
Ngeregong, Palau Is. 78 B o
Ngergoi, Palau Is. 78 A o
Ngesebus, Palau Is. 78 A o
Ngeuni, Sudan 119 L g
Ngobasangel, Palau Is. 78 B n
Ngong, Kenya 121 H e
Ngoring Nor, China 128 C d
Nguigmi, Niger 119 H f
Ngwasi, Tanzania 121 H f
Nha-Trang, S. Vietnam 132 D d
Nhill, Australia 134 H g
Niafounké, Mali 118 E e
Niagara Falls, Ontario 85 L j
Niagara on the Lake, Ont. 85 L j
Niah, Sarawak 129 F k
Niamey, Niger 118 F f
Nia Nia, Congo 121 F d
Niapa, Mt., Borneo 129 G k
Nias, I., Indonesia 129 C k
Nicaragua, Cent. Amer. 91 B d
Nicaragua L., Nicaragua 91 B d
Nicastro, Italy 111 F f
Nice, France 109 G e
Nichicun L., Quebec 81 M g
Nichinan, Japan 133 B j
Nicholson, Ontario 84 G e
Nickel Lake, Ontario 86 J b
Nicman, Quebec 82 G c
Nicobar Is., Indian Ocean 127 H g
Nicola, Br. Columbia 88 J e
Nicolet, Quebec 85 S f
Nicosia, Cyprus 123 B b
Nicoya & Pen., Costa Rica 91 B d
Nictau, New Brunswick 82 E f
Nictaux Falls, Nova Scotia 82 G j
Nidau, Switzerland 101 C a
Nidzica, Poland 105 J b
Niedere Tauern, Austria 104 E e
Niedersachsen, Germany 104 C b
Niellé, Ivory Coast 118 D f
Nielson B., Antarctica 136 Q e
Niére, Chad 119 K f
Nieuw Amsterdam, Surinam 93 F b
Nieuwendijk, Netherlands 100 C c
Nieuwersluis, Netherlands 100 C b
Nieuwkerke, Belgium 100 A d
Nieuwkoop, Netherlands 100 C b
Nieuw Nickerie, Surinam 93 F b
Nieuwpoort, Belgium 100 C c
Nieuwpoort, Netherlands 100 A c
Nieves, Mexico 90 D c
Nièvre, dep., France 108 E c
Nif, Yap I. 78 C m
Nigadoo, New Brunswick 82 G f
Nigde, Turkey 124 B b
Niger, W. Africa 118 G e
Nigeria, W. Africa 118 G g
Niger R., W. Africa 118 F f
Nighthawk L., Ontario 84 K d
Nigula, Estonia, U.S.S.R. 103 M g
Niigata, Japan 133 F f
Niitaka Chain, Taiwan 131 K l
Nijil, Jordan 123 D g
Nijkerk, Netherlands 100 D b
Nijmegen, Netherlands 100 D j
Nikaria. See Ikaría, I.
Nikel, U.S.S.R. 117 B b
Nikiforos, Greece 112 E d
Nikki, Dahomey 118 F g
Nikko Nat. Park, Japan 133 F f
Nikolayev, Ukraine, U.S.S.R. 116 G h
Nikolayevskiy, U.S.S.R. 117 G e
Nikolayevsk-na-Amure, U.S.S.R. 115 P c
Nikolo-Berezovka, U.S.S.R. 117 M b
Nikolo-Kozel'sk, Ukraine, U.S.S.R. 116 H h
Nikol'skaya Pestrovka, U.S.S.R. 117 G d
Nikopol, Ukraine, U.S.S.R. 116 J h
Niksar, Turkey 124 C a
Nikšić, Yugoslavia 112 B c
Nila, I., Indonesia 129 J m
Nile, R., N. Africa 119 M e
Nilgault, L., Quebec 85 N f
Nilgiri, India 127 G d
Nilgiri Hills, India 126 E f
Nimach (Neemuch), India 126 D d
Nîmes, France 109 F e
Nimgiri, Mt., India 127 F e
Nimrod Glacier, Antarctica 136 A b
Ninette, Manitoba 87 S j
Nineveh, Iraq 124 D b
Ningan, China 128 J b
Ninganpao, China 130 B d
Ningerh. See Puerh
Ninghai, China 131 K h
Ninghsien, China 131 F j
Ninghsien (Ningpo), China 131 K h
Ningi, Kwajalein Is. 79 U e
Ningkwo. See Suancheng
Ninglingting. See Kinki
Ningpo, China 131 K h
Ning-sia, China 130 C c
Ningsia Hui Aut. Reg., China 130 B d
Ningsiang, China 131 F h
Ningteh. See Yingchwan
Ning-wu-fu, China 130 F c
Ning-yüan chow, China 130 K b
Ning-yüan-ting, China 130 F b
Ninh-binh, N. Vietnam 132 D b
Ninh Hoa. See Nha Trang
Ninigo I., Admiralty Is. 78 E g
Ninnis Glacier, Antarctica 136 A e
Ninove, Belgium 100 C d
Nioro, Mali 118 D e
Niort, France 108 C c
Níos. See Ios, I.
Nipawin, Saskatchewan 87 N e
Nipawin Prov. Park, Saskatchewan 87 N d
Nipe, B. de, Cuba 91 D b
Nipigon, L. & R., Ontario 84 B c
Nipigon, Ontario 84 B c
Nipigon B., Ontario 84 B d
Nipin R., Saskatchewan 86 H c
Nipisiguit B., New Brunswick 82 G f
Nipisiguit R., New Brunswick 82 F f
Nipisi R., Alberta 86 C c
Nipissing, L., Ontario 85 L f
Nipissing Junc., Ontario 85 L f
Nipissis L. & R., Quebec 82 F c
Nipisso L., Quebec 82 G c
Niquelandia, Brazil 93 H f
Nirmal, India 126 E e
Nis, Yugoslavia 112 C c
Nischu, Kashmir 126 E b
Nish. See Nis
Nishapur. See Neyshābūr
Nishio, Japan 133 E g
Nishiwaki, Japan 133 D g
Nisiros, I., Greece 113 F f
Nissan, Solomon Is. 78 G h

Nissi, Estonia, U.S.S.R 103 L g
Nitchequon, Quebec 81 M g
Niterói, Brazil 93 J h
Nith R., Scotland 98 E e
Nitra, Czechoslovakia 105 H d
Nitrianske Pravno, Czechoslovakia 105 H d
Niue, I., Pacific Ocean 78 K j
Niut, Mt., Borneo 129 E k
Nivala, Finland 102 L e
Nivelles, Belgium 100 C d
Nivernais, prov., France 108 E c
Niverville, Manitoba 87 U j
Nizamabad, India 126 E e
Nizampatam, India 126 F e
Nizana, Israel 123 C g
Nizhne Udinsk, U.S.S.R 115 J c
Nizhniye Kresty, U.S.S.R. 115 R b
Nizhniy Lomov, U.S.S.R. 117 F d
Nizhniy Tagil, U.S.S.R. 117 P b
Nizhnyaya Pesha, U.S.S.R. 114 D b
Nizke Tatry, Czechoslovakia 105 H d
Njombe, Tanzania 121 G f
Nkonde, Tanzania 121 G f
N'Kongsamba, Cameroon 119 G h
Nmai R., Burma 127 J c
Noagarh, India 127 F d
Noakhali. See Sudharam
Noanama, Colombia 92 B c
Nobel, Ontario 84 K g
Nobleford, Alberta 86 D j
Nocera, Italy 111 E e
Nochistlán, Mexico 90 E d
Noel Paul's Brook, Newfoundland 83 Q e
Noelville, Ontario 84 K f
Noemfoor, I., New Guinea 129 K l
Nœrbö, Norway 103 A g
Nogaro, France 109 C e
Nogent-le-Rotrou, France 108 D b
Nogent-sur-Seine, France 108 E b
Noginsk, U.S.S.R. 116 L d
Noire, R., Quebec 85 N f
Noirmoutier, I. de, France 108 B c
Nokhtuysk, U.S.S.R. 115 L c
Nokomis, Saskatchewan 87 N g
Nokomis L., Saskatchewan 88 S b
Nola, Cent. Afr. Rep. 120 D d
Nola, Italy 111 E e
Nolalu, Ontario 87 N b
Nominingue, Quebec 85 P f
Nonancourt, France 108 D b
Nong-han, Thailand 132 C c
Nong Khai, Thailand 132 C c
Nongoma, South Africa 122 E e
Nonni (Nun), R., China 128 H a
Nonno, Ethiopia 121 H c
Nonoava, Mexico 90 C b
Nõo, Estonia, U.S.S.R. 103 M g
Noonkanbah, Australia 134 D c
Noordeloos, Netherlands 100 C c
Noordwolde, Netherlands 100 E b
Nootka & Sd., Br. Columbia 88 F f
Nootka I., Vancouver I., British Columbia 88 F f
Nora, Saskatchewan 87 O f
Nora, Sweden 103 F g
Noranda, Quebec 85 L d
Nord, dep., France 108 E a
Nord Cap. See Horn, Iceland
Norddal, Norway 102 B e
Nordegg R., Alberta 86 B f
Nordenshelda, Arch., U.S.S.R. 115 J a
Nordhausen, Germany 104 D c
Nordkapp, Norway 102 L a
Nordkinn Halvöya, Norway 102 M a
Nördlingen, Germany 104 D d
Nordreisa, Norway 102 J b
Nordrhein-Westfalen, Germany 104 B c
Nord Slesvig. See Jylland, S.
Nordstrand I., Germany 104 C a
Nordvik, U.S.S.R. 115 L a
Nore, Norway 103 C f
Norembego, Ontario 84 K d
Nore R., Eire 99 C h
Norfolk, co., England 99 H h
Norfolk I., Pacific Ocean 78 H k
Norgama, Pakistan 126 C c
Norheimsund, Norway 103 B f
Norily, U.S.S.R. 114 H b
Normanby I., Papua 135 K a
Normandie, prov., France 108 C b
Normandin, Quebec 85 S d
Normanton, Australia 135 H c
Norman Wells, N.-W. Terr. 80 G d
Normetal, Quebec 85 L d
Norquay, Saskatchewan 87 P g
Norquiñ, Argentina 95 B e
Norquiñco, Argentina 95 B f
Norris Arm, Newfoundland 83 R d
Norrköping, Sweden 103 G g
Norrsundet, Sweden 103 G f
Norrtalje, Sweden 103 H g
Norseman, Australia 134 D f
Norsholm, Sweden 103 F g
Northallerton, England 99 G f
Northam, Australia 134 C f
Northampton, Australia 134 B e
Northampton & co., England 99 G h
North Aulatsivik I., Labrador 81 N f
North Battleford, Saskatchewan 86 J f
North Bay, Newfoundland 83 O f
North Bay, Ontario 85 L f
North Berwick, Scotland 98 F d
North Borneo. See Sabah
North Branch, Ontario 86 H a
North Brook, Ontario 85 N h
North C., Antarctica 136 B d
North C., C. Breton I., Nova Scotia 83 M f
North C., New Zealand 135 Q j
North Caribou L., Ontario 81 K g
North Chan., Ontario 84 G f
North Chan., Scotland-Northern Ireland 98 D e
North Devon, New Brunswick 82 F h
North Downs, England 99 H j
North-East Foreland, Greenland 89 M a
Northeast I., Truk Is. 78 E m
Northeast Pt., Belle Isle, Newfoundland 83 R a
Northern Bight, Nfd. 83 S e
Northern Circars, India 126 F e
Northern Head, New Brunswick 82 F j
Northern Ireland, Brit. Isles 99 C f
Northern Light L., Ontario 87 M b
Northern Rhodesia. See Zambia
Northern Territory, Australia 134 F c
North French R., Ontario 84 J b
Northgate, Saskatchewan 87 P j
North Head, New Brunswick 82 F j
North Head, Newfoundland 83 O d
North I., New Zealand 135 R k
North Kent I., N.-W. Terr. 81 L b
North Knife L., Manitoba 87 V a
North Land. See Severnaya Zemlya
North McIntyre, Ontario 87 O b
North Magnetic Pole 89 S b
North Pole, Arctic Ocean 89 A a
Northport, Nova Scotia 82 J h
North Pt., Prince Edward I. 82 H f
North Riding, Yorkshire, England 99 F f
North River Bridge, C. Breton I., Nova Scotia 83 M g
North Ronaldsay, I., Orkney 98 F a
North Rustico, Prince Edward I. 82 J g
North Sea, W. Europe 96 G d
Northside, Canton I 79 S m
North Star, Alberta 88 L b
North Sydney, C. Breton I., Nova Scotia 83 M g
North Taranaki Bight, New Zealand 135 R k
Northumberland, co., England 98 F e
Northumberland Str., Nova Scotia 82 J g
North Vancouver, British Columbia 88 H f
North Vermilion, Alberta 88 L a
North Vietnam, S.E. Asia 131 B m
North West C., Australia 134 B d
North West River, Labrador 81 N g
North West St. Augustin R., Quebec 83 N b
Northwest Territories, political region, Canada 80 H d
North York, Ontario 84 C j
Norton, New Brunswick 82 G h
Norvegia, C., Antarctica 136 L d
Norway, North-West Europe 102-103
Norway House, Manitoba 80 K g
Norway I., N.-W. Terr. 80 G c
Norwegian B., N.-W. Terr 81 K b
Norwich, England 99 H h
Norwich, Ontario 84 K k
Norwood, Ontario 85 M h
Noshiro, Japan 133 F d
Nosseghem, Belgium 100 C d
Nossi Bé, I., Mal. Rep. 121 N j
Notikewin, R., Alberta 88 K b
Noto, Sicily 111 E g
Notodden, Norway 103 C g
Noto Pen., Japan 133 E f
Notre Dame, New Brunswick 82 H g
Notre Dame, Quebec 82 A h
Notre Dame B., Newfoundland 83 R d
Notre-Dame-de-Koartak, Quebec 81 N e
Notre Dame de la Dorée, Quebec 85 S d
Notre Dame-de-Lévis, Quebec 85 T c
Notre Dame de Lourdes, Manitoba 87 T j
Notre Dame de Rimouski, Quebec 82 D e
Notre-Dame-d'Ivugivic, Quebec 81 M e
Notre Dame du Lac, Quebec 82 D f
Notre Dame du Laus, Quebec 85 P f
Notre Dame Mts., Quebec 82 B g
Nottawasaga B., Ontario 84 K h
Nottaway R., Quebec 85 M b
Nottingham & co., England 99 G h
Nottingham I., North-West Territories 81 M e
Nouakchott, Mauritania 118 B e
Nouméa, Pacific Ocean 78 G k
Nouvelle, Quebec 82 F e
Nouvelle-France, C. de Quebec 81 M e
Nouvelle, L., Quebec 82 D c
Nova Bečej, Yugoslavia 112 C b
Nova Chaves, Angola 120 E g
Nova Cruz, Brazil 93 K e
Nova Freixo, Mozambique 121 H g
Nova Gaia, Angola 120 D g
Nova Goa, India 126 D e
Nova Iorque, Brazil 93 J e
Nova Lisboa, Angola 120 D g
Novara, Italy 110 B c
Nova Scotia, prov., Canada 81 N j
Nova Sofala, Mozambique 122 E d
Nova Venecia, Brazil 93 J g
Novaya Sibir, I., U.S.S.R. 115 Q a
Novaya Zemlya, I., U.S.S.R. 114 E a
Nové Zámky, Czechoslovakia 105 H e
Novgorod, U.S.S.R. 116 G b
Novi, Yugoslavia 110 E c
Novi Pazar, Bulgaria 112 F c
Novi Pazar, Yugoslavia 112 C c
Novi Sad, Yugoslavia 112 B b
Novocherkassk, U.S.S.R. 117 E g
Novokuznetsk, U.S.S.R. 114 H c
Novo Mesto, Yugoslavia 110 E c
Novomoskovsk, Ukraine, U.S.S.R. 116 J g
Novomoskovsk, U.S.S.R. 116 L d
Novo Redondo, Angola 120 C g
Novorossiysk, U.S.S.R. 114 C d
Novoshakhtinsk, U.S.S.R. 117 D g
Novosibirsk, U.S.S.R. 114 H c
Novosibirskaya Oblast, U.S.S.R. 114 G c
Novosibirskiye Ostrova, Is., U.S.S.R. 115 N a
Novo Troitsk, U.S.S.R. 117 P e
Novourgench. See Urgench
Novska, Yugoslavia 110 F c
Novy Jičín, Czechoslovakia 105 H d
Novyy Port, U.S.S.R. 114 G b
Nowa Wilejka. See Naujoji Vilnia
Nowgong, India 127 H c
Nowra, Australia 135 K f
Nowy Sacz, Poland 105 J d
Nowy Targ, Poland 105 J d
Nowy Tomysl, Poland 105 G b
Noya, Spain 106 A a
Noyrot, L., Quebec 83 O b
Nozay, France 108 C c
Nsanje, Malawi 122 F c
Ntungamo, Uganda 121 G e
Nuanetsi, Rhodesia 122 E d
Nuassuak Pen., Greenland 89 P b
Nueltin L., North-West Territories 81 K e
Nueva, I., Chile & Argentina 95 C j
Nueva Imperial, Chile 95 B e
Nueva Lennox, Chile-Arg. 95 C j
Nueva Lubecka, Argentina 95 B f
Nueve de Julio, Argentina 94 D e
Nuevitas, Cuba 91 D b
Nuevo, G., Argentina 95 D f
Nuevo Laredo, Mexico 90 E b
Nuevo León, state, Mexico 90 D b
Nui, I., Ellice Is. 78 H h
Nuits-St. Georges, France 108 F c
Nuku'alofa, Tonga Is. 78 J j
Nuku Hiva, I., Marquesas Is. 79 M h
Nukulaelae, I., Ellice Is. 78 J h
Nukunono, I., Tokelau Is. 78 J h
Nukuoro, I., Caroline Is. 78 F g
Nukus, Uzbek., U.S.S.R. 114 E d
Nules, Spain 107 E c
Nullagine, Australia 134 D d
Nullarbor, Australia 134 F f
Nullarbor Plain, Australia 134 E f
Numata, Japan 133 F f
Numazu, Japan 133 F g
Nunchía, Colombia 92 C b
Nunkiang, China 128 J a
Nuoro, Sardinia 111 B e
Nuquí, Colombia 92 B b
Nuremberg. See Nürnberg
Nurmes, Finland 102 N e
Nürnberg, Germany 104 D d
Nurri, Sardinia 111 B f
Nusaybin, Turkey 124 D b
Nushki, Pakistan 126 C c
Nutak, Labrador 81 N f
Nut L., Saskatchewan 87 O f
Nut Mountain, ra., Saskatchewan 87 P f
Nut Mountain, Saskatchewan 87 O f
Nutrias, Venezuela 92 D b
Nuu, Manua Is 79 R o
Nu'uli, Tutuila I. 79 U o
Nuvukjuak, N.-W. Terr 81 M d
Nuwara Eliya, Ceylon 126 F g
Nyada, Sweden 102 G e
Nyåker, Sweden 102 H e
Nyala, Sudan 119 K f
Nyalikungu, Tanzania 121 G e
Nyamlell, Sudan 119 L g
Nyandoma, U.S.S.R. 114 D b
Nyantakara, Tanzania 121 G e
Nyanza, Rwanda 121 F e
Nyasa, L., Malawi 121 G g
Nyasaland. See Malawi
Nyazepetrovsk, U.S.S.R. 117 P b
Nyda, U.S.S.R. 114 G b
Nyeri, Kenya 121 H e
Nyhammar, Sweden 103 F f
Nyiregyháza, Hungary 105 J e
Nykōbing, Denmark 103 C h
Nykōbing, I., Denmark 103 D j
Nyköping, Sweden 103 G g
Nylstroom, South Africa 122 D d
Nymagee, Australia 135 J f
Nyngan, Australia 135 J f
Nyon, Switzerland 101 B b
Nyonga, Tanzania 121 G f
Nyons, France 109 F d
Nysa, Poland 105 G c
Nysted, Denmark 103 D j
Nyurba, U.S.S.R. 115 L b
Nyuya, U.S.S.R. 115 L b
Nzega, Tanzania 121 G e
Oakan, Japan 133 J c
Oak Bay, New Brunswick 82 E h
Oakburn, Manitoba 87 R h
Oakham, England 99 G h
Oak L., Manitoba 87 R j
Oak Lake, Manitoba 87 R j
Oakland, Ontario 84 K j
Oakner, Manitoba 87 R h
Oak Point, Manitoba 87 T h
Oak River, Manitoba 87 R h
Oakville, Manitoba 87 T j
Oakville, Ontario 85 L j
Oamaru, New Zealand 135 Q m
Oates Coast, Antarctica 136 A d
Oates Ld., Antarctica 136 A d
Oaxaca & state, Mexico 90 E d
Ob, R., U.S.S.R. 114 F b
Oba, L., Ontario 84 F d
Oba, Ontario 84 F c
Obakamiga L., Ontario 84 E c
Obama, Japan 133 D g
Oban, New Zealand 135 P m
Oban, Saskatchewan 86 J f
Oban, Scotland 98 D d
Obatogamau L., Quebec 85 Q c
Obbia, Somali Republic 121 K c
Obed, Alberta 88 L d
Obeh, Afghanistan 125 H c
Oberammergau, Germany 104 D e
Oberhausen, Germany 104 B c
Oberriet, Switzerland 101 E a
Oberwald, Switzerland 101 D b
Obi, I., Indonesia 129 J l
Obidos, Brazil 93 F d
Obidos, Portugal 106 A c
Obihiro, Japan 133 H c
Obo, Cent. Afr. Rep. 119 L g
Obo, Mongolia 128 D b
Obock, Fr. Somaliland 121 J b
Obonga L., Ontario 87 O a
Oborona, U.S.S.R. 117 E d
Obrayera, Nicaragua 91 C d
O'Brien, Ontario 84 K e
Observatory Inlet, British Columbia 88 E c
Obskaya Guba, U.S.S.R. 114 G b
Ocampo, Mexico 90 E c
Ocana, Colombia 92 C b
Ocaña, Spain 106 D c
Occidental, Cord., Colombia 92 B c
Ocean Falls, Br. Columbia 88 F d
Oceania, Pacific Ocean 78-79
Ocean Park, Br. Columbia 88 E g
Ochil Hills, Scotland 98 E d
Ochre River, Manitoba 87 S g
Ocland, Romania 112 E a
Ocoa, B. de, Dom. Rep. 91 E c
Ocoña, Peru 92 C g
Ocos, Guatemala 90 F e
Ocotal, Nicaragua 91 B d
Octopus, Ontario 84 D c
Ocumare, Venezuela 92 D a
Ocussi Ambeno, Timor 134 D a
Oda, Ghana 118 E g
Odaka, Japan 133 G f
Odate, Japan 133 G d
Odawara, Japan 133 F g
Odemira, Portugal 106 A d
Ödemiş, Turkey 124 A b
Odense, Denmark 103 D j
Oder R., Germany 104 F b
Odessa, Manitoba 87 O h
Odessa, Ontario 85 O h
Odessa, Ukraine, U.S.S.R. 116 G h
Odhill, Manitoba 87 T c
Odienné, Ivory Coast 118 D g
Odom Inlet, Antarctica 136 J d
Odoorn, Netherlands 100 E b
Odorhei, Romania 112 E a
Odra R., Poland 104 F b
Odzala, Congo 120 C d
Oedelem, Belgium 100 B c
Oeiras, Brazil 93 J e
Oeno, I., Pacific Ocean 79 N k
Of, Turkey 124 D a
Offaly (Uí Failghe), co., Eire 99 B g
Offenbach, Germany 104 C c
Ofu, Manua Is. 79 R o
Ogahalla, Ontario 84 E b
Ogaki, Japan 133 E g
Ogascanan, L., Quebec 85 M e
Ogden, Mt., Alaska-B. C. 88 C a
Ogden, Nova Scotia 83 L h
Ogema, Saskatchewan 87 N j
Ogidaki, Ontario 84 F f
Ogilvie Ra., Yukon 80 F e
Ogimi, Okinawa 78 C a
Ogoja, Nigeria 118 G g
Ogoki, Ontario 81 L g
Ogoki, R., Ontario 84 D b
Ogoki L., Ontario 84 C b
Ogoki Res., Ontario 84 B b
Ogr, Sudan 119 L f
Ogulin, Yugoslavia 110 E c
Ohakune, New Zealand 135 R k
Ohaton, Alberta 86 E f
Ohau, L., New Zealand 135 P m
Ohey, Belgium 100 D d
O'Higgins, Mt., Chile 95 B g
Ohrid, Yugoslavia 112 C d
Ohridsko Jezero, Yugoslavia 112 C d
Oiapoque, R., Brazil, etc. 93 G c
Oignies, Belgium 100 C d
Oil Springs, Ontario 84 H k
Oirschot, Netherlands 100 D c
Oise, dep., France 108 E b
Oita, Japan 133 B h
Oiticica, Brazil 93 J e
Ojinaga, Mexico 90 D b
Ojiya, Japan 133 F f
Ojocaliente, Mexico 90 D c
Ojo de Agua, Argentina 94 D c
Ojo del Toro, Pico, Cuba 91 D c
Ojos del Salado, Mt., Chile-Argentina 94 C c
Oka, Quebec 85 Q g
Okahandja, S.W. Africa 122 B d
Okaihau, New Zealand 135 Q j
Okak Is., Labrador 81 N f
Okanagan Centre, British Columbia 88 K e
Okanagan Falls, British Columbia 88 K f
Okanagan L., Br. Columbia 88 K e
Okanagan Landing, British Columbia 88 K e
Oka R., U.S.S.R. 117 F c
Okau, Yap I. 78 D l
Okaukuejo, S.W. Africa 122 B c
Okavango, R., Angola 122 B c
Okayama, Japan 133 C g
Okehampton, England 99 E k
Okha, U.S.S.R. 115 P c
Okhansk, U.S.S.R. 117 M b
Okhotsk, Sea of, U.S.S.R. 115 P c
Okhotsk, U.S.S.R 115 P c
Oki gunto, Japan 133 C f
Okinawa, Ryukyu Is. 78 D d
Okotoks, Alberta 86 D h
Oktyabr'skiy, U.S.S.R. 117 L c
Oktyabrskoy Revolyutsiy, Os., U.S.S.R. 115 J a
Oku, Okinawa 78 C a
Okućani, Yugoslavia 110 F c
Okuma B., Antarctica 136 C c
Okuru, New Zealand 135 P e
Okushiri I., Japan 133 F c
Olaine, Latvia, U.S.S.R. 103 K h
Olamane R., Quebec 83 M c
Olanchito, Honduras 91 B c
Öland, I., Sweden 103 G h
Olasan, Ethiopia 121 K c
Olavarría, Argentina 94 D e
Oława, Poland 105 G c
Olbia, Sardinia 111 B e
Oldcastle, Eire 99 C g
Oldenburg, Germany 104 D a
Oldenburg, Germany 104 C b
Oldenzaal, Netherlands 100 E b
Old Fort Bay, Quebec 83 P b
Oldham, England 99 F g
Old Hogem, Br. Columbia 88 G c
Oldman R., Alberta 88 M f
Old Perlican, Newfoundland 83 T e
Old Post Pt., Quebec 83 L c
Olds, Alberta 86 C g
Old Wives & L., Saskatchewan 87 M h
O'Leary, Prince Edward I. 82 H g
Olecko, Poland 105 K a
Olekminsk, U.S.S.R. 115 M b
Olenek, R., U.S.S.R. 115 M a
Olenek, U.S.S.R. 115 L b
Olenekskiy Zaliv, U.S.S.R. 115 M a
Oléron, I. d', France 108 C d
Olga, U.S.S.R. 115 N d
Olga L., Quebec 85 N c
Olifants Kloof, Botswana 122 C d
Olimbos, Mts., Greece 113 D d
Oliva de Jerez, Spain 106 B c
Olivares, Cerro de, Argentina 94 C d
Olivares, Spain 107 D c
Oliveira, Brazil 93 J f
Olivenza, Spain 106 B c
Oliver, Br. Columbia 88 K f
Olivone, Switzerland 101 D b
Ollagüe, Chile 94 C b
Ollagüe, Mt., Bolivia 94 C b
Ollan, Truk Is. 78 D o
Olmedo, Spain 106 C b
Olomatimu, Manua Is. 79 S o
Olomouc, Czechoslovakia 105 G d
Olosega, Manua Is. 79 R o
Olot, Spain 107 G a
Olovyannaya, U.S.S.R. 115 L c
Olpe, Germany 104 B c
Olst, Netherlands 100 E b
Olsztyn, Poland 105 J b
Olten, Switzerland 101 C a
Oltu, Turkey 124 D a
Oltul R., Romania 112 E b
Olvera, Spain 106 C d
Olympia, Greece 113 C f
Olympus. See Olimbos
Olyutorskiy Zaliv, U.S.S.R. 115 R b
Omagh, N. Ireland 99 C f
Omaguas, Peru 92 C d
Oman, G. of, Saudi Arabia-Iran 125 G e
Oman, Muscat & Oman 125 G e
Omaok, Palau Is. 78 A o
Omaruru, S.W. Africa 122 B d
Ombabika B., Ontario 84 B b
Ombombo, S.W. Africa 122 A c
Omdurman, Sudan 119 M e
Omemee, Ontario 85 M h
Ometepec, Mexico 90 E d
Omin, Yap I. 78 D l
Omineca, R., Br. Columbia 88 G c
Omineca Mts., Br. Columbia 88 F b
Ommanney B., North-West Territories 80 J c
Ommen, Netherlands 100 E b
Omoa, Honduras 91 B c
Omsk, U.S.S.R. 114 G c
Omskaya Oblast, U.S.S.R. 114 G c
Omuta, Japan 133 B h
Omutninsk, U.S.S.R. 117 L a
Onakawana, Ontario 84 J b
Onakwahegan, R., Ontario 84 J a
Onaman L., Ontario 84 C b
Onamue, Truk Is. 78 D o
Onaping L., Ontario 84 J e
Onatchiway L., Quebec 82 A d
Öndör Hän, Mongolia 128 F a
Onega & R., U.S.S.R. 114 C b
Onehunga, New Zealand 135 R k
Onemak, Kwajalein Is. 79 U e
One Sided Lake, Ontario 86 J a
Onezhskoye Oz., U.S.S.R. 114 C b
Ongole, India 126 F e
Ongudai, U.S.S.R. 114 H c
Oniiba, S.W. Africa 122 B c
Onion Lake, Saskatchewan 86 H e
Onistagan L., Quebec 82 A c
Onitsha, Nigeria 118 G g
Onjūl, Mongolia 128 E a
Onna, Okinawa 78 B b
Onnaram, Truk Is. 78 F o
Onoto, Venezuela 92 D b
Onoway, Alberta 86 C e
Onslow, Australia 134 B d
Ontario, prov., Canada 81 K g
Onteniente, Spain 107 E c
Ontiñena, Spain 107 F b
Ooa, Jaluit I. 79 T j
Oodnadatta, Australia 134 G e
Ooldea, Australia 134 F f
Oostburg, Netherlands 100 B c
Oostcamp, Belgium 100 B c
Oostende. See Ostende
Ooster Schelde, Netherlands 100 B c
Oosterwolde, Netherlands 100 E b
Oosthuizen, Netherlands 100 D b
Oostmalle, Belgium 100 C c
Oostvoorne, Netherlands 100 C c
Ootacamund, India 126 E f
Ootsa L., Br. Columbia 88 G d
Opachuanau L., Manitoba 87 S b
Opal, Alberta 86 D e
Opala, U.S.S.R. 115 Q c
Opari, Sudan 119 M h
Opasatika, Ontario 84 H c
Opasatika L., Ontario 84 H c
Opataka L., Quebec 85 Q b
Opatija, Yugoslavia 110 E c
Opava, Czechoslovakia 105 G d
Opawica L. & R., Quebec 85 P c
Opemisca L., Quebec 85 Q c
Opemisha, Ontario 84 D b
Opeongo L., Ontario 85 M g
Ophir, Mt., Malaysia 132 C f
Ophoven, Belgium 100 D c
Opochka, U.S.S.R. 116 F c
Opocopa L., Quebec 82 F a
Opodepe, Mexico 90 B a
Opole, Poland 105 G c
Oporto. See Porto
Opotiki, New Zealand 135 R k
Oppa B., Japan 133 G e
Oppein. See Opole
Optic Lake, Manitoba 87 Q d
Oputo, Mexico 90 C a
Oqair. See Uqair
Ocnele, Romania 112 C a
Oran, Algeria 118 E a
Orán, Argentina 92 E h
Orange, France 109 F d
Orangedale, C. Breton I., Nova Scotia 83 L h
Orange Free State, prov., South Africa 122 D e
Orange R., S. Africa 122 B e
Orangeville, Ontario 84 K j
Oranje Geb., Mts., Surinam 93 F c
Oranjestad, Aruba, Dutch West Indies 91 E d
Oras, Philippines 129 J h
Orăştie, Romania 112 D b
Orasul Stalin. See Braşov
Oravita, Romania 112 C b
Oravská Magura, Czechoslovakia 105 H d
Orawia, New Zealand 135 P m
Orbe, Switzerland 101 B b
Orcera, Spain 107 D c
Ord, Mt., Australia 134 E c
Ordale, Saskatchewan 84 L e
Ordenes, Spain 106 A a
Ord River, Australia 134 E c
Ordu, Turkey 124 C a
Ordzhonikidze, U.S.S.R. 114 D d
Ordzhonikidzegrad. See Bezhitsa
Oreba, Kwajalein Is. 79 T d
Orebro, Sweden 103 F g
Öregrund, Sweden 103 H f
Orekhovo Zuyevo, U.S.S.R. 116 L d
Orel, U.S.S.R. 116 K e

Peiping. See Peking
Peipus, L. See Chudskoye Oz.
Peixe, Brazil 93 H f
Pekan, Malaysia 132 C f
Peking, China 130 H b
Pekisko, Alberta 88 N e
Pelagie Is., Mediterranean Sea 119 H a
Pélagos, I., Greece 113 D e
Peleduy, U.S.S.R. 115 L c
Pelee I. & Pt., Ontario 84 H k
Peleliu, Palau Is. 78 A o
Peleng, I., Indonesia 129 H l
Pelican B., Manitoba 87 R f
Pelican L., Alberta 86 D c
Pelican L., Manitoba 87 S j
Pelican L., Manitoba 87 R f
Pelican L., Saskatchewan 87 O c
Pelican Mts., Alberta 86 D c
Pelican Narrows, Saskatchewan 87 P c
Pelican Portage, Alberta 86 E c
Pelican Rapids, Manitoba 87 R f
Peljesac Pen., Yugoslavia 110 F d
Pelkosenniemi, Finland 102 M c
Pella, Greece 113 C d
Pellegrini, Argentina 94 D e
Pelletier L., Manitoba 87 U b
Pellworm I., Germany 104 C a
Pelly, Saskatchewan 87 Q g
Pelly Pt., British Columbia 88 C f
Peloponnisos, Greece 113 C f
Pelotas, Brazil 94 F d
Pemba Is., East Africa 121 H f
Pemberton, British Columbia 88 H e
Pembina Mt., ra., Manitoba 87 T j
Pembina Oil Fields & R., Alberta 86 B e
Pembroke, C., Falkland Is. 95 E h
Pembroke, Ontario 85 N g
Pembroke & co., Wales 99 D j
Penafiel, Portugal 106 A b
Peñafiel, Spain 106 C b
Penalva, Brazil 93 J d
Penambo Ra., Sarawak 129 F k
Peña Negra, Sa. de, Spain 106 B a
Penang, I., Malaysia 132 C e
Penápolis, Brazil 93 G h
Peñaranda de Bracamonte, Spain 106 C b
Peñarroya, Spain 106 C c
Penas, G. de, Chile 95 B g
Penck, C., Antarctica 136 R e
Penck Trough, Antarctica 136 L d
Pendembu, Sierra Leone 118 C g
Penedo, Brazil 93 K f
Penedono, Portugal 106 B b
Penetanguishene, Ontario 84 L h
Penggaram, Malaysia 132 C f
Penghu, Is., China 131 J l
Pengiai, China 130 K d
Pengpu, China 128 G d
Penguin Spit, Palmyra I. 79 T k
Penhalonga, Rhodesia 122 E c
Penhold, Alberta 86 D f
Penhurst, Ontario 84 F c
Peniche, Portugal 106 A c
Peñiscola, Spain 107 F b
Penn, Saskatchewan 86 K e
Pennant, Saskatchewan 86 J h
Pennant Pt., Nova Scotia 82 J j
Pennfield, New Brunswick 82 F h
Pennine, Alpi, Mts., Switzerland 101 C b
Pennine Chain, England 99 F f
Penny Ice Cap, North-West Territories 81 N d
Penobsquis, New Brunswick 82 G h
Penong, Australia 134 F f
Penonome, Panama 91 C e
Penrith, England 99 F f
Pensacola Mts., Antarctica 136 J b
Pense, Saskatchewan 87 N h
Pentecôte, L., Quebec 82 E d
Penticton, British Columbia 88 K f
Pentland Firth, Scotland 98 E b
Pentland Hills, Scotland 98 E e
Penza, U.S.S.R. 117 G d
Penzance, England 99 D k
Penzance, Saskatchewan 87 M g
Penzhino, U.S.S.R. 115 R b
Penzhinskaya Guba, U.S.S.R. 115 R b
Peperga, Netherlands 100 E b
Pepinster, Belgium 100 D d
Peqin, Albania 112 B d
Peralta, Spain 107 E a
Percé, Quebec 82 H e
Perdido, Mt., Spain 107 F a
Perdu, L., Quebec 82 B c
Perdue, Saskatchewan 86 K f
Pereira, Colombia 92 B c
Perello, Spain 107 F b
Pérez, Chile 94 C c
Pergamino, Argentina 94 D d
Perho, Finland 102 L e
Péribonca, Quebec 85 S d
Peribonca L., Quebec 82 A c
Peribonca R., Quebec 82 A d
Perico, Argentina 94 C b
Perigueux, France 109 D d
Perijá, Sa. de, Venezuela 92 C a
Peril Rock, Quebec 83 P b
Perim I., Red Sea 124 D g
Peristéra I., Greece 113 E e
Perlas, Arch. de las, Panama 91 D e
Perlas & L. de las, Nicaragua 91 C d
Perm, U.S.S.R. 117 N b
Pernambuco. See Recife
Péronne, France 108 E b
Péronnes, Belgium 100 C d
Perpignan, France 109 E e
Perron, Quebec 85 N d
Perry, Ontario 84 F e
Perry L., Ontario 84 D b
Perryvale, Alberta 86 D d
Persepolis, Iran 125 F d
Pershing, Quebec 85 O d
Persia. See Iran
Persian Gulf, Saudi Arabia, etc 124 E d
Perth, Australia 134 C f
Perth, New Brunswick 82 E g
Perth, Ontario 85 O h
Perth & co., Scotland 98 E d
Peru, South America 92 C f
Perufune, Japan 133 H c
Perugia, Italy 110 D d
Peruibe, Brazil 93 H h
Peruwelz, Belgium 100 B d
Pervijze, Belgium 100 A c
Pervomaysk, Ukraine, U.S.S.R. 116 G g
Perwez, Belgium 100 C d
Pesaro, Italy 110 D d
Pescadores, Is. See Penghu, Is.
Pescara, Italy 110 E d
Peschici, Italy 111 F e
Peshawar, Pakistan 126 D b
Pêso da Régua, Portugal 106 B b
Pesqueira, Brazil 93 K e
Pestravka, U.S.S.R. 117 J d
Petah Tiqva, Israel 123 C e
Petalioí, G. of, Greece 113 E f
Petalioí, I., Greece 113 E f
Petawaga, L., Quebec 85 P f
Petawawa, Ontario 85 N g
Peterbell, Ontario 84 G d
Peterborough, Australia 134 G f
Peterborough, England 99 G h
Peterborough, Ontario 85 M h
Peterhead, Scotland 98 F c
Peter I Island, Antarctica 136 G e
Petermann Fd., Greenland 89 P a
Petermann Pk., Greenland 89 N b
Petermann Ra., Australia 134 E e
Peter Pond L., Saskatchewan 86 H b
Peters Arm South, Newfoundland 83 R d
Petersfield, Manitoba 87 V h
Petitcodiac, New Brunswick 82 G h
Petite Matane, Quebec 82 E e
Petite Mecatina, R. du, Labrador-Quebec 83 L a
Petite Rivière, Quebec 82 B f
Petite Rivière Bridge, Nova Scotia 82 H j
Petit Etang, C. Breton I., Nova Scotia 83 L g
Petit Jardin, Newfoundland 83 N e
Petit Rocher, New Brunswick 82 G f
Petit Vallée, Quebec 82 H d
Peto, Mexico 90 G c
Petone, New Zealand 135 R l
Petorca, Chile 94 B d
Petra, Jordan 123 D g
Petras, Mt., Antarctica 136 E c
Petra Velikogo Zaliv, U.S.S.R. 115 N d
Petre, Pt., Ontario 85 N j
Petrich, Bulgaria 112 D d
Petrila, Romania 112 D b
Petrinja, Yugoslavia 110 F c
Petrodvorets, U.S.S.R 116 F b
Petrolândia, Brazil 93 K e
Petrolia, Ontario 84 H k
Petrolina, Brazil 93 J e
Petropavlovsk, Kazakh., U.S.S.R. 114 F c
Petropavlovsk, U.S.S.R. 115 Q c
Petrópolis, Brazil 93 J h
Petrovac, Yugoslavia 112 C b
Petrovsk, U.S.S.R. 117 N d
Petrovsk, U.S.S.R. 115 K c
Petrovsk, U.S.S.R. 117 G d
Petrozavodsk, U.S.S.R. 114 C b
Petsamo. See Pechenga
Petty Harbour, Newfoundland 83 T f
Pevek, U.S.S.R. 115 S b
Pézenas, France 109 E e
Pforzheim, Germany 104 C d
Phalodi, India 126 D c
Phanon Dang Raek, Thailand 132 C d
Phan Rang, S. Vietnam 132 D d
Phan-Thiet & B. of, South Vietnam 132 D d
Phatthalung, Thailand 132 B e
Phet Buri, Thailand 132 B d
Philippeville, Belgium 100 C d
Philippeville. See Skikda
Philippi, L., Australia 134 G d
Philippines, Is., East Indies 129 H h
Philippine Sea, Philippines 78 D e
Philippopolis. See Plovdiv
Philipsburg, Quebec 85 R g
Phillips B., N.-W. Territories 81 L a
Philomena, Alberta 88 O c
Philpots Pen., N.-W. Terr. 81 M c
Phippen, Saskatchewan 86 J f
Phitsanulok Muang, Thailand 132 C c
Phnom-Penh, Cambodia 132 C d
Phoenix I., Phoenix Is. 78 J h
Phoenix Is., Pacific Ocean 78 J g
Pho-mo-chang-thang Tso, Tibet 127 H c
Phou San, Mt., Laos 132 C c
Phu-dien, N. Vietnam 132 D c
Phuket, Thailand 129 C j
Phulji, Pakistan 126 C c
Phu Qui, N. Vietnam 132 D c
Phu-Quoc, I., S. Vietnam 132 C d
Piacenza, Italy 110 B c
Piakoudie L., Quebec 82 B b
Pianosa, I., Italy 110 C d
Piapot, Saskatchewan 86 H j
Pias, Portugal 106 B c
Piashti L., Quebec 82 K c
Piatra Neamt, Romania 112 F a
Piazza Armerina, Sicily 111 E g
Piazzi, I., Chile 95 B h
Pibor Post, Sudan 119 M g
Pibroch, Alberta 86 D d
Piccadilly, Newfoundland 83 O e
Pichanal, Argentina 94 D b
Pichilemu, Chile 94 B d
Pickardville, Alberta 86 D d
Pickerel, Ontario 84 K g
Pickerel L., Ontario 86 L b
Pickerel River, Ontario 84 K f
Pickering, England 99 G f
Pickle Lake, Ontario 81 K g
Pic R., Ontario 84 D d
Picton, Australia 135 K f
Picton, New Zealand 135 Q l
Picton, Ontario 85 N h
Pictou & I., Nova Scotia 82 K h
Picture Butte, Alberta 86 E j
Picun Leufú, Argentina 95 C e
Pidark, Pakistan 126 B c
Piedmont. See Piemonte
Piedrahita, Spain 106 C b
Piedras Negras, Mexico 90 D b
Piedra Sola, Uruguay 94 E d
Pie I., Ontario 87 O b
Pieksämäki, Finland 102 M e
Pielinen, Finland 102 N e
Piemonte, region, Italy 110 A c
Pierre L., Ontario 84 K c
Pierreville, Quebec 85 S f
Pierson, Manitoba 87 Q j
Pietarsaari, Finland 102 K e
Pietermaritzburg, South Africa 122 E e
Pietersburg, South Africa 122 D d
Pigeon B., Ontario 84 H k
Pigeon L., Alberta 86 D e
Pigeon L., Ontario 85 M h
Pigeon R., Manitoba 87 V f
Pigeon River, Ontario 87 N b
Pigüe, Argentina 95 D e
Pihtipudas, Finland 102 L e
Piirai, Eniwetok 79 S c
Pikangikum L., Ontario 81 K g
Pikwitonei, Manitoba 87 U c
Pila, Argentina 94 E e
Piła, Poland 105 G b
Pilão Arcado, Brazil 93 J f
Pilar, Argentina 94 D d
Pilar, C., Chile 95 B h
Pilar, Paraguay 94 E c
Pilcaniyeu, Argentina 95 B f
Pilger, Saskatchewan 87 M f
Pilibhit, India 126 E c
Pilley's I., Newfoundland 83 R d
Pílos, Greece 113 C f
Pilot Butte, Saskatchewan 87 N h
Pilot Mound, Manitoba 87 T j
Pilsen, Czechoslovakia 104 E d
Piltene, Latvia, U.S.S.R. 103 J h
Pi Mai, Thailand 132 C c
Pimentel, Peru 92 B e
Piña, Canal Zone 91 F b
Pina, Spain 107 E b
Pinarbasi, Turkey 124 C b
Pinar del Río, Cuba 91 C b
Pincher Creek, Alberta 86 D j
Pincher Station, Alberta 86 D j
Pinchi, British Columbia 88 G c
Pindhos, Mts., Greece 113 C e
Pine, C., Newfoundland 83 T g
Pinebluff L., Saskatchewan 87 P d
Pine Creek, Australia 134 F b
Pinedale, Alberta 88 L d
Pinehouse, Saskatchewan 86 L c
Pinehouse L., Saskatchewan 86 L c
Pinehurst L., Alberta 86 F d
Pine Island B., Antarctica 136 F d
Pine Portage, Ontario 84 B c
Pine R., Alberta 86 D d
Pine R., British Columbia 88 J c
Pine River, Manitoba 87 R g
Pine River, Saskatchewan 86 K c
Pinerolo, Italy 110 A c
Pines, I., Puerto Rico 54 D h
Pinery Prov. Pk., Ontario 84 H k
Pinetown, South Africa 122 E e
Pinewood, Ontario 86 H b
Piney, Manitoba 86 F a
Ping-chüan-chow, China 130 J b
Pingelap, I., Caroline Is. 78 F f
Pingelly, Australia 134 C f
Pingkiang, China 131 F h
Pinglap, I., Jaluit I. 79 T j
Pingliang, China 130 C e
Pinglo, China 131 E k
Pingrup, Australia 134 C f
Ping-tung-chow, China 130 F d
Pingwu, China 130 B f
Pingyang. See Linfen
Pingyüan, China 130 H d
Pinhel, Portugal 106 B b
Pini, I., Indonesia 129 C k
Pinjarra, Australia 134 B f
Pinkham, Saskatchewan 86 H g
Pinkiang, China 128 J a
Pink Mountain, British Columbia 88 H b
Pinnaroo, Australia 135 H g
Pinos, I. de, Cuba 91 C b
Pinos, Mexico 90 D c
Pinrang, Celebes 129 G l
Pins, Pte. aux, Ontario 84 J k
Pinsk, Belorussia, U.S.S.R. 116 E e
Pintados, Chile 94 C b
Pinto, Argentina 94 D c
Pinto Butte, Mt., Saskatchewan 86 K j
Pinware R. & B., Labrador 83 Q b
Pioneer, Os., U.S.S.R. 115 J a
Piotrkow, Poland 105 H c
Pipar, India 126 D c
Pipestone, Manitoba 87 R j
Pipestone Creek, Manitoba-Saskatchewan 87 Q j
Pipinas, Argentina 94 E e
Pipmuacan Res., Quebec 82 B d
Pippli, India 127 G d
Piracuruca, Brazil 93 J d
Piraeus. See Piraievs
Piraievs, Greece 113 D f
Pirámide, Mt., Chile 94 B g
Piranhaquara, Brazil 93 G d
Piranhas, Brazil 93 K e
Pirapora, Brazil 93 J g
Piratini, Brazil 94 F d
Piraube L., Quebec 82 A c
Piray, Argentina 94 F c
Pírgos, Crete 113 E g
Pírgos, Greece 113 D f
Pírgos, Greece 113 C f
Pirin Planina, Bulgaria 112 D d
Piripiri, Brazil 93 J d
Pirítu, Venezuela 92 E a
Pirmasens, Germany 104 B d
Pirna, Germany 104 E c
Pirot, Yugoslavia 112 D c
Pir Panjal Ra., Kashmir 126 D b
Pis, I., Truk Is. 78 E m
Pisa, Italy 110 C d
Pisagua, Chile 94 B a
Pisco, Peru 92 B f
Pisek, Czechoslovakia 104 F d
Pishin, Iran 125 H d
Pishin, Pakistan 126 C b
Pisticci, Italy 111 F e
Pistolet B., Newfoundland 83 R b
Pitaga, Labrador 82 G a
Pitangüi, Brazil 93 J g
Pitcairn I., Pacific Ocean 79 N k
Piteå, Sweden 102 J d
Pite Älv, Sweden 102 H d
Piterka, U.S.S.R. 117 H e
Piteşti, Romania 112 E b
Pithiviers, France 108 E b
Piti, I., Guam 78 A l
Pitlochry, Scotland 98 E d
Pitt I., British Columbia 88 D d
Pitt Meadows, British Columbia 88 E f
Pitt R., Br. Columbia 88 F f
Piuà-Petri, Romania 112 F b
Piumafua, I., Manua Is. 79 S o
Piura, Peru 92 A e
Pivabiska, R., Ontario 84 G b
Piza, Latvia, U.S.S.R. 103 J h
Pizeau, Pte., Quebec 83 Q j
Piz Sardona, Switzerland 101 E b
Pkulagalid, I., Palau Is. 78 B l
Pkulagasemieg, Palau Is. 78 B n
Pkulngril, I., Palau Is. 78 B m
Pkurengel, I., Palau Is. 78 B m
Placentia, Newfoundland 83 T f
Placentia B., Newfoundland 83 S f
Placer Guadalupe, Mexico 90 C b
Placetas, Cuba 91 D b
Plagua, I., Saipan-Tinian Is. 78 B d
Plain of Sharon, Israel 123 C e
Pláka B., Crete 113 E g
Plakoti, C., Cyprus 123 C b
Plamondon, Alberta 86 E d
Plana, Czechoslovakia 104 E d
Planaltina, Brazil 93 H g
Planina, Yugoslavia 110 E c
Plasencia, Spain 106 B b
Plaški, Yugoslavia 110 E c
Plassen, Norway 103 E f
Plaster Rock, New Brunswick 82 E g
Plastun, U.S.S.R. 115 N d
Plata, R. de la, Argentina 94 E d
Platamón, Greece 113 D d
Plate Cove, Newfoundland 83 T e
Platí, Greece 113 D d
Plato, Saskatchewan 86 J g
Platres, Cyprus 123 A c
Plauen, Germany 104 E c
Plav, Yugoslavia 112 B c
Plavnica, Yugoslavia 112 B c
Playas, Ecuador 92 A d
Playgreen L., Manitoba 87 T e
Plaza Huincul, Argentina 95 C e
Pleasantdale, Saskatchewan 87 N f
Pleasant Mt., New Brunswick 82 F h
Pleasant Point, Manitoba 87 S j
Pledger L., Ontario 84 G b
Pleiku, S. Vietnam 129 E h
Plenty, B. of, New Zealand 135 R k
Plenty, Saskatchewan 86 J g
Plessisville, Quebec 85 T f
Pletipi L., Quebec 82 B b
Plettenberg B., South Africa 122 C f
Pleven, Bulgaria 112 E c
Pljevlja, Yugoslavia 112 B c
Plock, Poland 105 H b
Ploeşti, Romania 112 F b
Plomarion, Greece 113 F e
Plön, Germany 104 D a
Plonge, L. la, Saskatchewan 86 K c
Płońsk, Poland 105 J b
Plovdiv, Bulgaria 112 E c
Plum Coulee, Manitoba 87 U j
Plumtree, Rhodesia 122 D d
Plunkett, Saskatchewan 87 M g
Plymouth & Sd., England 99 E k
Plympton, Nova Scotia 82 G j
Plynlimmon, Wales 99 E h
Plzeň. See Pilsen
Po, R., Italy 110 D c
Poai, China 130 F e
Pobedy, Mt., Kirgiz., U.S.S.R. 114 H d
Pobla de Segur, Spain 107 F a
Pochinki, U.S.S.R. 117 G c
Pochutla, Mexico 90 E d
Podkamennaya Tunguska, U.S.S.R. 114 H b
Podlubovo, U.S.S.R. 117 M c
Podolsk, U.S.S.R. 116 K d
Podporozh'ye, U.S.S.R. 116 J a
Pogamasing, Ontario 84 J f
Po Hai, G. of, China 130 J c
Pohai, Str. of, China 130 K c
Poincaré, L., Quebec 83 O b
Poinsett, C., Antarctica 136 S e
Point-à-Maurier, Quebec 83 N c
Point à Pitre, Leeward Is. 91 G c
Point du Chêne, New Brunswick 82 H g
Pointe au Baril Station, Ontario 84 K g
Pointe au Pic, Quebec 82 B f
Pointe aux Anglais, Quebec 82 E d
Pointe aux Trembles, Quebec 85 R g
Pointe Bleue, Quebec 85 S d
Pointe Claire, Quebec 85 R g
Point Edward, Ontario 84 H j
Pointe Gatineau, Quebec 84 D h
Pointe Verte, New Brunswick 82 G f
Point Leamington, Newfoundland 83 R d
Point Pelee Nat. Park, Ontario 84 H k
Poisson Blanc, L., Quebec 85 P f
Poitiers, France 108 D c
Poitoumarche, prov., France 108 C c
Poix, Belgium 100 D d
Poix, France 108 D b
Pok, I., Ponape I. 78 G o
Pokaran, India 126 D c
Pokhra, Nepal 127 F c
Pokka, Finland 102 L b
Pokrovsk (Engels), U.S.S.R. 117 H e
Pokrovsk, U.S.S.R. 117 F d
Pokrovsk, U.S.S.R. 117 D g
Pokrovskoe, U.S.S.R. 115 M b
Pola, I., Tutuila Is. 79 U o
Pola. See Pula
Pola de Laviana, Spain 106 C a
Poland, Central Europe 105 G c
Polesk, U.S.S.R. 103 J j
Polevskoi, U.S.S.R. 117 Q b
Polgahawela, Ceylon 126 F g
Polgar, Hungary 105 J e
Poli, Cameroon 119 H g
Políaigos, I., Greece 113 E f
Policastro, G. di, Italy 111 E f
Poligny, France 108 F c
Polillo Is., Philippines 129 H h
Pólinos. See Políaigos, I.
Polis, Cyprus 123 A b
Pollensa, Balearic Is. 107 G c
Pollet, L., Quebec 82 A a
Pollockville, Alberta 86 F g
Pollux, New Zealand 135 P m
Polotsk, Belorussia, U.S.S.R. 116 F d
Poltava, Ukraine, U.S.S.R. 116 J g
Poltimore, Quebec 85 P g
Põltsamaa, Estonia, U.S.S.R. 103 M g
Poluostrov Buzachi, Kazakh., U.S.S.R. 114 E d
Põlva, Estonia, U.S.S.R. 103 M g
Polwarth, Saskatchewan 86 L e
Polynesia, Pacific Ocean 78 K l
Pomán, Argentina 94 C c
Pombal, Brazil 93 K e
Pombal, Portugal 106 A c
Pombetsu, Japan 133 H c
Pomene, Mozambique 122 F d
Pommersche B., Germany 104 F a
Pomorie, Bulgaria 112 F c
Pomos, Pt., Cyprus 123 A b
Pomquet, Nova Scotia 83 L h
Ponape, I., Caroline Is. 78 F f
Ponape, Ponape I. 78 G n
Ponape Harb., Ponape I. 78 F n
Ponass L., Saskatchewan 87 O f
Ponce, Puerto Rico 54 C h
Pondicherry, India 126 E f
Pond Inlet, North-West Territories 81 M c
Ponente, Riviera di, Italy 110 A d
Pones, I., Truk Is. 78 F o
Ponferrada, Spain 106 B a
Ponhook L., Nova Scotia 82 H j
Ponoka, Alberta 86 D f
Ponoy, U.S.S.R. 114 D b
Pons, France 108 C d
Pons, Spain 107 F b
Ponta Grossa, Brazil 94 F c
Pont-Audemer, France 108 D b
Pontbriand B., Quebec 82 K c
Pont Château, France 108 B c
Pont d'Ain, France 108 F c
Ponte, Switzerland 101 E b
Ponte da Barca, Portugal 106 A b
Ponte de Sôr, Portugal 106 A c
Ponteix, Saskatchewan 86 K j
Ponte Nova, Brazil 93 J h
Pontevedra, Spain 106 A a
Pontianak, Borneo 129 E l
Pontivy, France 108 B b
Pont Lafrance, New Brunswick 82 H f
Ponto Berrío, Colombia 92 C b
Ponto Carreño, Venezuela 92 D b
Pontoise, France 108 E b
Ponton, Manitoba 87 S d
Ponto Piñasco, Paraguay 92 F h
Pontresina, Switzerland 101 E b
Pontrilas, Saskatchewan 87 N e
Pont Rouge, Quebec 85 T f
Pont Viau, Quebec 85 R j
Pontypool, Ontario 85 M h
Pontypool, Wales 99 E j
Pontypridd, Wales 99 E j
Ponza, I., Italy 111 D e
Poole, England 99 F k
Poona, India 126 D e
Pooncarie, Australia 135 H f
Poopo, Bolivia 92 D g
Poopo, L., Bolivia 92 D g
Popa Mt., Burma 127 J d
Popayán, Colombia 92 B c
Poperinge, Belgium 100 A d
Poplarfield, Manitoba 87 U h
Poplar Point, Manitoba 87 U h
Poplar Pt., Manitoba 87 U f
Poplar R., Manitoba 87 U f
Popocatapetl, Mt., Mexico 90 E d
Popokabaka, Congo 120 D f
Popovača, Yugoslavia 110 F c
Poppel, Belgium 100 D c
Porbandar, India 126 C d
Porcher I., Br. Columbia 88 D d
Porcupine Hills, Alberta 86 C h
Porcupine Hills, Manitoba-Saskatchewan 87 Q f
Porcupine Plain, Saskatchewan 87 O f
Poreč, Yugoslavia 110 D c
Pori, Finland 103 J f
Porjus, Sweden 102 H c
Porkhov, U.S.S.R. 116 F c
Porkkala, Finland 103 L g
Porlamar, Margarita I., Venezuela 92 E a
Pornic, France 108 B c
Poronaysk, U.S.S.R. 115 P d
Póros I., Greece 113 D f
Porpoise B., Antarctica 136 T e
Porquis Junction, Ontario 84 K d
Porsanger Fd., Norway 102 L a
Porsanger Halvöy, Norway 102 L a
Porsgrund, Norway 103 C g
Portachuelo, Bolivia 92 E g
Port Adelaide, Australia 135 G f
Portadown, N. Ireland 99 C f
Portage, Prince Edward I. 82 H g
Portage I., New Brunswick 82 G f
Portage la Prairie, Manitoba 87 T j
Portage Mountain Dam & Res. Br. Columbia 80 G f
Port Alberni, Vancouver I., British Columbia 88 G f
Port Albert, Ontario 84 J j
Portalegre, Portugal 106 B c
Port Alfred, Quebec 82 B e
Port Alice, Vancouver I., British Columbia 88 F e
Port Antonio, Jamaica 91 D c
Portarlington, Eire 99 C g
Port Arthur, Ontario 87 O b
Port Arthur (Lushun), China 128 H c
Port Augusta, Australia 134 G f
Port-au-Port & B., Newfoundland 83 O e
Port-au-Port Pen., Newfoundland 83 N e
Port-au-Prince, Haiti 91 E c
Port aux Basques, Newfoundland 83 N f
Port Blair, Andaman Is 127 H f
Port Blandford, Nfd. 83 S e
Port Borden, Prince Edward I. 82 J g
Port Bruce, Ontario 84 K k
Port Burwell, Ontario 84 K k
Port Carling, Ontario 85 L g
Port Cartier, Quebec 81 N g
Port Cartier, Quebec 82 F c
Port Chalmers, New Zealand 135 Q m
Port Clements, Queen Charlotte Is., Br. Columbia 88 C d
Port Colborne, Ontario 85 L k
Port Coquitlam, British Columbia 88 H f
Port Cornwallis, Andaman Is. 127 H f
Port Credit, Ontario 85 L j
Port Dalhousie, Ontario 85 L j
Port Daniel, Quebec 82 H e
Port Darwin, Falkland Is. 95 E h
Port de Paix, Haiti 91 E b
Port Dickson, Malaysia 132 C f
Port Douglas, Australia 135 J c
Port Dover, Ontario 84 K k
Port Dufferin, Nova Scotia 83 K j

Port Edward, *Br. Columbia* 88 D c
Portel, *Brazil* 93 G d
Port Elgin, *New Brunswick* 82 H g
Port Elgin, *Ontario* 84 J h
Port Elizabeth, *South Africa* 122 D f
Port Ellen, *Scotland* 98 C e
Porter L., *Saskatchewan* 88 Q b
Porter Landing, *Br. Columbia* 88 D a
Port Étienne, *Mauritania* 118 B d
Port Felix, *Nova Scotia* 83 L h
Port George, *Nova Scotia* 82 G j
Port Greville, *Nova Scotia* 82 H h
Port Guichon, *Br. Columbia* 88 D g
Port Harcourt, *Nigeria* 118 G h
Port Hardy, Vancouver I., *British Columbia* 88 F e
Port Hastings, C. Breton I., *Nova Scotia* 83 L h
Port Hawkesbury, C. Breton I., *Nova Scotia* 83 L h
Port Hedland, *Australia* 134 C d
Port Hood, C. Breton I., *Nova Scotia* 83 L h
Port Hope, *Ontario* 85 M j
Port Hope Simpson, *Labrador* 83 Q a
Portimão, *Portugal* 106 A d
Port Jackson, *Australia* 135 K f
Port Kells, *British Columbia* 88 E g
Port Kembla, *Australia* 135 K f
Portland, *Australia* 134 H g
Portland, *Ontario* 85 O h
Portland Bill, *England* 99 F k
Portland Can., *Alaska-British Columbia* 88 D c
Portland Creek Pond, *Nfd.* 83 P c
Portland Inlet, *Br. Columbia* 88 D c
Portland Point, *Jamaica* 91 D c
Portlaoise, *Eire* 99 C g
Port Lincoln, *Australia* 135 G f
Port Loko, *Sierra Leone* 118 C g
Port Loring, *Ontario* 84 L g
Port Lyautey. *See* Mina Hassan Tani
Port McNicoll, *Ontario* 84 L h
Port Macquarie, *Australia* 135 K f
Portmadoc, *Wales* 99 E h
Port Maitland, *Nova Scotia* 82 F k
Port Maitland, *Ontario* 85 L k
Port Manvers, *Labrador* 81 N f
Port Martin, *Antarctica* 136 A e
Port Medway, *Nova Scotia* 82 H j
Port Menier, Anticosti I., *Quebec* 82 H d
Port Moody, *British Columbia* 88 H f
Port Moody, inlet, *B.C.* 88 E f
Port Moody Conservation Reserve, *British Columbia* 88 E e
Port Moresby, *Papua* 135 J a
Port Morien, C. Breton I., *Nova Scotia* 83 N g
Port Mouton, *Nova Scotia* 82 H k
Portneuf, L., *Quebec* 82 B d
Portneuf, *Quebec* 85 T f
Portneuf, R., *Quebec* 82 C e
Portneuf sur Mer, *Quebec* 82 C e
Port Nicholson, *New Zealand* 135 R l
Port Nolloth, *South Africa* 122 B e
Port-Nouveau-Quebec, *Quebec* 81 N f
Porto, *Portugal* 106 A b
Pôrto Acre, *Brazil* 92 D e
Pôrto Alegre, *Brazil* 94 F d
Pôrto Alexandre, *Angola* 122 A c
Pôrto Amelia, *Mozambique* 121 J g
Portobello, *Panama* 91 D e
Porto Botte, *Sardinia* 111 B f
Pôrto Camargo, *Brazil* 93 G h
Porto d'Ascoli, *Italy* 110 D d
Pôrto de Mos, *Brazil* 93 G d
Pôrto de Moz, *Portugal* 106 A c
Porto Empedocle, *Sicily* 111 D g
Pôrto Esperança, *Brazil* 93 F g
Pôrto Espiridião, *Brazil* 92 F g
Pôrto Franco, *Brazil* 93 H e
Port of Spain, *Trinidad* 92 E a
Pôrto Guaira, *Brazil* 93 G h
Port Okha, *India* 126 C d
Pôrto Lucena, *Brazil* 94 F c
Pôrto Mendes, *Brazil* 93 G h
Pôrto Nacional, *Brazil* 93 H f
Porto Novo, *Dahomey* 118 F g
Porto Novo, *India* 126 E f
Pôrto Seguro, *Brazil* 93 K g
Porto Torres, *Sardinia* 111 B e
Porto Vecchio, *Corsica* 111 B e
Pôrto Velho, *Brazil* 92 E e
Portoviejo, *Ecuador* 92 A d
Portpatrick, *Scotland* 99 D f
Port Pegasus, *New Zealand* 135 P m
Port Perry, *Ontario* 85 M h
Port Phillip B., *Australia* 135 H g
Port Pirie, *Australia* 134 G f
Port Radium, *N.-W. Terr.* 80 H d
Portree, *Scotland* 98 C c
Portreeve, *Saskatchewan* 86 J h
Port Renfrew, *Br. Columbia* 88 G f
Port Rexton, *Newfoundland* 83 T e
Port Rowan, *Ontario* 84 K k
Port Royal, *Jamaica* 91 D c
Port Royal Nat. Hist. Park, *Nova Scotia* 82 G j
Portrush, *N. Ireland* 98 C e
Port Safaga, *Egypt* 119 M c
Port Said, *Egypt* 119 M b
Port St. John's, *South Africa* 122 D f
Port Saunders, *Nfd.* 83 P c
Port Shepstone, *South Africa* 122 E f
Port Simpson, *Br. Columbia* 88 D c
Portsmouth, *England* 99 G k
Portsmouth, *Ontario* 85 O h
Portsmouth Pt., *Palmyra I.* 79 U k
Port Stanley, *Ontario* 84 J k
Port Sudan, *Sudan* 119 N e
Port Swettenham, *Malaysia* 132 C f
Port Taufiq, *Egypt* 119 M c
Portugal, *W. Europe* 106 A c
Portugal Cove, *Nfd.* 83 T f
Portugalia, *Angola* 120 E f
Portuguese Guinea, *North-West Africa* 118 B f
Portumna, *Eire* 99 B g
Port Union, *Newfoundland* 83 T e
Port Union, *Ontario* 85 L j
Port Vendres, *France* 109 E e
Port Victoria, *Kenya* 121 G d
Port Williams, *Nova Scotia* 82 H h
Poru Tso, *Tibet* 127 F b
Porvenir, *Chile* 95 B h
Porvoo, *Finland* 103 L f
Posadas, *Argentina* 94 E c
Posadowsky B., *Antarctica* 136 R e
Poschiavo, *Switzerland* 101 F b
Poseh, *China* 131 C l
Posen. *See* Poznań
Poshan, *China* 130 H d
Poshkokagan L., *Ontario* 87 O a
Posht-e-Badam, *Iran* 125 G c
Poso, *Celebes* 129 H l
Poso Danau, *Celebes* 129 G l
Possession I., *Antarctica* 136 B d
Poste-de-Mistassini, *Quebec* 81 M g
Poste M. Cortier, *Algeria* 118 F d
Poste Weygand, *Algeria* 118 F d
Posušje, *Yugoslavia* 110 F d
Potapovo, *U.S.S.R.* 114 H b
Potchefstroom, *South Africa* 122 D e
Potemkino, *U.S.S.R.* 117 G e
Potenza, *Italy* 111 E e
Poti, *U.S.S.R.* 114 D d
Potiskum, *Nigeria* 119 H f
Potosí, *Bolivia* 92 D g
Potsdam, *Germany* 104 E b
Potter, *Ontario* 84 K d
Pouce Coupé, *Br. Columbia* 88 J c
Pouch Cove, *Newfoundland* 83 T f
Poulin-de-Courval, L., *Quebec* 82 B e
Poulo Condore, Is., *South China Sea* 129 E j
Pourquoi Pas I., *Antarctica* 136 H e
Pouso Alegre, *Brazil* 93 F f
Pouso Alegre, *Brazil* 93 H h
Poutrincourt, L., *Quebec* 85 Q c
Povenets, *U.S.S.R.* 114 C b
Poverty B., *New Zealand* 135 S k
Povoa de Varzim, *Portugal* 106 A b
Povorino, *U.S.S.R.* 117 F e
Povungnituk, *Quebec* 81 M f
Povungnituk, R., *Quebec* 81 M e
Powassan, *Ontario* 85 L f
Powell Creek, *Australia* 135 F c
Powell I., *Antarctica* 136 J f
Powell L., *British Columbia* 88 G e
Powell River, *British Columbia* 88 G f
Poyang, *China* 131 H h
Poyang Hu, *China* 131 H h
Poza de la Sal, *Spain* 106 D a
Požarevac, *Yugoslavia* 112 C b
Požega, *Yugoslavia* 112 A b
Poznań, *Poland* 105 G b
Pozo Almonte, *Chile* 94 C b
Pozoblanco, *Spain* 106 C c
Prachin Buri, *Thailand* 132 C d
Prado, *Brazil* 93 K g
Praga, *Poland* 105 J b
Prague (Praha), *Czechoslovakia* 104 F c
Praha. *See* Prague
Prai, *Malaysia* 132 C e
Praid, *Romania* 112 E a
Prainha, *Brazil* 92 E e
Prainha, *Brazil* 93 G d
Prairie, *Australia* 135 H d
Prairie River, *Saskatchewan* 87 P f
Prairies, L. des, *Quebec* 82 B c
Prairies, R. des, *Quebec* 85 R j
Prang, *Ghana* 118 E g
Prato, *Italy* 110 C d
Pratt, *Manitoba* 87 T j
Pravia, *Spain* 106 B a
Preeceville, *Saskatchewan* 87 P g
Pregolya, R., *U.S.S.R.* 103 J j
Preissac, *Quebec* 85 M d
Preissac L., *Quebec* 85 M d
Prelate, *Saskatchewan* 86 H h
Premio, *Quebec* 82 G b
Prenay, Lithuania, *U.S.S.R.* 103 K j
Prendergast, *Saskatchewan* 86 J d
Přerov, *Czechoslovakia* 105 G d
Presa Alvaro Obregon, *Mexico* 90 C b
Prescott, *Ontario* 85 P h
Preservation Inlet, *New Zealand* 135 P m
Presidencia R. Sáenz Pena, *Argentina* 94 D c
Presidente Hermes, *Brazil* 92 E f
Prešov, *Czechoslovakia* 105 J d
Prespansko, Jezero, *Albania, etc.* 113 C d
Presqu'ile Prov. Pk., *Ontario* 85 N j
Press, *Quebec* 85 O d
Pressburg. *See* Bratislava
Press L., *Ontario* 86 L a
Přeštice, *Czechoslovakia* 104 E d
Preston, *England* 99 F g
Preston, *Ontario* 84 K j
Prestrud Str., *Antarctica* 136 D c
Prestwick, *Scotland* 98 D e
Pretoria, *South Africa* 122 D e
Préveza, *Greece* 113 C e
Préville, *Quebec* 85 T k
Příbram, *Czechoslovakia* 104 F d
Price, *Quebec* 82 D e
Price I., *Br. Columbia* 88 E d
Priego, *Spain* 106 C d
Prieska, *South Africa* 122 C e
Prignitz, *Germany* 104 D b
Prijedor, *Yugoslavia* 110 F c
Prijepolje, *Yugoslavia* 112 B c
Prilep, *Yugoslavia* 112 C d
Priluki, Ukraine, *U.S.S.R.* 116 H f
Primate, *Saskatchewan* 86 H f
Primorskiy Kroy, *U.S.S.R.* 115 N d
Prim Pt., *Prince Edward I.* 82 J g
Primrose L., *Saskatchewan* 86 H d
Prince, *Saskatchewan* 86 J f
Prince Albert, *Saskatchewan* 87 M e
Prince Albert, *South Africa* 122 C f
Prince Albert Mts., *Antarctica* 136 A c
Prince Albert Nat. Park, *Saskatchewan* 86 L d
Prince Albert Pen., *North-West Territories* 80 H c
Prince Alfred C., *North-West Territories* 80 G c
Prince Charles I., *North-West Territories* 81 M d
Prince Charles Mts., *Antarctica* 136 Q d
Prince Charles Str., *Antarctica* 136 J g
Prince Edward B., *Ontario* 85 O j
Prince Edward I., prov., *Canada* 81 N h
Prince Edward I. Nat. Park, *Prince Edward I.* 82 J g
Prince Edward Pt., *Ontario* 85 O j
Prince Gustaf Adolf Sea, *North-West Territories* 80 J b
Prince Harald Ld., *Antarctica* 136 L d
Prince of Wales I., *Australia* 135 H b
Prince of Wales I., *North-West Territories* 80 J c
Prince of Wales Str., *North-West Territories* 80 H c
Prince Olav Coast, *Antarctica* 136 P e
Prince Olav Mts., *Antarctica* 136 C b
Prince Patrick I., *North-West Territories* 80 H b
Prince Regent Inlet, *North-West Territories* 81 K c
Prince Rupert, *British Columbia* 88 D c
Princes Lake. *See* Wallace
Princess Astrid Ld., *Antarctica* 136 M d
Princess Charlotte B., *Australia* 135 H b
Princess Martha Coast, *Antarctica* 136 L d
Princess Ragnhild Ld., *Antarctica* 136 N d
Princess Royal I., *British Columbia* 88 E d
Princeton, *Br. Columbia* 88 J f
Princeville, *Quebec* 85 T f
Principe Chan., *British Columbia* 88 E d
Princípe da Beira, *Brazil* 92 E f
Principe I., *G. of Guinea* 120 B d
Pringles, *Argentina* 95 D f
Prins Karls Forland, *Arctic Ocean* 114 A a
Prinsta B., Anticosti I., *Quebec* 83 L d
Prinzapolca, *Nicaragua* 91 C d
Pripyat (Pripet), R., *Belorussia, U.S.S.R.* 116 F f
Pripyat (Pripet) Marshes, *Belorussia, U.S.S.R.* 116 E e
Priština, *Yugoslavia* 112 C c
Pritzwalk, *Germany* 104 E b
Privolnoye, *U.S.S.R.* 117 H e
Prizren, *Yugoslavia* 112 C c
Prizzi, *Sicily* 111 D g
Proclamation I., *Antarctica* 136 P e
Procter, *Br. Columbia* 88 L f
Progreso, *Mexico* 90 G c
Prokop'yevsk, *U.S.S.R.* 114 H c
Prokuplje, *Yugoslavia* 112 C c
Prome, *Burma* 127 J e
Prophet, R., *Br. Columbia* 88 H a
Prophet River, *Br. Columbia* 88 H a
Propria, *Brazil* 93 K f
Prospector, *Manitoba* 87 Q e
Prosperine, *Australia* 135 J d
Provence, prov., *France* 109 F e
Providence, C., *New Zealand* 135 P m
Providence, *North-West Territories* 80 H e
Providence Bay, *Ontario* 84 H g
Provins, *France* 108 E b
Provost, *Alberta* 86 G f
Prozor, *Yugoslavia* 110 F d
Prudentópolis, *Brazil* 94 F c
Prudhoe Ld., *Greenland* 89 Q b
Prud'homme, *Saskatchewan* 87 M f
Prüm, *Germany* 104 B c
Prut, R., *U.S.S.R., etc.* 116 F j
Prydz B., *Antarctica* 136 Q e
Przasnysz, *Poland* 105 J b
Przemyśl, *Poland* 105 K d
Przhevalsk, Kirgiz., *U.S.S.R.* 114 G d
Psará, I., *Greece* 113 E e
Pskov, *U.S.S.R.* 116 F c
Pskovskoye Oz., *U.S.S.R.* 116 F b
Ptuj, *Yugoslavia* 110 E b
Puán, *Argentina* 95 D e
Pubnico, *Nova Scotia* 82 G k
Pucacuro, *Peru* 92 B d
Pucallpa, *Peru* 92 C e
Puchezh, *U.S.S.R.* 117 F b
Puchow. *See* Yungtsi
Puck, *Poland* 105 H a
Pudasjärvi, *Finland* 102 M d
Pudukkottai, *India* 126 E f
Puebla & state, *Mexico* 90 E d
Puebla de Alcocer, *Spain* 106 C c
Puebla de Sanabria, *Spain* 106 B a
Puebla de Trives, *Spain* 106 B a
Pueblo Hundido, *Chile* 94 C c
Puelches, *Argentina* 95 C e
Puenteareas, *Spain* 106 A a
Puente Caldelas, *Spain* 106 A a
Puentedeume, *Spain* 106 A a
Puerh, *China* 128 D f
Puerhken, *Mongolia* 115 J d
Puerto Aisen, *Chile* 95 B g
Puerto Armuelles, *Panama* 91 C e
Puerto Asis, *Colombia* 92 B c
Puerto Ayacucho, *Venezuela* 92 D b
Puerto Barriós, *Guatemala* 90 G d
Puerto Bermudez, *Peru* 92 C f
Puerto Berrio, *Colombia* 92 C b
Puerto Cabello, *Venezuela* 92 D a
Puerto Cabezas, *Nicaragua* 91 C d
Puerto Carreño, *Colombia* 92 D b
Puerto Casado, *Paraguay* 94 E b
Puerto Chicama, *Peru* 92 B e
Puerto Colombia, *Colombia* 92 C a
Puerto Córdoba, *Colombia* 92 D d
Puerto Cortes, *Honduras* 91 B c
Puerto Coyle, *Argentina* 95 C h
Puerto Cumarebo, *Venezuela* 92 D a
Puerto de Carrizal, *Chile* 94 B c
Puerto de Chañaral, *Chile* 94 B c
Puerto de Santa María, *Spain* 106 B d
Puerto Deseado, *Argentina* 95 C g
Puerto Gaiba. *See* Puerto Quijarro
Puerto Grether, *Bolivia* 92 E g
Puerto Harberton, *Argentina* 95 C h
Puerto Heath, *Bolivia* 92 D f
Puerto Juárez, *Mexico* 90 G c
Puerto La Cruz, *Venezuela* 92 E a
Puerto Leguizamo, *Colombia* 92 C d
Puerto Libertad, *Mexico* 90 B b
Puerto Libertad, *Salvador* 91 B d
Puertollano, *Spain* 106 C c
Puerto Lobos, *Argentina* 95 C f
Puerto Madryn, *Argentina* 95 C f
Puerto Maldonado, *Peru* 92 D f
Puerto Montt, *Chile* 95 B f
Puerto Morelos, *Mexico* 90 G c
Puerto Nuevo, *Colombia* 92 D b
Puerto Peñasco, *Mexico* 90 B a
Puerto Pilón, *Panama* 91 G a
Puerto Pirámides, *Argentina* 95 D f
Puerto Plata, *Dominican Republic* 91 E c
Puerto Princesa, *Philippines* 129 G j
Puerto Quellen, *Chile* 95 B f
Puerto Quijarro, *Bolivia* 92 F g
Puerto Rico, I., *W. Indies* 54 F c
Puerto Súarez, *Bolivia* 93 F g
Puerto Sucre, *Bolivia* 92 D f
Puerto Vallarta, *Mexico* 90 C c
Puerto Varas, *Chile* 95 B f
Puerto Victoria, *Peru* 92 C e
Puerto Villamizar, *Colombia* 92 C b
Puerto Visser, *Argentina* 95 C g
Puerto Wilches, *Colombia* 92 C b
Pueyrredón, L., *Argentina* 95 B g
Pugachev, *U.S.S.R.* 117 J d
Puget-Théniers, *France* 109 G e
Puglia, dep., *Italy* 111 F e
Pugwash & Harb., *Nova Scotia* 82 J h
Pugwash Junction, *Nova Scotia* 82 J h
Pühalepa, Estonia, *U.S.S.R.* 103 K g
Puigcerdá, *Spain* 107 F a
Puimro, *Brazil* 93 G c
Pukaki, L., *New Zealand* 135 Q m
Pukapuka, I., *Pacific Ocean* 78 K h
Pukatawagan & L., *Manitoba* 87 Q c
Pukchong, *Korea* 128 J b
Pukekohe, *New Zealand* 135 R k
Pukow, *China* 130 J f
Pula, *Yugoslavia* 110 D c
Pulacayo, *Bolivia* 94 C b
Pulap, I., *Caroline Is.* 78 E f
Pulicat I., *India* 126 F f
Pulkkila, *Finland* 102 L d
Puma, *Tanzania* 121 G e
Pumas, *Manitoba* 87 S h
Puná, I., *Ecuador* 92 A d
Punakha, *Bhutan* 127 G c
Punchaw, *Br. Columbia* 88 H d
Punjab, state, *India* 126 E b
Punnichy, *Saskatchewan* 87 N g
Puno, *Peru* 92 C g
Punta Alta, *Argentina* 94 D e
Punta Arenas, *Chile* 95 B h
Punta Cardón, *Venezuela* 91 E d
Punta Chirambirá, *Colombia* 92 B c
Punta Colorado, *Chile* 94 B c
Punta del Faro, *Sicily* 111 E f
Punta de Pedras, *Brazil* 93 H d
Punta Fijo, *Venezuela* 91 E d
Punta Gorda, *British Honduras* 91 B c
Punta Maceió, *Brazil* 93 K d
Puntan Gloria, *Saipan-Tinian Is.* 78 B e
Puntan Hagman, *Saipan-Tinian Is.* 78 B e
Puntan Masalog, *Saipan-Tinian Is.* 78 A e
Puntan Vincente, *Saipan-Tinian Is.* 78 A f
Puntarenas, *Costa Rica* 91 C e
Punta Salinas, *Venezuela* 92 C a
Punta Santa María, *Peru* 92 B f
Puolanka, *Finland* 102 M d
Puquio, *Peru* 92 C f
Purang Chaka, *Tibet* 127 F b
Purcell Mts., *British Columbia* 88 L e
Puri, *India* 127 G e
Purificación, *Colombia* 92 C c
Purna, *India* 126 E e
Purnea, *India* 127 G c
Purple Springs, *Alberta* 86 F j
Pursat, *Cambodia* 132 C d
Purulia, *India* 127 G d
Purús, R., *Brazil, etc.* 92 D e
Pusan, *S. Korea* 128 J c
Pushchino, *U.S.S.R.* 115 K c
Pusht-e-Kuh, Mts., *Iran* 124 E c
Pushthrough, *Newfoundland* 83 Q f
Puskitamika L., *Quebec* 85 O c
Putao. *See* Fort Hertz
Putaruru, *New Zealand* 135 R k
Putbus, *Germany* 104 E a
Putien, *China* 131 J k
Putignano, *Italy* 111 F e
Putnok, *Hungary* 105 J d
Putorana, Gory, *U.S.S.R.* 115 J b
Puttalam, *Ceylon* 126 E g
Putte, *Belgium* 100 C c
Putten, *Netherlands* 100 D b
Puttgarden, *Germany* 104 D a
Putumayo, R., *Colombia, etc.* 92 C d
Putussibau, *Borneo* 129 F k
Puula Vesi, *Finland* 103 M f
Puurs, *Belgium* 100 C c
Puy-de-Dôme, dep., *France* 108 E d
Pyapon, *Burma* 127 J e
Pyatistennoye, *U.S.S.R.* 115 R b
Pyhä Järvi, *Finland* 102 L e
Pyhä Järvi, *Finland* 103 K f
Pyhäntä, *Finland* 102 M d
Pyinmana, *Burma* 127 J e
Pyŏngyang, *N. Korea* 128 J c
Pyramid Pt., *Canton I.* 79 T n
Pyrénées, Mts., *France-Spain* 107 E a
Pyrénées-Orientales, dep., *France* 109 E e
Pyrzyce, *Poland* 104 F b
Pythonga, L., *Quebec* 85 O f
Pyu, *Burma* 127 J e
Pyzdry, *Poland* 105 G b
Qabatiya, *Israel* 123 D e
Qafar, *Saudi Arabia* 124 D d
Qaiya, *Saudi Arabia* 124 E e
Qala Mashiz, *Iran* 125 G d
Qal'at al Akhdhar, *Saudi Arabia* 124 C d
Qal'at Dar al Hamra, *Saudi Arabia* 124 C d
Qal'at de Dab'a, *Jordan* 123 E f
Qal'at el Marqah, *Syria* 123 D b
Qal'at Uneiza, *Jordan* 123 D g
Qalqiliya, *Jordan* 123 C e
Qamr, B., *S. Yemen* 125 F f
Qara, *Egypt* 125 L c
Qardaha, *Syria* 123 E b
Qartaba, *Lebanon* 123 D c
Qasab, *Trucial States* 125 G d
Qasim, *Saudi Arabia* 124 D d
Qasr Amij, *Iraq* 124 D c
Qasr el Azraq, *Jordan* 123 E f
Qasr e Qand, *Iran* 125 H d
Qasr Haiyaniya, *Saudi Arabia* 124 D d
Qasr ibn Aliya, *Saudi Arabia* 124 D d
Qasri-i-Shirin, *Iran* 124 E c
Qa'taba, *Yemen* 124 D g
Qatana, *Syria* 123 E d
Qatar, *Arabian Pen.* 125 F d
Qatif, *Saudi Arabia* 124 E d
Qayen, *Iran* 125 G c
Qazvin, *Iran* 125 F b
Qena, *Egypt* 119 M c
Qeshm I., *Iran* 125 G d
Qeys I., *Iran* 125 F d
Qishn, *S. Yemen* 125 F f
Qishran I., *Saudi Arabia* 124 C e
Qohoud, *Iran* 125 F c
Qom, *Iran* 125 F c
Qotur, *Iran* 124 D b
Qoz Bal 'Air, *Saudi Arabia* 124 D f
Quaco Hd., *New Brunswick* 82 G h
Quakenbruck, *Germany* 104 B b
Quang Tri., *S. Vietnam* 129 E g
Quantz L., *Ontario* 84 E a
Qu'Appelle, *Saskatchewan* 87 O h
Qu'Appelle R., *Saskatchewan* 87 P h
Qu'Appelle River Dam, *Saskatchewan* 86 L g
Quaraí, *Brazil* 94 E d
Quareau, L., *Quebec* 85 Q f
Quarryville, *New Brunswick* 82 G g
Quatre Bras, *Belgium* 100 C d
Quatsino, *Br. Columbia* 88 F e
Qubeiyat, *Lebanon* 123 E c
Quchan, *Iran* 125 G b
Quebec, prov., *Canada* 81 M g
Quebec, *Quebec* 82 A g
Québec Ouest, *Quebec* 85 R b
Quebec South, dist., *Que.* 83 P j
Québec Sud, *Quebec* 85 R c
Québec Sud, *Quebec* 85 T c
Quebradillas, *Puerto Rico* 54 C h
Queen, C., *N.-W. Terr.* 81 M e
Queen Alexandra Ra., *Antarctica* 136 A b
Queen Bess, Mt., *British Columbia* 88 G e
Queen Charlotte, *British Columbia* 88 C d
Queen Charlotte B., *Falkland Is.* 95 D h
Queen Charlotte Is., *British Columbia* 88 C d
Queen Charlotte Sd., *British Columbia* 80 G g
Queen Charlotte Str., *British Columbia* 88 F e
Queen Elizabeth Is., *North-West Territories* 80 J a
Queen Elizabeth Nat. Park, *Uganda* 121 G e
Queen Fabiola Mts., *Antarc.* 136 N d
Queen Mary Coast, *Antarc.* 136 R e
Queen Mary Ld., *Antarctica* 136 R e
Queen Maud G., *N.-W. Terr.* 80 J d
Queen Maud Ld., *Antarctica* 136 N d
Queen Maud Ra., *Antarctica* 136 C a
Queen's Chan., *Australia* 134 E b
Queensland, state, *Australia* 135 H d
Queensport, *Nova Scotia* 83 L h
Queenstown, *Alberta* 86 E h
Queenstown, *New Zealand* 135 P m
Queenstown. *See* Cobh
Queenstown, *South Africa* 122 D f
Queenstown, *Tasmania* 135 J h
Queimadas, *Brazil* 93 K f
Quelimane, *Mozambique* 122 F c
Quemú Quemú, *Argentina* 94 D e
Quequén, *Argentina* 95 E e
Querétaro, *Mexico* 90 D c
Quesnel, *Br. Columbia* 88 H d
Quesnel L., *Br. Columbia* 88 J d
Quetico, *Ontario* 87 M a
Quetico L., *Ontario* 86 L b
Quetico Prov. Park, *Ontario* 86 L b
Quetta, *Pakistan* 126 C b
Quévillon, L., *Quebec* 85 O c
Quévillon, *Quebec* 85 O c
Quezaltenango, *Guatemala* 90 F e
Quezon City, *Philippines* 129 H h
Quibdo, *Colombia* 92 B b
Quibell, *Ontario* 86 J a
Quiberon, B. de., *France* 108 B c
Quievrain, *Belgium* 100 B d
Quigley, *Alberta* 86 G b
Quila, *Mexico* 90 C c
Quilca, *Peru* 92 C g
Quilino, *Argentina* 94 D d
Quillabamba, *Peru* 92 C f
Quillan, *France* 109 E e
Quill Lake, *Saskatchewan* 87 N f
Quill Ls., *Saskatchewan* 87 N g
Quillota, *Chile* 94 B d
Quilon (Kollam), *India* 126 E g
Quilpie, *Australia* 135 H e
Quimper, *France* 108 A b
Quimperlé, *France* 108 B c
Quince Mil, *Peru* 92 C f
Quines, *Argentina* 94 C d
Quintana de la Serena, *Spain* 106 C c
Quintanar de la Orden, *Spain* 106 D c
Quintana Roo, state, *Mexico* 90 G d
Quinton, *Saskatchewan* 87 N g
Quipapa, *Brazil* 93 K e
Quiriquire, *Venezuela* 92 E a
Quirke L., *Ontario* 84 H f
Quiroga, *Spain* 106 B a
Quissanga, *Mozambique* 121 J g
Quissico, *Mozambique* 122 E d
Quitapa, *Angola* 120 D g
Quito, *Ecuador* 92 B d
Quixada, *Brazil* 93 K d
Quixeramobim, *Brazil* 93 K e
Qunsulye, *Saudi Arabia* 124 D e
Quoi, I., *Truk Is.* 78 E n
Quorn, *Australia* 134 G f
Quorn, *Ontario* 87 M a
Quryat, *Muscat & Oman* 125 G e
Qus, *Egypt* 119 M c
Qusaiba, *Saudi Arabia* 124 D d
Qusayar, *S. Yemen* 125 F g
Quseir, *Egypt* 119 M c
Qusuriya, *Saudi Arabia* 124 D e
Quteifa, *Syria* 123 E d
Quyon, *Quebec* 85 O g

Raahe, Finland 102 L d
Raanes Pen., N.-W. Terr. 81 L b
Raasay & Sd. of, Scotland 98 C c
Rab, I., Yugoslavia 110 E c
Raba, Sumbawa I., Indonesia 129 G m
Rabast, C., Anticosti I., Quebec 82 H d
Rabat, Morocco 118 D b
Rabat Kerim, Iran 125 F b
Rabaul, Bismarck Arch. 78 F h
Rabbit Lake, Saskatchewan 86 K e
Rabigh, Saudi Arabia 124 C e
Race, C., Newfoundland 83 T g
Rach-Gia, S. Vietnam 132 D d
Raciborz, Poland 105 H c
Racine-de-Bouleau, R., Quebec 82 D a
Racine, L., Ontario 84 G d
Rada, Yemen 124 D g
Rădăuti, Romania 116 D h
Radhanpur, India 126 D d
Radhwa, Jebel, Saudi Arabia 124 C e
Radisson, Saskatchewan 86 K f
Radium Hot Springs, British Columbia 88 L e
Radnevo, Bulgaria 112 E c
Radnor, co., Wales 99 E h
Radom, Poland 105 J c
Radomir, Bulgaria 112 D c
Radomsko, Poland 105 H c
Radstadt, Austria 104 E e
Radviliškis, Lithuania, U.S.S.R. 103 K j
Radville, Saskatchewan 87 N j
Radway, Alberta 86 E d
Radzyn, Poland 105 K c
Rae, Mt., Alberta 86 C h
Rae Isthmus, North-West Territories 81 L d
Rae L., N.-W. Territories 80 H l
Raeside, L., Australia 134 D e
Raetihi, New Zealand 135 R k
Rafaela, Argentina 94 D d
Rafah, Gaza Strip 123 C f
Rafsanjan, Iran 125 G c
Rafter, Manitoba 87 Q c
Raga, Sudan 119 L g
Ragaz, Bad, Switzerland 101 E a
Ragunda, Sweden 102 G e
Ragusa, Sicily 111 E g
Ragusa (Dubrovnik), Yugoslavia 110 G d
Rahaeng. See Tak
Raheita, Ethiopia 121 J b
Rahhyut, Muscat & Oman 125 F f
Raiatéa, I., Society Islands 79 L j
Raichur, India 126 E e
Raida, S. Yemen 124 E g
Rainy L., Ontario-Minnesota 87 K h
Rainy River, Ontario 86 H b
Raipur, India 126 F d
Rairik, I., Majuro Is. 79 U g
Raith, Ontario 87 N a
Raivavaé, I., Austral Is. 79 M k
Raja, Mt., Borneo 129 F l
Rajahmundry, India 126 F e
Rajang, R., Sarawak 129 F k
Rajapalaiyam, India 126 E g
Rajasthan, state, India 126 D c
Rajgarh, India 127 F c
Rajkot, India 126 D d
Rajmahal Hills, India 127 G d
Rajura, India 126 E e
Rakahanga, I., Pacific Ocean 78 K h
Rakaia R., New Zealand 135 Q l
Raka Tsangpo, R., Tibet 127 G c
Rakvere, Estonia, U.S.S.R. 103 M g
Raley, Alberta 86 D j
Ralik Chain, Marshall Is. 78 G f
Ram, Jordan 123 D h
Rama, Ethiopia 121 J b
Rama, Israel 123 D e
Rama, Saskatchewan 87 P g
Ramadi, Iraq 124 D c
Ramallah, Jordan 123 D f
Ramallo, Argentina 94 D d
Ramanthapuran, India 126 E g
Rambouillet, France 108 D b
Ramea Is., Newfoundland 83 P f
Rameswaram, India 126 E g
Ram Hormuz, Iran 124 E c
Ramkola, India 127 F d
Ramla, Israel 123 C f
Râmnicul Sărat, Romania 112 F b
Râmnicu Valcea, Romania 112 E b
Ramore, Ontario 84 K d
Ramoutsa, Botswana 122 D d
Rampur, India 126 F d
Ramree, Burma 127 H e
Ramscappelle, Belgium 100 A c
Ramsele, Sweden 102 G e
Ramsey, Isle of Man 99 E f
Ramsey, Ontario 84 H e
Ramsey I., Wales 99 D j
Ramsey L., Ontario 84 H e
Ramsgate, England 99 H j
Ramsjö, Sweden 103 F e
Ramtha, Jordan 123 E e
Ramtok, India 126 E d
Rancagua, Chile 94 B d
Rance, Belgium 100 C d
Ranch, Alberta 86 D c
Ranchi, India 127 G d
Randazzo, Sicily 111 E g
Randers, Denmark 103 D h
Random I., Newfoundland 83 T e
Randon, Algeria 111 A g
Randsfjord, Norway 102 D f
Ranenburg, U.S.S.R. 117 E d
Ran Fd., Norway 102 E c
Ranfurly, Alberta 86 F e
Ranfurly, New Zealand 135 Q m
Rangamati, E. Pakistan 127 H d
Rangaunu B., New Zealand 135 Q j
Ranger L., Ontario 84 G f
Rangiora, New Zealand 135 Q l
Rangitikei, R., New Zealand 135 R k
Rangitoto Ra., New Zealand 135 Q l
Rangoon & R., Burma 127 J e
Ranibennur, India 126 E f
Raniganj, India 127 G d
Ranikhet, India 126 E c
Rankin Inlet, North-West Territories 81 K e
Rannoch L., Scotland 98 E d
Ranoke, Ontario 84 J b
Rantauparapat, Sumatra 129 C k
Rantekombola, Mt., Celebes 129 G h
Rantsila, Finland 102 L d
Ranua, Finland 102 M d
Ranvik Mts., Antarctica 136 Q d
Raoul I., Pacific Ocean 78 J k
Rapa, I., Austral Is. 79 M k
Rapadama, Upper Volta 118 E f
Rapallo, Italy 110 B c
Raper, C., N.-W. Territories 81 N d
Rapid City, Manitoba 87 R h
Rapide Blanc, Quebec 85 R e
Rapides des Joachims, Quebec 85 N f
Rapid View, Saskatchewan 86 J d
Rapla, Estonia, U.S.S.R. 103 L g
Rapperswil, Switzerland 101 D a
Raqqa, Syria 124 C b
Rarotonga, I., Cook Is. 78 K j
Ras al Had, Muscat & Oman 125 G e
Ras al Khaymah, Trucial States 125 G d
Ras Dashan, Mt., Ethiopia 121 H b
Rashad, Sudan 119 M f
Rashadiya, Jordan 123 D g
Rasheiya, Lebanon 123 D d
Rashm, Iran 125 F b
Rasht, Iran 124 E b
Raška, Yugoslavia 112 C c
Rason, L., Australia 134 D e
Raşova, Romania 112 F b
Rasskazovo, U.S.S.R. 117 E d
Ratangarh, India 126 D c
Rat Buri, Thailand 132 B d
Rathlin I., N. Ireland 98 C e
Rathwell, Manitoba 87 T j
Ratibor. See Raciborz
Ratikon, Mts., Switzerland-Austria 101 E a
Rat L., Manitoba 87 S b
Ratnagiri, India 126 D e
Ratner, Saskatchewan 87 N e
Rat Rapids, Ontario 81 K g
Rattling Brook, Newfoundland 83 Q d
Rättvik, Sweden 103 F f
Ratz, Mt., Br. Columbia 88 C b
Rauch, Argentina 94 E e
Raudha, Yemen 124 D f
Raukumara Ra., New Zealand 135 R k
Rauma, Finland 103 J f
Rautas, Sweden 102 H b
Rautavaara, Finland 102 N e
Rautio, Finland 102 L d
Ravar, Iran 125 G c
Ravendal, Saskatchewan 87 O e
Ravenna, Italy 110 D c
Ravenscrag, Saskatchewan 86 H j
Ravensworth, Ontario 85 L g
Ravi R., Pakistan 126 D b
Rawaidha, Saudi Arabia 124 D e
Rawalpindi, Pakistan 126 D b
Rawandiz, Iraq 124 D b
Rawdon, Quebec 85 R f
Rawene, New Zealand 135 Q j
Rawlinna, Australia 134 E f
Rawson, Argentina 95 C f
Ray, C., Newfoundland 83 N f
Rayadrug, India 126 E f
Raymond, Alberta 86 E j
Raymora, Saskatchewan 87 N g
Rayon, Mexico 90 B b
Rayón. See Cárdenas
Razan, Iran 124 E b
Razelm L., Romania 112 G b
Razgrad, Bulgaria 112 F c
Ré, I. de, France 108 C c
Reader L., Manitoba 87 Q e
Reading, England 99 G j
Readlyn, Saskatchewan 87 M j
Real, Cord., Bolivia 92 D g
Real, Cord., Ecuador, etc. 92 B d
Real Castillo, Mexico 90 A a
Realico, Argentina 94 D e
Realp, Switzerland 101 D b
Reata, Mexico 90 D b
Rebun, I., Japan 133 G b
Recalada, Chile 95 A h
Recalde, Argentina 94 D e
Recherche Arch., Australia 134 D f
Recht, Belgium 100 E d
Recife, Brazil 93 L e
Récif Lancaster, Tubuai Is. 79 M k
Récif Président Thiers, Tubuai Is. 79 M k
Récifs d'Entrecasteaux, Pacific Ocean 78 G j
Reconquista, Argentina 94 E c
Recovery Glacier, Antarctica 136 K b
Recreio, Brazil 93 F e
Red Bay, Labrador 83 Q b
Red Bay, Ontario 84 J h
Redberry L., Saskatchewan 86 K f
Redcliff, Alberta 86 G h
Red Deer, Alberta 86 D f
Red Deer L., Manitoba 87 Q f
Red Deer R., Alberta 86 E g
Red Deer R., Saskatchewan 87 P f
Reddit, Ontario 86 H a
Red I., Newfoundland 83 S f
Red Indian L., Newfoundland 83 P e
Red Lake, Ontario 81 K g
Red Lodge Prov. Park, Alberta 86 C g
Redon, France 108 B c
Redondela, Spain 106 A a
Red Pass, Br. Columbia 88 K d
Red Pheasant, Saskatchewan 86 J f
Red R., Manitoba-North Dakota 81 K h
Red R. See Song-koi
Red Rapids, New Brunswick 82 E g
Red Rock, Ontario 84 B d
Red Sea, Africa-Asia 124 C e
Redstone, R., Ontario 84 J d
Redvers, Saskatchewan 87 Q j
Redwater, Alberta 86 D e
Redwater, Ontario 85 L f
Red Willow, Alberta 86 E f
Reed L., Manitoba 87 Q e
Reefton, New Zealand 135 Q l
Ree L., Eire 99 B g
Reesor, Ontario 84 G c
Reeves Glacier, Antarctica 136 A d
Refresco, Chile 94 C c
Regan, Ontario 84 E d
Regencia, Brazil 93 K g
Regensburg, Germany 104 E d
Regent, Manitoba 87 R j
Regent, Ontario 84 F e
Reggan, Algeria 118 F c
Reggio, Italy 111 E f
Reggio nell'Emilia, Italy 110 C c
Reghin, Romania 112 E a
Regina, Saskatchewan 86 N h
Regina Beach, Manitoba 86 N h
Registro do Araguaia, Brazil 93 G g
Rehoboth, S.W. Africa 122 B d
Rehovot, Jordan 123 C f
Reichenbach, Germany 104 E c
Reigate, England 99 G j
Reigi, Estonia, U.S.S.R. 103 K g
Reims, France 108 F b
Reina Adelaide, Arch. de la, Chile 95 B h
Reindeer I., Manitoba 86 U f
Reindeer L., Manitoba-Saskatchewan 80 J f
Reindeer L., Saskatchewan 88 S b
Reindeer R., Saskatchewan 88 S c
Reinosa, Spain 106 C a
Reitan, Norway 102 D e
Reitz, South Africa 122 D e
Rekinniki, U.S.S.R. 115 R b
Remanso, Brazil 93 J e
Rembang, Java 129 F m
Remedios, Cuba 91 D b
Remedios, Panama 91 C e
Remeshk, Iran 125 G d
Remic Rapids, Quebec-Ontario 84 C h
Rémigny, L., Quebec 85 L e
Rémigny, Quebec 85 L e
Remiremont, France 108 G b
Remoulins, France 109 F e
Remscheid, Germany 104 B c
Remüs, Switzerland 101 F b
Rena, Norway 103 D f
Renca, Argentina 94 C d
Rencontre East, Newfoundland 83 R f
Rendsburg, Germany 104 C a
Reneault, Quebec 85 L d
Renews, Newfoundland 83 T g
Renfrew, co., Scotland 98 E e
Renfrew, Ontario 85 O g
Rengat, Sumatra 129 D l
Renigunta, India 126 E f
Renison, Ontario 84 J b
Renk, Sudan 119 M f
Renkum, Netherlands 100 D c
Renmark, Australia 134 H f
Rennell, I., Solomon Is. 78 G h
Rennes, France 108 C b
Rennick B., Antarctica 136 B e
Rennie, Manitoba 86 F a
Renous, New Brunswick 82 G g
Renous R., New Brunswick 82 F g
Renown, Saskatchewan 87 M g
Renswoude, Netherlands 100 D b
Renwer, Manitoba 87 R f
Reo, Flores I., Indonesia 124 H m
Republic of South Africa, Africa 122 C e
Repulse B., Australia 135 J d
Repulse Bay, North-West Territories 81 L d
Requena, Peru 93 C d
Requena, Spain 107 E c
Reserve, Saskatchewan 87 P f
Resistencia, Argentina 94 E c
Reşita, Romania 112 C b
Resolute, N.-W. Territories 80 K c
Resolution Fort, North-West Territories 88 H e
Resolution I., New Zealand 135 P m
Resolution I., North-West Territories 81 N e
Resolution L., Quebec 81 N f
Restigouche, Quebec 82 F e
Restigouche R., New Brunswick 82 E f
Reston, Manitoba 87 Q j
Restoule, Ontario 85 L f
Rethel, France 108 F b
Réthimnon, Crete 113 E g
Rethy, Belgium 100 D c
Retlaw, Alberta 86 E h
Réunion, I., Indian Ocean 121 L a
Reusel, Netherlands 100 D c
Reutlingen, Germany 104 C d
Reutte, Austria 104 D e
Revda, U.S.S.R. 117 Q b
Revel. See Tallinn
Revelstoke, Br. Columbia 88 K e
Revenue, Saskatchewan 86 J f
Revilla Gigedo Is., Mexico 90 B d
Revivim, Israel 123 C f
Rewa, India 126 F d
Reward, Saskatchewan 86 H f
Rex, Mt., Antarctica 136 H d
Rexton, New Brunswick 82 H g
Rey, I. del, Panama 91 D e
Reydharfjord, Iceland 102 Z m
Reyes, Mexico 90 D d
Reykjavik, Iceland 102 U m
Reykjavik, Manitoba 87 T g
Reynaud, R. au, Quebec 82 H e
Reynaud, Saskatchewan 87 M f
Reynolds, Manitoba 86 F a
Reynosa, Mexico 90 E b
Rezā'īyeh, Iran 124 D b
Rēzekne, Latvia, U.S.S.R. 103 M h
Rheden, Netherlands 100 E b
Rhein, R. See Rhine
Rhein, Saskatchewan 87 P g
Rheine, Germany 104 B b
Rheinland-Pfalz, Germany 104 B c
Rhenen, Netherlands 100 D c
Rheydt, Germany 104 B c
Rhine (Rhein), R., Germany 104 B c
Rhodesia, Cent. Africa 122 D c
Rhodesia, N. See Zambia
Rhodesia, S. See Rhodesia
Rhodes (Rodhos), I., Greece 113 G f
Rhondda, Wales 99 E j
Rhône, dep., France 108 F d
Rhône, R., France, etc. 109 F d
Rhön Geb., Mts., Germany 104 C c
Rhyl, Wales 99 E g
Riaño, Spain 106 C a
Riau Arch., Indonesia 129 D k
Riaza, Spain 106 D b
Ribadeo, Spain 106 B a
Ribadesella, Spain 106 C a
Ribble, R., England 99 F g
Ribe, Denmark 103 C j
Ribeirão Prêto, Brazil 94 G b
Ribera, Sicily 111 D g
Riberalta, Bolivia 92 D f
Rib Lake, Ontario 85 L e
Ribstone, Alberta 86 G f
Ribstone Cr., Alberta 86 F f
Rice L., Ontario 85 M h
Rice L., Ontario 84 H l
Riceton, Saskatchewan 87 N h
Richard, Saskatchewan 86 K f
Richard Collinson Inlet, North-West Territories 80 H c
Richards C., Arctic Ocean 89 R a
Richards Landing, Ontario 84 F f
Richardson R., Alberta 88 O a
Richardson Sta., Saskatchewan 87 N h
Richdale, Alberta 86 F g
Richelieu, R., Quebec 85 R g
Riche Pt., Newfoundland 83 P c
Richibucto, New Brunswick 82 H g
Rich Lake, Alberta 86 F d
Richlea, Saskatchewan 86 J g
Richmond, Australia 135 H d
Richmond, co., British Columbia 88 C g
Richmond, New Zealand 135 Q l
Richmond, Ontario 85 P g
Richmond, Prince Edward I. 82 H g
Richmond, Quebec 85 S g
Richmond, South Africa 122 C f
Richmond Hill, Ontario 85 L j
Richmound, Saskatchewan 86 H h
Ricla, Spain 107 E b
Riddes, Switzerland 101 C b
Rideau, R., Ontario 85 P g
Rideau Can., Ontario 85 P h
Rideau L., Ontario 85 O h
Ridge, R., Ontario 84 F b
Ridgedale, Saskatchewan 87 N e
Ridgetown, Ontario 84 J k
Ridgeville, Manitoba 87 V j
Ridi, Nepal 127 F c
Riding Mt., ra., Manitoba 87 R h
Riding Mt. Nat. Park, Manitoba 87 R h
Ridpath, Saskatchewan 86 J g
Riesa, Germany 104 E c
Rietavas, Lithuania, U.S.S.R. 103 J j
Rieti, Italy 110 D d
Riga, G. of, Latvia, U.S.S.R. 103 K h
Riga, Latvia, U.S.S.R. 103 L h
Rigan, Iran 125 G d
Rigaud, Quebec 85 Q g
Rigili, I., Eniwetok 79 R c
Rigmati, Iran 125 G d
Rigolet, Labrador 81 O g
Rig-Rig, Chad 119 H f
Riiser-Larsen, Mt., Antarctica 136 P e
Riiser Larsen Pen., Antarctica 136 N d
Rijeka, Yugoslavia 110 E c
Rijswijk, Netherlands 100 C b
Rimatara, I., Austral Is. 79 L k
Rimbey, Alberta 86 C f
Rimini, Italy 110 D c
Rimouski & R., Quebec 82 D e
Rincón, Cuba 91 C b
Rincón, Puerto Rico 54 B h
Rindal, Norway 102 C e
Ringelspitz, Mt., Switzerland 101 E b
Ringköbing, Denmark 103 C h
Ringvassöy, I., Norway 102 H b
Rinihue, Chile 95 B e
Riobamba, Ecuador 92 B d
Rio Bonito, Brazil 93 J h
Rio Branco, Brazil 94 G c
Rio Branco, Brazil 92 D e
Río Branco, Uruguay 94 F d
Río Bueno, Chile 95 B f
Río Chico, Argentina 95 C g
Río Chico, Venezuela 92 D a
Río Colorado, Argentina 95 D e
Río Cuarto, Argentina 94 D d
Rio de Janeiro, Brazil 93 J h
Río de Oro. See Convención
Rio do Sul, Brazil 94 G c
Río Gallegos & R., Argentina 95 C h
Rio Grande, Brazil 94 F d
Río Grande, Mexico 90 D c
Río Grande, Puerto Rico 54 D h
Riohacha, Colombia 92 C a
Río Hondo, Argentina 94 D c
Río Muerto, Argentina 94 D c
Río Mulato, Bolivia 92 D g
Río Muni, Equatorial Guinea 120 C d
Rio Negro, Brazil 94 G c
Rionero in Vulture, Italy 111 E e
Rio Pardo, Brazil 93 G h
Rio Verde, Brazil 93 G g
Río Verde, Ecuador 92 B c
Río Verde, Mexico 90 E c
Rioz, France 108 G c
Ripats, Sweden 102 J c
Ripault, L., Quebec 82 K b
Ripley, Ontario 84 J h
Ripon, England 99 F f
Ripon, Quebec 85 P g
Risafe, Syria 124 C b
Risbäck, Sweden 102 J c
Rishiri, I., Japan 133 G b
Rishon-le-Zion, Israel 123 C f
Risör, Norway 103 C g
Ristijärvi, Finland 102 N d
Ritidian Pt., Guam 78 A k
Rivadavia, Argentina 94 D b
Rivas, Nicaragua 91 B d
Rivera, Argentina 94 D e
Rivera, Uruguay 94 E d
River Denys, Cape Breton I., Nova Scotia 83 L h
Riverhead, Newfoundland 83 T g
River Hébert, Nova Scotia 82 H h
Riverhurst, Saskatchewan 86 L h
River John, Nova Scotia 82 J h
Rivero, I., Chile 95 B g
River of Ponds, Newfoundland 83 P c
Riverport, Nova Scotia 82 H j
Rivers, L. of the, Saskatchewan 87 M j
Rivers, Manitoba 87 R h
Riverside, Ontario 84 H k
Rivers Inlet, Br. Columbia 88 F e
Riverton, Manitoba 87 U h
Riverton, New Zealand 135 P m
River Valley, Ontario 84 K f
Rivett, Mt., Antarctica 136 Q e
Riviera di Levante, Italy 110 B c
Riviera di Ponente, Italy 110 A d
Rivière-à-Claude, Quebec 82 G d
Rivière-a-la-Loatre, Anticosti I., Quebec 82 J d
Rivière à Pierre, Quebec 85 S f
Rivière-au-Renard, Quebec 82 H e
Rivière aux Graines, Quebec 82 G c
Rivière aux Rats, Quebec 85 S e
Rivière Bleue, Quebec 82 C f
Rivière-de-la-Chaloupe, Anticosti I., Quebec 82 K d
Rivière du Loup, Quebec 82 C f
Rivière du Milieu, Quebec 85 S e
Rivière du Moulin, Quebec 82 B e
Rivière Heva, Quebec 85 M d
Rivière la Madeleine, Que. 82 G d
Rivière Ouelle, Quebec 82 B f
Rivière Pentecôte, Quebec 82 E d
Rivière Pigou, Quebec 82 G c
Rivières des Prairies, Quebec 85 S h
Rivière St. Jean, Quebec 82 H c
Riviere Verte, New Brunswick 82 D f
Rivière Verte, Quebec 82 C f
Riyadh (Ar Riyadh), Saudi Arabia 124 E e
Riyaq, Lebanon 123 E d
Rizaiyeh. See Rezā'īyeh
Rize, Turkey 124 D a
Rizokarpaso, Cyprus 123 C b
Rizzuto, C., Italy 111 F f
Roa, Spain 106 D b
Roanne, France 108 F c
Roaringwater B., Eire 99 A j
Roatán, I., Honduras 91 B c
Robat Thana, Pakistan 126 B c
Robe Noire, L. de la, Quebec 82 K c
Robert English Coast, Antarctica 136 H d
Robert I., Antarctica 136 H f
Robertsfors, Sweden 102 J d
Robertsganj, India 127 F d
Robertson, Mt., Antarctica 136 H d
Robertson B., Antarctica 136 B d
Robertson I., Antarctica 136 J e
Robertson L., Quebec 83 N b
Robertsonville, Quebec 85 T f
Robertsport, Liberia 118 C g
Robertville, New Brunswick 82 G f
Roberval, Quebec 85 S d
Robeson Chan., Arctic Ocean 89 Q a
Robinson's, Newfoundland 83 O e
Robinsonville, New Brunswick 82 F f
Roblin, Manitoba 87 Q g
Robokaire, I., Majuro Is. 79 U f
Roboré, Bolivia 92 F g
Robsart, Saskatchewan 86 H j
Robson, Mt., Br. Columbia 88 K d
Rocafuerte, Ecuador 92 B d
Rocanville, Saskatchewan 87 Q h
Rocha, Uruguay 94 B d
Rochdale, England 99 F g
Rochebaucourt, Quebec 85 N d
Rochefort, Belgium 100 D d
Rochefort, France 108 C d
Roche Percée, Saskatchewan 87 P j
Rocher, L. du, Quebec 83 O b
Rochers, R. aux, Quebec 82 E c
Rochester, Alberta 86 D d
Rochester, England 99 H j
Rochfort Bridge, Alberta 86 B e
Rockall, I., Atlantic Ocean 96 D d
Rock Bay, Vancouver I., British Columbia 88 G e
Rockcliffe Airport, Ontario 84 D h
Rockcliffe Park, Ontario 84 D h
Rockefeller Mts., Antarctica 136 D c
Rockefeller Plat., Antarctica 136 E c
Rockglen, Saskatchewan 87 M j
Rockhampton, Australia 135 K d
Rockhaven, Saskatchewan 86 J f
Rock Island, Quebec 85 S g
Rockland, Ontario 85 P g
Rock Sound, Bahama Is. 91 D b
Rockstone, Guyana 92 F b
Rockwood, Ontario 84 K j
Rockyford, Alberta 86 D g
Rocky Island L., Ontario 84 G f
Rocky L., Manitoba 87 Q d
Rocky Mountain House, Alberta 86 C f
Rocroi, France 108 F b
Rödby, Denmark 103 D j
Rödbyhavn, Denmark 104 D a
Rodchevo, U.S.S.R. 115 Q b
Roddickton, Newfoundland 83 Q c
Rodez, France 109 E d
Rodhopi, Greece 112 E d
Rodhos & I., Greece 113 G f
Rodkhan, Pakistan 126 B c
Rodney, Ontario 84 J k
Rodopi Planina, Bulgaria-Greece 112 D d
Rodosto. See Tekirdag
Roebourne, Australia 134 C d
Roermond, Netherlands 100 D c
Roeselare (Roulers), Belgium 100 B d
Roes Welcome Sd., North-West Territories 81 L e
Roeulx, Belgium 100 C d
Rogachev, Belorussia, U.S.S.R. 116 G e
Roger, L., Quebec 85 M e
Rogers, Mt., Br. Columbia 88 L e
Rogersville, New Brunswick 82 G g
Rogliano, Corsica 110 B d
Roguron, I., Majuro Is. 79 T f
Rohault, L., Quebec 85 Q c
Rohi Ikhand, India 126 E c
Rohri, Pakistan 126 C c
Rohtak, India 126 E c
Roi, I., Kwajalein Is. 79 U d
Roi Et, Thailand 132 C c
Roisin, Belgium 100 B d
Rojas, Argentina 94 D d
Rojo, C., Puerto Rico 54 B j
Rojoa, I., Eniwetok 79 S c
Rokeby, Saskatchewan 87 P g
Rokiškis, Lithuania, U.S.S.R. 103 L j
Roland, Manitoba 87 U j
Rolde, Netherlands 100 E b
Rolla, British Columbia 88 J c
Rolle, Switzerland 101 B b
Rollet, Quebec 85 L e
Rolphton, Ontario 85 N f
Rolvsöy, Norway 102 K a
Roma, Australia 135 J e
Roma, I., Indonesia 129 J m
Roma. See Rome
Roma, Sweden 103 H h
Romaine R., Quebec 82 J c
Roman, Romania 112 F a
Romania, Central Europe 97 P g
Romans, France 109 F d
Romanshorn, Switzerland 101 E a
Rome (Roma), Italy 111 D e
Romerée, Belgium 100 C d
Romford, England 99 H j
Romny, Ukraine, U.S.S.R. 116 H f

Römö, I., *Denmark* 103 C j
Romont, *Switzerland* 101 B b
Romsdalshorn, *Norway* 102 B e
Ron, *N. Vietnam* 132 D c
Ronda, *Kashmir* 126 D a
Ronda, *Spain* 106 C d
Rondeau Prov. Park, *Ontario* 84 J k
Rondônia, *Brazil* 92 E f
Ronehamn, *Sweden* 103 H h
Rongelap, I., *Marshall Is.* 78 G f
Rongerik, I., *Marshall Is.* 79 T a
Ronkiti, I., *Ponape I.* 78 F o
Ronkiti Harb., *Ponape I.* 78 F o
Rönne, Bornholm I., *Denmark* 103 F j
Ronne B., *Antarctica* 136 H d
Ronne Ice Shelf, *Antarctica* 136 J b
Ronneby, *Sweden* 103 F h
Roosendaal, *Netherlands* 100 C c
Roosevelt, I., *Antarctica* 136 C h
Roosevelt, Mt., *British Columbia* 88 G a
Roper, R., *Australia* 134 F b
Roquefort, *France* 109 C d
Roquemaure, *Quebec* 85 L d
Rorketon, *Manitoba* 87 S g
Röros, *Norway* 102 D e
Rorschach, *Switzerland* 101 E a
Rosa, Monte, *Switzerland-Italy* 101 C c
Roseblanche, Mt., *Switzerland* 101 C b
Rosaire, *Quebec* 82 B g
Rosalind, *Alberta* 86 E f
Rosarinho. See Axinim
Rosario, *Argentina* 94 D d
Rosario, *Brazil* 93 J d
Rosario, *Chile* 94 B b
Rosario, *Mexico* 90 A a
Rosario, *Mexico* 90 C c
Rosario de la Frontera, *Argentina* 94 D c
Rosario Oeste, *Brazil* 93 F f
Rosario Tala, *Argentina* 94 E d
Rosas, G. de, *Spain* 107 G a
Rosas, *Spain* 107 G a
Roscommon & co., *Eire* 99 B g
Roscrea, *Eire* 99 B h
Rose, I., *Samoa* 78 K j
Rose Blanche, *Newfoundland* 83 O f
Rosebud, *Alberta* 86 E g
Rosebud R., *Alberta* 86 D g
Rosedale, *Alberta* 86 E g
Roseheath, *Ontario* 85 M h
Rose I., *Br. Columbia* 88 D g
Roseires, *Sudan* 119 M f
Rose Lynn, *Alberta* 86 F g
Rosemary, *Alberta* 86 E h
Rosenheim, *Germany* 104 E e
Rose Pt., Graham I., *British Columbia* 88 D c
Roseray, *Saskatchewan* 86 J h
Rosetown, *Saskatchewan* 86 K g
Rosetta (Rashid), *Egypt* 119 M b
Rose Valley, *Saskatchewan* 87 O f
Rosevear, *Alberta* 86 A e
Rosiers, C. des, *Quebec* 82 H e
Rosignano Marittamo, *Italy* 110 C d
Rosignol, *Guyana* 92 F b
Roslavl, *U.S.S.R.* 116 H e
Roslyn L., *Ontario* 84 C c
Rosport, *Luxembourg* 100 E e
Ross, *England* 99 F j
Ross, I., *Antarctica* 136 B c
Ross, *New Zealand* 135 Q l
Rossa, *Switzerland* 101 E b
Ross & Cromarty, co., *Scotland* 98 D c
Rossano, *Italy* 111 F f
Rosseau, *Ontario* 85 L g
Rossel I., *Papua* 135 K b
Rossendale, *Manitoba* 87 T j
Ross I., *Burma* 127 J f
Ross I., *Manitoba* 87 U d
Ross Ice Shelf, *Antarctica* 136 C b
Rossignol, *Belgium* 100 D e
Rossignol, L., *Nova Scotia* 82 G j
Rossland, *British Columbia* 88 L f
Rosslare Harb., *Eire* 99 C h
Rossport, *Ontario* 84 C d
Ross Sea, *Antarctica* 136 C d
Rossway, *Nova Scotia* 82 G j
Rosswood, *British Columbia* 88 E c
Rosta, *Norway* 102 H b
Rosthern, *Saskatchewan* 86 L f
Rostock, *Germany* 104 E a
Rostov, *U.S.S.R.* 117 D g
Rostov, *U.S.S.R.* 116 L c
Rös Vatn, *Norway* 102 F d
Rota, I., *Mariana Is.* 78 E e
Rothenburg, *Germany* 104 D d
Rotherham, *England* 99 G g
Rothesay, *New Brunswick* 82 G h
Rothesay, *Scotland* 98 D e
Rothschild I., *Antarctica* 136 H e
Roti, I., *Indonesia* 129 H n
Rotorua, *New Zealand* 135 R k
Rotterdam, *Netherlands* 100 C c
Rotuma, I., *Fiji Is.* 78 H h
Roubaix, *France* 108 E a
Rouen, *France* 108 D b
Rõuge, *Estonia, U.S.S.R.* 103 M h
Rouleau, *Saskatchewan* 87 N h
Roulers, *Belgium* 100 B d
Roumania. See Romania
Round Harbour, *Newfoundland* 83 R d
Round Hill, *Alberta* 86 E e
Round Pond, *Newfoundland* 83 R e
Rounthwaite, *Manitoba* 87 S j
Roura, *Fr. Guiana* 93 G c
Rous, Pen., *Chile* 95 C j
Rousay I., *Orkney, Scotland* 98 E a
Rousbrugge, *Belgium* 100 A d
Rouse, C., *Antarctica* 136 Q e
Roussillon Oriental, prov., *France* 109 E e
Routhierville, *Quebec* 82 E e
Rouveen, *Netherlands* 100 E b
Rouvray, L., *Quebec* 82 B d
Rouyn, *Quebec* 85 M d
Rovaniemi, *Finland* 102 L c
Roveredo, *Switzerland* 101 E b
Rovigo, *Italy* 110 C c
Rovinari, *Romania* 112 D b
Rovno, *Ukraine, U.S.S.R.* 116 E f
Rowan L., *Ontario* 86 J a
Rowley, *Alberta* 86 E g
Rowley I., *North-West Territories* 81 M d
Roxas, *Philippines* 129 H h
Roxburgh, co., *Scotland* 98 F e
Roxburgh, *New Zealand* 135 P m
Roxton, *Quebec* 85 S g
Roy, L., *Quebec* 82 C d
Royal, Mt., *Ontario* 84 B c
Royal Canal, *Eire* 99 C g
Royalties, *Alberta* 86 C h
Royan, *France* 108 C d
Rožňava, *Czechoslovakia* 105 J d
R. Scott Glacier, *Antarctica* 136 D a
Rtishchevo, *U.S.S.R.* 117 F d
Rua, I., *Jaluit I.* 79 T h
Ruac, I., *Truk Is.* 78 E m
Ruahine Ra., *New Zealand* 135 R k
Ruanda. See Rwanda
Ruanda-Urundi. See Rwanda, Burundi
Ruapehu, Mt., *New Zealand* 135 R k
Ruapuke I., *New Zealand* 135 P m
Rubtsovsk, *U.S.S.R.* 114 H c
Rudbar, *Afghanistan* 125 H c
Ruddell, *Saskatchewan* 86 K f
Ruddervoorde, *Belgium* 100 B c
Rudköbing, *Denmark* 103 D j
Rudok, *Tibet* 126 E b
Rudolf L., *Kenya* 121 H d
Ruel, *Ontario* 84 J e
Ruffec, *France* 108 D c
Rufino, *Argentina* 94 D d
Rugby, *England* 99 G h
Rügen, I., *Germany* 104 E a
Rui Barbosa, *Brazil* 93 J f
Rujiena, *Latvia, U.S.S.R.* 103 L h
Rujiyaru, I., *Eniwetok* 79 R c
Ruk, *Pakistan* 126 C c
Rukwa L., *Tanzania* 121 G f
Rum, I., *Scotland* 98 C d
Rumania. See Romania
Rumbek, *Sudan* 119 L g
Rumburk, *Czechoslovakia* 104 F c
Rum Cay, *Bahama Is.* 91 E b
Rumegies, *France* 100 B d
Rumigny, *France* 100 C e
Rumillies, *Belgium* 100 B d
Rum Jungle, *Australia* 134 F b
Rumoi, *Japan* 133 G c
Rumsey, *Alberta* 86 E g
Rumung, I., *Yap I.* 78 D l
Rumuruti, *Kenya* 121 H d
Runanga, *New Zealand* 135 Q l
Rungwa, *Tanzania* 121 G f
Rungwe Mt., *Tanzania* 121 G f
Runit, I., *Eniwetok* 79 S c
Runnymede, *Saskatchewan* 87 Q g
Runu, I., *Yap I.* 78 D l
Rupert, R., *Quebec* 81 M g
Rupert B., *Quebec* 85 L a
Rupert R., *Quebec* 81 N a
Ruppert Coast, *Antarctica* 136 D c
Rupshu, *India* 126 E b
Rurrenabaque, *Bolivia* 92 D f
Rurutu, I., *Austral Is* 79 L k
Rusape, *Rhodesia* 122 E c
Ruseifa, *Jordan* 123 E e
Rusele, *Sweden* 102 H d
Ruse (Ruschuk), *Bulgaria* 112 E c
Rush Lake, *Saskatchewan* 86 K h
Rusne, R., *Lithuania, U.S.S.R.* 103 J j
Russas, *Brazil* 93 K d
Russelkonda, *India* 127 F e
Russell, *Manitoba* 87 Q h
Russell, *New Zealand* 135 R j
Russell, *Ontario* 81 P g
Russell I., *North-West Territories* 81 K c
Russell L., *Manitoba* 87 Q b
Russell L., *Saskatchewan* 88 R b
Russia. See Union of Soviet Socialist Republics
Russkoye Ust'ye, *U.S.S.R.* 115 P a
Russo, *Switzerland* 101 D b
Rustak, *Afghanistan* 125 J b
Rutbah, *Iraq* 124 D c
Rutherglen, *Ontario* 85 L f
Rüthi, *Switzerland* 101 E a
Ruthilda, *Saskatchewan* 86 J g
Ruthin, *Wales* 99 E g
Rutland, co., *England* 99 G h
Rutland I., *Andaman Is* 127 H f
Rutland Station, *Saskatchewan* 86 H f
Rutter, *Ontario* 84 K f
Ruurlo, *Netherlands* 100 E b
Ruvuma R., *Mozambique* 121 H g
Ruweiba, *Sudan* 119 L e
Ruwenzori, Mt., *Uganda* 121 G d
Ružomberok, *Czechoslovakia* 105 H d
Rvazhsk, *U.S.S.R.* 116 M e
Rwanda, *Cent. Africa* 121 F e
Ryan, L., *Scotland* 98 D f
Ryazan, *U.S.S.R.* 116 L d
Rybachiy, Pol., *U.S.S.R* 114 C b
Rybinsk, *U.S.S.R.* 116 L b
Rybinskoye Vdkhr., *U.S.S.R.* 116 L b
Rybnoye, *U.S.S.R.* 115 K a
Rycroft, *Alberta* 88 K c
Rydal Bank, *Ontario* 84 G f
Ryde, Isle of Wight, *England* 99 G k
Rye, *England* 99 H k
Ryerson, *Saskatchewan* 87 Q j
Ryland, *Ontario* 84 G c
Ryley, *Alberta* 86 E e
Rymarov, *Czechoslovakia* 105 G d
Rypin, *Poland* 105 H b
Ryukyu Retto, Is., *Japan* 128 H j
Rzeszów, *Poland* 105 J c
Rzhev, *U.S.S.R.* 116 J c
Saalfeld, *Germany* 104 D c
Saanen, *Switzerland* 101 C b
Saanich, *Br. Columbia* 88 H f
Saarbrucken, *West Germany* 104 B d
Saaremaa, Os., *Lithuania, U.S.S.R.* 103 K g
Saari Selkä, *Finland* 102 N b
Saarland, *Europe* 104 B d
Saarlouis, *West Germany* 104 B d
Saas Grund, *Switzerland* 101 C b
Saavedra, *Argentina* 95 D e
Saavedra, *Chile* 95 B e
Šabac, *Yugoslavia* 112 B b
Sabadell, *Spain* 107 G b
Sabah, *Malaysia* 129 G j
Sabalan, Mt., *Iran* 124 E b
Sabalgarh, *India* 126 E c
Sabana, Arch. de, *Cuba* 91 C b
Sabanalarga, *Colombia* 92 C a
Sabancuy, *Mexico* 90 F d
Sab Biyar, *Syria* 123 F d
Sabha, *Jordan* 123 E e
Sabile, *Latvia, U.S.S.R.* 103 K h
Sabiñanigo, *Spain* 107 E a
Sabinas, *Mexico* 90 D b
Sabine, C., *N.-W. Terr.* 81 M b
Sabine Mt., *Antarctica* 136 B d
Sabi R., *India* 126 E c
Sable, C., *Nova Scotia* 82 G k
Sable, *France* 108 C c
Sable I., *Nova Scotia* 83 N k
Sable Island Bank, *Nova Scotia* 83 M k
Sable River, *Nova Scotia* 82 G k
Sables, R. aux, *Ontario* 84 H f
Sabrina Coast, *Antarctica* 136 S e
Sabzawar, *Iran* 125 G b
Sabzevar (Shindand), *Afghanistan* 125 H c
Sacaca, *Bolivia* 92 D g
Sacedón, *Spain* 107 D b
Săcele, *Romania* 112 E b
Sachigo, R., *Ontario* 81 K g
Sachs Harbour, *North-West Territories* 80 G c
Sackville, *New Brunswick* 82 H h
Sacramento, *Brazil* 93 H g
Sacré-Coeur Saguenay, *Quebec* 82 C e
Sada, *Yemen* 124 D f
Sádaba, *Spain* 107 E a
Sá da Bandeira, *Angola* 120 C g
Sadad, *Syria* 123 E c
Sadaich. See Sadīj
Sadīj, *Iran* 125 G d
Sadiya, *India* 127 J c
Sa 'diya, Jeb., *Saudi Arabia* 125 D e
Sadmarda, *Afghanistan* 125 J b
Sado, I., *Japan* 133 F e
Sadra, *India* 126 D d
Sadulpur, *India* 126 E c
Saeki, *Japan* 133 B h
Safad, *Israel* 123 E d
Safed Koh Ra., *Afghanistan-Pakistan* 126 C b
Safi, *Morocco* 118 D b
Safi, *Syria* 123 D f
Safidabeh, *Iran* 125 H c
Safita, *Syria* 123 E c
Safonovo, *U.S.S.R.* 116 H d
Safranbolu, *Turkey* 124 B a
Saga, *Japan* 133 B h
Sagaing, *Burma* 127 J d
Sagami, B., *Japan* 133 F g
Saganaga L., *Ontario* 87 M b
Saganash L., *Ontario* 84 H c
Sagar, *India* 126 E d
Saglek B., *Labrador* 81 N f
Sagone, G. de, *Corsica* 110 B d
Sagres, *Portugal* 106 A d
Sagua la Grande, *Cuba* 91 C b
Saguenay, R., *Quebec* 82 B e
Sagunto, *Spain* 107 E c
Saham, *Muscat & Oman* 125 G e
Sahand, Mt., *Iran* 124 E b
Sahara, reg., *Algeria* 118 E c
Sahara Des., *Africa* 118 D d
Saharanpur, *India* 126 E c
Saharien Atlas, Mts., *Algeria* 118 F b
Sahiadriparvat Ra., *India* 126 E d
Sahuaripa, *Mexico* 90 C b
Sahuayo, *Mexico* 90 D c
Sahugun, *Spain* 106 C a
Sahun, *S. Yemen* 124 E g
Sahy, *Czechoslovakia* 105 H d
Sahyadri Mts., *India* 124 D e
Saibai, I., *Australia* 135 H a
Saida. See Sidon
Saidabad, *Iran* 125 G d
Saidapet, *India* 124 F f
Said Bundas, *Sudan* 119 K g
Saidu Sharif, *Pakistan* 126 D b
Saignelégier, *Switzerland* 101 B a
Saigon, *S. Vietnam* 132 D d
Sailana, *India* 126 D d
Saimaa, L., *Finland* 103 M f
Saimaa Kanal, *Finland-U.S.S.R.* 103 N f
Saimbeyli, *Turkey* 124 B c
St. Abbs Hd., *Scotland* 98 F e
Ste. Adelaide, *Quebec* 82 H e
Ste. Adèle, *Quebec* 85 Q g
St. Affrique, *France* 109 E e
St. Agapit, *Manitoba* 85 T f
Ste. Agathe, *Manitoba* 87 U j
Ste. Agathe des Monts, *Quebec* 85 Q f
Ste. Agnes, *Quebec* 85 L d
St. Agrève, *France* 109 F d
St. Albans, *England* 99 G j
St. Alban's, *Newfoundland* 83 R f
St. Albert, *Alberta* 86 D e
St. Alexandre, *Quebec* 82 C f
St. Alexis des Monts, *Quebec* 85 R f
St. Ambroise, *Quebec* 85 T d
St. Amour, *France* 108 F c
St. Anaclet, *Quebec* 82 D e
St. André, C., *Mal. Rep.* 121 M k
St. Andrew's, *New Brunswick* 82 E h
St. Andrew's, *Newfoundland* 83 N f
St. Andrews, *Scotland* 98 F d
St. Andrew's Chan., Cape Breton I., *Nova Scotia* 83 M g
Ste. Ann, *Manitoba* 87 E a
St. Ann B., Cape Breton I., *Nova Scotia* 83 M g
Ste. Anne, L., *Quebec* 82 E c
Ste. Anne, R., *Quebec* 82 B f
Ste. Anne de Beaupré, *Quebec* 82 B f
Ste. Anne de Chicoutimi, *Quebec* 82 A e
Ste. Anne de la Pérade, *Que.* 85 S f
Ste. Anne de la Pocatière, *Quebec* 82 B f
Ste. Anne-des-Monts, *Que.* 82 F d
Ste. Anne du Lac, *Quebec* 85 P f
St. Anns, Cape Breton I., *Nova Scotia* 83 M g
St. Anns Bay, *Jamaica* 91 D c
St. Anthonis, *Netherlands* 100 D c
St. Anthony, *Newfoundland* 83 R b
St. Antönien, *Switzerland* 101 E b
St. Antonin, *Quebec* 82 C f
St. Arsène, *Quebec* 82 C f
St. Athanase, *Quebec* 82 C f
St. Aubert, *Quebec* 82 B f
St. Augustin, C. de., *Mal. Rep.* 121 M l
St. Augustin B., *Quebec* 83 O b
St. Augustin R., *Quebec* 83 N b
St. Augustin-Saguenay, *Quebec* 83 O b
St. Austell, *England* 99 D k
St. Barnabé Nord, *Quebec* 85 S f
St. Barthélemi, *Quebec* 85 R f
St. Barthélemy, I., *Leeward Is.* 91 G c
St. Béat, *France* 109 D e
St. Benedict, *Saskatchewan* 87 M f
St. Benoit Labre, *Quebec* 82 B g
St. Bernard, I., *Quebec* 85 Q k
St. Bernard Pass, Grand, *Switzerland-Italy* 110 A c
Ste. Blandine, *Quebec* 82 D e
St. Boniface, *Manitoba* 87 U j
St. Boswells, *Saskatchewan* 86 L h
St. Brendan's, *Newfoundland* 83 T e
St. Bride, Mt., *Alberta* 86 B g
St. Bride's, *Newfoundland* 83 S g
St. Bride's B., *Wales* 99 D j
St. Brieuc, *France* 108 B b
St. Brieux, *Saskatchewan* 87 N f
St. Bruno de Guigues, *Quebec* 85 L e
St. Calais, *France* 108 D c
St. Camille, *Quebec* 82 B g
St. Casimir, *Quebec* 85 S f
St. Catherine Lock, *Quebec* 85 S k
St. Catharines, *Ontario* 85 L j
St. Cécile, *Quebec* 82 B h
St. Césaire, *Quebec* 85 R g
St. Chamond, *France* 108 F d
St. Charles, *Quebec* 82 B g
St. Charles R., *Quebec* 83 P h
St. Chély d'Apcher, *France* 109 E d
St. Christopher (St. Kitts), I., *Leeward Is.* 91 G c
St. Clair, L., *Ontario-Michigan* 84 H k
St. Clair R., *Ontario-Michigan* 84 H j
St. Claude, *Manitoba* 87 T j
St. Clement, *Quebec* 82 C f
Ste. Clothilde, *Quebec* 85 S g
St. Coeur de Marie, *Quebec* 85 T d
St. Côme, *Quebec* 85 R f
St. Côme. See Linière
St. Croix, I., *West Indies* 54 E j
Ste. Croix, *New Brunswick* 82 E h
Ste. Croix, *Switzerland* 101 B b
Ste. Croix R., *Maine-New Brunswick* 82 E h
St. Cyprien, *Quebec* 82 C f
St. Cyrille, *Quebec* 85 S g
St. Cyr Lake, *Saskatchewan* 86 J d
St. Damien, *Quebec* 82 B g
St. David-de-Lévis, *Quebec* 85 S c
St. David's, *Newfoundland* 83 O e
St. David's Hd., *Wales* 99 D j
St. Denis, *France* 108 E b
St. Denis, *Quebec* 82 C f
St. di Nova Siri, *Italy* 111 F e
St. Dizier, *France* 108 F b
St. Donat, *Quebec* 85 Q f
Ste. Elisabeth, *Quebec* 85 S d
St. Eloi, *Quebec* 82 C e
St. Elzéar de Laval, *Quebec* 85 R h
Ste. Émélie de l'Energie, *Quebec* 85 R f
St. Ephrem, *Quebec* 82 B g
St. Etienne, *France* 108 F d
St. Eugène, *Quebec* 85 M d
St. Eusèbe, *Quebec* 82 D f
St. Eustache, *Quebec* 85 R g
St. Eustatius, I., *Leeward Is.* 91 G c
St. Fabien, *Quebec* 82 D e
Ste. Famille, *Quebec* 82 B g
Ste. Famille d'Aumond, *Quebec* 85 P f
St. Fargeau, *France* 108 E c
St. Félicien, *Quebec* 85 S d
Ste. Félicité, *Quebec* 82 E e
St. Félix de Valois, *Quebec* 85 R f
St. Filipsland, *Netherlands* 100 C c
St. Fintan's, *Newfoundland* 83 O e
St. Flavien, *Quebec* 85 T f
Ste. Florence, *Quebec* 82 E e
St. Florent & G. de, *Corsica* 110 B d
St. Florentin, *France* 108 E b
St. Flour, *France* 109 E d
St. Fortunat, *Quebec* 85 T g
St. Francis, C., *Newfoundland* 83 T f
St. Francis, L., *Quebec* 85 Q g
St. Francis B., *S.W. Africa* 122 A e
St. François, L., *Quebec* 85 T g
St. François, R., *Quebec* 85 S f
St. François Xavier, *Quebec* 85 S g
St. Fulgent, *France* 108 C c
St. Gabriel de Brandon, *Quebec* 85 R f
St. Gallen & canton, *Switzerland* 101 E a
St. Gaudens, *France* 109 D e
St. Gédéon, *Quebec* 82 B h
St. Gédéon, *Quebec* 85 T d
Ste. Geneviève B., *Newfoundland* 83 Q b
St. George, C., *Newfoundland* 83 N e
St. George, *New Brunswick* 82 F h
St. Georges, *Fr. Guiana* 93 G c
St. George's, *Nfd.* 83 O e
St. Georges, *Quebec* 82 B g
St. Georges, *Quebec* 82 H e
St. George's B., *Newfoundland* 83 N e
St. George's Chan., *Ireland-Wales* 99 C j
St. Gérard, *Belgium* 100 C d
St. Gérard, *Quebec* 85 M d
St. Gérard, *Quebec* 85 T g
St. Germain, *France* 108 E b
Ste. Germaine, *Quebec* 82 B g
St. Gervais, *Quebec* 82 B g
St. Gheorghe, I., *Romania* 112 G b
St. Ghislain, *Belgium* 100 B d
St. Giles, *Quebec* 85 T f
St. Gilgen, *Austria* 104 E e
St. Gilles, *Belgium* 100 C c
St. Gilles, *France* 109 F e
St. Gillis-Waas, *Belgium* 100 C c
St. Gingolph, *Switzerland* 101 B b
St. Girons, *France* 109 D e
St. Godefroy, *Quebec* 82 G e
St. Gotthard, pass, *Switzerland* 101 D b
St. Gregor, *Saskatchewan* 87 N f
St. Gregory, Mt., *Newfoundland* 83 O d
St. Guénolé, *France* 108 A c
St. Guillaume, *Quebec* 85 S g
St. Helena, I., *Atlantic Ocean* 120 A h
St. Helena B., *South Africa* 122 B f
Ste. Hélène, I., *Quebec* 85 S j
Ste. Hélène, *Quebec* 82 C f
St. Helens, *England* 99 E g
St. Helier, *Quebec* 82 H d
St. Hénédine, *Quebec* 82 B g
St. Henri, *Quebec* 82 A g
St. Herménégilde, *Quebec* 85 T g
St. Honoré, *Quebec* 82 C f
St. Honoré, *Quebec* 82 A e
St. Hubert, *Belgium* 100 D d
St. Hyacinthe, *Quebec* 85 S g
St. Ignace, *Ontario* 84 B d
St. Ignace du Lac, *Quebec* 85 R f
St. Imier, *Switzerland* 101 B a
St. Irénée, *Quebec* 82 B f
St. Isidore, *Quebec* 85 L e
St. Isidore, *Quebec* 85 T g
St. Ives, *England* 99 D k
St. Jacques, *New Brunswick* 82 D f
St. Jacques, *Quebec* 85 R g
St. James, C., *British Columbia* 88 D d
St. Janvier, *Quebec* 85 L d
St. Jean, *Belgium* 100 A d
St. Jean, *France* 108 G d
St. Jean, L., *Quebec* 85 S d
St. Jean, *Quebec* 85 R g
St. Jean, R., *Quebec* 82 H c
St. Jean Baptiste, *Manitoba* 87 U j
St. Jean Bosco, *Quebec* 85 S e
St. Jean d'Angély, *France* 108 C d
St. Jean de Dieu, *Quebec* 82 C e
St. Jean de Luz, *France* 109 C e
St. Jean de Matha, *Quebec* 85 R f
St. Jean Port Joli, *Quebec* 82 B f
St. Jérôme, *Quebec* 85 Q g
St. Jérôme, *Quebec* 85 T d
St. Joachim, *Quebec* 85 S g
St. Joachim, *Quebec* 82 B f
St. John, *New Brunswick* 82 F h
St. John B. & I., *Newfoundland* 83 P c
St. John I., *Virgin Is.* 54 E h
St. John R., *Maine-New Brunswick* 82 E g
St. John R., *Quebec* 82 G e
St. John's, *Newfoundland* 83 T f
St. John's I., *Red Sea* 124 C e
St. Joseph, L., *Ontario* 81 K g
St. Joseph, *Quebec* 82 B g
St. Joseph d'Alma. See Alma
St. Joseph de Lévis, *Quebec* 85 U b
St. Joseph I., *Ontario* 84 G f
St. Joseph's, *Newfoundland* 83 T f
St. Jovite, *Quebec* 85 Q f
St. Kilda, I., *Scotland* 98 B c
St. Lambert, *Quebec* 85 T f
St. Lambert, *Quebec* 85 R g
St. Laurent, *Fr. Guiana* 93 G b
St. Laurent, *Manitoba* 87 U h
St. Laurent, *Quebec* 85 R j
St. Laurent R., *Quebec* 83 Q j
St. Lawrence, *Australia* 135 J d
St. Lawrence, C., Cape Breton I., *Nova Scotia* 83 M f
St. Lawrence, G. of, *Canada* 82 K f
St. Lawrence, *Newfoundland* 83 R g
St. Lawrence I., *Bering Sea* 80 B e
St. Lawrence Islands Nat. Park, *Ontario* 85 O h
St. Lawrence R., *Canada-U.S.A.* 81 N h
St. Lawrence Seaway, *Quebec-New York* 85 P h
St. Lazare, *Manitoba* 87 Q h
St. Leger, *Belgium* 100 D e
St. Léon, *Quebec* 85 T d
St. Léon, *Quebec* 82 E e
St. Léonard, *Belgium* 100 C c
St. Léonard, *France* 108 D d
St. Leonard, *New Brunswick* 82 E f
St. Leonard, *Quebec* 85 S f
St. Léonard de Port Maurice, *Quebec* 85 R h
St. Léon-de-Standon, *Quebec* 82 B g
St. Lewis R., *Labrador* 83 P a
St. Liboire, *Quebec* 85 S g
St. Lin, *Quebec* 85 R g
St. Lô, *France* 108 C b
St. Louis, L., *Quebec* 85 R g
St. Louis, *Mauritania* 118 B e
St. Louis, *Prince Edward I* 82 H g
St. Louis, *Saskatchewan* 87 M f
St. Louis de Kent, *New Brunswick* 82 H g
St. Louis du Ha Ha, *Quebec* 82 D f
Ste. Louise, *Quebec* 82 B f
St. Lucia, C., *South Africa* 122 E e
St. Lucia, I., *Windward Is.* 91 G d
St. Lucia L., *South Africa* 122 E e
Ste. Lucie, *Quebec* 85 Q f
St. Ludger, *Quebec* 82 B h
St. Luke's I., *Burma* 127 J f
St. Lunaire B., *Newfoundland* 83 R b
St. Maartensdijk, *Netherlands* 100 C c
St. Magnus B., *Shetland* 98 H a
St. Maixent, *France* 108 C c
St. Malachie, *Quebec* 82 B g
St. Malo & G. de, *France* 108 B b
St. Marc, *Haiti* 91 E c
St. Marc des Carrières, *Quebec* 85 S f
St. Marcel, *Quebec* 82 B g
St. Mard, *Belgium* 100 D e
St. Margaret B., *Newfoundland* 83 P b
St. Margaret B., *Nova Scotia* 82 J j
Ste. Marguerite, R., *Quebec* 82 B e
Ste. Marguerite, R., *Quebec* 82 F c
Ste. Marie, *Quebec* 82 A g
Ste. Marie, C., *Mal. Rep.* 121 N m
Ste. Marie I., *Mal. Rep.* 121 N k
Ste. Marthe de Gaspé, *Quebec* 82 F d
St. Martin, I., *Leeward Is.* 91 G c
St. Martin L., *Manitoba* 87 T g
St. Martins, *New Brunswick* 82 G h
St. Mary, C., *Nova Scotia* 82 F j
St. Mary B., *Nova Scotia* 82 F j
St. Mary Is., *India* 126 D f
St. Mary Is., *Quebec* 83 N c
St. Mary Reefs, *Quebec* 83 N c
St. Mary Res., *Alberta* 86 D j
St. Mary's, *Newfoundland* 83 T g
St. Mary's, *Ontario* 84 J j

St. Mary's, Tasmania 134 J h
St. Mary's B., Newfoundland 83 T g
St. Mary's C., Newfoundland 83 S g
St. Mary's L., Scotland 98 E e
St. Mary's Pk., Australia 135 G f
St. Mary's R., Nova Scotia 83 K h
St. Mathieu, Quebec 82 D e
St. Mathieu, Quebec 85 M d
St. Matthew I., Bering Sea 80 B e
St. Matthew's I., Burma 127 J g
St. Maurice, R., Quebec 85 R e
St. Maurice, Switzerland 101 B b
St. Maximin, France 109 F e
St. Maxine, Quebec 82 A g
St. Meen, France 108 B b
St. Michel de Laval, Quebec 85 R j
St. Michel des Saints, Quebec 85 R f
St. Moritz, Switzerland 101 E b
St. Nazaire, France 108 B c
St. Nicolaasga, Netherlands 100 D b
St. Nicolas. See St. Niklaas
St. Niklaas, Belgium 100 C c
St. Niklau, Switzerland 101 C b
St. Norbert, Manitoba 87 U j
St. Odilienberg, Netherlands 100 E c
St. Omer, France 108 E a
St. Omer, Quebec 82 F e
St. Ours, Quebec 85 R g
St. Pacôme, Quebec 83 C f
St. Pamphile, Quebec 82 C g
St. Pascal, Quebec 82 C f
St. Patrice, L., Quebec 85 N f
St. Paul, Alberta 86 F d
St. Paul, Quebec 82 C f
St. Paul de Fenouillet, France 109 E e
St. Paul-de-Montminy, Quebec 82 B g
St. Paul du Nord, Quebec 82 C e
St. Paul I., Cape Breton I., Nova Scotia 83 M f
St. Paulin, Quebec 85 R f
St. Paul R., Quebec 83 P b
St. Pauls Inlet, Nfd. 83 P d
Ste. Perpétue, Quebec 82 C f
St. Peter, Pt., Quebec 82 H e
St. Peter B., Labrador 83 R a
St. Peter's, Cape Breton I., Nova Scotia 83 M h
St. Peter's, Prince Edward I. 82 K g
Ste. Pétronille, Quebec 85 U b
St. Philémon, Quebec 82 B g
St. Pie, Quebec 85 S g
St. Pierre, L., Quebec 85 S f
St. Pierre, Manitoba 86 E a
St. Pierre, Martinique, West Indies 91 G d
St. Pierre, Quebec 85 R k
St. Pierre & I., Atlantic Ocean 83 Q g
St. Pierre & Miquelon, Atlantic Ocean 83 P g
St. Pol, France 108 E a
St. Pölten, Austria 105 F d
St. Pons, France 109 E e
St. Pourçain, France 108 E c
St. Prime, Quebec 85 S d
St. Quentin, France 108 E b
St. Quentin, New Brunswick 82 E f
St. Raphaël, Quebec 82 B g
St. Raymond, Quebec 85 T f
St. Rémi, Quebec 85 R g
St. Robert, Quebec 85 R g
St. Romaine, Quebec 82 A h
Ste. Rose, Quebec 85 R g
Ste. Rose du Dégelé, Quebec 82 D f
Ste. Rose du Lac, Manitoba 87 S g
St. Samuel, Quebec 82 B h
St. Sauveur, Quebec 85 R b
St. Sébastien, C., Mal. Rep. 121 N j
St. Sernin-sur-Rance, France 109 E e
St. Servan, France 108 B b
St. Sever, France 109 C e
St. Shott's, Newfoundland 83 T g
St. Siméon, Quebec 82 C f
St. Simon, Quebec 82 C e
St. Stephen, New Brunswick 82 E h
St. Sylvestre, Quebec 85 T f
Ste. Thècle, Quebec 85 S f
St. Théophile, Quebec 82 B h
Ste. Thérèse, Quebec 85 R g
St. Thomas, I., Virgin Is. 54 E h
St. Thomas, Ontario 84 J k
St. Tite, Quebec 85 S f
St. Tite des Caps, Quebec 82 B f
St. Trond. See St. Truiden
St. Tropez, France 109 G e
St. Truiden, Belgium 100 D d
St. Urbain, Quebec 82 B f
St. Valéry, France 108 D a
St. Valéry-en-Caux, France 108 D b
St. Vallier, Quebec 82 B g
St. Veit, Austria 104 F e
Ste. Véronique, Quebec 85 Q f
St. Victor, Quebec 82 B g
St. Vincent, C., Mal. Rep. 121 M l
St. Vincent, G., Australia 135 G g
St. Vincent, Windward Is. 91 G d
St. Vincent de Paul, Quebec 85 R h
St. Vincent's, Newfoundland 83 T g
St. Vith, Belgium 100 E d
St. Walburg, Saskatchewan 86 H e
St. Williams, Ontario 84 K k
St. Yvon, Quebec 82 H d
Saintes, France 108 C d
Saintonge, prov., France 108 C d
Saipan, I., Mariana Is. 78 E e
Saipan Chan., Saipan-Tinian Is. 78 A e
Saiping. See Sinyang
Saiun (Saywūn), S. Yemen 124 E f
Saivomuotka, Sweden 102 K b
Saka Dzong, Tibet 127 G c
Sakai, Japan 133 D g
Sakakah, Saudi Arabia 124 D d
Saka Kalat, Pakistan 126 C c
Sakami L., Quebec 81 M g
Sakania, Congo 121 F g
Sakarya, R., Turkey 124 B b
Sakata, Japan 133 F e
Sakha, Saudi Arabia 124 D e
Sakhalin, U.S.S.R. 115 P c
Sakhalinskaya Oblast, U.S.S.R. 115 P c
Sakahlinskiy Zaliv, U.S.S.R 115 P c
Saki, U.S.S.R. 116 H j
Šakiai, Lithuania, U.S.S.R. 103 K j
Sakishima Gunto, Is., Japan 133 K k
Sakti, India 127 F d
Sakylä, Finland 103 K f
Sala, Czechoslovakia 105 G d
Sala, Sweden 103 G g
Salacgrīva, Latvia, U.S.S.R 103 L h
Sala Consilina, Italy 111 E e
Salada, L., Mexico 90 A a
Salado, R., Argentina 94 D c
Salaga, Ghana 118 E g
Salahiya, Syria 124 D c
Salajar, I., Indonesia 129 H m
Salala, Muscat & Oman 125 F f
Salama, Guatemala 90 F d
Salamanca, Mexico 90 D c
Salamanca, Spain 106 C b
Salamaua, New Guinea 135 J a
Salamina, Colombia 92 B b
Salamis & I., Greece 113 D f
Salangen, Norway 102 G b
Salas, Spain 106 B a
Salas de los Infantes, Spain 106 D a
Salat, I., Truk Is. 78 F o
Salat Pass, Truk Is. 78 F o
Salatsgriva. See Salacgrīva
Salaverry, Peru 92 B e
Sala-y-Gomez, I., Pacific Ocean 79 Q k
Salbris, France 108 E c
Saldaña, Spain 106 C a
Saldus, Latvia, U.S.S.R. 103 K h
Sale, Australia 135 J g
Salekhard, U.S.S.R 114 F b
Salem, India 126 E f
Salemi, Sicily 111 D g
Sälen, Sweden 103 E f
Salerno, G. di, Italy 111 E e
Salerno, Italy 111 E e
Salford, England 99 F g
Salgueiro, Brazil 93 K e
Salima, Malawi 121 G g
Salina, I., Italy 111 E f
Salina Cruz, Mexico 90 E d
Salinas, Ecuador 92 A d
Salinas, Mexico 90 D c
Salinas, Mexico 90 D b
Salinas, Pta., Puerto Rico 54 C h
Salinas, Puerto Rico 54 C j
Salinas. See Salinópolis
Salinas Grandes, Argentina 94 D c
Salinitas, Chile 94 B b
Salinópolis, Brazil 93 H d
Salins, France 108 F c
Salisbury, England 99 F j
Salisbury, L., Uganda 121 G d
Salisbury, New Brunswick 82 G g
Salisbury, Rhodesia 122 E c
Salisbury I., North-West Territories 81 M e
Salisbury Plain, England 99 F j
Salkhad, Syria 123 E e
Sallyana, Nepal 127 F c
Salmo, British Columbia 88 L f
Salmon, R., British Columbia 88 H c
Salmon Arm, British Columbia 88 K e
Salmon Bay, Quebec 83 P b
Salmon Gums, Australia 134 D f
Salmon R., Anticosti I., Quebec 82 K d
Salmon R., New Brunswick 82 G g
Salo, Finland 103 K f
Salon, France 109 F e
Salonica. See Thessaloníki
Salonta, Romania 112 C a
Salqin, Syria 123 E a
Salsette I. India 126 D e
Salta, Argentina 94 C b
Saltcoats, Saskatchewan 87 P g
Saltdal, Norway 102 F c
Saltee, Is., Eire 99 C h
Salt Fd., Norway 102 F c
Saltillo, Mexico 90 D b
Salt L., Australia 134 B d
Salt Ls., Australia 134 E e
Salto, Argentina 94 D d
Salto, Uruguay 94 E d
Salto da Divisa, Brazil 93 K g
Salt Ra., Pakistan 126 D b
Saltrou, Haiti 91 E c
Salûm & G. of, Egypt 119 L b
Salumaua, New Guinea 135 J a
Salur, India 127 F e
Salut, Is. du, French Guiana 93 G b
Saluzzo, Italy 110 A c
Salvador, El, Central America 91 B d
Salvador, Saskatchewan 86 H f
Salvador (Bahia), Brazil 93 K f
Salvage, Newfoundland 83 T e
Salvaterra, Portugal 106 A c
Salvatierra, Mexico 90 D c
Salvus, Br. Columbia 88 E c
Salzburg, Austria 104 E e
Salzgitter, Germany 104 D b
Salzwedel, Germany 104 D b
Samahala, Botswana 122 C c
Samalut, Egypt 119 M c
Samaná & B. de, Dominican Republic 91 F c
Samar, I., Philippines 129 J h
Samarai, Papua 135 K b
Samarinda, Borneo 129 G l
Samarkand, Uzbek., U.S.S.R. 114 F e
Samarra Balad, Iraq 124 D c
Samasala, India 126 D c
Samäwa, Iraq 124 E c
Sambalpur, India 127 F d
Sambava, Mal. Rep. 121 P j
Sambeek, Netherlands 100 D c
Sambhal, India 126 E c
Sambhar, India 126 D c
Sambor, Ukraine, U.S.S.R. 116 C g
Samborombón B., Argentina 94 E e
Sambre, R., Belgium 100 C d
Samedan, Switzerland 101 E b
Sameminato, Japan 133 G d
Sami, Pakistan 126 B c
Samira, Saudi Arabia 124 D d
Sam Ka, Burma 127 J d
Sam-nua, Laos 132 C b
Samoa, American & West Pacific Ocean 78 J h
Samokov, Bulgaria 112 D c
Samorogouan, Upper Volta 118 E f
Sámos, I., Greece 113 F f
Samothrace. See Samothráki, I.
Samothráki, I., Greece 113 E d
Sampacho, Argentina 94 D d
Sampit, Borneo 129 F l
Samrée, Belgium 100 D d
Samsat, Turkey 124 C b
Samshui, China 131 F l
Samsö, I., Denmark 103 D j
Samsu, N. Korea 128 J b
Samsun, Turkey 124 C a
San, Mali 118 E f
San'a, Yemen 124 D f
Sanam, Jebel, Iraq 124 E c
San Ambrosio I., Pacific Oc. 79 R l
Sanana, Moluccas 129 J l
Sanandaj, Iran 124 E b
San Antioco, I., Sardinia 111 B f
San Antonio, C., Argentina 94 E e
San Antonio, C., Cuba 91 C b
San Antonio, Chile 94 C c
San Antonio, Chile 94 B d
San Antonio, Mexico 90 C c
San Antonio Oeste, Argentina 95 D f
San Bartolomeu de Messines, Portugal 106 A d
San Benedetto del Tronto, Italy 110 D d
San Benito Is., Mexico 90 A b
San Bernardo, Chile 94 B d
San Blas, Argentina 95 D f
San Blas, G. de, Panama 91 D e
San Blas, Mexico 90 C c
San Blas, Mexico 90 C b
San Borja, Mexico 90 B b
San Carlos, Amazonas, Venezuela 92 D c
San Carlos, Argentina 94 C c
San Carlos, Argentina 94 C d
San Carlos, Argentina 94 C d
San Carlos, Chile 94 B e
San Carlos, Cojedes, Venezuela 92 D b
San Carlos, Mexico 90 E c
San Carlos, Nicaragua 91 C d
San Carlos de Bariloche, Argentina 95 B f
San Carlos del Zulia, Venezuela 92 C b
Sanchez, Dominican Republic 91 F c
San Clemente, Spain 107 D c
San Cosme, Paraguay 94 E c
San Cristóbal, Argentina 94 D d
San Cristóbal, I., Galápagos Is. 92 A h
San Cristóbal, I., Solomon Is. 78 G h
San Cristóbal, Mexico 90 F d
San Cristóbal, Venezuela 92 C b
Sancti Spíritus, Cuba 91 D b
Sanctuary, Saskatchewan 86 J g
Sand, Norway 103 B g
Sandakan, Sabah 129 G j
Sanday I., Orkney Is. 98 F a
Sandbank L., Ontario 84 H a
Sandefjord, Norway 103 D g
Sandfly L., Saskatchewan 86 L c
Sandgate, Australia 135 K e
Sand Hills, Great, Saskatchewan 86 H h
Sand Hills, Middle, Alberta 86 G h
Sandhornöy, Norway 102 E c
Sand I., Palmyra I. 79 T k
Sand I., Truk Is. 78 E n
Sandia, Peru 92 D f
San Diego, C., Argentina 95 C h
San Diego de Cabrutica, Venezuela 92 E b
Sandikli, Turkey 124 B b
Sandilands, Manitoba 86 F a
San Dimas, Mexico 90 C c
Sand L., Big, Manitoba 87 S a
Sand L., Little, Manitoba 87 T a
Sand L., Ontario 86 H a
Sand Lake, Ontario 84 F e
Sandnes, Norway 103 A g
Sandoa, Congo 120 E f
San Domingos, Portugal 106 B d
Sandoway, Burma 127 H e
Sand R., Alberta 86 F d
Sandspit, Moresby I., British Columbia 88 D d
Sandstone, Australia 134 C e
Sandtop, C., Anticosti I., Quebec 83 L d
Sandträsk, Sweden 102 J c
Sandvig, Bornholm I., Denmark 103 F j
Sandwich B., Labrador 81 O g
Sandwith, Saskatchewan 86 J e
Sandybeach L., Ontario 86 K a
Sandy C., Australia 135 K d
Sandy Creek, Quebec 85 O g
Sandy Falls, Ontario 84 J d
Sandy L., Newfoundland 83 Q d
Sandy L., Ontario 81 K g
Sandy Lake, Manitoba 87 R h
Sandy Lake, Saskatchewan 88 Q b
Sandy Narrows, Saskatchewan 87 O c
San Esteban de Gormaz, Spain 106 D b
San Felipe, Chile 94 B d
San Felipe, Guatemala 90 F e
San Felipe, Mexico 90 F d
San Felipe, Mexico 90 B a
San Felipe, Venezuela 92 D a
San Feliu de Guixols, Spain 107 G b
San Feliu de Llobregat, Spain 107 F b
San Félix, I., Pacific Ocean 79 R l
San Félix, Venezuela 92 E b
San Fernando, Chile 94 B d
San Fernando, Mexico 90 E c
San Fernando, Mexico 90 A b
San Fernando, Philippines 129 H g
San Fernando, Trinidad 92 E a
San Fernando de Apure, Venezuela 92 D b
San Fernando de Atabapo, Venezuela 92 D c
Sanford, Manitoba 87 U j
San Francisco del Chañar, Argentina 94 D d
San Francisco do Maranhão, Brazil 93 J e
Sanga, Angola 120 D g
Sangareddipet, India 126 E e
San Germán, Puerto Rico 54 B h
Sanggau, Borneo 129 F k
Sangihe Kep. (Sangi Is.), Indonesia 129 J k
Sangi Is. See Sangihe Kep.
San Giovanni in Fiore, Italy 111 F f
Sangkulirang, Borneo 129 G k
Sangre Grande, Trinidad 92 E a
Sangudo, Alberta 86 C e
Sanguin, Liberia 118 D g
San Ignacio, Bolivia 92 D f
San Ignacio, Bolivia 92 E g
San Ignacio, Mexico 90 C c
San Ignacio, Mexico 90 B b
San Ignacio, Paraguay 94 E c
San Javier, Argentina 94 E d
San Javier, Bolivia 92 E g
San Javier, Chile 94 B e
San João, Portugal 106 B b
San Joaquim, Bolivia 92 E f
San Jorge, G., Argentina 95 C g
San José, Bolivia 92 E g
San José, Colombia 92 C c
San José, Costa Rica 91 C e
San José, G., Argentina 95 D f
San José, Guatemala 90 F e
San José, I., Mexico 90 B b
San José, Uruguay 94 E d
San José Carpizo, Mexico 90 F d
San José de Amacuro, Venezuela 92 E b
San José de Feliciano, Argentina 94 E d
San José del Cabo, Mexico 90 C c
San José de Ocuné, Colombia 92 C c
San Juan, Bolivia 90 F g
San Juan, C., Argentina 95 D h
San Juan, Cabezas de, Puerto Rico 54 D h
San Juan, Peru 92 B g
San Juan, Puerto Rico 54 C h
San Juan, R., Mexico 90 E d
San Juan, R., Nicaragua 91 B d
San Juan, Venezuela 92 D a
San Juan & R., Argentina 94 C d
San Juan de Camarones, Mexico 90 C b
San Juan de Guadalupe, Mexico 90 D c
San Juan del Norte, Nicaragua 91 C d
San Juan de los Lagos, Mexico 90 D c
San Juan del Río, Mexico 90 E c
San Juan del Sur, Nicaragua 91 B d
San Julián, Argentina 95 C g
San Justo, Argentina 94 D d
Sankeimo, I., Okinawa 78 B b
Sankuri Post, Kenya 121 H e
San Lázaro, C., Mexico 90 B c
San Lorenzo, Argentina 94 D d
San Lorenzo, Ecuador 94 B c
San Lorenzo, Honduras 91 B d
San Lorenzo, Mexico 90 B a
San Lorenzo, Peru 92 D f
San Lorenzo, Puerto Rico 54 D h
San Lorenzo del Escorial, Spain 106 C b
San Lorenzo Is., Mexico 90 B b
Sanlucar la Mayor, Spain 106 B d
San Lucas, Bolivia 92 D h
San Lucas, C., Mexico 90 C c
San Luis, Argentina 94 E c
San Luis, Argentina 94 C d
San Luis, Cuba 91 D b
San Luis de la Paz, Mexico 90 D c
San Luis Potosí & state, Mexico 90 D c
Sanluri, Sardinia 111 B f
San Marcos, Colombia 92 B b
San Marino, rep., Italy 110 D d
San Martín, Argentina 94 C d
San Martín, Colombia 92 C c
San Martín, L., Chile-Argentina 95 B g
San Martín, R., Bolivia 92 E g
San Martín de los Andes, Argentina 95 B f
San Martín de Valdeiglesais, Spain 106 C b
San Martinho, Portugal 106 A c
San Mateo, Spain 107 F b
San Matías, Bolivia 92 F g
San Matías, G., Argentina 95 D f
San Maura. See Levkás, I.
Sanmenhsia, China 130 E e
San Miguel, B. de, Panama 91 D e
San Miguel, Bolivia 92 E g
San Miguel, Mexico 90 D c
San Miguel, Peru 92 C f
San Miguel, R., Bolivia 92 E g
San Miguel, Salvador 91 B d
San Miguel. See Rey, I. del
San Miguel de Tucumán, Argentina 94 C c
San Nicolás, Argentina 94 D d
San Pablo, Bolivia 92 D h
San Pablo, C., Argentina 95 C h
San Pedro, Argentina 94 E d
San Pedro, British Honduras 91 B c
San Pedro, Ivory Coast 118 D h
San Pedro, Mexico 90 D b
San Pedro, Paraguay 94 E b
San Pedro de Arimena, Colombia 92 C c
San Pedro del Gallo, Mexico 90 D b
San Pedro de Lloc, Peru 92 B e
San Pedro de Macoris, Dominican Republic 91 F c
San Pedro do Sul, Portugal 106 A b
San Pedro Sula, Honduras 91 B c
San Pietro I., Sardinia 111 B f
San Quintín & B., Mexico 90 A a
San Rafael, Argentina 94 C d
San Ramón, Peru 92 B f
San Remo, Italy 110 A d
San Roque, Argentina 94 E c
San Salvador, Angola 120 C f
San Salvador, Salvador 91 B d
San Salvador (Guanahani), Bahama Is. 91 E b
Sansanne Mango, Togo 118 F f
San Sebastián, Puerto Rico 54 C h
San Sebastián, Spain 107 D a
San Sebastián & B. de, Argentina 95 C h
San Severo, Italy 111 E e
Santa, Peru 92 B e
Santa Ana, Bolivia 92 D f
Santa Ana, Bolivia 92 F g
Santa Ana, Ecuador 92 A d
Santa Ana, Mexico 90 B a
Santa Ana, Salvador 91 B d
Santa Anna (do Bananal), I. de, Brazil 93 G f
Santa Bárbara, Honduras 91 B d
Santa Bárbara, Venezuela 92 E b
Santa Baturité, Brazil 93 K d
Santa Catalina, Chile 94 C c
Santa Catalina, I., Mexico 90 B b
Santa Catalina, Mt. See Encantada, Cerro de
Santa Catarina, I., Brazil 94 G c
Santa Catarina, Mexico 90 C c
Santa Clara, Brazil 92 D d
Santa Clara, Cuba 91 C b
Santa Clara, Sa., Mexico 90 B b
Santa Coloma de Farnes, Spain 107 G b
Santa Cruz, Argentina 95 C h
Santa Cruz, Bolivia 92 E g
Santa Cruz, Chile 94 B d
Santa Cruz, Mexico 90 B a
Santa Cruz, Peru 92 B e
Santa Cruz, Philippines 129 H h
Santa Cruz, R., Argentina 95 B h
Santa Cruz de la Zarza, Spain 106 D c
Santa Cruz del Sur, Cuba 91 D b
Santa Cruz de Tenerife, Canary Is. 118 B c
Santa Cruz Is., Pacific Ocean 78 G h
Santa de Unturán, Venezuela 92 D c
Santa dos Dois Irmãos, Brazil 93 J e
Santa Elena, Ecuador 92 A d
Santa Eufemia, G. di, Italy 111 F f
Santa Fé, Argentina 94 D d
Santa Fé, Cuba 91 C b
Santa Filomena, Brazil 93 H e
Santa Helena, Brazil 94 F b
Santa Helena, Brazil 93 H d
Santa Helena, Brazil 93 F e
Santai, China 130 B g
Santa Inés, B., Mexico 90 B b
Santa Inés, I., Chile 95 B h
Santa Isabel, Argentina 94 C e
Santa Isabel, Fernando Poo 118 G h
Santa Isabel, Puerto Rico 54 C j
Santa Isabel, Solomon Is. 78 F h
Santa Lucía, Cuba 91 D b
Santa Margarita, I., Mexico 90 B c
Santa María, Argentina 94 C c
Santa María, Brazil 94 F c
Santa Maria, I., Atlantic Ocean 118 B b
Santa María, I., Chile 95 B e
Santa María, Mexico 90 C b
Santa María, Mt., Argentina 94 C e
Santa María del Río, Mexico 90 D c
Santa Maria di Leuca, C., Italy 111 G f
Santa María la Real de Nieva, Spain 106 C b
Santa Marta, Colombia 92 C a
Santander, Colombia 92 B c
Santander, Spain 106 D a
Santa Quiteria, Brazil 93 J d
Santarém, Brazil 93 G d
Santarém, Portugal 106 A c
Santa Rita, Brazil 93 F e
Santa Rita, I., Guam 78 A l
Santa Rita, Venezuela 92 C a
Santa Rosa, Argentina 94 C d
Santa Rosa, Argentina 94 C d
Santa Rosa, Bolivia 92 E g
Santa Rosa, Brazil 94 F c
Santa Rosa, Honduras 91 B d
Santa Rosa de Toay, Argentina 94 D e
Santa Rosalía, Mexico 90 B b
Santa Rosa Mt., Guam 78 B k
Santa Sylvina, Argentina 94 D c
Santa Vitoria do Palmar, Brazil 94 F d
Santiago, Baja California, Mexico 90 C c
Santiago, Brazil 94 F c
Santiago, Cerro, Panama 91 C e
Santiago, Chile 94 B d
Santiago, Dominican Republic 91 E c
Santiago, Mexico 90 C c
Santiago, Panama 91 C e
Santiago, Sa. de, Bolivia 92 F g
Santiago de Compostela, Spain 106 A a
Santiago de Cuba, Cuba 91 D c
Santiago del Estero, Argentina 94 D c
Santillana, Spain 106 C a
Santis, Mt., Switzerland 101 E a
Santo Angelo, Brazil 94 F c
Santo António, Brazil 92 E f
Santo António da C., Brazil 93 G d
Santo António do Zaire, Angola 120 C f
Santo Corazón, Bolivia 92 F g
Santo Domingo, Cuba 91 C b
Santo Domingo, Dominican Republic 91 F c
Santo Domingo, Mexico 90 A a
San Tomé, Venezuela 92 E b
Santoríni. See Thíra, I.
Santos, Brazil 93 H h
Santo Tomás, Mexico 90 A a
Santo Tomás, Peru 92 C f
Santvliet, Belgium 100 C c
San Urbano, Argentina 94 D d
San Vicente, Salvador 91 B d
San Vicente del Caguán, Colombia 92 C c
San Vito, C., Italy 111 F e
São Antonio do Içá, Brazil 92 D d
São Bento do Norte, Brazil 93 K e
São Borja, Brazil 94 E c
São Carlos, Brazil 93 H h
São Cristovão, Brazil 93 K f
São Domingos, Brazil 93 H f
São Felix, Brazil 93 G e
São Francisco, Brazil 93 J e
São Francisco, Brazil 93 J g
São Francisco, R., Brazil 93 K e
São Francisco do Sul & I de, Brazil 94 G c
Sao Hill, Tanzania 121 H f
São Jerónimo, Brazil 94 F c
São João da Barra, Brazil 93 J h
São João da Boa Vista, Brazil 94 G b
São João del Rei, Brazil 93 J h
São João do Araguaya, Brazil 93 H e
São João do Piauí, Brazil 93 J e
São Joaquim, Brazil 92 D c
São José, Brazil 94 G c
São José, Brazil 92 D d
São José do Mipibú, Brazil 93 K e
São José do Norte, Brazil 94 F d
São José do Rio Prêto, Brazil 93 H h
São Lourenço & R., Brazil 93 F g
São Luis, Brazil 93 J d
São Luis, I. de, Brazil 93 J d
São Luiz Gonzaga, Brazil 94 F c

São Mateus, Brazil 93 K g
São Mateus do Sul, Brazil 94 F c
São Miguel, I., Atlantic Ocean 118 B a
Saona, I., Dominican Republic 91 F c
Saône, R., France 108 F c
Saône-et-Loire, dep., France 108 F c
São Paulo, Brazil 93 H h
São Paulo de Luanda, Angola 120 C f
São Paulo de Olivença, Brazil 92 D d
São Raimundo Nonato, Brazil 93 J e
São Romão, Brazil 92 D e
São Sebastião, Brazil 92 E e
São Sebastião & I. da, Brazil 93 H h
São Simão, Brazil 93 H h
São Tomé, I., G. of Guinea 120 B d
Saoura, Algeria 118 E c
São Vicente, Brazil 93 H h
Sapiéntza, I., Greece 113 C f
Saposoa, Peru 92 B e
Sapotnica, Yugoslavia 112 C d
Sapporo, Japan 133 G c
Sapri, Italy 111 E e
Saqqez, Iran 124 E b
Saragossa (Zaragoza), Spain 107 E b
Saraguro, Ecuador 92 B d
Saraikela, India 127 G d
Sarajevo, Yugoslavia 112 B c
Saraktash, U.S.S.R. 117 N e
Sarala, U.S.S.R. 114 H c
Sarandí del Yi, Uruguay 94 E d
Sarangarh, India 127 F d
Saransk, U.S.S.R. 117 G c
Sarapul, U.S.S.R. 117 L b
Saratov, U.S.S.R. 117 G e
Saratsi-ting, China 130 E b
Sarawak, Malaysia 129 F k
Sarbaz, Iran 125 H d
Sárbogárd, Hungary 105 H e
Sarco, Chile 94 B c
Sardarshahr, India 126 D c
Sardasht, Iran 124 E b
Sardegna. See Sardinia
Sardinia (Sardegna), Italy 111 B e
Sardoal, Portugal 106 A c
Sareks Nat. Park, Sweden 102 G c
Sargans, Switzerland 101 E a
Sari, Iran 125 F b
Sarikamis, Turkey 124 D a
Sarina, Australia 135 J d
Sariñena, Spain 107 E b
Sar-i-Pul, Afghanistan 125 J b
Sar-i-pul, Iran 124 E c
Sark, I., Channel Is. 108 B b
Sarkad, Hungary 105 J e
Sarlat, France 109 D d
Sarmi, W. Irian 129 L l
Sarmiento, Mt., Chile 95 B h
Sarna, Sweden 103 E f
Sarnen, Switzerland 101 D b
Sarnia, Ontario 84 H k
Sarno, Italy 111 E e
Saronic G., Greece 113 D f
Saronno, Italy 110 B c
Sar Passage, Palau Is. 78 B n
Sarpsborg, Norway 103 D g
Sarpul. See Shahsavar
Sarrebourg, France 108 G b
Sarreguemines, France 108 G b
Sarre Union, France 108 G b
Sarria, Spain 106 B a
Sart, Belgium 100 D d
Sartène, Corsica 111 B e
Sarthe, R. & dep., France 108 D c
Sarufutsu, Japan 133 H b
Saruru, Japan 133 H c
Sarvar, Hungary 105 G e
Sasa Baneh, Ethiopia 121 J c
Sasamat, L., Br. Columbia 88 E f
Sascumica L., Quebec 85 N b
Sasebo, Japan 133 A h
Saskatchewan, prov., Canada 80 J g
Saskatchewan R., N., Alberta-Saskatchewan 86 K f
Saskatchewan R., S., Saskatchewan 86 J h
Saskatoon, Saskatchewan 86 L f
Saskeram L., Manitoba 87 Q e
Saskylakh, U.S.S.R. 115 L a
Sasovo, U.S.S.R. 117 E c
Sassandra & R., Ivory Coast 118 D h
Sassari, Sardinia 111 B e
Sassnitz, Germany 104 E a
Sastre, Argentina 94 D d
Sas-van-Gent, Netherlands 100 B c
Satadougou, Mali 118 C f
Satara, India 126 D e
Satellite B., North-West Territories 80 H b
Säter, Sweden 103 F f
Satevo, Mexico 90 C b
Satka, U.S.S.R. 117 P c
Satoraljaujhely, Hungary 105 J d
Satpura Ra., India 126 D d
Satu Mare, Romania 105 K e
Satun, Thailand 132 C e
Sauda, Norway 103 B g
Saudhárkrókur, Iceland 102 W m
Saudi Arabia, South-West Asia 124 D e
Saugeen, R., Ontario 84 J h
Saugstad, Mt., Br. Columbia 88 F d
Saulieu, France 108 F c
Saulnierville, Nova Scotia 82 F j
Sault au Mouton, Quebec 82 C e
Sault-aux-Cochons, R., Quebec 82 C e
Sault Ste. Marie, Ontario 84 F f
Saumur, France 108 C c
Saumur, L., Quebec 82 K b
Saunders, Alberta 86 B f
Saunders, C., New Zealand 135 Q m
Saurashtra. See Kathiawar
Sauterelles, L. aux, Quebec 82 J b
Sava, R., Yugoslavia 112 B b
Savai'i, I., W. Samoa 78 J j
Savane R., Quebec 82 A b
Savannakhet, Laos 132 C c
Savanna la Mar, Jamaica 91 D c
Savant Lake, Ontario 87 M a
Savantvadi, India 126 D e
Savanur, India 126 E f
Save, Dahomey 118 F g
Saveh, Iran 125 F b
Savenay, France 108 C c
Save R., Mozambique 122 E d
Savoff, Ontario 84 F c
Savoie, dep., France 108 G d
Savoie, prov., France 108 G d
Savona, British Columbia 88 J e
Savona, Italy 110 B c
Savonlinna, Finland 102 N f
Savukoski, Finland 102 N c
Savu Sea, Indonesia 129 H m
Sawa, S. Yemen 124 E f
Sawahlunto, Sumatra 129 D l
Sawayan Pt., Quebec 85 L a
Sawbill, Manitoba 87 Q a
Sawdy, Alberta 86 D d
Sawle Pt., Palmyra I 79 T k
Sawqirah B., Muscat & Oman 125 G f
Sawyerville, Quebec 85 T g
Saxnäs, Sweden 102 F d
Saya, Syria 123 D b
Sayabac, Quebec 82 E e
Saya Buri. See Pak-lay
Sayán, Peru 92 B f
Sayan, Vostochnyy, U.S.S.R. 115 J c
Sayan, Zapadnyy, U.S.S.R. 115 J c
Sayhut, S. Yemen 125 F f
Sayula, Mexico 90 D d
Sayward, British Columbia 88 G e
Scafell Pike, England 99 E f
Scalea, Italy 111 E f
Scandia, Alberta 86 E h
Scânteia, Romania 112 F a
Scanterbury, Manitoba 87 V h
Scanzano, Italy 111 F e
Scapa, Alberta 86 F g
Scapa Flow, Orkney Is. 98 E b
Scarborough, England 99 G f
Scarborough, Ontario 84 E k
Scarborough Bluffs, Ontario 84 E k
Scărisoara, Romania 112 D a
Scarth, Manitoba 87 R j
Scatari I., Cape Breton I., Nova Scotia 83 N g
Sceptre, Saskatchewan 86 H h
Schaffhausen & canton, Switzerland 101 D a
Scharhörn, I., Germany 104 C b
Schefferville, Labrador 81 N g
Scheiben I., Truk Is. 78 E n
Schelde, Ooster & Wester, Netherlands 100 B c
Scheveningen, Netherlands 100 C b
Schiedam, Netherlands 100 C c
Schiermonnikoog I., Netherlands 100 E a
Schiphol, Netherlands 100 C b
Schleins, Switzerland 101 F b
Schleswig, Germany 104 C a
Schleswig-Holstein, Germany 100 C a
Schneidemühl. See Pila
Schönberg, Germany 104 D b
Schönbuhl, Switzerland 101 C a
Schönebeck, Germany 104 D c
Schongau, Germany 104 D e
Schoonhoven, Netherlands 100 C c
Schötz, Switzerland 101 D a
Schouwen I., Netherlands 100 B c
Schreiber, Ontario 84 C d
Schuchinsk, Kazakh., U.S.S.R. 114 G c
Schuler, Alberta 86 G h
Schull, Eire 99 A j
Schuls, Switzerland 101 F b
Schultz L., North-West Territories 80 K e
Schumacher, Ontario 84 J d
Schüpfheim, Switzerland 101 D b
Schwabach, Germany 104 D d
Schwäbisch Hall. See Hall
Schwägalp, Switzerland 101 E a
Schwandorf, Germany 104 E d
Schwaner Geb., Mts., Borneo 129 F l
Schwarzhorn, Mt., Switzerland 101 C b
Schwarzwald, Germany 104 C d
Schwedt, Germany 104 F b
Schweidnitz. See Swidnica
Schweinfurt, Germany 104 D c
Schwerin, Germany 104 D b
Schwyz & canton, Switzerland 101 D a
Sciacca, Sicily 111 D g
Scie, R. à la, Quebec 83 R k
Scilly, Is. of, England 99 C l
Sclater, Manitoba 87 R g
Scollard, Alberta 86 E g
Scoresby Ld., Greenland 89 N b
Scoresby Sd., Greenland 89 N b
Scotch Bay, Manitoba 87 T h
Scotia, Ontario 85 L g
Scotia Sea, Antarctica 136 K g
Scotland, Great Britain 98 D c
Scotsburn, Nova Scotia 82 K h
Scotsguard, Saskatchewan 86 J j
Scotstown, Quebec 85 T g
Scott, C., Vancouver I., British Columbia 88 E e
Scott, Saskatchewan 86 J f
Scott Glacier, Antarctica 136 S e
Scott I., Antarctica 78 K o
Scott Inlet, North-West Territories 81 M c
Scott Is., Br. Columbia 88 E e
Scottsdale, Tasmania 135 J h
Scottsville, Cape Breton I., Nova Scotia 83 L g
Scout Lake, Saskatchewan 87 M j
Scudder, Ontario 84 H k
Scugog, L., Ontario 85 M h
Scutari. See Shkodër
Scutari. See Uskudar
Seaforth, Ontario 84 J j
Seager Wheeler L., Saskatchewan 87 O d
Seahorse Pt., North-West Territories 81 L e
Sea I., British Columbia 88 C f
Seal Bight, Labrador 83 R a
Seal Cove, New Brunswick 82 F j
Seal Cove, Newfoundland 83 Q d
Sea Lion Is., Falkland Is. 95 E h
Seal R., Manitoba 81 K f
Searchmont, Ontario 84 F f
Searston, Newfoundland 83 N f
Seba Beach, Alberta 86 C e
Sebastián Vizcaino, B. de, Mexico 90 B b
Sebenico. See Sibenik
Sebha, Libya 119 H c
Sebin Karahisar, Turkey 124 C a
Séchelles, L., Quebec 82 C a
Sechelt, British Columbia 88 H f
Sečovce, Czechoslovakia 105 J d
Secretan, Saskatchewan 86 L h
Secretary I., New Zealand 135 P m
Secunderabad, India 126 E e
Seda, Lithuania, U.S.S.R. 103 K h
Sedalia, Alberta 86 G g
Sedan, France 108 F b
Sedano, Spain 106 D a
Seddonville, New Zealand 135 Q l
Sedgewick, Alberta 86 F f
Sedhiou, Senegal 118 B f
Sedley, Manitoba 87 O h
Sedom, Israel 123 D f
Sedrun, Switzerland 101 D b
Seebe, Alberta 88 C g
Seeheim, S.W. Africa 122 B e
Seeleys Bay, Ontario 85 O h
Seelisberg, Switzerland 101 D b
Sées, France 108 D b
Seewis, Switzerland 101 E b
Sefrou, Morocco 118 E b
Segorbe, Spain 107 E c
Ségou, Mali 118 D f
Segovia, R., Nicaragua 91 C d
Segovia, Spain 106 C b
Séguéla, Ivory Coast 118 D g
Sehkuheh, Iran 125 H c
Sehwan, Pakistan 126 C c
Seibo, Dominican Republic 91 F c
Seignelay, R., Quebec 82 C a
Seiland, Norway 102 K a
Seine, R., France 108 D b
Seine-et-Marne, dep., France 108 E b
Seine-et-Oise, dep., France 108 D b
Seine Maritime, dep., France 108 D b
Seitler, U.S.S.R. 116 J j
Seiyala, Egypt 119 M d
Sekenke, Tanzania 121 G e
Seki, Japan 133 E g
Sekieshan I., China 131 L g
Sekondi, Ghana 118 E g
Sektyakh, U.S.S.R. 115 M a
Selborne, C., Antarctica 136 B b
Selby, England 99 G g
Seldom, Newfoundland 83 S d
Selemiya, Syria 123 F b
Selenge, R., Mongolia-U.S.S.R. 115 K d
Selima Oasis, Sudan 119 L d
Selkirk, Manitoba 87 V h
Selkirk, Ontario 84 L k
Selkirk & co., Scotland 98 F e
Selkirk I., Manitoba 87 S e
Selkirk Mts., British Columbia-Montana 80 H g
Selle, Sa. de la, Haiti 91 E c
Selles, France 108 D c
Selva, Argentina 94 D c
Selwyn, Australia 135 H d
Selwyn Mts., Yukon 80 F e
Selwyn Ra., Australia 134 G d
Sem, Norway 103 D g
Semans, Saskatchewan 87 N g
Semarang, Indonesia 129 F m
Semawe, Jeb. See Har Sagī
Semipalatinsk, Kazakh., U.S.S.R. 114 H c
Semnan, Iran 125 F b
Semuida, I., Okinawa 78 B a
Senador Pompeu, Brazil 93 K e
Sena Madureira, Brazil 92 D e
Senate, Saskatchewan 86 H j
Sendai, Japan 133 G e
Senegal (Sénégal), W. Africa 118 B f
Sénégal R., W. Africa 118 C e
Senga Hill, Zambia 121 G f
Sengilei, U.S.S.R. 117 J d
Senhor do Bonfim, Brazil 93 J f
Senise, Italy 111 F e
Senj, Yugoslavia 110 E c
Senja, Norway 102 G b
Senlac, Saskatchewan 86 H f
Senneterre, Quebec 85 N d
Sens, France 108 E b
Senta, Yugoslavia 112 C b
Sentinel Pk., British Columbia 88 J c
Sentinel Ra., Antarctica 136 G c
Seoni, India 126 E d
Seoul, S. Korea 128 J c
Sepólno, Poland 105 G b
Sept Iles, Quebec 82 F c
Sept-Milles, L., Quebec 82 B b
Sepúlveda, Spain 106 D b
Sequeros, Spain 106 B b
Ser, Mt., India 126 E b
Serai, Syria 123 D b
Serakhs, Turkmen., U.S.S.R. 114 F e
Serbia (Srbija), Yugoslavia 112 C c
Serdeles, Libya 119 H c
Serdobsk, U.S.S.R. 117 G d
Serengeti Nat. Park, Tanzania 121 G e
Sergach, U.S.S.R. 117 G c
Sergiyevsk, U.S.S.R. 117 K c
Sérifos, I., Greece 113 E f
Sermata, I., Indonesia 129 J m
Serov, U.S.S.R. 114 F c
Serowe, Botswana 122 D d
Serpa, Portugal 106 B d
Serpent, R. au, Quebec 82 A d
Serpentine R., British Columbia 88 E g
Serpins, Portugal 106 A b
Serpukhov, U.S.S.R. 116 K d
Serra do Gurupí, Brazil 93 H d
Sérrai, Greece 112 D d
Serre San Bruno, Italy 111 F f
Serrezuela, Argentina 94 C d
Sertã, Portugal 106 A c
Sertañia, Brazil 93 K e
Sertão, Brazil 93 J e
Sertig, Switzerland 101 E b
Sérvia, Greece 113 D d
Seseganaga L., Ontario 87 N a
Sesekinika Lake, Ontario 84 K d
Seseko shima, Okinawa 78 A b
Sesheke, Zambia 122 C c
Sète, France 109 E e
Sete Lagoas, Brazil 93 J g
Sétif, Algeria 118 G a
Settee L., Manitoba 87 U a
Setting L., Manitoba 87 T c
Settlement, Wake I. 79 S e
Setubal, Portugal 106 A c
Seul, L., Manitoba 81 K g
Seul, Lac, Ontario 81 K g
Sevan, Oz., Armyanskaya 114 D d
Sevastopol, U.S.S.R. 116 H j
Sevelen, Switzerland 101 E a
Seven Islands. See Sept Iles
Seven Persons, Alberta 86 G j
Seventy Mile House, British Columbia 88 J e
Séverac-le-Château, France 109 E d
Severn, Ontario 81 L f
Severn, R., England 99 F j
Severn, R., Ontario 81 L f
Severn, South Africa 122 C e
Severnaya Dvina, U.S.S.R. 114 D b
Severnaya Zemlya, U.S.S.R. 115 K a
Sevilla. See Seville
Seville (Sevilla), Spain 106 C d
Seward Mts., Antarctica 136 H d
Sexsmith, Alberta 88 K c
Seybaplaya, Mexico 90 F d
Seychelles, Is., Indian Ocean 121 K a
Seydhisfjördhur, Iceland 102 Z a
Seyhan, Turkey 124 C b
Seymchan, U.S.S.R. 115 Q b
Seymour, Mt., British Columbia 88 D e
Seymour R., British Columbia 88 D e
Seyne, France 109 G d
Sézanne, France 108 E b
Sfakiá. See Khóra Sfakion
Sfântu Gheorghe, Romania 112 E b
Sfax, Tunisia 119 H b
Sfira, Syria 123 F a
Shaam, Trucial States 125 G d
Shabaqua, Ontario 87 N b
Shackleton, Saskatchewan 86 J h
Shackleton Glacier, Antarctica 136 C b
Shackleton Ice Shelf, Antarctica 136 R e
Shackleton Inlet, Antarctica 136 B b
Shackleton Ra., Antarctica 136 K b
Shadegan, Iran 124 E c
Shadrinsk, U.S.S.R. 117 R b
Shadwan, I., Egypt 119 M c
Shaftesbury, England 99 F j
Shag Rocks, Atlantic Ocean 136 J g
Shahba, Syria 123 E e
Shahbandar, Pakistan 126 C d
Shahdād, Iran 125 G c
Shahdadkot, Pakistan 126 C c
Shahdadpur, Pakistan 126 C c
Shahgarh, India 126 C c
Shahhat, Libya 119 K b
Shahidula, India 126 E a
Shahin, Iran 124 E b
Shahjahanpur, India 126 E c
Shahjui, Afghanistan 125 J c
Shāhpūr, Iran 124 D b
Shahpura, India 126 D c
Shahrakht, Iran 125 H c
Shahr-e-Babak, Iran 125 G c
Shahreza, Iran 125 F c
Shahr-i-Zabul. See Zabol
Shahrud, Iran 125 G b
Shahsavar, Iran 125 F b
Shahsien, China 131 H j
Shaiba, Saudi Arabia 124 D d
Shajara, Saudi Arabia 124 E e
Shakespeare I., Ontario 84 B c
Shakhty, U.S.S.R. 117 E g
Shakpets. See Shakubetsueki
Shakubetsueki, Japan 133 H c
Shala L., Ethiopia 121 H c
Shalasha, Sudan 119 L f
Shalath, Br. Columbia 88 H e
Shallow Lake, Ontario 84 J g
Shamil, Iran 125 G d
Shammar, Jabal, Saudi Arabia 124 D d
Shamrock, Saskatchewan 86 L h
Shanghai, China 130 K g
Shangjao, China 131 H h
Shangkiu, China 130 G e
Shangtu, China 130 F b
Shangtung, prov., China 130 H d
Shangyiu, China 131 G k
Shan-hai-kwan. See Linyu
Shanhsien. See Sanmenhsia
Shannah, Saudi Arabia 125 F f
Shannon, Eire 99 B h
Shannon, I., Greenland 89 M b
Shannon R., Eire 99 B g
Shansi, prov., China 130 E c
Shantarskiye Os., U.S.S.R. 115 N c
Shantou. See Swatow
Shantung Pen., China 118 H c
Shaohing, China 131 K g
Shaowu, China 131 H j
Shaoyang, China 131 E j
Shapinsay, I., Orkney Is. 98 F a
Shaqa, Saudi Arabia 124 D f
Shaqra, Saudi Arabia 124 E d
Sharbot Lake, Ontario 85 O h
Sharjah, Trucial States 125 G d
Shark B., Australia 134 B e
Sharqi, Jeb. esh, Lebanon-Syria 123 E d
Sharr, Jebel el, Saudi Arabia 124 C d
Sharya, U.S.S.R. 117 G a
Shasi, China 131 F g
Shatra, Iraq 124 E c
Shatt-al-Arab, Iraq 124 E c
Shaubek, Jordan 123 D g
Shaunavon, Saskatchewan 86 J j
Shawanaga, Ontario 84 K g
Shawbridge, Quebec 85 Q g
Shawinigan, Quebec 85 S f
Shawville, Quebec 85 O g
Shchors, Ukraine, U.S.S.R. 116 G f
Shebandowan L., Ontario 87 M b
Shedden, Ontario 84 J k
Shediac, New Brunswick 82 H g
Sheelin L., Eire 99 C g
Sheenborough, Quebec 85 N g
Sheenjik R., Alaska 80 E f
Sheep Cr., Alberta 88 K d
Sheep Haven, Eire 98 B e
Sheerness, Alberta 86 F g
Sheerness, England 99 H j
Sheet Harbour, Nova Scotia 82 K j
Sheffield, England 99 G g
Sheguindah, Ontario 84 J g
Sheho, Saskatchewan 87 O g
Shehuen. See Chalia, R.
Sheikh, Jeb. esh (Mt. Hermon), Syria 123 D d
Sheikh 'Abd er Rahman. See Arka, S. Yemen
Sheikh Miskin, Syria 123 E e
Sheikh 'Othman, S. Yemen 124 E g
Sheik Seraq, Syria 123 F d
Shekak, R., Ontario 84 F c
Shekha, S. Yemen 124 E f
Sheklung, China 131 F l
Shelburne, Nova Scotia 82 G k
Shelburne, Ontario 84 K h
Sheldrake, Quebec 82 H c
Shelikhova, Zaliv, U.S.S.R. 115 Q c
Shellbrook, Saskatchewan 86 L e
Shell Lake, Saskatchewan 86 K e
Shellmouth, Manitoba 87 Q h
Shelter Bay, Quebec 82 F c
Shenchow. See Yüanling
Shendam, Nigeria 119 G g
Shendi, Sudan 119 M e
Shëngjin, Albania 112 B d
Shenkursk, U.S.S.R. 114 D b
Shensi, prov., China 130 D e
Shenyang, China 130 L b
Sheopur, India 126 E c
Shepard, Alberta 86 D g
Shepard I., Antarctica 136 E d
Shepetovka, Ukraine, U.S.S.R. 116 E f
Sheppard, Mt., British Columbia 88 C b
Shepparton, Australia 135 J g
Sherada, Ethiopia 121 H c
Sherard, C., North-West Territories 81 L c
Sherard Osborn Fd., Greenland 89 P a
Sherbro I., Sierra Leone 118 C g
Sherbrooke, Nova Scotia 83 L c
Sherbrooke, Quebec 85 T g
Sherbrooke L., Nova Scotia 82 H j
Sher Dahan, Mt., India 126 C b
Sheridan, C., North-West Territories 81 N a
Sherridon, Manitoba 87 Q c
Sheslay, British Columbia 88 D a
Sheslay, R., British Columbia 88 D a
Shetland (Zetland), Is., Scotland 98 J a
Shevaroy Hills, India 126 E f
Shiant Is., Scotland 98 C c
Shibam, S. Yemen 124 E f
Shibarghan, Afghanistan 125 J b
Shibata, Japan 133 F f
Shibetsi, Japan 133 J c
Shibin el Kom, Egypt 119 M b
Shichiyo Is., Truk Is. 78 D n
Shickshock Mts., Quebec 82 F e
Shiel, L., Scotland 98 D d
Shigatse, Tibet 127 G c
Shigawake, Quebec 82 G e
Shihnan. See Enshih
Shih Pao Shan, China 128 E e
Shihshow, China 131 F h
Shihtao, China 130 L d
Shihtsien, China 131 D j
Shikag L., Ontario 87 M a
Shikarpur, Pakistan 126 C c
Shiki Is., Truk Is. 78 E n
Shikoku, I., Japan 133 C h
Shilka & R., U.S.S.R. 115 L c
Shillelagh, Eire 99 C h
Shillington, Ontario 84 K d
Shillong, India 127 H c
Shilongol. See Silinhot
Shimoga, India 126 E f
Shimo Jima, Japan 133 A h
Shimoni, Kenya 121 H e
Shimonoseki, Japan 133 B g
Shin, L., Scotland 98 E b
Shinapaaru, I., Rota I. 78 A h
Shinas, Muscat & Oman 125 G e
Shingshal & Pass, Kashmir 126 E a
Shingu, Japan 133 D h
Shining Tree, Ontario 84 J e
Shinjo, Japan 133 G e
Shinshar, Syria 123 E c
Shinyanga, Tanzania 121 G e
Ship Cove, Newfoundland 83 S f
Shipets. See Shibetsi
Shipman, Saskatchewan 87 N e
Shippegan & I., New Brunswick 82 H f
Shipshaw, R., Quebec 85 T d
Shipshaw Dam, Quebec 85 T d
Shiraishi, Japan 133 G f
Shiraz, Iran 125 F d
Shireza, Pakistan 126 C c
Shisur, Saudi Arabia 125 F f
Shiuchow. See Kukong
Shiuhing. See Koyiu
Shivpuri, India 126 E c
Shizugawa, Japan 133 G e
Shizuoka, Japan 133 F g
Shklov, Belorussia, U.S.S.R. 116 G d
Shkodër, Albania 112 B c
Shoal Harbour, Newfoundland 83 T e
Shoal L., Ontario 86 G a
Shoal Lake, Manitoba 87 R h
Shoal Ls., Manitoba 87 U h
Shoe Cove, Newfoundland 83 R d
Shoka. See Changhua
Sholapur, India 126 E e
Shonai. See Tsuruoka
Shonian Harb., Palau Is. 78 A o
Shortdale, Manitoba 87 R g
Shouldice, Alberta 86 E h
Shovo Tso, Tibet 127 F b
Shrewsbury, England 99 F h
Shropshire, co., England 99 F h
Shtora, Lebanon 123 D d
Shubenacadie, Nova Scotia 82 J h
Shubenacadie L., Nova Scotia 82 J j
Shuikow, China 131 J j
Shumaisa, Saudi Arabia 124 E e
Shumen. See Kolarovgrad
Shumerlya, U.S.S.R. 117 H c
Shunking. See Nanchung
Shunteh. See Singtai
Shuqra, S. Yemen 124 E g
Shurab, Iran 125 G c
Shuri, I., Okinawa 78 A c
Shurma, Saudi Arabia 124 D e
Shuru Tso, Tibet 127 G b
Shusf, Iran 125 H c
Shushal, Kashmir 126 E b
Shushtar, Iran 124 E c
Shuswap L., British Columbia 88 K e
Shuya, U.S.S.R. 117 E b
Shuyang, China 130 J e
Shwebo, Burma 127 J d
Shwedaung, Burma 127 J e
Shwegyin, Burma 127 J e
Shweli R., Burma 127 J d
Shyok, India 126 E b
Sialkot, Pakistan 126 D b

Siam, G. of, *S.-E. Asia* 132 C c
Siam. *See* Thailand
Sian, *China* 130 D e
Siangtan, *China* 131 F j
Siangyang, *China* 130 F f
Siangyin, *China* 131 F h
Siapu, *China* 131 J j
Siargao, I., *Philippines* 129 J j
Siaton, *Philippines* 129 H j
Šiauliai, *Lithuania, U.S.S.R.* 103 K j
Sib, *Muscat & Oman* 125 G e
Sibbald, *Alberta* 86 G g
Sibenik, *Yugoslavia* 110 E d
Siberut, I., *Indonesia* 129 C l
Sibi, *Pakistan* 126 C c
Sibiu, *Romania* 112 E b
Sibley Prov. Park, *Ontario* 84 B d
Sibolga, *Sumatra* 129 C k
Sibsagar, *India* 127 H c
Sibu, *Sarawak* 129 F k
Sicasica, *Bolivia* 92 D g
Sichang, *China* 128 D e
Sicié, C., *France* 109 F e
Sicilia, I. *See* Sicily
Sicilian Chan., *Mediterranean Sea* 111 C g
Sicily (Sicilia), I., *Italy* 111 D g
Sickle L., *Manitoba* 87 R b
Sicuani, *Peru* 92 C f
Šid, *Yugoslavia* 112 B b
Sideby, *Finland* 103 J e
Siderno Marina, *Italy* 111 F f
Sidewood, *Saskatchewan* 86 H h
Sidhout, *India* 126 E f
Sidi Barrani, *Egypt* 119 L b
Sidi-bel-Abbès, *Algeria* 118 E a
Sidi Ifni, Ifni, *North-West Africa* 118 C c
Sidlaw Hills, *Scotland* 98 E d
Sidley, Mt., *Antarctica* 136 E c
Sidney, *Manitoba* 87 S j
Sidney, Vancouver I., *British Columbia* 88 H f
Sidon, *Lebanon* 123 D d
Sidri, G. of, *Libya* 119 J b
Siedlce, *Poland* 105 K b
Siegen, *Germany* 104 C c
Siem Reap, *Cambodia* 132 C d
Siena, *Italy* 110 C d
Sieradz, *Poland* 105 H c
Siero, *Spain* 106 C a
Sierra Colorada, *Argentina* 95 C f
Sierra Grande, *Argentina* 95 C f
Sierra Leone, *W. Africa* 118 C g
Sierra Madre, *Mexico* 90 C b
Sierra Mojada, *Mexico* 90 D b
Sierra Rosada, *Argentina* 95 C f
Sífnos, I., *Greece* 113 E f
Sifton, *Manitoba* 87 R g
Sifton Pass, *Br. Columbia* 88 F b
Sigean, *France* 109 E e
Sighet, *Romania* 105 K e
Sighisoara, *Romania* 112 E a
Siglufjördhur, *Iceland* 102 W l
Sigmaringen, *Germany* 104 C d
Sigsig, *Ecuador* 92 B d
Sigüenza, *Spain* 106 D b
Siguiri, *Guinea* 118 D f
Sigulda, *Latvia, U.S.S.R.* 103 L h
Sihanoukville, *Cambodia* 129 D h
Sihl See, *Switzerland* 101 D a
Sihsien, *China* 131 J h
Siilinjärvi, *Finland* 102 M e
Sikanni Chief R., *B.C.* 88 H b
Sikar, *India* 126 E c
Sikasso, *Mali* 118 D f
Si Kiang, R., *China* 128 F f
Siking. *See* Sian
Sikinos, I., *Greece* 113 E f
Sikkim, *India* 127 G c
Silairsk, *U.S.S.R.* 117 N d
Silao, *Mexico* 90 D c
Silchar, *India* 127 H d
Silenen, *Switzerland* 101 D b
Silenrieux, *Belgium* 100 C d
Sil Garhi, *Nepal* 126 F c
Sili, I., *Manua Is.* 79 S o
Silifke, *Turkey* 124 B b
Silinhot, *China* 128 G b
Silistra, *Bulgaria* 112 F b
Siljan, L., *Sweden* 103 F f
Silkeborg, *Denmark* 103 C h
Sillery, dist., *Quebec* 85 S e
Silloth, *England* 98 E f
Sils, *Switzerland* 101 E b
Silsby L., *Manitoba* 87 W c
Silton, *Saskatchewan* 87 N h
Silvânia, *Brazil* 93 H g
Silvaplana, *Switzerland* 101 E b
Silva Porto, *Angola* 120 D g
Silver Centre, *Ontario* 85 L e
Silver Heights, *Alberta* 86 F f
Silver Islet, *Ontario* 84 B d
Silver Mt., *Newfoundland* 83 P d
Silver R., *Nova Scotia* 82 G j
Silver Star Prov. Park, *British Columbia* 88 K e
Silverthrone Mt., *British Columbia* 88 F e
Silves, *Brazil* 92 F d
Silves, *Portugal* 106 A d
Silvretta, Mts., *Austria-Switzerland* 104 C e
Simanggang, *Sarawak* 129 F k
Simard, L., *Quebec* 85 M e
Simcoe, *Ontario* 84 K k
Simcoe L., *Ontario* 85 L h
Simeulue, I., *Indonesia* 129 C k
Simferopol, *U.S.S.R.* 116 J j
Simi, I., *Greece* 113 F f
Simleul Silvaniei, *Romania* 105 K e
Simmie, *Saskatchewan* 86 J j
Simo, *Finland* 102 L d
Simö Järvi, L., *Finland* 102 M c
Simola, *Finland* 103 N f
Simonette, R., *Alberta* 88 K c
Simonhouse, *Manitoba* 87 Q d
Simon L., *Quebec* 85 P g
Simoom Sound, *British Columbia* 88 F e
Simpelveld, *Netherlands* 100 D d
Simplon & Pass, *Switzerland* 101 D b
Simpson, I., *Chile* 95 B g
Simpson, *Saskatchewan* 87 M g
Simpson Des., *Australia* 134 G e
Simpson I., *Ontario* 84 C d
Simpson Pen., *North-West Territories* 81 L d
Simuna, *Estonia, U.S.S.R.* 103 M g
Sinai, Pen., *Egypt* 119 M c
Sinaloa, state, *Mexico* 90 C b
Sinaloa & R., *Mexico* 90 C b
Sinamaica, *Venezuela* 92 C a
Sinbo, *Burma* 127 J d
Sinchang, *China* 131 K h
Sin-chow, *China* 130 G c
Sindel, *Bulgaria* 112 F c
Sindhi R., *India* 126 E c
Sind Sagar Doab, *Pakistan* 126 D b
Sines, *Portugal* 106 A d
Singa, *Sudan* 119 M f
Singapore, & Str., *S.-E. Asia* 132 C f
Singaradja, *Bali I., Indonesia* 129 G m
Singen, *Germany* 104 C e
Singida, *Tanzania* 121 G e
Singitic G., *Greece* 113 D d
Singkawang, *Borneo* 129 E k
Singkep, I., *Riau Arch., Indonesia* 129 D l
Singora. *See* Songkhla
Singsingsia, *China* 128 B b
Singtai, *China* 130 G d
Singtze, *China* 131 H h
Sinho, *China* 130 G d
Sinhsien, *China* 128 F c
Sinhwa, *China* 131 E j
Sining, *China* 128 D c
Siniscola, *Sardinia* 111 B e
Sinj, *Yugoslavia* 110 F d
Sinjar & Jebel, *Iraq* 124 D b
Sinjil, *Palestine* 123 D e
Sinkiang, *China* 114 H d
Sin-min-fu, *China* 130 L b
Sinnamary, *Fr. Guiana* 93 G b
Sinning, *China* 131 E j
Sinoe L., *Romania* 112 G b
Sinoia, *Rhodesia* 122 E c
Sinop, *Turkey* 124 C a
Sintaluta, *Manitoba* 87 O h
Sintang, *Borneo* 129 F k
Sintra, *Portugal* 106 A c
Sinuiju, *N. Korea* 128 H b
Sinyang, *China* 128 F d
Sion, *Switzerland* 101 C b
Sioux Lookout, *Ontario* 86 L a
Siparia, *Trinidad* 92 E a
Sipiwesk, *Manitoba* 87 U c
Sipiwesk L., *Manitoba* 87 U c
Siple, Mt., *Antarctica* 136 E d
Sipolilo, *Rhodesia* 122 E c
Sipora, I., *Indonesia* 129 C l
Siquisique, *Venezuela* 92 D a
Sira, *India* 126 E f
Sira. *See* Síros, I.
Siracusa. *See* Syracuse
Sirajganj, *E. Pakistan* 127 H d
Sir Alexander, Mt., *British Columbia* 88 J d
Sir Charles Hamilton Sd., *Newfoundland* 83 S d
Sir Douglas, Mt., *Alberta-British Columbia* 86 B h
Sir Edward Pellew Group, Is., *Australia* 134 G c
Siretul, R., *Romania* 112 F a
Siri, *Ethiopia* 121 H c
Sirjan, *Iran* 125 G d
Sirna, I., *Greece* 113 F f
Sironcha, *India* 126 E e
Sironj, *India* 126 E d
Síros, I., *Greece* 113 E f
Sirsa, *India* 126 D c
Sir Sanford, Mt., *British Columbia* 88 L e
Sirsi, *India* 126 D f
Sirte & G. of, *Libya* 119 J b
Sir Wilfred Laurier, Mt., *British Columbia* 88 K d
Sisak, *Yugoslavia* 110 F c
Sisaket, *Thailand* 132 C c
Sisal, *Mexico* 90 F c
Sisi, *Botswana* 122 D d
Sisib L., *Manitoba* 87 S f
Sisipuk L., *Manitoba-Saskatchewan* 87 Q c
Sisopon, *Cambodia* 132 C d
Sisteron, *France* 109 F d
Sitamau, *India* 126 E d
Sitapur, *India* 126 F c
Sitara, *Saudi Arabia* 124 E e
Sithonia, *Greece* 113 D d
Sitía, *Crete* 113 F g
Sittang, *Burma* 127 J e
Sittang, R., *Burma* 127 J e
Sittard, *Netherlands* 100 D d
Sitten. *See* Sion
Si'ufaga, I., *Manua Is.* 79 S o
Siulagi Pt., *Manua Is.* 79 S o
Sivand, *Iran* 125 F c
Sivas, *Turkey* 124 C b
Siverek, *Turkey* 124 C b
Sivrihisar, *Turkey* 124 B b
Sivry, *Belgium* 100 C d
Siwa, *Egypt* 119 L c
Siwalik Hills, *India* 126 E b
Sjælland, *Denmark* 103 D j
Sjötorp, *Sweden* 103 E g
Skadarsko Jezero, *Yugoslavia-Albania* 112 B c
Skagafjörd, *Iceland* 102 W l
Skagens, *Denmark* 103 D h
Skagerrak, Chan., *Norway-Denmark* 103 B h
Skara, *Sweden* 103 E g
Skardu, *Kashmir* 126 E a
Skarnes, *Norway* 103 D f
Skead, *Ontario* 84 K d
Skead, *Ontario* 84 K f
Skeena, R., *Br. Columbia* 88 E c
Skeena Crossing, *British Columbia* 88 F c
Skeena Mts., *Br. Columbia* 88 E b
Skegness, *England* 99 H g
Skellefte Älv, *Sweden* 102 H d
Skellefteå, *Sweden* 102 J d
Skelton Glacier, *Antarctica* 136 A e
Skiathos, I., *Greece* 113 D e
Skibbereen, *Eire* 99 A j
Skidegate, Graham I., *British Columbia* 88 C d
Skien, *Norway* 103 C g
Skierniewice, *Poland* 105 J c
Skiff, *Alberta* 86 F j
Skiftet Kihti, *Finland* 103 J f
Skikda (Philippeville), *Algeria* 109 Q h
Skipton, *England* 99 F g
Skíros, I., *Greece* 113 E e
Skive, *Denmark* 103 C h
Skofja Loka, *Yugoslavia* 110 E b
Skópelos, I., *Greece* 113 D e
Skopin, *U.S.S.R.* 116 L e
Skopje, *Yugoslavia* 112 C c
Skövde, *Sweden* 103 E g
Skovorodino, *U.S.S.R.* 115 M c
Skownan, *Manitoba* 87 S g
Skradin, *Yugoslavia* 110 E d
Skrunda, *Latvia, U.S.S.R.* 103 K h
Skudeneshavn, *Norway* 103 A g
Skuodas, *Lithuania, U.S.S.R.* 103 J h
Skye, I., *Scotland* 98 C c
Slagelse, *Denmark* 103 D j
Slamet, Mt., *Indonesia* 129 E m
Slaney R., *Eire* 99 C h
Slate Is., *Ontario* 84 D d
Slatina, *Romania* 112 E b
Slatina, *Yugoslavia* 112 A b
Slave L., Lesser, *Alberta* 86 B c
Slave Lake, *Alberta* 86 C c
Slăveni, *Romania* 112 E b
Slave R., Lesser, *Alberta* 86 C c
Slavgorod, *U.S.S.R.* 114 G c
Slavonia, *Yugoslavia* 112 A b
Slavonski Brod, *Yugoslavia* 112 A l
Slavyansk, *Ukraine, U.S.S.R.* 116 K g
Slea Hd., *Eire* 99 A h
Sleat, Sd. of, *Scotland* 98 D c
Sled L., *Saskatchewan* 86 K d
Sleeper Is., *North-West Territories* 81 L f
Slessor Glacier, *Antarctica* 136 K c
Sleydinge, *Belgium* 100 B c
Sliedrecht, *Netherlands* 100 C c
Slieve Aughty, Mts., *Eire* 99 B g
Slieve Bloom Mts., *Eire* 99 B g
Slieve Mish, Mts., *Eire* 99 A h
Sligo & co., *Eire* 99 B f
Sligo B., *Eire* 99 B f
Slite, *Sweden* 103 H h
Sliven, *Bulgaria* 112 F c
Slobodskoy, *U.S.S.R.* 117 K a
Slocan, *Br. Columbia* 88 L f
Slocan L., *Br. Columbia* 88 L f
Sloka, *Latvia, U.S.S.R.* 116 C c
Slonim, *Belorussia, U.S.S.R.* 116 D e
Sloten, *Netherlands* 100 D b
Slough, *England* 99 G j
Slovakia (Slovensko), reg., *Czechoslovakia* 105 H d
Slovenija, *Yugoslavia* 110 E c
Slovensko. *See* Slovakia
Sluis, *Netherlands* 100 B c
Sluiskil, *Netherlands* 100 B c
Slunj, *Yugoslavia* 110 E c
Słupsk, *Poland* 105 G a
Slussfors, *Sweden* 102 G d
Slutsk, *Belorussia, U.S.S.R.* 116 E e
Slyne Hd., *Eire* 99 A g
Slyudyanka, *U.S.S.R.* 115 K c
Small I., *Truk Is.* 78 F n
Small L., *Manitoba* 87 U a
Smeaton, *Saskatchewan* 86 N e
Smilde, *Netherlands* 100 E b
Smiley, *Saskatchewan* 86 H g
Smiltene, *Latvia, U.S.S.R.* 103 L h
Smith, *Alberta* 86 C c
Smith, I., *N.-W. Territories* 81 M e
Smith, I., *Quebec* 81 M e
Smith, I., *South Shetlands* 136 H f
Smith B., *N.-W. Territories* 81 M b
Smithers, *Br. Columbia* 88 F c
Smith Pt., *Nova Scotia* 82 J h
Smith Sd., *N.-W. Territories* 81 M b
Smiths Falls, *Ontario* 85 O h
Smithton, *Tasmania* 135 H h
Smoky C., C. Breton I., *Nova Scotia* 83 M g
Smoky Falls, *Ontario* 84 H b
Smoky Lake, *Alberta* 86 E d
Smoky R., *Alberta* 88 L c
Smoky R., Lit., *Alberta* 88 L c
Smöla, *Norway* 102 B e
Smolensk, *U.S.S.R.* 116 H d
Smooth Rock Falls, *Ontario* 84 J d
Smoothrock L., *Ontario* 84 A b
Smoothstone L., *Saskatchewan* 86 L d
Smoothstone R., *Saskatchewan* 86 L c
Smyley, C., *Antarctica* 136 H d
Smyrna (Izmir), *Turkey* 124 A b
Snaefell, *Isle of Man* 99 D f
Snare, L., *Saskatchewan* 88 Q a
Snåsa, *Norway* 102 E d
Snåsa Vatn, *Norway* 102 D d
Sneek, *Netherlands* 100 D a
Sneem, *Eire* 99 A j
Sneeuw Gebergte, Mts., *W. Irian* 129 L l
Snipe L., *Alberta* 86 A c
Snizort L., *Scotland* 98 C c
Snöhetta, Mt., *Norway* 102 C e
Snowden, *Saskatchewan* 87 N e
Snowdon, *Wales* 99 E g
Snowflake, *Manitoba* 87 T j
Snow Hill I., *Antarctica* 136 J f
Snow I., *Antarctica* 136 H f
Snow Lake, *Manitoba* 87 S d
Snow Road, *Ontario* 85 O h
Snowy Mts., *Australia* 135 J g
Soasiu, *Moluccas* 129 J k
Soazza, *Switzerland* 101 E b
Sobakin, *U.S.S.R.* 117 J d
Sobinka, *U.S.S.R.* 116 M d
Sobrado, *Brazil* 93 G e
Sobral, *Brazil* 93 J d
Sobrance, *Czechoslovakia* 105 K d
Sochi, *U.S.S.R.* 117 C d
Society Is., *Pacific Ocean* 79 L j
Socorro, *Colombia* 92 C b
Socorro I., *Mexico* 90 B d
Socotra I., *Indian Ocean* 121 L b
Soc-trang, *S. Vietnam* 132 D e
Soda Creek, *Br. Columbia* 88 H d
Sodankylä, *Finland* 102 M c
Söderfors, *Sweden* 103 G f
Söderhamn, *Sweden* 103 G f
Söderköping, *Sweden* 103 G g
Södertälje, *Sweden* 103 G g
Sodiri, *Sudan* 119 L f
Soepiori, I., *W. Irian* 129 L l
Soest, *Germany* 104 C c
Soest, *Netherlands* 100 D b
Soeurs, I. des, *Quebec* 85 S k
Sofia (Sofiya), *Bulgaria* 112 D c
Sofiya. *See* Sofia
Sogamoso, *Colombia* 92 C b
Sogndal, *Norway* 103 B g
Sogne Fd., *Norway* 103 A f
Söğüt, *Turkey* 124 B a
Sohag, *Egypt* 119 M c
Sohan R., *Pakistan* 126 D b
Sohar, *Muscat & Oman* 125 G e
Soheb, *S. Yemen* 124 E g
Soignies, *Belgium* 100 C d
Soissons, *France* 108 E b
Soke, *Turkey* 124 A b
Sok Gomba. *See* Pachen
Sok Karmalinsk, *U.S.S.R.* 117 L c
Sokode, *Togo* 118 F g
Sokol, *U.S.S.R.* 116 L b
Sokolo, *Mali* 118 D f
Sokoniya, I., *Okinawa* 78 C b
Sokota, *Ethiopia* 121 H b
Sokoto, *Nigeria* 118 F f
Solai, *Kenya* 121 H d
Solbad Hall, *Austria* 104 D e
Soledad, *Venezuela* 92 E b
Soledade, *Brazil* 92 D e
Solent, The, Chan., *England* 99 G k
Solenzara, *Corsica* 111 B e
Sol Iletsk, *U.S.S.R.* 114 E c
Solimões, R. *See* Amazonas
Solingen, *Germany* 104 B c
Sollefteå, *Sweden* 102 G e
Sollum. *See* Salûm
Solok, *Sumatra* 129 D l
Solomon Is., *Pacific Ocean* 78 G h
Solomon Sea, *Pacific Ocean* 135 K a
Solothurn & canton, *Switzerland* 101 C a
Solsona, *Spain* 107 F a
Solstad, *Norway* 102 D d
Soltau, *Germany* 104 C b
Solund, I., *Norway* 103 A f
Solway Firth, *England-Scotland* 98 E f
Solwezi, *Zambia* 120 F g
Soma, *Turkey* 124 A b
Somalia. *See* Somali Republic
Somali Republic (Somalia), *East Africa* 121 J d
Sombor, *Yugoslavia* 112 B b
Sombra, *Ontario* 84 H k
Sombreiro Chan., *Nicobar Is.* 127 H g
Sombrerete, *Mexico* 90 D c
Sombrero I., *Leeward Is.* 91 G c
Somcuța Mare, *Romania* 105 K e
Someren, *Netherlands* 100 D c
Somerset, *Australia* 135 H b
Somerset, co., *England* 99 E j
Somerset, *Manitoba* 87 T j
Somerset I., *North-West Territories* 81 K c
Somme, *Belgium* 100 D d
Somme, dep., *France* 108 E b
Somme, R., *France* 108 D a
Sommières, *France* 109 F e
Somoto, *Nicaragua* 91 B d
Somovit, *Bulgaria* 112 E c
Somzee, *Belgium* 100 C d
Sonaripur, *India* 126 F c
Sönderborg, *Denmark* 103 C j
Song-Cau, *S. Vietnam* 132 D d
Songea, *Tanzania* 121 H g
Songkhla, *Thailand* 132 C e
Song-koi, R., *China, etc.* 132 C b
Sonkajärvi, *Finland* 102 M e
Sonkovo, *U.S.S.R.* 116 K c
Sonmiani, *Pakistan* 126 C c
Sonneberg, *Germany* 104 D c
Sonningdale, *Saskatchewan* 86 K f
Sonogno, *Switzerland* 101 D b
Sonora, *Nova Scotia* 83 L h
Sonora, state & R., *Mexico* 90 B b
Sonoyta, *Mexico* 90 B a
Sonpur, *India* 127 F d
Sonsón, *Colombia* 92 B b
Sonsorol Is., *Pacific Ocean* 78 D g
Soochow, *China* 130 K g
Sooke, *Br. Columbia* 88 H f
Soping. *See* Yuyu
Soppero, *Sweden* 102 J b
Sopron, *Hungary* 110 F b
Sop's Arm, *Newfoundland* 83 Q d
Sora, *Italy* 111 D e
Sorata, *Bolivia* 92 D g
Sorbas, *Spain* 107 D d
Sorel, *Quebec* 85 R f
Sorell, *Tasmania* 135 J h
Sörenberg, *Switzerland* 101 D b
Sörfold, *Norway* 102 F c
Sorgono, *Sardinia* 111 B e
Soria, *Spain* 107 D b
Soriano, *Uruguay* 94 E d
Sornico, *Switzerland* 101 D b
Sorocaba, *Brazil* 93 H h
Soroka, *U.S.S.R.* 117 L d
Soroki, *Moldavia, U.S.S.R.* 116 F g
Sorol, I., *Caroline Is.* 78 E f
Soromesis, *Botswana* 122 C c
Soron, *India* 126 E c
Sorong, *W. Irian* 129 K l
Sororoca, *Brazil* 92 E c
Soroti, *Uganda* 121 G d
Söröya, I., *Norway* 102 K a
Sorrento, *Br. Columbia* 88 K e
Sorrento, *Italy* 111 E e
Sör-Rondane Mts., *Antarctica* 136 N d
Sorsele, *Sweden* 102 G d
Sortavala, *U.S.S.R.* 102 P f
Sosanjaya B., *Rota I.* 78 A j
Sosanlag B., *Rota I.* 78 A j
Sosnovka, *U.S.S.R.* 117 E d
Sosnovo, Ozerskoye, *U.S.S.R.* 115 L c
Sosnowiec, *Poland* 105 H c
Sosu, I., *Okinawa* 78 C a
Sosva, *U.S.S.R.* 114 F c
Soto la Marina, *Mexico* 90 E c
Sotra, I., *Norway* 103 A f
Sotuta, *Mexico* 90 G c
Souanke, *Congo* 120 C d
Soudan, *Australia* 134 G d
Souflíon, *Greece* 112 F d
Souillac, *France* 109 D d
Soulanges Can., *Quebec* 85 Q g
Sŏul. *See* Seoul
Sounding L., *Alberta* 86 G f
Soure, *Brazil* 93 H d
Soure, *Portugal* 106 A b
Sour el Ghozlane, *Algeria* 109 N h
Souris, *Manitoba* 87 R j
Souris, *Prince Edward I.* 83 K g
Souris R., *Manitoba-North Dakota* 80 J h
Sousel, *Brazil* 93 G d
Sousse, *Tunisia* 119 H a
South Africa, Rep. of, *Africa* 122 C e
South America 92-95
Southampton, C., *N.-W. Terr.* 81 L e
Southampton, *England* 99 F k
Southampton, I., *N.-W. Terr.* 81 L e
Southampton, *Nova Scotia* 82 H h
Southampton, *Ontario* 84 J h
Southard, C., *Antarctica* 136 T e
South Aulatsivik I., *Labrador* 81 N f
South Australia, state, *Australia* 134 F e
South B., *Ontario* 84 J g
South Baymouth, *Ontario* 84 H g
South Brook, *Newfoundland* 83 Q d
South Brookfield, *Nova Scotia* 82 H j
South Chan., *Eniwetok* 79 S d
South China Sea, *Asia* 78 B f
South Downs, *England* 99 G k
South-East C., *Tasmania* 135 J h
Southeast Pass, *Jaluit I.* 79 U j
Southend, *England* 99 H j
Southend, *Saskatchewan* 88 S b
Southern Alps, *New Zealand* 135 Q l
Southern Cross, *Australia* 134 C f
Southern Harbour, *Newfoundland* 83 S f
Southern Rhodesia. *See* Rhodesia
Southern Yemen, *S.W. Asia* 124 D g
Southey, *Saskatchewan* 87 N h
South Fork, *Saskatchewan* 86 J j
South Georgia, I., *Atlantic Ocean* 136 K g
South Harbour, Cape Breton I., *Nova Scotia* 83 M g
South Henik L., *N.-W. Terr.* 81 K e
South I., *New Zealand* 135 Q m
South Indian Lake, *Manitoba* 87 T b
South Inlet, *Antarctica* 136 B d
South Junction, *Manitoba* 86 F a
South Lochaber, *Nova Scotia* 83 K h
South Nelson, *New Brunswick* 82 G g
South Orkneys, Is., *Atlantic Ocean* 136 J f
South Pass, *Truk Is.* 78 E o
South Polar Plateau, *Antarc.* 136 C a
South Pole, *Antarctica* 136 A a
South Porcupine, *Ontario* 84 J d
Southport, *Australia* 135 K e
Southport, *England* 99 E g
South Pt., *Anticosti I., Que.* 83 K d
South Pt., *Jaluit I.* 79 U j
South River, *Ontario* 85 L g
South Ronaldsay I., *Orkney Is.* 98 F b
South Sask. Dam, *Sask.* 86 L g
South Seal R., *Manitoba* 87 S a
South Shetland Is., *Antarc.* 136 H f
South Shields, *England* 98 G f
Southside, *Canton I.* 79 S n
South Slocan, *Br. Columbia* 88 L f
South Taranari Bight, *New Zealand* 135 R k
South West Africa, *Southern Africa* 122 B d
Southwest C., Madeleine Is., *Quebec* 83 L f
South West C., *Tasmania* 135 J h
South Westminster, *British Columbia* 88 E g
Southwest Pass, *Jaluit I.* 79 T j
Southwest Passage, *Eniwetok* 79 R c
Southwest Pt., Anticosti I., *Quebec* 82 J a
Southwold, *England* 99 J h
Souza, *Brazil* 93 K e
Souzel, *Portugal* 106 B c
Sovereign, *Saskatchewan* 86 K g
Sovetsk, *U.S.S.R.* 103 J j
Sovetskaya Gavan, *U.S.S.R.* 115 P d
Sovietsk, *U.S.S.R.* 117 J b
Soviet Union (U.S.S.R.), *Europe-Asia* 114-115
Sowden L., *Ontario* 87 M a
Soy, *Kenya* 121 H d
Soya & B., *Japan* 133 G b
Soya Misaki, *Japan* 133 H b
Soya Str., *Japan* 133 G b
Soyopa, *Mexico* 90 C b
Spa, *Belgium* 100 D d
Spain, *W. Europe* 106-107
Spalato. *See* Split
Spalding, *England* 99 G h
Spalding, *Saskatchewan* 87 N f
Spandau, *Germany* 104 E b
Spaniard's Bay, *Nfd.* 83 T f
Spanish, *Ontario* 84 H f
Spanish R., *Ontario* 84 J f
Spanish Sahara, *W. Africa* 118 C c
Spanish Town, *Jamaica* 91 D c
Sparta, *Greece* 113 D f
Sparti. *See* Sparta
Spartivento, C., *Italy* 111 F g
Spassk, *U.S.S.R.* 117 F d
Spassk Dalniy, *U.S.S.R.* 118 K b
Spassk-Ryszanskiy, *U.S.S.R.* 117 E c
Spearhill, *Manitoba* 87 T g
Spedden, *Alberta* 86 F d
Speers, *Saskatchewan* 86 K f
Spence Bay, *N.-W. Terr.* 81 K d
Spencer G., *Australia* 134 G f
Spences Bridge, *British Columbia* 88 J e
Sperling, *Manitoba* 87 U j
Sperrin Mts., *N. Ireland* 99 C f
Spétsai I., *Greece* 113 D f
Speyer, *Germany* 104 C d
Spey R., *Scotland* 98 E c
Spezand, *Pakistan* 126 C b
Spinazzola, *Italy* 111 F e
Spiringen, *Switzerland* 101 D b
Spirit River, *Alberta* 88 K c
Spiritwood, *Saskatchewan* 86 K e
Spitsbergen, *Arctic Ocean* 114 A a
Spitsbergen, Vest, *Arctic Oc.* 114 A a
Spittal, *Austria* 104 E e
Split, C., *Nova Scotia* 82 H h
Split, *Yugoslavia* 110 F d
Split L., *Manitoba* 87 V b
Split Lake, *Manitoba* 87 V b
Splügen, Pass, *Switz.-Italy* 101 E b
Splügen, *Switzerland* 101 E b
Spoleto, *Italy* 110 D d
Spondin, *Alberta* 86 F g
Spontin, *Belgium* 100 C d
Sporadhes, Is., *Aegean Sea* 113 F f
Sporadhes, Voriai, Is., *Aegean Sea* 113 E e
Spragge, *Ontario* 84 H f
Sprague, *Manitoba* 86 F a
Spree, R., *Germany* 104 E b
Spremberg, *Germany* 104 F c
Sprimont, *Belgium* 100 D d

Springbok, South Africa 122 B e
Springburn, Alberta 88 L c
Spring Coulee, Alberta 86 D j
Springdale, Newfoundland 83 Q d
Springer, Mt., Quebec 85 Q c
Springfield, New Brunswick 82 G h
Springfield, Nova Scotia 82 H j
Springfield, Ontario 84 K k
Springfontein, South Africa 122 D f
Springhill, Nova Scotia 82 H h
Springhill, Quebec 82 A h
Springside, Saskatchewan 87 P g
Springsure, Australia 135 J d
Spring Valley, Saskatchewan 87 M j
Springwater, Saskatchewan 86 J g
Spruce Brook, Nfd. 83 O e
Sprucedale, Ontario 85 L g
Spruce Lake, Saskatchewan 86 H e
Spruga, Switzerland 101 D b
Spurfield, Alberta 86 C c
Spy Hill, Saskatchewan 87 Q h
Squamish, Br. Columbia 88 H f
Squattack, Quebec 82 D f
Squaw L., Quebec 83 L c
Squillace, G. di, Italy 111 F f
Srbija (Serbia), Yugoslavia 112 C c
Srebrenica, Yugoslavia 112 B b
Sredinnyy, Khrebet, Mts., U.S.S.R. 115 R c
Sredne Kamchatsk, U.S.S.R. 115 R c
Sredne Kolymak, U.S.S.R. 115 Q b
Sredne Vilyuysk, U.S.S.R. 115 M b
Śrem, Poland 105 G b
Srepok, Cambodia 132 D d
Sretensk, U.S.S.R. 115 L c
Srikakulam, India 127 F e
Sri Kolayatji, India 126 D c
Srinagar, Kashmir 126 D b
Srirangapatnar, India 126 E f
Srivilliputtur, India 126 E g
Srnetica, Yugoslavia 110 F c
Środa, Poland 105 G b
Stackpool, Ontario 84 J e
Staden, Belgium 100 A d
Staffa I., Scotland 98 C d
Stafford & co., England 99 F h
Stalingrad. See Volgograd
Stalin Mt., Br. Columbia 88 G a
Stallworthy, C., N.-W. Terr. 81 K a
Stalwart, Saskatchewan 87 M g
Stamprooi, Netherlands 100 D c
Stanchik, U.S.S.R. 115 Q a
Standard, Alberta 86 E g
Standerton, South Africa 122 D e
Stange, Norway 103 D f
Stanislav. See Ivano-Frankovsk
Stanley, Falkland Is. 95 E h
Stanley, New Brunswick 82 F g
Stanley Falls, Congo 120 F d
Stanley Mission, Saskatchewan 87 N c
Stanleyville. See Kisangani
Stanmore, Alberta 86 F g
Stann Creek, Brit. Honduras 91 B c
Stanovoy Khrebet, Mts., U.S.S.R. 115 M c
Stans, Switzerland 101 D b
Stansmore Ra., Australia 134 E d
Stanthorpe, Australia 135 K e
Staphorst, Netherlands 100 E b
Starachowice, Poland 105 J c
Stara Planina, Bulgaria 112 E c
Staraya Russa, U.S.S.R. 116 G c
Stara Zagora, Bulgaria 112 E c
Starbuck, I., Pacific Ocean 79 L h
Starbuck, Manitoba 87 U j
Star City, Saskatchewan 87 N f
Stargard, Poland 104 F b
Star'obelsk, Ukraine, U.S.S.R. 116 L g
Starodub, U.S.S.R. 116 H e
Starogard, Poland 105 H b
Staro Konstantinov, Ukraine, U.S.S.R. 116 E g
Staryy Oskol, U.S.S.R. 116 K f
Staten I. See Estados I
Stattlandet, Norway 102 A e
Stavanger, Norway 103 A g
Stave L., Br. Columbia 88 H f
Stavelot, Belgium 100 D d
Stavely, Alberta 86 D h
Stavenisse, Netherlands 100 C c
Staveren, Netherlands 100 D b
Stavern, Norway 103 D g
Stavropol, U.S.S.R. 114 D d
Stayner, Ontario 84 K h
Steckborn, Switzerland 101 D a
Steele I., Antarctica 136 J d
Steel L., Ontario 84 D c
Steel R., Ontario 84 D d
Steenbergen, Netherlands 100 C c
Steenkool, W. Irian 129 K l
Steensel, Netherlands 100 D c
Steenwijk, Netherlands 100 E b
Steep Creek, Saskatchewan 87 M e
Steephill L., Saskatchewan 87 O c
Steep Rock, Manitoba 87 T g
Steep Rock Lake, Ontario 86 L a
Stefanie L., Ethiopia 121 H d
Stefansson B., Antarctica 136 P e
Stefansson I., N.-W. Terr. 80 J c
Steiermark, prov., Austria 104 F e
Stein, Switzerland 101 D a
Steinbach, Manitoba 87 V j
Steinkjer, Norway 102 D c
Stekene, Belgium 100 C c
Stellarton, Nova Scotia 82 K h
Stenay, France 108 F b
Stendal, Germany 104 D b
Stenen, Saskatchewan 87 P g
Stenträsk, Sweden 102 H c
Stephenville, Newfoundland 83 O e
Stephenville Crossing, Nfd. 83 O e
Stepnyak, Kazakh., U.S.S.R. 114 G c
Steps Pt., Tutuila I. 79 U o
Sterea, Greece 113 C e
Sterlitamak, U.S.S.R. 117 M d
Sternberk, Czechoslovakia 105 G d
Sterrebeek, Belgium 100 C d
Stettin (Szczecin), Poland 104 F b
Stettler, Alberta 86 E f
Stevens, Ontario 84 E c
Stevenson, airfield, Man. 87 U j
Stevenson L., Manitoba 87 W e
Steveston, Lulu I., British Columbia 88 C g
Steveville Prov. Pk., Alberta 86 F h
Stewart, Br. Columbia 88 E c
Stewart Cr., Saskatchewan 87 N e
Stewart I., Chile 95 B h
Stewart Is., New Zealand 135 P m
Stewart River, Yukon 77 S e
Stewart Sd., Andaman Is. 127 H f
Stewart Valley, Sask. 86 K h
Stewiacke, Nova Scotia 82 J h
Steyr, Austria 104 F d
Stia, Italy 110 C d
Stikine, R., Br. Columbia 88 D b
Stimlje, Yugoslavia 112 C c
Štip, Yugoslavia 112 D d
Stirling, Alberta 86 E j
Stirling, Ontario 85 N h
Stirling, Quebec 85 S e
Stirling & co., Scotland 98 E d
Stirling Ra., Australia 134 C f
Stjernöy, Norway 102 K a
Stockholm, Saskatchewan 87 P h
Stockholm, Sweden 103 H g
Stockport, England 99 F g
Stockton, Manitoba 87 S j
Stockton-on-Tees, England 99 G f
Stoke-on-Trent, England 99 F g
Stokes Bay, Ontario 84 J g
Stolbovaya, U.S.S.R. 115 Q b
Stolp. See Słupsk
Ston, Yugoslavia 110 F d
Stonecliffe, Ontario 85 M f
Stoneham, Quebec 82 A g
Stonehaven, Scotland 98 F d
Stone Mountain Prov. Park, British Columbia 88 G a
Stonewall, Manitoba 87 U h
Stoney Beach, Saskatchewan 87 M h
Stoney Creek, Ontario 85 L j
Stony Mountain, Manitoba 87 U h
Stony Plain, Alberta 86 D e
Stora Lulevatten, Sweden 102 H c
Stora Sjöfallets Nat. Park, Sweden 102 G c
Storavan, Sweden 102 H d
Stord, I., Norway 103 A g
Stören, Norway 102 D e
Storforshei, Norway 102 F c
Stor I., N.-W. Territories 81 L b
Storkerson B., N.-W. Terr. 80 G c
Storlien, Sweden 102 D e
Stormy L., Ontario 86 K a
Stornoway, Saskatchewan 87 P g
Stornoway, Scotland 98 C b
Stor Sjön, Sweden 102 F e
Storsund, Sweden 102 J d
Storthoaks, Saskatchewan 87 Q j
Storuman, Sweden 102 G d
Storvik, Sweden 103 G f
Stouffville, Ontario 85 L j
Stoughton, Manitoba 87 O j
Stowmarket, England 99 H h
Strabane, N. Ireland 98 C f
Strachan, Mt., Br. Columbia 88 C e
Strachan I., Papua 135 H a
Strahan, Tasmania 135 H h
Stralsund, Germany 104 E a
Strand, Norway 103 B g
Stranda, Norway 102 B e
Strangford L., N. Ireland 99 D f
Strangways Springs, Australia 134 G e
Stranraer, Saskatchewan 86 J g
Stranraer, Scotland 98 D f
Strasbourg, France 108 G b
Strasbourg, Saskatchewan 87 N g
Stråssa, Sweden 103 F g
Stratford, New Zealand 135 R k
Stratford, Ontario 84 K j
Stratford, Quebec 82 A h
Stratford-on-Avon, England 99 F h
Strathclair, Manitoba 87 R h
Strathcona Prov. Park, Vancouver I., B.C. 88 G f
Strathlorne, C. Breton I., Nova Scotia 83 L g
Strathmore, Alberta 86 D g
Strathnaver, Br. Columbia 88 H d
Strathroy, Ontario 84 J k
Straubing, Germany 104 E d
Strawberry Hill, British Columbia 88 E g
Strawhat Depot, Quebec 85 R e
Strawn I., Palmyra I. 79 T k
Štrbské Pleso, Czechoslovakia 105 J d
Streaky B., Australia 134 F f
Streamstown, Alberta 86 G e
Strelka, U.S.S.R. 115 Q b
Strelka, U.S.S.R. 115 K b
Strelka, U.S.S.R. 115 J c
Strenči, Latvia, U.S.S.R. 103 L h
Střibro, Czechoslovakia 104 E d
Strickland, Ontario 84 J c
Strijbeek, Netherlands 100 C c
Strijen, Netherlands 100 C c
Strimón, G. of, Greece 113 E d
Stromboli, I., Italy 111 E f
Strome, Alberta 86 E f
Stromeferry, Scotland 98 D c
Stromness, Orkney Is. 98 E b
Strömsberg, Sweden 103 G f
Strömsbruk, Sweden 103 G f
Strömstad, Sweden 103 D g
Strömsund, Sweden 102 F e
Ströms Vattudal, Sweden 102 F d
Strömtorp, Sweden 103 F g
Strongfield, Saskatchewan 86 L g
Strongoli, Italy 111 F f
Stronsay I., Orkney Is. 98 F a
Stroud, England 99 F j
Struga, Yugoslavia 112 C d
Struma, R., Bulgaria-Greece 112 D d
Strumica, Yugoslavia 112 D d
Stryy, Ukraine, U.S.S.R. 116 C g
Strzelin, Poland 105 G c
Stuart Highway, Australia 135 F c
Stuart L. & R., Br. Columbia 88 G c
Stuart Ra., Australia 134 F e
Stugun, Sweden 102 F e
Stung-Treng, Cambodia 132 D d
Stupendous Mt., British Columbia 88 F d
Sturgeon B., Manitoba 87 U f
Sturgeon Falls, Ontario 84 L f
Sturgeon L., Alberta 88 L c
Sturgeon L., Ontario 85 M h
Sturgeon L., Ontario 87 L b
Sturgeon L., Ontario 87 M a
Sturgeon Landing, Sask 87 Q d
Sturgeon R., Alberta 86 C e
Sturgeon R., Ontario 84 K f
Sturgeon R., Saskatchewan 86 L e
Sturg I., Antarctica 136 B e
Sturgis, Saskatchewan 87 P g
Sturt Des., Australia 135 H e
Stuttgart, Germany 104 C d
Suakin, Sudan 119 N e
Suancheng, China 130 J g
Süan-hwa, China 130 G b
Suanwei, China 130 D e
Suaqui, Mexico 90 C b
Subeimanieh. See Karaj
Subh, Jebel, Saudi Arabia 124 C e
Subotica, Yugoslavia 112 B a
Success, Saskatchewan 86 J h
Sucha, Poland 105 H d
Suchan, U.S.S.R. 115 N d
Süchow. See Tungshan
Sucre, Bolivia 92 D g
Sudan, Africa 119 L f
Sudbury, England 99 H h
Sudbury, Ontario 84 J f
Suddie, Guyana 92 F b
Sudety, Mts., Czech., etc 105 F c
Sudharam, E. Pakistan 127 H d
Suez, Egypt 119 M c
Suez, G. of, Egypt 119 M c
Suez Canal, Egypt 119 M b
Sufeina, Saudi Arabia 124 D e
Suffield, Alberta 86 F h
Suffolk, co., England 99 H h
Suggi L., Saskatchewan 87 P d
Suhl, Germany 104 D c
Suifu. See Ipin
Suihwa, China 128 J a
Suining, China 130 H f
Suipacha, Bolivia 92 D h
Suiteh, China 130 E d
Sujica, Yugoslavia 110 F d
Sukadana, Borneo 117 F l
Sukarnapura, W. Irian 129 M l
Sukarno Pk., W. Irian 129 L l
Sukhothai, Thailand 132 B c
Sukhumi, U.S.S.R. 114 D d
Sukkiu, India 126 C c
Sukkur, Pakistan 126 C c
Sukow, China 130 F d
Sukumo, Japan 133 C h
Sukunka R., Br. Columbia 88 J c
Sulaiman Ra., Pakistan 126 D b
Sulaimiya, Saudi Arabia 124 E e
Sulaiyil, Saudi Arabia 124 E e
Sulawesi. See Celebes
Sulaymānīya, Iraq 124 E b
Sulęcin, Poland 104 F b
Sulgen, Switzerland 101 E a
Sulina, Romania 112 G b
Sulitelma, Mt., Norway 102 G c
Sullana, Peru 92 A d
Sullivan Bay, Br. Columbia 88 F e
Sullivan L., Alberta 86 F f
Sulmona, Italy 111 D d
Sultan, Ontario 84 H e
Sultan Bulak. See Razan
Sultan Dagh, Turkey 124 B b
Sultan Hamud, Kenya 121 H e
Sultaniyeh, Iran 124 E b
Sultanpur, India 127 F c
Sulu Arch., Philippines 129 H j
Sulu Kep., Is., Indonesia 129 J l
Sulu Sea, Philippines 129 G j
Sulzberger B., Antarctica 136 D c
Sumagawa, Japan 133 H c
Sumatra, I., Indonesia 129 C k
Sumba, I., Indonesia 129 G m
Sumbawa, I., Indonesia 129 G m
Sumbhar L., India 126 D c
Sumbur, Mongolia 128 E a
Sumburgh Hd., Shetland 98 J b
Sümeg, Hungary 105 G e
Sumiswald, Switzerland 101 C a
Summerford, Newfoundland 83 S d
Summerland, Br. Columbia 88 K f
Summerside, Prince Edward I. 82 J g
Summerville, Newfoundland 83 T e
Summit, Ontario 84 F e
Summit Lake, Br. Columbia 88 H c
Šumperk, Czechoslovakia 105 G d
Sumprabum, Burma 127 J c
Sumy, Ukraine, U.S.S.R. 116 J f
Suna, Tanzania 121 G f
Sunart L., Scotland 98 D d
Suncho Corral, Argentina 94 D c
Sunchow. See Kweiping
Sunda Is., Greater, Pacific Ocean 78 B g
Sunda Is., Lesser, Pacific Ocean 78 C h
Sundargarh, India 127 F d
Sunda Str., Indonesia 129 D m
Sunderland, England 98 G f
Sunderland, Ontario 85 L h
Sundown, Manitoba 86 F a
Sundre, Alberta 86 C g
Sundridge, Ontario 85 L g
Sundsvall, Sweden 102 G e
Sungari R., China 128 H a
Sungari Res., China 128 J b
Sungkiang, China 130 K g
Sunndal, Norway 102 C e
Sunnybrae, Nova Scotia 82 K h
Sunnybrook, Alberta 86 C e
Sunnynook, Alberta 86 F g
Sunnyside, Newfoundland 83 T f
Sunnyslope, Alberta 86 D g
Sunset House, Alberta 88 L c
Sunstrum, Ontario 86 K a
Suntar, U.S.S.R. 115 L b
Sunyani, Ghana 118 E g
Suomi, Ontario 87 M b
Suonenjoki, Finland 102 M e
Superb, Saskatchewan 86 H g
Suq ash Shuyukh, Iraq 124 E c
Sur, Muscat & Oman 125 G e
Sur. See Tyre
Surab, Pakistan 126 C c
Surabajo, Indonesia 129 F m
Surakarta, Indonesia 129 F m
Suran, Syria 123 E b
Surapur, India 126 E e
Sura R., U.S.S.R. 117 H c
Surat, India 126 D d
Suratgarh, India 126 D c
Surat Thani, Thailand 132 B e
Surendranagar, India 126 D d
Surf Inlet, Br. Columbia 88 E d
Surgères, France 108 C c
Surgut, U.S.S.R. 114 G b
Suri, India 127 G d
Suribachi yama, Iwo Jima 78 D b
Surigao Str., Philippines 129 J j
Surin, Thailand 132 C d
Surinam, S. America 93 F c
Suriname, R., Surinam 93 F c
Suriya, S. Yemen 124 E g
Surling, Mt. See Bonom Mhai, Mts.
Surprise L., Quebec 85 Q c
Surrey, co., Br. Columbia 88 E g
Surrey, co., England 99 G j
Surrey Centre, Br. Columbia 88 E g
Sursee, Switzerland 101 D a
Sursk, Ukraine, U.S.S.R. 116 J g
Surtsey, I., Iceland 102 V n
Suru, India 126 E b
Süs, Switzerland 101 F b
Susa, Iran 124 E c
Susak, Yugoslavia 110 E c
Sussex, co., England 99 G k
Sussex, New Brunswick 82 G h
Susteren, Netherlands 100 D c
Sustut Pk., Br. Columbia 88 F b
Sutherland, co., Scotland 98 D b
Sutherland, South Africa 122 C f
Sutherland Falls, New Zealand 135 P m
Suting. See Tahsien
Sutsien, China 130 J f
Suttej, R., India 126 D b
Sutton, Ontario 85 L h
Sutton, Quebec 85 S g
Sutton Bay, Ontario 85 L e
Suure Jaani, Estonia, U.S.S.R. 103 L g
Suva, Fiji Is. 78 H j
Suvavesi, Finland 102 N e
Suvorov, I., Pacific Ocean 78 K j
Suwair, Saudi Arabia 124 D c
Suwałki, Poland 105 K a
Suwannee L., Manitoba 87 R b
Suwayh, Muscat & Oman 125 G e
Suwayq, Muscat & Oman 125 G e
Suweilih, Jordan 123 D e
Suwo Nada, Japan 133 B h
Svalbard, Arctic Ocean 114 A a
Svanstein, Sweden 102 K c
Svappavaara, Sweden 102 J c
Svärholt, Halvöy, Norway 102 L a
Svartisen, Norway 102 E c
Svartvik, Sweden 102 G e
Švekšna, Lithuania, U.S.S.R. 103 J j
Svendborg, Denmark 103 D j
Svenner Is., Antarctica 136 Q e
Sverdlovsk, U.S.S.R. 117 Q b
Sverdrup, Os., U.S.S.R. 114 G a
Sverdrup Chan., N.-W. Terr. 81 K a
Sverdrup Is., N.-W. Terr. 80 J b
Svetogorsk, U.S.S.R. 103 N f
Svetozarevo, Yugoslavia 112 C c
Svishtov, Bulgaria 112 E c
Svitavy, Czechoslovakia 105 G d
Svlyazhsk, U.S.S.R. 117 J c
Svobodny, U.S.S.R. 115 M c
Svolvær, Norway 102 F b
Swain Reefs, Coral Sea 78 F k
Swains I., American Samoa 78 J j
Swakopmund, S.W. Africa 122 A d
Swale R., England 99 F f
Swalwell, Alberta 86 D g
Swan Hill, Australia 135 H g
Swan Hills, Alberta 86 B d
Swan L., Br. Columbia 88 E c
Swan L., Manitoba 87 R f
Swan Lake, Manitoba 87 T j
Swan Plain, Saskatchewan 87 Q f
Swan R., Alberta 86 B c
Swan R., Australia 134 C f
Swan R., Manitoba 87 Q f
Swan River, Manitoba 87 Q f
Swansea, Ontario 84 C k
Swansea, Tasmania 135 J h
Swansea & B., Wales 99 E j
Swanson, Saskatchewan 86 K g
Swarzewo, Poland 105 H a
Swastika, Ontario 84 K d
Swat & R., Pakistan 126 D a
Swatow, China 131 H l
Swaziland, Southern Africa 122 E e
Sweden, Northern Europe 102-103
Sweeney Mt., Antarctica 136 H c
Swellendam, South Africa 122 C f
Swidnica, Poland 105 G c
Swietochlowice, Poland 105 H c
Swift Current, Newfoundland 83 S f
Swift Current, Saskatchewan 86 K h
Swiftcurrent Cr., Sask. 86 J h
Swilly L., Eire 98 B e
Swindon, England 99 F j
Swinemünde. See Świnoujście
Świnoujście, Poland 104 F a
Switzerland, Central Europe 101
Swords, Eire 99 C g
Syas'stroy, U.S.S.R. 116 H a
Sydenham, Ontario 85 O h
Sydney, Australia 135 K f
Sydney, C. Breton I., N.S. 83 M g
Sydney Mines, C. Breton I., Nova Scotia 83 M g
Sydproven, Greenland 89 P d
Syeti Vrach, Bulgaria 112 D d
Syktyvkar, U.S.S.R. 114 E b
Sylhet, E. Pakistan 127 H d
Sylt, I., Germany 103 C j
Sylte, Norway 102 B e
Sylvania, Saskatchewan 87 N f
Sylvan Lake, Alberta 86 C f
Sylvester, Mt., Nfd. 83 R e
Sylvia, Mt., Br. Columbia 88 G a
Syracuse (Siracusa), Sicily 111 E g
Syr Darya, Kazakh., U.S.S.R. 114 F d
Syria, W. Asia 124 C b
Syrian Des., Iraq, etc. 124 C c
Sysert, U.S.S.R. 117 Q b
Syurkum, U.S.S.R. 115 P c
Syzran, U.S.S.R. 117 J d
Szarvas, Hungary 105 J e
Szczecin, Poland 104 F b
Szczecinek, Poland 105 G b
Szczecinski, L., Germany-Poland 104 F b
Szczytno, Poland 105 J b
Szechwan, prov., China 130 A g
Szeged, Hungary 102 C a
Székesfehérvar, Hungary 105 H e
Szekszard, Hungary 102 B a
Szemao, China 128 D f
Szenan, China 131 D j
Szengen, China 131 D l
Szentes, Hungary 105 J e
Szolnok, Hungary 105 J e
Szombathely, Hungary 110 F b
Szprotawa, Poland 105 F c
Szreńsk, Poland 105 J b
Taba, Saudi Arabia 124 D d
Tabala, Saudi Arabia 124 D f
Tabas, Iran 125 G c
Tabasará, Sierra de, Panama 91 C e
Tabasco, state, Mexico 90 F d
Tabas Sunnikhane, Iran 125 H c
Tabatière, La, Quebec 83 O c
Tabatinga, Brazil 92 D d
Tabelbala, Algeria 118 E c
Taber, Alberta 86 E j
Tabik, I., Kwajalein Is. 79 T e
Tabik Chan., Kwajalein Is. 79 T e
Table Mt., Newfoundland 83 N f
Table Mt., South Africa 122 B f
Taboieiro, Brazil 92 F e
Tábor, Czechoslovakia 104 F d
Tabora, Tanzania 121 G e
Tabora, Tanzania 121 G f
Tabor Prov. Park, Alberta 86 E j
Tabou, Ivory Coast 118 D h
Tabriz, Iran 124 E b
Tabuk, Saudi Arabia 125 C d
Tabunifi, I., Yap I. 78 D m
Tabusintac R., New Brunswick 82 G f
Tabut, S. Yemen 125 F f
Tacámbaro, Mexico 90 D d
Tacloban, Philippines 129 H h
Tacna, Peru 92 C g
Taco, Argentina 94 D c
Tacuarembo, Uruguay 94 E d
Tadjoura & G. of, French Somaliland 121 J b
Tadoussac, Quebec 82 C e
Tadzhikistan. See Tadzhikskaya
Tadzhikskaya (Tadzhikistan), U.S.S.R. 114 F e
Taegu, S. Korea 128 J c
Taejŏn, S. Korea 128 J c
Tafalla, Spain 107 E a
Taff R., Wales 99 E j
Tafila, Jordan 123 D g
Taft, Iran 125 F c
Taganrog & G., U.S.S.R. 116 L h
Tagawa, Japan 133 B h
Taga Zong, Bhutan 127 H c
Tagdempt, Algeria 109 M j
Taguá, Brazil 93 J f
Tagula, I., Papua 135 K b
Tagus (Tajo) R., Spain-Portugal 106 B c
Ta Hao, China 131 F l
Tahat Mt., Algeria 118 G d
Tahcheng, China 115 H d
Ta Hingan Ling, China 128 H a
Tahiti, I., Society Is. 79 M j
Tahltan, Br. Columbia 88 D a
Tahoua, Niger 118 G f
Tahsien, China 130 C g
Tahta, Egypt 119 M c
Tahuna, Indonesia 129 J k
Tai-an, China 130 H d
Taichung, Taiwan 131 K k
Taif, Saudi Arabia 124 D e
Tai-hang-shan, China 130 F d
Taihape, New Zealand 135 R k
Taiho, I., Okinawa 78 C a
Taihsien, China 130 F c
Tai Hu, China 130 J g
Taiku, China 130 F d
Taima, Saudi Arabia 124 C d
Tainan, Taiwan 131 K l
Taipale, Finland 102 N e
Taipei, Taiwan 131 K k
Taiping, Malaysia 132 C f
Taiping. See Tangtu
Taipingchwan, China 128 H b
Taipinght. See Wanyuan
Taipingot, I., Rota I. 78 A j
Taira, I., Okinawa 78 C b
Taira, Japan 133 G f
Tairadate Str., Japan 133 G d
Taishan I., China 131 L g
Taishet, U.S.S.R. 115 J c
Taishun, China 131 J j
Taitao, Pen. de, Chile 95 B g
Taiwan, I., China 131 K l
Taiwan Kaikyo, China 128 G f
Taiwara, Afghanistan 125 H c
Taiyetos, Mts., Greece 113 D f
Taiyiba, Jordan 123 D g
Taiyuan, China 130 F d
Ta'izz, Yemen 124 D g
Tajan, Borneo 129 F l
Tajo, R., Spain-Portugal 106 B c
Tajrish, Iran 125 F b
Tajumulco, Mt., Guatemala 90 F d
Tak, Thailand 132 B c
Taka, I., Marshall Is. 79 U a
Takabanare shima, Okinawa 78 B c
Takada, Japan 133 F f
Takahashi, Japan 133 C g
Takamatsu, Japan 133 D g
Takao. See Kaohsiung
Takaoka, Japan 133 E f
Takapuna, New Zealand 135 R k
Takasaki, Japan 133 F f
Takashiho, I., Okinawa 78 A c
Takatik, I., Ponape I. 78 G n
Takaungu, Kenya 121 H e
Takayama, Japan 133 E f
Takefu, Japan 133 E g
Takhta Bazar, Turkmen., U.S.S.R. 114 F e
Takht-i-Sulaiman, Pakistan 126 C b
Takingeun, Sumatra 129 C k
Takipy, Manitoba 87 Q c
Takiu, I., Ponape I. 78 G o
Takla L., Br. Columbia 88 G c
Takla Landing, Br. Columbia 88 G c
Takla Makan, Des., China 114 H e
Takoradi, Ghana 118 E h
Ta-ku, China 130 H c
Takuapa, Thailand 132 B e
Talafofo, I., Guam 78 B l
Talafofo B., Guam 78 B l
Talaimanar, Ceylon 126 E g
Talara, Peru 92 A d
Talar Ra., Pakistan 126 B c
Talasski Ala Tau, Kirgiz., U.S.S.R. 114 G d
Talaur Is., Pacific Ocean 78 C g
Talavera de la Reina, Spain 106 C c
Talbot Inlet, N.-W. Terr. 81 M b
Talbot L., Manitoba 87 S d
Talca, Chile 94 B e
Talcahuano, Chile 94 B e
Taldy Kurgan, Kazakh., U.S.S.R. 114 G d
Tali, China 130 D e
Tali, China 128 C e
Taliabu, I., Indonesia 129 H l
Taliwang, Sumbawa I., Indonesia 129 G m
Tallata-Mafara, Nigeria 118 G f
Tallinn, Estonia, U.S.S.R. 103 L g
Tall Pines, Saskatchewan 87 P f
Talmage, Manitoba 87 O j
Talmenka, U.S.S.R. 114 H c

Talou Shan, *China* 128 E e
Talsi, Latvia, *U.S.S.R.* 103 K h
Taltal, *Chile* 94 B c
Tamale, *Ghana* 118 E g
Tamanrasset, *Algeria* 118 G d
Tamarite de Litera, *Spain* 107 F b
Tamási, *Hungary* 105 H e
Tamatave, *Mal. Rep.* 121 N k
Tamaulipas, state, *Mexico* 90 E c
Tamaya, *Chile* 94 B d
Tamba, *Rhodesia* 122 D d
Tambach, *Kenya* 121 H d
Tambacounda, *Senegal* 118 C f
Tambo, *Australia* 135 J d
Tambo de Mora, *Peru* 92 B f
Tambohorano, *Mal. Rep.* 121 M k
Tamboril, *Brazil* 93 J d
Tambov, *U.S.S.R.* 117 E d
Tambura, *Sudan* 119 L g
Tame, *Colombia* 92 C b
Tamel Aiken, *Argentina* 95 B g
Tamiahua & L., *Mexico* 90 E c
Ta-ming, *China* 130 G d
Tamins, *Switzerland* 101 E b
Tamise, *Belgium* 100 C c
Tammisaari, *Finland* 103 K g
Tammu, *Burma* 127 H d
Tampere, *Finland* 103 K f
Tampico, *Mexico* 90 E c
Tamra, *Saudi Arabia* 124 E e
Tamsalu, Estonia, *U.S.S.R.* 103 M g
Tamtsak Bulak, *Mongolia* 128 G a
Tamworth, *Australia* 135 K f
Tamworth, *Ontario* 85 O h
Tana, I., *New Hebrides* 78 G j
Tana, L., *Ethiopia* 121 H b
Tana, R., *Norway* 102 M b
Tanabe, *Japan* 133 D h
Tanabu, *Japan* 133 G d
Tana Fd., *Norway* 102 N a
Tanah Merah, *Malaysia* 132 C e
Tanami, *Australia* 134 E c
Tananarive (Antananarivo), *Mal. Rep.* 121 N k
Tancha I., *Okinawa* 78 B b
Tancheng, *China* 130 J e
Tandil, *Argentina* 94 E e
Tandjung, *Indonesia* 129 E m
Tandjungpandan, Billiton I., *Indonesia* 129 E l
Tandjungredeb, *Borneo* 129 G k
Tandjungselor, *Borneo* 129 G k
Tanega Shima, *Japan* 133 B j
Tanegashima Kaikyo, *Japan* 133 B j
Tanen-taung-gyi Mts., *Thailand-Burma* 132 B c
Tanga, *Tanzania* 121 H f
Tanganyika. *See* Tanzania
Tanganyika, L., *Congo, etc.* 121 F f
Tangen, *Norway* 103 D f
Tanger, *Morocco* 118 D a
Tangermünde, *Germany* 104 D b
Tangier, *Nova Scotia* 82 K j
Tangier Grand L., *Nova Scotia* 82 K j
Tangier. *See* Tanger
Tang-shan, *China* 130 J c
Tangshan, *China* 130 H e
Tangtu, *China* 130 J g
Tangui, *U.S.S.R.* 115 K c
Tanimbar Kep., Is., *Indon* 129 K m
Tank, *Pakistan* 126 D b
Tankapirtti, *Finland* 102 M b
Tankse, *Kashmir* 126 E b
Tännäs, *Sweden* 102 E e
Tannin, *Ontario* 87 M a
Tanta, *Egypt* 119 M b
Tantallon, *Saskatchewan* 87 Q h
Tanzania (Tanganyika), *E. Africa* 121 G f
Tanzilla R., *Br. Columbia* 88 D a
Tao, *Burma* 127 H d
Taoan, *China* 128 H a
Taochow. *See* Kadiger
Taofu, *China* 128 D d
Taongi, I., *Marshall Is.* 78 G f
Taormina, *Sicily* 111 E g
Tapa, Estonia, *U.S.S.R.* 103 L g
Tapachula, *Mexico* 90 F e
Tapah, *Malaysia* 132 C f
Tapajós, R., *Brazil* 93 F d
Tapak, I., *Ponape I.* 78 G n
Tapalque, *Argentina* 94 D e
Tapan, *Sumatra* 129 D l
Tapanui, *New Zealand* 135 P m
Tapa Shan, *China* 130 D f
Tapauá, *Brazil* 92 E e
Taplang Dzong, *Nepal* 127 G c
Tapti R., *India* 126 E d
Tapuaenuku, Mt., *New Zealand* 135 Q l
Taputimu, I., *Tutuila I.* 79 T o
Taqa, *Muscat & Oman* 125 F f
Taquara, *Brazil* 94 F c
Taquaritinga, *Brazil* 93 K e
Tara, *Ontario* 84 J h
Tara, *U.S.S.R.* 114 G c
Taradale, *New Zealand* 135 R k
Tarahumare, Sa., *Mexico* 90 C b
Tarakan, *Borneo* 129 G k
Tarakli, *Turkey* 124 B a
Taranaki Bight, N., *New Zealand* 135 R k
Taranaki Bight, S., *New Zealand* 135 R k
Tarancón, *Spain* 106 D b
Taranto, G. di, *Italy* 111 F f
Taranto, *Italy* 111 F e
Tarapoto, *Peru* 92 B e
Taraqua, *Brazil* 92 D d
Tararua Ra., *New Zealand* 135 R l
Tarascon, *France* 109 D e
Tarasp, *Switzerland* 101 F b
Tarata, *Peru* 92 C g
Tarauaca, *Brazil* 92 C e
Tarawa, I., *Gilbert Is.* 78 H g
Tarawera, *New Zealand* 135 R k
Tarazona, *Spain* 107 E b
Tarazona de la Mancha, *Spain* 107 E c
Tarbagatai Khrebet, Kazakh., *U.S.S.R.* 114 H d
Tarbat Ness, *Scotland* 98 E c
Tarbert, *Scotland* 98 D e
Tarbert, *Scotland* 98 C c
Tarbes, *France* 109 D e
Tarchan, *Tibet* 126 F b
Tarcoola, *Australia* 134 F f
Taree, *Australia* 135 K f
Tärendö, *Sweden* 102 K c
Târgu Jiu, *Romania* 112 D b
Târgul Lapusul, *Romania* 105 K e
Târgul Ocna, *Romania* 112 F a
Târgu Mureş, *Romania* 112 E a
Tarija, *Bolivia* 92 E h
Tarik, I., *Truk Is.* 78 E o
Tarim, *Saudi Arabia* 124 E f
Tarlac, *Philippines* 129 H h
Tarma, *Peru* 92 B f
Tarn, dep. & R., *France* 109 E e
Tärna, *Sweden* 102 F d
Tarn-et-Garonne, dep., *Fr.* 109 D d
Tarnobrzeg, *Poland* 105 J c
Tarnopol, *Saskatchewan* 87 M f
Tarnów, *Poland* 105 J c
Tarnowskie Gory, *Poland* 105 H c
Tarnu Măgurele, *Romania* 112 E c
Taroom, *Australia* 135 J e
Taroudant, *Morocco* 118 D b
Tarragona, *Spain* 107 F b
Tarrega, *Spain* 107 F b
Tarsale, *U.S.S.R.* 114 G b
Tarso Muri, Mt. *See* Kegueur Tedi
Tarsus, *Turkey* 124 B b
Tartagal, *Argentina* 92 E h
Tartas, *France* 109 C e
Tartu, Estonia, *U.S.S.R.* 103 M g
Tartus, *Syria* 123 D c
Tarum, *Iran* 125 G d
Tarzwell, *Ontario* 84 K d
Taschereau, *Quebec* 85 M d
Taseevo, *U.S.S.R.* 115 J c
Taseko, Mt., *Br. Columbia* 88 H e
Taseko, R., *Br. Columbia* 88 H e
Tashi Bhup Tso, *Tibet* 127 F b
Tashihto, *China* 128 B b
Tashkent, Uzbek., *U.S.S.R.* 114 F d
Tashkurghan, *Afghanistan* 125 J b
Tashota, *Ontario* 84 C b
Tasil, *Syria* 123 D e
Taskan, *U.S.S.R.* 115 Q b
Tasman, Mt., *New Zealand* 135 Q l
Tasman B., *New Zealand* 135 Q l
Tasmania, I. & state, *Australia* 135 J h
Tasman Mts., *New Zealand* 135 Q l
Tasman Sea, *New Zealand, etc.* 78 G l
Tassgong, *Bhutan* 127 H c
Tast, L. du, *Quebec* 85 N a
Tata, *Hungary* 105 H e
Tataacho Pt., *Rota I.* 78 A h
Tatamagouche, *Nova Scotia* 82 J h
Tatarsk, *Iran* 114 G c
Tatarskaya, *U.S.S.R.* 114 E c
Tatarskiy Proliv, *U.S.S.R.* 115 P d
Tate, *Saskatchewan* 87 N g
Tating, *China* 131 B j
Tatla L., *Br. Columbia* 88 G e
Tatlayoko Lake, *British Columbia* 88 G e
Tatlow, Mt., *Br. Columbia* 88 H e
Tatnam, C., *Manitoba* 81 K f
Tatranská Lomnica, *Czechoslovakia* 105 J d
Tatry, Mts., *Poland-Czech* 105 H d
Tatta, *Pakistan* 126 C d
Tatu, R., *China* 128 D d
Tatuhí, *Brazil* 93 H h
Tatung, *China* 130 F b
Tatung Ho, R., *China* 128 D c
Ta'u, I., *Manua Is.* 79 S o
Tauá, *Brazil* 93 J e
Tauak Pass, *Ponape I.* 78 F o
Taualap Pass, *Truk Is.* 78 D n
Tauapeçaçú, *Brazil* 92 E d
Taubaté, *Brazil* 93 H h
Taulaga, I., *Swains I.* 79 Q o
Taumarunui, *New Zealand* 135 R k
Taungdwingyi, *Burma* 127 J d
Taung-gyi, *Burma* 127 J d
Taungup, *Burma* 127 H e
Taunton, *England* 99 E k
Taunus, Mts., *Germany* 104 C c
Taupo & L., *New Zealand* 135 R k
Tauragé, Lithuania, *U.S.S.R.* 103 K j
Tauranga & Harb., *New Zealand* 135 R k
Taureau L., *Quebec* 85 R f
Tauroa Pt., *New Zealand* 135 Q j
Tauste, *Spain* 107 E b
Tauysk, *U.S.S.R.* 115 P c
Tavani, *N.-W. Territories* 81 K e
Tavda, *U.S.S.R.* 114 F c
Taverne, *Switzerland* 101 D b
Taverner B., *N.-W. Terr.* 81 M d
Tavistock, *England* 99 E k
Tavistock, *Ontario* 84 K j
Tavolara, I., *Sardinia* 111 B e
Tävoy & R., *Burma* 127 J f
Tävoy I., *Burma* 127 J f
Tavrichanka, *U.S.S.R.* 117 B c
Tavsanli, *Turkey* 124 A b
Tawang, *India* 127 H c
Tawatinaw & R., *Alberta* 86 D d
Tawau, *Sabah* 129 G k
Tawitawi, I., *Philippines* 129 H j
Taxco, *Mexico* 90 E d
Tay, Firth of & R., *Scotland* 98 E d
Tayga, *U.S.S.R.* 114 H c
Tay L., *Scotland* 98 E d
Taylor, *Br. Columbia* 88 J b
Taymouth, *New Brunswick* 82 F g
Taymyr, Ozero, *U.S.S.R.* 115 K a
Taytay, *Philippines* 129 G h
Tayü, *China* 131 G k
Tayung, *China* 131 E h
Taza, *Morocco* 118 E b
Tazovskaya G., *U.S.S.R.* 114 G b
Tazovskoye, *U.S.S.R.* 114 G b
Tbilisi, *U.S.S.R.* 114 D d
Tchad. *See* Chad
Tchad, L. *See* Chad, L.
Tchaourou, *Dahomey* 118 F g
Tczew, *Poland* 105 H a
Te Anau, L., *New Zealand* 135 P m
Teano Ra., *Australia* 134 C d
Teapa, *Mexico* 90 F d
Te Aroha, *New Zealand* 135 R k
Tea Tree, *Australia* 134 F d
Te Awamutu, *New Zealand* 135 R k
Tebboursouk, *Tunisia* 119 G a
Tebyulyakh, *U.S.S.R.* 115 P b
Tecamachalco, *Mexico* 90 E d
Tecka & R., *Argentina* 95 B f
Tecolutla, *Mexico* 90 E c
Tecpan, *Mexico* 90 D d
Tecumseh, *Ontario* 84 H k
Tedzhen, Turkmen., *U.S.S.R.* 114 F e
Teema, I., *Okinawa* 78 B b
Tees, *Alberta* 86 D f
Tees, R., *England* 99 G f
Teeswater, *Ontario* 84 J j
Tefé, *Brazil* 92 E d
Tegerhi, *Libya* 119 H d
Tegucigalpa, *Honduras* 91 B d
Tehchow, *China* 130 H d
Tehek L., *N.-W. Territories* 81 K d
Teheran. *See* Tehran
Tehran, *Iran* 125 F b
Tehri, *India* 126 E b
Tehsien. *See* Tehchow
Tehuacán, *Mexico* 90 E d
Tehuantepec, G. of, *Mexico* 90 E d
Tehuantepec, Isthmus of, *Mexico* 90 E d
Tehuantepec, *Mexico* 90 E d
Teian, *See* Anlu
Teifi R., *Wales* 99 E h
Teign R., *England* 99 E k
Tekapo, L., *New Zealand* 135 Q l
Tekirdağ, *Turkey* 124 A a
Te Kuiti, *New Zealand* 135 R k
Tela, *Honduras* 91 B c
Tel Aviv-Yafo, *Israel* 123 C e
Telegraph Creek, *British Columbia* 88 H g
Telen, *Argentina* 94 C e
Telkalakh, *Syria* 123 E c
Telkwa, *Br. Columbia* 88 F c
Tell Bise, *Syria* 123 E c
Tellicherry, *India* 126 E f
Tellier, *Quebec* 82 F c
Telok Anson, *Malaysia* 132 C f
Teloloapan, *Mexico* 90 E d
Telpos-iz, *U.S.S.R.* 114 E b
Telsen, *Argentina* 95 C f
Telshyay, Lithuania, *U.S.S.R.* 103 K j
Teltaka, *Ontario* 84 E c
Telukbetung, *Sumatra* 129 E m
Tembeling, *Malaysia* 132 C f
Temblador, *Venezuela* 92 E b
Temesvar. *See* Timisoara
Temir, Kazakh., *U.S.S.R.* 114 E d
Temir Tau, *U.S.S.R.* 114 H c
Temiscamie L., *Quebec* 82 A b
Temiscamie R., *Quebec* 82 A b
Temiscouata, L., *Quebec* 82 D f
Témiskaming, *Quebec* 85 L f
Temnikov, *U.S.S.R.* 117 F c
Temosachic, *Mexico* 90 C b
Tempio, *Sardinia* 111 B e
Temta, *U.S.S.R.* 111 G b
Temuco, *Chile* 95 B e
Tenanzingo, *Mexico* 90 E d
Tenasique, *Mexico* 90 F d
Tenasserim, *Burma* 127 J f
Tenasserim R., *Burma* 127 J f
Tenby, *Wales* 99 D j
Tenby Bay, *Ontario* 84 G f
Ten Degrees Chan., *Andaman Is.* 127 H g
Tenerife, I., *Canary Is.* 118 B c
Ténès, *Algeria* 118 F a
Tengchow. *See* Penglai
Tengiz, Oz., Kazakh., *U.S.S.R.* 114 F c
Tenke, *Congo* 120 F g
Ten Mile L., *Newfoundland* 83 Q b
Tennant's Creek, *Australia* 134 F c
Tenterfield, *Australia* 135 K e
Teocaltiche, *Mexico* 90 D c
Teophilo Otoni, *Brazil* 93 J g
Tepatitlán, *Mexico* 90 D c
Tepehuanes, *Mexico* 90 C b
Tepelene, *Albania* 113 C d
Tepic, *Mexico* 90 D c
Teramo, *Italy* 110 D d
Ter Apel, *Netherlands* 100 E b
Terban, Jebel, *Saudi Arabia* 124 D f
Terborg, *Netherlands* 100 E c
Terence, *Manitoba* 87 R f
Teresina, *Brazil* 93 J e
Teressa, I., *Nicobar Is.* 127 H g
Terezin, *Czechoslovakia* 104 F c
Teri Nam Tso, *Tibet* 127 G b
Termez, Uzbek., *U.S.S.R.* 114 F e
Termini Imerese, *Sicily* 111 D f
Termoli, *Italy* 111 E e
Termonde, *Belgium* 100 C c
Ternate, *Halmahera I.* 129 J k
Terneuzen, *Netherlands* 100 B c
Terni, *Italy* 110 D d
Ternopol, Ukraine, *U.S.S.R.* 116 D g
Terpeniya, C., *U.S.S.R.* 115 P d
Terrace, *Br. Columbia* 88 E c
Terrace Bay, *Ontario* 84 C d
Terracina, *Italy* 111 D e
Terralba, *Sardinia* 111 B f
Terra Nova & R., *Nfd.* 83 S e
Terra Nova B., *Antarctica* 136 B c
Terra Santa, *Brazil* 93 F d
Terre Adélie, *Antarctica* 136 T e
Terrebonne, *Quebec* 85 R g
Terrence Bay, *Nova Scotia* 82 J j
Terrenceville, *Newfoundland* 83 S f
Terror Mt., *Antarctica* 136 B c
Terschelling I., *Netherlands* 100 D a
Teruel, *Spain* 107 E b
Tervola, *Finland* 102 L c
Tervueren, *Belgium* 100 C d
Tesecau L., *Quebec* 85 P a
Teshio, *Japan* 133 H b
Teslin, *Yukon* 77 V f
Tessaoua, *Niger* 118 G f
Tessenderloo, *Belgium* 100 D c
Tessier, *Saskatchewan* 86 K g
Tetachuck L., *Br. Columbia* 89 G d
Tetagouche R., *New Brunswick* 82 F f
Tetas, Pta., *Chile* 94 B b
Tete, *Mozambique* 122 E c
Tête à la Baleine, *Quebec* 83 N c
Tetreauville, *Quebec* 85 S h
Tetuan, *Morocco* 118 D a
Tetyukhe, *U.S.S.R.* 115 N d
Tetyushi, *U.S.S.R.* 117 J c
Teulada, *Sardinia* 111 B f
Teulada C., *Sardinia* 111 B f
Teulon, *Manitoba* 87 U h
Teutoburger Wald, *Germany* 104 B b
Tevere. *See* Tiber
Teviot R., *Scotland* 98 F e
Tevriz, *U.S.S.R.* 114 G c
Te Waewae B., *New Zealand* 135 P m
Texada I., *Br. Columbia* 88 G f
Texcoco, *Mexico* 90 E d
Texel I., *Netherlands* 100 C a
Tezpur, *India* 127 H c
Thachap Kangri, *Tibet* 127 F b
Thadiq, *Saudi Arabia* 124 E d
Thailand (Siam), *S.-E. Asia* 132 C c
Thakhek, *Laos* 132 C c
Thal, *Pakistan* 126 D b
Thale Sap, L., *Thailand* 132 C d
Thalkirch, *Switzerland* 101 E b
Thames, Firth of, *New Zealand* 135 R k
Thames, *New Zealand* 135 R k
Thames, R., *England* 99 H j
Thames, R., *Ontario* 84 H k
Thamesville, *Ontario* 84 J k
Thana, *India* 126 D e
Thanh-hoa, *N. Vietnam* 132 D c
Thanjavur, *India* 126 E f
Thann, *France* 108 G c
Thar Des., *India* 126 D c
Thargomindah, *Australia* 135 H e
Tharrawaddy, *Burma* 127 J e
Tharsis, *Spain* 106 B d
Thásos, I., *Greece* 113 E d
Thásos Str., *Greece* 113 E d
Thaton, *Burma* 127 J e
Thaungdut, *Burma* 127 H d
Thayetmyo, *Burma* 127 H e
Thazi, *Burma* 127 J d
Thedford, *Ontario* 84 J j
Theodore, *Australia* 135 K e
Theodore, *Saskatchewan* 87 P g
Therien, *Alberta* 86 F d
Thérmai, G. of, *Greece* 113 D d
Thermiá. *See* Kithnos, I.
Thermopylae, *Greece* 113 D e
Theron Mts., *Antarctica* 136 K c
Thesiger B., *N.-W. Terr.* 80 G c
Thesprotía, *Greece* 113 C e
Thessalía, *Greece* 113 D e
Thessalon, *Ontario* 84 G f
Thessaloníki, *Greece* 113 D d
Thetford, *England* 99 H h
Thetford Mines, *Quebec* 85 T f
Theux, *Belgium* 100 D d
Thicket Portage, *Manitoba* 87 U c
Thickwood Hills, *Alberta* 86 E b
Thiel Mts., *Antarctica* 136 G a
Thielt, *Belgium* 100 B c
Thiers, *France* 108 E d
Thiès, *Senegal* 118 B f
Thimbu, *Assam* 127 G c
Thingvalla vatn, *Iceland* 102 V m
Thio, *Ethiopia* 121 J b
Thionville, *France* 108 G b
Thíra, I., *Greece* 113 E f
Thirsk, *England* 99 G f
Thirty Thousand Is., *Ont.* 84 K g
Thisted, *Denmark* 103 C h
Thistilfjord, *Iceland* 102 Y l
Thityabin, *Burma* 127 J d
Thiviers, *France* 108 D d
Thjórsá, R., *Iceland* 102 W m
Thok Jalung, *Tibet* 126 F b
Thomas Mts., *Antarctica* 136 H c
Thomastown, *Eire* 99 C h
Thom Bay, *N.-W. Territories* 80 K c
Thompson, *Manitoba* 87 U c
Thompson R., *Br. Columbia* 88 J e
Thomson R., *Australia* 135 H d
Thongwa, *Burma* 127 J e
Thorburn, *Nova Scotia* 83 K h
Thorhild, *Alberta* 86 D d
Thorn. *See* Torun
Thornbury, *Ontario* 84 K h
Thorndale, *Ontario* 84 J j
Thorne Glacier, *Antarctica* 136 D a
Thornhill, *Ontario* 85 L j
Thornhill, *Scotland* 98 E e
Thorold, *Ontario* 85 L j
Thorsby, *Alberta* 86 C e
Thorshavn, *Faeroe Is.* 96 F c
Thórshöfn, *Iceland* 102 Y l
Thorsteinson, L., *Manitoba* 87 U a
Thorvard Nilsen Mts., *Antarctica* 136 C a
Thouars, *France* 108 C c
Thourout, *Belgium* 100 B c
Thraki, Dhitiki, *Greece* 112 E d
Three Hills, *Alberta* 86 D g
Three Kings Is., *New Zealand* 135 Q j
Threepoint L., *Manitoba* 87 T c
Three Points C., *Ghana* 118 E h
Three Rivers. *See* Trois Rivières
Three Rock Cove, *Nfd.* 83 N e
Throssel Ra., *Australia* 134 D d
Thueyts, *France* 109 F d
Thuin, *Belgium* 100 C d
Thule, *Greenland* 81 N b
Thule, I., *Antarctica* 136 K g
Thun, *Switzerland* 101 C b
Thunder B., *Ontario* 87 O b
Thunderhouse Falls, *Ont.* 84 G b
Thuner See, *Switzerland* 101 C b
Thur, R., *Switzerland* 101 D a
Thurgau, canton, *Switz.* 101 D a
Thüringer Wald, *Germany* 104 D c
Thurles, *Eire* 99 B h
Thursday I., *Australia* 135 H b
Thurso, *Quebec* 85 P g
Thurso, *Scotland* 98 E b
Thurston I., *Antarctica* 136 F d
Thusis, *Switzerland* 101 E b
Thutade L., *Br. Columbia* 88 F b
Tiassale, *Ivory Coast* 118 D g
Tibati, *Cameroon* 119 H g
Tiber, R., *Italy* 110 D d
Tiberias & L., *Israel* 123 D e
Tibet, *S. Asia* 127 G b
Tiblemont, *Quebec* 84 N d
Tiburon, *Haiti* 91 E c
Tiburón, I., *Mexico* 90 B b
Tichborne, *Ontario* 85 O h
Tichfield, *Saskatchewan* 86 K g
Ticino, canton, *Switzerland* 101 D b
Ticul, *Mexico* 90 G c
Tide Head, *New Brunswick* 82 F f
Tide L., *Alberta* 86 F h
Tidjikja, *Mauritania* 118 C e
Tidnish, *Nova Scotia* 82 J h
Tiébissou, *Ivory Coast* 118 D g
Tiefencastel, *Switzerland* 101 E b
Tieh-ling, *China* 130 L a
Tiel, *Netherlands* 100 D c
Tielt, *Belgium* 100 B c
Tien Chih, *China* 128 D f
Tien-ching. *See* Tientsin
Tien-chwang-tai, *China* 130 K b
Tienen. *See* Tirlemont
Tienpao, *China* 131 C l
Tienpaoshan, *China* 130 H b
Tienshai, *China* 130 B e
Tien Shan, *Central Asia* 114 G d
Tiensha Pass, *China* 130 C e
Tienshui, *China* 128 E d
Tientsin, *China* 130 H c
Tiermas, *Spain* 107 E a
Tierra del Fuego, *Chile-Argentina* 95 C h
Tigăneşti, *Romania* 112 F b
Tighina. *See* Bendery
Tigil, *U.S.S.R.* 115 Q c
Tignish, *Prince Edward I.* 82 H g
Tigris, R., *Iraq* 124 E c
Tijoca, *Brazil* 93 H d
Tika, *Quebec* 82 G c
Tikhvin, *U.S.S.R.* 116 H b
Tikrit, *Iraq* 124 D c
Tiksi, *U.S.S.R.* 115 M a
Tilburg, *Netherlands* 100 D c
Tilbury, *England* 99 H j
Tilbury, *Ontario* 84 H k
Tilbury I., *Br. Columbia* 88 D g
Tilcara, *Argentina* 94 C b
Tilichiki, *U.S.S.R.* 115 R b
Tillangchong I., *Nicobar Is.* 127 H g
Tilley, *Alberta* 86 F h
Tillsonburg, *Ontario* 84 K k
Tílos, I., *Greece* 113 F f
Tilsit. *See* Sovetsk
Tilston, *Manitoba* 87 Q j
Tilting, *Newfoundland* 83 S d
Timagami, *Ontario* 85 L e
Timagami L., *Ontario* 84 K f
Timanski Kryazh, *U.S.S.R.* 114 E b
Timaru, *New Zealand* 135 Q m
Timashevo, *U.S.S.R.* 117 K d
Timbuktu (Tombouctou), *Mali* 118 E e
Timiskaming, L., *Que.-Ont* 85 L e
Timisoara, *Romania* 112 C b
Timmins, *Ontario* 84 J d
Timoneng, I., *Guam* 78 B k
Timor, I. & Sea, *Indonesia* 129 H n
Timote, *Argentina* 94 D e
Tinaea Pt., *Philippines* 129 J j
Tindouf, *Algeria* 118 D c
Tineo, *Spain* 106 B a
Tingchow. *See* Changting
Tinghsien, *China* 130 G c
Tingnan, *China* 131 G k
Tingo María, *Peru* 92 B e
Tingri Dzong, *Tibet* 127 G c
Tingwick, *Quebec* 85 T g
Tinian & I., *Saipan-Tinian Is.* 78 A e
Tinian Chan., *Saipan-Tinian Is.* 78 A f
Tinian Harb., *Saipan-Tinian Is.* 78 A e
Tinnevelly. *See* Tirunelveli
Tinogasta, *Argentina* 94 C c
Tínos, I., *Greece* 113 E f
Tinsukia, *India* 127 J c
Tintigny, *Belgium* 100 D e
Tintina, *Argentina* 94 D c
Tioman, Pulau, I., *Malaysia* 132 C f
Tionaga, *Ontario* 84 H d
Tipperary & co., *Eire* 99 B h
Tip Top Hill, *Ontario* 84 D d
Tiracumbá, Sa. de, *Brazil* 93 H d
Tiran, I., *Saudi Arabia* 124 B d
Tirana. *See* Tiranë
Tiranë, *Albania* 112 B d
Tiraspol, Moldavia, *U.S.S.R.* 116 F h
Tire, *Turkey* 124 A b
Tireboli, *Turkey* 124 C a
Tiree I., *Scotland* 98 C d
Tirgovista, *Romania* 112 E b
Tirich Mir, *Pakistan* 126 D a
Tirlemont, *Belgium* 100 C d
Tirlyanski, *U.S.S.R.* 117 P c
Tirnavos, *Greece* 113 D e
Tirol (Tyrol), reg., *Austria* 104 D e
Tirua Pt., *New Zealand* 135 R k
Tiruchchendur, *India* 126 E g
Tiruchchirappalli, *India* 126 E f
Tiru Kona Malai. *See* Trincomalee
Tirunelvelei, *India* 126 E g
Tirupati, *India* 126 E f
Tiruvannamalai, *India* 126 E f
Tisa, R., *Yugoslavia* 112 C b
Tisdale, *Saskatchewan* 87 N f
Tisiye, *Syria* 123 E e
Tissa, *Nigeria* 119 H g
Tisza, R., *Hungary* 105 J e
Titicaca, L., *Bolivia-Peru* 92 D g
Titisee, *Germany* 104 C e
Titograd, *Yugoslavia* 112 B c
Titovo Užice, *Yugoslavia* 112 B c
Titov-Veles, *Yugoslavia* 112 C d
Titu, *Romania* 112 E b
Tiverton, *England* 99 E k
Tiverton, *Nova Scotia* 82 F j
Tiverton, *Ontario* 84 J h
Tivoli, *Italy* 111 D e
Tiwi, *Muscat & Oman* 125 G e
Tixkokob, *Mexico* 90 G c
Tixtla, *Mexico* 90 E d
Tizimín, *Mexico* 90 G c
Tizi Ouzou, *Algeria* 118 F a
Tjalang, *Sumatra* 129 C k
Tjilatjap, *Indonesia* 129 E m
Tjirebon, *Indonesia* 129 E m
Tjörn, I., *Sweden* 103 D g
Tlacotalpan, *Mexico* 90 E d
Tlaltenango, *Mexico* 90 D c
Tlapa, *Mexico* 90 E d
Tlaxcala, *Mexico* 90 E d
Tlaxiaco, *Mexico* 90 E d
Tlell, *Br. Columbia* 88 D d
Tlemcen, *Algeria* 118 E b
Tméssa, *Libya* 119 J c
Tmiet, I., *Jaluit I.* 79 U h
Toad R., *Br. Columbia* 88 G a
Toay, *Argentina* 94 D e
Toba, Donau, *Sumatra* 129 C k
Toba, *Japan* 133 E g
Tobago, I., *Windward Is.* 91 G d
Toba Inlet, *Br. Columbia* 88 G e
Tobarro, *Spain* 107 E c
Tobel, *Switzerland* 101 E a
Tobelo, *Halmahera I.* 129 J k
Tobermory, *Ontario* 84 J g
Tobermory, *Scotland* 98 C d
Tobi, I., *Pacific Ocean* 78 D g
Tobiishi hana, *Iwo Jima* 78 D b
Tobique R., *New Brunswick* 82 E f
Toboali, Bangka I., *Indon.* 129 E l
Tobol, *U.S.S.R.* 117 R d
Toboli, *Celebes* 129 H l
Tobolsk, *U.S.S.R.* 114 F c
Tobruk, *Libya* 119 K b
Tocantinópolis, *Brazil* 93 H e
Tocina, *Spain* 106 C d
Toco, *Chile* 94 C b
Tocopilla, *Chile* 94 B b
Tocoripa, *Mexico* 90 C b

Tocuyo, Venezuela 92 C b
Todd Mt., New Brunswick 82 F g
Todenvang, Kenya 121 H d
Todos Santos, B., Mexico 90 A a
Todos Santos, Mexico 90 B c
Tofield, Alberta 86 E e
Tofino, Vancouver I., British Columbia 88 G f
Togarakaikyo, Japan 133 A j
Toghraqbulaq, China 128 B b
Togo, Saskatchewan 87 Q g
Togo, West Africa 118 F g
Toguchi, I., Okinawa 78 B b
To Huping Tso, Tibet 127 F b
Tojo, Japan 133 C g
Tokachi Dake, Japan 133 H c
Tokanga, U.S.S.R. 114 D b
Tokanui, New Zealand 135 P m
Tokar, Sudan 121 H a
Tokara Retto, Japan 133 N n
Tokat, Turkey 124 C a
Tokelau Is., Pacific Ocean 78 K h
Toki Pt., Wake I. 79 S d
Tokmak, Kirgiz., U.S.S.R. 114 G d
Tokoto, China 130 E b
Tokushima, Japan 133 D h
Tokuyama, Japan 133 B g
Tokyo & B., Japan 133 F g
Tol, I., Truk Is. 78 D o
Tolaga Bay, New Zealand 135 S k
Tolbukhin, Bulgaria 112 F c
Toledo, Chile 94 B c
Toledo, Mts., Spain 106 C c
Toledo, Spain 106 C c
Tolen & I., Netherlands 100 C c
Tolmin, Yugoslavia 110 D b
Tolo, G. of, Celebes 129 H d
Toluca, Mexico 90 E l
Tolun, China 130 H a
Tölz, Bad, Germany 104 D e
Tomar, Portugal 106 A c
Tomari, U.S.S.R. 115 P d
Tomaszów Mazowiecki, Poland 105 J c
Tomatumari, Guyana 92 F b
Tombouctou. See Timbuktu
Tome, Chile 94 B e
Tomiko, Ontario 85 L f
Tomil, I., Yap I. 78 D l
Tomini, G. of, Celebes 129 H l
Tomkinson Ra., Australia 134 E e
Tommot, U.S.S.R. 115 M c
Tompkins, Saskatchewan 86 J h
Tomsk, U.S.S.R. 115 H c
Tomskaya Oblast, U.S.S.R. 114 G c
Tonala, Mexico 90 F d
Tönder, Denmark 103 C j
Tondern, Ontario 84 E c
Tondi, India 126 E g
Tonelik, I., Truk Is. 78 E m
Tonga, Is., Pacific Ocean 78 J j
Tonga, Sudan 119 M g
Tongareva, I., Pacific Ocean 78 K h
Tongatapu, I., Tonga Is. 78 J j
Tongeren, Belgium 100 D d
Tongking, N. Vietnam 131 B m
Tongobory, Mal. Rep. 121 M l
Tongoy, Chile 94 B d
Tongres. See Tongeren
Tongue, Scotland 98 E b
Tonichi, Mexico 90 C b
Tonk, India 126 E c
Tonkhil, Mongolia 128 B a
Tonking, G. of, China, etc. 132 D b
Tonkova, U.S.S.R. 114 H b
Tonle Sap, Cambodia 132 C d
Tonneins, France 109 D d
Tonnerre, France 108 F c
Tönsberg, Norway 103 D g
Toowoomba, Australia 135 K e
Topland, Alberta 86 B d
Topley Lodge, Br. Columbia 88 F c
Topolčany, Czechoslovakia 105 H d
Topolobampo & B., Mexico 90 C b
Top Oz, U.S.S.R.-Finland 114 C b
Tor B., Nova Scotia 83 L h
Torbat-e-Heydariyeh, Iran 125 G b
Torbat-e-Jam, Iran 125 H b
Torbay, Newfoundland 83 T f
Torhout. See Thourout
Toriñana, Spain 106 A a
Torino. See Turin
Tori Shima, Japan 133 J e
Torit, Sudan 119 M h
Torma, Estonia, U.S.S.R. 103 M g
Tornado Mt., Alberta-British Columbia 86 C j
Torne Älv, Sweden 102 K c
Torneträsk, L., Sweden 102 H b
Torneträsk, Sweden 102 H b
Torngat Mts., Labrador 81 N f
Tornio, Finland 102 L d
Tornquist, Argentina 95 D e
Törökszentmiklós, Hungary 105 J e
Toroni, G. of, Greece 113 D d
Toronto, Ontario 85 L j
Toronto Harb., Ontario 84 D k
Toronto Island Airport, Ontario 84 D k
Tororo, Uganda 121 G d
Toros Dağlari, Mts., Turkey 124 B b
Torquay, England 99 E k
Torquay, Saskatchewan 87 O j
Torrance, Ontario 85 L h
Torre Annunziata, Italy 111 E e
Torreblanca, Spain 107 F b
Torre del Greco, Italy 111 E e
Torrelaguna, Spain 106 D b
Torrelapaja, Spain 107 E b
Torrelavega, Spain 106 D a
Torrens, L., Australia 134 G f
Torrente, Spain 107 E c
Torreón, Mexico 90 D b
Torres, Mexico 90 B b
Torres Is., Pacific Ocean 78 G j
Torres Novas, Portugal 106 A c
Torres Str., Australia 135 H b
Torres Vedras, Portugal 106 A c
Torrevieja, Spain 107 E d
Torridon, L., Scotland 98 D c
Torrijos, Spain 106 C c
Torrington, Alberta 86 D g
Torrox, Spain 106 D d
Torsby, Sweden 103 E f
Tort, L. Le, Quebec 83 M b
Tortola, I., Virgin Is. 91 G c
Tortorici, Sicily 111 E f
Tortosa, Spain 107 F b
Tortue, I., Haiti 91 E b
Tortuga, I., Mexico 90 B b
Torud, Iran 125 G b
Torun, Poland 105 H b
Tõrva, Estonia, U.S.S.R. 103 M h
Tory, I., Eire 98 B e
Tory Hill, Ontario 85 M h
Torzhok, U.S.S.R. 116 J c
Tosa B., Japan 133 C h
Toscana, dep., Italy 110 C d
Tosco-Emiliano, Mts., Appennines, Italy 110 C c
Tossa, Spain 107 G b
Tostado, Argentina 94 D c
Totana, Spain 107 E d
Totling, Tibet 126 E b
Totma, U.S.S.R. 114 D c
Totnes, England 99 E k
Totolom, I., Ponape I. 78 G o
Totonicapán, Guatemala 90 F d
Totsk, U.S.S.R. 117 L d
Tottan Mts., Antarctica 136 L d
Totten Glacier Tongue, Antarctica 136 S e
Tottenham, Ontario 85 L h
Tottori, Japan 133 D g
Totzke, Saskatchewan 87 M f
Touba, Ivory Coast 118 D g
Toubkal, Mt., Morocco 118 D b
Touchwood Hills, reg., Saskatchewan 87 N g
Touggourt, Algeria 118 G b
Toul, France 108 F b
Toulnustouc R., Quebec 82 E c
Toulon, France 108 F e
Toulouse, France 109 D e
Toungoo, Burma 127 J e
Touraine, prov., France 108 D c
Tourakom, Laos 127 K e
Tourcoing, France 108 E a
Tournai, Belgium 100 B d
Tournon, France 109 F d
Tournus, France 108 F c
Tours, France 108 D c
Tourville, Quebec 82 B f
Toutes Aides, Manitoba 87 S g
Touwsrivier, South Africa 122 C f
Towada, Japan 133 G d
Towari, Celebes 129 H l
Townsville, Australia 135 J c
Towuti Danau, Celebes 129 H l
Towyn, Wales 99 E h
Towy R., Wales 99 E j
Toyama & B., Japan 133 E f
Tozeur, Tunisia 119 G b
Trabzon. See Trebizond
Tracadie, New Brunswick 82 H f
Tracadie, Nova Scotia 83 L h
Tracy, New Brunswick 82 F h
Trade L., Saskatchewan 87 O c
Tradom, Tibet 127 F c
Traiguén, Chile 95 B e
Traiguén, I., Chile 95 B g
Trail, Br. Columbia 88 L f
Traipú, Brazil 93 K e
Trairi, Brazil 93 K d
Tralee & B., Eire 99 A h
Tramore, Eire 99 C h
Tramping Lake, Sask 86 J f
Tranås, Sweden 103 F g
Trancas, Argentina 94 C c
Trancoso, Portugal 106 B b
Trang, Thailand 132 B e
Trangan, I., Indonesia 129 K m
Tranquebar, India 126 E f
Transcona, Manitoba 87 V j
Transilvania, Romania 112 D a
Transvaal, prov., S. Africa 122 D d
Transylvanian Alps, Romania 112 D b
Trapani, Sicily 111 D f
Traralgon, Australia 135 J g
Trasimeno, L., Italy 110 D d
Trasparga, Spain 106 B a
Traunstein, Germany 104 E e
Travers, Alberta 86 E h
Třebíč, Czechoslovakia 105 F d
Trebinje, Yugoslavia 112 B c
Trebizond (Trabzon), Turkey 124 C a
Tregarva, Saskatchewan 87 N h
Treherne, Manitoba 87 T j
Treinta-y-Tres, Uruguay 94 F d
Trelew, Argentina 95 C f
Trelleborg, Sweden 103 E j
Tremadoc B., Wales 99 E h
Trembleur L., Br. Columbia 88 G c
Tremiti Is., Italy 110 E d
Tremp, Spain 107 F a
Trenche, R., Quebec 85 S e
Trencin, Czechoslovakia 105 H d
Trenel, Argentina 94 D e
Trenque Lauquén, Argentina 94 D e
Trent, R., England 99 G g
Trent. See Trento
Trent Can., Ontario 85 L h
Trentino-Alto Adige, reg., Italy 110 C b
Trento (Trent), Italy 110 C b
Trenton, Nova Scotia 82 K h
Trenton, Ontario 85 N h
Trepassey & B., Nfd. 83 T g
Treptow L., Ontario 84 C c
Tres Arroyos, Argentina 95 D e
Tres Lomas, Argentina 94 D e
Tres Marias, Is., Mexico 90 C c
Tres Montes, Pen., Chile 95 A g
Três Rios, Brazil 93 J h
Tres Vírgenes, Las, Mexico 90 B b
Treves. See Trier
Treviso, Italy 110 D c
Trevna, Bulgaria 112 E c
Triana, Spain 106 B d
Triangle, Alberta 88 L c
Tribune, Saskatchewan 87 O j
Tricase, Italy 111 G f
Trichinopoly. See Tiruchchirappalli
Trichur, India 126 E f
Tricorn, Mt., Antarctica 136 H d
Trier, Germany 104 B d
Trieste, Italy 110 D c
Trikeri Str., Greece 113 D e
Tríkkala, Greece 113 C e
Trikomo, Cyprus 123 B b
Trilsbeck L., Ontario 84 F b
Trim, Eire 99 C g
Trincomalee, Ceylon 126 F g
Tring Junction, Quebec 82 B g
Trinidad, Bolivia 92 E f
Trinidad, Cuba 91 D b
Trinidad, I., Argentina 95 D e
Trinidad, I., West Indies 92 E a
Trinidad, Uruguay 94 E d
Trinity, Newfoundland 83 T e
Trinity B., Newfoundland 83 T e
Trinity Pen., Antarctica 136 J f
Trionto, C., Italy 111 F f
Tripoli, Lebanon 123 D c
Tripoli, Libya 119 H b
Tripolis, Greece 113 D f
Tripolitania, Libya 119 H c
Tripura, India 127 H d
Triquet, L., Quebec 83 N c
Triunfo, Mexico 90 B c
Trivandrum, India 126 E g
Trn, Bulgaria 112 D c
Trnava, Czechoslovakia 105 G d
Trobriand Is., Papua 135 K a
Trochu, Alberta 86 D g
Trogir, Yugoslavia 110 F d
Troilus, L., Quebec 85 Q b
Trois Pistoles, Quebec 82 C e
Trois Ponts, Belgium 100 D d
Trois Rivières, Quebec 85 S f
Troitsk, U.S.S.R. 117 Q c
Troitsk, U.S.S.R. 117 F c
Troitsko Pechorsk, U.S.S.R. 114 E b
Trollhättan, Sweden 103 E g
Trollheimen, Norway 102 C e
Tromen, Mt., Argentina 95 B e
Tromsö, Norway 102 H b
Tronchiennes, Belgium 100 B c
Trondheim & Fd., Norway 102 D e
Troödos, Cyprus 123 A c
Troon, Scotland 98 D e
Tropea, Italy 111 E f
Troppau. See Opava
Trosa, Sweden 103 G g
Trossachs, Saskatchewan 87 N j
Trousers L., New Brunswick 82 F f
Trout Creek, Ontario 85 L g
Trout L., Br. Columbia 88 L e
Trout L., Ontario 81 K g
Trout R., Alberta 86 C b
Trout R., Br. Columbia 88 G a
Trout River, Newfoundland 83 O d
Troy, Turkey 124 A b
Troyes, France 108 F b
Truax, Saskatchewan 87 N j
Truba, Saudi Arabia 124 D d
Trubia, Spain 106 B a
Trucial States, Arabian Pen. 125 F e
Truer Ra., Australia 134 F d
Truite, L. la, Quebec 85 M e
Trujillo, Ciudad. See Santo Domingo
Trujillo, Honduras 91 B c
Trujillo, Peru 92 B e
Trujillo, Spain 106 C c
Trujillo, Venezuela 92 C b
Truk Is., Caroline Is. 78 F f
Truksum, Tibet 127 F b
Truns, Switzerland 101 D b
Truro, England 99 D k
Truro, Nova Scotia 82 J h
Trutch, Br. Columbia 88 H b
Trutch Cr., Br. Columbia 88 H b
Trutnov, Czechoslovakia 105 F c
Trzebnica, Poland 105 G c
Tržič, Yugoslavia 110 E b
Tsabong, Botswana 122 C e
Tsagan Olom, Mongolia 128 C a
Tsahura, S. Yemen 124 E g
Tsamkong. See Chanchiang
Tsanghsien, China 130 H c
Tsangwu. See Wuchow
Tsaochow. See Hotseh
Tsaoking, China 130 G d
Tsaritsyn. See Volgograd
Tschenstochau. See Czestochowa
Tschiertschen, Switzerland 101 E b
Tsehchow. See Tsincheng
Tsengshing, China 131 F l
Tses, S.W. Africa 122 B e
Tsesis. See Cesis
Tshikapa, Congo 120 E f
Tsimlyanskoye Vdkhr., U.S.S.R. 117 F f
Tsinan, China 130 H d
Tsincheng, China 130 F e
Tsin-chow, China 130 G c
Tsinchow. See Tienshai
Tsingchow. See Yitu
Tsing Hai. See Ching Hai
Tsingkiang, China 131 G h
Tsingkiang, China 130 J f
Tsingkow, China 130 J e
Tsingtao, China 130 K d
Tsingyüan. See Paoting
Tsingyün, China 131 F l
Tsining, China 128 G g
Tsinkiang, China 131 J k
Tsinyang, China 130 F e
Tsis, I., Truk Is. 78 E o
Tsitsihar, China 128 H a
Tsitsutl Pk., Br. Columbia 88 G d
Tsivory, Mal. Rep. 121 N l
Tsivylsk, U.S.S.R. 117 H c
Tso-motre-tung, L., Tibet 127 G c
Tsu, Japan 133 E g
Tsugaru Str., Japan 133 G d
Tsugen jima, Okinawa 78 B c
Tsugitaka, Mt. See Tsukao Shan
Tsuha wan (Buckner B.), Okinawa 78 B c
Tsukao Shan, Mt., Taiwan 128 H f
Tsungfa, China 131 F l
Tsungming, China 130 K g
Tsungtso, China 128 E f
Tsunhwa, China 130 H b
Tsunyi, China 131 C j
Tsuruga, Japan 133 E g
Tsuruoka, Japan 133 F e
Tsuyama, Japan 133 D g
Tsuyung, China 128 D e
Tua, Congo 120 D e
Tua, Portugal 106 B b
Tuamotu Arch., Pacific Oc. 79 M j
Tuao, Philippines 129 H g
Tuapse, U.S.S.R. 114 C d
Tuba, R., U.S.S.R. 115 J c
Tubai, I., Society Is. 79 L j
Tubarão, Brazil 94 G c
Tubas, Jordan 123 D e
Tubeiq, Jeb. el, Saudi Arabia 123 F h
Tuberose, Saskatchewan 86 J h
Tübingen, Germany 104 C d
Tubize, Belgium 100 C d
Tubuai, I., Tubuai Is. 79 M k
Tubuai Is., Pacific Ocean 79 M k
Tubutama, Mexico 90 B a
Tucacas, Venezuela 90 D a
Tuchodi, R., Br. Columbia 88 G a
Tucker Inlet, Antarctica 136 B d
Tucuparé, Brazil 93 F e
Tucupita, Venezuela 92 E b
Tucuruí, Brazil 93 H d
Tudela, Spain 107 E a
Tudhope, Ontario 84 J d
Tufi, Papua 135 J a
Tug, Turkey 124 D b
Tugaske, Saskatchewan 86 L h
Tuguegarao, Philippines 129 H g
Tugur, U.S.S.R. 115 N c
Tuktoyaktuk, N.-W. Terr. 80 F d
Tukums, Latvia, U.S.S.R. 103 K h
Tula, Mexico 90 E c
Tula, U.S.S.R. 116 K d
Tulabi Lake, Saskatchewan 87 O d
Tulameen, Br. Columbia 88 J f
Tulan. See Dulan
Tulancingo, Mexico 90 E c
Tula Ra., Antarctica 136 P e
Tulcán, Ecuador 92 B c
Tulcea, Romania 112 G b
Tulchin, Ukraine, U.S.S.R 116 F g
Tuléar, Mal. Rep. 121 M l
Tuli, Rhodesia 122 D d
Tulkarm, Jordan 123 D e
Tullamore, Eire 99 C g
Tulle, France 109 D d
Tulsequah, Br. Columbia 88 C a
Tulua, Colombia 92 B c
Tulun, U.S.S.R. 115 K c
Tumaco & Rada de, Colombia 92 B c
Tumany, U.S.S.R. 115 Q b
Tumbes, Peru 92 A d
Tumkur, India 126 E f
Tummel R., Scotland 98 E d
Tummo, Libya 119 H d
Tumon B., Guam 78 A k
Tump, Pakistan 126 B c
Tumu, Ghana 118 E f
Tumucumaque, Sa., Brazil 93 G c
Tumupasa, Bolivia 82 D f
Tumu Pt., Ponape I. 78 F n
Tuna, Pta., Puerto Rico 54 D j
Tunas de Zaza, Cuba 91 D b
Tunbridge Wells, England 99 H j
Tundla, India 126 E c
Tundubai, Sudan 119 K f
Tunduru, Tanzania 121 H g
Tüngan, China 131 E j
Tungchang. See Liaocheng
Tungchwan. See Hweitseh
Tungchwan. See Santai
Tunghai, China 130 J e
Tungho, China 128 J a
Tunghsien, China 130 H c
Tunghwa, China 128 J b
Tungjen, China 131 D j
Tungkun, China 131 F l
Tungkwan, China 130 E e
Tungkwan, China 130 D e
Tungliao, China 128 H b
Tungshan (Süchow), China 130 H e
Tungtai, China 130 K f
Tung Ting Hu, China 131 F h
Tunguska, R., U.S.S.R. 115 J b
Tunhwang, China 128 B b
Tuni, India 127 F e
Tunis, Tunisia 119 H a
Tunisia, N. Africa 119 G b
Tunja, Colombia 92 C b
Tunnel Dam, Ontario 84 G f
Tunnsjö, Norway 102 E d
Tunungayualuk I., Labrador 81 N f
Tunuyán & R., Argentina 94 C d
Tuoy Khaya, U.S.S.R. 115 L b
Tupilco, Mexico 90 F d
Tupinambaranas, I., Brazil 92 F d
Tupiza, Bolivia 92 D h
Tupper, Br. Columbia 88 J c
Túquerres, Colombia 92 B c
Tura, India 127 H c
Turabah, Saudi Arabia 124 D e
Turan, Iran 125 G b
Turbo, Colombia 92 B b
Turda, Romania 102 D a
Tureia I., Tuamotu Arch. 79 M k
Turfan & Depression, China 128 A b
Turgay, Kazakh., U.S.S.R. 114 F d
Turgeon, R., Quebec 85 L c
Turgutlu, Turkey 124 A b
Türi, Estonia, U.S.S.R. 103 L g
Turia, R., Spain 107 E c
Turiaçu, Brazil 93 H d
Turiamo, Venezuela 92 D a
Turin, Alberta 86 E j
Turin (Torino), Italy 110 A c
Turkey, Europe-Asia 124 A a
Turkmenistan. See Turkmenskaya
Turkmenskaya, U.S.S.R. 114 E d
Turks Is., Bahamas Is. 91 E b
Turku, Finland 103 K f
Turnagain, C., New Zealand 135 R l
Turnagain R., Br. Columbia 88 E a
Turnberry, Manitoba 87 Q e
Turnbull, Manitoba 87 S d
Turneffe Is., Brit. Honduras 91 B c
Turner Valley, Alberta 86 C h
Turnhout, Belgium 100 C c
Turnor L., Saskatchewan 88 P b
Tŭrnovo, Bulgaria 112 E c
Turnu Severin, Romania 112 D b
Turquino, Pico de, Cuba 91 D c
Turrialba, Costa Rica 91 C e
Turshiz. See Kāshmar
Turtkul, Uzbek., U.S.S.R. 114 F d
Turtle Creek, New Brunswick 82 H h
Turtleford, Saskatchewan 86 J e
Turtle L., Saskatchewan 86 J e
Turtle Mountain Prov. Park, Manitoba 87 R j
Turukhansk, U.S.S.R. 114 H b
Turukta, U.S.S.R. 115 L b
Turzovka, Czechoslovakia 105 H d
Tus, Iran 125 G b
Tusket, Nova Scotia 82 G k
Tuticorin, India 126 E g
Tuttlingen, Germany 104 C e
Tutuila, I., American Samoa 78 K j
Tutuko, Mt., New Zealand 135 P m
Tuvinskaya Aut. Oblast, U.S.S.R. 115 J c
Tuwairifa, Saudi Arabia 124 E e
Tuxford, Saskatchewan 87 M h
Tuxpan, Mexico 90 E c
Tuxpan, Mexico 90 C c
Tuxtepec, Mexico 90 E d
Tuxtla & Vol. de, Mexico 90 E d
Tuxtla Gutiérrez, Mexico 90 F d
Tuy, Spain 106 A a
Tuyen-Quang, N. Vietnam 132 D b
Tuy-hoa, S. Vietnam 132 D d
Tuyun, China 131 C j
Tuz Gölü, Turkey 124 B b
Tuzla, Yugoslavia 112 B b
Tvärån, Sweden 102 J d
Tvurditsa, Bulgaria 112 E c
Twante, Burma 127 J e
Twawwassen, Br. Columbia 88 C o
Tweed, Ontario 85 N h
Tweedie, Alberta 86 F d
Tweed R., Scotland 98 F e
Tweedsmuir Hills, Scotland 98 E e
Tweedsmuir Is., N.-W. Terr. 81 M d
Tweedsmuir Provincial Park, British Columbia 88 F d
Twelve Mile L., Saskatchewan 86 L j
Twillingate, Newfoundland 83 S d
Twin City, Ontario 87 O b
Twin Ls., N. & S., Newfoundland 83 R d
Two Brothers, Is., North-West Territories 81 L f
Two Creeks, Manitoba 87 R h
Two Hills, Alberta 86 F e
Two Rivers, The, Saskatchewan 88 S c
Tygda, U.S.S.R. 115 M c
Tyndall, Manitoba 87 V h
Tyndinskiy, U.S.S.R. 115 M c
Tynemouth, England 98 G e
Tyne R., England 98 F f
Tyner, Saskatchewan 86 J g
Tyne Valley, Prince Edward I. 82 J g
Tynset, Norway 102 D e
Tyre (Sur), Lebanon 123 D d
Tyrol. See Tirol
Tyrone, co., N. Ireland 99 C f
Tyrrhenian Sea, Italy 111 C e
Tyul'gan, U.S.S.R. 117 N d
Tyumen, U.S.S.R. 114 F c
Tyumenskaya Oblast, U.S.S.R. 114 F b
Tyvan, Manitoba 87 O h
Tzechung, China 130 G d
Tzeli, China 131 E h
Tzeya Ho, China 128 G c
Tzeyang, China 130 G d
Tzeyun, China 131 C k
Uau el Chebir. See Wau el Kebir
Uaupés & R., Brazil 92 D c
Uba, Brazil 93 J h
Ubait, Saudi Arabia 124 C d
Ubari, Libya 119 H c
Uberaba, Brazil 93 H g
Uberlândia, Brazil 94 G a
Überlingen, Germany 104 C e
Ubsa Nur, Mongolia 115 J c
Ucayali, R., Peru 92 C e
Uchiura wan, Japan 133 G c
Uchiza, Peru 92 B e
Uckermark, Germany 104 E b
Ucluelet, Br. Columbia 88 G f
Udain, Yemen 124 D g
Udaipur, India 126 D d
Uddevalla, Sweden 103 D g
Udd Jaur, Sweden 102 G d
Uden, Netherlands 100 D c
Udidan, I., Truk Is. 78 E o
Udine, Italy 110 D b
Udon Thani, Thailand 132 C c
Udot, I., Truk Is. 78 E n
Udskaya Guba, U.S.S.R. 115 N c
Udzha. See Bor Yuryakh
Uelen, U.S.S.R. 115 T b
Ueno, Japan 133 E g
Ufa, U.S.S.R. 117 M c
Uganda, E. Africa 121 G d
Ugwashi-Uku, Nigeria 120 B c
Uherske Hradiště, Czechoslovakia 105 G d
Uhlman L., Manitoba 87 T b
Uí Failghe, co., Eire 99 B g
Uijec, I., Truk Is. 78 E o
Uist, North, I., Scotland 98 C c
Uist, South, I., Scotland 98 C c
Uitenhage, South Africa 122 D f
Uitgeest, Netherlands 100 C b
Ujae, I., Marshall Is. 79 S b
Ujpest, Hungary 105 H e
Uka, I., Okinawa 78 C a
Ukerewe Is., Tanzania 121 G e
Ukhta, U.S.S.R. 114 C b
Ukibaru shima, Okinawa 78 B c
Ukmerge, Lithuania, U.S.S.R. 103 J j
Ukraine, U.S.S.R. 116 E g
Ulalu, I., Truk Is. 78 D n
Ulan, Mongolia 115 J d
Ulan Bator, Mongolia 128 E a
Ulanhot, China 128 H a
Ulan Ude, U.S.S.R. 115 K c
Ulcinj, Yugoslavia 112 B d
Ulifauro Pass, Truk Is. 78 D o
Uliga, I., Marshall Is. 79 U g
Uligar Pass, Truk Is. 78 F o
Ulipero, I., Truk Is. 78 C o
Ullapool, Scotland 98 D c
Ullared, Sweden 103 E h
Ulldecona, Spain 107 F b
Ullswater, L., England 99 F f
Ullung Do, Sea of Japan 133 B f
Ulm, Germany 104 C d
Ulster, Eire-N. Ireland 98 B f
Ulua, R., Honduras 91 B c
Ulukişla, Turkey 124 B b
Ulverston, England 99 E f
Ulyanovsk, U.S.S.R. 117 J c
Ulzen, Germany 104 D b
Uman, Ukraine, U.S.S.R. 116 G g
Umanak Fd., Greenland 89 P b
Umarkot, Pakistan 126 C c
Umatac, I., Guam 78 A l
Umbria, dep., Italy 110 D d
Umeå, Sweden 102 J e
Umfreville, Ontario 86 L a
Umm ar Rusuys, Muscat & Oman 125 G e
Umm el Qulban, Saudi Arabia 124 D d
Umm Kuteira, Sudan 119 L f
Umm Lej, Saudi Arabia 124 C d
Umm Qasr, Iraq 124 E c
Umm Rasas. See Umm ar Rusuys
Umm Ruwaba, Sudan 119 M f
Umtali, Rhodesia 122 E c
Umtata, South Africa 122 D f
Umvuma, Rhodesia 122 E c
Una, Mt., New Zealand 135 Q l
Una, R., Yugoslavia 110 F c
Uncastillo, Spain 107 E a
Uncía, Bolivia 92 D g

Vlaardingen, *Netherlands* 100 C c
Vladimir, *U.S.S.R.* 116 M c
Vladimirovka, *U.S.S.R.* 117 H f
Vladivostok, *U.S.S.R.* 115 N d
Vlieland, I., *Netherlands* 100 C a
Vlissingen, *Netherlands* 100 B c
Vlone, *Albania* 113 B d
Vltava, R., *Czechoslovakia* 104 F c
Voghera, *Italy* 110 B c
Vohemar, *Mal. Rep.* 121 P j
Võhma, Estonia, *U.S.S.R.* 103 L g
Voi, *Kenya* 121 H e
Voiotía, *Greece* 113 D e
Voiron, *France* 108 F d
Voitsberg, *Austria* 104 F e
Voiviis, L., *Greece* 113 D e
Vojvodina, *Yugoslavia* 112 B b
Volcano B. *See* Uchiura wan
Volga, R., *U.S.S.R.* 114 D d
Volgograd, *U.S.S.R.* 117 G f
Volissos, *Greece* 113 E e
Volkhov, R., *U.S.S.R.* 116 G b
Vollenhove, *Netherlands* 100 D b
Volochanka, *U.S.S.R.* 115 J a
Volochisk, Ukraine, *U.S.S.R.* 116 E g
Vologda, *U.S.S.R.* 116 L b
Volokolamsk, *U.S.S.R.* 116 J c
Vólos, *Greece* 113 D e
Volovets, Ukraine, *U.S.S.R.* 116 C g
Volozhin, Belorussia, *U.S.S.R.* 116 E d
Volsk, *U.S.S.R.* 117 H d
Volta. *See* Upper Volta
Volta, L., *Ghana* 118 E g
Volta, White R., *Ghana* 118 E g
Voltveti, Estonia, *U.S.S.R.* 103 L g
Vonda, *Saskatchewan* 86 L f
Vonêche, *Belgium* 100 C d
Voorburg, *Netherlands* 100 C b
Voorschoten, *Netherlands* 100 C b
Voorst, *Netherlands* 100 E b
Voorthuizen, *Netherlands* 100 D b
Vopnafjordhur, *Iceland* 102 Y m
Vorab, Mt., *Switzerland* 101 E b
Vorarlberg, *Austria* 104 C e
Vorauen, *Switzerland* 101 D a
Vorkuta, *U.S.S.R.* 114 F b
Vormsi, I., Estonia, *U.S.S.R.* 103 K g
Voronezh, *U.S.S.R.* 116 L f
Vorposten Pk., *Antarctica* 136 M d
Vosges, dep. & Mts., *France* 108 G b
Voss, *Norway* 103 B f
Vostok I., *Pacific Ocean* 79 L h
Votkinsk, *U.S.S.R.* 117 L b
Vouvry, *Switzerland* 101 B b
Vouziers, *France* 108 F b
Voxna, *Sweden* 103 F f
Voyampolka, *U.S.S.R.* 115 Q c
Voyeykov Ice Shelf, *Antarctica* 136 T e
Voznesensk, Ukraine, *U.S.S.R.* 116 G h
Vrangelya Ostrov, *U.S.S.R.* 115 S a
Vranje, *Yugoslavia* 112 C c
Vranov, *Czechoslovakia* 105 J d
Vratsa, *Bulgaria* 112 D c
Vrbas, *Yugoslavia* 112 B b
Vrchovina Českomoravska, *Czechoslovakia* 105 F d
Vredefort, *South Africa* 122 D e
Vrin, *Switzerland* 101 E b
Vroomshoop, *Netherlands* 100 E b
Vršac, *Yugoslavia* 112 C b
Vrútky, *Czechoslovakia* 105 H d
Vryburg, *South Africa* 122 C e
Vučitrn, *Yugoslavia* 112 C c
Vukovar, *Yugoslavia* 112 B b
Vulcan, *Alberta* 86 D h
Vulcan, *Romania* 112 D b
Vulcano, I., *Italy* 111 E f
Vulpera, *Switzerland* 101 F b
Vuolijoki, *Finland* 102 M d
Vŭrbitsa, *Bulgaria* 112 F c
Vyatka, R., *U.S.S.R.* 114 D c
Vyatka. *See* Kirov
Vyatskiye Polyany, *U.S.S.R.* 117 K b
Vyazemskiy, *U.S.S.R.* 115 N d
Vyazma, *U.S.S.R.* 116 J d
Vyazniki, *U.S.S.R.* 117 F b
Vyborg, *U.S.S.R.* 116 F a
Vyrtsyarv Oz., Estonia, *U.S.S.R.* 103 M g
Vyru, Estonia, *U.S.S.R.* 103 M h
Vyshniy Volochek, *U.S.S.R.* 116 J c
Vyskov, *Czechoslovakia* 105 G d
Vytegra, *U.S.S.R.* 116 K a
Wa, *Ghana* 118 E f
Waalwijk, *Netherlands* 100 D c
Wababimiga L., *Ontario* 84 D b
Wabamun & L., *Alberta* 86 C e
Wabana, *Newfoundland* 83 T f
Wabasca, *Alberta* 86 D c
Wabasca L., North, *Alberta* 86 D b
Wabasca L., South, *Alberta* 86 D c
Wabasca R., *Alberta* 88 M b
Wabatongushi L., *Ontario* 84 F d
Wabigoon & L., *Ontario* 86 K a
Wabinosh L., *Ontario* 87 N a
Waboose Dam, *Ontario* 84 C b
Wabos, *Ontario* 85 F f
Wabowden, *Manitoba* 87 T d
Wabra, *Saudi Arabia* 124 E d
Wabuda, I., *Papua* 135 H a
Wachusett Shoal, *Pacific Ocean* 79 M l
Waco, *Quebec* 82 G b
Wacouno R., *Quebec* 82 G b
Wad, *Pakistan* 126 C c
Wadden Zee, *Netherlands* 100 D a
Waddington, Mt., *British Columbia* 88 G e
Wadena, *Saskatchewan* 87 O g
Wad Hamid, *Sudan* 119 M e
Wadham Is., *Newfoundland* 83 T d
Wadhams, *Br. Columbia* 88 E e
Wadi-es-Sir, *Jordan* 123 D f
Wadi Gemal I., *Egypt* 119 N d
Wadi Halfa, *Sudan* 119 M d
Wadi Musa, *Jordan* 123 D g
Wad Medani, *Sudan* 119 M f
Wadsley, *Br. Columbia* 88 C f
Wafi, *Saudi Arabia* 124 D e
Wagama L., *Quebec* 85 N b
Wagaming, *Ontario* 84 B b
Wageningen, *Netherlands* 100 D c
Wager B., *N.-W. Territories* 81 L d
Wager Bay, *N.-W. Territories* 81 K d
Wagga Wagga, *Australia* 135 J g
Wagin, *Australia* 134 C f
Wahla, *Saudi Arabia* 124 D f
Waiau, *New Zealand* 135 Q l
Waiau R., *New Zealand* 135 Q l
Waichow. *See* Waiyeung
Waigeo, I., *W. Irian* 129 K k
Waihi, *New Zealand* 135 R k
Waikaia, *New Zealand* 135 P m
Waikare, L., *New Zealand* 135 R k
Waikato, R., *New Zealand* 135 R k
Waimate, *New Zealand* 135 Q m
Waimes, *Belgium* 100 E d
Wainganga R., *India* 126 E d
Waingapu, *Indonesia* 129 H m
Wainwright, *Alberta* 86 G f
Waipapa Pt., *New Zealand* 135 P m
Waipara, *New Zealand* 135 Q l
Waipukurau, *New Zealand* 135 R k
Wairau R., *New Zealand* 135 Q l
Wairoa, *New Zealand* 135 R k
Waitaki, *New Zealand* 135 Q m
Waitara, *New Zealand* 135 R k
Waitomo, *New Zealand* 135 R k
Waitville, *Saskatchewan* 87 M f
Waiyeung, *China* 131 G l
Wajir, *Kenya* 121 J d
Wakamatsu, *Japan* 133 F f
Wakami L., *Ontario* 84 H e
Wakasa B., *Japan* 133 D g
Wakatipu, L., *New Zealand* 135 P m
Wakaw, *Saskatchewan* 87 M f
Wakayama, *Japan* 133 D g
Wakba. *See* El Jafr
Wakefield, *England* 99 G g
Wakefield, *Quebec* 85 P g
Wakefield Mts., *Antarctica* 136 H d
Wakomata L., *Ontario* 84 G f
Wakopa, *Manitoba* 87 S j
Wakrah, *Qatar* 125 F e
Wakuan Hu, *China* 130 H f
Wakwayowkastic R., *Ontario* 84 K b
Walachia, *Romania* 112 E b
Wałbrzych, *Poland* 105 G c
Walcheren I., *Netherlands* 100 B c
Walcott, *Br. Columbia* 88 F c
Wald, *Switzerland* 101 D a
Waldeck, *Saskatchewan* 86 K h
Waldheim, *Saskatchewan* 86 L f
Waldia, *Ethiopia* 121 H b
Waldo, *Br. Columbia* 86 B j
Waldron, C., *Antarctica* 136 S e
Waldron, *Saskatchewan* 87 P h
Walen See, *Switzerland* 101 E a
Walenstadt, *Switzerland* 101 E a
Wales, *Great Britain* 99 E h
Wales I., *N.-W. Territories* 81 L d
Walgett, *Australia* 135 J f
Walgreen Coast, *Antarctica* 136 F c
Walker L., *Manitoba* 87 V d
Walker L., *Quebec* 82 E c
Walker Mts., *Antarctica* 136 G d
Walkerton, *Ontario* 84 J h
Wallace, *Nova Scotia* 82 J h
Wallace, *Ontario* 85 M g
Wallaceburg, *Ontario* 84 H k
Wallace Mt., *Alberta* 86 B c
Wallacetown, *Ontario* 84 J k
Wallaroo, *Australia* 134 G f
Wallaston, Mt., *Australia* 134 F c
Wallis I., *Pacific Ocean* 78 J j
Walsall, *England* 99 F h
Walsh, *Alberta* 86 G j
Walsh, *Australia* 135 H c
Walsoorden, *Netherlands* 100 C c
Waltham, *Quebec* 85 O g
Walton, *Nova Scotia* 82 J h
Walton, *Ontario* 84 J j
Walvis Bay, *S.W. Africa* 122 A d
Walwale, *Ghana* 118 E f
Wamba, *Congo* 121 F d
Wamel, *Netherlands* 100 D c
Wana, *Pakistan* 126 C b
Wanaaring, *Australia* 135 H e
Wanaka & L., *New Zealand* 135 P m
Wanapital L., *Ontario* 84 K f
Wandering River, *Alberta* 86 E c
Wandiwash, *India* 126 E f
Wandoan, *Australia* 135 J e
Wandre, *Belgium* 100 D d
Wandsbek, *Germany* 104 D b
Wan Fou Shan, *China* 131 G h
Wangaratta, *Australia* 135 J g
Wanhsien, *China* 128 E d
Wankie, *Rhodesia* 122 D c
Wanless, *Manitoba* 87 Q d
Wanning, *Hainan* 131 E n
Wanping, *China* 130 H c
Wanup, *Ontario* 84 K f
Wanyuan, *China* 130 D f
Wapawekka Hills, *Saskatchewan* 87 N d
Wapawekka L., *Saskatchewan* 87 N d
Wapella, *Saskatchewan* 87 P h
Wapikamaski, *Ontario* 87 N a
Wapisu L., *Manitoba* 87 S c
Wapiti R., *Alberta* 88 K c
Wapus L., *Saskatchewan* 87 P b
Wapustagamau L., *Quebec* 83 O b
Warandab, *Ethiopia* 121 J c
Warangal, *India* 126 E e
Warburg, *Alberta* 86 C e
Wardair, *Ethiopia* 121 K c
Warden Junction, *Alberta* 86 E f
Wardha & R., *India* 126 E d
Ward Hunt I., *North-West Territories* 81 M a
Wardlow, *Alberta* 86 F h
Wardner, *Br. Columbia* 88 M f
Ware, *Br. Columbia* 88 G b
Ware, *England* 89 P e
Waremme, *Belgium* 100 D d
Warka, *Poland* 105 J c
Warkworth, *Ontario* 85 N k
Warkworth, *New Zealand* 135 R k
Warmbad, *S.W. Africa* 122 B e
Warmbaths, *South Africa* 122 D d
Warneford, *Ontario* 84 B c
Warnemünde, *Germany* 104 E a
Warner, *Alberta* 86 E j
Warneton, *Belgium* 100 A d
Warora, *India* 126 E d
Warragul, *Australia* 135 J g
Warren, *Ontario* 84 K f
Warren Landing, *Manitoba* 87 U e
Warrenpoint, *N. Ireland* 99 C f
Warri, *Nigeria* 118 G g
Warrington, *England* 99 F g
Warrnambool, *Australia* 134 H g
Warsaw (Warszawa), *Poland* 105 J b
Warspite, *Alberta* 86 E d
Warszawa. *See* Warsaw
Warta, *Poland* 105 H c
Warta R., *Poland* 105 H b
Wartime, *Saskatchewan* 86 J g
Warwick, *Australia* 135 K e
Warwick, *Quebec* 85 T g
Warwick & co., *England* 99 F h
Wasa, *British Columbia* 88 M f
Wasaga Beach, *Ontario* 84 K h
Waseca, *Saskatchewan* 86 H e
Wasekamio L., *Saskatchewan* 88 P b
Wasen, *Switzerland* 101 C a
Wash, The, *England* 99 H h
Washago, *Ontario* 85 L h
Washaw B., *Manitoba* 87 V g
Washikuti, *Quebec* 83 M c
Washington I., *Pacific Ocean* 78 K g
Washington Ld., *Greenland* 89 Q a
Washir, *Afghanistan* 125 H c
Washuk, *Pakistan* 126 B c
Waskada, *Manitoba* 87 R j
Waskaiowaka L., *Manitoba* 87 V b
Waskatenau, *Alberta* 86 E d
Waskesiu Lake, *Saskatchewan* 86 L e
Wasmes, *Belgium* 100 B d
Waspan, *Honduras* 91 C d
Wassen, *Switzerland* 101 D b
Waswanipi & L., *Quebec* 85 O c
Waswanipi R., *Quebec* 85 O c
Watabeag L., *Ontario* 84 K d
Watcomb, *Ontario* 86 L a
Waterdown, *Ontario* 84 L j
Waterford, *Ontario* 84 K k
Waterford Harb., *Eire* 99 C h
Waterford (Port Láirge), *Eire* 99 C h
Waterhen L., *Manitoba* 87 S f
Waterhen L., *Saskatchewan* 86 J d
Water I., *Virgin Is.* 54 E h
Waterloo, *Belgium* 100 C d
Waterloo, *Ontario* 84 K j
Waterloo, *Quebec* 85 S g
Waterton Park, *Alberta* 86 D j
Waterville, *Nova Scotia* 82 H h
Waterville, *Quebec* 85 T g
Waterways, *Alberta* 86 F b
Watford, *England* 99 G j
Watford, *Ontario* 84 J k
Watino, *Alberta* 88 L c
Watlings I., *Bahamas Is.* 91 E b
Watou, *Belgium* 100 A d
Watrous, *Saskatchewan* 87 M g
Watsa, *Congo* 121 F d
Watson, *Saskatchewan* 87 N f
Watson Lake, *Yukon* 77 X f
Watt Mts., *Alberta* 88 L a
Wau, *New Guinea* 135 J a
Wau, *Sudan* 119 L g
Waubamick, *Ontario* 84 K g
Waubaushene, *Ontario* 84 L h
Wauchope, *Australia* 134 F d
Wauchope, *Saskatchewan* 87 Q j
Wau el Kebir, *Libya* 119 J c
Waugh, *Manitoba* 86 G a
Wave Hill, *Australia* 134 F c
Waveney R., *England* 99 H h
Waverley, *Nova Scotia* 82 J j
Wavre, *Belgium* 100 C d
Wavy L., *Alberta* 86 E j
Wawagosic R., *Quebec* 85 M c
Wawaitin Falls, *Ontario* 84 J d
Wawanesa, *Manitoba* 87 S j
Wawota, *Saskatchewan* 87 P j
Way Archipelago, *Antarctica* 136 A e
Wayne, *Alberta* 86 E g
Wazirabad, *Pakistan* 84 D b
Weald, The, *England* 99 H j
Wear R., *England* 99 F f
Weaver L., *Manitoba* 87 V f
Webb, *Saskatchewan* 86 J h
Webbwood, *Ontario* 84 J f
Wechelderzande, *Belgium* 100 C c
Weda B., Halmahera, *Indonesia* 129 J k
Weddell I., *Falkland Is.* 95 D h
Weddell Sea, *Antarctica* 136 J d
Wedge Mt., *Br. Columbia* 88 H e
Wedgeport, *Nova Scotia* 82 F k
Weedon, *Quebec* 85 T g
Weekes, *Saskatchewan* 87 P f
Weert, *Netherlands* 100 D c
Weesen, *Switzerland* 101 E a
Weesp, *Netherlands* 100 D b
Weichang, *China* 130 J b
Weiden, *Germany* 104 E d
Weifang, *China* 130 J d
Wei-hai, *China* 130 L d
Wei Ho, R., *China* 128 E d
Weimar, *Germany* 104 D c
Weinfelden, *Switzerland* 101 E a
Weir, *Quebec* 85 Q g
Weirdale, *Saskatchewan* 87 M e
Wei Shan Hu, *China* 130 H e
Weissenfels, *Germany* 104 D c
Weisshorn, Mt., *Switzerland* 101 C b
Weissmies, Mt., *Switzerland* 101 D b
Weisstannen, *Switzerland* 101 E a
Weitzel L., *Saskatchewan* 88 Q b
Wejh. *See* Al Wajh
Wekusko & L., *Manitoba* 87 S d
Weldon, *Saskatchewan* 87 M f
Welford, *Australia* 135 H e
Welkom, *South Africa* 122 D e
Welland, *Ontario* 85 L k
Welland Can., *Ontario* 85 L k
Welles Harb., *Midway Is.* 79 P c
Wellesley Is., *Australia* 134 G c
Wellin, *Belgium* 100 D d
Wellingborough, *England* 99 G h
Wellington, *Newfoundland* 83 S e
Wellington, *New Zealand* 135 R l
Wellington, *Nova Scotia* 82 J j
Wellington, *Ontario* 85 N j
Wellington, *Prince Edward I.* 82 H g
Wellington B., *Ontario* 85 N j
Wellington Chan., *North-West Territories* 81 K b
Wellington I., *Chile* 95 B g
Wells, *England* 99 H h
Wells, *England* 99 F j
Wells Gray Provincial Park, *British Columbia* 88 J d
Wells L., *Manitoba* 87 R a
Wellwood, *Manitoba* 87 S h
Wels, *Austria* 104 E d
Welsford, *New Brunswick* 82 F h
Welshpool, *New Brunswick* 82 F j
Welshpool, *Wales* 99 E h
Welwyn, *Saskatchewan* 87 Q h
Wema, *Congo* 120 E e
Wembley, *Alberta* 88 K c
Wembo Niama, *Congo* 120 E e
Wemyss Bay, *Scotland* 98 D e
Wenchow, *China* 131 K h
Wenebegon L., *Ontario* 84 G e
Wenman I. *See* Wolf I.
Wenshan, *China* 131 B l
Wensi, *China* 130 E e
Wentworth Centre, *N. S.* 82 J h
Wernham L., *Ontario* 87 U b
Wernhout, *Netherlands* 100 C c
Wervershoof, *Netherlands* 100 D b
Wervica, *Belgium* 100 B d
Wesel, *Germany* 104 B c
Wesenberg, *Germany* 104 E b
Weser R., *Germany* 104 C b
Weslemkoon, *Ontario* 85 N h
Wesleyville, *Newfoundland* 83 T d
Wessel Is., *Australia* 134 G b
West Barra, *Shetland* 98 J a
West Bend, *Saskatchewan* 87 O g
West Bengal, *India* 127 G d
Westboro, *Ontario* 84 C j
Westbourne, *Manitoba* 87 T h
Westbridge, *Br. Columbia* 88 K f
West Bromwich, *England* 99 F h
West C., *New Zealand* 135 P m
Westende, *Belgium* 100 A c
Westerham, *Saskatchewan* 86 H h
Westerloo, *Belgium* 100 C c
Western Australia, state, *Australia* 134 D d
Western Head, *Nova Scotia* 83 H k
Western Is., *Ontario* 84 K g
Western Samoa, *Pacific Ocean* 78 H j
Wester Schelde, *Netherlands* 100 B c
Westfalen, *Germany* 104 C c
Westfield Beach, *New Brunswick* 82 F h
Westham I., *Br. Columbia* 88 C g
West Hartlepool, *England* 99 G f
West Hill, *Ontario* 85 L j
West Ice Shelf, *Antarctica* 136 R e
West Indies, *Caribbean Sea* 91 D b
West Irian, prov., *Indonesia* 129 L l
Westkapelle, *Netherlands* 100 B c
West Lagoon, *Palmyra I.* 79 T k
West Landing, *Majuro Is.* 79 T f
Westlock, *Alberta* 86 D d
West Lorne, *Ontario* 84 J k
West Lothian, co., *Scotland* 98 E e
West Magpie R., *Quebec* 82 H b
Westmeath, co., *Eire* 99 C g
Westmeath, *Ontario* 85 O g
Westmorland, co., *England* 99 F f
Westmount, *Quebec* 85 S j
West Nicholson, *Rhodesia* 122 D d
Weston, *Ontario* 84 C k
Weston, *Sabah* 129 G j
Weston-super-Mare, *England* 99 F j
West Pakistan, *S. Asia* 126 C c
Westport, *Eire* 99 A g
Westport, *Newfoundland* 85 Q d
Westport, *New Zealand* 135 Q l
Westport, *Ontario* 85 O h
West Prairie R., *Alberta* 86 A c
West Pt., Anticosti I., *Quebec* 82 H d
West Pt., *Jaluit I.* 79 T j
West Pt., *Marcus I.* 78 F a
West Pt., *Prince Edward I.* 82 H g
West Pt., Sable I., *Nova Scotia* 83 M k
West Pubnico, *Nova Scotia* 82 G k
Westray, *Manitoba* 87 Q e
Westray I., *Orkney Is.* 99 E a
Westree, *Ontario* 84 J e
West Riding, Yorkshire, *England* 99 F g
West Road R., *British Columbia* 88 G d
West St. John, *New Brunswick* 82 F h
West St. Modiste, *Labrador* 83 Q b
West Spit, *Eniwetok* 79 Q c
West Vancouver, *British Columbia* 88 C f
Westview, *Br. Columbia* 88 G f
Westville, *Nova Scotia* 82 K h
Westwoud, *Netherlands* 100 D b
Wetar, I. & Str., *Indonesia* 129 J m
Wetaskiwin, *Alberta* 86 D f
Wetetnagami, R., *Quebec* 85 O c
Wetterhorn, Mt., *Switzerland* 101 D b
Wexford & co., *Eire* 99 C h
Weyakwin L., *Saskatchewan* 86 L d
Weyburn, *Saskatchewan* 87 O j
Weymouth, *England* 99 F k
Weymouth, *Nova Scotia* 82 G j
Whakatane, *New Zealand* 135 R k
Whale I., *Quebec* 83 P b
Whale R., Gt., *Quebec* 81 M f
Whale R., *Quebec* 81 N f
Whales, B. of, *Antarctica* 136 C e
Whalsey I., *Shetland* 98 J a
Whangarei, *New Zealand* 135 Q j
Whatcheer, *Alberta* 86 F g
Wheeler R., *Saskatchewan* 88 R b
Whichaway Nunataks, *Antarctica* 136 K b
Whipple Pt., *Nova Scotia* 82 F j
Whiskey Gap, *Alberta* 86 D j
Whiskey Jack Landing, *Manitoba* 87 T d
Whitbourne, *Newfoundland* 83 T f
Whitby, *England* 99 G f
Whitby, *Ontario* 85 M j
White B., *Newfoundland* 83 Q c
White Bear, *Saskatchewan* 86 J h
White Brook, *New Brunswick* 82 E f
Whitecap L., *Manitoba* 87 W b
Whitecourt, *Alberta* 86 B d
White Fish, *Ontario* 84 J f
Whitefish Falls, *Ontario* 84 J f
Whitefish L., *Alberta* 86 E d
Whitefish L., *Ontario* 87 N b
White Fox, *Saskatchewan* 87 N e
Whitefox R., *Saskatchewan* 87 N e
Whitehaven, *England* 99 E f
Whitehorse, *Yukon* 77 U f
White I., *Antarctica* 136 B c
White I., *Antarctica* 136 P e
White I., *N.-W. Territories* 81 L d
White L., *Ontario* 85 O g
White L., *Ontario* 84 E d
White Lake, *Ontario* 85 O g
Whitemouth, *Manitoba* 86 F a
Whitemouth L. & R., *Manitoba* 86 F a
Whitemud, R., *Alberta* 88 L b
White Oil Springs. *See* Naft
White Otter L., *Ontario* 86 L a
White Point, Belle Isle, *Newfoundland* 83 R b
White R., *Br. Columbia* 86 B h
White R., *Ontario* 84 E d
White River, *Ontario* 84 E d
White Rock, *Br. Columbia* 88 E g
White Russia. *See* Belorussia
Whitesail L., *Br. Columbia* 88 F d
Whitesand R., *Saskatchewan* 87 P g
Whiteshell Prov. Park, *Manitoba* 86 F a
Whitestone L., *Manitoba* 87 U b
Whiteswan Ls., *Saskatchewan* 87 M d
White Volta, R., *Ghana* 118 E g
Whitewater L., *Ontario* 84 A b
Whitewood, *Saskatchewan* 87 P h
Whitgull L., *Quebec* 81 N f
Whitkow, *Saskatchewan* 86 K g
Whitla, *Alberta* 86 F j
Whitmore Mts., *Antarctica* 136 F a
Whitney, *Ontario* 85 M g
Whyalla, *Australia* 134 G f
Whycocomagh, C. Breton I., *Nova Scotia* 83 L h
Wiarton, *Ontario* 84 J h
Wick, *Scotland* 98 E b
Wickenden L., Anticosti I., *Quebec* 82 K d
Wickham West, *Quebec* 85 S g
Wicklow & co., *Eire* 99 C h
Wicklow Head, *Eire* 99 C h
Wicklow Mts., *Eire* 99 C g
Widdifield, *Ontario* 85 L f
Wielbark, *Poland* 105 J b
Wielen, *Poland* 105 G b
Wieliczka, *Poland* 105 J d
Wielun, *Poland* 105 H c
Wiener Neustadt, *Austria* 105 G e
Wien (Vienna), *Austria* 105 G d
Wiesbaden, *Germany* 104 C c
Wiesen, *Switzerland* 101 E b
Wigan, *England* 99 F g
Wight, Isle of, *England* 99 G k
Wigtown & co., *Scotland* 99 E f
Wigtown B., *Scotland* 99 E f
Wijhe, *Netherlands* 100 E b
Wijk, *Netherlands* 100 D d
Wijk, *Netherlands* 100 D c
Wikwemikong, *Ontario* 84 J g
Wil, *Switzerland* 101 E a
Wilberforce, *Ontario* 85 M g
Wilcannia, *Australia* 135 H f
Wilcox, *Saskatchewan* 87 N h
Wild Bight, *Newfoundland* 83 R d
Wilderness Prov. Park, *Alberta* 87 O j
Wild Goose, *Ontario* 87 O b
Wildhorn, Mt., *Switzerland* 101 C b
Wildnest L., *Saskatchewan* 87 P d
Wildstrubel, Mt., *Switzerland* 101 C b
Wildwood, *Alberta* 86 B e
Wilgar, *Ontario* 84 E b
Wilhelmsburg, *Germany* 104 D b
Wilhelmshaven, *Germany* 104 C b
Wilkes I., *Wake I.* 79 S e
Wilkes Land, *Antarctica* 136 S d
Wilkie, *Saskatchewan* 86 J f
Wilkins Coast, *Antarctica* 136 H d
Wilkins Sd., *Antarctica* 136 H d
Wilkin's Str., *Antarctica* 136 H d
Wilkolaz, *Poland* 105 K c
Willemsdorp, *Netherlands* 100 C c
Willemstad, *Curaçao I.* 92 D a
Willemstad, *Netherlands* 100 C c
Willesden Green, *Alberta* 86 C f
Willet, *Ontario* 84 B b
Williambury, *Australia* 134 B d
William Creek, *Australia* 134 G e
William L., *Manitoba* 87 S e
William R., *Saskatchewan* 88 P a
Williams, C., *Antarctica* 136 B e
Williamsford, *Ontario* 84 J h
Williams Lake, *British Columbia* 88 H d
Williamson Hd., *Antarctica* 136 A e
Williamsport, *Newfoundland* 83 Q c
Willingdon, *Alberta* 86 E e
Willingdon, Mt., *Alberta* 88 L e
Willis I., *Antarctica* 136 K g
Willis Is., *Coral Sea* 78 F j
Williston, *South Africa* 122 C f
Willmar, *Saskatchewan* 87 P j
Willowbrook, *Saskatchewan* 87 P g
Willow Bunch, *Saskatchewan* 87 M j
Willow Cr., *Alberta* 86 D h
Willowmore, *South Africa* 122 C f
Willow R., *Br. Columbia* 88 H d
Willows, *Saskatchewan* 87 M j
Wilma Glacier, *Antarctica* 136 P e
Wilnis, *Netherlands* 100 C b
Wilno, *Ontario* 85 N g
Wilson, C., *N.-W. Terr.* 81 L d
Wilson Hills, *Antarctica* 136 A e
Wiltshire, co., *England* 99 F j
Wiluna, *Australia* 134 D e
Wimapedi, L., *Manitoba* 87 S c
Wimborne, *Alberta* 86 D g
Winagami L., *Alberta* 86 A c
Winburg, *South Africa* 122 D e
Winchester, *England* 99 G j
Winchester, *Ontario* 85 P g
Windermere & L., *England* 99 F f
Windermere L., *Ontario* 84 G e
Windhoek, *S.W. Africa* 122 B d
Windorah, *Australia* 135 H e
Windsor, *England* 99 G j
Windsor, *Newfoundland* 83 R e
Windsor, *Nova Scotia* 82 H j
Windsor, *Ontario* 84 H k
Windsor, *Quebec* 85 S g
Windthorst, *Saskatchewan* 87 P h
Windward Is., *West Indies* 91 G d
Windward Pass, *West Indies* 91 E c

Windy L., Saskatchewan 87 P d
Winefred L. & R., Alberta 86 G c
Winfield, Alberta 86 C f
Wingham, Ontario 84 J j
Winghe-St. Georges, Belgium 100 C d
Winisk, Ontario 81 L f
Winisk L., Ontario 81 L g
Winisk R., Ontario 81 L g
Winkler, Manitoba 87 U j
Winnifred, Alberta 86 F j
Winning Pool, Australia 134 B d
Winnipeg, L., Manitoba 87 U f
Winnipeg, Manitoba 87 U j
Winnipeg Beach, Manitoba 87 U h
Winnipegosis, L., Manitoba 87 R f
Winnipegosis, Manitoba 87 S g
Winschoten, Netherlands 100 E a
Winter, Saskatchewan 86 H f
Winter Harb., N.-W. Terr 80 H c
Wintering L., Manitoba 87 U c
Winterswijk, Netherlands 100 E c
Winterthur, Switzerland 101 D a
Winterton, Newfoundland 83 T f
Winton, Australia 135 H d
Winton, New Zealand 135 P m
Wisbech, England 99 H h
Wiseton, Saskatchewan 86 K g
Wishart, Saskatchewan 87 O g
Wisła (Vistula), R., Poland 105 J c
Wismar, Germany 104 D b
Wistaria, Br. Columbia 88 F d
Witchai L., Manitoba 87 V c
Witchekan L., Saskatchewan 86 K e
Witham R., England 99 G g
Witless Bay, Newfoundland 83 T f
Witputs, S.W. Africa 122 B e
Witry, Belgium 100 D e
Witten, Germany 104 B c
Wittenberg, Germany 104 E c
Wittenberge, Germany 104 D b
Wittenoom, Australia 134 C d
Wittengen, Germany 104 D b
Wittstock, Germany 104 E b
Wivenhoe, Manitoba 87 W b
Włocławek, Poland 105 H b
Woerden, Netherlands 100 C b
Wognum, Netherlands 100 D b
Wohlen, Switzerland 101 D a
Wohlthat Mts., Antarctica 136 M d
Woito, Ontario 85 N g
Wokam, I., Indonesia 129 K m
Woking, Alberta 88 K c
Wolbrom, Poland 105 H c
Woleai, I., Caroline Islands 78 E f
Wolf B., Quebec 83 M c
Wolf Bay, Quebec 83 M c
Wolfe, Saskatchewan 86 J f
Wolfe Island, Ontario 85 O h
Wolfe's Cove, Quebec 85 S c
Wolf I., Madeleine Is., Quebec 83 L f
Wolf L., Alberta 86 G d
Wolfsberg, Austria 104 F e
Wolfville, Nova Scotia 82 H h
Wolgast, Germany 104 E a
Wolhusen, Switzerland 101 C a
Wollal, Australia 134 D c
Wollaston Foreland, Greenland 89 M b
Wollaston Is., Chile 95 C j
Wollaston L., Saskatchewan 80 J f
Wollaston Lake Post, Saskatchewan 88 S a
Wollongong, Australia 135 K f
Wolseley, Manitoba 87 O h
Wolstenholm, C., Quebec 81 M e
Wolvega, Netherlands 100 E b
Wolverhampton, England 99 F h
Wolverthem, Belgium 100 C d
Wolverton, England 99 G h
Woman R., Ontario 84 H e
Woman River, Ontario 84 H e
Wŏnsan, N. Korea 128 J c
Wonthaggi, Australia 135 J g
Wood B., Antarctica 136 B d
Woodbridge, Ontario 85 L j
Woodfibre, Br. Columbia 88 H f
Wood L., Manitoba 87 U a
Wood L., Saskatchewan 87 O c
Woodlands, Manitoba 87 U h
Woodlark I., Papua 135 K a
Wood Mountain, Saskatchewan 86 L j
Wood Mt., Saskatchewan 86 L j
Woodpecker, Br. Columbia 88 H d
Woodridge, Manitoba 86 F a
Woodroffe, Mt., Australia 134 F e
Woodrow, Saskatchewan 86 L j
Woods, L., Australia 134 F c
Woods, L. of the, Minnesota-Ontario 86 H a
Woodside, Australia 135 J g
Woodstock, New Brunswick 82 E g
Woodstock, Ontario 84 K j
Woodville, New Zealand 135 R l
Woodville, Ontario 85 M h
Woodwards Cove, New Brunswick 82 F j
Woody R., Manitoba 87 Q f
Woolaston L., Saskatchewan 88 S a
Woolford Prov. Park, Alberta 86 D j
Woomera, Australia 135 G f
Wooramel, Australia 134 B e
Worcester, South Africa 122 B f
Worcester & co., England 99 F h
Wordie Ice Shelf, Antarctica 136 H e
Wordsworth, Saskatchewan 87 P j
Workington, England 98 E f
Workum, Netherlands 100 D b
Worms, Germany 104 C d
Wostok, Alberta 86 E e
Wotho, I., Marshall Is. 78 G f
Wotje, I., Marshall Is. 79 U a
Wotton, Quebec 85 T g
Woudenberg, Netherlands 100 D b
Woudrichem, Netherlands 100 C c
Wour, Chad 119 J d
Wouw, Netherlands 100 C c
Wowoni, I., Indonesia 129 H l
Wrangel I. (Os. Vrangelya), Arctic Ocean 115 S a
Wrath, C., Scotland 98 D b
Wren, Oregon 86 B e
Wrentham, Alberta 86 E j
Wrexham, Wales 99 F g
Wright, Quebec 85 O f
Wrigley Gulf, Antarctica 136 E d
Writing-on-Stone Prov. Park, Alberta 86 F j
Wrocław, Poland 105 G c
Wrong L., Manitoba 87 V f
Wroxton, Saskatchewan 87 Q g
Wubin, Australia 134 C f
Wuchang, China 128 J b
Wuchang, China 131 G g
Wuchih, Hainan I. 128 E g
Wuchow, China 131 E l
Wuchwan, China 130 E b
Wudam, Muscat & Oman 125 G e
Wuestwezel, Belgium 100 C c
Wuhan, China 130 G g
Wuhsien. See Soochow
Wuhu, China 130 J g
Wukang, China 131 E j
Wukari, Nigeria 119 G g
Wukiang, China 130 G d
Wu Kiang, R., China 128 E e
Wuntho, Burma 127 J d
Wuppertal, Germany 104 B c
Wurttemberg, Germany 104 C d
Wurung, Australia 135 H c
Würzberg, Germany 104 C d
Wurzen, Germany 104 E c
Wusiang, China 130 F d
Wusih, China 130 K g
Wuti, China 130 H d
Wutsin, China 130 K g
Wuwei, China 130 A d
Wu Yi Shan, China 131 H j
Wuyüan, China 130 D b
Wuyun, China 128 J a
Wyandra, Australia 135 J e
Wye R., England 99 F h
Wyk, Germany 104 C a
Wymark, Saskatchewan 86 K h
Wyndham, Australia 134 E c
Wyndham, New Zealand 135 P m
Wynniatt B., N.-W. Terr. 80 H c
Wynghene, Belgium 100 B c
Wynyard, Saskatchewan 87 N g
Wyoming, Ontario 84 H k
Wysokie Mazowieckie, Poland 105 K b
Wyszkow, Poland 105 J b
Xánthi, Greece 112 E d
Xanxeré, Brazil 94 F c
Xapurí, Brazil 92 D f
Xavantes, Sa. dos, Brazil 93 H f
Xeró. See Peristéra I.
Xilókastron, Greece 113 D e
Xingú, Brazil 92 D e
Xique Xique, Brazil 93 J f
Xochimilco, vicinity México, Mexico
Yaan, China 128 D d
Yaate, Lebanon 123 E c
Yabbenohr, I., Kwajalein Is. 79 T e
Yablonovy Khrebet, U.S.S.R. 115 L c
Yabrud, Syria 123 E d
Yabucoa, Puerto Rico 54 D h
Yagvildino, U.S.S.R. 117 N c
Yahk, Br. Columbia 88 L f
Yakhtul, Yemen 124 D g
Yako, Upper Volta 118 E f
Yakoma, Congo 120 E d
Yaku Jima, Japan 133 A j
Yakutsk, U.S.S.R. 115 M b
Yale, Br. Columbia 88 J f
Yalgoo, Australia 134 C e
Yalinga, Cent. Afr. Rep 120 E c
Yalouke, Cent. Afr. Rep 120 D c
Yalta, U.S.S.R. 116 J j
Yalu, China 128 H a
Yalung R., China 128 D d
Yalu R., China, etc. 128 H b
Yalutorovsk, U.S.S.R. 114 F c
Yamada. See Ise
Yamagata, Japan 133 F e
Yamaguchi, Japan 133 B g
Yamal, Pol., U.S.S.R. 114 F a
Yamaska, Quebec 85 S f
Yamato Mts., Antarctica. See Queen Fabiola Mts.
Yambol, Bulgaria 112 F c
Yamdok Tso, Tibet 127 H c
Yamethin, Burma 127 J d
Yampol, Ukraine, U.S.S.R. 116 F g
Yampol, Ukraine, U.S.S.R. 116 E g
Yamsk, U.S.S.R. 115 Q c
Yanaha Shima, Okinawa 78 B a
Yanam, India 127 F e
Yanaoca, Peru 92 C f
Yanbu 'al Bahr, Saudi Arabia 124 C e
Yandoon, Burma 127 J e
Yangchow. See Kiangtu
Yang-kao, China 130 F b
Yangtze Kiang, China 130 E g
Yangyuan, China 130 G b
Yannina. See Ioánnina
Yaouiba, Bolivia 92 E h
Yaoundé, Cameroon 119 H h
Yap, I., Pacific Ocean 78 D f
Yaraka, Australia 135 H d
Yarda, Chad 119 J e
Yarensk, U.S.S.R. 114 D b
Yarim, Yemen 124 D g
Yarkhand R., India 126 E a
Yarmouth, Nova Scotia 82 F k
Yaroslavl, U.S.S.R. 116 L c
Yartsevo, U.S.S.R. 115 J b
Yarumal, Colombia 92 B b
Yarylgach, U.S.S.R. 116 H j
Yasin, Kashmir 126 D a
Yasothon, Thailand 129 D g
Yass, Australia 135 J f
Yatakala, Niger 118 F f
Yathkyed L., N.-W. Terr 81 K e
Yatsushiro, Japan 133 B h
Yatung, Tibet 127 G c
Yauca, Peru 92 C g
Yauco, Puerto Rico 54 C h
Yauri, Peru 92 C f
Yautepec, Mexico 90 E d
Yavi, Mt., Venezuela 92 D b
Yawata, I., Truk Is. 78 D n
Yawata, Japan 133 B h
Yazd, Iran 125 F c
Yazdan, Iran 125 H c
Yazd-e-Khrast, Iran 125 F c
Ybbs, Austria 104 F d
Ye, Burma 127 J e
Yecla, Spain 107 E c
Yecora, Mexico 90 C b
Yéfira, Greece 113 D d
Yefremov, U.S.S.R. 116 L e
Yegros, Paraguay 94 E c
Yehkiatsi, China 128 G d
Yehpaishow, China 130 J b
Yehsien, China 130 J d
Yelabuga, U.S.S.R. 117 L c
Yelan, U.S.S.R. 117 F e
Yelatma, U.S.S.R. 117 E c
Yeldyak, U.S.S.R. 117 N c
Yelets, U.S.S.R. 116 L e
Yelizarovo, U.S.S.R. 114 F b
Yellandu, India 126 F e
Yell I. & Sd., Shetland 98 J a
Yellow Creek, Saskatchewan 87 M f
Yellow Grass, Sask. 87 N j
Yellowhead Pass, Alberta 88 K d
Yellowknife, N.-W. Terr. 80 H e
Yellow R. See Hwang Ho
Yellow Sea, China 130 K e
Yelverton B., N.-W. Terr 81 L a
Yelwa, Nigeria 118 F f
Yemanzhelinka, U.S.S.R. 117 Q c
Yemen, S.-W. Asia 124 D f
Yenakiyevo, Ukraine, U.S.S.R. 116 L g
Yenan. See Fushih
Yenangyaung. See Kyaukpadating
Yen-Bay, N. Vietnam 132 C b
Yenbo. See Yanbu 'al Bahr
Yencheng, China 130 K f
Yenchih. See Mingshui
Yenchow. See Kienteh
Yenchow. See Tzeyang
Yenisey, R., U.S.S.R. 114 H b
Yeniseysk, U.S.S.R. 115 J c
Yeniseyskiy Zaliv, U.S.S.R. 114 H a
Yenki. China 133 A c
Yenkihsien, China 133 A c
Yenkishih, China 128 J b
Yenping. See Nanping
Yentai, China 130 K d
Yeovil, England 99 F k
Yeppoon, Australia 135 K d
Yeráki, Greece 113 D f
Yerbogachen, U.S.S.R. 115 K b
Yerevan, Armyanskaya, U.S.S.R. 114 D d
Yerofei Pavlovich, U.S.S.R. 115 M c
Yeropol, U.S.S.R. 115 R b
Yeshbum, S. Yemen 124 E g
Yessey, U.S.S.R. 115 K b
Yeste, Spain 107 D c
Yesud ha Ma'ala, Israel 123 D d
Ye-u, Burma 127 J d
Yeu, I. d', France 108 B c
Yeungkong, China 128 F f
Yevlakh, Azerbai., U.S.S.R. 124 E a
Yevreyskaya, Aut. Oblast, U.S.S.R. 115 N d
Yeysk, U.S.S.R. 114 C d
Yhu, Paraguay 94 E c
Yi, R., Uruguay 94 E d
Yianisadhes, Is., Crete 113 F g
Yiannitsá, Greece 113 D d
Yiáros. See Yioúra, I.
Yibna, Israel 123 C f
Yidha, Greece 113 D d
Yigo, I., Guam 78 B k
Yihsien, China 130 G c
Yingchow. See Fowyang
Yingchwan, China 130 C c
Yinghsien, China 130 F c
Yingkow, China 130 L b
Yingtak, China 131 F k
Yin Shan, China 130 C b
Yioúra, I., Greece 113 E f
Yithion, Greece 113 D f
Yitu, China 130 J d
Yiyang, China 131 F h
Yjig B., Guam 78 A l
Yocalla, Bolivia 92 D g
Yochow. See Yoyang
Yogovsk, U.S.S.R. 117 N b
Yoho Nat. Park, British Columbia 88 L e
Yokkaichi, Japan 133 E g
Yoko, Cameroon 119 H g
Yokohama, Japan 133 F g
Yokosuku, Japan 133 F g
Yokote, Japan 133 G e
Yola, Nigeria 119 H g
Yona, I., Guam 78 B l
Yona, I., Okinawa 78 C a
Yonabaru, I., Okinawa 78 A c
Yonago, Japan 133 C g
Yonaha, I., Okinawa 78 C b
Yone Zawa, Japan 133 G f
Yonker, Saskatchewan 86 H f
Yonne, dep., France 108 E c
York, Australia 134 C f
York, C., Australia 135 H b
York, C., Greenland 89 Q b
York, England 99 G g
Yorke Pen., Australia 134 G f
York Factory, Manitoba 81 K f
York Mills, Ontario 84 D j
York Pt., Labrador 83 R b
York R., Quebec 82 G e
York Sd., Australia 134 D b
Yorkshire Moors, England 99 G f
Yorkshire Wolds, England 99 G f
Yorkshire (York), co., England 99 F f
Yorkton, Saskatchewan 87 P g
Yoro, Honduras 91 B d
Yoshkar Ola, U.S.S.R. 117 H b
Youghal & Harb., Eire 99 B j
Youkadouma, Cameroon 119 J h
Young, Australia 135 J f
Young, Saskatchewan 87 M g
Young I., Balleny Is. 136 B e
Youngstown, Alberta 86 F g
Yoyang, China 131 F h
Yozgat, Turkey 124 B b
Ypres, Belgium 100 A d
Yssingeaux, France 109 F d
Ystad, Sweden 103 E j
Ytterhogdal, Sweden 102 F e
Yüanchow. See Chihkiang
Yüanchow. See Ichun
Yüanling, China 131 E h
Yubi, C., Morocco 118 C c
Yucamani, Mt., Peru 92 C g
Yucatán, state, Mexico 90 G c
Yucatan Chan., Mex.-Cuba 91 B b
Yugoslavia, Cent. Europe 112 B c
Yuhsien, China 130 G c
Yuhwan, China 131 K h
Yukhnov, U.S.S.R. 116 J d
Yukon R., Alaska-Yukon 80 D e
Yukon Territory, Canada 80 F e
Yuksekova, Turkey 124 D b
Yule B., Antarctica 136 B d
Yulin, China 130 D c
Yulin, Hainan 131 D n
Yumen, China 115 J d
Yungchow. See Lingling
Yungfu, China 131 E k
Yungkia. See Wenchow
Yungnien, China 130 G d
Yungning, China 128 D e
Yungping. See Lulung
Yungshun, China 131 D h
Yungsin, China 131 G j
Yungsui, China 131 D h
Yungtsi, China 130 E e
Yunhsien, China 130 E f
Yunsi, China 130 E f
Yurievets, U.S.S.R. 117 F b
Yurimaguas, Peru 92 B e
Yurlovka, U.S.S.R. 117 H d
Yurmysh, U.S.S.R. 117 R b
Yushu, China 118 C d
Yuta, Jordan 123 D f
Yuti, Bolivia 92 E g
Yütze, China 130 F d
Yuyang, China 131 D h
Yuyu, China 130 F b
Yverdon, Switzerland 101 B b
Zaachila, Mexico 90 E d
Zaandam, Netherlands 100 C b
Zabaykal'sk, U.S.S.R. 115 L d
Zabid, Yemen 124 D g
Zabol, Iran 125 H c
Zabrze, Poland 105 H c
Zacapa, Guatemala 90 G e
Zacapoaxtla, Mexico 90 E d
Zacatecas & state, Mexico 90 D c
Zader, Yugoslavia 110 E c
Zadonsk, U.S.S.R. 116 L e
Zafra, Spain 106 B c
Zagazig, Egypt 119 M b
Zagreb, Yugoslavia 110 E c
Zahedan, Iran 125 H d
Zahle, Lebanon 123 D d
Zahran, Saudi Arabia 124 D f
Zaidiya, Yemen 124 D f
Zainsk, U.S.S.R. 117 L c
Zaječar, Yugoslavia 112 D c
Zakho, Iraq 124 D b
Zakin, Afghanistan 125 H c
Zakinthos, I., Greece 113 C f
Zakroczyn, Poland 105 J b
Zákros, Crete 113 F g
Zălău, Romania 105 K e
Zalew Wislany, Poland 105 H a
Zaltbommel, Netherlands 100 D c
Zama L., Alberta 88 K a
Zambezi R., S.-E. Africa 122 E c
Zambia, Africa 122 D b
Zamboanga, Philippines 129 H j
Zamora, Ecuador 92 B d
Zamora, Mexico 90 D d
Zamora, Spain 106 C b
Zampa misaki, Okinawa 78 A b
Zandberg, Netherlands 100 E b
Zandvoort, Netherlands 100 C b
Zangla, Kashmir 126 E b
Zangla Kangmar, India 126 E b
Zanjan, Iran 124 E b
Zank, Muscat & Oman 125 G e
Zante. See Zakinthos, I.
Zanthus, Australia 134 D f
Zanzibar & I., Tanzania 121 H f
Zapala, Argentina 95 B e
Zapallar. See General José de San Martín
Zapata Pen., Cuba 91 C b
Zaporozhye, Ukraine, U.S.S.R. 116 J h
Zara. See Zader
Zara, Turkey 124 C b
Zaragoza, Colombia 92 C b
Zaragoza, Mexico 90 D b
Zaragoza, Spain 107 E b
Zarand, Iran 125 G c
Zarasai, Lithuania, U.S.S.R. 103 M j
Zarauz, Spain 107 D a
Zaraza, Venezuela 92 D b
Zaria, Nigeria 118 G f
Zarki, Poland 105 H c
Zarnuqa, Saudi Arabia 124 E d
Zarqa, Jordan 123 E e
Zaruma, Ecuador 92 B d
Zarzis, Tunisia 119 H b
Zaskar, India 126 E b
Zatec, Czechoslovakia 104 E c
Zativinsk, U.S.S.R. 115 M c
Zawiercie, Poland 105 H c
Zaysan, Kazakh., U.S.S.R 114 H d
Zaysan, Oz., Kazakh., U.S.S.R. 114 H d
Zbaszyn, Poland 105 F b
Zdúnska Wola, Poland 105 H c
Zealand. See Sjælland
Zealandia, Saskatchewan 86 K g
Zebak, Afghanistan 125 K b
Zeballos, Br Columbia 88 G e
Zebdani, Syria 123 E d
Zebid Qadhima, Saudi Arabia 124 C e
Zeebrugge, Belgium 100 B c
Zeeland, prov., Netherlands 100 B c
Zeerust, South Africa 122 D e
Zegharta, Lebanon 123 D c
Zeila, Somali Republic 121 J b
Zeist, Netherlands 100 D b
Zeitz, Germany 104 E c
Zele, Belgium 100 C c
Zelenogradsk, U.S.S.R. 103 J j
Železná Ruda, Czechoslovakia 104 E d
Zella, Libya 119 J c
Zelma, Saskatchewan 87 M g
Zelman, U.S.S.R. 117 G e
Zelzate, Belgium 100 B c
Zemio, Cent. Afr. Rep. 119 L g
Zemun, Yugoslavia 112 C b
Zenica, Yugoslavia 112 A b
Zenon Park, Saskatchewan 87 O e
Žepce, Yugoslavia 112 A b
Zermatt, Switzerland 101 C b
Zernez, Switzerland 101 F b
Zetland (Shetland), Scotland 98 J a
Zevenbergen, Netherlands 100 C c
Zeya, U.S.S.R. 115 M c
Zeyma, Saudi Arabia 124 D e
Zgierz, Poland 105 H c
Zgorzelec. See Görlitz
Zhdanov, Ukraine, U.S.S.R. 116 K h
Zheleznodrozhnyy, U.S.S.R. 58 E b
Zhigansk, U.S.S.R. 115 M b
Zhitomir, Ukraine, U.S.S.R. 116 F f
Zhmerinka, Ukraine, U.S.S.R. 116 F g
Zhob R., India 126 C b
Ziarat, Pakistan 126 C b
Ziba. See Dhaba
Zidani Most, Yugoslavia 110 E b
Zierikzee, Netherlands 100 B c
Zijpe, Netherlands 100 C c
Zikhron Ya'aqoy, Israel 123 C e
Zilaf, Syria 123 F e
Zile, Turkey 124 C a
Zilfi, Saudi Arabia 124 D d
Žilina, Czechoslovakia 105 H d
Zima, U.S.S.R. 115 K c
Zimapán, Mexico 90 E c
Zindajan, Afghanistan 125 H c
Zinder, Niger 119 G f
Zingst, Pen., Germany 104 E a
Zipaquira, Colombia 92 C b
Zirc, Hungary 105 G e
Zitácuaro, Mexico 90 D d
Zittau, Germany 104 F c
Zizers, Switzerland 101 E b
Zlatoust, U.S.S.R. 117 P c
Zmeinogorsk, U.S.S.R. 114 H c
Znin, Poland 105 G b
Znojmo, Czechoslovakia 105 G d
Zofingen, Switzerland 101 C a
Zōhab, Iran 124 E c
Zoisa, Tanzania 121 H f
Zolder, Belgium 100 D c
Zollino, Italy 111 G e
Zomba, Malawi 121 H h
Zonguldak, Turkey 124 B a
Zorita, Spain 106 C c
Zorra I., Canal Zone 91 G b
Zoute, Le, Belgium 100 B c
Zoutkamp, Netherlands 100 E a
Zrenjanin, Yugoslavia 112 C b
Zuara, Libya 119 H b
Zuevka, U.S.S.R. 117 K a
Zug & canton, Switzerland 101 D a
Zuger See, Switzerland 101 D a
Zuid Beijerland, Netherlands 100 C c
Zuider Zee. See IJssel Meer
Zuidland, Netherlands 100 C c
Zuidwolde, Netherlands 100 E b
Zuila, Libya 119 J c
Zukur, Jab., Yemen 124 D g
Zula, Ethiopia 121 H a
Zulfikar, Afghanistan 125 H b
Zumbo, Mozambique 122 E c
Zumpango, Mexico 90 E d
Zundert, Netherlands 100 C c
Zungeru, Nigeria 118 G g
Zurich, Ontario 84 J j
Zürich & canton, Switzerland 101 D a
Zürich See, Switzerland 101 D a
Zurzach, Switzerland 101 D a
Zutphen, Netherlands 100 E b
Zwai L., Ethiopia 121 H c
Zwartsluis, Netherlands 100 E b
Zweeloo, Netherlands 100 E b
Zweibrücken, W. Germany 104 B d
Zweisimmen, Switzerland 101 C b
Zwickau, Germany 104 E c
Zwoleń, Poland 105 J c
Zwolle, Netherlands 100 E b
Zyrardów, Poland 105 J b
Zyryanka, U.S.S.R. 115 P b
Zyryanovsk, Kazakh., U.S.S.R. 114 H d
Zyyi, Cyprus 123 B c

GENERAL INDEX

ORBIS TERRÆ COMPENDIOSA DESCRIPTIO
EVROPA
Polus 90 Arcticus
Circulus Arcticus
AMERICA
MEXICANA
Tropicus Cancri
MAR DEL ZUR
MAR DEL NORT
Circulus Aequinoctialis
Oceanus Peruuianus
PERVVIANA
Insulæ Salomonis
Tropicus Capricorni
EL MAR PACIFICO
TERRA AVSTRALIS
MAGALLANICA
Circulus Antarcticus
Terra del Fuego
Polus Antarcticus
AMERICA
Aries
Taurus
Auriga
Cepheus
Vrsa major
Vrsa minor
Gemini
Cancer
Leo
Corona A.
Ara
Fera Lupus
Corvus
Arnoldus, & Henricus